Gravel Edition / Pentagon Papers / Volume III

The Senator Gravel Edition

The Pentagon Papers

*The Defense Department
History of United States
Decisionmaking on Vietnam*

Volume III

Beacon Press *Boston*

The contents of this volume are drawn from the
official record of the U.S. Senate Subcommittee
on Public Buildings and Grounds. No copyright is claimed
in the text of this official Government document.

Library of Congress catalog card number: 75–178049

International Standard Book Number: 0–8070–0526–6 (hardcover)
0–8070–0527–4 (paperback)

Beacon Press books are published under the
auspices of the Unitarian Universalist Association

Printed in the United States of America

EXPLANATORY NOTE

The preparation of the subcommittee record was performed under the direction of Senator Gravel. No material was added to or changed in the study or appended documents and statements. In some cases, material was illegible or missing. If this occurred within a direct quotation, the omission was indicated with a bracketed statement. If it occurred in narrative text, it was bridged by removing the entire sentence in which it appeared, when it was evident that no substantive material would be lost by this procedure; otherwise, the omission was indicated by a bracketed statement. All other bracketed insertions appear in the original study.

Contents

[*At the end of each volume is a collection of documents, a section entitled
"Justification of the War—Public Statements," and a Glossary*]

Contents of Volume III

3. The Air War in North Vietnam: Rolling Thunder Begins, February–June, 1965   269

4. American Troops Enter the Ground War, March–July, 1965   389

Gravel Edition / Pentagon Papers / Volume III

1. U.S. Programs in South Vietnam, Nov. 1963–Apr. 1965

Summary and Analysis

During the period from the overthrow of the Diem government in November 1963 until the Honolulu Conference in April 1965, U.S. policymakers were concerned with a continuing, central dilemma in South Vietnam. An agonizing, year-long internal debate took place against the double backdrop of this dilemma and Presidential election year politics. Although the results of this debate could not be clearly seen until mid-1965, the seeds which produced those results are clearly visible in the official files at least a year earlier.

The basic problem in U.S. policy was to generate programs and other means adequate to secure the objectives being pursued. The central dilemma lay in the fact that while U.S. policy objectives were stated in the most comprehensive terms the means employed were both consciously limited and purposely indirect. That is, the U.S. eschewed employing all of its military might—or even a substantial portion of it—in a battle which was viewed in Washington as determinative of the fate of all of Southeast Asia, probably crucial to the future of South Asia, and as the definitive test of U.S. ability to counteract communist support for "wars of national liberation." Moreover, this limited U.S. resource commitment to practically unlimited ends took an indirect form. U.S. efforts were aimed at helping the Government of Vietnam (GVN) to win its own struggle against the insurgents. This meant that the newly established GVN had to somehow mobilize its human and other resources, improve its military performance against the Viet Cong, and shift the tide of the war.

As events in 1964 and 1965 were to demonstrate, the GVN did not succeed in achieving political stability. Its military forces did not stem the pattern of VC successes. Rather, a series of coups produced "revolving door" governments in Saigon. The military pattern showed, particularly by the spring of 1965, a precipitous decline in the fortunes of the Army of the Republic of Vietnam (ARVN). Yet there was no serious debate in Washington on the desirability of modifying U.S. objectives. These remained essentially fixed even as the means for their realization—limited U.S. material support for GVN—underwent one crisis and disappointment after another.

There were no immediate or forceful U.S. reactions in 1964 to this continuing political instability and military frustration in South Vietnam. Declaratory policy raced far ahead of resource allocations and use decisions. As events continued along an unfavorable course the U.S. pursued an ever-expanding number of minor, specific, programmatic measures which were inherently inadequate either to reverse the decline or to satisfy broad U.S. objectives. Concurrently, the U.S. began to make contingency plans for increasing pressures against NVN. It did not make similar plans for the commitment of U.S. ground forces in SVN.

In the aftermath of President Johnson's landslide electoral victory in November 1964, and in the face of persistent instability in SVN, the Administration finally expanded the war to include a limited, carefully controlled air campaign against the north. Early in 1965 it deployed Marine battalions to South Vietnam.

By April 1965, while continuing to follow the announced policy of efforts to enable GVN to win its own war, the U.S. had adumbrated a policy of U.S. military participation which presaged a high degree of Americanization of the war effort.

This evolving expansion and demonstration of commitment was neither continuous nor steady. The steps forward were warmly debated, often hesitant, sometimes reluctant.—But all of the steps taken were still forward toward a larger commitment; there were none to the rear.

THE INITIAL PERIOD: NOVEMBER 1963–MARCH 1964

The Diem coup preceded President Kennedy's assassination by less than a month. Thus, a new leader took the helm in the U.S. at a natural time to re-evaluate U.S. policies and U.S.–GVN relations. President Johnson's first policy announcement on the Vietnamese war, contained in NSAM 273 (26 November 1963), only three days after he had assumed the Presidency, was intended primarily to endorse the policies pursued by President Kennedy and to ratify provisional decisions reached in Honolulu just before the assassination. Even in its attempt to direct GVN's efforts toward concentration on the Delta area, NSAM 273 reflected earlier U.S. preferences which had been thwarted or ignored by Diem. Now was the time, many of the top U.S. policymakers hoped, when convincing U.S. support for the new regime in Saigon might allow GVN to start winning its own war.

Two developments—in addition to the VC successes which followed Diem's downfall—undercut this aura of optimism. First, it was discovered that the situation in SVN had been worse all along than reports had indicated. Examples of misleading reports were soon available in Washington at the highest levels. Second, the hoped-for political stability was never even established before it disintegrated in the Khanh coup in January 1964. By February MACV's year-end report for 1963 was available in Washington. Its gloomy statistics showed downward trends in almost every area.

Included in the MACV assessment was the opinion that military effort could not succeed in the absence of effective political leadership. A special CIA report, forwarded to Secretary McNamara at about the same time made the opposite point: military victories were needed to nourish the popular attitudes conducive to political stability. Assistant Secretary of State Roger Hilsman—who would shortly leave office after his views were rejected—stressed the need for physical security in the rural areas and the adoption of counterguerrilla tactics as the preconditions to success. These interesting reversals of nominal functional preferences indicate that there was at least a sufficiently broad awareness within U.S. Officialdom to permit a useful debate on U.S. actions which might deal more successfully with this seamless web of political-military issues. Certainly the intelligence picture was dark enough to prompt such a debate: the SNIE on short-term prospects in Southeast Asia warned that ". . . South Vietnam has, at best, an even chance of withstanding the insurgency menace during the next few weeks or months."

The debate did begin, but in hobbles. The generally agreed necessity to work through GVN and the felt imperative to strengthen GVN left the U.S. in a position of weakness. It was at least as dependent on GVN leaders as were the latter on U.S. support. Moreover, mid-1964 was not an auspicious time for new departures in policy by a President who wished to portray "moderate" alternatives to his opponent's "radical" proposals. Nor was any time prior to or immediately following the elections very appealing for the same reason. Thus, while the debate in high official circles was very, very different from the public debate it still reflected the existence of the public debate.

LIMITED MEASURES FOR LIMITLESS AIMS

The first official internal pronouncement to reflect this difficult policymaking milieu was NSAM 288, in March 1964. Approved verbatim from the report of the most recent McNamara-Taylor visit to Vietnam, it was virtually silent on one issue (U.S. troops) and minimal in the scale of its recommendations at the same time that it stated U.S. objectives in the most sweeping terms used up to that time. The U.S. objective was stated to be an "independent, non-communist South Vietnam, free to accept assistance as required to maintain its security" even though not necessarily a member of the Western alliance. The importance of this objective was underscored in a classic statement of the domino theory:

> Unless we can achieve this objective in South Vietnam, almost all of Southeast Asia will probably fall under Communist dominance (all of Vietnam, Laos, and Cambodia), accommodate to Communism so as to remove effective U.S. and anti-Communist influence (Burma), or fall under the domination of forces not now explicitly Communist but likely then to become so (Indonesia taking over Malaysia). Thailand might hold for a period with our help, but would be under grave pressure. Even the Philippines would become shaky, and the threat to India to the west, Australia and New Zealand to the south, and Taiwan, Korea, and Japan to the north and east would be greatly increased.

The present situation in SVN was painted in somber tones of declining GVN control and deterioration within ARVN while VC strength and NVN-supplied arms were on the rise. To introduce U.S. combat troops for the protection of Saigon under these circumstances, McNamara stated, would create "serious adverse psychological consequences and should not be undertaken." A U.S. movement from the advisory role to a role which would amount to command of the war effort was similarly rejected without discussion because of anticipated adverse psychological effects. Thus, the fear of undesirable impacts upon a weak GVN caused at least one major course of action to be ruled out. Although fears of adverse impacts in domestic U.S. politics were not mentioned it is inconceivable that such fears were not present.

Having ruled out U.S. active leadership and the commitment of U.S. troops, Secretary McNamara analyzed three possible courses of action: (1) negotiations leading to the "neutralization" of SVN; (2) the initiation of military actions against NVN; and (3) measures to improve the situation in SVN. The first of these was incompatible with the U.S. objective stated at the beginning of the NSAM; the time was not propitious for adoption of the second; the third was recommended for adoption. Additionally, Secretary McNamara recommended NSAM 288 proclaimed that plans be made so that the U.S. would be in a position at a later date to initiate military pressures against NVN within a relatively brief time after any decision to do so might be made.

Many of the steps approved in NSAM 288 were highly programmatic. It should be observed that they were also palliative, both in scope and degree. Of the twelve approved actions, two addressed possible future actions beyond the borders of South Vietnam. Of the remaining ten, three were declaratory in nature (e.g., "To make it clear that we fully support the Khanh government and are opposed to any further coups"). The seven actions implying additional U.S. assistance (some of it advice) dealt with such matters as exchanging 25 VNAF aircraft for a newer model, replacing armored personnel carriers with a more reliable model, and trebling the fertilizer program within two years. The additional cost of the programs was only slightly more than $60 million at the most: $30–$40 million to support a 50,000 man increase in RVNAF and to raise pay scales; $1.5 million to support an enlarged civil administrative cadre; and a one time cost of $20 million for additional and replacement military equipment.

It is clear with the advantage of hindsight that these steps were grossly inadequate to the magnitude of the tasks at hand—particularly if the broad U.S. objectives stated in the NSAM were to be realized. But such hindsight misses the policymakers' dilemma and the probable process by which the approved actions were decided upon. President Johnson had neither a congressional nor a popular mandate to Americanize the war or to expand it dramatically by "going north." U.S. hopes were pinned on assisting in the development of a GVN strong enough to win its own war. Overt U.S. leadership might undercut the development of such a government in Saigon. The course of policy adopted was not the product of an attempt to select the "best" alternative by means of examining expected benefits; it resulted from a determination of the "least bad" alternative through an examination of risks and disadvantages. It reflected what was politically feasible rather than what was desirable in relation to stated objectives. The practical effect of this understandable—perhaps inescapable and inevitable—way of deciding upon U.S. policy was to place almost complete responsibility in the hands of the GVN for the attainment of U.S. objectives—it being assumed that GVN's objectives were compatible with ours.

Midway through 1964 President Johnson changed the entire top level of U.S. leadership in Saigon. General Maxwell D. Taylor, Chairman of the Joint Chiefs of Staff, retired from active military duty (for the second time) to become the U.S. Ambassador. An experienced and highly regarded career diplomat, U. Alexis Johnson, was appointed deputy to Taylor. General William C. Westmoreland stepped up from deputy to commander of U.S. military forces in Vietnam. The new "first team" was not without knowledge about Vietnam but it inescapably lacked the close personal knowledge of leading GVN figures which only time and close association can develop. It set about attempting to help the Khanh government to help itself.

General Khanh, in the event, proved unable to marshal SVN's resources and to establish his regime in a position of authority adequate either to stem or to turn the VC tide. Khanh's failure was, however, neither precipitous nor easily perceivable at the time. As the U.S. entered and passed through a Presidential campaign in which the proper policy to pursue in Vietnam was a major issue, it sometimes appeared that the GVN was making headway and sometimes appeared that it was not.

U.S. policy remained virtually unchanged during this period although significant planning steps were accomplished to permit the U.S. to exercise military pressures against NVN should it appear desirable (and politically feasible) to do so. Thanks to such planning, the Tonkin Gulf incidents of 2–4 August 1964 were answered by "tit-for-tat" reprisal raids with considerable dispatch. The cost was minimal in terms of world opinion and communist reaction. Moreover, President Johnson used the Tonkin Gulf incidents as the springboard to a broad endorsement by the Congress of his leadership and relative freedom of action.

When this was followed in November by what can only be described as a smashing victory at the polls, the President's hands were not completely untied but the bonds were figuratively loosened. His feasible options increased.

LIMITED ESCALATION LEADS TO OPEN-ENDED INTERVENTION

Immediately following his election, the President initiated an intense, month-long policy review. An executive branch consensus developed for a two phase expansion of the war. Phase I was limited to intensification of air strikes in Laos and to covert actions in NVN. Phase II would extend the war to a sustained, escalating air campaign against North Vietnamese targets. The President approved Phase I for implementation in December 1964 but approved Phase II only "in principle."

The effect of this decision was to increase the expectation that the air campaign against NVN would be undertaken if the proper time arose. What conditions were proper was the subject of considerable disagreement and confusion. Tactically, the U.S. desired to respond to North Vietnamese acts rather than to appear to initiate a wider war. But the strategic purposes of bombing in NVN were in dispute. The initiation of an air campaign was deferred early in 1964 as a prod to GVN reform. By 1965 such initiation was argued for as a support for GVN morale. Some adherents claimed that bombing in NVN could destroy the DRV's will to support the war in South Vietnam. Others expected it to raise the price of North Vietnam's effort and to demonstrate U.S. commitment but not to be decisive in and of itself. The only indisputable facts seem to be that the long planning and debate over expanding the air war, the claimed benefits (although disputed), and the relatively low cost and risk of an air campaign as compared to the commitment of U.S. ground forces combined to indicate that the bombing of NVN would be the next step taken if nothing else worked.

Nothing else was, in fact, working. General Khanh's government was reorganized in November 1964 to give it the appearance of civilian leadership. Khanh finally fell in mid-February 1965 and was replaced by the Quat regime. Earlier that month the insurgents had attacked the U.S. base at Pleiku, killing eight Americans. Similar attacks late in 1964 had brought about recommendations for reprisal attacks. These had been disapproved because of timing. On this occasion, however, the President approved the FLAMING DART retaliatory measures.

Presidential assistant McGeorge Bundy was in SVN when the Viet Cong attacked the U.S. facilities in Pleiku. He recommended to the President that, in addition to retaliatory measures, the U.S. initiate phase II of the military measures against NVN. The fall of the Khanh regime a week later resurrected the worst U.S. fears of GVN political instability. The decision to bomb north was made, announced on 28 February, and strikes initiated on 2 March. A week later, after a request from Generals Taylor and Westmoreland which was debated little if at all, two battalion landing teams of Marines went ashore at DaNang to assume responsibility for security of the air base there. U.S. ground combat units were in an active theater on the mainland of Asia for the first time since the Korean War. This may not have been the Rubicon of the Johnson administration's Vietnam policy but it was a departure of immeasurable significance. The question was no longer one of whether U.S. units should be deployed to SVN; rather, it was one of how many units should be deployed and for what strategic purposes.

The Army Chief of Staff, General Harold K. Johnson, went to Saigon in mid-

March and recommended that bombing restrictions be lifted and that a U.S. division be deployed to SVN for active combat. General Taylor strongly opposed an active combat—as distinct from base security—role for U.S. ground forces. But the President decided on 1 April to expand the bombing, to add an air wing in SVN, and to send two more Marine battalions ashore. These decisions were announced internally on 6 April in NSAM 328.

General Taylor continued to voice strong opposition to a ground combat role for U.S. forces but his voice was drowned out by two developments. First, the air campaign against NVN (ROLLING THUNDER) did not appear to be shaking the DRV's determination. Second, ARVN experienced a series of disastrous defeats in the spring of 1965 which convinced a number of observers that a political-military collapse within GVN was imminent.

As the debate in Washington on next steps revealed, something closely akin to the broad objectives stated over a year earlier in NSAM 288 represented a consensus among U.S. policymakers as a statement of proper U.S. aims. The domestic political situation had changed materially since early 1964. President Johnson was now armed with both a popular mandate and broad Congressional authorization (the extent of which would be challenged later, but not in 1965). Palliative measures had not been adequate to the task although they had continued and multiplied throughout the period. As General Taylor wryly remarked to McGeorge Bundy in a back channel message quoted in the following paper, the U.S. Mission in Saigon was charged with implementing a 21-point military program, a 41-point non-military program, a 16-point USIS program, and a 12-point CIA program ". . . as if we can win here somehow on a point score."

As fears rose in Washington it must have seemed that everything had been tried except one course—active U.S. participation in the ground battle in SVN. Palliative measures had failed. ROLLING THUNDER offered little hope for a quick decision in view of the rapid deterioration of ARVN. The psychological barrier against the presence of U.S. combat units had been breached. If the revalidated U.S. objectives were to be achieved it was necessary for the U.S. to make quickly some radical departures. It was politically feasible to commit U.S. ground forces and it seemed desirable to do so.

Secretary McNamara met in Honolulu on 20 April with the principal U.S. leaders from Saigon and agreed to recommend an enclave strategy requiring a quantum increase above the four Marine battalions. An account of the rapidity with which this strategy was overtaken by an offensively oriented concept is described in Chapter 4. The present volume describes the situational changes, the arguments, and the frustrations as the U.S. attempted for over a year to move toward the realization of ambitious objectives by the indirect use of very limited resources and in the shadow of a Presidential election campaign.

End of Summary and Analysis

CHRONOLOGY

20 Nov 1963   *Honolulu Conference*
                Secretaries McNamara and Rusk and their party meet with the entire US country team and review the South Vietnamese situation after the Diem coup.

22 Nov 1963   *Kennedy Assassination*
                President Kennedy is assassinated in Dallas. Lodge confers with the new President, Johnson, in Washington, during the next few days.

26 Nov 1963   NSAM 273

Drawing on the Honolulu Conference and Lodge's conversations with the President, NSAM 273 established US support for the new Minh government and emphasized that the level of effort, economic and military, would be maintained at least as high as to Diem. All US and GVN efforts were to be concentrated on the Delta where the VC danger was greatest. But the war remained basically a South Vietnamese affair to win or lose.

6 Dec 1963   *Report on Long An Province*

A report by a USOM provincial representative on Long An Province, adjacent to Saigon, describes the near complete disintegration of the strategic hamlet program. The basic problem is the inability or unwillingness of the ARVN to provide timely support when villages are under attack. Hamlets are being overrun by the VC on an almost daily basis. Ambassador Lodge forwards the report to Washington.

17 Dec 1963   *NSC Meeting*

After hearing a briefing by General Krulak that falls short of giving an adequate explanation for the Long An report, the President decides to send McNamara on another fact-finding trip.

18–20 Dec 1963   *SecDef Trip to Vietnam*

During this quick visit to South Vietnam, McNamara ordered certain immediate actions to be taken by the US Mission to improve the situation in the 13 critical provinces. He returns directly to Washington to report to the President.

21 Dec 1963   *McNamara Report to the President*

McNamara's report substantiates the existence of significant deterioration in the war since the preceding summer. He recommends strengthened ARVN formations in the key provinces, increased US military and civilian staffs, the creation of a new pacification plan, and better coordination between Lodge and Harkins. His report is especially pessimistic about the situation in the Delta.

7 Jan 1964   *McCone Proposes Covert Reporting*

The serious failure of the reporting system to indicate the critical state of deterioration of the war prompts McCone to recommend to McNamara a special TDY covert CIA check on the in-country reporting system to make recommendations for improving it.

16 Jan 1964   *McNamara Accepts Revised McCone Proposal*

McNamara accepts a revised form of McCone's proposal, specifically ruling out any IG-like aspects to the study.

28 Jan 1964   *Khanh Warns US Aide of Pro-Neutralist Coup*

General Khanh, I Corps Commander, warns his US advisor, Colonel Wilson that pro-neutralist members of the MRC—Xuan, Don, and Kim—are plotting a coup.

29 Jan 1964   *Khanh Warns Lodge*

Khanh repeats to Lodge the warning that pro-neutralist elements are planning a coup. Lodge recommends an intervention with Paris to get DeGaulle to restrict his activity in Saigon. Khanh's efforts are really a screen for his own planned coup.

30 Jan 1964   *Khanh Coup*
Early in the morning, Khanh acts to take over control of the government in a bloodless internal coup that removes the civilian government and puts him in power.

2 Feb 1964   *MACV Personal Assessment of 4th Qtr CY 1963*
The Diem coup and the subsequent political instability in the fall of 1963 are given by MACV as the main reasons for the rise in VC activity and the decline in GVN control of the country. The tempo of GVN operations was good but the effectiveness low. Military failures were largely attributed to political problems.

10 Feb 1964   *CAS Group's Preliminary Report*
The preliminary report of the special CAS group cross-checking the reporting system confirms the deterioration of the strategic hamlet program. It documents the decline in rural security and the increase in VC attacks.

12 Feb 1964   *SNIE 50–64*
This intelligence community evaluation of the short-term prospects for Vietnam confirms the pessimism now felt in all quarters. The political instability is the hard core problem.

18 Feb 1964   *Final CAS Group Report*
The final CAS group report confirms the black picture of its initial estimate in greater detail and further confirms the previous failings of the reporting system.

JCSM 136–64
In addition to a long list of recommendations for GVN action, the JCS propose to SecDef major US escalatory steps including bombing of the North.

21 Feb 1964   *MACV Comment on CAS Group Findings*
General Harkins takes issue not with the specific factual reporting of the CAS Group, but with their broader conclusions about the direction the war is going, and the respective effectiveness of the VC and GVN.

2 Mar 1964   *JCSM-174-64*
The JCS outline their proposal for punitive action against the DRV to halt Northern support for the VC insurgency. Bombing is specifically called for.

8 Mar 1964   *SecDef and CJCS Begin Five-Day Trip to SVN*
The President sends Secretary McNamara and General Taylor on another fact-finding trip to prepare for a major re-evaluation of the war and US involvement. While there, a set of recommendations to the President is decided upon.

12 Mar 1964   *McNamara-Taylor see Khanh*
Prior to their departure, McNamara and Taylor present their principal conclusions to General Khanh who is responsive to their suggestions and, in particular, declares his readiness to move promptly on a national mobilization and increasing ARVN and Civil Guard.

14 Mar 1964   *Hilsman sends Final Memos to SecState*
Having resigned over policy disagreement, Hilsman sends Rusk parting memos on SEA and SVN. He describes two principles basic to success in guerrilla warfare: (1) the oil blot approach to progressive rural security; and (2) the avoidance of large-scale operations. He further opposes redirecting the war effort against the North. Political stability is absolutely essential to eventual victory.

JCSM-222-64
The JCS, in commenting on McNamara's proposed recommendations to the President, reiterate their views of 2 March that a program of actions against the North is required to effectively strike at the sources of the insurgency. The overall military recommendations proposed by McNamara are inadequate, they feel.

16 Mar 1964   *SecDef Recommendations to the President*
Largely ignoring the JCS reclama, McNamara reports on the conclusions of his trip to Vietnam and recommends the full civilian and military mobilization to which General Khanh has committed himself. This is to be accompanied by an extensive set of internal reforms and organizational improvements. Some increases in US personnel are recommended along with increased materiel support for the GVN.

17 Mar 1964   *NSAM 288*
The President accepts McNamara's full report and has it adopted as NSAM 288 to guide national policy. The importance of South Vietnam to US policy and security is underlined and the extent of the US commitment to it increased. While significant increases in actual US participation in the war are rejected as not warranted for the moment, the JCS are authorized to begin planning studies for striking at the sources of insurgency in the DRV.

1 Apr 1964   *Embassy Saigon Msg 1880*
Lodge reports per State request that Khanh's proposed mobilization measures call for both civilian and military build-ups.

4 Apr 1964   *Khanh Announces Mobilization*
Khanh announces that all able-bodied males aged 20 to 45 will be subject to national public service, etiher military or civilian.

W. P. Bundy Letter to Lodge
In a letter to Lodge, Bundy asks him to comment on a scenario for mobilizing domestic US political support for action against the DRV.

15 Apr 1964   *Lodge reports on Mobilization*
Lodge reports that Khanh's 4 April announcement was only the precursor of the legal decrees the essence of which he described.

15–20 Apr 1964	*General Wheeler, CofS/USA, Visits Vietnam*
	The Army Chief of Staff, General Earl Wheeler visits Vietnam to make a survey and represent the SecDef during the visit of Secretary Rusk. On 16 April, he meets with Khanh who first mentions his view that the war will eventually have to be taken to the North.
17–20 Apr 1964	*Rusk Visits Saigon*
	Secretary Rusk and party visit Saigon. On 18 April, Rusk sees Khanh who again mentions the eventual necessity of carrying the fight to the North. Rusk replies that such a significant escalation of the war would require much thought and preparation. At the 19 April meeting with the Country Team, much of the discussion is devoted to the problem of pressures against the North.
25 Apr 1964	*President Names General Westmoreland to Succeed General Harkins*
	General William Westmoreland is named to succeed General Harkins in the summer.
29 Apr 1964	*JCS Msg 6073 to MACV*
	The JCS, worried at the GVN delay, ask MACV to submit the force plan for 1964 by 7 May.
30 Apr 1964	*Lodge, Brent and Westmoreland See Khanh*
	In a showdown with Khanh, Lodge, Brent and Westmoreland state that the fundamental problem is lack of administrative support for the provincial war against the VC, particularly the inadequacy of the piastre support for the pacification program. Khanh promises more effort.
	Embassy Saigon Msg 1889 EXDIS for the President
	Lodge informs the President that Khanh has agreed to US advisors in the pacified areas if we are willing to accept casualties. Lodge recommends one advisor for each corps area and one for Khanh, all reporting to Lodge.
2 May 1964	*Lodge Reports on Delay in Mobilization*
	Lodge reports that the draft mobilization decrees have still not been signed or promulgated.
4 May 1964	*Embassy Saigon Msg 2112*
	Having asked to see Lodge, Khanh asks him whether he, Lodge, thinks the country should be put on a war footing. Khanh wants to carry the war to the North and sees this as necessary preliminary.
6 May 1964	*NSC Meeting*
	The NSC confirms Rusk's caution to Khanh on any moves against the North. The President asks McNamara to make a fact-finder to Vietnam.
7 May 1964	*MACV, US/GVN 1964 Force Level Agreement*
	MACV informs the JCS that agreement has been reached with the GVN on the level of forces to be reached by year's end.
12–14 May 1964	*McNamara-Taylor Mission*
	McNamara-Taylor visit SVN. They are briefed on 12–13 April by

the Mission. On 14 April they see Khanh who again talks of going North. McNamara demurs, but insists on more political stability and program effectiveness.

30 May 1964   *Honolulu Conference*
Rusk, McNamara, McCone and aides meet in Honolulu with the Country Team. A full dress discussion of pressures takes place, but no decisions or recommendations are approved. Rather, more emphasis on the critical provinces is approved, along with an expanded advisory effort.

5 Jun 1964   *Department of State Msg 2184*
Lodge is informed of the President's approval of the expanded effort in the critical provinces.

15 Jun 1964   *W. P. Bundy memo to SecState and SecDef*
Attached to a Bundy memo for consideration at a meeting later the same day, are six annexes each dealing with a different aspect of the problem of getting a Congressional resolution of support for the current US Southeast Asian policy. One of the important themes is that an act of irreversible US commitment might provide the necessary psychological support to get real reform and effectiveness from the GVN.

23 Jun 1964   *President Announces JCS Chairman Taylor as New Ambassador*
President Johnson announces the appointment of JCS Chairman, Maxwell Taylor, to succeed Lodge, who is returning to engage in Republican Presidential politics.

30 Jun 1964   *Taylor Succeeds Lodge*
Lodge leaves Saigon and Taylor takes over as US Ambassador with U. Alexis Johnson as Deputy.

7 Jul 1964   *Taylor Forms Mission Council*
In an effort to streamline the Embassy and increase his policy control, Taylor forms the Mission Council at the Country Team level.

8 Jul 1964   *Taylor Calls on Khanh*
Taylor calls on Khanh who expresses satisfaction with the new personnel, approves the Mission Council idea and offers to create a counter part organization.

10 Jul 1964   *Department of State Msg 108*
The President asks Taylor to submit regular month-end progress reports on all aspects of the program.

15 Jul 1964   *Taylor reports increased VC strength, Embassy Saigon Msgs 107 and 108*
Taylor raises the estimate of Viet Cong strength from the previous total of 28,000 to 34,000. This does not represent a sudden increase, but rather intelligence confirmation of long suspected units.

17 Jul 1964   *USOM Meets With GVN NSC*
As he had promised, Khanh creates a coordinating group within the GVN to deal with the new Mission Council and calls it the NSC.

19 Jul 1964   *Khanh Makes Public Reference to "Going North"*
In a public speech, Khanh refers to the "March to the North." In a separate statement to the press, General Ky also refers to the "march North."

23 Jul 1964   *Taylor Meets with Khanh and NSC*
In a meeting with Khanh and the NSC, Taylor is told by Khanh that the move against the North is indispensable to the success of the counterinsurgency campaign in the South.

24 Jul 1964   *Taylor and Khanh discuss Coups*
In a discussion of coup rumors, Khanh complains that it is US support of Minh that is behind all the trouble, Taylor reiterates US support for Khanh.

2 Aug 1964   USS Maddox *Attacked in Tonkin Gulf*
The destroyer *USS Maddox* is attacked in the Tonkin Gulf by DRV patrol craft while on a DE SOTO patrol off the DRV coast. Several patrol boats sunk.

4 Aug 1964   Maddox *and* C. Turner Joy *Attacked*
In a repetition of the 2 August incident, the *Maddox* and the *C. Turner Joy* are attacked. After strenuous efforts to confirm the attacks, the President authorizes reprisal air strikes against the North.

5 Aug 1964   *US Reprisals*
US aircraft attack several DRV patrol boat bases, destroying ships and facilities.

7 Aug 1964   *Tonkin Gulf Resolutions*
At the time of the attacks, the President briefed leaders of Congress, and had a resolution of support for US policy introduced. It is passed with near-unanimity by both Houses.

Khanh Announces State of Emergency
Khanh announces a state of emergency that gives him near-dictatorial powers.

10 Aug 1964   *Taylor's first Monthly Report*
In his first monthly report to the President, Taylor gives a gloomy view of the political situation and of Khanh's capacities for effectively pursuing the war. He is equally pessimistic about other aspects of the situation.

11 Aug 1964   *President Signs Tonkin Resolution*
The President signs the Tonkin Gulf Resolution and pledges full support for the GVN.

12 Aug 1964   *Taylor and Khanh Meet*
Khanh discusses with Taylor his plan to draw up a new constitution enhancing his own powers. Taylor tries to discourage him.

14 Aug 1964   *Khanh shows Taylor Draft Charter*
At GVN NSC meeting, Khanh shows Taylor his proposed draft Constitution. Taylor dislikes its blatant ratification of Khanh as dictator.

16 Aug 1964   *Khanh Names President*
With the promulgation of the new constitution, Khanh is elected President by the MRC.

27 Aug 1964   *MRC Disbands*
After ten days of political turmoil and demonstrations, Khanh withdraws the constitution, the MRC names Khanh, Minh and Khiem to rule provisionally and disbands itself.

4 Sep 1964   *Khanh Resumes Premiership*
Khanh returns from Dalat and ends the crisis by resuming the Premiership.

6 Sep 1964   *Embassy Saigon Msg 768*
Taylor cables an assessment that ". . . at best the emerging governmental structure might be capable of maintaining a holding operation against the Viet Cong."

7 Sep 1964   *Washington Conference*
Taylor meets with the President and the NSC Principals and decisions are made to resume DE SOTO operations, resume 34A operations, and prepare for further tit-for-tat reprisals.

10 Sep 1964   *NSAM 314*
The 7 September decisions are promulgated.

13 Sep 1964   *Abortive Phat Coup*
General Phat launches a coup but it is defeated by forces loyal to Khanh. This establishes the power of younger officers such as Ky and Thi.

18 Sep 1964   *DE SOTO Patrol Attacked*
The first resumed DE SOTO patrol comes under apparent attack. To avoid future incidents, the President suspends the patrols.

26 Sep 1964   *Vietnam High National Council*
The MRC names a High National Council of distinguished citizens to prepare a constitution.

20 Oct 1964   *New Constitution Revealed*
The MRC presents the new constitution drafted by the High National Council. A prompt return to civilian government is promised.

1 Nov 1964   *Huong Names Premier*
Tran Van Huong, a civilian, is named Premier after the appointment of Phan Khac Suu as Chief of State, thus returning the government to civilian control.

1 Nov 1964   *VC Attack Bien Hoa Airport*
The VC launch a mortar attack on the Bien Hoa airfield that kills Americans and damages aircraft. The military recommend a reprisal against the North; the President refuses.

3 Nov 1964   *Johnson re-elected*
Lyndon Johnson is re-elected President with a crushing majority.

Task Force Begins Policy Review
At the President's request, W. P. Bundy heads an inter-agency Task

Force for an in-depth review of US Vietnam policy and options. The work goes on throughout the month.

26 Nov 1964   *Bundy Group Submits Three Options*
The Bundy Task Force submits its draft conclusions to the Principals. They propose three alternative courses of action: (1) continuation of current policy with no escalation and a resistance to negotiations; (2) a significant set of pressures against the North accompanied by vigorous efforts to start negotiations; (3) a modest campaign against the North with resistance to negotiations.

30 Nov 1964   *NSC Principals Modify Bundy Proposals*
The NSC Principals reject the pure form of any of the recommendations and instead substitute a two-phase recommendation for the President: the first phase is a slight intensification of current covert activities against the North and in Laos, the second after 30 days would be a moderate campaign of air strikes against the DRV.

1 Dec 1964   *President Meets with NSC and Taylor*
The President, in a meeting with the NSC Principals, and Taylor, who returned on 23 November, hears the latter's report on the grave conditions in SVN, then approves Phase I of the proposal. He gives tentative approval to Phase II but makes it contingent on improvement by the GVN.

3 Dec 1964   *President Confers with Taylor*
In a last meeting with Taylor, the President stresses the need to get action from the GVN before Phase II.

8 Dec 1964   *Taylor Sees Huong*
Taylor presents the President's requirements to Premier Huong who promises to get new action on programs.

14 Dec 1964   *BARREL ROLL Begins*
BARREL ROLL armed reconnaissance in Laos begins as called for in Phase I of the program approved 1 December.

20 Dec 1964   *Military Stage Purge*
The struggle within the MRC takes the form of a purge by the younger officers Ky and Thi. They are seeking to curb the power of the Huong Government.

21 Dec 1964   *Khanh Declares Support for Purge*
Khanh declares his support of the purge and opposes the US, Taylor in particular. He states he will not "carry out the policy of any foreign country." Rumors that Taylor will be declared *personna non grata* circulate.

24 Dec 1964   *US Billet in Saigon Bombed*
The VC bomb a US billet in Saigon on Christmas Eve, killing several Americans. The President disapproves military recommendations for a reprisal against the North.

31 Dec 1964   *Embassy Saigon Msg 2010*
Taylor recommends going ahead with the Phase II air campaign against the North in spite of the political instability and confusion

in the South. He now argues that the strikes may help stabilize the situation.

6 Jan 1965   *Bundy Memo to SecState*
In a memo to the Secretary of State, Wm Bundy urges that we consider some additional actions short of Phase II of the December plan in spite of the chaos is Saigon. It is the only possible course to save the situation.

8 Jan 1965   *ROK Troops go to SVN*
South Korea sends 2,000 military advisors to South Vietnam.

27 Jan 1965   *McNaughton Memo to SecDef*
In a memo to SecDef, McNaughton underscores the importance of SEA for the US and then suggests that we may have to adopt Phase II as the only way to save the current situation.

27 Jan 1965   *Khanh Ousts Huong Government*
Khanh and the younger officers oust the civilian Huong government. Khanh nominates General Oanh to head an interim regime the next day.

7 Feb 1965   *VC Mortar Attack Pleiku*
The VC launch a mortar attack on a US billet in Pleiku and an associated helicopter field. Many Americans are killed and helos damaged. The President, with the unanimous recommendation of his advisors, authorizes a reprisal.

FLAMING DART I
The reprisal strikes involve both US and VNAF planes. A second mission is flown the following day.

McGeorge Bundy Memo to the President
In an influential memo to the President after a fact-finding trip to Vietnam, Bundy concludes that the situation can only be righted by beginning sustained and escalating air attacks on the North à la Phase II. He had telephoned his concurrence in the FLAMING DART reprisal to the President from Vietnam.

8 Feb 1965   *McNamara Memo to JCS*
In a memo to the JCS, McNamara requests the development of a limited bombing program against the North. The JCS later submit the "Eight-week Program."

10 Feb 1965   *VC Attack Qui Nhon*
Thumbing their noses at the US reprisal, the VC attack a US billet in Qui Nhon and kill 23.

11 Feb 1965   *FLAMING DART II*
The second reprisal strikes authorized by the President attack targets in the North.

18 Feb 1965   *Coup Fails, but Khanh Ousted*
A coup against the new Premier, Quat, fails when the Armed Forces Council intervenes. They seize the opportunity to remove Khanh and he is forced to leave the country several days later.

24 Feb 1965   ROLLING THUNDER *Approved*
The President approves the first strikes for the ROLLING THUNDER sustained, escalating air campaign against the DRV.

2 Mar 1965   ROLLING THUNDER *Begins*
After being once postponed, the first ROLLING THUNDER strikes take place.

6 Mar 1965   *Marines to DaNang*
The President decides to send two US Marine Battalion Landing Teams to DaNang to take up the base security function. They arrive two days later.

14 Mar 1965   *General H. K. Johnson Report*
After a trip to Vietnam, the Army Chief of Staff, General Johnson, recommends a 21-point program to the President. Included are increased attacks on the North and removal of restrictions on these missions.

29 Mar 1965   *US Embassy Bombed*
Just as Ambassador Taylor is leaving for a policy conference in Washington, the US Embassy in Saigon is bombed by VC terrorists with loss of life and extensive property damage.

31 Mar 1965   *State Memo to the President*
In a 41-point non-military recommendation to the President, State elaborates on a Taylor proposal.

1 Apr 1965   *President Meets With NSC and Taylor*
At a meeting with Taylor and the NSC Principals, the President approves the 41-point non-military proposal, plus General Johnson's 21-point proposal. In addition, he decides to send two more Marine battalions and an air wing to Vietnam and to authorize an active combat role for these forces. He also authorizes 18,000–20,000 more support forces.

2 Apr 1965   *McCone Dissents from 1 Apr Decisions*
In a memo to SecState, SecDef, and Ambassador Taylor, CIA Director John McCone takes exception to the decision to give US troops a ground role. It is not justified unless we take radically stronger measures against North Vietnam.

6 Apr 1965   *NSAM 288*
NSAM 288 promulgates the decisions of the 1 April meeting.

7 Apr 1965   *President's Johns Hopkins Speech*
The President, in a speech at John Hopkins, offers unconditional talks with the DRV plus help in rebuilding after the war if they will cease aggression.

8 Apr 1965   *Pham Van Dong Announces 4 Points*
DRV Foreign Minister, Pham Van Dong, announces his four points for a Vietnam settlement. They are a defiant, unyielding repudiation of Johnson's offer.

15 Apr 1965   *State Department Msg 2332*
McGeorge Bundy informs Taylor that further increments of troops are being considered, plus use of US Army civil affairs personnel.

17 Apr 1965   *Embassy Saigon Msg 3419*
Taylor takes angry exception to the proposal to increase troops and to introduce military civil affairs personnel into the provinces. He did not think he had agreed on 1 April to a land war in Asia.

20 Apr 1965   *Honolulu Conference*
In a hastily called conference, McNamara informs Taylor in detail of the new policy directions and "brings him along." An attempt is made to mollify him.

I.   NSAM-273

A.   NSAM-273—THE AFTERMATH OF DIEM

NSAM 273 of 26 November 1963 came just four days after the assassination of President Kennedy and less than a month after the assassination of the Ngo brothers and their replacement by the Military Revolutionary Committee (MRC). NSAM 273 was an interim, don't rock-the-boat document. Its central significance was that although the two assassinations had changed many things, U.S. policy proposed to remain substantially the same. In retrospect, it is unmistakably clear, but it was certainly not unmistakably clear at that time, that this was a period of crucial and accelerated change in the situation in South Vietnam. NSAM 273 reflected the general judgment of the situation in Vietnam that had gained official acceptance during the previous period, most recently and notably during the visit of Secretary McNamara and General Taylor to Vietnam in late September of that year.

This generally sanguine appraisal had been the basis for the recommendation in that report to establish a program to train Vietnamese to carry out, by the end of 1965, the essential functions then performed by U.S. military personnel —by which time "it should be possible to withdraw the bulk of U.S. personnel." As an immediate gesture in this direction, the report recommended that "the Defense Department should announce in the very near future, presently pre- pared plans to withdraw one thousand U.S. military personnel by the end of 1963." The latter recommendation was acted upon the same day (2 October 1963) by making it part of a White House statement of *U.S. Policy on Vietnam.* This White House statement included the following pronuncement.

> Secretary McNamara and General Taylor reported their judgment that the major part of the U.S. military task can be completed by the end of 1965, although there may be a continuing requirement for a limited number of U.S. training personnel. They reported that by the end of this year the U.S. program for training Vietnamese should have progressed to the point where one thousand U.S. personnel assigned to South Vietnam can be withdrawn.

The visit of the Secretary of Defense and the Chairman of the Joint Chiefs to Saigon at the end of September was followed by the report to the President in early October and agreements reached with the President at the White House early in October following the Diem coup, a special meeting on Vietnam was held at CINCPAC headquarters on 20 November. Although this Honolulu meet- ing was marked by some concern over the administrative dislocation that had resulted from the coup of three weeks before, the tone remained one of optimism along the lines of the October 2 report to the President. Ambassador Lodge took note of what he called the "political fragility" of the new regime, but he was on the whole optimistic, and even mentioned that the statement on U.S. military withdrawal was having a continued "tonic" effect on the Republic of Vietnam (RVN). General Harkins in his report mentioned a sharp increase in Viet Cong (VC) incidents right after the coup, but added that these had dropped to normal within a week, and that there had, moreover, been compensating events such as additional Montagnards coming out of the hills to get government protection. All in all there was some uneasiness, perhaps, about unknown effects of the coup, but nothing was said to suggest that any serious departure was contemplated from the generally optimistic official outlook of late September and early October. And so, with reference to the statements of October 2, NSAM 273 repeated:

> The objectives of the United States with respect to the withdrawal of U.S. military personnel remain as stated in the White House statement of October 2, 1963.

Before examining further the background of NSAM 273—especially the appraisals of the Vietnam situation that it reflected—it is well to review some of the main provisions of that policy statement of 26 November 1963.

NSAM 273 was not comprehensive, as the McNamara–Taylor report of 2 October (discussed below) had been, nor as NSAM 288 was later to be. Mainly it served to indicate continuance by the new President of policies already agreed upon, and to demonstrate full support by the United States of the new government of Vietnam (GVN). Both military and economic programs, it was emphasized, should be maintained at levels as high as those in the time of the Diem regime. In addition, there was an unusual Presidential exhortation—reflecting the internal U.S. dispute over policy concerning Diem and Nhu that had made embarrassing headlines in October—that:

> The President expects that all senior officers of the government will move energetically to insure the full unity of support for established U.S. policy in South Vietnam. Both in Washington and in the field, it is essential that the government be unified. It is of particular importance that express or implied criticism of officers of other branches be assiduously avoided in all contacts with the Vietnamese government and with the press.

NSAM 273 was specifically programatic so far as SVN was concerned only in directing priority of effort to the Delta.

> (5) We should concentrate our efforts, and insofar as possible we should persuade the government of South Vietnam to concentrate its effort, on the critical situation in the Mekong Delta. This concentration should include not only military but political, economic, social, educational and informational effort. We should seek to turn the tide not only of battle but of belief, and we should seek to increase not only the controlled hamlets but the productivity of this area, especially where the proceeds can be held for the advantage of anti-Communist forces.

In general, the policies expressed by NSAM 273 were responsive to the older philosophy of our intervention there, which was that the central function of the U.S. effort was to help the South Vietnamese to help themselves because only if they did the major job themselves could that job in reality be done at all. We would assist stabilization of the new regime and head it in that direction.

(3) It is a major interest of the United States government that the present provisional government of South Vietnam should be assisted in consolidating itself in holding and developing increased public support.

Definition of the central task in South Vietnam as that of winning the hearts and minds of the people and of gaining for the GVN the support of the people had been the central consideration in the late summer and early fall of what to do about Diem and Nhu. The argument concerning the Diem government centered on the concept that the struggle in South Vietnam could not be won without the support of the South Vietnamese people and that under the Diem regime —especially because of the growing power and dominance of Nhu—the essential popular base was beyond reach. In the 2 October report to the President as well as in the discussions later at Honolulu on 20 November this theme was prominent. The U.S. could not win the struggle, only the Vietnamese could do that. For instance, in the report to the President of 2 October, there were these words in the section on "the U.S. military advisory and support effort."

> We may all be proud of the effectiveness of the U.S. military advisory and support. With few exceptions, U.S. military advisors report excellent relations with their Vietnamese counterparts, whom they characterize as proud and willing soldiers. The stiffening and exemplary effect of U.S. behavior and attitudes has had an impact which is not confined to the war effort, but which extends deeply into the whole Vietnamese way of doing things.
> *The U.S. advisory effort, however, cannot assure ultimate success. This is a Vietnamese war and the country and the war must in the end be run solely by the Vietnamese. It will impair their independence and development of their initiative if we leave our advisors in place beyond the time they are really needed* . . . [emphasis supplied]

Policy concerning aid to the Vietnamese may be considered to range between two polar extremes. One extreme would be our doing almost everything difficult for the Vietnamese, and the other would consist of limiting our own actions to provision of no more than material aid and advice while leaving everything important to be done by the Vietnamese themselves. Choice of a policy at any point on this continuum reflects a judgment concerning the basic nature of the problem; i.e. to what extent political and to what extent military; to what extent reasonable by political means and to what extent resolvable by military means even by outsiders. But in this case the choice of policy also reflected confidence that success was being achieved by the kind and level of effort that had already been devoted to this venture. The policy of NSAM 273 was predicated on such confidence. It constituted by its reference to the 2 October statement an explicit anticipation, with tentative time phases expressly stated, of the assumption by the Vietnamese of direct responsibility for doing all the important things themselves sometime in 1965, the U.S. thereafter providing only material aid and non-participating advice at the end of that period. That optimism was explicit in the report to the President of 2 October wherein the conclusion of the section on "The US Military Advisory and Support Effort" consisted of this paragraph:

> Acknowledging the progress achieved to date, there still remains the question of when the final victory can be obtained. If, by victory, we mean the reduc-

tion of the insurgency to something little more than sporadic banditry in outlying districts, it is the view of the vast majority of military commanders consulted that success may be achieved in the I, II, and III Corps area by the end of CY 1964. Victory in IV Corps will take longer—at least well into 1965. *These estimates assume that the political situation does not significantly impede the effort.* [emphasis supplied]

B. FIRST REAPPRAISALS OF THE SITUATION IN SOUTH VIETNAM

The caveat given expression in the last sentence of the conclusions cited above offered an escape clause, but it was clearly not employed as a basis for planning and for programming. It was not emphasized, and the lack of emphasis was consistent with the general tone of optimism in the report as a whole. This general optimism in fact reflected the judgments proferred by most of the senior officials upon whom the Secretary of Defense and the Chairman of the Joint Chiefs had principally relied for advice. It is obvious, however, that the optimism was scarcely consistent with the grave apprehension with which the political situation was viewed at the time.

Ever since the Buddhist crisis began in early summer, the fear had been felt at the highest U.S. policy levels that the explosiveness and instability of the political situation in Vietnam might undermine completely our efforts there. This apprehension had been the reason why the President first dispatched the Mendenhall–Krulak mission to Vietnam in early September, and then, a fortnight later, sent the McNamara–Taylor mission. The political crisis existing in Vietnam was indeed a subject of great concern at the very time of the latter visit. During this visit a decision was made that a proposed Presidential letter of remonstrance to Diem for his repressive policies concerning the Buddhists was tactically unwise and that, instead, a letter over the signature of the Joint Chiefs, ostensibly directed primarily to the military situation, should be delivered to Diem carrying a somewhat modified expression of protest. That letter dated October 1 was delivered to Diem on October 2 and included these judgments:

> Now, as Secretary McNamara has told you, a serious doubt hangs over our hopes for the future. Can we win together in the face of the reaction to the measures taken by your government against the Buddhists and the students? As a military man I would say that we can win provided there are no further political setbacks. The military indicators are still generally favorable and can be made more so by actions readily within the power of your government. If you allow me, I would mention a few of the military actions which I believe necessary for this improvement.

And, in closing the letter the CJCS expressed himself in these words:

> In closing, Mr. President, may I give you my most important overall impression? Up to now the battle against the Viet Cong had seemed endless; no one has been willing to set a date for its successful conclusion. After talking to scores of officers, Vietnamese and American, I am convinced that the Viet Cong insurgency in the North and Center can be reduced to little more than sporadic incidents by the end of 1964. The Delta will take longer but should be completed by the end of 1965. But for these predictions to be valid, certain conditions must be met. Your government should be prepared to energize all agencies, military and civil, to a higher output of activity than up to now. Ineffective commanders and province officials must

be replaced as soon as identified. Finally, there should be a restoration of domestic tranquility on the homefront if political tensions are to be allayed and external criticism is to abate. Conditions are needed for the creation of an atmosphere conducive to an effective campaign directed at the objectives, vital to both of us, of defeating the Viet Cong and of restoring peace to your country.

This letter was a policy instrument, of course, rather than exclusively an expression of an appraisal. As a matter of tactics it was softened considerably from the first proposed letter which was to say that the United States would consider disassociating itself from the Vietnam Government and discontinue support unless the GVN altered its repressive policies. It is cited here mainly to indicate the concern, made explicit by the senior members of the U.S. Mission in late September, concerning the possible effect upon military effectiveness of the political unrest.

About a week later, in testimony before the House Committee on Foreign Affairs, Secretary McNamara repeated the theme that the military situation was good, that the political situation was bad, that the political situation *could* have a bad effect on the military situation, but it had not had such a bad effect yet.

Following an appraisal of the military situation by Gen. Taylor, Chairman Morgan asked the SecDef "Mr. Secretary, then you feel and I am sure the General feels, that the military effort is going very well?" To this the SecDef's response was:

> *Secretary McNamara.* Yes we do. I think Gen. Taylor has emphasized and I would like to emphasize again, that while we believe the serious political unrest has not to date seriously and adversely affected the military effort, it may do so in the future, if it continues.
> *Chairman Morgan.* General, or Mr. Secretary, could we say that the military situation is moving well, but the political situation is not—the political situation is bad?
> *Secretary McNamara.* Yes, I think that is a fair summary.
> *Chairman Morgan.* Mr. Secretary, then, from your observations, both you and the General, from the 8 days you spent in the country, you can't see any deterioration in the military effort of SVN because of the political situation in the country?
> *Secretary McNamara.* This is a fair statement.
> *Chairman Morgan.* You feel that the Vietnamese Army is moving ahead and is cooperating with our forces in there?
> *Secretary McNamara.* Yes. Certain of the affairs of the Vietnamese Army have been affected by the political unrest of recent months. As Gen. Taylor pointed out, some of their relatives have been arrested and subjected to a violation of their personal freedoms and liberties, and undoubtedly this has tended to turn some of the officers away from support of their government.
> But they are strongly motivated by the desire to resist the Communist encroachment . . . and their anti-Communist feelings are stronger than their distrust of government. So to date there has been no reduction in the effectiveness of their military operations.

There is no record that this express recognition that the bad political situation might affect the military capability was considered a contingency to be foreseen in the program, or that anyone suggested it should be.

Nearly four months later Secretary McNamara had an explanation to offer concerning his view of the situation at the time of this testimony. Appearing once more in Executive Session to testify on the authorization bill for the fiscal year 1965, before the House Committee on Armed Services on 27 January 1964, the Secretary was asked by Mr. Chamberman of the House Committee to explain why

> his press conference comments on the situation the day before were clearly more optimistic than those in his Congressional statement. Both were more optimistic than recent news reports from Viet Nam.

In response, the Secretary went back to his Joint Report to the President of 2 October, to cite again the caveat which had been expressed as follows.

> The political situation in South Viet Nam remains deeply serious. The United States has made clear its continuing opposition to any repressive actions in South Viet Nam. While such actions have not yet significantly affected the military effort, they could do so in the future.

In further amplification of this point the Secretary almost claimed, in effect, to have foreseen and to have forecast the degradation of capability that it was then clear (in January 1964) had occurred and, had, in fact continued ever since November. These were his words,

> We didn't say—but I think you could have predicted that what we had in mind was—that (1) either Diem would continue his repressive measures and remain in power, in which case he would continue to lose public support and, since that is the foundation of successful counter guerilla operations, the military operations would be adversely affected, or (2) alternatively he would continue his repressive measures and build so much resistance that he would be thrown out, then a coup would take place, and during the period of reorganization following . . . there would be instability and uncertainty and military operations would be adversely affected.

No fully persuasive explanation has been discovered of the apparent discrepancy between this foresight concerning the possible ill effects of political instability and the generally optimistic prognosis and the program based upon that optimism. The Secretary had had no enthusiasm for the coup. Possibly he adjusted, though reluctantly, to the idea and decided that the political difficulties would either be overcome by means he did not feel it was his duty to explore, or would not be serious or lasting enough to be critical. However, all of the thinking then in vogue about counterinsurgency insisted that favorable political circumstances were essential to success. Therefore, unless it was assumed that favorable political circumstances could be brought about, the counterinsurgency effort was bound to fail. So long as the adverse case was not proved one had to assume ultimately favorable political conditions because it was unthinkable to stop trying.

Even before NSAM 273 was adopted, evidence began to accumulate that the optimistic assumptions underlying it were suspect. First, there was unmistakable and accumulating evidence that, in the period immediately after the coup, the situation had deteriorated in many places as a direct result of the coup. Then came increasing expression of a judgment that this deterioration was not merely an immediate and short lived phenomenon, but something, rather, that continued well after the worst administrative confusions immediately after the coup had been reduced. Finally, the impression, developed in many quarters, and eventually spread to all, that *before* the coup, the situation had been much more adverse than we had recognized officially at the time. Before the end of December, we decided to institute a system of covert checks on the accuracy of our basic intelligence—a large part of which came from Vietnamese sources. (There was suspicion that the interests of these officials were often served by reporting to us or to their superiors within the GVN what we or the GVN high officials *wanted* to hear.) As December and January and February passed, the situation reports trended consistently downward, the accumulating evidence seemed to indicate quite clearly that appreciation of setbacks and of adverse developments was regularly belated. The result was that programs tended commonly to be premised upon a more optimistic appraisal of the situation than was valid for the time when they were adopted, whether or not they were valid for an earlier period.

Judgments of the trend of events in Vietnam and of the progress of our program had long been a subject of controversy, both public and within the councils of government. That there had been an undercurrent of pessimism concerning the situation in Vietnam was no secret to the responsible officials who visited Vietnam in September and who reported to the President on 2 October, or to the larger group that convened at CINCPAC HQ on 20 November. Most of the qualifications in their minds related to imponderables of the political situation, which it was always hoped and assumed would be successfully resolved. The focus of the disagreement had generally been the policies of Diem and Nhu especially with respect to the Buddhists. During the summer of 1963, disagreement over the state of affairs in Vietnam had not only been aired in closed official councils, but had flared into open controversy in the public press in a manner that seemed to many to be detrimental to the U.S. It was possible to get directly conflicting views from the experts. One of the better known illustrations of this bewildering diversity of opinions among those with some claim to know is the instance recounted by both Schlesinger and Hilsman of the reports to President Kennedy on 10 September 1963 by General Victor Krulak and Mr. Joseph A. Mendenhall upon their return from their special mission to Vietnam. General Krulak was a specialist in counterinsurgency and Mr. Mendenhall had, not long before, completed a tour of duty in Saigon as Deputy Chief of Mission under Ambassador Durbrow. After hearing them both out (with Krulak painting the rosy picture and Mendenhall the gloomy one), the President, in the words of the Hilsman account, "looked quizzically from one to the other. You two did visit the same country, didn't you?"

Much of the disagreement concerning the progress of the anti-Viet Cong effort during the middle of 1963 was related intimately to issues posed by the Buddhist revolt. Where there was pessimism or scepticism about the progress of the war in general or the success of the pacification program, the attitude was generally associated with the judgment that Diem and Nhu were not administering affairs right and were alienating rather than winning the support of the masses of South Vietnamese people. Aside from Diem and Nhu and the Buddhist revolt, the major center of controversy was the situation in the Delta. The fact that NSAM 273 called for priority effort in the Delta reflected official recognition that the situation in the Delta demanded it. The ground work for this was laid during the McNamara–Taylor visit, but recognition of the serious problem there had come slowly and not without controversy.

A public controversy on the subject was touched off by an article filed in Saigon on 15 August 1963 by David Halberstam of the *New York Times*. The Halberstam article said that the RVN military situation in the Delta had deteriorated seriously over the past year, and was getting increasingly worse. The VC had been increasing greatly in number, were in possession of more and better arms and had larger stores of them, and their boldness to operate in large units—up to 600 or even 1,000 men—had become marked. The VC weapon losses were down, and the GVN weapon losses were up. U.S. military men and civilian officials in the field, according to this article, were reported to be very apprehensive of the effect of all this upon the Strategic Hamlet Program, and the whole future of GVN control in the Delta was in doubt. But, it was hinted strongly, higher echelon authorities were unwilling to perceive the dangers. "Some long-time observers are comparing official American optimism about the Delta to the French optimism that preceded France's route from Indochina in 1954. They warn of high-level self-deception."

The official refutation of the Halberstam article, prepared for the Secretary of Defense and the Chairman of the Joint Chiefs by SACSA, categorically denied everything. Based upon what it termed "the most reliable and accurate data available from both classified and unclassified sources" the analysis showed, in the language of its summary, that "the military situation is improving throughout the Republic of Vietnam, not as rapidly in the Mekong Delta as in the North, but improving markedly none the less. *The picture is precisely the opposite of the one painted by Mr. Halberstam.*" In the body of the refutation, 13 of the principle charges in the Halberstam article were analyzed, one-by-one, and battered by an array of percentages, statistics presented both tabularly and in graphs, and all of the numbers were very impressive and persuasive if taken at face value. They showed, for instance, that the VC armed attacks and VC initiated incidents (not armed), in mid-summer 1963 were below the 1962 average, that the average net weekly loss of GVN weapons to the VC had fallen from 62 in 1961 to 12 in 1962 to only 6 of 1963, and that the rate of both company-sized and battalion-sized VN attacks had fallen markedly, in 1963 from the 1962 level.

Generalizations about how the different groups, agencies, and echelons sided on the issue of the Vietnam situation tend to oversimplify because however they are made, there are exceptions. Most of the senior officers in-field in the direct line of operational responsibility tended to accept the more optimistic interpretation. Examples in this category would include CINCPAC (Admiral Felt), COMUSMACV (General Harkins), Ambassador Nolting (who was soon to be replaced, however, by Ambassador Lodge, who tended to be less optimistic), and CIA Station Chief Richardson. Nolting and Richardson had been charged to develop a close and friendly relationship with Diem, and this involved necessarily a special sort of sympathy for his outlook. The lives of most senior officers charged with operating responsibility have been pointed to giving leadership in situations of stress. This leadership includes setting an example of high morale, by their own conduct, to encourage enthusiastic *esprit de corps* among subordinates, and to project an unfailing image of confidence to the outside world. Such men are likely to find it almost impossible to recognize and to acknowledge existence of a situation seriously adverse to their assigned mission. It is contrary to their lifetime training never to be daunted. This characteristic makes them good leaders for difficult missions but it does not especially qualify them for rendering dispassionate judgments of the feasibility of missions or of the progress they are making. Admiral Felt and General Harkins in the field, and General Krulak in Washington, appear to have been more the *gung ho* type of leaders of men in combat situations than the cautious reflective weighers of complex circumstances and feasibilities, including political complications.

Officials and agencies in Washington who depended directly or primarily upon these officers for an understanding of the situation tended, very naturally, to put their greatest faith in the judgment of those in the field who were administratively responsible and who had access to the most comprehensive official reports and data. If there were disadvantages in the position of these people, a major one was that most of their information was supplied by GVN officials, who often had a vested interest in making things look good. Moreover, the U.S. officials in positions of operational responsibility had a professional commitment to programs which, often, they had had a hand in establishing. This normally inhibited them from giving the worst interpretation to evidence that was incomplete, ambiguous or inconclusive—and most evidence was one or more of these. Moreover, the public relations aspects of most positions of operating responsibility make it seem necessary to put a good face on things as a part of that operating responsibility. The morale of the organization seems to demand it. Finally, the intelligence provided on an official basis generally followed formats devised for uniform formal compilation and standard statistical treatment. All along the line, lower echelons were judged, rewarded or penalized by higher echelons in terms of the progress revealed by the reports they turned in. This practice encouraged and facilitated feeding unjustifiably optimistic data into the reporting machinery.

The darker view was easier for those who lacked career commitment to the success of the programs in the form in which they had been adopted. The more pessimistic interpretations were generally based, also, upon sources of information which were intimate, personal, out-of-channels, and with non-official personages. They were particularistic rather than comprehensive, intimate and intuitive rather than formal, impressionistic rather than statistical.

Moreover, some of the principal Cassandras were newsmen whose stories, whether correct or incorrect, made the front page and sometimes even the headlines. This suggested a vested interest in what for one reason or another was sensational. Other Cassandras were military advisors of junior grades, or lesser USOM officers especially those in the provinces, whose views were easy to discount by higher officials because, however familiar the junior officers might be with local acts or particular details, they generally lacked knowledge of the overall picture.

There was unquestionable ambivalence in U.S. official attitudes concerning progress and prospects. Despite the repeatedly expressed qualifications concerning the potentially grave effect of the political instability in Vietnam, the programming and policy formulation, as already noted, was without qualification based on optimistic assumptions. In an over-view of the Vietnam War (1960–1963) prepared by SACSA and delivered to the Secretary shortly after his return from South Vietnam, the mission's assessment of military progress was summarized in these terms:

> The evidences of overall military progress were so unmistakably clear that the mission, acknowledging the implications and uncertainties of the power crisis underway in Vietnam, concluded that the GVN military effort had achieved a momentum of progress which held further promise of ultimate victory over the Viet Cong; further, that victory was possible within reasonable limits of time and investment of U.S. resources.

The high priority of the Delta problem was recognized, in this same over-view, with the statement that "the mission was impressed with the evidence that the decisive conflict of the war was approaching in the Mekong Delta." The major difficulty there was identified somewhat euphemistically as due to the fact that "the mission found evidences that the Government of Vietnam had overextended its hamlet construction program in these southern provinces."

Not long before this, however, Michael Forrestal in the White House had sent to Secretary McNamara a copy of a *Second Informal Appreciation of the Status of the Strategic Hamlet Program* dated 1 September 1963, and prepared by USOM Regional Affairs officers. This *Appreciation* gave province by province summaries that were far from encouraging concerning the Delta. In addition to Long An and Dinh Tuong provinces which were the worst, it was said of Kien Tuong that

> the program continues to be slow . . . few hamlets are completed and a fraction of planned militia trained . . . the one bright spot . . . remains the Pri Phap area, which is, however, vulnerable militarily should the VC decide to concentrate their efforts against it. The Chief of Province . . . we feel is totally unqualified. *Vinh Binh,* although the hamlet program continued to increase in numbers . . . the security situation deteriorated in July and August. The removal of a recently introduced RVN battalion damaged the effort, and a change in leadership dislocated projects underway . . . Nhi Long has been severely threatened in August, the route to Vinh Long is again insecure . . . elsewhere the hamlet program appears to be over-extended and with insufficient troop support is under serious threat in former VC strongholds. Security in southernmost Long Toan District, the province VC haven, continues to be very poor . . . Major Thao, an extremely competent leader, . . . was replaced in late July . . .
> *Vinh Long:* Although most signs indicate progress . . . evaluation of Vinh Long remains largely an evaluation of Lt. Col. Phuoc, Chief of Province . . . whose idea had previously led him to construct through corvee labor kilometer after kilometer of useless walls, and whose insensitivity to the population had led to considerable popular antipathy. An apparent change of attitude has taken place . . . and Phuoc now says that the strategic hamlet is a state of mind rather than a fortification. Phuoc's sincerity and commitment to the program are still problematical, however, as is public acceptance of him and of the program . . . some pessimists feel that this may well prove . . . the most difficult province in the Delta to pacify.
> *Chuong Thien:* The Communists still control most of the people and land in Chuong Thien . . . [the] new province chief . . . has been evasive and has shown no desire really to cooperate . . . the large relocation effort . . . risks loss of the province to the VC because the people involved have been alienated.
> *Ba Xuyen:* Shortcoming in the implementation of the hamlet program, as well as a lack of confidence in the province chief . . . led to the recall in late August of the USOM provincial representative and possible unofficial suspension of USOM . . . in an effort to build statistics, the province had constructed a number of vulnerable and non-viable hamlets. There has been a forced wholesale relocation, insufficiently justified, poorly financed . . . numerous occurrences have convinced us that there is venality . . . and lack of good faith. A new province chief (not presently in prospect) might permit progress in this rich and important area . . . a major effort to gain popular support for government is needed in this as in many other Delta provinces.
> *An Xuyen:* The province remains under VC control with the exception of a handful of widely separated government strong points . . . An Xuyen,

comprising much of the enemy's main Delta power center, is a primary source of men, money and supplies for the Communists.

Whether or not the full seriousness of the situation in the Delta was appreciated at the time of the McNamara–Taylor mission in September 1963, it is entirely clear that the Delta was recognized as a high priority problem. The recommendations set forth in their joint Report to the President of 2 October called for "the training and arming of hamlet militia at an accelerated rate, especially in the Delta" and for "a consolidation of the Strategic Hamlet Program, especially in the Delta, and action to insure that in the future strategic hamlets are not built until they can be protected and until civic action programs can be introduced." And in the appraisal of overall progress, the judgments were rendered that

The Delta remains the toughest area of all, and now requires top priority in both GVN and U.S. efforts. Approximately 40 percent of the people live there; the area is rich and has traditionally resisted central authority; it is the center of Viet Cong strength—over one-third of the "hard-core" are found there; and the maritime nature of the terrain renders it much the most difficult region to pacify.

During the Honolulu meeting of 20 November when Gen. Harkins presented a summary of the situation in 13 critical provinces, 7 were in the Delta. Secretary McNamara in a detailed discussion on that occasion of the situation on these provinces suggested that there were three things to be done in the Delta: (1) to get the Chieu Hoi program moving; (2) to get the fertilizer program going in order to increase the output of rice, and (3) most important, to improve the security of strategic hamlets by arming and training and increasing the numbers of the militia. It is recorded that at this point General Taylor made a suggestion that perhaps we needed joint U.S.–Vietnamese province teams to attack problems at the province level because the problems were in fact different in each province. This latter seems worth noting in view of the emphasis that was to be placed, some months later, upon getting more Americans into a supervisory or advisory capacity in the provincial areas.

When General Harkins presented his review of the military situation at this meeting, he indicated that weapon losses were quite high, particularly in November when the government forces lost nearly 3 weapons to every one captured from the VC. The losses were incurred largely by the Civil Guard, the Self-Defense Corps and the hamlet militia. It was also indicated at the meeting that the greatest single difficulty of a pacification program was in the problem of security in the hamlets. The assumptions were retained that: (1) the Communist insurgency would be brought under control in the Northern two-thirds of the country by the end of calendar year '64, the phase down of the RVNAF could be started at the beginning of calendar year 1965 (instead of the previous estimate of calendar year '66); and this resulted in a reduction from previous estimates of funding for the RVNAF (excluding para-military and police) as follows: (in millions of dollars)

Fiscal year '65	225.2–213.3
Fiscal year '66	225.5–197.4
Fiscal year '67	143.5–131.2
Fiscal year '68	122.7–119.7
Fiscal year '69	121.9–119.5

While those from Washington who were attending the conference at Honolulu, and Ambassador Lodge, were returning to Washington, President Kennedy was assassinated. The following day, on 23 November, a memorandum was prepared to guide the new President for his meeting with Ambassador Lodge. The main points of this guidance stressed the need for teamwork within this U.S. mission.

> It is absolutely vital that the whole of the country team, and particularly Ambassador Lodge and General Harkins, work in close harmony and with full consultation, back-and-forth. There must be no back-biting or sniping at low levels such as may have contributed to recent news stories about General Harkins being out of favor with the new regime . . .

C.   FIRST ACTIONS ON NSAM–273 AND FIRST MISGIVINGS

In response to the call for priority of effort to turn the tide in the Delta, an additional ARVN division was shifted to the Delta, and directives were issued to COMUSMACV to effect an increase in military tempo there, especially to improve tactics, to maintain full strength in combat elements, in arming and training hamlet militia. Along with this, he was to consolidate strategic hamlet programs to bring the pace of construction to a level consistent with GVN capabilities both to provide essential protection and to introduce civic action programs. AID actions to increase production in the Delta were also initiated and accelerated—fertilizer, pesticides, rice seed, the hamlet school program and hamlet medics, generators and radio sets, etc. USOM had, further, conveyed to the GVN its assurance that, subject to Congressional appropriations, the U.S. fully intended to maintain the level of aid previously given to the Diem Government.

Scarcely more than a week after the formalization of NSAM 273 on 26 November 1963, the adverse trend of events that previously had been only rumored or feared moved much closer to being acknowledged to be an unmistakable and inescapable reality. On 7 December (Saigon time), Ambassador Lodge forwarded a report of USOM provincial representative Young on the situation in Long An province as of 6 Demember. Part of that report was as follows:

> (1) The only progress made in Long An province during the month of November, 1963 has been by the Communist Viet Cong. The past thirty days have produced a day-by-day elimination of US/Vietnamese sponsored strategic hamlets and the marked increase in Viet Cong influence, military operations, physical control of the countryside and Communist controlled combat hamlets.
>
> (2) At the end of September, 1963 province officials stated that 219 strategic hamlets were completed and met the 6 criteria. Effective 30 November 1963 this figure has been reduced to about 45 on the best estimates of MAAG, USOM and new province chief, Major Dao. Twenty-seven hamlets were attacked in November compared with a figure of 77 for June. This would appear to be an improvement. However, the explanation is a simple one: so many strategic hamlets have been rendered ineffective by the Viet Cong that only 27 were worth attacking this month . . .
>
> (4) The reason for this unhappy situation is the failure of the government of Vietnam to support and protect the hamlets. The concept of the strategic hamlet called for a self-defense corps capable of holding off enemy

attack for a brief period until regular forces (ARVN, Civil Guard, or SDC) could come to the rescue. In hamlet after hamlet this assistance never came, or in most cases, arrived the following morning during daylight hours . . .

(5) Two explanations are presented for the lack of assistance: (a) there are not sufficient troops to protect key installations and district headquarters and at the same time go to the assistance of the hamlet. (b) Both official orders and policy prohibit the movement of troops after dark to go to the assistance of hamlets or isolated military posts . . .

(9) The strategic hamlet program in this province can be made workable and very effective against the Viet Cong. But help must come immediately in the form of additional troops and new concepts of operation, not in the same reheated French tactics of 1954, beefed up with more helicopters and tanks. The hamlets must be defended if this province is not to fall under complete control of the Viet Cong in the next few [material missing]

(11) See also General Don's statement to me on Long An, notably his statement that totally useless and impractical hamlets were built with forced labor so that grafters would receive the money allocated to strategic hamlets . . .

(12) I am asking MACV and USOM to find out how the above and the scandalous conditions described by General Don escaped inspection.

This report on Long An province reached Washington about the same time that a Cabinet level meeting at the Department of State was being held to review the situation in Vietnam and discuss possible further actions. A briefing on the situation was presented, on behalf of the Defense Department and the Secretary, by General Krulak. General Krulak's briefing included the following conclusions:

a. The new GVN shows a desire to respond to U.S. advice and improve its military effectiveness and has the capability to do so. Its plans are basically sound but it is in a state of organizational turmoil which cannot fail to affect its capabilities adversely for the short term.

b. The VC are making an intensive although loosely coordinated effort to increase their hold on the countryside while the new government is shaking down.

c. The VC have exhibited a powerful military capability for at least a brief period of intensified operations and their skill at least in counter airborne operations is improving.

d. There is ground for concern that infiltration of materiel support has increased in the Delta area but there is little hard proof. This is a prime intelligence deficiency since it affects not only the military tactics but our overall Southeast Asia strategy.

The prevailing view at this time seems to have been more apprehensive than Gen. Krulak's briefing would suggest. It was immediately decided that the Secretary should have another look at the situation by returning from the December NATO meeting *via* Saigon.

The Backup Book for the Secretary of Defense's Saigon trip of 18–20 December contains indications of the major questions that he proposed to look into during his brief projected visit to Vietnam. The Young Report on Long An Province as of 6 December had evidently made a strong impression, and it seems the Secretary was especially anxious to safeguard against being misled in the future about the status of programs. With respect to the Strategic Hamlet Program generally, it is evident that there was apprehension concerning the questionable statistics that had been used in the Diem regime's portrayal of the program. It was hoped that it would be possible to identify the requirements for a program of on-going current assessments of the program as quickly as possible. There was also an intention to publish an appropriate set of new guidelines for the coordination of construction, civic action and military programs, and, perhaps more important, to accomplish the consolidation and correction of hamlet programs in the shortest possible time. Five problem areas with respect to the strategic hamlet program were identified prior to the trip, these were:

a. What progress is being achieved by the surveys and when will the reports be available?
b. What specific actions were then underway to coordinate the companion military, political and social programs?
c. When would the new guidelines be published?
d. What action was underway to indoctrinate the newly assigned province officials to enable them to pursue the program effectively?
e. Was it plain that one big problem would be to insure that the province and district officials understood and executed vigorously their revised programs? Had any thought been given to adding an additional advisor or two, in the critical provinces, to work at the district level and to insure that the officials actually drove programs forward.

A point to be noted in these is the growing idea of placing an increasing number of advisors at the province and district level.

The Secretary made certain decisions of an immediate nature concerning programs in Vietnam while he was still in Saigon; and immediately upon his return he made his report to the President in which he described the situation as he had found it, and made further recommendations that he had evidently not felt empowered to enact without Presidential approval.

Among the actions agreed upon during the visit to Saigon on 19–20 December were the following:

1. The GVN should be pressed to increase troop density in six provinces in III Corps by about 100% (ten infantry and three engineering batallions), in accordance with plans discussed at a meeting with COMUSMACV and the Ambassador.
2. Revise the pacification plans for critical provinces to insure that they reflect scheduling and programming "based on a realistic appraisal of the actual status of the hamlets, the SDC and Civil Guard and ARVN as well as the rehabilitation materials available."
3. Increase U.S. military advisory strength in the thirteen critical provinces (agreed to be critical at Honolulu) in accordance with a table submitted by COMUSMACV.
4. Reinforce USOM representation in thirteen critical provinces starting with Long An in accordance with a proposal from USOM Saigon.
5. Provide uniforms for the SDC with priority on the Delta area.
6. Press the GVN for a clear statement, in form of orders to province chiefs, for continuance and reshaping of the hamlet program.

7. Press the GVN to provide for a Joint General Staff (JCS) chief, and for a III Corps commander with no other responsibilities.

8. Continue to stress to the GVN the need for forceful central leadership and effective and visible popular leadership.

The Secretary's report for the President dated 21 December '63 [Doc. 52] was gloomy and expressed fear that the situation had been deteriorating long before any deterioration had been suspected (officially). The report began by saying that the situation was "very disturbing," and that unless current trends were reversed within two or three months they would "lead to neutralization at best and more likely to a Communist-controlled state." The new government of Big Minh was identified as the greatest source of concern because it seemed indecisive and drifting. There seemed to be a clear lack of administrative talent and of political experience. While on the other hand generals who should have been directing military affairs were preoccupied with political matters [i.e., working to assure or to increase their own political power within the RMC].

A second major weakness seemed to the Secretary to be the Country Team. He felt that it lacked leadership and had been "poorly informed" and was "not working according to a common plan." He had found as an example of confusion conflicts between USOM and military recommendations, in cases of recommendations to the government of Vietnam and Washington concerning the size of the military budget. "Above all, Lodge has virtually no official contact with Harkins." The Ambassador, the Secretary felt, simply could not conduct a coordinated administration—not because he did not wish to, but because he had "operated as a loner all his life and cannot readily change now." Concerning enemy progress, the report said

> Viet Cong progress has been great during the period since the coup, *with my best guess being that the situation has in fact been deteriorating in the countryside since July to a far greater extent than we realized because of undue dependence on distorted Vietnamese reporting.* The Viet Cong now control very high proportions of the people in certain key provinces, particularly those directly South and West of Saigon. [Doc. 52] [emphasis supplied]

As remedial measures he recommended that the government of Vietnam be required to reallocate its military forces so that its effective strength in these key provinces would be essentially doubled. There would also have to be major increases in both the U.S. military staff and the USOM staff, to the point where the numbers of Americans assigned in the field would give the U.S. a reliable independent U.S. appraisal of the status of operations. (This was a clear enough indication of the Secretary's unhappiness with past reporting.) Third, he stated that a "realistic pacification plan" would have to be prepared. Specifically, they should allocate adequate time to make the remaining government controlled areas secure, and only then work from them into contiguous surrounding areas.

The Secretary stressed that the situation was worst in the Delta and surrounding the capitol, and that in the North things were better, and that General Harkins remained hopeful that the latter areas could be made reasonably secure late in the year. The report expressed considerable concern over the increasing infiltration of men and equipment from North Vietnam. Various proposals to counter this infiltration had been discussed in Saigon, but the Secretary was not yet convinced that there were means that were politically acceptable and militarily feasible of stopping that infiltration.

Minh had strongly opposed any ideas of possible neutralization of Vietnam. (This was taken to dispose of proposals suggested by Senator Mansfield, President DeGaulle, the *New York Times,* columnist Walter Lippman and others).

Concerning a possible escalation of U.S. effort, the Secretary indicated that he had directed supply of a modest increase in artillery, but, "US resources and personnel cannot usefully be substantially increased."

In concluding, the Secretary said that his appraisal might be overly pessimistic, and that Lodge, Harkins and Minh, while agreeing on specific points, seemed to feel that January might bring a significant improvement.

Following his report to the President, the Secretary made the following remarks to the press, at the White House:

> . . . We have just completed our report to the President . . . We observed the results of the very substantial increase in VC activity, an increase which began shortly after the new government was formed, and has extended over a period of several weeks.
> During this time, the Viet Cong have attacked and attacked successfully, a substantial number of the strategic hamlets. The rate of that VC activity, however, has substantially dropped within the past week to ten days.
> This rapid expansion of activity, I think, could have been expected. It was obviously intended to take advantage of the period of organization in the new government . . . We received in great detail the plans of the South Vietnamese and the plans of our military advisors for operations during 1964. We have every reason to believe they will be successful. We are determined that they shall be.

D. EFFORTS TO IMPROVE INTELLIGENCE ON PROGRESS OF THE WAR

The Secretary had made evident in his memo of 21 December to the President that he had become seriously disturbed at the failure of the reporting system in Vietnam to alert him promptly to the deterioration of the situation there. CIA Director McCone had accompanied him on the trip to Saigon and, immediately upon his return, Mr. McCone initiated efforts to improve the reporting system. On 23 December he wrote the Secretary:

> . . . information furnished to us from MACV and the Embassy concerning the current Viet Cong activities in a number of provinces and the relative position of the SVN Government versus the Viet Cong forces was incorrect, due to the fact that the field officers of the MAAG and USOM had been grossly misinformed by the province and district chiefs. It was reported to us, and I believe correctly, that the province and district chiefs felt obliged to "create statistics" which would meet the approbation of the Central Government.
> I believe it is quite probable that the same practice might be repeated by the new province and district chiefs appointed by the MRC . . .

McCone, therefore, proposed development of a new, covert method of checking on the information supplied by these regular reporting authorities on the progress of the war and on pacification and other counterinsurgency efforts. A plan was developed within CIA by 3 January 1964 which called for the formation of a mission of 10 to 12 experienced intelligence officers, all drawn from CIA, to proceed to Saigon for a 60 to 90 day TDY beginning about 12 January. There, under the direction of the CAS Station Chief, they would undertake:

1. A survey of Vietnamese/American counterinsurgency reporting machinery;
2. Develop, assess, and recruit new covert sources of information, to serve as a check, and finally,
3. Assist the station chief in developing recommendations, for submission to Washington through the Saigon country team, on means of improving overall GVN and US reporting machinery.

McCone forwarded these plans to McNamara on 7 January for discussion at a meeting that same day. Following the meeting of 7 January on this original proposal, a revised proposal was drawn up and submitted by McCone to McNamara for concurrence on 9 January. The revision was largely responsive to a fear of the Secretary that, as originally proposed, the TDY team would serve as a sort of Inspector General functioning independently of both the Country Team and the CAS Station/Saigon. Accordingly the new draft expressly specified that a separate reporting system would *not* be established, nor a reorganization of the existing reporting system attempted. It would attempt, however, to develop through covert techniques a method of spot checking the accuracy of regular reporting and develop also new covert sources of information on the progress of the war.

In accepting the proposal in a written reply dated 16 January, Secretary McNamara expressed insistence on making this a team effort, first by emphasizing that "I do not believe that the team should have an inspectoral function for the overall reporting system," and second by adding to the draft submitted for his signature the clause, "but it should be a joint program involving all of the affected members of the country team." When the definitive messages went out to Saigon they had the concurrence of State, Defense and CIA.

It is understandable enough from an administrative point of view that a formally coordinated unified effort seemed preferable. There had been notable discords, and failures of communication, and policy disagreement within the Mission in the past and these had caused serious problems. Important sources of disagreement remained, and anything resembling an IG inquiry might have brought about morale problems that it was well to avoid. The reverse of the coin was that formalized coordination of intelligence stood the chance of stifling or concealing minority dissent. It was indeed the basic mission of the group to set up checks. But in the extent to which this system of checks was to be coordinated with the system as a whole, it risked losing some part of its independence of the accepted view. And it had been the accepted view that had been proved wrong.

By the time full agreement was reached on the terms of reference for the team, the team was already in Saigon. A month later it submitted a report evaluating the situation in Viet Nam at about the same time that the CAS station chiefs submitted two other evaluations which were apparently for a time mistakenly attributed to the TDY team. These evaluations caused enough uneasiness within the country team to indicate that interpretation of intelligence and situation appraisals remained the touchy matter that the Secretary had foreseen. The "Initial Report of CAS Group Findings in SVN," dated 10 February 1964 began by acknowledging that the group activities had been temporarily disrupted by the Khanh Coup of 30 January (which will be described later), and did not attempt to report on the covert cross checks because before covert cross checks could be established it was necessary to learn the pattern and nature of the reporting system then in use, both American and Vietnamese. The first appraisals, therefore, were expressly based solely on a new look at what the existing system reported. The first impression of the group was that for the most part the Vietnamese had been reporting honestly to their American counterparts since the 1 November coup and that if current reporting was indeed biased it was biased against the Diem regime.

The first general impression of the situation, expressly subject to further inquiry, was that "the momentum of the strategic hamlet program has slowed practically to a halt." More specific evaluations, which focused on local situations north and east of Saigon and took up most of this initial report, were more pessimistic than the "general impression." Within Binh Long Province, security had deteriorated rapidly during January and the VC now controlled route 13. Well planned and viciously executed VC attacks on hamlets had caused wide fear, and produced doubt among the populace that the GVN could protect them. The former province chief and deputy chief for military operations had been replaced just two days before the Khanh coup. The response to the Khanh coup had been one of disgust. Phuoc Thanh Province, according to the province chief, was 80% controlled by the VC. The VC controlled the roads, making GVN travel impossible without large armed escorts. The VC were moving freely in battalion size units with heavy weapons throughout the province. COMUSMACV had reported that the one to one GVN/VC ratio in the province was misleading because many of the GVN units were tied down in static positions whereas the VC were mobile.

When the Special CAS group turned in its final appraisal on 18 February, Gen. Harkins was asked by the CGCS to comment. Gen. Harkins offered, 3 days later, a paragraph by paragraph commentary, much of which agreed with the CAS group findings. There were a few minor points of fact that were in disagreement. Where General Harkins pointedly disagreed was in the matter of interpretation and emphasis and where both the CAS group and Gen. Harkins agreed that past performance had not been good, Gen. Harkins tended to emphasize the hope, as the CAS group did not, that under Khanh the situation would perhaps improve. Beyond this, Gen. Harkins was, in general, somewhat disturbed that the CAS group might be exceeding its terms of reference by reporting unilaterally, and misleading the national decision process by forwarding information not coordinated and cleared with other elements of the U.S. reporting mechanism in Vietnam. Perhaps most significant of all, at the very beginning of his comments he offered an observation that, internationally or otherwise, raised very basic issues of the nature, function, and limitations of the intelligence and estimation process.

> Except for the spectacular and eye catching lead sentence ["Tide of insurgency in all four corps areas appears to be going against GVN"], I have no quarrel with most of the statements contained in the CAS Survey Team appraisal. Where the statements are *clean-cut*, the supporting information was usually provided by my field personnel and reflected in reports already sent to Washington by this headquarters. Where the statements are sweeping, they are based on opinion or an *unfortunate penchant for generalizing from the specific*. My detailed comments follow and are geared to the specific paragraphs of the CAS message. [emphasis supplied.]

If we examine this statement with particular reference to the words and phrases underlined, the large, epistemological problem of the junction of intelligence and national decision-making is pointedly indicated. By "clean-cut," Gen. Harkins undoubtedly referred to phenomena that were concrete, highly specific and narrowly factual. These were the sort of phenomena about which there could seldom or never be any serious dispute. By "sweeping" statements, and by "unfortunate penchant for generalizing from the specific," he was referring to the mental process of bridging the gap from the small concrete detail —which was seldom or never by itself a basis for large decision—to the interpretation of that detail—to the judgment of the significant of that detail. Only upon the basis of interpretations (judgments) of the importance, meaning and relevance of things could policy decisions be made. And that judgment or interpretation was seldom or never inescapably inherent in the measurable, sharply definable, completely unarguable concrete detail. It might be derived from or directly reflect such data, but its form would be determined equally, or even more, from the perspective in which it was viewed. And this perspective was comprised of the whole context of incompletely described, not fully identified values, and imperfectly defined priorities, that determined the weight and place given to that factual detail in the mysterious calculus of the decision-maker. If this were not the case, any bright college boy given the same set of "facts" would inevitably derive from them the same judgments of what national policy should be, as the canniest, most generally knowledgeable and experienced veteran.

E. THE UNREALIZED JANUARY UPTURN AND THE KHANH COUP

There was hope that as January 1964 wore on the situation would take a turn for the better. But, as the CAS reports cited in the foregoing section suggest, things did not get better. The hope was that the Minh regime would find itself, but before it did the Khanh coup of 30 January came as another blow to progress in the operating program and as a disillusioning surprise to the hopes for the stable political situation generally agreed to the prerequisite to ultimate success.

Despite the unfavorable news—which was beginning to excite the first serious proposals within the JCS for carrying the war to the north by expanded clandestine operations and finally by overt bombing—the Secretary managed to maintain the earlier philosophy that the U.S. involvement would remain limited and that in fact the counterinsurgency effort could not really attain its goals unless the U.S. role continued to be limited and the South Vietnamese did the main job themselves.

Just before the Khanh coup, in testimony on 27 and 29 January before the House Armed Services Committee, the Secretary encountered some sharply probing questions on the continuing costs of the war. The questions centered on the inconclusiveness of the efforts to date and upon the apparent discrepancies between autumnal optimism and the winter discouragements, and between official optimism and the pessimistic reports appearing in newspaper stories. Even Mr. Mendel Rivers, evidently impatient that the VC had not already been subdued and perhaps suspecting that this was due to lack of vigor in our prosecution of the war, asked during these hearings if we were planning to "do anything to bring this war to the VC, any more than what we have done already . . ." The Secretary tried to explain that ". . . It is a Vietnamese war. They are going to have to assume the primary responsibility for winning it. Our policy is to limit our support to logistical and training support." To this, Mr. Rivers replied with the following question: "There are no plans to change the modus operandi of this war, so far as the bleeding of this country is concerned?"

A little later, Representative Chamberlain asked the Secretary if he continued to be as "optimistic" about the scheduled withdrawal of U.S. personnel as he had been in October. The Secretary in reply reaffirmed that he believed that:

> . . . the war in South Vietnam will be won primarily through the South Vietnamese efforts; it is a South Vietnamese war. It is a war of the counter guerrillas as against the guerrillas. We are only assisting them through training and logistical support.
>
> We started the major program of assistance in training and logistical support toward the latter part of 1961. I think it is reasonable to expect that after four years of such training we should be able gradually to withdraw certain of our training personnel.

Following this, Representative Stratton addressed an inquiry to the Secretary:

> Mr. Secretary, I am a little bit worried about your statement in answer to Mr. Chamberlain, that you still contemplate continuing withdrawal of our forces from Vietnam, in line with your previously announced plan. Isn't this a little unrealistic, in view of the fact that when you first made the announcement things were going a bit better than they appear to be going at the moment? And wouldn't you say that in the event that things do not go as well as you hope they will, that unquestionably we can't continue to withdraw any more of our forces?

Secretary McNamara's reply:

> No Sir, I would not. I don't believe that we as a nation should assume the primary responsibility for the war in South Vietnam. It is a counter-guerrilla war, it is a war that can only be won by the Vietnamese themselves. Our responsibility is not to substitute ourselves for the Vietnamese, but to train them to carry on the operations that they themselves are capable of.

The theme was next picked up by Representative Cohelan. He said that "One of the things that some of us are quite concerned about is this constant tendency toward a sanguine approach to the problem of Southeast Asia." He went on to recall that when he and other committee members had been out to South Vietnam in November of 1962, when General Harkins was saying the war would be won in 2 years and Admiral Felt said it would be won in 3 years—although Halberstam and other newsmen were pessimistic at that time and now seemed, to Representative Cohelan, to have been right

[material missing]

transport anything for fear of ambush by ground, although the Vietnamese themselves could move the freight by some kind of pay-off to the Viet Cong.

In response to this the Secretary said that we were in a very different position than the French had been and that in this sort of war improvement was bound to be slow—a matter of years. But this did not mean we should retain all of our existing personnel in South Vietnam. It would be a waste to do so, and by "keeping the crutch there too long we would weaken the Vietnamese rather than strengthen them."

Within a day or two after this testimony was given there came the Khanh coup, which constituted not only another hard blow to our efforts in Vietnam but also to our confidence that we knew what was going on there. The Khanh coup of 30 January 1964 came as an almost complete surprise to the mission and to Washington. What may be considered in retrospect, but only in retrospect, as the first very general danger signal came in the form of a conversation between the US/DCM in Saigon and Italian Ambassador D'Orlandi, on 20 January, and reported that same evening to Washington. In discussing the current French initiative in Asia (recognition of Communist China and advocacy of neutralization of SEA), the Italian Ambassador had said that the greatest danger to the U.S. position in Southeast Asia lay in the effect it might have upon certain pro-French and potentially neutralist members of the MRC. When asked to clarify, D'Orlandi named Generals Tran Van Don and Ton Thap Dinh as potential leaders of a group that might accept a French neutralization formula, especially if the U.S. position on that issue were not clarified immediately. In reporting the incident the Embassy commented it had no hard evidence of either of these two flirting with neutralization, although because of French training they were frequently cited as pro-French.

A few days later Ambassador Lodge issued a public statement which acknowledged existence of neutralization rumors and proceeded to affirm that U.S. policy remained unchanged and that the U.S., "In solidarity with the Government of the Republic of Vietnam, firmly rejects the spurious idea of 'neutralizing' South Vietnam since 'neutralization' would simply be another means of Communist take-over."

The first warning of the coup that may be considered specific and definite, however, did not come until 28 January, when General Khanh told Colonel Jasper Wilson, U.S. Senior MAAG advisor for I Corps, that pro-French, pro-neutralist members of the MRC—Generals Xuan, Don, and Kim—were planning a palace coup that would take place as early as 31 January. Once the coup was effected, they would call for neutralization of South Vietnam. It was not reported that in the conversation with Wilson, Khanh had expressly suggested that he might try a counter coup action. He did say, however, that he planned to go to Saigon that day or on the morrow. In reporting this conversation to Lodge and Harkins in Saigon and to CIA/Washington, CAS cited four other recent intelligence items, from other sources, which might have lent some credence to the Khanh allegations (although in the course of time Khanh's allegations were discounted almost entirely). These were (1) Tran Van Ly gained impression in conversation with Xuan that Xuan favored a coup. (2) Lt. Col. Tran Dinh Lam, recently brought back from Paris at the request of Generals Tran Van Don and Le Van Kim, was reported to have French authorization to spend 2 billion piastres to achieve a neutralization of South Vietnam. (3) An American had observed several military trucks bringing weapons and ammunition to Xuan's police headquarters at Camp DuMare. (4) Generals Kim, Don, Nguyen Van Vy, and Duong Van Duc had been identified by Major General Le Van Nghiem as pro-French and privately in favor of neutralization. Nevertheless, Khanh's charges along with other reports were described by CAS as difficult to evaluate; and it was speculated that he and others making similar charges might be motivated by disgruntlement over failure to obtain better positions for themselves within the MRC.

The next move in this sequence of events was when General Khanh talked to Ambassador Lodge in Saigon on the afternoon of 29 January. The striking thing is that although Khanh evidently made his intentions clear, the Ambassador's first thought was to protest to DeGaulle rather than to warn the GVN. That evening at 8:00 p.m., Ambassador Lodge filed a NODIS (Embtel 1431) suggesting that representations should be made to DeGaulle against French clandestine plotting to upset the GVN and set it thereby upon a neutralist course. General Khanh had apparently made an impression on the Ambassador with his allegations of French machinations, asking for assurance that the U.S. opposed neutralization and if necessary would help him, Khanh, get his family, then in Da Nang, out of the country. He claimed that he had the support of General Khiem of III Corps and General Tri of II Corps as well as 90 percent of the army and 70 percent of the existing government. Lodge further reported that Khanh made a special point of wanting to continue to use Colonel Jasper Wilson as his exclusive contact with the U.S. Khanh refused absolutely to deal with any other than Wilson because he had had "an unfortunate experience with a CIA representative named Spera, before the 31 October coup." Lodge went on to say that although he had no great faith in Xuan, he believed that Don and Kim were patriotic Vietnamese and "therefore, what General Khanh says about them goes against my deepest instincts." Lodge sensed the intent of a coup, but evidently did not appreciate its imminence; for although he said he expected that there would be more to report later, he decided not to alter the government of Vietnam and had confided the news from Wilson only to Harkins and DeSilva.

However, it was a matter of only about seven hours after reporting this first Khanh feeler that Lodge at 3:15 a.m. of 30 January (Saigon time) advised Secretaries Rusk and McNamara that:

> General Khanh has informed us through his contact, Colonel Jasper Wilson, MAAG advisor I Corps, that he together with General Phat and Khiem intend to move at 0400 this morning to secure changes in the composition of the MRC. General Khiem states that General Minh has been informed of his move and agrees. The only definite statement we have as yet is that Premier Tho must go.

Over the next two or three days Ambassador Lodge altered considerably his first opinions about the justification for the coup. The U.S. chose to view the act as merely a change of personnel within the same MRC format; and the Ambassador's first attempt to explain the affair revealed his hope that an effort to put a good face on it might not be amiss. (There was little else he could do.)

> Herewith my preliminary assessment of the new Government in Viet Nam. It is very much subject to change as we move along.
>
> 1. General Khanh's coup was obviously extremely disconcerting at first blush. We felt we were beginning to make real progress here with the Minh Government—in the conduct of the effort against the Viet Cong; and in making General Minh into a popular figure. To overthrow a Government which was progressing fairly satisfactorily seemed like a violent and disorderly procedure . . .
>
> 2. On second thought, however, one realized the Generals Don and Kim had never at any time foresworn the possibility of a neutral solution at which might seem to them to be the proper time. They had clearly been working, and working effectively, to strengthen the effort against the Viet Cong. But none of us had ever discussed what the next step would be after the Government of Viet Nam had reached a position of strength. Perhaps they did favor the French neutrality solution at that time. We had all con-

centrated exclusively on winning . . . Finally, Ambassador D'Orlandi of Italy, who is one of the shrewdest men here, has thought ever since November that the Minh Government was actively in support of General De Gaulle's ideas and would turn overtly neutralist at the proper time. He had said this to me several times and had made much of the fact that both Don and Kim were still French citizens, had been aides to Marshal de Lattre when he was here, and had actively worked in the French Secret Service in the past. Therefore, opinion of the French intentions for neutralization coup might be correct . . .

4. Finally, in this country it rarely occurs to anyone that an election is an efficient or appropriate way to get anything important accomplished. The traditional way of doing important things here is by well planned, well thought out use of force. What General Khanh has done does not appear to have shocked the Vietnamese . . . However, numerous Vietnamese have expressed the opinion to members of my staff that it was a pity that General Minh was removed because he is a "good man."

5. The real question is, therefore: Is Khanh able? Will he really supply some drive in connection with the effort against the Viet Cong? The evidence to date is that he is able, that he has a lot of drive, and that he is not tolerating any delay . . .

6. If Khanh is able, his advent to power may give this country one-man command in place of a junta. This may be good. We have everything we need in Viet Nam. The U.S. has provided military advice, training, equipment; economic and social help; and political advice. The Government of Viet Nam has put relatively large number of good men into important positions and has evolved civil and military procedures which appear to be workable. Therefore, our side knows how to do it; we have the means with which to do it; we simply need to do it. This requires a tough and ruthless commander. Perhaps Khanh is it.

Privately we continued, however, to be deeply chagrined and even shaken that we had not seen the coup coming. We recognized it was a severe blow to the stability of government that we had believed was so necessary for South Vietnam, and we doubted the charges that Khanh used as a justification for his actions. But we accepted his explanations, promised to support him, and hoped for the best. About all we could do was threaten to withhold aid and that was ineffective because it was increasingly apparent that *we* were as committed to the struggle as our clients were—possibly even more committed. Whatever the real possibilities of influence may have been, we accepted as inescapable the fact that there was nothing we could do but go along with it. The President of the United States quickly offered his public expression of recognition and strong support. And one of our strongest resolves was to see what we might hit upon as a means to assure that we would not be taken again by a similar surprise.

F. DEEPENING GLOOM IN FEBRUARY

Among the flood of SitReps that came in soon after the coup was "Commander's Personal Military Assessment of the Fourth Quarter, CY-63." This was a report that MACV had been directed to establish at the end of the September 1963 visit of the Secretary and the CJCS in order to establish checkpoints by which to measure progress toward achievement of the goals agreed upon at that time. It is not essential here to review all of MACV's report but there are interesting details that are worth noting. MACV's report gave central attention to the fact that the political turbulence during the last quarter of 1963 had been reflected in a regression in government control, and corresponding opportunities for the VC. The political instability had resulted, especially, in a decline of GVN control within the 13 provinces listed as critical at Honolulu on 20 November. The strategic hamlet program had received setbacks which forced the GVN's military forces to adopt a defensive posture. After this there came a somewhat equivocal statement that:

> Analysis disclosed that, in spite of political turbulence, a satisfactory tempo of operation was maintained during this quarter. On the other hand, statistics clearly supported previous convictions that GVN operations were not effective when judged by reasonable standards of results versus effort expended. The immediate response to this analysis is to focus the advisory effort at all levels on the need for radical improvement in the effectiveness of operations.

What this seems to say is that GVN operations were satisfactory by the criteria which had been adopted for judging them, yet they did not achieve results. This seems to amount to an admission that the criteria by which operations were judged did not lead to good judgments concerning the results that were being achieved by these operations.

This appears, indeed, to have been very near the truth. Throughout this report there was a recognition of the effect of political and psychological and motivational factors upon real and effective capabilities. On the matter of training, the assessment was that it had "proven to be quantitatively satisfactory and flexible enough to meet the pressures and accelerated time schedules." But this expression of satisfaction that the nominal goals of training had been met was followed by the qualification that "the degree to which training can, in fact, develop combat aggressiveness or compensate for the lack of other motivation remains a matter for concern and continuing scrutiny." The anomaly was expressed *in words,* but the *fact* of it seems to have gone almost unrecognized.

When he turned to the two major areas of military action, first in the north and center and later in the Delta, MACV was obliged to admit that "there was little substantial progress toward completing the military progress in either of the two major regions." But he seemed to have been so thoroughly imbued with a chin-up, never-say-die spirit that he rejected the pessimistic implications which he explicitly acknowledged were present.

> If the military aspects of the fourth quarter of calendar year 1963 were viewed in isolation, or could in any way be considered typical, the forecast would be pessimistic in nature and a complete reappraisal of U.S. effort, approach, and even policy would be indicated. However, viewed in the light of January operational improvements, the forecast remains one of potential long term military progress.

The improvements cited as grounds for not accepting the pessimistic implications were a new military plan to support the pacification program; adoption of U.S. advice concerning GVN management to cope with increasing VC threats, especially around Saigon; and some government operations that seemed to demonstrate improved military leadership, and what he called "victories" while admitting they were not decisive. The difficulty here was that the judgment did not include consideration that these happier signs had come under the regime which had just been overturned by the Khanh coup a day or two before this report was dispatched, which coup, it was acknowledged, would have a disturbing and disruptive effect upon GVN capabilities as they had existed before the coup. Although it was still too soon to predict the full impact of the coup, it seemed "likely that at least part of the operational momentum which was being slowly generated earlier this month will be slowed for a time . . ."

In closing this assessment, MACV philosophized, in words with which few would disagree, that experiences of the last quarter of calendar year 1963 disclosed "the extent to which military opportunities are dependent upon political and psychological policies and accomplishments in a counter-insurgency environment." And he found the big lesson—"the broad implication"—was, that

> no amount of military effort or capability can compensate for poor politics. Therefore, although the prospects for an improved military posture are good, the ultimate achievement of the established military goal depends primarily upon the quality of support achieved by the political leadership of the government of Vietnam at all levels.

Here again was an explicit judgment that the *sine qua non* of an effective counter-insurgency operation was a stable, broadly based, popular and effective government. It was acknowledged at this time, as it had been acknowledged before concerning other governments, that a government of these qualities did not exist. But along with the acknowledgment that what was described as the *sine qua non* did not exist, there was apparently always the hope that fate would not close in before something happened to change the situation.

The U.S. mission Monthly Status Report, dated 9 February 1964, agreed with MACV that it was too soon to judge the effects of the Khanh coup. In the "overall evaluation," there was the following key paragraph:

> January witnessed distinct, if limited, progress in GVN's organization and action, both on political front in Saigon and on counter-insurgency front in countryside. Nevertheless, by January 30, when General Khanh moved swiftly and bloodlessly to take over reins of government, GVN had still not achieved sufficient momentum either to stem growing tide of popular criticism against it or to register meaningful gains against VC. In retrospect, greatest single positive achievement during three months of post-Diem regime was measurable success of General Minh in establishing himself as popular national leader. Measure of his success reflected in General Khanh's obvious effort to keep Minh on his side and exploit Minh's growing popularity for benefit of second post-Diem regime.

On the same day that the Mission Report was dispatched, CIA addressed to the Secretary of Defense a special report which had just been received by the Director of CIA by Mr. Peer de Silva (CAS station chief in Saigon) and Mr. Lyman D. Kirkpatrick, concerning the situation in Vietnam with particular respect to the conduct of the war and the prognosis of the stability of the Khanh regime. The de Silva judgment was that

> The situation at this moment must be characterized as one in which the population at large appears apathetic, without enthusiasm either for the GVN or the VC sides but responsive to the latter because it fears the VC. The most important single factor appears to be whether or not the rural population will be willing to defend itself against the VC and to support GVN actions against the VC. In this sector there now seems to be less conviction and resolution, and a more widespread inclination to avoid the problems of opposing the VC, and to play both sides in hopes of somehow getting on peacefully and without personal commitment.

. . . What is needed in this regard and very soon are a series of GVN successes in the military sphere which would go toward implanting and nourishing a popular attitude that the GVN has the means of bringing security and a sense of ease to the rural population and is clearly determined to do so on an ever broadening front throughout the countryside. Only within some such atmosphere of hopefulness can the will and resolve to oppose the VC be strengthened, and it must be if this war is to be won.

Mr. Kirkpatrick's comment was based upon his recent trip to South Vietnam:

I agree with the above but must note that even armed with your pessimistic comments following your last visit, I have been shocked by the number of our (CIA) people and of the military, even those whose jobs is always to say we are winning, who feel that the tide is against us. Admittedly, this is based on a limited number of discussions here and in Danang in three days. There are ominous indications that the VC are able to mount larger operations than in the past using bigger arms, including antiaircraft. Vietnamese government reactions are still slow, defensive and reminiscent of French tactics here a decade ago. There are still really no fundamental internal security measures of any effectiveness such as identity cards, block wardens, travel controls, etc. . . . It is evident that a major factor in VC victories is their superior intelligence based on nationwide penetrations and intimidations at all levels. . . . Finally, with the Laos and Cambodia borders opened, this entire pacification effort is like trying to mop the floor before turning off the faucet.

Two days later the Secretary received an advance copy of SNIE 50–64, "Short-term Prospects in Southeast Asia." Its leading conclusion was:

(a) That the situation in South Vietnam is very serious and prospects uncertain. Even with U.S. assistance as it is now, we believe that, unless there is a marked improvement in the effectiveness of the South Vietnamese government and armed forces, South Vietnam has, at best, an even chance of withstanding the insurgency menace during the next few weeks or months.

In further explanation of this judgment, it was stated that the situation had been serious for a long time and in recent months it had deteriorated further. The VC had exploited dislocations caused by the November coup and then more recently by the January coup. Just as Minh's reorganization was beginning to be established, Khanh's coup upset everything, and Khanh's regime was not yet assessable. Meanwhile, the VC had improved in their organization and armament, were increasingly aggressive and acting in larger units.

G.   TWO GENERAL ALTERNATIVE DIRECTIONS OF POLICY

Thus as winter drew to an end in February–March 1964, it was recognized, as it had never been fully recognized before, that the situation in Vietnam was deteriorating so rapidly that the dimensions and kinds of effort so far invested could not hope to reverse the trend. This was indeed a turning point. The proposals for neutralization that had been loosely suggested in late fall and early winter having been rejected, the issue to be resolved was what kinds of new efforts, and what new dimensions of U.S. effort, would be decided upon. One direction of effort which might have been chosen had, as its most articulate advocate, the Assistant Secretary of State for Far Eastern Affairs, Roger Hilsman. This was the policy line that, for better or for worse, was largely rejected. Mainly because of this policy disagreement, Mr. Hilsman left his post at almost the time it became evident that his views were conclusively overruled. At the time of his departure he wrote two memos to the Secretary of State (dated 14 March 1964); one on the Southeast Asia problem generally, one on South Vietnam. The latter of the two affords not only a good summary of his views on the subject, but also a statement of the policy alternatives that were, in significant measure, rejected. (The rejection was of course by no means total. It was a matter of degree and a question of where emphasis should lie among some programs that were not in dispute generically. But the matter of degree and emphasis was in dispute, and it was sufficient not only to induce Hilsman to resign but to alter drastically the course of U.S. involvement.) Hilsman wrote:

In my judgment, the strategic concept that was developed for South Vietnam remains basically sound. If we can ever manage to have it implemented with vigor, the result will be victory.

The concept is based on the assumption that villages in Southeast Asia are turned inward on themselves and have little or no sense of identification with either the national government or Communist ideology—that the villagers are isolated physically, politically, and psychologically. In such circumstances it is not difficult to develop a guerrilla movement . . .

A corollary . . . is that the villagers' greatest desire is security and that if the villagers are given security, some simple progress towards a better life, and—most important of all—a sense that the government cares about them and their future, they will respond with loyalty . . .

On the basis of . . . [this] assumption, the strategic concept calls for primary emphasis on giving security to the villagers. The tactics are the so-called oil-blot approach, starting with a secure area and extending it slowly, making sure no Viet Cong pockets are left behind, and using police units to winkle out [sic] the Viet Cong agents in each particular village. This calls for the use of military forces in a different way from that of orthodox, conventional war. Rather than chasing Viet Cong, the military must put primary emphasis on clear-and-hold operations and on rapid reinforcement of villages under attack. It is also important, of course, to keep the Viet Cong regular units off balance by conventional offensive operations, but these should be secondary to the major task of extending security . . .

At the heart of this strategic concept are two basic principles:

The first is that of the oil blot. In the past the GVN sought to blanket the whole country with so-called strategic hamlets . . . The result was to blanket the Delta with little Dienbienphus—indefensible, inadequately armed hamlets far from reinforcements . . . In effect these were storage places of arms for the Viet Cong which could be seized at any time. After November first, the military began to demobilize some of these vulnerable villages . . . and a race developed between the government and the Viet Cong. The race may have ended in a tie, but . . . the Viet Cong now have much better weapons and greater stocks of ammunition than they ever had before.

The second basic principle is that the way to fight a guerrilla is to adopt the tactics of a guerrilla . . . In spite of all our pressures, this has never been done in Vietnam. Instead, the emphasis has been on large operations . . .

As to the question of operations against North Vietnam, I would suggest that such operations may at a certain stage be a useful *supplement* to an effective counterinsurgency program, but . . . not be an effective *substitute . . .*

My own preference would be to continue the covert, or at least deniable operations . . . Then, after we had made sufficient progress in the Delta so that all concerned began to realize that the Viet Cong were losing the support of the population, and that their ability to continue the war depended solely on North Vietnamese support, I think we should indicate as much privately to the North Vietnamese and follow this by selected attacks on their infiltration bases and training camps.

In my judgment, significant action against North Vietnam that is taken before we have demonstrated success in our counterinsurgency program will be interpreted by the Communists as an act of desperation, and will, therefore, not be effective in persuading the North Vietnamese to cease and desist. What is worse, I think that premature action will so alarm our friends and allies and a significant segment of domestic opinion that the pressures for neutralization will become formidable.

In sum, I believe that we can win in Vietnam with a number of provisos. The first proviso is that we do not over-militarize the war—that we concentrate not on killing Viet Cong . . . but on an effective program for extending the areas of security gradually, systematically, and thoroughly . . .

My second proviso is that there be political stability in Saigon . . .

Some of the Hilsman recommendations were to be adopted, none rejected out-of-hand. The so-called oil blot principle had many adherents, and was in fact already coming into vogue. Over the ensuing months, the phrase was much honored, though the execution may have faltered. No one disputed the principle that the hamlets needed security above all else, nor that everything depended on a stable government in Saigon. Nevertheless, emphasis shifted toward greater emphasis on military operations, perhaps for the pressing reason that the VC were out now in increasing numbers, with more and better weapons, seeming to invite, if not to require, conventional military operations if the VC threatening the hamlets were to be destroyed or reduced to powerlessness. And, above all, the more elusive the VC were, the stronger they grew, and the more unstable and unpopular the GVN became, the more tempting the idea of attacking the north seemed to be.

Much more influential than these Hilsman views were those of the JCS, especially as set forth in the memorandum of 18 February 1964 to the SecDef from the CJCS:

1. Reference is made to the memorandum by the Joint Chiefs of Staff, dated 22 January 1964 . . . It sets forth a number of actions which the United States should be prepared to take in order to ensure victory . . . the Joint Chiefs of Staff have reviewed the situation in South Vietnam with the view of determining additional actions which can be recommended for implementation immediately.

2. The Government of Vietnam has developed, with the close collaboration of the U.S. Military Assistance Command, a new National Pacification Plan which provides for the orderly pacification of the insurgency in accordance with a realistic phasing schedule . . . and it provides for consolidation of secure areas and expansion of them (the "spreading oil drop"). U.S. military assets in Vietnam will fully support this plan. What is now

required is implementation of additional actions which will insure an integrated political, socio-economic, and psychological offensive to support more fully the military effort. Accordingly, the Joint Chiefs of Staff recommend that the Country Team be directed to implement the following actions at the earliest practicable time:

a. Induce the GVN (General Khanh) military to accept U.S. advisors at all levels considered necessary by COMUSMACV. (This is particularly applicable in the critical provinces) . . .

b. Intensify the use of herbicides for crop destruction against identified Viet Cong areas as recommended by the GVN.

c. Improve border control measures . . .

d. Direct the U.S. civilian agencies involved in Vietnam to assist the GVN in producing a civilian counterpart package plan to the GVN National Pacification Plan . . .

e. Provide U.S. civilian advisors to all necessary echelons and GVN agencies . . .

f. Encourage early and effective action to implement a realistic land reform program.

g. Support the GVN in a policy of tax forgiveness for low income population in areas where the GVN determines that a critical state of insurgency exists . . .

h. Assist the GVN in developing a National Psychological Operations Plan . . . to establish the GVN and Khanh's "images," create a "cause" which can serve as a rallying point for the youth/students of Vietnam, and develop the long term national objectives of a free Vietnam.

i. Intensify efforts to gain support of U.S. news media representatives in Washington . . .

j. Arrange U.S. sponsored trips to Vietnam by groups of prominent journalists and editors.

k. Inform all GVN military and civilian officials . . . that the United States (a) considers it imperative that the present government be stabilized, (b) would oppose another coup, and (c) that the United States is prepared to offer all possible assistance in forming a stable government . . . all U.S. intelligence agencies and advisors must be alert to and report cases of dissension and plotting in order to prevent such actions.

3. The Joint Chiefs of Staff recognize that the implementation of the foregoing measures will not be sufficient to exercise a decisive effect on the campaign against the Viet Cong. They are continuing study of the actions suggested in the memorandum of 22 January 1964, as well as other proposals . . . Among the subjects to be studied as a matter of urgency are the following:

a. Intensified operations against North Vietnam to include air bombings of selected targets.

b. Removal of restrictions for air and ground cross-border operations.

c. Intelligence and reporting.

d. U.S. organizational changes.

e. Increased U.S. Navy participation in shore and river patrol activities.

f. Introduction of jet aircraft into the Vietnamese Air Force and the U.S. Air Commando unit . . .

Except for 2f, 2g, 2i, 2j, and the escalatory military actions of paragraph 3 that had been suggested previously by the JCS, this memorandum outlined much of the program that was to be adopted by the SecDef in March after his trip to Saigon, and approved by the President thereafter as NSAM 288.

H. THE FACT FINDING MISSION AND NSAM–288

Before the Secretary left for Vietnam, trip books were prepared for his use and the use of others in his official party. In this trip was an appraisal of the Vietnam situation, dated 3 March 1964, prepared especially for this occasion by the normally optimistic SACSA. It began with this summary:

> The RVN faces the most critical situation in its nearly 10 years of existence. This situation is the result of political erosion, culminating in two changes of government within three months and in a nationwide revamping of civil administrators, and of the continued growth of a well-organized, dedicated Communist insurgency movement.

This was followed by a political discussion wherein there was mention of the chronic shortage of competent administrators. The government was credited with superior material resources, but, "unless it is able to demonstrate the willpower and political skill to bring this potential to bear, the political and security situation will continue to deteriorate." It was considered hopeful that Khanh seemed determined to provide dynamic leadership, but it was observed that he would have to overcome "widespread public and official apathy, lack of confidence, low morale, and factionalism among key personnel."

Khanh's efforts and attributes were catalogued approvingly, but this only led to a concluding paragraph as follows:

> Encouraging as Khanh's performance has been to date, he has not been able to counteract the overall trend of events in South Vietnam. In many of the most critical provinces, pacification programs remain at a virtual standstill and there is an evident lack of urgency and clear direction.

This was followed by a section entitled "Military and Security Situation." This section contained an interesting judgment, which represented a reversal by SACSA of opinions expressed six months or more before concerning the time when the situation had begun to deteriorate.

> By the final quarter of 1963, the conclusion was inescapable that despite the considerable improvement in the offensive capabilities of the RVN's counter-insurgency forces, the VC likewise had improved their own capabilities. *It became apparent that a gradual erosion of the government's position throughout the country had been underway since at least August 1963.* This erosion became progressively worse after the November coup, although late in January 1964, the Minh government exhibited some signs of assuming the initiative. This initiative dissolved with the Khanh coup on 30 January. Organizational dislocations brought about by coups have weakened the national direction of most of the counter-insurgency programs underway throughout the country. The large number of personnel changes, both locally and nationally, have played a crucial role in the indecision and lack of energetic direction of the government's programs.
> Despite General Khanh's expressed determination to prosecute the war vigorously, available statistics since his coup reflect a gradual decline in small-scale ARVN operations. In addition, Communist forces continue to

enjoy the initiative and to execute disruptive operations at times and places of their own choosing . . .

All available evidence points to a steady improvement in the VC's military posture, both quantitatively and qualitatively, throughout 1963 and the first two months of 1964 . . . [Emphasis supplied.]

In advising the Embassy in Saigon of the intended visit of Secretary Mc-Namara and General Taylor in March, a Joint State/Defense message outlined the issues that it was hoped would be taken up during the visit. Five major subject areas were named, each of which was divided into parts. Objectives were described, in general, as "to produce best possible evaluation of situation, assist you in measures to improve it, and help Washington make future policy decisions."

The first subject area was a Review of Situation, in three parts: *political, economic,* and *military.* It was suggested that the *political* review should be in executive session limited to the three principals (McNamara, Lodge and Taylor) and the DCM, Harkins, Brent, de Silva, and perhaps Zorthian. The subjects of prime interest were how Khanh was taking hold, and the dangers of further coups. Next in importance were the effectiveness of the civil administration and the morale of major religious and political groups, and measures to strengthen and buttress the Khanh regime. On the *economic* side, the Secretary hoped to get a full review of the economy, the budget, price and supply trends, AID operations, and, finally, the possibility of land reform and tax forgiveness. On the *military* side, it was suggested they begin with the broad picture, and later proceed to selected critical provinces and specific provincial plans.

The main interest, with respect to intelligence and reporting, was to review Country Team recommendations concerning periodic assessments and joint reporting requirements. After this the interest centered on intelligence concerning the VC—specifically the extent of their control and activities in the provinces, intentions and tactics, and indicators thereof. Then, clearly in anticipation of possible requirement for public relations materials for us in U.S.:

4. Handling of intelligence bearing on control and direction of Viet Cong from North Vietnam including infiltration of personnel and weapons and operation of communications net. One of our basic projects here is preparing strongest possible material on this subject for use as appropriate to support stronger measures. We need to be sure your intelligence effort is geared to furnish such information promptly in usable form.

5. Review of draft (which we will supply) of control and support of VC by North Vietnam.

Concerning current operational problems, the items foreseen to be of interest were policy on possible evacuation of dependents, review of GVN national and provincial plans, rural rehabilitation plans, adequacy and deployment of ARVN, status and problems of paramilitary forces, current status and possible expansion of the U.S. Special Forces' role in connection with Civilian Irregular Defense Groups (CIDG), status of plans to reduce or reorganize U.S. forces as GVN became capable of performing functions currently performed by U.S., review of political and psywar progress, and of military tactics against VC, and "possible modification of existing operation [al] restrictions."

The special third country problems of French activities in RVN, and of Cambodia and Laos, would be dealt with in executive session.

The last item listed for special consideration was to review Operations Plan 34A-64, for feasibility, adequacy, and possible expansion, with special consideration to advantages derivable from making it an overt Vietnamese program with participation by U.S. as required to obtain adequate results."

The language and the tone of this message suggest that, however pessimistic may have been the appraisals of the situation, there was no disposition to recognize any doubt that the struggle could be won or that we would undertake whatever measures were necessary to win it. Previously unprecedented escalatory measures of a military nature were beginning to be studied tentatively as a response to the bad news that kept coming. Most of these were to be rejected, for the time being, except for moves to convey to NVN that an exchange of air blows between NVN and SVN was a possibility. This, it was hoped, might exploit NVN fears that if they persisted aiding the VC they faced the loss of their industrial establishment. The inferential significance of our considerations at this time seems to have been that we were already committed, by the momentum of our past actions, to a course which forbade turning back, however reluctant we might be about taking any forward step.

A schedule for the trip was set up extending from the planned arrival on 8 March 1964 through 12 March. In the course of five days of briefings, conferences, and field trips, most of the details of a program, to implement policies already evidently largely agreed upon, were decided upon in the light of views and information elicited from our own and GVN officials. In the final meeting with General Khanh and his GVN associates, most of the programs for Vietnam which were later to be recommended to the President by Secretary McNamara were discussed. The exchange of views at that time was made a matter of record by a memcon, a summary of which was transmitted the next day by Ambassador Lodge.

> General Khanh . . . proposed National Service Act for SVN. Khanh said his government prepared embark upon program to mobilize all human and material resources to fight VC. As envisaged by General Khanh proposed National Service Act would have two major components: military service and civil defense . . .
>
> Military service comprised of: RVNAF . . . (actual strength: 227,000; planned: 251,683); Civil Guard (actual: 90,032; planned: 119,636). SDC & Hamlet Militia . . . (actual: 257,960; planned: 422,874). Civil Defense comprised of Civil Service Corps, Cadre Corps, National Youth, and Political-Administration Corps . . .
>
> Civil Defense component included Civil Administration Corps for work in countryside. Khanh emphasized that in civil defense sector all civilians would be included . . .
>
> Khanh emphasized figures were planning figures only and designed give idea of number of military and civilians required and indicate financial implications of plan . . .
>
> McNamara stated that U.S. . . . would wish to study strength figures carefully; however, his first impression was that figure of 422,874 SDC and Hamlet Militia appeared unduly large and would be difficult to support. Khanh responded that in actual practice total numbers may not reach this level. In fact, number may not exceed 300,000 SDC and Hamlet Militia actually deployed against VC . . .
>
> Thieu stated that all men from age 18 through 40 would be required to participate in national pacification effort. Most of them . . . would

serve in same positions they now occupy. Others, such as National Youth Group up to age 40, would be required serve in city and countryside and would be organized into small groups to assist ARVN and Civil Guard. Category of Political-Administration Corps would consist of cadres planned for assignment to villages and hamlets. General Thieu estimated that 125,-000 such cadre would be required . . . McNamara stated that general approach appeared excellent but he questioned whether GVN would need 125,000 cadre . . . This number added to total figures for Civil Guard, SDC and Hamlet Militia, constituted an extremely large figure . . . population appeared disproportionate . . . desirable to look most closely at planning figures.

Khanh replied that he intended make maximum effort in first instance in 8 critical provinces surrounding Saigon . . . However, a National Service Act would have a very good effect in Saigon and the other urban areas.

McNamara inquired whether upon his return to Washington he could tell President Johnson that General Khanh's government was prepared embark on a program of national mobilization of human and material resources and whether President Johnson in turn could inform the American people . . . Khanh replied in the affirmative . . . McNamara indicated that he viewed concept favorably and . . . Ambassador stated that he favored general concept but thought that detailed figures should be looked into carefully. Ambassador also believed that emphasis should be placed first on 8 critical provinces surrounding Saigon . . .

General Harkins noted that a mobilization law was in fact in existence but that few people know about it. He pointed out that ARVN, CG and SDC were not up to their authorized military strengths. Khanh said that he realized this but believed it still desirable to have a new law setting forth a national service or mobilization program. Harkins stated that MACV and other elements of U.S. Mission would like to work closely with Khanh . . . in developing such a law. Khanh replied this well understood. McNamara said it was agreed on American side that general concept was a wise one and that we should proceed on this basis.

Khanh then inquired whether it was desirable to raise CG to same relative status as ARVN as regards salary, pensions, survivors benefits, etc. He estimated that total cost would be in neighborhood of one billion piasters. McNamara thought this was highly desirable . . .

McNamara inquired how long . . . it would take to recruit and train administrative cadre for 8 critical provinces near Saigon. Khanh estimated approximately one month, in any event he believed cadres could be in place by end of April. Khanh said GVN would aim for volunteers for this effort and it was not necessary to await promulgation of National Service Act.

In response Taylor's question as to how long Khanh anticipated it would take to draft and promulgate National Service Law, Khanh observed that . . . law could be ready for his signature in very short time. Taylor pointed to necessity give due regard to democratic forms in developing and announcing a National Service Act. Khanh agreed and said that at same time a major effort was being made to pacify the countryside. He intended push for concurrent development of democratic institutions and forms. McNamara suggested that when Khanh ready announce a National Service Act that he also re-emphasize related actions . . . such as those for expansion of national economy, for increased educational opportunities in hamlets, for increased production of rice, for marketing of fish, and so forth. McNamara believed a well publicized announcement of this nature would find ready response among people and would materially assist Khanh to obtain and hold support of Vietnamese people. . . .

I. NSAM–288

The program formulated in March 1964 in connection with the trip to Vietnam was reported orally to the President by the Secretary of Defense and the Chairman of the Joint Chiefs on their return, then presented formally to the President and the NSC by memorandum to the President dated 16 March. [Doc. 54] It was finally approved as NSAM 288 dated 17 March 1964. As such NSC documents go, NSAM 288 was comprehensive and programmatic. It reviewed U.S. objectives, appraised the situation, discussed various alternative courses of action, and finally recommended a rather detailed program intended to serve the defined objectives and to meet the situation as it had been described. It consisted of seven parts. The first was a discussion and definition of objectives, the second a description of U.S. policy, the third an appraisal of the present situation, the fourth a discussion of alternative courses of action, the fifth a consideration of possible actions, the sixth a mention of other actions considered but rejected, and seventh and last, a statement of specific recommendations.

NSAM 288, being based on the official recognition that the situation in Vietnam was considerably worse than had been realized at the time of the adoption of NSAM 273, outlined a program that called for considerable enlargement of U.S. effort. It involved an assumption by the United States of a greater part of the task, and an increased involvement by the United States in the internal affairs of South Vietnam, and for these reasons it carried with it an enlarged commitment of U.S. prestige to the success of our effort in that area.

In tacit acknowledgement that this greater commitment of prestige called for an enlargement of stated objectives, NSAM 288 did indeed enlarge these objectives. Whereas, in NSAM 273 the objectives were expressly limited to helping the government of South Vietnam win its contest against an externally directed Communist conspiracy, NSAM 288 escalated the objectives into a defense of all of Southeast Asia and the West Pacific and redefined American foreign policy and American security generally. In NSAM 273 the statement of objectives was comparatively simple and limited:

> It remains the central object of the United States in South Vietnam to assist the people and the government of that country to win their contest against the externally directed and supported Communist conspiracy. The test of all U.S. decisions and actions in this area should be the effectiveness of their contribution to this purpose.

In contrast to this, the statement of "U.S. Objectives in South Vietnam" in NSAM 288 was considerably more extensive and more central to U.S. security interests:

> We seek an independent non-Communist South Vietnam. We do not require that it serve as a Western base or as a member of a Western alliance. South Vietnam must be free, however, to accept outside assistance as required to maintain its security. This assistance should be able to take the form not only of economic and social measures but also police and military help to root out and control insurgent elements.

Unless we can achieve this objective in South Vietnam, almost all of Southeast Asia will probably fall under Communist dominance (all of Vietnam, Laos, and Cambodia), accommodate to Communism so as to remove effective U.S. and anti-Communist influence (Burma), or fall under the domination of forces not now explicitly Communist but likely then to become so (Indonesia taking over Malaysia). Thailand might hold for a period without help, but would be under grave pressure. Even the Philippines would become shaky, and the threat to India on the West, Australia and New Zealand to the South, and Taiwan, Korea, and Japan to the North and East would be greatly increased.

All of these consequences would probably have been true even if the U.S. had not since 1954, and especially since 1961, become so heavily engaged in South Vietnam. However, that fact accentuates the impact of a Communist South Vietnam not only in Asia but in the rest of the world, where the South Vietnam conflict is regarded as a test case of U.S. capacity to help a nation to meet the Communist "war of liberation."

Thus, purely in terms of foreign policy, the stakes are high . . .

The argument in the next to last paragraph of NSAM 288 that "all these consequences would probably have been true even if the U.S. had not since 1954, and especially since 1961, become so heavily engaged in SVN" is clearly debatable. But the logic that the increasing U.S. involvement led to increasing commitment of U.S. prestige is probably beyond argument. And it is probably also true that, in the extent to which we defined the issues simply and centrally as a symbolic confrontation with Communism, wherein far more is at stake than the immediate battlefield (in South Vietnam) on which we fought—and acted upon this definition and proclaimed it as the issue—we tended more and more to endow the issue with that significance whether or not it had in fact been the issue in the first place. And this point, if closely examined, might logically have raised the question of whether it is absolutely necessary to accept any challenge put to us, and if so what advantage this confers upon our enemies in granting them the choice of issue and of battleground. Finally, a struggle so defined came close to calling for war *à outrance*—not the centrally political war, with severe restriction upon violent means, following counter-guerrilla warfare theory.

Despite the encompassing nature of the definition of objectives, and although NSAM 288 proposed a marked increase in U.S. involvement, our implementing programs remained comparatively limited as if we did not fully believe these strong words. We even expressed agreement with the older idea of helping the Vietnamese help themselvs.

We are now trying to help South Vietnam defeat the Viet Cong, supported from the North, by means short of the unqualified use of U.S. combat forces. We are not acting against North Vietnam except by a modest "covert" program operated by South Vietnamese (and a few Chinese Nationalists)—a program so limited that it is unlikely to have any significant effect . . .

There was a further statement of this older policy theme:

There were and are some sound reasons for the limits imposed by the present policy—the South Vietnamese must win their own fight; U.S. intervention on a larger scale, and/or GVN actions against the North, would disturb key allies and other nations; etc. In any case, it is vital that we continue to take every reasonable measure to assure success in South Vietnam. The policy choice is not an "either/or" between this course of action and possible pressures against the North; the former is essential and without regard to our decision with respect to the latter. The latter can, at best, only reinforce the former.

At the end of this section, which described measures that we would take to assist the Khanh government in administering internal programs, there was a final admonition:

Many of the actions described in the succeeding paragraphs fit right into the framework of the [Pacification] plan as announced by Khanh. *Wherever possible, we should tie our urgings of such actions to Khanh's own formulation of them, so that he will be carrying out a Vietnamese plan and not one imposed by the United States.* [Emphasis supplied]

The discussion of the situation in Vietnam began with the statement that the military tools and concepts that had been adopted were sound and adequate. But much needed to be done in terms of a more effective employment both of military forces and of the economic and civic action means already available. This improved effort might require some selective increases in the U.S. presence. These increases were not considered to be necessarily major in nature and not in contradiction to "the U.S. policy of reducing existing military personnel where South Vietnamese are in a position to assume the functions . . ."

No major reductions of U.S. personnel in the near future were expected, but it continued to be the basic policy that there would be gradual U.S. withdrawal from participation. This was considered to be sound because of its effect "in portraying to the U.S. and the world that we continue to regard the war as a conflict the South Vietnamese must win and take ultimate responsibility for." And along this line there was the continued hope that "substantial reductions in the numbers of U.S. military training personnel should be possible before the end of 1965. (The language here suggested a beginning retreat from NSAM 273).

It was conceded, however, that "the situation has unquestionably been growing worse, at least since September . . ." Forty percent of the territory was then under the Viet Cong control or predominant influence, and twenty-two of the forty-three provinces were controlled fifty percent or more by the Viet Cong. Other indications of the continuing deterioration were that large groups of the population displayed signs of apathy and indifference, while frustration was evident within the U.S. contingent. Desertion rates within the ARVN and the Vietnamese paramilitary were particularly high and increasing—especially in the latter. Draft-dodging was high; but the Viet Cong were recruiting energetically and effectively. The morale of the hamlet militia and of the SDC, upon which the security of the hamlets depended, was poor and falling. The position of the government within the provinces was weakening.

The machinery of political control extending from Saigon down to the hamlets had virtually disappeared following the November coup. Of forty-one incumbent province chiefs on November 1, thirty-five had been replaced. Nine provinces had had three province chiefs in three months, and one province had had four. Lesser officials had been replaced by the score. Almost all major military commands had changed hands twice since the November coup and the faith of the peasants had been shaken by disruptions in experienced leadership and loss of physical security.

There was an increase in North Vietnamese support, and communication between Hanoi and the Viet Cong had increased. CHICOM 75 millimeter recoilless rifles and heavy machine guns were increasingly in evidence among the Viet Cong.

The greatest source of weakness in the present situation was the uncertain viability of the Khanh government. The greatest need, therefore, was to do the things that would enhance the stability of that government, and at the same time provide the advice and assistance that was necessary to increase its capabilities to deal with the problems confronting it.

Among the alternatives considered, but rejected for the time being (along with complete adoption of the Hilsman formulations), were overt military pressure on North Vietnam, neutralization, return of U.S. dependents, furnishing of a U.S. combat unit to secure the Saigon area, and a full takeover of the command in South Vietnam by the U.S. With respect to this last proposal, it was said that

> . . . the judgement of all senior people in Saigon, with which we concur, was that the possible military advantages of such action would be far outweighed by adverse psychological impact. It would cut across the whole basic picture of the Vietnamese winning their own war and lay us wide open to hostile propaganda both within South Vietnam and outside.

The areas of action that were favored and that formed the basis of the specific recommendations to which the paper led, fell under two major and two minor headings. The two major headings were, (1) civil and military mobilization and (2) improvement of military forces. The two minor headings were (1) additional military equipment for the GVN and (2) economic actions.

The first point under civil and military mobilization was to put the whole country on a war footing. The purpose was to maintain and strengthen the armed forces, to assist other national efforts, and to remedy the recognized inequities and under-utilization of current manpower policies. Specifically, there was proposed a new national mobilization plan including a national service law, which was to be developed on an urgent basis by the Country Team in collaboration with the Khanh Government. To this end the third of the several recommendations at the conclusion of the report called for the U.S. to "support a program of national mobilization (including a national service law) to put South Vietnam on a war footing."

A second measure under this heading was to strengthen the armed forces, both regular and paramilitary by at least 50,000 men. Of these, about 15,000 would be required to fill the regular armed forces (ARVN) to their current authorized strength, 5,000 would be needed to fill the existing paramilitary forces to their authorized strengths, and the remaining 30,000 would be to increase the strength of the paramilitary forces. To this end it was specifically recommended that the U.S. "assist the Vietnamese to increase the armed forces (regular plus paramilitary) by at least 50,000 men."

The third measure of mobilization was to assist in an increase of the civil administrative corps of Vietnam by an additional 7,500 in 1964, with the ultimate target of at least 40,000 men for service in 8,000 hamlets and 2,500 villages, and in 3 provincial centers. It was specified that in accomplishing this the United States should work with the GVN to devise necessary recruiting plans, training facilities, financing methods and organizational arrangements, and should furnish training personnel at once under the auspices of the AID mission. The specific recommendation was "to assist the Vietnamese to create a greatly enlarged civil administrative corps for work at province, district and hamlet levels."

The improvement of SVN military forces was to be accomplished not only by the increase in numbers specified above, but also by internal reforms and organizational improvements. What remained of the current hamlet militia and related forces of part-time nature for hamlet defense should be consolidated with the self-defense corps into a single force which would be compensated by the national government. The pay and collateral benefits of the paramilitary groups should be substantially improved. Strength of the forces should be maintained and expanded by effectively enforced conscription measures and by more centrally directed recruitment policies. It was recommended that U.S. personnel should be assigned to the training of the paramilitary forces. The National Police required further special consideration. An offensive guerrilla force should be created to operate along the border and in areas where VC control was dominant. These measures were included in specific recommendations to "assist the Vietnamese to improve and reorganize the paramilitary forces and to increase their compensation" and "to assist the Vietnamese to create an offensive guerrilla force."

Under the last two headings there were recommendations to provide the Vietnamese Air Force with 25 A–1H aircraft in exchange for their T–28s and to provide the Vietnamese Army additional M–113 APCs (withdrawing the M–114s there) and also to provide additional river boats and approximately 5 to 10 million dollars worth of related additional materiel. A fertilizer program to increase the production of rice in areas safely controlled by the government was to be expanded and announced very soon.

Although VC successes in rural areas had been the prime feature of the downswing over the past half year or more, pacification was to receive less comparative emphasis, in fact, in the next year or so than it had before. Nevertheless, Khanh's statement of a pacification strategy—which was later to form a conceptual basis for the ill-fated *Hop Tac* program—was approved in principle, and a critique of it was accorded a place as Annex B of NSAM 288.

In simplified outline, the plan was based on a "clear and hold" concept, including for each area these steps:

1. Clearing organized VC units from the area by military action;

2. Establishing permanent security for the area by the Civil Guard, Self Defense Corps, hamlet militia, and national police;

3. Rooting out the VC "infrastructure" in the hamlets (particularly the VC tax collector and the chief of the VC political cadre);

4. Providing the elements of economic and social progress for the people of the area: schools, health services, water supply, agricultural improvements, etc.

These general ideas were to be (1) adapted and applied flexibly . . . (2) applied under the clear, undivided and decentralized control of the province chief; and (3) applied in a gradually spreading area moving from secure to less secure areas and from more populated to less populated areas (the "oil drop" principle) . . .

The major *requirements for success* of the Pacification Plan were:

First, and of by far the greatest importance, clear, strong, and continuous political leadership . . .

General Khanh and his top colleagues were to supply this requirement. Their ability to do so was as yet untested, but some early evidence was good . . .

A *second* major requirement for success of the Pacification Plan was the adoption of government policies which would give greater promise of economic progress and greater incentives to rural people. The three key areas were:

—the price of rice to farmers, which was artifically depressed and held substantially below the world market price;

—uncertain or oppressive tenure conditions for many farmers (a land reform program was half completed some years ago); the VC had been exploiting the situation very effectively;

—oppressive marketing conditions for fishermen (fisheries accounted for 25 per cent of the rural product of SVN).

General Khanh's initial statement about the land reform problem was not very encouraging; Mr. Oanh was not even aware of the rice problem until a conversation with U.S. visitors on March 10th.

A *third* major requirement for success of the Pacification Plan was to improve greatly the leadership, pay, training, and numbers of some of the kinds of personnel needed, notably:

—pay and allowances for Civil Guards and S.D.C. . . .

—recruitment and training for more civilian technicians . . . also increased pay and supporting costs for them; and recruitment and training of a new kind of rural worker—"hamlet action teams"—to move into newly cleared hamlets and start improvement programs . . .

The real problems were managerial: to develop concepts, training schools, action programs, and above all, leadership at the provincial level and below.

Other requirements for success of the Pacification Plan included: improvement in the leadership and attitudes of the ARVN particularly at levels which came into contact with villagers; greatly increased military civic action programs by the ARVN; much more flexibility and decentralization of authority in the administration of GVN civilian agencies; and a far clearer and more consistent pattern of rewarding excellence and penalizing poor performance in the management of both military and civilian agencies of the GVN.

Finally, there was one predominant recommendation (it was in fact the second of twelve): that the U.S. "make it clear that we fully support the Khanh government and are opposed to any further coups." This reflected our deep concern over the political instability and our dismay at having been surprised by the Khanh coup at the end of January.

An immediate measure to provide this kind of support to Khanh was the issuance on the following day (17 March) of a White House release which gave Presidential public blessing to the Khanh regime, saying in part that, to meet the difficulties and setbacks that had arisen since last October, "General Khanh and his government are acting vigorously and effectively . . . [having] produced a sound central plan for the prosecution of the war, recognizing to a far greater degree than before the crucial role of economic and social, as well as military action . . ."

This statement helped to solidify the Khanh regime by giving it explicit assurance of continuing U.S. support. It did not fully take care of our dismay over the surprise that the Khanh coup had been, and our fear that such a coup might be repeated. In addition to making it clear that we fully supported the incumbent regime, therefore, it seemed necessary that we should discourage attempted coups, or, getting wind of them, head them off before they passed the point of no return. On 18 March, W. H. Sullivan of State sent out a message to Saigon as follows:

Point 2 . . . [of NSAM 288] stipulated that U.S. government agencies should make clear our full support for Khanh government and our opposition to any further coups. While it is recognized that our chances of detecting coup plotting are far from fool-proof . . . all elements [of] U.S. mission in Vietnam should be alerted against coup contingencies.

Mission should establish appropriate procedure which will assure that all rumors of coup plotting which come to attention [of] any U.S. government personnel in Vietnam will be brought to attention of Ambassador without delay. This is not, repeat not, a responsibility solely for intelligence elements [of the] U.S. mission.

The program embodied in NSAM 288 was by no means judged adequate by all concerned. One major dissent had been registered by the JCS, who tended to view the problem primarily in its military dimensions, and who believed that the source of VC strength in the North must be neutralized. In a memorandum dated 14 March 1964, the CJCS had provided the Secretary of Defense with comments on the SecDef's draft memo to the President (NSAM 288). The general view of the JCS was that the program being recommended by the Secretary of Defense was inadequate militarily, and that much more aggressive policies, mainly against NVN, but also against the Cambodian sanctuaries of VC forces, were necessary.

a. The JCS do not believe that the recommended program in itself will be sufficient to turn the tide against the Viet Cong in SVN without positive action being taken against the Hanoi government at an early date. They have in mind the conduct of the kind of program designed to bring about cessation of DRV support for operations in SVN and Laos outlined in JCSM–174–64, subject "Vietnam," dated 2 March 1964. Such a program would not only deter the aggressive actions of the DRV but would be a source of encouragement to SVN which should significantly facilitate the counterinsurgency program in that country. To increase our readiness for such actions, the U.S. Government should establish at once the political and military bases in the U.S. and SVN for offensive actions against the North and across the Laotian and Cambodian borders, including measures for the control of contraband traffic on the Mekong.

b. In view of the current attitude of the Sihanouk Government in Cambodia, the JCS recommend authorizing now hot pursuit into that country . . .

As already noted, however, this sort of escalation had already been rejected for the time being. And in any event, there were both a new regime in Vietnam and an enlarged program of U.S. aid to support it, although not as enlarged militarily, as the JCS would wish. (That form of enlargement would not come until later.) But it was the first program since 1961 enlarged in explicit recognition that the programs preceding it had not succeeded, had indeed fallen far short of their goals. And in that sense at least it was the end of one period and the beginning of another.

II. NSAM–288—TONKIN GULF

B. GENERAL CHARACTER OF THE PERIOD FROM NSAM–288 TO TONKIN GULF

In enunciating the policies of NSAM–288 we had rhetorically committed ourselves to do whatever was needed to achieve our stated objectives in South

Vietnam. The program decided upon and spelled out in NSAM–288 reflected our recognition that the problem was greater than we had previously supposed and that the progress that we had previously thought we were making was more apparent than real. The program constituted a larger effort than we had undertaken before; it corresponded to our increased estimates of the magnitude of the task before us. Nevertheless, we might have chosen to do more along the lines of what we did decide to do, and above all we might have chosen to do some things that we specifically chose not to do at this time (although we began to plan for some of these on a contingency basis). If there were to be new or greater problems in the future it was because we did not correctly appraise the magnitude of the problem nor fully foresee the complexity of the difficulties we faced. There were indeed some who believed that the program we decided upon was not enough, notably the JCS who had gone on record that until aid to the VC from outside of South Vietnam was cut off, it would be impossible to eliminate the insurgency there. But the program as decided upon in 288 did correspond to the official consensus that this was a prescription suited to the illness as we diagnosed it.

There were many inhibitions that discouraged doing more than the bare necessity to get the job done. There inhibitions related to the image of the U.S. in world affairs, to possible risks of over-action from the Communist side, to internal American hesitancies about our operations there, and finally to a philosophy concerning the basic social nature of what was happening in Vietnam and how wise it was for the U.S. to become very deeply involved. We had given serious thought to a program of pressures upon the North, largely covert and intended more to persuade them to compel. This was on the theory that the heart of the problem really lay not in South Vietnam but in North Vietnam. But these measures, although far from forgotten, were put on the shelf in the belief, or at least the hope, that they would not be needed.

The long year from March 1964 to April 1965 is divisible into three periods that correspond to major modifications or reformulations of policy. The first would be from March (NSAM–288) to the Tonkin Gulf affair in early August 1964, the second would be from August 1964 to February of 1965, and the third would be from February to April 1965.

From March to August 1965 we tried to make a go of it with the program approved in NSAM–288, in hope that that program would carry us toward our objectives by increasing the amount of aid and advice we gave to the South Vietnamese in order to enable them better to help themselves. But almost from the beginning there were signs that this program would not be enough. And as time passed it became more and more evident that something more would be needed. Soon we began to be turned from full concentration upon the NSAM–288 program by a major distraction—instability and inefficiency of the GVN. This was a distraction that from the first we had feared but had hoped against hope would not grow to major proportions.

A year before, in 1963, it had become more and more evident as time wore on that the unpopularity and inefficiencies of the Diem–Ngu regime destroyed the hope of permanent progress in the pacification program and the ultimate chance of success of the whole counter-insurgency effort. This time it was the increasing instability of the Khanh regime and the inefficiency of *his* government—the regime that had supplanted the regime that had suupplanted Diem and Ngu. Now we feared the inability of the Khanh government to attract and hold the loyalties of the politically active groups within the cities, and we had no confidence in its competence to administer the pacification programs, and thereby win the support of the politically inert peasantry in the rural areas.

But we wanted no more coups. Although Khanh's coup had surprised us and even shaken our confidence somewhat, we quickly made him our boy, put the best possible face on the matter, and made it a prime element of U.S. policy to support Khanh and his colleagues, and discourage any further coups. Each coup that occurred, it seemed, greatly increased the possibility of yet another coup.

Through the first period from March until July, we concentrated upon making the NSAM–288 program work. In addition to the increases in U.S. aid and advice, we sought to strengthen Khanh by patching things up with Big Minh and mollifying the other Generals he had thrown out. We hoped he could somehow subdue the politically active Buddhists, the Catholic political activists, the Dai Viet, and the miscellaneous ambitious colonels and generals.

But execution of the 288 program began to fall behind the plans. The GVN administration of the program had troubles. There were troubles getting piastres —which the U.S. government in effect provided—from the central government to the provinces and districts where they were needed. Agreed pay increases and force increases in the GVN armed forces were only tardily and partially met. Civil servants needed to operate the program in the provinces and districts were not available, were not trained, or, if available and trained, were often not paid, or were insufficiently or tardily paid, or were not provided with necessary expenses. Funds for the provision of necessary goods in the provinces and districts were not met. Payments to peasants for relocation as a part of the pacification program were tardy or inadequate or not made at all. There seemed to be a business as usual attitude in the central government, and the strength of the RVNAF declined. Viet Cong depredations continued and pacification efforts fell behind.

As we pressured Khanh to adopt reforms to remedy the deficiencies of the GVN administration of programs within South Vietnam, his frustrations over these difficulties and failures were increased. He had no taste for the long, unspectacular social reform and social rebuilding that were the tasks of pacification. He soon began to talk increasingly of a scapegoat—a march to the North. He wanted to get the struggle over with. This corresponded to the means that we had considered but had for the time being rejected—seeking escape from our own frustrations in South Vietnam by pressure on the North. We moved gradually in this direction, impelled almost inevitably to ultimate actions of this sort, but always reluctantly and always hesitant to commit ourselves to more than very minor moves, until suddenly and dramatically the Tonkin Gulf affair of early August provided an occasion to make a move of the sort we had long been anticipating but had until then always deferred. But during this period the debate over possible measures of this sort, and the instability of the Khanh government, increasingly distracted attention from programs focussed directly on the problems of pacification and of winning the loyalties of the Vietnamese for the GVN.

In the immediate aftermath of the Tonkin Gulf affair, Khanh, feeling his position strengthened, took ill advised measures to consolidate the gains that he believed had been made thereby, and quickly precipitated an overriding governmental crisis. Thereafter, the stability of the regime became the dominant factor in all considerations. Atttention had to shift from pacification of the millions of rural Vietnamese, who made up the vast majority of the people, to the very few in Saigon, Hue and Danang who were struggling for power.

B. NSAM–288 PROGRAMS MID-MARCH TO MID-MAY 1964

Recommendation #13 of NSAM—288 was "to support a program for national mobilization (including a national service law) to put South Vietnam on a war footing." Responsibility for this was shared between ASD/ISA and AID.

A first step was taken on 20 March when the country team was asked to report on the status of GVN plans and also country team views concerning the adoption of a national service act. The points of greatest concern were what would be the main provisions of the act, and what would be the administrative machinery set up to implement it. The Country Team was also advised that economic mobilization measures should be deferred until after a joint U.S.–GVN survey had been completed.

On 1 April Ambassador Lodge replied, with MACV concurrence, that Premier Khanh planned two categories of mobilization, one civil and one military. The Ambassador said that proposed decrees had been prepared and that if promulgated they would give the GVN adequate power. Details were not included, however, in the Ambassador's report. The Ambassador proposed, on a personal basis, that, if Washington approved, he would try to persuade Khanh to proceed with a mass media presentation of it. Washington agreement to the Embassy evaluation came three days later, although only the general concept had been explained. On that same day, 4 April 1964, Khanh publicly proclaimed a basic decree prescribing broad categories of national service. Its main terms were that all able-bodied males ages 20–45 were subject to national public service. This national public service was to consist of either (a) military service or (b) civil defense service.

This initial decree of 4 April 1964 amounted evidently to nothing more than a statement of intention by the Prime Minister. This was quite short of a law that would go into effect, be administered and thereby made to accomplish something.

On 10 April, the Embassy was informed by a telegram from State that Khanh's decrees had received little publicity in the United States, and the Embassy was asked for a text of the implementing decrees. Five days later on 15 April 1964, Ambassador Lodge reported in more detail on the basic terms of the national public service decree, to wit:

(1) All able-bodied males 20–45 would be subject to national public service and females would be permitted to volunteer.

(2) National public service would consist of either military service or civil defense service.

(3) Civil defense service would be managed by the Ministry of Interior.

(4) The duration of military service would be three years of RVNAF or four years in Regional Forces (Civil Guard) and Popular Forces (Civil Defense Corps and Hamlet Militia).

(5) Call-up priority would be based on age and number of dependents.

(6) Drafted personnel were to be paid by the force to which they were assigned.

This came closer to a law to be administered, but on 28 April Washington told the Embassy that the status of implementation of the recommendations was still not clear. Four days later, on 2 May, Ambassador Lodge reported that draft decrees were still not signed in fact, and that the final nature of the Civil Defense Decree was still in doubt. However, he reported agreement on the principle that the objectives of the National Mobilization Plan should give priority to: (1) bringing the armed forces to authorized strength, (2) improving their morale, (3) carrying out conscription more effectively, and (4) obtaining qualified civilian workers.

Before he was able to make this report of 2 May, however, Ambassador Lodge had a showdown meeting with Khanh over the failure of the GVN to carry out many of the necessary actions called for by the NSAM-288 programs. On 30 April, accompanied by Westmoreland and Brent (USOM chief), Lodge met with Khanh, Oanh, Khien, and Thieu, to discuss the GVN failure to provide operating funds to provincial and lower local levels, and to correct manpower deficiencies.

Lodge opened the meeting with a prepared statement which he read in French. He said that direct observation by U.S. provincial advisors throughout Vietnam proved that nowhere was there an adequate effort to provide piastres to Corps, Division and sectors, to increase the pay of ARVN and paramilitary forces, to bring these troops to authorized strength, to recruit added forces, or to compensate incapacitated soldiers or families of those killed. In fact, he said, there were confirmed reports from Corps and Division headquarters of deceased soldiers being kept on the roles as the only means of compensating their families and preventing further deterioration of ARVN and paramilitary morale. There had been a steady decline in the strength of RVNAF since October 1963, notably including a decrease of 4,000 in March alone; and the current strength was almost 20,000 below the authorized figure agreed necessary by both governments. Likewise, the force level of SDC had decreased in the same period by almost 13,000, leaving that force 18,000 below its authorized strength. The Civil Guard was almost 5,000 below the required strength. The ARVN and CG desertion rate was double what it had been in February, and SDC desertion rate was up 40%. Only 55% of the conscription quotas were being met and volunteers were below the expected level.

Failure to provide funds was blamed as a major reason for these military manpower deficiencies. The shortage was so great that the current trend in effectives could not be reversed before August in any event. Lodge went on to say that USOM and MACV visits to the provinces also confirmed that failure to provide piastres to local headquarters also led to shortages of resources for pacification efforts. The result was that most of the McNamara program of reforms and improvements (of NSAM-288) was failing, not due to lag in support promised by the United States, but simply because the Saigon government did not provide piastre support for the joint pacification program agreed upon by the two governments. The war, Lodge concluded, was being lost for want of administrative initiative in printing and distributing the necessary local funds for the agreed programs. Lodge conceded that the government had made a forward step in announcing its intentions to decentralize procurement authority from the Director General of the Budget and Foreign Aid to the ministries, but further decentralization to provincial and district authorities was advisable.

Khanh passed the buck to Oanh, who explained that the MRC had inherited enormously complicated bureaucratic procedures based on older French practices, with checks and counterchecks before actions could be effected, and that these practices were being reformed. New regulations were about to go into effect and it was hoped that they would improve the situation.

Recommendation #5 of 288 had been "to asist the Vietnamese to create a greatly enlarged administrative corps." Effective action upon this recommendation was considered essential to effective progress in the pacification program, as is clearly implied by the following list of the lines of action that were to be strengthened by the enlarged administrative corps. These were:

1. Training and pay of new hamlet action cadres, of new village secretaries, of district chiefs and other district staff, of a new assistant for pacification for each Province Chief, and of hamlet school teachers, health workers, district agricultural workers, and rural information officers.
2. Special incentive pay for government workers in rural areas.
3. Selective pay raises for some civil servants.
4. Increasing enrollment in the National Institute of Administration (NIA) to full capacity (this was a training school for civil servants), including provision of short term in-service training by NIA.
5. Organization of a joint U.S.-GVN Committee on governmental reform to review, recommend, and install needed provisions in governmental procedures.
6. Expanding and training National Police especially for rural areas consistent with other recommendations to strengthen military and paramilitary forces.

Along with this increase in Vietnamese administrative personnel there was to be increase in U.S. advisory personnel to assist them. On 2 April the Mission advised Washington that a general agreement had been reached with the GVN and estimated that 12 additional USOM public administration personnel were needed. On the following day, however, the Ambassador expressed his reservations over the large increase in staff. On 30 April in an EXDIS to the President, Lodge said that Khanh was willing to accept U.S. administrators in pacified areas provided the U.S. felt willing to accept casualties. Lodge recommended a high level civil administrative advisor to Khanh himself; and on 4 May in an EXDIS to the Secretary of State he recommended four AID public administrative advisors, one to each of the four Corps areas, all to be directly under the Ambassador.

As of mid-May, however, while there were some accomplishments, on the whole there had been more discussion than action. Before the mid-May meeting for Secretary McNamara in Saigon the status of progress was summarized for him in the Mid-May Briefing Book as follows:

1. The initiation of a two-week training program for district chiefs had started and the first class had graduated.
2. Assignment had been made of one entire graduating class, 82 of them with three full years of training, to be district chiefs.
3. Training of 75 hamlet action cadres for use in the Pacification Plan had been initiated.
4. Assignment of 700 Saigon civil servants to the III Corps area had been completed (but two-thirds of them had returned by mid-May as either unfit or in excess of needs).
5. The long standing training programs for hamlet workers had continued.
6. A course to train 2500 new village secretaries had been initiated.
7. Assurance that all future graduates of NIA would be assigned to the countryside had been made.

8. There was a promise to undertake to double the output of graduates from the NIA.

No action had been taken, however, on other measures. The most salient inaction was the failure to set up the promised U.S.–GVN committee on government reform. Further, the GVN was not inclined to provide incentive pay to key rural workers.

At the time that Secretary McNamara and his party went to Saigon in the middle of May, the problem areas with respect to implementation of NSAM-288 recommendations were identified as follows:

1. Inadequate provision of piastres for proper utilization of already trained officials and technicians.
2. Possible inability of GVN to get the job done without direct U.S. participation.
3. Lack of information from the field on plans for aggressive implementation of all aspects of this recommendation.

Recommendation 4, 6, and 7 of NSAM-288 concerned increases in GVN military forces and capabilities and were generally considered together:

4. To assist the Vietnamese to increase the armed forces (regular plus paramilitary) by at least 50,000 men.
6. To assist the Vietnamese to improve and reorganize the paramilitary forces and to increase their compensation.
7. To assist the Vietnamese to create an offensive guerrilla force.

On 23 March 1964 a joint State-Defense-AID message asked the country team to refine (and elaborate) these concepts and recommend a program of implementing actions. The mission was authorized to initiate appropriate first steps without waiting for final agreement between the USG and the GVN. There followed, as already noted, the pertinent proclamations of early April, but they were only proclamations, nothing more. On 27 April General Harkins reported that GVN planning for reorganization of paramilitary forces and development of a concept for programs was still in process. General Phat, the Minister of Interior, was considering a merger of SDC and Combat Youth into a single organization (the Popular Forces) under the Ministry of Interior. The Civil Guard would go under the Army high command. Operational control of Popular Forces would be vested in sector and sub-sector commanders at province and district levels. At village levels, Popular Forces would encompass the total local security force and would include both full-time and part-time personnel. Details of compensation and the logistic mechanism were not clear. Harkins judged that the concept was consistent with the Pacification Plan, but the total anticipated strength of Popular Forces could not be projected until more detailed planning had been accomplished. Detailed negotiations with the GVN were continuing and a further report was to be made on 10 May.

Two days later, on 29 April 1964, the JCS commented on the slowness of the GVN in implementing recommendations for 6 and 7 and pointed out an apparent divergence between MACV and GVN on the strength and organization of the GVN forces. They explained that the 50,000 figure was an *interim* planning figure, and that further increases should be recommended when and as necessary. COMUSMACV was asked to submit his detailed plan for implementing 4, 6, and 7 by the 7th of May.

Almost simultaneously with this JCS message, Harkin's deputy, General West-moreland, was accompanying Ambassador Lodge to see Khanh on the occasion, already described, when Ambassador Lodge made his strong demarche with the Vietnamese Premier. Westmoreland expatiated on the military aspects of the Ambassador's complaint, especially the RVNAF deficiencies, specifying increased desertion rates and inadequate enlistments and draft callups. He calculated that at the current rates of desertion, casualties and recruitment the RVNAF at the end of the year would be smaller not larger than at present.

Finally, on 7 May, Harkins was able to report that a USG–GVN agreement had been reached on calendar year 1964 force goals for the RVNAF, Civil Guard and the National Police, although there was not yet an agreement on the SDC and Combat Youth. The agreement on the RVNAF, CG, and SDC force levels were as shown in the tabulation below:

	Current Authorized Strength	Recommended Strength CY 64	Amount Increase	Estimated Cost
RVNAF	227,000	237,600	10,600	1. GVN = 1.4 billion piastres 2. U.S. = $18 million for pay; $5 million MAP
Civil Guard	90,015	97,615	7,600	1. .8 billion piastres 2. $2.2 million MAP (no estimate of cost of pay increase)
SDC	110,000	110,000	—	No estimates of cost (no agreement yet)
Combat Youth	180,000 (trained) 80–90,000 (trained and armed)	200,000	20,000	No estimates of cost (no agreement yet)
National Police	24,250	34,900	10,650	500,000 million piastres $1.2 million

With respect to the perennial problem of assisting the Vietnamese to develop their own offensive guerrilla force, in mid-May there was some progress to report, although the accomplishments were less than had been hoped. Efforts were continuing to improve the distribution of Ranger battalions for use against VC base areas and in border areas of I and II Corps. Plans also were being developed at that time for better border control, and for intelligence integration, coordination of Vietnamese Special Forces operations, and air surveillance. Efforts were also being made towards integration of Vietnamese Special Forces and U.S. Special Forces staffs at all command echelons. Vietnamese junior officers and NCO's, including Montagnards, were being initiated to training and guerrilla warfare techniques in the new VNSF/USSF Center at Nha Trang. This was expected to encourage the VNSF to adopt bolder and more confident tactics.

Recommendations 8, 9, and 10 were accomplished rather simply and expeditiously because they consisted entirely of supplying the South Vietnamese materials that they needed. It did not involve our inducing the Vietnamese themselves to do anything. Recommendation 8 was to provide the Vietnamese Air Force 25 A1H aircraft in exchange for present T-28's. Recommendation 9 was to provide the Vietnamese army additional M-113 APC's (withdrawing the M-114's there), additional riverboats and approximately $5–10 million worth of additional materiel. Recommendation 10 was to announce publicly the fertilizer program and to expand it with a view to trebling within two years the amount of fertilizer currently made available.

MAP funding for Recommendation 8 was approved by ISA on 25 March 1964 following approval of the delivery schedule on 22 March. On 1 May 1964, 19 A1H's were delivered and six more scheduled for delivery 10 days later. A Navy unit of 4 support officers, 8 instruction pilots and 150 men arrived on 30 April 1964 to train Vietnamese crews until they could assume full responsibility, which was estimated to be in three to six months. By early May planning and funding action for the provision of the M-113's had been completed. According to the schedule developed in response to the request for this materiel made by CINCPAC and COMUSMACV, 17 M-113's were shipped to arrive in Saigon 17 April, 16 were due to arrive 29 April, 30 were shipped to arrive by 1 June, and 30 more were to arrive by 10 July. There was an agreement between CINCPAC and COMUSMACV that no additional howitzers, riverboats or AN/PRC/41s were to be recommended at that time. Eighty-five thousand tons of fertilizer had been requested and procured by early May for spring planting, and this had been publicized by the GVN and in Washington. A distribution scheme was being developed and refined in early May with provision for further expansion including a probable 18,000 tons requirement in the fall.

There were two important visitations to Saigon during April. The first was by General Earle G. Wheeler, then Chief of Staff, USA, who visited Saigon from 15–20 April and represented Secretary McNamara and the JCS during the visit of the Secretary of State to Saigon 17–20 April. It was during these meetings that Khanh's desire to shift the emphasis of the struggle to an attack on the North first become emphatically evident. In the meeting with Khanh on 16 April, Wheeler, in company with General Harkins, was informed by Khanh that eventually the war must be moved north. Harkins later told Wheeler that this was the first time Khanh had ever said that extending operations to the North was inevitable. Khanh explained that when the move to the North occurred MACV would have to take over all the logistics. He further said he was ready to start planning for an extension of operations to the North.

Two days later on 18 April Khanh again brought the matter up, this time with Secretary of State Rusk. Rusk replied that this was a big problem, that political preparation would be needed, and that while the U.S. was prepared to take any action necessary to win the war, it had to be very clear that such action was indeed necessary before the U.S. would embark on it.

A fortnight before on 4 April 1964 W. P. Bundy had written a letter to Ambassador Lodge with enclosures which concerned a possible political scenario to support action against North Vietnam and for the earlier, so-called "Blue Annex" (considerations of extended actions to the North) completed during the McNamara-Taylor visit in March 1964. In Washington there was considerable theorizing, in this period, about the best manner of persuading North Vietnam to cease aid to the NLF-VC by forceful but restrained pressures which would convey the threat of greater force if the North Vietnamese did not end their support of the insurgency in South Vietnam. In certain circles in Washington at least, there was what appears now to have been an amazing level of confidence that we could induce the North Vietnamese to abandon their support of the SVN insurgency if only we could convince them that we meant business, and that we would indeed bomb them if they did not stop their infiltration of men and supplies to the South.

This confidence, although ultimately accepted as the basis for decision, was neither universal nor unqualified. This was evident, for instance in the meeting of 19 April, when the subject was discussed in Saigon with Rusk, Lodge, Harkins, Nes, Manfull, DeSilva, Lt. Col. Dunn, General Wheeler, W. P. Bundy, and Solbert of ISA. Much of the discussion on that occasion centered on the political context, objectives, and risks, of increasing military pressure on North Vietnam. It was understood that it would be first exerted solely by the Government of Vietnam, and would be clandestine. Gradually both wraps and restraints would be removed. A point on which there was a good deal of discussion was what contact with the DRV would be best in order to let Hanoi know the meaning of the pressures and of the threats of greater pressures. Ambassador Lodge favored a Canadian ICC man who was about to replace the incumbent. The new man he had known at the UN. While Lodge was willing to participate in discussions of the mechanisms, he was explicitly unsure of Hanoi's reaction to any level of pressure. Lodge was not always fully consistent in his views on this subject, and it is not clear that his reservations on this score led him to counsel against the move or to express other cautions. However, he did say he doubted that we could meet massive intervention by the DRV by purely conventional measures. Rusk hoped that the threatened pressures against Hanoi would induce her to end her support for the VC. Rusk emphasized the importance of obtaining the strongest possible evidence of DRV infiltration. It was during this discussion that the question of the introduction of U.S. Naval forces—and hints of Cam Ranh Bay—arose as a measure which it was hoped would induce increased caution in Hanoi. The presence of military power there, it was hoped, might induce Hanoi to be more restrained in its actions toward South Vietnam. There was speculation about whether the use of nuclear weapons against North Vietnam would bring in the Russians. Rusk had been impressed, so he said, by Chiang Kai-shek's recent, strongly expressed opposition to any use by the United States of nuclear weapons. There was mention that Khiem had sought Chinese Nationalist military forces but their utility was generally deprecated. Bundy conjectured, for argument's sake, that nukes used in wholly unpopulated areas solely for purposes of interdiction might have a different significance than if used otherwise. It is not reported that any examination of effectiveness or of obviously possible countermeasures was essayed; and no decisions were made. But the direction of thinking was clearly away from measures internal to Vietnam, and clearly headed toward military actions against the North.

At the conclusion of his visit to Vietnam in mid-April Secretary Rusk drew up the two-part summary list of added steps that he believed necessary. The first part, composed of actions presenting no substantive policy problems listed the following actions:

    1. Engage more flags in South Vietnam.
    2. Increase GVN diplomatic representation, and GVN information activity (to widen support of the GVN cause).
    3. Enlist General Minh in the war effort.
    4. Mobilize public support for war effort by civilian groups.
    5. Improve the psychological warfare effort.

6. Discreetly cooperate with Khanh for the expulsion of "undesirable characters."

7. Empower Ambassador Lodge to make on-the-spot promotions to U.S. civilians in Vietnam.

Among the actions the Secretary felt should be considered, but which involved policy problems, were:

1. Maintain U.S. naval presence at either Tourane or Cam Ranh Bay, as a signal to Hanoi (to suggest to them our deep interest in affairs in Vietnam).

2. Spend more money in developing pacified provinces instead of concentrating efforts almost exclusively on trouble spots.

3. Push GVN anti-junk operations gadually north of the DMZ.

4. Remove inhibitions on the use of Asian intelligence agents in Cambodian-Laos border areas.

By the end of another fortnight Khanh's mood had turned much more strongly toward insistence upon his march to the North. On the morning of 4 May 1964, Khanh asked Lodge to call, and Khanh began by asking if he should make a declaration putting the country on a war footing. This, he said would involve getting rid of "politicians" in the government and having a government composed frankly of technicians. It would involve suspension of civil rights ("as had been the case under Lincoln in your civil war"). There would be a curfew, Saigon would cease to be a city of pleasure, and plans laid to evacuate the diplomatic corps and two million people. Khanh then said that an announcement should be made to Hanoi that any further interference with South Vietnam's internal affairs would lead to reprisals, and Khanh specifically asked if the U.S. would be prepared to undertake tit-for-tat bombing each time there was such interference.

Continuing, Khanh talked further, somewhat wildly, of defying Cambodia and breaking diplomatic relations with France; and he even mentioned a declaration of war against the DRV at one point. He conveyed the impression of a desperate desire to press for an early military decision by outright war with the DRV. Lodge sought to discourage this sort of adventurism, but acknowledged that if the DRV invaded South Vietnam with its Army, that act would raise a host of new questions of acute interest to the U.S. Possible entry of Chinese forces would have to be considered. The question then would be whether such an Army could be made ineffective by interdicting its supply lines. He could not envision the U.S. putting into Asia an Army the size of the U.S. Army in Europe in World War II. Khanh said that he understood this but that an "Army Corps" of U.S. Special Forces numbering 10,000 could do in Asia as much as an Army group had done in Europe. "One American can make soldiers out of 10 Orientals." [Sic!] It was illogical, wasteful, and wrong to go on incurring casualties "just in order to make the agony endure."

Near the end of his report of this conversation, the Ambassador inserted this comment, "this man obviously wants to get on with the job and not sit here indefinitely taking casualties. Who can blame him?" Then he added, as a further comment:

His desire to declare a state of war . . . seems wholly in line with our desire to get out of a "business as usual" mentally. He is clearly facing up to all the hard questions and wants us to do it, too.

Lodge's report of Khanh's impatient wish to strike north drew an immediate flash response from Rusk, which began with a statement that made it clear that the message had been considered carefully at the White House. Extremely grave issues were raised by the conversation, and reactions had to be developed with great care. There would still be another meeting with the President on the matter, on 6 May, before McNamara departed for the trip that would take him to Saigon (after Bonn). McNamara would take up issues with Lodge upon his arrival there. But before the 6 May meeting with the President, would Lodge please answer seven questions as a contribution to the Washington consideration of the issue.

The questions raised by the Secretary and the answers provided later by the Embassy follow:

1. What were Khanh's motivations? Does he believe that mobilization makes sense *only* as a preparation for military action against North Vietnam? *Reply:* Khanh as professional soldier thinks in terms of victory. Not a matter of pique. Honestly seeking a means of putting country on war footing.

2. Is there a trace of despair in Khanh's remarks? Does he think he can win without attacking north? *Reply:* No.

3. Previously Khanh told McNamara it would be necessary to consolidate a base in South Vietnam for attacking North Vietnam. Previous counter-guerrilla experience in Greece, Malaya, and Korea supports this judgment. *Reply:* Khanh does *not* want to move regardless of progress in the South.

4. Khanh's talk of evacuating seems fantastic. *Reply:* Agree. Khanh's concern was an ability to administer the city if attacked. (This referred to Khanh's discussion of evacuating the city.)

5. Were Khanh's talks of warning to Hanoi and Cambodia and action against the French integral parts of mobilization? *Reply:* Yes. But he should have *evidence* against French nationals.

6. How to interpret Khanh's remarks about U.S. "Army Corps?" *Reply:* Loose talk. This reaction came after (Lodge's) discouraging reply about the possibility of the U.S. bringing in large numbers of forces.

7. Was the GVN capable of administering limited mobilization? *Reply:* Question is a puzzler. However, some such thing might be a way of over-coming "business as usual."

The response to Khanh's proposal that came out of the 6 May meeting was that the Secretary of Defense was to tell Khanh, when he was in Saigon, that the U.S. did "not intend to provide military support nor undertake the military ob-jective of rolling back Communist control in North Vietnam."

C.   THE SECRETARY'S VISIT TO SAIGON MAY 1964

Accompanied by General Wheeler, and MM. Sylvester and McNaughton, and his military aide, the Secretary of Defense made a brief visit to Saigon 12–14 May enroute home from Bonn. In informing Saigon on 4 May of his projected visit he said that his primary objective was to get full information as to the current status and future plans, with targets and dates, for the following items for the rest of calendar year 1964:

1. Augmentation of GVN military and paramilitary forces, with a break-down by area and service category.

2. Increased compensation for GVN military and paramilitary personnel.
3. Reorganization of military and paramilitary forces.
4. Creation of the Civil Administrative Corps.
5. Implementation of the national mobilization plan.
6. The steps and timetables, both military and civil, for our implementation of the oil-spot concept of pacification.

Additionally, it was further specified that he wanted information on the following:

1. A map of population and areas controlled by the VC and the GVN.
2. Progress of military operations in extending control by the oil-spot theory.
3. Brief reports on the critical provinces.
4. The Country Team's appraisal of Khanh's progress in strengthening national, provincial and district governments.
5. The Country Team's evaluation of Khanh's support by various groups (constituting Vietnamese political power centers).
6. MACV's forecast of likely VC and GVN military activity for the rest of 1964.
7. Recommendations on cross-border intelligence operations.
8. Report on the extent to which the U.S. contribution of added resources or personnel (either military or civilian) for civil programs could strengthen the GVN counterinsurgency program.

The trip books prepared for the members of the Secretary's party also indicated that one major concern was to reinforce Lodge's demarche of 30 April concerning facilitating the flow of piastres to the provinces for counterinsurgency support. It was suggested that possibly the rigid and conservative director of the budget, Luu Van Tinh might have to be dismissed if Oanh couldn't make him do better. A list of problems that were created by lack of piastres in the provinces followed:

1. Health workers trained by AID were not employed for lack of piastres.
2. Provincial and district officers (both health and agricultural extension workers) were severely restricted in travel to villages for lack of *per diem* and gasoline.
3. Bills for handling AID counterinsurgency cargo at the port of Danang were not paid, resulting in refusal and threat of refusal, by workers and groups, to handle more cargo.
4. Several categories of GVN workers had not been paid salaries owed to them for months.
5. Truckers were threatening to refuse to handle AID counterinsurgency cargo because they had not been paid for past services by the Government of Vietnam.
6. There were inadequate funds to compensate villages for food, lodging, water and services provided by peasants to the ARVN, the CG, and the SDC.
7. There had been nonpayment or delayed or only partial payment of promised relocation allowances to relocated authorities.

In the light of these problems it was considered that two USOM piastre cash funds might be established: (1) a petty cash fund to support the Ministry of Education; and (2) a substantial USOM-controlled piastre fund to break bottlenecks in such matters as transportation of goods, spare parts, *per diem* payment of immobilized Vietnamese personnel, and emergency purchases on the local market. AID Administrator Bell in Washington had made commitments to Secretary McNamara that all piastres necessary for counterinsurgency would be forthcoming even if deficit financing were needed. But because there were plenty of commodity imports at hand, that posed no problem. USOM and MACV and the public administration advisors who were then being recruited should review carefully whether U.S. civil administration advisors to the provincial chiefs could facilitate the flow of funds and commodities, and expedite paper work. Finally, the use of rural affairs provincial staffs should be increased by one or more per province, perhaps using Filipinos or Chinese Nationals.

The first day of the Secretary's stay in Saigon was spent in briefings, and not all of what he heard was encouraging. There was first a briefing from the Ambassador, who said the administrative mechanism of the central GVN was not functioning smoothly, that Khanh overcentralized authority, and that although the situation might work out the prospects were not good. One bit of encouragement was that Khanh was requesting more U.S. advisors—this was taken as a token of good intentions and of willingness to cooperate with the U.S. The provincial government would continue to be weak, and the corps commanders' authority handicapped the provinces. Khanh's 23 new province chiefs and 80 new district chiefs had improved the quality of leadership, he thought. But the Buddhists, although fragmented, remained politically active and Thich Tri Quang was agitating strongly against Khanh. The Catholics were about to withdraw their chaplains from the Army. The students supported Khanh but the intellectuals did not. Lodge thought that the current U.S. program was of about the right size but that better leadership was needed. He would like U.S. civilian advisors in each corps area. When USOM Director Brent gave his briefing he made the point that USOM was 25 percent short of authorized personnel strength. This led the Secretary to ask about the use of U.S. military personnel, FSOs, or Peace Corps personnel to fill the shortage. Forrestal was asked to look into the problem and report. The NIA was short of faculty because seven instructors had been assigned elsewhere and there was, moreover, and inadequate budget.

In the afternoon briefing, General Harkins said he was guardedly optimistic in spite of the fact that 23 province chiefs, 135 district chiefs, and practically all senior military commanders had been replaced since the last coup. In discussing "Population Control" (pacification), it was decided to use 1 April 1964 as a base for statistical measurements of pacification progress. When he came to the subject of the planned augmentation of ARVN and the paramilitary forces, the figures presented by General Harkins showed that achievement lagged behind the agreed goals. Although the agreed MAP program called for 229,000 RVNAF personnel at that time and 238,000 for the end of calendar year 1964, there were actually only 207,000 currently in RVNAF. (This showed no improvement over March.) The strength of RVNAF had in fact been decreasing consistently from a high of 218,000 in July 1963 because of increased activity (hence losses through casualties), desertions, budget problems and miscellaneous lesser causes.

Among the topics receiving considerable attention during the meeting on the morning of the 13th of May was that of VNAF pilot training program. This subject assumed special importance for three reasons. First, the March program of providing helicopters to the Vietnamese Air Force called also for the provision of pilots to fly them. Second, there had just previously been some embarrassing publicity concerning the participation of USAF pilots in covert combat roles, an activity that had not been publicly acknowledge. Third, the meeting with the President on 6 May had led to the instructions to the Secretary, already noted, to discourage Khanh's hopes of involving the United States in his March to the North. In this discussion of VNAF pilot training, it was revealed that there were 496 VNAF pilots currently at hand, but that 666 were required by 1 July. Thirty helicopter pilots were to finish by 1 July, 30 liaison pilots to finish by 27 June, and 226 cadet pilots were in the United States whose status was not known at the time of the meeting. The Secretary emphasized that it had never been intended that the USAF participate in combat in Vietnam, and current practices that belied this were exceptions to that policy. The Administration had been embarrassed because of the Shank affair—letters which had complained that U.S. boys were being killed in combat while flying inferior aircraft. The Secretary emphasized that that VNAF should have a better pilot-to-aircraft ratio. It should be 2 to 1 instead of 1.4 to 1 as at present. And, as a first priority project, VNAF pilots should transition from other aircraft to the A-1Hs to bring the total to 150 qualified to fly that aircraft. It was tentatively agreed to fix that objective for 120 days and accept the consequent degradation of transport capability.

Following this there was a discussion of offensive guerrilla operations and cross-border operations, both of which were agreed to be inadequate. Creation of an offensive guerrilla force had been one of the Secretary's March recommendations. General Westmoreland said that Special Forces of both the U.S. and the GVN were over-extended, and he added he believed that they should be expanded. As a result of this conversation MACV was directed to study the six-month duty tour of the U.S. Special Forces. The Secretary considered it possibly too short and thought it might have to be extended to a full year. On the subject of cross-border operations, the concept was to drop six-man teams in each of authorized areas in North Vietnam and Laos and pick them up, 30 days later, by helicopter. The objective was two teams by 15 June; and this potential was to be doubled each month thereafter. It was decided that operations should begin approximately 15 June 1964.

In his subsequent report on this second SecDef-MACV conference, MACV reported that the Secretary of Defense had expressed disappointment that the civil defense decree of the GVN did not constitute a counterpart to military conscription. Furthermore, MACV recorded that in the course of the discussion of means of strengthening the VNAF the Secretary of Defense had reaffirmed basic U.S. policy that fighting in Vietnam should be done by Vietnamese. The FARM-GATE concept was explained as a specific, reluctantly approved exception, a supplementary effort transitory in nature.

The Secretary's military aide, Lt. Col. Sidney B. Berry, Jr., recorded the decisions taken by the Secretary at Saigon. They were these:

1. Have the first group of six-man reconnaissance teams for cross-border operations ready to operate by 15 June 1964, then double the number of teams each month thereafter. The Secretary was anxious to get hard information on DRV aid to the VC. The Secretary was to get authority for additional cross-border operations in addition to the operations already authorized in two locations.

2. Concerning the VNAF training program, there was never any intent, nor was it the policy of the USG to have USAF pilots participate in combat. Exception to this should be considered undesirable and not setting a precedent. MACV was therefore to give first priority to manning 75 A1Hs with two Vietnamese pilots per aircraft, for a total of 150 Vietnamese pilots; and he was also to determine the optimum size of the VNAF, tentatively using a figure of 125 to 150 A1H aircraft. In connection with this the

Secretary approved assignment to the VNAF of 25 more A1Hs by 1 October 1964 to replace 18 RT-28s on hand.

3. When the Secretary asked Harkins if he needed additional Special Forces, Harkins replied, "Yes." The Secretary then said that when COMUS-MACV stated requirements he would approve them if they were valid. He said that a six-month duty tour was too short and the normal tour should be extended to one year, reserving the right, of course, to make exceptions for special cases.

4. When General Harkins handed the Secretary a shopping list for items and funds totalling about $7 million, the Secretary immediately approved the list.

5. The Secretary directed COMUSMACV to submit in writing requirements for South Vietnamese military housing.

6. Concerning MACV needs, the "SecDef made unequivocal statement that MACV should not hesitate to ask for anything they need. SecDef gives first priority to winning the war in SVN. If necessary he will take weapons and equipment from U.S. forces to give the VNAF. Nothing will be spared to win the war. But U.S. personnel must operate in compliance with USG policies and objectives."

Near the end of the Secretary's stay General Khanh met with McNamara, Lodge, Taylor and Harkins; and judging from the report of the meeting sent in by the Ambassador, Khanh put on a masterful performance. Khanh began his talk by reviewing the recent course of the war claiming to have established control, in the last three months, over some three million Vietnamese citizens [sic]. However, the danger of reinfiltration by the Communists still existed. Khanh said that the biggest and most time-consuming problems were political, and he was unskilled in such things and wanted to lean for advice on Ambassador Lodge. But religious problems were also pressing. There was religious conflict between Catholics and Buddhists and within the Buddhist movement. The Government of Vietnam was in the middle. The real trouble-maker was Thich Tri Quang. Lodge was trying to help Khanh in this. There was also a problem with the press, and with "parlor politicians" (civilians). Khanh said that he was a soldier, not a politician, and wished he could spend his time mounting military operations and in planning long-term strategy instead of dealing with political intrigues and squabbles. But he had to think about the security of his regime.

The Secretary then referred to the Ambassador's report of Khanh's desire not to "prolong the agony," and said that he, the Secretary, wanted to hear more about this. Khanh said that in speaking of not wanting to "make the agony endure" he did not mean he would lose patience, but rather wanted to speed up the effort by something like a proclamation that South Vietnam was being attacked from the north and was therefore being put on a war footing. The statement would also say that if this attack from the north did not stop within a specified period of time, South Vietnam would strike back in ways and degrees comparable to the North Vietnamese attacks on South Vietnam.

> Whereas the north attacks us with guerrillas that squirm through the jungle, we would attack them with guerrillas of our own, only ours would fly at treetop level and blow up key installations or mine the Port of Haiphong.

The Secretary asked in return if Khanh judged it wise to start operations at that time. Khanh replied that he needed first to consider the enemy's probable reaction, including the reaction of Communist China. The NLF and VC were only arms and hands of the monster whose head was in Hanoi "and maybe further north." To destroy the thing it was necessary to strike the head. The purpose of going on a war footing was to prepare for ultimate extension of the war to the north. Taylor asked how best to attack the North. It had been noted that small-scale operations had had no success. With respect to RVNAF capabilities, Khanh said that they either were equal to the task already, or soon would be—the problem was to be sure of enjoying full U.S. support. Khanh conceded that there were always unknowns that created uncertainties. Taylor recalled that in March Khanh had favored holding off the attack on North Vietnam until there was a stabler base in South Vietnam. Khanh hedged on this point at first; then, after conceding some GVN weakness, said an attack on the North was the best way to cure that weakness. It would be a cure for weakness to draw clear lines of battle and thereby engage men's hearts in an all-out effort.

The Secretary at a later point reminded Khanh of the 72,000-man increase in ARVN, and another 72,000-man increase in paramilitary forces, that had been agreed upon in March; and pointed out that accomplishments in April did not suggest that the GVN was on schedule. The Secretary emphasized he made the observation only to introduce his main point, which was that the U.S. Government would help in any way it could to get the program back on schedule. Then he produced a chart showing what should have been achieved and what actually had been achieved. The USG would supply any needed funds, and fighter-type aircraft, but the GVN must emphasize to the provinces that program funds must be disbursed. Khanh blamed the piastre disbursal difficulties on inherited French budget practices, and promised to pressure the province chiefs further on the matter. There was talk about incompetent personnel within the GVN and of the problems of replacing them.

D. THE HONOLULU CONFERENCE OF 30 MAY 1964

The next landmark of policy formation for Vietnam was the Honolulu Conference of 30 May 1964. On 26 May, the President sent out to Lodge his call for the Honolulu Conference:

> I have been giving the most intense consideration to the whole battle for Southeast Asia, and I have now instructed Dean Rusk, Bob McNamara, Max Taylor and John McCone to join Felt in Honolulu for a meeting with you and a very small group of your most senior associates in Southeast Asia to review for my final approval a series of plans for effective action.
>
> I am sending you this message at once to give you private advance notice because I hope this meeting can occur very soon—perhaps on Monday. Dean Rusk will be sending you tomorrow a separate cable on the subjects proposed for the meeting, and Bob McNamara will put a plane at your disposal for the trip . . .

Other parts of the message referred to matters related to imepnding changes in the mission in Saigon—the retirement of General Harkins and his replacement by General Westmoreland and the strengthening of the civilian side of the country team.

The promised policy guidance followed promptly. It constituted both an appraisal of the current situation and a statement of the needs—flowing from that appraisal—that it seemed evident had to be met, along with some proposals for meeting those needs.

> I. You will have surmised from yesterday's telegram from the President and the Secretary that we here are fully aware that gravest decisions are in

front of us and other governments about free world's interest in and commitment to security of Southeast Asia. Our point of departure is and must be that we cannot accept overrunning of Southeast Asia by Hanoi and Peiping. Full and frank discussion of these decisions with you is purpose of Honolulu meeting . . .

2. President will continue in close consultation with Congressional leadership (he met with Democratic leadership and Senate Republicans yesterday) and will wish Congress associated with him on any steps which carry with them substantial acts and risks of escalation. At that point there will be three central questions:

a. Is the security of Southeast Asia vital to the U.S. and of the free world?

b. Are additional steps necessary?

c. Will the additional steps accomplish their mission of stopping the intrusions of Hanoi and Peping into the south?

Whether approached from b or c above, it seems obvious that we must do everything within our power to stiffen and strengthen the situation in South Vietnam. We recognize that . . . the time sequence of Communist actions may force the critical decisions before any such preparatory measures could achieve tangible success.

II. Nevertheless, in Honolulu, we would like you . . . to be prepared to discuss with us several proposals . . perhaps the most radical . . . is the one which . . . would involve a major infusion of U.S. efforts into a group of selected provinces where Vietnamese seem currently unable to execute their pacification programs . . .

We would therefore propose that U.S. personnel, both civilian and military, drawn from the U.S. establishment currently in Vietnam, be "encadred" into current Vietnamese political and military structure . . .

Specifically, this would involve the assignment of civilian personnel, alternatively military personnel with a civilian function, to work in the provincial administration, and insofar as it is feasible, down to the logistic level of administration. On the military side it would mean the introduction of mobile training teams to train, stiffen and improve the state of the Vietnamese paramilitary forces and district operation planning . . .

In order to test the utility of such a proposal, we would suggest that seven provinces be chosen for this purpose. We would offer the provinces of Long An, Dinh Tuong, Kien Hoa, Tay Ninh, Hau Nghia, which are five critical provinces in the immediate vicinity of Saigon. Additionally, we would propose Quang Ngia. . . . and finally Phu Yen. . . .

. . . U.S. personnel assigned to these functions would not appear directly in the chain of command. . . . They would instead be listed as "assistants" to the Vietnamese officials. In practice, however, we would expect them to carry a major share of the burden of decision and action . . .

. . . This proposal might also require a close integration of U.S. and Vietnamese pacification activities in Saigon. . . .

III. In addition to these radical proposals . . . we continue gravely concerned about the differences between Khanh and the generals, the problem of Big Minh, and the religious differences. . . .

IV. Finally, we wish to consult with you on the manner in which we can . . . eliminate the business as usual attitude in Saigon. . . . We will also wish to examine the best means of reducing the problems of dependents. . . .

On the same day that the foregoing policy guidance went out to Ambassador Lodge, a meeting was held in Washington at William Sullivan's suggestion. Attended by Mr. McGeorge Bundy, John McNaughton, General Goodpastor and William Colby, it considered a policy memo drawn up by Mr. Mendenhall covering most of the same points raised in the message to Lodge. The gist of the memo was that the GVN was not operating effectively enough to reverse the adverse trend of the war against the VC, that the Khanh government was well intentioned but its good plans were not being translated into effective action, and that it was necessary therefore to find means of broadening the U.S. role in Vietnam in order to infuse efficiency into the operations of the GVN. In general, the memo argued the U.S. should become more deeply involved both militarily and otherwise, abandoning the passive advisor role but avoiding visibility as a part of the chain of command. Vietnamese sensitivities imposed limitations, and if it should appear that the United States intruded, the Vietnamese might come to resent our presence. The memo proposed, nevertheless, that the meeting carefully consider a phased expansion of the U.S. role. First, military advisors might be placed in paramilitary units in seven provinces—about 300 added advisors would be needed for this purpose. Second, in the same seven provinces—Long An, Dinh Tuong, Kien Hoa, Tay Ninh, Hau Nghia, Quang Ngia, and Phu Yen— U.S. civilian and military personnel should be interlarded in the *civil* administration, about 10 per province for a total of 70. Third, as an experiment, the U.S. might try civilians at district levels to supplement the U.S. military personnel being assigned there. "In view of the traditional distrust of the Vietnamese peasants for military personnel, it is of considerable importance to begin an introduction of American civilian presence at this level to help win support of the peasant population." [Sic] To back up these field operations it was suggested that a joint Vietnamese-American Pacification Operations Committee be established, with high level representation from MACV and USOM on the U.S. side, and from the Defense Ministry, the Joint General Staff (JGS), the Vice President for Pacification, and the Directorate of the Budget and Foreign Aid on the Vietnamese side. This Joint Pacification Operations Committee should be concerned *not* with policy but with *implementation* of policies. (This was judged the weak side of the GVN.) U.S. personnel might, in addition, be introduced at reasonably high levels into the Ministries of Rural Affairs, Interior, Information, Education, Health, Public Works, and, in fact, into any other agency concerned with pacification. Finally, the U.S. personnel so assigned should come from among those Americans already on the spot—partly from civilians and partly from military officers already on assignment there—and the vacancies caused by these reassignments should be filled by recruitment from the U.S.

A cable from the Chairman of the Joint Chiefs to CINCPAC and COMUSMACV indicated that (in addition to some questions on Laos) the Secretary of Defense wanted the views of the two senior commanders in the Pacific (CINCPAC and MACV) on a series of questions largely but not exclusively military in nature:

> 1. What military actions, in ascending order of gravity, might be taken to impress Hanoi with our intentions to strike North Vietnam?
> 2. What would be the time factors and force requirements involved in achieving readiness for such actions against North Vietnam?
> 3. What should be the purpose and pattern of the initial air strike against North Vietnam?

4. What was their concept of the actions and reactions which might arise from progressive implementation of CINCPAC plans 37–64 and 32–64?

5. How might North Vietnam and Communist China respond to these escalating pressures?

6. What military help should be sought from SEATO nations?

There was a second group of queries which referred not to the possibility of military pressures of one sort or another against North Vietnam, but rather were directed mainly to the counterinsurgency efforts within South Vietnam.

1. What were their views on providing four-man advisory teams, at once, for each district in the seven selected provinces, and later in all of the 239 districts in SVN?

2. In what other ways could military personnel be used to advantage in forwarding the pacification program in the seven selected provinces?

3. What was the current status of:

a. The proposed increase in regular *and* paramilitary forces of the GVN, including the expansion of the VNAF, the reorganization of paramilitary forces and the increased compensation for GVN military forces?

b. Formation of an intelligence net of U.S. advisors reporting on conditions in the RVNAF?

c. Development of a capability for offensive guerrilla operations?

d. Progress under decrees for national mobilization?

e. Progress in detailing and in carrying out operational plans for clear-hold operations (the oil-spot concept)?

Along with the solicitation of opinion from COMUSMACV and CINCPAC, summary proposals were developed by SACSA on the "feasiblility of strengthening RVNAF, CG and SDC by increased advisory efforts and/or encadrement." SACSA's proposals, intended for consideration at the Honolulu meeting, centered on three subjects. The first elaborated a concept which was called "U.S. Advisory Assistance to the Vitenamese Civil Guard" which consisted of a phased program of U.S. detachments at the district level to provide operational assistance to paramilitary forces. About one and one-half years (or until the end of calendar year 1965) would be needed to expand the current effort—which consisted of two-man teams for only 13 districts—to 239 districts with larger advisory teams (one officer and 3 NCO specialists). Thus, by the end of 1965, according to this plan, approximately 1,000 men would be assigned to the districts. To support this effort in the districts about 500 more personnel would be needed, raising the total to 1500. The limiting factor on this effort would be a shortage of interpreters.

The second program proposed for consideration by SACSA was a "Pilot Program for Provision of Advisory Assistance to Paramilitary Forces in Seven Provinces." This was directed exclusively to the seven critical provinces, namely, Long An, Dinh Tuong, Kien Hoa, Hau Nghia, Tay Ninh, Quang Ngia and Phu Yen. The concept in this case was to assign one advisory detachment with one company grade officer and three NCOs to each of the 49 districts in the seven provinces. In addition to this total of 200 persons, a 35 percent manpower overhead slice plus some augmentation at the province level (70 + 30) would be required. This would mean about 100 men in addition to the 4 × 49 in the districts, or an overall total of about 300. In addition, a minimum of 49 interpretors would be needed.

The third proposal for discussion was a suggestion that U.S. advisors be placed at company level in regular ARVN units. In investigating this proposal, CINCPAC, COMUSMACV and advisors on the spot had been asked their judgment, and all were reported to believe that this extension of advisors to company level was not necessary, and that the current advisory structure to ARVN was adequate.

The problem areas cited in all of these proposals to extend the advisory system were the questionable acceptability to the Vietnamese of further intrusion by American advisors, the shortage of interpretors, and finally the inevitable increase in U.S. casualties.

The political problems demanding solutions in order to permit the GVN to proceed effectively in its struggle against the VC were identified in the U.S preparations for the Honolulu Conference as:

> a. The disposition of the senior political and military prisoners from the two coups (there was resentment by some groups over the detention of prisoners at Dalat; on the other hand, there was possible danger to the Khanh regime if they were released).
>
> b. The rising religious tension both Catholic and Buddhist.
>
> c. The split between Buddhists under Thich Tam Chau (moderates and under Thich Tri Quang (extremists).
>
> d. Petty politicking within the GVN.
>
> e. GVN failure to provide local lectures.
>
> f. GVN failure to appoint Ambassadors to key governments.
>
> g. Inadequate GVN arrangements to handle third country aid.
>
> h. RVNAF failure to protect the population.

It was not within the competence of the Honolulu Conference to come to any decisions concerning the touchy matter of additional pressures against the North; this could be done only at the White House level. Agreement was reached, however, on certain specific actions to be taken with respect to the critical provinces and very shortly after the return of major participants to Washington these actions were approved and instructions were sent to the field accordingly.

On 5 June the Department notified the Embassy in Saigon that actions agreed upon at Honolulu were to be taken with respect to the critical provinces as follows:

> 1. Move in added South Vietnamese troops to assure numerical superiority over the VC.
>
> 2. Assign contol over all troops in each province to the province chief.
>
> 3. Execute clear-and-hold operations on a hamlet-by-hamlet basis following the "oil spot" theory for each of the approximately 40 districts within the seven critical provinces.
>
> 4. Introduce population control programs (curfews, ID papers, intelligence networks, etc.).
>
> 5. Increase the number of provincial police.
>
> 6. Expand the information program.
>
> 7. Develop special economic programs for each province.
>
> 8. Add U.S. personnel as follows:
>
> > a. 320 military advisors in provinces and districts.
> >
> > b.   40 USOM advisors in provinces and districts.
> >
> > c.   74 battalion advisors (2 for each of 37 battalions).
> >
> > 434 TOTAL

9. Transfer military personnel as needed to fill USOM shortages.
10. Establish joint US/GVN teams to monitor the program at both National and Provincial levels.

E. PREPARATION FOR INCREASED PRESSURE ON NORTH VIETNAM

The critical question of pressures against North Vietnam remained theoretically moot. The consensus of those formulating policy proposals for final approval by highest authority appears to have been that these pressures would have to be resorted to sooner or later. But the subject was politically explosive, especially in a presidential election year. Accordingly, not only did the basic foreign policy issues involved need careful exploration, but the domestic political framework needed preparation before any binding commitments to serious actions could be decided upon.

On 15 June 1964, McGeorge Bundy addressed a memorandum to the Secretaries of State and Defense announcing a meeting in the Secretary of State's Conference room that same day at 6:00 p.m.

> The principal question for discussion will be to assess the desirability of recommending to the President that a Congressional resolution on Southeast Asia should be sought [material missing]
> The second question is what the optimum recommendation for action should be if in fact a congressional resolution is not recommended. . . .

There were six enclosures included for the consideration of those attending the conference. The first was a memorandum on the subject of "Elements of a Southeast Asia Policy That Does Not Include a Congressional Resolution." The second was a Sullivan memorandum summarizing the current situation in South Vietnam. The third was a memorandum by W. P. Bundy dated 12 June 1964 on "Probable Developments and [the] Case for Congressional Resolution on Southeast Asia." The fourth was a draft resolution on Southeast Asia for Congressional approval. The fifth suggested basic themes to be employed in presenting the resolution to the Congress. The sixth and last consisted of a long series of questions and answers regarding the resolution of the public relations sort that it was thought should surround the effort.

The proposed "Elements of a Policy That Does Not Include a Congressional Resolution" consisted largely of an elaboration of the covert measures that were already either approved or nearing approval. This included RECCE STRIKE and T-28 Operations all over Laos and small-scale RECCE STRIKE Operations in North Vietnam after appropriate provocation. Apparently the sequence of actions was thought of as beginning with VNAF Operations in the Laotian corridor, followed by limited air and sea deployments of U.S. forces toward Southeast Asia, and still more limited troop movements in that general area. Military actions were to be accompanied by political actions which would maximize diplomatic support for Laos and maximize the support and visible presence of allies in Saigon. This last was explicitly stated to be particularly desired by "higher authority." Diplomatic moves, it was hoped, would also intensify support of Souvanna. In Vietnam, the paper argued, we should emphasize the critical province program, strengthen the Country Team, shift the U.S. role from advice to direction, discourage emphatically any further coup plots, and give energetic support to Khanh. In the U.S. there should be expanded publicity for opposition to both aggressive adventure and withdrawal. It is probably significant that the last words of this study were that "this outline does not preclude a shift to a higher level of action, if actions of other side should justify or require it. It does assume that in the absence of such drastic action, defense of U.S. interests is possible within these limits over the next six months."

The Sullivan memorandum warrants special attention because, although nominally a report on this situation, it speculated on policy and courses of action in a way very significant to the policy formulation processes at this time. In discussing the role of morale as a future consideration it approached a level of mysticism over a pathway of dilettastism. It was stated that at Honolulu both Lodge and Westmoreland had said the situation would remain in its current stalemate unless some "victory" were introduced. Westmoreland defined victory as determination to take some new military commitments such as air strikes against the Viet Cong in the Laos corridor; while Lodge defined victory as willingness to make punitive air strikes against North Vietnam. "The significant fact . . . was that they [both Westmoreland and Lodge] looked toward some American decision to undertake a commitment which the Vietnamese would interpret as a willingness to raise the military ante and eschew negotiations begun from a position of weakness." Although Khanh had had some success, Vietnamese morale was still not good and needed leadership had not been displayed.

> If we can obtain a breakthrough in the mutual commitment of the U.S. in Vietnam to a confident sense of victory, we believe that we can introduce this sort of executive involvement into the Vietnamese structure. . . . No one . . . can define with precision just how that breakthrough can be established. *It could come from the external actions of the U.S., internal leadership in Vietnam, or from an act of the irreversible commitment by the United States.*

The "logic" of this seemed to be that Khanh had not been able to provide the necessary leadership, despite all the aid and support the U.S. had given. No level of mere aid, advice, and support short of full participation could be expected to supply this deficiency, because Khanh would remain discouraged and defeated until he was given full assurance of victory. He would not be able to feel that assurance of victory until the U.S. committed itself to full participation in the struggle, even to the extent of co-belligerency. If the U.S. could commit itself in this way, the U.S. determination would somehow be transfused into the GVN. The problem before the assembled U.S. policy-makers, therefore, was to find some means of breakthrough into an irreversible commitment of the U.S.

The actions contemplated in this memorandum were not finally decided upon at this juncture, as we know. But we were gravitating inexorably in that direction in response to forces already at work, and over which we had ceased to have much real control. The situation in Vietnam had so developed, by this time, that by common consent the success of our programs in Vietnam—and indeed of our whole policy there, with which we had publicly and repeatedly associated our national prestige—depended upon the stability of the GVN. Conditions being what they were, the GVN equated, for the future to which plans and actions applied, with the Khanh regime. We were therefore almost as dependent upon Khanh as he was beholden to us. Circumstances had thus forced us into a situation wherein the most immediate and pressing goal of our programs in Vietnam was recognized to be using our resources and prestige to perpetuate a regime that we knew was only one faction—opposed by other factions—and without any broad base of popular support. We were aware of that weakness, and fully intented, whenever it was expedient, to find ways to broaden that basis of popular support. But that was something that could be—and indeed *had* to be—deferred. Meantime we had to do first things first—we had to bolster the Khanh regime, and since this could only be done by endowing it with some of our own sense of purpose and determination for the cause that was in the first instance theirs, not ours, we would prepare to do the things Khanh indicated were necessary to give him courage.

F. INCREASING U.S. INVOLVEMENT AND GROWING GVN INSTABILITY

The changing of the guard in the U.S. mission in Saigon at the half year point, when Ambassador Lodge returned to the U.S. to participate in election year politics, symbolized the growing importance attached by the U.S. to its Southeast Asia commitment. The combination of the Chairman of the Joint Chiefs as Ambassador, backed up by a Deputy Ambassador in the person of U. Alexis Johnson, a former Under Secretary of State who had been U.S. Ambassador to Thailand and was well known in SEA, made a prestigious and impressive team. Moreover, in sending the new Ambassador, the President endowed him with unusual powers.

> Dear Ambassador Taylor: As you take charge of the American effort in South Vietnam, I want you to have this formal expression not only of my confidence, but of my desire that you have and exercise full responsibility for the effort of the United States government in South Vietnam. In general terms this authority is parallel to that set forth in President Kennedy's letter of May 29, 1961, to all American Ambassadors; specifically, I wish it clearly understood that this overall responsibility includes the whole military effort in South Vietnam and authorizes the degree of command and control that you consider appropriate.
>
> I recognize that in the conduct of the day-to-day business of the military assistance command, Vietnam, you will wish to work out arrangements which do not burden you or impede the exercise of your overall direction.
>
> At your convenience I should be glad to know of the arrangements which you propose for meeting the terms of this instuction, so that appropriate supporting action can be taken in the Defense Department and elsewhere as necessary.
>
> This letter rescinds all conflicting instructions to US officers in Vietnam.
>
> Sincerely,
> Lyndon B. Johnson

The new U.S. team set out immediately to systematize U.S. operations in Vietnam, including reorganization of the upper echelons of the Mission. Added to this was an effort to improve the efficiency of the GVN and USG–GVN cooperation by developing a coordinate, parallel GVN organization. On 7 July Ambassador Taylor reported that, following recommendations from Deputy Ambassador Johnson and agency heads there, he had organized U.S. mission operations under the direction of a U.S. Mission Council, over which he would preside. The Council was to consist of himself, Johnson, Westmoreland, Killen (temporarily Hurt), Zorthian, DeSilva and Sullivan. This group was to meet once a week as an executive organization. To support this council he also established a Coordinating Committee to be chaired by Sullivan. This would carry out Mission Council decisions and prepare the agenda for Council meetings. On the following day, 8 July, Ambassador Taylor reported that he had called upon Khanh, and that Khanh had expressed satisfaction over the new U.S. personnel, and noted the rising morale their appointments had caused within the government. Taylor told Khanh about the formation of the Mission Council and Khanh asked for an organization chart so that he could develop a coordinate set-up within the GVN. Khanh said moreover that the U.S. should not merely advise, but should actually participate in GVN operations and decisions. "We should do this in Saigon (as well as in the provinces), between GVN ministries and offices and their American counterparts."

The new Ambassador did not delay in plunging into the substance of the problems that were plaguing Vietnam. In his first conversations with Khanh he asked about the status of the religious problem, and according to Taylor's report of the conversation, Khanh said the situation was still delicate, that the Catholics were better organized and were the aggressors, that Thich Tri Quang appeared reasonable when in Saigon but less so when in Hue. When the Ambassador queried Khanh about the progress of the recruiting effort, Khanh said that it was not going as well as he would like. With respect to the new pacification plan, HOP TAC, that had been agreed upon, the Ambassador expressed his approval of the general idea because paramilitary forces existed in this area to relieve ARVN. The Ambassador next took up the question of high desertion rates to which Khanh appears to have replied rather fuzzily. He said that the problem was complicated by many factors, that the Vietnamese liked to serve near home and sometimes left one service to join another. He implied that the figures might not mean exactly what they seemed to mean.

The lively interest of the President at this time was indicated by his 10 July request directly to the Ambassador for a coordinated Country Team report at the end of each month to show "where we stand in the process of increasing the effectiveness of our military, economic, information, and intelligence programs, just where the Khanh government stands in the same fields, and what progess we are making in the effort to mesh our work with theirs along the lines of your talk with General Khanh.

Five days later on 15 July, Ambassador Taylor transmitted estimates (not the monthly report) of VC strength which raised the previous estimate from 28,000 to 34,000. In so doing he explained that this was not a sudden and dramatic increase, but rather amounted to acceptance of the existence of units that had been suspected for two or three years but for which confirming evidence had only recently been received.

> This increased estimate of enemy strength and recent upward trend in VC activity in the North should not occasion over-concern. We have been coping with this strength for some time without being accurately aware of its dimensions.

The figures were interpretable as a reminder, however, of the growing magnitude of the problem, and of the need to raise the level of GVN/US effort. As a result the Ambassador commented that he was expediting formulation of additional requirements to support the plans in the ensuing months.

For a while, there was a serious effort to coordinate USOM-GVN planning, and on 17 July 1964, USOM met with Khanh, Hoan, Oanh and others—a group Khanh called the National Security Council. This cooperation was approved, as well as cooperation between USIS and the GVN information office—a more sensitive problem. On 23 July 1964, Taylor and Khanh discussed this co-operation in another NSC meeting and it was agreed that, to facilitate things, mutual bureaucratic adjustments would be made. In this same meeting of 23 July, Khanh revived his pressure for offensive operations against North Vietnam and expressed again his impatience with the long pull of counterinsurgency and pacification programs.

This reopening of the "march to the north" theme on 23 July was not the first revival. On 19 July, General Ky had talked to reporters about plans for operations in Laos, and on the same day Khanh himself had made indiscreet remarks about "march to the north" at a unification rally in Saigon. This led to stories and editorials in the Saigon press. The Ambassador protested the campaign as looking like an effort to force the hand of the U.S. This became a central pre-occupation of Ambassador Taylor thereafter. He firmly opposed Khanh's pressure on the one hand, and on the other had argued for patience with the GVN even though the GVN defense ministry put out an embarrassing press release immediately after the long Taylor-Khanh talk which followed on 24 July 1964.

The political pressures in Saigon were at that time increasing vastly. Both Khanh and other top Vietnamese politicians and political generals were reacting in increasingly strong ways. The very evident instability of the current regime increased rapidly and at the same time there was a tendency to try to escape from the dilemmas posed within South Vietnam by actions against North Vietnam, actions which it had been hoped would lead to a unity within South Vietnam impossible under the current circumstances. There was a CAS report, for instance, of coup plotting on 24 July that said a decision had been made by the generals to remove Khanh, but that it was not clear who would replace him or whether the planned removal would be opposed. This was the same day that the Ambassador, who had scarcely been in Saigon a fortnight, had first protested to Khanh concerning his indiscreet remarks about a march to the north. The Ambassador also talked to Khanh, following the Mission Council meeting, concerning the rumors of a possible coup. Khanh said that because he (Taylor—i.e., the U.S.) had imposed Minh on the MRC as Chief of State, and because of Minh's support of Generals Kim and Xuan and other partisans of French neutralist policies, Defense Minister Khiem and Chief of State Thieu were leading a group that was pressing Khanh to get rid of Minh. This Khiem block was permeated by Dai Viet political influence. Khanh asked Taylor if he should resign. Taylor said the USG could not contemplate the consequences of another change of government. Because no other leader was in sight, Khanh had our support and he must continue in the face of adversity. "Could we help?" Taylor inquired. Khanh asked that we let it be known that we wanted no more changes of government and asked Taylor to talk to Khiem and his supporters about the bad effects of politics in the armed forces.

One means of demonstrating U.S. support of Khanh was to let Khanh make the first announcement of increased U.S. aid, followed by a background statement by the Ambassador. To carry this out, the Ambassador submitted a draft statement for Khanh to use. One part of this draft statement mentioned the increase of U.S. military advisors and their extension "to the district level." When Taylor and Johnson discussed this with Khanh at Dalat two days later, Khanh saw advantages to the proclamation in general, but preferred to change the reference "advisors at the district level" to read "advisors throughout the provinces," because the original suggested an undesirably deep penetration of the GVN by the U.S.

When Ambassador Taylor on 25 July reported further on Khanh's revival of the march to the north theme, he interpreted it as response to political and morale problems within South Vietnam. The Ambassador suggested several possible motivations, and commented that if Khanh had been reasonably sincere his objective probably was to:

> . . . talk "march north" but really have in mind getting U.S. committed to program of reprisal bombing. Such a limited program could be first step to further escalation against Hanoi.   [Doc. 58]

On 10 August, when the storm clouds had already appeared but before the gale had begun to blow, Ambassador Taylor filed his first monthly U.S. mission report. The report began by expressing surprise that the first sampling of advisor-level opinion revealed more optimism than among the senior U.S. officials in Saigon. Following this preliminary flourish, the report gave an introductory definition of the problem which was, in simplest terms, that the Hanoi/NLF startegy was not to defeat GVN military forces in battle but rather to harass and terrorize the SVN population and leadership into a state of such demoralization that a political settlement favorable to NVN would ensue. At that point they could proceed by stages to the full attainment of their goals. To oppose this strategy, the Khanh government had a complex not only of military programs, but of social, economic, psychological and above all administrative programs. This complex of programs Taylor reported on under three captions: "Political," "Military" and "Overall." On the political side he reported:

> The most important and most intractable internal problem of South Vietnam in meeting the Viet Cong threat is the political structure at the national level. The best thing that can be said about the Khanh government is that it has lasted six months and has about a 50–50 chance of lasting out the year, although probably not without some changed faces in the Cabinet. Although opposed by Minh and resisted less openly by Dai Viet sympathizers among the military, Prime Minister Khanh seems for the time being to have the necessary military support to remain in power. However, it is an ineffective government beset by inexperienced ministers who are also jealous and suspicious of each other . . .
> On the positive side, Khanh seems to have allayed the friction between Buddhists and Catholics at least for the moment, has won the cooperation of the Hoa Hao and Cao Dai, and has responded to our suggestions for improved relations between the GVN and the U.S. mission . . .
> . . . Khanh has not succeeded in building any substantial body of active popular support in the countryside. In the countryside . . . that support for the GVN exists in direct proportion to the degree of security established by government forces . . .
> The intriguing inside his government and the absence of dramatic military or political successes react upon Khanh . . . moody . . . subjective to fits of despondency. Seeing the slow course of the counterinsurgency campaign frustrated by the weakness of his government, Khanh has turned to the "march north" theme to unify the home front and to offset the war weariness which he asserts is oppressing his people and his forces. . . .
> The state of mind of Khanh and his colleagues would be an important factor in the future conduct of the war, Taylor judged.

They found slow, hard-slugging contest fatiguing to their spirits. The reprisals of 5 August (Tonkin Gulf) had given them a lift, but if indecisive bloodshed with the VC continued, they would probably exert continuing and increasing pressure for direct attack upon Hanoi.

Concerning pacification, the Ambassador observed that the most difficult part of the program was the civilian follow-up after the clearing operation in the clear-and-hold program. The difficulty stemmed from the inefficiency of the ministries. To energize these civilian functions, USOM had increased its provincial representation from 45 in March to 64 in July, but this was still insufficient, despite the judgment of critical inefficiency in the ministries. Taylor next reported that "U.S. observers reported in July that in about ¾ of the provinces GVN provincial and district officers were performing effectively. . . ." It was too soon to go into details regarding Hop Tac, and the report on that program was in effect a description of its objectives and rationale rather than a progress report.

The Ambassador reported that on the military side, the personnel strength of RVNAF and of the paramilitary forces was slowly rising and by January should reach about 98 percent of the target strength of 446,000. COMUSMACV had reported at the end of July that the actual GVN strength stood at 219,954 RVNAF, 88,560 Regional Forces (formerly Civil Guard), and 127,453 Popular Forces (formerly Self Defense Corps).

III.   FROM TONKIN TO NSAM-328

A.   *TONKIN GULF AND FOLLOWING POLITICAL CRISES*

As already noted, the Ambassador's first monthly report was filed just before the internal Vietnamese political storm broke in full force. Through the late spring and into July of 1964, the Buddhist-Catholic quarrel intensified. Students again began to demonstrate in Saigon and Hue. By July a coup plot was developing against Khanh led by his disgruntled Vice Premier, Dr. Nguyen Ton Hoan, who was backed by the Dai Viet and several top military leaders. But according to one of the best authorities, known U.S. opposition to a coup made its leaders hesitate and nothing immediately developed. Then came the Tonkin Gulf affair of 2–4 August, and the U.S. retaliatory strikes of 4–5 August.

An immediate effect of the raids was to shore up Khanh's weakening position. But contrary to prevailing theories and hopes, stability was very short-lived. Khanh sought to exploit the affair by a radio appeal for unity and national discipline. He did not arrest the coup plotters however, which many Vietnamese—but not the U.S. Embassy—advised. Instead, on 7 August, he announced a state of emergency, reimposed censorship and other prescriptions and restrictions on liberties and movements of the Vietnamese people.

Apparently hoping to further exploit the opportunity, Khanh hurriedly sought to draw up a new charter to centralize and increase his powers. On 12 August he discussed this for the first time with Ambassador Taylor. The Ambassador made two comments, one suggesting caution lest "renewed instability . . . result from these sweeping changes," the other urging a public explanation of the need for the changes because of a state of emergency.

Two days later at a joint NSC planning session, Khanh showed Ambassador Taylor a rough translation of the proposed draft of a new charter. It was hastily drawn and included both dubious provisions and gruff language. The Ambassador was immediately afraid this would lead to criticism in the U.S. and the world press; he assigned Sullivan and Manfull to work on a revision. But they had little time and were unable to exert much influence. A day later, August 15, the Ambassador reported the document still did not satisfy him but that the MRC fully intended to impose it and he saw no alternative to trying to make the best of it. Certain passages evidently had been toned down and something resembling a bill of rights inserted. Nevertheless the charter gave virtually complete power to Khanh. A special session of the MRC approved Khanh's new charter and elected him President. Minh was expediently removed: the charter abolished his job as Chief of State. Since his overthrow at the end of January Minh had been inactive and sulky; but whatever his faults he had a considerable following within South Vietnam. It had been American policy to convince Khanh to bring Minh into his government thereby endowing the Khanh regime with some of Minh's popularity. Khanh had acceded to U.S. wishes. But Minh's presence had not yielded the hoped for unity. Ambassador Taylor, Minh's friend for several years, had attempted to patch up the deteriorating relations between the two generals but these efforts only incurred Khanh's suspicion of Taylor.

In the period immediately following the Tonkin Gulf affair, Washington officials sought agreement on Southeast Asian policies. We were entering a new era. On 14 August, State cabled a summary of a tentative policy paper to Saigon, Vientiane and CINCPAC for comment. The paper began by stating that during the next fortnight no precipitate actions that might relieve the Communists of the onus of further escalation should be taken. DESOTO patrols should be held up; there should be no extra 34A operations. But low morale and lost momentum in SVN had to be treated. The best means to improve morale in South Vietnam and at the same time pressure North Vietnam at the lowest level of risk had to be found. This was the guiding philosophy. Basically required were military pressures plus other actions to convince Hanoi and Peking to cease aggression. Negotiation without continued military pressure would not achieve these objectives. The paper listed seven [words illegible] those already exerted, then discussed more serious actions. Lesser pressures, it was stated, were to relay the threat of systematic, military action against the DRV. Hanoi was to be informed that incidents arising from the lesser actions or deterioration in South Vietnam —particularly clear evidence of increased infiltration from the North—could trigger that sustained action. In any case, for planning purposes the paper looked to 1 January 1965 as the starting point for the more serious systematic pressures.

The Mission comment took the form of an alternative draft. It began by agreeing with the assumption of the proposed Department paper, that the present pacification plan, by itself, was insufficient to maintain national morale or to offer reasonable hope of eventual success. Something more was clearly needed. The main problem in the immediate future was to gain time for the Khanh regime to achieve a modicum of stability and thereby provide a viable base for operations.

> In particular, if we can avoid it, we should not get involved militarily with North Vietnam or possibly with Red China if our base in South Vietnam is insecure and Khanh's Army is tied down by the VC insurgency.

A second objective was to maintain the morale of the GVN. The mission judged that this would not be difficult if we could assure Khanh of our readiness to bring added pressure on Hanoi in return for evidence of his ability and willingness to do his part. A third objective would be to hold the DRV in check and restrain further infiltration to aid the VC buildup.

1 January 65 was agreed upon, for planning purposes, as the date to begin the escalating pressure on the DRV. Three aspects of these pressures were considered

by the Mission: first, actions to be taken with the Khanh government; second, actions against Hanoi; and third, after a pause, "initiation of an orchestrated air attack against North Vietnam." The first of these involved a commitment. "We should express our willingness to Khanh to engage in planning and eventually to exert intense pressure on North Vietnam providing certain conditions are met in advance." Thus, before we would agree to go all out against the North, Khanh must stabilize his government and make progress in cleaning out his own backyard. Specifically, he would be required to execute the initial phases of the HOP TAC plan successfully. This would have to succeed to the extent of pushing the VC away from the doors of Saigon. Moreover, the overall pacification program, including HOP TAC, should progress sufficiently to allow earmarking at least three division equivalents for the defense of the I Corps area should the DRV step up military operations in that area.

In making these commitments to Khanh, the Mission would make clear to Khanh the limited nature of our objectives—that we were not ready to join in a crusade to unify the North and the South, nor to overthrow Ho Chi Minh. Our objective was to be limited to inducing Hanoi to cease its subversive efforts in the South. Pursuant of this philosophy, the Mission draft proposed a program roughly comparable to that suggested by Washington. The specific difference was the emphasis in the Mission draft on the need for a stable base in South Vietnam before beginning overt pressures on the North; and, to effect this, the policy of a *quid pro quo*—getting Khanh to clean up his house and make some progress in pacification as the price of our commitment to pressures against the North.

During the fast moving events of the third week of August, the President decided to bring Ambassador Taylor back to Washington for consultation early in September. In a joint State-Defense message on 20 August, Taylor was advised of questions that officials in various departments would want to ask during his forthcoming visit. The visit was first scheduled for the end of the month, but along with the draft policy paper of mid-month, the original plans were overtaken by political events (turmoil) in Vietnam, and the meeting was postponed about two weeks, from late August to mid-September. It is worth noting, nevertheless, that among the items still prominent in the intended discussions with Taylor, at the time of the first notice of the meeting, were the status of pacification programs—HOP TAC especially—Corps, division and provincial plans; the joint US/GVN committees; the newly established operations center; the role of Popular Forces and of Regional Forces; and the RVNAF police and local security plans. Pacification was the first item, and detailed interest was indicated.

Shaplen calls the week from 16 August—when Khanh publicly announced the new charter—to 23 August critical, because of Khanh's failure to establish a broadly based civilian government under the authority of the new charter. He had been warned by many Vietnamese that the pressures of civilian and religious demands for a voice in the government were building up, but nothing was done and major demonstrations began again on 21 August.

This account will not detail the political events that occurred from 21 August on. However, to keep our American concern with programs in Vietnam in context it is necessary to keep in mind the general sequence of political events during the turmoil of the next several weeks. On 21 August the first serious student demonsration following the proclamation of the 16 August charter occurred. Khanh met with the students, but did not satisfy their demands. The same day Thich Tam Chau, President of the Buddhist Institute for Secular Affairs, demanded that Khanh take action against the Diemist Can Lao Party, whom the Buddhists alleged to be their oppressors. Both Buddhists and Viet Cong began to infiltrate the fringes of the student demonstrations about this time. A confused, many-sided contest developed with Catholics, Viet Cong and Buddhists seeking to manipulate or exploit the student demonstrations. On 23 August the Buddhists in Hue formed a new Movement for the Salvation of Buddhism in Danger (similar to the organization against Diem).

On the night of 24 August another coup rumor spread. It was later suspected that Dai Viet generals had indeed been ready to move that night, but that Khiem, who had been wavering between Khanh and the Dai Viet, told them to wait. That same night Khanh asked three top bonzes to come to Cap St. Jacques for consultation. They refused, and Khanh for his part rushed back to Saigon. He met with them and they demanded, first, abolition of the 16 August charter, second establishment of government councils to assure full freedom of religion and expression, and third, free elections by 1 November 1965. Khanh made the mistake of telling them he wanted to consult with the Americans. At 1:00 a.m. on 25 August, Ambassador Taylor and Deputy Ambassador Johnson met with Khanh and they "unofficially" advised him to accept the Buddhist demands in principle, but otherwise to be tough and not to knuckle under to any minority. The conference lasted until about 3:00 a.m.

At 5:00 a.m. of 25 August, Khanh issued a communique promising to revise the new constitution, reduce press censorship, rectify local abuses by arranging special courts, and permit continued demonstrations, with the proviso that those responsible for actions of disorder be punished.

But these concessions again were not enough to satisfy the students. Later that morning a crowd of 25,000 gathered in front of Khanh's office. Khanh appeared before them and denied that he wanted to be a dictator, but refused to make further concessions. He did not, however, have the crowd dispersed. Instead, he withdrew and then, without warning, issued an announcement from his military headquarters that the 16 August charter would be withdrawn and that he, Khanh, was quitting. Further, he announced that the MRC would meet the next day, 26 August, to choose a new Chief of State.

The MRC met on 26 and 27 August. Khanh brought in the three generals he had accused of participating in the pro-French neutralist plot, as a ploy to forestall a power bid by Minh. But the Council refused to seat them and they were returned to their protective custody at Dalat. While these maneuvers were going on street demonstrations continued. Within the MRC Khiem failed in an attempt to name himself Chief of State and Minh Prime Minister. Next Khanh was named Prime Minister, but refused to accept either Khiem or Minh as President. Finally, when he refused to be installed alone, the triumvirate of Khanh, Minh and Khiem was chosen.

Anarchy in the streets of Saigon intensified. Khanh again nominally Prime Minister, was by this time back in Dalat in a state of exhaustion. The troika of Khanh, Minh and Khiem never met, and Nguyen Xuan Oanh was made acting Prime Minister. Rumors of coups continued—one supposedly by the Dai Viet, another by the so-called "colonels' Group."

On 29 August 1964 Vietnamese paratroopers with bayonets were used to restore order in Saigon. At this time Khanh was in Dalat. On 1 September General Westmoreland went to see Khanh in Dalat to urge him to keep ARVN on the offensive against the Viet Cong and to press on with HOP TAC and the other pacification programs. As a *quid pro quo* for this, Westmoreland revised his previous position, and promised that U.S. advisors throughout MACV would alert Khanh to unusual troop movements (movements which might be an indication of a coup).

Meanwhile, because of this turmoil, Ambassador Taylor's trip to Washington had been postponed until the end of the first week of September. There was further excitement on the night of 2 September, when dissident troops, mostly aligned with Dai Viet leaders, began to converge on the city. But some of the Colonels' Group got wind of the movement and stopped the advance before midnight, stringing along with Khanh for the time being. Meanwhile, a new group had been formed in Hue called the People's Revolutionary Committee, which, according to Shaplen, had "distinct tones of separatism," and was verbally attacking the temporary government. On 4 September Khanh returned to Saigon from his Dalat retreat, and announced a tentative formula for new administrative machinery to take over for the next two months, after which a new government of civilians would replace the government of the military. Khanh was welcomed, and produced a letter, signed by both Thich Tri Quang and Thich Tam Chau, pledging support and unity. Reportedly this had been paid for by a sum equalling $230,000. Deals of this kind were by no means unknown in Vietnam. Khanh at this time finally got rid of Dr. Hoan, who had been plotting against him for a long time, by forcing his resignation and exile to Japan. Following this there was enough of a lull to permit the Ambassador to return to Washington. He would not complete the round trip, however, before turmoil erupted again in Saigon.

B. POLICIES IN THE PERIOD OF TURMOIL

On the eve of his 6 September departure for Washington, Ambassador Taylor cabled a review of the Vietnamese situation

> . . . At best the emerging governmental structure might be capable of maintaining a holding operation against the Viet Cong. This level of effort could, with luck and strenuous efforts, be expanded to produce certain limited pacification successes, for example, in the territory covered by the HOP TAC Plan. But the willingness and ability of such a government to exert itself or to attempt to execute an allout pacification plan would be marginal. It would probably be incapable of galvanizing the people to the heightened levels of unity and sacrifice necessary to carry forward the counterinsurgency program to final success. Instead, it would look increasingly to the United States to take the major responsibility for prying the VC and the North Vietnamese off the backs of the South Vietnamese population. . . . In the cold light of recently acquired facts, we need 2 to 3 months to get any sort of government going which has any chance of being able to maintain order in the cities and to continue the pacification efforts of past levels. There is no present urge to march north . . . the leadership is exhausted and frustrated . . . and not anxious to take on any new problems or obligations. Hence, there is no need to hasten our plans to satisfy an impatinece to close with the enemy . . .

On 4 September the Acting Assistant Secretary of Defense for International Security Affairs, Peter Solbert, forwarded to the Secretary of Defense a memorandum including a set of summary recommendations for a program of overall social development called "stability for the GVN." Copies of this memorandum were seen by both Vance and McNamara, but there is no documentary evidence that it was given serious consideration. The program was based on a longer RAND study by C. J. Zwick, and it proposed a series of measures to broaden popular support of the Government of Vietnam. The measures were divided into an Urban Program and a Rural Program. Summarily, under the Urban Program, there were six major areas of development:

1. a reduction of consumer prices for selected commodities;
2. an increase in government salaries;
3. mass low cost public housing;
4. urban public works;
5. expanded educational programs; and
6. an improved business climate to foster private business.

Under the proposed Rural Program there were four items:

1. an elimination of corvée labor and provision for paid public works;
2. subsidized credit to peasants under GVN control;
3. an increase in military pay and benefits; and
4. educational assistance to rural youths.

This memorandum further suggested that involving in the program the leaders of the various political factions in Vietnam who were currently causing trouble would indirectly enlist them in what amounted to stabilizing efforts, and the current plague of factionalism might be reduced.

The policy decisions reached in the high level discussions of 7 September were formalized in NSAM-314. These decisions were approved:

1. Resumption of U.S. Naval patrols (DESOTO) in the Gulf of Tonkin, following the return to Saigon of the Ambassador.

2. 34A operations by the GVN to be resumed after completion of the first DESOTO patrol.

3. Discussions with the government of Laos of plans for a limited GVN air-ground operation in the Laos corridor areas.

4. Preparation to respond against the DRV to any attack on U.S. units or any spectacular DRV/VC acts against South Vietnam.

Following the statement of these specific action decisions, NSAM-314 reemphasized the importance of economic and political actions having immediate impact on South Vietnam such as pay raises to civilian personnel and spot projects in cities and selected rural areas. The emphasis on *immediate* impact should be noted. Finally, it was emphasized that all decisions were "governed by a prevailing judgment that the first order of business at present is to strengthen the fabric of the Government of South Vietnam . . ."

In the period immediately after the August crisis, Minh, acting, in effect, as Chief of State, although he did not actually hold the title, appointed a new High National Council to represent all elements of the population and prepare a new constitution for the return of civilian government.

But there was no real stability. On 13 September, while Ambassador Taylor was on his way back to Saigon from his visit to Washington, a bloodless coup was staged in Saigon by General Lam Van Phat (who had been scheduled to be removed as Commander of IV Corps). Soon after the coup began the U.S. announced its support for the "duly constituted" troika regime of Khanh, Minh and Khiem. This plus a counter-coup by a group of younger officers including Nguyen Cao Ky and Nguyen Chanh Thi, put Khanh back in power. One result of the Phat coup attempt, however, was that it established the power of the younger general officers headed by Ky and Thi. Nguyen Van Thieu, who was close to the Dai Viet party, was reported to be a major behind-the-scenes manipulator of the coup, mainly by neutralizing his immediate boss, General Khiem.

The next several weeks amounted to a period of suspended animation for the GVN (but not for the VC) while the new constitution was being prepared. Except for some debatable progress in HOP TAC, little was accomplished in pacification. Moreover, infusing an interim government with an efficiency that neither it nor any predecessor had had was too much to expect. In Saigon, much attention was given to establishing a policy coordination center for covert military operations—i.e., 34A, Cross-Border, Yankee Team, Lucky Dragon, etc. These operations, and the political problems of the central government, appear to have been the principal immediate concerns of the Embassy during this period.

In October, Washington queried the Embassy as to whether greater progress in pacification might result from further decentralization of the program, even raising the question of whether aid might not bypass the GVN in Saigon and go directly to the provinces. In reply, the Mission conceded that a good deal of decentralization was already in effect and that in some provinces local initiative was paying off. Progress was continuing despite the turmoil in Saigon. Nevertheless, recent U.S. advisor reports showed that the number of provinces where pacification was *not* going satisfactorily had doubled since July—from 7 to 14. This in part was due to concentration of most of the pacification efforts on HOP TAC, and in part to the political turmoil in Saigon. However, the Mission did not believe that further decentralization was either feasible or advisable. The central problem in administering pacification, in the considered view of the Mission, was to establish justified requirements at the provincial level and then fill pipelines to meet these provincial needs. This required overall coordination.

Two weeks after the 13 September coup, the High National Council, composed of 17 elderly professional men, was inaugurated. Despite the continuing air of crisis, the Council fulfilled its promise to deliver a new constitution by the end of October and selected Phan Khac Suu (an older, non-aligned politician) as the new Chief of Staff. Suu immediately chose a civilian, Tran Van Huong, as new Premier. Huong almost immediately came under fire from several factions and it soon became apparent that Khanh was still the real power behind the throne. Khanh got rid of Khiem, sending him to Washington, and Minh went abroad on a "goodwill tour."

As the year moved toward a close it came time again for the Ambassador to return to Washington for policy consultations. Progress in the program within South Vietnam had been spotty at best, and in many areas retrogression could not be denied. The efforts to develop efficient administration within the GVN had made no progress at all—the game of musical chairs at the top made this impossible. It was generally conceded that pacification had fallen back, at best marking time in some areas. As for the HOP TAC area immediately surrounding Saigon, opinions were divided. The official view reflected in the statistical analysis was that slow but steady progress was being made. Most of the informal and local judgments, however, were less sanguine. Some increases in RVNAF recruitment had been registered, but this did not mean that action against the VC had improved, that capabilities had increased, that lost ground was being retaken, or that control of the rural population was being wrested from the Viet Cong.

C. THE PERIOD OF INCREASING PRESSURES ON NVN

In anticipation of the Ambassador's forthcoming visit to Washington, General Westmoreland provided an assessment of the military situation. On 24 November General Westmoreland observed that in September the Mission had been preoccupied with the problem of keeping RVNAF intact in the face of internal dissention and political and religious purges but by late November he was pleased at the way the RVNAF had weathered the political storm and encouraged by increased RVNAF strength because of volunteers and enlistments. RVNAF strength of 31 October was compared to figures for 30 April: 230,474 RVNAF, up from 207,410; 92,265 Regional Forces, up from 85,660; 159,392 Popular Forces, up from 96,263. During September and October, RVNAF and Regional Forces officers and NCOs to the rank of first corporal had received a 10% increase in basic pay; the lowest three enlisted grades in these forces—plus all Popular Force personnel—had received 300 more piastres per month. Cost of living increases to NCOs matched those given to officers. Subsector U.S. advisory teams (two officers, three enlisted men) were operating in some 75 districts. General Westmoreland reported HOP TAC was progressing slowly. Civil-military-political planners were working together; the Saigon-level coordinating group, the HOP TAC Council, was operating.

General Westmoreland summarized the key issues as he viewed them at the time. First, there was a need to establish concrete but attainable shortrange goals to give momentum; second, more effective means of asserting U.S. policy and plans for the pacification program at the Saigon level was needed; third, the U.S. should take a positive position against external support of the insurgency.

Also on 24 November, Westmoreland recommended an increase in RVNAF force structure and requested its early approval to permit official negotiations with the GVN, to facilitate MAP planning. This recommendation followed a joint U.S./GVN survey and a COMUSMACV staff study. Two alternative levels of increase were proposed:

	Already Authorized	Increase		New Total	
		Alt 1	Alt 2	Alt 1	Alt 2
RVNAF	243,599	30,309	47,556	273,908	291,155
Para Mil		*No* alt. for Para. Mil.		322,187	
		212,246		109,941	

The increase in U.S. advisors for the two alternative programs would be 446 and 606, respectively. The first (the lower) alternative was supported by the JCS on 17 December 1964 and approved by Secretary McNamara on 13 January 1965. This January decision raised the total U.S. military personnel in Vietnam from 22,309 to 22,755.

Both the tenor of the thinking and the policies that emerged from the meetings of early December are reflected in the draft instructions from the President to Ambassador Taylor possibly written by Taylor himself. These were first drawn up on 30 November 1964, revised on 2 December and used at the meeting of the principals on 3 December.

During the recent review in Washington of the situation in South Vietnam, it was clearly established that the unsatisfactory progress being made in the pacification of the VC was the result of two primary causes from which many secondary causes stemmed; first, the governmental instability in Saigon and the second, the continued reinforcement and direction of the VC by the North Vietnamese government. To change the downward trend of events, it will be necessary to deal adequately with both of these factors.

It is clear however that these factors are not of equal importance. There must be a stable, effective government to conduct a campaign against the VC even if the aid of North Vietnam for the VC should end. While the elimination of North Vietnamese intervention will raise morale on our side and make it easier for the government to function, it will not in itself end the war against the VC. It is rather an important contributory factor to the creation of conditions favoring a successful campaign against the VC within South Vietnam. Since action against North Vietnam is contributory, not central, we should not incur the risks which are inherent in expansion of hostilities until there is a government in Saigon capable of handling the serious problems involved in such an expansion and of exploiting the favorable effects which may be anticipated from an end of support and direction by North Vietnam.

It is this consideration which has borne heavily on the recent deliberations in Washington and has conditioned the conclusions reached. There have been many expressions of admiration for the courage being shown by the Huong government which has the complete support of the U.S. government in its resistance to the minority pressures which are attempting to drag it down. However, the difficulties which it is facing raise inevitable questions as to its capacity and readiness to discharge the responsibilities which it would incur if some of the new measures under consideration were taken.

There are certain minimum criteria of performance in South Vietnam which must be met before any new measures against North Vietnam would be either justified or practicable. At a minimum the government should be able to speak for and to its people who will need guidance and leadership throughout the coming critical period. It should be capable of maintaining law and order in its principal centers of population, make plans for the conduct of operations and assure their efficient execution by military and police forces completely responsive to its authority. It must have the means to cope with the enemy reactions which must be expected to result from any change in the pattern of our operations.

I (the President) particularly request that you and your colleagues in the American Country Team develop and execute a concerted effort to bring home to all groups in South Vietnam the paramount importance of national unity against the Communist enemy at this critical time. It is a matter of the greatest difficulty for the U.S. government to require great sacrifice of American citizens when reports from Saigon reportedly give evidence of heedless self-interest and shortsightedness among nearly all major groups in South Vietnam . . .

While effectiveness is largely a subjective judgement, progress in certain specific areas such as those listed below provide some tangible measure. The U.S. mission should urge upon the GVN particular efforts in these fields. . . .

(1) Improve the use of manpower for military and pacification purposes.

(2) Bring the armed forces and police to authorized strength and maximize their effectiveness.

(3) Replace incompetent officials and commanders; freeze the competent in place for extended periods of service.

(4) Clarify and strengthen police powers of arrest, detention, and interrogation of VC suspects.

(5) Clarify and strengthen the authority of provincial chiefs.

(6) Make demonstrable progress in the HOP TAC operation around Saigon.

(7) Broaden and intensify the civic action program using both military and civilian resources to produce tangible evidence of the desire of the government to help the hamlets and villages.

(8) Carry out a sanitary clean up of Saigon.

While progress was being made toward these goals, the U.S. would be willing to strike harder at infiltration routes in Laos and at sea and, in conjunction with the Lao Government, add U.S. air power to operations to restrict the use of Laotian territory for infiltration into South Vietnam. The U.S. would also favor intensification of MAROPS (covert activities against the DRV). In the meantime, GVN and U.S. armed forces should be ready to execute prompt reprisals for any unusual hostile action. When these conditions were met (and after the GVN had demonstrated its firm control) the U.S. would be prepared to consider a program of direct military pressure on the DRV. These second phase operations would consist of a series of air attacks on the DRV progressively mounting in scope and intensity for the purpose of convincing DRV leaders that it was in their interest to cease aid to the VC, to respect the independence and security of the South. The prospective participants in such attacks were the Air Forces of the U.S., South Vietnam and Laos. The U.S. Mission was to be authorized to initiate planning with the GVN for such operations immediately, with the understanding that the U.S. had not committed itself to them.

Immediately after the Ambassador's return to Saigon the U.S. began to increase its covert operations against infiltration from the North. On 14 December U.S. aircraft began Operation BARREL ROLL (armed reconnaissance against infiltration routes in Laos). This and other signs of increased American commitment against North Vietnam's involvement in the South showed no results in terms of increasing GVN stability. Jockeying among generals behind the scenes continued. The younger generals who had saved Khanh in the 13 September coup demanded the High National Council fire nine generals and 30 other officers, notably Generals Minh, Don, Xuan and Kim, who had been in the original post-Diem junta. The Council refused and the young generals began a life and death struggle against the Huong regime. On 20 December Generals Thi and Ky led their group in a purge—or virtual coup—of the Council. This was followed immediately by formation of an Armed Forces Council (AFC). Nominally headed by Khanh, the young generals aimed to curb his powers through the new council. AFC offered to mediate conflicts between Buddhist dissidents and the Huong government. These actions exacerbated already unhappy relations between Khanh and politically motivated young generals and the American Ambassador who was striving to foster a representative civilian government and discourage coups by small-time military dictators. The struggle (described in detail in other papers) was intensified at this time and continued for several weeks.

Throughout January and February 1965 the weekly Vietnam Sitreps published by the Intelligence and Reporting Subcommittee of the Interagency Vietnam Coordinating Committee warned generally and repeatedly that progress concerning pacification was "slow" or that there was a "slow down" or said there was "little progress to report." The Vietnamese commander of the HOP TAC area generally continued to report "a favorable situation"—but this was accompanied frequently by a statement of increased Viet Cong activity in these favorable areas.

After BARREL ROLL, U.S. pressure upon North Vietnam was notably increased by the FLAMING DART attacks of 7–12 February following the

Pleiku incident. The McGeorge Bundy group (MacNaughton, Cooper, Unger and Bundy) were in Saigon at the time. On the return trip to Washington shortly after Pleiku, the group drafted a memorandum for the President. Intended to reflect the consensus of policy discussions with the Mission, the memorandum really reflects Bundy's point of view, particularly in presentation of a rationale for ROLLING THUNDER operations—soon to begin. Analysis of this memo and the ROLLING THUNDER annex is part of another report in this series. For present purposes it is sufficient to note that the memo reported the situation in Vietnam was deteriorating and said defeat was inevitable unless the United States intervened military by bombing the North to persuade Hanoi to cease and desist. South Vietnam was to be rescued not by measures in South Vietnam but by pressures against the North.

The idea that victory could be achieved quickly was explicitly dismissed: perhaps "the next year or so" would be enough to turn the tide. And this, hopefully, could be accomplished by the persuasive power of aerial bombardment.

ROLLING THUNDER was to be a program of sustained, continuous, increasing reprisal beginning at a low level and becoming increasingly violent. The level of violence would vary according to the North Vietnamese response: if they persisted in infiltration, violence would continuously increase; if they reduced their meddling, we would respond in kind and degree.

This subject had been discussed at considerable length in Saigon. The Bundy memorandum was followed by a cable from Taylor which presented generally similar recommendations under the heading of "graduated reprisals." CINCPAC commented on the Taylor proposals, urging that the levels of attack should be forceful enough to be militarily effective, not merely politically persuasive. On 8 February, McNamara requested the JCS to develop a program; shortly thereafter they produced their "Eight-week-Program" of bombing.

In Saigon, the FLAMING DART bombings of 7–12 February—the first reprisal bombings since August 1964—were promptly followed by the Armed Forces Council selection on 16 February of a new cabinet; headed by Dr. Pham Huy Quat, the cabinet was installed on 18 February. Another coup was attempted on 19 February but thwarted by the AFC. And General Khanh (whose actions against Huong in January had lost him Taylor's confidence) was removed on the 20th. Four days later, 24 February, Khanh left for foreign parts and ROLLING THUNDER began. Any positive correlation between U.S. pressure on North Vietnam and the stability of the GVN remained to be established.

During these first two months of 1965 almost no progress was made toward increasing RVNAF strength. Goals were raised but actual force levels were not. MACV data on RVNAF strength were later provided the Secretary:

RVNAF IN THOUSANDS

	Jan 65	Feb 65	Mar 65	Apr 65	May 65
Objective	—	252.1	259.5	266.9	274.3
Actual	244.7	245.5	248.5	252.3	256.9
Shortfall	—	(6.6)	(11.0)	(14.6)	(17.4)
KIA	.35	.32	.27	.27	.42
Desertions	2.4	2.5	5.0	3.6	3.1

Although the conditions stipulated in December had not been met, although the program continued to fall further behind, we were fully committed to pressure on the North by this time. On 1 March 1965, in a memorandum to all Service Secretaries, Chairman of the Joint Chiefs, Chief of Naval Operations, Army and Air Force Chiefs of Staff and Commandant of the Marine Corps, the Secretary of Defense pledged unlimited funds to the support of the Vietnam effort.

> Over the past two or three years I have emphasized the importance of providing all necessary military assistance to South Vietnam, whether it be through MAP or through application of U.S. forces and their associated equipment.
>
> Occasionally instances come to my attention indicating that some in the Department feel restraints are imposed by limitations of funds.
>
> I want it clearly understood that there is an unlimited appropriation available for the financing of aid to Vietnam. Under no circumstances is a lack of money to stand in the way of aid to that nation.
>
> signed/Robert S. McNamara

Early in March the Chief of Staff of the Army, General Harold K. Johnson, evaluated the need for added supporting actions in Vietnam. On 5 March his party was briefed by the Ambassador. Taylor saw the basic unresolved problem as the provision of adequate security for the population. Without it, other programs were either impossible or of marginal effectiveness at best. Given security and reasonable time, however, these other programs would fall into place. The three primary causes of insecurity were (1) lack of satisfactory progress in destroying the VC, (2) the continuing capability of the VC to replace losses and increase their strength, and (3) our inability to establish and maintain an effective government.

Inability to suppress the insurgency was considered largely the consequence of insufficient trained paramilitary and police manpower. A numerical superiority in excess of five to one over the VC had never been obtained; historical example suggested a 10-to-1 or 20-to-1 ratio was prerequisite to effective operations against guerrilla forces. It was therefore essential to raise new forces and improve those already in being.

Why was the pacification program of such limited effectiveness? In many provinces the reason was poor—or non-existent—civil action after military clearing operations. The Ministries of Interior, Health, Agriculture, Public Works and Rural Affairs were responsible for civilian "follow-up" but these departments had been impotent throughout 1964, largely because of general government instability. Programs lacked continuity; personnel were constantly rotating. Occasional military successes achieved in clearing operations too frequently went unexploited. Areas were cleared but not held. Other areas were cleared and held—but were not developed; the VC infra-structure remained in place, ready to emerge when the troops moved on.

Counterinsurgency was plagued by popular apathy and dwindling morale, some the consequences of a long and seemingly endless war. There was no sense of dedication to the GVN comparable to that instilled in the VC.

Secondly, South Vietnam's open frontiers could not be sealed against infiltration. Continued DRV support to the VC, the heart of the infiltration problem, could not be eliminated by closing the frontiers from inside South Vietnam so the only way to stop infiltration was to make Hanoi order it stopped. Such was the fundamental justification for BARREL ROLL and ROLLING THUNDER operations. These, plus 34A, constituted the principal hope for ending infiltration.

It was conceded that even without its support from the North the VC could continue to recruit in the South, especially in areas lacking security and commitment to Saigon. However, it was hoped that pressure on Hanoi would help to change many conditions unfavorable to the GVN. For example, offensive action against NVN would raise national morale in South Vietnam and might provide at least a partial antidote against the willingness of country boys to join the VC.

There were many causes of the failure to establish and maintain an effective government. South Vietnam had never been a nation in spirit; a government which the people could call their own was new to them. Even now their instinct said any government was intrinsically their enemy. The people had long been divided by racial and religious differences which over the centuries their alien rulers had sought to perpetuate. No cement was present to bind together the heterogeneous elements of this society. Since the fall of Diem and the sudden removal of the restraints imposed by his dictatorial regime, the natural tendency to disunity and factionalism had been given free play; demonstrations, bonze immolations and military coups had been rife. These had produced the political turbulence of the last fifteen months.

The Ambassador closed his briefing by suggesting the possibility of increased activities in several areas:

    a. improvement in training and mobility of existing forces;

    b. establishment of priorities in the use of existing forces;

    c. expansion of the capacity of the training establishment;

    d. means to give greater attractiveness to military service;

    e. use of U.S. manpower to offset the present shortage in the Vietnamese armed forces;

    f. use of U.S. Navy resources to strengthen surveillance of coastal and inland waterways;

    g. increased tempo for BARREL ROLL and ROLLING THUNDER;

    h. expanded use of peoples action teams;

    i. increased U.S. aid in combatting economic ills;

    j. preparations to cope with the mounting refugee problem in central Vietnam;

    k. improved procedures and equipment for resource control;

    l. vitalization of public information programs, provision of a 250-kilowatt transmitter for Saigon; and

    m. prompt response to all personnel requests supporting the U.S. mission.

General Johnson returned on 12 March, submitted his report on the 14th. The guts of the report, a series of 21 recommendations plus an indication of marginal comments Secretary McNamara scribbled on his copy follow (the Secretary's comments are in parentheses):

    1. Provide increased mobility for existing forces by introducing more Army helicopter companies. (OK)

    2. Deploy more 0-1 type aircraft to give saturation surveillance capability to improve intelligence. (OK)

    3. Establish Joint U.S.–RVNAF Target Research and Analysis Center to utilize increased info effectively. (OK)

    4. Evaluate effects of COMUSMACV's unrestricted employment of U.S. fighter-bombers within SVN. (?)

5. Increase scope and tempo of U.S. air strikes against NVN. (Discuss with Chiefs.)

6. Remove self imposed restrictions on conduct of U.S. air strikes against North Vietnam. (Some already removed. Views of Chiefs.)

7. Increase tempo and scope of special operations activities against North Vietnam. (Ask Max for plan.)

8. Increase Naval and air RECCE and harassing operations against North Vietnam. (Ask Max for plan.)

9. Re-orient BARREL ROLL to increase effectiveness. (OK)

10. Commit elements of 7th Fleet to air/surface patrol of coastal areas. (OK, ask Max for plan.)

11. Program of cash awards for capture of DRV junks. (OK, ask Max for plan.)

12. Streamline procedure to give MACV quick authority and funds for construction projects in VN. (See 13)

13. Establish stockpile of construction materials and equipment within 3 to 4 sailing days of VN controlled by MACV. (Applicable to both 12 and 13—John to work with Paul and Charlie.) [ASD/ISA, SecDef and SecArmy respectively]

14. Get Australian/New Zealand agreement to take responsibility for establishing regional forces training center. (Ask State to try.)

15. Integrated U.S./GVN psychological warfare operations organization. (USIA job,—DOD will help.)

16. Accelerate positioning of remaining sub-sector advisory teams. (OK—ask Max his requirements.)

17. Provide cash contingency fund to each sub-sector advisory group. (OK—ask Max for his plan.)

18. Establish procedure for sub-sector advisory groups to draw on USOM food stuffs and building materials. (OK—ask Max for his plan.)

19. Initiate dredging projects at Danang, Qui Nhon and Nha Trang. (OK—ask Max for his requirements.)

20. Provide 4 LSTs and 6 LSVs for logistic support along east-west supply axis. (OK—ask Max for his requirements.)

21. Accelerate program for jet applicable airfield. (What is the program?—John will follow.)

To the measures the Secretary added one of his own: "extend tours." It was incorporated into later versions of the list.

In addition to the above the Johnson report suggested two alternative deployments of a tailored division force to assist Vietnamese units in offensive action in II Corps. One was to deploy U.S. combat units to assume responsibility for security of the Bien Hoa-Tan Son Nhut air base complex, Nha Trang, Qui Nhon and Pleiku. The second was to deploy U.S. combat units to assume responsibility for defense of Kontum, Pleiku and Darlac provinces in II Corps. On the first alternative the Secretary noted: "Johnson does not recommend this"; he suggested that JCS should study, and "Max's and Westy's views" toward the second alternative should be sought.

On 8 March, when Johnson was in Vietnam, the first two Marine battalions landed at Danang. Almost all of the intelligence reports during that month indicated our programs in Vietnam were either stalemated or failing. Not only was RVNAF strength considerably below the goals set and agreed upon, it was in considerable danger of actually decreasing. The situation on this score was indicated by the following table included in the March MACV report.

	Authorized Strength	*28 Feb 65 Audited Strength*	*31 March 65 Estimates*
Regular Force	274,163	245,453	246,500
Regional Force	137,187	99,143	100,000
Popular Force	185,000	162,642	160,000
Coastal Force	4,640	4,137	4,150
CIDG	20,100	19,152	19,500
National Police	51,500	33,599	34,500
Armed Combat Youth	—	44,244	44,500

Although some HOP TAC progress was occasionally reported the pacification situation otherwise was quite gloomy. The Vietnam Sitreps of 3 March 1965 reported the nationwide pacification effort remained stalled. The HOP TAC program "continues but personnel changes, past and future, may retard the future success of this effort." The 10 March Sitrep called the national pacification effort "stagnated" and objectives in some areas "regressing." In the I and II Corps pacification has "all but ceased." Only a few widely scattered places in the rest of the country could report any achievement. In the HOP TAC area the anticipated slow-down in pacification had arrived—the result of shifting military commanders and province and district chiefs. On 17 March, pacification was virtually stalled, refugee problems were mounting in I and II Corps. Only in the HOP TAC area were there "modest gains . . . in spite of increased VC area activity." By 24 March the word used for pacification efforts generally was "stalled," and the effort had now become increasingly devoted to refugee centers and relief. However, the Sitrep said 356 hamlets in the HOP TAC area had been reported—by Vietnamese authorities—as meeting agreed criteria and 927,000 persons were living in zones that had been declared clear.

At the time of the Johnson Mission, concern over the evident failures of the pacification program was such that proposals to change the framework within which it was conducted—proposals to put the USOM, USIS and CIA pacification operations all under MACV—were examined at length. Ambassadors Taylor and Alexis Johnson as well as General Westmoreland were advocating sweeping changes of this sort. All apparently conceded the need for greater coordination of the different kinds of programs, military and aid, [words illegible] into pacification but senior mission officials strongly opposed any major revision of the non-military effort.

IV. NSAM-328

Near the end of March Ambassador Taylor returned to Washington for policy conferences. Four sets of proposals had been specifically developed for consideration at the 1 April meeting. One of these was General Johnson's report which has already been described in detail. Another was a suggested program of 12 covert actions submitted by the Director of Central Intelligence. A third was an information program developed by USIS. The fourth was a proposed program of 41 non-military measures initially suggested, by Ambassador Taylor, then worked on by State during the third week of March, and finally incorporated in a memorandum to the President dated 31 March.

The 41 possible non-military actions proposed for consideration by Ambassador Taylor were arranged in 9 groups. The first group was entitled "Decentralization In The GVN and The Rural Program." This group included measures to urge the GVN to increase the power and responsibility of individual province chiefs, and to persuade the peasants they had a stake in the GVN by giving rural pacification a positive label, "new rural life hamlet program," and complexion.

The second group of non-military actions concerned "Youth, Religion, and Other Special Groups." Within this group were a series of actions to expand the support of the GVN Ministry of Youth and Sports, to reduce the draft age from 20 to 18 or 17, to persuade the GVN to meet Montagnard grievances, and to increase aid to the Vietnamese labor movement.

Under the heading "Economic and Social Measures," there were specific proposals to support a better coastal water transportation system and to urge the GVN to promulgate and put into effect an equitable land reform program. By sending U.S. and possibly nationalist Chinese experts it was hoped the GVN could be assisted in combating the growing VC capability to extract financial and material support from GVN resources. Measures were also urged to expand and accelerate slum clearance and low cost housing in troublesome urban areas and to improve the water supply.

Specific measures advocated under the heading "Education" included a general increase in U.S. assistance, expansion of the program to translate American textbooks into Vietnamese and to establish secondary schools on American principles for Vietnamese students.

Among the five specific measures under the rubric "Security and Intelligence," one urged promulgation of an effective arrest and detention law, another asked for a great increase in intelligence funds, a third called for a system of rewards for information leading to the capture or death of VC leaders, and the last was a suggestion for a national counterespionage organization.

The "Psychological Operations" proposed were mainly additions to proposals already made in the USIS report of Mr. Rowan.

The specific measures under "GVN Personnel" (and its systems of recruiting and training officials for the rural program) were to urge the GVN to establish rewards for outstanding performance, and give double or triple pay to rural school teachers and officials.

There were two measures to aid "Refugees in Emergency Situations": one to provide additional U.S. support for the refugee program, and the other to establish a joint U.S./GVN reaction team for quick survey and immediate action in war disaster situations.

The last group of proposals was a revision of the old idea of encadrement of U.S. officers at key spots within the GVN. The administrative measures to increase U.S. effectiveness included such suggestions as allowing U.S. officers to work directly with special interest groups including Buddhists, Catholics, the sects, Montagnards, students, labor, etc.; and assigning other U.S. officers to work directly within the GVN, including the Prime Minister's office and key ministries. Another suggestion was for the establishment of a U.S. inter-agency group on pacification to be directed by a senior Mission officer reporting directly to the Ambassador. (This suggestion was evidently directed at the same problem as the suggestion for establishing all U.S. pacification effort under MACV that had arisen during the visit of General Johnson.)

A feature of this proposed program that should be noted is that many if not most of the suggestions began with such phrases as "urge the GVN" or "persuade the GVN." This was of course not the first time that our assistance took this form. This had been going on for a long time. But the difference between merely supplying aid and also trying to supply initiative is significant.

In preparation for the important 1 April meeting a White House paper entitled "Key Elements For Discussion, Thursday, April 1, at 5:30 P.M." was circulated to participants. In summarizing the situation the paper said that morale had improved in South Vietnam and that, although the government had not really settled down, it seemed "hopeful both in its capacity and its sense of political forces." The South Vietnamese armed forces were in reasonably good shape although its top leadership was not really effective and the ratio of ARVN to VC (whose members were increasing) was not good enough. The situation in many parts of the countryside continued to go in favor of the VC although there was, at that writing, what was believed to be a temporary lull. Turning to the matter of the bombing this statement said that:

> Hanoi has shown no signs of give, and Peiping has stiffened its position within the last week. We still believe that attacks near Hanoi might substantially raise the odds of Peiping coming in with air.

Hanoi was expected to continue stepping up its infiltration both by land through Laos and by sea. There were clear indications of different viewpoints in Hanoi, Peiping, and Moscow with respect to "so-called wars of liberation," as well as continued friction between Moscow and Peiping.

> However, neither such frictions nor the pressure of our present slowly ascending pace of air attacks on North Vietnam can be expected to produce a real change in Hanoi's position for some time, probably two to three months at best.

The argument then proceeded to the key question of whether or not Hanoi would continue to make real headway in the South. If it continued to make such headway, even a major step-up in our air attacks would probably not make them much more reasonable. On the other hand if the situation in South Vietnam began to move against the VC and the going became increasingly tough, then the "situation might begin to move on a political track—but again not in less than two to three months, in our present judgment." This was a significant departure from the theory for ROLLING THUNDER propounded when that bombing pressure was inaugurated.

Following some considerations on immediate international moves and more general political posture, the memo turned to "actions within South Vietnam." Employing every useful resource to improve the efforts in the South was defined as crucial. The paper indicated that the 41-point program of non-military measures developed mainly by Ambassador Taylor included promising elements and that the mission as well as agencies in Washington should develop additional points. McCone's suggestions for largely covert actions were recommended for further study. Both the Rowan (USIS) and the 21-point program of General Johnson were viewed favorably, as well as an increase in U.S. military support forces in Vietnam from 18,000 to 20,000 men. An increase in GVN manpower was also approved with increased pay scales to be used as an inducement regardless of the monetary costs. On one copy of this document that went to OSD, there was a handwritten additional point that was, "change mission of Marine force." This significant addition was later adopted in NSAM-328.

The remainder of the paper was devoted, first, to U.S. and third country combat forces in South Vietnam, and second, to actions against North Vietnam and in Laos. These are of interest here only in the extent to which they distracted from or supplanted counterinsurgency actions within South Vietnam. So far as U.S. combat forces within South Vietnam were concerned, there was cautious consideration of a small and gradual buildup. But it was emphasized that because the reaction of the GVN and of the South Vietnamese people to any major U.S. combat deployment was uncertain, and because the net effectiveness of U.S. combat forces in the Vietnamese environment was also uncertain, the Secretary of State and the Secretary of Defense had recommended that action of this sort be limited. Only the deployment of two additional Marine battalions, one Marine air squadron and certain logistical forces over the ensuing sixty-day period was approved. Continuation of ROLLING THUNDER operations on a slowly ascending scale was assumed. It was also assumed that preparations would be made for additional strikes and for a response to any higher level of VC operations, as well as, correspondingly, to slow the pace in the unlikely event that VC actions slacked off sharply.

In the NSC meeting of 1 April 1965, the President gave his formal approval, "subject to modifications in the light of experience," to the 41-point program of non-military actions submitted by Ambassador Taylor and described above. He gave general approval to the USIS recommendations, except that no additional funds were to be supplied for this work—the program was to be funded and supported by other agencies. The President further approved the urgent exploration of the covert actions proposed by the Director of Central Intelligence. Finally, he repeated his previous approval of the 21-point program of military actions recommended by General Johnson. On the exclusively military side the President authorized the 18,000 to 20,000-man increase in U.S. military support forces, the deployment of two additional Marine battalions, and the change of mission for all Marine battalions to permit their use in active combat under conditions to be established and approved by the Secretary of Defense in consultation with the Secretary of State. However, because this last decision was contingent upon future agreements between the Secretary of State and the Secretary of Defense its full significance was not immediately apparent. It was left to the Ambassador to seek South Vietnamese government approval and coordination for all of these measures.

NSAM-328 did not last long as a full and current statement of U.S. policy. There were some responsible officials who had misgivings about increasing our involvement in South Vietnam or about increasing it more rapidly than might be necessary. There were others who apparently felt that NSAM-328 risked falling between two stools. One such was John A. McCone, Director of CIA (who was perhaps also unhappy about the increasing involvement *per se*). The day after the 1 April meeting he addressed a memorandum expressing second thoughts to the Secretary of State, the Secretary of Defense, the Special Assistant to the President for National Security Affairs and Ambassador Taylor. The change in the U.S. role from merely giving advice and static defense, to active combat operations against Viet Cong guerrillas, appeared to bother him. He felt our ground force operations would very possibly have only limited effectiveness against guerrillas, and above all, he felt the conduct of active combat operations in South Vietnam should be accompanied by air strikes against the North sufficiently heavy and damaging to really hurt the North. If the U.S. were to combine combat operations in the South with air strikes of any kind in the North, the attacks on the North should be heavy and do great damage. Without expressly saying so, his point seems to have been that the air war against the North should not be an attempt to persuade, but an effort to compel. He said that he had already reported that:

> The strikes to date have not caused a change in the North Vietnamese policy of directing Viet Cong insurgency, infiltrating cadres and supplying materials. If anything, the strikes to date have hardened their attitude.

Although the memo as a whole conveys Mr. McCone's serious doubt that the ground operations in the South would in any event serve their purpose, he clearly advocated bombing more heavily if we decided to engage in ground operations. Unless they were supported by really strong actions against North Vietnam, he felt such ground operations would be doomed to failure:

> I believe our proposed track offers great danger of simply encouraging Chinese Communists and Soviet support of the DRV and VC cause if for no other reason than the risk for both will be minimum. I envision that the reaction of the NVN and the Chinese Communists will be to deliberately, carefully, and probably gradually, build up the Viet Cong capabilities by covert infiltration of North Vietnamese and, possibly, Chinese cadres and thus bring an ever increasing pressure on our forces. In effect, we will find ourselves mired down in combat in the jungle in a military effort we cannot win, and from which we will have extreme difficulty in extracting ourselves.

McCone argued that if we were going to change the mission of the U.S. ground forces we also needed to change the ground rules of the strikes against North Vietnam, and he concluded:

> If we are unwilling to take this kind of a decision now, we must not take the actions concerning the mission of our ground forces for the reasons I have mentioned above.

McCone's views notwithstanding, U.S. policy was promptly and sharply reoriented in the direction of greater military involvement with a proportionate de-emphasis of the direct counterinsurgency efforts. It is not fully clear to this writer exactly how and why this rapid re-orientation occurred. On 7 April the President made his famous Johns Hopkins speech in which he publicly committed the United States more than ever before to the defense of South Vietnam, but also committed himself to engage in unconditional discussions. The following day, Pham Van Dong published his Four Points in what seemed a defiant, and unyielding response. This sharp DRV rebuff of the President's initiative may well have accelerated the re-orientation. The re-orientation of policy itself, however, was expressed not in an explicit restatement of formal policy, but in a series of action decisions over the following fortnight that caught the Saigon Mission very much by surprise.

The Ambassador's NODIS to the President on 13 April had a comparatively optimistic tone. It began, "We have just completed another quite favorable week in terms of losses inflicted upon the Viet Cong. . . ." The critical conditions in Bien Dinh Province had been considerably relieved and the province, it was believed, was about back to normal. Although a large part of the province remained under Viet Cong control, many areas had been restored to government control and the fear of the loss of major towns seemed past. There had been aggressive action by a new division commander, and there seemed to be improved morale attributable to the air actions against North Vietnam. There was a possibility that the Viet Cong were regrouping and they would probably soon engage in some new kind or phase of offensive action. But, then as now, there were what some interpreted as indications that the Viet Cong morale might be dropping. Furthermore, estimates—not audited figures—indicated that the government military and paramilitary forces had been increased by some 10,000 during the month of March as against the target of 8,000 per month. Prime Minister Quat was continuing his program of visiting the provinces, and in addition to making himself and the Saigon government known to the hinterlands, he had expressed particular interest in such projects as rural electrification, agricultural development, water supply and school construction. Quat's principal worry continued to be the unruly generals and there was continued evidence of disunity within the senior officers corps.

Within two days, however, messages went out from Washington indicating that decisions had been made at the highest level to go beyond the measures specified in NSAM-328. On 15 April, McGeorge Bundy sent a personal *nodis* to Ambassador Taylor saying that the President had just approved important future military deployments and that some personal explanation might be helpful.

> The President has repeatedly emphasized his personal desire for a strong experiment in the encadrement of U.S. troops with the Vietnamese. He is also very eager to see prompt experiments in use of energetic teams of U.S. officials in support of provisional governments under unified U.S. leadership. These desires are the source of corresponding paragraphs in our message.
>
> On further troop deployments, the President's belief is that current situation requires use of all practical means of strengthening position in South Vietnam and that additional U.S. troops are important if not decisive reinforcements. He has not seen evidence of negative result of deployments to date, and does not wish to wait any longer than is essential for genuine GVN agreement.
>
> President always intended these plans be reviewed with you and approved by Quat before final execution, and we regret any contrary impression given by our messages in recent days.

The message stated that "highest authority" believed that, in addition to the actions against the North, something new had to be added in the South, to achieve victory.

> 1. Experimental encadrement by U.S. forces of South Vietnamese ground troops both to stiffen and increase their effectiveness and also to add to their fire power. Two approaches were to be carried out concurrently, one involving integration of a substantial number of U.S. combat personnel in each of several ARVN battalions, the other involving the combined operation of approximately three additional Army/Marine battalions with three or more South Vietnamese battalions for use in combat operations.
>
> 2. Introduction of a brigade force into the Bien Hoa-Vung Tau area to act both as a security force for installations and to participate in counterinsurgency combat operations.
>
> 3. Introduction of a battalion or multi-battalion forces into three additional locations along the coast, such as Qui Nhon. The purpose here would

be to experiment further with using U.S. forces in counterinsurgency role in addition to providing security for the base.

In addition to these three steps, which were intended basically to increase the military effectiveness of the counterguerrilla campaign, a series of other steps was proposed. One was a substantial expansion of the Vietnamese recruiting campaign using U.S. recruiting experts, techniques and procedures. A second was an experimental program to provide expanded medical services to the countryside utilizing mobile dispensaries.

The next one—and the one that caused considerable subsequent discussion—was the experimental introduction into the provincial government structure of a team of U.S. Army civil affairs personnel to assist in the establishment of stable provincial administration and to initiate and direct the necessary political, economic and security programs. It was proposed that teams be introduced first into only one or two provinces. General Peers was being sent to work with COMUSMACV in developing detailed plans.

The last non-military measure was an experimental plan for distributing food directly to regular and paramilitary personnel and their families.

Hot on the heels of this message came another on 16 April explaining in some further detail the proposition to experiment with U.S. civil affairs officers in the pacification program. Major General W. R. Peers' party was scheduled to arrive in Saigon on 19 April. According to the proposal COMUSMACV was to designate a senior officer to direct the overall U.S. Army Civil Affairs effort in the one or two test provinces. Within these, the responsibility for all U.S. activities would be vested in the senior U.S. Army sector advisor.

This last message was, for Taylor, the straw that broke the camel's back. Immediately upon receiving it the Ambassador dispatched a NODIS to McGeorge Bundy:

> . . . . Contrary to the firm understanding which I received in Washington, I was not asked to concur in this massive visitation. For your information, I do not concur.
>
> Based on the little I know of the proposed civil affairs experiment, I am opposed to beginning any extensive planning exercise which, because of its controversial and divisive concept, is going to shake this mission and divert senior members from their important daily tasks. If GVN gets word of these plans to impose U.S. military government framework on their country (as this new concept seems to imply), it will have a very serious impact on our relations here.
>
> We are rocking the boat at a time when we have it almost on an even keel. I recommend that we suspend action on this project until we have time to talk over its merits and decide how to proceed with order.

Shortly after dispatching this telegram, the Ambassador sent another to McGeorge Bundy, this one dealing more generally with the defense message of 15 April which had laid out the new program of added measures decided upon by the President.

> I am greatly troubled by DoD 15 April 15. First, it shows no consideration for the fact that, as a result of decisions taken in Washington during my visit, this mission is charged with securing implementation by the two-month old Quat government of a 21-point military program, a 41-point non-military program, a 16-point Rowan USIS program and a 12-point CIA program. Now this new cable opens up new vistas of further points as if

we can win here somehow on a point score. We are going to stall the machine of government if we do not declare a moratorium on new programs for at least six months. Next, it shows a far greater willingness to get into the ground war than I had discerned in Washington during my recent trip . . .

My greatest concern arises over para 6 reftel [the civil affairs experiment proposal] which frankly bewilders me. What do the authors of this cable think the mission has been doing over the months and years? We have presumably the best qualified people the Washington agencies (State, AID, DoD, USIA and CIA) can find working in the provinces seven days a week at precisely the task described in paragraph 6. Is it proposed to withdraw these people and replace them by Army civil affairs types operating on the pattern of military occupation? If this is the thought, I would regard such a change in policy which would gain wide publicity, as disastrous in its likely efforts upon pacification in general and on US/GVN relations in particular.

Mac, can't we be better protected from our friends? I know that everyone wants to help, but there is such a thing as killing with kindness. In particular, we want to stay alive here because we think we're winning—and will continue to win unless helped to death.

Shortly after sending this cable, the Ambassador sent still a third message, this one suggesting certain steps that might be taken in Washington to facilitate his implementation of the many and rapidly changing policies and programs that had been decided upon in Washington since his visit. The problem was winning not only the acquiescence, but the support and active cooperation of the South Vietnamese government. He suggested the kind of instruction that Washington should provide him to present to the GVN—the new policy of third country participation in ground combat. Taylor's proposed instructions are quoted in full here because they provide, for better or worse, an internally consistent rationale for the shifting policies of that month:

The USG has completed a thorough review of the situation in South Vietnam both in its national and international aspects and has reached certain important conclusions. It feels that in recent weeks there has been a somewhat favorable change in the overall situation as the result of the air attacks on the DRV, the relatively small but numerous successes in the field against the VC and the encouraging progress of the Quat government. However, it is becoming increasingly clear that, in all probability, the primary objective of the GVN and the USG of changing the will of the DRV to support the VC insurgency cannot be attained in an accpetable time frame by the methods presently employed. The air campaign in the North must be supplemented by signal successes against the VC in the South before we can hope to create that frame of mind in Hanoi which will lead to the decisions we seek.

The JCS have reviewed the military resources which will be available in SVN by the end of 1965 and have concluded that even with an attainment of the highest feasible mobilization goals, ARVN will have insufficient forces to carry out the kind of successful campaign against the VC which is considered essential for the purposes discussed above. If the ground war is not to drag into 1966 and even beyond, they consider it necessary to reinforce GVN ground forces with about twenty battalion equivalents in addition to the forces now being recruited in SVN. Since these reinforcements cannot be raised by the GVN they must inevitably come from third country sources.

The USG accepts the validity of this reasoning of the JCS and offers its assistance to the GVN to raise these additional forces for the purpose of bringing the VC insurgency to an end in the shortest possible time. We are prepared to bring in additional U.S. ground forces provided we can get a reasonable degree of participation from other third countries. If the GVN will make urgent representations to them, we believe it will be entirely possible to obtain the following contributions: Korea, one regimental combat team; Australia, one Infantry battalion; New Zealand, one battery and one company of tanks; Philippine Islands, one battalion. If the forces of the foregoing magnitude are forthcoming, the USG is prepared to provide the remainder of the combat reinforcements as well as the necessary logistic personnel to support the third country contingents. Also, it will use its good offices as desired in assisting the GVN approach to these governments.

You (the Ambassador), will seek the concurrence of the GVN to the foregoing program, recognizing that a large number of questions such as command relationships, concepts of employment and disposition of forces must be worked out subsequently.

The message concluded that, armed with an instruction of this kind, he, Taylor, would be adequately equipped to initiate what might be a sharp debate within the GVN. Something of this sort was needed before taking up the matter of troop arrangements with Quat.

Later the same day, Deputy Ambassador U. Alexis Johnson sent Washington his personal observations on the recent decision to introduce third country troops. He had just returned from one day at Pleiku with Premier Quat, and two days in the Danang-Hue area, where he had had "extended visits and informal conversations with all of the senior Marine officers ashore."

I fully appreciate considerations both internal and external to SVN which impel move on our part to bring this war to successful conclusion as quickly as possible . . . However, I gravely question whether this result can be achieved at this time by massive input of non-Vietnamese military forces. As we have learned, we are dealing with volatile and hyper-sensitive people with strong xenophobic characteristics never far below the surface. We have thus far deployed our Marine battalions to minimize direct contact with local population. This not only from our choice but that of GVN, especially General Thi. On this I think Thi is right. Hasty and ill conceived deployment of non-Vietnamese in combat roles where they are substantially involved with local population could badly backfire on U.S. and give rise to cries by Buddhists . . . and others to "throw out foreigners" and "return Vietnam to the Vietnamese . . ."

The message went on to say that in the next few weeks the Marines at Danang would have a chance to test their success as a reaction force in support of ARVN initiated contact with the enemy, and in patrolling thinly populated areas. The Deputy Ambassador recommended that we await the outcome of this testing before engaging any more forces.

A hastily arranged meeting in Honolulu on 20 April was evidently called to soothe Taylor's temper over the hasty decisions to deploy third country troops, and to get agreement to them by the senior U.S. policy officials concerned—not to reverse or alter those policies or to shift the direction of our commitments. By that point we were inexorably committed to a military resolution of the insurgency. The problem seemed no longer soluble by any other means.

2. Military Pressures Against North Vietnam, February 1964–January 1965

Summary

February–June, 1964

The first half of 1964 saw the unfolding of an intensive debate and planning effort within the Johnson Administration concerning the desirability, limitations, and risks of mounting major military pressures against North Vietnam. Actual U.S. involvement in SEA increased only slightly during this period.

The single notable element of actual increased U.S. involvement during this period was a program of covert GVN operations, designed to impose "progressively escalating pressure" upon the North, and initiated on a small and essentially ineffective scale in February. The active U.S. role in the few covert operations that were carried out was limited essentially to planning, equipping, and training of the GVN forces involved, but U.S. responsibility for the launching and conduct of these activities was unequivocal and carried with it an implicit symbolic and psychological intensification of the U.S. commitment. A firebreak had been crossed, and the U.S. had embarked on a program that was recognized as holding little promise of achieving its stated objectives, at least in its early stages. Thus, a demand for more was stimulated and an expectation of more was aroused.

The demands came—mostly from U.S. officials in Saigon and Washington and mostly because of the felt need to do something about a deteriorating situation in SVN—to increase the intensity of the covert operations and to change from covert to overt action. The Khanh government, it should be noted, opposed these demands on the grounds that it would expose the vulnerable GVN to greater pressures from the enemy. With each successive "crisis"—recognition of insufficient intelligence on the nature and scope of the infiltration (December through May), realization of dramatic communist gains in SVN (February), threats of major communist advances in Laos (late May)—the demands were redoubled and intensified. The basic assumption underlying these demands was that the DRV, faced with the credible prospect of losing its industrial and economic base through direct attack, would halt its support of the insurgencies in Laos and South Vietnam.

Beginning in early February, a series of valuable studies and planning exercises were undertaken, with participation of all national security agencies, to examine the whole panoply of problems—objectives, options, effects, costs, and risks—of mounting overt coercive pressures against the North. The planning effort served to develop consensus on some issues, including the recognition that punitive action in the North would be, at best, complementary to successful counterinsurgency in the South. It also surfaced significant differences among the participants in the planning effort and in the broader debate that ensued, in their respective approaches to "pressure planning" as well as in the substantive content of their recommendations. Thus, the JCS viewed the planning task as preparation of an action program for near-term implementation, and their recommendations tended toward immediate and forceful military measures. The State-ISA planning group, on the other hand, viewed it as a contingency planning exercise and its scenarios and recommendations stressed a more deliberate, cautious approach, carefully tailoring proposed U.S. actions in SEA to the unique political context of each country. Ambassador Lodge, in turn, developed yet a third "carrot and stick" approach, stressing a diplomatic effort at persuasion, *i.e.*, combining a threat of punitive strikes with an offer of some economic assistance to the DRV. These divergences in approach and concept persisted, though varying in degree and emphasis, throughout the planning period.

By June, with increasing recognition that only relatively heavy levels of attack on the DRV would be likely to have any signoficant compelling effect, with a greater awareness of the many imponderables raised by the planning effort, and with the emergence of a somewhat more hopeful situation in SVN and Laos, most of the President's advisers favored holding off on any attempts to pressure North Vietnam through overt military operations. Only the JCS, Ambassador Lodge, and Walt Rostow continued to advocate increased military measures, and even Rostow qualified his recommendations with the claim that a firm public stance, and supporting actions giving the impression of increased military operations, would be the best assurance of avoiding having to employ them. Moreover, most of the advisers recognized the necessity of building firmer public and congressional support for greater U.S. involvement in SEA before any wider military actions should be undertaken.

Accordingly, with the political conventions just around the corner and the election issues regarding Vietnam clearly drawn, the President decided against actions that would deepen the U.S. involvement by broadening the conflict in Laos, Cambodia or North Vietnam. In his view, there were still a number of relatively mild military and intensified political actions in the South open to him that would serve the national interest better than escalation of the conflict.

July–October, 1964

During the spring and summer of 1964, there was disquiet about the situation in South Vietnam and disillusion with on-going U.S. actions to right that situation. During the third quarter of 1964, a consensus developed within the Johnson Administration that some form of continual overt pressures mounting in severity against North Vietnam soon would be required. The purpose of these pressures was twofold: (1) to effect DRV will and capabilities in order to persuade and force the leadership in Hanoi to halt their support and direction of the war in the South; and (2) to induce negotiations at some future point in time on our terms after North Vietnam had been hurt and convinced of our resolve. This consensus was in an early formative stage—it had become an idea, not a program for action; it was a belief, not as yet fully staffed and considered. Because of this and because of important tactical considerations (the impending U.S. elections, the instability of the GVN, and the need to produce further evidence of VC infiltration into the South) implementation of such a policy was deferred. Nevertheless, the groundwork was being laid. The Tonkin Gulf reprisal constituted an important firebreak, and the Tonkin Gulf Resolution set U.S. public suport for virtually any action.

Since the fall of Diem in November 1963, the political situation in South Vietnam had been deteriorating. The Khanh Government had succeeded Minh in January 1964, but had demonstrated only greater capacity for survivability, not more capacity for reversing the trend toward collapse. In the wake of the Tonkin Gulf reprisals, when South Vietnamese morale was still temporarily inflated, Khanh made a bold bid to consolidate his personal power and impose semi-dictatorial rule. He was brought to heel, however, in less than a month by the military junta which continued to operate behind the scenes. By September, the most salient aspect of the confused political situation in South Vietnam was the likelihood that it would continue its downward slide into the foreseeable future.

In this setting, a program of covert military pressures against North Vietnam already had been set in process. These were basically of three kinds: (1) low level recce with armed escort over Laos; (2) De Soto patrols within 4 n.m. of the NVN coast to acquire visual, electronic, and photographic intelligence; and (3) Oplan 34-A which included a variety of anti-infiltration, sabotage, and psywar measures. The portent of these actions was being conveyed to the North Vietnamese through private and public channels. A Canadian, Blair Seaborn, was sent to Hanoi to state that U.S. objectives were limited but that our commitment was deep, and that "in the event of escalation the greatest devastation would of course result for the DRVN itself."

Neither the situation in SVN nor the failure of Hanoi to acquiesce to our threats diminished the basic U.S. commitment. NSAM 288 expounding the need to do what was necessary to preserve an "independent non-communist South Vietnam" was the guiding policy document. At no time in this period was the NSAM 288 commitment brought into question. Rather, American concern was focused on how the U.S. could retrieve the situation. The usual palliatives—more aid, more advice, more pressure on the GVN to reform, and more verbal threats to Hanoi—were no longer seen as satisfactory. Nor did it appear to U.S. decision-makers that we faced a stark choice between complete U.S. withdrawal from the struggle or a large scale introduction of U.S. ground forces. Nor did the leadership in Washington believe that a massive bombing campaign against the North need be seriously considered—although such a program was proposed by the JCS. With all these alternatives implicitly ruled out at this time, the choice was both obvious and inevitable. Although it did not take the form of decision, it was agreed that the U.S. should at an unspecified date in the future begin an incremental series of gradually mounting strikes against North Vietnam. The only real questions were precisely what actions should be taken and when? None of these early fall discussions in Washington really confronted the hard issues of what a bombing campaign would buy and what it would cost. These hardheaded discussions, to some extent, took place in the last few months of 1964.

The key events in this period were the Tonkin Gulf incidents of August 2nd and 4th and the U.S. reprisal on North Vietnam PT boats and bases on August 5th. The explanation for the DRV attack on U.S. ships remains puzzling (perhaps it was simply a way of warning and warding off U.S. patrols close to North Vietnam borders). The swift U.S. reaction was to be expected. While there was some momentary uncertainty about the actuality of the second attack on August 4th, confirming evidence of the attack was received before the U.S. reprisal was launched. The U.S. reprisal represented the carrying out of recommendations made to the President by his principal advisers earlier that summer and subsequently placed on the shelf. The existence of these previous recommendations with planning down to detailed targeting made possible the immediate U.S. reaction when the crisis came.

At the same time as U.S. reprisals were taken, President Johnson decided to act on another recommendation that had been under consideration since at least May—a Congressional resolution of support for U.S. policy. Whereas in the earlier discussions, such a resolution had been proposed as a vehicle for mobilizing Congressional and public support behind an escalating campaign of pressures against the North, the President, in the midst of an election campaign, now felt impelled to use it to solidify support for his overall Vietnam policy. On August 5th he sent a message to Congress on the Tonkin incidents and asked for passage of a joint resolution endorsing his policy. The resolution itself was one prepared by the Administration and introduced on its behalf by the Chairmen of the Foreign Affairs Committees in the two Houses. It was passed with near unanimous support on August 7th.

The net effect of the swift U.S. reprisals and the Congressional Resolution was to dramatically demonstrate, publicly state and formally record the commitments to South Vietnam and within Southeast Asia that had been made internal U.S. policy by NSAM 288 in March 1964. They were also conceived and intended as a clear communication to Hanoi of what it could expect if it continued to pursue its current course of action. They were portents of the future designed to demonstrate the firmness of U.S. resolve and the direction its policy was tending. The psychological impact of the raids on the Administration and the American public is also significant. They marked the crossing of an important threshhold in the war, and it was accomplished with virtually no domestic criticism, indeed, with an evident increase in public support for the Administration. The precedent for strikes against the North was thus established and at very little apparent cost. There was a real cost, however. The number of unused measures short of direct military action against the North had been depleted. Greater visible commitment was purchased at the price of reduced flexibility.

But, a worried Administration went to some lengths to insure that the strikes did not bind or commit it to any future policies or actions and to have it understood that the strikes had been pure and simple reprisals of the one of a kind variety. Yet, for all these reasons, when a decision to strike the North was faced again, it was much easier to take.

The Tonkin reprisals were widely regarded within the Administration as an effective, although limited demonstration of the firmness of American resolve. However, they also served to stiffen that resolve and to deepen the commitment. Several officials within the Administration, including Ambassador Taylor, felt that to have any lasting impact this demonstration of resolve would have to be followed up by other continuing actions, in an increasing tempo. The positive short-term effect of the reprisals in raising South Vietnamese morale was noted as an important by-product of the strikes and offered as one justification for continuing pressures against the North. Also figuring importantly in calculation of resolve and intent was the appreciable improvement in our position in Laos as a result of the vigorous spring offensive by Laotian Government forces. This improvement had led us to oppose a 14-nation conference on Laos for fear of placing the new gains in jeopardy, and convinced many that only military measures were unambiguously understood by Hanoi's communist rulers. This, however, was tempered by a countervailing concern not to provoke by U.S. action any communist military escalation in Laos.

Quite another set of arguments for strikes against the North were advanced by Walt Rostow, then Counselor of the State Department, in a paper that circulated widely through the Administration in August 1964. The "Rostow Thesis" argued that externally supported insurgencies could only be successfully dealt with by striking at their sources of support and neutralizing them. The objective of such attacks would be psychological rather than purely military. They would be designed to alter the aggressor's calculation of interests in supporting the insurgency through the fear of further military and economic damage, the fear of involvement in a wider conflict, the fear of internal political upheaval and the fear of greater dependence on a major communist power. Any incidental improvement in morale in the country troubled by insurgency or improvement in bargaining leverage were to be regarded as bonuses. To achieve the desired effect, a carefully orchestrated series of escalating military measures, coupled with simultaneous political, economic and psychological pressures was called for. The "thesis" was articulated in general terms, but the immediate case in everyone's mind was, of course, Southeast Asia.

A thorough critique of Rostow's paper was prepared in OSD/ISA with inputs from State's Policy Planning Council. This analysis argued that the validity of the "thesis" would depend on two variables: (1) the extent of the commitment of the nation supporting the insurgency; and (2) the degree to which vital U.S. interests were at stake in the conflict. The latter question having been settled with respect to South Vietnam by NSAM 288, the remaining problem was whether the kinds of actions Rostow recommended could succeed given the level of determined commitment of the North Vietnamese. For the Rostow approach to succeed, the DRV would have to be persuaded that: (1) the U.S. was taking limited action to achieve limited goals; (2) the U.S. commitment was total; and (3) the U.S. had established a sufficient domestic consensus to see the policy through. If the DRV was not so convinced, the approach would fail unless there were a major U.S. military involvement in the war. The critique concluded that the public opinion problems of such an approach, both domestic and international, would be very great, and that in view of the inherent problems of implementing and managing such a discriminating policy, it had poor chances of success. These reservations notwithstanding, the outlook embodied in the "Rostow thesis" came to dominate a good deal of Administration thinking on the question of pressures against the North in the months ahead.

All of the pressures-against-the-North thinking came to a head in the strategy meeting of the principals on September 7th. It appears that a rather narrow range of proposals was up for consideration. One program proposal came from the JCS. It was a repeat of the 94-target list program which the JCS had recommended on August 26th. The JCS called for deliberate attempts to provoke the DRV into taking acts which could then be answered by a systematic U.S. air campaign. The JCS argued that such actions were now "essential to preventing complete collapse of the U.S. position in the RVN and SEA," because "continuation of present or foreseeable programs limited to the RVN will not produce the desired result." The Chiefs were supported by ISA in their provocation approach. For ISA, ASD McNaughton argued that our acts and the DRV response "should be likely to provide good grounds for us to escalate if we wished." McNaughton's approach was for a "gradual squeeze," not simply a tit-for-tat contingency and unlike the quick, all-out proposals of the JCS.

The principal conferees at this September meeting did not believe that deliberate acts of provocation should be undertaken "in the immediate future while the GVN is still struggling to its feet." However, they apparently reached a consensus that they might recommend such actions—"depending on GVN progress and communist reaction in the meantime"—by early October. This deferral decision was strongly supported by Mr. McCone of the CIA and Ambassador Taylor. Ambassador Taylor, revising his previous position, believed that the conflict should not be escalated to a level beyond South Vietnamese capacities to manage it. He opposed overt actions against North Vietnam as too risky and urged instead that further measures to strengthen the GVN be taken first. Similarly, Secretary McNamara affirmed his understanding that "we are not acting more strongly because there is a clear hope of strengthening the GVN." McNamara went on to urge, however, that the way be kept open for stronger actions even if the GVN did not improve or in the event the war were widened by the communists. In notes taken at this meeting the President asked: "Can we really strengthen the GVN?"

It is important to differentiate the consensus of the principals at this September meeting from the views which they had urged on the President in the preceding spring. In the spring the use of force had been clearly contingent upon a major reversal—principally in Laos—and had been advanced with the apparent assumption that military actions hopefully would not be required. Now, however, their views were advanced with a sense that such actions were inevitable.

The results of the September meeting were recorded in NSAM 314. The actions that were approved against the DRV for the next three month period were highly limited and marginal in character. They included resumption of the offshore U.S. naval patrols, resumption of covert GVN coastal operations against the North, limited air and ground operations in the Laotian corridor, and a preparedness to respond to any further DRV attacks on a tit-for-tat basis.

From the September meeting forward, there was little basic disagreement among the principals on the need for military actions against the North. What prevented action for the time being was a set of tactical considerations. The President was in the midst of an election campaign in which he was presenting himself as the candidate of reason and restraint as opposed to the quixotic Barry Goldwater. Other concerns were the aforementioned shakiness of the GVN, the uncertainty as to China's response to an escalation, the desire not to upset the delicate Laotian equation, the need to design whatever actions were taken so as to achieve the maximum public and Congressional support, and the implicit belief that overt actions at this time might bring pressure for premature negotiations —that is, negotiations before the DRV was hurting. In summary, the period saw the development of the consensus on military pressures against the North and the decision to defer them for temporary reasons of tactics.

November 1964–January 1965

In the late fall of 1964, President Johnson made a tentative decision in favor of limited military pressures against North Vietnam. He acted on the consensus recommendation of his principal advisors, a consensus achieved by a process of compromising alternatives into a lowest-common-denominator proposal at the sub-cabinet and cabinet level, thereby precluding any real Presidential choice among viable options. The choices he was given all included greater pressures against North Vietnam. The Presidential decision itself was for a limited and tightly controlled two-step build-up of pressures. The first phase involved an intensification of existing harassment activities with reprisals; the second, which was approved in principle only, was to be a sustained, slowly escalating air campaign against the North. The spectrum of choice could have run from (a) a judgment that the situation in the South was irretrievable and, hence, a decision to begin the withdrawal of U.S. forces; to (b) a judgment that the maintenance of a non-communist South Vietnam was indispensable to U.S. strategic interests and, therefore, required a massive U.S. intensification of the war both in the North and in the South. The extreme withdrawal option was rejected almost without surfacing for consideration since it was in direct conflict with the independent, noncommunist SVN commitments of NSAM 288. The opposite option of massive involvement, which was essentially the JCS recommendation at an early point in these deliberations, was shunted aside because both its risks and costs were too high.

Short of those extremes, however, were two other alternatives that were briefly considered by the Working Group as fallback positions but rejected before they were fully explored. While both came into some conflict with the commitments to South Vietnam of NSAM 288, they could have been justified as flowing from another long-standing U.S. conviction, namely that ultimately the war would have to be won in the South by the South Vietnamese. These fallback positions were outlined in the following manner:

1. To hold the situation together as long as possible so that we have time to strengthen other areas of Asia.
2. To take forceful enough measures in the situation so that we emerge from it, even in the worst case, with our standing as the principal helper against Communist expansion as little impaired as possible.
3. To make clear . . . to nations, in Asia particularly, that failure in South Vietnam, if it comes, was due to special local factors that do not apply to other nations we are committed to defend. . . .

In operational terms the first would have meant holding the line—placing an immediate, low ceiling on the number of U.S. personnel in SVN, and taking vigorous efforts to build on a stronger base elsewhere, possibly Thailand. The second alternative would have been to undertake some spectacular, highly visible supporting action like a limited-duration selective bombing campaign as a last effort to save the South; to have accompanied it with a propaganda campaign about the unwinnability of the war given the GVN's ineptness and; then, to have sought negotiations through compromise and neutralization when the bombing failed. Neither of these options was ever developed.

The recommendation of the Principals to the President left a gap between the maximum objective of NSAM 288 and the marginal pressures against the North being proposed to achieve that objective. There are two by no means contradictory explanations of this gap.

One explanation is the way in which pressures and the controlled use of force were viewed by the Principals. There is some reason to believe that the Principals thought that carefully calculated doses of force could bring about predictable and desirable responses from Hanoi. The threat implicit in minimum but increasing amounts of force ("slow squeeze") would, it was hoped by some, ultimately bring Hanoi to the table on terms favorable to the U.S. Underlying this optimistic view was a significant underestimate of the level of the DRV commitment to victory in the South, and an overestimate of the effectiveness of U.S. pressures in weakening that resolve. The assumption was that the threat value of limited pressures coupled with declarations of firm resolve on our part would be sufficient to force the DRV into major concessions. Therefore, the U.S. negotiating posture could be a tough one. Another factor which, no doubt, commended the proposal to the Administration was the relatively low-cost—in political terms—of such action. Furthermore, these limited measures would give the GVN a temporary breathing spell, it was thought, in which to regroup itself, both politically and militarily should stronger action involving a direct confrontation between the two Vietnams be required at some future date. And lastly, it was the widely shared belief that the recommendation was a moderate solution that did not foreclose future options for the President if the measures did not fully achieve their intended results. The JCS differed from this view on the grounds that if we were really interested in affecting Hanoi's will, we would have to hit hard at its capabilities.

A second explanation of the gap between ends and means is a more simple one. In a phrase, we had run out of alternatives other than pressures. The GVN was not reforming, ARVN was being hit hard, further U.S. aid and advice did not seem to do the trick, and something was needed to keep the GVN afloat until we were ready to decide on further actions at a later date. Bombing the North would fit that bill, and make it look like we tried.

The President was cautious and equivocal in approaching the decision. Indicative of his reluctance to widen the U.S. commitment and of his desire to hedge his bets was the decision to make phase II of the new policy contingent on GVN reform and improvement. Ambassador Taylor was sent back to Saigon in December after the White House meetings with the understanding that the U.S. Government did not believe:

> that we should incur the risks which are inherent in any expansion of hostilities without first assuring that there is a government in Saigon capable of handling the serious problems involved in such an expansion and of exploiting the favorable effects which may be anticipated. . . .

As with the discussions of the preceding six months, the decisions at the end of 1964 marked another step in the U.S. involvement in Vietnam. The following is a summary of the November–December, 1964 and January, 1965 deliberations.

On the eve of the November election, and after the decision not to retaliate against the North for the VC attack on the Bien Hoa airbase on November 1, the President appointed an inter-agency working group and asked it to conduct a thorough re-examination of our Vietnam policy and to present him with alternatives and recommendations as to our future course of action. That such a review should have been undertaken so soon after the policy deliberations and decisions of September is at first glance surprising. The President, however, was now being elected in his own right with an overwhelming mandate and all the sense of opportunity and freedom to reconsider past policy and current trends that such a victory invariably brings. In retrospect, there appears to have been, in fact, remarkably little latitude for reopening the basic questions about U.S. involvement in the Vietnam struggle. NSAM 288 did not seem open to question. In Vietnam, our now substantial efforts and our public affirmation of resolve to see the war through to success had failed to reverse either the adverse trend of the war or the continuing deterioration of South Vietnamese political life. The September deliberations had produced only a decision against precipitate action and had done nothing to redress the situation. Significantly, however, they had revealed the existence of an Administration consensus that military pressures against the North would be required at some proximate future date for a variety of reasons. Now, in November, with a new electoral mandate and the abundant evidence of the inadequacy of current measures, the President was once again looking for new ideas and proposals—a low-cost option with prospects for speedy, positive results.

The Working Group's first job had been to examine U.S. interests and objectives in South Vietnam. This subject stirred some of the most heated debate of the entire Working Group Project. At the outset, the maximum statement of U.S. interests and objectives in South Vietnam was accompanied by two fallback positions—the first a compromise, the second merely rationalizations for withdrawal. The JCS representative took testy exception to including the fallback positions in the Group's paper and cited JCS Memoranda on the critical importance of South Vietnam to the U.S. position in Asia. His forceful objections were effective and they were downgraded in the final paper which, while also pointedly rejecting the "domino theory" as over-simplified, nevertheless, went on to describe the effect of the fall of South Vietnam in much the same terms. Specifically pointing up the danger to the other Southeast Asian countries and to Asia in general, the paper concluded:

> There is a great deal we could still do to reassure these countries, but the picture of a defense line clearly breached could have serious effects and could easily, over time, tend to unravel the whole Pacific and South Asian defense structures.

In spite of these concessions, the JCS refused to associate itself with the final formulation of interests and objectives, holding that the domino theory was perfectly appropriate to the South Vietnamese situation.

One of the other important tasks assigned to the Working Group was the intelligence assessment of the effectiveness of measures against the North in improving the situation in the South. The initial appraisal of the intelligence community was that "the basic elements of Communist strength in South Vietnam remain indigenous," and that "even if severely damaged" the DRV could continue to support a reduced level of VC activity. While bombing might reduce somewhat the level of support for the VC and give the GVN a respite, there was very little likelihood that it would break the will of Hanoi. The estimate was that Hanoi was confident of greater staying power than the U.S. in a contest of attrition. These views were challenged by the JCS member who stressed that the military damage of air strikes would appreciably degrade DRV and VC capabilities. In deference to this view, the final Working Group estimate gave greater emphasis to the military effectiveness of strikes, although it was pessimistic about the extent of damage the DRV leaders would be willing to incur before reconsidering their objectives. It concluded with the assessment that there was very little likelihood of either Chinese or Soviet intervention on behalf of the DRV if pressures were adopted by the U.S.

As the Working Group toiled through November in its effort to develop options, it focused on three alternative courses of action. Option A was essentially a continuation of military and naval actions currently underway or authorized in the September decisions, including prompt reprisals against the North for attacks on U.S. forces and VC "spectaculars." It also included a resistance to negotiations until the North had agreed in advance to our conditions. Option B augmented current policies with systematic, sustained military pressures against the North and a resistance to negotiations unless we could carry them on while continuing the bombing. Option C proposed only a modest campaign against the North as compared with option B and was designed to bring the DRV to the negotiating table. If that occurred the pressures were to be suspended—although with the threat of resumption should negotiations break down.

In the course of the month, these options converged and the distinctions between them blurred. In particular, option A was expanded to include some low-level pressures against the North; the negotiations element of option B was, in effect, dropped and the pressures were to be applied at a faster, less flexible pace; and option C was stiffened to resemble the first incarnation of option B—the pressures would be stronger and the negotiating position tougher. Thus, by the end of the month when the Working Group's proposals were presented to the NSC Principals for consideration before a recommendation was made to the

President, all options included pressures against the North, and, in effect, excluded negotiations in the short-run, since the terms and pre-conditions proposed in all three options were entirely unrealistic. The policy climate in Washington simply was not receptive to any suggestion that U.S. goals might have to be compromised. And, in proposing pressures against the North, the Working Group was conscious of the danger that they might generate compelling world-wide pressure on the U.S. for negotiations. How large a role the specific perception of the President's views, validated or unvalidated, may have played in the Working Group's narrowing of the options is not clear. It seems likely, however, that some guidance from the White House was being received.

During the last week in November, the NSC Principals met to consider the Working Group's proposals. They were joined on November 27 by Ambassador Taylor. Taylor's report on conditions in South Vietnam was extremely bleak. To improve South Vietnamese morale and confidence, and to "drive the DRV out of its reinforcing role and obtain its cooperation in bringing an end to the Viet Cong insurgency," he urged that military pressures against the North be adopted. His report had a considerable impact on the Principals and later on the President. As the discussions continued through the several meetings of that week, opinion began to converge in favor of some combination of an "extended option A" and the first measures against the North of option C.

In the end, the Principals decided on a two-phase recommendation to the President. Phase I would be merely an extension of current actions with some increased air activity by the U.S. in Laos and tit-for-tat reprisals for VC attacks on U.S. forces or other major incidents. During this period, the GVN would be informed of our desires for its reform and when these were well underway, phase II, a campaign of gradually escalating air strikes against the North, would begin. This proposal was presented to the President on December 1. He approved phase I and gave assent, at least in principle, to phase II. In approving these measures, the President appears to have been reluctant to grant final authorization for phase II until he felt it was absolutely necessary.

If a consensus was reached within the Administration in favor of military pressures against the North, it certainly reflected no commonly held rationale for such action. Generally speaking the military (MACV, CINCPAC, JCS) favored a strong campaign against the North to interdict the infiltration routes, to destroy the overall capacity of the North to support the insurgency, and to destroy the DRV's will to continue support of the Viet Cong. The State Department (with the exception of George Ball) and the civilian advisors to Secretary McNamara favored a gradually mounting series of pressures that would place the North in a slow squeeze and act as both carrot and stick to settling the war on our terms. As would be expected, State was also concerned with the international political implications of such steps. Bombing the North would demonstrate our resolve, not only to the South Vietnamese but also to the other Southeast Asian countries and to China, whose containment was one of the important justifications of the entire American involvement. Walt Rostow, the Chairman of State's Policy Planning Council, took a slightly differently view, emphasizing the importance of pressures as a clear signal to the North and to China of U.S. determination and resolve and its willingness to engage the tremendous power at its disposal in support of the 1954 and 1962 Geneva agreements. Ambassador Taylor supported strikes against the North as a means of reducing infiltration and as a way of bolstering South Vietnamese morale.

As is readily apparent, there was no dearth of reasons for striking North. Indeed, one almost has the impression that there were more reasons than were required. But in the end, the decision to go ahead with the strikes seems to have resulted as much from the lack of alternative proposals as from any compelling logic advanced in their favor. By January, for example, William Bundy, while still supporting the pressures, could only offer the following in their favor:

> on balance we believe that such action would have some faint hope of really improving the Vietnamese situation, and, above all, would put us in a much stronger position to hold the next line of defense, namely Thailand. [And it would put us in a better position in our Asian relations] since we would have appeared to Asians to have done a lot more about it.

It is interesting to note that during the deliberations of September one of the preconditions to such strikes had been generally acknowledged as a unity of domestic American opinion in support of such Presidentially authorized action. During the November debates, this is no longer an important factor. Indeed, it is openly conceded that such action is likely to evoke opposition in both domestic and international public opinion. Another interesting aspect of this policy debate was that the question of Constitutional authority for open acts of war against a sovereign nation was never seriously raised.

Phase I of the newly approved program went into effect in mid-December. The BARREL ROLL "armed recce" by U.S. aircraft in the Laotian panhandle began on a limited scale on December 14. It had been foreseen that the number of sorties would slowly increase with each succeeding week. However, once the first week's level of two missions of four aircraft each was determined by Secretary McNamara, it became the guideline for the remainder of December and January. Covert GVN operations along the North Vietnamese coast were continued at about the level of the previous months and JCS proposals for direct U.S. air and naval support were rejected. Furthermore, the public disclosure of information on DRV infiltration into the South was deferred at the request of Secretary McNamara. On December 24, the Viet Cong bombed a U.S. officers' billet in Saigon killing two Americans. MACV, CINCPAC, the JCS, and Ambassador Taylor all called immediately for a reprisal strike against the North of the kind authorized under phase I. For reasons still not clear, the Administration decided against such a reprisal. Thus, in purely military terms, the phase I period turned out to be little more than a continuation of measures already underway. (The BARREL ROLL activity apparently was not differentiated by the DRV from RLAF strikes until well into January.)

One of the explanations for this failure to fully implement the December 1 decisions was the political crisis that erupted in South Vietnam. Ambassador Taylor had returned to South Vietnam on December 7 and immediately set about getting the GVN to undertake the reforms we desired, making clear to both the civilian and military leaders that the implementation of phase II was contingent on their efforts to revive the flagging war effort and morale in the South. For his efforts, he was rewarded with a military purge of the civilian government in late December and rumored threats that he would be declared *persona non grata*. The political crisis boiled on into January with no apparent solution in sight in spite of our heavy pressure on the military to return to a civilian regime. And, while Taylor struggled with the South Vietnamese generals, the war effort continued to decline.

At the same time that Taylor had been dispatched to Saigon a vigorous U.S. diplomatic effort had been undertaken with our Asian and NATO allies to inform them of the forthcoming U.S. intensification of the war, with the expected eventual strikes against the North. The fact that our allies now came to expect this action may have been a contributing reason in the February decision to proceed with phase II in spite of the failure of the South Vietnamese to have complied with our requirements. In any case, it added to the already considerable momentum behind the policy of striking the North. By the end of January 1965, William Bundy, McNaughton, Taylor and others had come to believe that we had to proceed with phase II irrespective of what the South Vietnamese did.

Clear indication that the Administration was considering some kind of escalation came on January 25. Ambassador Taylor was asked to comment on a proposal to withdraw U.S. dependents from Saigon so as to "clear the decks." Previously, this action, which was now approved by the JCS, was always associated with pressures against the North. While there is no indication of any decision at this point to move into phase II, it is clear that the preparations were already underway.

[*End of Summary*]

CHRONOLOGY

11 May 63   *NSAM 52*
Authorized CIA-sponsored covert operations against NVN.

9 Sep 63   *CINCPAC OPLAN 34-63*
JCS approved this program for non-attributable "hit and run" GVN covert operations against NVN, supported by U.S. military advisory materiel and training assistance.

1 Nov 63   *Diem overthrown*
Military junta led by General Minh assumed control.

20 Nov 63   *Vietnam Policy Conference, Honolulu*
During high-level USG discussions of the probable consequences, political and military, of Diem's downfall, conferees agreed military operations against the Viet Cong had not been and would not be particularly upset by the changed political situation. Development of a combined MACV–CAS program for covert operations against NVN was directed.

23 Nov 63   *President Kennedy Assassinated*

26 Nov 63   *NSAM 273*
Authorized planning for specific covert operations, graduated in intensity, against the DRV.

11 Dec 63   *State Department Views on Operations in Laos*
State (and ISA) opposed overt military operations in Laos. Extension of CIA-sponsored covert activity in Laos was okayed: this neither threatened Souvanna's sovereignty nor openly violated the Geneva Accords which State termed basic to eventual political stability in the region.

19 Dec 63   *OPLAN 34A Submitted by CINCPAC*
The MACV-CAS plan providing a "spectrum of capabilities for the RVNAF to execute against North Vietnam" was forwarded to the JCS with CINCPAC's comment that only air attacks and a few other "punitive or attritional" operations were likely to achieve the stated objective of convincing Hanoi to cease supporting insurgents in SVN and Laos.

30 Dec 63   *Memo for the Director, CIA*
Assessing "Probable Reactions to Various Courses of Action with Respect to North Vietnam" the Board of National Estimates studied 13 proposed covert operations. The BNE did not think any would convince NVN to change its policies. Hanoi's reaction to them was forecast as mild.

2 Jan 64   *Krulak Committee Report*
"Least risk" activities drawn from the 2062 in OPLAN 34A formed the basis of a 12-month, three-phase program of covert operations. MACV would exercise operational control, CAS and CINCPAC would train and equip the GVN or third-nation personnel involved. Phase One (February–May) included intelligence collection (through U-2 and special intelligence missions), psychological operations and some 20 "destructive" undertakings. Similar operations would be increased in number and intensity during Phases Two and Three; destructive acts would be extended to targets "identified with North Vietnam's economic and industrial well-being." Committee members reasoned that Hanoi attached great importance to economic development, that progressive damage to the economy—or its threatened destruction—would convince Hanoi to cancel support of insurgency. But the committee cautioned, even successful execution of the program might not induce Hanoi to "cease and desist."

22 Jan 64   *JCSM 46–64*
Criticizing "self-imposed restrictions" on operations in Laos, arguing that Laotian security depended on that of South Vietnam, the JCS requested authority to initiate reconnaissance operations over and into Laos. Without them the task in Vietnam was made "more complex, time consuming . . . more costly."

30 Jan 64   *Coup in Saigon*
Minh's junta was ousted by one headed by General Khanh.

Early   *Situation in Laos and South Vietnam*
Feb 64   NVA troop influx into Laos rose significantly and a similar rise was feared in SVN; Viet Cong terrorism continued to increase.

1 Feb 64   *OPLAN 34A*
Phase One of the covert activities program began.

20 Feb 64   *Lodge Msg. to McGeorge Bundy*
Ambassador Lodge urged adoption of a "carrot and stick" approach to North Vietnam (first presented to Governor Harriman on 30 October 1963). Lodge envisaged secret contact with Hanoi to demand NVN cease supporting the Viet Cong. In exchange the U.S. would offer economic aid (especially food imports). If Hanoi refused the offer, previously threatened punitive strikes would be initiated. The U.S. would not publicly admit to the attacks.

20 Feb 64   *NSC Meeting*
President Johnson ordered more rapid contingency planning for pressures—covert and overt—against North Vietnam and ordered

pressures shaped to produce the maximum credible deterrent effect on Hanoi.

This decision reflects the convergence of (1) fear that the Laos situation could get worse; (2) knowledge that this would affect U.S. operations and policies in Vietnam; (3) recognition that more U.S. military assistance to the GVN was required to execute OPLAN 34A; (4) and the increasing articulation by policy makers (JCS, SecState) of a direct relationship between the challenge of halting NVN assistance to insurgents and broader U.S. strategic interests. Together, these factors increased the attractiveness of proposals for punitive, overt actions against NVN.

25 Feb 64   *Draft Presidential Memorandum*
State recommended 12 F-100's be deployed to Thailand to deter further NVN activity in Laos and to signal U.S. determination.

26 Feb 64   *JCSM 159-64*
"Steps to Improve the Situation in Southeast Asia with Particular Reference to Laos" asked authority to initiate low-level reconnaissance flights over Laos for intelligence collection and to visibly display U.S. power. The JCS argued the "root of the problem is in North Vietnam and must be dealt with there," but if operations against NVN had to be ruled out, operations in Laos must not be. They urged that Laos and South Vietnam be treated as an integrated theatre.

29 Feb 64   *Director, DIA Memorandum for the Secretary*
Reporting on "North Vietnamese Support to the Viet Cong and Pathet Lao," DIA said certain "intelligence gaps" related to kinds and amounts of arms, supplies and men infiltrating SVN through Laos. The JCS favored closing such gaps by overt military operations; State opposed.

1 Mar 64   *Interim Report: "Alternatives for the Imposition of Measured Pressure against NVN"*
An Interagency Study Group under State's Vietnam Committee listed these as U.S. objectives: make Hanoi cease support of the Viet Cong; strengthen GVN and Asian morale and reduce VC morale; prove to the world U.S. determination to oppose Communist expansion.

Military means to attain those objectives were explored—ranging from the air defense of Saigon and US/GVN cross-border operations to the massive deployment of U.S. ground troops and air strikes against North Vietnam. The group believed unilateral U.S. actions would not compel Hanoi to call off the Viet Cong (and doubted Hanoi could do that anyway); operations against NVN were termed no substitute for successful counterinsurgency in SVN.

However, expanded activity could demonstrate U.S. power, determination and restraint to the world, reduce somewhat NVN support to the Viet Cong, cause "some reduction" Viet Cong morale, and possibly improve the U.S. negotiating position. "New U.S. bolstering actions" in South Vietnam and considerable improvement of the situation there were required to reduce VC activity and make victory on the ground possible, according to the report.

1 Mar 64   *Embassy Vientiane Message 927 for SecState*
Reasoned that if current USG policy toward Laos is changed (e.g., if the Geneva Accords were openly violated), large numbers of U.S. troops will eventually be required to enforce political stability.

2 Mar 64   *JCSM 168-64*
Requesting "Removal of Restrictions for Air and Ground Cross Border Operations," the Joint Chiefs said direct action had to be taken to convince NVN the U.S. was determined to eliminate the insurgents' Laotian sanctuary. ". . . The time has come to lift the restrictions which limit the effectiveness of our military operations."

2 Mar 64   *JCSM 174-64*
The Chiefs recommended direct strikes against North Vietnam. In line with their view (JCSM 159-64) that the root of the problem was North Vietnam, the JCS justified the need for overt action against NVN on two grounds: first, to support the short-term policy objective of stopping Hanoi's aid to the insurgents; second, to support the long-range objective of forcing a change in DRV policy by convincing Hanoi the U.S. was determined to oppose aggression in Southeast Asia.

15 Mar 64   *Lodge Msg. for the President (State 1757)*
Reiterating his preference for the "carrot and stick" approach to Hanoi, Lodge opposed initiation of overt actions against North Vietnam.

16 Mar 64   *SecDef Memo for the President*
Reporting on his recent trip to Honolulu and Saigon, McNamara recommended against overt actions (U.S. or GVN) against NVN "at this time" because of the problems of justification, communist escalation and pressures for premature negotiations. McNamara felt the practical range of overt actions did not allow assured achievement of practical U.S. objectives. (Like the Interagency Group, the Secretary distinguished between the stated aim of eliminating Hanoi's control of the Viet Cong and the practical objective of building the morale of the Khanh regime while eroding VC morale.)
The Secretary did favor military action against NVN in Laos. He recommended initiation by GVN forces of "hot pursuit" and small-scale operations across the Laotian border, plus continuation of U.S. high-level reconnaissance flights over Laos. He recommended the U.S. prepare planning for 72-hour readiness to initiate Laos and Cambodian border control actions and prepare plans for "retaliatory actions" (overt high and/or low level reconnaissance flights, "tit-for-tat" bombing strikes, commando raids) against NVN. He also recommended planning for 30 days' readi-

ness to initiate the "program of Graduated Overt Military Pressure" against North Vietnam.*

17 Mar 64   NSAM 288
Approved Mr. McNamara's report and his twelve recommendations to improve the military situation. Planning was to "proceed energetically."

17 Mar 64   *President's Message to Lodge* (*State 1454*)
On North Vietnam, the President indicated agreement with Lodge's "carrot and stick" approach and said he had reserved judgment on overt U.S. measures against NVN.
On Laos, the President said he was reluctant to inaugurate overt activities unless or until he had Souvanna's support and a stronger case had been made for the necessity of overt operations. Otherwise the President felt such action ". . . might have only limited military effect and could trigger wider Communist action in Laos."

17 Mar 64   *Lodge Message to SecState* (*State 1767*)
Reported GVN-RLG agreement on political and military issues. Diplomatic relations had been reestablished. Laos granted free passage into southern Laos to GVN forces, the right to bomb infiltration areas with unmarked T-28s and to conduct hot pursuit, commando raids and sabotage operations "without limit" into Laotian territory to combined RLG-GVN units. A combined Laotian-Vietnamese staff was to be created.

18 Mar 64   *JCS Message 5390 to CINCPAC*
The JCS directed CINCPAC to begin "Planning Actions, Vietnam" in line with Recommendations 11 and 12 of NSAM 288. The program was to "permit sequential implementation" of three actions (border controls, retaliatory cross-border operations with 72-hour responsiveness, graduated overt military pressures against NVN with 30-days responsiveness).

20 Mar 64   *President's Message to Lodge* (*State 1484*)
Confirmed that actions with North Vietnam as the target mentioned in NSAM 288 were regarded strictly as contingency planning and that interagency study was so oriented.

31 Mar 64   *State/ISA Draft Scenarios*
State/ISA planners presented three papers. The first was a scenario for current actions (political steps to increase Congressional and international understanding of U.S. aims plus continued military action by GVN with U.S. advisory assistance). The second scenario called for overt GVN/covert U.S. action against NVN (characterized by the GVN-USAF FARMGATE operation); it emphasized political initiatives which would surface in Saigon and thus retain credibility for GVN sovereignty. The third

---

* Here McNamara probably referred to the various plans for graduated pressure against NVN then being discussed; no actual "program" had yet been finalized or approved.

scenario—associated with overt U.S. response to DRV-CHICOM escalation—also included diplomatic and political preparations for overt U.S. activity.

13 Apr 64   *J-5 Memorandum for the ASD(ISA)*
Commenting on the 31 March scenario, the Joint Staff outlined a continually intensifying program of military pressures—and gradually increasing U.S. military involvement. J-5 urged the 31 March scenario be fused with OPLAN 37-64 and border control operations be moved into the scenario for the current time period. Approximate time-phasing of the draft's then separate scenarios was recommended.

8 and 17   *Scenario Drafts*
Apr 64   Reflecting the JCS influence toward development of a continuous scenario, current political activities were treated in a separate section, "Steps Which Should be Taken Now." The other political-military scenarios included increased FARMGATE operations, separate Laotian and Cambodian border control actions, separate GVN retaliatory actions against NVN, and graduated overt U.S. military pressures against NVN. The detailed scenario for GVN/FARMGATE operations was given D-Day minus X time-phasing; apparently it was the basis for discussions held in Saigon on 19–20 April.

18–20   *Saigon Conference*
Apr 64   Scenarios and other issues were discussed by Lodge, William Bundy, Rusk, Wheeler, and others. Lodge objected to planning for—or adopting—massive publicity and massive destruction actions before trying a well-reasoned, well-planned diplomatic effort to convince Hanoi to "call off the VC." His "carrot/stick" approach was expanded: Lodge suggested a third country interlocuteur be selected to tell Hanoi of U.S. resolve, that the threat of air strikes be combined with an economic assistance offer and that as part of the "carrot" the U.S. offer to withdraw some personnel from South Vietnam.
Rusk wanted the extent of NVN infiltration and support to be satisfactorily proved to U.S. citizens, allies and neutrals; he wanted Asian military support for the U.S. Rusk did not think China would intervene militarily without Soviet support and thought we could pressure the Chinese economically through our allies. He doubted elimination of DRV industrial targets would have much adverse impact on any NVN decision to stop aiding the insurgency.
Results: Canada would be asked to act as interlocuteur. Also, Secretary Rusk recommended the U.S. seek "more flags" to support the GVN, deploy a carrier task force to Cam Ranh Bay to establish a permanent U.S. Naval presence, initiate anti-junk operations to "inch northward" along the coast and enlist SEATO support in isolating the DRV from economic or cultural relations with the Free World.

23 Apr 64   *SecDef Memorandum to CJCS*
This forwarded the 20 April scenario which contained three

stages: uncommitting steps to be taken now; graduated overt pressures on the DRV (FARMGATE); and a contingency plan for overt U.S. response to DRV/CHICOM escalation. The first stage could stand alone, but stage two could not be launched unless the U.S. was prepared to take the third step—perhaps within 10 days of the previous "D-Day."

23 Apr 64   *Rostow Memorandum for SecState*
Reasoning that deterioration in Laos and SVN would make it very difficult to win Hanoi's adherence to the Geneva Accords and predicting deterioration was imminent, Rostow implied necessary (U.S.) actions should be taken soon.

30 Apr 64   *Rusk Visit to Ottawa*
Set up the Seaborn Mission (interlocuteur) to Hanoi for mid-June.

4 May 64   *Lodge to SecState (State 2108)*
This reflects the deliberate, cautious approach then dominant. In talking with General Khanh (who suggested putting SVN fully on a war footing and wanted to tell NVN that further interference in GVN affairs would bring reprisals), Lodge urged Khanh to keep cool and asked that McNamara similarly emphasize the need to avoid such drastic measures during his 12 May meeting with Khanh.

7 May 64   *Talking Paper for the Secretary*
In addition to the Lodge suggestions, McNamara was to tell Khanh the U.S. did "not intend to provide military support nor undertake the military objective of 'rolling back' communist control in NVN."

12–13 May 64   *McNamara/Sullivan Trip to Vietnam*
Khanh and McNamara met and apparently discussed the issues mentioned above.

16 May 64   *JCSM 422-64*
JCS criticized the final draft scenario for omitting the immediate actions mentioned in NSAM 288 (border control and retaliatory operations); advocated incorporating retaliatory and overt military pressures against NVN in the second stage, as well as battalion-size border control operations in Laos to include striking bridges and armed route reconnaissance. These were justified in JCS eyes because military operations against the DRV to help stabilize either the Laos or SVN situation involved attacking the same target systems and to a large extent, the same targets. JCS felt attacks would assist ". . . in the achievement of the objective" and offer ". . . the possibility of a favorable long-term solution to the insurgency problem in Southeast Asia."

17 May 64   *Pathet Lao Offensive*
The Pathet Lao seized a significant portion of the Plaine des Jarres in Laos—a major setback for RLG forces.

19 May 64   *JCSM 426-64*
Clearly indicating the crisis management aspects of the scene

created by Pathet Lao gains, the JCS now called for new, more intensive covert operations during the second phase of OPLAN 34A.

21 May 64   *At the UN . . .*
Adlai Stevenson's major speech explaining U.S. policy toward Southeast Asia was the first such U.S. move at the UN.

21 May 64   Baltimore Sun *Report*
With Souvanna's permission, the U.S. began low-level reconnaissance operations over enemy-occupied areas in Laos.

21 May 64   *Rusk Message to Lodge* (*State 2027*)
Rusk said Washington saw the fragility of the SVN situation as an obstacle to further U.S. military involvement in Southeast Asia. He asked Lodge to suggest ways to achieve greater solidarity in SVN saying, "we need to assure the President that everything humanly possible is being done both in Washington and the Government of Vietnam to provide a solid base of determination from which far-reaching decisions could proceed."

23 May 64   *JCSM 445–64*
The JCS renewed their plea for prompt "Readiness to Implement NSAM 288." Larger border control and retaliatory operations were called for; prompt consultations with the GVN and immediate joint operations were said to be needed.

23 May 64   *Draft Presidential Memorandum*
The crisis in Laos had focused interest on but one stage of earlier scenarios: overt operations against NVN. The scenario for steps to be taken now had been dropped (as Rusk explained to Lodge on 22 May—State 2049—because initial attacks without acknowledgement were not feasible; publicity seemed inevitable). The scenario called for 30 days of graduated military/political pressures (including initiatives to enter negotiations with Hanoi). A Congressional Resolution supporting U.S. resistance to DRV aggression was called for; air strikes would continue—despite negotiations—until it was clear that NVN had ceased subversion. Negotiating objectives were: terrorism, armed attack and armed resistance would stop; "communications on networks out of the North would be conducted entirely in uncoded form."

25 May 64   *SNIE 50-2-64*
An estimate of the likely consequences of actions proposed in the 23 May DPM (discussed by the Executive Committee, or ExCom, on 24, 25 and 26 May). NVN might order guerrillas to reduce "the level of insurrections for the moment" in response to U.S. force deployments or FARMGATE attacks; with Peking and Moscow, Hanoi might count on international actions to end the attacks and stabilize communist gains. If attacks continued, Hanoi might intensify political initiatives and possibly increase the tempo of insurgency. If these failed to bring a settlement and if attacks damaged NVN considerably, the SNIE estimated NVN would lower negotiating demands to preserve its regime—and plan to renew insurgency later. The SNIE saw "significant danger" that

Hanoi would fight because (1) NVN did not think the U.S. would commit ground forces and (2) even if U.S. troops were sent, NVN believed they could be defeated à la 1954. Affecting the *will* of NVN leaders was emphasized. None of the actions forecast in the DPM would affect enemy *capabilities* because the major sources of "communist strength in SVN are indigenous." The SNIE said the DRV must (be made to) understand that the U.S.—not seeking to destroy NVN—is willing to "bring ascending pressure to bear to persuade Hanoi to reduce the insurrections." The report added ". . . retaliatory measures which Hanoi might take in Laos and South Vietnam might make it increasingly difficult for the U.S. to regard its objectives as attainable by limited means. Thus difficulties of comprehension might increase on both sides as the scale of action mounted."

25 May 64   *McGeorge Bundy Memorandum to Rusk, et al.*
The ExCom abandoned the scenario approach—perhaps because entering into escalating conflict might obscure the limited U.S. objectives. The ExCom recommended the President decide that the U.S. will use graduated military force against NVN after appropriate diplomatic and political warning and preparation; evident U.S. determination to act—combined with other efforts— "should produce a sufficient improvement of non-communist prospects in South Vietnam and in Laos to make military action against North Vietnam unnecessary."
OR: The ExCom explicitly assumed that a decision to use force if necessary—backed by resolute deployment and conveyed every way possible ". . . gives the best present chance of avoiding the actual use of such force." Other actions recommended were: communicate U.S. resolve through the Canadian interlocuteur; call a high-level Southeast Asian strategy conference; begin diplomatic efforts at the UN to present the case for DRV aggression; consult with SEATO allies and obtain allied force commitments; seek a Congressional Resolution in support of U.S. resistance to NVN in SEA; deploy forces periodically to the region; consider an initial strike against NVN "designed to have more deterrent than destructive impact" and accompany it by an active diplomatic offensive to restore stability—including an agreement to a Geneva Conference.

26 May 64   *Lodge Message to Rusk (State 2318)*
Lodge said only firm action against North Vietnam by the U.S. and GVN could lead to a significant improvement in the GVN effort. (A "new wrinkle" in Lodge's view.)

27 May 64   *Polish Initiative*
Poland proposed a Laos conference format which avoided many undesirable aspects of those formerly supported by communist governments.

29 May 64   *State Message to Rusk (TOSEC 36)*
The ExCom, preferring to initially treat Laos independently of Vietnam, recommended the President accept the Polish proposal.

The U.S. would not be willing to write off Laos to the communists and would assure Souvanna: "We would be prepared to give him prompt and direct military support if the Polish Conference . . ." failed.

30 May 64   *JCSM 460-64*

Advocating "Air Strikes Against North Vietnam," the JCS felt NVN support to insurgents could be reduced by armed reconnaissance of highways leading into Laos, striking airfields identified with supporting insurgents, striking supply, ammunition and POL storage sites and military installations connected with PL/VC support. The JCS said Hanoi's "military capability to take action against Laos and the RVN" would result from hitting "remaining" airfields, important railroad and highway bridges, depots in northern NVN and from aerial mining and bombing of POL stores in Hanoi and Haiphong. The Chiefs also outlined the capability to effectively destroy the entire NVN industrial base.

2 Jun 64   *JCSM 461-64 (CJCS non-concurred)*

Recommended the U.S. seek to destroy Hanoi's will and capabilities, as necessary, to support the insurgency. They called for "positive, prompt and meaningful military action"—mainly air strikes—to show NVN "we are now determined that (its support to insurgency) will stop" and to show NVN we can and will make them incapable of rendering such support.

2 Jun 64   *SECTO 37*

Rusk reported General Khanh's views: Khanh felt the GVN could not win against the Viet Cong without some military action outside its borders; he wanted insurgent forces in eastern Laos cleaned out—by GVN forces and U.S. air support; he recommended selected air attacks against NVN "designed to minimize the chances of a drastic communist response."

1–2 Jun 64   *Honolulu Conference*

Conferees assessing overall U.S. policy toward Southeast Asia agreed with State that the point of departure ". . . is and must be that we cannot accept (the) over-running of Southeast Asia by Hanoi and Peking." "Operational"—not policy—aspects of air operations against NVN were the main points of discussion, with attention centered on the effect of pressures in Laos, preparatory steps necessary for a Laotian contingency and probable repercussions.

Evaluating possible communist reaction to pressures against NVN, Mr. McNamara said the "best current view" was an appropriately limited attack against NVN, which would not bring CHICOM air or NVN/CHICOM ground forces. Westmoreland felt there was no significant unused capability left to the VC; Lodge said the VC had a major capability for terrorism, even for military action against Saigon. Like Khanh, Lodge also felt selective bombing would build morale and unity in South Vietnam.

Results: The U.S. would seek international (beginning with U.S.–Thai consultations) and domestic support (through a Congressional Resolution) for wider U.S. actions. ("Wider" could mean committing up to seven U.S. divisions and calling up the reserves ". . . as the action unfolds.") But actual expansion of the U.S. role would be postponed for these and other politico-military reasons.

3 Jun 64   *William Bundy Memorandum for SecState*
The report to the President on Honolulu was probably based on this paper in which Bundy recapped talks there and called for time to "refine" plans and estimates, to "get at" basic doubts about the value of Southeast Asia and the importance of the U.S. stake there.

Mid-Jun 64   *Post-Honolulu Military Actions*
Mr. McNamara discussed NVN targets, troop movement capabilities with the JCS (8 June); he wanted facts and statistics on Haiphong traffic, existing plans for and estimated impact of mining the harbor, alternative DRV importation facilities. He ordered immediate improvement in effectiveness and readiness plus some expansion of prepositioned stocks in Thailand and Okinawa.

Mid-Jun 64   *Post-Honolulu Non-Military Activity*
State began gathering information on prevalent public questions about the U.S. in Vietnam, in Southeast Asia; interagency groups studied implications of a Congressional Resolution; Rusk (14 June), President Johnson (23 June) and others spoke publicly on U.S. goals in Asia, U.S. determination to support its Southeast Asian allies.

9 Jun 64   *Memorandum for the Director, CIA*
President Johnson asked: "Would the rest of Southeast Asia necessarily fall if Laos and South Vietnam came under NVN control?" The CIA response said Cambodia "might" but no other nation "would quickly succumb." U.S. prestige, credibility and position in the Far East would be profoundly damaged but the wider U.S. interest in containing overt military attacks would not be affected. All of this was predicated on a clear-cut communist victory in Laos and South Vietnam and U.S. withdrawal from the area. The Agency called results of a "fuzzy" outcome harder to evaluate.

10 Jun 64   *SecDef Memorandum to CJCS (Response to CM-1451-64, 5 June 64)*
McNamara supported Taylor's criticism of JCSM 461-64 (2 June), agreeing that the two courses of action presented by the Chiefs were neither accurate nor complete. Taylor saw three ways in which air power could be used to pressure NVN—and opted for the least dangerous. He recommended demonstrative strikes against limited military targets to show U.S. readiness and intent to move up the scale if NVN did not reduce insurgent support. Up the scale meant moving from demonstrative strikes to attacks against a significant part of the DRV military target system and ultimately, to massive attacks against all significant military targets in NVN. By destroying them the U.S. would destroy NVN's capacity to support insurgency.

12 Jun 64   *William Bundy Memorandum*
Called for a Congressional Resolution right away to demonstrate U.S. resolve (especially to Souvanna and Khanh) and provide flexibility for executive action.

15 Jun 64   *McGeorge Bundy Memorandum to SecState, SecDef, et al.*
One subject was made the agenda for final talks about a Congressional Resolution: actions still open to the U.S. if both major military operations and a Congressional Resolution are rejected at this time. White House guidance indicated that by taking limited military and political actions, the U.S. could demonstrate firm resistance without risking major escalation or loss of policy flexibility.

McGeorge Bundy suggested these possible limited actions, military: reconnaissance, strike, T-28 operations in all of Laos; small-scale reconnaissance strikes—after appropriate provocation—in NVN; VNAF strikes in Laotian corridors; limited air and sea, more limited ground deployments. (Bundy said major ground force deployments seem more questionable without a decision "to go north" in some form.) Political: "Higher authority" wants a maximum effort to increase allied real and visible presence in support of Saigon; make intensive efforts to sustain Souvanna; rapidly develop province and information programs, strengthen the country team, shift the U.S. role from advice to direction; opposing both aggressive adventure and withdrawal, explain the above lines of action (especially in the U.S.) and leave the door open to selected military actions.

Unless the enemy provoked drastic measures, the ExCom agreed that defense of "U.S. interests . . . over the next six months" is possible within limits. Both a Congressional Resolution and wider U.S. action were deferred.

17 Jul 1964   *DESOTO naval patrols off North Vietnam reauthorized*
Authority was given to resume the DESOTO destroyer patrols off North Vietnam. They had been suspended since March.

30 Jul 1964   *Covert GVN attack on North Vietnam*
The night before the USS MADDOX is to resume her patrols off the North Vietnamese coast, South Vietnamese commandos raid two North Vietnamese islands.

31 Jul 1964   *USS MADDOX resumes patrol off North Vietnam*
After a six month suspension, the USS MADDOX resumed the DESOTO patrols off the coast of North Vietnam.

1 Aug 1964   *British seek meeting of three Laotian princes*
Acting on Souvanna Phouma's request, the British government urged the ICC members to arrange a meeting among the three Laotian political factions as represented by the three rival princes.

2 Aug 1964   *China urges USSR not to resign Geneva co-chairmanship*
The Chinese Communists urged the USSR not to carry out its threat to abandon its co-chairman role in the Geneva settlements, apparently viewing such a development as jeopardizing the possibilities of a Geneva settlement of the current Laotian crisis.

DRV PT boats attack MADDOX

Apparently mistaking the MADDOX for South Vietnamese, three DRV patrol boats launched a torpedo and machine gun attack on her. Responding immediately to the attack, and with the help of air support from the nearby carrier TICONDEROGA, the MADDOX destroyed one of the attacking boats and damaged the other two. The MADDOX, under 7th Fleet orders, retired to South Vietnamese waters where she is joined by the C. TURNER JOY.

3 Aug 1964 ### U.S. protest through ICC

A stiff U.S. protest of the attack on the MADDOX is dispatched to Hanoi through the ICC. It warns that "grave consequences" will result from any future attacks on U.S. forces.

DESOTO patrol resumed

The JCS approved a CINCPAC request to resume the DESOTO patrol at 1350 hours, ordered the C. TURNER JOY to be added to it and authorized active defensive measures for the destroyers and their supporting aircraft. The President announced the action later that day.

GVN again attacks North Vietnam

The Rhon River estuary and the Vinh Sonh radar installation were bombarded under cover of darkness.

4 Aug 1964 ### Second DRV naval attack on DESOTO patrol

At about 2140 hours, after several hours of shadowing, a second PT boat attack on the augmented DESOTO task force was launched. This engagement in the dark lasted about three hours and resulted in two patrol boats destroyed.

Reprisal alerts

At 0030 hours (5 Aug 1964 Vietnam time), "alert orders" for possible reprisal air strikes were given to the TICONDEROGA and a second carrier, the CONSTELLATION, that had been steaming toward the area from Hong Kong since Aug 3.

NSC meeting

At 1230, Washington time, the NSC convened after a brief meeting of the JCS with the President. The JCS, McNamara and others recommended reprisals against the patrol craft and their bases. This the President approved.

2nd NSC meeting

After a confusing afternoon in which the attacks were double-checked and verified, the NSC met again at 1700, confirmed the reprisal order, and discussed incremental force deployments to the Western Pacific.

Congressional briefing

At 1845 the President met with 16 Congressional leaders, briefed them on the proposed attacks and informed them of his intention to ask for a joint Congressional resolution of support. None raised objections.

5 Aug 1964   *U Thant calls for 14-nation conference on Laos*
In an unrelated development, UN Secretary General U Thant
called for the rescheduling of the 14-nation conference to deal
with the Laotian situation.

Presidential message to Congress
In a formal message to both houses of Congress, the President
requested passage of a joint resolution of support for U.S. policy
in Southeast Asia. Concurrently, identical draft resolutions prepared by the executive branch were introduced in the Senate by
Senator Fulbright, and in the House, by Representative Morgan.

6 Aug 1964   *Tonkin Gulf Resolutions discussed in committee*
Both houses heard top Administration officials, including Secretary
McNamara, testify in behalf of the pending resolutions.

Force deployments
The additional forces deployments, particularly air forces, begin
to move to the theatre.

7 Aug 1964   *Tonkin Gulf Resolution passes Congress*
The Tonkin Gulf resolution was passed in both houses by near
unanimous vote.

Khanh proclaims himself President
Declaring a state of emergency, General Khanh proclaimed himself President of South Vietnam and claims virtual dictatorial
powers.

State message 136, Rusk to Vietiane and others
Concern over not provoking a communist military escalation in
Laos, particularly in view of the Tonkin Gulf reprisals, prompted
State to defer temporarily approval of air and ground initiatives
in the Laotian panhandle.

9 Aug 1964   *Embassy Saigon message 363, Taylor to Rusk*
Taylor opposes a 14-nation Geneva Conference as likely to undermine the little stability the fragile GVN still has. He further states
that the reprisals, while effective in the short run, do not deal
with the continuing problem of DRV infiltration which must be
confronted. He felt there was need for follow-up action to demonstrate to the DRV that the rules of the game had changed.

10 Aug 1964   *U.S. message to Hanoi through Canadian ICC representative*
Through the Canadian representative on the ICC, the U.S. communicated its uncertainty about DRV motives in the Aug 4
Tonkin Gulf raids, that additional air power deployed to SEA
was precautionary, that U.S. official and public patience was wearing thin, that the Congressional resolution demonstrated U.S.
determination in SEA, and that if the DRV pursued its present
course, it could expect to suffer the consequences.

11 Aug 1964   *William Bundy memo to SecDef, "Next Courses of Action in
Southeast Asia"*
Assistant Secretary of State Bundy felt that only a continuous
combination of military pressure and communication would con-

vince Hanoi that they were facing a determined foe and that they should get out of South Vietnam and Laos.

14 Aug 1964   *CJCS memo to SecDef, "Next Courses of Action in Southeast Asia"*
Positive assessment of the impact of the reprisal actions was given and a continuation of strikes against the North was recommended.

State message 439 to Vientiane, Saigon, CINCPAC, "Southeast Asia, August 1964"
In opposing both a new 14-nation Geneva Conference on Southeast Asia, and U.S. air operations against the North, State stressed the shakiness of the GVN and the need to shore it up internally before any such actions were started. For planning purposes, the message suggested that Ambassador Taylor's suggested date of January 1, 1965, be used for any sustained U.S. air campaign against the North.

15 Aug 1964   *JCS message 7947 to CINCPAC, "Rules of Engagement"*
U.S. forces were authorized to attack any vessels or aircraft that attack or give positive indication of intent to attack, and to pursue such attackers into territorial waters or air space of all Southeast Asian countries, including North Vietnam.

16 Aug 1964   *COMUSMACV message to CINCPAC, "Cross-Border Operations"*
MACV requested authority to begin the Phase I of the covert cross-border operations into Laos and North Vietnam.

17 Aug 1964   *CINCPAC message to JCS, "Next Courses of Action in Southeast Asia"*
The positive impact of the reprisals on South Vietnamese morale is noted, and a strong argument made for continuing actions against the North to make clear to Hanoi and Peking the cost of their aggression.
The momentum of the Aug 5 raids must not be lost or the benefits of the initial attacks will disappear.

18 Aug 1964   *Embassy Saigon message 465*
Taylor reiterates his belief that the reprisals must be followed up with other actions against the North.

21 Aug 1964   *Henry Rowen memo to JCS, et al, "The Rostow Thesis"*
Initially presented in Dec 1963, the "Rostow Thesis" was recirculated within the Administration in mid-August. Its fundamental argument was that military pressure against the external sources of an insurgency would bring the aggressor to an appreciation of the costs of his interference and he would reduce or eliminate his support for the insurgents. The exercise was primarily psychological, not necessarily strategic. The measures should greatly increase his uncertainty about the consequences of continued support of the insurgency. Rowen's critique raised serious questions about the general validity of the thesis, pointing out the requirement for solid public and political support for such actions, and doubting that anywhere but in Southeast Asia U.S. interests were so critically at stake. Even in that area, it doubted the effectiveness of the proposal.

26 Aug 1964 **JCSM-746-64**
In response to State's Aug 14 analysis, the JCS proposed a continuous and escalating air campaign against the North designed to both the physical resources and the psychological will to support the insurgency in the South. It called for deliberate attempts to provoke the DRV into actions which could then be answered by a systematic air campaign.

27 Aug 1964 *Three Laotian Princes meet*
The three Laotian Princes met in Paris as a result of the British initiative to begin discussions on the current crisis.

31 Aug 1964 *CINCPAC message to JCS, "Immediate Actions to be taken in South Vietnam"*
CINCPAC reiterates the request for approval of covert cross-border operations.

3 Sep 1964 *McNaughton paper, "Plan of Action for South Vietnam"*
In anticipation of the 7 September strategy meeting, McNaughton prepared a paper calling for actions that would provoke a DRV response that could be used as grounds for a U.S. escalation.

Khanh reverts to Premiership
His bid for dictatorial power having been rebuffed by the Army with popular support, Khanh reverted to his former title of Premier with greatly reduced power. Minh is to play a larger role.

7 Sep 1964 *JCS Talking Paper for CJCS, "Next Courses of Action for RVN"*
The JCS repeated its recommendations of 26 Aug and detailed it with a list of 94 targets for air strikes.

White House strategy meeting; decisions in William Bundy memo to SecDef, et al., "Courses of Action for South Vietnam," 8 Sep 1964
With Ambassador Taylor returned from Saigon, a full dress strategy review of actions against the North is held at the White House. The Pentagon spokesmen, both military and civilian, favored immediate initiation of an escalatory air campaign against the North. But this was rejected on the grounds that the GVN was too weak to sustain the expected intensification of the war in the South it would evoke. This was the view of CIA, State and the White House. But a decision was made to resume the DESOTO patrols, the covert GVN coastal operations against the North, and to authorize limited cross-border operations into Laos when Souvanna approved. It was further agreed that we would respond to any future DRV attacks on U.S. units on a tit-for-tat basis. These latter measures were to bolster GVN morale.

10 Sep 1964 **NSAM 314**
Formal approval of the 7 September decision was given in NSAM 314.

11 Sep 1964 *Saigon meeting on cross-border operations*
At a Saigon meeting of representatives of the U.S. missions in Laos, Thailand, and Vietnam, it was agreed that the air operations in Southern Laos would be carried out by RLAF aircraft

for the present. As to ground operations, while their desirability was recognized, they were disapproved because of the flagrant violation of the Geneva Accords they would constitute. This objection by Vientiane was subsequently removed and company-size operations up to 20 kilometers into Laos were approved.

12 Sep 1964   *DESOTO patrols resumed*
The destroyers USS MORTON and USS EDWARDS resumed the DESOTO patrols off North Vietnam.

18 Sep 1964   *3rd Tonkin Gulf incident*
On the night of the 18th, the third incident in the DESOTO patrols occurred. The two destroyers fired on radar identified attackers and apparently scored a number of hits. No return fire was received from the "attackers." Later on the 18th the President suspended the DESOTO patrols which were not to be resumed until February 1965.

30 Sep 1964   *CJCS memo to SecDef, "Cross-Border Operations"*
The CJCS endorsed the proposals of the mission representatives and requested immediate authority to implement air operations in the Laotian panhandle with RLAF T-28s and U.S. aircraft for suppressive fire and attacking heavily defended targets. Authority for GVN ground intelligence acquisition patrols in the Laotian corridor was also sought.

1 Oct 1964   *SNIE 53-2-64*
The deterioration of GVN morale and effectiveness continued unabated and this intelligence estimate did not think that the hoped for civilian government would be able to reverse it. The VC were not, however, expected to make an overt military effort to capture the government.

4 Oct 1964   *Covert GVN coastal operations against DRV again authorized*
The President authorized reactivation of the covert coastal strikes by the GVN against the DRV, under very tight controls with each action to be cleared in advance by OSD, State and the White House.

6 Oct 1964   *Joint State/Defense message 313 to Vientiane*
The Embassy is authorized to urge the Laotian Government to begin T-28 strikes as soon as possible against a 22-target list which excluded the Mu Gia pass. Some of the targets were designed for U.S. YANKEE TEAM strikes.

9 Oct 1964   *SNIE 10-3-64*
In the evaluation of the likely North Vietnamese reactions to the actions approved in the September 7 meeting, CIA concluded that these would probably be limited to defensive and propaganda measures with possibly some scaling down of operations in the South. China was not expected to enter the war as a result of even a systematic U.S. air campaign against the North.

Embassy Saigon message 1068, Taylor to Rusk
Taylor reported that the ARVN would be unable to conduct ground operations in the Laotian corridor in the foreseeable future and therefore U.S. air operations are urged. At a minimum,

combat air patrols supporting RLAF strike missions were requested.

13 Oct 1964   *Embassy Vientiane message 609, Unger to Rusk and McNamara*
U.S. air strikes against four defended targets are requested to accompany RLAF T-28 strikes in the northern panhandle.

Washington approves only combat air patrols
Washington, responding to Unger's request, authorized only U.S. combat air patrols in support of the RLAF operations, not the U.S. strikes. U.S. air strikes against communist LOCs in the panhandle are not authorized until much later.

14 Oct 1964   *RLAF makes initial U.S. supported attacks*
The RLAF, with U.S. aircraft in combat air patrol support, make the first strikes against the communist LOCs in the panhandle.

16 Oct 64   *Embassy Saigon Message, JPS 303, Taylor to the President*
Ambassador Taylor reports greatly increased infiltration from the North, including North Vietnamese regulars, and a steadily worsening situation in the South.

21 Oct 64   *JCSM 893-64*
The JCS urge Secretary McNamara to back military measures to seize control of the border areas of South Vietnam and to cut off the supply and direction of the Viet Cong by direct measures against North Vietnam.

27 Oct 64   *JCSM 902-64*
On the basis of the new intelligence on infiltration levels, the JCS again recommend direct military pressures against the North.

1 Nov 64   *Viet Cong Attack Bien Hoa Airbase*
In a daring strike, the Viet Cong staged a mortar attack on the large U.S. airbase at Bien Hoa, killing four Americans, destroying five B-57s, and damaging eight others.

White House Decides Not to Retaliate
Concerned about possible further North Vietnamese escalation and the uncertainty of the Red Chinese response, the White House decides, against the advice of Ambassador Taylor, not to retaliate in the tit-for-tat fashion envisaged by NSAM 314. As a result of the attack, however, an interagency Working Group of the NSC is established to study future courses of U.S. action under the Chairmanship of William Bundy, Assistant Secretary of State for Far Eastern Affairs.

3 Nov 64   *Civilian Named Premier*
Tran Van Huong is named Premier in SVN.

First Meeting of NSC Working Group
The NSC Working Group held its first meeting. Other members are Michael Forrestal and Marshall Green from State, John McNaughton from ISA, Harold Ford for CIA, and Admiral Lloyd Mustin from JCS. Work continues for three weeks.

President Re-elected
In a landslide victory, President Johnson is re-elected with a new
Vice President, Hubert Humphrey.

4 Nov 64 *JCSM 933–64*
The JCS place in writing their request for reprisal action against
North Vietnam in retaliation for the Bien Hoa attack. Failure to
act may be misinterpreted by the North Vietnamese as a lack of
will and determination in Vietnam.

14 Nov 64 *CGCS Memorandum to SecDef, CM 258-64; and JCSM 955-64*
In separate memos to the Secretary, the JCS recommend covert
GVN air strikes against North Vietnam and additional U.S. de-
ployments to South East Asia to make possible implementation of
U.S. strikes should these be approved.

17 Nov 64 *Working Group Circulates Draft "Options" for Comment*
The Working Group circulates its draft paper on the "Options"
available to the U.S. in South Vietnam. They are three: (A)
continuation of present policies in the hope of an improvement in
the South but strong U.S. resistance to negotiations; (B) strong
U.S. pressures against the North and resistance of negotiations
until the DRV was ready to comply with our demands; and (C)
limited pressures against the North coupled with vigorous efforts
to get negotiations started and recognition that we would have to
compromise our objectives. Option B is favored by the Working
Group.

18 Nov 64 *JCSM 967-64*
The JCS renews its recommendation for strikes against the North
tempering it slightly in terms of "a controlled program of systematically increased military pressures."

21 Nov 64 *Revised Working Group Draft*
Having received comments from the different agencies, the Working Group revises its draft slightly, takes note of different viewpoints and submits its work to the NSC Principals for their consideration.

23 Nov 64 *Rostow Memo to SecState*
Taking a somewhat different tack, the then Director of State's
Policy Planning Staff, W. W. Rostow, proposes military pressures
against the North as a method of clearly signaling U.S. determination and commitment to the North.

24 Nov 64 *NSC Principals Meeting*
No consensus is reached, but Option A is generally rejected as
promising only eventual defeat. Option B is favored by the JCS
and CIA, while State and OSD favor Option C. No firm conclusion is reached on the issue of sending ground troops to South
Vietnam.

27 Nov 64 *Taylor Meets with Principals*
Having returned for consultations, Ambassador Taylor meets with

the NSC Principals and after giving a gloomy report of the situation in South Vietnam, recommends that to shore up the GVN and improve morale we take limited actions against the North but resist negotiations until the GVN is improved and the DRV is hurting. He proposed an extended Option A with the first stages of Option C. This proposal was adopted by the Principals as the recommendation to be made to the President.

28 Nov 64   *NSC Principals Meeting*
In a follow-up meeting, the Principals decide to propose a two phase program to the President. The first phase would be a thirty-day period of slightly increased pressure such as the resumption of the DE SOTO patrols and U.S. armed recce on the Laotian corridor while we tried to get reforms in South Vietnam. The second phase would involve direct air strikes against the North as in Option C. William Bundy was charged with preparing a draft NSAM to this effect and an infiltration study was commissioned.

30 Nov 64   *NSC Principals Meeting*
Meeting to review the draft prepared by Bundy, the Principals decided not to call it a NSAM. Its provisions are those recommended on 28 Nov. Phase II would be a graduated and mounting set of primarily air pressures against the North coupled with efforts to sound out the DRV on readiness to negotiate on U.S. terms. A recommendation on linking U.S. actions to DRV infiltration is deleted.

1 Dec 64   *White House Meeting*
While the exact decisions made at this meeting of the Principals with the President are not available, it is clear that he approved in general terms the concept outlined in the Bundy paper. He gave his approval for implementation of only Phase I, however. The President stressed the need for Taylor to get improvement from the GVN and the need to brief our allies on our new course of action, and to get more assistance from them in the conflict.

3 Dec 64   *Taylor Meets President*
The President meets privately with Taylor and gives him instructions that he is to explain the new program to the GVN, indicate to its leaders that the Phase II U.S. strikes against the North are contingent on improvement in the South, and explain that these will be cooperative efforts.

4 Dec 64   *Cooper Report on Infiltration*
A thorough study on North Vietnamese infiltration as commissioned by the Principals is submitted to the NSC and later forwarded to Saigon. Decisions on its release are continually deferred.

7 Dec 64   *Taylor Meets with Premier Huong*
The day after his return to Saigon, Taylor meets with Premier Huong and with General Khanh and outlines the new U.S. policy and states the requirements this places on the GVN.

7–9 Dec 64   *Prime Minister Wilson briefed*
In Washington on a state visit, British Prime Minister Wilson is thoroughly briefed on the forthcoming U.S. actions. On 4 Dec.,

William Bundy had gone to New Zealand and Australia to present the new policy and seek support. Other envoys were meeting with the remaining Asian allies.

9 Dec 64   *Second Taylor-Huong-Khanh Meeting*
At a second meeting with Huong and Khanh, Taylor presents a detailed set of actions he desires the GVN to take to improve the situation and receives agreement from the two leaders.

10 Dec 64   *Souvanna Phouma Approves U.S. Laos Strikes*
The U.S. proposal for armed air recce over the Laotian corridor is presented to Souvanna Phouma who gives his assent.

11 Dec 64   *GVN Announces Greater Efforts*
Complying with Taylor's request, the GVN announces stepped-up efforts to improve the campaign against the VC and to reform the government.

12 Dec 64   *SecDef Approves JCS Proposal for Naval Actions*
The Secretary approves a JCS proposal for shore bombardment, naval patrols and offshore aerial recce for the first thirty days. A decision on the Phase II was deferred.

NSC Principals Approve Armed recce in Laos
As planned, the NSC approved armed air recce over the Laotian corridor with the exact number and frequency of the patrols to be controlled by SecDef.

14 Dec 64   *BARREL ROLL Begins*
The first sorties of U.S. aircraft in the "armed recce" of the Laotian corridor, known as BARREL ROLL, take place. They mark the beginning of the thirty-day Phase I of the limited pressures.

18 Dec 64   *Level of Laotian Missions Set*
Secretary McNamara sets two missions of four aircraft each as the weekly level of BARREL ROLL activity.

19 Dec 64   *NSC Principals Meeting*
The NSC Principals approve McNamara's recommendation that BARREL ROLL missions be held at constant levels through Phase I. It is revealed that adverse sea conditions have brought maritime operations against the DRV to a virtual halt. At McNamara's insistence it is agreed that the infiltration study will not be made public.

Khanh Purges Civilian Government
Late in the evening, the military high command, led by Khanh, moved to remove all power from the civilian regime of Premier Huong by dissolving the High National Council. Khanh assumes power.

20 Dec 64   *Taylor Meets With ARVN Leaders*
In a meeting with the leading South Vietnamese military officers, Taylor once again outlined the actions required from the GVN by the U.S. before Phase II could be started.

22 Dec 64   *Khanh Publicly Repudiates Taylor*
After having given initial appearances of understanding the dif-

ficulty that the military purge placed the U.S. in, Khanh on Dec. 22 holds a news conference and states that the military is resolved not to carry out the policy of any foreign power.

24 Dec 64   *Rumors of Taylor's Expulsion*
Rumors are received by the Embassy that Khanh intends to have Taylor declared *persona non grata.* Vigorous U.S. efforts to dissuade him and the use of Phase II as leverage cause Khanh to reconsider.

U.S. BOQ Bombed; Embassy Saigon Message 1939; CINCPAC Message to JCS, 26 Dec; JCSM 1076-64
In a terror attack this Christmas Eve, the VC bomb a U.S. BOQ in Saigon. Two U.S. officers are killed, 58 injured. Taylor urges reprisals against the North. He is supported by CINCPAC and the JCS.

29 Dec 64   *NSC Principals Meeting*
At the meeting of the NSC Principals, a decision against reprisals for the barracks bombing is taken in spite of the strong recommendations above. At the same meeting, ISA reported the readiness of the Philippines, ROK, and GRC to send military assistance to South Vietnam.

31 Dec 64   *Embassy Saigon Message 2010*
Taylor proposes going forward with the Phase II U.S. strikes against the North in spite of the political crisis in the South and under any conceivable U.S. relations with the GVN short of complete abandonment.

CJCS Memo to DepSecDef, CM 347-64
The JCS recommend the addition of several air missions to already approved operations, including two air strikes by unmarked VNAF aircraft against the North, and U.S. air escort for returning GVN naval craft.

3 Jan 65   *Rusk TV Interview*
Secretary Rusk appears on a Sunday TV interview program and defends U.S. policy, ruling out either a U.S. withdrawal or a major expansion of the war. The public and Congressional debate on the war had heated up considerably since the Army take-over in South Vietnam in December. The debate continues through January with Senator Morse the most vocal and sharpest critic of the Administration.

4 Jan 65   *Soviets call for new Conference on Laos*
Renewing their earlier efforts, the Soviets call again for a conference on the Laotian problem.

5 Jan 65   *NSC Principals Meet*
The Principals disapprove the JCS recommendation for VNAF strikes with unmarked aircraft against the North. The JCS voice concern at the failure to begin planning for Phase II of the pressures program. But no decision to go ahead is taken.

6 Jan 65   *William Bundy Memo to Rusk*
In view of the continued deterioration of the situation in the South and the prevailing view that the U.S. was going to seek a way out,

Bundy recommended some limited measures, short of Phase II (i.e. recce, a reprisal, evacuation of U.S. dependents, etc.), to strengthen our hand. There were risks in this course but it would improve our position with respect to the other SEA nations if things got rapidly worse in SVN and we had to contemplate a withdrawal.

8 Jan 65 **First Korean Troops Go to South Vietnam**
The first contingent of 2,000 South Korean troops leave for South Vietnam.

9 Jan 65 **Generals Announce Return to Civilian Government**
Under U.S. pressure, the South Vietnamese generals announce that matters of state will be left in the future in the hands of a civilian government. The joint Huong-Khanh communique promises to convene a constituent assembly.

11 Jan 65 **US–GVN Aid Discussions Resume**
With the return to civilian government, the U.S. resumes its discussions with the GVN on aid and measures to improve the military situation.

14 Jan 65 **U.S. Laotian Operations Revealed**
A UPI story reveals the U.S. BARREL ROLL armed recce missions in Laos and tells the story of the YANKEE TEAM armed escort for the RLAF.

17 Jan 65 **Buddhist Riots**
Shortly after the GVN announcement of increased draft calls, Buddhist protest riots break out in several cities against the allegedly anti-Buddhist military leaders. Disturbances continue through the month.

22 Jan 65 **Soviets Affirm Support of DRV**
In letters to Hanoi and Peking, Gromyko affirms Soviet support for the DRV struggle against American imperialism.

23 Jan 65 **USIS Library Burned in Hue**
Rioting Buddhists burn the USIS library in Hue.

27 Jan 65 **McNaughton paper, "Observations re South Vietnam After Khanh's 'Re-Coup'"**
The U.S. stakes in South Vietnam were defined as holding buffer land for Thailand and Malaysia and maintaining our national honor. They required continued perseverance in a bad situation, taking some risks such as reprisals. It was important to remember that our objective was the containment of China not necessarily the salvation of South Vietnam. In this effort, however, we should soon begin reprisal strikes against the North. They would not help the GVN much but would have a positive overall effect on our policy in SEA.

Generals Withdraw Support from Huong
The generals under Khanh's leadership act once again to eliminate the civilian government. This time they succeed in their coup and the U.S. only protests.

28 Jan 65 **General Oanh Named Premier**
General Nguyen Xuan Oanh is named acting Premier by General Khanh.

DECISIONS REGARDING MILITARY PRESSURE AGAINST
NORTH VIETNAM

9 Mar 1961   NSAM 28 conveys President Kennedy's instructions that "we make
every possible effort to launch guerrilla operations in Viet-Minh
territory at the earliest possible time." SecDef and Director, CIA,
asked to furnish views re actions to be taken in the near and "the
longer" future periods.

11 May 1961   President Kennedy approves program for covert actions proposed
by Vietnam Task Force. Program includes: (1) dispatch of agents
into NVN, (2) aerial resupply of agents in NVN through use of
civilian mercenary air crews, (3) infiltration of special GVN
forces into SE Laos to locate and attack Communist bases and
LOC's, (4) formulation of "networks of resistance, covert bases
and teams of sabotage and light harrassment "inside NVN, and
(5) conduct of overflights of NVN for purpose of dropping leaflets.
(NSAM 52)

11 Oct 1961   State Department proposes concept for U.S. intervention in Viet-
nam/Laos situation. Concept would require deployment of SEATO
ground force of 11,000 men along Laos and portion of Cambodian
borders, along with options for "hot pursuit" of VC across borders.
Proposal sought to achieve political objective of responding to an
appeal by Diem to help protect his borders from infiltrated guerrilla forces "inspired, directed and supported from NVN." Supplemental Note, appended to the proposal by OSD/ISA recommended (among other measures) that the U.S. encourage GVN
guerrilla action against communist aerial resupply missions in the
Tchepone area of Laos, through the commitment of U.S. advisers
if necessary. Operation was to include employment of indigenous
forces equipped with .50 calibre AA weapons.

13 Oct 1961   President Kennedy directs (among other measures) that we "initiate guerrilla ground action, including the use of U.S. advisers if
necessary" against Communist aerial resupply missions in the vicinity of Tchepone. He also directed the Department of State to
prepare to publish its White Paper on DRV responsibility for aggression in SVN. (NSAM 104)

8 Dec 1961   Department of State publishes 1st White Paper on DRV aggression in violation of the 1954 Geneva Accords.

Mid-Decem-   GVN augments its CIA-sponsored programs of infiltration and
ber 1961   covert operations through recruiting candidates "to form an underwater demolition team (to operate) . . . in strategic maritime
areas of NVN." ("Status Report on Covert Actions in Vietnam,"
21 Dec. '61)

2 Jun 1962   I.C.C. report states that DRV has violated 1954 Geneva Agreement through its encouragement and support of SVN insurgency.
GVN also criticized, on two counts.

1962   Signing of Geneva Accords on Laos reduces considerably the scope
of covert operations against Communist forces outside SVN.

25 Jun 1963   President Kennedy rejects portion of State Department's plan of actions to deal with a deteriorating situation in Laos, which called for actions to be taken against NVN. While approving two other phases of the proposal (one only for planning purposes), he urges that this final phase be reviewed to determine whether "additional U.S. actions should be taken in Laos before any action be directed against NVN." (NSAM 249)

9 Sep 1963   JCS approve CINCPAC OPLAN 34-63, which called for MACV and CAS, Saigon to provide advice and assistance to the GVN in certain operations against NVN. Phase I of the plan was to consist of "Psychological Operations"; Phase II of "Hit and Run Attacks." The latter included "amphibious raids using Vietnamese UDT/SEAL Team, Rangers, Airborne, and Marine units against selected targets south of the Tonkin Delta having little or no security." Apparently, the plan was not forwarded to the White House by SecDef.

30 Oct 1963   Ambassador Lodge recommends a political-military initiative directed at NVN. In the context of a scheme to "neutralize NVN," he urges "an essentially diplomatic carrot and stick approach, backed by covert military means."

Mid-November 1963   Cross-border operations into Laos reported to be resumed by CAS, Saigon. On 19 November, CAS reported "first results just coming in." (CAS Saigon 2540)

26 Nov 1963   In a review of discussions of Vietnam policy held at Honolulu, 20 November 63, newly installed President Johnson directs (among other measures) that "planning should include different levels of possible increased activity, and in each instance there should be estimates of such factors as:
  a. Resulting damage to NVN;
  b. The plausibility of denial;
  c. Possible NVN retaliation;
  d. Other international reaction."
The directive also called for a plan, to be submitted for approval, for military operations "up to a line up to 50 km. inside Laos, together with political plans for minimizing the international hazards of such an enterprise." (NSAM 273)

15 Dec 1963   In response to JCS request of 26 Nov 63, MACV and CAS, Saigon forward a joint plan of combined GVN/USG operations against NVN. Designated OPLAN 34A, the proposal providing "a spectrum of capabilities for RVNAF to execute against NVN" that would "convince the DRV leadership that they should cease to support insurgent activities in the RVN and Laos. It contained 72 actions, many of which were covert and only 16 of which were considered "punitive or attritional." In forwarding letter, CINCPAC urges that Category IV actions, largely air attacks, "appear to have the highest probability of success." (CINCPAC letter to JCS, 19 Dec 63)

Feb 1964   Interagency study group chaired by Robert Johnson, Department of State Policy Planning Council, begins examination of various ways of applying pressure directly to NVN, as director and supplier of SVN insurgency.

20 Feb 1964 Ambassador Lodge recalls his recommendation of 30 October 63, urging President Johnson to apply "various pressures" to NVN and eliminate the sanctuary for guerrilla support. (Saigon Embassy Msg./State 1954)

21–25 Feb 1964 Both President Johnson and Secretary Rusk (dates respectively) make public statements that "those engaged in external direction and supply [of the SVN insurgency] would do well to be reminded and to remember that this type of aggression is a deeply dangerous game." (*Dept. of State Bulletin,* March 16, 1964)

15 Mar 1964 Ambassador Lodge urges President Johnson to begin reconnaissance flights over NVN and covert actions against NVN before considering any "overt U.S. measures."

17 Mar 1964 President Johnson approves Secretary McNamara's report resulting from an inspection trip to South Vietnam and culminating an extensive policy review by the Administration. Report recommended against overt military measures directly against SVN for the present and stressed numerous internal actions in support of the GVN's progam to combat the VC insurgency. Report did urge immediate preparation of a capability to "mount new and significant pressures against NVN," to include a 72-hour capability for a full range of SVN "border control" operations and "retaliatory actions against NVN," and a capability to initiate "graduated overt military pressure" within 30 days of notification. It further urged authority for "continued high-level U.S. overflights of SVN's borders," and "hot pursuit" and GVN ground operations into Laos for purposes of border control. (NSAM 288)

17 Mar 1964 President Johnson requests that "political and diplomatic preparations be made to lay a basis for "high- or low-level reconnaissance over NVN" if it seems necessary or desirable after a few weeks." He asks Secretaries Rusk and McNamara to further study and make recommendations in concert on "questions of further U.S. participation and of air and ground strikes against Laos," and reserves judgement on overt U.S. measures against NVN. The President authorizes Ambassador Lodge "to prepare contingency recommendation for specific tit-for-tat actions in the event attacks on Americans are renewed." (White House Msg. to Amb. Lodge/ State 1454)

19 Apr 1964 Secretary Rusk decided to go ahead with plan suggested by Ambassador Lodge to have new Canadian I.C.C. Commissioner selected and briefed, in part, for purpose of conveying to Hanoi the seriousness of U.S. purpose and the limited nature of U.S. objectives in Vietnam. Decision was made in the context of a Saigon conference to discuss the categories of action against NVN developed by the interagency study group. It reflected the Ambassador's feeling that a diplomatic attempt to persuade NVN to call off the insurgency (using the carrot and stick approach) should precede any program involving "massive publicity" or "massive destructive actions."

30 Apr 1964 In **Ottawa,** Secretary Rusk obtains Canadian agreement to cooperate in the proposed diplomatic initiative toward Hanoi. J. Blair Seaborn named as I.C.C. Commissioner and given preliminary instructions.

14 May 1964 In conversation with Secretary McNamara, General Khanh expresses his concern that the GVN will not be ready for greater actions against the North for some time. However, he states his belief that they will be inevitable at some later date. (Saigon Embassy Msg. to Secretaries Rusk and McNamara/State 2203)

15 May 1964 In answer to President Johnson's query, Ambassador Lodge confirms his backing of the idea to initiate promptly the Hanoi mission of the Canadian I.C.C. Commissioner. Further, he urges that "if . . . there has been a terroristic act of the proper magnitude . . . a specific target in NVN 'should be struck' as a prelude to his arrival."

23 May 1964 Assistant Secretary of State William Bundy (designated as coordinating executive by President Johnson in NSAM 288) presents members of SEA ExCom. with proposed 30-day scenario for exerting graduated military and political pressure on NVN. Involving a planned sequence of diplomatic moves and public statements from both Saigon and Washington, the scenario culminated with GVN, and eventually US, air strikes against NVN war-supporting targets and a call for international conference on Vietnam. Included in the sequence would be a Joint Congressional Resolution affirming the President's freedom of action to use force if necessary in protecting the security of SEA. (Ambassador Lodge had previously expressed strong dissent at the overt nature of the actions included in the scenario.) (Draft Memo for the President)

25 May 1964 ExCom. decided not to recommend the 30-day scenario—apparently because of the estimated high probability of escalation and the countervailing diplomatic image of larger objectives that such escalation would create. Instead, it recommends a Presidential decision to use force if "appropriate diplomatic and political warning and preparation" and "other efforts" fail to "produce a sufficient improvement of non-Communist prospects in South Vietnam and in Laos." Recommendation was based on the premises that included: "that a decision to use force if necessary, backed by resolute and extensive deployment, and conveyed by every possible means to our adversaries, gives the best present chance of avoiding the actual use of such force." The ExCom. further recommends that all parts of Southeast Asia be treated as part of a single problem and that a sequence of diplomatic and public actions similar to those in the scenario and including a well-publicized strategy conference in Honolulu, be set in motion. (Draft Memo to the President)

26 May 1964 Ambassador Lodge cables Secretary Rusk that he is "coming to the conclusion that we cannot reasonably . . . expect a much better performance out of the GVN than what we are now getting unless something [like US retaliation for terrorist acts] is brought into the picture." (State 2318)

31 May 1964 In Saigon, General Khanh tells Secretary Rusk (on way to Honolulu Conference) that SVN can not win against the VC without military actions outside its borders. He urges immediate actions by ARVN, with air support (US or GVN not clear), to eliminate Communist forces in E. Laos and end the VC threat to cut SVN in half across the Highlands. Secretary Rusk tells Khanh "We are purposely giving the Sino-Soviet bloc many indicators that we are about to react to recent aggressions." But that he could say nothing about specific American intentions in the immediate future "because he simply did not know. The Honolulu meeting would produce some firm recommendations to the President and some plans, but ultimately only the President could decide. His decision would be influenced by consideration of all implications of escalation . . ." (CINCPAC Msg. 1 June 64/SECTO 37)

2 Jun 1964 JCS question military adequacy "for the present situation" of the currently dominant objective to "cause the North Vietnamese to decide to terminate their subversive support of activity in Laos and SVN," but agree to it as "an initial measure." They state their opinion that termination of the DRV's support of the insurgencies can be assured only by "military actions to accomplish destruction of the NVN will and capabilities as necessary to compel the DRV to cease providing support." In case national authority opts for the lesser (and former) objective, the JCS propose two target complexes significantly associated with support of the effort in Laos and SVN, the destruction of which can be achieved quickly and precisely and "with minimum impact on civilian populations." (JCSM–471–64)

At Honolulu, Secretaries McNamara and Rusk and CIA Director McCone agree "emphatically," in response to Ambassador Lodge's questioning, that a Congressional Resolution was a necessary element in any preparations for wider US participation against . . . NVN. The possibilities of (1) having to deploy as many as seven divisions, (2) having to call up reserves, and (3) having to protect SVN from possible NVN and CHICOM reprisals were cited as reasons why special confirmation of the Presidential authority was needed. Its deterrence effects were also cited. As a result of discussions of current military plans and posture for SEA, the principals acknowledge numerous factors that make prompt military action by the US undesirable. These included: (1) force build-up necessary to support current plans, (2) the possible interference of such build-ups with our intended signal of limited objective, (3) the need for more precise targeting studies, (4) the need for a larger ARVN reserve, (5) the need for a stronger GVN base, (6) the need to prepare allied governments and US public opinion, and (7) the impact of the rainy season, inhibiting offensive operations in the Laos panhandle. (Memo of Record, 3 June 64)

5 Jun 1964 CJCS Taylor sends Secretary McNamara a view contrary to that in 2 June 64 JCS memo, urging three, rather than two, general alternative patterns for putting military pressure on NVN. To alternatives roughly corresponding to the two posed by the JCS he adds a third "demonstrative" alternative "to show US readiness and intent to pass to [the harsher] alternatives." Though stating his preference for the middle alternative, he states feeling "that it is highly probable that political consideration will incline our responsible civilian official to opt for [the mildest] alternative," and that, therefore, the JCS should develop a plan for implementing it.

9 Jun 1964   In answer to the President's question whether control of SVN and Laos by NVN would necessarily mean the loss of SEA, CIA replies negatively. It asserts, however, that such an eventuality "would be profoundly damaging to the US position in the Far East . . . would be damaging to US prestige, and would seriously debase the credibility of US will and capability to contain the spread of Communism elsewhere in the areas [sic] [by later elaboration, the SEA mainland]." The US deterrence posture vis-a-vis overt military aggression by Peking and Hanoi was viewed as not suffering appreciably from such a loss," as long as the US can effectively operate from [its island] bases." The Department of State view agreed and, if different, was slightly more alarmist. (Memo for the Director, CIA)

11 Jun 1964   Laotian Premier Souvanna Phouma reaffirms original agreement (8 June) to US armed escort of reconnaissance flights over "South Laos" and the Plaine des Jarres, with authority to attack ground units first firing on them. Situation in Laos has become fairly stabilized and non-threatening, with the US entered on a "negotiating track" hopefully leading to "the convening of the Polish consultations in the next 3–4 weeks and their continuation over a period of time." This State Department assessment opines, "We do not expect at the present time to move in the near future to military action against NVN." (Memo on the SEA Situation, 12 June 64)

23 Jun 1964   Presidential news conference, cited in State Dept. messages to embassies as "significant and precise statement of the US position in SEA." Previously, military posturing actions including: (1) deployment of a B–57 wing from Japan to the Philippines, (2) reinforcement of military contingency stockpiles in Thailand, and (3) development of a network of new air bases and operational facilities in SVN and Thailand had been given extensive press coverage.

Jul 1964   President Johnson directs all government agencies to "seek to identify actions which can be taken to improve the situation in Vietnam: actions which would produce maximum effect with minimum escalation."   [words missing]

2–5 Aug 1964   Tonkin Gulf incident and US reprisals against NVN targets.

6 Aug 1964   Congress passes a joint resolution stating that international peace and security in SEA were "vital to" the national interest. The resolution authorized President Johnson "to take all necessary

steps, including the use of armed force," to assist any SEATO "member of protocol state" requesting US help in defending its freedom. (Dept. of State Bulletin August 24, 1964)

Aug 1964   In response to Secretary McNamara's request for NVN targets, the JCS submits initial "94-target list."

14 Aug 1964   Department of State cables Saigon and Vietnam embassies and CINCPAC requesting comment on key points in a "tentative high level paper on next courses of action in SEA." In summary of points, is included statement, "the next ten days to two weeks should be short holding phase in which we would avoid action that would in any way take onus off Communist side for escalation." Cable then specifies that DESOTO patrol will not be resumed and new 34A operations will not be undertaken. After sketching "essential elements of the political and military situations in both SVN and Laos, as well as respective strategies re negotiations, the cable then lists proposed "limited pressures" to be exerted on the DRV in Laos and in NVN during the period, "late August tentatively through December." (State Msgs. to Saigon 439; Vietnam 157)

Aug 1964   At a meeting at Udorn, Ambassadors Unger and Taylor agree that MACV should work out a division of targets in the Laotian panhandle area between RLAF and RVNAF aircraft and US suppressive strikes. In principle, the concept of cross-border operations into Laos by GVN ground forces, is agreed to within specific limits, for planning purposes.

24 Aug 1964   After re-examining initial targeting proposals, the JCS recommend a course of action for SEA. They call for a "sharp sudden blow" as the most effective way "to bring home . . . the intent of the US "to bring about cessation of the DRV's support of insurgency in the South. They present a revised 94-target list" as the basis for their recommended course of actions. (JCSM 729/64)

Late August through October 1964   Joint State and ISA effort to develop new scenario for graduated pressures against NVN apparently in progress

10 Sep 1964   President authorizes resumption of DESOTO patrols and MAROPS portion of the 34A operations.

18 Sep 1964   President suspends DESOTO patrol operation, in the wake of a third incident (18 Sep 64) involving NVN patrol boat threats to US destroyer in the Tonkin Gulf.

3 Oct 1964   President Johnson authorizes resumption of the MAROPS program, involving (during October) two probes, an attempted junk capture and ship-to-shore bombardment of radar sites.

16 Oct 1964   Ambassador Taylor cables President Johnson regarding increased infiltration and worsening situation in SVN.

27 Oct 1964   The JCS express judgement that "strong military actions are required now in order to prevent the collapse of the US position in Southeast Asia," "making specific reference to SNIE 53–2–64 and the Taylor cable. They recommend a program of actions designed to support a strategy of:

> a. Depriving the Viet Cong (VC) of out of country assistance by applying continuously increasing military pressures on the Democratic Republic of North Vietnam (DRV) to the extent necessary to cause the DRV to cease support and direction of the insurgency.
> b. Depriving the VC of assistance within SVN by expanding the counterinsurgency effort—military, economic and political—within SVN.
> c. Continuing to seek a viable effective government in SVN based on the broadest possible consensus.
> d. Maintaining a military readiness posture in Southeast Asia that:

>> (1) Demonstrates the US will and capability to escalate the action if required.
>> (2) Deters a major communist aggression in the area."

Further, they request authority "to implement now" six actions within SVN and eight actions outside SVN, including GVN and US FARMGATE, also attacks on the infiltration LOC's in Southern NVN. (JCSM–902–64)

1 Nov 1964 Viet Cong forces attack the US air base and billeting at Bien Hoa.

3 Nov 1964 Assistant Secretary of State Bundy convenes newly established NSC Working Group on SVN/SEA, with membership from State, OSD/ISA, the JCS, and CIA.

Group work allocated into the following categories:
I. The Situation in SVN; II. US Objectives and Stakes in SVN and SEA: III. The Broad Options; IV. Alternative Forms of Negotiations; V. Analysis of Option A; VI. Analysis of Option B; VII. Analysis of Option C; VIII. Immediate Actions in the Period Prior to Decision; IX. Conclusions and Recommendations. Initial drafts of statements covering many of these sections were underway prior to establishment of the group. (Memo to Working Group Members.)

4 Nov 1964 The JCS urge "prompt and strong" military actions in reprisal for the Bien Hoa attacks. The actions include B-52 night strikes on Phue Yen airfield, attacks on Hanoi and Haiphong POL storage and other high-value targets. (JCS 2339/153)

14 Nov 1964 In response to Secretary McNamara's request to examine possible DRV/CHICOM military reactions to US air strikes on NVN, the JCS also reiterate their recommendation for "specific actions" made on 4 Nov 64. They link prepared actions to the "underlying objective . . . of causing the DRV to cease supporting and directing the insurgencies in RVN and Laos" and call them "equally applicable and appropriate for other serious provocations in SEA." (JCSM–955–64)

17 Nov 1964   NSC Working Group circulates draft working papers for each of the topics included in its study to the principal participating agencies for comment. The objective of the group is to prepare recommended courses of action prior to the arrival of Ambassador Lodge for a high-level SEA policy meeting. Papers present three alternative courses of action: A—Continued emphasis on counterinsurgency in SVN with provision for reprisals for provocations like Bien Hoa along with somewhat intensified 34A operations and air operations against the Ho Chi Minh Trail in Laos; B—Graduated but steadily escalating air operations against LOCs and high-value targets in NVN; C—Graduated but variably paced military actions against infiltration routes in Laos and NVN. C would differ from the others also by including an overt willingness to negotiate a settlement based on the Geneva Accords.

23 Nov 1964   The JCS criticize the NSC Working Group's alternatives and some of its supporting rationale. Arguing that the loss of SEA "would lead to grave political and military consequences in the entire Western Pacific," the JCS urge stronger military options than those of the Working Group. They state that only two of five they describe give promise of achieving the stated US objectives: that recommended in JCSM–967–64, dated 18 Nov 64 and the stronger (and preferred) option recommended in JCSM–955–64, dated 14 Nov 64. (JCSM–98Z–64)

24 Nov 1964   At a meeting of the NSC Principals for SEA, consensus is reached that:

1. If the DRV did withdraw its effort, the security situation in the South could be handled in time if the government could maintain itself. However, the struggle would still be long.

2. The South Vietnam situation would deteriorate further under Option A even with reprisals, but that there was a significant chance that the actions proposed under Option B or Option C would improve GVN performance and make possible an improvement in the security situation.

3. Any negotiating outcome under Option A (with or without US negotiating participation) was likely to be clearly worse than under Option C or Option B.

4. It was *not* true, as the draft paper states, that Option B, in the light of all factors, has the best chance of attaining our full objectives.

5. The loss of South Vietnam would be somewhat more serious than stated in Section II of the draft paper, and it would be at least in the direction of the Joint Staff view as stated in the footnote to page 7 of the draft.

6. The requirement of Option C—maintaining military pressure and a credible threat of major action while at the same time being prepared to negotiate—*could* in practice be carried out.

7. Under Option C, our early military actions against the DRV should be determined, but low in scale, but that some higher-damage actions should be included under the reprisal heading. Other points achieve less than consensus, and various aspects of executing Options B and C are discussed, including the merits of committing ground forces in various roles. (Memo of ExCom Meeting)

27 Nov 1964   At a meeting of the NSC Principals with Ambassador Taylor, consensus is expressed that it would be difficult for the US to continue its policies in SEA "if the GVN collapsed or told us to get out." Westmoreland's advice to delay wider actions for about six months is rejected on grounds that the situation may not hold together that long. Agreement is reached that although stronger action by the US would "have a favorable effect on GVN . . . performance and morale," it may not really improve the situation, and "the strengthening effect of Option C could at least buy time, possibly measured in years." The Principals recommend "that over the next two months we adopt a program of Option A plus the first stages of Option C," and that "we needed a more precise and fully spelled out scenario . . . with or without a decision to move into the full Option C program at some time thereafter." (Memo of Meeting)

1 Dec 1964   President Johnson approves Principals' recommendation to initiate immediate actions like those proposed under Option A. Principals conceive first phase of pressures against NVN as continuing 30 days or more, depending on GVN progress along specified lines. Should such progress be made, they see US entering a second-phase program consisting "principally of progressively more serious air strikes," as in Option C, "possibly running from two to six months." The President also grants US Mission in Saigon authority to work out reprisal plans with the GVN. Ambassador Taylor is instructed to tell the GVN that SVN's national unity and firm leadership are necessary prerequisites to US consideration of second phase operations. (Attach to Memo for SEA Principals, 29 Nov 64)

14 Dec 1964   JCS order initiation of armed reconnaissance operations in Laos and doubling of MAROPS incident rate—also initiate deployment of WESTPAC force augmentations necessary for reprisal actions (All Phase I operations).

I.   FEB–JUNE 1964

A.   INITIATION OF COVERT OPERATIONS

On 1 February 1964, the United States embarked on a new course of action in pursuance of its long-standing policy of attempting to bolster the security of Southeast Asia. On that date, under direction of the American military establishment, an elaborate program of covert military operations against the state of North Vietnam was set in motion. There were precedents: a variety of covert activities had been sponsored by the American CIA since 1961. Intelligence agents, resupplied by air, had been dispatched into North Vietnam; resistance and sabotage teams had been recruited inside the country; and propaganda leaflets had been dispensed from "civilian mercenary" aircraft. But the program that began in February 1964 was different, and its impact on future U.S. policy in Southeast Asia was far-reaching.

1. *Covert Action Program: Scope and Character*

The covert action program beginning in February 1964 was different, first of all, because it was a *program.* Designed to extend over a period of 12 months, it was divided into three phases distinguished by the character and intensity of their respective operations. The first phase (February through May) called for intelligence collection through U-2 and communications intelligence missions and psychological operations involving leaflet drops, propaganda kit deliveries, and radio broadcasts. It also provided for about "20 destructive undertakings, all within . . . early prospective [GVN] capabilities . . . [and] designed to result in substantial destruction, economic loss and harassment." The second and third phases involved the same categories of action, but of increased tempo and magnitude, and with the destructive operations extending to "targets identified with North Vietnam's economic and industrial well-being." Once started, the program was intended to inflict on North Vietnam increasing levels of punishment for its aggressive policies.

The 1964 program was different also because it was placed under control of an operational U.S. military command. Though the program was designed to be carried out by GVN or third country personnel, plans were developed by COMUSMACV and the GVN jointly and given interagency clearance in Washington through a special office under the JCS. CINCPAC and the appropriate CIA station furnished the necessary training and equipment support and COMUSMACV exercised operational control. Since subsequent phases of the covert program were to be based on a continuous evaluation of actions already taken, operation reports were submitted periodically through JCS staff channels for review by various Washington agencies.

Normally such routine staffing arrangements tend to encourage expectations of continued program actions. Moreover, they foreshadow bureaucratic pressures for taking stronger measures should previous ones fail to produce desired results. In the case of the covert operations program, these tendencies were reinforced through the evocation of a GVN policy commitment and the involvement of GVN officials in its implementation.

2. *Origins and Development: Presidential Support and Approval*

The covert program was spawned in May of 1963, when the JCS directed CINCPAC to prepare a plan for GVN "hit and run" operations against NVN. These operations were to be "non-attributable" and carried out "with U.S. military materiel, training and advisory assistance." Approved by the JCS on 9 September as CINCPAC OPLAN 34–63, the plan was discussed during the Vietnam policy conference at Honolulu, 20 November 1963. Here a decision was made to develop a combined COMUSMACV-CAS, Saigon plan for a 12-month program of covert operations. Instructions forwarded by the JCS on 26 November specifically requested provision for: "(1) harassment; (2) diversion; (3) political pressure; (4) capture of prisoners; (5) physical destruction; (6)

acquisition of intelligence; (7) generation of intelligence; and (8) diversion of DRV resources." Further, that the plan provide for "selected actions of graduated scope and intensity to include commando type coastal raids." To this guidance was added that given by President Johnson to the effect that "planning should include . . . estimates of such factors as: (1) resulting damage to NVN; (2) the plausibility of denial; (3) possible NVN retaliation; and (4) other international reaction." The MACV-CAS plan, designated OPLAN 34A, and providing for "a spectrum of capabilities for RVNAF to execute against NVN," was forwarded by CINCPAC on 19 December 1963.

The idea of putting direct pressure on North Vietnam met prompt receptivity on the part of President Johnson. According to then Assistant Secretary of State, Roger Hilsman, it was just a few days before the military-CIA submission that State Department Counselor, Walt Rostow passed to the President "a well-reasoned case for a gradual escalation." Rostow was well-known as an advocate of taking direct measures against the external sources of guerrilla support, having hammered away at this theme since he first presented it at Fort Bragg in April 1961. In any event, on 21 December, President Johnson directed that an interdepartmental committee study the MACV-CAS plan to select from it those least risk." This committee, under the chairmanship of Major General Krulak, USMC, completed its study on 2 January 1964 and submitted its report for review by the principal officials of its various member agencies. The report recommended the 3-phase approach and the variety of Phase I operations described earlier. President Johnson approved the committee's recommendations on 16 January and directed that the initial 4-month phase of the program be implemented beginning 1 February.

3. *Concept and Rationale: Convince DRV to Desist by Raising the Cost*

In view of program performance and later decisions, the conceptualization underlying the program of covert operations against North Vietnam is particularly significant. JCS objectives for the initial CINCPAC formulation were to increase the cost to the DRV of its role in the South Vietnamese insurgency. The catalogue of operations submitted from Saigon was intended to "convince the DRV leadership that they should cease to support insurgent activities in the RVN and Laos." Although, in its forwarding letter, CINCPAC expressed doubt that all but a few of the 2062 separate operations detailed by MACV-CAS could have that kind of effect. In his view, only air attacks and a few other "punitive or attritional" operations had any probability of success in achieving the stated objectives.

Rationale accompanying the interdepartmental committee's program recommendations, apparently accepted by higher authority, reflected both the coercive objectives and the reservations associated with the earlier documents. Through its recommended program of "progressively escalating pressure," the committee aimed "to inflict increasing punishment upon North Vietnam and to create pressures, which may convince the North Vietnamese leadership, in its own self-interest, to desist from its aggressive policies." However, it expressed the caution that "it is far from clear whether even the successful conduct of the operations . . . would induce Hanoi's leaders to cease and desist." Still, after enumerating a number of specific risks involved, it expressed the opinion that they were "outweighed by the potential benefits of the actions [it] recommended." In selecting these actions, the committee stated the assumption that the DRV's current strategy was to support the Viet Cong "at little cost to itself and at little risk to its industrial complex, while counting for victory upon U.S. and South Vietnamese war weariness . . ." It calculated:

> The importance attached by Hanoi's leaders to the development of North Vietnam's economy suggests that progressive damage of its industrial projects, attrition of its resources and dislocation of its economy might induce a decision to call off its physical support of the Viet Cong. This reaction might be intensified by the traditional Vietnamese fear of Chinese domination, where expanded operations by our side could arouse concern in Hanoi over the likelihood of direct Chinese Communist intervention in North Vietnamese affairs.

Interagency commentary on the proposed operations provides additional insight into the rationale and expectancies associated with the initial 4-month program. After reviewing 13 of these operations, the Board of National Estimates concluded that "even if all were successful," they would not achieve the aim of convincing the DRV to alter its policies. The Board thought it possible that North Vietnamese leaders might view these operations "as representing a significant increase in the vigor of U.S. policy, potentially dangerous to them," but with a likely reaction no more significant than a DRV effort to try to arouse greater international pressure for a Geneva-type conference on Vietnam. In addition, it cautioned that at least three operations proposed for the initial period were too large and complex to be plausibly denied by the GVN. The committee noted this CIA caution but suggested it might provide a psychological advantage "for South Vietnam to acknowledge publicly its responsibility for certain of the retaliatory acts taken against the aggressor." However, the State Department member demurred, urging that only those operations that were covert and deniable by both the GVN and the United States be undertaken. His caution reflected recognition "of the risks and the uncertainty as to whether operations against North Vietnam will materially contribute to our objective of ending the war."

4. *Implications: Greater Pressure on Hanoi*

Thus, by early February 1964, the United States had committed itself to a policy of attempting to improve the situations in South Vietnam and Laos by subjecting North Vietnam to increasing levels of direct pressure. Despite explicit assessments that the contemplated early steps could not achieve its objectives, it had embarked on a program which demanded a significant commitment for its South Vietnamese allies and which in its expected later stages could expose them to considerable risk. Moreover, by initiating a program recognized as giving little promise of achieving its stated objectives through early actions, it raised expectancies for continued and intensified operations in later stages. It can be concluded that *either* the Administration (1) intended to continue to pursue the policy of pressuring North Vietnam until these pressures showed some propensity for success, *or* (2) sought through the covert operations program to achieve objectives different from those anticipated during the initial planning.

B. *PLANNING FOR LARGER PRESSURES*

As indicated by reservations expressed by an *ad hoc* interdepartmental committee on "pressures" against North Vietnam chaired by General Krulak, covert operations were seen as possessing several shortcomings with respect to influencing decisions in Hanoi. In appraising these operations, attention was drawn increasingly to the potential for undertaking punitive measures that appeared likely to be more compelling. The Krulak committee assessed the likely North Vietnamese response as follows:

> Toughened, as they have been, by long years of hardships and struggle, they will not easily be persuaded by a punitive program to halt their support of the Viet Cong insurgency, unless the *damage* visited upon them is of great magnitude.

Moreover, the committee rationale reflected the idea generally held that the DRV would be responsive to more damaging actions. For example, Walt Rostow pressed the view on Secretary Rusk that "Ho [Chi Minh] has an industrial complex to protect: he is no longer a guerrilla fighter with nothing to lose."

1. *Conceptual Origins and Motivations*

In early February, several conceptual elements converged to focus Administration attention on the question of whether U.S. policy should embrace readiness to undertake larger punitive actions against North Vietnam. One element was the realization that the GVN would be incapable of increasing the number or size of its maritime operations beyond the modest "pin pricks" included in the Phase I covert actions program. Should stronger pressures be called for before May or June, they would have to be applied through direct air strikes, probably with USAF/FARMGATE assistance. Another element was the prospect of serious deterioration within Laos and South Vietnam, resulting from recent North Vietnamese troop influxes into Laos, fear of similar trends in South Vietnam, and heightened VC activity in the wake of the latest GVN coup of 30 January. Concern within the State Department was such that discussions were held on the desirability of the President's requesting a congressional resolution, drawing a line at the borders of South Vietnam.

A third element was the increasing articulation of a direct relation between the challenge of halting North Vietnam's assistance to the Southeast Asian insurgents and broader U.S. strategic interests. Stopping Hanoi from aiding the Viet Cong virtually became equated with protecting U.S. interests against the threat of insurgency throughout the world. For example, in support of their recommendation to "put aside many of the self-imposed restrictions which now limit our efforts" and "undertake a much higher level of activity" than the covert actions against external assistance to the Viet Cong, the JCS argued:

> In a broader sense, the failure of our programs in South Vietnam would have heavy influence on the judgment of Burma, India, Indonesia, Malaysia, Japan, Taiwan, the Republic of Korea, and the Republic of the Philippines with respect to U.S. durability, resolution, and trustworthiness. Finally, this being the first real test of our determination to defeat the Communist wars of national liberation formula, it is not unreasonable to conclude that there would be a corresponding unfavorable effect upon our image in Africa and in Latin America.

Similarly, in Secretary Rusk's perception.

> We must demonstrate to both the Communist and the non-Communist worlds that the wars of national liberation formula now being pushed so actively by the Communists will not succeed.

2. *Interagency Study, February–March 1964*

The immediate effect of the heightened interest in causing Hanoi to alter its policies by exerting greater punitive pressures was to stimulate a variety of planning activities within the national security establishment. For example, on 20 February, at a meeting with the Secretaries of State and Defense, CIA Director McCone, CJCS Taylor and members of the Vietnam Committee, the President directed:

> Contingency planning for pressures against North Vietnam should be speeded up. Particular attention should be given to shaping such pressures so as to produce the maximum credible deterrent effect on Hanoi.

Underway at the time was a detailed interagency study intended to determine ways of bringing measured pressures to bear against the DRV. Directed by Robert Johnson, of the Department of State Policy Planning Council, the study group was assembled under the auspices of State's Vietnam Committee. Its products were funneled through William Sullivan, head of the committee, to its members and thence to the principal officials of the agencies represented. However, the papers produced by the study group did not necessarily represent coordinated interdepartmental views.

The study examined three alternative approaches to subjecting North Vietnam to coercive pressures: (1) non-attributable pressures (similar to the advanced stages of the covert actions program); (2) overt U.S. deployments and operations not directed toward DRV territory; and (3) overt U.S. actions against North Vietnam, including amphibious, naval and air attacks. In addition, it encompassed a number of "supporting studies" on such subjects as U.S. objectives, problems of timing, upper limits of U.S. action, congressional action, control arrangements, information policy, negotiating problems, and specific country problems. By addressing such a range of subjects, participants in the study came to grips with a number of broader issues valuable for later policy deliberations (e.g., costs and risks to the U.S. of contemplated actions; impact of the Sino-Soviet split; possible face-saving retreats).

In support of this study and in order to permit necessary political evaluations concerning the military alternatives available, the JCS were asked to furnish their views on the following issues: (1) the overall military capabilities of the DRV and Chinese Communists with respect to logistical capacity, geographical areas of operation, time required to initiate operations, and capacity for concurrent reactions in different regions; (2) military actions against NVN, using air and naval power only, which the GVN might undertake alone or which the U.S. might undertake both with and without public acknowledgment; (3) NVN targets, attack on which would be most effective in inhibiting particular DRV military capabilities; (4) course of action likely to bring about cessation of DRV support for the conflicts in Laos and South Vietnam; (5) action most likely to deter communist attacks on various parts of Asia in the event of a large-scale communist reaction to attacks on NVN; (6) the extent to which the United States could counter such reactions, using only air and naval operations and different ordnance combinations; and (7) modifications needed in current contingency plans to provide for U.S. responses depending "primarily upon air activities rather than the intervention of substantial U.S. ground forces."

The work of the study group resulted in an interim report on 1 March 1964, just prior to Secretary McNamara's and CJCS Taylor's visit to South Vietnam.

This they carried with them in the form of a summary analysis of the group's findings. During a brief stopover in Honolulu, these findings and the issues raised by the Secretary's memorandum to the JCS were discussed. Particular emphasis was given to the possible advantage to be derived from converting the current operations into an "overt Vietnamese program with participation by [the] U.S. as required to obtain adequate results."

3. *Study Group Analysis of Proposed Actions*

The study group had given considerable attention to overt U.S. actions against North Vietnam. Its analysis was based on a concept of exploiting "North Vietnamese concern that their industrialization achievements might be wiped out or could be defended (if at all) only at the price of Chicom control" and of demonstrating "that their more powerful communist allies would not risk their own interests for the sake of North Vietnam." The actions it proposed were aimed at accomplishing five objectives: (1) induce North Vietnam to curtail its support of the Viet Cong in South Vietnam; (2) reduce the morale of the Viet Cong; (3) stiffen the Khanh government and discourage moves toward neutralism; (4) show the world that we will take strong measures to prevent the spread of communism; and (5) strengthen morale in Asia. However, the study group cautioned that "public justification of our actions and its expressed rationale must be based primarily upon the fact of Northern support for and direction of the war in the South in violation of the independence of South Vietnam." It then outlined a series of public informational, domestic political, and international diplomatic steps desirable for establishing this justification.

In seeking to achieve the objective cited above, the study group suggested military actions with the best potential and raised some vital policy issues. In ascending order of the degree of national commitment, the study group believed each would entail, the military actions were as follows: (1) "deploy to Thailand, South Vietnam, Laos and elsewhere the forces, sea, air and land, required to counter a North Vietnamese or Chicom response of the largest likely order"; (2) "initiate overt air reconnaissance activities as a means of dramatizing North Vietnamese involvement"; beginning with high-level flights and following with low-level missions; (3) "take limited air or ground action in Cambodia and Laos, including hot pursuit across the Cambodian border and limited operations across the Laos border"; (4) "blockade Haiphong," which would "have dramatic political effect because it is a recognized military action that hits at the sovereignty of North Vietnam and suggests strongly that we may plan to go further"; (5) "establish a limited air defense capability around Saigon"; and (6) conduct air strikes on key North Vietnamese LOC's, infiltrator training camps, key industrial complexes, and POL storage. It is important to note that the order of commitment perceived in early 1964 was considerably different from the order which most observers would assign to such actions at the time of this writing. The ground force deployments (Item 1) were primarily deterrent deployments to Thailand, on the model of those made during the 1961–62 Laotian crisis. Blockading (Item 4) was considered a low-commitment, low-risk action through most of 1964. Significantly, the last set of actions "in any number" was cited as implying "a U.S. commitment to go all the way if necessary." Thus, the group cautioned that before embarking on such steps the Administration should consider how far it would be willing to go in the event of possible reactions. For example, how long would we persist "in defiance of international pressures for a cease-fire and conference"? Or, how far would we go, either within the proposed concept or by escalating beyond it, in continuing military pressures if the DRV did not comply—or if it decided to escalate?

Although warning of the need to be prepared "to follow through against Communist China if necessary," the study group estimated that neither China nor the Soviet Union would intervene militarily, other than to supply equipment. In view of these estimates and the study group's basic assumption of DRV sensitivity to industrial losses, its assessments of the likely outcomes of the actions it discussed are significant. Asserting that pressures against North Vietnam were "no substitute for successful counterinsurgency in South Vietnam," the group listed the probable positive gains: (1) U.S. action could demonstrate U.S. power and determination, along with restraint, to Asia and the world at large; (2) U.S. action would lead to some reduction in Viet Cong morale; and (3) U.S. action if carefully planned and executed might improve our negotiating position over what it would otherwise be. (The group saw negotiation as "virtually inevitable.") However, it then countered with the following judgment:

> It is not likely that North Vietnam would (if it could) call off the war in the South even though U.S. actions would in time have serious economic and political impact. Overt action against North Vietnam would be unlikely to produce reduction in Viet Cong activity sufficiently to make victory on the ground possible in South Vietnam unless accompanied by new U.S. bolstering actions in South Vietnam and considerable improvement in the government there. The most to be expected would be reduction of North Vietnamese support of the Viet Cong for a while and, thus, the gaining of some time and opportunity by the government of South Vietnam to improve itself.

When he returned from his visit to South Vietnam, Secretary McNamara recommended against either the United States or the GVN undertaking overt actions against North Vietnam "at this time." One compelling reason was General Khanh's expressed wish not to engage in overt operations until a firmer GVN political base had been established, but there were others as well. Mr. McNamara regarded such actions as "extremely delicate . . . both from the military and political standpoints," because of specific problems. These were identified as: (1) the problem of justifying such actions; (2) the problem of "communist escalation"; and (3) the problem of pressures for premature negotiations. Moreover, he stated the judgment that the practical range of our overt options did not permit assured achievement of our practical objectives. In identifying these, he drew a distinction similar to that made by the interagency study group—between the stated objective of eliminating Hanoi's control of the VC insurgency and the "practical" objectives of "collapsing the morale and the self-assurance of the Viet Cong cadres . . . and bolstering the morale of the Khanh regime." [Doc. 158]

What Mr. McNamara did recommend for military actions outside South Vietnam reflected the contemporary concerns over Laos. Prior to his visit, the increased NVA activity in eastern Laos had prompted several recommendations for military measures to thwart new communist territorial gains in that country and to interrupt the flow of men and materiel into South Vietnam along the Laotian infiltration routes. In particular, elements within the Department of Defense urged efforts to lift existing restrictions on cross-border pursuit of engaged forces into Laos, including accompaniment of GVN air and ground forces by U.S. advisory personnel. They also sought authorization for both GVN and U.S. aircraft to overfly Laos for reconnaissance purposes. The JCS urged low-level reconnaissance flights over Laos as advantageous both for collecting badly needed intelligence and for visibly displaying U.S. power. The State Department recommended deploying twelve F-100's to Thailand, with a view toward its potential deterrence and signalling impacts on communist activities in Laos. On his return from South Vietnam, two of the actions for which Secretary McNamara sought Presidential authority dealt with activities affecting Laos: (1) (Recommendation 11) "hot pursuit" and small-scale operations across the Laotian border by GVN ground forces "for the purpose of border control" and "continued high-level U.S. overflights" of the border; and (2) (Recommendation 12) preparations to be ready "to initiate the full range of Laotian and Cambodian border control actions" within 72 hours.

Actions recommended by the Secretary to provide measures aimed directly at North Vietnam (Recommendation 12) fell into two categories: (1) preparation for "retaliatory actions," defined to include "overt high and/or low level reconnaissance flights . . . over North Vietnam" as well as "tit-for-tat" bombing strikes and commando-type raids; and (2) planning and preparations "to be in a position on 30 days' notice to initiate the [sic] program of 'Graduated Overt Military Pressure' against North Vietnam." The wording of the latter recommendation is notable because, at the time, there apparently was no planned overt "program" in existence; the discussion of overt pressures appended to the Secretary's report was considerably less than even a recommendation for such a program. The concept of retaliatory actions was more explicitly defined, but here too, it was apparent that important questions like, "Retaliation for what?" and "Under what circumstances?" had yet to be answered clearly. The scenario described in the report's appended "Illustrative Program" of retaliatory pressure seemed to mix elements appropriate for a continuous program of military actions against North Vietnam with those suitable as tit-for-tat response to specific provocations.

Each of the Secretary's recommendations was approved by President Johnson at a National Security Council meeting on 17 March, with the directive for all agencies "to proceed energetically" in executing them. Subsequent planning activities by different implementing agencies indicate that they did not share a common view of the policy implications and assumptions contained in these recommendations.

C. DIFFERENT POLICY PERCEPTIONS IN PLANNING

1. *Two Basic Approaches: JCS and State-ISA*

The principal planning agencies responding to the President's directive regarding Recommendations 11 and 12 were the Joint Chiefs of Staff and the Department of State together with OSD/ISA, and the two efforts took rather different approaches. The JCS responded literally to the instructions and tasked CINCPAC to prepare an action program of border control and retaliatory operations with 72-hour responsiveness and one of "graduated overt military pressure by GVN and U.S. forces" against North Vietnam with 30-day responsiveness. The JCS preparation for near-term implementation of these recommendations went beyond the usual contingency planning as indicated by their instruction that CINCPAC's plan "permit sequential implementation" of the three actions. The JCS approved the CINCPAC submission, as OPLAN 37–64, on 17 April 1964.

The State–ISA planning activity proceeded under the apparent belief that the actions included in Secretary McNamara's Recommendation 12 were approved as contingency options, one or more or none of which might be selected for implementation at some time in the future. In fact, State believed the Secretary's categories of action were not in keeping with likely developments—"that [cross-border] actions against Cambodia and Laos are dependent heavily on the political position in these countries at the time, and that, in general, it seems more likely that we would wish to hold off in hitting Cambodia until we had gone ahead hard against North Vietnam itself . . . there appear to be reasons not to open up other theaters until we have made clear that North Vietnam is the main theater and have not really started on it." Further, it questioned the utility of tit-for-tat retaliatory actions because of (1) the difficulty of responding in kind, or in a fitting manner, to the most likely—terrorist—variety of VC provocations and (2) their inappropriateness for conveying "the picture of concerted and steadily rising pressures that reflect complete U.S. determination to finish the job." Accordingly, the State-ISA effort began by developing a political scenario designed to accommodate only the graduated military pressures referred to in Recommendation 12. These were divided into three major categories: (1) covert GVN action against North Vietnam with covert U.S. support; (2) overt GVN action with covert U.S. support; and (3) overt joint GVN and U.S. action. The two categories involving overt activities were conceived of as possible future developments, contingent upon a Presidential decision that clearly had not been made.

2.   Different Approaches: Perceptions of the Strategic Problem in Southeast Asia

The differences in approach taken in the two planning efforts cannot be explanned simply by the obvious military and political division of labor. It is clear from documents of the period that there was considerable coordination between the two groups, with the JCS planners looking to State and ISA for political guidance and the latter group looking to the former for recommendations for appropriate military actions. During the early months of 1964, these are well illustrated in the different approaches taken to the problem of determining the extent and implications of the movement of men and supplies through Laos.

At the end of 1963 and early in 1964, there was general agreement among all Washington agencies that we lacked adequate information concerning the nature and magnitude of whatever movement of men and materiel was occurring along the Laotian infiltration routes. For example, citing the "lack of clarity" on the "role of external intrusion" in South Vietnam, Walt Rostow urged William Sullivan on the eve of his March visit to attempt to "come back from Saigon with as lucid and agreed a picture" as possible on the extent of the infiltration and its influence on the Viet Cong. A few days later, the Defense Intelligence Agency informed Secretary McNamara that "certain intelligence gaps" were "related primarily to the types and amounts of weapons and materiel coming into South Vietnam, [and] the number of Viet Cong personnel infiltrating into South Vietnam . . ." To alleviate this situation, the JCS favored such measures as ground probes into Laos by GVN reconnaissance teams and low-level reconnaissance flights over the trail areas by GVN and U.S. aircraft. The State Department, supported by OSD/ISA, opposed such operations as potentially damaging to our relations with the Laotian government.

In supporting its recommendations and in its comments on State-ISA proposals, the JCS argued that an integrated approach should be taken to the security of Southeast Asia, with our actions in Laos closely related to those taken on behalf of South Vietnam. They saw the key problem for all of Southeast Asia as the DRV's aggressive intent. As they stated, "the root of the problem is in North Vietnam and must be dealt with there." Moreover, they felt that reconnaissance operations into and over Laos were justified because they saw Laotian security as dependent on that of South Vietnam. "Laos," they argued, "would not be able to endure the establishment of a communist—or pseudo neutralist—state on its eastern flank." They criticized our "self-imposed restrictions" as tending to make the task in Vietnam "more complex, time-consuming, and in the end, more costly" and for possibly signalling "irresolution to our enemies." Accordingly, they implied that the United States should convince the Laotian Premier of the need to take direct action against the Viet Minh infiltration through low-level reconnaissance and other cross-border operations— but above all, to *carry out* these actions in order to impress the DRV with our resolve to deny its insurgents a sanctuary. In the specific context of recommending these kind of actions, they stated "that the time has come to lift the restrictions which limit the effectiveness of our military operations."

The State-ISA policy view also regarded Laos and Vietnam as parts of the overall Southeast Asian problem, but in early 1964 their conception of how U.S. objectives might be achieved extended beyond the need to thwart the communist guerrilla threat. In this view, policy success meant "bolstering the capability of all free countries in the area to resist communist encroachment." This required cooperating with the foreign governments of these countries and being careful not to erode their authority or contribute to their instability. Thus, instead of cross-border ground probes or low-level reconnaissance missions, which might prove politically embarrassing to the shaky regime of Laotian Premier Souvanna Phouma, the State-ISA view favored extending the mission of Laotian ground reconnaissance teams, which had been sponsored covertly by the CIA with the Premier's support. Moreover, this approach to policy included the view that, within the scope of broad regional policy goals, solutions to problems in individual countries should be tailored to the unique political context of each country. Insofar as Laos was concerned, this meant not only being sensitive to Souvanna Phouma's political status, but also adhering to the letter and spirit of the 1962 Geneva Accords, on which it was conceded the structure of a stable political future must be erected. In the State-ISA view, the only alternative to this approach would be an eventual large-scale deployment of U.S. ground forces to drive out the Pathet Lao/NVA forces.

The meaning of these different overall policy conceptions for the planning processes of April and early May 1964 was that the U.S. Government was faced with a dilemma—whether to take remedial military actions which might ease the short-term problems in South Vietnam or whether to dramatize our commitment to all of Southeast Asia with the long-term solution in mind. The dilemma was particularly complex because elements of one alternative were needed to enable progress toward the other. Specifically, three accomplishments were considered vital to our long-term objectives in Southeast Asia: (1) to convince Hanoi, whose direction of the insurgencies was certain, of our resolve to prevent the success of its aggressive policies; (2) to maintain the cooperation of Souvanna Phouma and the Laotian neutralist political structure (which also required the support of the Geneva members) and thereby preserve the framework of the 1962 Geneva Accords; and (3) to build a stable, effective political authority in South Vietnam. Vital to the third accomplishment was our major short-term objective—of permanently reversing the trends in the guerrilla war in South Vietnam. These, in turn, were believed to be sustained in their currently deteriorating direction by the infiltration of men and supplies from North

Vietnam. The possibility was recognized that determining the extent of this infiltration and eliminating it, if necessary, might be a decisive element in a solution of the short-term problem.

However, the short-term solution involved potential threats to the long-term policy elements: the most effective measures for obtaining the necessary intelligence involved actions likely to alienate Souvanna and damage the political structure in Laos. Yet, some of this same kind of intelligence would be important in convincing the Premier of the need to permit low-level reconnaissance flights and other kinds of operations. On the other hand, the impact of the infiltration on the war in South Vietnam was far from certain. For example, Ambassador Unger reported in December that the recent use of the Laotian corridor was not extensive enough to have influenced significantly the then intensive VC efforts in South Vietnam. Hence, if the desired military operations were undertaken without Souvanna's approval, and it was discovered that the infiltration was not really crucial to the war in the South, a long-term interest would have been compromised without receiving any real short-term advantage.

To further complicate the picture, direct strikes against North Vietnam were being advocated as a means to obtain both long and short-term goals. On the one hand, overt military actions had been recommended to convince the DRV of our resolve. On the other hand, they were proposed as a means to force Hanoi to stop the flow of material assistance to the South. Moreover, it was generally agreed within policy circles that such actions must be supported by public disclosures of the kind of convincing evidence of Hanoi's support for the VC that the Administration did not yet possess.

By the end of March, one aspect of policy puzzle had been resolved. On 17 March, Ambassador Lodge reported a long conversation between General Khanh and a Laotian representative, with Souvanna's permission, at which a working agreement between military forces of the two governments was obtained. Khanh and Phoumi Nousavan, Laotian rightist military commander, arranged to resume diplomatic relations between the two countries during that week and came to other more specific agreements as follows:

> 1. Laotians agreed to allow South Vietnam to have free passage in Southern Laos, to create a combined Laotian–Vietnamese staff to use all the bases including Tchepone, and to conduct bombardment with unmarked T–28 planes (in the areas where FAR (Phoumi's) forces were engaged).
> 2. The 10-kilometer limit on hot pursuit is abrogated; commando raids and sabotage can be undertaken without limit by combined Laotian and South Vietnamese units; South Vietnamese officers will serve the Laotian units to provide added leadership.

Previously, President Johnson had indicated approval of cross-border ground penetrations into Laos "along any lines which can be worked out between Khanh and Phoumi with Souvanna's endorsement." Although asking Secretaries Rusk and McNamara to develop a joint recommendation concerning U.S. participation in air strikes within Laos, the President went on to state a position consonant with that of the State-ISA view:

> My first thought is that it is important to seek support from Souvanna Phouma and to build a stronger case before we take action which might have only limited military effect and could trigger wider Communist action in Laos.

3. *Planning Overt Actions on Contingency Basis (April–May)*

The planning efforts of April and early May attempted to accommodate the remaining contradictory aspects of the policy dilemma. On the same day he signed NSAM 288 approving Secretary McNamara's visit report, the President sent the first of two closely spaced messages to Ambassador Lodge that could have set the tone for the planning ahead. (Presumably the President's views were communicated to the principal officials in the agencies involved in planning for Southeast Asia.) Commenting on Lodge's critique of the McNamara report, he indicated favor for the Ambassador's expressed preference for "carrot and stick" pressures short of overt military action, and specifically "reserve[d] judgment on overt U.S. measures against North Vietnam." Three days later he cabled confirmation that actions being studied with North Vietnam as a target were regarded strictly as contingency planning.

Principal focus for the planning during April was OSD/ISA, with assistance from the Far Eastern Bureau and the Vietnam Committee, in the Department of State, and from the JCS. During the first three weeks of April, it developed three or four versions of scenarios of political actions "to set the stage and to develop support both at home and abroad" for different categories of military action against North Vietnam. Initially, the categories, and their scenarios, were regarded separately, although the first "Covert SVN action against the North (with U.S. covert support)," was recognized as the stage of political-military activity in which the United States was currently engaged. The others, (1) covert U.S. support of overt GVN aerial mining and air strike operations and (2) overt joint U.S. and GVN aerial reconnaissance, naval displays, naval bombardments and air attacks, would necessarily have to follow. In subsequent versions, the planning evolved more explicitly toward a continuous scenario in three sequential phases.

In each version, however, the "current" scenario included such political measures as: (1) a speech by General Khanh stating GVN war aims; (2) a briefing for "friendly" senators and congressmen on our aims in Southeast Asia and the problem of DRV directions of the VC; (3) public explanations of U.S. policy toward South Vietnam; and (4) diplomatic discussions with the United Kingdom and the North Atlantic Council. Each of the second scenarios, which came to be characterized by GVN–USAF/FARMGATE air operations, contained similar actions but placed emphasis on political initiatives that would surface in Saigon rather than in Washington, "so as to maintain the credibility of the sovereignty of the GVN." This stage also included such measures as: (1) another trip to Saigon by Secretary McNamara for the specific purpose of obtaining General Khanh's agreement to begin overt GVN actions against the North; (2) consultations with Thailand and the Philippines; (3) Presidential consultations with key congressional leaders; and (4) public release of a new State Department White Paper on North Vietnamese involvement in the insurgency. Each of the final scenarios, which came to be associated with our overt responses to DRV/CHICOM escalations, included diplomatic and political preparations for direct U.S. actions. Significantly, the scenarios also incorporated initiatives leading to an international conference on Vietnam at Geneva.

The evolution toward a continuous sequential scenario reflects the influence of the JCS. Their response to the 31 March draft: (1) called for approximate time-phasing of the various steps in "the scenario"; (2) urged a fusion of the scenario with CINCPAC operational planning (OPLAN 37/64); and (3) attempted to incorporate Secretary McNamara's requested border control operations into the political actions recommended for the current time period. Moreover, the JCS developed a "political/military scenario" for graduated overt military pressure against North Vietnam, as called for in Secretary McNamara's Recommendation No. 12, 16 March 1964. Within this scenario the JCS included "expanded U.S. overt military pressures" against the DRV. In effect, they outlined a continually intensifying program of military pressures which increasingly involved U.S. military participation.

Complementing the thrust of JCS advice, the next draft, 8 April, removed current political actions from the list of political scenarios and treated them in a section entitled "Steps Which Should be Taken Now." The current scenarios included: (1) GVN/FARMGATE graduated overt military pressures against North Vietnam; (2) separate Laotian and Cambodian border control actions; (3) separate GVN retaliatory actions against North Vietnam; and (4) overt U.S. graduated military pressures against North Vietnam. The detailed scenario for the GVN/FARMGATE operations was reviewed by Mr. McNaughton with William Sullivan of the Department of State and Michael Forrestal of the White House staff. The scenario version resulting from this conference, contains the JCS-recommended time-phasing, in terms of D-Day minus X approximations. It also incorporates specific military actions recommended by the JCS submission. Apparently, only this scenario and the detailed description of "Steps Which Should be Taken Now" were circulated for comment by other agencies. Apparently, this draft provided the basis for scenario discussions held in Saigon among Secretary Rusk, Assistant Secretary William Bundy, CJCS Wheeler, Ambassador Lodge and certain military and civilian members of the Country Team on 19–20 April 1964.

A later version was prepared on 20 April and forwarded to the Chairman, Joint Chiefs of Staff, on 23 April. Significantly, it contained only three scenarios: I. "Uncommitting" steps which should be taken now; II. GVN/FARMGATE graduated overt pressures on DRV; III. Contingency Plan for U.S. overt response to DRV/CHICOM reactions. It also carried the following comment concerning their relationship:

> It should be noted that carrying out Scenario I does not necessarily commit the U.S. to commence Scenario II; and that Scenario II may be carried out without requiring resort to Scenario III. However, since Scenario II cannot be launched without our being prepared to carry out Scenario III, you should assume that it may be necessary for the D-Day of Scenario III to occur as soon as 10 days after the D-Day of Scenario II. Scenario III is a contingency plan of action which we would contemplate putting into effect only if the DRV's or Chicom's reaction to Scenario II was judged by the President to require overt U.S. response.

At the Saigon meeting, the concerns of the local officials for initiating some immediate measures to relieve the situation in South Vietnam came into conflict with the longer-range scenario approach. Ambassador Lodge "questioned the wisdom both of massive publicity and of massive destruction actions before a well-planned and well executed diplomatic attempt had been made to persuade NVM to call off the VC." He went on to propose communicating to Hanoi, through a third-country "interlocutor," our intent to embark on a "carrot and stick program," combining the threat of increasing air strikes with the granting of some assistance to the DRV. His supporting rationale explicitly cautioned that the VC reaction to large-scale measures against the North might be violent and damaging to the South Vietnamese economy. More significant may have been the fact that the "large-scale measures" proposed in the scenario came quite late in the second stage, a stage that may not have been entered—at least for some time.

What the Ambassador had in mind regarding a carrot and stick approach was not entirely new. It had first been proposed in his memorandum to Governor Harriman on 30 October 1963. It was raised again in cables to the White House on 20 February and 15 March 1964. Initially proposed in the context of a scheme to encourage the neutrality of North Vietnam, the carrot and stick concept envisioned a secret contract with Hanoi at which an ultimatum would be delivered demanding the DRV's cessation of support for the VC insurgency. Rewards for compliance would include our making available food imports, to help alleviate the known shortages affecting North Vietnam in late 1963 (and early '64). In the case of non-compliance, we would undertake previously threatened punitive strikes to which we would not admit publicly. What was new in the proposal of 19 April were: (1) the suggestion for using a third country intermediary and (2) that one element of the "carrot" might be our pledge to withdraw some U.S. personnel from South Vietnam. The latter suggestion was criticized by William Bundy on the basis that we didn't yet know how many and what types of American military personnel were needed in South Vietnam. Lodge countered with the comment that "it would be very hard indeed for Ho Chi Minh to provide a salable package for his own people and for other communist nations unless we can do something that Hanoi can point to, even though it would not be a real concession on our part."

The ensuing discussion, on a variety of points, provided an indication of some of Secretary Rusk's paramount concerns, which may shed important light on later policy decisions. For example, he sought opinions on the likely GVN reaction to a Geneva Conference specifically for Laos. In another context, he stated "his concern that the extent of infiltration and other provisions of support from the North be proven to the satisfaction of our own public, of our allies, and of the neutralists." During a discussion of the availability of other Asian troops to fight in Vietnam, Secretary Rusk stated "that we are not going to take on the masses of Red China with our limited manpower in a conventional war." He also stated the opinion that the Chinese would not opt to intervene militarily unless they felt they could count on Soviet support and that we could bring great economic pressure to bear on the Chinese through our allies. While expressing the opinion that Hanoi's renunciation of the Viet Cong would "take the heart out of the insurgency," he indicated doubt that elimination of North Vietnam's industrial targets would have much of an adverse impact on it. Moreover, the Secretary acknowledged the possibility that such an act "would have forfeited the 'hostage' which we hold in the North . . . without markedly affecting the fight against the Viet Cong, at least in the short run."

The major immediate outcome of the meeting was a decision to go ahead with the suggestion to arrange for the visit of a third country interlocutor to Hanoi. On 30 April, Secretary Rusk visited Ottawa and obtained an agreement from the Canadian Government to include such a mission among the instructions for its new I.C.C. representative. According to the agreement, the new official, J. Blair Seaborn, would: (1) try to determine Ho's attitude toward Chinese support, whether or not he feels over-extended, and his aims in South Vietnam; (2) stress U.S. determination to see its objectives in South Vietnam achieved; (3) emphasize the limits of U.S. aims in Southeast Asia and that it wanted no permanent bases or installations there; and (4) convey U.S. willingness to assist North Vietnam with its economic problems. Other results of the Saigon meeting consisted of a variety of actions recommended by Secretary Rusk. Of these, only four were related to the issue of military pressures against North Vietnam. These were recommendations to (1) engage "more flags" in efforts directly supporting the GVN; (2) deploy a carrier task force to establish a permanent U.S. naval presence at Cam Ranh Bay; (3) initiate anti-junk operations that would "inch northward" along the Vietnam coast; and (4) enlist SEATO countries in an effort to isolate the DRV from economic or cultural relations with the Free World.

4.   Conflict of Short and Long Term Views: Caution Prevails

During the last week of April and the early weeks of May, the contention between those urging prompt measures and those counseling a deliberate, cautious pacing of our actions continued. For example, Walt Rostow urged Secretary Rusk to consider how difficult it would be to make a credible case in support of actions to force Hanoi's adherence to the Geneva Accords if political deterioration took place in Laos and South Vietnam. Predicting such an eventuality in the coming months, he implied that the necessary actions should be taken soon. Similarly, Ambassador Lodge continued to advocate prompt implementation of his carrot and stick approach including, if VC provocations warranted, a well-timed reprisal just prior to Commissioner Seaborn's arrival in Hanoi. These views were communicated to Secretary McNamara and William Sullivan during their visit to Saigon, 12–13 May, and confirmed in a cable to the President three days later.

The JCS commented on the final version of the State-ISA political-military scenarios and criticized them for not including the more immediate actions requested in NSAM 288: namely, border control and retaliatory operations. Making a distinction between border operations already arranged for (Recommendation 11) and those intended by Recommendation 12, they advocated incorporating in the second-stage scenario retaliatory operations and overt military pressures against North Vietnam. They also urged including border control operations of battalion-size or larger, low-level reconnaissance by U.S. aircraft, and VNAF air operations in Laos that include strikes on bridges and armed route reconnaissance. In justifying such actions, they stated:

> . . . military operations against the DRV to help stabilize the situation in the Republic of Vietnam, and other operations planned to help stabilize the situation in Laos, involve the attack of the same target systems and to a considerable extent the same targets. Assistance in the achievement of the objective in the Republic of Vietnam through operations against NVN could likewise have a similar result in Laos, offering the possibility of a favorable long-term solution to the insurgency problem in Southeast Asia.

However, the deliberate, cautious approach continued to hold sway. Secretary McNamara's trip to Saigon, called for early in the second-stage scenario as a means to obtain General Khanh's agreement to initiate overt operations against the North, did not include this purpose. On the contrary, a week prior to the visit General Khanh had raised with Ambassador Lodge the issue of putting his country on a fully mobilized war footing—accompanying it with a declaration that further interference by Hanoi in South Vietnamese affairs would bring reprisals—and Secretary McNamara was instructed to impress upon

Khanh that such drastic measures and threatening gestures were unnecessary at the moment. More important, it was stressed that the GVN "systematically and aggressively demonstrate to the world that the subversion of the South is directed from Hanoi," through sending "capable ambassadors to the important capitals of the world to convince governments of this fact." Moreover, while assuring General Khanh that our commitment to his country and Laos "does not rule out the use of force . . . against North Vietnam," the Secretary was advised to remind him that "such actions must be supplementary to and not a substitute for successful counterinsurgency in the South"—and that "we do not intend to provide military support nor undertake the military objective of 'rolling back' communist control in North Vietnam."

D. DEALING WITH THE LAOTIAN CRISIS

1. Laos in Danger: "Pressure Planning"

In mid-May 1964, a new factor entered the policy-shaping process—a factor which cast a shadow of crisis management over the entire decision making environment. On 17 May, pro-communist forces in Laos began an offensive which led to their control of a significant portion of the Plaine des Jarres. On the 21st, the United States obtained Souvanna Phouma's permission to conduct low-level reconaissance operations over the occupied areas. For several weeks the offensive threatened to destroy the security of the neutralist-rightist position—and with it the political underpinning of U.S.–Laotian policy. These developments lent a greater sense of urgency to the arguments of those advisers favoring prompt measures to strengthen the U.S. position in Southeast Asia.

The most avid of those urging prompt action were the JCS. On 19 May they had recommended a new, more intensive series of covert operations for the four-month Phase II under OPLAN 34–A. [Doc. 161] On the 23rd, referring to their earlier recommendations to incorporate larger border contol and retaliatoy operations and overt graduated pressures in the next-phase scenario, they expressed opinions on the urgency of preparing for such actions. Particular emphasis was placed on the need to consult with the GVN so that the necessary training and joint operational preparations could take place. The JCS prodded State with the comment, "The Department of State should take the lead on this but as yet has not," at the same time recalling that the operations in question had been provided for under the approved CINCPAC OPLAN 37–64 (17 April 1964). In another plea for prompt implementation, they argued that since these operations were to be plausibly deniable by the United States, "efforts to create the necessary climate of opinion should not be, of necessity, too time consuming."

Figuring prominently in the retaliatory operations and the graduated pressures advocated by the JCS against North Vietnam were air strikes—some by the VNAF alone and some in cooperation with USAF/FARMGATE and other U.S. air units. What they thought these kinds of operations could accomplish varied according to the targets struck and the composition of the attacking force. Assuming an air campaign ordered for the purpose of: (1) causing the DRV to stop supporting the Viet Cong and Pathet Lao and (2) reducing its capability to renew such support, the JCS perceived the following categories of accomplishment: *Category A*—They believed that undertaking "armed reconnaissance along highways leading to Laos," striking "airfields identified with supporting" the insurgents, and destroying "supply and ammunition depots, petroleum storage and military (installations) connected with PL/VC support" would result in "a *reduction of DRV support.*" *Category B*—They believed that striking the "remaining airfields," destroying "important railroad and highway bridges" and "depots in northern NVN," conducting aerial mining operations, and bombing "petroleum storage in Hanoi and Haiphong" would result in a reduced "DRV military capability to take action against Laos and the RVN." *Category C*—They cited the remaining capability for effectively destroying the North Vietnamese industrial base.

In the same appraisal, the JCS went on to estimate the time required to achieve 85% damage against the various target categories, using different force combinations in continuous operations. For Category A, they estimated, it would take the VNAF alone more than seven months, *if* they could sustain combat operations that long; the VNAF plus FARMGATE B–57's would require over two months. By using, in addition, U.S. land and carrier-based air units readily available in the Western Pacific, they claimed that targets in Category A could be eliminated in only twelve days; those in all categories could be destroyed in 46 days. They added that sustaining this destruction on LOC targets would require restrikes "conducted for an indeterminate period."

The JCS were not the only Presidential advisers to sense the urgency created by the situation in Laos. Referring to "recent steps with regard to bombing operations in Laos and reconnaissance which step up the pace," Secretary Rusk cabled Ambassador Lodge to seek suggestions for ways to achieve greater solidarity in South Vietnam. He explained that in Washington, the fragility of the situation in South Vietnam was seen as an obstacle to further U.S. military involvement in Southeast Asia. As he stated, "We need to assure the President that everything humanly possible is being done both in Washington and by the government of Vietnam to provide a solid base of determination from which far-reaching decisions could proceed." Lodge's reply reflected a new wrinkle in his usual proposals for prompt, but carefully masked actions. He expressed the attitude that some kind of firm action against North Vietnam by U.S. and South Vietnamese forces was the only way to bring about a significant improvement in the GVN effort. This view complemented an apparently growing belief among Presidential advisers "that additional efforts within South Vietnam by the U.S. will not prevent further deterioration there."

This belief, together with the threat presented by the Pathet Lao offensive, led to a resumption of scenario development. However, in the new "crisis management" atmosphere, several new elements affected the process. One was the fact that the latest scenario was prepared as a draft memorandum for the President. Another was the expectation that it would be presented to and discussed among the principal officials of the participating agencies, serving as an Executive Committee of the National Security Council. And finally, the crisis in Laos apparently had focused advisory interest primarily on one stage—that dealing with overt operations against North Vietnam. The scenario no longer contained a section devoted to "uncommitting steps which should be taken now." The rationale behind this shift of emphasis was explained to Ambassador Lodge, an outspoken critic of both the overt approach and the scenario, by Secretary Rusk:

> It is our present view here that [substantial initial attacks without acknowledgment] would simply not be feasible. Even if Hanoi itself did not publicize them, there are enough ICC and other observers in North Viet-

nam who might pick them up and there is also the major possibility of leakage at the South Vietnam end. Thus, publicity seems almost inevitable to us here for any attack that did significant damage.

2. *A New Scenario: 30 Days of Sequential Politico-Military Action*

On the same day that the JCS urged that the GVN be consulted regarding preparations for border control and retaliatory operations, the new scenario of political and military actions was completed. The scenario called for a 30-day sequence of military and political pressures coupled with initiatives to enter negotiations with Hanoi (see Table 1). Military actions would not start until after "favorable action on a U.S. Congressional Joint Resolution" supporting U.S. resistance to DRV aggressions in Southeast Asia. Initially, the strikes would be carried out by GVN aircraft, but as they progressed, USAF/FARMGATE and other U.S. air units would join in. These "would continue despite negotiations, until there was clear evidence that North Vietnam had stopped its subversion of the South." The negotiating objectives would be to obtain both agreement and evidence that (1) "terrorism, armed attacks, and armed resistance stop" and (2) "communications on the networks out of the North are conducted entirely in uncoded form."

Presented along with the scenario were assessments of likely communist reactions and the possible U.S. responses to these moves. The most likely military reactions to the scenario actions were seen as expanded insurgency operations, including possible "sizeable infiltration" of North Vietnamese ground forces, and a drive toward the Mekong by Pathet Lao and North Vietnamese forces. The Soviet Union was expected to intensify its diplomatic opposition to U.S. policies and China was expected to (1) augment North Vietnamese air defense capabilities, and (2) successfully dissuade Hanoi from any willingness (particularly after U.S. air operations began) to reduce its support of the Viet Cong. To counter communist reactions, the proposal specified in each contingency that intensified operations against North Vietnam would be the most effective option. In response to intensified insurgency, considered the least intense (though most likely) alternative available to the communist powers, the proposal included provision for augmenting South Vietnamese forces "by U.S. ground forces prepositioned in South Vietnam or on board ship nearby."

The May 23, 1964 scenario read as follows: (Table 1)

1. Stall off any "conference on [Laos or] Vietnam until D-Day."
2. Intermediary (Canadian?) tell North Vietnam in general terms that U.S. does not want to destroy the North Vietnam regime (and indeed is willing "to provide a carrot"), but is determined to protect South Vietnam from North Vietnam.
3. (D–30) Presidential speech in general terms launching Joint Resolution.
4. (D–20) Obtain Joint Resolution approving past actions and authorizing whatever is necessary with respect to Vietnam.
    Concurrently: An effort should be made to strengthen the posture in South Vietnam. Integrating (interlarding in a single chain of command) the South Vietnamese and U.S. military and civilian elements critical to pacification, down at least to the district level, might be undertaken.
5. (D–16) Direct CINCPAC to take all prepositioning and logistic actions that can be taken "quietly" for the D-Day forces and the forces described in Paragraph 17 below.

6. (D–15) Get Khanh's agreement to start overt South Vietnamese air attacks against targets in the North (see D-Day item 15 below), and inform him of U.S. guarantee to protect South Vietnam in the event of North Vietnamese and/or Chinese retaliation.

7. (D–14) Consult with Thailand and the Philippines to get permission for U.S. deployments; and consult with them plus U.K., Australia, New Zealand and *Pakistan,* asking for their open political support for the undertaking and for their participation in the re-enforcing action to be undertaken in anticipation of North Vietnamese and/or Chinese retaliation.

8. (D–13) Release an expanded "Jordan Report," including recent photography and evidence of the communications nets, giving full documentation of North Vietnamese supply and direction of the Viet Cong.

9. (D–12) Direct CINCPAC to begin moving forces and making specific plans on the assumption that strikes will be made on D-Day (see Attachment B* in backup materials for deployments).

10. (D–10) Khanh makes speech demanding that North Vietnam stop aggression, threatening unspecified military action if he does not. (He could refer to a "carrot.")

11. (D–3) Discussions with Allies not covered in Item 7 above.

12. (D–3) President informs U.S. public (and thereby North Vietnam) that action may come, referring to Khanh speech (Item 10 above) and declaring support for South Vietnam.

13. (D–1) Khanh announces that all efforts have failed and that attacks are imminent. (Again he refers to limited goal and possibly to "carrot.")

14. (D–Day) Remove U.S. dependents.

15. (D–Day) Launch first strikes (see Attachment C** for targets). Initially, mine their ports and strike North Vietnam's transport and related ability (bridges, trains) to move South; and then against targets which have maximum psychological effect on the North's willingness to stop insurgency—POL storage, selected airfields, barracks/training areas, bridges, railroad yards, port facilities, communications, and industries. Initially, these strikes would be by South Vietnamese aircraft; they could then be expanded by adding FARMGATE, or U.S. aircraft, or any combination of them.

16. (D–Day) Call for conference on Vietnam (and go to UN). State the limited objective: Not to overthrow the North Vietnam regime nor to destroy the country, but to stop DRV-directed Viet Cong terrorism and resistance to pacification efforts in the South. Essential that it be made clear that attacks on the North will continue (*i.e.,* no cease-fire) until (a) terrorism, armed attacks, and armed resistance to pacification efforts in the South stop, and (b) communications on the networks out of the North are conducted entirely in uncoded form."

The scenario was circulated among members of the ExCom and discussed during their meetings of 24 and 25 May. Apparently, modifications were made in the course of these meetings, as notations in the SecDef files indicate scenario versions of 24, 25 and 26 May. In addition to the assessments that accompanied the scenario proposal, the discussants had available to them an estimate of likely consequences of the proposed actions, prepared by the Board of National Estimates, CIA, with State and DIA assistance, and concurred in by the U.S. Intelligence Board.

The national estimate agreed essentially with the proposal's assessment of

Soviet and Chinese reactions and concluded that Hanoi's would vary with the intensity of the U.S./GVN actions. The national intelligence boards believed that Hanoi "would order the Viet Cong and Pathet Lao to refrain from dramatic new attacks, and might reduce the level of the insurrections for the moment" in response to U.S. force deployments or GVN-USAF/FARMGATE attacks. The expected DRV rationale, supported by Peking and Moscow, would be to bank on "a new Geneva Conference or UN action . . . [to] bring a cessation of attacks" and to stabilize communist gains in Vietnam and Laos. Communist agitation of world opinion would be employed to bring on the conference. If attacks on North Vietnam continued, the intelligence boards saw Hanoi intensifying its political initiatives, but also possibly increasing "the tempo of the insurrections in South Vietnam and Laos." If these tactics failed to produce a settlement "and North Vietnam began to suffer considerable destruction," the boards estimated:

> We incline to the view that [DRV leaders] would lower their terms for a negotiating outcome; they would do so in the interests of preserving their regime and in the expectation of being able to renew the insurrections in South Vietnam and Laos at a later date. There would nevertheless be a significant danger that they would fight, believing that the U.S. would still not be willing to undertake a major ground war, or that if it was, it could ultimately be defeated by the methods which were successful against the French.

In its discussion of the problem of compelling Hanoi to halt the VC insurgency, the national estimate emphasized that this depended on affecting the *will* of the DRV leaders. It stressed that the measures called for in the scenario "would not seriously affect communist *capabilities* to continue that insurrection," stating that "the primary sources of communist strength in South Vietnam are indigenous." On the other hand, it predicted that withdrawal of material assistance from North Vietnam would badly hurt the Pathet Lao capability. Because of the crucial importance of Hanoi's *will,* the estimate argued that the DRV "must understand that although the U.S. is not seeking the destruction of the DRV regime, the U.S. is fully prepared to bring ascending pressures to bear to persuade Hanoi to reduce the insurrections." But, while comprehending U.S. purposes in the early phase of the scenario actions, they may "tend increasingly to doubt the limited character of U.S. aims" as the scale of the attacks increases. The report adds:

> Similarly, the retaliatory measures which Hanoi might take in Laos and South Vietnam might make it increasingly difficult for the U.S. to regard its objectives as attainable by limited means. Thus difficulties of comprehension might increase on *both* sides as the scale of action mounted.

3.   *Rejection of Scenario: "Use Force If Necessary"*

At its meeting on 25 May, the ExCom apparently decided not to retain the scenario approach in the courses of action it would recommend to the President. At least, it abandoned the time-phasing aspects of the series of actions contained in the scenario proposal, and it made explicit its purpose not to embark on a series of moves "aimed at the use of force as an end in itself." The available evidence is far from conclusive on the reasons why the scenario approach was cast aside, but it seems clear that the potential for entering into an escalating conflict in which our limited objectives might become obscured weighed heavily in the decision.

In addition to the evidence already cited, a strong indication of the ExCom's desire to avoid the possibility of escalation is contained in the draft memorandum prepared for President Johnson, as a result of the 25 May meeting. In this memorandum, it was recommended that the President decide:

> . . . that the U.S. will use selected and carefully graduated military force against North Vietnam, under the following conditions: (1) after appropriate diplomatic and political warning and preparation, (2) and unless such warning and preparation—in combination with other efforts— should produce a sufficient improvement of non-Communist prospects in South Vietnam and in Laos to make military action against North Vietnam unnecessary.

The recommendation was based on an explicit assumption "that a decision to use force if necessary, backed by resolute and extensive deployment, and conveyed by every possible means to our adversaries, gives the best present chance of avoiding the actual use of such force." Reflecting the influence of the national intelligence boards' rationale concerning "U.S. preparatory and low-scale action," the ExCom also stated the belief that "selective and carefully prepared military action against North Vietnam will not trigger acts of terror and military operations by the Viet Cong which would engulf the Khanh regime." What the ExCom meant by "selective and carefully prepared military actions" is suggested by its request, on the same day, for JCS views on the feasibility of telegraphing intended action through military deployments.

Despite its abandonment of the paced scenario approach, the ExCom proposed that many of the actions incorporated in the scenario be undertaken. Although proposing a particular order for these actions, the committee suggested that the sequence may need to be modified in reaction to specific developments, especially in view of different choices available to the enemy. In addition to the Presidential decision, the recommended actions included: (1) communication of our resolve and limited objectives to Hanoi through the Canadian intermediary; (2) conducting a high-level Southeast Asian strategy conference in Honolulu; (3) diplomatic initiatives at the UN to present the case for DRV aggression; (4) formal and bilateral consultation with SEATO allies, including the question of obtaining allied force commitments; (5) seeking a Congressional Resolution in support of U.S. resistance to communist aggression in Southeast Asia; (6) periodic force deployments toward the region; and (7) an initial strike against North Vietnam, "designed to have more deterrent than destructive impact" and accompanied by an active diplomatic offensive to restore peace in the area—including agreement to a Geneva Conference. Further, the ExCom recommended that in the execution of these actions, all functional and geographic elements "should be treated as parts of a single problem: the protection of [all] Southeast Asia from further communist encroachment."

If all of the decisions and actions contained in the draft memorandum were in fact recommended to the President, all of them were not approved immediately. It is doubtful that the President made the decision to use force if necessary, since some advisers were still urging the same kind of decision on him in the weeks to follow. The plan to convey a message to Hanoi by Canadian channels was carried out on June 18, but it may have been decided on already before the meeting, given the earlier negotiations with Ottawa. The President did approve the calling of a conference in Honolulu "to review for [his] final approval a series of plans for effective action" in Southeast Asia. U.S. policy toward Southeast Asia was explained by Ambassador Stevenson in a major UN speech on 21 May. He did not address the Security Council on this subject again until 6 August, after the Tonkin Gulf episode. It is doubtful if less publicized statements at the UN contained the "hitherto secret evidence" suggested in the ExCom sessions as "proving Hanoi's responsibility" before the world diplomats. It is likely that questions of consulting with SEATO allies, deploying additional forces to Southeast Asia, and requesting a congressional resolution were held in abeyance pending that meeting.

One of the kinds of developments which the ExCom thought would necessitate a flexible approach to its proposed action sequence occurred prior to the Honolulu meeting. Its effect was to remove some of the "crisis management" pressure from further policy deliberations. On 27 May, the Polish Government proposed a conference format for Laos that avoided many of the undesirable features of the Geneva proposals which had been supported by communist governments in the past. After two days of deliberations, during which time Secretary Rusk departed for Nehru's funeral in New Delhi, a policy group composed of several ExCom members determined that the United States should attempt initially "to treat [the] Lao question separately from [the] SVN–NVN problem." Reasoning that "if [a] satisfactory Lao solution [were] not achieved, [a] basis should have been laid for possible subsequent actions that would permit our dealing more effectively with NVN with respect [to] both SVN and Laos," the group decided to recommend to the President that he accept the Polish proposal. Integral to the approach would be a "clear expression of U.S. determination . . . that U.S. [is] not willing [to] write off Laos to [the] communists," and assurances to Souvanna Phouma "that we would be prepared to give him prompt and direct military support if the Polish Conference was [sic] not successful." With respect to our larger objectives in Southeast Asia, the proposed discussions among representatives of Laos, the I.C.C. and the Geneva co-chairmen would have the advantage of permitting Souvanna to continue to insist upon his preconditions for any resumed 14-nation conference, and would avoid the issue of Vietnam.

E. THE QUESTION OF PRESSURES AGAINST THE NORTH

With the policy line and the courses of action for dealing with Laos determined, and with the Laotian military situation having become somewhat stabilized, the Administration turned to the broader issues of its Southeast Asian policy. These were among the principal concerns of the Honolulu Conference, 1–2 June 1964.

1. The Honolulu Conference: Defining the U.S. Commitment

The Honolulu Conference was approached with the realization that the "gravest decisions are in front of us and other governments about [the] free world's interest in and commitment to [the] security of Southeast Asia." The State Department saw such decisions focusing on three "central questions": (1) Is the security of Southeast Asia vital to the United States and the Free World? (2) Are additional steps which carry risks of escalation necessary? (3) Will the additional steps accomplish our goals of stopping intrusions of Hanoi and Peking into South Vietnam? The Conference apparently began with the answer to the first question as a basic assumption. Again State:

Our point of departure is and must be that we cannot accept [the] over-running of Southeast Asia by Hanoi and Peiping.

In addition to considering specific proposals for improving conditions in South Vietnam (Administration officials entered the Conference with another assumption that "we must do everything in our power to stiffen and strengthen the situation in South Vietnam"), the discussions in Honolulu were intended to help clarify issues with respect to exerting pressures against North Vietnam.

2.   *At Honolulu: Exerting Pressure on NVN*

In preparation for the conference, CINCPAC and COMUSMACV had been asked by JCS Chairman Taylor to develop their views on such questions as:

(1) What military actions might be taken in ascending order of gravity to impress Hanoi with our intention to strike NVN?

(2) What should be the purpose and pattern of the initial air strikes against NVN?

(3) What is your concept of the actions and reactions which may arise from the progressive implementation of CINCPAC 37-64 and 32-64? How may NVN and Communist China respond to our escalating pressures?

(4) If at some point Hanoi agrees to desist from further help to VC & PL, how can we verify fulfillment? How long should we be prepared to maintain our readiness posture while awaiting verification?

(5) What help should be sought from SEATO nations in relation to the situation (a) in Laos? (b) in SVN?

Just prior to the conference, the JCS also submitted their views, to which General Taylor did not subscribe. Expressing concern over "a lack of definition" of U.S. objectives, the JCS asserted that it was "their first obligation to define a militarily valid objective for Southeast Asia and then advocate a desirable military course of action to achieve that objective." With its basis identified as "military considerations," they then made the recommendation that:

. . . the United States should seek through military actions to accomplish destruction of the North Vietnamese will and capabilities as necessary to compel the Democratic Government of Vietnam (DRV) to cease providing support to the insurgencies in South Vietnam and Laos. Only a course of action geared to this objective can assure that the North Vietnamese support of the subversive efforts in Laos and South Vietnam will terminate.

However, the JCS went on to note that "some current thinking appears to dismiss the objective in favor of a lesser objective, one visualizing limited military action which, hopefully, would cause the North Vietnamese to decide to terminate their subversive support . . ." Drawing a distinction between destroying DRV capability to support the insurgencies and "an enforced changing of policy . . . which, if achieved, may well be temporary," they stated their opinion that "this lesser objective" was inadequate for the current situation. They agreed, however, to undertake a course of action to achieve this lesser objective as an "initial measure."

What the JCS proposed as this "initial measure" were a pair of sustained attacks to destroy target complexes directly associated with support of the communist efforts in Laos and South Vietnam. Military installations at Vinh, which served as a major resupply facility for transshipping war materiel into Laos, and a similar facility at Dien Bien Phu were recommended. In support of these operations, which would require U.S. participation to achieve "timely destruction" as necessary to achieve the objectives, the JCS stated a need to demonstrate forcefully that our pattern of responses to Hanoi's aggression had changed. They argued:

> We should not waste critical time and more resources in another protracted series of "messages," but rather we should take positive, prompt, and meaningful military action to underscore our meaning that after more than two years of tolerating this North Vietnamese support we are now determined that it will stop.

Aside from the JCS, whose views were not shared by their spokesman at Honolulu, the main voices in support of the idea of attacking the North in early June 1964 seemed to come from Saigon. But this source of advocacy seemed to anticipate short-term impacts on South Vietnam, rather than ultimate effects on the DRV. On the way to Honolulu, Secretary Rusk had talked with General Khanh, who argued that South Vietnam could not win against the Viet Cong without some military action outside its borders. In particular, the General urged clearing out the communist forces in eastern Laos, who might move across the border and attempt to cut South Vietnam in two, with the implication that GVN forces could carry out the task if given air support. He also favored attacks directly on North Vietnam, but said that they "should be selective and designed to minimize the chances of a drastic communist response."

At the conference's initial plenary session, Ambassador Lodge also argued in favor of attacks on the North. In answer to Secretary Rusk's query about South Vietnamese popular attitudes, which supported Hanoi's revolutionary aims, the Ambassador stated his conviction that most support for the VC would fade as soon as some "counter-terrorism measures" were begun against the DRV. He urged "a selective bombing campaign against military targets in the North" and predicted this would "bolster morale and give the population in the South a feeling of unity." When asked by Mr. McCone how the political differences among Vietnamese leaders might be overcome, he stated the opinion that "if we bombed Tchepone or attacked the [NVN motor torpedo] boats and the Vietnamese people knew about it, this would tend to stimulate their morale, unify their efforts and reduce [their] quarreling."

If other comments, either pro or con, were made at the plenary session about the desirability of attacking North Vietnam, they were not reflected in the record. General Westmoreland discussed the "military and security situation" in South Vietnam and apparently did not mention the potential impact of measures against the North. Similar discussions of the military situations in Laos and Cambodia apparently did not include the subject either. The discussion of North Vietnam, as indicated by the record, was limited to assessments of the DRV's military capabilities, particularly its air defenses, and their implications for the feasibility of an air attack. Policy aspects of air operations against the North were not mentioned.

On the second day of the conference, possible pressures to be applied against North Vietnam were a prominent subject. However, as reported by William

Bundy, the main context for the discussion was Laos—what might have to be done in the event the current diplomatic track failed or the military situation deteriorated. Not contemplated, it seems, were initiatives against the North to relieve the current levels of pressure on Laos or South Vietnam. Rather, considerable attention was given to preliminary steps that would need to be taken in order to prepare for actions necessary within the context of a Laotian military contingency.

One such step would be consultation with allies who might contribute to a ground force contingent needed for the defense of Laos. The UK and other SEATO nations were cited as particularly important contributors. The conferees agreed, however, that contingency preparations for Laos should be undertaken outside the SEATO framework. As Secretary Rusk pointed out, "Souvanna Phouma might well call on individual SEATO nations for help, but was less likely to call on SEATO as an organization." Besides, the French and Pakistani were expected to be obstructive and the Philippines Government was regarded as presenting a constant threat of untimely leaks. Consensus was reached that the starting point for our bilateral consultations should be Thailand, since that government's confidence in the sincerity of the U.S. commitment seemed particularly needful of being shored up. At the meeting, Ambassador Martin echoed the themes which he had reported earlier in cables—that the Thais were not convinced that we meant to stop the course in Southeast Asia and probably would not participate in or permit allied troop build-ups in their country without firmer assurances than had been given in the past.

Another preliminary step discussed by the conferees was the desirability of obtaining a Congressional resolution prior to wider U.S. action in Southeast Asia. Ambassador Lodge questioned the need for it if we were to confine our actions to "tit-for-tat" air attacks against North Vietnam. However, Secretaries McNamara and Rusk and CIA Director McCone all argued in favor of the resolution. In support, McNamara pointed to the need to guarantee South Vietnam's defense against retaliatory air attacks and against more drastic reactions by North Vietnam and Communist China. He "added that it might be necessary, as the action unfolded . . . to deploy as many as seven divisions." Rusk noted that some of the military requirements might involve the calling up of reserves, always a touchy Congressional issue. He also stated that public opinion on our Southeast Asian policy was badly divided in the United States at the moment and that, therefore, the President needed an affirmation of support.

Next, the discussion turned to present estimates of communist reaction to attacks on North Vietnam:

> General Taylor summarized the present Washington view, to the effect that there would certainly be stepped-up Viet Cong activity in South Vietnam, Communist Chinese air might be sent to North Vietnam, Hanoi itself might send some ground forces south (though probably only on a limited scale), and there was the final possibility that the Communist Chinese would respond with significant military action. As to the last, he made clear that he did not visualize a "yellow horde" of Chinese pouring into Southeast Asia, and that air interdiction could have a significant effect in reducing the number of forces the Communist Chinese could send down and support . . . In any case, he said that the military judgment was that seven ground divisions would be needed if the Communist Chinese employed their full capabilities in the dry season, and five divisions even in the wet season. The needed five–seven divisions could come in part from

the Thai and others, but a major share would have to be borne by the U.S.

Secretary McNamara said that before we undertook attacks against the North, we certainly had to be prepared to meet threats at the level stated by General Taylor. Mr. McCone agreed with this point, but when on to say that there was a serious question about the effect of major deployments on Communist Chinese reactions. The intelligence community was inclined to the view that the more substantial the deployment, the greater the possible chance of a drastic Communist Chinese reaction. General Taylor commented that under present plans it was not contemplated that we should have deployment of all the potentially necessary forces at the outset. We were thinking along the lines of a brigade to the northern part of South Vietnam, two to three brigades to Thailand, considerable naval deployments, and some alerting of other forces in the U.S. and elsewhere. Even this, however, added up to a significant scale of activity . . .

Secretary McNamara noted that all this planning was on the basis that a really drastic communist reaction was possible, and was not based on any judgment that it was probable. The best current view was that appropriately limited attacks on the North would *not* bring in Communist Chinese air or North Vietnam or Communist Chinese ground forces. However, it was still essential that we be prepared against these eventualities.

Ambassador Lodge asked whether the Communist Chinese could not in fact mount almost any number of forces they chose. General Taylor and Admiral Felt said they could not do so and support them to the extent required . . . Secretary McNamara then went on to say that the possibility of major ground action also led to a serious question of having to use nuclear weapons at some point. Admiral Felt responded emphatically that there was no possible way to hold off the communists on the ground without the use of tactical nuclear weapons, and that it was essential that the commanders be given the freedom to use these as had been assumed under the various plans. He said that without nuclear weapons the ground force requirement was and had always been completely out of reach. General Taylor was more doubtful as to the existence or at least to the degree of the nuclear weapon requirement, and again the point was not really followed up.

Secretary Rusk said that another possibility we must consider would be the Soviets stirring up trouble elsewhere. We should do everything we could to minimize this risk, but it too must be considered. He went on to stress the nuclear question, noting that in the last ten years this had come to include the possibility of a nuclear exchange, with all that this involved.

General Taylor noted that there was a danger of reasoning ourselves into inaction. From a military point of view, he said that the U.S. could function in Southeast Asia about as well as anywhere in the world except Cuba. Mr. McCone made the point that the passage of the Congressional resolution would in itself be an enormous deterrent. This led to brief discussion of the text of the resolution, which was read by Mr. Sullivan . . .

Discussion then shifted to what the Viet Cong could do in South Vietnam if we struck the North. General Westmoreland thought there was not a significant unused Viet Cong capability, but Ambassador Lodge thought there was a major capability for terrorism and even for military action against Saigon, and that in sum the Viet Cong 'could make Saigon uninhabitable.'

Finally, the conferees dealt with the crucial question of how soon the United States and the GVN would be prepared to engage in wider military actions should the need arise. For several reasons, the consensus seemed to be that such actions should be delayed for some time yet. "Secretary Rusk thought we should not be considering quick action unless the Pathet Lao lunged toward the Mekong." Discussion yielded several things we could do in the interim to strengthen the current government position in Laos (*i.e.*, re-equip Kong Le's neutralist forces as an aid to Phouma's FAR; back Souvanna's demand for pre-conditions before any reconvening of the Geneva Conference; support the RLAF T–28 operations). General Taylor pointed to the prior need to educate the American public regarding U.S. interests in Southeast Asia. Secretary McNamara thought this would require at least 30 days.

Generals Taylor and Westmoreland then listed a number of military factors that affected the question of timing, although stating that these referred to "an optimum military posture":

1. The additional Vietnamese aircraft would not be available until July for two squadrons and September for another. However, B–57's could be introduced at any time and operated on a FARMGATE basis.
2. There were logistic factors, shipping requirements, and the call-up of some logistic reserve units involved in having five–seven divisions ready for action, and these would take two months to be sorted out properly.
3. It was desirable if not essential to build up military manpower in South Vietnam. He would like to be in a position to have 12 battalions that could be freed for deployment along the Laos border.
4. The rainy season was a factor precluding any substantial offensive in the panhandle area until mid-November.

They added that General Khanh's political base was not as strong as we wished and that it might not be so until the end of the year. This factor was also cited by other conferees as being a reason for delay.

3.   *The Need to Refine Plans and Resolve Issues*

Immediately following the Honolulu Conference, its Chairman, Secretary Rusk, reported to President Johnson, presumably making some recommendations. Although a record of this discussion is not available, Ass't Secretary Bundy's brief to Rusk just prior to his White House meeting may provide a clue to the thrust of the Secretary's remarks. Citing a "somewhat less pessimistic estimate" of conditions in South Vietnam, the "somewhat shaky" but hopeful situation in Laos, and the military timing factors reported above, Bundy counseled taking more time "to refine our plans and estimates." Criticizing CINCPAC's presentation on military planning, he stated that it "served largely to highlight some of the difficult issues we still have." These he identified as: "(1) the likely effects of force requirements for any significant operations against the [Laotian] Panhandle"; (2) the trade-off between the precautionary advantages of a major build-up of forces prior to wider action and the possible disadvantages of distorting the signal of our limited objectives; (3) the sensitivity of estimates of communist reactions to different levels and tempos of a military build-up; and (4) the need for "more refined targeting and a clearer definition of just what should be hit and how thoroughly, and above all, for what objective."

In particular, Bundy emphasized to Secretary Rusk the need for immediate efforts in the information and intelligence areas. These were needed, he said, "both for the sake of refining our plans and for preparing materials to use for eventual support of wider action if decided upon"—particularly to support the diplomatic track in Laos. He called for "an urgent U.S. information effort" to "get at the basic doubts of the value of Southeast Asia and the importance of our stake there . . ." However, noting the problem of "handling the high degree of expectations flowing from the conference itself," Bundy recommended "careful guidance and consideration of high-level statements and speeches in the next two weeks" to assure that our posture appeared firm.

Rusk was accompanied at the White House meeting by other high-ranking Honolulu conferees. Bundy's reactions to Honolulu were forwarded to Secretary McNamara, Mr. McCone and General Taylor prior to the meeting. Events which followed the late afternoon meeting of 3 June provide an indication of the discussion that probably occurred.

4.   *The Aftermath of Honolulu*

The importance of combining appearances of a firm posture with efforts to reduce public doubts on U.S. interests in Southeast Asia apparently struck a responsive chord in the White House. In the military area, the President apparently recognized the need for more and better information, but did not convey a sense of urgency regarding its acquisition. Possibly just following the meeting, Secretary McNamara expressed his wish to discuss North Vietnamese targets and troop movement capabilities with the JCS on 8 June. The following day, he communicated interest to the Joint Staff in obtaining "facts and statistics" on Haiphong harbor traffic; existing plans for mining the harbor; impacts of such operations on different import categories; and alternative DRV importation facilities. On the other hand, non-committing military actions which could improve our image in Southeast Asia were given immediate approval. On the same day he received the request for Haiphong mining information, the Director of the Joint Staff informed the Army of a McNamara directive calling for "immediate action . . . by the Army to improve the effectiveness and readiness status of its materiel prestocked for possible use in Southeast Asia." Specifically, the Secretary ordered (1) augmenting the stockage at Korat, in Thailand, to support a ROAD Infantry Brigade and (2) giving first priority at the Okinawa Army Forward Depot to stocking non-air-transportable equipment required by an airlifted ROAD Infantry Brigade. In keeping with the Administration's current policy rationale, the augmentation of contingency war stocks in Thailand was given extensive press coverage.

In non-military areas, the President apparently encouraged further examination of the vital issues which impacted on national commitment and public support. Soon after the 3 June meeting, work was begun under State Department guidance to assemble information in answer to some of the prevalent public questions on Southeast Asian involvement. For example, on 10 June, the Department of Defense was asked to furnish responses to 27 questions developed in State, as a fall-out of the discussions in Honolulu. Similar questions became a frequent focus for interdepartmental correspondence and meetings in the coming weeks. Paralleling this effort was an examination of the desirability of requesting a Congressional resolution. On the same day that OSD received State's request to furnish information, an interagency meeting was held to discuss the implications which a resolution would have for the U.S. policy position and the public rationale which its acceptance would demand. The relative advantages of having or not having a resolution were also considered.

To supplement recommendations coming from Honolulu, the President apparently sought additional guidance to help sort out the alternatives available to him. Soon after receiving reports from the Honolulu conference, he sent a request to Walt Rostow to prepare a public statement for him, detailing a Governmental view of U.S. policy and commitments in Southeast Asia. As most likely expected, the rationale and discussion which resulted took a more aggressive approach than the prevailing views at Honolulu and were not used. In fact, President Johnson did not deliver a major policy address during the coming weeks, relying on news conferences and speeches by other officials to state the official view. In contrast to the Rostow approach, his news conference of 23 June and Secretary Rusk's speech at Williams College, 14 June, emphasized the U.S. determination to support its Southeast Asian allies, but avoided any direct challenge to Hanoi and Peking or any hint of intent to increase our military commitment.

In addition, the President asked his advisers the basic question, "Would the rest of Southeast Asia necessarily fall if Laos and South Vietnam came under North Vietnamese control?" On 9 June, the Board of National Estimates, CIA, provided a response, stating:

> With the possible exception of Cambodia, it is likely that no nation in the area would quickly succumb to communism as a result of the fall of Laos and South Vietnam. Furthermore, a continuation of the spread of communism in the area would not be inexorable, and any spread which did occur would take time—time in which the total situation might change in any of a number of ways unfavorable to the communist cause.

The statement went on to argue that the loss of South Vietnam and Laos "would be profoundly damaging to the U.S. position in the Far East," because of its impact on U.S. prestige and on the credibility of our other commitments to contain the spread of communism. It did not suggest that such a loss would affect the wider U.S. interest in containing overt military attacks. Our island base, it argued, would probably still enable us to employ enough military power in the area to deter Hanoi and Peking from this kind of aggression. It cautioned, however, that the leadership in Peking (as well as Hanoi) would profit directly by being able to justify its militant policies with demonstrated success and by having raised "its prestige as a leader of World Communism" at the expense of the more moderate USSR.

5.   *Sources of Moderate Advice*

The strength of the Board's warning was weakened by two significant caveats. The first linked the estimate's less-than-alarmist view to a clearly "worst case":

> This memorandum assumes a clear-cut communist victory in these countries, *i.e.*, a withdrawal of U.S. forces and virtual elimination of U.S. presence in Indochina, either preceded or soon followed by the establishment of communist regimes in Laos and South Vietnam. The results of a fuzzier, piecemeal victory, such as one staged through a "neutralist" phase, would probably be similar, though somewhat less sharp and severe.

The second indicated that even in the worst case, the United States would retain some leverage to affect the outcome. They argued that "the extent to which individual countries would move away from the U.S. towards the communists would be significantly affected by the substance and manner of U.S. policy in the period following the loss of Laos and South Vietnam."

The largely moderating tone of this estimate of the degree to which U.S. vital interests were in jeopardy in Southeast Asia tended to be reinforced by the views of the President's highest-level advisers on military matters. On his way to the Honolulu Conference, CJCS Taylor had forwarded without detailed comment the JCS recommendation for courses of action in Southeast Asia. On 5 June, after his return, he submitted highly critical comments, together with his preferred alternative to the JCS proposal, to Secretary McNamara. Five days later, the Secretary communicated his approval of General Taylor's views and no doubt conveyed the flavor, if not the details, of them to the White House.

The nature of these views shared by the President's two top military advisers indicates a rejection of the concept of trying to force the DRV to reverse its policies by striking North Vietnam with punishing blows. The JCS had stated the view that only by initiating military actions designed to destroy the DRV's will and capabilities could we reasonably expect to compel it to terminate its support of the insurgencies in South Vietnam and Laos. But they had expressed their support of certain recommended limited actions as "an initial measure" directed toward causing the DRV "to decide to terminate their subversive support." General Taylor argued that these two alternatives were not "an accurate or complete expression of our choices." He suggested three patterns from which the United States "may choose to initiate the attack on North Vietnam," in descending order or weight:

> a. A massive air attack on all significant military targets in North Vietnam for the purpose of destroying them and thereby making the enemy incapable of continuing to assist the Viet Cong and the Pathet Lao.
>
> b. A lesser attack on some significant part of the military target system in North Vietnam for the dual purpose of convincing the enemy that it is to his interest to desist from aiding the Viet Cong and the Pathet Lao, and, if possible, of obtaining his cooperation in calling off the insurgents in South Vietnam and Laos.
>
> c. Demonstrative strikes against limited military targets to show U.S. readiness and intent to pass to alternatives *b* or *a* above. These demonstrative strikes would have the same dual purpose as in alternative *b*.

Stating a personal preference for the second, he noted the probability that "political considerations will incline our responsible civilian officials to opt for [the third] alternative." Therefore, his recommendation to the Secretary was that the JCS be asked to develop a strike plan based on the assumption that a decision was made to implement the third alternative.

It is clear that the JCS not only preferred the larger attacks—directed against both DRV capabilities and will—but intended that they be implemented in the near future. However, there is no indication that the CJCS urged prompt implementation—even of the limited measures he linked with pressures against DRV will alone. Neither view was supported with an explanation of *why* it was expected that the preferred course of action might be successful or with any analysis of what lesser results might lead to in the way of next steps by either side or of likely public reactions.

6. *The President Decides*

The Presidential reaction to these various patterns of advice and the different assessments of national interest is not evident in the available documents. However, it can be surmised from the pattern of events surrounding the effort to obtain a Congressional resolution. As will be recalled, a resolution was recommended to the President in late May as one of a series of events to include the Canadian's mission to Hanoi, the Honolulu Conference, and consultations with allies. It also fit in with the emphasis on public information and a firm posture that stemmed from the Honolulu meeting. Its intended purpose was to dramatize and make clear to other nations the firm resolve of the United States Government in an election year to support the President in taking whatever action was necessary to resist communist aggression in Southeast Asia.

The week of 8 June saw the planning for a Congressional resolution being brought to a head. By 10 June there was firm support for it on the part of most agencies, despite recognition that obtaining it would require a vigorous public campaign, a likely requirement of which would be a "substantial increase in the commitment of U.S. prestige and power to success in Southeast Asia." Therefore, at the meeting held on that day, five basic "disagreeable questions" were identified for which the Administration would have to provide convincing answers to assure public support. These included: (1) Does this imply a blank check for the President to go to war in Southeast Asia? (2) What kinds of force could he employ under this authorization? (3) What change in the situation (if any) requires the resolution now? (4) Can't our objectives be attained by means other than U.S. military force? (5) Does Southeast Asia mean enough to U.S. national interests?

By June 12, after a temporary diversion caused by Souvanna Phouma's withdrawal and reaffirmation of permission to continue the reconnaissance flights, much of the rationale in support of the resolution was formulated. Even though the Administration did not expect "to move in the near future to military action against North Vietnam," it recognized that significant changes in the local situations in both Laos and South Vietnam were beyond our control and could compel us to reconsider this position." Although our diplomatic track in Laos appeared hopeful, and our now firm escorted reconnaissance operations provided an image of U.S. resolve to complement the Polish negotiating scheme, we needed to be able to augment this posture in the event negotiations stalemated. If Souvanna were to become discouraged, or if Khanh were to view our efforts to obtain a Laotian settlement as a sign of willingness to alter our objectives, we would need additional demonstrations of our firmness to keep these leaders from being demoralized. Since additional military actions in Laos and South Vietnam did not hold much promise, actions or the strong threat of actions against the North might need to be considered. For these reasons, an immediate Congressional resolution was believed required as "a continuing demonstration of U.S. *firmness* and for complete *flexibility* in the hands of the Executive in the coming political months."

A crucial interagency meeting was held at the State Department on 15 June to hold final discussions on the recommendation for a resolution to be sent to the President. The meeting was scheduled from the White House and included Secretaries Rusk and McNamara, their principal advisers on the subject, and

McGeorge Bundy. On the afternoon of the meeting, a memorandum was distributed by Bundy to the participants, which provided a rather clear picture of current White House attitudes toward the resolution—and by implication, of the President's judgment on the issue of preparing to take harder measures against North Vietnam.

The memorandum dealt with one subject only—"actions that would remain open to us in varying combinations in the event that we do not now decide on major military operations against North Vietnam and do not now decide to seek a Congressional resolution." It then listed under the categories of "military" and "political," those actions which were within an acceptable range of U.S. capability, as follows:

Possible military actions

a. Reconnaissance, reconnaissance-strike, and T–28 operations in all parts of Laos.

b. Small-scale reconnaissance strike operations, after appropriate provocation, in North Vietnam (initially VNAF?).

c. VNAF strike operations in Laotian corridors.

d. Limited air and sea deployments toward Southeast Asia, and still more limited ground troop movements. (Major ground force deployments seem more questionable, without a decision "to go north" in some form.)

Political actions

a. Internationally—a continued and increased effort to maximize support for our diplomatic track in Laos and our political effort in South Vietnam. Higher authority particularly desires a maximum effort with our allies to increase their real and visible presence in support of Saigon.

b. Laos—an intensive effort to sustain Souvanna and to restrain the right wing from any rash act against the French. Possible increase of direct support and assistance to Kong Le in appropriate ways.

c. South Vietnam—rapid development of the critical province program and the information program, strengthening of country team, and shift of U.S. role from advice toward direction; emphatic and continued discouragement of all coup plots; energetic public support for Khanh Government.

d. In the U.S.—continued reaffirmation and expanded explanation of the above lines of action, with opposition to both aggressive adventure and withdrawal, and a clear open door to selected action of the sort included in above *Possible military actions*.

The files contain no record of the discussion that occurred at the 15 June meeting, but in this memorandum, the guidance provided from the White House was evident: Unless drastic measures were provoked from "the other side," there were still a number of political and military actions available which appeared to enable the United States to demonstrate an increasingly *firm* resistance without the need to risk major escalation. Moreover, such actions would not risk embarking on a depth or direction of commitment in which the United States would sacrifice policy *flexibility*. As the White House memorandum concluded, the actions were listed with the assumption that "defense of U.S. interests is possible, within these limits, over the next six months."

II.   JULY–OCTOBER 1964 *

A.   PROLOGUE: ACTIONS AND PROGRAMS UNDERWAY

Several forms of pressure were already being applied against North Vietnam by July of 1964. Moreover, contingency plans for other forms—should political and military circumstances warrant a decision to use them—were continually being adjusted and modified as the situation in Southeast Asia developed.

The best known of these pressures was being applied in Laos. Since 21 May, U.S. aircraft had flown low-level reconnaissance missions over communist-occupied areas. In early June Premier Souvanna Phouma both gave and reaffirmed his permission for armed escort of these missions, which included the right to retaliate against hostile fire from the ground. This effort was supplemented at the end of the month when the United States decided to conduct transport and night reconnaissance operations and furnish additional T–28 aircraft and munitions to support a Royal Laotian counteroffensive near Muong Soui. This decision came in response to Souvanna's request, in which he equated the protection of Muong Soui with the survival of the Laotian neutralist army. Air strikes conducted by the Royal Lao Air Force, with T–28s obtained from the United States, were later credited with playing a major role in the success of the RLG's operations.

Other actions obviously designed to forestall communist aggressive intentions were taken in different parts of Southeast Asia. In June, following the Honolulu strategy conference, State and Defense Department sources made repeated leaks to the press affirming U.S. intentions to support its allies and uphold its treaty commitments in Southeast Asia. U.S. contingency ground-force stockages in Thailand were augmented and publicly acknowledged. Revelations were made that USAF aircraft were operating out of a newly constructed air base at Da Nang. Moreover, the base was characterized as part of a network of new air bases and operational facilities being developed in South Vietnam and Thailand. On 10 July, the Da Nang base was the site of a well-publicized Air Force Day display of allied airpower, including aircraft from a B–57 wing recently acknowledged to have been permanently deployed to the Philippines from Japan.

Less known were parallel actions taken within the Government. U.S. resolve to resist aggression in Southeast Asia was communicated directly to North Vietnam by the newly appointed Canadian member of the International Control Commission, Blair Seaborn. Stressing that U.S. ambitions were limited and its intentions were "essentially peaceful," Seaborn told Pham Van Dong that the patience of the U.S. Government was not limitless. He explained that the United States was fully aware of the degree to which Hanoi controlled the Viet Cong.

[Several paragraphs missing]

The next DE SOTO Patrol did not occur until 31 July, on which the *U.S.S. Maddox* was restricted to a track not closer than 8 n.m. off the North Vietnamese mainland. Its primary mission, assigned on 17 July, was "to determine DRV coastal activity along the full extent of the patrol track." Other specific intelligence requirements were assigned as follows:

---

* A number of pages were missing from the manuscript for Subsections A, B, and C. However, the available material has been included, in spite of these gaps, to give the reader at least the flavor of the material contained therein.

(a) location and identification of all radar transmitters, and estimate of range capabilities; (b) navigational and hydro information along the routes traversed and particular navigational lights characteristics, landmarks, buoys, currents and tidal information, river mouths and channel accessibility, (c) monitoring a junk force with density of surface traffic pattern, (d) sampling electronic environment radars and navigation aids, (e) photography of opportunities in support of above. . . .

Separate coastal patrol operations were being conducted by South Vietnamese naval forces. These were designed to uncover and interdict efforts to smuggle personnel and supplies into the South in support of the VC insurgency. This operation had first been organized with U.S. assistance in December 1961; to support it a fleet of motorized junks was built, partially financed with U.S. military assistance funds. During 1964 these vessels operated almost continually in attempts to intercept communist seaborne logistical operations. As Secretary McNamara told Senate committees:

In the first seven months of this year [1964], they have searched 149,000 junks, some 570,000 people. This is a tremendous operation endeavoring to close the seacoasts of over 900 miles. In the process of that action, as the junk patrol has increased in strength they [sic] have moved farther and farther north endeavoring to find the source of the infiltration.

In addition to these acknowledged activities, the GVN was also conducting a number of operations against North Vietnam to which it did not publicly admit. Covert operations were carried out by South Vietnamese or hired personnel and supported by U.S. training and logistical efforts. Outlined within OPLAN 34A, these operations had been underway theoretically since February but had experienced what the JCS called a "slow beginning." Despite an ultimate objective of helping "convince the North Vietnamese leadership that it is in its own self-interest to desist from its aggressive policies," few operations designed to harass the enemy were carried out successfully during the February–May period. Nevertheless, citing DRV reactions tending "to substantiate the premise that Hanoi is expending substantial resources in defensive measures," the JCS concluded that the potential of the OPLAN 34A program remained high and urged its continuation through Phase II (June–September).

[Several paragraphs missing]

B. THE TONKIN GULF CRISIS

Several of the pressuring measures recommended to the White House in May or June were implemented in conjunction with or in the immediate aftermath of naval action in the Tonkin Gulf. It is this fact and the rapidity with which these measures were taken that has led critics to doubt some aspects of the public account of the Tonkin incidents. It is also this fact, together with later Administration assessments of the Tonkin Gulf experience, that give the incidents greater significance than the particular events seemed at first to warrant.

1. The First Incident

What happened in the Gulf? As noted earlier, U.S.S. MADDOX commenced the second DE SOTO Patrol on 31 July. On the prior night South Vietnamese coastal patrol forces made a midnight attack, including an amphibious "commando" raid, on Hon Me and Hon Nieu Islands, about 19° N. latitude. At the time of this attack, U.S.S. MADDOX was 120–130 miles away just heading into waters off North Vietnam. On 2 August, having reached the northernmost point on its patrol track and having headed South, the destroyer was intercepted by three North Vietnamese patrol boats. Apparently, these boats and a fleet of junks had moved into the area near the island to search for the attacking force and had mistaken *Maddox* for a South Vietnamese escort vessel. (Approximately eleven hours earlier, while on a northerly heading, *Maddox* had altered course to avoid the junk concentration shown on her radar; about six hours after that— now headed South—*Maddox* had altered her course to the southeast to avoid the junks a second time.) When the PT boats began their high-speed run at her, at a distance of approximately 10 miles, the destroyer was 28 miles from the coast and heading farther into international waters. Two of the boats closed to within 5,000 yards, launching one torpedo each. As they approached, *Maddox* fired on the boats with her 5-inch batteries and altered course to avoid the torpedoes, which were observed passing the starboard side at a distance of 100 to 200 yards. The third boat moved up abeam of the destroyer and took a direct 5-inch hit; it managed to launch a torpedo which failed to run. All three PT boats fired 50-caliber machine guns at *Maddox* as they made their firing runs, and a bullet fragment was recovered from the destroyer's superstructure. The attacks occurred in mid-afternoon, and photographs were taken of the torpedo boats as they attacked.

Upon first report of the PT boats' apparently hostile intent, four F-8E aircraft were launched from the aircraft carrier *Ticonderoga,* many miles to the south, with instructions to provide air cover but not to fire unless they or *Maddox* were fired upon. As *Maddox* continued in a southerly direction, *Ticonderoga*'s aircraft attacked the two boats that had initiated the action. Both were damaged with Zuni rockets and 20mm gunfire. The third boat, struck by the destroyer's five-inch guns . . .

[Several paragraphs missing]

Vietnamese coastal targets—this time the Rhon River estuary and the Vinh Sonh radar installation, which were bombarded on the night of 3 August. The more controversial of the two, this incident occurred under cover of darkness and seems to have been both triggered and described largely by radar and sonar images. After the action had been joined, however, both visual sightings and intercepted North Vietnamese communications confirmed that an attack by hostile patrol craft was in progress.

At 1940 hours, 4 August 1964 (Tonkin Gulf time), while "proceeding S.E. at best speed," Task Group 72.1 (*Maddox and Turner Joy*) radioed "RCVD INFO indicating attack by PGM P-4 iminent." Evidently this was based on an intercepted communication, later identified as "an intelligence source," indicating that "North Vietnamese naval forces had been ordered to attack the patrol." At the time, radar contacts evaluated as "probable torpedo boats" were observed about 36 miles to the northeast. Accordingly, the Task Group Commander altered course and increased speed to avoid what he evaluated as a trap. At approximately 2035 hours, while west of Hainan Island, the destroyers reported radar sightings of three unidentified aircraft and two unidentified vessels in the patrol area. On receiving the report, *Ticonderoga* immediately launched F-8s and A-4Ds to provide a combat air patrol over the destroyers. Within minutes, the unidentified aircraft disappeared from the radar screen, while the vessels maintained a distance of about 27 miles. Actually, surface contacts on a parallel course had been shadowing the destroyers with radar for more than three hours. ECM contacts maintained by the *C. Turner Joy* indicated that the radar was that carried aboard DRV patrol boats.

New unidentified surface contacts 13 miles distant were reported at 2134 hours. These vessels were closing at approximately 30 knots on the beam and were evaluated as "hostile." Six minutes later (2140) *Maddox* opened fire, and at 1242, by which time two of the new contacts had closed to a distance of 11 miles, aircraft from *Ticonderoga*'s CAP began their attacks. Just before this, one of the PT boats launched a torpedo, which was later reported as seen passing about 300 feet off the port beam, from aft to forward, of the *C. Turner Joy*. A searchlight beam was observed to swing in an arc toward the *C. Turner Joy* by all of the destroyer's signal bridge personnel. It was extinguished before it illuminated the ship, presumably upon detection of the approaching aircraft. Aboard the *Maddox*, Marine gunners saw what were believed to be cockpit lights of one or more small boats pass up the port side of the ship and down the other. After approximately an hour's action, the destroyers reported two enemy boats sunk and no damage or casualties suffered.

In the meantime, two patrol craft from the initial surface contact had closed to join the action, and the engagement was described for higher headquarters— largely on the basis of the destroyers' radar and sonar indications and on radio intercept information.

[Several paragraphs missing]

Returning from this session shortly after 1500, Secretary McNamara, along with Deputy Secretary Vance, joined with the JCS to review all the evidence relating to the engagement. Included in this review was the communications intelligence information which the Secretary reported, containing North Vietnamese reports that (1) their vessels were engaging the destroyers, and (2) they had lost two craft in the fight. In the meantime, however, messages had been relayed to the Joint Staff indicating considerable confusion over the details of the attack. The DE SOTO Patrol Commander's message, expressing doubts about earlier evidence of a large-scale torpedo attack, arrived sometime after 1330 hours. Considerably later (it was not sent to CINCPACFLT until 1447 EDT), another message arrived to the effect that while details of the action were still confusing, the commander of Task Group 72.1 was certain that the ambush was genuine. He had interviewed the personnel who sighted the boat's cockpit lights passing near the *Maddox*, and he had obtained a report from the *C. Turner Joy* that two torpedoes were observed passing nearby. Accordingly, these reports were discussed by telephone with CINCPAC, and he was instructed by Secretary McNamara to make a careful check of the evidence and ascertain whether there was any doubt concerning the occurrence of an attack. CINCPAC called the JCS at least twice more, at 1723 and again at 1807 hours, to state that he was convinced on the basis of "additional information" that the attacks had taken place. At the time of the earlier call Secretary McNamara and the JCS were discussing possible force deployments to follow any reprisals. On the occasion of the first call, the Secretary was at the White House attending the day's second NSC meeting. Upon being informed of CINCPAC's call, he reports:

> I spoke to the Director of the Joint Staff and asked him to make certain that the Commander in Chief, Pacific was willing to state that the attack had taken place, and therefore that he was free to release the Executive Order because earlier in the afternoon I had told him that under no circumstances would retaliatory action take place until we were, to use my words, 'damned sure that the attacks had taken place.'

At the meeting of the National Security Council, proposals to deploy certain increments of OPLAN 37–64 forces to the Western Pacific were discussed, and the order to retaliate against North Vietnamese patrol craft and their associated facilities were confirmed. Following this meeting, at 1845, the President met with 16 Congressional leaders from both parties for a period of 89 minutes. Reportedly, he described the second incident in the Gulf, explained his decisions to order reprisals, and informed the legislators of his intention to request a formal statement of Congressional support for these decisions. On the morning following the meeting, *The Washington Post* carried a report that none of the Congressional leaders present at the meeting had raised objections to the course of action planned. Their only question, the report stated, "had to do with how Congress could show its agreement and concern in the crisis."

[Several paragraphs missing]

increase pressures for an international conference *or* that the DRV was testing U.S. reactions to a contemplated general offensive—have lost some credibility. Subsequent events and DRV actions have appeared to lack any consistent relationship with such motives. Perhaps closer to the mark is the narrow purpose of prompt retaliation for an embarrassing and well-publicized rebuff by a much-maligned enemy. Inexperienced in modern naval operations, DRV leaders may have believed that under cover of darkness it would be possible to even the score or to provide at least a psychological victory by severely damaging a U.S. ship. Unlike the first incident, the DRV was ready (5 August) with a propaganda blast denying its own provocation and claiming the destruction of U.S. aircraft. Still, regardless of motive, there is little question but that the attack on the destroyers was deliberate. Having followed the destroyers for hours, their course was well known to the North Vietnamese naval force, and its advance units were laying ahead to make an ambushing beam attack fully 60 miles from shore.

The reality of a North Vietnamese attack on 4 August has been corroborated by both visual and technical evidence. That it may have been deliberately provoked by the United States is belied to a considerable degree by circumstantial evidence. Operating restrictions for the DE SOTO Patrol were made more stringent following the first attack. The 11 n.m., rather than 8 n.m., off-shore patrolling track indicates an intention to avoid—not provoke—further contact. On 4 February the rules of engagement were modified to restrict "hot pursuit" by the U.S. ships to no closer than 11 n.m. from the North Vietnamese coast; aircraft were to pursue no closer than 3 n.m. Given the first attack, the President's augmentation of the partol force was a normal precaution, particularly since both *Ticonderoga* and *C. Turner Joy* were already deployed in the immediate vicinity as supporting elements. Moreover, since the augmentation was coupled with a clear statement of intent to continue the patrols and a firm warning to the DRV that repetition would bring dire consequences, their addition to the patrol could be expected to serve more as a deterrent than a provocation.

The often alleged "poised" condition of the U.S. reprisal forces was anything but extraordinary. *U.S.S. Constellation* was well out of the immediate operating area as the patrol was resumed on 3 August. In fact, one reason for delaying the launching of retaliatory air strikes (nearly 1100 hours, 5 August—Tonkin Gulf time) was to permit *Constellation* to approach within reasonable range of the targets. Target lists from which to make appropriate selections were already available as a result of routine contingency planning accomplished in June and July. In preparation for the resumed DE SOTO Patrol of 3–5 August, the patrol track was moved farther north to make clearer the separation between it and the 34-A operations. The ways in which the events of the second Tonkin Gulf incident came about give little indication of a deliberate provocation to provide opportunity for reprisals.

2.   *Broadening the Impact*

[Several paragraphs missing]

bomber squadrons have been transferred from the United States into advance bases in the Pacific. Fifthly, an antisubmarine task force group has been moved into the South China Sea.

It is significant, relative to the broader purpose of the deployments, that few of these additional units were removed from the Western Pacific when the immediate crisis subsided. In late September the fourth attack aircraft carrier was authorized to resume its normal station in the Eastern Pacific as soon as the regularly assigned carried completed repairs. The other forces remained in the vicinity of their August deployment.

Other actions taken by the Administration in the wake of Tonkin Gulf were intended to communicate to various audiences the depth and sincerity of the U.S. commitment. On the evening of 4 August, in conjunction with his testing of Congressional opinion regarding reprisal action, President Johnson disclosed his intention to request a resolution in support of U.S. Southeast Asian policy. This he did through a formal message to both houses on 5 August. Concurrently, identical draft resolutions, the language of which had been prepared by executive agencies, were introduced in the Senate by J. William Fulbright (D., Ark.) and in the House by Thomas E. Morgan (D., Pa.) and co-sponsored by bipartisan leadership. Discussed in committee on 6 August, in response to testimony by leading Administration officials, the resolution was passed the following day—by votes of 88 to 2 in the Senate and 416 to 0 in the House.

Despite the nearly unanimous votes of support for the Resolution, Congressional opinions varied as to the policy implications and the meaning of such support. The central belief seemed to be that the occasion necessitated demonstrating the nation's unity and collective will in support of the President's action and affirming U.S. determination to oppose further aggression. However, beyond that theme, there was a considerable variety of opinion. For example, in the House, expressions of support varied from Congressman Laird's argument, that while the retaliation in the Gulf was appropriate such actions still left a policy to be developed with respect to the land war in Southeast Asia, to the more reticent viewpoint of Congressman Alger. The latter characterized his support as being primarily for purposes of showing unity and expressed concern over the danger of being dragged into war by "other nations seeking our help." Several spokesmen stressed that the Resolution did not constitute a declaration of war, did not abdicate Congressional responsibility for determining national policy commitments, and did not give the President carte blanche to involve the nation in a major Asian war.

Similar expressions were voiced in the senior chamber. For example, Senator Nelson sought assurances that the resolution would not tend to commit the United States further than . . .

[Several paragraphs missing]

addition to repeating points made earlier, Seaborn's second message conveyed the U.S. Government's uncertainty over DRV intentions in the 4 August attack and explained that subsequent U.S. deployments of additional airpower to South Vietnam and Thailand were "precautionary." In addition, the new message stressed: (1) that the Tonkin Gulf events demonstrated that "U.S. public and official patience" was wearing thin; (2) that the Congressional Resolution reaffirmed U.S. determination "to continue to oppose firmly, by all necessary means, DRV efforts to subvert and conquer South Vietnam and Laos"; and (3) that "if the DRV persists in its present course, it can expect to suffer the consequences."

Thus, in the immediate aftermath of the provocation handed the U.S. Government in the Tonkin Gulf, the Administration was able to carry out most of the actions recommended by its principal officials early in the summer. By the same token, it was reducing the number of unused measures short of direct military action that had been conceived as available for exerting effective pressure on the DRV. In effect, as it made its commitments in Southeast Asia clearer it also deepened them, and in the process it denied itself access to some of the uncommitting options which it had perceived earlier as offering policy flexibility. Meanwhile, other events were also having the effect of denying options which had been considered useful alternatives to strikes against the North.

C. 1. [Title and several paragraphs missing]
over Southeast Asia and the likelihood that back-corridor discussions of the Vietnamese problem would be an almost inevitable by-product. In time such a procedure might be useful, but for the balance of 1964 it was to be avoided in order to promote GVN stability and encourage a more vigorous GVN war effort.

The pressure for a Geneva-type conference had been building ever since the resumption of fighting in Laos in May. The chief protagonist in the quest for negotiations was France, who first proposed reconvening the 14-Nation Conference to deal with the crisis on 20 May. What made French policy so dangerous to U.S. interests, however, was that its interest in a Geneva solution applied to Vietnam as well. On 12 June, DeGaulle publicly repeated his neutralization theme for all Indo-China and called for an end to all foreign intervention there; on 23 July he proposed reconvening the 1954 Geneva Conference to deal with the problems of Vietnam.

The Soviet Union's return to the 14-Nation formula in July (it had endorsed the original French proposal before indicating willingness to support the 6-Nation approach) indicated solidarity in the communist camp. The call was endorsed by North Vietnam on the following day. Communist China first announced support for a 14-Nation Conference (on Laos) on 9 June, repeating this through notes to the co-chairman calling on the 13th for an "emergency meeting." On 2 August, the Chinese urged the USSR not to carry out its threat to abandon its co-chairman role, apparently viewing such a development as jeopardizing the possibilities for a Geneva settlement.

Great Britain also urged the Russians to stay on, and during the last days of July it attempted to make arrangements in Moscow to convene a 14-Nation assembly on Laos. The negotiations failed because Britain insisted on Souvanna's prerequisite that the communists withdraw from positions taken in May and was unable to gain Soviet acquiescence. However, U.S. leaders were aware that Britain's support on this point could not be counted on indefinitely in the face of increasing pressure in the direction of Geneva.

In the meantime, however, Laotian military efforts to counter the communist threat to key routes and control points west of the Plaine des Jarres were showing great success. As a result of a counteroffensive (Operation Triangle), government forces gained control of a considerable amount of territory that gave promise of assuring access between the two capitals (Vientiane and Luang Prabang) for the first time in three years.

In effect, the government's newly won control of territory and communication routes in central Laos created a new and more favorable balance of power in that country, which in the perceptions of the administration should not be jeopardized.

[Several paragraphs missing]

firmness in the event negotiating pressure should become compelling.

Reactions to this tentative policy change were unfavorable. It was seen as likely to have a demoralizing impact on the GVN. It was also seen as possibly eroding the impression of strong U.S. resolve, which the reprisal air strikes were believed to have created. For example, Ambassador Taylor cabled:

> . . . rush to conference table would serve to confirm to CHICOMS that U.S. retaliation for destroyer attacks was transient phenomenon and that firm CHICOM response in form of commitment to defend NVN has given U.S. "paper tiger" second thoughts. . . .
>
> In Vietnam sudden backdown from previously strongly held U.S. position on [Plaine des Jarres] withdrawal prior to conference on Laos would have potentially disastrous effect. Morale and will to fight and particular willingness to push ahead with arduous pacification task . . . would be undermined by what would look like evidence that U.S. seeking to take advantage of any slight improvement in non-Communist position as excuse for extricating itself from Indo-China via [conference] route. . . .
>
> Under circumstances, we see very little hope that results of such a conference would be advantageous to us. Moreover, prospects of limiting it to consideration of only Laotian problem appear at this time juncture to be dimmer than ever. . . .

2. *Concern Over Tonkin Reprisal Signals*

Contained in Ambassador Taylor's views was yet another of the Administration's reflections on the impact of the Tonkin Gulf incidents. Officials developed mixed feelings regarding the effect of the Tonkin reprisals for signaling firm U.S. commitments in Southeast Asia. On one hand, it was conceded that the reprisals and the actions which accompanied them represented the most forceful expression of U.S. resolve to date. Improvements were perceived in South Vietnamese morale, and the combination of force and restraint demonstrated was believed effective in interrupting communist momentum and forcing a reassessment of U.S. intentions. On the other hand, they reflected concern that these effects might not last and that the larger aspects of U.S. determination might still be unclear.

Several officials and agencies indicated that our actions in the Tonkin Gulf represented only one step along a continually demanding route for the United States. They expressed relief that if a persuasive impression of firmness were to be created relative to the general security of Southeast Asia, [words illegible]

> It should be remembered that our retaliatory action in Gulf of Tonkin is in effect an isolated U.S.–DRV incident. Although this has relation . . . to [the] larger problem of DRV aggression by subversion in Viet-Nam and Laos, we have not (repeat not) yet come to grips in a forceful way with DRV over the issue of this larger and much more complex problem.

Later, he described a need for subsequent actions that would convey to Hanoi that "the operational rules with respect to the DRV are changing." Assistant

Secretary of State Bundy believed that Hanoi and Peking had probably been convinced only "that we will act strongly where U.S. force units are directly involved . . . [that] in other respects the communist side may not be so persuaded that we are prepared to take stronger action. . . ." He saw the need for a continuous "combination of military pressure and some form of communication" to cause Hanoi to accept the idea of "getting out" of South Vietnam and Laos. CINCPAC stated that "what we have not done and must do is make plain to Hanoi and Peiping the cost of pursuing their current objectives and impeding ours. . . . Our actions of August 5 have created a momentum which can lead to the attainment of our objectives in S.E. Asia. . . . It is most important that we not lose this momentum." The JCS urged actions to "sustain the U.S. advantage [recently] gained," and later cautioned: "Failure to resume and maintain a program of pressure through military actions . . . could signal a lack of resolve."

What these advisors had in mind by way of actions varied somewhat but only in the extent to which they were willing to go in the immediate future. Bundy stressed that policy commitments must be such that U.S. and GVN hands could be kept free for military actions against DRV infiltration routes in Laos. Ambassador Taylor, CINCPAC and the JCS urged prompt air and ground operations across the Laotian border to interrupt the current (though modest) southward flow of men and supplies. Both Taylor and CINCPAC indicated the necessity of building up our "readiness posture" to undertake stronger actions—through additional deployments of forces and logistical support elements and strengthening of the GVN political base.

The mood and attitudes reflected in these viewpoints were concrete and dramatic expressions of the increased U.S. commitment stemming from the Tonkin Gulf incidents. They were candidly summed up by CINCPAC in his statement:

> . . . pressures against the other side once instituted should not be relaxed by any actions or lack of them which would destroy the benefits of the rewarding steps previously taken. . . .

Increasingly voiced by officials from many quarters of the Administration and from the professional agencies were arguments which said, in effect, now that we have gone [words missing] go no further;
[Several paragraphs missing]
destruction of specific targets by aerial bombardment or naval gunfire. They could be supported by such non-destructive military actions as aerial reconnaissance, harassment of civil aviation and maritime commerce, mock air attacks, and timely concentrations of U.S. or allied forces at sea or near land borders. Following a line of reasoning prevalent in the Government during the early 60's, Rostow observed that a target government might well reduce its insurgency supporting role in the face of such pressures because of the communists' proverbial "tactical flexibility."

The thesis was subjected to a rather thorough analysis in OSD/ISA and coordinated with the Department of State. The nature of this review will be discussed on later pages and in a different context.

3. *Accompanying Pause in Pressures*

The foregoing policy assessments were conducted in an atmosphere relatively free of even those pressure measures that preceded the Tonkin Gulf crisis. Since the force deployments of 6 August, little military activity had been directed at the DRV. U-2 flights over North Vietnam and reconnaissance of the Laotian Panhandle were continued. Military operations within Laos were limited to the consolidation of gains achieved in Operation Triangle. A deliberate stand-down was adopted for all other activities—including DE SOTO Patrols and the GVN's covert harassing operations. The purpose of this "holding phase," as it was called, was to "avoid actions that would in any way take the onus off the Communist side for [the Tonkin] escalation."

However, during the "holding phase" some of the administrative impediments to wider military action were cleared away. One measure that was taken was to relax the operating restrictions and the rules of engagement for U.S. forces in Southeast Asia. This was accomplished in response to JCS urging that attacking forces not be permitted sanctuaries from which to regroup and perhaps repeat their hostile acts. Prior rules had not permitted pursuit of hostile aircraft outside South Vietnam or authorized intercept of intruders over Thailand. Under the revised rules of 15 August 1964, U.S. forces were authorized to attack and destroy any vessel or aircraft "which attacks, or gives positive indication of intent to attack" U.S. forces operating in or over international waters and in Laos, to include hot pursuit into the territorial waters or air space of North Vietnam and into the air space over other countries of Southeast Asia. "Hostile aircraft over South Vietnam and Thailand" could be engaged as well and pursued into North Vietnam, Laos and Cambodia.

Another prerequisite to wider military action that was accomplished was the combined GVN-U.S. planning for cross-border ground operations. By 16 August, this had proceeded to such an extent that COMUSMACV believed it necessary to seek approval of the concept. MACV made the request despite explicit comment that the concept was "an overly ambitious scheme." Presumably, he considered it likely to be ineffective militarily, but perhaps important in stimulating more vigorous GVN efforts. Whatever his particular reasons at the time, MACV repeated the recommendations later in the month as part of several measures to be taken inside and outside South Vietnam. These were designed "to give the VC a bloody nose," to steady the newly reformed South Vietnamese government, and to raise the morale of the population. However, the earlier MACV cable had already acknowledged what must have been one of the Administration's key inhibitions against undertaking cross-border actions: General Westmoreland stated, "It should be recognized that once this operation is initiated by the GVN, U.S. controls may be marginal."

The period of the "holding phase" was also a period of significant developments within South Vietnam. Ambassador Taylor's initial report (10 August) made clear that the political situation was already precarious, giving Khanh only a 50–50 chance of staying in power and characterizing the GVN as ineffective and fraught with conflicting purposes. In Taylor's view, the leadership in Saigon showed symptoms of "defeatism" and a hesitancy to prosecute the pacification campaign within South Vietnam. Meanwhile, however, its popular support in the countryside seemed to be directly proportional to the degree of protection which the government provided. In view of this shaky political base, General Khanh seized upon the occasion of post-Tonkin euphoria—apparently with Ambassador Taylor's encouragement—to acquire additional executive authority. On 7 August, announcing the necessity for certain "emergency" powers to cope with any heightened VC activity, he proclaimed himself President and promulgated the Vung Tau Charter. This action, which gave him virtually dictatorial power over several aspects of South Vietnamese life, met with hostile reactions.

In late August, Khanh's authority was challenged in the streets of Saigon, Hue and Da Nang, during several days of student protest demonstrations and clashes between Buddhist and Catholic groups. In response to student and Buddhist pressures primarily, he resigned his recently assumed post as President and promised that a national assemblage would be called to form a more popularly based government. On 3 September, Khanh returned to assume the premiership, but clearly with weaker and more conditional authority than before the government crisis.

Meanwhile, as the GVN's lack of cohesion and stability was being demonstrated, the infiltration of communist forces into South Vietnam may have been on the increase. At least, belief in an increase in the rate of this infiltration apparently gained currency in various U.S. agencies at this time. The documents available to this writer from the period neither refute nor substantiate the increase, but several of them contained references to this perception. For example, a State Department memorandum, dated 24 August, acknowledged a "rise and change in the nature of infiltration in recent months." Later analyses confirmed that increases had taken place, but the precise period when this [words illegible].

Possibly influencing the judgments of August was the fact that increased communist movement of men and supplies to the South was expected, resulting in part from a DIA assessment (7 August) of the most likely DRV reactions to the Tonkin reprisals. Moreover, the State Department's analysis of next courses of action in Southeast Asia had made "clear evidence of greatly increased infiltration from the North" an explicit condition for any policy judgment that "systematic military action against DRV" was required during the balance of 1964. And leading officials from several agencies were beginning to feel that such action might be inevitable.

The combined effects of the signs of increased VC infiltration and of continuing upheaval in Saigon caused great concern in Washington. The central perception was one of impending chaos and possible failure in South Vietnam. Among several agencies, the emerging mood was that some kind of action was urgently needed—even if it had the effect merely of improving the U.S. image prior to pulling out. It was this mood that prevailed as the period of "pause" drew to a close.

D.   Next Courses of Action

By early September a general consensus had developed among high-level Administration officials that some form of additional and continuous pressure should be exerted against North Vietnam. Though Laos was relatively stabilized, the situation there was recognized as dependent ultimately on the degree of success achieved in solving the problems of Vietnam. Pacification efforts within South Vietnam were regarded as insufficient by themselves to reverse the deteriorating trends in that country. As a result, officials from both civilian and military agencies were anxious to resume and to extend the program of military actions against communist forces outside its borders.

1.   Strategy Meeting In September

How to go about this was a problem of great concern to top-level officials (the President, Secretary Rusk, Secretary McNamara, General Wheeler, Ambassador Taylor, CIA Director McCone) as they assembled in Washington on 7 September. The main purpose of the meeting was to discuss with Ambassador

Taylor future courses of U.S. and GVN action, particularly as related to the implications of the recent political upheaval in Saigon.

The alternatives presented for discussion were based largely on responses to the tentative analysis circulated by the State Department in mid-August. Replies from CINCPAC and the Saigon and Vientiane embassies had been circulated, and they provided the basis for a number of questions which Ambassador Taylor's party was asked to be ready to discuss. JCS reactions to the analysis and to the earlier replies were submitted to the Secretary of Defense with the specific intent that they be considered at the meeting and presumably were passed to other participating agencies. OSD/ISA views were prepared by Assistant Secretary McNaughton on 3 September and were known at least to Assistant Secretary of State Bundy. [Doc. 188]

Just prior to the meeting, the JCS urged that General Wheeler, their Chairman, propose a course of action involving air strikes against targets in North Vietnam appearing on the JCS-approved, 94-target list. This kind of action had been recommended before—most recently on 26 August, in response to the Department of State analysis—as a means of "destroying the DRV will and capabilities, as necessary, to continue to support the insurgencies in South Vietnam and Laos." What made this proposal particularly significant was that it called for deliberate attempts to provoke the DRV into taking action which could then be answered by a systematic U.S. air campaign. According to the JCS scheme, the campaign "would be continuous and in ascending severity," with its tempo and intensity varied as required by enemy reactions. Targets would eventually include airfields, bridges, railroads, and military installations.

Whether or not or in what form General Wheeler presented this proposal to the assembled officials on 7 September is not indicated in the documentary sources available. The JCS belief in the necessity of bombing North Vietnam was discussed, as was some of their rationale. Made explicit, for example, was their argument that there was no reason to delay the bombing since (in their view) the situation in South Vietnam would only become worse. That the idea of deliberately provoking a DRV reaction was discussed in some form is indicated in a record of the consensus arrived at in the discussions. [Doc. 191] However, the JCS were not the only officials who favored such an idea. Assistant Secretary McNaughton's "Plan of Action" (3 September 1964) also called for actions that "should be likely at some point to provoke a military DRV response." The latter, in turn, "should be likely to provide good grounds for us to escalate if we wished."

The principal conferees did not believe that deliberately provocative actions should be undertaken "in the immediate future while the GVN is still struggling to its feet." However, they apparently reached a consensus that they might recommend such actions—"depending on GVN progress and Communist reaction in the meantime"—by early October.

The reasons cited for their opposition to provocative acts were also applied in rejecting proposals for an immediate bombing campaign. The GVN was expected to be too weak for the United States to assume the "deliberate risks of escalation that would involve a major role for, or threat to, South Vietnam." In the discussion, Mr. McCone observed that undertaking a sustained attack on the DRV would be very dangerous, due to the weakness and unpredictability of the political base in South Vietnam. Secretary Rusk stated the view that every means short of bombing must be exhausted. Secretary McNamara affirmed his understanding that "we are not acting more strongly because there is a clear hope of strengthening the GVN." But he went on to urge that the way be kept open for stronger actions even if the GVN did not improve or in the event the war were widened by the communists. It is interesting to note that the President asked specifically, "Can we really strengthen the GVN?"

Even though the principals did not accept the JCS proposal and apparently did not agree with their assessment of the chances for improvement in South Vietnam, they did indicate accord with the JCS sense of the gravity of the U.S. predicament. In response to General Wheeler's statements that "if the United States loses in South Vietnam, it will lose all of Southeast Asia" and that its position throughout all of Asia would be damaged, both McCone and Rusk indicated agreement. Ambassador Taylor stated the view that the United States could not afford to let Ho Chi Minh win in South Vietnam. Secretary Rusk added the consideration that the whole world doubted our ability to pull it off.

The meeting resulted in consensus among the principals on certain courses of prompt action to put additional pressure on North Vietnam. The following measures were recommended to the President for his decision:

> 1. U.S. naval patrols in the Gulf of Tonkin should be resumed immediately (about September 12). They should operate initially beyond the 12-mile limit and be clearly dissociated from 34A maritime operations. . . .
> 2. 34A operations by the GVN should be resumed immediately thereafter (next week). The maritime operations are by far the most important. . . .
> 3. Limited GVN air and ground operations into the corridor areas of Laos should be undertaken in the near future, together with Lao air strikes as soon as we can get Souvanna's permission. These operations will have only limited effect, however.
> 4. We should be *prepared* to respond on a tit-for-tat basis against the DRV [against specific and related targets] in the event of any attack on U.S. units or any *special* DRV/VC action against SVN.

The purposes for these measures were conceived as: (1) "to assist morale in SVN," (2) to "show the Communists we still mean business," and (3) "to keep the risks low and under our control at each stage."

2. *Implementing Actions*

These recommendations (and presumably the purposes) were approved by the President and became the basis for a program of limited (though not continuous) pressures exerted against North Vietnam from mid-September to mid-December 1964. On 10 September, the White House issued a National Security Action Memorandum [Doc. 195] which authorized immediate resumption of the DE SOTO Patrols and prompt discussions with the Government of Laos to develop plans for cross-border operations. It also authorized resumption of 34A operations following completion of the DE SOTO Patrol, with the additional guidance that "we should have the GVN ready to admit that they are taking place and to justify and legitimize them on the basis of the facts of VC infiltration by sea." It is significant that although this order, in effects authorized the initiation of Phase III (October through December) of the covert operations under OPLAN 34A, it specified contrary to the provisions of Phase III that "we should not consider air strikes under 34A for the present."

Naval Operations. The resumption of naval patrol and covert maritime operations off the coast of North Vietnam did not proceed exactly as planned. The destroyers *U.S.S. Morton* and *U.S.S. Edwards* embarked on the third DE SOTO Patrol on 12 September. On the night of 14 September [words illegible]

Approximately 40 minutes after first contact and after firing a warning shot, *Morton* and *Edwards* opened fire, both scoring hits. Subsequently, on two separate occasions after the target images had disappeared from the radar, new contacts appeared and were fired on at a range of approximately 8,500 yards, hits again being indicated for both vessels. In all, *Morton* fired 56 five-inch and 128 three-inch rounds; *Edwards* fired 152 five-inch and 6 three-inch rounds. There were no rounds or torpedoes reported coming from the radar contacts. Later on the 18th (Washington time), President Johnson suspended the DE SOTO Patrols; they were not to be resumed until February 1965.

In the aftermath of the third destroyer incident in the Tonkin Gulf, covert GVN maritime operations were not resumed until October. President Johnson authorized reactivation of this program on the 4th, under very tight controls. The proposed schedule of maritime operations had to be submitted at the beginning of each month for approval. Each operation was approved in advance by OSD (Mr. Vance), State (Mr. L. Thompson or Mr. Forrestal) and the White House (Mr. McGeorge Bundy). During October, these included two probes, an attempted junk capture, and ship-to-shore bombardment of North Vietnamese radar sites. Later, they included underwater demolition team assaults on bridges along coastal LOC's. Unlike the DE SOTO Patrols, these unacknowledged operations continued throughout the year.

Actions in Laos. Operations in the Laotian Panhandle took shape with fewer unpredictable developments. On 11 September, representatives of the U.S. missions in Laos, Thailand and Vietnam met in Saigon to discuss implementation of the NSAM 314 provisions for cross-border air and ground operations. [Doc. 196] Regarding air operations, they agreed that if their primary objective was military in nature, "sharp, heavy" and concentrated attacks would be needed and that U.S. and/or VNAF/FARMGATE forces would be required. If their impact was intended to be primarily psychological (presumably affecting both communists and the GVN), they believed that the operations could be more widely spaced, relying primarily on Laotian T-28s with some U.S. strikes on harder targets. In view of Souvanna Phouma's reported opposition to VNAF strikes in the Panhandle, the representatives conceded that the slower paced operation with RLAF aircraft offered the best course. However, they saw a joint Lao, Thai, RVN and U.S. operation as particularly desirable, were it not for the time required to arrange it. As one means of symbolizing four power support for the operation, they recommended that the Thai Government be approached regarding use of the Korat base by participating U.S. aircraft.

Regarding cross-border ground operations, the representatives agreed that the southern and central Panhandle offered terrain and targets consistent with the available GVN assets. Although it was recognized that accompanying U.S. advisers might be necessary to assure the success of the operations, the planners acceded to Vientiane's objections that such a flagrant violation of the Geneva Accords would endanger the credibility of our political stance in Laos. Subsequent to the meeting, the Vientiane Embassy removed a reservation expressed earlier and cleared the way for company-size penetrations of up to 20 km along Route 9, near Tchepone. At the conference this operation was considered of high priority with respect to infiltration traffic into South Vietnam.

The mission representatives agreed that, once the operations began, they should not be acknowledged publicly. In effect, then, they would supplement the other covert pressures being exerted against North Vietnam. Moreover, while the Lao Government would of course know about the operations of their T-28s,

Souvanna was not to be informed of the GVN/U.S. operations. The unacknowledged nature of these operations would thus be easier to maintain. Accordingly, the representatives recommended to Washington that Vientiane be authorized to approach the Laotian Government regarding initiation of T-28 operations. On the other hand, the Administration was asked to approve ground operations in three specified areas of the Panhandle.

Over two weeks passed before these recommendations were acted on. In the meantime, the JCS also submitted proposals for implementing NSAM 314, requesting immediate authority to implement air operations in the Panhandle. Endorsing the main theme of the mission representatives, they called for combined action by RLAF T-28s and U.S. aircraft which would provide "suppressive fire" and attack heavily defended bridges. The JCS also sought authority to initiate GVN ground intelligence collection and target reconnaissance patrols in the Laotian corridor.

On 6 October, authority was given to Vientiane Embassy to urge the Laotian Government to begin T-28 air strikes "as soon as possible." The RLAF targets were to be selected from a previously coordinated 22-target list, a few of which were designed for U.S. YANKEE TEAM strikes, but they were to exclude Mu Gia Pass. The latter mission was known to require U.S. escort and suppressive fire, and a decision on whether to authorize such U.S. operations had not yet been made in Washington. Moreover, neither had the Administration authorized YANKEE TEAM strike missions against the tougher Panhandle targets. [Doc. 204]

Administration rationale on the issue of U.S. participation in the Panhandle air strikes is not clear from the sources available to this writer. Contemporary intelligence estimates indicated the communist responses were likely to be limited to (1) increases in antiaircraft deployments in the area, (2) propaganda attacks and (3) possible sabotage of U.S./GVN supporting bases. However, Washington's viewpoint on another Laotian request for air support may be significant. With respect to air strikes against targets along Route 7, in support of the RLG campaign to consolidate its holdings west of the Plaine des Jarres, Administration rationale was as follows:

[material missing]
[to] defer decision on Route 7 strikes until we have strong evidence [of] Hanoi's preparation for new attack in [the Plaine des Jarres], some of which might come from RLAF operations over the Route.

On 13 October, one day before the initial RLAF attacks, U.S. strikes were again requested on four defended targets near Nape and Tchepone. They were to accompany T-28 strikes on communist military installations and supply points in the northern part of the Panhandle. The significance of these operations, and U.S. participation in them, was indicated a few days earlier in another meeting among representatives of the three missions. It was reported at this time that it was probable "that ARVN will be unable [to] afford detachment [of] any significant ground capability for [the Laotian] Corridor in [the] foreseeable future." Therefore, air operations would offer the only dependable means of combatting VC infiltration through Laos. The participants recorded "unanimous agreement that U.S. participation in air operations in [the] corridor is essential if such operations are to have desired military and psychological impact." Emphasizing that the initiative for these operations came from the United States Government, they pointed out that failure to participate could result in loss of control over them and could even jeopardize their continuation. At minimum the group recommended that U.S. aircraft fly CAP (combat air patrol) over the RLAF aircraft, as requested by the Laotian Government and as permitted by a "relatively minor extension" of existing U.S. rules of engagement.

CAP missions were approved, but U.S. air strikes against communist LOCs in the Laotian Panhandle were not authorized until much later in the year. Cross-border ground operations did not receive authorization at any time during the period covered in this study.

3. *Negotiating Posture in Laos*

One reason for the delay in requesting Laotian air strikes in the Panhandle was the need to await the uncertain outcome of discussions in Paris among leaders of the three Laotian political factions. Since 27 August, when they first met, the three Princes (Souvanna Phouma, Souphanouvang, and Boun Oum) had reached an impasse on conditions to accompany a ceasefire. Souvanna Phouma insisted on communist withdrawal from positions won in the May offensive and had proposed neutralization of the Plaine des Jarres under I.C.C. supervision. On 15 September, when it seemed that further negotiations had become fruitless, Prince Souphanouvang offered to withdraw communist forces from the Plaine in return for discussions leading to a new 14-Nation Conference. The following day, Souvanna countered with a proposal that a cease-fire begin on 1 October and attempted to verify and make more explicit the mutual concessions. The pro-communist leader balked over stipulated guarantees, such as I.C.C. supervision, that pro-communist forces would in fact withdraw and be replaced by neutralists. However, on the 21st, the leaders arrived at [words illegible] and preliminary conditions for reconvening a Geneva conference.

The narrow margin by which the cease-fire agreement failed to come about dramatized the delicate nature of the Administration's diplomatic position in Laos. Having agreed to support the tripartite discussions prior to the Tonkin Gulf incidents and prior to the political upheaval in Saigon, it felt constrained to go along with them—particularly if they served to forestall movement toward a Geneva-type negotiation. However, a Laotian cease-fire was not compatible with current perceptions of U.S. interest even if it resulted in communist withdrawal from the Plaine des Jarres. Ambassador Unger pointed out the contradictory nature of our position in his reply to the State Department's mid–August analysis of future U.S. courses of action. Ambassador Taylor emphasized the need to maintain the option of operations in the Panhandle in his reply also, and the September discussions in Washington confirmed that his view was shared by most of the President's advisors. One could conclude that the United States was fortunate that Prince Souphanouvang was so intransigent on the issue of I.C.C. supervision. It is also possible that in insisting on this provision to the leftist prince Souvanno Phouma "knew his man"—perhaps reflecting perceptive American advice.

Certainly the course of the tripartite discussion followed a pattern commensurate with prior U.S. calculation. In an assessment of future courses of action used as the basis for the policy analysis cabled to affected interested embassies and CINCPAC by the State Department, Assistant Secretary Bundy characterized U.S. strategy with the statement, "We would wish to slow down any progress toward a conference. . . ." He then referred to a specific negotiating position proposed by Ambassador Unger (a proposal for tripartite administration of the Plaine des Jarres) as "a useful delaying gambit." Significantly, this proposal was advanced at Jaris by Souvanna Phouma on 1 September—illustrating the fact that Souvanna was carefully advised by U.S. diplomats both prior to and during the Paris meetings. Other features of Souvanna's negotiating posture which apparently were encouraged as likely to have the effect of drawing out the discussions were insistence on communist acceptance of (1) Souvanna's political status as premier and (2) unhampered operations by the I.C.C. It will be recalled that the latter point was the issue on which progress toward a cease-fire became stalled.

It is important to note here that the State Department recognized that Souvanna Phouma might well act on his own and feel compelled to move toward a conference, even at the price of a cease-fire. In such an event, our position was to be dependent on conditions in South Vietnam:

[quotation illegible]

It is apparent from this and other documents that GVN stability and morale were perceived by the Administration as the principal pacing elements for Southeast Asian policy in the post-Tonkin period.

4. *Anticipation of Wider Action*

Through most of the strategy discussions of early autumn, South Vietnam was the main focus of attention. However, with increasing frequency its political and military conditions were referred to in a new way. More and more it was being evaluated in terms of its suitability as a base for wider action. Ambassador Taylor cautioned that "we should not get involved militarily with North Vietnam and possibly with Red China if our base in South Viet Nam is insecure and Khanh's army is tied down everywhere by the VC insurgency." At the September meeting, Mr. McCone criticized the actions recommended by the JCS as being very dangerous because of the current weakness of the GVN base. On 23 September, Walt Rostow wrote to Ambassador Taylor of the need for building a more viable political system in South Vietnam "which will provide us with an adequate base for what we may later have to do."

General Scheme. The kind of operations for which "an adequate base" was increasingly considered essential is evident in a number of strategy discussions of the period. Moreover, it is clear that several officials shared the expectation that these operations would begin early in the new year. It will be recalled that the series of actions recommended to President Johnson by his top advisers at the end of May—most of which had been completed within a few days of the Tonkin Gulf incidents—were intended to culminate, if necessary, in a strike against North Vietnam accompanied by an active diplomatic offensive that included agreement to a negotiated settlement. Further, Phase III of the approved contingency OPLAN 37–64, developed in response to NSAM 288, provided for the application of overt graduated pressures against North Vietnam—primarily air strikes. These were to be carried out by the GVN, but which would also include operations by U.S. air and naval forces. Deployments of additional forces to Southeast Asia in early summer and in the immediate aftermath of the Tonkin Gulf incidents were based on force requirements identified to support this plan. Its perceived significance during the post-Tonkin period was indicated when Ambassador Taylor reported that the objectives of the U.S. Mission in Saigon included preparation to implement OPLAN 37–64 "with optimum readiness by January 1, 1965."

Subsequent strategy discussions reflected the extent to which the new year was anticipated as the occasion for beginning overt military operations against North Vietnam. Both the State Department's mid-August strategy analysis and the working paper on which it was based indicated that the "limited pressures" (subsequently authorized by NSAM 314) would extend "tentatively through December." However, these actions were perceived as "foreshadowing systematic military action against the DRV," which "we might at some point conclude . . . [was appropriate, depending on the] situation in South Vietnam, particularly if there were to be clear evidence of greatly increased infiltration from the north.") Should specific provocations not occur, a contingency target of 1 January 1965 was indicated:

> . . . in [the] absence of such major new development [incidents or increased infiltration], we should probably be thinking of a contingency date for planning purposes, as suggested by Ambassador Taylor, of 1 January 1965.

The working paper elaborated more fully than the cable the kind of preliminary actions considered necessary to set the stage. Some of this elaboration was provided in suggested language changes penciled-in by OSD prior to an interagency meeting called to discuss its contents. Referring to air strikes in the Panhandle (proposed to begin in September), a suggested OSD addition stated: "The strike should probably be timed and plotted on the map to bring them to the borders of North Vietnam at the end of December." The main body of the text suggested that the January operations include "action against infiltration routes and facilities" as "probably the best opening gambit." It explained that "the family of infiltration-related targets starts with clear military installations near the borders [and] can be extended almost at will northward." The "next upward move" was suggested to include action against "military-related targets," such as "POL installations and the mining of Haiphong Harbor" and "key bridges and railroads." The purposes perceived for these operations was "to inflict progressive damage that would have a meaningful cumulative effect."

Ambassador Taylor viewed 1 January 1965 as a "target D-Day" before which the U.S. Mission and the GVN should develop "a posture of maximum readiness for a deliberate escalation of pressure against North Viet Nam." The nature of this escalation was perceived as "a carefully orchestrated bombing attack on NVN, directed primarily at infiltration and other military targets." It would consist of

> U.S. reconnaissance planes, VNAF/FARMGATE aircraft against those targets which could be attacked safely in spite of the presence of the MIGs, and additional U.S. combat aircraft if necessary for the effective execution of the bombing program.

He qualified this assessment with the observation, "We must always recognize, however, that events may force [the] U.S. to advance D-Day to a considerably earlier date." The reason for this qualification was Taylor's concern that the GVN might not be able to sustain its authority until January. Thus, in order to "avoid the probable consequences of a collapse of national morale" it would be necessary, he felt, "to open the campaign against the DRV without delay."

Similar assessments of timing in relation to more vigorous military action against North Vietnam were made in OSD/ISA. The immediate measures proposed in McNaughton's draft "Plan of Action for South Vietnam" (3 September) were conceived not only as means to provoke North Vietnam into responses justifying U.S. punitive actions. They were also believed to make possible the postponement "probably until November or December" of a decision regarding the more serious escalation. In McNaughton's terminology the latter were referred to as "a crescendo of GVN-U.S. military actions against the DRV," but they included a variety of possibilities:

> The escalating actions might be naval pressures or mining of harbors; or they might be made up of air strikes against North Vietnam moving from southern to northern targets, from targets associated with infiltration and by-then-disclosed DRV-VC radio command nets to targets of military then industrial importance, and from missions which could be handled by the VNAF alone to those which could be carried out only by the U.S.

It is clear, however, that what was contemplated was a pattern of gradually mounting pressures intended to impress the DRV with the increasing gravity of its situation.

Records of the September conference do not indicate that a decision was made relative to an explicit January contingency date. In several respects they do make clear that the possibility of escalation at the end of the year was considered. For example, hope was expressed that the GVN would grow stronger over the following two to three months—by implication, strong enough to permit "major deliberate risks of escalation" or "deliberately provocative" U.S. actions. Directly related to this hope was the intention of having the GVN admit publicly to its conduct of maritime operations against North Vietnamese coastal installations and communications. The aim was "to justify and legitimize them on the basis of the facts of VC infiltration by sea." It was believed that this step would be useful in establishing a climate of opinion more receptive to expanded (air) operations against North Vietnam when they should become necessary.

Reservations. By October 1964, therefore, there was a general belief among the President's top advisors that it would probably be necessary eventually to subject North Vietnam to overt military pressure. Many were convinced, however reluctantly, that it would not be possible to obtain an effective solution to the problem of DRV sponsorship of the insurgency in South Vietnam or a practical solution to the political strife in Laos without such direct pressure on the instigators of these problems. The earlier views of most of the principal advisors had been clearly contingent upon a major reversal—principally in Laos— and had been advanced with the apparent assumption that military actions hopefully would not be required. Now, however, their views were advanced with a sense that such actions were inevitable. Moreover, they were advanced despite the perspective afforded by a number of critical evaluations of the use of military pressure. In addition to the studies made during the first half of 1964, all of the principal advisory agencies had reviewed a detailed critique of the so-called "Rostow thesis" just prior to the September strategy conference.

The critique was accomplished in OSD/ISA with inputs and coordination from State's Policy Planning Council. The assigned task was to make "a thorough analysis of and report on the Rostow thesis that covert aggression justifies and must be fought by attacks on the source of the aggression." Copies were distributed to the Washington recipients of the Rostow paper, including the White House, Department of State, Department of Defense, the JCS and each of the services.

In their summary analysis of the thesis, the critiquers emphasized two variables which would determine its utility: (1) the extent of the commitment of the nation furnishing external support and (2) the extent to which the insurgency affected vital U.S. interests. With regard to the former variable, they described "three fundamental conditions" which would have to exist to achieve success "in cases where the external opponent is committed to the extent of the North Vietnamese." The opponents would have to be persuaded that: (1) the United States was "taking limited actions to achieve limited objectives;" (2) "the commitment of the military power of the United States to the limited objective is a total commitment—as total as our commitment to get the missiles out of Cuba in October 1962;" (3) the United States has "established a sufficient consensus to see through this course of action both at home and on the world scene." Further, unless such an opponent were so persuaded, "the approach might well fail to be effective short of a larger U.S. military involvement."

Essential to creating the necessary conviction of U.S. intent on the part of the opposing government, the analysis argued, was a firm image that the President and the U.S. public were in agreement that vital national interests were at stake. Unless vital interests were clearly at stake,

> the limited military actions envisaged would not only involve much greater political costs at home and abroad . . . but there would be much greater risk that the program would not be effective except at high levels of involvement and risk, and that it might be allowed to fall short of such levels.

Assuming that vital U.S. interests were assessed as being at stake by an Administration in some unspecified case, the critiquers went on to outline some additional "conditions for success." First, an Administration would have to present a solid case to the U.S. Congress and public and to our allies that the external support provided by the target nation was instrumental in sustaining the insurgency. In the interest of making its public case conclusive, "the U.S. would have to be prepared to expose intelligence data." Second, it would have to identify enemy targets "such that limited attacks and the threat of further attacks would bring great pressure on him to comply." Third, the U.S. Government would have to be able to communicate its case to the target nation "including the high degree of U.S. commitment and the limited nature of our objective." This would involve controlling both the U.S. and its ally's actions "to convey limited objectives, minimizing incentives to comply." Finally, it would have to be capable of determining enemy compliance with our demands.

The critiquers' analysis included an assessment of the costs and risks to be incurred in applying the thesis and cautioned against its adoption as a general declaratory policy:

> Given present attitudes, application of the Rostow approach risks domestic and international opposition ranging from anxiety and protest to condemnation, efforts to disassociate from U.S. policies or alliances, or even strong countermeasures. . . .
>
> Currently, then, it is the Rostow approach, rather than the measures it counters that would be seen generally as an "unstabilizing" change in the rules of the game, an escalation of conflict, an increasing of shared, international risks, and quite possibly, as an open aggression demanding condemnation . . . particularly in general terms or in abstraction from a specific, immediately challenging situation.

On the other hand, the controlled, limited military actions implied in the Rostow approach would be far more acceptable to the extent that they were seen to follow from Presidential conviction of vital national *necessity* in a specific context, and even more to the extent that this conviction were shared by Congress and the U.S. public.

An attempt to legitimize such actions in general terms, and in advance of an emergency situation, would not only be likely to fail, but might well evoke public expression of domestic and allied opposition and denunciation . . . from opponents that would make it much *more* difficult for the President to contemplate this approach when an occasion actually arose. . . .

They went on to point out that accepting the Rostow thesis as a principle of U.S. declaratory policy would *require* making it public before applying it. The need to be assured of "Congressional and other public support in carrying through the thesis in a given case" would require this. Therefore, the analysts concluded, "It would be exceedingly unwise to make the Rostow thesis a declaratory policy unless the U.S. were prepared to act on it"—but then only if we were assured of the public commitment and the capability to achieve success.

With regard to the applicability of the thesis to the contemporary situation in Southeast Asia, the critiquers summarized their views as follows:

> . . . the situation in Vietnam and Laos is the only one in which a strong case can be made that the two major indications for the Rostow approach are made: the ineffectiveness of alternatives and vital U.S. interests. Even in this case the degree of U.S. interest, the degree and acceptability of the risks, and the potential effectiveness of this approach are subject to question. In particular, the likelihood and the political costs of *failure* of the approach, and the *pressures for U.S. escalation* if early moves should fail, require serious examination.

5. Differing Agency Policy Views

In describing the evolution of Administration strategy, this account has previously emphasized the points of general agreement among the President's advisors. Its purpose has been to describe the existence and sense of a policy consensus that had emerged by mid-October. However, significant differences of opinion existed among the various advisory agencies regarding *what* actions should be taken and *how soon* they should be initiated. These differences can be discerned with respect to five issues: (1) whether and how soon the GVN maritime operation should be acknowledged; (2) the desirability of tit-for-tat reprisals; (3) how best to cope with enemy reactions to increased pressures on the DRV; (4) the degree of GVN/U.S. readiness required before increasing the pressures; and (5) the relationship perceived between increased pressures and negotiations.

JCS views. Senior military officials differed among themselves on the first three issues. CINCPAC apparently perceived difficulties resulting from official acknowledgments of GVN maritime operations and sugested that press leaks would [words illegible]. General Wheeler [words illegible] operations and thereby enable their scope and effectiveness to be increased. However, he was not supported by the service chiefs. They opposed surfacing the GVN operations until they could become associated with the DE SOTO Patrols "or until the United States is prepared openly to support MAROPS militarily." All of these officials agreed that it was necessary to undertake reprisals for a variety of hostile VC or DRV actions. In particular they wanted U.S. responses to be greater in degree, not necessarily matching in kind, than the provocations. Where they came to differ was on the desirability of deliberately provoking DRV actions to which we could then respond. After the September White House meeting only the Air Force Chief of Staff and the Marine Commandant favored this approach.

Differences with respect to preparation for coping with enemy reactions to harsher pressures centered around the issue of committing greater numbers of U.S. ground forces to South Vietnam. CINCPAC, supporting General Westmoreland's request, urged provision for deployment of Marine and Army units to provide security for U.S./GVN operating bases. The JCS disagreed and disapproved a request to make such adjustments in OPLAN 37–64, on grounds that since VC capabilities were still questionable it was preferable not to precommit U.S. forces in the manner urged. At issue concurrently was an Air Force proposal to reduce the number of ground forces provided for in the event of a large scale DRV/CHICOM intervention in Southeast Asia and to reply more heavily on tactical air capabilities. The other chiefs disagreed, but the controversy concerning the relative emphasis on ground and air forces for the defense of Southeast Asia was to occupy JCS attention for several months to come.

Regarding the issue of readiness to increase pressures on North Vietnam and the role of negotiations, the military chiefs were in agreement throughout the period. Soon after the Tonkin Gulf incidents they urged prompt implementation of more serious pressures using U.S. air capabilities. They opposed B-57 training for the VNAF, citing its limited pilot and supporting technical resources which would be needed for counterinsurgency missions. In response to warnings that we should not get deeply involved in a conflict in Southeast Asia until we were surer of the GVN's commitment, they replied that "the United States is already deeply involved." They went on to recommend preparations for deploying the remaining OPLAN 37–64 forces needed for mounting a U.S. air strike program against North Vietnam. While the JCS did not address the subject of negotiations explicitly during this period, their statements implied a lack of interest in a negotiated solution to the Vietnam problem. At every opportunity they reiterated their recommendation that we should attack North Vietnamese will and capabilities as necessary to force a DRV decision to halt its support and direction of the insurgency.

Saigon Embassy views. Ambassador Taylor opposed the views of his former military colleagues on most issues. Prior to the September meeting, he expressed objections to the idea of surfacing or leaking to the press the nature of GVN maritime operations. He also opposed tit-for-tat retaliation bombing for the reason that it was "likely to release a new order of military reaction from both sides, the outcome of which is impossible to predict." He saw enemy ground assaults as a greater threat to U.S. bases in South Vietnam than enemy air attacks and supported the deployment of U.S. ground force units for base security purposes. This was to occur after the beginning of GVN/U.S. ground and air cross-border operations into Laos. However, not unlike the Chiefs, one of the criteria he employed in shaping his recommendation was the avoidance of a major U.S. ground force commitment.

Ambassador Taylor's views were apparently based on an underlying rationale that actions to counter the VC/DRV aggression should not outstrip the GVN and that if it could be avoided, the conflict should not be escalated to a level beyond South Vietnamese capacities to manage it. Although believing firmly that the United States would have to apply direct pressure against North Vietnam eventually, to force her to abandon her objectives, he felt that the major burden of this effort should be borne by the GVN. Thus, his support for U.S. base security deployment was based in part on concern lest ARVN units be tied down in such roles and, thus, unavailable for more free-ranging combat. Similarly, in August, the Embassy favored immediate initiation of B-57 training for the VNAF to enable it to play a substantial role in the overt air attacks envisioned for 1965.

This training—like Saigon's discouragement of U.S. eagerness to negotiate in Laos—was also advocated for its value in bolstering the GVN's morale and determination to continue fighting against its communist enemies. This same consideration was at the root of the Ambassador's belief that any negotiations which affected South Vietnam should be avoided until North Vietnam was subjected to more forceful military pressures. He also felt that communication with Hanoi should be preceded by a thorough discussion and understanding of our limited war aims with the GVN.

The Ambassador's basic concern that the GVN be capable of and committed to supporting the evolving levels of war effort against the communists was indicated in his response to the political upheaval in Saigon. Earlier, his recommendations had included the option of opening "the [air] campaign against the DRV without delay," in the event of threatened collapse of the Khanh Government. The objective was to have been "to avoid the possible consequences of a collapse of national morale." At the September meeting and subsequently, however, after Khanh had already been forced to step down from GVN leadership once and his new government had [words illegible] the Ambassador opposed overt action [words illegible] urged instead [words illegible].

OSD views. OSD and OSD/ISA views were clearer on some issues than on others. For example, the source documents indicate their consistent support for surfacing the GVN maritime operations. Similarly, it is clear that OSD continually regarded negotiations as a necessary process for terminating the insurgency in South Vietnam and a program of increased pressures against the DRV as a means of improving the U.S. bargaining position. Like other agencies, it saw negotiations as something that should not be entered into until the pressures were hurting North Vietnam, but it emphasized that the pattern of pressures should make clear our limited aims.

Equally consistent but less explicit were OSD views on GVN/U.S. readiness to mount overt attacks on North Vietnam. Secretary McNamara was concerned that too early initiation of air action against North Vietnam might find the United States unprepared to cope with the consequences. At the end of August he directed the JCS to study and report on POL and ordnance stocks available to carry out approved contingency plans to combat a large-scale communist intervention *after* the expenditures required for the pattern of attacks which they proposed against North Vietnam. He also asked for specific recommendations on next steps to be taken in the event destruction of the proposed JCS targets did not destroy the DRV will and capability to continue. Mr. McNaughton's "Plan of Action" was intended to make unnecessary any decision concerning larger operations until late in the autumn. Morever, it was designed explicitly "to create as little risk as possible of the kind of military action which would be difficult to justify to the American public and to preserve where possible the option to have no U.S. military action at all." In September, OSD/ISA was on record as favoring the initiation of bombing against North Vietnam—after suitable provocation by Hanoi. But by mid-October the OSD view was apparently that overt actions against the North should be held off at least until the new year.

With respect to the other issues, the most consistent aspect of OSD views was their prudence. Its attitudes toward tit-for-tat reprisals are not really clear. Soon after Tonkin Gulf, OSD notified the JCS that the events there precluded any further need for their work on retaliation scenarios in support of NSAM 288. Then, just three weeks later, the McNaughton "Plan of Action" proposed deliberate provocation of DRV actions to permit U.S. retaliation—but as a means to begin a gradual squeeze on North Vietnam, not merely tit-for-tat reprisals. Mr. McNamara's own views do not appear except by implication, in that he did not indicate any opposition to them when shown William Bundy's draft summation of the September meeting consensus. Prudence was again the dominant feature of OSD views on preparations to cope with possible enemy reactions to the harsher pressures. For example, "on several occasions" Secretary McNamara expressed to the JCS his interest in the possibility of countering a massive Chinese intervention in Southeast Asia without the need to introduce large numbers of U.S. ground forces.

[material missing]

proposal to reduce provisional ground force levels for Southeast Asian defense concluded that the issue remained "open." It was critical of that particular study because of its methodology and assumptions. Later, however, Mr. McNamara supported the JCS in their disapproval of the MACV request for allocation of additional ground force units for base security purposes.

State views. Various documents make it clear that there were several different points of view prevalent within the State Department during the period in question. Reflected here are those channeled through the Secretary of State or communicated to the Department of Defense, usually through the Assistant Secretary for Far Eastern Affairs. With few exceptions, the courses of action followed by the Administration were those advocated by State. Its proposal for B-57 training for the VNAF was apparently overruled on the basis of JCS recommendations, but otherwise its support for measures to further strengthen the GVN and for pressuring actions other than overt military attacks throughout 1964 prevailed. Its support for the acknowledgement of GVN maritime operations failed to materialize only because of objections on the part of the GVN itself.

State Department views on the other issues, likewise, were reflected in U.S. policy positions. Reprisals for VC acts that could be matched with fitting responses were favored in principle but were not necessarily to be carried out in all instances. Escalation through such responses was seen as useful for purposes of assisting GVN morale, but State did not believe that steps should be taken to bring about such situations just yet. It did, however, acknowledge that deliberate provocations might be useful in the future. Negotiation of a Vietnam solution through an international conference was viewed as inevitable, but it should be permitted only after hurting North Vietnam and convincing South Vietnam of U.S. resolve to achieve its objectives. Moreover, Secretary Rusk, Assistant Secretary Bundy and Counselor Rostow were each known to view avoidance of a commitment of U.S. ground forces to Southeast Asia as an important element in policy.

CIA views. With the exception of Mr. McCone's opinions rendered in the September strategy meeting, available CIA documents provide no policy recommendations. However, they do contain assessments bearing directly on the policy issues discussed previously—particularly with respect to enemy reactions to the measures contemplated. For example, intelligence estimates indicated little likelihood that intensified maritime operations would result in retaliation against GVN naval bases. Similarly, they predicted few serious consequences in response to U.S. limited tit-for-tat reprisal strikes. Rather, the CIA believed that communist responses would be limited to defensive measures, increased propaganda, and additional logistical assistance from China. In the event our reprisal actions were "heavier and sustained," the DRV was expected first to attempt to dissuade the United States through international political moves, [words illegible]

CIA estimates of communist reaction to systematic U.S./GVN air attacks on North Vietnam were less certain. While acknowledging "substantial danger" that the DRV might decide to send its own armed forces on a large scale to Laos and South Vietnam,

> ("Hanoi might assume that United States would be unwilling to undertake a major ground war, or that if it was, it could ultimately be defeated by the methods which were successful against the French.")

they thought it more likely that Hanoi would choose a more conservative course. They reasoned that "the DRV might calculate that it would be better to stop VC activity temporarily than risk loss of its military facilities and industry," but that they would make no meaningful concessions "such as agreeing to effective international inspection of infiltration routes." In any event, the CIA did not believe that Chinese intervention was likely unless the United States should strike the Chinese mainland or unless U.S./GVN forces should attempt to "occupy areas of the DRV or communist-held territory in Northern Laos." It indicated that both North Vietnam and Communist China wished to avoid direct conflict with the United States and would probably "avoid actions that would in their view unduly increase the chances of a major U.S. response" against them.

Rather than outright military victory in South Vietnam, CIA estimates indicated belief that the communists expected to gain control through a "neutralist coalition government dominated by pro-Communist elements" that would come about "soon." This concern over the threat of neutralism had been voiced at the September meeting by Mr. McCone and was quite prevalent among intelligence discussions of the period. Altogether, it created a rather gloomy impression of GVN readiness to support sustained overt operations against North Vietnam and absorb likely VC countermeasures. In October the picture became even gloomier as a result of an intelligence assessment which described continuing deterioration of the South Vietnamese political situation and predicted even more:

> . . . we believe that the conditions favor a further decay of GVN will and effectiveness. The likely pattern of this decay will be increasing defeatism, paralysis of leadership, friction with Americans, exploration of possible lines of political accommodation with the other side, and a general petering out of the war effort.

II. NOVEMBER 1964–JANUARY 1965

A. POLICY DEBATE IN NOVEMBER

In their Southeast Asia policy discussions of August–October 1964, Administration officials had accepted the view that overt military pressures against

North Vietnam probably would be required. Barring some critical developments, however, it was generally conceded that these should not begin until after the new year. Preparations for applying such pressures were made in earnest during November.

1. *Immediate Antecedents*

In Administration policy discussions, the two developments most often cited as perhaps warranting implementation of overt military pressures before 1965 were: (1) increased levels of infiltration of guerrillas into South Vietnam and (2) serious deterioration of the GVN. Evidence of both was reported to Washington during October.

National intelligence estimates gave the GVN little hope of surviving the apathy and discouragement with which it was plagued. They reported, "Government ministries in Saigon are close to a standstill, with only the most routine operations going on." U.S./GVN planning was not being followed by GVN action. A coup by disgruntled South Vietnamese military figures was believed imminent (one had been attempted unsuccessfully on 13 September). Moreover, the civilian government which General Khanh had promised for the end of October was seen as unlikely to bring about any real improvement.

A threat of GVN capitulation to the NLF, in the form of accepting a coalition government, was also seen as a real possibility. Citing "numerous signs that Viet Cong agents have played a role in helping sustain the level of civil disorder . . . in the cities," intelligence reports estimated that it was the Communist intention to seek victory through a "neutralist coalition" rather than by force of arms. Perhaps straining a bit, an estimate stated, "The principal GVN leaders have not to our knowledge been in recent contact with the Communists, but there has been at least one instance of informal contact between a lesser governmental official and members of the NLF." Another estimate portrayed the DRV and Chinese as regarding South Vietnam as a "developing political vacuum," soon to be filled "with a neutralist coalition government dominated by pro-Communist elements."

Reports of increasing infiltration began arriving in mid-October. Ambassador Taylor cabled on the 14th [Doc. 210] that he had received indications of a "definite step-up in infiltration from North Vietnam, particularly in the northern provinces . . ." He went on to report:

> A recent analysis suggests that if the present rate of infiltration is maintained, the annual figure for 1964 will be of the order of 10,000. Furthermore . . . we are finding more and more "bona fide" North Vietnamese soldiers among the infiltrees. I feel sure that we must soon adopt new and drastic methods to reduce and eventually end such infiltration if we are ever to succeed in South Vietnam.

A similar report was cabled directly to the White House on 16 October. In it, Ambassador Taylor repeated his comments on infiltration and advised the President of the steadily worsening situation in South Vietnam. The Ambassador reported the infiltration of northern-born conscripts and relayed GVN claims that they were coming in organized units. He pointed out that with the advent of the dry season, the problem would assume even greater magnitude and urged that it be given immediate attention.

The Taylor estimates of end-year infiltration totals probably were quite alarming. If accurate they indicated that the rate had risen sharply during September and early October: The total number of infiltrees for 1964 as of 1 September was then estimated as 4,700. Of particular concern, no doubt, was the apparent emphasis on reinforcing Communist units in the Central Highlands and in the northern provinces of South Vietnam. These warnings came hard on the heels of widespread press reports of badly weakened GVN control in three portions of the country.

The JCS seized on these fresh reports and resubmitted their proposals for taking prompt measures against North Vietnam. On 21 October, they argued:

> Application of the principle of isolating the guerrilla force from its reinforcement and support and then to fragment and defeat the forces has not been successful in Vietnam. . . . The principle must be applied by control of the national boundaries or by eliminating or cutting off the source of supply and direction.

On the 27th they submitted a major proposal for "strong military actions" to counteract the trends cited in the national intelligence estimates and in the Taylor cables. In language identical to that used in two August memoranda and at the September strategy meeting, they stated that such actions were "required now in order to prevent the collapse of the U.S. position in Southeast Asia." They then recommended a program of actions to support the following strategy:

a. Depriving the Viet Cong of out of country assistance by applying military pressures on the . . . DRV to the extent necessary to cause the DRV to cease support and direction of the insurgency.

b. Depriving the VC of assistance within SVN by expanding the counterinsurgency effort—military, economic, and political—within SVN.

c. Continuing to seek a viable effective government in SVN based on the broadest possible consensus.

d. Maintaining a military readiness posture in Southeast Asia that:

> (1) Demonstrates the U.S. will and capability to escalate the action if required.
> (2) Deters a major Communist aggression in the area.

The program recommended by the JCS included a list of actions to be taken within South Vietnam and a separate list of actions outside. The Chiefs had listed them in order of increasing intensity, and they requested authority "to implement now" the first six actions within the country and the first eight outside. The latter included air strikes by GVN/FARMGATE aircraft against Communist LOC's in Laos and in the southern portion of North Vietnam.

In the context of the reported worsening situation in South Vietnam, the JCS proposal was given serious consideration in OSD. Since Ambassador Taylor had expressed concern over initiating overt pressures against North Vietnam "before we have a responsible set of authorities to work with in South Vietnam," a copy of the JCS paper was forwarded to him for review and comment. The OSD's stated intention was to consider the Ambassador's views before developing a proposal to present to President Johnson.

While this proposal was still under consideration (1 November 1964), Viet Cong forces attacked U.S. facilities at the Bien Hoa airbase with 81mm. mortar fire. Four American servicemen were killed, and five B–57 tactical bombers were destroyed, and major damage was inflicted on eight others.

Administration attention was focused immediately on the question of what the United States should do in response to the Bien Hoa provocation. It will be recalled that such an eventuality had been discussed at the September strategy meeting. The Presidential directive which resulted from it stated: "We should be prepared to respond as appropriate against the DRV in the event of any attack on U.S. units or any special DRV/VC action against SVN." As of the end of October (in anticipation of resumed DE SOTO Patrols), elements of our Pacific forces were reported as "poised and ready" to execute reprisals for any DRV attacks on our naval vessels. Thus, there was a rather large expectancy among Administration officials that the United States would do something in retaliation.

Apparently, the decision was made to do nothing—at least not of a retaliatory nature. At a White House meeting to discuss possible courses of action, on 1 November, "concern was expressed that proposed U.S. retaliatory punitive actions could trigger North Vietnamese/CHICOM air and ground retaliatory acts." Questions were raised about "increased security measures and precautionary moves of U.S. air and ground units to protest U.S. dependents, units and installations against such retaliation. [Doc. 215] Following the meeting, a White House news release announced that the President had ordered the destroyed and badly damaged aircraft replaced. Administration officials stated that "the mortar attack must be viewed in the light of the Vietnamese war and of the whole Southeast Asian situation. If the United States is to retaliate against North Vietnam in the future," they reportedly said, "it must be for broader reasons than the strike against the Bien Hoa base." Moreover, they drew a contrast between this incident and the Tonkin Gulf attacks where our destroyers were "on United States business."

Source documents available do not indicate that any further decisions were made on the Bien Hoa matter. A second meeting to discuss possible U.S. actions was "tentatively scheduled" for 2 November, but the available materials contain no evidence that it was held. President Johnson was scheduled to appear in Houston that afternoon, for his final pre-election address, and it may be that the second White House meeting was called off. In any event, unofficial reports from Saigon, two days later, stated that most of the B–57s had been withdrawn from the Bien Hoa base. While acknowledging that "some" had been removed to Clark Air Base, in the Philippines, official spokesmen in Saigon refused to comment on whether or not a wholesale withdrawal had taken place. One thing is certain; there were no retaliatory strikes authorized following the attack on the U.S. bomber base.

However, retaliatory measures were proposed. On 1 November, the JCS suggested orally to Secretary McNamara that air strikes be authorized on key Communist targets in both Laos and North Vietnam. According to the JCS plan, those in Laos would be hit within 24–36 hours after approval, with forces already in place, and these attacks would divert attention from the preparation necessary for the stronger actions to follow. The latter would include a B–52 night attack on Phuc Yen airfield (outside Hanoi), to be followed by a dawn strike by USAF and Navy tactical aircraft against other airfields and POL storage in the Hanoi-Haiphong area.

Ambassador Taylor immediately cabled a Saigon Embassy-MACV recommendation for "retaliatory bombing attacks on selected DRV targets by combined U.S./VNAF air forces and for a policy statement that we will act similarly in like cases in the future." In a later cable he made specific reference to "the retaliatory principle confirmed in NSAM 314," stating that, if his initial recommendation was not accepted, at least a lesser alternative should be adopted. This he described as "intensifying 34A operations and initiating air operations against selected targets as an interim substitute for more positive measures."

On 4 November, the JCS repeated in writing their recommendations of the 1st, adding some explanatory comment and taking issue with certain aspects of the Taylor recommendations. They explained that they considered the VC attack on Bien Hoa airfield "a deliberate act of escalation and a change of the ground rules under which the VC have operated up to now." They cautioned against "undue delay or restraint" in making a response, since it "could be misinterpreted by our allies in Southeast Asia, as well as by the DRV and Communist China" and "could encourage the enemy to conduct additional attacks. . . ." Referring to Ambassador Taylor's recommendation to announce a policy of reprisal bombing, the JCS denounced a "tit-for-tat" policy as "unduly restrictive" and tending to "pass to the DRV substantial initiatives with respect to the nature and timing of further U.S. actions." They concluded:

> Early U.S. military action against the DRV would lessen the possibility of misinterpretation by the DRV and Communist China of U.S. determination and intent and thus serve to deter further VC attacks such as that at Bien Hoa.

In the meantime, there had been created what may have been the only concrete result from the high-level policy deliberations following the Bien Hoa incident. An interagency task force, known as the NSC Working Group, had begun an intensive study of future U.S. courses of action. Recommendations from the JCS and others were passed on to that group for incorporation in their work.

2. *Formation of the NSC Working Group*

The "NSC Working Group on SVN/SEA" held its first meeting at 0930 hours, 3 November, thus placing the decision to organize such a group at sometime earlier—probably on 2 November or perhaps even at the high-level meeting on 1 November. Its charter was to study "immediately and intensively" the future courses of action and alternatives open to the United States in Southeast Asia and to report as appropriate to a "Principals Group" of NSC members. In turn, this group of senior officials would then recommend specific courses of action to the President. Initially, the working group was given approximately one week to ten days to complete its work. Actually, it developed and recast its reports over a period of three weeks or more.

Four agencies were represented in the formal membership of the group. The Department of State contingent included Assistant Secretary Bundy (Chairman), Marshall Green, Michael Forrestal (both of the Bureau of Far Eastern Affairs), and Robert Johnson (of the Policy Planning Council). Assistant Secretary (ISA) McNaughton represented OSD. Vice Admiral Lloyd Mustin was the JCS member. The CIA was represented by Harold Ford. Other staff members from these agencies assisted in work on specific topics.

The Working Group's efforts were apportioned among seven tasks, the initial input for each being accomplished by a particular member or subcommittee, as shown on p. 211. [Doc. 216]

Most inputs were made in the form of either (1) draft papers treating fully a topic intended for inclusion in the Working Group's final submission or (2)

TOPIC	RESPONSIBILITY
Assessment of the current situation in South Vietnam, including policy direction of interested powers.	Intelligence community
U.S. objectives and stakes in South Vietnam and Southeast Asia.	William Bundy
Broad options (3) available to the United States.	Bundy and ISA
Alternative forms of possible negotiation.	State/Policy Planning Council
Analyses of different options *vis-a-vis* U.S. objectives and interests.	JCS to propose specific actions; Policy Planning Council to examine political impacts of the most violent option first.
Immediate actions in the period prior to Presidential decision on options.	State/Far East Bureau

memoranda commenting on an initial draft paper and suggesting alterations. Because of the unique responsibilities and advisory processes of the JCS, their member apparently chose to make initial inputs largely through references to or excerpts from regular JCS documents; he also contributed to the redrafting of the option analyses. The initial papers on each of the topics were circulated among the Working Group members, reviewed in consultation with their parent organizations and modified. Some positions passed through as many as three drafts before being submitted to the Principals.

3. *Working Group Assessments of the Utility of Pressures*

The NSC Working Group approached its work with the general assessment that increased pressures against North Vietnam would be both useful and necessary. However, this assessment embraced a wide range of considerations stemming from the developing situation in South Vietnam and a variety of viewpoints concerning what kinds of pressures would be most effective.

a. *Sense of Urgency.* As the working group began its deliberation, an awareness that another Bien Hoa could occur at any time was prominent in both the official and the public mind. The tenuous security of U.S. bases in South Vietnam had received wide publicity. Moreover, the news services were reporting the threat of civil protest against the new Saigon government, and the increased level of guerrilla infiltration from the North was being publicly aired. These developments lent an added sense of urgency to the Group's work. The Chairman of the Working Group was sensitive to these developments and to related attitudes within the Administration. For example, he indicated that the intelligence agencies were "on the verge of . . . agreement that infiltration has in fact mounted," and that the Saigon mission was "urging that we surface this by the end of this week or early next week." He stressed that "the President is clearly thinking in terms of maximum use of a Gulf of Tonkin [reprisal] rationale." The nature of such a decision was expected to be:

either for an action that would show toughness and hold the line till we can decide the big issue, or as a basis for starting a clear course of action under . . . broad options.

He implied that our intention to stand firm in South Vietnam was being communicated to the USSR ("Secretary Rusk is talking today to Dobrynin") and indicated the desirability of President Johnson signalling something similar rather soon through the public media. This was seen as particularly important "to counter any SVN fears of a softening in our policy," presumably in view of our not responding to the Bien Hoa attack. [Doc. 219]

Chairman Bundy was aware also of the significance attached by some observers to the first U.S. actions after the Presidential election. As was pointed out to him, "all Vietnamese and other interested observers" would be watching carefully to "see what posture the newly mandated Johnson Administration will assume." For this reason, William H. Sullivan, head of the interagency Vietnam Coordinating Committee (and soon to be appointed the new U.S. Ambassador to Laos), urged "that our first action be . . . one which gives the appearance of a determination to take risks if necessary to maintain our position in Southeast Asia." An immediate retaliation for any repetition of the Bien Hoa attack and armed reconnaissance missions in the Laotian Panhandle were cited as specific examples. He went on to recommend to Mr. Bundy:

> I feel that it is important . . . that the Administration go on record fairly soon placing our policy in Viet Nam within the larger perspective of our policies in the Western Pacific, especially as they involve confrontation with Communist China. [Doc. 220]

A sense of urgency for the Working Group's efforts was also derived from assessments of the trends within South Vietnam. For example, the intelligence panel composed of CIA, DIA, and State/INR members saw little prospect for an effective GVN despite an acknowledged slowing of "adverse political trends." In their view the political situation was "extremely fragile," with the Saigon administration "plagued by confusion, apathy and poor morale" and the new leadership hampered by the older factionalism. The security situation in the countryside was assessed as having continued to deteriorate, with "Viet Cong control . . . spreading over areas heretofore controlled by the government." Although indicating "better than even" chances that the GVN could "hang on for the near future and thus afford a platform upon which . . . [to] prosecute the war and attempt to turn the tide," the panel painted a grim picture of its prospects. This assessment was probably instrumental in prompting Assistant Secretary McNaughton's cryptic observation that "progress inside SVN is important, but it is unlikely despite our best ideas and efforts." Besides, he observed, if it came at all, it would take "at least several months." In his view, the efforts of the Working Group could in some measure compensate for this slow progress inside South Vietnam:

> Action against North Vietnam is to some extent a substitute for strengthing the government in South Vietnam. That is, a less active VC (on orders from DRV) can be handled by a less efficient GVN (which we expect to have.

b. *Views of DRV Susceptibility.* The extent to which "action against North Vietnam" might affect that nation's support of the conflicts in South Vietnam and Laos was a matter on which members of the Working Group did not fully agree. The intelligence panel members tended toward a pessimistic view. They pointed out that "the basic elements of Communist strength in South Vietnam remain indigenous," and that "even if severely damaged" the DRV could continue to support the insurrection at a lessened level. Therefore, they stressed that the U.S. ability to compel a halt to the DRV support depended on eroding Hanoi's will and persuading the DRV:

> that the price of mounting the insurrection in the South at a high level would be too great and that it would be preferable to reduce its aid . . . and direct at least a temporary reduction of V.C. activity.

As the panel members saw it, this respite would then provide an opportunity to stabilize and improve the GVN. But, in their words, "Even so, lasting success would depend upon a substantial improvement in the energy and effectiveness of the RVN government and pacification machinery."

However, the intelligence panel did not concede very strong chances for breaking the will of Hanoi. They thought it quite likely that the DRV was willing to suffer damage "in the course of a test of wills with the United States over the course of events in South Vietnam." To support this view, they cited Hanoi's belief that international pressures would develop against deliberate U.S. expansion of the war. Further, that given present trends in South Vietnam, both Hanoi and Peking had good reason to expect success without having to initiate actions carrying the risk of the kind of war which would expose them to "the great weight of superior U.S. weaponry." The panel also viewed Hanoi as estimating that the U.S. will to maintain resistance in Southeast Asia could in time be eroded—that the recent U.S. election would provide the Johnson Administration with "greater policy flexibility" than it previously felt it had.

This view was challenged by the Working Group's JCS member as being too "negative." Interpreting the panel's non-specific reference to "policy flexibility" in an extreme sense, he wrote:

> If this means that Hanoi thinks we are now in position to accept worldwide humiliation with respect to our formerly stated objectives in Vietnam, this is another reason why it is desirable that we take early measures to disabuse their thinking.

Moreover, he indicated the JCS view that the slightly improved hopes for government stability (acknowledged by the panel) were good reason why "early and positive actions" should be taken. This point was reinforced by his judgment that (in contrast with its impact on esprit and political effectiveness) the GVN's "principal task is to afford the platform upon which the RVN armed forces, with U.S. assistance, prosecute the war."

In criticism of the intelligence panel's emphasis on the need to influence DRV will, Admiral Mustin indicated that enemy capabilities represented a more appropriate target. He stated the JCS assessment that:

> a. The actual U.S. requirement with respect to the DRV is reduction of the *rate of delivery* of support to the VC, to levels below their minimum necessary sustaining level . . .
> b. In the present unstable situation something far less than total destruction may be all that is required to accomplish the above. A very modest

change in the government's [GVN] favor . . . *may* be enough to turn the tide and lead to a sucessful solution. Of course it is not possible to predict in advance . . . the precise level of measures which will be required to achieve the above. This is the reason for designing a program of progressively increasing squeeze.

One of the factors encouraging JCS optimism, he pointed out, was the assessment accepted by the panel that both Hanoi and Peking wanted to avoid direct conflict with the United States. This would act as a deterrent to Communist persistence, particularly if by a program of military pressures we were able to revise their assessment that they could win "without much risk of having to feel the weight of U.S. response."

Apparently as a result of these criticisms and their influence on other Working Group members, the Group's final assessment of DRV susceptibility to military pressures was somewhat modified. While continuing to emphasize that affecting Hanoi's will was important, the criticality of it was obscured by concessions to the possible impact of damage to DRV capabilities and by greater reliance on conditional phrasing. For example:

the nature of the war in Vietnam is such that U.S. ability to compel the DRV to end or reduce the VC insurrection rests essentially upon the effect of the U.S. sanctions on the will of DRV leadership to sustain and enlarge that insurrection, and to a lesser extent upon the effect of sanctions on the capabilities of the DRV to do so.

Although giving explicit recognition to "a rising rate of infiltration," and continuing to acknowledge limits to U.S. abilities to prevent the DRV's material support for the VC, the assessment stated that "U.S.-inflicted destruction in North Vietnam and Laos would reduce these supporting increments and damage DRV/VC morale." It qualified this statement, however, by pointing out that the degree to which such damage would provide the GVN with a breathing spell would depend largely on "whether any DRV 'removal' of its direction and support of the VC were superficial or whole." If superficial or "limited to gestures . . . that removed only the more visible evidences of the DRV increment," the report continued, "it would probably not be possible to develop a viable and free government in South Vietnam."

In general, the final assessment of DRV susceptibility to pressures was less discouraging than the intelligence panel's initial submission, although it could not be considered particularly encouraging either. The reference to U.S. "policy flexibility," to which the JCS took such violent objection, was removed, and the following non-committing statement was used instead: "Hanoi's immediate estimate is probably that the passing of the U.S. election gives Washington the opportunity to take new military actions against the DRV and/or new diplomatic initiatives." If new military pressures were applied, the report indicated that Hanoi's leaders would be faced with a basic question: "Is the U.S. determined to continue escalating its pressures to achieve its announced objectives . . . or is the U.S. escalation essentially a limited attempt to improve the U.S. negotiating position?" It continued:

Their decision . . . would be affected by the U.S. military posture in the area, by the extent and nature of the U.S. escalation, the character of the U.S. communication of its intentions, and their reading of domestic

U.S. and international reactions to the inauguration of U.S. attacks on the North.

The report [words illegible] not to predict how the DRV might answer the "basic question" given alternative assessments of the variables in the quoted paragraph. However, it did offer the caveat that "comprehension of the other's intentions would almost certainly be difficult on both sides, and especially so as the scale of hostilities mounted."

In assessing Hanoi's ability and willingness to sustain U.S. attacks in order to pursue its goals, the report continued its balanced but slightly pessimistic approach:

> We have many indications that the Hanoi leadership is acutely and nervously aware of the extent to which North Vietnam's transportation system and industrial plan is vulnerable to attack. On the other hand, North Vietnam's economy is overwhelmingly agriculture and, to a large extent, decentralized. . . . Interdiction of imports and extensive destruction of transportation facilities and industrial plants would cripple DRV industry. These actions would also seriously restrict DRV military capabilities, and would degrade, though to a lesser extent, Hanoi's capabilities to support guerrilla warfare in South Vietnam and Laos. . . . We do not believe that attacks on industrial targets would so greatly exacerbate current economic difficulties as to create unmanageable control problems. . . . DRV leaders . . . would probably be willing to suffer some damage to the country in the course of a test of wills with the U.S. over the course of events in South Vietnam.

The assessment concluded with estimates of likely Chinese Communist and Soviet efforts to offset pressures directed toward North Vietnam. The Working Group recorded its belief "that close cooperation exists between Hanoi and Peiping and that Hanoi consults Peiping on major decisions regarding South Vietnam." Because the VC insurrection served "Peiping's interests in undermining the U.S. position in Asia" and because of the Sino-Soviet dispute, the group thought it likely that the Chinese would "feel compelled to demonstrate their readiness to support" Hanoi in maintaining pressure on South Vietnam. However, it was noted that "Chinese Communist capabilities to augment DRV offensive and defensive capabilities are slight," being limited largely to modest quantities of air defense equipment, additional jet fighters and naval patrol craft. On the other hand, the group believed "Moscow's role in Vietnam is likely to remain a relatively minor one." Khrushchev's successors were believed unwilling to run substantial risks to undermine the GVN. Citing Hanoi's desire for continuing Soviet military and economic aid, the report stated an ironic judgment concerning the less-militant of the large Communist powers:

> Moscow's *ability* to influence decisions in Hanoi tends consequently to be proportional to the North Vietnamese regime's fears of American action against it, rising in moments of crisis and diminishing in quieter periods. Moscow's *willingness* to give overt backing to Hanoi, however, seems to be in inverse proportion to the level of threat to North Vietnam.

4. *Perceptions and Development of U.S. Pressure Options*

The NSC Working Group began its deliberations with a variety of U.S. actions in mind and with an apparently flexible approach to the objectives that the Administration might reasonably seek to achieve. As ideas were exchanged and debated, however, objectives became somewhat less flexible and options seemed to narrow. Such a process could have resulted from either: (1) preconceptions on the part of particularly influential members; (2) a bureaucratic tendency to compromise; or (3) simply the limited availability of practical alternatives. A combination of these factors may even have been at work in the case of the Working Group. An assessment of this nature is beyond the scope of this primarily documentary research effort. Still, the question is an important one to reflect on in tracing the development of Working Group recommendations.

a. *Perception of U.S. Objectives and Interests.* National objectives in Southeast Asia were regarded in two categories: existing (sometimes called "initial") policy objectives and those comprising a possible fallback position. The former did not change and did not undergo any reinterpretation during the course of the Working Group's study. These were seen as (1) "helping a government [of South Vietnam] defend its independence," and (2) "working to preserve [in Laos] an international neutralized settlement." Three basic "factors" were recognized as "standing behind" these policy objectives:

> a. The general principle of helping countries that try to defend their own freedom against communist subversion and attack.
> b. The specific consequences of communist control of South Vietnam and Laos for the security of, successively, Cambodia, Thailand (most seriously), Malaysia, and the Philippines—and resulting increases in the threat to India and—more in the realm of morale effects in the short term—the threat to [other nations in Asia].
> c. South Vietnam, and to a lesser extent, Laos, as test cases of communist "wars of national liberation" world-wide.

Current U.S. objectives in South Vietnam and Laos were seen as an integral part of the "overall policy of resisting Communist expansion world-wide," and particularly a part of the "policy of resisting the expansion of Communist China and its allies, North Vietnam and North Korea." Thus, for South Vietnam to come under Communist control, "in any form," was seen as

> a major blow to our basic policies. U.S. prestige is heavily committed to the maintenance of a non-Communist South Vietnam, and only less heavily so to a neutralized Laos.

Unlike the current objectives, those comprising a fall-back position dealt only with South Vietnam. Moreover, they were modified during the course of the Working Group's effort. The modifications occurred in the way the objectives were presented—in the context of the presentation—rather than in their specific phrasing. The words remained the same throughout:

> 1. To hold the situation together as long as possible so that we have time to strengthen other areas of Asia.
> 2. To take forceful enough measures in the situation so that we emerge from it, even in the worst case, with our standing as the principal helper against Communist expansion as little impaired as possible.
> 3. To make clear . . . to nations in Asia particularly, that failure in

South Viet-Nam, if it comes, was due to special local factors that do not apply to other nations we are committed to defend—that, in short, our will and ability to help those nations defend themselves is not impaired.

At first, these fall-back objectives for South Vietnam were presented as possible alternatives—to be considered in conjunction with a reassessment of the costs and risks associated with currently acknowledged objectives. Following its recognition of the extent to which U.S. prestige had been committed, even the second draft (8 November) stated:

> Yet . . . we cannot guarantee to maintain a non-Communist South Vietnam short of committing ourselves to whatever degree of military action would be required to defeat North Vietnam and probably Communist China militarily. Such a commitment would involve high risks of a major conflict in Asia, which could not be confined to air and naval action but would almost inevitably involve a Korean-scale ground action and possibly even the use of nuclear weapons at some point.

Despite all this, it was acknowledged, South Vietnam "might still come apart," leaving the United States deeply committed but with much of its initial justification disintegrated. "Hence," the evaluation continued,

> . . . we must consider realistically what our over-all objectives and stakes are, not just what degree of risk and loss we should be prepared to make to hold South Vietnam, or alternatively, to gain time and secure our further lines of defense in the world and specifically in Asia.

Significant, in shedding light on the subtle changes that occurred in this rationale during the ensuing three or four weeks, was its treatment of the third fall-back objective. Observing that "most of the world had written off" both South Vietnam and Laos in 1954, an early draft acknowledged that neither had acquired the international standing of such former targets of Communist aggression as Greece, Iran and South Korea. It went on to point out several historical characteristics of South Vietnam and Laos that made them such unique cases, including: (1) "a bad colonial heritage" and inadequate preparation for self-government; (2) a "colonialist war fought in half-baked fashion and lost"; and (3) "a nationalist movement taken over by Communists ruling in the other half of an ethnically and historically united country. . . ." It then added:

> The basic point, of course, is that we have never thought we could defend a government or a people that had ceased to care strongly about defending themselves, or that were unable to maintain the fundamentals of government. And the overwhelming world impression is that these are lacking elements in South Viet-Nam. . . .

Moreover, the commentary noted that there was widespread expectancy that if South Vietnam were lost it would be due to its lack of these elements.

Subsequent to circulation of the initial draft of the "objectives and national interest" Section, a number of critical or related comments were directed toward Group Chairman Bundy. On 4 November, Michael Forrestal suggested that "an important flavor" was lacking in the original analysis—namely, "the role of China" and her need for "ideological successes abroad." In his view, given Chinese policy, "the effect of our withdrawal from a situation in which the people we were trying to help seemed unable to help themselves" would be more politically pervasive in Asia than if China did not exist. He thought the U.S. object should be to "contain" Chinese political and ideological influence "for the longest possible period," thus providing time to create, "at the very least, Titoist regimes on the periphery of China . . . ." [Doc. 218] On 6 November, William Sullivan also urged placing U.S. policy in Vietnam in the "larger perspective" of the political confrontation with Communist China. In an attached, larger exposition of policy rationale for the Western Pacific, he presented conceptions of the U.S. problem quite similar to those advocated by Forrestal. The political future of the peoples of East Asia was portrayed as depending largely on a struggle between Washington and Peking. Chinese political and ideological aggressiveness was viewed as a threat to the ability of these peoples to determine their own futures, and hence to develop along ways compatible with U.S. interests. The U.S. commitment to defeat North Vietnamese aggression, even at the risk of "direct military confrontation" with Communist China, was perceived as part of the longer-term policy of establishing conditions which permit the independent nations of the region to develop the ability and confidence "to cope with the emerging and expanding power of China." These comments may have influenced that part of the 8 November version which referred to current U.S. objectives as part of the broader policy of "resisting the expansion of Communist China and its allies. . . ."

The JCS member also stressed the importance of not falling back from current policy aims. [Doc. 228] He stated that "in the eyes of the world" the United States was committed to its initial objectives "as matters of national prestige, credibility, and honor." Further, that U.S. retention of "a measure of free-world leadership" required "successful defense" in South Vietnam against the wars of national liberation strategy. Admiral Mustin criticized the Bundy draft for overstating "the degree of difficulty associated with success for our objectives in SVN." He asserted:

> Our first objective is to cause the DRV to terminate support of the SEA insurgencies. . . . To achieve this objective does not necessarily require that we "defeat North Viet-Nam," and it almost certainly does not require that we defeat Communist China. Hence our commitment to SVN does not involve a high probability, let alone "high risks," of a major conflict in Southeast Asia.

He characterized the draft's expression of concern over risks and costs as an inference "as though the harder we try the more we stand to risk and to lose. On the contrary, he stated, the "best hope for minimizing risks, costs, and losses in achieving our objectives" could be attained though "a resolute course of action."

Admiral Mustin also attacked the implication that there was "some alternative to our holding South Vietnam. There is none," he stated, adding: "We have no further fall-back position in Southeast Asia in the stated view of the Joint Chiefs of Staff." Specifically, he warned that to attempt to strengthen other areas of Asia, "in the context of our having been pushed out of SVN, would be a thoroughly non-productive effort militarily. . . ." Moreover, characterizing the draft's concessions to the unique difficulties in Laos and South Vietnam as "sour grapes," he attacked its assumptions that we could convince other nations that failure in South Vietnam was due to strictly local factors. He warned that other nations would regard any such explanation on our part as "completely transparent." Concerning any lack of GVN will to defend itself, he commented, "A resolute United States would ensure . . . that this lack were cured, as the alternative to accepting the loss." The JCS member portrayed a U.S. failure in South Vietnam as shaking the faith and resolve of the non-Communist nations who rely on the United States for major help against Communist aggression. In that event, he saw little possibility for effective U.S. reassurances.

The impact of these criticisms can be seen in the working Group's final assessment of U.S. interests in Southeast Asia. In explaining the need to consider a fall-back position, the statement stressed the need merely to assess "the drawbacks" associated with it. Lending to this judgment were admissions that "there is some chance that South Vietnam might come apart under us whatever course of action we pursue" and "strong military action necessarily involves some risks of an enlarged and even conceivably major conflict in Asia." Then followed the statement:

> These problems force us to weight in our analysis the *drawbacks and possibilities of success* of various options, including *the drawbacks* of accepting only the fall-back objectives set forth below. (Italics added)

Missing was the earlier draft's reference to potential costs and risks involved in pursuing current objectives. Missing also was any suggestion that the Administration might find some advantage in seeking an alternative to these objectives.

The Working Group went on to assess, in terms almost identical to those in the initial draft, the likely consequence of Communist control of South Vietnam for different world areas of interest to the United States. The group saw important distinctions between the likely impact on U.S. interests in Asia and those in the world at large. For the latter, the most significant variable was seen as the degree to which adverse developments in Southeast Asia might produce domestic public revulsion against all U.S. commitments overseas:

> Within NATO (except for Greece and Turkey to some degree), the loss of South Vietnam probably would not shake the faith and resolve to face the threat of Communist aggression or confidence in us for major help. This is so provided we carried out any military actions in Southeast Asia without taking forces from NATO and without generating a wave of "isolationism" in the U.S. In other areas of the world, either the nature of the Communist threat or the degree of U.S. commitment or both are so radically different than in Southeast Asia that it is difficult to assess the impact. The question would be whether the U.S. was in fact able to go on with its present policies.

For Asia, other than Southeast Asia, the Working Group's assessment went as follows:

> The effect on Asia generally would depend heavily on the circumstances in which South Vietnam was lost and on whether the loss did in fact greatly weaken or lead to the early loss of other areas in Southeast Asia. Nationalist China . . . , South Korea, and the Philippines would need maximum reassurance. While Japan's faith in our military posture and determination may not be shaken, the growing feeling that Communist China must somehow be lived with might well be accentuated. India and Iran appear to be

the Asian problem cases outside the Far East. A U.S. defeat could lead to serious repercussions in these countries. There is a great deal we could still do to reassure these countries, but the picture of a defense line clearly breached could have serious effects and could easily, over time, tend to unravel the whole Pacific and South Asian defense structures.

The consequences for Southeast Asia of Communist control in South Vietnam were seen as highly differentiated and by no means automatic. The "domino theory" was viewed as "over-simplified." The Working Group felt that it might apply "if, but only if, Communist China . . . entered Southeast Asia in force and/or the United States was forced out of South Vietnam, in circumstances of military defeat." Nevertheless, the group judged that "almost immediately," Laos would become extremely hard to hold and Cambodia would be "bending sharply to the Communist side." These developments were seen as placing great pressure on Thailand and encouraging Indonesia to increase its pressure on Malaysia. Thailand, it was noted, had "an historic tendency to make 'peace' with the side that seems to be winning," and Malaysia's "already serious Malay–Chinese problem" was cited. The Working Group concluded:

> We could do more in Thailand and with the British in Malaysia to re-inforce the defense of these countries, the initial shock wave would be great [sic] . . .

This assessment was quite close to that made in the 8 November draft in which Bundy had gone on to point out that even if we succeeded in overcoming the shock wave in Thailand and Malaysia, "the struggle would be uphill for a long time to come." But in neither case was much credence placed in the domino theory.

It should be noted that Admiral Mustin and the JCS did not agree with this assessment. The Admiral commented that the JCS believed the so-called domino theory "to be the most realistic estimate for Cambodia and Thailand, probably Burma, possibly Malaysia." In the context of late 1964, these nations were expected to collapse "plainly and simply as the corollary to our withdrawal." Accordingly, a specific notation of the differing viewpoint of the JCS was placed in the Working Group's final report.

In describing its assessment of the consequences of Communist control in South Vietnam, the Working Group stated:

> There are enough "ifs" in the above analysis so that it cannot be concluded that the loss of South Vietnam would soon have the totally crippling effect in Southeast Asia and Asia generally that the loss of Berlin would have in Europe; but it could be that bad, driving us to the progressive loss of other areas or to taking a stand at some point [so that] there would almost certainly be a major conflict and perhaps the great risk of nuclear war.

  b. *Evolution of Options.* The alternative courses of action perceived by the Working Group went through a fairly rapid evolution. As conceived by Chairman Bundy and John McNaughton, who apparently collaborated in their initial formulation, the options would offer a wide range of military actions and diplomatic postures. [Doc. 224] As the views of other members and interested officials were expressed, and as it became more apparent how little flexibility was perceived with respect to national objectives, subtle changes occurred. The effect was to narrow somewhat the range of effects which the different options might achieve and to tend to blur the distinctions between them. However, the process occurred so early in the life of the Working Group that it is difficult to pin-point the changes and somewhat presumptuous, relying only on documentary evidence, to explain them.

The perceived options were three in number, labeled A, B, and C. Option A essentially was a continuation of military and naval actions currently underway or previously authorized, to include prompt reprisals for attacks on U.S. facilities or other VC "spectaculars" in South Vietnam. These were to be accompanied by continued resistance to a negotiated settlement unless stringent preconditions, amounting to agreement to abide by U.S. interpretations of the Geneva Accords, were met. Option B consisted of current policies plus a systematic program of progressively heavy military pressures against North Vietnam, to be continued until current objectives were met. Negotiations were to be resisted, as in A, although to be entered ultimately, but they were to be carried on in conjunction with continued bombing attacks. Option C combined current policies with (1) additional—but somewhat milder—military pressures against North Vietnam and (2) a declared willingness to negotiate. Once negotiations were begun, the military pressures were to stop, although the threat to resume was to be kept alive.

In a general sense, these distinctions remained constant throughout the Working Group effort. However, subtle changes occurred. In the initial conception of B, it was perceived as "meshing at some point with negotiation," based on an underlying assumption that negotiations would probably be unavoidable. The full analysis of this earliest form of B (discussed more fully later) makes it clear that some kind of international discussions would probably begin fairly early in time as the intensity of our military pressures increased. These would be applied deliberately to permit evaluation of results at each step. Yet, the initial form of B was intended to embrace high intensity options—in McNaughton's terminology, a "full squeeze." It will be recalled from the discussions earlier in the fall, that this term was applied to graduated operations that included mining harbors, bombing bridges and LOC targets and eventually attacking industries. As Option B developed, however, it became associated with prolonged resistance to a negotiated settlement. Moreover, although the intensity of the military operations it embraced remained about the same, they were perceived as being applied at a faster, less flexible pace. For example, in a comment about this option on 14 November, Admiral Mustin wrote:

> . . . while the Joint Chiefs of Staff offer the capability for pursuing Option B as defined, they have not explicitly recommended that the operations be conducted on a basis necessarily that inflexible. All implementing plans . . . would permit suspension whenever desired by national authority.

Perceptions of Option C became more like B. Initially, the additional pressures in C were conceived as "additional forceful measures and military moves." They included such operations as extension of the current armed escort of reconnaissance flights in Laos to full-fledged armed route reconnaissance—gradually leading to similar attacks against infiltration routes in the southern border regions of North Vietnam. The initial Option C also provided for authorization of the already planned for cross-border ground operations in Laos and possibly in Cambodia. By 8 November, however, the pressure portion of this option was perceived as (1) including eventual attacks against other-than-infiltration targets in North Vietnam and (2) giving "the impression of a steady deliberate approach," the pace of which could be quickened if necessary. Moreover, in this later development of C, the U.S. negotiating position would be to insist from the outset on full acceptance of the current U.S. objectives. Initially this position would incorporate certain additional bargaining elements that could drop out in the course of discussion.

This modification of the pressure and negotiation aspects of C led other members of the Working Group to express reservations. Robert Johnson stated that this "proposed stiffer version" was little different from B. He argued that the only real differences now were (1) a declared willingness to negotiate and (2) our unwillingness under C to carry the action through to its ultimate conclusion. He cautioned that the new version was unlikely to produce the hoped-for advantages of "pure C" and that it could convince the Communists that our negotiatory spirit was not sincere. Enclosed with his comments were the views of the CIA member, who also believed there would be confusion between B and the new C—particularly as observed by the DRV. Other reservations were expressed by Assistant Secretary McNaughton, who urged that the proposed pace of the new C be slowed down. This would be accomplished by dividing the additional pressure [words illegible] in Laos as part of the first phase. The OSD representative also urged not yielding to pressures to participate in a Geneva conference until after several military actions had been taken against the DRV. Of all the reservations stated above, only the last (delaying Geneva participation) was reflected in subsequent descriptions of Option C.

Even Option A was altered to some extent. The main emphasis for A continued to be the currently adopted policies. At some time prior to 8 November (when the final analysis was drafted), interest was shown in an "extended A." This version retained the policy of resisting negotiations in hope that the situation would improve, but it incorporated low-level pressure action akin to the early stages of C. The type and intensity of the action "would vary in direct proportion to our success in convincing the world and our own public of the truth about Hanoi's support, direction and control of the VC." It might begin with armed reconnaissance in Laos, include greater naval activity along the coast, and gradually phase into strikes against LOC targets in North Vietnam. In terms of military actions alone, extended A resembled closely the initial version of C. However, it was conceded that even an extended Option A did not offer a very promising means for moving toward negotiations.

Why did these changes take place? The available documentary materials do not make this entirely clear. One factor which may have influenced the modifications in all three of the options was recognition of the problem of conflicting signals that could result from reprisal actions. If reprisals were designed to be forceful and punitive and intended to match the seriousness of VC provocations, they might be so strong as to interfere with the messages to Hanoi which it was originally intended would be conveyed by the graduated pressures. Indeed, it was pointed out that operations orders already developed by CINCPAC for retaliation in response to attacks on DE SOTO Patrols (should they be resumed) were "of magnitude which would not be politically viable" except under extremely serious provocations. Moreover, it was feared that improperly orchestrated reprisals might create undue international pressures for negotiations that could upset the negotiating strategy appropriate for the selected option.

Both A and B may have been altered as a result of changes made in C. The objections raised to the new C may have encouraged Chairman Bundy to include an extended A that was closer in the military sense to his and Mc-

Naughton's original concept of graduated pressures. Moreover, it had been pointed out that the same negotiating situations seen as appropriate for C (to include discussions of Laos and/or Cambodia as well as South Vietnam) could also apply to eventual negotiations arrived at through A. Besides, with the stiffening of the C negotiating formula, the distinctions between the respective bargaining positions for A and C had become somewhat blurred. Option B's faster pace in expanding operations may have been an attempt to make a clear distinction between it and the new C. Use of the term "fast/full squeeze" in reference to Option B began concurrently with descriptions of the stiffer version of Option C.

In addition, it is possible that the emphasis on a fast-paced B, with its harsher measures, was motivated in part by a desire to make this option unattractive to higher authority. This may explain the rather perplexed tone of the previously cited Mustin comment comparing the JCS and Working Group approaches. Other than the JCS member, most of the Working Group members appear to have favored less intensive measures than those being advocated by the military. Despite a sense of high stakes in Southeast Asia, which was shared by several members and other interested officials, many of these persons did not want the United States to plunge ahead with deeply committing actions as long as there was some doubt about the GVN's durability and commitment.

Not incompatible with the foregoing argument is a possible additional explanation for the stiffening of Option C. As U.S. objectives came to be viewed somewhat less flexibly, it is possible that dominant elements in the Working Group thought it advisable to make C into a tougher position. There is little question that Option C was the natural heir of the concept of graduated pressures coupled with a negotiated settlement advocated at several points earlier in the year. Several of the Working Group members had been instrumental in shaping those proposals and were quite naturally attached to them conceptually. Now, advocates of the graduated approach were confronted with: (1) greater pressures from the JCS and their like-thinkers in the Congress; (2) recognition of little flexibility among Administration officials regarding interpretations of national interest and objectives; and (3) an increasingly critical situation in South Vietnam. It is likely that these individuals viewed it necessary to stiffen their preferred approach in order to improve its compatibility with the current policy climate.

Whatever the reasons, the options for review and discussions were somewhat more closely alike than the original conceptions had been. Option A provided for intensified efforts to improve the situation in South Vietnam, and for somewhat intensified military action in line with current policy. Inside South Vietnam, it provided for improvement in the GVN administrative performance and for strengthening different elements of the pacification program. These internal actions were stressed as necessary regardless of whatever other measures were decided on. Option A's provisions for measures outside the country included: (1) continuing and increasing the GVN's covert maritime harassment program; (2) resuming the DE SOTO Patrol operations; (3) increasing the scope of Laotian T-28 attacks on infiltration targets in Laos and (4) when feasible, undertaking small-scale cross-border GVN ground and air operations into the Laotian Panhandle. The option also included individual U.S. reprisal action "not only against such incidents as the Gulf of Tonkin attacks but also against any recurrence of VC 'spectaculars' such as Bien Hoa." The aim of these actions would be to deter repetitions of and to punish for such actions in South Vietnam, "but not to a degree that would create strong international negotiating pressures."

Basic to Option A was its provision for "continued rejection of negotiation in the hope that the situation will improve." However, it included recognition that "the GVN itself, or individual South Vietnamese in potentially powerful positions" might initiate "discussions with Hanoi or the Liberation Front." If a coalition government were thus arranged, the Working Group believed, the odds were that it would eventually "be taken over by the Communist element." In the event of such discussions, the U.S. response under Option A might be either (1) "stand aside," thus disassociating the United States from such a settlement, or (2) "seek to cover a retreat by accepting negotiations" through something like a Geneva conference, which might buy additional time.

Option B provided for everything included in A plus a program of U.S. military pressures against North Vietnam. These were to continue "at a fairly rapid pace and without interruption" until the DRV agreed to stop supporting and directing the war in South Vietnam and Laos. The pressures were to begin with attacks on infiltration targets and increase in intensity; however, the option included provision that an early attack on Phuc Yen airfield and certain key bridges in the northern part of North Vietnam might be required "to reduce the chances of DRV interference with the spectrum of actions" that were contemplated.

Although our public position on negotiations would be "totally inflexible" under Option B, it provided for recognition of the need to negotiate eventually. Under B, this would occur simultaneously with a continuation and escalation of the pressures and would be based on "inflexible insistence on our present objectives." Nevertheless, B acknowledged the need "to deal with channels of [international] communication, the UN, and perhaps—despite our strong opposition— a reconvened Geneva Conference of some sort" even before we agreed to enter into settlement talks. Moreover, while resisting negotiations, the option provided for (1) making "the strongest possible public case of the importance, increase, and present intolerable level of DRV infiltration" and (2) "strengthening the picture of a military situation in South Vietnam requiring the application of systematic military force."

Option C provided for every military action included in A plus "graduated military moves against infiltration targets, first in Laos and then in the DRV, and then against other targets in North Vietnam." The air strikes on infiltration routes within North Vietnam were to be preceded by low-level reconnaissance flights over the same general area. Advantage was seen in initiating such measures "following either additional VC 'spectaculars' or at least strong additional evidence of major infiltration." Moreover, Option C made provision for the possibility of making a "significant ground deployment to the northern part of South Vietnam, either in the form of a U.S. combat force or a SEATO-members force" as an additional bargaining counter. In any event, C was intended to "give the impression of a steady deliberate approach" and "designed to give the U.S. the option at any time to proceed or not, to escalate or not, and to quicken the pace or not."

In C, military pressures were to be accompanied by "communications with Hanoi and/or Peiping" indicating in essence "a willingness to negotiate in an affirmative sense." From the outset "we would be . . . accepting the possibility that we might not achieve our full objectives." Accordingly, the concept for C included provision for an initial negotiating position that added "certain bargaining elements" to the basic U.S. objectives. Once negotiations started the military pressures would cease. As in B, these would be preceded by a vigorous program of public information efforts and political consultations with Congressional leaders and foreign allies, surfacing information on DRV infiltration and explaining our rationale for action. The latter would be "that documented DRV illegal infiltration of armed and trained insurgents, and over-all DRV direction and control of VC insurgency, had now reached an intolerable level and that it was now necessary to hit at the infiltration . . . and to bring pressure on Hanoi to cease this infiltration and direction."

c. *Significance of Negotiations.* One of the most significant aspects of the NSC Working Group's analyses was its emphasis on a negotiated settlement as the final outcome of contemplated U.S. actions. Regardless of the option selected or the pressure actions employed, international negotiations in some form were perceived as the means by which the situation in Southeast Asia would ultimately be relieved. Even in the event of a unilateral GVN or a South Vietnamese splinter negotiation with the NLF, under circumstances of a relatively shallow U.S. commitment (Option A), negotiation under a Geneva format was regarded as a preferable outcome. However, it is also clear that a parallel aim was to insure that pressures on behalf of such negotiations did not become compelling before the U.S. bargaining position could be improved.

Also significant is the fact that the kind of settlement which was seen as the purpose of negotiation was one which would end North Vietnam's participation in the conflicts in Southeast Asia—and concurrently, also end the United States' direct participation (as it was in 1964) in those conflicts. In view of the prevalent Administration perception of North Vietnam as instigator and aggressor in the conflict within South Vietnam, it is ironic that the Working Group's considerations of a negotiated settlement did not include the problems of a political settlement in the South. In the available source materials, this subject was raised only once and even then was not dealt with further. The one instance was in the context of Robert Johnson's [words illegible] resulted (one to which the DRV in fact complied with our demands to the extent that we ceased our pressure actions) "we would then have to consider . . . whether or not to make compromises—such as, for example, accept less than perfection for international supervisory mechanism, agree to permit the NLF to become a legitimate political party in the South, or agree to political consultations between GVN and DRV." In other words, at the level of the Working Group's analysis, the political stakes for which the game in Vietnam was really being played and the very powerful and relevant cards held by the DRV and the VC were not really considered. To continue the analogy, the Working Group concerned itself only with the various opening bids the United States might make in order to achieve a position from which it could attempt a finesse.

The main problem apparently recognized by the Working Group was that, given its current objectives, the United States had few bargaining points with which to negotiate. In essence, it was primarily to fill this lack that many group members and Administration officials favored initiation of direct military pressures against North Vietnam. To some, bombing attacks were something that might then be removed as an inducement for the DRV to stop or to reduce its support of the military operations in South Vietnam and Laos. To others, such vigorous measures might at least serve as a demonstration of U.S. resolve to combat external aggression but also as a screen behind which to extract ourselves should the situation in South Vietnam deteriorate further.

Gaining maximum bargaining advantage from the military measures contemplated under each of the options was one of the major emphases in the Working Group's analyses. For example, under A, emphasis was placed on obtaining maximum leverage from exploiting the threat of further escalation—to be demonstrated primarily through reprisal actions and deployments. Under B, a similar kind of psychological leverage was to be achieved through the clearly ascending nature of the actions, particularly if some time were permitted to assess results. Under C, the effect was to be achieved by the combined effects of (1) maximizing the threat of impending escalation after each graduated and carefully paced step and (2) minimizing the Communist governments' problems of "face" as they moved toward negotiation.

It was the recognized lack of strong bargaining points that led the Working Group to consider the introduction of ground forces into the northern provinces of South Vietnam. In advancing this proposal, the State Policy Planning Council member pointed out that "whatever the stated U.S. intentions," the Communists would probably expect to put an end to all air and naval attacks on North Vietnam merely by agreeing to enter negotiations. In that event, he pointed out, the United States could not use these pressures (or the promised relief from them) as a bargaining counter during negotiations. If ground forces were deployed prior to an obvious need to combat invading enemy troops, this disposition could be read as such a counter. Their deployment, "would, moreover, carry with it the threat of subsequent air and naval attacks against North Vietnam. And," he continued, "threat may be as important as execution . . . in producing desired Communist reactions."

Although initially advocated as a valuable bargaining piece for all the options, the concept of deploying ground forces for this purpose became associated with Options A or C. In the former case, it was urged with recognition that A offered little leverage for bargaining other than hoped-for improvement in the GVN's internal administration and pacification efforts. For C, it was perceived much in the sense in which it was originally proposed—serving as an additional negotiating ploy before it might be needed as an operational military capacity. Such a force was seen as taking either of two forms: (1) a U.S. combat force, probably of division strength, or (2) a force composed of contingents from certain SEATO members (Australia, New Zealand, the UK, Thailand and the Philippines). Interesting, in view of subsequent events, is the fact that participation by South Korea and the Republic of China specifically was not to be sought. (This may also have been significant of the Administration's tendency at the time to view Communist China as co-instigator of the Vietnamese aggression.) The contemplated ground force deployment also was seen as serving some auxiliary functions: (1) to deter DRV ground force deployment into South Vietnam; (2) by taking blocking positions, to reduce the infiltration into the South through Laos; and (3) (in the case of the multi-national force) to improve the internal picture of our actions in South Vietnam by virtue of visible international participation.

As stated previously, the primary bargaining element in Option B was the application of clearly ascending military strikes against North Vietnam. These would be halted only in return for demonstrated DRV compliance with demands that it stop supporting and directing military operations in South Vietnam and Laos. It was pointed out that DRV compliance under pressure would be tantamount to surrender. Further, if we insisted that compliance include calling off all acts of VC terrorism and of resistance to pacification efforts in South Vietnam, it would mean "virtual unconditional surrender." To obtain such high stakes, the group recognized that intensive pressures would be required. However, it also recognized that the combination of extreme demands and harsh actions would be most likely to produce adverse international reaction and increased pressures for an early cease-fire and negotiations.

The basic political objective perceived for Option B was to "prevent international consideration . . . from interfering with our continuing pressures against the DRV until the DRV has taken the actions we desire of it." In view of the expected demands for an early cease-fire, it was believed advisable to present the U.S. case in the United Nations at the time B military operations were initiated. The ensuing discussions would likely consume considerable time. Moreover, taking such initiatives would avoid the defensive posture that the United States would be placed in if our military actions were introduced for condemnatory purposes by another government. The Working Group stressed that under Option B, the United States should firmly resist a Geneva-type conference until it had obtained assurances of DRV compliance with its demands. Should the pressures for negotiation become too formidable to resist and discussions begin before a Communist agreement to comply, it was stressed that the United States should define its negotiating position "in a way which makes Communist acceptance unlikely." In this manner it would be made "very likely that the conference would break up rather rapidly," thus enabling our military pressures to be resumed.

The only option that provided for bargaining in the usual sense of the word was Option C. The Working Group intended that with the initiation of this option and the U.S. declaration of willingness to negotiate, the Administration would have embarked on a bargaining course. In the group's view, we would stick to our full objectives at the outset "but we would have to accept the possibility that, as the whole situation developed, we might not achieve those full objectives unless we were prepared to take the greater risks envisaged under Option B." In such circumstances, it acknowledged, "it might become desirable to settle for less than complete assurances on our key objectives."

Accepting in principle the possible need to compromise the initial U.S. position under Option C, the Working Group specified a somewhat hardened definition of that position. The initial negotiating objective ("the complete termination of DRV support to the insurgency . . .") was refined to specify that it incorporated three fundamentals: (a) that the DRV cease its assistance to and direction of the VC; (b) that an independent and secure GVN be reestablished; and (c) that there be adequate international supervisory machinery." Specific areas of "give" for the bargaining process were identified as the question of free elections and the degree of verification we would require. The group further provided that during negotiations the intensity with which the United States would pursue its initial objectives would vary with the extent of improvement within the GVN. If the situation in South Vietnam got better, the United States would press harder for acceptance of its initial position. If the situation grew worse, "we would have to decide whether to intensify our military actions, modify our negotiating positions, or both."

Because of a declared willingness to negotiate from the outset, the approach to a negotiating situation under Option C was viewed by the Working Group as considerably different from that under Option B. Whereas, in the latter case it was believed that the UN would provide the most useful medium for discussions, the preferred approach under Option C was through a Geneva-type meeting. The channels, both direct and indirect, to Hanoi were not believed useful for negotiating. The UN was viewed as presenting a special problem because of the approaching annual issue of Communist China's membership. For this reason the Working Group felt that it would not provide an effective negotiating forum until late February or March 1965, although it acknowledged the necessity of presenting the U.S. case before the Security Council. In view of these considerations, the Working Group viewed it most desirable to yield to the expected pressure for a Geneva conference—but only after conducting "a number of military actions against the DRV."

d. *Perceived Reactions to Options.* The Working Group evaluated the relative advantages and disadvantages of the three options and concluded that Option C provided the most promising course of action. The evaluation was based on three general criteria: (1) likely reactions of allied and non-aligned foreign governments; (2) reactions within South Vietnam; and (3) effectiveness in bringing desired responses from the Communist government. With respect to the first, the group reported:

> Option A would cause no adverse reactions but if it failed it would leave a considerable after-taste of U.S. failure and ineptitude; Option B would run major risks of sharply expressed condemnation, which would be erased only if the course of action succeeded quite clearly and in reasonable time; Option C would probably be in between in both respects.

With respect to the remaining criteria, Option A seemed likely to achieve little more than buying some time, and in some respects it appeared counterproductive. While Option B was viewed as standing "a greater chance than either of the other two of attaining our objectives," it also was seen as running "considerably higher risks of major military conflict with Hanoi and possibly Communist China." On balance, Option C was considered "more controllable and less risky of major military action" than B and more likely "to achieve at least part of our objectives" than A.

The Working Group reported that Option A appeared to offer "little hope of getting Hanoi out or an independent South Vietnam re-established." It was recognized that the actions included in this option could not physically affect the extent of infiltration from the North and would not be likely to affect Hanoi's determination to continue its policies. At best, the group believed, "they might . . . keep the DRV from engaging in further spectaculars, and thus keep the scale of the conflict in the south within some limits." However, Option A was conceded little chance of contributing to an improved GVN, in the short period of additional time its effects might possibly make available. The group recognized sagging morale and doubts concerning U.S. intentions as the "most immediate problem" in South Vietnam. Several members felt that without further U.S. actions, political collapse was imminent—that to add only reprisals for VC spectaculars might lift morale immediately, but would not have lasting effect. At best, under A, it was believed that the gradual deterioration in the countryside of South Vietnam would continue.

Although the Working Group viewed a decision to continue Option A indefinitely as ruling out either B or C, it did suggest the possibility of extending A to its limits and gradually phasing into operations like those in Option C. It was suggested that this might, over time, generate "favorable, or at least not unfavorable," domestic and international reaction which along with the increasing cost of gradual disruption in North Vietnam might cause Hanoi to slow down its infiltration. However, the result of this process, at best, would be a gradual improvement of the U.S. position without advancement toward a meaningful settlement. Lacking a deliberate attempt to phase into something like C, Option A was viewed as "an indefinite course of action." As such, its "sole advantages" were seen as:

(a) defeat would be clearly due to GVN failure, and we ourselves would be less implicated than if we tried Option B or Option C, *and failed;*

(b) the most likely result would be a Vietnamese-negotiated deal, under which an eventually unified Communist Vietnam would reassert its traditional hostility to Communist China and limits its own ambitions to Laos and Cambodia.

The group's assessment went on to indicate that should this occur, Thailand would likely conclude that "we simply could not be counted on, and would accommodate somehow to Communist China even without any marked military move by Communist China."

The Working Group reported that the actions in Option B offered a number of unique advantages relative to the other options:

1. Option B probably stands a greater chance than either of the other two of attaining our objectives vis-a-vis Hanoi and a settlement in South Vietnam.

2. Our display of real muscle in action would undoubtedly have a salutary effect on the morale of the rest of non-Communist Asia.

3. The course of military events vis-a-vis Communist China *might* give us a defensible case to destroy the Chinese Communist nuclear production capability.

However, Option B was also seen to present some unique problems and to possibly lead to some undesirable results. For example, most of the group believed Option B would risk an impairment of the "U.S. standing in NATO and European framework." The option was believed likely to produce a major conflict, and these effects were seen as quite probable if it "produced anything less than an early and completely satisfactory outcome." Problems were also perceived at home. It was pointed out that any U.S.-initiated military pressures against North Vietnam should be consistent with the provisions of the Joint Congressional Resolution passed following the Tonkin Gulf incidents, but that Option B would be difficult to justify under the authorities cited in this resolution.

Characterizing the use of force in the context of this alternative as a legitimate exercise of the right of individual or collective self-defense in response to an "armed attack" from the North would be a major public relations effort.

Moreover, given the pace and likely intensity of escalation in this option, it was suggested that "the constitutional prerogatives of the Congress, for example, to declare war [would] become pertinent."

As seen by the Working Group, the most disturbing aspect of Option B was its almost irreversible commitment to a major military effort, the ultimate nature of which was difficult to predict. That Hanoi would yield to U.S. demands at an early stage of B was considered unlikely. The chances were considered "significantly greater" that the DRV would retaliate, either by air attacks on the South or a ground offensive either in Laos or into South Vietnam. It was considered *most* likely, however, that Hanoi would continue to hold firm, thus requiring the United States to "up the ante militarily." With further increases in our military pressure, the group argued, "the odds would necessarily start to increase that Hanoi . . . would either start to yield by some real actions to cut down, or would move itself to a more drastic military response." The Working Group then cautioned:

> We could find ourselves drawn into a situation where such military actions as an amphibious landing in the DRV—proposed as one of our further actions—moved us very far toward continuing occupation of DRV soil. Alternatively, the volume of international noise . . . could reach the point where, in the interest of our world-wide objectives, we would have to consider accepting a negotiation on terms that would relatively but not necessarily be wholly favorable to the attainment of our full objectives.

Option C was particularly attractive to the Working Group because it was believed to be more controllable and, therefore, less deeply committing than B. The reactions to C expected by the Working Group differed from B primarily as a result of the U.S. negotiating posture. The initial strikes against targets in North Vietnam were seen as a "first break-point," marking the beginning of major international pressures for negotiation. Communist reactions to the early pressures were regarded as little different from B. Some change of military response was conceded, but it was thought more likely that the DRV would "hold firm while stimulating condemnation of [the United States] by world opinion, and, if in negotiations, take a tough position." Under C, however, our response would not necessarily be an immediate increase in pressure. If the GVN situation had improved, "we would try to capitalize on [it] . . . by pressing harder for acceptance of our initial negotiating position." Barring success, the pressures would continue, and the Working Group recognized that the likely dragging out of the war at this point would probably lead to a resumption of deteriorating trends in South Vietnam. It stated: "In this case, we would have to decide whether to intensify our military actions, modify our negotiating positions or both." If U.S. military measures were increased at this point, it was expected that "there would be a progressively increasing chance of major Communist military response," such as those considered under B. If the U.S. negotiating position were modified at this point, the group perceived a "major problem, in that key nations on both sides would suspect that we were getting ready for a way out." Therefore, it suggested that additional military actions, possibly including greater deployments to Southeast Asia, would need to accompany the modifying moves.

The major disadvantages of Option C acknowledged by the Working Group was its tendency to "stretch-out" the confrontation and expose the United States to an increasing variety of pressures and criticism. For example, the group acknowledged that GVN morale and effectiveness were likely to suffer at several points in the course of the options: (1) upon initial U.S. agreement to enter negotiations; (2) as it became clear that the war was dragging on; and (3) with modification of the U.S. negotiating position. It also recognized several measures that the Communists might take during a prolonged, indecisive period to reduce our initial advantage: (1) improving air defenses in North Vietnam; (2) deploying Chinese ground forces southward; and (3) hardening their propaganda. While increasing the enemy's public commitment to its current line of policy, these measures would not serve as clear acts of escalation.

These difficulties and other uncertainties encompassed by Option C illustrate the intensity with which most members of the NSC Working Group wanted the United States to couple limited military commitments with a negotiated settlement to relieve our position in Vietnam.

United States policy in Southeast Asia was fraught with real contradictions. For example, the one feature that gave Option C its most distinctive character —early willingness to negotiate without the concurrent effects of continually mounting military pressures—was its most uncertain aspect. This particular part of the analysis was revised twice between the final drafting of the group's findings and their considerations by the Principals. Moreover, the Working Group had received at least one informed judgment to the effect that, given Hanoi's high stakes in South Vietnam and its perceived opportunity to deal the United States a major blow, the DRV would not be likely to negotiate in response to any of the options. On the eve of the initial meeting with the Principals, Chairman Bundy called early negotiations "the least satisfactory part of the present script." In particular, it was recognized as difficult to "keep up our show of determination and at the same time listen for nibbles."

In many respects Option C seems to have been favored primarily for what it incorporated—for the means it employed—rather than for what it might achieve. It certainly was not presented as an optimistic alternative. Under C, the group perceived that "at best . . . the DRV might feign compliance and settle for an opportunity to subvert the South another day." This stood in marked contrast to what it perceived as the "at best" outcome of B, namely that Hanoi "might be ready to sit down and work out a settlement in some form that would give a restoration of the 1954 agreements," hopefully with firmer guarantees. Moreover, with C, the group believed that in between the best and worst outcomes, the United States "might be faced with no improvement in the internal South Vietnam situation and with the difficult decision whether to escalate on up to major conflict with China." This kind of outcome promised little more than the group perceived as available through A—and without the additional commitment of national prestige and military force. But it was an outcome readily perceivable from a policy that clung tenaciously to rather major objectives but was reticent to accept major risks.

5. *Views from Outside the NSC Working Group*

While the NSC Working Group was preparing its findings for submission to the Principals, other sources of influential opinion were communicating their views to these individuals. In addition, it is important to consider that members of the Working Group were most likely communicating their respective impressions of group progress to the principal official in the agencies they represented. Thus, William Bundy no doubt shared ideas with Secretary Rusk; John McNaughton with Secretary McNamara; Harold Ford with CIA Director McCone; and Admiral Mustin with General Wheeler. Some of these Principals no doubt had injected particular ideas into the group's deliberations. Whatever the source, these high officials were exposed to a variety of suggestions and viewpoints before reacting directly to the Working Group.

The following sections deal with two rather significant sources of ideas whose communications reached Secretary MacNamara. However, their views were known to other members of the Principals Group as well, through the normal inter-departmental coordination procedures. These proposals are significant also because of their rather contending viewpoints on the subject of U.S. courses of action.

a. *JCS Views.* On four different occasions during the period of the Working Group's existence, the JCS submitted formal proposals for direct military strikes against North Vietnamese targets. On each occasion they took pains to remind the Secretary of Defense and other readers of their earlier recommendation for a preferred course of action, which involved a systematic pattern of air attacks on major targets.

On 14 November, two such recommendations were made. One was intended to bring about expansion of the GVN's covert operations, to include "air strikes by unmarked aircraft" of the VNAF. It specified that these were to be "separate and distinct from larger (more decisive) air strike actions recommended . . . on 1 November 1964." The JCS stated that such smaller attacks would be useful in: (1) continuing the pressure on the DRV; (2) encouraging GVN leaders; (3) providing useful air defense data; and (4) demonstrating patterns of DRV/ Chinese reactions that could be helpful in planning larger operations. The other recommendations came in response to Secretary McNamara's request to examine possible DRV/CHICOM military reactions to U.S. air strikes against North Vietnam. In answer, they discussed various Communist military alternatives and U.S. means to counter them, and they described what they viewed as the most likely enemy reactions. These, they felt, would be primarily in the propaganda and diplomatic spheres because of what was perceived as China's general reluctance to become directly involved in conflict with the United States. In addition, the JCS repeated their recommendations of 4 November (with respect to the VC attacks on Bien Hoa) as retaliatory actions equally applicable to any other serious provocations. They went on to recommend deployments "to improve capabilities to conduct the program of air strikes" recommended on 4 November 1964.

Four days later they submitted another proposal, in response to Secretary McNamara's interest in a possible program of graduated U.S. pressures against North Vietnam. [Doc. 234] This possibility was described as "a controlled program of systematically increased military pressures against the Democratic Republic of Vietnam (DRV) applied in coordination with appropriate political pressures." (Interestingly, the Secretary's interest was expressed on the same day as McNaughton's reactions to the draft analysis of Option C.) The JCS referred to their statements of 4 and 14 November, describing their preferred course of action for causing the DRV "to cease supporting and directing the insurgencies" in South Vietnam and Laos. However, they also proposed an alternative series of specific actions, "should a controlled program of systematically increased pressures . . . be directed." This would:

"a. [Word illegible] the willingness and determination of the United States to employ increasing force in support of . . . an independent and stable noncommunist government in RVN and a free and neutral Laos. . . .

"b. Reduce, progressively, DRV support of the insurgencies in RVN and Laos to the extent necessary to tip the balance clearly in favor of the Governments of RVN and Laos by:

  (1) Reduction of the amount of support available through destruction of men, material, and supporting facilities;
  (2) . . . [and] through diversion of DRV resources to increased homeland defenses and alerts; and
  (3) Reduction of the rate of delivery of available support through destruction of bridges and other LOC choke points . . . and through interruption of movements. . . .

"c. Punish the DRV for DRV-supported military actions by the Viet Cong/ Pathet Lao. . . .

"d. Terminate the conflict in Laos and RVN only under conditions which would result in the achievement of U.S. objectives."

The final JCS proposal to be submitted relative to the "courses of action" debate in November 1964 came in direct response to the NSC Working Group's draft papers, circulated to interested agencies for comment on 17 November. Criticizing the group's assessment of U.S. stakes and interests, the JCS called Southeast Asia "an area of major strategic importance to the United States, the loss of which would lead to grave political and military consequences in the entire Western Pacific, and to serious political consequences world-wide." They reiterated their view that the best probability of success in attaining the currently recognized U.S. objectives in that region would be "by achieving the prerequisite objective of causing the cessation of DRV support and direction of the insurgencies in RVN and Laos."

The JCS also criticized the three options described by the Working Group and outlined five alternatives to them, in an ascending order of intensity:

1. Terminate commitments in South Vietnam and Laos and withdraw as gracefully as possible. The JCS called this "implicit in the context of the Working Group paper.

2. Continue actions contained within present policies, including reprisals for VC provocations. The JSC identifies this as the group option A but stated that the added demands it placed on the DRV were "not commensurate with those proposed by DRV on RVN." In essence, they agreed with the Working Group's evaluation that this alternative would neither accomplish our objectives nor alleviate the critical situation in South Vietnam.

3. Undertake graduated military and political initiatives to apply additional pressures against the DRV

> without necessarily determining in advance to what degree we will commit ourselves to achieve our objectives, or at what point we might stop to negotiate, or what our negotiating objectives might be.

The JCS stated that this alternative corresponded to the NSC Working Group's Option C, which they criticized for its "uncertain pace" and because it did not include "a clear determination to see things through in full." They argued that such an "inconclusive" option "could permit and encourage enemy build-ups to counter our own," and thus "raise the risks and costs to us of each separate military undertaking."

4. Undertake a "controlled program" of graduated military and political pressures, based on an "advanced decision to continue military pressures, if necessary, to the full limit of what military actions can contribute toward U.S. national objectives." The JCS called this "a variant and logical extension" of Option C and cited their proposal of 18 November as a detailed description of it.

5. Undertake a "controlled program of intense military pressures . . . designed to have major military and psychological impact from the outset, and accompanied by appropriate political pressures." The JCS offered this alternative in lieu of the Working Group's Option B which they stated "is not a valid formulation of any authoritative views known to the JCS." In particular, they specified that their intensive program would

> be undertaken on the basis that it would be carried through, if necessary, to the full limit of what military actions can contribute toward national objectives; it would be designed, however, for suspension short of those limits if objectives were earlier achieved.

For a full description of this alternative, they referred to their proposal of 14 November.

The last two alternatives provided for sizable force build-ups that "should make miscalculation of U.S. resolve less likely." Option C was objectionable in their view because it did not provide "a clear set of agreed military objectives" and because it provided for "the contingency that as developments are analyzed, it may be thought expedient to settle for less than completed achievement of our objectives for RVN and Laos." It is important to note that in outlining the last two options, the JCS stressed that they called for "controlled" programs. In the mode of Admiral Mustin's memorandum, referred to earlier, they were apparently attempting to combat the Working Group's inferences that the more intensive actions which the JCS advocated were not controllable. It is fairly clear that group members favoring Option C had tagged the extreme Option B with a JCS label.

b. *Rostow Views.* Whereas the JCS emphasized damaging actions, designed to affect Hanoi's will by destroying a significant portion of their capability, Walt Rostow urged a different approach. [Doc. 238] In his view, emphasis should have been placed on signalling to Hanoi and Peking our commitment to use our vast resources to whatever extent required to reinstate effectively the provisions of the 1954 and 1962 Geneva Accords.

With respect to military moves most useful for this purpose, Rostow communicated to Secretary McNamara his concern that "too much thought is being given to the actual damage we do in the North, not enough thought to the signal we wish to send." Outlining a concept similar to the earliest Option C, he urged that the initial use of additional force against North Vietnam "should be as limited and unsanguinary as possible" and that it

> should be designed merely to install the principle that [the DRV] will, from the present forward, be vulnerable to . . . attack . . . for continued violations of the 1954 and 1962 Accords. In other words, we would signal a shift from the principle involved in the Tonkin Gulf response.

Even more important, in his view, would be the signals communicated by additional military moves in the Southeast Asia region. He urged deploying U.S. ground forces to South Vietnam and large-scale retaliatory forces into the Western Pacific. Besides their value as a bargaining counter, Rostow saw a ground force commitment as a clear signal that "we are prepared to face down any form of escalation North Vietnam might mount on the ground." He argued that such a move would rule out "the possibility of [the Communists] radically extending their position on the ground at the cost of air and naval damage alone." He stated that the increased retaliatory forces would signal:

> that we are putting in place a capacity subsequently to step up [words illegible] be required; [and] that we are putting forces into place to exact retaliation directly against Communist China, if Peiping should join in an escalatory response from Hanoi.

The broader context of Rostow's views on military action was described for Secretary Rusk on the eve of the first meeting of the Principals to discuss the Working Group's findings. Stating his agreement with those portions of the latest intelligence estimate which stressed the Asian Communist powers' desire not to become involved in a direct conflict with the United States, he framed the "most basic" U.S. problem as follows:

> . . . how to persuade [the Communists] that a continuation of their present policy will risk major destruction in North Vietnam; that a preemptive move on the ground as a prelude to negotiation will be met by U.S. strength on the ground; and that Communist China will not be a sanctuary if it assists North Vietnam in counter-escalation.

He then repeated his prescription of military moves earlier urged on Secretary McNamara. However, he stressed that these moves would not, "in themselves, constitute a decisive signal." More significant in Communist eyes, he felt, would be signals to answer the question:

> Is the President of the United States deeply committed to reinstalling the 1954–62 Accords; or is he putting on a demonstration of force that would save face for, essentially a U.S. political defeat at a diplomatic conference?

In Rostow's view, the Communists would not accept a setback until they were absolutely certain that the United States really meant business—an assessment that could only come as a result of firm public commitments on the part of the President and appropriate follow-through actions. He stated:

> I have no doubt we have the capacity to achieve a reinstallation of the 1954–1962 Accords if we enter the exercise with the same determination and staying power that we entered the long test on Berlin and the short test on the Cuba missiles. But it will take that kind of Presidential commitment and staying power.

Acknowledging that the kind of conflict we faced lent itself to prolonged uncertainties and that the Communists could pretend to call off the guerrilla war, only to revive it again, he stressed the need to maintain pressure on them for some time. The installation of ground forces and a "non-sanguinary" naval blockade were suggested for this purpose. Rostow urged trying "to gear this whole operation with the best counter-insurgency effort we can mount with our Vietnamese friends . . . and not withdraw U.S. forces from Vietnam until the war is truly under control."

In closing, Rostow outlined a scenario of action that would follow from the kind of Presidential decision described above. This would include, in sequence:

(1) Immediate movement of relevant forces to the Pacific.
(2) Immediate direct communication to Hanoi . . . including a clear statement of the limits of our objectives but our absolute commitment to them.
(3) Should this first communication fail (as is likely) installation of our ground forces and naval blockade, plus first attack in North, to be accompanied by publication [of a report on infiltration] and Presidential speech.

Thus, in their communications to senior officials in the latter half of November, both Walt Rostow and the JCS stressed a similar point. Although advocating different solutions, they both emphasized that the Administration could not expect to dissuade Hanoi and Peking from continued pursuit of the DRV's important and strongly-held commitments without making correspondingly strong commitments to resist them. The JCS, for their own reasons, sought to avoid a commitment of ground forces to Vietnam and argued instead for punitive air and naval actions. Rostow felt that by forceful and meaningful demonstrations of national resolve, including the commitment of ground forces to South Vietnam, direct use of force against the Communist nations need be minimal.

B. POLICY DECISIONS

The efforts of the NSC Working Group were intended to be completed in preparation for a major policy review late in November 1964. Plans were made for Ambassador Taylor to return to Washington from Saigon to join in a series of strategy meetings. The expectations were that the meetings would result in a Presidential action order to supersede the one issued following the high-level conference in September (NSAM 314).

Meetings with the President were scheduled for the week following Thanksgiving, when he returned from his working holiday at the ranch. Preliminary meetings between Ambassador Taylor and the principal officials from agencies with national security interests in Southeast Asia were held during the preceding weekend, 27–29 November. The whole episode took place amid widespread speculation that a major policy change was imminent and rumors that Taylor had returned to insist on the bombing of infiltration targets in North Vietnam and Laos. Public and Congressional speculation ran so high on the eve of the meetings that the White House and State Department sought to dampen it with statements that Taylor's reported comments "were not policy" and that his return did not mean that "any great, horrendous decision" would result.

1. Reactions of Principals to Working Group Analyses

Before their meetings with Taylor and the President, the Principals in Washington met to consider the Working Group's findings and to assess the major issues affecting future U.S. courses of action. Just prior to their initial gathering, on 24 November, William Bundy had forwarded a list of questions and comments pertaining to the Working Group's findings, and these served as a kind of agenda. [Doc. 239] Included were such issues as: (1) whether the relative advantages among the three options were actually as evident as the group had found; (2) whether or not the papers' assessment of U.S. stakes in Southeast Asia should be revised in the direction of JCS attitudes; (3) whether the actions associated with the various options could in fact be carried out to achieve the results expected; and (4) whether a deployment of ground forces to South Vietnam would in fact provide any advantages.

a. *Consensus Among NSC Officials.* As the Principals' meeting opened, Secretary Rusk raised an issue that was high among Administration concerns— namely, that the American public was worried about the chaos in the GVN, and particularly with respect to its viability as an object of an increased U.S. commitment. Secretary McNamara and General Wheeler conceded the propriety of this concern but warned that the situation in the GVN would only get worse if additional steps were not taken to reverse present trends. Rusk then presented a question which addressed the whole rationale for contemplated U.S. courses of action. He asked whether the situation in South Vietnam could be improved in time to save it if the DRV were not to withdraw its support. CIA Director McCone conceded that the VC would still have plenty of capability remaining but expressed the view that the situation could be coped with from the stand-point of internal security criteria. At this point Under Secretary of State George Ball asked if bombing North Vietnam could improve the situation in South Vietnam directly. McNamara replied that it could not unless the bombing ac-tually cut down infiltration into the South. After agreeing with the Rusk com-ment that the struggle would be a long one, even with the DRV out of it, the group reached consensus that South Vietnam could be made secure, provided the Saigon government could maintain itself. This was the *first* of several major policy judgments reached in the course of the meeting.

Other points of clear consensus (with no more than a single dissenting opinion) were as follows:

(2) That the situation in South Vietnam would deteriorate further under Option A even with reprisals, but that there was a "significant chance" that the actions proposed under B or C would result in an improved GVN performance and "make possible" an improved security situa-tion (George Ball indicated doubt).

(3) That any negotiating outcome under Option A (with or without U.S. negotiating participation) probably would be clearly worse than under Option B or C.

(4) That it was doubtful (contrary to the view expressed in the Working Group papers) that Option B would have the best chance of achieving the full U.S. objectives (General Wheeler expressed agreement with the Working Group statement).

(5) That the requirement of Option C, "that we maintain a credible threat of major action while at the same time seeking to negotiate," could be carried out despite acknowledged public pressures.

(6) That the Administration could safely assume that South Vietnam could "only come apart for morale reasons, and not in a military sense," as a result of intensified VC effort.

(7) That early military actions against North Vietnam under Option C should be determined, but low in scale (General Wheeler disagreed, stating that our losses might be higher in the long run with such an approach).

(8) That the loss of South Vietnam would be more serious than stated in Section II of the Working Group's draft papers and that the Adminis-tration's assessment should be revised at least in the direction of the JCS viewpoint (George Ball argued against this judgment).

The context of the Principals' discussion of this last point contained some significant expressions of opinion. Secretary Rusk stated the viewpoint that the confidence of other nations in the United States would be affected by the loss of South Vietnam despite their possible indifference to the political struggle in Southeast Asia. He added that if we did nothing to affect the course of events in Vietnam it would have the effect of giving more to De Gaulle. However, Rusk did not accept the Working Group's rationale that we would obtain inter-national credit merely for trying. In his view, the harder we tried and then failed, the worse our situation would be. McGeorge Bundy disagreed with this last point, except to acknowledge that to attempt something like Option B and then quit would clearly be damaging. Secretary McNamara seemed to support the

(McGeorge) Bundy view, stating that B followed by failure would clearly be worse than Option C followed by a compromise settlement. George Ball expressed strong agreement with the last Rusk point, saying that De Gaulle would portray us as being foolish and reiterating that the damage to U.S. prestige would worsen if we tried either B or C and failed. General Wheeler stated the opinion that to do little or nothing at this point would be an act of bad faith. Mr. McCone pointed out a perpetual dilemma if the Administration continued to act despite South Vietnamese deterioration; hence, he urged great care.

It is interesting to note the views and associations of the two occasional dissenters in the series of consensus judgments rendered by the Principals. General Wheeler, Chairman of the JCS, expressed viewpoints consistent throughout with the recorded JCS views of future courses of action. On the other hand, George Ball, Under Secretary of State, had no obvious jurisdictional or institutional influences to affect his judgments. Nevertheless, known to Administration observers as "the devil's advocate," he had developed something of a reputation as an independent thinker. At about the time of the Working Group deliberations, for example, he developed a paper suggesting U.S. diplomatic strategy in the event of imminent GVN collapse. In it, he advocated working through the UK, who would in turn seek cooperation from the USSR, in arranging an international conference (of smaller proportions than those at Geneva) at which to work out a compromise political settlement for South Vietnam. In addition, Ball's prevalent occupation with European affairs may have influenced him to view Southeast Asia as of lesser importance to the U.S. national interest.

b. *Views Backing Consensus.* Also discussed at the 24 November Principals' meeting were several issues on which consensus was not reached. Most of these related to immediate U.S. actions that would need to be taken irrespective of the option selected, or to problems faced in carrying out a particular option. Since earlier agreements had indicated little interest in Option A, only B and C were examined further.

Discussion of Option B dealt primarily with questions of the intensity of blows that might be struck in North Vietnam. With respect to whether DRV airfields should be struck early or as a part of a more gradual sequence, General Wheeler pointed out that early strikes on airfields were what made B operations so different. It was these strikes at potential DRV capabilities to interfere with U.S. attacks, or to retaliate, that made systematic, intensive air operations possible. In response to a specific question from the Working Group, the possibility of using nuclear weapons was also discussed. Secretary McNamara stated that he could not imagine a case where they would be considered. McGeorge Bundy observed that under certain circumstances there might be great pressure for their use both from the military and from certain political circles. General Wheeler stated that he would not normally vote for their use—never, for example, in an interdiction role. However, he suggested that they might be considered *in extremis*—for example, to hold off an enemy to save a force threatened with destruction, or to knock out a special target like a nuclear weapons facility. In response to Secretary Rusk's query as to their potential for cordoning off an area, both McNamara and Wheeler answered negatively.

Discussions of Option C dealt with the problem of early negotiations and, at greater length, with that of deploying ground forces to South Vietnam. On the former, there was little interchange noted in the proceedings. Despite the Working Group's admitted frustration with this particular issue, only two Principals' comments were recorded. McGeorge Bundy stated the view that we should let negotiations come into play slowly. Secretary Rusk expressed concern that the GVN would be very sensitive on the issue of a negotiating conference. Earlier, however, he indicated his opinion that pressure for a conference would not be a serious problem as long as military actions continued.

On the issue of sending ground forces to South Vietnam in the early stages of Option C, there was no firm conclusion. Secretary McNamara stated that there was no military requirement for ground forces and that he would prefer a massive air deployment. In response to General Wheeler's suggestion that some ground forces could be justified for air defense and base security purposes, he acknowledged that "we might do both." Mr. McCone stated the opinion that U.S. ground forces would help stabilize South Vietnam, similar to their effect on Lebanon in 1958. They might even provide a general security force in the South. McNamara disagreed. Secretary Rusk and McGeorge Bundy suggested their utility in proving a "preemptive effect," presumably equipped in ways to show our determination. In the end, it was agreed to raise this issue with Ambassador Taylor, at the Principals' next meeting. Significantly, the value of ground forces as a bargaining counter apparently was not discussed, thus providing one more indication of the Principals' reticence to deal with the issue of negotiation. (It is interesting to note in this respect that William Bundy's memorandum, formally summarizing the points of consensus and disagreement, does not deal with the early negotiating problem—despite its being a specific agenda item which he had suggested as Chairman of the Working Group.)

The only basic issue between the options on which the Principals did not arrive at a consensus was the question of the relative risks of major conflict entailed by Options B and C. General Wheeler stated that there was less risk of a major conflict before achieving success under Option B than under Option C. Secretary McNamara believed the opposite to be true. Secretary Rusk argued that if B were selected, there would be no chance to apply the JCS variant of C, whereas under the Working Group's C, this would still be left available. He observed that entry into the JCS variant of C would feel something like the Cuban Missile Crisis. McNamara then suggested a four-week program of actions following the general pattern of Option C. Mr. McCone stated that they sounded "fine," but that in his opinion the "negotiating mood" interfered with their potential effect. He agreed to attempt a paper to deal more directly with the relation of risk to likely success, as between the two options. In the end, the only conclusion that could be drawn was that there was not complete agreement that B ran a higher risk of major conflict than C, as alleged by the Working Group.

During the meeting of 24 November there was no clear decision as to which option was favored by the Principals. It seems likely that A was favored by Ball. Wheeler clearly favored B, and he may have had support from McCone, although this was far from clear. On the basis of either their participation in the Working Group or from statements of preference made at the meeting, it is clear that C was favored by McNamara, McNaughton, Rusk, and the Bundy brothers. However, McGeorge Bundy and McNamara apparently preferred a "firm C," whereas the other three wanted a more restrained, incremental approach.

c. *Policy Views from Saigon.* The same group of Principals that met on the 24th reassembled on 27 November for their first meeting with Ambassador Taylor. Present also was Michael Forrestal who had gone to Saigon to help prepare Taylor for the forthcoming strategy meeting and to apprise him of the Working Group efforts. Taylor led off with a prepared briefing on the current state of affairs within South Vietnam. [Doc. 242]

Ambassador Taylor's estimate of the situation in South Vietnam was rather bleak. He reported continued deterioration of the pacification program and continued weakness in the central government. The former was portrayed as related to increased direction and support of VC operations from Hanoi and increasing VC strength despite "very heavy losses inflicted almost daily" by the ARVN. Particular areas of concern were identified as the area surrounding Saigon and the northern provinces which were "now in deep trouble." Taylor related GVN weakness to political factionalism, mounting war weariness and hopelessness, "particularly in the urban areas," and a lack of "team play or mutual loyalty" among many central and provincial officials. Calling such chronic weakness "a critical liability to future plans," he warned that lack of an effective central government caused U.S. efforts to assist South Vietnam to have little impact.

To alter the course of what Taylor called "a losing game in South Vietnam," he recommended three measures: (1) "establish an adequate government"; (2) improve the counterinsurgency effort; and (3) "persuade or force the DRV" to stop aiding and directing the insurgency. With respect to the first, Taylor allowed that it was "hard to decide what is the minimum government which is necessary to permit reasonable hope" of success. However, he stated:

> . . . it is hard to visualize our being willing to make added outlays of resources and to run increasing political risks without an allied government which, at least, can speak for and to its people, can maintain law and order in the principal cities, can provide local protection for the vital military bases and installations, can raise and support Armed Forces, and can gear its efforts to those of the United States. Anything less than this would hardly be a government at all, and under such circumstances, the United States Government might do better to carry forward the war on a purely unilateral basis.

With regard to the counterinsurgency effort, he opined, "We cannot do much better than what we are doing at present until the government improves."

Ambassador Taylor saw U.S. military actions directed at the DRV as fulfilling a twofold purpose. On the one hand, he believed that even if an effective government were established, "we will not succeed in the end unless we drive the DRV out of its reinforcing role and obtain its cooperation in bringing an end to the Viet Cong insurgency." On the other hand, he saw actions outside South Vietnam as a means to improve GVN morale and confidence. Acknowledging that using our aid, advice and encouragement on behalf of programs to stabilize the government would probably be insufficient for this purpose, he suggested additional measures:

> One way to accomplish this lift . . . would be ground and air assault counterinfiltration attacks within the Laotian corridor. While the former would be covert . . . knowledge of their occurrence could be made known . . . to give the morale lift which is desired. Additionally we could engage in reprisal bombings, to repay outrageous acts of the Viet Cong in South Viet Nam. . . .

However, he added that even all these actions might not be sufficient "to hold the present government upright," in which case we would have to reconsider our policies. Our alternatives, he said, would be either to support one form or another of a replacement government or to "limit our contribution to military action directed at North Viet Nam."

In addition to the military actions already identified with morale-raising purposes, Taylor suggested:

> . . . we could begin to escalate progressively by attacking appropriate targets in North Viet Nam. If we justified our action primarily upon the need to reduce infiltration, it would be natural to direct these attacks on infiltration-related targets such as staging areas, training facilities, communications centers and the like. . . . In its final forms, this kind of attack could extend to the destruction of all important fixed targets in North Viet Nam and to the interdiction of movement on all lines of communication.

Ambassador Taylor's views regarding the circumstances under which such escalatory actions should be initiated were not entirely clear in his briefing to the Principals. After reiterating the necessity of stepping up the 34A operations, increasing those in Laos, and undertaking reprisals as part of the efforts to raise morale and strengthen the GVN, he stated two somewhat different, although not necessarily contradictory, viewpoints on the question of stronger military actions:

> If this course of action is inadequate, and the government falls, then we must start over again or try a new approach. . . . In any case, we should be prepared for emergency military action against the North if only to shore up a collapsing situation.
>
> If, on the other hand . . . the government maintains and proves itself, then we should be prepared to embark on a methodical program of mounting air attacks in order to accomplish our pressure objectives vis-a-vis the DRV. . . .

He then proposed a scenario for controlled escalation, the actions in which were quite similar to an extended Option A or a low-order Option C without declared negotiating willingness.

The implication is that Taylor visualized graduated air operations having primarily psychological impact on the North following logically from successful political efforts in the South—but that he also wanted an (perhaps somewhat stronger) air campaign held in readiness as a punitive measure in the event of a critical reversal in the South. This impression is strengthened by his earlier comment about U.S. alternatives and by the second of "three principles" which he recommended to the Principals:

> a. Do not enter into negotiations until the DRV is hurting.
> b. Never let the DRV gain a victory in South Viet Nam without having paid a disproportionate price.
> c. Keep the GVN in the forefront of the combat and the negotiations.

Involving the GVN in all phases of our operations was an important aspect of the Ambassador's thinking about next courses of action. He stressed that before making a final decision on the course we would follow, it would be necessary to obtain the reaction of Prime Minister Huong and General Khanh to our various alternatives. He explained:

> They will be taking on risks as great or greater than ours so that they have a right to a serious hearing. We should make every effort to get them to

ask our help in expanding the war. If they decline, we shall have to rethink the whole situation.

"If, as is likely, they urge us," Taylor added, we should take advantage of their enthusiasm "to nail down certain important points" on which we want their agreement. Included were GVN pledges to maintain military and police strength, to replace incompetent officials, and to suppress disorder and agreements to stipulated divisions of responsibility for conducting military operations.

Taylor's briefing made clear his commitment to limited U.S. objectives in Southeast Asia and his belief in the necessity of assuring the DRV of this limitation. Further, he made explicit his expectation that the DRV would not accept U.S. offensive actions without some intensified military reaction in the South and that any DRV submission to our demands might well be temporary.

d. *Discussions with Ambassador Taylor.* Following the briefing, the Principals commented on a number of the Ambassador's observations and discussed further the question of future courses of action. [Doc. 244] Secretary Rusk asked what could be done to make the GVN perform better. Taylor replied that he must be able to convey a strong message, but that we couldn't threaten the Saigon government. For example, a threat to "withdraw unless" would be "quite a gamble." The issue of neutralism was raised and "Ambassador Taylor noted that neutralism' as it existed in Saigon appeared to mean throwing the internal political situation open and thus inviting Communist participation." Mr. Ball observed that a neutralist state could not be maintained unless the VC were defeated and that the GVN must continue to be free to receive external aid until that occurred. Therefore, "neutralism in the sense of withdrawal of external assistance" did not seem to be a hopeful alternative. In apparent reply to Taylor's briefing comments to the effect that the United States might continue military action against North Vietnam despite a GVN collapse, Rusk commented that he "couldn't see a unilateral war" in this event. Taylor indicated that he meant "only punitive actions." Secretary McNamara agreed with Rusk, but added that if the GVN continued to weaken we would need to try Option C or A. "The consensus was that it was hard to visualize continuing in these circumstances [if the GVN collapsed or told us to get out], but that the choice must certainly be avoided if at all possible."

After a discussion of some of the administrative problems in the GVN, "Ambassador Taylor noted that General Westmoreland had prepared a report of the military situation" in South Vietnam. (The report was later distributed to the group.) He indicated that "Westmoreland was generally more optimistic than he (Taylor)" and that he saw better morale, increased defections and the like as signs of improvement in the military situation. Further, he stated that Westmoreland would be inclined to wait six months before taking further action in order to have a firmer base for them. However, Taylor added that "he himself did not believe that we could count on the situation holding together that long, and that we must do something sooner than this." Secretary McNamara also disagreed with Westmoreland's view, expressing doubts that the military situation would improve. In answer to specific questions, McNamara stated his opinion that (1) no, the political situation would not become stronger, but (2) yes, we would be justified in undertaking Option C even if the political situation did not improve. Taylor replied that "stronger action would definitely have a favorable effect" in South Vietnam, "but he was not sure this would be enough really to improve the situation." Others, including McNamara, agreed with Taylor's evaluation, but the Secretary added that "the strengthening effect of Option C could at least buy time, possibly measured in years."

Ambassador Taylor then urged that "over the next two months we adopt a program of Option A plus the first stages of Option C." He argued that the GVN was badly in need of some "pulmotor treatment," that any other alternative would probably result in a worsened situation—perhaps militarily. He added that the likelihood of GVN improvement seemed so doubtful that "we should move into C right away." Secretary Rusk asked if Option C would give Taylor the "bargaining leverage" needed with the GVN. The Ambassador replied by suggesting certain details of the message he would propose passing to the Saigon government. In effect these called for the GVN to agree to the kind of internal policies and command arrangements suggested in his briefing, in return for a prompt U.S. implementation of "Option A plus" and acknowledgment of the intention to go further if the GVN stabilized itself. It is important to note that the official memorandum of the foregoing discussion implied agreement among the Principals that Option A plus early stages of C should be recommended. The memorandum states, "It was urged that . . ." and "to get what improvements we could it was thought that we should move into some parts of C soon."

There followed a discussion of the infiltration evidence, during which Mr. McCone indicated that an intelligence team had made a further investigation of it.

It was agreed that State and Defense should check statements made by Secretary Rusk, Secretary McNamara, and General Wheeler on this subject, so that these could be related to the previous MACV and other estimates and a full explanation developed of how these earlier estimates had been made and why they had been wrong in the light of fuller evidence.

Before the meeting adjourned (with agreement to meet again the next day), Ambassador Taylor raised a number of questions which he thought the Working Group papers had not covered adequately. Only a few received answers during the meeting, and he agreed to furnish the Principals with the complete list. However, it was indicated that Option B or C could be initiated from a "standing start"—presumably with no incidents necessarily occurring first. The GVN were acknowledged to have "plenty of capabilities" to participate—even before arriving at the intended four-squadron strength of A-1 aircraft. It was stressed that the VNAF role would be in North Vietnam only—not in Laos—and Secretary McNamara indicated a strong role for them against targets below the 19th Parallel. Finally, a time-span of three to six months was indicated as the expected duration for Option C.

On the following day, when the Principals reassembled, William Bundy circulated a draft scenario of actions proposed in the event a decision were made to undertake measures like those contained in Option A. [Doc. 245] It had been agreed at the end of the initial meeting that these would be reviewed by the group with the assumption that they could be implemented "with or without a decision to move into the full Option C program at some time thereafter." (It is important to note how readily the attention of the Principals focused on the similarity of prepartory actions and early military measures in the various options, apparently without regard to the particular negotiating rationale which each option incorporated.) Bundy's scenario of early military, political and diplomatic actions was based on a similar assumption. He indicated, however, that the Working Group believed "that at least a contingent decision to go on *is* now required." To facilitate discussion on the part of the Principals, worksheets indicating proposed language or procedures were described, to include the following action categories:

1. U.S. public action
   a. White House statement following 1 December meeting
   b. Background briefing on infiltration
   c. Congressional consultation
   d. Major Presidential speech
   e. Public report on infiltration
2. Consultation with the GVN
3. Consultation with key allies
4. Communications with Communist nations
5. Existing forms of military actions (including reconnaissance and RLAF strikes in Laos, GVN maritime operations, etc.)
6. Reprisal actions resulting from DE SOTO Patrols and "spectaculars"
7. Added military and other actions

Certain of these topics received more attention than others in the course of the meeting, with emphasis being placed on "spelling out" the exact steps that the Principals would be asking the President to approve. With respect to actions aimed at the U.S. public, McGeorge Bundy stressed that the Presidential speech must both (1) affirm U.S. determination and (2) be consistent with the infiltration evidence. General Wheeler stated that earlier infiltration reports could be defended because of their small data base and suggsted that the discrepancies could be used to explain how the VC operated. It was determined that one man should be put in charge of assembling the available infiltration data for public release, and Chester Cooper was suggested for the job. With respect to coordination with the GVN, Ambassador Taylor pointed out the need to prepare a draft statement to the GVN for the President's review and agreed to prepare a table of the specific GVN actions needed. Secretary Rusk acknowledged the possible desirability of delaying until GVN leadership issues were resolved, but that "anything now would cause problems." Mr. Ball reminded that it would be necessary to query the GVN regarding release of some of the infiltration evidence.

Military and other related actions were also discussed: Secretary Rusk indicated the need to surface the GVN maritime operations, and Ambassador Taylor suggested that they and other morale-raising actions could be made public "in one package." In discussing the possible need for additional airfields in the northern part of South Vietnam, it was pointed out that a new jet field might take two years. Secretary McNamara said he thought there were enough fields to support Option C now if certain readily accessible improvements were added. He and the generals (Wheeler and Taylor) reminded the group that stopping the movement of U.S. dependents to South Vietnam or withdrawing those already there could not be concealed and that this problem must be resolved promptly—certainly within the initial 30 days. Taylor cautioned that actions regarding dependents could not be taken until our full course was decided, presumably because of potential GVN fears of a U.S. withdrawal. The question of resumed DE SOTO Patrols was raised with the reminder that CINCPAC wanted them for intelligence purposes. Taylor, McNamara and McGeorge Bundy opposed the idea, while General Wheeler strongly supported it. Notes of the meeting indicate resolution to the effect that the patrols should *not* be resumed during the first 30-day period. It was also agreed to recommend joint U.S./GVN planning of reprisal actions and of further escalatory measures.

At some point during the meeting it was determined that William Bundy would undertake preparation of a draft national security action paper containing policy guidance for the approaching period. The paper was to describe the strategic concept, outline the actions to be taken during the initial 30-day period, and indicate likely follow-on measures and the conditions under which they might be implemented. It was decided that the paper would be reviewed at another meeting of the Principals on 30 November, before submission to the President. A White House meeting had been scheduled for the following day.

On the afternoon of the 30th, in Secretary Rusk's conference room, the Principals met again. Bundy's draft paper had been distributed to them earlier after being generally approved (re format) by Rusk and reviewed for substance by Messrs. McNaughton and Forrestal. [Doc. 246]

In describing the basic concept, the paper presented U.S. objectives as "unchanged," although giving primary emphasis to our aims in South Vietnam. However, getting the DRV to remove its support and direction from the insurgency in the South, and obtaining their cooperation in ending VC operations there, were listed among the basic objectives—not presented as a strategy for attaining them. The objectives were to be pursued in the first 30 days by measures including those contained in Option A, plus U.S. armed route reconnaissance operations in Laos. They were linked with Ambassador Taylor's rationale that these actions would be intended primarily "to help GVN morale and to increase the costs and strain on Hanoi." The concept also included Taylor's emphasis on persuading the GVN to make itself more effective and to push forward its pacification efforts. For the period beyond the first 30 days, the concept provided that

. . . first-phase actions may be continued without change, or additional military measures may be taken including the withdrawal of dependents and the possible initiation of strikes a short distance across the border against the infiltration routes from the DRV. In the latter case this would become a transitional phase.

The kind of actions that the transition would lead to were described in a carefully qualified manner:

. . . if the GVN improves its effectiveness to an acceptable degree and Hanoi does not yield on acceptable terms, or if the GVN can only be kept going by stronger action, the U.S. is prepared—at a time to be determined —to enter into a second phase program . . . of graduated military pressures directed systematically against the DRV.

The concept continued with a mixture of suggested actions and rationale similar to that in Option C. The air strikes would be "progressively more serious" and "adjusted to the situation." The expected duration was indicated as "possibly running from two to six months." "Targets in the DRV would start with infiltration targets south of the 19th Parallel and work up to targets north of that point." The approach would be steady and deliberate, to give the United States the option "to proceed or not, to escalate or not, and to quicken the pace or not." It concluded with the following:

Concurrently, the U.S. would be alert to any sign of yielding by Hanoi, and would be prepared to explore negotiated solutions that attain U.S. objectives in an acceptable manner. The U.S. would seek to control any negotiations and would oppose any independant South Vietnamese efforts to negotiate.

Bundy's draft NSAM also included a summation of the recommended JCS alternative concept and a brief description of the various military, political and diplomatic measures to be taken during the first 30 days following implementation of the concept. Significantly, the latter included reprisal actions "preferably within 24 hours" for a wide range of specified VC provocations. It also contained a specific provision that DE SOTO Patrols would *not* be resumed during the initial 30-day period, but would be considered for the follow-on period.

In the documents available there was no record of the proceedings of the meeting on 30 November. The only evidence available is the notes and comments on the original draft NSAM, filed with other papers from the NSC Working Group at the State Department. Therefore, the following assessment of what occurred is limited to inferences from that sparse evidence. Moreover, based on this evidence, it is not absolutely certain that the changes indicated came as a result of the Principals meeting.

Several changes apparently were made in order not to ask the President to commit himself unnecessarily (e.g., the language was changed from "take" to "resume" a specific action in the second phase, to "be prepared to take," etc.). Others had policy implications. The only significant change in the first category was to remove any reference in the title to NSAM and to call it merely a "position paper." In the latter category, several changes seem significant. For example, keeping the GVN going through the effects of stronger U.S. action was deleted as one of the circumstances under which we might initiate a program of "graduated military pressures" against the DRV. Apparently based on Secretary McNamara's comment, reference to the United States seeking to control the negotiations and blocking South Vietnamese efforts in this direction was removed. The summary of JCS views was also removed from the concept, in effect presenting a united front to the President. From the description of 30-day actions, all reference to the intent to publicize infiltration evidence or present it to allied and Congressional leaders was eliminated, including the intention to link reprisal actions to DRV infiltration to develop "a common thread of justification." Also removed was reference to a major Presidential speech, apparently on the advice of McGeorge Bundy.

Although there is a bare minimum of rationale or explanation for these changes in the available evidence, the pattern described by the changes themselves is significant. In effect, Option A along with the lowest order of Option C actions were being recommended by the Principals in a manner that would represent the least possible additional commitment. This represented a considerable softening of the positions held at the end of the first Principals meeting, on the 24th.

It also represented a substantial deviation from the findings of the Working Group. It will be recalled that the group conceded Option A little chance of contributing to an improved GVN and saw its likely impact on South Vietnamese morale as no more lasting than the effects of the Tonkin Gulf reprisals. Moreover, even extended A was believed "at best" to be capable of little more than an improved U.S. position—certainly not of a meaningful settlement. In effect, the Principals were returning to the initial concept of Option C held in the Working Group by Bundy, Johnson and McNaughton—but without the initially flexible attitude toward national interest and objectives in Southeast Asia.

It is of interest to consider the factors that may have brought about the change. (1) It may have resulted as a reaction to the persuasiveness of General Taylor's arguments. (2) It may have represented a genuine mellowing of individual viewpoints after the opportunity to consider other judgements and weigh all the factors. (3) It may have resulted from the Principals' uneasiness with the negotiating track included in Option C. (4) It may have reflected concern over public pressure for harsher measures that could have resulted from too much public emphasis on the increased infiltration. (5) It may have represented an attempt to enhance the chances of the President's approving some kind of stepped up U.S. action outside of South Vietnam. With regard to the latter, McGeorge Bundy, as the President's Assistant for National Security Affairs, was in a position to convey President Johnson's mood to the group. Moreover, notes taken at the White House meeting tend to confirm that the President's mood was more closely akin to the measures recommended than to those in Option B or full Option C. Then again, it may be that all of these factors operated on the Principals in some measure.

Also significant, in the series of discussions held by the Principals, was their apparent lack of attention to the policy issues related to negotiations. Despite the fact that Option C measures were stipulated for the second phase of U.S. actions, the early negotiating posture intended to accompany that option was apparently paid little heed. According to the meeting notes, the only reference to our bargaining capability was Secretary Rusk's concern as to whether Option C actions would enable Ambassador Taylor to bargain in Saigon. Among the documents from the Principals meetings, the only reference to Hanoi's interest in negotiating occurred in Bundy's draft NSAM, where he reflected apparent Administration expectations that after more serious pressures were applied the DRV would move first in the quest for a settlement.

In retrospect, the Principals appear to have assumed rather low motivation on the part of the DRV. Either this or they were overly optimistic regarding the threat value of U.S. military might, or both.

For example, Ambassador Taylor's perception of how a settlement might be reached—which apparently produced little unfavorable reaction among the others—indicated the assumption that DRV concessions to rather major demands could be obtained with relatively weak pressures. In his suggested scenario (acknowledged as "very close" to the concept accepted by the Principals), the U.S. negotiating posture accompanying a series of attacks, limited to infiltration targets "just north of the DMZ," was intended to be as follows:

> . . . in absence of public statements by DRV, initiate no public statements or publicity by ourselves or GVN. If DRV does make public statements, confine ourselves and GVN to statements that GVN is exercising right of self-defense and we are assisting . . . . disclose to selected allies, and possibly USSR, U.S./GVN *terms for cessation of attacks* as follows:
> A. Demands:
>   1. DRV return to strict observance of 1954 Accords with respect SVN—that is, stop infiltration and *bring about a cessation of VC armed insurgency*.
> B. In return:
>   1. U.S. will return to 1954 Accords with respect to military personnel in GVN and GVN would be willing to enter into trade talks looking toward normalization of economic relations between DRV and GVN.
>   2. Subject to faithful compliance by DRV with 1954 Accords, U.S. and GVN would give assurances that they not use force or sup-

port the use of force by any other party to upset the Accords with respect to the DRV.

3. . . . the GVN would permit VC desiring to do so to return to the DRV without their arms or would grant amnesty . . .

Taylor went on to suggest that "if and when Hanoi indicates its acceptance," the United States should avoid (1) the danger of a cease-fire accompanied by prolonged negotiations and (2) "making conditions so stringent" as to be impracticable.

Significantly, the terms were to be conveyed to Hanoi privately. They did not constitute a declaratory policy in the usual sense of that term. Hence, it must be assumed that they would be presented to the DRV with the attitude of "acceptance or else"—that they were not perceived primarily as conveying a firm public image. Moreover, the terms were designed to accompany what became known as "phase two," the graduated pressures of Option C—not the 30-day actions derived from Option A. They were meant to represent the "early negotiating" posture of the United States—not the "no-negotiation" posture associated with Option A.

This general attitude toward negotiations was apparently shared by other Principals. This is indicated by changes made in Option C procedures. Essentially, these involved an adamant resistance to any formal "Geneva Conference on Vietnam." Formerly, such a conference was regarded as the "best forum"—after conducting a number of military actions against the DRV. Under the revised approach, the U.S. Government would merely "watch and listen closely" for signs of weakening from Hanoi and Peking. If the DRV held firm in response to initial military actions against North Vietnam and if, along with these actions, an improvement had occurred in the GVN, the Administration would press harder for acceptance of the initial negotiating position. Thus, it is fairly clear that the policy position formulated by the Principals before presentation to the President included no provision for early bargaining at the conference table.

2. *Courses of Action Approved in the White House*

On 1 December, the Principals met with President Johnson and Vice President-elect Humphrey in the White House. During a meeting that lasted two-and-one-half hours, Ambassador Taylor briefed the President on the situation in South Vietnam, and the group reviewed the evidence of increasing DRV support for the conflicts in South Vietnam and Laos. Ways of countering the impact of infiltration and of improving the situation were discussed. At the conclusion of the meeting Secretary McNamara was reported to have been overheard saying to the President, "It would be impossible for Max to talk to these people [waiting reporters] without leaving the impression that the situation is going to hell." Accordingly, Ambassador Taylor slipped out the White House rear entrance, and only a brief, formal statement was given to the press.

The source documents available at the time of this writing do not indicate the precise nature of the President's decisions. Since a NSAM was not issued following the meeting, one would have to have access to White House case files and National Security Council meeting notes to be certain of what was decided. Even then, one might not find a clear-cut decision recorded. However, from handwritten notes of the meeting, from instructions issued to action agencies, and from later reports of diplomatic and military actions taken, it is possible to reconstruct the approximate nature of the discussion and the decisions reached.

The revised "Draft Position Paper on Southeast Asia," containing the two-phase concept for future U.S. policy and the proposed 30-day action program, provided the basis for the White House discussions. Handwritten notes of the proceedings refer to various topics in approximately the same order as they are listed in that portion of the position paper dealing with the 30-day action program. There is no indication that the over-all concept was discussed. However, it is evident from the notes that the various actions under discussion were considered in terms of the details of their implementation. The instructions to Ambassador Taylor make it clear that, in general outline at least, the concept submitted by the Principals was accepted by the President. However, as will be seen, it is also clear that he gave his approval to implement only the first phase of the concept.

In addition to Ambassador Taylor's report, the meeting dealt mainly with two subjects: (1) Taylor's consultations with South Vietnamese leaders and (2) conversations with other U.S. allies who had an interest in the Vietnamese situation.

The President made it clear that he considered that pulling the South Vietnamese together was basic to anything else the United States might do. He asked the Ambassador specifically which groups he might talk to and what more we might do to help bring unity among South Vietnam's leaders. He asked whether we could not say to them "we just can't go on" unless they pulled together. To this, Taylor replied that we must temper our insistence somewhat, and suggested that we could say that "our aid is for the Huong government, not necessarily for its successor." The President asked whether there was not some way we could "get to" such groups as the Catholics, the Buddhists and the Army. Possible additional increments of military aid were then discussed as means of increasing U.S. leverage among military leaders. The President also asked about "the Communists" in South Vietnam. Taylor's reply was noted rather cryptically, but the impression given is that the Communists were being used already, but that he questioned the desirability of trying to pressure them. He apparently stated that they were "really neutralists," but that the French were "not really bothering" to use them. The President observed that the situation in South Vietnam "does look blacker" to the public than it apparently was. He wondered if something could not be done to change the impression being given in the news.

Toward the end of the discussion of consultations with the South Vietnamese, President Johnson stated his conviction that the GVN was too weak to take on the DRV militarily. He acknowledged that the South Vietnamese had received good training, but emphasized that we "must have done everything we can" to strengthen them before such a conflict occurred. This attitude was reflected in the guidance given to Ambassador Taylor and in the statement he was authorized to make to the GVN. The statement contained a passage asserting that the U.S. Government did not believe

> that we should incur the risks which are inherent in any expansion of hostilities without first assuring that there is a government in Saigon capable of handling the serious problems involved in such an expansion and of exploiting the favorable effects which may be anticipated. . . .

The White House discussions of U.S. consultation with other allies were prefaced by the President's strong affirmation that we needed "new dramatic, effective" forms of assistance from several of these countries. Australia, New Zealand, Canada and the Philippines were specifically mentioned. Secretary Rusk added that the U.K. also could do more. A possible Republic of China contribution was discussed, but the Secretary expressed concern that introduction of GRC combat units would tend to merge the problem of Vietnam with the conflict between the two Chinese regimes. Apparently, the Principals' proposal to end a representative to the governments of Australia, New Zealand, and the Philippines was approved. In each case, the representative was to explain our concept and proposed actions and request additional contributions by way of forces in the event the second phase of U.S. actions were entered. Vice President-elect Humphrey was suggested for consultations with the Philippine government. The President asked about the possibility of a West German contribution, but Secretary McNamara emphasized that German political problems would inhibit such a pledge from Bonn. Finally, it was agreed that Ambassador Taylor would cable the particular kind of third country assistance that would be welcomed after he had a chance to consult with the GVN.

At the close of the meeting, the White House released a press statement which contained only two comments regarding any determinations that had been reached. One reaffirmed "the basic United States policy of providing all possible and useful assistance" to South Vietnam, specifically linking this policy with the Congressional Joint Resolution of 10 August. The other stated:

> The President instructed Ambassador Taylor to consult urgently with the South Vietnamese government as to measures that should be taken to improve the situation in all its aspects.

During the subsequent press briefing, George Reedy indicated to reporters that Taylor would be working on the specific details of his forthcoming conversations in Saigon "for another two to three days" and would have at least one more meeting with the President before his return. However, it seems clear that most of what he would say to GVN officials was settled during the initial White House meeting. A proposed text was appended to the Principals' draft position paper, and it is clear that this was discussed on 1 December. Apparently, the only change made at that time was to remove a proposed U.S. pledge to furnish air cover for the GVN maritime operations against the North Vietnamese coast.

The statement was recast in the form of Presidential instructions to Ambassador Taylor—with specific authorization for the Ambassador to alter the phrasing as he thought necessary to insure effective communications with the GVN. However, the concept and the specific points for communication were unchanged. The instructions made specific provision for him to inform senior GVN officials of the U.S. willingness (1) to cooperate in intensifying the GVN maritime operations and (2) "to add U.S. airpower as needed to restrict the use of Laotian territory as an infiltration route into SVN." These pledges were prefaced by statements to the effect that U.S. actions directly against the DRV could not be taken until GNV effectiveness was assured along certain specified lines. The statements made explicit the policy view that "we should not incur the risks which are inherent in such an expansion of hostilities" until such improvements were made. As evidence of our desire to encourage those developments, however, the rationale stressed that the Administration was "willing to strike harder at the infiltration routes in Laos and at sea."

The instructions also included specific provision that the U.S. Mission in Saigon was to work with the GVN in developing joint plans for reprisal operations and for air operations appropriate for a second phase of new U.S. actions. The general relationship between the two contemplated phases was explained, and the Phase Two purpose "of convincing the leaders of DRV that it is to their interest to cease to aid the Viet Cong" was stated. The joint character of the "progressively mounting" air operations against North Vietnam, should they be decided on later, was emphasized.

As indicated earlier, there was no NSAM issued following the strategy meeting of 1 December. The reasons why are clear. In effect, the actions recommended by the Principals and approved by the President did not constitute a significant departure from the actions authorized in NSAM 314 (9 September 1964). That document had already provided for discussions with the Laotian government leading to possible U.S. armed reconnaissance operations along the infiltration routes. Further, it had provided for resumption of the 34A maritime operations, which had continued throughout the fall. In effect, the December strategy meeting produced little change except to make more concrete the concept of possible future operations against North Vietnam and to authorize steps to include the GVN in preparations for these possibilities.

It is clear that the President did not make any commitment at this point to expand the war through future operations against North Vietnam. The assurances intended for the GVN in this regard were conditional at best. The extent to which the President was committed to such a course in his mind, or in discussions with his leading advisers, was not made explicit in the sources available. It is implied, however, in brief notes which were apparently intended to summarize the mood of the meeting on 1 December. These were (1) [illegible] (2) it may be necessary to act from a base not as strong as hoped for; (3) it is not certain, however, how public opinion can be handled; and (4) it is desirable to send out a "somewhat stronger signal. "In addition, a comment not entirely legible stated "Measures can't do as much ——— (1) UN and (2) international [negotiations?]." In the context of the discussions, the impression left by these notations is that the White House was considerably less than certain that future U.S. actions against North Vietnam would be taken, or that they would be desirable.

C. IMPLEMENTING THE POLICY

When Ambassador Taylor next met with the President on the afternoon of 3 December, McGeorge Bundy was the only other official present. Prior to this occasion, Taylor had sat with the other Principals to review specific features of the Administration's position and to work out details of the scenario that was about to go into production. When he left the President's office, presumably having received the final version of his instructions, the Ambassador told reporters that he was going to hold "across-the-board" discussions with the GVN. Asserting that U.S. policy for South Vietnam remained the same, he stated that his aim would be to improve the deteriorating situation in South Vietnam. Although he hinted of changes "in tactics and method," he quite naturally did not disclose the kind of operations in which the United States was about to engage or any future actions to which immediate activities could lead.

1. Early Actions

Phase One actions to exert additional pressures against North Vietnam were quite limited. Only two, the GVN maritime operations and U.S. armed reconnaissance missions in Laos, were military actions. The others involved stage-managing the public release of evidence of the increased Communist infiltration into South Vietnam and the acquisition of additional assistance for that country from other governments.

a. *GVN Maritime Operations.* Maritime operations under OPLAN 34A represented nothing new. These had been underway steadily since 4 October, and their November schedule was in the process of being carried out at the time the decisions on immediate actions were being made. On 25 November, six PTF craft bombarded a barracks area on Tiger Island with 81mm mortars, setting numerous fires. Moreover, a proposed schedule for December had been submitted to COMUSMACV on 27 November. This included a total of 15 maritime operations involving shore bombardments, a junk capture, a kidnap mission, and a demolition sortie against a coastal highway bridge. According to the concept, these were to be intensified during Phase One.

Soon after the decisions had been made to begin Phase One, the JCS tasked COMUSMACV with developing a revised December 34A schedule to better reflect the newly adopted pressure concept. CINCPAC was requested to submit revised 34A plans so as to arrive in Washington not later than 8 December. The instructions specified that these were "to include proposed sequence and timing for increased frequency of maritime operations" in two packages. The first was to begin on 15 December, extend over a period of 30 days and provide for "shallow penetration raids . . . on all types of targets which would provide the greatest psychological benefits . . ." Destructive results and military utility were to be strictly secondary considerations. Package Two was to add four to six U.S. aircraft to afford protective cover and incorporate action against certain North Vietnamese coastal targets above the 19th Parallel. This package was intended to begin approximately 30 days following initiation of the first, although the instructions cautioned that the plans should be "prepared to provide for an indefinite period" of operations under Package One.

MACV's new proposal for maritime operations was submitted on 5 December, with proposals for psychological operations and aerial resupply/reinforce missions following close behind. On the 10th, approval for the latter two was communicated back to the field. At the time, the MAROPS proposals were still under consideration within the JCS. On the 12th, the JCS submitted their two-package proposal. Included in their first 30-day package were coastal bombardment of radar sites, barracks, and PT boat bases plus a maritime equivalent of aerial armed reconnaissance. Patrol boats would make "fire sweeps" along the coast against "targets of opportunity." In addition, upon their return from bombardment missions, it was proposed that the GVN PT boats attempt the capture of NVN junks and SWATOW craft. With the single exception of the coastal fire sweeps, all of these initial package operations were approved by OSD, and instructions were issued to implement the initial increment of such operations on or about 15 December.

In accord with the instructions initially issued regarding intensified maritime operations, OSD decisions on the proposed second package were deferred. The JCS indicated that the addition of U.S. air cover, and the necessary command and control procedures needed to support such operations, could be implemented on or about 15 January. They went on to recommend that if this were decided, the "maritime operations should be surfaced . . . prior to [implementation of] Package Two."

The JCS were disconcerted over disapproval of the fire sweeps along the North Vietnamese coast. However, their concern stemmed not so much from the lack of support for these particular operations as from their view that the disapproval removed from the package the only significant intensification beyond the level already attained before the President's Phase One decision. At a Principals meeting on 19 December, acting JCS chairman, General Harold H. Johnson, pointed out that with the modifications now made to it, the 34A program was, in effect, not intensified at all. Moreover, as discussion revealed, seasonal sea conditions were now so severe that no maritime operation had been completed successfully during the previous three weeks. In effect, therefore, the "intensified" December schedule of approved maritime operations still remained to be implemented as the month drew to a close.

[Words illegible] JCS urged that several air missions be added to the kinds of operations already approved. Included were the VNAF air strikes, using unmarked aircraft and U.S. air escort for returning surface craft. However, both of these items were disapproved; only the air operations in support of psychological and resupply operations gained acceptance. Apparently there was little additional MAROPS activity during January, 1965; the normal documentary sources include very little for this period.

b. *Armed Reconnaissance in Laos.* Like the maritime operations, armed reconnaissance in Laos was, in some respects, a continuation of operations that had been underway for some time. At least, U.S. aircraft had been operating over Laos since the previous May, performing reconnaissance functions and providing armed escort for these and (since October) the RLAF strike missions. Of course, armed escort was carried out under strict rules of engagement that permitted attacking ground targets only in response to hostile fire. Given the operational code YANKEE TEAM, these carrier and land-based missions had been following a constant pattern for several months. This pattern included roughly four daylight reconnaissance flights in the Plaine des Jarres–Route 7 area every two weeks, and during a like period, approximately ten reconnaissance flights in the Panhandle, and two night-reconnaissance flights along Route 7. Complimenting these efforts were those of the RLAF, whose T-28's harassed the Pathet Lao, gave tactical air support to Royal Laotian Army units, interdicted Route 7 and the Panhandle, and performed armed route reconnaissance in central Laos. During the period 1 October–30 December, there were a total of 724 T–28 sorties in the Panhandle alone. These had already precipitated several complaints from the DRV, alleging U.S.-sponsored air attacks on North Vietnamese territory.

The intended U.S. policy was discussed with Premier Souvanna Phouma on 10 December by the new U.S. Ambassador to Laos, William Sullivan. He reported that Souvanna "Fully supports the U.S. pressures program and is prepared to cooperate in full." The Premier particularly wanted interdiction of Routes 7, 8, and 12, but he insisted on making no public admission that U.S. aircraft had taken on new missions in Laos. The Administration had indicated to the Vientiane Embassy a few days earlier that it wished the RLAF to intensify its strike program also, particularly "in the Corridor area and close to the DRV border."

In the meantime, the JCS developed an air strike program to complement the YANKEE TEAM operation in accordance with current guidance, and had instructed CINCPAC to be prepared to carry it out. The program included missions against targets of opportunity along particular portions of Route 8 and Routes 121 and 12. It also included secondary targets for each mission that included barracks areas and military strongpoints. The second mission was to be flown not earlier than three days following the first. The program was briefed at a 12 December meeting of the Principals by Deputy Secretary Vance and was approved by them with one exception. They amended the ordnance instructions which had been prepared for CINCPAC to specifically exclude the use of napalm. For its first use against targets in Laos, they felt, the RLAF would be the only appropriate user. McGeorge Bundy stated that the amended program "filled precisely the President's wishes," and that he (Bundy) would so inform the President. He further stated that, barring separate advice to the contrary, the program should be executed. It was also agreed at this meeting that there would be no public statements about armed reconnaissance operations in Laos unless a plane were lost. In such an event, the Principals stated, the Government should continue to insist that we were merely escorting reconnaissance flights as requested by the Laotian government.

Armed reconnaissance operations in Laos, called BARREL ROLL, got underway on 14 December. This first mission was flown by USAF jet aircraft along Route 8. It was followed on the 17th by carrier-based A-1 and jet aircraft, striking along Routes 121 and 12. On the 18th, this pattern of two missions by four aircraft each was determined by Secretary of Defense or higher authority to be the weekly standard—at least through the third week. Just a day earlier, the JCS had proposed a second week's program that included repetition of the first week's operation plus missions along Routes 7, 9 and 23. Their proposals were prepared with a statement of JCS understanding "that a gradual increase in intensity of operations is intended for the second week." Recalling Souvanna Phouma's reported request for such operations, they also included a strong recommendation that Route 7 be struck as part of the second week's mission.

This same rationale was voiced by General Johnson in the Principals meeting on 19 December. He pointed out that the BARREL ROLL program briefed there by Deputy Secretary Vance did not represent any intensification beyond the previous week's effort. Vance confirmed that not intensifying the program had been one of the criteria applied in selecting the second week's missions. Consensus was reached by the Principals that the program should remain about the same for the next two weeks, in accordance with the most recent guidance.

At the end of December, when there was serious question about the efficacy of maintaining the direction of U.S. policy in South Vietnam, Defense officials requested an evaluation of the BARREL ROLL program. In particular, they were concerned as to "why neither the DRV nor the Communist Chinese had made any public mention of or appeared to have taken cognizance of our BARREL ROLL operations." In response, a DIA assessment indicated that the Communists apparently had made no "distinction between BARREL ROLL missions on the one hand and the Laotian T-28 strikes and YANKEE TEAM missions on the other." Attributing all stepped up operations in Laos to the United States and its "lackeys," they had lumped all operations together. DIA observed that "it would be most difficult to distinguish between YANKEE TEAM with its flat suppression aircraft from the BARREL ROLL missions." Further, the assessment observed that "BARREL ROLL strikes have followed T-28 strikes by varying periods of time and have been of lesser intensity. They probably appear to be a continuation of the Laotian program." It concluded:

> On balance, therefore, while the Communists are apparently aware of some increased use of U.S. aircraft, they probably have not considered the BARREL ROLL strikes to date as a significant change in the pattern or as representing a new threat to their activities.

Despite the lack of discernible Communist reaction to BARREL ROLL by the end of the year and considerable concern among the JCS, there was little change in the operation during early January. On the 4th, CINCPAC was authorized to go ahead with the fourth week's program:

> One U.S. armed reconnaissance/pre-briefed air strike mission in Laos for the week of 4–10 January 1965, is approved. Additional *missions* will be the subject of later message. (Italic added)

The approved mission called for *night* armed reconnaissance along Route 7, the first of its kind. At the time, the JCS were awaiting a decision on their proposals for a complementary mission, but the Department of State had objected to their choice of a secondary target because it was located near Cambodian territory. Earlier in the series, the Tchepone barracks had been deleted as a secondary mission by the White House because a Hanson Baldwin article had named it as a likely target. On 5 January, the JCS representative reminded the Principals that the currently approved BARREL ROLL mission constituted the fourth week of these operations and, therefore, would terminate the initial 30-day period of Phase One pressures. The JCS were quite concerned that there had not yet been plans made for a "transition phase" of stepped up attacks to begin around mid-January.

c. *Surfacing Infiltration Evidence.* An integral part of the Administration's pressures policy, porticularly if U.S. forces were to be involved in direct attacks on North Vietnam, was the presentation to the public of convincing evidence of DRV responsibility for the precarious situation in South Vietnam. As seen earlier, a former intelligence specialist, Chester Cooper, was selected to compile a public account of the infiltration of trained cadre and guerrilla fighters, to be used for this purpose. His account was to be developed from the various classified reports that had been produced and was to lay particular stress on the alarming increase in the rate of infiltration in [words illegible] 1964.

[Words illegible] his paper on 4 December. It was based on (1) a State-sponsored updating of the so-called Jorden Report, which described also the DRV's direction, control and materiel support of the insurgency (this had been discussed during the policy discussions in the Spring and initiated during the Summer); (2) the MACV infiltration study, based on interrogations of VC prisoners and completed in October; and (3) reports from a DIA/CIA/INR team who went to Saigon in mid-November to evaluate the MACV report (they confirmed its validity). His report consisted of four items: (1) a summary statement and a more detailed public discussion of VC infiltration; (2) a list of possible questions and suggested answers for use with the press or the Congress; (3) "a reconciliation, or at least an explanation of past low estimates of infiltration given in Congressional testimony and to the press"; and (4) a listing of available documentary evidence and graphic materials to aid in public presentations. In his covering memorandum, Cooper urged that the materials be forwarded to Saigon so as to make MACV and Embassy officials fully aware of the proposed approach and to make consistent its use by U.S. and GVN personnel.

The Cooper materials were forwarded for review to the Saigon Embassy on 8 December, and to the Principals on the 9th. Shortly thereafter, Secretary Rusk cabled Ambassador Taylor, expressing his concern that early release of the infiltration data "would generate pressures for actions beyond what we now contemplate." He sought Taylor's advice as to whether release would be wise. In the Ambassador's reply, he urged early release. He stated, "I do not feel that, at this point, the substance of the release will generate pressure for extreme action." Moreover, he expressed the view that release would serve to quiet the currently rife speculation among news correspondents and parts of the GVN concerning what the United States was intending to do in SVN. Citing a *New York Daily News* article (7 December) as an example of what he felt were increasingly likely leaks, he expressed his desire to make planned deliberate announcements of what the United States was now doing and what might be done in the future. He expressed his intention to have the GVN release the report on infiltration, complete with press briefings and statements, between 10–17 December.

Despite strong recommendations from the field to release the infiltration data, the Principals determined that it should not yet be made public. During the first part of December, the chief advocate for not releasing it was Secretary McNamara. At their meeting on 12 December, Mr. Vance stated that Mr. McNamara wanted to withhold the infiltration data for the time being. His rationale was not recorded in the minutes. The State Department opinion in response was that the Department "did not consider it of any great moment." Thereafter, the Principals decided that release should be withheld, at least until their next meeting, on 19 December. By the time they met again Ambassador Taylor had reported that the ARVN intelligence chief had reviewed the original infiltration report and the proposed press release and had "concurred in commending declassification." On the 16th Ambassador Sullivan praised the Cooper report and suggested passing it to Souvanna Phouma prior to what he hoped would be a prompt public release. At the Principals meeting these views were cited in a strong statement by William Bundy concerning the problems of keeping the infiltration evidence out of the press. General Johnson, Acting Chairman, JCS, favored release as a morale boost to U.S. personnel in South Vietnam. McGeorge Bundy and Carl Rowan (USIA) favored gradual or piecemeal release. However, Mr. Vance repeated Secretary McNamara's wish to continue suppression of the infiltration report—possibly for an indefinite period. This view finally prevailed, as the Principals agreed not to release the Cooper report either in Saigon or Washington. Instead, they felt that the President might disseminate some of the information through such vehicles as his State of the Union message or in a contemplated Christmas address to U.S. forces in Saigon.

Following the meeting, but before receiving reports concerning the current political upheaval in Saigon, the State Department cabled the Administration's decision not to make a formal GVN/U.S. release of the infiltration data. It gave as rationale the feeling that formal release "could be misinterpreted and become vehicle [for] undesirable speculation" and suggested alternative procedures. Stating that "general background briefings . . . should continue to indicate infiltration has increased without getting into specifics," it indicated that under pressure, the Saigon Embassy "could have one or more deep background sessions with [the] American forces." The cable cautioned, however, that specific numbers and comparisons with previous years' estimates should be avoided. These would not be released, it was advised, until late in January after senior Administration officials had testified to Congress in a scheduled inquiry. The current aim was stated "to get general picture into survey stories such as Grose article of November 1 rather than as spot news commanding wide attention." The cable concluded by acknowledging a "just received" Taylor message and approving his stated judgment to proceed with periodic background briefings in Saigon, along lines outlined above.

Following the rift between the South Vietnamese military leaders and the

American Embassy, resistance to the release of infiltration data hardened. In cables of 24 December, Ambassador Taylor was instructed to avoid background briefings on the infiltration increases until the political situation clarified. He was counseled that release of the data would be "unwise" unless he were to obtain evidence that the South Vietnamese military was planning to go ahead with a unilateral release. These instructions prevailed until well into January, 1965.

d. *Consultations with "Third Countries."* In the days immediately following the policy decisions of 1–3 December, several U.S. allies were consulted concerning the intended U.S. approach to Southeast Asia. In accord with the Principals' views, the governments of Thailand and Laos were briefed by the respective U.S. Ambassadors to those countries. Foreign minister Thanat Khoman later visited the President in Washington and presumably pursued the matter further. The Canadians were contacted in both Ottawa and Washington. William Bundy held discussions in New Zealand and Australia on 4–5 December. Prime Minister Wilson of the United Kingdom was thoroughly briefed during a series of meetings in Washington, 7–9 December. Later, William Bundy told the Principals that the U.K., Australia and New Zealand received the full picture of immediate U.S. actions and its stipulations to the GVN and the potential two-phased concept of graduated pressures on North Vietnam. The Canadian government was told slightly less. The Philippines, South Korea and the Republic of China were briefed on Phase One only.

One of the aims stressed by President Johnson in the meeting of 1 and 3 December, and continually thereafter, was obtaining increased assistance for the GVN and for our efforts on its behalf from our allies. During the 12 December Principals meeting, for example, William Bundy related the President's recent wish to obtain assistance even from governments without strong Southeast Asia commitments, like Denmark, West Germany, and India. This was mentioned in the context of a summary report on current "third-country assistance of all kinds to South Vietnam."

At the time, however, not only general assistance from many countries but specifically military assistance from a select few was particularly sought. During the consultations with allied governments, both Australia and New Zealand were pressed to send troop units to assist ARVN. Both supported the U.S. policy decisions as probably necessary, but neither was willing at the time to make a commitment. New Zealand officials expressed grave doubts that Phase Two would lead to negotiations, predicting instead that the DRV would only increase the clandestine troop deployments to the South. They expressed doubts about the advisability of sending allied ground forces into South Vietnam.

The concept under which the allied troop deployments were believed desirable was related to that which the NSC Working Group had recommended as deserving further study. Contemplated was an international force built around one U.S. division to be deployed just south of the DMZ in conjunction with stepped-up U.S./GVN air operations against North Vietnam. In essence, therefore, it was a Phase Two concept, dependent in some respects on the degree of success achieved during Phase One activities. The concept was examined in detail by the Joint Staff in early December, and their staff study was forwarded to the services and the Joint Pacific Headquarters "for comment and recommendations" on 10 December. The purposes cited for such a force deployment by the Joint Staff were stated as follows: (1) to deter ground invasion by the DRV; (2) to hold a "blocking position against DRV attacks to down the coastal plain and make more difficult DRV efforts to bypass"; and (3) to be "capable of holding the defensive positions against attack [words illegible] While the State Department and other non-military agencies apparently favored it, the Department of Defense was less than enthusiastic. At the 19 December Principals meeting, for example, all of those present agreed that "suitable planning toward such a force should go forward" except Assistant Defense Secretary McNaughton. He stated that he thought the idea had been shelved. Later, in their review of the Joint Staff's study, the services expressed reservations concerning the concept. They questioned its military utility, due to deployments being framed essentially within a narrow deterrent contour. They recommended instead a continued adherence to the deployment concept in the approved SEATO plans, which in their totality were aimed at the military defense of all Southeast Asia. The Army, in particular, expressed concern regarding routes and modes of possible DRV advance into South Vietnam that differed from those assumed by the study's below-the-DMZ concept. The Air Force pointed out that the international force concept conflicted with the JCS concept for deterring and dealing with overt DRV/CHICOM aggression as submitted on 14 December (JCSM-955-64).

Mr. McNaughton's comments on 19 December seem to have been correct. The case files containing the service comments in the international force concept indicate no further action by the JCS after mid-January.

In the meantime, however, a different approach to attracting wider allied participation in the military defense of South Vietnam appeared promising. On 29 December, OSD/ISA reported readiness on the part of the Philippine, ROK and GRC Governments to provide various forms of assistance to South Vietnam. Included in the available Philippine and Korean packages were an assortment of military forces. The ROK Joint Chiefs of Staff offered a combat engineer battalion, an engineer field maintenance team, an Army transportation company, and a Marine Corps combat engineer company. The Philippine Government stated its willingness to send a reinforced infantry battalion, an engineer construction battalion, and some Special Forces units.

2.   *Relations with the GVN*

Following his second meeting with President Johnson, Ambassador Taylor returned to Saigon. He arrived on 6 December amid press speculation concerning the details of his instructions and subsequent U.S. actions. The basic charge given him by the President had been well publicized since their meeting on the 1st: "to consult urgently with the government of Prime Minister Tran Van Huong as to measures to be taken to improve the situation in all its aspects." However, such a diplomatically worded statement left much room for imaginative interpretation—particularly in view of the Ambassador's "unannounced stopover in Hong Kong to get a briefing by U.S. 'China Watchers' in that listening post." Several correspondents speculated on the likelihood of air action. An apparent inside source even reported that these would be held in abeyance pending the outcome of strikes in Laos and the GVN reaction to U.S. suggestions for improvement.

a. *Joint Planning.* In the days immediately following his return, Ambassador Taylor's schedule precipitated press reports of frantic activity within the Embassy and other parts of the U.S. Mission in Saigon. Taylor first briefed his Embassy Council and the Embassy staff on the policy discussions in Washington and the joint U.S./GVN courses of action which it was hoped would be followed in South Vietnam during ensuing weeks. On 7 December, he met with Premier Huong and his senior ministers and with General Khanh. On these occasions he outlined the military and diplomatic actions which the U.S. Government intended to take during Phase One and explained how the Administration related the possibilities of Phase Two actions to GVN performance. The Ambassador described in general terms the kinds of administrative improvements and joint planning activities which U.S. officials thought the GVN should undertake.

Similar sessions were held during the next few days, as the details for the joint GVN/U.S. efforts were worked out. On the evening of the 8th, Ambassador Taylor held a reception for members of the high National Council, and General Westmoreland hosted the top ARVN generals at dinner. At both occasions, Taylor briefed the assembled on U.S. attitudes toward the GVN and, presumably, on the Administration's calculations of U.S. risk relative to GVN capability. On the following day, he held a lengthy session with Premier Huong, Deputy Premier Vien and General Khanh. On this occasion, he distributed a paper outlining nine specific actions which the U.S. Government believed were needed to strengthen the GVN and in which the local U.S. Mission was committed to help. Taylor reported that the "paper was generally well received" and that "specific joint action responsibilities" had been agreed on. These were to be confirmed in writing on the following day. On that same day, he submitted a proposed GVN press release, describing in general terms the nature of the new U.S. assistance to be given and the new areas of GVN and joint GVN/U.S. planning, designed to improve the situation in South Vietnam.

On the 11th, having obtained Administration approval, an official GVN statement was released to the press. It related that "a series of discussions with the U.S. Mission" had just been completed and that the U.S. Government had offered additional assistance "to improve the execution of the Government's program and to restrain [not 'offset' as originally worded] the mounting infiltration of men and equipment" from North Vietnam. Among military measures, it specified that U.S. support would enable "increased numbers of [South Vietnamese] military, paramilitary and police forces" and would permit "the strengthening of the air defense of South Vietnam." It also mentioned assistance "for a variety of forms of industrial, urban and rural development" and promised a GVN effort to emphasize security and local government in the rural areas." The statement closed with the following two paragraphs, which subsequent events made to appear ironic but which were juxtaposed with great care:

> Together, the Government of Vietnam and the United States Mission are making joint plans to achieve greater effectiveness against the infiltration threat.
> In the course of the discussions, the United States representatives expressed full support for the duly constituted Government of Prime Minister Huong.

As the following section will show, the joint planning that had just gotten under way for reprisal action and Phase Two operations was soon to be halted. It was deferred for a period of about three weeks during the forthcoming GVN crisis. However, as implicit in the quoted paragraphs above, its resumption provided effective U.S. leverage to help bring about an accommodation between the military dissidents and the civilian regime.

b. *GVN Crises.* Late in the evening of 19 December, high-ranking South Vietnamese military leaders, led by General Khanh, moved to remove all power from the civilian regime of Premier Huong. The move came in the announced dissolution of the High National Council, which had been serving as a provisional legislature pending adoption of a permanent constitution, and the arrest of some of its members. Air Commodore Ky, acting as spokesman for the military, claimed that their intent was "to act as a mediator [to resolve] all differences in order to achieve national unity." The immediate apparent conflict was with the Buddhists who had been demonstrating and threatening to provoke civil disorders in protest against the Huong government. In Ambassador Taylor's view, however, the underlying motive was growing antipathy with particular members of the High National Council, brought to a head by the Council's refusal to approve a military plan to retire General (Big) Minh from active service (and thus remove him from a position to contend with the ruling military clique). Moreover, the military had become quite impatient with the civilian officials.

The general consensus among the Ambassador, General Westmoreland and State Department officials was that General Khanh's relationship with the other influential generals and younger officers was rather uncertain. Therefore, they sought to bolster Premier Huong's resolve to remain in office on the basis of an understanding with the generals—even to the extent of seeking Khanh's resignation or dismissal. When presented with U.S. views, Khanh gave initial appearances of recognizing that the military seizure had directly defied the U.S. policy position and the stipulated basis for continuing joint GVN/U.S. efforts, and of accepting the need to withdraw. However, he quickly attempted to turn the crisis into a direct confrontation between himself and Ambassador Taylor. On the 22th, he issued a strong public affirmation of the military leaders' actions, [words illegible] views "favorable to the common enemies [communism and colonialism in any form]," and of the military's resolve "not to carry out the policy of any foreign country." On the 24th, information was received that he intended to pressure Premier Huong into declaring Ambassador Taylor *persona non grata.*

Administration reaction to this challenge indicated that it considered Khanh's defiance as a threat to the foundations of U.S. policy in South Vietnam. Ambassador Taylor was instructed to inform Huong that the U.S. Government regarded the PNG issue as a "matter of gravest importance," and that "any acceptance of [Khanh's] demand or hesitation in rejecting it would make it virtually impossible . . . to continue support [of the] GVN effort." Suggesting that Huong might be asked if he thought the "American people could be brought to support continued U.S. efforts in SVN in face [of] PNG action against trusted Ambassador," the Administration urged persistence in encouraging Huong to seek an accommodation with the other military leaders. Moreover, high-ranking MACV personnel were urged to exploit their close relationships with South Vietnamese counterparts to encourage such an arrangement. As leverage, Taylor was encouraged to emphasize the intended directions of U.S. policy, subsequent to a strengthened and stable GVN. Specifically, he was urged to point out that joint reprisals for unusual VC actions and "any possible future decision to initiate [the] second phase" were impossible as long as current conditions persisted. He was told, "without offering anything beyond terms of your instructions, you could use these to their fullest to bring [Ky and the other generals] around."

There is no indication in the available sources that this advice was directly employed. It is evident, however, that Ambassador Taylor had explained the dependency of further U.S. actions on GVN progress very clearly to the key military leaders on 8 and 20 December. Therefore, they were well aware that continued U.S. assistance along the policy line explained to them was predicated on their cooperation, and this was demonstrated early in the crisis. Even before Khanh's public declaration of independence from U.S. policy, it became known that joint talks concerning increased aid to the South Vietnamese war effort had been suspended. A few days later that fact was given additional circulation, with emphasis that this suspension included particularly any discussions of measures to reduce the infiltration from Laos and North Vietnam.

The degree to which the suspensions of joint planning actions affected the judgments of the South Vietnamese generals is, of course, not clear. What is apparent, however, is that this factor together with careful Embassy and Administration efforts to clarify possible misunderstandings, led the generals to reconsider. By 28 December, Ambassador Taylor was reporting encouraging signs of an accommodation. On the 29th, Secretary Rusk advised the President that the "generals were having second thoughts" and that "he hoped to see signs of political unity in Saigon soon." Finally, on the 9th, the generals pledged to return to terms agreed to during the previous August whereby matters of state would be left in the hands of a civilian government. The joint communique issued by Huong and Khanh also promised to speedily convene a representative constituent assembly to replace the High National Council.

The general's reassessments were no doubt helped by a strong U.S. public statement directed toward the South Vietnamese press, explaining the U.S. policy position toward that country's political situation. In language strikingly similar to the President's draft instructions to Taylor, it included the following:

> The primary concern of the United States Government and its representatives is that there be in Saigon a stable government in place, able to speak for all its components, to carry out plans and to execute decisions. Without such a government, United States cooperation with and assistance to South Vietnam cannot be effective.
>
> . . . The sole object of United States activities has been and continues to be the reestablishment as quickly as possible of conditions favorable to the more effective prosecution of the war against the Vietcong."

Consistent with the expressed U.S. policy position, discussions between U.S. and GVN officials concerning explained assistance to the South Vietnamese war effort were resumed on 11 January.

However, the aparent reconciliation of South Vietnam's military and civilian leadership was short-lived. Close on the heels of an announced GVN decision (17 January) to increase its military draft calls—long advocated by the U.S. Mission—student and Buddhist riots swept through Hue and Dalat. On the 20th, as arrangements were completed to appoint four leading generals to Premier Huong's cabinet, a leading Buddhist official issued a proclamation accusing the Huong Government of attempting to split the Buddhist movement. On the 21st, Tri Quang issued a statement charging that the Huong Government could not exist without U.S. support, a charge that gained in intensity in the days to follow. On the 23rd, Buddhist leaders ordered a military struggle against the United States. Denouncing Premier Huong as a lackey of the U.S. Ambassador, they accused Taylor of seeking to wipe out Buddhism in Vietnam. In Hue, student-led demonstrators sacked the USIA library and destroyed an estimated 8,000 books. Two days later, riots and strikes were in progress in Hue, Saigon and Da Nang, and Hue was placed under martial law. Meanwhile, military leaders were attempting to convince Buddhist spokesmen to call off their demonstrations against the GVN and the United States. Finally, on the 27th, the generals [words illegible] issued a statement that he was resuming power "to resolve the political situation." Soon after, the Buddhist leaders issued orders to their followers to halt their demonstrations, at least until they had sufficient opportunity to observe the performance of the new regime.

Thus, in late January the United States Government was faced with a dilemma. In December, it had spoken out quite clearly to the effect that its continued assistance along previously determined policy lines was dependent upon the effective functioning of a duly constituted South Vietnamese government. By its actions and statement during the initial December crisis, it had indicated that what it had in mind was a civilian regime governing without interference from any particular group. Now, less than a month from the settlement of the former crisis along lines compatible with the preferred U.S. solution, it was faced with another military coup. A time for reassessing former policy decisions and taking stock of the shifting debits and assets in the U.S. position had arrived.

c. *Joint Reprisals.* Meanwhile, an issue of great significance to the Administration, as well as to future relations with the GVN, was adding to the growing dissatisfaction with progress achieved in other Phase One actions. One of the basic elements in Phase One policy was to have been joint GVN/U.S. reprisal actions in response to any "unusual actions" by the VC. When faced with a significant provocation at the end of December, the Administration failed to authorize such actions. At the time, the circumstances in South Vietnam provided cogent reasons for not doing so, but it nevertheless represented a significant departure from the agreed policy position.

At the height of the first government crisis, on Christmas Eve, the Brink U.S. officers billet in downtown Saigon was bombed and severely damaged. Two Americans were killed and 38 injured; 13 Vietnamese also were injured. No suspicious person was observed near the building, so the responsible party was unknown. In reporting the incident, Ambassador Taylor treated it as an occasion for reprisal action. The immediate administration assessment was that under current political circumstances, neither the American public nor international opinion might believe that the VC had done it. Moreover, with clear evidence lacking, it felt that a reprisal at this time might appear as though "we are trying to shoot our way out of an internal political crisis." Given the political disorder in Saigon, the administration believed it would be hard for [the] American public to understand action to extend [the] war." Therefore, so the reasoning went, it would be undesirable to undertake reprisals at this time.

Calls for reprisal action came from several quarters. Citing what it called "a further indication" of Viet Cong responsibility, and cautioning against adding the Brink affair to the Bien Hoa instance of unreciprocated enemy provocation, CINCPAC urged a reprisal attack. He argued that the "bombing of Brink BOQ was an act aimed directly at U.S. armed force in RVN" and that failure to respond would only encourage further attacks. Ambassador Taylor forwarded what he termed "a unanimous recommendation" by himself and members of the U.S. Mission Council "that a reprisal bombing attack be executed [as soon as possible]" on a specified target "accompanied by statement relating this action to Brink bombing." He stated that "no one in this part of the world has [the] slightest doubt of VC guilt" and pointed out that the NLF was publicly taking credit for the incident. Citing Taylor's request and concurring in his recommendation, even to the specific target selection, the JCS added their voices to those arguing for reprisals. In their proposed execute message to CINCPAC, they proposed a one-day mission by 40 strike aircraft against the Vit Thu Lu Army barracks. Further, they recommended that the VNAF should participate if their state of readiness and time permitted.

In spite of these strong recommendations, the decision was made not to retaliate for the Brink bombing incident. On 29 December, the following message was dispatched to the U.S. embassies in Southeast Asia and to CINCPAC:

> Highest levels today reached negative decision on proposal . . . for reprisal action for BOQ bombing. We will be sending fuller statement of reasoning and considerations affecting future actions after Secretary's return from Texas tonight.

Available materials do not include any further explanation.

3. *Policy Views in January*

As the new year began, the Administration was beset with frustration over an apparent lack of impact from Phase One operations, over its failure to take reprisals after an attack on U.S. personnel, and over the still troublesome crisis within the GVN. In this mood, U.S. policy was subjected to various kinds of criticism and comment. Some came from within the Administration, various reactions came from outside it.

a. *Public Debate.* At the height of the GVN crisis, a number of newspapers and periodicals joined with the already committed (in opposition) and influential *New York Times* and *St. Louis Post Dispatch* in questioning U.S. objectives in Southeast Asia and/or advocating U.S. withdrawal from the entanglement of South Vietnam. In the midst of this kind of public questioning a major debate arose among members of Congress.

In a particularly active television day, Sunday 3 January, Secretary Rusk defended Vietnam policy in the context of a year-end foreign policy report. Ruling out either a U.S. withdrawal or a major expansion of the war, Rusk gave assurances that, with internal unity, and our aid and persistence, the South Vietnamese could themselves defeat the insurgency. On another network, three Senators expressed impatience with U.S. policy in Vietnam and urged a public reevaluation of it. Senator Morse criticized our involvement in South Vietnam on a unilateral basis, while Senators Cooper and Monroney spoke in favor of a full-fledged Senate debate to "come to grips" with the situation there. Senator Mansfield also appeared on the 3rd to urge consideration of Church's neutralization idea as an alternative to current policy but in keeping with the President's desire neither to withdraw nor carry the war to North Vietnam. On the 6th, in response to an Associated Press survey, the views in the Senate were shown to be quite divided. Of 63 Senators commenting, 31 suggested a negotiated settlement after the anti-communist bargaining positions were improved, while 10 favored negotiating immediately. Eight others favored commitment of U.S. forces against North Vietnam, 3 urged immediate withdrawal of U.S. advisers and military aid, and 11 stated that they didn't know what should be done other than to help strengthen the GVN. On 11 January, Senator Russell reacted to a briefing by CIA Director McCone with a statement that "up until now we have been losing ground instead of gaining it." He urged reevaluation of the U.S. position in South Vietnam, cautioning that unless a more effective government developed in Saigon the situation would become a prolonged stalemate at best.

On 14 January, as a result of reports of the loss of two U.S. jet combat aircraft over Laos, accounts of U.S. air operations against Laotian infiltration routes gained wide circulation for the first time. One in particular, a U.P.I. story by Arthur Dommen, in effect blew the lid on the entire YANKEE TEAM operation in Laos since May of 1964. Despite official State or Defense refusal to comment on the nature of the Laotian air missions, these disclosures added new fuel to the public policy debate. In a Senate speech the following day, in which he expressed his uneasiness over "recent reports of American air strikes in Laos and North Vietnam," Senator McGovern criticized what he called "the policy, now gaining support in Washington, of extending the war to the North." He denied that bombing North Vietnam could "seriously weaken guerrilla fighters 1,000 miles away" and urged seeking a "political settlement" with North Vietnam. Senator Long and Congressman Ford indicated on a TV program that they didn't feel that such operations were "a particularly dangerous course" for the nation to follow and that they were the kind of actions that could help protect our forces in South Vietnam. Senator Morse criticized the bombings as part of the Administration's "foreign policy of concealment in Southeast Asia." On the 19th, in the Senate, he repeated his blast, charging that the air strikes ignored the 1962 Geneva accord and violated the nation's belief in "substituting the rule of law for the jungle law of military might." Broadening his attack, he warned that "there is no hope of avoiding a massive war in Asia" if the U.S. policy toward Southeast Asia were to continue without change.

b. *Policy Assessments.* The intensifying public debate and the events and forces which precipitated it brought about an equally searching reassessment of policy within the Administration. While there is little evidence in the available materials that shows any serious questioning of foreign policy decisions among the Principals, questioning did occur within the agencies which they represented. It is clear that some of the judgments and alternative approaches were discussed with these NSC members, and presumably, some found their way into discussions with the President.

One very significant and probably influential viewpoint was registered by the Saigon Embassy. In a message described as the reflections of Alexis Johnson and Ambassador Taylor on which General Westmoreland concurred, the thrust of the advice seemed to be to move into Phase Two, almost in spite of the political outcome in Saigon. After listing four possible "solutions" to the then-unsettled GVN crisis, Taylor identified either a military takeover coupled with Huong's resignation or a successor civilian government dominated by the military as equally the worst possible outcomes. (It is important to note here that, depending on how one interprets the structure of the January 27th regime, one or the other of these was in fact the case at the beginning of the air strikes in February, 1965). In the event of such an outcome, Taylor argued that the United States could either "carry on about as we are now" or "seek to disengage from the present intimacy of relationship with the GVN" while continuing "to accept responsibility for [its] air and maritime defense . . . against the DRV." In the case of disengagement, he argued, the United States could offset the danger of South Vietnamese leaders being panicked into making a deal with the NLF "if we were engaged in reprisal attacks or had initiated Phase Two operations against DRV." The message then summarized the *three* different conditions under which the Mission officials thought Phase Two operations could be undertaken.

A. In association with the GVN after the latter had proved itself as a reasonably stable government able to control its armed forces.

B. Under a situation such as now as an emergency stimulant hopefully to create unity at home and restore failing morale.

C. As a unilateral U.S. action to compensate for a reduced in-country U.S. presence.

In other words, under any conceivable alliance condition short of complete U.S. abandonment of South Vietnam, Ambassador Taylor and his top level associates in Saigon saw the graduated air strikes of Phase Two as an appropriate course of action. As they concluded, "without Phase Two operations, we see slight chance of moving toward a successful solution."

Within the more influential sections of the State Department, policy re-examination took a similar, though not identical, tack. Rather than adjust the substance or projected extent of the pressures policy, the tendency was to re-calculate and adjust the conditions under which it was considered appropriate to apply it. The motivation for a reassessment was the sense of impending disaster in South Vietnam. What the Saigon Embassy reports appear to have portrayed at the time as concrete instances of foot-dragging, political maneu-vering, and sparring for advantage among political and military leaders seem to have been interpreted in Washington as an impending sell-out to the NLF. For example, the Assistant Secretary for Far Eastern Affairs, who had been an important participant in the policy and decision-making processes through most of 1964, offered the following prognosis [Doc. 248]:

> . . . the situation in Vietnam is now likely to come apart more rapidly than we had anticipated in November. We would still stick to the estimate that the most likely form of coming apart would be a government or key groups starting to negotiate covertly with the Liberation Front or Hanoi. perhaps not asking in the first instance that we get out, but with that necessarily following at a fairly early stage.

The perceived impact of a collapse in Saigon on other nations—perhaps even more than the political fortunes of South Vietnam itself—were a significant part of the State Department calculations. If a unilateral "Vietnam solution" were to be arranged, so the thinking went in January 1965, not only would Laos and Cambodia be indefensible, but Thailand's position would become unpredictable. Bundy wrote:

> Most seriously, there is grave question whether the Thai in these circum-stances would retain any confidence at all in our continued support. . . . As events have developed, the American public would probably not be too sharply critical, but the real question would be whether Thailand and other nations were weakened and taken over thereafter.

There was also a perceived lack of reaction or effectiveness in U.S. policies during the late autumn. Bundy reflected an apparently widely shared concern that Administration actions and statements since the election had convinced the Vietnamese and other Asians that the U.S. Government did not intend to take stronger action and was "possibly looking for a way out." Moreover, he saw this impression being created by our "insisting on a more perfect government than can reasonably be expected, before we consider any additional action—and that we might even pull out our support unless such a government emerges."

To change this impression and reverse the disturbing trends, Bundy and others in State suggested stronger actions, even though recognizing that these actions incurred certain risks. However, the immediate actions suggested fell somewhat short of Phase Two (a term that was *now* used in the correspondence). They included: (1) "an early occasion for reprisal action . . ."; (2) "possibly beginning low-level reconnaissance of DRV . . ."; (3) "an orderly withdrawal of our dependents," which was termed "a grave mistake in the absence of stronger action"; and (4) "introduction of limited U.S. ground forces into the northern area of South Vietnam . . . concurrently with the first air attacks into the DRV." They downgraded the potential of further intensifying the air operations in Laos, indicating that such actions "would *not* meet the problem of Saigon morale" and might precipitate a "Communist intervention on a substantial scale in Laos. . . ." The perceived risks of the suggested actions were: (1) a deepened U.S. commitment at a time when South Vietnamese will appeared weak; (2) the likelihood of provoking open opposition to U.S. policies in nations like India and Japan; (3) the uncertainty of any meaningful stiffening effort on the GVN; and (4) the inability of "limited actions against the southern DRV" to sharply reduce infiltration or "to induce Hanoi to call it off."

If the graduated, "progressively mounting," air operations of Phase Two were implied by these suggestions, it appears that they were perceived as being entered rather gingerly and with little intent to intensify them to whatever extent might be required to force a decision in Hanoi. Rather, the expectancies in State were quite different: "On balance we believe that such action would have some faint hope of really improving the Vietnamese situation, and, above all, would put us in a much stronger position to hold the next line of defense, namely Thailand." Moreover, Bundy and others felt that even with the stronger actions, the negotiating process that they believed was bound to come about could not be expected to bring about a really secure and independent South Vietnam. Still, despite this shortcoming, they reasoned that their suggested "stronger actions" would have the desirable effect in Southeast Asia: ". . . we would still have appeared to Asians to have done a lot more about it."

High among the State Department's concerns over the impact of U.S. Vietnam policy on the rest of Southeast Asia were current developments in the communist world. For one thing, the Soviet Union had re-entered Southeast Asian politics in an active way, after a period of nearly three years of diligent detachment. Following a reported Soviet pledge in November to increase economic and military aid to North Vietnam, the Administration held a series of conversations in December with representatives of the new Soviet regime. During at least one of these—in addition to exchanging the now standard respective lines about who violated the Geneva Accord—Secretary Rusk stressed the seriousness of the situation created by Hanoi's and Peking's policies, implying strongly that we would remain in South Vietnam until those policies had changed or had resulted in "a real scrap." Soviet Foreign Minister Gromyko replied that if the United States felt so strongly about improving the situation in Vietnam, it should be willing to attend an international conference to discuss Laos and Vietnam. However, he would not agree with Rusk's request for assurances that Laos would be represented by Souvanna Phouma.

Within a few weeks of this conversation, Mr. Gromyko sent assurances to the DRV that the Soviet Union would support it in the face of aggressive actions by the United States. Further, he expressed the official Soviet view that it was the duty of all participants in the Geneva agreements to take the steps necessary to frustrate U.S. military plans to extend the war in Indo-China. This note, sent on 30 December, was made public in a renewed call on 4 January for a conference on Laos, to be convened without preconditions. On 17 January, Pravda carried an authoritative statement warning that "the provocations of the armed forces of the United States and their Saigon puppets against North Vietnam" carried dangers of "large armed conflict," and citing naval attacks on the DRV coast and U.S. air attacks in Laos as examples. On the 22nd, in letters to both Hanoi and Peking, Gromyko reiterated the Soviet pledge to aid North Vietnam in resisting any U.S. military action.

In addition to renewed Soviet activity in Southeast Asia, that of Communist China also appeared ominous. Fanned by Sukarno's abrupt withdrawal of Indonesia's participation in the U.N., some U.S. officials voiced concern over the development of a "Peking-Jakarta axis" to promote revolution in Asia. North Vietnam, together with North Korea, were seen as natural allies who might join in to form an international grouping exerting an attraction on other Asian states to counter that of the U.N. Peking was viewed as the instigator and prime benefactor of such a grouping.

Complementing the State Department policy assessments, were those in OSD. For example, in early January, Assistant Secretary McNaughton regarded U.S. stakes in South Vietnam as [Doc. 247]: (1) to hold onto "buffer real estate" near Thailand and Malaysia and (2) to maintain our national reputation; and the latter was the more important of the two. Sharing the State view that South Vietnam was being lost ("this means that a government not unfriendly to the DRV would probably emerge within two years"), he believed that the U.S. reputation would suffer least "if we continue to support South Vietnam and if Khanh and company continue to behave like children as the game is lost." However, he pointed out that "dogged perseverance" was also recommended because the situation might possibly improve.

In specific terms, McNaughton defined perseverance as including the following course of action:

> a. Continue to take risks on behalf of SVN. A reprisal should be carried out soon. (Dependents could be removed at that time.)
>
> b. Keep slugging away. Keep help flowing, BUT do not increase the number of U.S. men in SVN. (Additional U.S. soldiers are as likely to be counter-productive as productive.)
>
> c. Do not lead or appear to lead in any negotiations. Chances of reversing the tide will be better and, if we don't reverse the tide, our reputation will emerge in better condition.
>
> d. If we leave, be sure it is a departure of the kind which would put everyone on our side, wondering how we stuck it and took it so long.

In the event of inability to prevent deterioration within South Vietnam, he urged the development of plans to move to a fallback position by helping shore-up Thailand and Malaysia.

An OSD assessment made immediately after the Khanh coup in late January adds perspective to this viewpoint. [Doc. 249] In it, McNaughton stated and Secretary McNamara agreed, "U.S. objective in South Vietnam is not to 'help friend' but to contain China." In particular, both Malaysia and Thailand were seen as the next targets of Chinese aggressiveness. Neither official saw any alternative to "keep plugging," insofar as U.S. efforts inside South Vietnam were concerned. However, outside the borders, both favored initiating strikes against North Vietnam. At first, they believed, these should take the form of reprisals; beyond that, the Administration would have to "feel its way" into stronger, graduated pressures. McNaughton doubted that such strikes would actually help the situation in South Vietnam but thought they should be carried out anyway. McNamara believed they probably would help the situation, in addition to their broader impacts on the U.S. position in Southeast Asia.

Though different in some respects, all of these policy views pointed in a similar direction. In his own way, each Principal argued that it was unproductive to hold off on further action against North Vietnam until the GVN began to operate in an effective manner. Each suggested broader benefits that could be gained for the United States if firmer measures were taken directly against the DRV.

The impact of these views can be seen in the policy guidance emanating from Washington in mid and late January 1965. For example, on the 11th, Ambassador Taylor was apprised of Administration doubts that General Khanh had put aside his intentions to stage a coup and was given counsel for such an eventuality. Essentially, the guidance was to avoid actions that would further commit the United States to any particular form of political solution. The underlying rationale expressed was that if a military government did emerge, "we might well have to swallow our pride and work with it." Apparently, the Administration's adamant insistence on an effective GVN along lines specified by the United States had been eroded. However, on the 14th guidance to Taylor indicated that the Administration had not yet determined to move into a phase of action more vigorous than the current one. In the immediate wake of public disclosures concerning the bombing operations in Laos, Secretary Rusk concurred in Taylor's proposal to brief the GVN leaders on these operations, but cautioned against encouraging their expectations of new U.S. moves against the North. Rusk considered it "essential that they not be given [the] impression that [BARREL ROLL, etc.] represents a major step-up of activity against the DRV or that it represents an important new phase of U.S. operational activity." The immediate matter for speculation was the striking of a key highway bridge in Laos, but the program still called for two missions per week.

Clear indication that the Administration was contemplating some kind of increased military activity came on 25 January. Ambassador Taylor was asked to comment on the "Departmental view" that U.S. dependents should be withdrawn to "clear the decks" in Saigon and enable better concentration of U.S. efforts on behalf of South Vietnam. Previously, the JCS had reversed their initial position on this issue and requested the removal, a view which was forwarded to State "for consideration at the highest levels of government" in mid-January. Recalling the Bundy policy assessment of 6 January, it will be noted that clearing the decks by removing dependents was recommended only in association with "stronger actions." However, there is no indication of any decision at this point to move into Phase Two. The Rusk cable made specific reference to a current interest in reprisal actions. Moreover, consideration of later events and decisions compels the judgment that it was only reprisals which the Administration had in mind as January drew to a close.

3.   The Air War in North Vietnam:
Rolling Thunder Begins, February–June, 1965

Summary and Analysis

The United States decisions, in the early months of 1965, to launch a program of reprisal air strikes against North Vietnam, evolving progressively into a sustained bombing campaign of rising intensity, were made against a background of anguished concern over the threat of imminent collapse of the Government of South Vietnam and of its military effort against the Viet Cong. The air war against the North was launched in the hope that it would strengthen GVN confidence and cohesion, and that it would deter or restrain the DRV from continuing its support of the revolutionary war in the South. There was hope also that a quite modest bombing effort would be sufficient; that the demonstration of US determination and the potential risks and costs to the North implicit in the early air strikes would provide the US with substantial bargaining leverage; and that it would redress the "equation of advantage" so that a political settlement might be negotiated on acceptable terms.

Once set in motion, however, the bombing effort seemed to stiffen rather than soften Hanoi's backbone, as well as to lessen the willingness of Hanoi's allies, particularly the Soviet Union, to work toward compromise. Moreover, compromise was ruled out in any event, since the negotiating terms that the US proposed were not "compromise" terms, but more akin to a "cease and desist" order that, from the DRV/VC point of view, was tantamount to a demand for their surrender.

As Hanoi remained intractable in the face of a mere token demonstration of U.S. capability and resolve, U.S. policy shifted to a more deliberate combination of intensified military pressures and modest diplomatic enticements. The carrot was added to the stick in the form of an economic development gesture, but the coercive element remained by far the more tangible and visible component of U.S. policy. To the slowly but relentlessly rising air pressures against the North was added the deployment of US combat forces to the South. In response to public pressures, a major diplomatic opportunity was provided Hanoi for a quiet backdown through a brief bombing pause called in mid-May, but the pause seemed to be aimed more at clearing the decks for a subsequent intensified resumption than it was at evoking a reciprocal act of de-escalation by Hanoi. The U.S. initiative, in any event, was unmistakably rebuffed by North Vietnam and by its Communist allies, and the opposing positions were more hopelessly deadlocked than ever before.

It is the purpose of this study to reconstruct the immediate circumstances that led up to the U.S. reprisal decision of February 1965, to retrace the changes in rationale that progressively transformed the reprisal concept into a sustained graduated bombing effort, and to chronicle the relationship between that effort and the military-political moves to shore up Saigon and the military-diplomatic signals to dissuade Hanoi, during the crucial early months of February through May of 1965.

*   *   *   *   *   *   *

Background to Pleiku. The growing realization, throughout 1964, that the final consolidation of VC power in South Vietnam was a distinct possibility, had led to a protracted US policy reassessment and a determined search for force- ful military alternatives in the North that might help salvage the deteriorating situation in the South. The proposed program of graduated military pressures against North Vietnam that emerged from this reassessment in late 1964 had three major objectives: (1) to signal to the Communist enemy the firmness of U.S. resolve, (2) to boost the sagging morale of the GVN in the South, and (3) to impose increased costs and strains upon the DRV in the North. Under- lying the rationale of the program was the hope that it might restore some equi- librium to the balance of forces, hopefully increasing the moment of US/GVN bargaining leverage sufficiently to permit an approach to a negotiated solution on something other than surrender terms.

Throughout the planning process (and even after the initiation of the pro- gram) the President's principal advisors differed widely in their views as to the intensity of the bombing effort that would be desirable or required, and as to its likely effectiveness in influencing Hanoi's will to continue its aggression. The JCS, for example, consistently argued that only a most dramatic and forceful application of military power would exert significant pressure on North Vietnam, but firmly believed that such application could and would affect the enemy's will. Most civilian officials in State, OSD, and the White House, on the other hand, tended to favor a more gradual, restrained approach, "progressively mounting in scope and intensity," in which the prospect of greater pressure to come was at least as important as any damage actually inflicted. But these officials also tended, for the most part, to have much less confidence that such pressures would have much impact on Hanoi's course, making such equivocal assessments as: "on balance we believe that such action would have some faint hope of really im- proving the Vietnamese situation."

Reprisal Planning. In spite of these rather hesitant judgments, the graduated approach was adopted and a program of relatively mild military actions aimed at North Vietnam was set in motion beginning in December 1964. At the same time, detailed preparations were made to carry out bombing strikes against tar- gets in North Vietnam in reprisal for any future attacks on U.S. forces. These preparations were made chiefly in connection with the occasional DESOTO Patrols that the US Navy conducted in the Gulf of Tonkin which had been fired upon or menaced by North Vietnamese torpedo boats on several previous oc- casions during 1964. In order to be prepared for an attack on any future patrol, a pre-packaged set of reprisal targets was worked up by CINCPAC on instruc- tions from the JCS, and pre-assigned forces were maintained in a high state of readiness to strike these targets in accordance with a detailed strike plan that provided a range of retaliatory options.

In late January, a DESOTO Patrol was authorized to begin on Feb. 3 (later postponed to Feb. 7) and Operation Order FLAMING DART was issued by CINCPAC, providing for a number of alternative US air strike reprisal actions in the eventuality that the DESOTO Patrol were to be attacked or that any other provocation were to occur, such as a spectacular VC incident in South Vietnam. At the last moment, however, the Patrol was called off in deference to Soviet Premier Kosygin's imminent visit to Hanoi. U.S. officials hoped that the USSR might find it in its interest to act as an agent of moderation vis a vis Hanoi in the Vietnam conflict, and wished to avoid any act that might be inter- preted as deliberately provocative. Nevertheless, it was precisely at the beginning of the Kosygin visit, during the early morning hours of February 7, that the VC launched their spectacular attack on US installations at Pleiku, thus triggering FLAMING DART I, the first of the new carefully programmed US/GVN reprisal strikes.

Imperceptible Transition. By contrast with the earlier Tonkin strikes of August, 1964 which had been presented as a one-time demonstration that North Vietnam could not flagrantly attack US forces with impunity, the February 1965 raids were explicitly linked with the "larger pattern of aggression" by North Vietnam, and were a reprisal against *North* Vietnam for an offense committed by the *VC* in *South* Vietnam. When the VC staged another dramatic attack on Qui Nhon on Feb. 10, the combined US/GVN response, named FLAMING DART II, was not characterized as an event-associated reprisal but as a generalized response to "continued acts of aggression." The new terminology reflected a conscious U.S. decision to broaden the reprisal concept as gradually and imperceptibly as possible to accommodate a much wider policy of sustained, steadily intensifying air attacks against North Vietnam, at a rate and on a scale to be determined by the U.S. Although discussed publicly in very muted tones, the second FLAMING DART operation constituted a sharp break with past US policy and set the stage for the continuing bombing program that was now to be launched in earnest.

Differences in Advocacy. While all but one or two of the President's principal Vietnam advisors favored the initiation of a sustained bombing program, there were significant differences among them. McGeorge Bundy and Ambassador Maxwell Taylor, for example, both advocated a measured, controlled sequence of raids, carried out jointly with the GVN and directed solely against DRV military targets and infiltration routes. In their view, the intensity of the attacks was to be varied with the level of VC outrages in SVN or might be progressively raised. But whereas McGeorge Bundy's objective was to influence the course of the struggle in the *South* (boosting GVN morale, improving US bargaining power with the GVN, exerting a depressing effect on VC cadre), Ambassador Taylor's principal aim was "to bring increasing pressure on the DRV to cease its intervention." It was coercion of the North, rather than a rededication of the GVN to the struggle in the South that Taylor regarded as the real benefit of a reprisal policy. CINCPAC, on the other hand, insisted that the program would have to be a very forceful one—a "graduated pressures" rather than a "graduated reprisal" philosophy—if the DRV were to be persuaded to accede to a cessation on U.S. terms. The Joint Chiefs, in turn (and especially Air Force Chief of Staff General McConnell), believed that the much heavier air strike recomendations repeatedly made by the JCS during the preceding six months were more appropriate than the mild actions proposed by Taylor and Bundy.

Initiating ROLLING THUNDER. A firm decision to adopt "a program of measured and limited air action jointly with the GVN against selected military targets in the DRV" was made by the President on February 13, and communicated to Ambassador Taylor in Saigon. Details of the program were deliberately left vague, as the President wished to preserve maximum flexibility. The first strike was set for February 20 and Taylor was directed to obtain GVN concurrence. A semi-coup in Saigon, however, compelled postponement and cancellation of this and several subsequent strikes. Political clearance was not given until the turbulence was calmed with the departure of General Nguyen Khanh from Vietnam on Feb 25. U.S. reluctance to launch air attacks during this time was further reinforced by a UK–USSR diplomatic initiative to reactivate the Cochairmanship of the 1954 Geneva Conference with a view to involving the members of that conference in a consideration of the Vietnam crisis. Air strikes executed at that moment, it was feared, might sabotage that diplomatic gambit, which Washington looked upon not as a potential negotiating opportunity, but as a convenient vehicle for public expression of a tough U.S. position. The Co-Chairmen gambit, however, languished—and eventually came to naught. The first ROLLING THUNDER strike was finally rescheduled for Feb 26. This time adverse weather forced its cancellation and it was not until March 2 that the first of the new program strikes, dubbed ROLLING THUNDER V, was actually carried out.

In the closing days of February and during early March, the Administration undertook publicly and privately to defend and propound its rationale for the air strikes, stressing its determination to stand by the GVN, but reaffirming the limited nature of its objectives toward North Vietnam. Secretary Rusk conducted a marathon public information campaign to signal a seemingly reasonable but in fact quite tough US position on negotiations, demanding that Hanoi "stop doing what it is doing against its neighbors" before any negotiations could prove fruitful. Rusk's disinterest in negotiations at this time was in concert with the view of virtually all the President's key advisors, that the path to peace was not then open. Hanoi held sway over more than half of South Vietnam and could see the Saigon Government crumbling before her very eyes. The balance of power at this time simply did not furnish the U.S. with a basis for bargaining and Hanoi had not reason to accede to the hard terms the U.S. had in mind. Until military pressures on North Vietnam could tilt the balance of forces the other way, talk of negotiation could be little more than a hollow exercise.

Evolving a Continuing Program. Immediately after the launching of the first ROLLING THUNDER strike, efforts were set in motion to increase the effectiveness, forcefulness and regularity of the program. US aircraft loss rates came under McNamara's scrutiny, with the result that many restrictions on the use of U.S. aircraft and special ordnance were lifted, and the air strike technology improved. Sharp annoyance was expressed by Ambassador Taylor over what he considered an unnecessarily timid and ambivalent US stance regarding the frequency and weight of U.S. air attacks. He called for a more dynamic schedule of strikes, a several week program, relentlessly marching North, to break the will of the DRV. Army Chief of Staff General Johnson, returning from a Presidential survey mission to Vietnam in mid-March, supported Taylor's view and recommended increasing the scope and tempo of the air strikes as well as their effectiveness. The President accepted these recommendations and, beginning with ROLLING THUNDER VII (March 19), air action against the North was transformed from a sporadic, halting effort into a regular and determined program.

Shift to Interdiction. In the initial U.S. reprisal strikes and the first ROLLING THUNDER actions, target selection had been completely dominated by political and psychological considerations. With the gradual acceptance, beginning in March, of the need for a militarily more significant sustained bombing program, a refocusing of target emphasis occurred, stressing interdiction of the DRV's lines of communication (LOC's)—the visible manifestations of North Vietnamese aggression. The JCS had called the SecDef's attention to this infiltration target complex as early as mid-February, and an integrated counter-infiltration attack plan against LOC targets south of the 20th parallel began to be developed by CINCPAC, culminating at the end of March in the submission of the JCS 12-week bombing program. This program was built around the "LOC-cut" concept developed by the Pacific Command and was strongly endorsed by General Westmoreland and Ambassador Taylor. The JCS recommended that only the first phase (third through fifth weeks) of the 12-week program be adopted, as they had not reached agreement on the later phases. The JCS submission, however, was not accepted as a program, although it strongly influenced the new interdiction-oriented focus of the attacks that were to follow. But neither the SecDef nor the President was willing to approve a multi-week program in advance. They preferred to retain continual personal control over attack concepts and individual target selection and to communicate their decisions through weekly guidance provided by the SecDef's ROLLING THUNDER planning messages.

April 1 Reassessment. By the end of March, in Saigon's view, the situation in South Vietnam appeared to have rebounded somewhat. Morale seemed to have been boosted, at least temporarily, by the air strikes, and Vietnamese forces had not recently suffered any major defeats. Washington, on the other hand, continued to regard the situation as "bad and deteriorating," and could see no signs of "give" on the part of Hanoi. None of the several diplomatic initiatives that had been launched looked promising, and VC terrorism continued unabated, with the March 29 bombing of the US embassy in Saigon being by far the boldest provocation.

Ambassador Taylor returned to Washington to participate in a Presidential policy review on April 1 and 2, in which a wide range of possible military and non-military actions in South and North Vietnam were examined. The discussions, however, did not deal principally with the air war, but focused mainly on the prospect of major deployments of US and Third Country combat forces to South Vietnam. As a result of the discussions, the far-reaching decision was made, at least conceptually, to permit US troops to engage in offensive ground operations against Asian insurgents. With respect to future air pressures policy, the actions adopted amounted to little more than a continuation of "roughly the present slowly ascending tempo of ROLLING THUNDER operations," directed mainly at the LOC targets that were then beginning to be struck. The Director of Central Intelligence John McCone demurred, arguing that a change in the US ground force role in the South also demanded comparably more forceful action against the North. He felt that the ground force decision was correct only "if our air strikes against the North are sufficiently heavy and damaging really to hurt the North Vietnamese."

A "Carrot" at Johns Hopkins. Although devoting much effort to public explanation and private persuasion, the President could not quiet his critics. Condemnation of the bombing spread and the President was being pressed from many directions to make a major public statement welcoming negotiations. He found an opportunity to dramatize his peaceful intent in his renowned Johns Hopkins address of April 7, in which he (1) accepted the spirit of the 17-nation Appeal of March 15 to start negotiations "without posing any preconditions," (2) offered the vision of a "billion dollar American investment" in a regional Mekong River basin development effort in which North Vietnam might also participate, and (3) appointed the illustrious Eugene Black to head up the effort and to lend it credibility and prestige. The President's speech evoked much favorable public reaction throughout the world, but it failed to silence the Peace Bloc and it failed to move Hanoi. Premier Pham Van Dong responded to the President's speech by proposing his famous Four Points as the only correct way to resolve the Vietnam problem and, two days later, denounced the President's proposal as simply a "carrot" offered to offset the "stick" of aggression and to allay public criticism of his Vietnam policy. But this is as far as the President was willing to go in his concessions to the Peace Bloc. To the clamor for a bombing pause at this time, the Administration responded with a resounding "No."

Consensus at Honolulu. By mid-April, communication between Washington and Saigon had become badly strained as a result of Ambassador Taylor's resentment of what he regarded as Washington's excessive eagerness to introduce US combat forces into South Vietnam, far beyond anything that had been approved in the April 1–2 review. To iron out differences, a conference was convened by Secretary McNamara at Honolulu on April 20. Its main concern was to reach specific agreement on troop deployments, but it also sought to reaffirm the existing scope and tempo of ROLLING THUNDER. The conferees agreed that sufficient pressure was provided by repetition and continuation of the strikes, and that it was important not to "kill the hostage" by destroying the valuable assets inside the "Hanoi do-not." Their strategy for victory was to "break the will of the DRV/VC by denying them victory." Honolulu apparently succeeded in restoring consensus between Washington and Saigon. It also marked the relative downgrading of pressures against the North, in favor of more intensive activity in the South. The decision, at this point, was to "plateau" the air strikes more or less at the prevailing level, rather than to pursue the relentless dynamic course ardently advocated by Ambassador Taylor and Admiral Sharp in February and March, or the massive destruction of the North Vietnamese target complex consistently pressed by the Joint Chiefs.

Following Honolulu, it was decided to publicize the fact that "interdiction" was now the major objective of the bombing, and Secretary McNamara devoted a special Pentagon briefing for the press corps to that issue.

First Bombing Pause. Pressure for some form of bombing halt had mounted steadily throughout April and early May and, although the President did not believe that such a gesture would evoke any response from Hanoi he did order a brief halt effective May 13, "to begin" as he expressed it "to clear a path either toward restoration of peace or toward increased military action, depending on the reaction of the Communists." The political purpose of the pause—to test Hanoi's reaction—was kept under very tight wraps, and the project was given the code name MAYFLOWER. A great effort was made to inform Hanoi of the fact of the pause and of its political intent. Soviet Ambassador Dobrynin was given an oral explanation by Secretary Rusk, confirmed by a tough written statement, reasserting Rusk's public position that the cessation of the DRV's attacks upon South Vietnam was the only road to peace and that the US would be watchful, during the pause, for any signs of a reduction in such attacks. A similar statement was sent to U.S. Ambassador Kohler in Moscow, for personal transmittal to the DRV Ambassador there. Kohler, however, met with refusal both from the DRV Ambassador to receive, and from the Soviet Foreign Office to transmit, the message. A written note, sent to the DRV embassy, was returned ostensibly unopened. Nevertheless, it is quite clear that Hanoi was more than adequately advised of the contents of the U.S. message through the various diplomatic channels that were involved.

Given the "rather strenuous nature" of the U.S. note to Hanoi and the briefness of the pause, it is hardly surprising that the initiative encountered no receptivity from the Soviet government and evoked no positive response from Hanoi. The latter denounced the bombing halt as "a worn out trick of deceit and threat . . ." and the former, in the person of Soviet Foreign Minister Gromyko in a conversation with Rusk in Vienna, branded the U.S. note to Hanoi as "insulting."

Having thus been unmistakably rebuffed, the President ordered the resumption of the bombing raids effective May 18. The entire pause was handled with a minimum of public information, and no announcement was made of the suspension or of the resumption. But prime ministers or chiefs of state of a half dozen key friendly governments were briefed fully after the event. A still somewhat ambiguous diplomatic move was made by Hanoi in Paris on May 18, a few hours after the bombing had been resumed, in which Mai Van Bo, the DRV economic delegate there seemed to imply a significant softening of Hanoi's position on the Four Points as "prior conditions." But subsequent attempts at clarification left that issue as ambiguous as it had been before.

End of Summary and Analysis

CHRONOLOGY FEBRUARY–JUNE, 1965

6 Jan 1965   *William Bundy Memorandum for Rusk*
Taking note of the continued political deterioration in SVN, Bundy concludes that, even though it will get worse, the US should probably proceed with Phase II of the December pressures plan, the escalating air strikes against the North.

8 Jan 1965   *2,000 Korean troops arrive in SVN*
South Korea sends 2,000 military advisors to SVN, the first such non-US support.

27 Jan 1965   *Huong Government ousted*
General Khanh ousts the civilian government headed by Huong and assumes powers of government himself.

McNaughton Memorandum for Secretary of Defense
McNaughton is as pessimistic as William Bundy about prospects in the South. He feels the US should evacuate dependents and respond promptly at the next reprisal opportunity. McNamara's penciled notes reveal more optimism about the results of air strikes than McNaughton.

28 Jan 1965   *JCS message 4244 to CINCPAC*
A resumption of the DESOTO Patrols on or about 3 February is authorized.

29 Jan 1965   *JCSM-70-65*
The JCS urge again that a strong reprisal action be taken immediately after the next DRV/VC provocation. In particular, they propose targets and readiness to strike should the forthcoming resumption of the DESOTO Patrols be challenged.

4 Feb 1965   *CJCS message 4612 to CINCPAC*
In view of Kosygin's impending visit to Hanoi, authority for the DESOTO Patrol is cancelled.

SNIE 53–65 "Short Term Prospects in South Vietnam"
The intelligence community does not see the conditions of political instability in SVN improving in the months ahead. The political base for counterinsurgency will remain weak.

6 Feb 1965   *Kosygin arrives in Hanoi*
Soviet Premier Kosygin arrives in Hanoi for a state visit that will deepen Soviet commitment to the DRV, and expand Soviet economic and military assistance.

7 Feb 1965   *VC attack US base at Pleiku*
Well-coordinated VC attacks hit the US advisors' barracks at Pleiku and the helicopter base at Camp Holloway.

President decides to retaliate
The NSC is convened in the evening (6 Feb. Washington time) and with the recommendation of McGeorge Bundy, Ambassador Taylor and General Westmoreland from Saigon, decides on a reprisal strike against the North in spite of Kosygin's presence in Hanoi.

McGeorge Bundy Memorandum to the President: "The Situation in South Vietnam"
Completing a fact-gathering trip to SVN on the very day of the Pleiku attack, Bundy acknowledges the bad state of the GVN both politically and militarily, but nevertheless recommends that the US adopt a policy of "sustained reprisal" against the North and that we evacuate US dependents from Saigon. The reprisal policy should begin from specific VC attacks but gradually escalate into sustained attacks as a form of pressure on the DRV to end its support of the VC and/or come to terms with the US.

8 Feb 1965   *FLAMING DART I*
49 US Navy jets conduct the first FLAMING DART reprisal attack on the Dong Hoi army barracks; a scheduled VNAF attack is cancelled because of bad weather.

13 Feb 1965   *B-52s sent to area*
Approval is given for the dispatch of 30 B-52s to Guam and 30 KC-135s to Okinawa for contingency use in Vietnam.

ROLLING THUNDER approved by President; DEPTEL to Saigon 1718
The President decides to inaugurate ROLLING THUNDER sustained bombing of the North under strict limitations with programs approved on a week-by-week basis.

17 Feb 1965   *CINCPAC message 170217 February to JCS*
Admiral Sharp urges that the strikes be conceived as "pressures" not "reprisals" and that any premature discussions or negotiations with the DRV be avoided. We must convince them that the cost of their aggression is prohibitive.

UK reports Soviet interest in Geneva Talks
The UK Ambassador, Lord Harlech, informs Rusk that the Soviets have approached the UK about reactivating the 1954 Geneva Conference in the current Vietnam crisis. After an initial US interest, the Soviets back off and the matter dies.

18 Feb 1965   *President schedules ROLLING THUNDER*
President Johnson sets February 20 as the date for the beginning of ROLLING THUNDER and informs US Ambassadors in Asia.

SNIE 10-3/1-65
The intelligence community gives its view that sustained attacks on the DRV would probably cause it to seek a respite rather than to intensify the struggle in the South.

19 Feb 1965   *Thao "semi-coup"*
Colonel Thao, a longtime conspirator, launches a "semi-coup" against Khanh, designed to remove him but not the Armed Forces Council. He is quickly defeated but the AFC decides to use the incident to remove Khanh itself. The events drag on for several days.

Embassy Saigon message 2665
Taylor recommends urgently that the ROLLING THUNDER strike be cancelled until the political situation in Saigon has clarified. The President agrees.

CM-438-65
In a memo to McNamara, Wheeler proposes a systematic attack on the DRV rail system as the most vulnerable link in the transportation system. Military as opposed to psychological value of targets is already beginning to enter discussions.

21 Feb 1965   *Khanh resigns*
Unable to rally support in the Armed Forces Council, Khanh resigns.

24 Feb 1965   *U.S. reassures Peking*
In a meeting in Warsaw the Chinese are informed that while the U.S. will continue to take those actions required to defend itself and South Vietnam, it has no aggressive intentions toward the DRV.

27 Feb 1965   *State Dept. issues "White Paper" on DRV aggression*
The State Department issues a "White Paper" detailing its charges of aggression against North Vietnam.

28 Feb 1965   *ROLLING THUNDER announced*
U.S. and GVN make simultaneous announcement of decision to open a continuous limited air campaign against the North in order to bring about a negotiated settlement on favorable terms.

2 Mar 1965   *First ROLLING THUNDER strike*
104 USAF planes attack Xom Bang ammo depot and 19 VNAF aircraft hit the Quang Khe Naval Base in the first attacks of ROLLING THUNDER.

President decides to send CSA, H.K. Johnson, to Vietnam
The President decides to send Army Chief of Staff, Gen. H. K. Johnson, to Saigon to explore with Taylor and Westmoreland what additional efforts can be made to improve the situation in the South, complementarily to the strikes against the North.

3 Mar 1965   *Tito letter to Johnson*
Yugoslav President Tito, in a letter to Johnson, urges immediate negotiation on Vietnam without conditions on either side.

5–12 Mar   Gen. Johnson trip to Vietnam
1965   Army Chief of Staff, Gen. H. K. Johnson, tours Vietnam on a
mission for the President.

6 Mar 1965   Marines sent to Da Nang
Two Marine Battalion Landing Teams are ordered to Da Nang
by the President to take up base security functions in the Da
Nang perimeter.

8 Mar 1965   Marines land at Da Nang
The two Marine battalions land at Da Nang and set up defensive
positions.

Embassy Saigon msgs. 2888, and 2889
Taylor expresses sharp annoyance at what seems to him an unnecessarily timid and ambivalent U.S. stance on air strikes. The
long delay between strikes, the marginal weight of the attacks, and
the great ado about diplomatic feelers were weakening our signal
to the North. He calls for a more dynamic schedule of strikes, a
multiple week program relentlessly marching North to break
Hanoi's will.

U Thant proposes big power conference
U Thant proposes a conference of the big powers with North and
South Vietnam to start preliminary negotiations.

9 Mar 1965   U.S. rejects Thant proposal
The U.S. rejects Thant's proposal until the DRV stops its aggression.

Some bombing restrictions lifted
The President lifts the restriction on the use of napalm in strikes
on the North, and eliminates the requirement for Vietnamese co-
pilots in FARMGATE missions.

10 Mar 1965   CJCS memo to SecDef CM-469-65
In a memo to SecDef with preliminary reports on U.S. aircraft
losses in hostile action, Wheeler requests better ordnance, more
recce, and greater field command flexibility in alternate target
selection for weather problems.

12 Mar 1965   State msg. 1975 to Saigon
ROLLING THUNDER VI is authorized for the next day; it is
subsequently delayed until the 14th because of weather.

President replies to Tito
In his reply to Tito the President indicates the only bar to peace
is DRV aggression which must stop before talks can begin.

13 Mar 1965   Embassy Saigon msg. 2949
Taylor complains about the postponement of RT VI, stating that
too much attention is being paid to the specific target, any target
will do since the important thing is to keep up the momentum of
the attacks.

13–18 Mar   Conference of non-aligned nations in Belgrade
1965   Tito calls a meeting of 15 non-aligned nations in Belgrade. The
declaration calls for negotiations and blames "foreign intervention" for the aggravation of the situation.

14–15 Mar   *ROLLING THUNDER VI*
1965   The delayed RT VI is carried out and is the heaviest attack thus far with over 100 U.S. aircraft and 24 VNAF planes hitting two targets.

14 Mar 1965   *Gen. Johnson submits his report to SecDef*
Gen. Johnson submits a 21-recommendation report including a request that the scope and tempo of strikes against the North be increased and that many of the restrictions on the strikes be lifted.

15 Mar 1965   *President approves most of Johnson report*
Having reviewed the Johnson report, the President approves most of his recommendations including those for expanding and regularizing the campaign against the North. The new guidelines apply to RT VII on 19 Mar.

19 Mar 1965   *ROLLING THUNDER VII*
The first week's program of sustained bombing under the name ROLLING THUNDER VII begins.

20 Mar 1965   *STEEL TIGER Begins*
Acting on a CINCPAC recommendation the Administration had approved the separation of the anti-infiltration bombing in the Laotian panhandle from the BARREL ROLL strikes in support of Laotian forces. The former are now called STEEL TIGER.

21 Mar 1965   *CINCPAC msg. to JCS 210525 Mar.*
In a long cable, CINCPAC proposes a program for cutting, in depth, the DRV logistical network, especially below the 20th parallel. The plan calls for initial intensive strikes to cut the system and then regular armed recce to eliminate any residual capacity, or repair efforts.

24 Mar 1965   *McNaughton memo "Plan of Action for South Vietnam"*
McNaughton concludes that the situation in SVN probably cannot be improved without extreme measures against the DRV and/or the intervention of US ground forces. He gives a thorough treatment to the alternatives and risks with particular attention to the strong air campaign on the North. He takes note of the various escalation points and tries to assess the risks at each level. He evaluates the introduction of US troops and a negotiations alternative in the same manner.

27 Mar 1965   *JCSM-221-65*
The JCS formally propose to SecDef a plan already discussed with him for an escalating 12-week air campaign against the North with a primarily military-physical destruction orientation. Interdiction is the objective rather than will-breaking.

29 Mar 1965   *VC bomb US Embassy*
In a daring bomb attack on the US Embassy, the VC kill many Americans and Vietnamese and cause extensive damage. Taylor leaves almost simultaneously for talks in Washington.

31 Mar 1965   *CINCPAC msg. to JCS 310407 Mar.*
CINCPAC recommends a spectacular attack against the North

to retaliate for the bombing of the Embassy. The President rejects the idea.

NSC meeting with Taylor
The President meets with Taylor and the NSC to begin a major policy review.

1 Apr 1965   *McGeorge Bundy memo*
Bundy recommends little more than a continuation of the on-going modest RT program, gradually hitting the LOC choke points. He does, however, recommend removing the restriction on the Marines to static defense. Focus is on winning in SVN.

NSC meeting
The White House policy review continued with another meeting of the principals.

Rostow memo to SecState
In a memo to Rusk, Walt Rostow proposes knocking out the DRV electric power grid as a means of bringing her whole urban industrial sector to a halt.

2 Apr 1965   *NSC meeting*
At the NSC meeting the President approves the Bundy recommendations including the proposal to allow US troops in Vietnam a combat role.

McCone dissents from Presidential decision
CIA director McCone circulates a memo dissenting from the Presidential decision to have US troops take part in active combat. He feels that such action is not justified and wise unless the air attacks on the North are increased sufficiently to really be physically damaging to the DRV and to put real pressure on her.

Canadian Prime Minister suggests pause
Canadian Prime Minister Lester Pearson in a speech in Philadelphia suggests that the US call a halt to the bombing in the interests of getting negotiations started.

5 Apr 1965   *JCSM-265-65*
The JCS report confirmation of the construction of a SAM missile site near Hanoi and request authority to strike it before it becomes operational. Their request is not acted on at the time.

6 Apr 1965   *NSAM 328*
The Presidential decisions of April 2 are promulgated using the verbatim language of the Bundy memo.

7 Apr 1965   *President's Johns Hopkins Speech*
In a major speech at Johns Hopkins University, the President outlines his hope for a peaceful, negotiated settlement in Vietnam. He names Eugene Black as the US negotiator and offers to assist both North and South Vietnam on a regional basis to the tune of $1 billion in the post-war reconstruction and economic development of SEA.

8 Apr 1965   *Pham Van Dong's "Four Points"*
Rejecting the President's initiative, the DRV Foreign Minister, Pham Van Dong announces his famous "Four Points" for the settlement of the war. Each side sees settlement in the capitulation of the other. Peking denounces the President's speech also.

17 Apr 1965   *Presidential press conference*
In a press conference the President acknowledges the failure of his most recent peace overtures.

Rusk press conference
Secretary Rusk rejects suggestions from Canada and others to suspend the bombing in order to get peace talks started. He reiterates the President's view that Hanoi does not want peace.

18 Apr 1965   *Taylor opposes the ground build-up*
Having been bombarded with cables from Washington about a build-up in ground forces to carry out NSAM 328, Taylor reacts opposing the idea in a cable to McGeorge Bundy.

19 Apr 1965   *Hanoi rejects 17-nation appeal*
Hanoi rejects the proposal of the 17 non-aligned nations for a peace conference without pre-conditions by either side.

20 Apr 1965   *Honolulu Conference*
Secretary McNamara meets with Taylor, Westmoreland, Sharp, Wm. Bundy, and McNaughton in Honolulu to review the implementation and interpretation of NSAM 328. A plateau on air strikes, more effort in the South, and the specifics of force deployments are agreed to.

21 Apr 1965   *SecDef memo to the President*
Secretary McNamara reports the results of the Honolulu Conference to the President and indicates that harmony has been restored among the views of the various advisors.

22 Apr 1965   *Intelligence assessment TS #185843-c*
The intelligence community indicates that without either a massive increase in the air campaign or the introduction of US combat troops, the DRV would stick to its goal of military victory.

23 Apr 1965   *Rusk Speech*
In a speech before the American Society of International Law, Rusk makes first public mention of interdiction and punishment as the purposes of the US bombing rather than breaking Hanoi's will.

24 Apr 1965   *U Thant calls for pause*
U Thant asks the US to suspend the bombing for three months in an effort to get negotiations. The proposal is rejected in Washington.

25 Apr 1965   *McGeorge Bundy memo*
In an effort to clarify internal government thinking about negotiations, Bundy outlines his view of US goals. His exposition is a maximum US position whose acceptance would amount to surrender by the other side.

26 Apr 1965   *McNamara press briefing*
In a special briefing for the press complete with maps and charts, McNamara goes into considerable depth in explaining the interdiction purposes of the US strikes against the North.

28 Apr 1965   *McCone resigns and submits last memo*
McCone who is leaving his post as CIA Director (to be replaced

by Admiral Raborn) submits a last memo to the President opposing the build-up of ground forces in the absence of a greatly
intensified campaign against the North.

4 May 1965   *President denies DRV willingness to negotiate*
In a speech at the White House, the President indicates that the
DRV has turned back all peace initiatives, either from the US or
from neutral parties.

Embassy Saigon msg. 3632
Taylor confirms the President's view about the DRV by noting
that in Hanoi's estimates they are still expecting to achieve a
clear-cut victory and see no reason to negotiate.

6 May 1965   *CIA Director Raborn assessment*
Commenting, at the President's request, on McCone's parting
memo on Vietnam, Raborn agrees with the assessment that the
bombing had thus far not hurt the North and that much more
would be needed to force them to the negotiating table. He suggests a pause to test DRV intentions and gain support of world
opinion before beginning the intensive air campaign that he believes will be required.

CM-600-65
The Chairman of the JCS recommends to the Secretary that the
SAM sites already identified be attacked.

10 May 1965   *State Department msg. 2553*
The President informs Taylor of his intention to call a temporary
halt to the bombing and asks Taylor to get PM Quat's concurrence. The purpose of the pause is to gain flexibility either to
negotiate if the DRV shows interest, or to intensify the air strikes
if they do not. He does not intend to announce the pause but
rather to communicate it privately to Moscow and Hanoi and
await a reply.

11 May 1965   *Embassy Saigon msg. 3731*
Taylor reports Quat's agreement but preference not to have the
pause linked to Buddha's birthday.

State Department msg. 2557
State confirms the decision, agrees to avoid reference to the Buddhist holiday, and indicates that the pause will begin on May 13
and last for 5–7 days.

Department of State msg. 3101
Kohler in Moscow is instructed to contact the DRV Ambassador
urgently and convey a message announcing the pause. Simultaneously, Rusk was transmitting the message to the Soviet Ambassador in Washington.

12 May 1965   *Embassy Moscow msg. 3391*
In Moscow, the DRV Ambassador refuses to see Kohler or receive the message. A subsequent attempt to transmit the message
through the Soviet Foreign Office also fails when the Soviets decline their assistance.

13 May 1965   *Presidential speech*
The President avoids reference to the pause in a major public

speech, but does call on Hanoi to consider a "political solution" of the war.

14 May 1965 *Embassy Moscow msg. 3425*
Kohler suggests that the language of the message be softened before it is transmitted to Hanoi via the British Consul in the DRV capital.

British Consul–Hanoi transmits the pause msg.
Having rejected Kohler's suggestion, State has the British Consul in Hanoi transmit the message. The DRV refuses to accept it.

MACV msg. 16006
Westmoreland, with Taylor's concurrence, recommends the use of B-52s for patterned saturation bombing of VC headquarters and other area targets in South Vietnam.

15 May 1965 *Rusk-Gromyko meet in Vienna*
In a meeting between the two men in Vienna, Gromyko informs Rusk that the Soviet Union will give firm and full support to the DRV as a "fraternal socialist state."

16 May 1965 *Embassy Saigon msg. 3781*
Taylor suggests that the DRV's cold response to our initiative warrants a resumption of the bombing. The level should be linked directly to the intensity of VC activity in the South during the pause.

President decides to resume bombing
The President decides that Hanoi's response can be regarded as negative and orders the bombing to resume on May 18.

17 May 1965 *Allies informed of impending resumption*
US Asian and European allies are forewarned of the impending resumption of bombing. In a separate msg. the President authorizes the radar recce by B-52s of potential SEA targets.

18 May 1965 *Bombing resumes*
After five days of "pause" the bombing resumes in the North.

Hanoi denounces the pause
On the evening of the resumption, the DRV Foreign Ministry issues a statement describing the pause as a "deceitful maneuver" to pave the way for further US acts of war.

Hanoi's Paris demarche
Somewhat belatedly the DRV representative in Paris, Mai Van Bo discusses the "four points" with the Quai somewhat softening their interpretation and indicating that they are not necessarily preliminary conditions to negotiations.

20 May 1965 *Rostow memo "Victory and Defeat in Guerilla Wars"*
In a memo for the Secretary of State Rostow argues that a clearcut US victory in SVN is possible. It requires mainly more pressure on the North and effective conduct of the battle in the South.

21 May 1965 *Peking denounces the pause*
Declaring its support for the DRV, Peking denounces the President's bombing pause as a fraud.

2 Jun 1965 *SNIE 10-6-65*
The intelligence community gives a pessimistic analysis of the

likelihood that Hanoi will seek a respite from the bombing through negotiation.

3 Jun 1965   *ICC Commissioner Seaborn sees Pham Van Dong*
In a meeting in Hanoi with DRV Foreign Minister Pham Van Dong, ICC Commissioner Seaborn (Canada) confirms Hanoi's rejection of current US peace initiatives.

12 Jun 1965   *SVN Premier Quat resigns*
SVN Premier Quat hands his resignation to the Armed Forces Council.

15 Jun 1965   *SecDef memo to JCS*
McNamara disapproves the JCS recommendation for air strikes against the SAM sites and IL 28s at DRV air bases since these might directly challenge the Soviet Union.

24 Jun 1965   *Ky assumes power*
Brig. Gen. Nguyen Cao Ky assumes power and decrees new measures to strengthen GVN prosecution of the war.

A CHRONOLOGY OF ROLLING THUNDER MISSIONS FEBRUARY–JUNE, 1965*

ROLLING THUNDER 1 was scheduled on 20 February 1965 as a one-day reprisal strike by U.S. and VNAF forces, against Quang Khe Naval Base and Vu Con Barracks. Two barracks and an airfield were authorized as weather alternates. ROLLING THUNDER 1 was cancelled because of a coup in Saigon and diplomatic moves between London and Moscow. ROLLING THUNDER 2, 3, and 4 were planned as reprisal actions, but subsequently cancelled because of continued political instability in Saigon, during which VNAF forces were on "coup alert." Joint participation with VNAF was desired for political reasons.

The first actual ROLLING THUNDER strike was ROLLING THUNDER 5, a one-day, no recycle strike on 2 March 1965. Targets were one ammo depot and one naval base as primary U.S. and VNAF targets. Four barracks were authorized as weather alternates. VNAF participation was mandatory. The approved effort for the week was substantially below the level recommended by the Joint Chiefs of Staff.

ROLLING THUNDER 6 (14–15 March) was a far more forceful one-day fixed-target program representing a week's weight of attack. Napalm was authorized for the first time, but aircraft recycle was prohibited.

ROLLING THUNDER 7 (19–25 March) relaxed the mandatory one-day strike execution to a week's period, with precise timing being left to field commanders. It included five primary targets with weather alternates. The requirement for concurrent timing of U.S. and VNAF strikes was removed. One U.S. and two VNAF armed recce missions were authorized during the seven-day period. Specified route segments were selected in southern North Vietnam. Authority was given to strike three fixed radar sites located one each route. The strikes were no longer to be specifically related to VC atrocities and publicity on them was to be progressively reduced.

ROLLING THUNDER 8 (26 March–1 April) included nine radar sites for

* Based on information in JCS compilations and ROLLING THUNDER execute messages.

U.S. strike, and a barracks for VNAF. The radar targets reflected primarily policy-level interest in additional purely military targets in southern NVN. Three armed recce missions were again authorized, against specified route segments with U.S. armed recce conducted against NVN patrol craft, along the coast from Tiger Island north to 20° and authority granted to restrike operational radar sites. VNAF armed recce was conducted along Route 12 from Ha Tinh to two miles east of Mu Gia Pass.

ROLLING THUNDER 9 (2–8 April) inaugurated a planned LOC interdiction campaign against NVN south of latitude 20°. The Dong Phuong (JCS target No. 18.8) and Thanh Hoa bridges (JCS target No. 14) were the northernmost fixed-target strikes in this campaign to be followed by additional armed reconnaissance strikes to sustain the interdiction. ROLLING THUNDER 9 (2–8 April) through ROLLING THUNDER 12 (23–29 April) completed the fixed-target strikes against 26 bridges and seven ferries.

a. ROLLING THUNDER 9 permitted three armed recce missions on specified route segments. Sorties were increased to not more than 24 armed recce strike sorties per 24-hour period in ROLLING THUNDER 10 through ROLLING THUNDER 12. This effort was still far short of the level considered by the JCS to be "required for significant effectiveness."

b. Prior to ROLLING THUNDER 10, armed recce targets were limited to locomotives, rolling stock, vehicles, and hostile NVN craft. For ROLLING THUNDER 10 through ROLLING THUNDER 12 the rules were changed to provide day and night armed recce missions to obtain a high level of damage to military movement facilities, ferries, radar sites, secondary bridges, and railroad rolling stock. It also included interdiction of the LOC by cratering, restriking and seeding choke-points as necessary.

c. From the beginning, armed recce geographical coverage was limited to specified segments of designated routes. By ROLLING THUNDER 9 it had increased to one-time coverage of Routes 1 (DMZ to 19–58–36N), 7, 8, 15, 101, and lateral roads between these routes.

d. The dropping of unexpended ordnance on Tiger Island was authorized in this period. Prior to this time, ordnance was jettisoned in the sea.

ROLLING THUNDER 13 (30 April–May 1965) through ROLLING THUNDER 18 (11–17 June) continued U.S. and VNAF strikes against 52 fixed military targets (five restrikes) as follows: six ammo depots, five supply depots, 21 barracks, two airfields, two POL storages, two radio facilities, seven bridges, two naval bases, one railroad yard, two thermal power plants, one port facility, and one ferry. It was argued by the JCS that, as some barracks and depots had been vacated, political insistence on hitting only military targets south of latitude 20° was "constraining the program substantially short of optimum military effectiveness."

a. During this six-week period armed recce sorties were expanded to a maximum allowable rate of 40 per day and a maximum of 200 per week (60 additional armed recce sorties were authorized for ROLLING THUNDER 17). Although this period saw a significant increase in armed recce, the new level was well below existing capabilities and, so the JCS argued, "the increase was authorized too late to achieve tactical surprise."

b. With ROLLING THUNDER 13 armed recce authorizations changed from stated routes, etc., to more broadly defined geographical areas, in this case the area south of 20°.

c. Air strikes against fixed targets and armed recce were suspended over NVN during the five-day and twenty-hour bombing pause of 13–17 May.

d. Authority was requested to strike the first SAM site during the ROLLING THUNDER 15 period (immediately following the bombing pause) but it was denied.

e. Armed recce targets were expanded during this six-week period to include railroad rolling stock, trucks, ferries, lighters, barges, radar sites, secondary bridges, road repair equipment, NVN naval craft, bivouac and maintenance areas. Emphasis was placed on armed recce of routes emanating from Vinh in order to restrict traffic in and out of this important LOC hub. ROLLING THUNDER 18 added the provision that authorized day armed route recce sorties could include selected missions to conduct small precise attacks against prebriefed military targets not in the JCS target list, and thereafter conduct armed route recce with residual capability.

f. ROLLING THUNDER 14 added authority for returning aircraft to use unexpended ordnance on Hon Nieu Island Radar Site, Hon Matt Island Radar Site, Dong Hoi Barracks, or rail and highway LOC's targets, in addition to Tiger Island previously authorized for this purpose.

I.   INTRODUCTION—PLEIKU PULLS THE TRIGGER

At 2:00 a.m. on the morning of February 7, 1965, at the end of five days of Tet celebrations and only hours after Kosygin had told a cheering crowd in Hanoi that the Soviet Union would "not remain indifferent" if "acts of war" were committed against North Vietnam, Viet Cong guerrillas carried out well-coordinated raids upon a U.S. advisers' barracks in Pleiku and upon a U.S. helicopter base at Camp Holloway, some four miles away. Of the 137 American soldiers hit in the two attacks, nine eventually died and 76 had to be evacuated; the losses in equipment were also severe: 16 helicopters damaged or destroyed and six fixed-wing aircraft damaged, making this the heaviest communist assault up to that time against American installations in South Vietnam.

The first flash from Saigon about the assault came on the ticker at the National Military Command Center at the Pentagon at 2:38 p.m. Saturday, February 6, Washington time. It triggered a swift, though long-contemplated Presidential decision to give an "appropriate and fitting" response. Within less than 14 hours, by 4:00 p.m. Sunday, Vietnam time, 49 U.S. Navy jets—A-4 Skyhawks and F-8 Crusaders from the Seventh Fleet carriers USS *Coral Sea* and USS *Hancock* —had penetrated a heavy layer of monsoon clouds to deliver their bombs and rockets upon North Vietnamese barracks and staging areas at Dong Hoi, a guerrilla training garrison 40 miles north of the 17th parallel. On the following afternoon, a flight of 24 VNAF (A-1H Skyraiders, cancelled the previous day because of poor weather, followed up the attack by striking a military communications center in the Vinh Linh area just north of the border.

Though conceived and executed as a limited one-shot tit-for-tat reprisal, the dramatic U.S. action, long on the military planners' drawing boards under the operational code name FLAMING DART, precipitated a rapidly moving sequence of events that transformed the character of the Vietnam war and the U.S. role in it. It was also the opening move in what soon developed into an entirely new phase of that war: the sustained U.S. bombing effort against North Vietnam. It is the purpose of this paper to reconstruct the immediate circumstances that led up to the FLAMING DART decision, to retrace the changes in rationale that progressively transformed the reprisal concept into a sustained graduated bombing effort, and to chronicle the relationship between that effort and the military-political moves to shore up Saigon and the military-diplomatic signals to dissuade Hanoi, during the crucial early months of February through May of 1965.

II. THE LONG ROAD TO PLEIKU—A RETROSPECTIVE VIEW

A. 1964: YEAR OF POLITICAL AND MILITARY DECLINE

The year 1964 was marked by a gradual American awakening to the fact that the Viet Cong were winning the war in South Vietnam. Almost uninterrupted political upheaval in Saigon was spawning progressive military dissolution in the countryside. Constant changes within the Vietnamese leadership were bringing GVN civil administration into a state of disarray and GVN military activities to a near-standstill. ARVN forces were becoming more and more defensive and demoralized. At the same time, the communists were visibly strengthening their support base in Laos, stepping up the rate of infiltration of men and supplies into South Vietnam, and mounting larger and more aggressive attacks. The GVN was still predominant, though not unchallenged, in the urban population centers; there were also a few areas where traditional local power structures (the Hoa Hao, the Cao Dai, etc.) continued to exercise effective authority. But the rest of the country was slipping, largely by default, under VC control. By the end of 1964, all evidence pointed to a situation in which a final collapse of the GVN appeared probable and a victorious consolidation of VC power a distinct possibility.

Ironically, it was left to Senator Fulbright to state the harsh realities in terms which set the tone for much of Administration thinking as it was to emerge in the months to come—though his views then were hardly consistent with the opposition role he was increasingly to take later on. As early as March 1964, in a celebrated speech entitled "Old Myths and New Realities" he observed that "the hard fact of the matter is that our bargaining position is at present a weak one; and until the equation of advantage between the two sides has been substantially altered in our favor, there can be little prospect of a negotiated settlement."

B. EVOLUTION OF A NEW POLICY

With the growing realization that the ally on whose behalf the United States had steadily deepened its commitment in Southeast Asia was in a near state of dissolution, Washington launched a protracted reassessment of the future American role in the war and began a determined search for new pressures to be mounted against the communist enemy, both within and outside of South Vietnam. High level deliberations on alternative U.S. courses of action in Southeast Asia were started as early as March 1964, and a military planning process was set in motion in which much attention was given to the possibility of implementing some sort of pressures or reprisal policy against North Vietnam.

The first of these planning efforts, authorized by the President on 17 March 1964 (NSAM 288), led to the development of CINCPAC OPLAN 37-64, a three-phase plan covering operations against VC infiltration routes in Laos and Cambodia and against targets in North Vietnam. Phase I provided for air and ground strikes against targets in South Vietnam and hot pursuit actions into Laotian and Cambodian border areas. Phase II provided for "tit-for-tat" air strikes, airborne/amphibious raids, and aerial mining operations against targets in North Vietnam. Phase III provided for increasingly severe air strikes and other actions against North Vietnam, going beyond the "tit-for-tat" concept. According to the plan, air strikes would be conducted primarily by GVN forces, assisted by U.S. aircraft.

As part of OPLAN 37-64, a detailed list of specific targets for air attack in North Vietnam was drawn up, selected on the basis of three criteria: (a) reducing North Vietnamese support of communist operations in Laos and South Vietnam, (b) limiting North Vietnamese capabilities to take direct action against Laos and South Vietnam, and finally (c) impairing North Vietnam's capacity to continue as an industrially viable state. Detailed characteristics were provided for each target, together with damage effects that could be achieved by various scales of attack against them. This target list, informally called the "94 Target List," became the basic reference for much of the subsequent planning for air strikes against North Vietnam, when target selection was involved.

The Tonkin Gulf incident of 4–5 August, which precipitated the first U.S. reprisal action against North Vietnam, had enabled the Administration to obtain a broad Congressional Resolution of support and had brought with it a prompt and substantial forward deployment of U.S. military forces in Southeast Asia, to deter or deal with possible communist reactions to the U.S. reprisal strike. Encouraged somewhat by the fact that no such reaction occurred, U.S. officials began to look more hopefully toward forceful military alternatives that might help salvage the deteriorating situation in South Vietnam. A new wave of disorders and governmental eruptions in Saigon gave added impetus to a succession of JCS proposals for intensified harassing and other punitive operations against North Vietnam. Their recommendations included retaliatory actions for stepped up VC incidents, should they occur, and initiation of continuing air strikes by GVN and U.S. forces against North Vietnamese targets.

A Presidential decision was issued on 10 September. Besides some modest additional pressures in the Lao panhandle and covert actions against North Vietnam, it authorized only *preparations* for retaliatory actions against North Vietnam in the event of any attack on U.S. units or any extraordinary North Vietnamese/VC action against South Vietnam. The forward deployments that had been carried out in connection with the Tonkin incident and in accordance with OPLAN 37-64 were kept in place, but the forces involved were precluded from action in South Vietnam and no decision was made to utilize them in operations in Laos or North Vietnam.

Throughout September and October, the JCS continued to urge stronger U.S. action not only in North Vietnam, but also in Laos, where infiltration was clearly on the increase, and in South Vietnam, where GVN survival was becoming precarious and time seemed to be running out.

These urgings reached a crescendo on 1 November 1964 when, just three days prior to the U.S. Presidential elections, the VC executed a daring and dramatic mortar attack on the U.S. air base at Bien Hoa, killing five Americans, wounding 76, and damaging or destroying 27 of the 30 B-57's that had been deployed to South Vietnam to serve notice upon Hanoi that the United States had readily at hand the capacity to deliver a crushing air attack on the North. The attack was the most spectacular anti-American incident to date and was viewed by the JCS as warranting a severe punitive response. Their recommendation, accordingly, went far beyond a mere reprisal action. It called for an initial 24–36 hour period of air strikes in Laos and low-level air reconnaissance south of the 19th parallel in North Vietnam, designed to provide a cover for the introduction of U.S. security forces to protect key U.S. installations, and for the evacuation of U.S. dependents from Saigon. This would be followed, in the next three days, by a B-52 strike against Phuc Yen, the principal airfield near Hanoi, and by strikes against other airfields and major POL facilities in the Hanoi/Haiphong area; and subsequently by armed reconnaissance against infiltration routes in Laos, air strikes against infiltration routes and targets in North Vietnam, and progressive PACOM and SAC strikes against remaining military and industrial targets in the 94 Target List.

That the JCS recommendations were not accepted is hardly surprising, considering the magnitude and radical nature of the proposed actions and the fact that these actions would have had to be initiated on the eve of the election by a President who in his campaign had plainly made manifest his disinclination to lead the United States into a wider war in Vietnam, repeatedly employing the slogan "we are not going North." In any event, as subsequent developments indicate, the President was not ready to approve a program of air strikes against North Vietnam, at least until the available alternatives could be carefully and thoroughly re-examined.

Such a re-examination was initiated immediately following the election, under the aegis of a NSC interagency working group chaired by Assistant Secretary of State William Bundy. After a month of intensive study of various options, ranging from an intensification of existing programs to the initiation of large-scale hostilities against North Vietnam, the working group recommended a *graduated* program of controlled military pressures designed to signal U.S. determination, to boost morale in the South and to increase the costs and strains upon the North. A basic aim of the program was to build a stronger bargaining position, to restore an "equilibrium" in the balance of forces, looking toward a negotiated settlement.

The recommended program was in two phases: Phase I, which was to last about 30 days, consisted of little more than an intensification of earlier "signals" to Hanoi that it should cease supporting the insurgency in the South or face progressively higher costs and penalties. Coupled with these military measures was to be a continuous declaratory policy communicating our willingness to negotiate on the basis of the Geneva accords. It was recommended that successive actions would be undertaken only after waiting to discern Hanoi's reactions to previous actions, with the commitment to later stages, such as initiation of air strikes against infiltration targets across the 17th parallel, kept unspecific and dependent upon enemy reactions.

The recommended program also included a Phase II, a continuous program of progressively more serious air strikes possibly running from two to six months. The attacks would at first be limited to infiltration targets south of the 19th parallel, but would gradually work northward, and could eventually encompass all major military-related targets, aerial mining of ports, and a naval blockade, with the weight and tempo of the action being adjusted to the situation as it developed. The approach would be steady and deliberate, "progressively mounting in scope and intensity," with the U.S. retaining the option to proceed or not, escalate or not, or quicken the pace or not, at any time. It was agreed, however, that this second phase would not be considered for implementation until after the GVN had demonstrated considerable stability and effectiveness.

As part of this "progressive squeeze," the working group recommended that the U.S. be willing to pause to explore negotiated solutions, should North Vietnam show any signs of yielding, while maintaining a credible threat of still further pressures. In the view of the working group, the prospect of greater pressures to come was at least as important as any damage actually inflicted, since the real target was the *will* of the North Vietnamese government to continue the aggression in the South rather than its *capability* to do so. Even if it retained the capability, North Vietnam might elect to discontinue the aggression if it anticipated future costs and risks greater than it had bargained for.

The JCS dissented from the working group's program on the grounds that it did not clearly provide for the kinds and forms of military pressures that might achieve U.S. objectives. They recommended instead a more accelerated program of intensive air strikes from the outset, along lines similar to the actions they had urged in response to the Bien Hoa incident. Their program was in consonance with the consistent JCS view that the way to exert significant military pressure on North Vietnam was to bring to bear the maximum practicable conventional military power in a short time.

The working group's proposals for a graduated approach were hammered out in a series of policy conferences with Ambassador Taylor, who had returned to Washington for this purpose at the end of November, and were then presented to the President, who approved them conditionally on 1 December, without, however, setting a timetable or specifying precise implementing actions. Allies had to be brought in line, and certain other diplomatic preliminaries had to be arranged, before the program could be launched. More important, it was feared that possible enemy reactions to the program might subject the GVN to severe counter-pressures which, in its then enfeebled state, might be more than it could bear. Thus securing some GVN leadership commitment to improved perform-ance was made a prerequisite to mounting the more intensive actions contem-plated. In fact, Ambassador Taylor returned to Saigon with instructions to hold out the prospect of these more intensive actions as an incentive to the GVN to "pull itself together" and, indeed, as a *quid pro quo,* for achieving, in some manner, greater stability and effectiveness. The instructions, however, contained no reference to U.S. intentions with respect to negotiations. Any mention of U.S. interest in a negotiated settlement before the initiation of military operations against North Vietnam was regarded as likely to have the opposite effect from the desired bolstering of GVN morale and stamina, as well as being premature in terms of the hoped-for improvement in the U.S. bargaining position vis-a-vis Hanoi that might result from the actions.

The President's 1 December decisions were extremely closely held during the ensuing months. The draft NSAM that had been prepared by the working group was never issued and the decisions were only informally communicated. Ambas-sador Taylor, upon returning to Saigon, began his discussions of the proposed actions with the GVN, and received certain assurances. Several allies, including the UK, Canada, Australia, and New Zealand, were given a fairly complete description of U.S. intentions. Others, such as Thailand and Laos, were informed about Phase I only. Still others, like Nationalist China, Korea, and the Philippines, were simply given a vague outline of the projected course of action.

The first intensified military pressures in the program—more high level recon-naissance missions over North Vietnam, more extensive 34A maritime operations with VNAF cover south of the 18th parallel, and RLAF air strikes against PL/ NVA forces in Laos—were begun on 14 December, along with a new program of limited USAF-Navy armed reconnaissance missions against infiltration routes and facilities in Northern Laos under the code name BARREL ROLE. The strikes were not publicized and were not expected to have a significant military interdiction effect. They were considered useful primarily for their political value as another of a long series of signals to Hanoi to the effect that the U.S. was prepared to use much greater force to frustrate a communist take-over in South Vietnam.

C. SIGNALS TO HANOI

Throughout 1964, a basic U.S. policy in Vietnam was to severely restrain any expansion of the direct U.S. combat involvement, but to carry out an essentially psychological campaign to convince Hanoi that the United States meant business. The campaign included repeated reaffirmations of the U.S. commitment to the defense of Southeast Asia, made both in public and in diplomatic channels; hints and warnings that the U.S. might escalate the war with countermeasures against North Vietnam, such as guerrilla raids, air attacks, naval blockade, or even land invasion, if the aggression persisted; and a number of overt military actions of a precautionary nature, intended more to demonstrate U.S. resolve than to affect the military situation. Taken together, however, the signals were somewhat ambiguous.

Among the more important *military-political* actions, carried out with considerable publicity, were the accelerated military construction effort in Thailand and South Vietnam, the prepositioning of contingency stockpiles in Thailand and the Philippines, the forward deployment of a carrier task force and land-based tactical aircraft within close striking distance of relevant enemy targets, and the assignment of an unprecedentedly high-level "first team" to man the U.S. Diplomatic Mission in Saigon. These measures were intended both to convince Hanoi and to reassure the GVN of the seriousness and durability of the U.S. commitment.

In addition, the U.S. undertook a number of unpublicized and more provocative actions, primarily as low-key indications to the enemy of the U.S. willingness and capability to employ increased force if necessary. Chief among these were the occasional DE SOTO Patrols (U.S. destroyer patrols conducted deep into the Gulf of Tonkin along the cost of North Vietnam), both as a "show of strength" and as an intelligence gathering device; Laotian air strikes and limited GVN cross-border operations against VC infiltration routes in Laos; GVN maritime raids and other harassing actions against North Vietnam; YANKEE TEAM, low-level photo reconnaissance missions over Laos, conducted by U.S. jet aircraft with fighter escorts for suppressive or retaliatory action against enemy ground fire; and finally, the initiation at the very end of 1964 of BARREL ROLL, armed reconnaissance missions by U.S. jet fighters against VC infiltration routes and facilities in Laos.

The fact that these actions were not publicized—although most of them eventually became public knowledge—stemmed in part from a desire to communicate an implicit threat of "more to come" for Hanoi's benefit, without arousing undue anxieties domestically in the United States in a Presidential election year in which escalation of the war became a significant campaign issue.

Within this general pattern of subtle and not-so-subtle warning signals, the U.S. reprisal strike, following the controversial Gulf of Tonkin incident of 4–5 August, stands out as a single forceful U.S. reaction, the portent of which could hardly have escaped Hanoi. Its effect, however, may have been gradually diluted, first by the care that was taken to allay public fears that it represented anything more than an isolated event, and subsequently by the failure of the U.S. to react to the November 1 attack at Bien Hoa or to the Christmas Eve bombing of the Brink BOQ. Even this signal, therefore, may not have been, in Hanoi's reading, entirely unambiguous.

For Hanoi, the U.S. *public declaratory policy* during most of 1964 must have been a major source of confusion. Presidential statements alternated between hawk-like cries and dove-like coos. Thus, in February 1964, in a University of California speech, the President issued the thinly veiled threat that "those engaged in external direction and supply would do well to be reminded and to remember that this type of aggression is a deeply dangerous game." But for the rest of the year and particularly during the election campaign, the President was saying, emphatically and repeatedly, that he did not intend to lead the United States into a wider war in Vietnam. He ridiculed the pugnacious chauvinism of Barry Goldwater and contrasted it with his own restraint. "There are those that say I ought to go north and drop bombs, to try to wipe out the supply lines, and they think that would escalate the war," he said in a speech on September 25. "But we don't want to get involved in a nation with seven hundred million people and get tied down in a land war in Asia."

But if there was reason for confusion in Hanoi's reading of the public declaratory signals, there was no shortage of opportunities for transmitting more unequivocal signals through quiet diplomatic channels. The clearest explanations of U.S. policy, and warnings of U.S. intent, were communicated to Hanoi on June 18, 1964, by the Canadian International Control Commissioner Seaborn. In a long meeting with Premier Pham Van Dong, Seaborn presented a carefully prepared statement of U.S. views and intentions to the North Vietnamese Premier, clearly warning him of the destructive consequences for the DRV of a continuation of its present course. Pham Van Dong fully understood the seriousness and import of the warning conveyed by Seaborn. But in this, as in a subsequent meeting with Seaborn on August 15, Pham Van Dong showed himself utterly unintimidated and calmly resolved to pursue the course upon which the DRV was embarked to what he confidently expected would be its successful conclusion.

On balance, while U.S. words and actions were not always in consonance, while public and private declarations were much in conflict, and while U.S. reactions fluctuated between the unexpectedly forceful and the mystifyingly hesitant, the action-signals were sufficiently numerous and the warnings sufficiently explicit to have given Hanoi a fair awareness that the U.S. was likely to respond to the deteriorating situation by intensifying the conflict. How far this intensification would go, neither Hanoi nor the U.S. could have foreseen.

D. OMINOUS DEVELOPMENTS IN SAIGON

The first of the new military pressures against the North—BARREL ROLL air strikes in Laos—authorized in the 1 December decision, went into effect on 14 December. The hoped-for improvement in GVN stability, however, did not materialize. To the contrary, on 20 December the erratic SVN Premier Lt. Gen. Nguyen Khanh abruptly dissolved the High National Council.

The crisis of confidence that developed was one reason for the lack of a U.S. response to the bombing of the Brink BOQ in Saigon on Christmas Eve. As pointed out earlier, it was the kind of incident which had been contemplated in the approved Phase I guidelines as warranting a U.S. reprisal action, and the JCS did recommend such an action. They proposed an immediate air strike against Vit Thu Lu army barracks just north of the 17th parallel, employing up to 40 aircraft sorties, with Vietnamese participation if feasible. It was to be a one-day strike, on a much smaller scale than those recommended by the JCS on earlier occasions. However, both because of the unsettled situation in Vietnam and because of the Christmas Season—which caught the President and the

Secretary of Defense out of town and Congress in recess—Washington was hesitant and reluctant to press for a prompt reaction. By the time the issue was discussed with the President on 29 December, it seemed too late for an event-associated reprisal and the decision was negative.

In the meantime, GVN forces had experienced major reverses. ARVN as well as the Regional and Popular Forces had been seriously weakened by defeat and desertions in the last few months of 1964. A highly visible setback occurred from 26 December to 2 January 1965 at Binh Gia, where the VC virtually destroyed two Vietnamese Marine battalions. Viet Cong strength, augmented by infiltrating combat forces from North Vietnam, increased, and their hit-and-run tactics were increasingly successful.

The government of Tran Van Huong came to an abrupt end on 27 January 1965 when the Vietnamese Armed Forces Council ousted him, leaving only a facade of civilian government. The continuing power struggle clearly impeded military operations. Large elements of VNAF, for example, were maintained on constant "coup alert."

Washington reacted to these developments with considerable anguish. "I think we must accept that Saigon morale in all quarters is now very shaky indeed. . . ." wrote Assistant Secretary of State William P. Bundy on January 6, and he continued:

> We have not yet been able to assess the overall impact of the continuing political crisis and of the Binh Gia military defeat, but there are already ample indications that they have had a sharp discouraging effect just in the last two weeks. By the same token, it is apparent that Hanoi is extremely confident, and that the Soviets are being somewhat tougher and the Chinese Communists are consolidating their ties with Hanoi . . . they see Vietnam falling into their laps in the fairly near future. . . . The sum total of the above seems to us to point . . . to a prognosis that the situation in Vietnam is now likely to come apart more rapidly than we had anticipated in November.

A similarly gloomy view was taken by Assistant Secretary of Defense John McNaughton. In a February 1965 memorandum (no exact date), he characterized the situation as "deteriorating":

> The new government will probably be unstable and ineffectual, and the VC will probably continue to extend their hold over the population and territory. It can be expected that soon (6 months? two years?) (a) government officials at all levels will adjust their behavior to an eventual VC take-over, (b) defections of significant military forces will take place, (c) while integrated regions of the country will be totally denied to the GVN, (d) neutral and/or left-wing elements will enter the government, (e) a popular-front regime will emerge which will invite the US out, and (f) fundamental concessions to the VC and accommodations to the DRV will put South Vietnam behind the Curtain.

These views were fully consistent with USIB-approved national intelligence estimates which, as early as October 1964, predicted:

> . . . a further decay of GVN will and effectiveness. The likely pattern of this decay will be increasing defeatism, paralysis of leadership, friction with Americans, exploration of possible lines of political accommodation with the other side, and a general petering out of the war effort. . . .

By February 1965, the intelligence community saw "the present political arrangements in Saigon [as] avowedly temporary" and detected no more than "a faint chance that the scenario announced for the ensuing weeks [would] hold promise for improved political stability in SVN." It judged the odds as "considerably less than even . . . [that] the spring and summer might see the evolution of a stronger base for prosecuting the counter-insurgency effort than has heretofore existed."

These views were most authoritatively endorsed by the President's highest national security staff advisor, McGeorge Bundy, who undertook an urgent fact-finding trip to South Vietnam at the beginning of February. In a pivotal memorandum to the President (which will be referred to in greater detail subsequently) he characterized the general situation as follows:

> For the last year—and perhaps for longer—the overall situation in Vietnam has been deteriorating. The Communists have been gaining and the anti-Communist forces have been losing. As a result there is now great uncertainty among Vietnamese as well as Americans as to whether Communist victory can be prevented. There is nervousness about the determination of the U.S. Government. There is recrimination and fear among Vietnamese political leaders. There is an appearance of weariness among some military leaders. There is a worrisome lassitude among the Vietnamese generally. There is a distressing absence of positive commitment to any serious social or political purpose. Outside observers are ready to write the patient off. All of this tends to bring latent anti-Americanism dangerously near to the surface.
>
> To be an American in Saigon today is to have a gnawing feeling that time is against us. Junior officers in all services are able, zealous and effective within the limits of their means. Their morale is sustained by the fact that they know that they are doing their jobs well and that they will not have to accept the responsibility for defeat. But near the top, where responsibility is heavy and accountability real, one can sense the inner doubts of men whose outward behavior remains determined.

Interestingly, McGeorge Bundy saw the military situation as moderately encouraging and the Vietnamese people still remarkably tough and resilient, though the social and political fabric was stretched thin. "Nevertheless," he warned, ". . . extremely unpleasant surprises are increasingly possible—both political and military."

E. MORE AGONIZING OVER ADDITIONAL PRESSURES

In the face of these uniformly discouraging appraisals, both Saigon and Washington continued their long debate over ways and means of mounting new or more intensive pressures against the enemy—and most notably over the desirability and likely effectiveness of reprisal strikes and "Phase II operations" against the DRV. But enthusiasm for these operations was far from boundless.

The intelligence community, for example, had expressed, ever since May of 1964, very little confidence that such added pressures would have much impact on Hanoi's course. The 9 October 1964 national estimate considered probable communist reactions to "a systematic program of gradually intensifying US/GVN [air] attacks against targets in the DRV. . . ." The estimate tended only very hesitantly to the judgment that such a program of air attacks, if protracted, might "on balance" cause the DRV to stop its military attacks in SVN, to press for a negotiated cease-fire in the South, and to try to promote an international conference to pursue their ends, expecting, however, to fight another day. State dissented from even this ambivalent judgment, believing that the DRV would carry on the fight regardless of air attacks.

In February 1965, they reiterated this hesitant view, again with State dissenting:

> If the United States vigorously continued in its attacks and damaged some important economic or military assets, the DRV . . . might decide to intensify the struggle, but . . . it seems to us somewhat more likely that they would decide to make some effort to secure a respite from US attack. . . .

Parenthetically, even this equivocal judgment was reversed in effect, though not explicitly, in a June, 1965 estimate, this time with USAF ACS/I dissenting:

> Our present estimate is that the odds are against the postulated US attacks leading the DRV to make conciliatory gestures to secure a respite from the bombing; rather, we believe that the DRV would persevere in supporting the insurgency in the South.

On top of these by no means reassuring estimates, Ambassador Taylor's hopes for a more stable GVN had been badly shaken by his abrasive experiences with General Khanh during the late-December episode. The Ambassador-Premier relationship was now ruptured beyond repair, and highest-level contacts between the USG and the GVN had to be carried on through Deputy Ambassador U. Alexis Johnson. For the first time Maxwell Taylor talked seriously of possible U.S. disengagement, and even suggested a new role for air attacks on the North in such a context.

In a year-end joint Taylor-Johnson cable to the Secretary of State, the Mission leadership actually suggested, as one possible alternative, "disengaging from the present intimacy of relationship with the GVN, withdrawing the bulk of our advisers . . . while continuing sufficient economic and MAP aid to keep the GVN going." In such a situation, they would shrink MACV to the status of a MAAG and USOM to that of an economic-budgetary advisory group, but continue to accept responsibility for air and maritime defense of South Vietnam against the DRV. The danger in such a course, however, would be that "panicked by what would be interpreted as abandonment, the [GVN] leaders here would rush to compete with each other in making deals with the NLF." Taylor and Johnson, however, believed that this danger could be offset by an energetic U.S. program of reprisal attacks and Phase II operations against the DRV.

Thus, in the Taylor/Johnson view, there were now three conditions in which reprisal attacks and Phase II operations might be conducted:

(i) In association with the GVN after the latter had proven a reasonably stable government "able to control its armed forces"—the condition originally laid down in the President's 1 December decision, but which now appeared unlikely to be attained.

(ii) Under the prevailing acutely unstable conditions "as an emergency stimulant hopefully to create unity at *home* and restore failing morale."

(iii) As a unilateral U.S. action "to compensate for reduced in-country U.S. presence," if such reduction were to be undertaken.

A similarly unprepossessing view of "stronger [words illegible] was probably presented to the President by Rusk. There is no direct record of the Secretary's presentation to the President during this period, but a set of notes put together in preparation for a Rusk meeting with the President on January 6 by Assistant Secretary William Bundy, Special Assistant Michael Forrestal and Deputy Assistant Secretary Leonard Unger, laid out the alternatives in some detail. Recognizing that a "coming apart" of the GVN would most likely take the form of covert negotiations by key governmental groups with the NLF, leading eventually to the U.S. being invited out, Rusk's principal Vietnam advisers argued that this was one possible "Vietnamese solution," but hardly a desirable one:

> It would still be virtually certain that Laos would then become untenable and that Cambodia would accommodate in some way. Most seriously, there is grave question whether the Thai in these circumstances would retain any confidence at all in our continued support. In short, the outcome would be regarded in Asia, and particularly among our friends, as just as humiliating a defeat as any other form. As events have developed, the American public would probably not be too sharply critical, but the real question would be whether Thailand and other nations were weakened and taken over thereafter.
>
> The alternative of stronger action obviously has grave difficulties. It commits the US more deeply, at a time when the picture of South Vietnamese will is extremely weak. To the extent that it included actions against North Vietnam, it would be vigorously attacked by many nations and disapproved initially even by such nations as Japan and India, on present indications. Most basically, its stiffening effect on the Saigon political situation would not be at all sure to bring about a more effective government, nor would limited actions against the southern DRV in fact sharply reduce infiltration or, in present circumstances, be at all likely to induce Hanoi to call it off.
>
> Nonetheless, on balance we believe that such action would have some faint hope of really improving the Vietnamese situation, and, above all, would put us in a much stronger position to hold the next line of defense, namely Thailand. Accepting the present situation—or any negotiation on the basis of it—would be far weaker from this latter key standpoint. If we moved into stronger actions, we should have in mind that negotiations would be likely to emerge from some quarter in any event, and that under existing circumstances, even with the additional element of pressure, we could not expect to get an outcome that would really secure an independent South Vietnam. Yet even on an outcome that produced a progressive deterioration in South Vietnam and an eventual Communist takeover, we would still have appeared to Asians to have done a lot more about it.

Turning then to specific alternatives, Bundy and his colleagues envisioned five proposals:

> a. An early occasion for reprisal action against the DRV.
> b. Possibly beginning low-level reconnaissance of the DRV at once.
> c. Concurrently with *a* or *b*, an early orderly withdrawal of our dependents. We all think this would be a grave mistake in the absence of stronger action, and if taken in isolation would tremendously increase the pace of deterioration in Saigon. If we are to clear our decks in this way—and we are more and more inclined to think we should—it simply *must* be, for this reason alone, in the context of *some* stronger action.

d. Intensified air operations in Laos may have some use, but they will *not* meet the problem of Saigon morale and, if continued at a high level, may raise significant possibilities of Communist intervention on a substantial scale in Laos with some plausible justification. We have gone about as far as we can go in Laos by the existing limiting actions, and, apart from cutting Route 7, we would not be accomplishing much militarily by intensifying US air actions there. This form of action thus has little further to gain in the Laos context, and has no real bearing at this point on the South Vietnamese context.

e. Introduction of limited US ground forces into the northern area of South Vietnam still has great appeal to many of us, concurrently with the first air attacks into the DRV. It would have a real stiffening effect in Saigon, and a strong signal effect to Hanoi. On the disadvantage side, such forces would be possible attrition targets for the Viet Cong. For your information, the Australians have clearly indicated (most recently yesterday) that they might be disposed to participate in such an operation. The New Zealanders are more negative and a proposal for Philippine participation would be an interesting test.

Whether and how these alternatives were posed for the President is not recorded, but at least two of the actions—getting the U.S. dependents out of Vietnam and reacting promptly and firmly to the next reprisal opportunity—were also recommended to another top presidential advisor, namely to Secretary McNamara, by Assistant Secretary John McNaughton, in a McNaughton memorandum that he discussed with McNamara on January 27. The memorandum contains McNaughton's pencil notations of McNamara's comments on various points, which suggest that the Secretary of Defense was dissatisfied with the way U.S. Vietnam policy was "drifting" and seemed a good deal less dubious than was McNaughton about the potential benefits to be derived from initiating air strikes against the DRV.

In the meantime, a 7 January 1965 conference of SEACORD (the coordinating mechanism of the U.S. ambassadors and military commanders in Southeast Asia) had reviewed the accomplishments of the first few weeks of Phase I—the 30-day program of mild BARREL ROLL, YANKEE TEAM and other operations—and had concluded that the results were militarily negligible. SEACORD recommended an extension of the operations for another 30 days, and their intensification as "an effective tonic [for the GVN], particularly if accompanied by serious joint preparations and timely initiation of retaliatory and Phase II operations against the DRV."

The most forceful restatement of the reprisal policy, however, came from the Joint Chiefs of Staff at the end of January, in the form of a memorandum to the Secretary of Defense reviewing earlier JCS recommendations on reprisals and noting that the continued lack of a U.S. response to major enemy provocations risked inviting more such actions. They urged that the next significant provocation be met with a "positive, timely, and appropriate response . . . undertaken preferably within twenty-four hours, against selected targets in the DRV." They appended to their memorandum a resume of possible reprisal actions of varying intensities, for which plans were available and the strike forces at hand to carry out these actions. The most intensive preparations had already been made, particularly in connection with the forthcoming resumption of the DESOTO Patrols, to which a reprisal operation was explicitly linked as a contingency option, under the code name FLAMING DART. These preparations and the evolution of the readiness posture associated with this and other potential reprisal actions is reviewed briefly in the next section.

III. DESOTO PATROL AS A REPRISAL OPPORTUNITY—AND THE DECISION TO SUSPEND

Detailed and specific reprisal preparations had been under way for many months prior to February 1965, most prominently in connection with the periodic DESOTO Patrols in the Gulf of Tonkin. The patrols were suspended after the August 2 and 4, 1964 incidents, when the destroyer patrol group had been fired upon, giving rise to the first U.S. retaliatory strikes. They were resumed on 12 September, and at that time were believed to have been again attacked, or at least "menaced," by unfriendly vessels on the night of 18 September. That incident, however, was considered as too ambiguous by Washington officials to justify a reprisal action. The patrol was once more suspended on 20 September.

In order to be properly prepared for an attack on any future patrol, military authorities began to work up a pre-packaged set of reprisal targets that might be politically acceptable, with pre-assigned forces that would be in a high state of readiness to strike these targets, and with a detailed strike plan that would provide a range of retaliatory options. Accordingly, CINCPAC, on instructions from the JCS, developed appropriate plans and issued a series of Fragmentary Operations Orders under the colorful caption, "Punitive and Crippling Reprisal Actions on Targets in NVN." The orders provided for air strikes to be conducted against selected targets in North Vietnam in retaliation for DRV attacks against the DESOTO Patrol, if the patrol were resumed and attacked. Two levels of retaliation response were prescribed, with two target options each (all located south of the 19th parallel), with the various options scaled to the extent and severity of damage inflicted upon the patrol. A high alert posture was to be maintained during the days the patrol was in progress, such that the strikes could be launched within one hour after receipt of the execution order. The retaliatory forces were to be carefully prepositioned and rules of engagement were meticulously spelled out.

While these preparations were initially associated exclusively with the DESOTO Patrol, it was recognized that reprisals might also be called for in retaliation for any type of serious provocation which could occur without warning, could be caused by the DRV or by the VC, and might be directed against US or GVN forces. But the high alert status ordered in connection with the DESOTO Patrols could be maintained for only short periods of time. A more sustained capability was also needed, and the JCS prepared an outline plan for further elaboration by CINCPAC, calling for a more limited reprisal action that could be launched with the least possible delay with forces in place and with a readiness posture normally maintained. The forces expected to be available for such strikes were one CVA air wing, two squadrons of B–57, two squadrons of F–105, three squadrons of F–100, and approximately one squadron of VNAF A–1H; and the targets considered most suitable were:

> Target No. 33—Dong Hoi Barracks
> 36—Vit Thu Lu Army Barracks
> 39—Chap Le Army Barracks
> 52—Vinh Army Supply Depot E
> 71—Ben Thuy Port Facilities

All of these preparations came to a head at the end of January, when a tentative decision had evidently been reached in Washington to authorize resumption of the DESOTO Patrols on or about 3 February. A JCS directive to that effect went out to CINCPAC on 28 January, requesting CINCPAC to issue the necessary Operational Plan, covering a two destroyer Patrol Group with on-line Crypto RATT and Star Shell illumination capabilities. Interestingly, the instructions were explicit to the effect that the "Patrol track shall not be provocative with the Patrol Group remaining 30 nautical miles from both NVN mainland and Hainan Island and South of 20 degrees North latitude." The Patrol was to be continued for a period of three days, during which time SP–2 aircraft with searchlight and flare capability were to support the Patrol Group during hours of darkness by assisting in contact investigation and clarification, and a Combat Air Patrol was to be airborne in the vicinity of the Patrol during daylight and to be on immediate call during darkness. Instructions also called for carefully dissociating the Patrol from OPLAN 34A operations in and over the Gulf of Tonkin 48 hours before, during, and 48 hours following completion of the Patrol.

Rules of engagement, in the event of attack, were as follows:

a. The Patrol ships and aircraft are authorized to attack with the objective of insuring destruction of any vessel or aircraft which attacks, or gives positive indication of intent to attack, US forces operating in international waters or airspace over international waters.

b. In event of hostile attack, the Patrol ships and aircraft are directed to fire upon the hostile attacker with the objective of insuring destruction. Ships are authorized to pursue the enemy to the recognized three mile territorial limit. Aircraft are authorized hot pursuit inside territorial waters (three miles) against surface vessels and into hostile air space (includes DRV, Hainan Island and Mainland China) against attack aircraft when necessary to achieve destruction of identified attack forces. Ships and aircraft will confine their actions to the attacking ships and/or aircraft.

In the days following, attention centered on plans for the reprisal strike. A number of last-minute changes were made in the targets that had been recommended by CINCPAC and the JCS, in order to reduce the risk of aircraft losses and to reduce sortie requirements. The launching date for the DESOTO Patrol was postponed from the 3rd to the 7th of February, and the JCS asked CINCPAC to re-order its reprisal raids into three attack options, consisting respectively of three, five, and seven specified targets, and to plan to conduct the air strikes against them, as directed, by option or by target, in any combination. The options and targets, together with estimated sorties, were as follows:

			Strike	*Flak*	*CAP*	*Total*
Option One						
Tgts	33	Dong Hoi Barracks	24	8	8	40
	36	Vit Thu Lu Barracks	24	8	4	36
	39	Chap Le Barracks	40	12	4	56
		Total....	80	28	16	132

	Strike	Flak	CAP	Total
Option Two				
Tgts 33, 36, 39 of Option One, plus:				
24 Chanh Hoa Barracks	28	12	12	52
32 Vu Con Barracks	10	8	4	22
Total	126	48	32	206
Option Three				
Tgts 33, 36, 39, 24, 32 of Option Two, plus:				
14 Thanh Hoa Bridge	32	12	4	48
74 Quang Khe Naval Base	22	4	2	28
Total	180	64	38	282

Of these seven targets, six were south of the 19th parallel, and on the November working group's reprisal target list; one, the Thanh Hoa Bridge, Target 14 in Option Three, was north of the 19th parallel.

The strikes against these targets were to employ the US forces then in mainland Southeast Asia in their alerted and augmented state (with an additional F105 squadron from the Philippines at Da Nang), plus up to 3 CVAs; but they would also provide for strikes from a non-alert status, i.e., with US forces normally in-country, plus CVA normally on station. Strikes from a non-alert status, if ordered, would be simultaneous, launched within the minimum feasible reaction time, and as near as practicable to first light following the reprisal incident. CINCPAC was also asked to make "preliminary provisions" for a strike at Target 32—Vu Con Barracks in Option Two above—to be conducted by VNAF, with assistance from US flak suppression, CAP, pathfinder, and SAR. These provisions were not to be revealed to the GVN at that time, since the inclusion of this VNAF strike might or might not be ordered, depending on the circumstances.

CINCPAC responded the following day by issuing Operation Order FLAMING DART, directing its Air Force and Navy Component Commands to be prepared to conduct air strikes when directed, against the above targets by option, or against any combination of the above targets within or between options, in retaliation for attacks on the DESOTO Patrol. CINCPACFLT was assigned Targets 33 and 36 of Option One, 24 of Option Two, and 74 of Option Three. CINCPACAF was assigned Targets 39 of Option One, 32 of Option Two, and 14 of Option Three. Aircraft would be armed with optimum conventional ordnance for the target to be attacked, excluding napalm.

Operation Order FLAMING DART placed the US in a highly flexible position. It provided a vehicle for a quick reprisal decision in the eventuality of an attack on the DESOTO Patrol or of any other provocation, such as a dramatic VC incident in South Vietnam. The particular targets involved had been briefed to the principal decision-makers, had the virtue of being known and understood by them, and even had their tentative approval. Moreover, nearly all the targets were in the far south of North Vietnam and all could be associated with infiltration, which were two of the conditions laid down in the guidelines for retaliating against the North for spectacular incidents in the South. The Operation Order therefore served well as a generalized pre-planned reprisal target package, offering a wide spectrum of choices.

The DESOTO Patrol, however, which had been the major focus for the reprisal planning, was never to carry out its assigned role. On 4 February, three days before the Patrol was to begin its operation, the Chairman of the JCS informed CINCPAC and all interested posts and commands that authority to execute DESOTO was cancelled, in view of Soviet Premier Kosygin's imminent four-day visit to Hanoi that was to begin on 6 February. "DESOTO patrol concurrent with Kosygin visit or immediately thereafter," wrote the CJCS, "could be interpreted as reaction to visit, thereby impairing and complicating US–Soviet relations."

The decision to call off the Patrol in deference to Kosygin's visit, reflected a growing feeling in some parts of the Administration that the renewed involvement of the Soviet Union in Southeast Asia, after its hands-off policy of almost three years' standing, might, on balance, be a good thing for the U.S. While some American experts interpreted Moscow's November, 1964 pledge of military assistance to Hanoi and Kosygin's visit in February 1965 as a sure sign that the Soviet Union saw the collapse of the US venture in SVN as imminent and wanted merely to stake its claim in apposition to Peking before it was too late, others believed that the USSR might well find it in its interest to act as an agent of moderation and compromise, providing the U.S. with an avenue of graceful retreat from a seemingly irretrievable situation.

This view was certainly held by some State Department experts, particularly in the Office of Asian Communist Affairs (ACA) and in the Office of Intelligence and Research (INR). In an interesting memorandum of February 5, 1965 to William Bundy, Lindsay Grant of ACA saw the implications for American policy of the Kosygin visit to Hanoi as "enormous."

> It is possible to hypothesize that the Soviet initiative may be intended to present the United States with an acceptable, albeit difficult, choice. They may presume that the situation in the South would deteriorate to the point where we could foresee ourselves confronted with the possibility of:
>
> 1) a series of defeats on the ground and/or total collapse of authority in Saigon, or
>
> 2) a rapid movement in the direction of neutralism, leading to our being invited out, or
>
> 3) some kind of negotiated settlement which would permit us to reduce our commitment to the bare bones, and thereby at least minimize a generally distasteful loss. The last prospect, which would represent the best of a bad choice, could possibly result from an increased Soviet presence in North Viet-Nam.
>
> Thus, the Soviets might find it in their own interest to propose to Hanoi a solution of the war in Viet-Nam along the following lines:
>
> 1) North Viet-Nam would remain untouched, with the Soviet Union guaranteeing to provide major economic and other help;
>
> 2) South Viet-Nam would be neutralized, with some sort of paper guarantee offered by outside powers, including the Soviet Union;
>
> 3) The National Front for the Liberation of South Viet-Nam would participate in a neutralist coalition government.
>
> (The Soviet Union would, presumably, give North Viet-Nam private assurances that it would not stand in the way of further Front and Viet Cong efforts to gain a complete political victory in the South.)

The author of the memorandum, of course, recognized that it would be only under the prospect of a collapse of the GVN or of being requested to leave that the U.S. would be willing to accede to the solutions suggested. But he stressed, as the major benefit of this course, that:

. . . the Soviet presence would represent [words missing]

A somewhat similar view was echoed subsequently in a SEACORD conference, the sense of which was reported in a Saigon message to the Secretary of State. The relevant arguments were to the effect that:

> (1) The DRV is almost entirely dependent both economically and militarily upon the Chinese Communists who see great value in having the DRV continue this exclusive dependence;
>
> (2) The Soviet Union is the only alternative source of economic and military support to Hanoi which would enable the DRV to remain viable if it decided to cease its aggression;
>
> (3) It is therefore important that the Soviets receive accurate indications that we would *not* oppose a continuing Soviet role in the DRV, although this is not a matter on which the U.S. can take an initiative.

Subsequent events on the negotiating front, and the role we believed the USSR could play on that front, also lend support to the view that, at least in the early part of 1965, there was a fairly widespread belief among U.S. policymakers that the Soviet Union could and probably would exert a benign influence upon Hanoi.

There is, indeed, some evidence that the USSR itself had some such thought in mind in connection with Kosygin's February visit. Peking, at least, has charged that Kosygin had tried at that time to persuade both Hanoi and Peking to negotiate some kind of settlement with the United States, reportedly involving a "face-saving" U.S. withdrawal.

In any event, there seems little doubt that the decision to forego the DESOTO Patrol was inspired by the hope, if not expectation, that Kosygin would, from the US point of view, weigh in constructively in the Vietnam struggle.

IV. FLAMING DART I AND II
—THE IMPERCEPTIBLE TRANSITION

A. THE FIRST REPRISAL

The long months of contingency planning, hesitation, and agonized debate were suddenly cut short on February 7th, when the VC struck the American installations at Pleiku and Camp Holloway. This time the President showed the same decisiveness and swift reaction that he had displayed six months earlier in the Gulf of Tonkin. The decision to strike back was reached in a 75 minute meeting of the National Security Council on the evening of February 6 (Washington time) in the Cabinet Room of the White House, and in the presence of Senate Majority Leader Mike Mansfield and House Speaker John McCormack. McGeorge Bundy, on his mission to Saigon at the time, had joined Ambassador Taylor and General Westmoreland in recommending prompt retaliation in telecoms with the President from the communications center in Saigon.

The strike, carried out during the early morning hours of the 7th (Washington time) was, at least militarily, something of a fizzle. The mildest of the three attack options was selected for the strike, but when the executive order was flashed, only one of the three CVA's (USS Ranger) was on station at Point Yankee. The other two (Hancock and Coral Sea) had been stood down to a 96-hour alert after the cancellation of the DESOTO Patrol and were enroute to assignments elsewhere. They were urgently recalled by CINCPAC to participate in the strike, which had to be delayed until the CVA's returned to points from which their aircraft could reach the assigned targets. The weather, however, was very adverse, causing a large number of sorties to abort, with the result that only one of the three assigned targets was struck in force. In order to stiffen the reprisal and to make it clearly a joint US–GVN response, the target was restruck the following day (February 8) by the US carrier aircraft that had aborted the previous day, and a VNAF strike by 24 A-1H's supported by USAF pathfinder, flak suppression and CAP aircraft, was carried out against target 32 (Vu Con Barracks) concurrently.

B. TIMING OF PLEIKU AND THE KOSYGIN VISIT

As was indicated earlier, the U.S. had put off the DESOTO Patrol that had been scheduled for February 7 so as to avoid any appearance of provocativeness *vis-a-vis* Kosygin, who was to arrive in Hanoi on February 6. And yet it was precisely then, at the very beginning of the Kosygin visit, that the VC launched their spectacular attack on the US installations. This had led many to conjecture that the raid was deliberately organized and timed by the hardliners in Hanoi so as to nip in the bud any possible Soviet peace initiative or in other ways to put Kosygin on the spot.

Whether Hanoi specifically ordered the Pleiku attack or whether the VC merely received Hanoi's blessing for the attack remains speculative. There can be little doubt, however, that Hanoi had full [words missing] ample reason to favor the notion [words missing]

> . . . it had more to gain than lose by having the attack take place while Kosygin was present, even though it might embarrass him, as it very likely did. If the Americans failed to respond, the North Vietnamese could argue that the United States was indeed a paper tiger, and that all that was needed for the war to be brought to a successful conclusion in the south was some additional military assistance. If the United States did respond, the North Vietnamese could claim that more aid was necessary to prosecute the war under more difficult circumstances, and they could then reasonably ask for planes and defensive missiles with which to protect their own cities, too. Since Kosygin was wooing North Vietnam for Russia's own purposes as much as Hanoi was wooing him to help it regain some balance between Moscow and Peking, the Russian Premier was hardly in a position to leave Hanoi in a huff, which besides would have made him look foolish.

Although the onset of the bombing no doubt took the Russians by surprise, they probably viewed it as a futile last-ditch effort by Washington to strengthen its bargaining position rather than as a prelude to new escalation. In any event, Kosygin's reaction in Hanoi was restrained. He pointed out that the situation was "fraught with serious complications" and seemed to be favoring a negotiated termination. In any event, in keeping with the view held in several influential Administration quarters that the USSR might be a valuable moderating influence upon Hanoi, Washington took pains to assure Moscow that Kosygin's presence in Hanoi during the US reprisal strikes of February 7–8 was an unfortunate coincidence and no affront to the Soviet Union was intended.

C. THE REPRISAL RATIONALE AND ITS PUBLIC HANDLING

On the morning after the reprisal order had been issued (February 7), a second NSC meeting was convened at the White House to agree on an appropriate text for the White House statement and to discuss the content of a

McNamara press briefing at the Pentagon, called for that afternoon. The public handling of the raids was of crucial importance in conveying to Hanoi some inkling of what the implications of the reprisal action were for future U.S. responses and for the future U.S. role in the Vietnamese war, without at the same time arousing undue anxieties at home and in the rest of the world.

It is worth noting that there were important differences between the February 7–8 raids and the earlier strikes in the Gulf of Tonkin incident. The August Tonkin strikes had clearly been presented as a one-time retaliatory action in response to a North Vietnamese attack on US naval power in international waters.

Publicly, the Tonkin strikes had ben depicted as a "positive reply"—one which was "limited but fitting"—to an unprovoked attack on US vessels operating within their rights on the high seas. The "one-shot" nature of the strikes was stressed, and it was explicitly stated that, provided there were no further enemy attacks, the US considered the incident closed. Together with declarations that the US strikes were not intended to expand or escalate the guerrilla war in Southeast Asia, this tended to make the strikes appear as an isolated action, bearing only incidental relationship to the war itself. The war continued to be officially pictured as one being fought by the South Vietnamese, with the US in a strictly limited supporting role. It is true that stiff warnings were sent to Hanoi through discrete diplomatic channels (ICC Commissioner Seaborne's August visit), stressing that US patience was wearing thin and that the DRV could expect to suffer the consequences if it persisted in its aggressive course, but U.S. public statements made it clear that the strikes were not intended to change the basic ground rules of the conflict at that time. The strikes were intended primarily to demonstrate that North Vietnam could not flagrantly attack U.S. forces with impunity; but nothing was said publicly to imply that the North could not continue its activities in the South without fear that its own territory would be placed in jeopardy.

By contrast with the Tonkin strikes, the February 1965 raids, while also initiated as reprisals, were intended to be explicitly linked with the "larger pattern of aggression" by North Vietnam, and were designed to signal a change in the ground rules of the conflict in the South. By retaliating against North Vietnam for a VC incident in the South, the US consciously made its first open break with self-imposed ground rules which had permitted the North to direct and support the war in the South, but which had precluded direct US countermeasures against the North's territory. The strikes thus were to serve clear notice upon all concerned that the US would not abide by such rules in the future.

But the change in ground rules also posed serious public information and stage managing problems for the President. Until the February raids, and especially throughout the election campaign of 1964, the case had regularly been made that the insurrection in the South was essentially a home-grown affair and largely self-supporting; now the argument had to be turned around and public opinion persuaded that there really wouldn't be much difficulty cleaning up the South if infiltrators from the North would just go home and "leave their neighbors alone."

In the White House press release immediately following the reprisal, therefore, major emphasis was placed on Hanoi's role in the South:

> . . . these attacks were only made possible by the continuing infiltration
> of personnel and equipment from North Vietnam . . . infiltration mark-

edly increased during 1964 and continues to increase. . . . "The key to the situation remains the cessation of infiltration from North Vietnam and the clear indication that it is prepared to cease aggression against its neighbors."

Another major new departure of the 7–8 February strikes was that they were intended to be at least a first step in more directly and actively associating the US with the South Vietnamese in "their" war. Thus while the retaliation was precipitated by the Pleiku incident, it was considered essential to justify it in broader terms—not merely as a response to a single outrage committed against Americans, but as a response to a series of outrages, committed against South Vietnamese as well as Americans.

Thus, the White House press release and, even more explicitly, the McNamara press briefing of February 7 spoke of three VC attacks, all "ordered and directed by the Hanoi regime," but only one of these was the Pleiku–Camp Holloway raid against U.S. installation. The two others cited in justification of the reprisal were attacks on Vietnamese villages in which, it was carefully pointed out, no American casualties were sustained.

Thtis effort to link the reprisal to VC offenses against both parties was reinforced by having the reprisal strikes conducted by both South Vietnamese and US forces. McNamara's statement heavily stressed the fact that "elements of the U.S. and South Vietnamese Air Forces were directed to launch joint retaliatory attacks . . ."

By demonstrating that the US was prepared to join with the South Vietnamese in military reprisals against North Vietnam for actions committed against either or both parties in the South, the strikes tended to weaken the policy line, assiduously adhered to up to that time, that the war was essentially a Vietnamese war with US involvement confined to advice and support. Once the US began participating in such military reprisals on a regular basis, it would unavoidably begin to appear as more of a co-belligerent, along with South Vietnam, against the VC and their sponsors in North Vietnam.

The practical significance of this point is obvious. As long as the U.S. maintained the policy line that it was not really directly engaged in the war, it had to deny its forces many proposed military actions in Southeast Asia, and had to impose on itself severe political constraints in its military operations. The abandonment of this policy line as a result of reprisal actions like FLAMING DART would open the way to a much wider range of politically acceptable US military options in Vietnam.

The 7–8 February strikes, however, were only a limited and tentative first step, and far from an irrevocable commitment to a broader course of action. US action was still "tit-for-tat." The White House statement stressed the phrase "appropriate reprisal action" and, likening it to the Gulf of Tonkin incident, characterized the response as similarly "appropriate and fitting."

The idea of equivalent punishment was conveyed by confining the strikes to a quite limited number of targets plausibly associated with infiltration. Thus the possibility was left open that these reprisals were strictly one-shot operations that would be carried out only in the event of spectacular enemy actions. But the public language was both ominous and ambiguous: "As the U.S. Government has frequently stated, we seek no wider war. Whether or not this course can be maintained lies with the North Vietnamese aggressors." In fact, however, there was little expectation, that the North Vietnamese would "cease their aggression," and every expectation that the U.S. would go beyond a policy of event-associated reprisals. For immediately following the first press release, the White

House issued another significant presidential statement, ordering what had long been recommended:

> . . . I have directed the orderly withdrawal of American dependents from South Vietnam . . . We have no choice now but to clear the decks and make absolutely clear our continued determination to back South Vietnam . . .

And as further indication that much more than a mere occasional reprisal was in the offing, McNamara met with the JCS on the following day to request that they prepare and submit to him their recommendations for an eight-week air strike campaign against infiltration-associated targets in the lower portion of North Vietnam as a sustained reply to any further provocations.

D. AN ACT OF DEFIANCE

The flashing red warning signals—if that is what they were—were not heeded by Hanoi. On the contrary, in what was regarded by some observers as a calculated act of defiance, the VC staged another dramatic attack on 10 February, this one against a US enlisted men's billet in Qui Nhon, inflicting the heaviest single loss of American personnel yet. Within 24 hours, US and South Vietnamese aircraft executed the largest retaliatory air strike of the war up to that time. Named FLAMING DART II, 28 VNAF A–1H's and 20 USAF F–100's hit Chap Le. Simultaneously, Navy aircraft struck Chanh Hoa not far from Dong Hoi, just north of the DMZ.

This time, significantly, the strikes were not characterized as a reprisal linked to the immediate incident. Instead, the White House release of February 11, listed a long series of VC incidents and attacks that had occurred since February 8, most of which were not "spectacular" but quite normal features of the Vietnam war. The statements moreover characterized the US air strikes as a response to these "further direct provocations by the Hanoi regime," and to these "continued acts of aggression." The words "retaliation" and "reprisal" were carefully avoided and the joint US/GVN statement released in Saigon the same day actually characterized the air attack action for the first time as "air operations."

The change in terminology from "retaliation" or "reprisal" to "response," from a specific set of incidents to "continued aggression," and from a single attack to "air operations" was clearly deliberate. A strict reprisal policy, although permitting the US to strike the North, would have left the initiative in the enemy's hands and would have restricted the US to the kinds of responses that could be represented as equivalent or "fitting." But, more important, the new terminology reflected a conscious U.S. decision to broaden the reprisal concept as gradually and as imperceptibly as possible to accommodate a much wider policy of sustained, steadily intensifying air attacks against North Vietnam, at a rate and on a scale to be determined by the U.S. As will be discussed further in the next section, that decision was being forcefully pressed upon the President by his principal advisers immediately after FLAMING DART I (February 7). Whether the President had tacitly or explicitly accepted this course before FLAMING DART II (February 11), is not recorded. But it would have been important to him politically in any event to play it with a minimum of drama and to preserve maximum flexibility. It seemed sensible to make it all appear as a logical sequence of almost unavoidable steps, to avoid portraying any single move as a watershed or any single decision as irreversible. The February 11 strikes did constitute a much sharper break with past policy than any previous US action in Vietnam; they set the stage for the continuing bombing program that was now to be launched in earnest; but they were presented and discussed publicly in very muted tones.

Some of the President's private comments on the attacks are reported by one of his more perceptive biographers, Philip Geyelin, in the following terms:

> His discussion of the first two retaliatory attacks, following Pleiku and Qui Nhon, was almost offhand. To one visitor, he lampooned the "crisis" tones of the television broadcasters, the long faces, and the grim talk of big, black limousines assembled for weighty policy-making.
>
> They woke us up in the middle of the night, and we woke them up in the middle of the night. Then they did it again, and we did it again, was the way he described it. If he suspected he was on the front edge of a major plunge into a fair-sized ground war in Asia, he hid his concern masterfully, dismissing all the excitement as the sort of thing that happens periodically.

Geyelin gives the President very high marks for his performance:

> . . . his handling of Vietnam in the early months of 1965 was more than skillful, it was a triumph of international and domestic politics. For if one accepts the need to right the "equilibrium," then it cannot be denied that Lyndon Johnson moved to do so with a bare minimum of dissent at home and less foreign opposition than might have been expected. And he did it, at least for a good many months, without giving the Communist Chinese or the Russians provocation in such intolerable degree that they felt obliged to move in any drastic way to the defense of Hanoi.

E.   REACTIONS AT HOME AND ABROAD

Official and public reactions to the retaliatory strikes were fairly predictable. *In the U.S.,* as *Newsweek* put it, the decision "touched off a wave of national concern and international jitters unequalled since the US–Soviet confrontation over the Cuban missile build-up." Much of the US press expressed serious doubts about where the US was heading in Vietnam. A great majority of the nation's newspapers regarded the strikes as necessary and justified and the notion that Pleiku was a deliberate VC provocation was widely accepted. But many admitted to confusion as to just what U.S. policy in Vietnam was: (e.g., *Kansas City Star*: "Do we have a specific, unwavering policy or are we improvising from crisis to crisis?" *St. Louis Post-Dispatch*: "A strike for strike strategy . . . without any ultimate objective except to hang on in Vietnam, is not much of a policy." *New York Times* (James Reston): "We do not know what the President has in mind . . . For the moment we seem to be standing mute in Washington, paralyzed before a great issue and merely digging our thought deeper into the accustomed military rut.")

In Western Europe reactions were less uniform. To the dismay of leftist members of his own Labor Party, the U.K.'s Harold Wilson phoned a message of solid support to President Johnson. Moreover, the London *Economist* saw the bombing as part of a drama acted out for the benefit of Mr. Kosygin as a warning to all communist countries "that there are limits beyond which the Viet Cong cannot push things in the South without bringing down American reprisals on the North. There is no call to specify exactly what these limits are; but to make it clear that they exist, the shot across Mr. Kosygin's bow was essential." By contrast, de Gaulle issued a cool statement that the Southeast Asia crisis "cannot be settled by force of arms" and called again for a new Geneva conference to end the war—a recommendation that was echoed by India's Prime Minister Shastri and U.N. Secretary General U Thant.

The pro-Western nations in *Southeast Asia* that live in the shadow of Communist China were visibly cheered. In South Vietnam, General Nguyen Khanh proclaimed that the VNAF reprisal strike after Pleiku marked "the happiest day of my life."

The most interesting reactions, of course, were those of the *Bloc countries*. As predicted in CIA's October 1964 estimate, the reactions of the three principal Communist powers to the limited US reprisal strikes were relatively restrained, with both Moscow and Peking promptly and publicly pledging unspecified support and assistance to Hanoi. Beneath the verbiage of condemnation of the U.S. "provocation," however, there was a measure of caution in both pledges. Neither raised the specter of a broad conflict or portrayed the U.S. actions as a threat to "world" peace. *Peking's* propaganda, though full of bellicosity and bluster, and publicizing huge anti-U.S. rallies organized in China's major cities, carefully avoided threatening any direct Chinese intervention. Thus it warned that, if the U.S. spread the flames of war to the DRV, "the *Vietnamese people* will, most assuredly, destroy the U.S. aggressors lock, stock, and barrel on their own soil." The propaganda line also suggested that only actual U.S. invasion of North Vietnam would precipitate direct Chinese intervention in the war.

Moscow's response was even more restrained. "In the face of U.S. actions" the Soviet statement said, the USSR "will be forced, together with its allies and friends, to take further measures to safeguard the security and strengthen the defense capability of the DRV." And it added that "no one should doubt that the Soviet people will fulfill its international duty to the fraternal socialist country." Like Peking, however, it derided U.S. statements that the air strikes were retaliatory, and Soviet media widely publicized international expressions of indignation and popular protests in the USSR. While indicating that "DRV defenses" would be strengthened, some Moscow broadcasts took note of growing interest in the United States and elsewhere for a negotiated settlement in Vietnam.

Hanoi's voluble, heated propaganda reaction to the air strikes pictured the incident as a sequel to previous air and naval "provocations" against the DRV rather than as a move which essentially altered either America's or North Vietnam's positions in the conflict. DRV propaganda hailed the "heroic exploit" of the antiaircraft units and claimed that, in the first raid, 12 planes were downed.

Officially, Hanoi responded in a more carefully worded fashion. A Defense Ministry statement on the 7th warned that the United States must "bear the responsibility" for the "consequences" of its "aggression" and demanded an end to "provocative and war-seeking acts against the DRV and the aggressive war in South Vietnam." Implying that the air raids would not deter future rebel aggression in the South, the DRV Government declared that "the Vietnamese people will never shrink before any threat of the United States" and will "further increase their forces and step up their struggle."

V. "SUSTAINED REPRISAL" AND ITS VARIANTS —ADVOCACY SHIFTS INTO HIGH GEAR

A. THE MCGEORGE BUNDY RECOMMENDATION

Pleiku, and the first FLAMING DART reprisal, caught the McGeorge Bundy group (which also included Assistant Secretary of Defense John McNaughton,

White House Aide Chester Cooper, and Chairman of the Vietnam Coordinating Group Leonard Unger) in the midst of intensive discussions with the US Mission in Saigon. These discussions covered the whole range of US-Vietnam policy options, particularly the complex issue of future pressures on the North. Immediately following the reprisal decision of February 7, the group returned to Washington via Air Force One. Enroute and airborne, they drafted a memorandum to the President which was intended to reflect in some degree the consensus reached among the Bundy group and with the U.S. Mission in Saigon. But in an unmistakable way, the memorandum also represents a highly personal Bundy assessment and point of view. For this reason, and because of its unique articulation of a rationale for the ROLLING THUNDER policy, it is reproduced here in considerable detail.

The Summary Conclusions, presented at the very outset of the memorandum, set the tone of the more detailed elaboration that is to follow:

> The situation in Vietnam is deteriorating, and without new U.S. action defeat appears inevitable—probably not in a matter of weeks or perhaps even months, but within the next year or so. There is still time to turn it around, but not much.
>
> The stakes in Vietnam are extremely high. The American investment is very large, and American responsibility is a fact of life which is palpable in the atmosphere of Asia, and even elsewhere. The international prestige of the United States, and a substantial part of our influence, are directly at risk in Vietnam. There is no way of unloading the burden on the Vietnamese themselves, and there is no way of negotiating ourselves out of Vietnam which offers any serious promise at present. It is possible that at some future time a neutral non-Communist force may emerge, perhaps under Buddhist leadership, but no such force currently exists, and any negotiated U.S. withdrawal today would mean surrender on the installment plan.
>
> The policy of graduated and continuing reprisal outlined in Annex A is the most promising course available, in my judgment. That judgment is shared by all who accompanied me from Washington, and I think by all members of the country team.
>
> The events of the last twenty-four hours have produced a practicable point of departure for this policy of reprisal, and for the removal of U.S. dependents. They may also have catalyzed the formation of a new Vietnamese government. If so, the situation may be at a turning point.
>
> There is much that can and should be done to support and to supplement our present effort, while adding sustained reprisals. But I want to stress one important general conclusion which again is shared by all members of my party: the U.S. mission is composed of outstanding men, and U.S. policy within Vietnam is mainly right and well directed. None of the special solutions or criticisms put forward with zeal by individual reformers in government or in the press is of major importance, and many of them are flatly wrong. No man is perfect, and not every tactical step of recent months has been perfectly chosen, but when you described the Americans in Vietnam as your first team, you were right.

After a brief description of the general situation in Vietnam as the Bundy group found it, the memorandum explains the crucial question of whether and to what degree a stable government is a necessity for the successful prosecution of U.S. policy in Vietnam. It is well to bear in mind that the achievement of considerable government stability had been made, in all previous "pressure guidance," a *sine qua non* of any transition to Phase II action against the North. And yet GVN stability continued to be a most elusive goal. Bundy now seemed to be arguing that the U.S. may have been insisting on a more perfect government than was really necessary, at least in the short run:

> For immediate purposes—and especially for the initiation of reprisal policy, we believe that the government need be no stronger than it is today with General Khanh as the focus of raw power while a weak caretaker government goes through the motions. Such a government can execute military decisions and it can give formal political support to joint US/GVN policy. That is about all it can do.
>
> In the longer run, it is necessary that a government be established which will in one way or another be able to maintain its political authority against all challenges over a longer time than the governments of the last year and a half.
>
> The composition and direction of such a government is a most difficult problem, and we do not wholly agree with the mission in our estimate of its nature . . .
>
> We believe that General Khanh, with all his faults, is by long odds the outstanding military man currently in sight—and the most impressive personality generally. We do not share the conclusion of Ambassador Taylor that he must somehow be removed from the military and political scene.
>
> There are strong reasons for the Ambassador's total lack of confidence in Khanh. At least twice Khanh has acted in ways that directly spoiled Ambassador Taylor's high hopes for December. When he abolished the High National Council he undercut the prospect of the stable government needed for Phase II action against the North. In January he overthrew Huong just when the latter, in the Embassy's view, was about to succeed in putting the bonzes in their place. . .
>
> . . . our principal reasons for opposing any sharp break with Khanh is that we see no one else in sight with anything like his ability to combine military authority with some sense of politics.

Bundy also differed from the Embassy on the necessity of "facing down" the Buddhist leaders, believing instead that they should be "incorporated" into GVN affairs rather than being "confronted." He stressed the significance of these differences, but then generously endorsed the Mission's overall relationship to and handling of the GVN.

> Having registered these two immediate and important differences of emphasis, we should add that in our judgment the mission has acted at about the right level of general involvement in the problem of Vietnamese government-making. American advice is sought by all elements, and all try to bend it to their own ends. The mission attempts to keep before all elements the importance of stable government, and it quietly presses the value of those who are known to be good, solid, able ministerial timber . . .
>
> . . . It is important that the mission maintain a constant and active concern with the politics of government-making. This it is doing.

Bundy then went on to pay obeisance to the need for a stronger pacification program and for greater recognition that the Vietnamese need "a sense of positive hope":

If we suppose that new hopes are raised—at least temporarily—by a reprisal program, and we suppose further that a government somewhat better than the bare minimum is established, the most urgent order of business will then be the improvement and broadening of the pacification program, especially in its non-military elements . . .

. . . there is plainly a deep and strong yearning among the young and the unprivileged for a new and better social order. This is what the Buddhist leaders are groping toward; this is what the students and young Turk generals are seeking. This yearning does not find an adequate response in American policy as Vietnamese see it. This is one cause of latent anti-American feeling. We only perceived this problem toward the end of our visit. We think it needs urgent further attention. We make no present recommendations. We do believe that over the long pull our military and political firmness must be matched by our political and economic support for the hopes that are embodied to Vietnamese in the word "revolution."

Bundy harbored no illusions concerning the enemy's ability and determination:

The prospect in Vietnam is grim. The energy and persistence of the Viet Cong are astonishing. They can appear anywhere—and at almost any time. They have accepted extraordinary losses and they come back for more. They show skill in their sneak attacks and ferocity when cornered. Yet the weary country does not want them to win.

There are a host of things the Vietnamese need to do better and areas in which we need to help them. The place where we can help most is in the clarity and firmness of our own commitment to what is in fact as well as in rhetoric a common cause.

Finally, Bundy explained the central rationale of his recommendations:

There is one grave weakness in our posture in Vietnam which is within our own power to fix—and that is a widespread belief that we do not have the will and force and patience and determination to take the necessary action and stay the course.

This is the overriding reason for our present recommendation of a policy of sustained reprisal. Once such a policy is put in force, we shall be able to speak in Vietnam on many topics and in many ways, with growing force and effectiveness.

One final word. At its very best the struggle in Vietnam will be long. It seems to us important that this fundamental fact be made clear and our understanding of it be made clear to our own people and to the people of Vietnam. Too often in the past we have conveyed the impression that we expect an early solution when those who live with this war know that no early solution is possible. It is our own belief that the people of the United States have the necessary will to accept and to execute a policy that rests upon the reality that there is no short cut to success in South Vietnam.

Appended to the Bundy memorandum as Annex A [Doc. 250] is a detailed, carefully formulated explanation of his "sustained reprisal" policy, including specific action recommendations. Because of its explicitness and clarity, it is reproduced in full:

A POLICY OF SUSTAINED REPRISAL

I. Introductory

We believe that the best available way of increasing our chance of success in Vietnam is the development and execution of a policy of *sustained reprisal* against North Vietnam—a policy in which air and naval action against the North is justified by and related to the whole Viet Cong campaign of violence and terror in the South.

While we believe that the risks of such a policy are acceptable, we emphasize that its costs are real. It implies significant U.S. air losses even if no full air war is joined, and it seems likely that it would eventually require an extensive and costly effort against the whole air defense system of North Vietnam. U.S. casualties would be higher—and more visible to American feelings—than those sustained in the struggle in South Vietnam.

Yet measured against the costs of defeat in Vietnam, this program seems cheap. And even if it fails to turn the tide—as it may—the value of the effort seems to us to exceed its cost.

II. Outline of the Policy

1. In partnership with the Government of Vietnam, we should develop and exercise the option to retaliate against *any* VC act of violence to persons or property.

2. In practice, we may wish at the outset to relate our reprisals to those acts of relatively high visibility such as the Pleiku incident. Later, we might retaliate against the assassination of a province chief, but not necessarily the murder of a hamlet official; we might retaliate against a grenade thrown into a crowded cafe in Saigon, but not necessarily to a shot fired in a small shop in the countryside.

3. Once a program of reprisals is clearly underway, it should not be necessary to conect each specific act against North Vietnam to a particular outrage in the South. It should be possible, for example, to publish weekly lists of outrages in the South and to have it clearly understood that these outrages are the cause of such action against the North as may be occurring in the current period. Such a more generalized pattern of reprisal would remove much of the difficulty involved in finding precisely matching targets in response to specific atrocities. Even in such a more general pattern, however, it would be important to insure that the general level of reprisal action remained in close correspondence with the level of outrages in the South. We must keep it clear at every stage both to Hanoi and to the world, that our reprisals will be reduced or stopped when outrages in the South are reduced or stopped—and that we are not attempting to destroy or conquer North Vietnam.

4. In the early stages of such a course, we should take the appropriate occasion to make clear our firm intent to undertake reprisals on any further acts, major or minor, that appear to us and the GVN as indicating Hanoi's support. We would announce that our two governments have been patient and forbearing in the hope that Hanoi would come to its senses without the necessity of our having to take further action; but the outrages continue and now we must react against those who are responsible; we will not provoke; we will not use our force indiscriminately; but we can no longer sit by in the face of repeated acts of terror and violence for which the DRV is responsible.

5. Having once made this announcement, we should execute our reprisal

policy with as low a level of public noise as possible. It is to our interest that our acts should be seen—but we do not wish to boast about them in ways that make it hard for Hanoi to shift its ground. We should instead direct maximum attention to the continuing acts of violence which are the cause of our continuing reprisals.

6. This reprisal policy should begin at a low level. Its level of force and pressure should be increased only gradually—and as indicated above it should be decreased if VC terror visibly decreases. The object would not be to "win" an air war against Hanoi, but rather to influence the course of the struggle in the South.

7. At the same time it should be recognized that in order to maintain the power of reprisal without risk of excessive loss, an "air war" may in fact be necessary. We should therefore be ready to develop a separate justification for energetic flak suppression and if necessary for the destruction of Communist air power. The essence of such an explanation should be that these actions are intended solely to insure the effectiveness of a policy of reprisal, and in no sense represent any intent to wage offensive war against the North. These distinctions should not be difficult to develop.

8. It remains quite possible, however, that this reprisal policy would get us quickly into the level of military activity contemplated in the so-called Phase II of our December planning. It may even get us beyond this level with Hanoi and Peiping, if there is a Communist counteraction. We and the GVN should also be prepared for a spurt of VC terrorism, especially in urban areas, that would dwarf anything yet experienced. These are the risks of any action. They should be carefully reviewed—but we believe them to be acceptable.

9. We are convinced that the political values of reprisal require a *continuous* operation. Episodic responses geared on a one-for-one basis to "spectacular" outrages would lack the persuasive force of sustained pressure. More important still, they would leave it open to the Communists to avoid reprisals entirely by giving up only a small element of their own program. The Gulf of Tonkin affair produced a sharp upturn in morale in South Vietnam. When it remained an isolated episode, however, there was a severe relapse. It is the great merit of the proposed scheme that to stop it the Communists would have to stop enough of their activity in the South to permit the probable success of a determined pacification effort.

III. Expected Effect of Sustained Reprisal Policy

1. We emphasize that our primary target in advocating a reprisal policy is the improvement of the situation in South Vietnam. Action against the North is usually urged as a means of affecting the will of Hanoi to direct and support the VC. We consider this an important but longer-range purpose. The immediate and critical targets are in the South—in the minds of the South Vietnamese and in the minds of the Viet Cong cadres.

2. Predictions of the effect of any given course of action upon the states of mind of people are difficult. It seems very clear that if the United States and the Government of Vietnam join in a policy of reprisal, there will be a sharp immediate increase in optimism in the South, among nearly all articulate groups. The Mission believes and our own conversations confirm—that in all sectors of Vietnamese opinion there is a strong belief that the United States could do much more if it would, and that they are suspicious of our failure to use more of our obviously enormous power. At least in the short run, the reaction to reprisal policy would be very favorable.

3. This favorable reaction should offer opportunity for increased American influence in pressing for a more effective government—at least in the short run. Joint reprisals would imply military planning in which the American role would necessarily be controlling, and this new relation should add to our bargaining power in other military efforts—and conceivably on a wider plane as well if a more stable government is formed. We have the whip hand in reprisals as we do not in other fields . . .

4. The Vietnamese increase in hope could well increase the readiness of Vietnamese factions themselves to join together in forming a more effective government.

5. We think it plausible that effective and sustained reprisals, even in a low key, would have a substantial depressing effect upon the morale of Viet Cong cadres in South Vietnam. This is the strong opinion of CIA Saigon. It is based upon reliable reports of the initial Viet Cong reaction to the Gulf of Tonkin episode, and also upon the solid general assessment that the determination of Hanoi and the apparent timidity of the mighty United States are both major items in Viet Cong confidence.

6. The long-run effect of reprisals in the South is far less clear. It may be that like other stimulants, the value of this one would decline over time. Indeed the risk of this result is large enough so that we ourselves believe that a very major effort all along the line should be made in South Vietnam to take full advantage of the immediate stimulus of reprisal policy in its early stages. Our object should be to use this new policy to effect a visible upward turn in pacification, in governmental effectiveness, in operations against the Viet Cong, and in the whole US/GVN relationship. It is changes in these areas that can have enduring long-term effects.

7. While emphasizing the importance of reprisals in the South, we do not exclude the impact on Hanoi. We believe, indeed, that it is of great importance that the level of reprisal be adjusted rapidly and visibly to both upward and downward shifts in the level of Viet Cong offenses. We want to keep before Hanoi the carrot of our desisting as well as the stick of continued pressure. We also need to conduct the application of the force so that there is always a prospect of worse to come.

8. We cannot assert that a policy of sustained reprisal will succeed in changing the course of the contest in Vietnam. It may fail, and we cannot estimate the odds of success with any accuracy—they may be somewhere between 25% and 75%. What we can say is that even if it fails, the policy will be worth it. At a minimum it will damp down the charge that we did not do all that we could have done, and this charge will be important in many countries, including our own. Beyond that, a reprisal policy—to the extent that it demonstrates U.S. willingness to employ this new norm in counter-insurgency—will set a higher price for the future upon all adventures of guerrilla warfare, and it should therefore somewhat increase our ability to deter such adventures. We must recognize, however, that that ability will be gravely weakened if there is failure for any reason in Vietnam.

IV. *Present Action Recommendations*

1. This general recommendation was developed in intensive discussions in the days just before the attacks on Pleiku. These attacks and our reaction to them have created an ideal opportunity for the prompt development and execution of sustained reprisals. Conversely if no such policy is now developed, we face the grave danger that Pleiku, like the Gulf of Tonkin, may be a short-run stimulant

and a long-term depressant. We therefore recommend that the necessary preparations be made for continuing reprisals. The major necessary steps to be taken appear to us to be the following:

(1) We should complete the evacuation of dependents.

(2) We should quietly start the necessary westward deployments of back-up contingency forces.

(3) We should develop and refine a running catalogue of Viet Cong offenses which can be published regularly and related clearly to our own reprisals. Such a catalogue should perhaps build on the foundation of an initial White Paper.

(4) We should initiate joint planning with the GVN on both the civil and military level. Specifically, we should give a clear and strong signal to those now forming a government that we will be ready for this policy when they are.

(5) We should develop the necessary public and diplomatic statements to accompany the initiation and continuation of this program.

(6) We should insure that a reprisal program is matched by renewed public commitment to our family of programs in the South, so that the central importance of the southern struggle may never be neglected.

(7) We should plan quiet diplomatic communications of the precise meaning of what we are and are not doing, to Hanoi, to Peking and to Moscow.

(8) We should be prepared to defend and to justify this new policy by concentrating attention in every forum upon its cause—the aggression in the South.

(9) We should accept discussion on these terms in any forum, but we should *not* now accept the idea of negotiations of any sort except on the basis of a stand down of Viet Cong violence. A program of sustained reprisal, with its direct link to Hanoi's continuing aggressive actions in the South will not involve us in nearly the level of international recrimination which would be precipitated by a go-North program which was not so connected. For this reason the international pressures for negotiation should be quite manageable.

B.   THE TAYLOR CONCEPTION OF "GRADUATED REPRISALS"

At about the same time that the McGeorge Bundy memorandum was being submitted to the President, Ambassador Taylor in Saigon conveyed his own views concerning a future reprisal program to Washington. Not surprisingly (since they had exchanged ideas extensively in Saigon) Taylor's concept closely paralleled Bundy's in many of its features. But in at least one significant respect it diverged sharply. Whereas Bundy's main objective was to influence the course of the struggle in the *South* (providing a boost to GVN morale and cohesion, affording an opportunity for increased American influence upon and bargaining power with the GVN, and exerting a depressing effect upon VC cadres), Taylor's principal aim was "to bring increasing pressure on the DRV to cease its intervention."

The areas of agreement between Taylor and Bundy were considerable. Like Bundy, he recommended "a measured, controlled sequence of actions against the DRV taken in reprisal for DRV-inspired actions in South Vietnam . . . carried out jointly with the GVN and . . . directed solely against DRV military targets and infiltration routes. . ." The reprisals could be "initiated on the basis of a general catalogue or package of VC outrages, no one particularly grave itself. . . ." and could be varied "with the general level of VC outrages in SVN or, if we so desired, progressively raised. . . . Thus it would be tantamount to the so-called Phase II escalation, but justified on the basis of retaliation." Like Bundy, he believed "that we should limit US/GVN publicity to the bare minimum . . ." and he also cautioned that "we should attempt to avoid in the present situation a general letdown in morale and spirit which followed our action in the Tonkin Gulf."

But Taylor's concept was much more directly aimed at bringing pressures to bear against the DRV, to give them "serious doubts as to their chances for ultimate success" and to cause them to cease their aggression and to accede to a rigorously enforced 1954/1962 Geneva-type settlement. It was this focus on the *North,* rather than a rededication of the GVN to the struggle in the *South,* that Taylor considered to be the real benefit of a reprisal policy. Integrating the Vietnamese in a program against the DRV, he believed, would have an exhilarating effect which, if exploited early "could lead to a greater sense of purpose and direction both in the government and the military and awaken new hope for eventual victory on the part of the Vietnamese people."

In a subsequent cable, Taylor spelled out his "graduated reprisal" concept in a more orderly fashion:

> In review of the rationale for concept of graduated reprisals we are of the opinion that, in order of importance, it should have the following objectives:
>
> (a) The will of Hanoi leaders;
> (b) GVN morale; and
> (c) Physical destruction to reduce the DRV ability to support the VC.

Of these three, the first appears to us by far the most imporant, since our effectiveness in influencing Hanoi leadership will, in the long run, determine the success or failure of our efforts in both North and South Vietnam. Second objective, effect on GVN morale, is also important and fortunately the requirements for building morale in the South are roughly the same as those for impressing Hanoi leaders with the rising costs of their support of the VC. In this case, what is bad for Hanoi is generally good for Saigon.

Effect of the physical destruction of material objects and infliction of casualties will not, in our judgment, have a decisive bearing upon the ability of DRV to support VC. However, degree of damage and number of casualties inflicted gauge the impact of our operations on Hanoi leadership and hence are important as a measure of their discomfort.

. . . We should keep our response actions controllable and optional to maximum degree possible so that we can act or withhold action when and as we choose. This need for flexibility argues strongly for vagueness in defining criteria for situations justifying retaliation and for retention of freedom of action to make *ad hoc* decisions in light of our interests at the moment. But in any case, complete flexibility will not be possible . . .

Assuming that we have achieved control and flexibility, we will then need to think of the tempo which we wish to communicate to the retaliatory program, with primary consideration given to effect of the program on Hanoi leadership. It seems clear to us that there should be a gradual, orchestrated acceleration of tempo measured in terms of frequency, size, number and/or geographical location of the reprisal strikes and of related activities such as BARREL ROLL and 34-A. An upward trend in any or all of these forms of intensity will convey signals which, in combination, should present to the DRV leaders a vision of inevitable, ultimate destruction if they do not change their ways. The exact rate of acceleration is a matter of judgment but we consider, roughly speaking, that each successive week should include some new act on our part to increase pressure on Hanoi . . .

We do not believe that our reprisal program will lead the GVN to believe that we have taken over their war and that they can reduce their anti-VC activities. We hope that the opposite will be the effect and the retaliatory actions in the North will give impulsion to the defensive efforts in the South. However, the Dept's fear can certainly not be ruled out and we shall watch closely the GVN reaction to the program.

One of Ambassador Taylor's major concerns was that, if a graduated reprisals program were adopted, it would be necessary to begin discussions with the GVN to seek agreement on mutually acceptable terms for the ultimate settlement of the conflict. Taylor thought of this as a process of education by which he would guide the GVN towards formulating a "framework of demands to be made on the DRV as well as the general negotiating procedures." He outlined his proposed "terms for cessation of our reprisal attacks" as follows:

  A. Demands
    1. DRV return to strict observance of 1954 accords with respect SVN and the 1962 agreement with respect to Laos—that is, stop infiltration, and bring about a cessation of VC armed insurgency. (With respect to Laos strictly observe the 1962 accords with respect to Laos, including the withdrawal of all Viet Minh forces and personnel from Laos and recognize that the freedom of movement granted therein in Laos under those accords is not subject to veto or interference by any of the parties in Laos.)
  B. In return and subject in each instance to a judgment that DRV is complying faithfully and effectively:
    1. U.S. will return to 1954 accords with respect to military personnel in SVN and GVN would be willing to enter into trade talks looking toward normalization of economic relations between DRV and GVN.
    2. Subject to faithful compliances by DRV with 1954 accords, U.S. and GVN would give assurances that they would not use force or support the use of force by any other party to upset the accords with respect to the DRV.
    3. Within the framework of the 1954 accords, the GVN would permit VC desiring to do so to return to the DRV without their arms and would grant amnesty to those peacefully laying down their arms and desiring to remain in SVN.
  C. If and when Hanoi indicates its acceptance of foregoing conditions, careful consideration must be given to immediate subsequent procedures which will avoid danger of: (a) becoming involved in a cease fire *vis-a-vis* the DRV and/or the VC accompanied by strung-out negotiations; (b) making conditions so stringent as to be unworkable from practical point of view. Probably best procedure would be to have the GVN and DRV meet in the DMZ at the military level under ICC auspices with U.S. observers to reach agreement mechanics of carrying out understanding while action against the VC and DRV continues at least in principle. RLG would have to be associated with these negotiations at some point.

It is evident from these and similar tough settlement terms and cessation "demands" that were being discussed between Saigon and Washington at that time that there was a real expectation that the kinds of reprisal pressures contemplated would inflict such pain or threat of pain upon the DRV that it would be compelled to order a stand-down of Viet Cong violence and accept conditions that, from their point of view, were tantamount to surrender. Such a view is even more clearly implicit in the comments and proposals on reprisal programs emanating from the U.S. military leadership.

C.   CINCPAC'S "GRADUATED PRESSURES" PHILOSOPHY

Admiral Sharp, commenting on Ambassador Taylor's reprisal and negotiating concepts, called attention to the need to make the reprisal program a very forceful one, if the DRV was to be persuaded to accede to a cessation on US terms:

> While it may be politically desirable to speak publicly in terms of a "graduated reprisal" program, I would hope that we are thinking, and will act, in terms of a "graduated pressures" philosophy which has more of a connotation of steady, relentless movement toward our objective of convincing Hanoi and Peiping of the prohibitive cost of them of their program of subversion, insurgency and aggression in SEAsia.
>
> If a firm decision is made to embark upon a graduated pressures program, the recommendation contained in [Taylor's Feb 11 message] to undertake discussions with the RVN reference joint US/GVN military actions is most necessary. Failure to develop firm arrangements concerning roles and responsibilities could result in over reliance on the U.S. contribution to the war effort, and perhaps GVN resorting to rash military actions from which we would have to bail them out.
>
> There is no question of the desirability of concurrently educating the GVN, as also proposed in Ref b, toward formulation of war objectives, demands and negotiating procedures to be employed against the DRV. I believe that such an educational process, combined with a graduated military pressures program will further contribute to GVN stability.
>
> We must be certain that we are dealing from a posture of strength before we sit down at the bargaining table. Successful direct increasing military pressures against NVN must be complemented by a reversal of the trend toward VC success within RVN. We must also exhibit complete confidence in ability to win in Vietnam and so indicate by our willingness to rely on our military superiority if need be.
>
> We must not be driven to premature discussions with the DRV in our eagerness to find a solution to the Southeast Asian problem. We should continue our military pressures, making (our) general objectives publicly known, while awaiting some sign that the DRV is ready to negotiate towards achievement of those objectives . . .
>
> . . . Finally, any political program which is designed to formulate terms and procedures for reaching agreement on cessation of a graduated military pressures program, will be successful in proportion to the effectiveness of the military pressures program itself.

D.   JCS EIGHT-WEEK PROGRAM

As these discussions continued, the Joint Chiefs of Staff, responding to a McNamara request of 8 February, sent to the Secretary of Defense their recommendations for an initial program of military actions against the DRV, extending over a period of eight weeks. In accordance with McNamara's instructions, the program was to be confined generally to targets along Route 7 and south of the 19th parallel, was to employ both RVN and US forces, and was to be primarily a plan for air strikes. Since it was so constrained, the JCS program does not fully reflect the preferences of the Joint Chiefs. But it does reveal something of their thinking. The context in which the program would be undertaken is described as follows:

> It is visualized that the initial overt air strikes of this program will have been undertaken as a retaliation in response to a provocative act by Viet Cong or DRV forces against US or RVN personnel or installations. Successive overt operations to provide sustained pressures and progressive destruction will be continued on the plausible justification of further provocations, which on the basis of recent past experience seem quite likely to exist. As this program continues the realistic need for precise event-association in this reprisal context will progressively diminish. A wide range of activities are within the scope of what may be stated to be provocations justifying reprisal.

The program called for two to four US–VNAF strikes per week, initially against targets along Route 7 south of the 19th parallel and near the Laos border. Specifically, the program was conceived as follows:

> The air attacks are scheduled for the first eight weeks at the rate of four fixed targets a week . . . These initial targets are located South of the 19th parallel with the exception of Target 89, an Armed Route Reconnaissance of Route 7, in the DRV close to the Laos border. BARREL ROLL missions in Laos will be coordinated with air strikes in the DRV near the Laos border to ensure maximum effectiveness.
>
> a. The targets are attacked in the order of ascending risk to attacking forces and are attacked at a frequency that assures that continuous and regular pressure is maintained against the DRV. Authority should be delegated to CINCPAC to select alternate weather targets from the list of previously approved targets for the eight weeks program. Subsequent weekly operations would be adjusted as appropriate when alternate targets are attacked.
>
> b. Airfields north of the 19th parallel are not scheduled for attack in the first eight weeks. However, if, during the scheduled attacks in this program, DRV or CHICOM aircraft attempt intercept of US/RVN forces, the communist air threat involved should be eliminated. The program of graduated pressures would then have reached a higher scale of escalation and would require reorientation.

The program also provided for naval gunfire bombardment and for continuation of already ongoing activity, including 34A operations, resumption of DESOTO Patrols, and authorization for ground cross border operations.

To carry out this program, the JCS wished to deploy about 325 more aircraft to the Western Pacific to deter or cope with any escalation that might result. This would include dispatch of 30 B-52's to Guam, deployment of 9 more USAF tactical fighter squadrons and a fourth aircraft carrier. Some Marine and Army units would go to Thailand, and other units would be alerted.

As for the risks of escalation, the JCS considered these as manageable:

> The Joint Chiefs of Staff believe that the DRV, Communist China, and the Soviet Union will make every effort through propaganda and diplomatic moves to halt the US attacks. The DRV also will take all actions to

defend itself, and open, overt aggression in South Vietnam and Laos by the DRV might occur. In addition, the mere initiation of the new US policy almost certainly would not lead Hanoi to restrain the Viet Cong; Hanoi would probably elect to maintain the very intense levels of activity of the past few days. However, if the United States persevered in the face of threats and international pressures, and as the degree of damage inflicted on North Vietnam increased, the chances of a reduction in Viet Cong activity would rise. They further believe that the Chinese communists would be reluctant to become directly involved in the fighting in Southeast Asia; however, as the number and severity of US attacks against the DRV increase, they probably would feel an increased compulsion to take some dramatic action to counter the impact of US pressures. There is a fair chance that Peiping would introduce limited numbers of Chinese ground forces as "volunteers" into North Vietnam, and/or northern Laos, intending to raise the specter of further escalation, to underline its commitment to assist the North Vietnamese, and to challenge the Soviets to extend corresponding support. They also believe that the probable Soviet response to these US courses of action would consist both of a vigorous diplomatic and propaganda effort to bring the United States to the conference table and the provision of military support to North Vietnam. While the extent and nature of the latter are difficult to predict, it almost certainly would include anti-aircraft artillery and radars. In order to provide a more effective defense against the US air attacks, North Vietnam would probably press for surface-to-air missiles. The chances are about even that the Soviets would agree to provide some SA-2 defenses, but they would do so in ways calculated to minimize the initial risks to them. By providing the necessary Soviet personnel in the guise of "technicians," the USSR could preserve the option of ignoring any Soviet casualties. In the event the DRV and Communist Chinese openly undertake aggressive actions, the United States and its allies can deal with them adequately. . . .

It is the opinion of the Joint Chiefs of Staff that the program herein proposed will demonstrate to the DRV that continuation of its direction and support of insurgencies will lead progressively to more serious punishment. If the insurgency continues with active DRV support, strikes against the DRV will be extended with intensified efforts against targets north of the 19th parallel.

While the Joint Chiefs recommended approval of the recommendations, not all considered them adequate. General McConnell, Air Force Chief of Staff, believed that the much heavier air strike recommendations made by the JCS in late 1964 were more appropriate than the mild actions now proposed. General Wheeler backed deployment of more USAF and other air units but pressed for an integrated air program against the North's transportation system, especially railroads. He also believed, along with General Harold K. Johnson, Army Chief of Staff, that three U.S. ground divisions might have to be sent to Southeast Asia. The JCS chairman directed the Joint Staff to examine the possibility of placing one or two of these divisions in northeast Thailand and a third, augmented by allied personnel, south of the demilitarized zone in South Vietnam. Some of these JCS recommendations were quickly accepted, particularly those having to do with Air Force deployments. Thus the Administration approved the dispatch, from 11 to 13 February, of 30 B-52's to Guam and 30 KC-135's to Okinawa. Designated Arc Light, these bombers and tankers of the Strategic Air

Command (SAC) initially were earmarked (though never used) for high-altitude, all-weather bombing of important targets in the *North*.

The particular JCS air strike program, on the other hand, was never adopted. The detailed JCS target proposals did figure prominently in the intensive highest-level reprisal and pressures planning that continued during the succeeding weeks and months, but that planning was conducted essentially on an *ad hoc* basis, strike by strike, and did not at this stage embrace a multi-week program.

VI. INITIATION OF "ROLLING THUNDER"—18 DAYS OF MANEUVER AND DELAY

A. *THE PRESIDENTIAL DECISION AND TAYLOR'S RESPONSE*

The formal Presidential decision to inaugurate what eventually emerged as the ROLLING THUNDER program was made on Sunday, February 13. It was reported to Ambassador Taylor in a NODIS cable drafted in the White House and transmitted to Saigon late that afternoon. The full text of the message follows:

> The President today approved the following program for immediate future actions in follow-up decision he reported to you in Deptel 1653. [The first FLAMING DART reprisal decision.]
>
> 1. We will intensify by all available means the program of pacification within SVN.
>
> 2. We will execute a program of measured and limited air action jointly with GVN against selected military targets in DRV remaining south of 19th parallel until further notice.
>
> FYI. Our current expectation is that these attacks might come about once or twice a week and involve two or three targets on each day of operation. END FYI.
>
> 3. We will announce this policy of measured action in general terms and at the same time, we will go to UN Security Council to make clear case that aggressor is Hanoi. We will also make it plain that we are ready and eager for "talks" to bring aggression to an end.
>
> 4. We believe this 3-part program must be concerted with GVN, and we currently expect to announce it by Presidential statement directly after next authorized air action. We believe this action should take place as early as possible next week.
>
> 5. You are accordingly instructed to seek immediate GVN agreement on this program. You are authorized to emphasize our conviction that announcement of readiness to talk is stronger diplomatic position than awaiting inevitable summons to Security Council by third parties. We would hope to have appropriate GVN concurrence by Monday [Feb 14th] if possible here.
>
> In presenting above to GVN, you should draw fully, as you see fit, on following arguments:
>
> a. We are determined to continue with military actions regardless of Security Council deliberations and any "talks" or negotiations that may ensue, unless and until North Vietnam [words missing] its aggression to an end. Our demand would be that they cease infiltration and all forms of support and also the activity they are directing in the south.
>
> b. We consider the UN Security Council initiative, following another

strike, essential if we are to avoid being faced with really damaging initiatives by the USSR or perhaps by such powers as India, France, or even the UN.

c. At an early point in the UN Security Council initiative, we would expect to see calls for the DRV to appear in the UN. If they failed to appear, as in August, this will make doubly clear that it is they who are refusing to desist, and our position in pursuing military actions against the DRV would be strengthened. For same reason we would now hope GVN itself would appear at UN and work closely with US.

d. With or without Hanoi, we have every expectation that any "talks" that may result from our Security Council initiative would in fact go on for many weeks or perhaps months and would above all focus constantly on the cessation of Hanoi's aggression as the precondition to any cessation of military action against the DRV. We further anticipate that any detailed discussions about any possible eventual form of agreement returning to the essentials of the 1954 Accords would be postponed and would be subordinated to the central issue.

For your private guidance, the following draft language is under consideration for Presidential announcement:

BEGIN QUOTE:

The aggression has continued. It has continued against the Vietnamese, and it has continued against Americans. In support of the independence of Vietnam, in the service of our nation, and in fulfillment of the solemn public obligation of our nation, and in our individual and collective self-defense, the Government of the United States, with the Government of Vietnam, has now decided that further action must be taken.

The actions we have agreed upon are three:

First and most important, we will continue and will intensify still further our campaign against terror and violence in South Vietnam itself. The establishment of civil peace and the disarming of the Communist forces are the first order of business for both our Governments. Our military and police actions will be increasingly energetic and effective. We will also strengthen and enlarge our efforts to move forward with the peaceful development of a society set free from [words illegible] the mistake of assuming that there is any substitute for victory against aggression where it shows its open face—inside the borders of South Vietnam itself.

Second—and at the same time—we will carry out measured but effective actions against military targets in North Vietnam. These actions will be reported to the United Nations Security Council under the Provisions of Article 51 of the United Nations Charter—and each such report will include a full account of the continuing acts of aggression which make our actions necessary. These actions will stop when the aggression stops.

Third, we will press with urgency for talks designed to bring an end to the aggression and its threat to peace. I have today instructed Ambassador Stevenson to seek such action urgently, in the Security Council of the United Nations, and if that body should be hamstrung by any veto, we shall then press for talks in another appropriate forum. We believe that in any such talks the first object must be an end of aggression, and we believe that the government in Hanoi must be brought to the conference room. Our common purpose—and our only purpose—is to restore the peace and domestic tranquility which others have so savagely attacked. END QUOTE

Several aspects of the message are of interest. First, it features intensified pacification as the first order of business and as a major point in the contemplated Presidential announcement. This stress on action in the South reflected a serious concern at high levels in the White House and the State Department at that time, that a growing preoccupation with action against the North would be likely to cause the US Mission and the GVN leadership to neglect the all-important struggle within the borders of South Vietnam. Second, the description of the air strike program in the message is extremely cursory, suggesting that the President at this time still wished to preserve as much flexibility as possible concerning the future scope and character of the program. And third, the message reveals the President's intention, as of that date, to take the DRV aggression issue and the US bombing response promptly before the UN Security Council—an intention that was dropped several days later in favor of a quite different approach, namely the UK/USSR Co-Chairmen initiative recounted below. In actuality, instead of mounting a major UN approach, the President contented himself initially with a brief public statement of US objectives in Vietnam, which formed the keynote of the official line, and was to be frequently quoted by Administration officials in subsequent weeks:

> As I have said so many, many times, and other Presidents ahead of me have said, our purpose, our objective there is clear. That purpose and that objective is to join in the defense and protection of freedom . . .
> We have no ambition there for ourselves. We seek no dominion. We seek no conquest. We seek no wider war. But we must all understand that we will persist in the defense of freedom and our continuing actions will be those which are justified and those that are made necessary by the continuing aggression of others.
> These actions will be measured and fitting and adequate. Our stamina and the stamina of the American people is equal to the task.

Ambassador Taylor received the news of the President's new program with enthusiasm. In his response, however, he explained the difficulties he faced in obtaining authentic GVN concurrence "in the condition of virtual non-government" which existed in Saigon at that moment. The Vietnamese Armed Forces Council had arrogated unto itself the authority of appointing the Chief of State and the Premier, and had left him to his own devices in trying to form a cabinet. Any GVN concurrence that Taylor could obtain would have to be a consensus of a lame-duck acting prime minister, a widely mistrusted military commander-in-chief, a prime-minister-designate with uncertain prospects, and assorted other power figures in a foundering caretaker government. This Alice-in-Wonderland atmosphere notwithstanding, Taylor was undaunted:

> It will be interesting to observe the effect of our proposal on the internal political situation here. I will use the occasion to emphasize that a dramatic change is occurring in U.S. policy, one highly favorable to GVN interests but demanding a parallel dramatic change of attitude on the part of the GVN. Now is the time to install the best possible government as we are clearly approaching a climax in the next few months. The U.S. Mission and the GVN will have serious problems to work out together, many of them complicated matters in the field of foreign affairs where the GVN must strengthen its professional representation. We need the first team and we need it fast.

There is just a chance that the vision of possible victory may decide Khanh to take over the government at this juncture. Alternately, it may create some measure of national unity which will facilitate the task of Quat or of any other Prime Minister who succeeds in forming a new government.

Quat's chances for creating national unity—even with the assist of an imminent "dramatic change in US policy"—were slim indeed. Quat's government was the ninth attempt to form a viable structure since the overthrow of Diem. It was obvious from the outset that it would be under the domination of the Armed Forces Council which had publicly declared that it would "act as a mediator until the government [words illegible]. The mediator himself, however, was to be rent asunder within days of Quat's assumption of office in one of these explosions that had become so typical in Vietnam since Diem's demise. That political explosion was particularly unfortunate in its timing in relation to the "dramatic" new ROLLING THUNDER program just then set to get under way.

B. *ROLLING THUNDER I IS LAID ON—AND CANCELLED*

A refinement of the February 13 decision on ROLLING THUNDER, including determination of the timing and character of the first air strike, was evidently made by the President on February 18. A NODIS cable of that date informed nine American posts in the Far East of the decisions in the following words:

Policy on Viet-Nam adopted today calls for following:
1. Joint program with GVN of continuing air and naval action against North Viet-Nam whenever and wherever necessary. Such action to be against selected military targets and to be limited and fitting and adequate as response to continuous aggression in South Viet-Nam directed in Hanoi. Air strikes will be jointly planned and agreed with GVN and carried out on joint basis.
2. Intensification by all available means of pacification program within South Viet-Nam, including every possible step to find and attack VC concentrations and headquarters within SVN by all conventional means available to GVN and US.
3. Early detailed presentation to nations of world and to public of documented case against DRV as aggressor. Forum and form this presentation not yet decided, but we do not repeat not expect to touch upon readiness for talks or negotiations at this time. We are considering reaffirmation our objectives in some form in near future.
4. Careful public statements of USG, combined with fact of continuing air action, are expected to make it clear that military action will continue while aggression continues. But focus of public attention will be kept as far as possible on DRV aggression; not on joint GVN/US military operations. There will be no comment of any sort on future actions except that all such actions will be adequate and measured and fitting to aggression. (You will have noted President's statement of yesterday, which we will probably allow to stand.)
Addressees should inform head of government or State (as appropriate) of above in strictest confidence and report reactions . . .
You may indicate that we will seek to keep governments informed, subject to security considerations, of each operation as it occurs; as we did with respect to operations of February 7 and 11.

Although the cable does not indicate it, the first air action under the new program was set for February 20th. Dubbed ROLLING THUNDER I, it called for US strikes against Quang Khe Naval Base and concurrent VNAF strikes against Vu Con Barracks, with appropriate weather alternates provided. The above cable was sent from Washington at 8:00 p.m. on February 18th. Five hours later, at 1:00 p.m., February 19 (Saigon time), Colonel Pham Ngoc Thao, a conspiratorial revolutionary figure who had been active in the coup against Diem, began his infamous semi-coup to oust General Khanh—but not to overthrow the Armed Forces Council. Aided by General Phat, his forces succeeded in occupying the ARVN military headquarters and other key government buildings in Saigon, including the radio station. Until the coup was defeated and Khanh's resignation submitted some 40 hours later, pandemonium reigned in Saigon. Ambassador Taylor promptly recommended cancellation of the February 20 air strike and his recommendation was equally promptly accepted. In a FLASH message to all recipients of the cable quoted above, Washington rescinded the instructions to notify respective heads of state until further notice "in view of the disturbed situation in Saigon."

The "disturbed situation" was not to settle down completely for almost a week. Even though the semi-coup failed quickly and the Armed Forces Council reasserted its full authority, the AFC continued the anti-Khanh momentum of the coup-plotters by adopting a "vote of no confidence" in Khanh. The latter made frantic but unsuccessful efforts to rally his supporters. Literally running out of gas in Nha Trang shortly before dawn on February 21, he submitted his resignation, claiming that a "foreign hand" was behind the coup. No one, however, could be quite certain that Khanh might not "re-coup" once again, unless he were physically removed from the scene. This took three more days to accomplish. On the afternoon of February 25, after some mock farewell performances designed to enable Khanh to save face, he left Vietnam to become an Ambassador-at-Large. At the airport to see him off and to make sure that he was safely dispatched from the country, was Ambassador Taylor, glassily polite. It was only then that Taylor was able to issue, and Washington would accept, clearance for the long postponed and frequently rescheduled first ROLLING THUNDER strike.

C. THE UK/USSR CO-CHAIRMEN GAMBIT

Political turbulence in Saigon was not the only reason for delaying the air action. Even before the semi-coup broke out, forcing cancellation of the February 20 strike, a diplomatic initiative was taken by the Soviet Foreign Office in Moscow that was eagerly picked up by London and Washington. . . .

On February 7, the UK Ambassador to Washington, Lord Harlech, informed Secretary Rusk that the Soviet Foreign Office had approached the British with the suggestion that the UK–USSR Co-Chairmanship of the 1954 Geneva Conference might be reactivated in connection with the current Vietnam crisis. Secretary Rusk described the possibilities of such a gambit in a message to Ambassador Taylor as follows:

> British apparently expect that next Soviet step might be to propose a joint statement by two Co-Chairmen on bombings in North Viet-Nam as reported to Co-Chairmen by regime in Hanoi. Interest of Soviet Government in co-chairmanship, though not yet confirmed, might also reflect some relief for Moscow regarding dilemma in which they may find themselves

in dealing with Hanoi, Peiping and Southeast Asia issues. It may prove desirable for us to provide to UK and USSR full statement of facts as we see them, US purposes in Southeast Asia and our concept of necessary solution . . . We would stop short of ourselves proposing formal systematic negotiations but assumption of 1954 co-chairmanship by two governments would imply that they might themselves explore with interested governments possibilities of solution, which we could encourage or otherwise as we see fit. If message is made to two Co-Chairmen, which would be made public, it may mean that better procedure would be to present full documentation on North Viet-Namese aggression to [U.N. Secretary General] in writing for circulation to members rather than make oral presentation in meeting of Security Council which might require Soviets to act as defense counsel for Hanoi.

Obviously, this has bearing on timing of next strike. Hope to be in touch with you within next several hours on our further reflection on this problem. Do not believe a Thursday [February 18] strike therefore feasible because of this time factor and because these possibilities have not been explored here at highest level.

With encouragement from Rusk, the British Foreign Office showed itself eager to pick up the Soviet hint. London proposed to make a formal approach to the Soviet Government, through UK Ambassador Trevelyan in Moscow. Specifically, they wished to instruct the Ambassador to propose to the Soviet Government that the Co-Chairmen of the 1954 Geneva Conference request the Governments which were members of that Conference and those represented on the International Control Commission "to furnish the Co-Chairmen without delay with a statement of their views on the situation in Viet-Nam and, in particular, on the circumstances in which they consider that a peaceful settlement could be reached.

In a further discussion with Lord Harlech on February 19, Secretary Rusk agreed to the proposed British action and Ambassador Trevelyan was duly instructed to approach the Soviet Foreign Office on February 20.

[material missing]

What were US expectations with respect to this initiative, and how did it relate to the new policy of pressures against the DRV? An excellent indication of State Department thinking on these matters at that moment is contained in an unfinished draft memorandum dated February 18, prepared by William P. Bundy and entitled "Where Are We Heading?" Because it is addressed to the relevant issues of that moment and surveys the political-diplomatic scene, it is reproduced here in full:

This memorandum examines possible developments and problems if the US pursues the following policy with respect to South Viet-Nam:

a. Intensified pacification within South Vietnam. To meet the security problem, this might include a significant increase in present US force strength.

b. A program of measured, limited, and spaced air attacks, jointly with the GVN, against the infiltration complex in the DRV. Such attacks would take place at the rate of about one a week, unless spectacular Viet Cong action dictated an immediate response out of sequence. The normal pattern of such attacks would comprise one GVN and one US strike on each occasion, confined to targets south of the 19th parallel, with variations in severity depending on the tempo of VC action, but with a slow upward trend in severity as the weeks went by.

    c. That the US itself would take no initiative for talks, but would agree to cooperate in consultations—*not* a conference—undertaken by the UK and USSR as Co-Chairmen of the Geneva Conferences. As an opening move, the British would request an expression of our views, and we would use this occasion to spell out our position fully, including our purposes and what we regard as essential to the restoration of peace. We would further present our case against the DRV in the form of a long written document to be sent to the President of the United Nations Security Council and to be circulated to members of the UN.

*   *   *   *

    1. *Communist responses.*

    a. *Hanoi* would almost certainly not feel itself under pressure at any early point to enter into fruitful negotiations or to call off its activity in any way. They would denounce the continued air attacks and seek to whip up maximum world opposition to them. Within South Viet-Nam, they might avoid spectacular actions, but would certainly continue a substantial pattern of activity along past lines, probably with incidents we have seen this week, in which Communist agents stirred up a village protest against government air attacks, and against the US. Basically, they would see the situation in South Viet-Nam as likely to deteriorate further (crumble, as they have put it), and would be expecting that at some point someone in the GVN will start secret talks with them behind our backs.

    b. *Communist China* might supply additional air defense equipment to the DRV, but we do not believe they would engage in air operations from Communist China, at least up to the point where the MIGs in the DRV were engaged and we had found it necessary to attack Fukien or possibly —if the MIGs had been moved there—Vinh.

    c. *The Soviet* would supply air defense equipment to the DRV and would continue to protest our air attacks in strong terms. However, we do not believe they would make any new commitment at this stage, and they would probably not do so even if the Chicoms became even more deeply involved—provided that we were not ourselves attacking Communist China. At that point, the heat might get awfully great on them, and they would be in a very difficult position to continue actively working as Co-Chairmen. However, their approach to the British on the Co-Chairmanship certainly suggests that they would find some relief in starting to act in that role, and might use it as a hedge against further involvement, perhaps pointing out to Hanoi that the Co-Chairman exercise serves to prevent us from taking extreme action and that Hanoi will get the same result in the end if a political track is operating and if, in fact, South Viet-Nam keeps crumbling. They might also argue to Hanoi that the existence of the political track tends to reduce the chances of the Chicoms having to become deeply involved—which we believe Hanoi does not want unless it is compelled to accept it.

    2. *Within South Viet-Nam* the new government is a somewhat better one, [Note: this was written one day before the semi-coup] but the cohesive effects of the strikes to date have at most helped things a bit. The latest MACV report indicates a deteriorating situation except in the extreme

south, and it is unlikely that this can be arrested in any short period of time even if the government does hold together well and the military go about their business. We shall be very lucky to see a leveling off, much less any significant improvement, in the next two months. In short, we may have to hang on quite a long time before we can hope to see an improving situation in South Viet-Nam—and this in turn is really the key to any negotiating position we could have at any time.

3. *On the political track* we believe the British will undertake their role with vigor, and that the Soviets will be more reserved. The Soviets can hardly hope to influence Hanoi much at this point, and they certainly have no leverage with Communist China. In the opening rounds, the Soviets will probably fire off some fairly sharp statements that the real key to the situation is for us to get out and to stop our attacks, and the opposing positions are so far apart that it is hard to see any useful movement for some time to come. We might well find the Soviets—or even the Canadians —sounding us out on whether we would stop our attacks in return for some moderation in VC activity. This is clearly unacceptable, and the very least we should hold out on is a verified cessation of infiltration (and radio silence) before we stop our attacks. Our stress on the cessation of infiltration may conceivably lead to the Indians coming forward to offer policing forces—a suggestion they have made before—and this would be a constructive move we could pick up. But, as noted above, Hanoi is most unlikely to trade on this basis for a long time to come.

4. In sum—the most likely prospect is for a prolonged period without major risks of escalation but equally without any give by Hanoi.

In retrospect, Bundy's expectations appear appropriately sober and realistic in comparison with more euphoric views held by some of his contemporaries. Particularly with respect to the Co-Chairmen gambit; his predictions were strikingly close to the mark. The British did in fact "undertake their role with vigor" and, as it turned out, the Soviets were indeed "more reserved." So much so, that the Co-Chairman initiative eventually came to naught.

At this point in time, however (in the days following February 20th), the Co-Chairman proposal was in orbit and real hopes were held out for it. Trevelyan had approached Soviet Deputy Foreign Minister Lapin with the proposal and the Soviet officials had agreed to take it under advisement, warning Trevelyan that absolute secrecy was essential. U.S. Ambassador to Moscow Foy Kohler, upon learning of the UK/Soviet undertaking, expressed his concern that the air strikes on the DRV planned for February 20 would put the Soviets on the spot, and would cause them to reject the British proposal.

Washington reassured Kohler by advising him that the scheduled strikes were being postponed and also informed him that, when rescheduled, the strikes would be tied to a major DRV aggressive act which had just come to light. It appears that, on February 16, an armed ocean-going North Vietnamese vessel, carrying large quantities of arms and ammunition, was intercepted and captured as it was infiltrating into Vung Ro Bav in South Vietnam, to deliver its cargo to the VC. By pegging the strikes primarily to that boat incident, and by directing the strikes in part against a DRV naval base, the risk of an adverse Soviet reaction would be minimized.

During the next several days, Washington was in almost continuous communication (1) with Taylor in Saigon—to ascertain whether the political situation had stabilized sufficiently to permit rescheduling the postponed air strikes;

(2) with Kohler in Moscow—to feel the pulse of the Soviet government and its likely reaction to the upcoming air operation; and (3) with Ambassador Bruce in London—to monitor the progress of the Trevelyan approach to the Soviet Foreign Office concerning the Co-Chairman process. Throughout this time, Secretary Rusk was visibly torn on the question of whether or not to proceed with the air strikes. He wanted very much to push ahead immediately, in order to exploit promptly the DRV arms ship incident which seemed to beg for some response. But he hesitated to launch a strike on behalf of and in concert with a government that was teetering and whose Commander-in-Chief was in the process of being deposed; he also wished to avoid angering the Soviets, thus possibly sabotaging their Co-Chairmen effort. On the other hand, he wanted to make it clear that the U.S. would not indefinitely accept a "unilateral ceasefire" while the Co-Chairman effort dragged on.

It is important to note that the Co-Chairmen gambit was not viewed by anyone involved on the US side as a negotiating initiative. On the contrary, every effort was made to avoid giving such an impression. Instead, the gambit was intended to provide a vehicle for the public expression of a tough U.S. position. This was clearly implied in Washington messages to Saigon and London on this issue, as, for example, in a cable from Unger to Taylor:

> You should not reveal possibility this UK/USSR gambit to GVN for time being. We naturally wish have it appear entirely as their initiative, so that our reply would not be any kind of initiative on our part and would, in its content, make clear how stiff our views are.

Finally, by February 24th, since no reply had as yet been received from Moscow and the situation in Saigon had begun to settle down, Secretary Rusk felt he could hold off no longer. In a message to Bruce in London, he wrote:

> We have decided that we must go ahead with next operation Feb. 26 unless there should be further political difficulties in Saigon. Taylor will be seeking political clearance afternoon Feb. 25 Saigon time once Khanh is off the scene.
> We told Harlech this decision today stating that while we recognized British concern and possibly some Soviet reaction we cannot even by implication get into [words illegible] continuation of program. We may hear further from London following his report but would now expect to maintain decision and indeed Taylor would probably have gone ahead on political side. If matter comes up you may of course note that we have held off five days but that British have not had any indication of Soviet response so that further delay now appeared unwise. We continue of course attach major importance to UK/Soviet gambit . . .

Confidence that the Co-Chairman initiative would pay off was beginning to wane, and the air strikes were indeed being rescheduled for February 26. A continuous readiness to launch had in fact been maintained ever since February 20, by simply postponing the strikes for 24 hours at a time and laying on new strikes whenever a change in targets or in operating rules had been decided upon. The February 26 operation was the fourth reprogramming of the strikes and thus went by the code designation ROLLING THUNDER IV, even though RT's I through III had been scratched.

Fully expecting that the February 26 air operation would go off as planned,

State sent out a cable to thirteen posts, quoting the probable text of a joint GVN/US announcement that was to be made at about 2:00 a.m. Washington time on February 26, and instructing all addressees to contact their respective host governments as soon as FLASH notification was received that the mission had in fact been executed. The execution messages however, never came. Weather over the entire target area in North Vietnam had closed in, forcing another postponement and, ultimately, cancellation of the strikes. The weather remained adverse for four more days. It was not until March 2 that the first of the new program strikes, dubbed ROLLING THUNDER V was actually carried out.

D. EFFORTS AT JUSTIFICATION AND PERSUASION

The need to communicate the new policy promptly and persuasively to the public had been recognized throughout the 1964 planning process as an essential ingredient of any graduated pressures campaign. Now the time had come to put the information and education plans into effect.

Over the weekend of February 12, serious work was begun in the State Department on the preparation of a "White Paper" on the infiltration of men and supplies from the North. Such a public report was considered essential to justifying any program of U.S. military operations against North Vietnam. The compilers of the exhibits for the public record were handicapped however, by the fact that the most persuasive evidence on DRV infiltration and support was derived from Special Intelligence sources which could not be revealed without embarrassment and detriment to other U.S. security interests. The White Paper that was submitted to the U.S. public and to the United Nations on February 27, therefore, did not make as strong a case as it might have of the extent and nature of DRV involvement in the war in the South.

Concurrently, the Administration undertook to communicate to both foreign and domestic audiences its determination to prevent Communist destruction of the Government of South Vietnam and to underline the limited character of its objectives in Southeast Asia. A series of "leaked" press analyses suggested that the most recent and the anticipated air strikes constituted a clear threat of extensive future destruction of North Vietnam's military assets and economic investments. They inferred that such consequences could be avoided if Hanoi would agree to cease its direct support of the insurgency in the South.

At the same time, privately the State Department asked the Canadian ICC representative Blair Seaborn again to act as a discreet intermediary with Hanoi, conveying to the DRV leadership the same statement on Vietnam that had been handed by U.S. Ambassador Cabot to Chicom Ambassador Wang Kuo-chuan in Warsaw on February 24, reaffirming that the United States had no designs on the territory of North Vietnam, nor any desire to destroy the DRV. On his March visit to Hanoi, Seaborn sought an appointment with Prime Minister Pham Van Dong, but was forced to settle for a meeting with the chief of the North Vietnamese Foreign Liaison Section, to whom he read the statement. This officer commented that it contained nothing new and that the North Vietnamese had already received a briefing on the Warsaw meeting from the Chicoms. The Canadian Government publicly noted in April that Seaborn had two important conversations with DRV officials in recent months, but did not go into details.

In the closing days of February and continuing through the first week of March, Secretary Rusk conducted a marathon public information campaign to explain and justify the new U.S. policy and to signal a seemingly reasonable but in fact quite tough U.S. position on negotiations. In part, the Rusk campaign was precipitated by a press conference comment by U Thant at the United Nations on February 24, implying that the U.S. had perhaps not been as zealous in its quest for peace as it might have been. Thant went so far as to assert that "the great American people, if they only knew the true facts and the background to the developments in South Vietnam, will agree with me that further bloodshed is unnecessary." The suggestion that the U.S. Government wasn't leveling with the U.S. public produced a sharp retort from Secretary Rusk:

> We have talked over the past 2 years informally and on a number of occasions with the Secretary-General . . . as well as with many governments in various parts of the world . . . But the proposals that I know about thus far have been procedural in nature. The missing piece continues to be the absence of any indication that Hanoi is prepared to stop doing what it is doing against its neighbors. . . . This question of calling a conference, under what circumstances—these are procedural matters. What we are interested in, what is needed to restore peace to Southeast Asia, is substance, content, and indication that peace is possible . . .

This and similar themes were endlessly reiterated in the ensuing days:

> The key to peace in Southeast Asia is the readiness of all in that area to live at peace and to leave their neighbors alone. . . . A negotiation aimed at the confirmation of aggression is not possible. And a negotiation which simply ends in bitterness and hostility merely adds to the danger.
> South Viet-Nam is being subjected to an aggression from the North, an aggression which is organized and directed and supplied with key personnel and equipment by Hanoi. The hard core of the Viet Cong were trained in the North and have been reinforced by North Vietnamese from the North Vietnamese army . . . Our troops would come home tomorrow if the aggressors would go north—go back home, and stay at home . . . The missing piece is the lack of an indication that Hanoi is prepared to stop doing what it is doing, and what it knows that it is doing, to its neighbors.

But when asked under what circumstances the U.S. might sit down to talk to Hanoi, Rusk was clearly as yet unwilling to appear publicly receptive:

> I am not getting into the details of what are called preconditions, because we are not at that point—we are not at that point. Almost every postwar negotiation that has managed to settle in some fashion some difficult and dangerous question has been preceded by some private indication behind the scenes that such a negotiation might be possible. That is missing here— that is missing here.

Rusk's disinterest in negotiation—except on "absolutist" terms—was, of course, in concert with the view of virtually all the President's key advisors, that the path to peace was not open. Hanoi, at about that time, held sway over more than half of her southern neighbor and could see the Saigon Government crumbling before her very eyes. The balance of power in South Vietnam simply did not furnish the United States with a reasonable basis for bargaining and the signals from Hanoi and Moscow—or lack thereof—did not encourage optimism about the sort of hard settlement the U.S. had in mind. All this pointed directly to military pressures on North Vietnam and to other urgent measures to tilt the balance of forces the other way. Until these measures could have some visible and tangible effect, talk of negotiation could be little more than a hollow exercise.

At the same time, while neither Moscow nor Hanoi seemed in the least interested in U.S. style "conciliation," the likelihood of explosive escalation also seemed remote. So far there were no signs of ominous enemy countermoves. An assessment of probable Soviet responses to the evolving U.S. "pressures" policy, cabled to the Department by Foy Kohler in Moscow, was moderately reassuring and indeed quite perceptive:

1. Soviets will make noises but not take decisive action in response to specific retaliatory strikes in southern areas DRV, probably including—after publication "White Paper"—strike against DRV sealift capabilities in this area. Indeed, Soviets likely to read our failure to continue carry out such strikes as confirmation their estimates re weakness our basic position in SVN.

2. Soviet military aid program in DRV is probably defensive in nature and Soviets would wish to keep it that way. However, if attacks on DRV become general, particularly if they are extended to industrial or urban targets and areas beyond border zone. Soviets will reassess our intent as well as basic politico-military situation. If reassessment leads them to see U.S. aim as ending existence of DRV as socialist state, Soviets will not only step up defensive aid but supply means of counterattack, e.g., aircraft for raids on SVN cities and heavy ground equipment. While aware of risk that this might bring Peiping actively into picture, Soviets will not hold back if existence of DRV seems threatened.

3. There seems no possibility of change in present hard Soviet posture at least until after March 1 CP meeting and its aftermath or until they somehow convinced of real danger of major escalation and direct confrontation.

4. Major factor underlying Soviet position is conviction that in Vietnam situation, unlike Cuban crisis, we are almost alone among allies and even U.S. public opinion seriously divided; any real and publicized improvement in this picture would correspondingly influence Soviet policy.

5. Apart their estimate as to our relative isolation, Soviet failure move toward negotiations on any basis conceivably acceptable to USG also reflects DRV and CPR posture and Moscow's unwillingness or inability to impel DRV to call off activities in SVN or yield control of territory they now hold. To extent Soviets can influence communist attitude toward negotiations, they might in face of increasingly dangerous situation decide to work toward settlement based on coalition Govt in SVN, convincing own allies that this only temporary situation.

6. Major Soviet Dilemma—[words illegible] If they consider necessary to protect position in own camp, Soviets are probably prepared to see relations with US suffer for indefinite period.

With the immediate fear of escalation thus somewhat allayed and the public concern temporarily pacified, attention began to shift toward developing ROLLING THUNDER into a more forceful continuous program.

VII.   ROLLING THUNDER BECOMES A CONTINUING PROGRAM

A.   *MCNAMARA'S CONCERN OVER COST-INEFFECTIVENESS OF STRIKES*

As has been indicated, ROLLING THUNDER was finally inaugurated, after much delay and postponement, on March 2. On that day, 104 USAF aircraft

(B-52's F-100's F-105's and refueling KC-135's) struck the Xom Bang Ammo Depot, while 19 VNAF A-1H's hit the Quang Khe Naval Base. This was the first strike on the North in which USAF aircraft played the dominant role. Although the attack was officially proclaimed "very successful," the loss of four USAF aircraft, three to antiaircraft fire, intensified earlier OSD concern over the effectiveness of the strikes and over the vulnerability of US aircraft.

Shortly after the first two February reprisal raids, the Secretary of Defense had received some disturbing bomb damage assessment reports that indicated that,

> . . . with a total of 267 sorties (including flak suppression, etc.) directed against 491 buildings, we destroyed 47 buildings and damaged 22.

The reports caused McNamara to fire off a rather blunt memorandum to the CJCS, dated 17 February 1965, which stated in part:

> Although the four missions left the operations at the targets relatively unimpaired, I am quite satisfied with the results. Our primary objective, of course, was to communicate our political resolve. This I believe we did. Future communications of resolve, however, will carry a hollow ring unless we accomplish more military damage than we have to date. Can we not better meet our military objectives by choosing different types of targets, directing different weights of effort against them, or changing the composition of the force? Surely we cannot continue for months accomplishing no more with 267 sorties than we did on these four missions.

The Chairman of the JCS promptly asked his staff to look into the matter and reported back a few days later on some initial points of interest:

> (1) We do not have sufficient or timely information about the results of the strikes;
> (2) In light of prior detailed study of the targets (94 Target Study), the weight of effort expended against at least two of them is open to question;
> (3) The weaponeering [words illegible] open to question.
> In view of these deficiencies, the CJCS continued,
> . . . I intend to ask the Joint Staff, in drafting its proposals for future strikes, to insure that the critical elements of target selection and weight of effort are evaluated as carefully as possible against specific and realistic military objectives. At the same time, I believe the commander of the operating force should have a degree of flexibility with respect to the weaponeering of the strikes and their timing. My concern here is that the operational commander be given adequate latitude to take advantage of his first-hand knowledge of the target and its defenses as well as of the changing conditions of weather and light.
> 2. I am also asking the Director, DIA, to propose a standardized and streamlined system of after-action reporting so that prompt and responsive analysis of strike results can be made available to those who require it.

Immediately after the first ROLLING THUNDER strike on March 2, Deputy Secretary of Defense Cyrus R. Vance convened a meeting attended by Air Force Secretary Eugene M. Zuckert and other USAF officials to consider using the high-flying B-52's for pattern bombing in either North or South Vietnam to avoid Communist ground fire. The Air Staff and SAC recommended reserving

B-52's for use against major targets in the North. The idea of B-52 pattern bombing was not again seriously considered until April. On the same date (March 2) Secretary McNamara asked that the Joint Staff prepare as soon as possible an analysis of US aircraft losses to hostile action in Southeast Asia. An expedited review and analysis of this subject was promptly undertaken, covering the experience in YANKEE TEAM (Reconnaissance), BARREL ROLL (Armed Reconnaissance/Interdiction), BLUE TREE (Photo Reconnaissance), PIERCE ARROW (Tonkin Gulf Reprisal), FLAMING DART and ROLLING THUNDER operations. The results were reported to the Secretary of Defense on March 10, and, aside from presenting some early and not too revealing statistical findings, the report urged that consideration be given to several measures that, the Chairman felt, might help minimize loss rates:

(1) Authorize use of NAPALM.
(2) Provide "optimum" strike ordnance not yet available in the theater.
(3) Allow the operational commander flexibility in strike timing and selection of alternate targets so as to minimize weather degradations and operational interferences at target.
(4) Conduct random and frequent weather reconnaissance and medium and low-level photo reconnaissance, over prospective strike areas of North Vietnam to reduce the likelihood of signaling our intentions.
(5) Improve security and cover and deception measures at US/VNAF air bases.

These and other measures were explored in greater depth in a USAF Study Team effort launched on March 15 and reported on in late May. Many of the recommendations to lift restrictions and improve air strike technology were being acted upon during this period and in subsequent days and weeks. For example, the restrictions on the use of FARMGATE and PACOM aircraft were lifted, permitting their use in combat operations in South Vietnam with USAF markings and without VNAF personnel aboard, effective 9 March; and use of napalm against North Vietnamese targets was approved by the President on the same date.

B.   *TAYLOR'S CONCERN OVER FEEBLE, IRRESOLUTE ACTION*

Sharp annoyance over what seemed to him an unnecessarily timid and ambivalent US stance on air strikes was expressed by Ambassador Taylor. The long delays between strikes, the marginal weight of the attacks, and the great ado about behind-the-scenes diplomatic feelers, led Taylor to complain:

> I am concerned from standpoint our overall posture vis-a-vis Hanoi and communist bloc that current feverish diplomatic activities particularly by French and British tends to undercut our ability to convey a meaningful signal to Hanoi of USG determination to stick it out here and progressively turn the screws on DRV. Seaborn's estimate of mood of confidence characterizing DRV leadership despite our joint air strikes to date almost identical our estimate . . . It appears to me evident that to date DRV eaders believe air strikes at present levels on their territory are meaningless and that we are more susceptible to international pressure for negotiations than are they. Their estimate may be based in part on activities of "our friends" to which we seem to be active party.

In my view current developments strongly suggest that we follow simultaneously two courses of action: (1) attempt to apply brakes to British and others in their headlong dash to conference table and leave no doubt in their minds that we do not intend to go to conference table until there is clear evidence Hanoi (and Peking) prepared to leave neighbors alone; and (2) step up tempo and intensity of our air strikes in southern part of DRV in order convince Hanoi [words missing] face prospect of progressively severe punishment. I fear that to date ROLLING THUNDER in their eyes has been merely a few isolated thunder claps.

The same general considerations apply re our urging British to undertake further early soundings re Article 19 Laos Accords as Ambassador Martin so cogently states in his EXDIS 1278 to Dept. [in which Martin expresses concern over the risks of moving to the conference table too soon]. Many of the problems which worry him are also applicable to Vietnamese here and I share his reasoning and concern.

It seems to me that we may be in for a tough period ahead but I would hope we will continue to do whatever is required and that we try to keep fundamental objectives vis-a-vis Hanoi clear and simple.

In a separate cable of the same date, Taylor, with General Westmoreland's explicit concurrence, offered his specific recommendations for increasing the tempo and intensity of the air strikes. In effect, he called for a more dynamic schedule of strikes, a several week program relentlessly marching North to break the will of the DRV:

We have a sense of urgent need for an agreed program for the measured and limited air action against military targets in DRV [previously] announced. The rate of once or twice a week for attacks involving two or three targets on each day appears to us reasonable as to frequency, and leaves open the possibility of increasing the effect on Hanoi by adding to the weight of the strikes (in types of ordnance and sorties per target) and by moving northward up the target system. What seems to be lacking is an agreed program covering several weeks which will combine the factors, frequency, weight and location of attack into a rational pattern which will convince the leaders in Hanoi that we are on a dynamic schedule which will not remain static in a narrow zone far removed from them and the sources of their power but which is a moving growing threat which cannot be ignored.

I have seen the JCS proposed eight-week program which has much to recommend it but, I believe, remains too long South of the 19th parallel. [It is] Seaborn's opinion that Hanoi has the impression that our air strikes are a limited attempt to improve our bargaining position and hence are no great cause for immediate concern. Our objective should be to induce in DRV leadership an attitude favorable to US objectives in as short a time as possible in order to avoid a build-up of international pressures to negotiate. But our efforts to date are falling far short of anticipated necessary impact. In formulating a more effective program of future attacks, I would be inclined to keep the rate as indicated, maintain the weight on target as for recent strikes, but begin at once a progression of US strikes North of 19th parallel in a slow but steadily ascending movement. The targets in the area South thereof could be reserved largely for VNAF and FARMGATE. It is true that the MIG threat will grow as we move North but we have the means to take care of it. If we tarry too long in the South, we will give Hanoi a weak and misleading signal which will work against our ultimate purpose. General Westmoreland concurs.

Taylor's dissatisfaction with the tempo of the air campaign was by no means mitigated by the decision to launch the next scheduled attack, ROLLING THUNDER VI on March 13, as another isolated, stage-managed joint US/GVN operation. Notification of the decision to strike came to him in the following FLASH message:

Decision has been taken here to execute ROLLING THUNDER VI during daylight hours Saturday 13 March Saigon time. If weather precludes effective strike Phu Qui ammo depot (Target 40) on this date, US portion of ROLLING THUNDER VI will be postponed until 14 March Saigon time or earliest date weather will permit effective US strike of Target 40. However if US strike weathered out, VNAF strike (with US support) on its own primary or alternate targets is still authorized to go. Request you solicit Quat's agreement this arrangement.

If joint US/GVN strike goes . . . would expect GVN/US press announcement be made in Saigon. NMCC has furnished time of launch in past and this has proven eminently satisfactory. Will continue this arrangement.

If US strike weathered out and GVN strike goes, recommend that GVN make brief unilateral press statement which would not detract from already agreed US/GVN statement, which we would probably wish use at time of US strike against Target 40. GVN unilateral press announcement should indicate strike made by GVN aircraft supported by US aircraft. Would hope that announcement, although brief, could also mention target, identifying it as military installation associated with infiltration.

Request reply by flash cable.

Washington's anticipation that the strike might be weathered out proved correct, and Taylor's pique at the further delay is reflected in his reply:

As reported through military channels, VNAF is unable to fly today. Hence, there will be no ROLLING THUNDER Mission and no present need to see Quat. I am assured that VNAF will be ready to go tomorrow, 14 March.

With regard to the delays of ROLLING THUNDER VI, I have the impression that we may be attaching too much importance to striking target 40 because of its intrinsic military value as a target. If we support the thesis (as I do) that the really important target is the will of the leaders in Hanoi, virtually any target North of the 19th parallel will convey the necessary message at this juncture as well as target 40. Meanwhile, through repeated delays we are failing to give the mounting crescendo to ROLLING THUNDER which is necessary to get the desired results.

When the strike finally came off, however, on March 14 and 15, it was the most forceful attack on the North launched to date. 24 VNAF A1-H's supported by US flak, CAP and pathfinder aircraft, struck weapon installations, depots, and barracks on Tiger Island, 20 miles off the North Vietnamese coast, and more than 100 US aircraft (two-thirds Navy, one-third USAF) hit the ammunition depot near Phu Qui, only 100 miles southwest of Hanoi. Some of the earlier hesitancy about bombing the North was beginning to wear off.

C. PRESIDENT'S CONCERN OVER INSUFFICIENT PRESSURE IN SOUTH VIETNAM

While attention was being increasingy focused on pressures against the North, disturbing assessments continued to come to the President's attention concerning developments in the South. One such estimate was Westmoreland's analysis, dated February 25, of the military situation in the four corps area. It was essentially in agreement with a grave CIA appraisal issued the same day. Observing that the pacification effort had virtually halted, Westmoreland foresaw in six months a Saigon government holding only islands of strength around provincial and district capitals that were clogged with refugees and beset with "end the war" groups asking for a negotiated settlement. The current trend presaged a Viet Cong takeover in 12 months, althought major towns and bases, with U.S. help, could hold out for years. To "buy time," permit pressure on North Vietnam to take effect, and reverse the decline, he proposed adding three Army helicopter companies, flying more close support and reconnaissance missions, opening a "land line" from Pleiku in the highlands to the coast, and changing U.S. policy on the use of combat troops.

There was now real concern at the highest Administration level that the Vietnamese military effort might collapse in the South before pressures on the North could have any significant impact. On March 2, therefore, the President decided to dispatch Army Chief of Staff General Harold K. Johnson to Saigon with a high-ranking team. In an exclusive message for Ambassador Taylor, Secretary McNamara described General Johnson's mission as follows:

> After meeting with the President this morning, we believe it wise for General Johnson to go to Saigon to meet with you and General Westmoreland . . . Purpose of trip is to examine with you and General Westmoreland what more can be done within South Vietnam. He will bring with him a list of additional actions which has been developed for your consideration. Would appreciate your developing a similar list for discussion with him. In developing list, you may, of course, assume no limitation on funds, equipment or personnel. We will be prepared to act immediately and favorably on any recommendations you and General Johnson may make. The President is continuing to support such action against North as is now in progress but does not consider such actions a substitute for additional action within South Vietnam. The President wants us to examine all possible additional actions—political, military, and economic—to see what more can be done in South Vietnam . . .

General Johnson returned from his survey mission on March 14 with a 21-point program which he submitted to the JCS and the Secretary of Defense and which was reviewed by the President on March 15. General Johnson's recommendations included but went beyond Westmoreland's prescriptions. With respect to the use of air power in South Vietnam, he proposed more helicopters and 0–1 aircraft, possibly more USAF fighter-bombers (after further MACV evaluation), better targeting, and accelerated airfield expansion. These proposals were in keeping with recommendations that had been made previously by COMUSMACV, and especially insistently by CINCPAC, to expand the use of US airpower in SVN. For example, on February 26, in an exclusive message to General Wheeler, Admiral Sharp had written: ". . . the single most important thing we can do to improve the security situation in South Vietnam is to make full use of our airpower.

For Laos, General Johnson favored reorienting BARREL ROLL operations to allow air strikes on infiltration routes in the Lao Panhandle to be conducted as a separate program from those directed against the Pathet Lao and North Vietnamese units. This program was subsequently authorized under the nickname STEEL TIGER (see below, p. 341).

With respect to air action against the North, the Army Chief of Staff made two recommendations (designated as points 5 and 6 in his 21-point program):

5. Increase the scope and tempo of US air strikes against the DRV. This action could tend to broaden and escalate the war. However, it could accomplish the US objective of causing the DRV to cease its support and direction of the Viet Cong aggression. To date, the tempo of punitive air strikes has been inadequate to convey a clear sense of US purpose to the DRV.

6. Remove self-imposed restrictions on the conduct of air strikes against North Vietnam which have severely reduced their effectiveness and made it impossible to approach the goal of 4 missions per week. Restrictions which should be lifted are:

a. Requirement that a US strike be conducted concurrently with a VNAF strike.

b. Requirement that US aircraft strike the primary target only.

c. Ban on use of classified munitions.

d. Narrow geographical limitations imposed on target selection.

e. Requirement to obtain specific approval from Washington before striking alternate targets when required by adverse weather conditions or other local conditions.

After reviewing these recommendations, the President approved most of General Johnson's program. In regard to the air strikes against the North, the President authorized important new actions, as subsequently described by the JCS:

Action (paras 5 & 6): The scope and tempo of air strikes against NVN is being increased in current plans. Depots, LOCs, and air defense ground environment facilities will be stressed in operations in the near future. The requirement for concurrent US–VNAF strikes has been removed. Only prime targets will be designated as primary or alternates for US aircraft, thus lifting restriction in 6b above. Greater timing flexibility will be provided for weather and other delays. Tactical reconnaissance has been authorized at medium level for targets south of the 20th parallel to support the expanded program. Specific recommendations on para 6c, quoted above, are requested. Restrictions in 6d and e, quoted above, have been lifted in ROLLING THUNDER SEVEN and will so remain in subsequent programs.

The Presidential decision marked a major turning point in the ROLLING THUNDER operation. Air action against the North was being transformed from a sporadic, halting effort into a regular and determined program.

D.   ROLLING THUNDER VII—ENTER "REGULARITY"
AND "DETERMINATION"

The March 15 Presidential guidelines were clearly reflected in the instructions that Washington sent Saigon describing the new character of ROLLING THUN-

DER to begin with RT VII [words illegible] the instructions contain at least six novel ideas:

    (1) The strikes were to be packaged in a week's program at a time;
    (2) precise timing of the strikes were to be left to field commanders;
    (3) the requirement for US–VNAF simultaneity was to be dropped;
    (4) the strikes were no longer to be specifically related to VC atrocities;
    (5) publicity on the strikes was to be progressively reduced; and
    (6) the impression henceforth to be given was one of regularity and determination.

Here is the full text of the Secretary of State's message to Ambassador Taylor, describing the new program:

Having in mind considerations raised your reftel [Taylor's Saigon 2889 of March 8th,] and recommendations of General Johnson following his return, longer range program of action against North Viet Nam has been given priority consideration here and program for first week for ROLLING THUNDER VII, has been decided, for execution this week. Details this program which includes one US and one VNAF strike together with one US and two VNAF route armed recce is subject of instructions being sent through military channels. You will note these instructions leave to military commands in field decisions as to specific timing within period covered. Execution of first action under ROLLING THUNDER VII may take place anytime from daylight March 19 Saigon time. Although program contains full measure VNAF participation, requirement that US and VNAF operations proceed simultaneously is dropped.

You are requested to see Pri Min ASAP in order to outline to him this further program we have in mind and to solicit GVN participation as specified therein. You should convey to PriMin that proposed program, on which you will be providing him with further information in successive weeks, is designed to maintain pressure on Hanoi and persuade North Vietnamese regime that costs of continuing their aggression becoming unacceptably high. At same time Quat should understand we continue seek no enlargement of struggle and have carefully selected targets with view to avoiding undesirable provocation. Further objective is to continue reassure Government and people [words missing] and will continue fight by their side and we expect they will also be making maximum efforts in South Viet Nam where a real setback to Viet Cong would do more than perhaps anything else to persuade Hanoi stop its aggression.

With initiation ROLLING THUNDER VII we believe publicity given US and VNAF strikes should be progressively reduced, although in its place there should be picture of GVN and US pursuing with regularity and determination program against the North to enable South restore its independence and integrity and defend itself from aggression from North. Larger strikes (ROLLING THUNDER VII A and VII B) be announced as before but suggest in future that such announcements not contain references to Viet Cong atrocities, etc. Instead, these matters, which should get full attention, might be subject of separate and perhaps regular press briefings by GVN with full US support.

As regards route recce, we question whether we should take initiative to announce these missions since this could contribute to impression of substantial increase in activity. At same time we presume reporters will get wind of these missions, Hanoi will report them and VNAF may not wish maintain silence. Therefore seems difficult avoid replying to inevitable press questions. Request PIO meeting opening tomorrow Honolulu to look into this one and give us and Saigon its recommendations; possibility it should consider passing off all route recce missions in low key replies to queries as "routine recce."

ROLLING THUNDER had thus graduated to the status of a regular and continuing program. What now remained to be more carefully re-examined—though hardly resolved—was the problem of target emphasis.

VIII.   TARGET RATIONALE SHIFTS TOWARD INTERDICTION

Late February and early March, 1965 saw a significant refocusing of target emphasis. Up to that time—in the initial U.S. reprisal strikes and the first ROLLING THUNDER actions—target selection had been completely dominated by political and psychological considerations. Paramount in the Administration's target choices were such complex and often conflicting objectives as boosting the GVN's morale, evidencing the firmness of U.S. resolve, demonstrating the potential for inflicting pain upon the DRV, providing a legal rationale for our actions, and so forth. Relatively little weight was given to the purely physical or more directly military and economic implications of whatever target destruction might be achieved.

With the gradual acceptance, beginning in March, of the need for a militarily more significant, sustained bombing program, serious attention began to be paid to the development of a target system or systems that would have a more tangible and coherent military rationale. The first and most obvious candidate for such a target concept was that of interdicting the flow of men and supplies into South Vietnam by striking the lines of communication (LOC's) of the DRV. Since North Vietnamese "aggression" was the principal legal justification for U.S. bombing raids upon the DRV, attacking and impeding the visible manifestations of this aggression—the infiltration—also seemed logical and attractive from this international legality point of view.

The Secretary of Defense's attention was called to this target concept as early as 13 February, when the Joint Chiefs briefed McNamara in the Chairman's office on an analysis of the southern portion of the North Vietnamese railway system. It was pointed out in the briefing that South of the 20th parallel there exists about 115 miles of operable rail systems and that the vulnerable points on this southern portion of the system are five bridges of 300 feet or greater length and the railway classification yards at Vinh. It was argued that the bridges were very lightly defended and that only the rail yards at Vinh would pose any serious anti-aircraft defense problem. The CJCS felt that:

> There is no doubt but that the six targets mentioned comprise an attractive, vulnerable and remunerative target system which would hurt the North Vietnamese psychologically, economically and militarily. As regards the latter, the destruction of the southern bridge system would hamper and delay the movement of DRV/CHICOM ground forces to the south and, likewise, would place a stricture on the quantities of materiel and personnel which can be infiltrated through Laos and South Vietnam. A minimum of 201 strike sorties would be required to attack with a high degree of assurance

the six targets simultaneously which would be militarily the most desirable timing of attack.

In a follow-up memorandum, the CJCS forwarded to the Secretary of Defense a DIA analysis of VC attacks on the *South* Vietnamese railway system during 1963 and 1964, and indicated his concurrence with Ambassador Taylor that these attacks justified US/GVN strikes against the rail system in North Vietnam. The CJCS then added the following recommendation:

> As discussed with you on 13 February, while I strongly recommend that we attack the North Vietnamese rail system as soon as possible, I would recommend against first striking the southern elements thereof. Should we do so I would anticipate that the DRV would take both passive and active defense measures to protect rolling stock and bridges and, probably, would start work on train ferries or truck by-passes in order to ameliorate the effects of our strike. As pointed out earlier I would advocate militarily that the entire southern segment of the rail system be struck simultaneously. Should this be politically objectionable, I would recommend that two northern targets—Dong Phuong rail/highway bridge and Thanh Hoa bridge (prestige bridge)—be the first targets attacked in order to trap the maximum quantity of rolling stock south of the 20th parallel where we could destroy it at least.

The Secretary of Defense responded to this recommendation by inviting the JCS to develop a detailed plan for an integrated attack on the DRV rail system south of the 20th parallel, with the option of attacking the targets individually on an incremental basis rather than all at once. This request set in motion a planning effort by the Joint Staff and by U.S. military commands in the Pacific area, and gave rise to spirited discussions and recommendations that culminated at the end of March in the submission of the JCS 12-week bombing program, essentially built around the LOC interdiction concept.

General Westmoreland, with Ambassador Taylor's concurrence, strongly endorsed the interdiction rationale in mid-March. In a LIMDIS cable to Admiral Sharp and General Wheeler, he called attention to the mounting VC attacks on transportation targets in *South* Vietnam, and argued that:

> The Viet Cong's intensive efforts against lines of communications would make strikes against DRV LOC's highly appropriate at this time. In view heavy traffic recently reported moving south, such strikes would also be military desirable. Moreover, these attacks by interrupting the flow of consumer goods to southern DRV would carry to the NVN man in the street, with minimum loss of civilian life, the message of U.S. determination. Accordingly, early initiation of ROLLING THUNDER strikes and armed reconnaissance is recommended against DRV [words missing]

Counter-infiltration operations also received a boost from the recommendation in General Johnson's report to the effect that BARREL ROLL be re-oriented to increase its military effectiveness against Lao Panhandle infiltration routes into South Vietnam. Acting upon that recommendation and upon a Presidential directive to make a maximum effort to shut off infiltration into SVN, a new program, nicknamed STEEL TIGER, was developed, for the conduct of greatly intensified air operations against routes and targets in Laos associated with infiltration.

At about the same time, a Pacific Command study group developed a more comprehensive concept of air operations "to attrit, harass, and interdict the DRV south of 20 degrees." In a lengthy cable to the Joint Chiefs excerpted below, Admiral Sharp described the concept as follows:

> The program calls for an integrated strike, armed recce and recce program designed to cut, in depth, the NVN logistic network south of 20 degrees, and to continually attrit and harass by-pass and repair reconstitution efforts.
>
> This program provides for primary bridge/ferry cuts and highway blockage/take out cuts on major long-haul road and rail routes. It additionally cuts the full road network including all feeder and by-pass routes which develop into 4 main entry/funnels to Laos and SVN. All targets selected are extremely difficult or impossible to by-pass. The program also provides for concurrent disruption of the sea-carry to SVN with strikes against suspect coastal staging points supporting end-running shipping into the area, as well as SVN.
>
> LOC network cutting in this depth will degrade tonnage arrivals at the main "funnels" and will develop a broad series of new targets such as backed-up convoys, off-loaded materiel dumps, and personnel staging areas at one or both sides of cuts. Coupling these strikes with seeding and re-seeding missions to hamper repairs, wide ranging armed recce missions against "developed" targets, and coastal harass and attrit missions against coastal staging facilities, may force major DRV log flow to sea-carry and into surveillance and attack by our SVN coastal sanitization forces . . .
>
> In summary: recommend concerted attacks against LOC targets recommended herein be initiated concurrently with interdiction targets programmed for ROLLING THUNDER 9-13. Preferentially, recommend a compressed "LOC cut program" similar to my proposal for a "Radar Busting Day." This should be followed by completion of attacks on other than LOC targets in ROLLING THUNDER 10-13, Phase II armed recce would be conducted concurrently with these actions and would be continued indefinitely to make DRV support to the VC in SVN and PL/VM in Laos as difficult and costly as possible.

As these recommendations reached the JCS, the Joint Chiefs were intensely pre-occupied with an interservice division over the issue of the nature and extent of proposed large-scale U.S. troop deployments to South Vietnam, requiring adjudication among at least 10 separate proposals, and among widely differing views of the several Service Chiefs. There were also substantial differences over the future character of the bombing program. On this latter issue, Air Force Chief of Staff General McConnell took a maverick position, opting for a 28-day air program against North Vietnam to destroy all targets on the 94-target list. He proposed beginning the air strikes in the southern part of North Vietnam and continuing at two- to six-day intervals until Hanoi itself was attacked. "While I support appropriate deployment of ground forces in South Vietnam," McConnell wrote, "it must be done in concert with [an] overall plan to eliminate the source of [the] insurgency." McConnell believed that his proposal was consistent with previous JCS views on action against the North and would be a strong deterrent against open Chinese intervention.

General McConnell withdrew his 28-day proposal from JCS consideration when it became apparent that the Joint Chiefs were inclined to accept much of the CINCPAC recommendation for a "LOC-cut program" as summarized above, and to incorporate some of McConnell's concepts in a 12-week air strike program that the Joint Staff was preparing in response to the Secretary of Defense's request and in accordance with his guidance. The JCS 12-week program was briefed to the Secretary of Defense conceptually on March 22 and submitted to him formally on March 27 under cover of a JCS memorandum of that date.

The program is described in a detailed Annex to the memorandum as follows:

1. *Concept.* The concept, simply stated, is to conduct an air strike program during the remaining 10 weeks of a 12-week program which increases in intensity and severity of damage over the period. The program can be considered in four phases.

a. The initial phase consists of a three-week interdiction campaign against the vulnerable Democratic Republic of Vietnam (DRV) LOCs south of the 20th parallel. The concept of this campaign is to conduct strikes against a number of interrelated but separated choke points which will disrupt the flow of military supplies and equipment and tax the DRV capability to restore these facilities. Essential to the success of this phase is the initial attacks on targets No. 14 and 18. The dropping of at least one span in either and preferably both of these bridges will sever the main north-south railroad and highway routes in sufficient depth for an effective follow-on program. This initial action would be accompanied by an intense armed reconnaissance mission to destroy the isolated transport equipment. Subsequent strikes against choke points throughout the isolated area are designed to make the program effective and to complicate the DRV recovery program. Day and night armed reconnaissance would be conducted at random intervals to harass these recovery efforts and to sustain the interdiction, including armed reconnaissance against junk traffic over sea LOCs. This initial program should bring home to the population the effects of air strikes since consumer good will be competing with military supplies for the limited transport. An effective interdiction in this area will also impede the DRV capability to mass sizeable military forces and to deploy air defense resources. The remaining few installation targets in this area would be left for later strikes by VNAF. Also, the interdiction in this area would be sustained by VNAF as US strikes moved to the north.

b. The second phase, the launching of the interdiction campaign north of the 20th parallel, introduces a consideration which was not a major factor in the campaign in the southern DRV; i.e., the possibility of MIG intervention as strikes are made against targets progressively closer to the Hanoi–Haiphong area. In order to reduce this possibility to a minimum, the first week of air operations north of the 20th parallel includes strikes against the radar net in the delta area to blind or minimize DRV early warning and intercept capability. Following these preparatory attacks, operations against the LOCs north of the 20th parallel are scheduled with the primary objective of isolating the DRV from external overland sources; i.e., rail and highway supply routes from Communist China. Subsequent to cutting these primary LOCs, the initial phase of the interdiction campaign would be completed by striking LOC targets in depth throughout the area of the DRV north of the 20th parallel.

c. Having completed the primary interdiction program in the delta area, a substantially lower effort should maintain its effectiveness. With his overland LOC cut, blocked, and harassed, the enemy can be expected to turn more and more to his port facilities and sea LOC. The ninth week air strikes will include attacks against these port facilities and the mining of seaward approaches to block the enemy from relieving his resupply problems over the sea LOC. Strikes will be initiated during the tenth week against ammunition and supply dumps to destroy on-hand stores of supplies and equipment to further aggravate his logistic problems.

d. In the wind-up phase of the 12-week program (during the eleventh and twelfth week), strikes against on-hand supplies, equipment, and military facilities will be continued, attacking remaining worth-while targets throughout the DRV. As a part of this phase, industrial targets outside of population areas will be struck, leading up to a situation where the enemy must realize that the Hanoi and Haiphong areas will be the next logical targets in our continued air campaign.

2. [The program includes] an anti-MIG strike package; however, as provided in the policy guidance furnished the Joint Chiefs of Staff, this mission will not be executed unless the DRV MIG aircraft are able to impair the effectiveness of the strike forces. Combat air patrol aircraft, in sufficient numbers to deter MIG attack, will accompany all missions and will engage these DRV aircraft as required to protect the force. Strike forces and armed reconnaissance aircraft may persist in their missions but other reconnaissance missions will break off mission to avoid contact with MIG aircraft if feasible. Heavily populated areas will be avoided by both strike and armed reconnaissance missions.

3. Strike sorties for the next ten weeks would total approximately 3,000 or roughly 300 per week. CINCPAC has reported a capability to conduct approximately 1,600 strike sorties per week on a sustained basis. This leaves ample margin for US air support within South Vietnam and Laos and substantial armed reconnaissance to sustain the LOC interdiction . . .

Interestingly, the Joint Chiefs did *not* endorse the entire air strike program they submitted to the Secretary of Defense. They recommended that only the first phase (third, fourth, and fifth weeks of the program) be approved for execution. They had evidently failed to reach agreement on the later phases (weeks six through twelve), and indicated to the Secretary of Defense that they were still in the process of "considering alternatives for a follow-on program of air strikes beginning with the sixth week. They will advise you further in this regard, taking account of the developing situation, the current policy considerations, and military measures available to us."

As matters developed, however, even the three-week program endorsed by the JCS was not approved by the Secretary of Defense, 'though it strongly influenced the new interdiction-oriented focus of the attacks that were to follow, as well as the particular targets that were selected. But neither the Secretary of Defense nor the President was willing to approve a multi-week program in advance. They clearly preferred to retain continual personal control over attack concepts and individual target selection. Consequently, although the Joint Chiefs strongly urged that "the field commander be able to detect and exploit targets of opportunity . . . ," action in the air war against the DRV continued to be directed at the highest level and communicated through weekly guidance provided by the Secretary of Defense's ROLLING THUNDER planning messages.

IX. REASSESSMENT AS OF APRIL 1 AND THE NSAM 328
DECISIONS

A. THE SITUATION IN SOUTH VIETNAM

A curious phenomenon concerning the period of late March and early April 1965 was the great divergence among views that were being expressed about the then prevailing state of affairs in South Vietnam. Some quite favorable assessments emanated from Saigon. For example, MACV's Monthly Evaluations for March and April were most reassuring:

> *March, 1965:* Events in March were encouraging . . . RVNAF ground operations were highlighted by renewed operational effort . . . VC activity was considerably below the norm of the preceding six months and indications were that the enemy was engaged in the re-supply and re-positioning of units possibly in preparation for a new offensive . . . In summary, March has given rise to some cautious optimism. The current government appears to be taking control of the situation and, if the present state of popular morale can be sustained and strengthened, the GVN, with continued U.S. support, should be able to counter future VC offensives successfully.
> *April, 1965:* Friendly forces retained the initiative during April and a review of events reinforces the feeling of optimism generated last month . . . In summary, current trends are highly encouraging and *the GVN may have actually turned the tide at long last.* However, there are some disquieting factors which indicate a need to avoid overconfidence. A test of these trends should be forthcoming in the next few months if the VC launch their expected counter-offensive and the period may well be one of the most important of the war.

Similarly encouraging comments were contained in Ambassador Taylor's NODIS weeklies to the President—e.g., in Saigon 2908, March 11, 1965:

> The most encouraging phenomenon of the past week has been the rise in Vietnamese morale occasioned by the air strikes against North Vietnam on March 2, the announcement of our intention to utilize U.S. jet aircraft within South Vietnam, and the landing of the Marines at Danang which is still going on. The press and the public have reacted most favorably to all three of these events.

And in Saigon 2991, March 17, 1965:

> With the growing pressure on North Vietnam, the psychological atmosphere continues to be favorable. What is still missing in this new atmosphere is the image of a Vietnamese Government giving direction and purpose to its [words missing].

On the other hand, a much more sobering assessment was contained in General Westmoreland's *Commander's Estimate of the Situation in South Vietnam,* dated 26 March 1965, which bluntly asserted that RVNAF would not be able to build up their strength rapidly and effectively enough to blunt the coming VC

summer offensive or to seize the initiative from them. The document also estimated that the program of air activity against the North, while it might ultimately succeed in causing the DRV to cease its support of the war, would not
in the short run have any major effect on the situation in the South.

The view from Washington was even less hopeful. Assistant Secretary of Defense John McNaughton summed up the situation in the following words:

> The situation in general is bad and deteriorating. The VC have the initia-
> tive. Defeatism is gaining among the rural population, somewhat in the
> cities, and even among the soldiers—especially those with relatives in rural
> areas. The Hop Tac area around Saigon is making little progress; the Delta
> stays bad; the country has been severed in the north. GVN control is
> shrinking to enclaves, some burdened with refugees. In Saigon we have a
> remission: Quat is giving hope on the civilian side, the Buddhists have
> calmed, and the split generals are in uneasy equilibrium.

A more complete and balanced overview was prepared by McGeorge Bundy
in a memorandum outlining "Key Elements for Discussion" for an April 1
meeting with the President:

> Morale has improved in South Vietnam. The government has not really
> settled down, but seems to be hopeful both in its capacity and in its sense
> of political forces. The armed forces continue in reasonably good shape,
> though top leadership is not really effective and the ratio of armed forces
> to the VC build-up is not good enough.
>
> The situation in many areas of the countryside continues to go in favor
> of the VC, although there is now a temporary lull. The threat is particu-
> larly serious in the central provinces, and the VC forces may be regrouping
> for major efforts there in the near future.
>
> Hanoi has shown no signs of give, and Peiping has stiffened its position
> within the last week. We still believe that attacks near Hanoi might sub-
> stantially raise the odds of Peiping coming in with air. Meanwhile, we
> expect Hanoi to continue and step up its infiltration both by land through
> Laos and by sea. There are clear indications of different viewpoints in
> Hanoi, Peiping, and Moscow (and even in the so-called Liberation Front),
> and continued sharp friction between Moscow and Peiping. However,
> neither such frictions nor the pressure of our present slowly ascending pace
> of air attack on North Vietnam can be expected to produce a real change
> in Hanoi's position for some time, probably 2–3 months, at best.
>
> A key question for Hanoi is whether they continue to make real headway
> in the south, or whether the conflict there starts to move against them or
> at least appear increasingly tough. If the former, even a major step-up in
> our air attacks would probably not cause them to become much more rea-
> sonable; if the latter, the situation might begin to move on a political track
> —but again in not less than 2–3 months, in our present judgment.

B. INTERNATIONAL DIPLOMATIC MOVES

On the diplomatic front, there had been no indication of any desire for talks
from Hanoi, Peking, or Moscow. The British Co-Chairmen initiative had been
turned down by the Soviet Goverment, which first floated a totally unacceptable
counterproposal—in the form of a statement condemning the U.S. "gross violation of the Geneva Accords" and calling on the U.S. "to immediately cease their
aggressive acts against the DRV and to withdraw their troops . . ."—and then

totally rejected the British proposal. By March 16, when Gromyko met with UK Foreign Secretary Michael Stewart in London, it had become quite clear that the two Geneva Co-Chairmen would not be able to agree on a message sufficiently objective to be mutually acceptable to other members of the Conference. Gromyko had made a public statement after the meeting in London to the effect that the United States would have to deal directly with Hanoi on the Vietnam situation, to which Secretary Rusk had replied.

> I agree with Mr. Gromyko that Hanoi is the key to peace in Southeast Asia. If Hanoi stops molesting its neighbors, then peace can be restored promptly and U.S. forces can come home. I regret that the Soviet Union, which was a signatory of the 1954 and 1962 accords, appears disinclined to put its full weight behind those agreements.

A second initiative had been launched by President Tito of Yugoslavia in early March. Tito had written to President Johnson on March 3, urging immediate negotiations on Vietnam without either side imposing conditions. The President had replied on March 12, describing the background of our involvement in Vietnam and stating that there would be no bar to a peaceful settlement if Hanoi ceased "aggression against South Vietnam."

Tito's concern prompted him to convene a conference of 15 nonaligned nations which met in Belgrade from March 13 to 18. The resulting declaration blamed "foreign intervention in various forms" for the aggravation of the Vietnam situation and repeated Tito's call for negotiations without preconditions.

Yet another third-party peace initiative came from U.N. Secretary General U Thant. U Thant proposed a three-month period in which there would be "a temporary cessation of all hostile military activity, whether overt or covert, across the 17th parallel in Vietnam."

McGeorge Bundy commented on these propositions in his April 1 "Key Elements for Discussion" Memorandum in a manner suggesting that he had very little expectation that any of these initiatives would lead to an early conference:

> We think the U Thant proposal should be turned off. (Bunche tells us U Thant will not float it publicly if we reject it privately). It is not clear that the trade-off would be to our advantage, even if it could be arranged, and in any case, we prefer to use U Thant for private feelers rather than public proposals. We can tell U Thant that we have no objection on his sounding out Hanoi on this same point, however, and that if he gets a response, we would ge glad to comment on it.
>
> The 17 nation proposal is more attractive. We are inclined to propose to Quat that both South Vietnam and the U.S. should accept it with a covering statement of our good, firm, clear objectives in any such negotiation. The President has already made it clear that he will go anywhere to talk with anyone, and we think the 17 nation proposal is one to which we can make a pretty clear response. Tactically, it will probably not lead to any early conference, because the position of Hanoi and Peking will be that they will not attend any meeting until our bombings stop. The Secretary of State will elaborate on these propositions.

C. AN END TO "REPRISAL"

In mid-morning of March 29, VC terrorists exploded a bomb outside the U.S. embassy in Saigon, killing and wounding many Americans and Vietnamese. It was the boldest and most direct Communist action against the U.S. since the attacks at Pleiku and Qui Nhon which had precipitated the FLAMING DART reprisals. Almost simultaneously, Ambassador Taylor enplaned for talks in Washington—and both cities were instantly abuzz with speculation that the war had entered a new and perhaps critical phase.

Indeed, Admiral Sharp promptly urged the JCS to make a forceful reply to the VC outrage [words missing] spectacular bombing attack upon a significant target in the DRV outside of the framework of ROLLING THUNDER. The plea, however, did not fall on responsive ears. At this point, the President preferred to maneuver quietly to help the nation get used to living with the Vietnam crisis. He played down any drama intrinsic in Taylor's arrival by having him attend briefings at the Pentagon and the State Department before calling at the White House; and he let it be known that the U.S. had no intention of conducting any further specific reprisal raids against North Vietnam in reply to the bombing of the embassy. Instead, he confined himself to a public statement:

> The terrorist outrage aimed at the American Embassy in Saigon shows us once again what the struggle in Viet-Nam is about. This wanton act of ruthlessness has brought death and serious injury to innocent Vietnamese citizens in the street as well as to American and Vietnamese personnel on duty." He added that the Embassy was "already back in business," and that he would "at once request the Congress for authority and funds for the immediate construction of a new chancery.

After his first meeting with Taylor and other officials on March 31, the President responded to press inquiries concerning dramatic new developments by saying, "I know of no far-reaching strategy that is being suggested or promulgated."

But the President was being less than candid. The proposals that were at that moment being promulgated, and on which he reached significant decisions the following day, did involve a far-reaching strategy change: acceptance of the concept of U.S. troops engaged in offensive ground operations against Asian insurgents. This issue greatly overshadowed all other Vietnam questions then being reconsidered.

D.   NSAM 328—ISSUES POSED AND DECISIONS MADE

The underlying question that was being posed for the President at this time was well formulated by Assistant Defense Secretary John McNaughton in a draft memorandum of March 24, entitled "Plan of Action for South Vietnam." The key question, McNaughton thought, was:

> Can the situation inside SVN be bottomed out (a) without extreme measures against the DRV and/or (b) without deployment of large numbers of US (and other) combat troops inside SVN? And the answer, he believed, was perhaps—but probably no.

To get closer to an answer, McNaughton began by restating U.S. objectives in Vietnam, and by attempting to weigh these objectives by their relative importance:

70%—To avoid a humiliating US defeat (to our reputation as a guarantor).

20%—To keep SVN (and then adjacent) territory from Chinese hands.

10%—To permit the people of SVN to enjoy a better, freer way of life.

ALSO—To emerge from crisis without unacceptable taint from methods
used.

NOT—To "help a friend," although it would be hard to stay in if asked
out.

McNaughton then proceeded to enumerate some twenty-odd ways in which the
GVN might collapse, and noted that in spite—or perhaps precisely because—
of the imminence of this collapse and the unpromising nature of remedial action,
U.S. policy had been drifting. As he saw it, the "trilemmas" of U.S. policy was
that the three possible remedies to GVN collapse—(a) heavy will-breaking air
attacks on the DRV, (b) large U.S. troops deployments to SVN, and (c) exit
by negotiations—were all beset with difficulties and uncertainties. Strikes against
the North, he felt, were balked "(1) by flash-point limits, (2) by doubts that the
DRV will cave and (3) by doubts that the VC will obey a caving DRV.
(Leaving strikes only a political and anti-infiltration nuisance.)" Deployment
of combat forces, he believed, was blocked "by French-defeat and Korea syn-
dromes, and Quat is queasy. (Troops could be net negatives, and be besieged.)"
And negotiations he saw as "tainted by the humiliation likely to follow."

McNaughton then proceeded to review in detail the purposes, alternatives, and
risks of the bombing program as it then stood, treating the issue more compre-
hensively and systematically than it has been considered elsewhere. His schematic
exposition is, therefore, reproduced here in full:

Strikes on the North (program of progressive military pressure)
a. *Purposes:*
　　(1) Reduce DRV/VC activities by affecting DRV will.
　　(2) To improve the GVN/VC relative "balance of morale."
　　(3) To provide the US/GVN with a bargaining counter.
　　(4) To reduce DRV infiltration of men and materiel.
　　(5) To show the world the lengths to which US will go for a friend.
b. *Program:* Each week, 1 or 2 "mission days" with 100-plane high damage US–VNAF strikes each "day" against important targets, plus 3
armed recce missions—all moving upward in weight of effort, value of
target or proximity to Hanoi and China.

　　ALTERNATIVE ONE:　12-week DRV-wide program shunning only
　　　　　　　　　　　　"population" targets.
　　ALTERNATIVE TWO:　12-week program short of taking out Phuc
　　　　　　　　　　　　Yen (Hanoi) airfield.
c *Other actions:*
　　(1) Blockade of DRV ports by VNAF/US-dropped mines or by ships.
　　(2) South Vietnamese-implemented 34A MAROPS.
　　(3) Reconnaissance flights over Laos and the DRV.
　　(4) Daily BARREL ROLL armed recce strikes in Laos (plus T–28s).
　　(5) Four-a-week BARREL ROLL choke-point strikes in Laos.
　　(6) US/VNAF air & naval strikes against VC ops and bases in SVN.
　　(7) Westward deployment of US forces.
　　(8) No DeSoto patrols or naval bombardment of DRV at this time.

d. *Red "flash points."* There are events which we can expect to imply substantial risk of escalation:
(1) Air strikes north of 17°. (This one already passed.)
(2) First US/VNAF confrontation with DRV MIGs.
(3) Strike on Phuc Yen MIG base near Hanoi.
(4) First strikes on Tonkin industrial/population targets.
(5) First strikes on Chinese railroad or near China.
(6) First US/VNAF confrontation with Chicom MIGs.
(7) First hot pursuit of Chicom MIGs into China.
(8) First flak-suppression of Chicom- or Soviet-manned SAM.
(9) Massive introduction of US ground troops into SVN.
(10) US/ARVN occupation of DRV territory.

e. *Blue "flash points."* China/DRV surely are sensitive to events which might cause us to escalate:
(1) All of the above "Red" flash points.
(2) VC ground attack on Danang.
(3) Sinking of a US naval vessel.
(4) Open deployment of DRV troops into South Vietnam.
(5) Deployment of Chinese troops into North Vietnam.
(6) Deployment of FROGs or SAMs in North Vietnam.
(7) DRV air attack on South Vietnam.
(8) Announcement of Liberation Government in 1/11 Corps area.

f. *Major risks:*
(1) Losses to DRV MIGs, and later possibly to SAMs.
(2) Increased VC activities, and possibly Liberation Government.
(3) Panic or other collapse of GVN from under us.
(4) World-wide revulsion against us (against strikes, blockade, etc.).
(5) Sympathetic fires over Berlin, Cyprus, Kashmir, Jordan waters.
(6) Escalation to conventional war with DRV, China (and USSR?).
(7) Escalation to the use of nuclear weapons.

g. *Other Red Moves:*
(1) More jets to NVN with DRV or Chicom pilots.
(2) More AAA (SAMs?) and radar gear (Soviet-manned?) to NVN.
(3) Increased air and ground forces in South China.
(4) Other "defensive" DRV retaliation (e.g., shoot-down of a U–2).
(5) PL land grabs in Laos.
(6) PL declaration of new government in Laos.
(7) Political drive for "neutralization" of Indo-China.

h. *Escalation control.* We can do three things to avoid escalation too-much or too-fast:
(1) *Stretch out:* Retard the program (e.g., 1 not 2 fixed strikes a week).
(2) *Circuit breaker.* Abandon at least temporarily [words missing] "plateau" them below the "Phuc Yen airfield" flash point on one or the other of these tenable theories: (a) That we strike as necessary to interdict infiltration. (b) That our level of strikes is generally responsive to the level of VC/DRV activities in South Vietnam.
(3) *Shunt.* Plateau the air strikes per para (2) and divert the energy into: (a) a mine-and/or ship-blockade of DRV ports. (b) Massive deployment of US (and other?) troops into SVN (and Laos?): (1) To man the "enclaves," releasing ARVN forces. (2) To take over Pleiku, Kontum, Darlac provinces. (3) To create a 16+° sea-Thailand infiltration wall.

i. *Important Miscellany:*
  (1) Program should appear to be relentless (i.e., possibility of employing "circuit-breakers" should be secret).
  (2) Enemy should be kept aware of our limited objectives.
  (3) Allies should be kept on board.
  (4) USSR should be kept in passive role.
  (5) Information program should preserve US public support.

McNaughton's memorandum dealt in similar detail with the two other forms of remedial action that were then being considered: US troop deployments and exit negotiations. Neither of these, however, is a matter of prime concern within the scope of this paper. It is well to remember, however, that the April 1 Presidential policy review was not confined to the air campaign against the DRV. It embraced the whole panoply of military and non-military actions that might be undertaken in South and North Vietnam, but the main focus was clearly on actions within *South* Vietnam, and the principal concern of Administration policy makers at this time was with the prospect of major deployments of US and Third Country combat forces to SVN.

Unlike McNaughton's memorandum, the McGeorge Bundy discussion paper of April 1 which set forth the key issues for consideration and decision by the President, gave only the most superficial treatment to the complex matter of future air pressures policy. In fact, the Bundy paper merely listed a series of action recommendations, seemingly providing little room for debate or for consideration of alternatives. The actions proposed amounted to little more than a continuation of the ongoing modest ROLLING THUNDER program, directed, with slowly rising intensity, at the LOC targets that were then beginning to be hit. Recommendations were not subjected to any searching debate when they were discussed with the President on April 2, since the wording of the President's decision in the NSAM issued on April 6, is verbatim identical with the wording of the McGeorge Bundy recommendation that was circulated to the Principals before the meeting:

> Subject to continuing review, the President approved the following general framework of continuing action against North Vietnam and Laos:
>
> We should continue roughly the present slowly ascending tempo of ROLLING THUNDER operations, being prepared to add strikes in response to a higher rate of VC operations, or conceivably to slow the pace in the unlikely event VC slacked off sharply for what appeared to be more than a temporary operational lull.
>
> The target systems should continue to avoid the effective GCI range of MIGs. We should continue to vary the types of targets, stepping up attacks on lines of communication in the near future, and possibly moving in a few weeks to attacks on the rail lines north and northeast of Hanoi.
>
> Leaflet operations should be expanded to obtain maximum practicable psychological effect on the North Vietnamese population.
>
> Blockade or aerial mining of North Vietnamese ports needs further study and should be considered for future operations. It would have major political complications, especially in relation to the Soviets and other countries, but also offers many advantages.
>
> Air operation in Laos, particularly route blocking operations in the Panhandle area, should be stepped up to the maximum remunerative rate.

E.   THE DIRECTOR OF CENTRAL INTELLIGENCE DEMURS

As has been indicated, the dramatic element in the President's decisions of April 2 was not in the sphere of air strikes against the North, but in the area of the mission of US ground forces in South Vietnam. NSAM 328 promulgated the significant decision to change the role of the Marine battalions deployed to Vietnam from one of advice and static defense to one of active combat operations against the VC guerrillas. The fact that this departure from a long-held policy had momentous implications was well recognized by the Administration leadership. The President himself was greatly concerned that the step be given as little prominence as possible. In NSAM 328 his position in this regard was stated as follows:

> The President desires that with respect to (these) actions . . . premature publicity be avoided by all possible precautions. The actions themselves should be taken as rapidly as practicable, but in ways that should minimize any appearance of sudden changes in policy, and official statements on these troop movements will be made only with the direct approval of the Secretary of Defense, in that these movements and changes should be understood as being gradual and wholly consistent with existing policy.

Whether and to what extent there was support or opposition to this step among top Administration advisers is not recorded in the documentation available to this writer. But one interesting demurrer was introduced by the Director of Central Intelligence, John A. McCone, in a memorandum he circulated on April 2 to Secretary Rusk, Secretary McNamara, McGeorge Bundy, and Ambassador Taylor.

McCone did not inherently disagree with the change in the U.S. ground force role, but felt that it was inconsistent with the decision to continue the air strike program at the feeble level at which it was then being conducted. McCone developed his argument as follows:

> I have been giving thought to the paper that we discussed in yesterday's meeting, which unfortunately I had little time to study, and also to the decision made to change the mission of our ground forces in South Vietnam from one of advice and static defense to one of active combat operations against the Viet Cong guerrillas.
>
> I feel that the latter decision is correct only if our air strikes against the North are sufficiently heavy and damaging really to hurt the North Vietnamese. The paper we examined yesterday does not anticipate the type of air operation against the North necessary to force the NVN to reappraise their policy. On the contrary, it states, "We should continue roughly the present slowly ascending tempo of ROLLING THUNDER operations ——," and later, in outlining the types of targets, states, "The target systems should continue to avoid the effective GCI range of MIG's," and these conditions indicate restraints which will not be persuasive to the NVN and would probably be read as evidence of a U.S. desire to temporize.
>
> I have reported that the strikes to date have not caused a change in the North Vietnamese policy of directing Viet Cong insurgency, infiltrating cadres and supplying material. If anything, the strikes to date have hardened their attitude.

I have now had a chance to examine the 12-week program referred to by General Wheeler and it is my personal opinion that this program is not sufficiently severe or [words illegible] the North Vietnamese to [words illegible] policy.

On the other hand, we must look with care to our position under a program of slowly ascending tempo of air strikes. With the passage of each day and each week, we can expect increasing pressure to stop the bombing. This will come from various elements of the American public, from the press, the United Nations and world opinion. Therefore time will run against us in this operation and I think the North Vietnamese are counting on this.

Therefore I think what we are doing is starting on a track which involves ground force operations which, in all probability, will have limited effectiveness against guerrillas, although admittedly will restrain some VC advances. However, we can expect requirements for an ever-increasing commitment of U.S. personnel without materially improving the chances of victory. I support and agree with this decision but I must point out that in my judgment, forcing submission of the VC can only be brought about by a decision in Hanoi. Since the contemplated actions against the North are modest in scale, they will not impose unacceptable damage on it, nor will they threaten the DRV's vital interests. Hence, they will not present them with a situation with which they cannot live, though such actions will cause the DRV pain and inconvenience.

I believe our proposed track offers great danger of simply encouraging Chinese Communist and Soviet support of the DRV and VC cause, if for no other reason then the risk for both will be minimum. I envision that the reaction of the NVN and Chinese Communists will be to deliberately, carefully, and probably gradually, build up the Viet Cong capabilities by covert infiltration on North Vietnamese and, possibly, Chinese cadres and thus bring an ever-increasing pressure on our forces. In effect, we will find ourselves mired down in combat in the jungle in a military effort that we cannot win, and from which we will have extreme difficulty in extracting ourselves.

Therefore it is my judgment that if we are to change the mission of the ground forces, we must also change the ground rules of the strikes against North Vietnam. We must hit them harder, more frequently, and inflict greater damage. Instead of avoiding the MIG's, we must go in and take them out. A bridge here and there will not do the job. We must strike their airfields, their patroleum resources, power stations and their military compounds. This, in my opinion, must be done promptly and with minimum restraint.

If we are unwilling to take this kind of a decision now, we must not take the actions concerning the mission of our ground forces for the reasons I have mentioned.

The record does not show whether this memorandum was ever submitted to or discussed with the President. In any event, the President had already made his decision by the time the above memorandum reached the addressees. McCone, however, persisted in his concern over what he felt was an inadequately forceful air strike program and he did subsequently make his views known to the President, by way of a personal memorandum and a coordinated intelligence estimate he handed to the President on April 28, the date on which his successor,

Admiral Raborn, was sworn in. The memorandum itself is not available to this writer, but both the estimate and Admiral Raborn's reaction to the two documents are at hand. They are discussed in Section XIII below.

X.   APRIL 7TH INITIATIVE—THE BILLION DOLLAR CARROT

A.   MOUNTING PUBLIC CRITICISM

During the latter half of March and the beginning of April, from near and far more and more brickbats were being hurled at the Administration's position on Vietnam. At home, columnist Walter Lippman raised his voice to observe that U.S. policy "is all stick and no carrot. We are telling the North Vietnamese that they will be very badly hurt if they do not quit . . . But we are not telling the North Vietnamese what kind of future there would be for them and the rest of Indochina if the war ended as we think it should end."

Abroad, in an empty but well-publicized gesture, philosopher Jean-Paul Sartre canceled a lecture trip to the U.S. on the ground that Gallup polls indicated most Americans are in favor of the air raids into North Vietnam. "Where contradictory opinions thus have hardened," said the reluctant Nobel Prize winner, "dialogue is impossible." And in a considerably more potent gesture, the government of Charles de Gaulle chose this particular juncture to renew its annual trade agreement with North Vietnam and to extend Hanoi medium-term credits for the purchase of French goods.

Within the Administration there was a growing feeling that somewhere along the line the hand had been misplaced, that somehow the mix of increased military pressure and increased diplomatic efforts for settlement had not been right. In late March, therefore, the President began to try to alter the mix. He began by spending much time on efforts at personal persuasion, talking to Congressmen and other visitors in his office about the restraint and patience he was showing in operation ROLLING THUNDER. Evans and Novak describe one of these sessions as follows:

> To illustrate his caution, he showed critics the map of North Vietnam and pointed out the targets he had approved for attack, and to the many more targets he had disapproved. As for Communist China, he was watching for every possible sign of reaction. Employing a vivid sexual analogy, the President explained to friends and critics one day that the slow escalation of the air war in the North and the increasing pressure on Ho Chi Minh was seduction, not rape. If China should suddenly react to slow escalation, as a woman might react to attempted seduction, by threatening to retaliate (a slap in the face, to continue the metaphor), the United States would have plenty of time to ease off the bombing. On the other hand, if the United States were to unleash an all-out, total assault on the North—rape rather than seduction—there could be no turning back, and Chinese reaction might be instant and total.

But despite the full use of his power to influence, the President could not stop the critics. Condemnation of the bombing spread to the campuses and to a widening circle of Congressmen. From many directions the President was being pressed to make a major public statement welcoming negotiations.

Up to this time, the official U.S. position had been unreceptive to negotiations, although the President had paid lip-service to his willingness to "do anything and go anywhere in the interests of peace." Past inaction he blamed entirely on Hanoi. It was, he said, Hanoi that would not talk peace, Hanoi that was subverting South Vietnam, Hanoi that was making it possible for the war to continue by funneling supplies and manpower over the Ho Chi Minh trail. Washington was not to blame. But now the formula no longer seemed adequate, and the President began to look for a more spectacular way of dramatizing his peaceful intent. He found it in three ingredients which he combined in his renowned Johns Hopkins address of April 7th.

B. INGREDIENTS FOR JOHNS HOPKINS

Three elements combined to make the President's Johns Hopkins speech an important initiative: *First,* a new formulation of U.S. readiness to negotiate, in the shape of an acceptance by the President of the spirit of the 17-Nation Appeal of March 15, which had called upon the belligerents to start negotiations as soon as possible "without posing any preconditions." Here are the words of the speech which the President hoped would satisfy the principal demand of the doves:

> We will never be second in the search for . . . a peaceful settlement in Viet-Nam.
> There may be many ways to this kind of peace: in discussion or negotiation with the governments concerned; in large groups or in small ones; in the reaffirmation of old agreements or their strengthening with new ones.
> We have stated this position over and over again 50 times and more to friend and foe alike. And we remain ready with this purpose for unconditional discussions.

A *second* key element of the speech was drawn from ideas long propounded by such old Southeast Asia hands as former U.S. Ambassador to Thailand Kenneth Young, involving a massive regional development effort for the area, based on the Mekong River basin. This was precisely the kind of hopeful and positive gesture the President needed to put a bright constructive face on his Vietnam policy. Painting the picture of a potentially peaceful five-nation area, the President said:

> The first step is for the countries of Southeast Asia to associate themselves [words illegible] take its place in the common effort just as soon as peaceful cooperation is possible.
> And the President then offered his munificant carrot:
> For our part I will ask the Congress to join in a billion-dollar American investment in this effort as soon as it is underway.

And he underlined the grandioseness of the vision by characterizing the effort as being conceived "on a scale to dwarf even our TVA."

There was a *third* key element to the Johns Hopkins speech which the President added almost literally at the last minute—an illustrious name, a person of unquestioned stature, to lend some credibility and prestige to the somewhat improbable peaceful development gambit in the midst of war. The President found that ingredient in the person of Eugene Black, former President of the World Bank, a figure of high prominence in international finance, and a politician enjoying Congressional confidence and open lines to both Democrats and Republicans. In a whirlwind performance, the President recruited Black just a few short hours before his scheduled appearance at Johns Hopkins, and was able to announce that appointment in his speech.

C. HANOI AND PEKING "CLOSE THE DOOR"

While the President's speech evoked a good press and much favorable public reaction throughout the world, its practical consequences were meager. It failed to silence the Peace Bloc and it failed to bring the Communists to the negotiating table.

It is worth noting that the President's initiative of April 7 was in accord with the "pressures-policy" rationale that had been worked out in November, 1964, which held that U.S. readiness to negotiate was not to be surfaced until after a series of air strikes had been carried out against important targets in North Vietnam. Significantly, during the two weeks prior to the President's address, ROLLING THUNDER VIII (the "Radar Busting Week") and IX (the first week of the "anti-LOC" campaign) had inaugurated an almost daily schedule of bombing. Thus the U.S. was now attempting to achieve, through a deliberate combination of intensified military pressures and diplomatic enticements, what it had hoped would result from a mere token demonstration of capability and resolve. The carrot had been aided to the stick, but the stick was still the more tangible and visible element of U.S. policy.

But neither pressures nor blandishments succeeded in moving Hanoi. On the day following the President's speech, North Vietnamese Premier Pham Van Dong published his famous "Four Points," recognition of which he made clear, was the sole way in which "favorable conditions" could be created for peaceful settlement of the war. Two days later, in a telling denunciation of the President's Johns Hopkins speech, North Vietnam said that the United States was using the "peace" label to conceal its aggression and that the Southeast Asia development proposal was simply a "carrot" offered to offset the "stick" of aggression and to seek to allay domestic and international criticism of U.S. policy in Vietnam. The following day, an article in a Chinese Communist newspaper denounced President Johnson's proposal for unconditional discussions as "a swindle pure and simple." To complete the rejection of Western initiatives, Hanoi turned down the appeal of the seventeen non-aligned nations on April 19, reiterating that Pham Van Dong's "Four Points" were the "only correct way" to resolve the Vietnam problem; and three days later Peking's *Peoples' Daily* gave the coup-de-grace to the 17-nation appeal, saying that it amounted to "legalizing the United States imperialist aggression" and that "the Viet-Namese people will never agree to negotiations 'without any preconditions.' "

D. PRESIDENT'S REPRISE: TRAGEDY, DISSAPPOINTMENT— BUT NO BOMBING PAUSE

The rejection of the President's initiative had been total. And other Western peace feelers were equally bluntly turned away. British former Foreign Secretary Patrick Gordon Walker who sought to visit Peking and Hanoi on a self-appointed peace mission to sound out both governments on the possibilities of negotiations was unceremoniously denied entry to both Mainland China and North Vietnam.

In the light of these developments, the President made another public statement, opening with the words, "This has been a week of tragedy, disappointment, and progress."

"We tried to open a window to peace," the President said, "only to be met with tired names and slogans and a refusal to talk." But he tried once more:

> They want no talk with us, no talk with a distinguished Briton, no talk with the United Nations. They want no talk at all so far. But our offer stands. We mean every word of it . . .
>
> To those governments who doubt our willingness to talk the answer is simple—agree to discussion, come to the meeting room. We will be there. Our objective in Viet-Nam remains the same—an independent South Vietnam, tied to no alliance, free to shape its relations and association with all other nations. This is what the people of South Vietnam want, and we will finally settle for no less.

But this is as far as the President was willing to go in his concessions to the Peace Bloc at this time.

To the clamor from many directions, including from Senator Fulbright and from Canada's Prime Minister Lester Pearson, that the U.S. should pause in its air strikes to bring about negotiations, the Administration responded with a resounding "No." Secretary Rusk made the U.S. position clear on this, in a statement read to news correspondents on April 17:

> We have thought long and soberly about suspending, for a period, the raids on North Viet-Nam. Some have suggested this could lead to an end of aggression from the North. But we have tried publicly and privately to find out if this would be the result, and there has been no response. Others say such a pause is needed to signal our sincerity, but no signal is needed. Our sincerity is plain.
>
> If we thought such action would advance the cause of an honorable peace, we would order it immediately, but now our best judgment tells us it would only encourage the aggressor and dishearten our friends who bear the brunt of battle.

XI. HONOLULU, APRIL 20—IN SEARCH OF CONSENSUS

A. BACKGROUND AND CONCLUSIONS OF CONFERENCE

By the middle of April, communications between Washington and Saigon were becoming increasingly strained, as it began to dawn upon Ambassador Taylor that Washington was determined, with the President's sanction, to go far beyond the agreements to which Taylor had been a party at the beginning of April and that had been formalized in NSAM 328. From April 8 onward, Taylor had been bombarded with messages and instructions from Washington testifying to an eagerness to speed up the introduction to Vietnam of U.S. and Third County ground forces and to employ them in a combat role, all far beyond anything that had been authorized in the April 2 NSC decisions. Ambassador Taylor's ill-concealed annoyance at these mounting pressures and progressively more radical proposals changed to outright anger and open protest when, on April 18, he received another instruction, allegedly with the sanction of "highest authority," proposing seven additional complicated measures having to do with combat force deployment and employment, on the justification that "something new must be added in the South to achieve victory." Taylor's exasperated response to McGeorge Bundy the same day made it clear that meaningful communication between Washington and Saigon had all but broken down and that something needed to be done quickly to restore some sense of common purpose and to provide Taylor with a revised set of instructions.

It was with this background that Secretary McNamara convened a conference in Honolulu on very short notice, bringing together most of the key personalities involved in Vietnam policy-making: Chairman Wheeler of the JCS, General Westmoreland, COMUSMACV, Admiral Sharp, CINCPAC, Ambassador Taylor from Saigon, William Bundy of State, and John McNaughton of Defense.

Precisely what transpired during the one-day meeting in Honolulu on April 20th is not known to this writer. But clearly the meeting was called for the explicit purpose of ironing out differences and smoothing ruffled feathers. The immediate concern was to reach specific agreement on troop deployments; but an underlying objective was to restore a semblance of consensus about assessments and priorities.

The record contains two documents that report on the results of the meeting. (1) The minutes of the meeting prepared by John McNaughton, and (2) a Memorandum for the President prepared by the Secretary of Defense on April 21 which is almost, but not quite, identical with McNaughton's minutes. The differences are significant in that they suggest an effort on McNamara's part to stress even more than did McNaughton the unanimity of view that was achieved at Honolulu.

Sections of the two documents relevant to the air war are quoted below. Where the two texts differ, both versions are shown—McNamara's in brackets [   ], McNaughton's in parentheses (   ):

(Secretary McNamara, accompanied by) Mr. William Bundy (and) Mr. McNaughton [and I] met with Ambassador Taylor, General Wheeler, Admiral Sharp and General Westmoreland in Honolulu on Tuesday, April 20. (The minutes of that meeting follow:)
[Following is my report of the meeting:]
1. (There was consensus that) [None of them expect] the DRV/VC (cannot be expected) to capitulate, or come to a position acceptable to us, in less than six months. This is because they believe that a settlement will come as much or more from VC failure in the South as from DRV pain in the North, and that it will take more than six months, perhaps a year or two, to demonstrate VC failure in the South.
2. With respect to strikes against the North, (it was agreed) [they all agree] that the present tempo is about right, that sufficient increasing pressure is provided by repetition and continuation. All of them envisioned a strike program continuing at least six months, perhaps a year or more, avoiding the Hanoi–Haiphong–Phuc Yen areas during that period. There might be fewer fixed targets, or more restrikes, or more armed reconnaissance missions. Ambassador Taylor stated what appeared to be a (shared) [majority] view, that it is important not to "kill the hostage" by destroying the North Vietnamese assets inside the "Hanoi do-nut." (It was agreed) [They all believe] that the strike program is essential to our campaign—both psychologically and physically—but that it cannot be expected to do the job alone. [They] All considered it very important that strikes against the North be continued during any talks.
3. None of (the participants) [them] sees a dramatic improvement in the South in the immediate future. (The) [Their] strategy for "victory" (proposed by Ambassador Taylor, General Wheeler, Admiral Sharp and Gen-

eral Westmoreland) [however] is to break the will of the DRV/VC by denying them victory. Ambassador Taylor put it in terms of a demonstration of Communist impotence, which will lead eventually to a political solution. They see slow improvement in the South, but all (participants) emphasized the critical importance of holding on and avoiding—for psychological and moral reasons—a spectacular defeat of GVN or US forces. And they all suspect that the recent VC lull is but the quiet before a storm . . .

The documents continue with specific force deployment recommendations that were agreed upon at the meeting. In addition, McNaughton's minutes contain the following concluding item:

It was agreed that tasks within *South* Vietnam should have first call on air assets in the area [words illegible] necessary tasks, more air should be brought in. Secretary McNamara directed that this policy be implemented at once.

From this evidence, it seems apparent that Honolulu marked the relative downgrading of pressures against the North, in favor of more intensive activity in the South. The key to success, it was now felt, was not to destroy or defeat the enemy, but to frustrate him—"to break the will of the DRV/VC by denying them victory" and, above all, to avoid, for our part, a dramatic defeat. Thus the decision at this point was to "plateau" the air strikes more or less at the prevailing level, relying on "repetition and continuation" to provide increasing pressure, rather than to pursue the relentless dynamic course that had been so ardently advocated by Ambassador Taylor and Admiral Sharp in February and March, or the massive destruction of the North Vietnamese target complex so consistently advocated by the Joint Chiefs. If Honolulu represented more than a "shotgun wedding," if it reflected in fact a relatively uncoerced expression of views, the leading U.S. actors in the Vietnam drama must have undergone, in the intervening weeks, a reordering of expectations with respect to the results that bombing might achieve. Their views at this point, in any event, were strikingly more restrained on the bombing issue than they had been previously.

An alternative—and less charitable—explanation might be that, in the meantime, attention had shifted from the air war to the subject of U.S. combat force deployments, and had thus generated a need to concentrate on issues, arguments and rationalizations that would serve to promote and justify these new actions. Preoccupation with pressures against the North had long been viewed as something of a competitor, something of a distraction, by many advocates of a more forceful U.S. role in the South. Thus it seems logical that, with the decision to begin a major U.S. ground force commitment, the air campaign should have been reduced in rank to second billing.

B. INTERDICTION IS SURFACED

Along with the levelling-off of the air strikes and a reordering of expectations as to their likely effectiveness came the decision to publicize the fact that "interdiction" was now a major objective of the strikes. It will be recalled that LOC interdiction had become a key element in the U.S. target rationale beginning with ROLLING THUNDER IX (week of April 2). After Honolulu, with the prospective deepening of the U.S. involvement on the ground and the need to justify that involvement in terms of "resisting NVN aggression," it seemed desirable to stress that aspect of U.S. action more explicitly in public. Whereas previously there had been only passing reference to the fact that U.S. air attacks on North Vietnam had been aimed at targets "associated with infiltration," it was now decided to feature interdiction as *the* objective of U.S. bombing.

Secretary Rusk made first public mention of this on April 23, when he stated:

> The bombing is designed to interdict, as far as possible, and to inhibit, as far as may be necessary, continued aggression against the Republic of Viet-Nam.

Three days later, Secretary McNamara gave a special briefing to the press corps at the Pentagon, complete with maps and photographs, driving home the point of massive infiltration from the North:

> Now the current [VNAF and U.S.] strikes against North Vietnam have been designed to impede this infiltration of men and materiel, and infiltration which makes the difference between a situation which is manageable and one which is not manageable internally by the Government of South Vietnam.
>
> The air strikes have been carefully limited to military targets, primarily to infiltration targets. To transit points, to barracks, to supply depots, to ammunition depots, to routes of communication, all feeding the infiltration lines from North Vietnam into Laos and then into South Vietnam.
>
> More recently there has been added to this target system railroads, highways, and bridges which are the foundation of the infiltration routes . . .
>
> The strikes have been designed to increase the dependence on an already over-burdened road transport system by denying the use of the rail lines in the South. In summary, our objectives have been to force them off the rails onto the highways and off the highways onto their feet . . .
>
> Supplementing the bridge strikes, armed reconnaissance is being conducted along truck convoy routes against maritime traffic and rolling stock on the rail lines . . .
>
> These carefully controlled rail strikes will continue as necessary to impede the infiltration and to persuade the North Vietnamese leadership that their aggression against the south will not succeed . . .

C.   POLITICAL OBJECTIVES ARE REVIEWED

Now that interdiction was being publicly embraced as a major objective of the bombing, at least one high-ranking Administration official began to realize that insufficient attention had been paid to the U.S. political posture in the event that the DRV became persuaded "that their aggression will not succeed."

As early as April 1, McGeorge Bundy expressed his concern that the eventual bargaining tradeoffs had not received the careful consideration that they deserved. As he saw it:

> We have three cards of some value: our bombing of North Vietnam, our military presence in South Vietnam, and the political and economic carrots that can be offered to Hanoi. We want to trade these cards for just as much as possible of the following: an end to infiltration of men and supplies, an end of Hanoi's direction, control, and encouragement of the

Viet Cong, a removal of cadres under direct Hanoi control, and a dissolution of the organized Viet Cong military and political forces. We do not need to decide today just how we wish to mesh our high cards against Communist concessions. But we will need to be in such a position soon, if only to exchange views with Quat. On this more general point, we believe more exploratory conversation with the President is needed today. [April 1]

Apparently, however, any exploratory conversation that took place on that and other occasions failed to lead to a clarification of what the U.S. and the GVN could regard as "a satisfactory outcome" in Vietnam. McGeorge Bundy continued to feel a sense of urgency about beginning discussions with the Saigon Government on this matter. Thus on April 25 he circulated a Memorandum to the Principals, lamenting the lack of progress toward such discussions:

> We have had a lot of discussion among ourselves and with Embassy Saigon on the negotiating track, but we have not yet had serious discussions with the Republic of Vietnam. Such serious discussions are the necessary preliminary of any substantial improvement in our political posture, because our whole position depends on the legitimacy of that *independent* government.
>
> But we have had great difficulty in talking to Quat so far because our thinking has focused so sharply on the complexities of the bargaining problem itself:
>
> At what stage would we stop bombing?
>
> At what point and with what guarantees could we begin to withdraw?
>
> What are the real terms of an effective cease-fire?
>
> These are very difficult questions and the truth is that they cannot be answered today. They are precisely the problems which will have to be settled [words illegible] on the ground and hard bargaining. Moreover, it is very hard for us to look these questions in the eye with Quat & Company lest each of us begins to suspect the determination of the other.

It is perhaps worth observing that these very same questions were still as difficult to answer and as devisive in April, 1968 as they seemed to Bundy in April, 1965. But at that time Bundy felt that a different approach might be more productive. Thus the main purpose of his memorandum was:

> . . . to suggest that there is a better place to begin on this problem: namely, by getting a clearer and more comprehensive statement of the elements of a good eventual solution inside South Vietnam. We can and should work out with Quat a program whose elements could include:
>
> 1. Internationally validated free elections, first locally, than regionally, and finally on a national basis.
>
> 2. A broad and generous offer of political amnesty to all who abandon the use of force, coupled with the right of repatriation to the North, or opportunities for peaceful resettlement in the South.
>
> 3. A clear opportunity for the people of South Vietnam themselves to express themselves directly on the peaceful presence of Americans and other foreigners in helping with the peaceful progress of Vietnam.
>
> 4. Reciprocal guarantees against any border violation with all neighbors of South Vietnam, and a readiness to accept international patrols along these borders.

5. A declaration of intent to work for the unification of all Vietnam by the free choice of its people and a readiness to accept nationwide free elections for this purpose if this position is:

a. Supported by the people of South Vietnam in appropriate constitutional process.

b. Accepted by the Government of North Vietnam, and

c. Validated by effectively guaranteed rights of free political activity for all parties in both parts of the country.

There are other elements to a strong GVN [words missing] our own political position needs now to be built on a clearer and stronger statement of objectives from Saigon itself.

Once this stronger position of Saigon is established, the US could add its own support and its own determination to be guided by the freely expressed wishes of the people of South Vietnam. It could express its readiness to give peaceful help to such a settled country, and it could reaffirm its readiness to participate in appropriate international guarantees. It could also reaffirm its determination to support the GVN until this program is accepted.

But the "strong GVN program" Bundy had in mind clearly did not contemplate any serious compromise with the NLF. It was a politically strengthened, internationally guaranteed, Western-oriented government Bundy was seeking to create —at least in appearance if not in reality. The grinding problem of the ultimate role of the NLF was left unaddressed and in limbo:

The probability is that any such program would and should leave open the exact opportunities open to the Liberation Front and its members in the new politics of South Vietnam. This is as it should be, since this point is precisely the one which can only be settled by events and bargaining.

It is a striking fact that, in April, 1968, three years later, this crucial point was still viewed as one which can only be settled by events and bargaining.

XII. PROJECT MAYFLOWER—THE FIRST BOMBING PAUSE

A. THE BACKGROUND

Pressure for some form of bombing halt had mounted steadily throughout April and early May. As early as April 2, Canada's Prime Minister Lester Pearson, on his way to meet with President Johnson, had stopped off to make a speech in Philadelphia in which he suggested that the President should order a "pause" in the bombing of North Vietnam.

Pearson's gratuitous advice was particularly galling to the President because the pause had become the battle slogan of the anti-Vietnam movement. Students had picketed the LBJ Ranch in Texas, demanding a cessation of bombing. A massive teach-in had been scheduled for May 15 in Washington, with academicians who wanted withdrawal of American influence from the Asian mainland, ready to demand as a first step an immediate end of the bombing. Pressure for a pause was building up, too, in Congress among liberal Democrats. The U.N. Secretary General was on a continual bombing pause kick, with a proposal for a three month suspension of bombing in return for Hanoi's agreement to cease infiltration in South Vietnam. U Thant had told Ambassador Stevenson on April

24 that he believed such a gesture would facilitate renewed non-aligned pressure upon Hanoi to negotiate.

Evidently, however, the President was not impressed with the widespread clamor that such a gesture would evoke any response from Hanoi. He had responded favorably to the 17-Nation appeal in his April 7th speech, only to be answered with blunt rejection by Hanoi and Peking. The US. had responded favorably to the idea of a Cambodian Conference that would provide opportunities for "corridor contacts" with Communist powers on the Vietnam problem, but Peking had apparently blocked that initiative. Encouragement had been given to a UK approach to the Soviets in February looking toward consultations under Article 19 of the 1962 Geneva Accords, but no response from the USSR had been received. The Radhakrishnan proposal for a cease-fire along the 17th parallel, supervised by an "Afro-Asian Force" was being favorably considered by the U.S. only to be denounced as a "plot" by Peking and as an "offense" by Hanoi. Publicly, the President was plaintive:

> There are those who frequently talk of negotiations and political settlement and that they believe this is the course we should pursue, and so do I. When they talk that way I say, welcome to the club. I want to negotiate. I would much rather talk than fight, and I think everyone would. Bring in who you want us to negotiate with. I have searched high and wide, and I am a reasonably good cowboy, and I can't even rope anybody and bring them in who is willing to talk and settle this by negotiation. We send them messages through allies—one country, two countries, three countries, four or five countries—all have tried to be helpful. The distinguished British citizen, Mr. (Patrick Gordon) Walker, has been out there, and they say, we can't even talk to you. All our intelligence is unanimous in this one point, that they see no need for negotiation. They think they are winning and they have won and why should they sit down and give us something and settle with us.

But while the public clamor persisted and became more and more difficult to ignore, the President was receiving intelligence assessments from Saigon and from Washington that tended to confirm his reading of Hanoi's disinterest in negotiations, but that provided him with a quite different argument for a bombing pause at this time: if the conflict was going to have to be expanded and bombing intensified before Hanoi would "come to reason," it would be easier and politically more palatable to do so *after* a pause, which would afford an opportunity for the enemy's intentions to be more clearly revealed.

On May 4, in response to an urgent request from Washington, Ambassador Taylor submitted a U.S. Mission "Assessment of DRV/VC Probable Courses of Action During the Next Three Months." The assessment confirmed the Washington view that Hanoi continued to have a very favorable view of its prospects for victory:

> . . . Tone of statements emanating from Hanoi since [February and March] indicate that the DRV has not weakened in its determination to continue directing and supporting Viet Cong and seeking further intensification of war in the South.
>
> From DRV viewpoint, outlook is probably still favorable despite air strikes on North. Although their general transportation system in North has been significantly damaged, thus somewhat reducing their infiltration

capability, Hanoi may calculate it can accept level of damage being inflicted as reasonable price to pay for chance of victory in South. Viet Cong forces in south retain capability of taking local initiatives on ground, although they must accept cost of heavier losses from tactical air support, and their morale possibly has been reduced by recent developments. GVN force levels still are not adequate to cope with these Viet Cong capabilities. Despite relative longevity of Quat Govt., which marks improvement over previous recent Govts., political situation is still basically unstable. While military and civilian morale has risen, rumblings among generals continue, suspicion among political and religious groups persist and are subject to exploitation by communists. On balance, Hanoi probably believes it has [words illegible] for expectation that Viet Cong, who were clearly making progress as recently as February, can regain the initiative and, by the application of offensive power, can create an atmosphere in which negotiations favorable to the DRV can be instituted.

Given this situation, the report argued, the most probable course of action that Hanoi would pursue is to continue its efforts to expand its military action in the South, "including covert introduction of additional PAVN units on order of several regiments. This course offers . . . the prospect of achieving major military gains capable of offsetting US/GVN application of air power. Such gains would expand Viet Cong areas of control and might lead to political demoralization in South Vietnam."

A similarly unencouraging assessment had been submitted to the President by the Board of National Estimates on April 22. In a "highly sensitive, limited distribution" memorandum, the leading personalities of the U.S. intelligence community concurred in the prediction that:

> If present US policies continue without the introduction of large additional forces or increased US air effort, the Communists are likely to hold to their existing policy of seeking victory in the local military struggle in South Vietnam. They will try to intensify that struggle, supporting it with additional men and equipment. At the same time, DRV air defenses will be strengthened through Soviet and perhaps Chinese aid.

If, however, the U.S. deepens its involvement by increasing its combat role and intensifying its air effort, the intelligence officers believed:

> . . . that the Viet Cong, North Vietnam, and China would initially . . . try to offset the new enemy strength by stepping up the insurgency, reinforcing the Viet Cong with the men and equipment necessary. They would likely count on time being on their side and try to force the piecemeal engagement of US troops under conditions which might bog them down in jungle warfare, hoping to present the US with a de facto partition of the country. The Soviet Union . . . would almost certainly acquiesce in a decision by Hanoi to intensify the struggle.

This lack of any real prospect of "give" on the enemy's part was also confirmed by Admiral Raborn, shortly after he had succeeded John McCone as Director of Central Intelligence. On the day of Raborn's swearing-in (April 28), the President had given him a letter from McCone (apparently worded along the lines of his memorandum described in Section IX.E. of this study) which

McCone had handed to the President as his last official act. The President had asked Raborn for his own comments on McCone's views. Raborn's comments, circulated to Secretaries Rusk and McNamara on May 6, included the following:

> Our limited bombing of the North and our present ground-force build-up in the South are not likely to exert sufficient pressure on the enemy to cause him to meet our present terms in the foreseeable future. I note very recent evidence which suggests that our military pressures are becoming somewhat more damaging to the enemy within South Vietnam, but I am inclined to doubt that this damage is increasing at a rate which will bring him quickly to the conference table.

With particular reference to McCone's recommendation that the US add much heavier air action against the North to its planned combat force deployment to the South, Raborn indicated his agreement, and expressed his belief that such an action would have the following consequences:

> The DRV is, in my view, unlikely to engage in meaningful discussions at any time in coming months until US air attacks have begun to damage or destroy its principal economic and military targets. I thus concur with the USIB's judgment of 18 February 1965, that, given such US punishment, the enemy would be "somewhat more likely" to decide to make some effort to secure a respite, rather than to intensify the struggle further and accept the consequent risks.

And then he added the following advice:

> Insofar as possible, we should try to manage any program of expanded bombings in ways which (1) would leave the DRV an opportunity to explore negotiations without complete loss of face, (2) would not preclude any Soviet pressures on Hanoi to keep the war from expanding, and (3) would not suddenly produce extreme world pressures against us. In this connection, timing and circumstances in which the bombings were extended northward could be of critical importance, particularly in light of the fact that there have been some indications of differing views between Moscow, Peiping, and Hanoi. For example, it would probably be advantageous to expand bombings after, not before, some major new VC move (e.g., obvious concentration for imminent attack on Da Nang or Kontum) and *after, not before, any current possibilities of serious negotiations have been fully tested*. And such bombings should not be so regular as to leave no interval for the Communists to make concessions with some grace. Indeed, *we should keep in mind the possibility of a pause at some appropriate time, which could serve to test the Communist intentions and to exploit any differences on their side*. (Emphasis supplied)

One other consideration may have entered into the President's bombing pause calculus at this time. On April 5, a TROJAN HORSE photography mission had revealed the first SA-2 SAM site under construction fifteen miles SSE of Hanoi, confirming the long-rumored shipment of Soviet surface-to-air missiles to North Vietnam. Moreover, the SAMs were only the most dramatic form of considerably increased quantities of modern military equipment beginning to be furnished to the DRV by the Soviet Union. The Soviet Union was now in the process of becoming visibly committed to assisting North Vietnam in resisting U.S. attacks on its territory, and a more direct confrontation of US and USSR military force was rapidly approaching. Indeed, the Joint Chiefs had indicated, on April 14, their desire to obtain approval for air strikes against the sites on short notice as they become operational, had estimated, on May 6, that the first site construction could be completed by May 15, and had instructed CINCPAC to commence planning to conduct air strikes against that site. A decision involving a major Soviet "flashpoint," therefore, would soon have to be faced, and the President may well have wished to provide a prior opportunity for a quiet Hanoi backdown, before proceeding with more forceful military activity.

B. SETTING THE STAGE

On the evening of May 10 the President sent a personal FLASH message to Ambassador Taylor, informing him that he (the President) had decided to call a brief halt to air attacks in the North and instructing him to obtain Premier Quat's agreement to the plan. The text of the message follows:

I have learned from Bob McNamara that nearly all ROLLING THUN-DER operations for this week can be completed by Wednesday noon, Washington time. This fact and the days of Buddha's birthday seem to me to provide an excellent opportunity for a pause in air attacks which might go into next week and which I could use to good effect with world opinion.

My plan is not to announce this brief pause but simply to call it privately to the attention of Moscow and Hanoi as soon as possible and tell them that we shall be watching closely to see whether they respond in any way. My current plan is to report publicly after the pause ends on what we have done.

Could you see Quat right away on Tuesday and see if you can persuade him to concur in this plan. I would like to associate him with me in this decision if possible, but I would accept a simple concurrence or even willingness not to oppose my decision. In general, I think it important that he and I should act together in such matters, but I have no desire to embarrass him if it is politically difficult for him to join actively in a pause over Buddha's birthday.

We have noted your [recent cables] but do not yet have your appreciation of the political effect in Saigon of acting around Buddha's birthday. From my point of view it is a great advantage to use Buddha's birthday to mask the first days of the pause here, if it is at all possible in political terms for Quat. I assume we could undertake to enlist the Archbishop and the Nuncio in calming the Catholics.

You should understand that my purpose in this plan is to begin to clear a path either toward restoration of peace or toward increased military action, depending upon the reaction of the Communists. We have amply demonstrated our determination and our commitment in the last two months, and I now wish to gain some flexibility.

I know that this is a hard assignment on short notice, but there is no one who can bring it off better.

I have kept this plan in the tightest possible circle here and wish you to inform no one but Alexis Johnson. After I have your report of Quat's reaction I will make a final decision and it will be communicated promptly to senior officers concerned.

Ambassador Taylor promptly relayed the President's plan to Quat, whose major objection was to the notion of linking the pause in any way with Buddha's birthday. Taylor reported this objection to Washington and received the following additional instructions from the Department in return.

We have decided here to go ahead commencing on Thursday [May 13] for period of approximately 5–7 days. Orders through military channels will place stand-down on basis "in order to observe reaction of DRV rail and road transportation systems" and will order increase in photo recce of DRV and bombing within SVN. You should tell Westmoreland true basis for his personal use only so that you and he and Alex Johnson remain the only three Americans in Saigon aboard. We have informed Dobrynin tonight and are instructing Kohler to convey message to Hanoi through DRV Ambassador in Moscow. I will also be telling British and Canadian Foreign Ministers personally tomorrow and we will convey message to Menzies through Embassy here. However, each of these being informed only at highest levels and their Saigon representatives will not repeat not be witting.

You should take following actions:

1. Inform Quat we are going ahead. You should not specify period but let us know if he raises question or still insists on as short a period as 4–5 days [words illegible] refrain at all times from associating action with Buddha's birthday and that our initial plan will be to refer all press queries to Washington and to hold as long as possible simply to operational factors as explanation. You should raise with him question of what he will tell generals urging in strongest terms that he tell them only what we are saying through military channel and preferably delay even this until question arises. If Quat raises question of what we are saying to Communist side, you will have copies tonight's talk with Dobrynin and instructions to Kohler by septels and may draw generally on these for his personal use only.

2. To deal with any possibility adverse Catholic reaction you should inform Archbishop and/or Nuncio very privately that any variation in actions in forthcoming period will be USG decisions not related in any way to Buddha's birthday or any appeal or issue connected with it. You may of course also reiterate that any such variations have no effect whatever on our determination as clearly shown in recent months. We leave timing this approach to you but believe it should be done earliest before any speculation arises.

3. At appropriate time you should instruct Zorthian to report simply that no operations other than reconnaissance were conducted on each day and to refer press queries, preferably by indirection, to Washington.

A few hours later, Secretary McNamara, with the concurrence of Secretary Rusk and McGeorge Bundy, sent the following FLASH joint State/Defense message through military channels to Ambassador Taylor, CINCPAC and COMUSMACV:

In order to observe reaction of DRV rail and road transportation systems, bombing (including armed recce and other strike operations) of targets within DRV will cease for several days effective 2400 12 May Saigon time. CINCPAC should issue the necessary instructions to US forces and Ambassador should seek to obtain compliance of VNAF.

During the period in which bombing operations are suspended, photo and eyeball reconnaissance flights over DRV, in so far as they can be carried out without flak suppression escorts and within currently approved rules relating to altitudes and latitudes, will be increased to the level required to permit a thorough study of lines of communication. The bombing sorties which would have been directed against the DRV during this period, to the extent practical, will be targeted against appropriate targets in South Vietnam.

ROLLING THUNDER 15 as outlined in JCS 1736 has been approved. It is to be executed upon receipt of appropriate execution orders.

Press guidance for the period during which bombing operations are suspended will be furnished in a separate message.

Acting on these instructions, Taylor saw Quat in Saigon on the morning of May 12, and reported back as follows:

Along with Alex Johnson, I called this morning to convey to Quat the information contained in Department's instructions. I told him that his views with regard to linking the pause with Buddha's birthday had been accepted and that this element had been removed from the plan. I explained that the pause begins tomorrow (Saigon time) and will continue for several days. As he did not raise any question with regard to the precise duration, I did not elaborate. He liked the military justification for the pause as explained in REFTEL and undertook to remain within this language in dealing with his generals. I assured him that General Westmoreland would do the same in his military contacts.

We explained to Quat how the message was being conveyed to the USSR and Hanoi. He had no comment except to express doubt that any detectable change in DRV conduct will take place during the suspension of attacks.

As for comment to the press, he repeated his intention to ward off queries by references to "Operational Requirements."

While securing Quat's support has been somewhat easier than I had anticipated, I am sure that he and his colleagues will become uneasy very quickly if this pause runs beyond the "four to five days" which Quat has indicated to be acceptable from his point of view. I would hope that our purposes can have been fulfilled within the five day period.

With regard to paragraph 2 [of Department's instructions], Johnson and I feel that it is unnecessary and probably undesirable to approach Archbishop Binh or the Nuncio at this time. We will watch closely the local reaction to the suspension and convey the message to the Catholic leadership, if necessary, at a timely moment.

Much additional attention was lavished by Washington upon maintaining near-absolute secrecy, preserving a plausible front *vis-a-vis* the press, and other aspects of stage management. On May 12, the operation was given the codeword MAYFLOWER, and all communications on it were thenceforth to be slugged with that indication. [words illegible] Johnson, the only Americans [words illegible] of MAYFLOWER were William Sullivan in Vientiane, Foy Kohler in Moscow, and Winthrop Brown in Seoul—the latter only for the purpose of informing President Park Chung Hee who was about to embark on a state visit to Washington and who, the Department felt, should be forewarned so that he might more effectively fend off press probings.

On the evening of May 11, Secretary Rusk made two moves designed to inform "the other side" of the fact that a bombing halt was being called and of its political purpose:

1. He sent a cable to Foy Kohler in Moscow, instructing him to make urgent contact with the DRV Ambassador in Moscow to convey a carefully prepared message to him, as quoted below. The cable set forth the instructions and rationale as follows:

> . . . We are using you as channel to avoid using Soviets as intermediaries and also to insure that message is accurately and directly delivered. We leave appropriate method of arranging contact to you and are not concerned if Soviets should become aware you are making such contact. You should of course make maximum effort avoid any attention by any third party.

> Message you should deliver should be oral but confirmed by written piece of paper which you should hand to Ambassador with request he deliver message to Hanoi. Message is as follows:

> BEGIN TEXT. The highest authority in this Government has asked me to inform Hanoi that there will be no air attacks on North Viet-Nam for a period beginning at noon, Washington time, Wednesday, May 12, and running into next week.

> In this decision the United States Government has taken account of repeated suggestions from various quarters, including public statements by Hanoi representatives, that there can be no progress toward peace while there are air attacks on North Viet-Nam. The United States Government remains convinced that the underlying cause of trouble in Southeast Asia is armed action against the people and Government of South Vietnam by forces whose actions can be decisively affected from North Vietnam. The United States will be very watchful to see whether in this period of pause there are significant reductions in such armed actions by such forces. (The United States must emphasize that the road toward the end of armed attacks against the people and Government of Vietnam *is the only road which will permit the Government of Vietnam* (and the Government of the United States) to bring a permanent end to their attacks on North Vietnam.) . . . [words illegible] be misunderstood as an indication of weakness, and it is therefore necessary for me to point out that if this pause should be misunderstood in this fashion, by any party, it would be necessary to demonstrate more clearly than ever, after the pause ended, that the United States is determined not to accept aggression without reply in Vietnam. Moreover, the United States must point out that the decision to end air attacks for this limited trial period is one which it must be free to reverse if at any time in the coming days there should be actions by the other side in Vietnam which required immediate reply.

> But my Government is very hopeful that there will be no such misunderstanding and that this first pause in the air attacks may meet with a response which will permit further and more extended suspension of this form of military action in the expectation of equally constructive actions by the other side in the future. END TEXT.

2. He summoned Soviet Ambassador Anatol Dobrynin to his office in the State Department and made virtually the same oral statement to him, confirmed by a parallel written version handed to him. Rusk, that same evening described the meeting to Foy Kohler in a second cable, sent immediately after the message quoted above:

I explained we were not indicating any precise number of days, that we retained freedom of action, and that we would convey similar message to Hanoi. I also said we would make no announcement although we expected press pressures, and made clear our action related only to strikes of any sort and not to continued reconnaissance. (Paper itself makes clear action confined to DRV and does not include Laos or SVN.)

I also said we did not know what to expect but that Hanoi knows what it is doing and can find a way to make its response clear.

Dobrynin noted we were merely informing Soviets and was clearly relieved we not asking them to act as intermediary. Asked about my trip to Vienna and indicated there might be further conversations there Saturday with Gromyko. Asked basically whether action represented any change in fundamental US position.

I replied that it did not and that this should be no surprise.

I reviewed recent indications that Cambodia conference blocked by Peiping despite favorable mention in DRV-Moscow communique and that three-party talks on Laos likewise in abeyance apparently following Peiping and perhaps Hanoi pressure. President on April 7 had tried open up discourse but thus far channels blocked. If attacks on DRV were part of problem, Communist response to present action might open up channels.

Dobrynin said he thought we would get some answer but could not predict what.

I underscored importance action not be misunderstood in Hanoi. Hanoi appears to have impression they may succeed, but US will not get tired or be affected by very small domestic opposition or by international pressures, Hanoi cannot rely on Saigon instability. They may have wrong ideas on these points and important they not misunderstand our action.

Dobrynin responded he saw no danger of misunderstanding but problem was to find way.

Parallel with the Secretary's diplomatic moves, the President made a major public address on the first day of the bombing pause, in which he made no reference to the pause, but in which he urged Hanoi to consider a "political solution." The speech, embracing the theme of the "three faces of war" (1. armed conflict, 2. diplomacy and politics, and 3. human need) contained the following passage:

> The second face of war in Viet-Nam is the quest for a political solution —the face of diplomacy and politics—of the ambitions and the interests of other nations. We know, as our adversaries should also know, that there is no purely military solution in sight for either side. We are ready for unconditional discussions. Most of the non-Communist nations of the world favor such unconditional discussions. And it would clearly be in the interest of North Vietnam to now come to the conference table. For them the continuation of war, without talks, means only damage without conquest. Communist China apparently desires the war to continue whatever the cost to their allies. Their target is not merely South Viet-Nam; it is Asia. Their objective is not the fulfillment of Vietnamese nationalism; it is to erode and to discredit America's ability to help prevent Chinese domination over all of Asia.

In this domination they will never succeed.

C. TRANSMITTING THE MESSAGES

Foy Kohler in Moscow, upon receiving the Secretary's instructions, directed his Deputy Chief of Mission to telephone the North Vietnamese Embassy on the morning of May 12 to request an urgent appointment for Ambassador Kohler with the North Vietnamese Ambassador. The latter declined to receive the American Ambassador "in view of the absence of diplomatic relations between our two countries," and suggested instead that the "important, high level private message" from the US Government which Ambassador Kohler wished to communicate to the NVN Ambassador be sent to the Soviet Government "in its capacity as Co-Chairman of the Geneva Conference."

Kohler felt it would not be productive to press the NVN embassy further, and cabled the Department for instructions as to which of two alternatives he should pursue: "(1) Transmit message by letter via messenger to NVN ambassador; or (2) seek appointment with Acting Foreign Minister Kuznetsov to convey message."

The Department's reply was as follows:

> Believe you should pursue both alternatives urgently, explaining to Kuznetsov (who will by now have heard from Dobrynin) that you recognize reluctance of Soviets to act as intermediary and are asking solely that Soviets transmit message to DRV Ambassador in accordance with DRV suggestion.

Kohler acted promptly on both alternatives. He transmitted the "oral" communication to the DRV Ambassador under cover of a letter signed by Kohler, which read as follows:

> In accordance with the suggestion made by a member of your staff today, I am attempting to reach the Acting Foreign Minister tonight.
> Since this may not be possible and because of its importance, I enclose the message I had hoped to be able to convey to you personally earlier today.

However, though hand-delivered by an American embassy employee to a DRV employee, the communication was returned the following morning in a plain envelope addressed simply Embassy of US of A.

At the same time, Kohler sought an urgent appointment with Acting Foreign Minister Kuznetsov (Gromyko being out of town) but Kuznetsov was not available and Kohler was able to see only Deputy Foreign Minister Firyubin. The latter, after some temporizing, flatly refused his government's services as an intermediary and lectured Kohler at length upon the US misconception of the real nature of the conflict in Vietnam. Kohler's account of the conversation follows:

> I informed Firyubin that as he must know from report of Dobrynin's conversation with Secretary, US Government has made decision which we hoped would be both understood and not misunderstood. I had been informally [words illegible] Soviet agreed that decision we had taken was precisely what was called for but none had been in position to predict reaction. Our purpose in reaching this significant decision was to attempt to ascertain if a way could be found to peaceful solution of current crisis in Southeast Asia. We had hoped we would be able to deliver oral communication conveying this decision to DRV authorities and I had attempted

to do so today through DRV Ambassador. Unfortunately Ambassador let it be known that he did not wish to receive me personally and when his embassy was informed that the message I sought to deliver was of extreme importance, it was suggested that we transmit the message through the Soviet Government in its capacity as Geneva Co-Chairman. It was because of these circumstances that I had found it necessary to disturb Mr. Firyubin tonight. I pointed out that although DRV Ambassador had refused to receive me, embassy had succeeded in delivering a copy of oral communication to employee of DRV embassy earlier this evening (2015 Local) who agreed to bring it to attention of Ambassador (communication as set forth in DEPTEL 3103 then translated in full for Firyubin with sole interruption being Firyubin's inquiry if cessation attacks applied only to those from air —which I confirmed). After receiving confirmation from me that communication was of oral nature, Firyubin said he viewed communication as based on old erroneous conception on which US has proceeded, a conception which precludes US recognizing that the South Vietnamese people are fighting for their freedom and are struggling against aggression and control by Saigon puppets. Furthermore it indicated to Firyubin that we continued to view the picture incorrectly when we referred again to the struggle in South Vietnam as being organized and directed by the DRV. The absurdity of this view, he said, is obvious and naturally the Soviet Government cannot agree with it as it has made clear in numerous statements. Firyubin could only view the communication as repetition of the threat against the DRV —now a threat of renewed and expanded aggression. This was the only way he could interpret the reference to the risk that a suspension of attacks involved. Obviously we are suffering from a gross misunderstanding if we think that such aggression will go unpunished, without response. The only constructive approach to a peaceful settlement of the situation in South Vietnam was to end the aggression, recall troops from South Vietnam and give the Vietnamese people the right to choose their own form of Government—a choice which can be made freely only if the so-called specialists should be withdrawn and their opportunity of exercising influence on the Vietnamese thus removed. Firyubin said that he well acquainted with the countries and peoples of Southeast Asia; he therefore was aware and could understand the feelings caused by our actions there as well as in many other parts of the world.

I told Firyubin I had asked to see him to put a very simple question to him. Does the Soviet Government agree to transmit the oral communication to the DRV? I said this was the whole purpose of my visit.

Firyubin said the DRV embassy had not put such a request to the Soviet Government. I must agree that for Soviets to act as intermediary between us and DRV is very unusual. Naturally he would report my request to his Government and if the DRV should request this service he would not exclude the possibility of transmitting the communication to the DRV Government. Meanwhile he would be interested in knowing just how the DRV embassy had responded to our approach.

I again described for Firyubin our efforts to deliver the message to the DRV through its embassy in Moscow and told him that the end result was a suggestion by the embassy that we transmit the message through the Soviet Government in its capacity as Geneva Co-Chairman. Firyubin repeated his promise to report my request to his Government and to inform me of the results.

While the conversation continued in this vein, Firyubin had passed a note to a Foreign Office assistant, Kornienko, who attended him, and the latter left the room. After some time, Kornienko reappeared and handed a note to Firyubin, which the latter read carefully. After reading the note, Firyubin said flatly that the Soviet Government would not transmit the U.S. Government's message to the DRV, that the DRV embassy had not requested this service and that it was the U.S. responsibility to find a convenient way of passing the message. Kohler's account continues:

> I said I wished to understand him correctly. Was he rejecting my request to transmit the communication to the DRV?
>
> He said this was a correct understanding of the Soviet Government position. We must ourselves find the way.
>
> I said that what I was seeking was the cooperation of the Soviet Government and Firyubin's remarks indicated clearly that the Soviet Government was refusing this. Firyubin said, "I am not a postman" and again said we could find our own ways of transmitting messages.
>
> I pointed out to Firyubin that the cooperation I had requested is a well-known and not unprecedented process in international diplomacy. I had great difficulty in reconciling Soviet Government refusal to cooperate with its declaration in support of peaceful settlement of all questions.
>
> Kornienko chimed in that he had recalled statement by both the President and Secretary of State on several occasions that the U.S. Government has channels for transmitting messages direct to Hanoi. On this the conversation ended but it should be noted that Firyubin made no effort to return to me the text of the oral communication which I had handed him at the outset of the conversation.

After further reflection on his meeting with Firyubin, Kohler sent a follow-on message to Washington that afternoon, in which he sought to present the Soviet position with some sympathy and to promote an understanding of the Soviet rebuff in the light of the "rather strenuous nature" of the document we were asking them to transmit. Kohler's comments were as follows:

> I came away from my meeting with Firyubin last night with mixed feelings. On the one hand, I was annoyed at the apparent Soviet rebuff of an effort to take heat out of admittedly dangerous situation in SEA and impatient with flimsy rationale for Soviet refusal offered by Firyubin. On the other hand, I could understand, if not sympathize with, Soviet sensitivity, given Chicom eagerness to adduce proof of their charges of collusion against Soviets and, frankly, given rather strenuous nature of document they were being asked to transmit to DRV.
>
> Implicit in latter view, of course, is assumption that Soviets in fact want bombing to stop, are genuinely concerned at possibilities escalation, and are interested in working out some sort of modus vivendi which would take heat out of situation while not undercutting their own position in Commie world as loyal socialist ally. We cannot be sure that this is way Soviets view situation, and it entirely possible they so confident our ultimate defeat in Vietnam that no gesture on our part would meet with encouraging response. Believe at this point, however, we lose nothing assuming Soviets have not completely forgotten lesson Cuba and there is some flexibility in Soviet position which we should seek to exploit.

I would hope, therefore, we would not regard Firyubin's reaction last night as evidence conscious hardening of Soviet attitude. It may simply be reflection of bind Soviets find themselves in at moment. Meanwhile, we can feel sure message is already in DRV hands—copies now available thru Dobrynin, Firyubin, and DRV embassy here—and I would suggest we go through with original plan and be on alert, both here and on the scene for any signs reaction from other side. Seen from here, we would lose nothing by doing so; and we gain at least with our friends and the unaligned.

By this time (1:00 p.m. March 13, Moscow time), though Kohler was not aware of it, the bombing pause had already been in effect for seventeen hours. It had gone into effect as planned at 2400 on May 12, Saigon time, and the Department so informed Kohler. The Department also decided, in spite of Kohler's confidence that the U.S. "oral" communication had reached Hanoi, to make doubly sure by asking the U.K. Government to instruct its Consul in Hanoi to transmit the same message, in writing, to his normal contact in the DRV. Informed by the Department that this step was about to be taken, Kohler expressed his dissatisfaction with the character and tone of the communication by recommending that, in any resubmission, the message be shortened and softened:

> . . . I would recommend we shorten and revise wording of "oral" communication to DRV if we plan resubmit through British Consul Hanoi. If cast is present form, I think we are simply inviting rebuff, and exercise-Hanoi would prove as fruitless as our efforts in Moscow. Something along lines following would get essential message across:
> BEGIN TEXT. The highest authority in this Government has asked me to inform Hanoi that there will be no air attacks on North Vietnam for a period beginning at noon, Washington time, Wednesday, May 12 and running into next week.
> In this decision the United States Government has taken account of repeated suggestions from various quarters, including public statements by Hanoi representatives, that there can be no progress toward peace while there are air attacks on North Vietnam.
> The United States Government expects that in consequence of this action the DRV will show similar restraint. If this should not prove to be the case, then the United States Government will feel compelled to take such measures as it feels are necessary to deal with the situation in Vietnam. END TEXT.

Kohler's recommendation was not accepted, and the message was transmitted to the DRV by the British Consul in Hanoi in its original form. As in the Moscow case, the message was shortly thereafter returned to the sender, ostensibly unopened.

As a footnote to the "unopened letter" episodes, it may be worth noting that Canadian ICC Commissioner Blair Seaborn, on an early-June visit to Hanoi, was approached by the Czech Ambassador to the DRV, who recounted to him the story of Kohler's unsuccessful effort to deliver the message to the DRV Ambassador in Moscow, with the message having been returned ostensibly unopened. The Czech Ambassador said "everybody" in Hanoi knew the story.

D. AWAITING A RESPONSE

While the Administration expected little in the way of a positive Hanoi response, a watchful eye was kept for any signals or actions that might suggest North Vietnamese or Soviet receptivity to any further diplomatic explorations. Such signals as were received, however, were entirely negative. On May 15 a Hanoi English language broadcast noted Western news reports of the bombing cessation, terming them "a worn out trick of deceit and threat . . ." On the same day, in a conversation with British Foreign Secretary Michael Stewart in Vienna, Soviet Foreign Minister Andrei Gromyko indicated the USSR's disinclination to participate in any negotiations on Indochina.

In the meantime, in Saigon, the U.S. Mission was hard at work trying to clarify its own thinking—and that of Washington—on the persuasive, or rather coercive, possibilities of bombing pauses. In particular, the Mission was hoping to link the intensity of US bombing after the resumption closely to the level of VC activity during the pause. The purpose would be to make it clear to Hanoi that what we were trying to accomplish with our bombing was to get the DRV to cease directing and supporting the VC *and* to get VC units to cease their military activities in the South. In this approach, a downward trend in VC activities would be "rewarded" in a similar manner by decreasing US bombing. Thus it was hoped that, during the bombing pause, the DRV would offer the first step in a series of events which might ultimately "lead to the termination of hostilities on satisfactory [i.e., U.S.] terms, without engaging in formal negotiations."

Ambassador Taylor described this approach to Washington in a lengthy cable concurred in by Deputy Ambassador Johnson and General Westmoreland. The Ambassador recognized that there were one or two minor pitfalls in the scheme, but seemed undaunted in his confidence that US bombing could be designed to have powerful coercive effects. Taylor admitted that:

> Any success in carrying out such a scenario [would] obviously depend on a considerable amount of cooperation from the DRV side based on a conviction arising from self-interest that the DRV must accept a settlement which excludes the conquest of SVN by NVN. There is little likelihood that the Hanoi leaders are yet ready to reach such a conclusion, but a rigorous application of air attacks at a tempo related to Hanoi/VC activities accompanied by pressure on the ground to compel the VC to engage in incidents or retreat appears to us to have possibilities. Conceivably, these ground operations might eventually result in herding VC units into "safe havens" . . . Whatever its other weaknesses, such a program would eliminate in large measure the danger which we may now be facing of equating our bombing activity to VC initiated incidents . . .

A quite different approach to a settlement was proposed in a rather puzzling informal contact between Pierre Salinger and two somewhat shadowy Soviet officials in Moscow. On the evening of May 11 (i.e., one full day prior to the inauguration of the bombing pause) Salinger, who was in Moscow at the time on private movie production business, was invited to dinner by Mikhail Sagatelyan, whom Salinger had known in Washington during the Kennedy years as the TASS Bureau Chief, and who was at this time assigned to TASS headquarters in Moscow. Salinger reported his conversation to Ambassador Kohler who related it to Secretary Rusk in a cable as follows:

Sagatelyan probed Salinger hard as to whether he was on some kind of covert mission and seemed unconvinced despite latter's reiterated denials. In any case, Sagatelyan, protesting he was speaking personally, talked at length about Viet-Nam. He wanted Salinger's opinion on hypothetical formula for solution approximatey on following lines:

1. US would announce publicly temporary suspension of bombing DRV;

2. DRV or USSR or both would make statement hailing suspension as step toward reasonable solution;

3. Soviet Union would intercede with Viet Cong to curtail military activities;

4. De facto cease fire would thus be accomplished.

5. Conference would be called on related subject (not specifically Viet-Nam). Viet Cong would not be participant but have some kind of observer or corridor status (this followed Salinger's expression of opinion US Government would never accept Viet Cong as participant in any conference).

6. New agreement would be worked out on Viet-Nam providing for broader-based SVN Government not including direct Viet Cong participation but including elements friendly to Viet Cong.

In a follow-up dinner conversation between Salinger and Sagatelyan two nights later, in which a Foreign Office representative, identified only as "Vassily Sergeyevich" also participated, the Soviet interlocutors generally confirmed the proposal quoted above, modifying points three and four by suggesting that an actual cease fire could take place only after initiation of negotiations and that a cease fire would in fact be the first item on the agenda of any negotiations. Additional items of interest were reported by Kohler as follows:

> Soviet interlocutors talked at length about President Kennedy's forebearance post-Cuba period and broadly implied that Soviets now interested in reciprocating such forebearance. It was clear from their remarks that Soviets assume we would welcome some avenue of withdrawal so long as this would not involve loss of American prestige.
>
> Soviets informed Salinger that Soviet Government had received a "Rusk proposal" with regard Vietnam but would not answer proposal or act on it in any way until Soviet Government had some idea as to how current exercise with Salinger would turn out . . .
>
> As to mechanics of carrying on exercise, Sagatelyan suggested Salinger might convey proposal to US Government through embassy Paris and he himself would fly immediately Paris in order receive from Salinger there any official reaction. Alternatively, if Salinger wished to proceed direct Washington, contact could be designated there, probably either Zinchuk (Soviet embassy counselor) or Vadvichenko (TASS Washington Bureau).
>
> Throughout conversation Soviets made clear to Salinger that because of sensitive Soviet position any progress toward political settlement Vietnam problem must be initiated and carried through, at least in preliminary stages, on basis unofficial contacts, clear implication being if leak should occur or if scheme should go awry, Soviet Government would be in position disavow whole affair. At same time, it was clear from remarks as well as presence of Foreign Office representative that proposal by Sagatelyan had official backing.

Salinger had one further contact with Sagatelyan and Vassily the following day, where it became apparent that the Soviet officials' interest in the proposal had waned. By the time Salinger had returned to Washington and saw Ambassador Thompson at the State Department on May 18, the Soviet disinterest in any role for themseves during the current bombing pause had been made clear through other channels, and Salinger's contacts were not further pursued.

Of these other channels, the most important (and also the most casual) was a brief Kaffeeklatsch between Secretary Rusk and Foreign Minister Gromyko at the Austrian Chancelor's residence in Vienna on May 15. The proceedings are described in a Rusk cable to Undersecretary Ball as follows:

> Have just returned from Chancellor's lunch for visiting dignitaries. After lunch Gromyko and I [words illegible] were in something of a dilemma about Southeast Asia. We felt there might be some value in a serious exchange of views between our two Governments but that we did not know whether they themselves wished to discuss it.
>
> He commented with considerable seriousness that the Soviets will not negotiate about Viet-Nam. He said there were other parties involved in that situation and that the United States woud have to find ways of establishing contact with them, and he specifically mentioned the DRV. He said they will continue to support North Viet-Nam and will do so "decisively." He then made reference to a fellow socialist country under attack.
>
> I interrupted to point out that the problem was not that a socialist country was subject to attack but that a socialist country was attacking somone else. I said that American military forces are in South Vietnam solely because North Vietnam has been sending large numbers of men and arms into the South.
>
> He denied these facts in the usual ritual fashion but added that in any event it was not up to the United States to be the judge between Vietnamese. I reminded him that he must know by now that a North Korean attack against South Koreans would not be accepted merely because both were Korean. He merely commented that there were important differences between those two situations.
>
> He referred to Dobrynin's talk with me and said that the temporary suspension of bombing was "insulting." I said I could not understand this in view of the fact that Hanoi, Peiping and Moscow have all talked about the impossibility of discussions while bombing was going on.
>
> At this point Chancellor Klaus joined the table to express great happiness that Gromyko and I were sitting together. Neither one of us dispelled his illusion.
>
> I do not know whether Gromyko will pursue the matter further when the four foreign ministers meet briefly with Quaison–Sackey this afternoon or when we all assemble for the opera tonight.
>
> Thompson and I both have the impression that Gromyko's attitude clearly means that the Salinger talk was of little substance and that we should now merely consider what kind of signal we wish to get back by way of Salinger as a part of the closing out process.
>
> I do not believe that we should assume from Gromyko's remarks that we ourselves should not put to Moscow our own most serious views of the situation, whether they are willing to discuss them or not. It is quite clear, however, that Gromyko wanted me to believe that they are not prepared to work toward a settlement in Hanoi and Peiping and that, indeed, unless we abandon our effort in South Viet-Nam there will be very serious consequences ahead.

E. RESUMING THE BOMBING

Having thus been unmistakably rebuffed by Moscow, Hanoi, and Peking, the President determined on the evening of May 16 that the bombing raids should be resumed, beginning on the morning of May 18 Saigon time. In addition to the ROLLING THUNDER XV execute message sent by the JCS to CINCPAC on the 16th, Secretary Rusk sent messages of a political nature to Saigon, London, and Ottawa on May 17, so that the action could be cleared with Premier Quat (which Taylor promptly accomplished), and so that the foreign ministers of the Commonwealth countries would be informed beforehand.

> You should see Fon Min immediately to inform that beginning Tuesday morning, Saigon time, bombing of North Viet-Nam will be resumed by US and South Vietnamese forces, marking the end of a five-day suspension.
> You should convey message from me that we regret that the reception of the other side to the idea of a pause was not merely negative but hostile. Gromyko told Rusk that our message to Dobrynin on subject was "insulting." Nevertheless we do not exclude possibility of other such attempts in future.
> There will be no public announcement of the resumption of bombing. When press questions are asked, it will be pointed out that there have been and may again be periods when no bombing will take place in response to operational factors and that we do not discuss these operational questions.

Ambassador Kohler, upon receiving word of the resumption, suggested that the US might inform the NATO Council and the 17 non-aligned nations of our actions, in advance of any resumption, to underline the seriousness of the President's response to the Unaligned Appeal. The Department, however, responded negatively to Kohler's suggestion:

> There will be no official public statement from here concerning suspension or resumption. Decision at highest levels is to avoid any discussion Project MAYFLOWER [words illegible] concluded, outside of resricted circle designated when Project begun. Despite disappointing response, we wish to keep open channel with Soviets on this subject and we hope eventually with DRV via Soviets. We feel that use of this channel another time might be precluded if we appear to have carried through Project MAYFLOWER solely for credit it might earn us with third parties and public opinion in general. Therefore we would not now wish inform NATO Council and 17 Non-aligned countries.
> Only British, Canadians, Australians, UN Secreary General and Korean President Park (here on state visit) were in fact informed in advance of resumption bombing and also of negative outcome of soundings of other side.

In addition to this limited circle of allied intimates, a larger circle of friendly governments was provided with Ambassadorial briefings on the bombing pause *after* the resumption. An instruction to this effect went out to American ambassadors in New Delhi, Tokyo, Bangkok, Vientiane, Manila, Wellington, and Paris:

> You should take first opportunity see Pri. Minister, Fon Min, or other appropriate high level official to inform him that the U.S. and South Viet-

namese Governments suspended bombing against North Viet-Nam for a period of five days which ended on May 18. The initiation of this pause in bombing was accompanied by an approach by us to the Governments of the Soviet Union and North Viet-Nam which took note of repeated calls from that side for cessation of bombing and their statements that discussions could not take place while bombing continued. Unfortunately the reception of our approach was not merely negative but hostile . . . In view of the complete absence of any constructive response, we have decided the bombing must be resumed. Nevertheless we do not exclude possibility of other such attempts in the future.

You should add that the record of the past several weeks is discouraging in that Communists and particularly Peking appear intent on rejecting every effort from whatever quarter to open up contacts and conversations which might lead to a resolution of the Viet-Nam situation. The rejection of President Johnson's April 7 proposals for unconditional discussions, of the appeal of the Seventeen Non-aligned countries and of President Radhakrishnan's proposal all illustrate the point together with Peking and Hanoi's obvious efforts to obstruct the convening of a conference on Cambodia. We will nevertheless continue to explore all possibilities for constructive discussion, meanwhile maintaining with the Government of South Viet-Nam our joint military efforts to preserve that country's freedom.

On the evening of May 16, the DRV Foreign Ministry issued a statement denouncing the gesture as a "deceitful maneuver designed to pave the way for new U.S. acts of war," and insisted U.S. planes had, since May 12, repeatedly intruded into DRV airspace "for spying, provocative and strafing activities."

Communist China's Foreign Ministry issued a statement May 21 fully endorsing Hanoi's position and denouncing the suspension with characteristic intemperateness.

F. AFTERMATH

A still somewhat ambiguous diplomatic move was made by Hanoi on May 18, shortly after the bombing had been resumed.

It appears that in Paris, on the morning of May 18, Mai Van Bo, head of the DRV economic delegation there, approached the Asian Direction of the Quai d'Orsay to explain the reasons for the DRV's rejection of the Radhakrishnan proposals (involving a *cordon sanitaire* by Afro–Asian troops along the 17th parallel). More important, however, Bo explained with text in hand that the Pham Van Dong Four Points, enunciated on April 8, should not be isolated from the declaration that had followed the four points. He then softened the language of that declaration by pointing out that the four points constituted the "best basis" from which to find the "most just" solution, and that recognition of these principles would create favorable conditions for a solution of the problem and would open the possibility of convoking a conference.

When asked if Hanoi recognized that realization of its proposed "principle of withdrawal" of American forces would depend upon the "conclusions of a negotiation," Bo responded "exactly," and indicated that if there were agreement on the "bases," the "ways and means" of application of "principles" would be found and in a peaceful manner; the possibilities were many; a way out (porte de sortie) should be found for the US; "our suggestion humiliates no one."

This happening, which occurred on May 18, was first reported by a Quai official to the US Embassy's Political Counsellor in Paris unofficially on May 19, in a highly glossed version, making it appear that the DRV was clearly responding to the bombing pause by a significant softening of its position on "prior conditions." In the official version that Lucet, the Director of Political Affairs of the French Foreign Office conveyed to the DCM on May 20, however, the continued ambiguity of the DRV position—as to whether or not recognition of the four points remained a precondition to talks of any sort—was fully revealed.

This ambiguity was in no sense resolved a few weeks later, when Blair Seaborn raised this question with the DRV Foreign Minister in Hanoi. The U.S. had asked Seaborn in late May to seek a meeting with Pham Van Dong and on its behalf reiterate the March message and U.S. determination to persist in the defense of South Vietnam, to regret that Hanoi had not responded positively to the various recent initiatives, including the bombing pause, and to state that, nevertheless, the United States remained ready "to consider the possibility of a solution by reciprocal actions on each side." If the Vietnamese brought up Pham Van Dong's four points, Seaborn was authorized to endeavor to establish whether Hanoi insisted that they be accepted as the condition for negotiations. On June 3, Seaborn succeeded in gaining an audience with the DRV Foreign Minister (and concurrent Deputy Premier) Nguygen Duy Trinh, who reluctantly heard him out after stating that the U.S. position was too well known to require restatement. Trinh's reaction to the message was totally negative, and in the exchange preceding its recitation he studiously avoided going beyond the vague statement that Pham Van Dong's four points were the "basis for solution of the Vietnam question."

As there was considerable misunderstanding concerning the Mai Van Bo approach of May 18, and misleading accounts of it were circulating, the State Department informed several U.S. ambassadors (Saigon, Paris, Bonn) of what it considered the true facts in the case.

> Facts are that bombing was actually resumed on morning May 18 Saigon time. Subsequently on morning May 18, Paris time, but undoubtedly on antecedent instructions, DRV economic delegate in Paris, Mai Van Bo, approached Quai urgently for appointment. His message was to explain negative Hanoi attitude toward Indian proposal (cessation of hostilities on both sides and Afro–Asian force) but second, and more important, to discuss Pham Van Dong's four points originally stated April 8 and later included in Hanoi statement referring to appeal of 17 Non-aligned nations . . . Bo repeated four points with slight variations from public statements, apparently softening language by indicating that four points might be "best basis" for settlement and apparently insisting less strongly that their recognition was required as condition to negotiations. During course of conversations, French asked whether withdrawal US forces visualized as prior condition or as resulting from negotiations, and Bo responded that latter was correct.
>
> French passed us this message on May 20 (delaying two days) so that we had in fact resumed well before we heard of it. More important, message still left ambiguity whether recognition of four points remained precondition to talks of any sort. Accordingly, we saw no reason to alter conclusion based on Hanoi propaganda denunciation of pause, plus fact that pace of Hanoi-directed basic actions in South had continued and even

increased—that Hanoi not ready to respond to pause and that we must resume.

Subsequently, Canadian ICC Representative, Seaborn, visited Hanoi commencing May 31. He himself raised same questions with DRV Foreign Minister and response indicated DRV evasive, and in effect negative, apparently taking position recognition four points, plus some element US withdrawal, were preconditions to any talks.

XIII. DEBATE OVER BOMBING STRATEGY AND EFFECTIVENESS CONTINUES

A. THE ROSTOW "VICTORY" THESIS

With the resumption of the bombing at 0600 on 18 May (Saigon time), the arguments over the usefulness and intensity of the U.S. air attacks against the North were taken up again with full energy.

ROLLING THUNDER XV (week of 18–24 May) was designed to attack principally fixed military installations, while continuing the interdiction of LOC's south of the 20th parallel. The attacks were carried out with a weight of effort similar to the pre-pause level, i.e., 40 sorties per day, with a maximum of 200 sorties for the entire week.

It was at this time that Walt W. Rostow, then State Department Counselor and Chairman of the Policy Planning Council, floated a memorandum entitled "Victory and Defeat in Guerrilla Wars: The Case of South Vietnam," in which he argued that a clear-cut victory for the U.S. in Vietnam *was* a possibility and that what it required mainly was more pressure on the North and effective conduct of the battle in the South. Rostow's memo follows:

> In the press, at least, there is a certain fuzziness about the possibility of clear-cut victory in South Viet-Nam; and the President's statement that a military victory is impossible is open to misinterpretation.
>
> 1. Historically, guerrilla wars have generally been lost or won cleanly: Greece, China, mainland, North Viet-Nam, Malaya, Philippines. Laos in 1954 was an exception, with two provinces granted the Communists and a *de facto* split imposed on the country.
>
> 2. In all the cases won by Free World forces, there was a phase when the guerrillas commanded a good part of the countryside and, indeed, placed Athens, Kuala Lumpur, and Manila under something close to siege. They failed to win because all the possible routes to guerrilla victory were closed and, in failing to win, they lost. They finally gave up in discouragement. The routes to victory are:
>
> > a) Mao Stage Three: going to all-out conventional war and winning as in China in 1947–49;
> > b) Political collapse and takeover: North Viet-Nam;
> > c) Political collapse and a coalition government in which the Communists get control over the security machinery; that is, army and/or police. This has been an evident Viet Cong objective in this war, but the nearest precedents are Eastern European takeovers after 1945, rather than guerrilla war cases.

d) Converting the bargaining pressure generated by the guerrilla forces into a partial victory by splitting the country: Laos. Also, in a sense, North Viet-Nam in 1954 and the Irish Rebellion after the First World War.

3. If we succeed in blocking these four routes to victory, discouraging the Communist force in the South, and making the continuance of the war sufficiently costly to the North there is no reason we cannot win as clear a victory in South Viet-Nam as in Greece, Malaya, and the Philippines. Unless political morale in Saigon collapses and the ARVN tends to break up, case c), the most realistic hope of the VC, should be avoidable. This danger argues for more rather than less pressure on the North, while conducting the battle in the South in such a way as to make VC hopes of military and political progress wane.

4. The objective of the exercise is to convince Hanoi that its bargaining position is being reduced with the passage of time; for, even in the worst case for Hanoi, it wants some bargaining position (rather than simply dropping the war) to get U.S. forces radically reduced in South Viet-Nam and to get some minimum face-saving formula for the VC.

5. I believe Hanoi understands its dilemma well. As of early February it saw a good chance of a quite clean victory via route c). It now is staring at quite clear-cut defeat, with the rising U.S. strength and GVN morale in the South and rising costs in the North. That readjustment in prospects is painful; and they won't, in my view, accept its consequences unless they are convinced time has ceased to be their friend, despite the full use of their assets on the ground in South Viet-Nam, in political warfare around the world, and in diplomacy.

6. Their last and best hope will be, of course, that if they end the war and get us out, the political, social, and economic situation in South Viet-Nam will deteriorate in such a way as to permit Communist political takeover, with or without a revival of guerrilla warfare. It is in this phase that we will have to consolidate, with the South Vietnamese, a victory that is nearer our grasp than we (but not Hanoi) may think.

Rostow had long been a strong bombing advocate, and an outspoken proponent of air attack on elements of the North Vietnamese industrial target system. As early as April 1, he had expressed a conviction that Hanoi attaches a high premium to the maintenance of its industrial establishment and that the optimum U.S. bombing objective should be not the destruction, but the paralysis of the DRV's industrial and urban life. By taking out all the major electric power stations, he believed, Hanoi would be presented "with an immediate desperate economic, social, and political problem which could not be evaded."

In the May memorandum, however, he was not confining his confident expertise to the sphere of targeting strategy, but extending it to the much larger sweep of the U.S. policy objectives in Vietnam. Rostow's grand historic perspective of the road to victory, unfortunately, never focused down upon the nagging practical problem of how the U.S. might "make VC hopes of military and political progress wane" when compelled to fight in behalf of a long-besieged, teetering GVN that was, by this time, hopelessly incapable of coping with the military and political tasks required of it. The critical problem of how to preserve and restore political effectiveness in the GVN never engaged Rostow's serious attention nor, for that matter, that of his contemporaries in the administration.

B. *"ARC LIGHT" COMES TO* SOUTH *VIETNAM—ATTACKS* ON THE NORTH *EDGE UPWARD*

In line with the April decision to give priority to South Vietnam over North Vietnam in the employment of U.S. air power, a major administration decision was taken after the bombing pause to assign saturation bombing missions in the South to SAC B–52 bombers which had long been alerted, but never used, to attack North Vietnam. General Westmoreland, with Ambassador Taylor's political endorsement, presented his case to CINCPAC in the following terms:

1. During recent months firm intelligence has been collected using all possible sources which confirms existence of various VC headquarters complexes and troop concentrations in RVN. Each of these targets (COSVN, NAMBO, Military Region Hqs, VC battalions in jungle assembly areas, etc.) is spread over a relatively large area and consists of groups of buildings or huts, foxholes, trenches, tunnels, etc., connected by trails. General topography is more suitable for area carpet bombing than for pinpoint tactical fighter weapon delivery. In most areas two and three canopy jungle growth hides surface target. Even if accurate coordinates fixed on maps (with inherent map inaccuracies) or photos, solid jungle canopy provides few reasonable aiming points for delivery aircraft.

2. Operation Black Virgin 1 on 15 April 1965 was an attack on the military component of the Central Office South Vietnam (COSVN), (the main VC military headquarters). 443 sorties were applied against an area of approximately 12 square kilometers, dropping approximately 900 tons of ordnance. As a result of this effort, the existence of the target complex was confirmed by the uncovering of over 100 buildings and the occurrence of several large secondary explosions. We have determined that the attack created a drastic effect within the VC military headquarters. Individual components were disrupted for several days, and even though these components now appear to be functioning again, they have not re-assembled into an integrated headquarters complex as they were before the attack. In spite of the apparent success of the attack we still have no information concerning the number of casualties caused and have only fragmentary information concerning other damage accomplished.

3. During the attack the target area became completely covered by smoke and resulting bomb pattern was spotty. BDA photography shows that as a result, the distribution of bombs throughout the target was poor. Some areas received a heavy concentration of bomb impacts while other parts of the target area received no hits. If an attack could have been launched in which the bombs were evenly distributed, results would have been far more effective. An attack compressed into a shorter period of time would also have been much more likely to kill VC before they could evacuate the area and would have allowed ground troops to enter the area the same day.

4. It is essential that we keep these selected VC headquarters and units under attack. We are developing target information on the headquarters of

the 325th PAVN Division, Headquarters Military Region V and Headquarters Military Region VII where current reports indicated a large VC troop build-up. We know from interrogation of VC captives and from agent reports that VC fear air attacks. We also know that their plans can be upset by unexpected events. The best way for us to keep them off balance and prevent large-scale VC attacks is to keep them under constant pressure in their base areas.

5. Continued use of tactical fighters for pattern bombing does not get the job done properly; it diverts them from other important work for which they are better suited; it creates an unacceptable drain on ordnance assets; and it disrupts all SEA air programs in and out of country. We will, of course, continue to use tactical fighters as the major punch against tactical targets which constitute the vast majority of the in-country air requirements, but for attacks on VC base areas, we must provide a capability which will permit us to deliver a well planned pattern of bombs over large areas and preferably within a short period of time.

6. The problem has been discussed with representatives of the Strategic Air Command and believe that their conventional bombing tactics based on pattern bombing techniques are ideally suited to meet this requirement. I strongly recommend, therefore, that as a matter of urgency, we be authorized to employ SAC B–52 aircraft against selected area targets in RVN . . .

Washington first authorized the use of ARC LIGHT B–52 forces for night photography over target areas in the Kontum and War Zone D regions on May 1. A month later, despite the misgivings of the Air Staff and the SAC commander, the first B–52 bombing raid was authorized (ARC LIGHT I, June 18, 1965) attacking the War Zone D VC stronghold near Saigon. On July 4 and 7 further attacks were undertaken, and ARC LIGHT became a regular bombing program in South Vietnam.

As the weight of air attacks increased significantly in *South* Vietnam, there was also some rise in the level of air strikes in the North. Combined U.S.–VNAF combat sorties totaled about 3,600 in April, 4,000 in May, and 4,800 in June. USAF aircraft flew less than half the mission. But an analysis by JCS Chairman Wheeler on 4 April and another by the CIA and the Defense Intelligence Agency (DIA) early in July showed that the strikes had not reduced appreciably North Vietnam's ability to defend its homeland, train its forces, and infiltrate men and supplies into South Vietnam and Laos.

But this rising level of attacks did not satisfy the Air Staff. At the end of June, General McConnell continued to stress the need for more air pressure on Hanoi, saying he was:

more convinced than ever that these [air] operations cannot be divorced from and are the essential key to the eventual defeat of the Viet Cong. In November 1964 . . . [the] JCS unanimously agreed that direct, decisive, action against the DRV was needed immediately. This course of action was not adopted and intelligence reports indicate that the current air strike program, while inconveniencing the DRV had done little to curtail or destroy their will and capability to support the insurgency, largely due to the restraints on the air strike program. In fact, the restraints have provided the DRV with the incentive and opportunity to strengthen both their offensive and defensive capabilities.

So [the] C/S USAF considers an intensified application of air power against key industrial and military targets in North Vietnam essential to the result desired. During the period of time required to introduce more forces, any build-up of and support for the Viet Cong offensive should be denied. . . . Failing this, more serious difficulties and casualties for U.S. and allied troops can be expected.

McConnell urged again that the Air Force be allowed to strike targets in the 94 target list, as well as others.

C. MCNAMARA REVIEWS THE PROGRAM

At the end of July, in response to a Presidential request, Secretary McNamara undertook a review and evaluation of the bombing program against North Vietnam. The results of this review were forwarded to the President in a memorandum, dated July 30, 1965. Since it represents an effective wrap-up, the memorandum is reproduced in full.

1. *Rationale for bombing the North.* The program of bombing RVN began in an atmosphere of reprisal. We had had the August Tonkin Gulf episode; we had absorbed the November 1 attack on Bien Hoa Airfield and the Christmas Eve bombing of the Brinks Hotel in Saigon. The attacks at U.S. installations at Pleiku on February 7 and Qui Nhon on February 10 were the immediate causes of the first strikes against North Vietnam. The strike following Pleiku was announced as a "response"—a "reprisal"; our strike following Qui Nhon was called a response to more generalized VC terrorism. The major purposes of the bombing program, however, were:

a. *To promote a settlement.* The program was designed (1) to influence the DRV to negotiate (explicitly or otherwise), and (2) to provide us with a bargaining counter within negotiations.
b. *To interdict infiltration.* The program was calculated to reduce the flow of men and supplies from the North to the South—at the least, to put a ceiling on the size of war that the enemy could wage in the South. [Author's Note: This is not entirely accurate; interdiction did not become a program rationale within the Administration until late March, and publicaly not until late April (see Sections VIII and XI.B).] Supplemental purposes of the program were (c) to demonstrate to South Vietnam, North Vietnam and the world the U.S. commitment to see this thing through, (d) to raise morale in South Vietnam by punishing North Vietnam, the source of the suffering in the South, and (e) to reduce criticism of the Administration from advocates of a bombing program.

2. *Achievement of major purposes.* The potential targets, targets struck and per cent of destruction are shown at Tab A. In terms of the purposes of the program, its results have been as follows:

a. *To promote a settlement.* Obviously, this objective has not yet been attained. We recognized at the start of the program, as we do now, that the influence of the bombing on a settlement would not be great until the North Vietnamese had been disappointed in their hopes for a quick military success in the South. There is no doubt that the bombing program has become an important counter in the current tacit and explicit bargaining process and will be an important counter in any future bargaining.

b. *To interdict infiltration.* It is believed that regular North Vietnamese units now in South Vietnam (estimated to be one division) require about 4 tons of supplies daily for the "current" level of combat but would require 67 tons of supplies daily for "light" combat. ("Current" levels are operations conducted largely in small units; "light" combat would involve larger elements in action on the average of every third day, with expenditures of one-third of each unit's basic load of ammunition on each action.) It is believed that regular North Vietnamese units and Pathet Lao forces in the Laos Panhandle require about 21 and 51 tons daily respectively for the two levels of combat. Viet Cong arms, ammunition and other supply requirements are estimated at 8 tons daily for "current" combat and 115 tons for "light" combat. The effect of the interdiction program on the movement of supplies is summarized below:

The 440-ton per day rail traffic from Hanoi south to Vinh has been cut off at Ninh Binh (40 miles south of Hanoi). Supplies still move by sea and over the parallel highway system. The latter has been badly damaged and is subject to armed reconnaissance; sea traffic into SVN is under surveillance. At a minimum, supply is slower and less regular and delivered at increased cost in resources and energy expended. Roads into Laos have been subjected to similar interdiction and armed recce. Only limited interdiction has been imposed on the key rail and road net northwest of Hanoi, and none on the railway net northeast of Hanoi; and port destruction has been minimal. Thus, substantially uninterrupted supply continues from China by rail into Hanoi and by sea into Haiphong to meet major North Vietnamese military, industrial and civilian needs.

The effect of the bombing on military operations is estimated to have been as follows:

(1) *For regular North Vietnamese and Pathet Lao forces.* The interdiction program has caused North Vietnam increasing difficulty in supplying their units in Laos and South Vietnam. How severe this difficulty is or how stretched North Vietnam's supply capabilities are cannot be estimated precisely. Our interdiction efforts may have either prevented or deterred the North from sending more troops than they already have. The interdiction programs in North Vietnam and Laos also may have influenced a Communist decision to forego a 1965 offensive in Laos.

(2) *For Viet Cong forces.* Because the VC require significantly less infiltrated arms and ammunition and other supplies than do the North Vietnamese and Pathet Lao forces, the interdiction program probably has had less of an adverse effect on their operations. By raising VC fears concerning adequacy of supplies, however, the program may have caused the VC summer offensive to be less intense, aggressive and unrelenting than it would otherwise have been.

It should be noted that the program has not been a "strategic" bombing program; it has been limited to selected targets of fairly direct military relevance. Populations and targets such as dikes and basic industries have not been struck. Furthermore, the immediate vicinities of Hanoi and Haiphong have been avoided, partly because the targets there are primarily of the "strategic" type and partly because strikes there would involve even more serious risks of confrontations with the Soviet Union and China.

3. *Other effects of the program.*

a. *Deterrence of VC terrorism.* There is no evidence that strikes against North Vietnam have affected one way or another the level or kind of VC incidents of terror in South Vietnam.

b. *Morale in South Vietnam.* Morale in South Vietnam was raised by the initiation of the bombing program (as, later, by the deployment of additional troops). Now—with the bombing programs having become commonplace and with the failure of the situation to improve—morale in South Vietnam is not discernibly better than it was before the bombing program began. In a sense, South Vietnam is now "addicted" to the program; a permanent abandonment of the program would have a distinct depressing effect on morale in South Vietnam.

c. *Reduction of criticism of the Administration.* Some critics, who advocated bombing, were silenced; others are now as vocal or more vocal because the program has been too limited for their taste. The program has generated a new school of criticism among liberals and "peace" groups, whose activities have been reflected especially in teach-ins and newspaper criticisms.

d. *Damage to peaceful image of the US.* The price paid for improving our image as a guarantor has been damage to our image as a country which eschews armed attacks on other nations. The hue and cry correlates with the kind of weapons (e.g., bombs vs. napalm), the kind of targets (e.g., bridges vs. people), the location of targets (e.g., south vs. north), and not least the extent to which the critic feels threatened by Asian communism (e.g., Thailand vs. the UK). Furthermore, for a given level of bombing, the hue and cry is less now than it was earlier, perhaps to some extent helped by Communist intransigence toward discussions. The objection to our "warlike" image and the approval of our fulfilling our commitments competes in the minds of many nations (and individuals) in the world, producing a schizophrenia. Within such allied countries as UK and Japan, popular antagonism to the bombings per se, fear of escalation and belief that the bombings are the main obstacle to negotiation, have created political problems for the governments in their support of US policy.

e. *Pressures to settle.* More countries are now, as a consequence of the bombing program, more interested in taking steps to help bring the war to an end.

f. *Impact on US–Soviet detente.* The bombing program—because it appears to reject the policy of "peaceful co-existence," because it involves an attack on a "fellow socialist country," because the Soviet people have vivid horrible memories of air bombing, because it challenges the USSR as she competes with China for leadership of the Communist world, and because US and Soviet arms are now striking each other in North Vietnam—has strained the US–Soviet detente, making constructive arms-control and other cooperative programs more difficult. How serious this effect will be and whether the detente can be revived depend on how far we carry our military actions against the North and how long the campaign continues. At the same time, the bombing program offers the Soviet

Union an opportunity to play a role in bringing peace to Vietnam, by gaining credit for persuading us to terminate the program. There is a chance that the scenario could spin out this way; if so, the effect of the entire experience on the US–Soviet detente could be a net plus.

g. *Risk of escalation.* The bombing program—especially as strikes move toward Hanoi and toward China and as encounters with Soviet/ Chinese SAMs/MIGs occur—may increase the risk of escalation into a broader war.

4. *The future of the program.* Even with hindsight, I believe the decision to bomb the DRV was wise and I believe the program should be continued. The future program should:

a. *Emphasize the threat.* It should be structured to capitalize on fear of future attacks. At any time, "pressure" on the DRV depends not upon the *current* level of bombing but rather upon the credible threat of *future* destruction which can be avoided by agreeing to negotiate or agreeing to some settlement in negotiations.

b. *Minimize the loss of DRV "face."* The program should be designed to make it politically easy for the DRV to enter negotiations and to make concessions during negotiations. It may be politically easier for North Vietnam to accept negotiations and/or to make concessions at a time when bombing of their territory is not currently taking place.

c. *Optimize interdiction vs. political costs.* Interdiction should be carried out so as to maximize effectiveness and to minimize the political repercussions from the methods used. Physically, it makes no difference whether a rifle is interdicted on its way into North Vietnam, on its way out of North Vietnam, in Laos or in South Vietnam. But different amounts of effort and different political prices may be paid depending on how and where it is done. The critical variables in this regard are (1) the type of targets struck (e.g., port facilities involving civilian casualties vs. isolated bridges), (2) type of aircraft (e.g., B–52s vs. F–105s), (3) kind of weapons (e.g., napalm vs. ordinary bomb), (4) location of target (e.g., in Hanoi vs. Laotian border area), and (5) the accompanying declaratory policy (e.g., unlimited vs. a defined interdiction zone).

d. *Coordinate with other influences on the DRV.* So long as full victory in the South appears likely, the effect of the bombing program in promoting negotiations or a settlement will probably be small. The bombing program now and later should be designed for its influence on the DRV at that unknown time when the DRV becomes more optimistic about what they can achieve in a settlement acceptable to us than about what they can achieve by continuation of the war.

e. *Avoid undue risks and costs.* The program should avoid bombing which runs a high risk of escalation into war with the Soviets or China and which is likely to appall allies and friends.

4.   American Troops Enter the Ground War, March–July 1965

Summary

MARINE COMBAT UNITS GO TO DA NANG, MARCH 1965

On March 8, 1965, two United States Marine Corps Battalion Landing Teams arrived at Da Nang with the Mission to help secure the air base and associated installations. What was the rationale behind the decision to put the first U.S. ground combat units into Vietnam? Was this a conscious prelude to U.S. assumption of a ground combat role in the Vietnam war?

On February 22, 1965, COMUSMACV, General Westmoreland, recommended the landing and the mission. The United States at the time was already conducting Flaming Dart airstrikes against the DRV. Since Da Nang was supporting those strikes in addition to concomitant air activity within SVN, there was concern in many quarters that Da Nang might suffer the same fate as had Bien Hoa the previous November. Ambassador Taylor supported Westmoreland's request for the Marines, but with serious reservations. He saw this deployment as the removal of the last barrier to U.S. assumption of the ground war. In addition, he argued that two Marine BLTs would not be able to guarantee base security and that "white-faced" troops would be unable to assimilate and would have great difficulty identifying the enemy.* There is no documentary

---

* Back in August 1964, when he was less well-acquainted with the Vietnamese war and the proclivities of the side we were supporting, Ambassador Taylor was more readily inclined to recommend prudent actions involving the deployment of U.S. ground forces to Vietnam. He is on record in Embtel 465 of 18 August 1964, as being in favor of "taking such visible measures as introducing U.S. HAWK units to Da Nang and Saigon, [and] landing a Marine Force at Da Nang for defense of the airfield and beefing up MACV's support base. . . ."
There is no agonizing over "white-faced" soldiers and their difficulties in Embtel 465. The cable contains the discussion of two specific courses of action, labeled appropriately A and B, aimed at increasing the pressure on North Vietnam through the use of American air and naval power primarily. Course of Action A presumed that the government of General Nguyen Khanh would respond to the input of increased American assistance, get itself organized and make enough military progress to "free Saigon from the VC threat which presently rings it and assure that sufficient GVN ground forces will be available to provide a reasonable measure of defense against any DRV ground reaction which may develop in the execution of our program and thus avoid the possible requirement for a major U.S. ground force commitment." Course of Action B was based upon the inability of Khanh government to overcome its difficulties or make any significant military progress in the South. Course of Action B presumed that the U.S. would go ahead with its program to increase pressure on the DRV notwithstanding; "however, it increases the likelihood of U.S. involvement in ground action, since Khanh will have almost available ground forces which can be released from pacification employment to mobile resistance of DRV attacks."

evidence to indicate that any of the other decision-making principals shared Ambassador Taylor's reservations.

Approval to send the Marines, contingent on GVN concurrence, came on February 26, 1965, and, except for an abortive attempt by the Defense Department to substitute Army airborne troops for the Marines at the last minute, all progressed smoothly through the landing of the Marines and the preparation of their defensive positions.

Estimates of the political/military situation in SVN in early 1965, both from the official viewpoint and from other observers, were universally gloomy. No one foresaw ultimate US/GVN victory without reversal of the then-current trend. The GVN was seen to be well on its way to complete collapse. The most optimistic estimate was that the VC would take over within a year.

Prior to the request for Marines, the principal advisors to the President had, for some time, been debating possible U.S. courses of action in SVN. The possible use of ground forces for security and as deterrent or reaction forces against possible DRV/CPR ground action in SEA was included in these discussions, and indeed both CINCPAC and COMUSMACV had prepared detailed contingency plans in expectation of a decision to so employ ground forces. However, no plan to engage U.S. ground forces in offensive action against the Viet Cong had been considered. From the documentary record, it appears that the U.S. offensive role was to be limited to airpower. On February 7, 1965, for example, McGeorge Bundy sent to the President a memorandum which outlined the policy of graduated reprisal airstrikes against the DRV. There is no reference in that memorandum to the use of ground troops in SVN, despite the fact that it was a major document outlining what was to become U.S. strategy.

While it appears as though all the principals in the decision-making process, including Ambassador Taylor and CINCPAC, chose to view the Marine deployment as an isolated phenomenon rather than as part of a sequence, there is evidence to indicate that COMUSMACV saw it as the first step presaging a U.S. ground force build-up in SEA. A fair proportion of the newspaper writers at the time were equally prescient.

Regardless of what was said or believed at the time the Marines were landed, it was obvious to them from the outset that they had neither the capability nor the flexibility to adequately secure the airbase at Da Nang, and they believed that the restrictions placed on them were ill-considered.

PHASE I IN THE BUILD-UP OF U.S. FORCES, MARCH–JULY 1965

The U.S. decision to deploy 44 US/FW battalions to Vietnam was the product of a debate over strategy, but more basically, a debate over objectives. Once the consensus developed that the U.S. would neither opt out of the conflict nor settle for a stalemate, 44 BLT's made more sense than 17 BLT's (agreed to at Honolulu in April) or fewer. When it emerged that the U.S. objective was to defeat the VC/NVA on the ground in order to assure an "independent, non-

---

In anticipation of having to proceed with Course of Action B, Taylor recommended "raising the level of precautionary military readiness" by deploying forces as described above. He did not address the involvement of U.S. ground forces in the war against the insurgents in the South, but rather was concerned with the possibility of provoked DRV aggression from the North, and the necessity to counter it if it occurred.

communist South Vietnam," an aggressive search and destroy strategy had to prevail over the more experimental and cautionary enclave approach.

The decision was made swiftly and in an atmosphere of crisis. After almost three months of euphoria (RVNAF was holding together and the Saigon government was stable), four factors converged in late May and early June to set the decision full speed in motion: (1) Rolling Thunder was recognized *in itself* as insufficient to convince Hanoi to negotiate; (2) on 12 June, the Quat government fell, and all the nightmares about no Saigon political authority reappeared; (3) the Viet Cong, it was supposed, was about to launch an all-out offensive, cut the country in two, and establish an alternate government-in-country; and (4) RVNAF, faced with an unfavorable force ratio, quickly demonstrated that it could not cope.

The major participants in the decision knew the choices and understood the consequences. The strategy of base security for the air war against North Vietnam and the strategy of coastal enclaves were rejected with the knowledge that a quick solution was no longer possible. Unlike the sending of Marines to Da Nang, the 44 BLT decision was perceived as a threshold—entrance into Asian land war. The conflict was seen to be long, with further U.S. deployments to follow. The choice at that time was not whether or not to negotiate, it was not whether to hold on for a while or let go—the choice was viewed as winning or losing South Vietnam. Should negotiations come, should North Vietnam or the Viet Cong elect to settle before this victory, the U.S. would then be in a position of strength.

I. EVOLUTION OF THE SITUATION

In the history of the Vietnam War, the Year 1965 is notable for momentous and fateful U.S. decisions. In February, after a dramatic increase in activity initiated by the Viet Cong, the United States responded by increasing its own level of commitment to the Republic of Vietnam. For the first time, U.S. jet aircraft were authorized to support the RVNAF in ground operations in the South without restriction. In immediate retaliation for guerrilla raids on U.S. installations in the South, U.S aircraft also began bombing targets in the southern reaches of North Vietnam. In early March, the latter program evolved into Rolling Thunder, the sustained bombing of the North. Also, during March, two U.S. Marine battalions were landed at Da Nang on the coast of Central Vietnam. The airbase at Da Nang was a major supporter of the Rolling Thunder bombing, and the mission of the Marines was to strengthen its defenses. Those troops represented the first U.S. ground combat commitment to the Asian mainland since Korea.

While the pace of military activity in 1965 was on the rise, the political situation in South Vietnam remained as unpredictable as it had been throughout the previous year. A very confusing series of events in the middle of February culminated in the departure from Vietnam of the volatile General Nguyen Khanh. Left in his stead were two civilians, Prime Minister Phan Huy Quat and Chief of State Phan Khac Suu.

The rate of ground combat activity dropped off in March and remained low for the next month and a half. The Viet Cong eased the pressure on the GVN considerably and yielded the initiative to the government armed forces. The performance of the RVNAF, whose effectiveness was called into question with the deployment of U.S. troops to look after major bases, began to improve according to the statistical indicators used to measure the progress of the war.

Whenever the RVNAF succeeded in locating and fixing the Viet Cong, the government troops and their officers seemed to demonstrate more offensive spirit and willingness to engage.

Parallel to hopeful signs on the military side, Premier Quat, a quietly determined man, showed promise that for the first time the Vietnamese might be close to solving their frustrating political problems. Under Quat, the progressive deterioration in governmental stability seemed at long last to have halted.

The reaction of the U.S. community to the period of quiescence in the spring of 1965 was mixed. Pessimistic predictions in March as to the capability of the RVNAF to withstand the next wave of Viet Cong offensive activity were offset by convictions that ongoing U.S. aid programs were adequate to meet the situation provided the GVN resolved its internal contradictions and devoted its energies to the war. Expressions of cautious optimism, and of conviction that radical changes to U.S. strategy were unwarranted—Ambassador Taylor's notable among them—continued to reach Washington from Saigon through April and May. Among the less sanguine, even General Westmoreland expressed hope that perhaps, with the aid of increased U.S. air activity and signs of greater RVNAF resolve, a corner had indeed been turned. In the absence of dramatic action in Vietnam, most observers were prepared to wait and see what was to transpire when the military hiatus ended.

The drop in activity during the spring of 1965 was not unprecedented. The Viet Cong had traditionally yielded the initiative to the more highly mobile RVNAF during the dry season, and they were expected to reappear with the advent of the summer season, or rainy season, in May and June. The official estimates of the Viet Cong Order of Battle, including in April confirmed presence in the South of at least one battalion of the North Vietnamese Army, provided little cause for comfort. Coupled with reports that the Viet Cong were concentrating their forces in a few critical areas, the estimates of enemy capability were a sure indication that the coming summer monsoon in 1965 would provide a sore test of the RVNAF's ability.

The test began in earnest in May as the Viet Cong mounted a regiment-sized attack on the capital of Phuoc Long Province. The enemy scored again with the successful ambush of an ARVN infantry battalion and its rescue force near Quang Ngai in I Corps later that month. The Quang Ngai action left two ARVN battalions decimated, and American officers who had witnessed the battle went away with the distinct impression that the RVNAF were close to collapse. The impression was confirmed during the battle of Dong Xoai in mid-June. In a textbook display of tactical ineptitude, battalions of ARVN's finest reserves were frittered away piecemeal during the fighting. The violence of the action at Dong Xoai and the level of RVNAF casualties during the second week of June 1965 were both unprecedented.

As the summer wore on, the focus of the enemy campaign shifted to the highlands of the II Corps. By early July, Viet Cong successes in taking remote District Headquarters heralded the expected loss of the entire highlands area and the possible establishment there of a National Liberation Front government.

General Westmoreland responded immediately to the marked upsurge in Viet Cong activity by requesting in June U.S. and Third Country reinforcements to spell the RVNAF during their time of trial and to blunt the Viet Cong offensive by conducting operations throughout the country against them. The collapse of the Quat government in mid-June and its succession by an untested military regime further increased the urgency associated with Westmoreland's request.

The debate in U.S. official circles over the extent of American involvement in the war—a debate which had followed a devious course all through the spring of 1965—moved onto a higher plane at this juncture.

II. THEMES GERMANE TO THE STRATEGY DEBATE

Official hopes were high that the Rolling Thunder program begun in March would rapidly convince Hanoi that it should agree to negotiate a settlement to the war in the South. After a month of bombing with no response from the North Vietnamese, optimism began to wane. In the middle of April it was recognized that in addition to the bombing some manifestation of the Viet Cong's inability to win in the South was needed before the Communists would agree to negotiate. By the end of April, the North Vietnamese showed signs of preparing for a long seige under the bombing, while they waited for what they saw as the inevitable victory of the Viet Cong in the South. Indeed, the North Vietnamese proved their intractability when they failed to respond meaningfully to overtures made during a week-long pause in the bombing in May. By June, U.S. officials recognized that something dramatic was going to have to be added to the bombing program if the Communists were ever to be persuaded to call off their campaign in the South.

All through early 1965, officials in the U.S. Government debated the level of effort required of the United States in order to achieve its objectives in South Vietnam. Generally stated, those objectives were to insure that the Communist insurgents were defeated in their efforts to take over the government of South Vietnam and that a stable and friendly government was maintained in their place. The U.S. embarked on the Rolling Thunder bombing program in order to convince the North Vietnamese to cease their direction and support of the insurgency in the South. When the bombing program, which could have been halted almost as easily as it was initiated, gave indication that it was not going to succeed by itself, the U.S. was presented essentially with two options: (1) to withdraw unilaterally from Vietnam leaving the South Vietnamese to fend for themselves, or (2) to commit ground forces in pursuit of its objectives. A third option, that of drastically increasing the scope and scale of the bombing, was rejected because of the concomitant high risk of inviting Chinese intervention.

This paper deals essentially with the decision by the U.S. Government to intervene on the ground in South Vietnam. The debate over ground strategy was characterized by an almost complete lack of consensus throughout the first half of 1965. Proposals for levels of commitment ranging from a couple of battalions to several divisions were under consideration simultaneously. For each identifiable strategy—and there are three discussed in this paper—security, enclave, and search and destroy—there were many proponents, some of them quite vociferous. The announcements of decisions regarding the ground build-up were invariably couched in terms which gave clear indication to more aggressive proponents that their turn might yet come.

The initial steps in ground build-up appear to have been grudgingly taken, indicating that the President of the United States and his advisers recognized the tremendous inertial implications of ground troop deployments. Halting ground involvement was seen to be a manifestly greater problem than halting air or naval activity. In addition, the early build-up may have been permitted some leisure because of the lack of immediate urgency in the situation in Vietnam and the necessity to improve on an inadequate logistical base there.

III. STRATEGIES FOR GROUND FORCE EMPLOYMENT

A. STRATEGY OF SECURITY

The strategy of security arose with the beginning of the bombing programs and was designed simply to increase security of U.S. bases and installations supporting those programs. It was conceived at a time when enthusiasm for the bombing programs was high and its proponents were at pains to insure that U.S. troops did not get involved in the ground war. All 9 of the U.S. battalions deployed to Vietnam by June 1965 had base security as their primary mission, and 21 of the 44 U.S. and Third Country battalions deployed by the end of 1965 were so oriented. In part, however, most of those units were deployed for far more ambitious reasons. At a maximum, four Marine and possibly two Army battalions were recommended for deployment solely under the provisions of the security strategy, and the strategy was a dead letter by the time most of those deployments had been approved.

The strategy of security expired along with the early hopes that Rolling Thunder could succeed by itself. The non-involvement of the "security troops" in the ground war was designed to keep U.S. casualties to a minimum and to facilitate withdrawal. By deploying its own troops to secure bases, the U.S. showed lack of confidence in the RVNAF, but by keeping U.S. troops out of the fighting it demonstrated at the same time belief that the RVNAF would be able to hold on until the other side decided it had had enough. Because of the well-known shibboleth about U.S. involvement in an Asian ground war and because of the ponderous nature of ground force deployments, it was inevitable that some observers would see in the strategy of security the crossing of a threshold.

B. ENCLAVE STRATEGY

The President decided during NSC meetings on 1 and 2 April 1965 to get U.S. ground combat units involved in the war against the insurgents. He did this in the sober awareness that Rolling Thunder was unlikely to produce immediate results, but also with the caveat that U.S. troops might not do too well in an Asian insurgency environment. The enclave strategy, which had been presented by Ambassador Taylor as a way to get U.S. troops engaged at relatively low risk, was implicitly endorsed by the President. The strategy proposed that U.S. troops occupy coastal enclaves, accept full responsibility for enclave security, and be prepared to go to the rescue of the RVNAF as far as 50 miles outside the enclave. Initially, the U.S. was to experiment with four Marine battalions in two coastal enclaves to see if the concept and the rules for operating with the RVNAF (which were to be worked out with the GVN) were feasible.

Without the benefit of any experimentation the number of battalions was increased at Honolulu in mid-April to 17 and the number of enclaves to 5. The enclave strategy as formalized at Honolulu was designed to frustrate the Viet Cong in the South while Rolling Thunder continued to hammer the North. The intent was not to take the war to the enemy but rather to deny to him certain critical areas while simultaneously providing ready assistance to the RVNAF if they should run into difficulty. The RVNAF were expected to continue aggressively prosecuting the war against the enemy's main forces, thereby bearing the brunt of the casualties.

The enclave strategy was controversial and expectations for it ran the gamut from extreme optimism to deep pessimism. The Ambassador expected it to buy some time for the Vietnamese to eventually save themselves. General Westmoreland and other military men expected it to guarantee defeat for the U.S. and the RVNAF, who were already demonstrating that they were incapable of defeating the enemy.

A masterpiece of ambiguity, the enclave strategy implied a greater commitment to the war on the part of the U.S., but simultaneously demonstrated in the placing of the troops with their backs to the sea a desire for rapid and early exit. While purporting to provide the basis for experimentation with U.S. soldiers in an unfamiliar environment, it mitigated against the success of the experiments by placing those troops in close proximity to the Vietnamese people, where the greatest difficulty would be encountered. In order to prove the viability of its reserve reaction foundation, it required testing; but the rules for commitment were not worked out until the strategy was already overtaken by events. As a consequence of this delay, several opportunities were passed up when the RVNAF really needed help and U.S. troops were available. The whole enclave concept implied that the RVNAF would ultimately prevail, but in any case the Viet Cong could never win as long as certain areas were denied to them. The enclave strategy tacitly yielded the initiative to the enemy, but the initiative was not seen as the vital factor. The key was to be able to outlast the enemy at lowest cost to the United States.

C. SEARCH AND DESTROY STRATEGY

Almost in reaction to the dearth of proposals to seize the initiative from the enemy, General Westmoreland provided consistent pressure for a free hand to maneuver U.S. and Third Country forces in South Vietnam. His search and destroy strategy, which was given Presidential sanction during the summer of 1965, was articulated by both Westmoreland and the JCS in keeping with sound military principles garnered by men accustomed to winning. The basic idea behind the strategy was the desire to take the war to the enemy, denying him freedom of movement anywhere in the country and taking advantage of the superior firepower and maneuverability of U.S. and Third Country forces to deal him the heaviest possible blows. In the meantime, the RVNAF, with superior knowledge of the population and the role of the Viet Cong, would be free to concentrate their efforts in populated areas.

The strategy of search and destroy was given approval at a time when there was very little hope for results from the Rolling Thunder program. The bombing became, therefore, an adjunct to the ground strategy as the war in the South assumed first priority. Accompanying the strategy was a subtle change of emphasis—instead of simply denying the enemy victory and convincing him that he could not win, the thrust became defeating the enemy in the South. This was sanctioned implicitly as the only way to achieve the U.S. objective of a non-communist South Vietnam. It was conceivable, of course, that sometime before total defeat the North Vietnamese and the Viet Cong might decide that they had had enough. In this event, the U.S. could halt its efforts short of complete defeat of the insurgents and negotiate a settlement to the conflict from a much stronger position than that offered by any of the alternate strategies.

The strategy described above with all its implications evolved in piecemeal fashion during June and July 1965. Westmoreland was first given authority in June to commit U.S. ground forces anywhere in the country when, in his judgment, they were needed to strengthen the relative position of the RVNAF. His first major operation with U.S. troops under the new aegis was on 27 June, and that force made a deep penetration into the Viet Cong base area of War Zone "D" NW of Saigon. Once the forces had been liberated from the restrictions of the coastal enclaves, the next step was to decide how much reinforcement was needed in order to insure that the Viet Cong and their North Vietnamese allies could not win. The force decided upon was 44 U.S. and Third Country battalions, and the President approved that number sometime in mid-July. Finally, the amount of additional force required to seize the initiative from the enemy and to commence the "win" phase of the strategy was the next topic of discussion after the 44 battalions had been approved. Secretary McNamara received Westmoreland's first estimate during talks in Saigon, 16 to 20 July 1965. Based on what he knew then of Viet Cong and DRV intentions and capabilities, Westmoreland asked for 24 additional maneuver battalions and a healthy support package. The figure was revised upward several times later in the year as increased intelligence revealed the extent of DRV infiltration and Viet Cong build-up.

Force levels for the search and destroy strategy had no empirical limits. The amount of force required to defeat the enemy depended entirely on his response to the build-up and his willingness to continue the fight. The 44 battalions seen in mid-summer 1965 as the amount required to deny victory to the Viet Cong exceeded the amount forecast by the enclavists to achieve that end for two reasons. First, the enemy had by the end of June revealed that he was much stronger than had originally been surmised. Second, the 44 battalions had a dual mission: they were not only to hold the fort, but were also to lay the groundwork for the subsequent input of forces to implement the next phase of the strategy.

Ambassador Taylor expected the search and destroy strategy and the force associated with it to accomplish little more than would have been accomplished by the enclave strategy at less cost. He was convinced that only the Vietnamese could save their own country, and too aggressive use of foreign troops might even work against them in that regard. George Ball of the State Department wrote that there was no assurance no matter what the U.S. did that it could defeat the enemy on the battlefield or drive him to the conference table. The larger force associated with the search and destroy strategy signified to Ball no more than acceptance by the U.S. of a higher cost to ultimately be incurred. The 44 battalion force seemed to William Bundy of State to be an ultimatum presented to the DRV which would in all probability trigger some sort of dire response. Westmoreland expected the 44 battalions and the search and destroy strategy to hold things together long enough to prepare the way for later input of greater force. With enough force to seize the initiative from the Viet Cong sometime in 1966, Westmoreland expected to take the offensive and, with appropriate additional reinforcements, to have defeated the enemy by the end of 1967. Exactly what the President and his Secretary of Defense expected is not clear, but there are manifold indications that they were prepared for a long war.

The acceptance of the search and destroy strategy and the eclipse of the denial of victory idea associated with the enclave strategy left the U.S. commitment to Vietnam open-ended. The implications in terms of manpower and money are inescapable. Written all over the search and destroy strategy was total loss of confidence in the RVNAF and a concomitant willingness on the part of the U.S. to take over the war effort. U.S. involvement in an Asian ground war was a reality.

IV. CAVEATS

The bulk of this paper is taken up in describing the various proposals put forward by exponents of the strategies. The numerous decision points are identified and the expectations of decision-making principals involved are analyzed. Ancillary reasons for advancing proposals are identified as such and discussed. The position of each of the principals is described only as clearly as it emerges from the files of the Secretary of Defense. Thus, the JCS are treated as a monolith, although it is common knowledge that there is always considerable dissension and debate amongst the Chiefs themselves. While they might have been unanimous in their recognition that U.S. bases needed securing, the Chiefs did not see eye to eye during ensuing debates over enclave or search and destroy. The Chief of Staff of the Air Force and the Commandant of the Marine Corps were known proponents of the enclave concept, but the Chairman of the JCS and the Chief of Staff of the Army were equally determined to see the deployment of several divisions of troops for unlimited combat operations. The record of their debate, interesting though it may be, remains in the JCS files.

Through all of the strategy debate in early 1965 ran a common thread—the concern with possible intervention in the conflict by elements of the North Vietnamese Army or the Communist Chinese Army or a combination of both. A variety of CINCPAC contingency plans were in existence at the time which addressed the problem and called for various deployments, some of them preemptive, to deal with it. The JCS consistently mentioned the problem as an *additional* justification for deployments they were advocating, but the National Intelligence Board just as consistently discounted the possibility of such intervention. Covert infiltration of elements of the North Vietnamese Army, however, was another matter. It was recognized early in the debate as something to be reckoned with even though the real extent of the infiltration was not confirmed for some time. In any case, contingency deployments were not intended to deal with the latter type of provocation.

V. ISSUES

In conclusion, it seems clear that the debate over ground commitments and accompanying strategy followed closely the course of expectations about the Rolling Thunder bombing program and the development of the situation in South Vietnam itself. The strategy of security was eclipsed because Rolling Thunder was taking too long. The enclave strategy was never unanimously endorsed and it never got off the ground. It was based on the assumption that victory could be denied to the enemy in the South while Rolling Thunder punished him in the North. Eventually, the U.S. would achieve its objectives because the enemy in frustration would give up. The whole enclave idea was conceived in a period of relative quiet, and certainly the experimentation aspect of it presupposed a relatively stable situation. In the heat of the summer monsoon offensive, it became a moot question whether or not a negative approach like the enclave strategy *could* deny victory, and more important, whether or not there would be an RVNAF left to shore up.

In June, Rolling Thunder and the ground strategy switched places in the order of priorities as far as achieving U.S. objectives was concerned. First, a positive strategy for the employment of the forces, the search and destroy strategy, was approved. Secondly, a force of 44 battalions was recognized as sufficient to prevent collapse while the stage was being set for further deployments. 44 battalions was probably about the maximum the traffic would have borne at that juncture in any case. Final acceptance of the desirability of inflicting defeat on the enemy rather than merely denying him victory opened the door to an indeterminate amount of additional force.

The 44 battalions, or Phase I as they were later called, were supposed to stem the tide of the Viet Cong insurgency and enable the friendly forces to assume the offensive. As the GVN did not collapse, it can reasonably be concluded that they did stem the tide. It is just possible, however, that rather than stem the tide, they increased it through provocation of greater infiltration from North Vietnam. In any case, it is debatable whether the allied forces actually did assume the offensive the following year.

No further proof of the monumental implications of the endorsement in the summer of 1965 of the search and destroy strategy, the 44 battalions, and the "win" concept is required beyond the present state of the war in Vietnam. At this writing, the U.S. has reached the end of the time frame estimated by General Westmoreland in 1965 to be required to defeat the enemy. It has committed 107 battalions of its own forces and a grand total of 525,000 men. The strategy remains search and destroy, but victory is not yet in sight.

End of Summary

CHRONOLOGY

MARINE COMBAT UNITS GO TO DA NANG, MARCH 1965

18 Aug 64   EMBTEL 465
In a discussion of proposed U.S. air and naval action to increase pressure on North Vietnam, Taylor told State that as a hedge against the failure of the GVN to do its part, the U.S. "should raise the level of precautionary military readiness (if not already done) by taking such visible measures as introducing U.S. Hawk units to Da Nang and Saigon, [and] landing a Marine force at Da Nang for defense of the airfield and beefing up MACV's support base. . . ."

1 Oct 64   SNIE
The National Intelligence Board expected the political situation in South Vietnam to continue to decay, the war effort gradually peter out and the Vietcong to seek a neutralist coalition which they could easily dominate. Two latent strengths of the GVN were cited: the endurance of the people and the ability of administrators to carry out routine tasks without guidance from Saigon.

3 Nov 64   William Bundy Memorandum for the NSC Working Group
Convening a new group on Southeast Asia, Bundy mentioned three courses of action open to the U.S. in Vietnam—none of which involved the use of U.S. ground troops except in response to overt CHICOM/DRV attacks as called for by CINCPAC OPLANS 32-64 and 39-65.

13 Nov 64   Draft Memorandum
William Bundy said he did "not envisage the introduction of

substantial ground forces into South Vietnam or Thailand in conjunction with these initial actions"—the three courses of action then under study. The use of U.S. ground troops for base security was not mentioned although sending a multilateral force to northern SVN was suggested.

23 Nov 64 *JCSM 982-64*
This first JCS proposal for sending U.S. ground troops to Vietnam suggested Marines go to Da Nang, other ground troops to Tan Son Nhut Airbase for security and deterrence.

30 Nov 64 *"Alternatives to Air Actions on North Vietnam"*
(State Dept) A proposal to use ground troops "in support of diplomacy": deploy them to prove U.S. resolve, then launch a major diplomatic offensive. This paper was considered by the NSC Working Group, but went no further.

1 Dec 64 *Presidential Decision*
President Johnson approved the recommendation of Ambassador Taylor and NSC principals to implement the Working Group's "Course of Action A"; after about a month and after GVN progress in certain areas, Course C—a program "principally of progressively more serious air strikes" against NVN would be initiated. Again, ground troop commitment was not discussed.

1 Jan 65 *OPLAN 32-64*
The "alert" or first phase of the plan in effect. (MACV Command History shows planning had begun for the dispatch of U.S. ground troops into South Vietnam in connection with this and other contingency plans.)

Jan and Feb *MACV Monthly Evaluation Reports; CIA Situation Reports*
1965 General Westmoreland said recently initiated "Flaming Dart" air campaign against the North was beneficial for morale in South Vietnam. He called GVN social and political institutions "remarkably intact" despite the "disintegrating blows" of political upheaval. (Huong's government fell in January; Premier Quat's regime was shaky.) But enemy gains continued. The Viet Cong struck Pleiku and other bases in early February; 12 battalions (6000 men) had reportedly moved into the I Corps. Westmoreland hoped air attacks in North and South Vietnam would be enough to reverse the trend.
CIA assessments were more pessimistic. In February Binh Dinh Province was said to be just about lost to the enemy. Intelligence indicated the Viet Cong might try to take Kontum Province and split the GVN through II Corps during the rainy season.

7 Feb 65 *McGeorge Bundy Memorandum for the President*
Bundy felt the GVN would collapse by 1966 without substantially more U.S. help and action. To avert collapse and to counter latent anti-Americanism and the growing feeling among Vietnamese that U.S. was going to quit, Bundy recommended a policy of graduated, continuing air strikes against North Vietnam. He did not mention a base security problem; he did not suggest deployment of U.S. ground troops—then or in the future.

(This document—and the absence of others—supports the interpretation that the forthcoming Marine deployment to Da Nang was intended as a one-shot response to a particularly serious security problem, not as the first in a planned series of U.S. troop commitments.)

7 Feb 65   *McNamara News Conference*
The Secretary announced elements of a USMC HAWK missile battalion would be deployed to Da Nang to improve security against air attack.

11 Feb 65   *JCSM 100-65*
A proposal for the first eight weeks of military action against North Vietnam. As expected, air strikes were paramount but the JCS recommended collateral deployment of a Marine Expeditionary Brigade (MEB) to Da Nang and an Army brigade to Thailand—not for counterinsurgency duties but to deter overt DRV/CHICOM retaliation to the air strikes, to improve U.S. ability to respond if retaliatory attacks were launched.

18 Feb 65   *SNIE*
A new ingredient in the still critical situation in South Vietnam was to be the inauguration of the Rolling Thunder air campaign. This evaluation showed Viet Cong attacks against U.S. bases would probably continue at about their present level of intensity despite increased air action against North Vietnam.

22 Feb 65   *MACV Msg to CINCPAC 220743Z*
General Throckmorton, Deputy COMUSMACV, visited Da Nang, called the situation grave, and doubted ARVN's ability to provide adequate security. Throckmorton recommended that the entire 9th MEB be sent to Da Nang, but General Westmoreland cut this to two Battalion Landing Teams (BLTs) with a third to be held off-shore in reserve. The troops were to assist GVN forces in guarding Da Nang against enemy ground attacks.

22 Feb 65   *EMBTEL 2699*
Ambassador Taylor voiced several strong reservations to the idea of sending Marines to Da Nang:
It reversed a long-standing policy of avoiding commitment of ground combat forces in SVN. Taylor was sure the GVN would "seek to unload other ground force tasks upon us"; he was sure this deployment would invite requests for more troops to meet additional and ultimately defensive offensive requirements.
Two BLTs would not release significant numbers of ARVN for mobile operations against the Viet Cong; the Marines would simply be performing static defense tasks inadequately done by ARVN in the past.
Anticipating that using U.S. troops for active operations would grow more attractive, Taylor warned against it. The "white-faced" soldier cannot be assimilated by the population, he cannot distinguish between friendly and unfriendly Vietnamese; the Marines are not armed, trained or equipped for jungle guerrilla

warfare. Taylor prophesied that the U.S.—like France—would fail to adapt to such condition.

Two BLTs could help but could not make Da Nang secure. The entire MEB might significantly improve things, but no force could prevent surprise mortar attacks, a favorite VC tactic.

However, because Westmoreland was so concerned about Da Nang's safety and because Taylor felt security was a legitimate mission for U.S. troops although he objected to it, the Ambassador would support MACV's recommendation for one BLT. He suggested GVN approval be sought prior to the Marine deployment.

22 Feb 65 *MACV Message to JCS*
Claimed the Marine deployment to Da Nang would free four Regional Force companies, one tank platoon and another RF battalion then being formed for active anti-VC operations. (The March MACV Evaluation Report showed only two RF companies had been released.)

24 Feb 65 *CINCPAC Message to JCS*
Recommended immediate deployment of two BLTs; recommended one squadron of F–4s be sent to Da Nang for close air support of the troops and "for other missions along with the primary mission." The tone was urgent: deploy now "before the tragedy" of a Viet Cong attack.
CINCPAC disagreed with Taylor; called attention to the Marine Corps' distinguished record in counterinsurgency operations; claimed U.S. presence would free ARVN for mobile patrol operations and make Da Nang a tougher target for enemy forces.

24 Feb 65 *JCSM 130-65*
Forwarded and supported CINCPAC's recommendations.

26 Feb 65 *DEPTEL 1840*
Approved the deployment; said the Marines were on their way and instructed Taylor to secure GVN approval.

28 Feb 65 *EMBTEL 2789*
Taylor agreed to seek GVN concurrence to the deployment—and planned an approach designed to stress U.S. reluctance to deploy any men even temporarily, emphasize the limited mission of the Marines and discourage GVN hopes for further commitments. Taylor would open by discussing the severe security problem at Da Nang and USG concern about it. Although he wished more GVN battalions could be sent there, Taylor would say he knew ARVN troops were chronically short in I Corps and he knew any redeployment would impose prohibitive costs to security in other areas. Thus, he would say "the USG has been driven to consider a solution which we have always rejected in the past: the introduction of U.S. ground combat forces to reinforce the defense of Da Nang until GVN forces become available for the purpose."

1 Mar 65 *CJCS Letter to SecDef (forwarding JSOP-70)*
General Wheeler said the JCS were addressing Southeast Asia

force levels separately because that was a "specific problem area" requiring a "near term and long term solution." This suggests the JCS probably had been considering deployment of U.S. troops to Vietnam—perhaps for active operations—before the Marine deployment to Da Nang.

2 Mar 65   *DOD Tel 6166*
ASD (ISA) McNaughton cabled Taylor that the 173d Airborne Brigade (then on Okinawa) would be deployed to Da Nang instead of the Marines. (This last minute change may have been Mr. McNaughton's attempt to emphasize the limited, temporary nature of the U.S. troop deployment and to reduce the conspicuousness of the U.S. presence. Airborne troops carry less equipment and look less formidable than the Marines plus they have no history of peace-keeping intervention in foreign wars.)

2 Mar 65   *EMBTEL 1954*
Taylor and Westmoreland—who argued that the Marines were more self-sustaining than the airborne—objected to the proposed substitution of Army airborne for Marine troops.

3 Mar 65   *CINCPAC Message to JCS 030230Z*
CINCPAC strongly objected to Mr. McNaughton's proposal. It denied him the only airborne assault force in the theater and, more importantly, completely upset his contingency plans for combat operations in Southeast Asia. CINCPAC said that since 1959 when OPLAN-32 was approved, the Marines had been scheduled for deployment to Da Nang; seven CINCPAC and SEATO contingency plans plus many supporting plans rested on this. All the preparations had been made for the landing of the BLTs—and some forces were already embarked. CINCPAC concluded: "The situation in Southeast Asia has now reached a point where the soundness of our contingency planning may be about to be tested." Some 1300 Marines were then in Da Nang; tasking of new forces had been completed; logistics, communications, command arrangements had been set. It would be "imprudent to shift forces in a major sector and to force changes in U.S. contingency posture for other parts of Southeast Asia." (The McNaughton proposal was killed.)

3 Mar 65   *DEPTEL 1876*
State requested Taylor's views on the possible use of an international force in Vietnam.

3 Mar 65   *EMBTELs 2014*
and 3112
Taylor first reported the views of the Australian envoy to the GVN on a multilateral force—views which Taylor supported. It would heighten Vietnamese xenophobia; it might cause the GVN to "shuck off greater responsibility onto the USG." In his second message Taylor said he had no idea what the GVN attitude toward a MLF might be, said many problems were involved which had yet to be faced. (The MLF was just a concept at the time—but Taylor readily looked beyond immediate tactical needs

to the long-term ramifications of such a move just as he had in evaluating the proposal to deploy Marines to Da Nang.)

4 Mar 65 *JCSM 100-65*
The proposal for an eight-week air strike program (and possible deployment of some ground troops) was resubmitted to the Secretary. Again, the use of U.S. troops for active anti-insurgent operations was not mentioned.

5 Mar 65 *CINCPAC Eyes Only Message to Wheeler*
This said the 9th MEB was needed as soon as possible for base security, to boost the GVN war against the Viet Cong, to provide insurance in case the GVN was unable to resist collapse in the critical Da Nang area where so much was already committed. CINCPAC said the "single most important thing we can do quickly to improve the security situation in South Vietnam is to make full use of our air power."

6 Mar 65 *OSD(PA) News Release*
Announced two USMC Battalion Landing Teams—3500 men— were being deployed to Vietnam on a limited mission: to provide base security and relieve GVN forces for pacification and offensive operations against the Viet Cong.

6 Mar 65 *JCS Message to CINCPAC*
Ordered the BLTs to commence landing.

7 Mar 65 *Statement by Secretary of State to National TV Audience*
Secretary Rusk said the Marines would shoot back if shot at, but their mission was to put a tight security ring around Da Nang— not to kill Viet Cong.

11 Mar 65 *"Estimate of the Situation in SVN" Saigon Airgram to State*
The Mission Council reported insurgency would grow unless ". . . NVN support is checked, GVN military and paramilitary resources increased, pacification goals and concepts refined, administrative efficiency improved and an adequate political-psychological base created. . . . Only U.S. resources can provide the pressures on NVN necessary to check Hanoi's support although some measure of GVN armed forces participation will be required for psychological reasons; the other measures and programs required to stem the tide . . . are largely internal to SVN but even here success will require a marked increase in U.S. support and participation."

14 Mar 65 *General Harold Johnson's "Report on Trip to South Vietnam"*
General Johnson, in SVN from 5–12 March, was as impressed by the gravity of the situation—particularly in I Corps—as were Saigon officials. He submitted several proposals—including deployment of additional U.S. ground troops—for attaining U.S. objectives (persuade NVN to abandon support and direction of the insurgency, defeat the insurgents, create a stable GVN). He said more U.S. action was necessary because "what the situation requires may exceed what the Vietnamese can be expected to do." To release ARVN for offensive action, General Johnson proposed sending a U.S. division either to the Bien Hoa/Tan Son Nhut

area plus some coastal enclaves or to Kontum, Pleiku and Darlac Provinces in the highlands. Both General Johnson and Mr. McNamara preferred the second alternative—but McNamara found neither efficient in terms of ARVN released per U.S. input and he also favored a ROK division rather than U.S. troops. General Johnson recommended the SEATO Treaty be invoked and a four-division MLF be deployed across the DMZ "from the South China Sea to the Mekong River" to counter infiltration. Finally he said to evaluate MACV's requests properly a policy decision "must be made now to determine what the Vietnamese should be expected to do for themselves and how much more the U.S. must contribute directly to the security of South Vietnam." Mr. McNamara noted in the margin: "Policy is: anything that will strengthen the position of the GVN will be sent. . . ."

20 Mar 65   JCSM 204-65
The JCS proposed that U.S. troops be deployed to South Vietnam for active operations against the Viet Cong.

27 Mar 65   MACV Message to CINCPAC
Westmoreland submitted his estimate of the situation and his request for U.S. troops for offensive action against the Viet Cong. Preparation of both estimate and troop input recommendation had began on 13 March (five days after the Marines arrived; one day after General Johnson completed his trip).

6 Apr 65   NSAM 328
President Johnson approved General Johnson's specific proposals for more U.S. action. This meant more U.S. involvement in terms of money, ships, aircraft, materiel and advisors, but deployment of ground combat units of division size was not approved at this time (2 additional Marine BLTs were approved).

BUILD-UP ACTIVITY: PHASE I

11 Feb 65   JCSM 100-65
JCS recommended in conjunction with program for the 1st eight weeks of air activity against NVN the collateral action of landing one MEB at Da Nang for security of the air base.

20 Feb 65   JCSM 121-65
JCS reiterated CINCPAC recommendation to land MEB at Da Nang. Presence of the Marines would serve to deter VC/DRV action against the base and would enhance readiness posture for other contingencies.

22 Feb 65   MACV 220743Z
Westmoreland recommended landing of ⅔ of MEB to secure base and installations at Da Nang.

22 Feb 65   Embtel 2699
Taylor concurred in MACV's request to the extent of ⅓ MEB for security but warned against further foreign troop deployments.

23 Feb 65   MACV 231230Z
Westmoreland backed down to ⅓ MEB with proviso that more could follow after 1st battalion was in place.

24 Feb 65   CINCPAC 240315Z
Sharp recommended ⅔ MEB for security at Da Nang.

24 Feb 65   JCSM 130–65
JCS recommended ⅔ MEB for security. Approved 25 Feb.

26 Feb 65   Deptel 1840
State told *Ambassador* ⅔ MEB *approved* for landing contingent on GVN approval. [Dep SecDef approval on 25 Feb.] Remaining elements of MEB deferred.

28 Feb 65   Embtel 2789
Taylor told *State* he'd get GVN approval for 2 BLTs to land at Da Nang. He said that should be all we send and that they would eventually be relieved by Viet forces.

2 Mar 65   Deptel 6166
McNaughton told *Taylor* that it would be desirable to substitute 173d Airborne for the Marines at Da Nang.

2 Mar 65   Embtel 1954
Taylor supported *Westmoreland* in opposing substitution of 173d.

3 Mar 65   CINCPAC 030230Z
CINCPAC opposed attempted substitution citing seven OPLANS calling for Marines into Da Nang.

4 Mar 65   JCSM 121–65
JCS recommended deployment of entire MEB to Da Nang, one Army Bde to Thailand, reconstitution of MEB in WestPac, and alert of III MEF (-) and 25 Inf Div as insurance in support of deterrence deployments.

4 Mar 65   JCSM 144–65
JCS urged *SecDef* to reconsider deferred funds for Chu Lai airstrip. Facility was needed to "prepare for a wide variety of courses of action." Approved by SecDef 18 Mar 65.

6 Mar 65   Press Release
DOD said U.S. at request of GVN will put 2 BLTs at Da Nang for security.

7 Mar 65   JCS 070001Z
JCS ordered *CINCPAC* to commence landing Marines and build up to two battalions ashore.

8 Mar 65   3500 Marines landed at Da Nang. (Totals bns. in SVN:2)

14 Mar 65   CSA Memo for SecDef & JCS
Gen Johnson recommended 21 separate measures for increased support of the GVN. Measures merely were increases in the same vein as previous steps. He also proposed deployment of up to a full U.S. division for security of various bases with the concomitant release of Viet troops from security mission for combat. The U.S. Division could go either to coastal enclaves and Saigon or into the II Corps highlands. Finally, Johnson proposed a four-division force comprised of U.S. and SEATO troops along the DMZ and into Laos to contain NVN infiltration of men and

supplies. President approved 21 parts 15 Mar & again on 1 Apr; deferred the rest.

15 Mar 65   JCS met w/Pres.
President urged the *JCS* to come up with measures to "kill more VC"; he approved most of Gen Johnson's recommendations.

17 Mar 65   "Strength of VC Military Forces in SVN"
Joint *CIA, DIA, State* Memo showing VC Order of Battle (confirmed) as follows:
37,000 Regular Forces
100,000 ± Irregulars and Militia
Confirmed strength up 33% over 1964.
　　5 Regimental Hq
　　50 Battalions
　145 Separate Companies

17 Mar 65   MACV 170747Z
Westmoreland recommended landing one Marine BLT at Phu Bai, near Hue, to secure airfield there and enable thereby movement of helicopters from congested area at Da Nang to Phu Bai. Recommended a 4th BLT within a month.

18 Mar 65   Embtel 3003
Taylor supported *Westmoreland's* Phu Bai request above and went on to discuss pro's and con's of introduction of U.S. Division without offering a recommendation.

19 Mar 65   CINCPAC 192207Z
Sharp recommended to *JCS* that remainder of MEB be landed within a month and one BLT at Phu Bai be landed ASAP.

20 Mar 65   JCSM 204–65
JCS proposed sending 2 US and 1 ROK division to SVN for active operations against VC. Marines to I CTZ could be had quickly in concert with US/SEATO contingency plans for DRV/ Chicom aggression. (A portion of this proposal could have been construed as a deterrent measure to Chicom aggression.) All forces were to engage in offensive operations with or without centralized command structure. Location for ROK Div not specified, but Army Div was to go to II CTZ highlands to release ARVN battalions for operations along the coast. The JCS proposed resupplying it by air until Rte 19 could be opened. This recommendation considered by the JCS to be an essential component of the broader program to put pressure on the DRV/VC.

25 Mar 65   JCSM 216–65
JCS reiterated *CINCPAC's* recommendation that 1 BLT and remaining MEB elements be landed at Da Nang and one BLT be landed at Phu Bai—all to improve security situation. Approved by Pres. 1 Apr & in NSAM 328 6 Apr.

26 Mar 65   "Commander's Estimate of The Situation in SVN"
Westmoreland predicted that air activity would not bear fruit in the next six months, and in the interim, RVNAF needed 3d country reinforcements to enable it to offset VC/DRV build-up and

enjoy favorable force ratios while permitting an "orderly" build-up of its own forces. MACV wanted the equivalent of two divisions by June '65 and possibly more thereafter if bombing failed. Westmoreland proposed deploying Marines as described in JCSM 216–65, an Army brigade in Bien Hoa/Vung Tau, and an Army division to the II CTZ highlands with a couple of battalions to protect coastal bases. The mission of these forces was to be defense of vital installations and defeat of VC efforts to control Kontum, Pleiku, Binh Dinh region.

27 Mar 65   *Embtel 3120*
Taylor told *State* that if U.S. forces were to come in for combat, he favored offensive enclave—mobile reaction concept of employment rather than territorial clear and hold in highlands or defensive enclave.

29 Mar 65   *SecDef & JCS met with Amb Taylor*
JCS three division plan presented to *Taylor*. The latter inclined to disfavor it because too many troops were involved, the need wasn't manifest, and the Viets would probably resent it. *SecDef* was inclined to favor the proposal but desired more information in reference to the Taylor qualifications.

1–2 Apr 65   *NSC meetings with Amb Taylor present*
President Johnson decided to send two more Marine battalions to Da Nang and Phu Bai and to alter the mission of U.S. combat forces "to permit their more active use" under conditions to be established by the Secy of State in consultation with SecDef. He also approved 18 to 20,000 man increase in U.S. forces to fill out existing units and provide needed logistic personnel. (All of these changes were to be contingent on GVN concurrence.) A slowly ascending tempo in response to rises in enemy rates of activity was approved for the Rolling Thunder program. The President agreed to overtures to GOA, GNZ, and to ROK, seeking combat support from them.

2 Apr 65   *CIA Director Memo to SecDef & others*
McCone said present level of RT not hurting DRV enough to make them quit. He warned against putting more U.S. troops into SVN for combat operations, since that would merely encourage the USSR and China to support the DRV/VC at minimum risk. He predicted covert infiltration of PAVN and the U.S. getting mired down in a war it could not win.

2 Apr 65   *JCSM 238–65*
JCS asked *SecDef* to clear the decks of "all administrative impediments that hamper us in the prosecution of this war." Specifically, they asked for: increases in funds, a separate MAP for SEA, improved communications systems, quicker response to CINCPAC's requests, exemption of SEA from balance of payments goals, authority to extend military terms of service and to consult with Congress on the use of Reserves, relaxation of civilian and military manpower ceilings, and a substantial increase in military air transport in and out of SVN.

4 Apr 65   *CINCPAC 042058Z (For Taylor)*
Taylor told *State* that in absence of further guidance, he will tell GVN that Marine mission is now mobile counterinsurgency, plus reserve, in support of ARVN up to 50 miles of base.

5 Apr 65   *SecDef Memo to CJCS*
McNamara told *Wheeler* that he understood the JCS to be planning for the earliest practicable introduction of 2–3 Div into SVN.

8 Apr 65   *JCSM 265–65*
JCS recommended RVNAF build-up be accelerated through an additional 17,247 MAP-supported spaces plus 160 advisors. SecDef approved 12 Apr.

9–10 Apr 65   *Planning Conference in Honolulu*
PACOM and JCS representatives recommended deployment of 173d Airborne Brigade to Bien Hoa/Vung Tau for security of the installations there and an Army brigade to Qui Nhon/Nha Trang to prepare for the later introduction of a division. They also recommended that the 173d be replaced by a CONUS brigade ASAP. They treated the two Marine BLTs of NSAM 328 as approved and described as "in planning" the remainder of the JCS's three-division force (III MEF (-), ROK Div, and U.S. Army Div). They recommended that I MEF be deployed to WESTPAC to improve readiness posture.

11–14
Apr 65   Two Marine BLTs land at Phu Bai and Da Nang. (Total bns. in SVN:4)

11 Apr 65   *MACV 110825Z*
Westmoreland told *CINCPAC* that he still wanted a U.S. division in the highlands, even though it was apparent Washington was not of a mind to approve it. He also reaffirmed the need for an Army brigade in the Bien Hoa/Vung Tau area for security, to strengthen the eastern flank of the Hop Tac area, and to act as a mobile reserve in case needed in the highlands. To forestall political difficulty, Westmoreland said he'd like to see a joint staff with the RVNAF and an international Military Assistance Force under U.S. hegemony in the Da Nang area.

12 Apr 65   *Meeting, SecDef & JCS*
McNamara agreed with *JCS* that Marines' "Enclave" build-up plan would be adopted. Concept was to initially provide base security and then phase into combat operations from logistically supportable base areas. The logistics base extant at that juncture was recognized to be inadequate.

12 Apr 65   *Embtel 3372*
Taylor told *State* that with the 18 to 20,000 man increase in support forces authorized by NSAM 328, "some preliminary work in anticipation of the arrival of additional U.S. forces" could be accomplished but that for "significant progress toward the establishment of a logistic base to support additional forces," about 5000 more engineers would be required. He went on to say that despite studies dealing with ambitious plans for reinforcement, he

hoped that "they do not interfere with essential work in preparation for less ambitious but more probable deployments." He indicated favorable disposition toward the establishment of brigade-sized enclaves at Qui Nhon and Bien Hoa/Vung Tau "if the Marines demonstrate effectiveness . . ."

13 Apr 65 *McNamara* approved deployment of 173d Airborne to Bien Hoa/Vung Tau subject to GVN concurrence (with Presidential sanction).

14 Apr 65 *JCS 140050Z*
JCS asked *CINCPAC* to deploy the 173d to SVN as soon after GVN concurrence as possible. Their mission would be to initially secure Bien Hoa/Vung Tau and then phase into counterinsurgency operations.

14 Apr 65 *Embtel 3373*
Taylor surprised at decision to deploy the 173d. He requested a hold.
Embtel 3374
Taylor & *Westmoreland* both embarrassed at amount of heavy equipment, not appropriate for counterinsurgency, brought ashore in Da Nang by Marines.
Embtel 3384
Taylor advised Washington to keep additional U.S. forces *out* of SVN, perhaps just offshore, until need for them is incontrovertible.

15 Apr 65 *JCSM 281–65*
JCS replied to *Taylor's* traffic of the previous day. They said the 173d was needed for security of air operations and logistic bases and for subsequent phasing into counterinsurgency operations. They added that the security of existing or proposed bases at Chu Lai, Qui Nhon and Nha Trang required a battalion each. They added that to deploy the Marines without their full complement of equipment would be imprudent. They (the Marines) were now prepared to meet any contingency.

15 Apr 65 *Deftel 9164*
McNaughton told Saigon that "highest authority" felt situation in SVN was deteriorating, and proposed seven actions to help remedy the situation, including: (1) encadrement of U.S. troops in ARVN units either 50 U.S. to each of 10 ARVN battalions or combined operations of 3 U.S. and 3 ARVN battalions; (2) a brigade force into Bien Hoa/Vung Tau for security and subsequent combat operations; (3) battalions into coastal enclaves for further experimentation with U.S. forces in counterinsurgency role; (4) application of U.S. recruiting techniques in RVN; (5) expansion of MEDCAP; (6) pilot experimentation in 2 or 3 provinces with a team of U.S. civil affairs personnel integrated into gov't structure; and (7) provision of food directly to RVNAF troops.

17 Apr 65 *Embtel 3419 & 3421*
Taylor told *McGeorge Bundy* that 7-point program plus all visiting firemen were rocking the boat and asked for respite.

17 Apr 65   *Embtel 3423*
Taylor sent to Washington the kind of guidance he felt he should have received in order to carry out all that Washington had proposed in the past week.

17 Apr 65   *JCSM 288–65*
JCS proposed sending one Marine BLT to Chu Lai to secure the CB's constructing the airstrip there.

17 Apr 65   *JCS 171847Z*
JCS described to *CINCPAC* the concept for U.S. combat units deploying to SEA as assistance in arresting the deteriorating situation against the VC and as an assurance that the U.S. would be ready to counter overt DRV or Chicom action should such occur.

20 Apr 65   *Honolulu Conference*
McNamara, McNaughton, W. Bundy, Taylor, Wheeler, Sharp and *Westmoreland* reached consensus that: (1) the DRV was unlikely to quit in the next six months and probably would only give up because of VC "pain" in the South rather than bomb damage in the North; (2) RT was about right but wouldn't do the job alone; (3) best strategy would be to break the DRV/VC will by effectively denying them victory and bringing about negotiations through the enemy's impotence. They proposed establishing four brigade-sized enclaves, in addition to Da Nang–Hue/Phu Bai, at Bien Hoa/Vung Tau (3 Army battalions plus 1 GOA battalion); Chu Lai (3 BLTs plus 3 Marine TFS); Qui Nhon (3 Army battalions); and Quang Ngai (3 ROK battalions). Added on to the 4 USMC BLTs (33,000 U.S. troops) and 2000 ROK troops already in Vietnam, the total was to be 82,000 U.S. and 7250 3d country troops. Mentioned for possible later deployment were: a U.S. Airmobile Division, a Corps Hq, an ROK Div (-), and the remainder of the III MEF (2 battalions). It was agreed that ARVN and U.S. units would be "brigaded" for operations, that the U.S. would try single managers of U.S. effort in 3 provinces as an experiment, that MEDCAP would be expanded, and that a study of fringe benefits for RVNAF would be undertaken.

21 Apr 65   *SecDef Memo for The President*
McNamara sent the Honolulu recommendations to the *President* essentially as described above.

21 Apr 65   *CIA Memo to SecDef & others*
McCone said the communists still saw the tide going their way. They would see in the Honolulu expansions of U.S. involvement the acceptance by the U.S. of a greater commitment, but they would assume U.S. was reluctant to widen the war. The DRV and Chicoms might reinforce with men and equipment, but would not intervene.

21 Apr 65   *CIA–DIA Memo "An Assessment of Present VC Military Capabilities"*
The presence in Kontum Province since February 1965 of one regiment of the 325th PAVN Division confirmed. As of late 1964 the supply of repatriated southerners infiltrated back from NVN had dried up and NVN volunteers were coming down the trail.

22 Apr 65   *Deptel 2397*
Unger told *Taylor* that if Quat agrees to the Honolulu program, the U.S. intention was not to announce the whole thing at once "but rather to announce individual deployments at appropriate times."

23 Apr 65   *CINCPAC 230423Z*
Sharp recommended replacing the 173d, if it deployed, with a CONUS brigade.

23 Apr 65   *Embtel 2391*
Taylor told *State* that Quat was extremely reluctant to discuss foreign reinforcements. Taylor feared GVN reaction.

30 Apr 65   *Deftel 1097*
Saigon informed by *McNaughton* that the 173d and 3 BLTs to Chu Lai approved for deployment at Ambassador's call.

30 Apr 65   *JCSM 321–65*
JCS as a result of Honolulu and subsequent discussions recommended a detailed program to deploy 48,000 U.S. and 5250 Free World troops to SVN. The forces included two Army brigades, one MEB, an ROK Regt. Combat Team, and an ANZAC battalion. They were to bolster GVN forces during their continued build-up, secure bases and installations, conduct combat operations in co-ordination with the RVNAF, and prepare for the later introduction of an airmobile division to the central plateau, the remainder of III MEF to the Da Nang area, and the remainder of an ROK division to Quang Ngai. 173d & MEB appr. 30 Apr.

5 May 65   *ISA Memo to Dep SecDef*
McNaughton informed *Vance* that a portion of the force package listed as "approved" by the JCS in JCSM 321–65 was in fact a part of the not-yet sanctioned three-division plan.

5 May 65   Main body of 173d Airborne Brigade arrived at Vung Tau. (Total bns. in SVN: 6)

7 May 65   Marines began landing at Chu Lai (Total bns. in SVN: 9)

7 May 65   *CINCPAC 072130Z*
Sharp reminded *JCS* that he wanted to reconstitute WESTPAC reserve after deployment of 173d and additional Marines. Movement of I MAF to WESTPAC approved by SecDef 15 May.

8 May 65   *MACV 15182*
Westmoreland with *Taylor* concurrence forwarded concept of operations by U.S./allied ground combat forces in support of RVNAF:
Stage I—Security of base area (extended TAOR out to light artillery range).
Stage II—Deep patrolling and offensive operations (with RVNAF coordination and movement out of TAORs).
Stage III—Search and destroy plus reserve reaction operations. Westmoreland saw the U.S. role in the Vietnam war evolving through four phases:
Phase I—Securing and improving coastal enclaves

Phase II—Operations from the enclaves
Phase III—Securing inland bases and areas
Phase IV—Operations from inland bases after occupying and improving them.

Westmoreland recommended locations for various forces then being discussed for future deployment:
III MEF—Da Nang, Hue, Chu Lai Airmobile Division—Qui Nhon, Nha Trang ROK Division—Quang Ngai, Chu Lai (relieve USMC) 173d—Bien Hoa/Vung Tau (already landing)

11 May 65   *Embtel 3727*
Taylor described arrival of 173d and Marines; predicted boredom would be a problem.

14 May 65   *JCS 142228Z*
JCS told *CINCPAC* that *SecDef* approved combined coordinating staff with RVNAF and knew that MACV was planning a Joint General Staff.

15 May 65   *MACV 150900Z*
Westmoreland told *DA* he was preparing concept for employment of a division-sized force, possibly the airmobile division, and requested experts to help plan.

17 May 65   *Embtel 3788*
Taylor told *State* Quat was agreeable to deployment of an Army brigade to Qui Nhon/Nha Trang. If build-up of Cam Ranh Bay as a base were to be approved, he said, Westmoreland wanted to divert one battalion there for security.

19 May 65   *Embtel 3808*
Taylor told *State* that RVN could absorb 80,000 US/3d country troops. He recommended a pause before considering further expansion and wanted to hold off logistics support for contingency follow-on until there was a case of clear and indisputable necessity.

21 May 65   *JCSM 634–65*
JCS recommended to *SecDef* that Cam Ranh Bay be developed to either (1) enable further contingency deployments, or (2) to fully support troops already there. Approved by SecDef 8 Jun.

24 May 65   *Embtel 3855*
Taylor told *State* that joint command structure was repugnant to Viets and should not be raised at that time. Problem of command needed to be sorted out, however, prior to input of large numbers of U.S. forces.

24 May 65   *MACV 17292*
Westmoreland told *CINCPAC* that despite SecDef approval of joint planning staff, the Viets were cool to the idea.

27 May 65   *JCSM 417–65*
JCS recommended approval of 2369 MAP supported spaces for RVNAF to organize a tenth division using assets of three existing regiments. Approved by SecDef 4 Jun.

June 65   1st battalion, Royal Australian Regiment, closed RVN in early June and joined the 173d at Vung Tau. (Total bns. in SVN:10)

5 June 65   *Embtel 4074*
Mission Intelligence Committee with concurrence of Taylor, Johnson, and Westmoreland told *State* that a series of recent ARVN defeats raised the possibility of collapse. To meet a shortage of ARVN reserves, U.S. ground troops would probably have to be committed to action.

7 June 65   *MACV 19118 070335Z*
Westmoreland told *CINCPAC* that a summer offensive was under way to destroy GVN forces and isolate and attack district and province towns. The enemy had yet to realize his full potential, and RVNAF's capability to cope was in grave doubt. RVNAF build-up was halted because of recent losses. No choice but to reinforce with additional US/3d country forces as rapidly as possible. Westmoreland asked that all forces then in the planning stages be approved for deployment, plus he identified more forces (9 maneuver battalions in a division (−) and one MEB) which might be required later and for which planning should begin. He asked that the 173d be held in SVN until the Airmobile Division was operational.

7 June 65   *CINCPAC 072325Z*
Sharp supported *Westmoreland's* request for more troops but added that he felt the airmobile division should go to Qui Nhon rather than inland and should operate in Binh Dinh instead of up in the highlands. He felt 600 to 800 tons of aerial resupply for the division if it went to the highlands was asking too much of air facilities. He also felt the ROK division should go to Quang Ngai rather than to Qui Nhon, where it would be unproductive, or to Cam Ranh as Westmoreland had suggested.

8 June 65   *Press Conference*
McCloskey, State Dept Press Officer, told the press that U.S. troops would be made available to fight alongside Viet forces when and if necessary.

9 June 65   *White House Press Release*
Statement released which said that there had been no recent change in mission of U.S. combat units. They would help the Viets if help was requested and COMUSMACV felt U.S. troops were required.

11 June 65   *CINCPAC 112210Z*
Sharp elaborated on his earlier objections to airmobile division going into highlands and clarified his views on employment of the ROKs in either Quang Ngai, Nha Trang, or the Delta.

11 June 65   *JCSM 457–65*
JCS, after discussing *MACV* and *CINCPAC* requests with *Taylor,* recommended that the airmobile division go to Qui Nhon, and recommended everything else that Westmoreland had requested. Total strengths recommended were: U.S.—116,793; FW—19,750.

11 June 65   JCS 112347Z
JCS told *Sharp* that somewhat less than MACV's 19118 was close to being approved as an alternative. Force described amounted to one additional Army brigade instead of the airmobile division. JCS wanted to know where Westmoreland would put the brigade were it to be approved.

13 June 65   MACV 131515Z
Westmoreland objected to *Taylor's* questioning of the seriousness of the situation and pointed out that to date ARVN had lost 5 battalions and the end was not in sight. He justified his request for troops by Corps area and asked for a free hand in maneuvering units. He included his concept for the employment of ROK and ARVN troops.

15 June 65   *McNamara* gave the green light for planning to deploy the airmobile division to SVN by 1 September.

16 June 65   *Press Conference*
McNamara announced deployments to SVN that would bring U.S. strength there to between 70,000 and 75,000 men. 20,000 of these would be combat troops and more would be sent if necessary. He said U.S. troops were needed because the RVNAF to VC force ratio of less than 4 to 1 was too low to enable the GVN to cope with the threat. Total U.S. Bns after deployments would be 15.

17 June 65   *Embtel 4220*
Taylor confirmed to *State* the seriousness of the military situation in SVN. GVN had to either give up outlying outposts or face being ambushed trying to reinforce them.

18 June 65   *White House Memo to SecDef*
McGeorge Bundy passed on to *McNamara* the President's concern that "we find more dramatic and effective actions in SVN . . ."

18 June 65   JCSM 482–65
JCS further refined recommended troop list showing the airmobile division to deploy by 1 September 1965 along with its support and the brigade of the 101st airborne division to return to CONUS when the airmobile division was operational. Total strength recommended was:

U.S.—120,839; FW—19,750

22 June 65   *Unsigned Memo to SecDef*
McNamara told that the President could wait until 10 July to approve the deployment of the airmobile division if SecDef is immediately given the go-ahead for readiness preparation. The question of removal of the two Army brigades was to be reconsidered in August.

22 June 65   JCS 2400
JCS told *CINCPAC* and *Westmoreland* that a force of 44 battalions was being considered for deployment to Vietnam. The Chairman wished to know if that would be enough to convince the DRV/VC they could not win.

23 June 65 Deptels 3078 & 3079
Approval for landing of one Marine BLT at Qui Nhon for security and an additional BLT at Da Nang sent to Saigon.

24 June 65 MACV 3320
Westmoreland told *CINCPAC* and the *JCS* that there was no assurance the DRV/VC would change their plans regardless of what the U.S. did in the next 6 months. The 44 battalions, however, should be enough to prevent collapse and establish a favorable balance of power by year's end.

26 June 65 Memo, SecArmy to SecDef
Resor told *McNamara* that Air Cav Div must have its movement directive by 8 July at the latest in order to meet its readiness deadlines. Security would be impossible after issuing the directive.

26 June 65 Deptel 3057
W. Bundy told *Taylor* that Westmoreland could commit U.S. troops to combat "in any situation in which the use of such troops is required by an appropriate GVN commander and when, in COMUSMACV's judgment, their use is necessary to strengthen the relative position of GVN forces."

26 June 65 ISA Memo of Conversation w/Dep Amb.
On 25 June *Alexis Johnson* told *McNaughton* that in many respects the situation in SVN was no worse than the previous year. Even if it were, large numbers of foreign troops could do no more than hold a few enclaves. The Vietnamese feared massive inputs of foreign troops would degrade their control over the country.

1 July 65 Memo for The President
Ball of State described the Vietnam war as one the U.S. cannot win regardless of effort. Rather than have the U.S. pour its resources down the drain in the wrong place, he recommended that U.S. force levels be held to 15 battalions and 72,000 men announced by SecDef in June. The combat role of the U.S. forces should be restricted to base security and reserve in support of ARVN. As rapidly as possible and in full realization of the diplomatic losses which might be incurred, the U.S. should exit from Vietnam and thereby cut its losses.

1 July 65 Memo for The President
W. Bundy of State proposed a "middle way" to the *President* which would avoid the ultimatum aspects of the 44 battalions request and also the Ball withdrawal proposal, both of which were undesirable. Bundy offered further experimentation with U.S. troops from coastal enclaves. The numbers would be held to planned deployments of 18 battalions and 85,000 men. The airmobile division and the 1st Infantry Division would be got ready but not deployed. Furious diplomatic activity concomitantly should find a gracious exit for the U.S.

1 July 65 One Marine BLT landed at Qui Nhon to strengthen security there. (Total bns. in SVN: 11)

2 July 65 JCSM 515–65
Pursuant to their meeting with *SecDef* on 28 June, the *JCS* for-

warded a program for the deployment of "such additional forces at this time as are required to insure that the VC/DRV cannot win in SVN at their present level of commitment." Concurrently, the JCS recommended expansion of the air activity against NVN as an indispensable part of the overall program. Total U.S. strength at completion of these deployments was to be 175,000.

6 July 65   One Marine BLT landed at Da Nang to strengthen the defenses there. (Total bns in SVN: 12)

7 July 65   *Deftel 5319*
McNamara informed *Westmoreland* that the purpose of the forthcoming visit to Saigon scheduled for 16–20 July was to "get your recommendations for forces to year's end and beyond."

10 July 65   *Deftel 5582*
McNaughton told *Taylor* that it had been decided to deploy 10,400 logistic and support troops by 15 August to support current force levels and to receive the airmobile division, if deployed. GVN concurrence sought.

11 July 65   *Embtel 108*
Estimate of the situation prepared by the *Mission Intelligence Committee* reaffirmed the need for U.S./3d country forces to stem the tide then flowing against the RVNAF.

12 July 65   2d Brigade, 1st Infantry Division arrived in Vietnam (Total bns in SVN: 15)

16–20
July 65   *Conference in Saigon*
McNamara and *Wheeler* met with *Westmoreland* and *Taylor*, heard presentation of COMUSMACV's concept for operations in SVN. The 44 battalions were to be the Phase I of the build-up and were enough to prevent defeat. In order to move to Phase II and seize the initiative, Westmoreland told SecDef he'd require a further 24 battalions in 1966.

17 July 65   *NMCC 172042Z*
Vance told *McNamara* that the President had decided to go ahead with the plan to deploy 34 U.S. battalions and that he was favorably disposed to the call-up of reserves and extension of tours of active duty personnel.

28 July 65   *Presidential Press Conference*
The President told *the press* that he had ordered the airmobile division and other units to SVN. Strength after these deployments would be 125,000 and more would be sent if required. He also said he'd decided not to call up reserve at that juncture.

29 July 65   1st Brigade, 101st Airborne Division arrived in Vietnam. (Total bns. in SVN: 18)

30 July 65   *JCSM 590–65*
Annex showed 34 battalions and 193,587 men as planned for deployment to RVN.

14–15
Aug 65   Marine BLTs landed at Chu Lai and Da Nang. Coupled with the SLF BLT, they brought USMC maneuver strength in RVN to 12 battalions, 9 from III MAF and 3 from I MAF. (Total bns. in SVN: 21)

28 Sept 65   1st Air Cavalry Division closed in RVN and assumed responsibility for its TAOR. (Total bns. in SVN: 29)

7 Oct 65   Remainder of the 1st Infantry Division closed in RVN. (Total bns. in SVN: 35)

8 Nov 65   A full division of ROK forces closed into RVN. (Total bns. in SVN: 44)

10 Nov 65   *JCSM 811–65*
After numerous adjustments in required support for Phase I deployments, the *JCS* proposed a final ceiling of 219,000 on that portion of the build-up and then addressed on-going Phase II proposals.

31 Dec 65   Phase I U.S. strength in RVN at year's end was 184,314.

I.   MARINE COMBAT UNITS GO TO DA NANG, MARCH 1965

A.   *INTRODUCTION*

At approximately nine o'clock on the morning of 8 March 1965, the United States Marine Corps' Battalion Landing Team 3/9 splashed ashore at Da Nang on the mainland of Southeast Asia. Although there were already over 20,000 American servicemen in Vietnam, this was the first time that U.S. ground combat units had been committed to action. The mission assigned 3/9 and its companion battalion 1/3 (which landed by air later the same day) was "to occupy and defend critical terrain features in order to secure the airfield and, as directed, communications facilities, U.S. supporting installations, port facilities, landing beaches and other U.S. installations against attack. The U.S. Marine Force will not, repeat will not, engage in day to day actions against the Viet Cong." The overall responsibility for the security of that base complex was to remain within the purview of the ARVN Commander of the I Corps Tactical Zone, General Nguyen Chanh Thi. It was hoped that with the provision of reinforcements for Da Nang security, General Thi would be able to release some of his own troops from that mission to undertake offensive action against the Viet Cong. In light of subsequent events, it would be facile to conclude that the modest input of some 3,500 Marines at this juncture presaged the massive buildup of U.S. fighting power in Vietnam which brought American military strength in country to over 180,000 by the end of 1965. Except for COMUSMACV who did see it as a first step and welcomed it and Ambassador Taylor who saw it as an unwelcome first step, official Washington regarded the deployment as a one shot affair to meet a specific situation.

B.   *THE MAKING OF THE DECISION*

1.   *COMUSMACV's Request*

On 22 February 1965, after a visit to Da Nang by General Throckmorton, then Deputy COMUSMACV, General Westmoreland cabled CINCPAC requesting two Marine BLT's to assist in protecting the base against Viet Cong raids, sabotage, and mortar attacks. As a result of his visit, General Throckmorton told General Westmoreland that he questioned the capability of the

Vietnamese to protect the base and recommended the deployment of the entire 9th Marine Expeditionary Brigade. General Westmoreland concurred with the security evaluation but requested only two of the three BLT's organic to the 9th MEB with the third BLT to be held offshore as a reserve.

2. *The Ambassador's Opinion*

Ambassador Taylor sent to the State Department on the same day the following cable:

> The ref cable requests CINCPAC, MACV and Ambassador's views as to requirement for force deployments to this area in view of security situation of SVN. General Westmoreland and I agree that there is no need to consider deployments to SVN at this time except possibly for protection of airfield at Da Nang.
>
> As I analyze the pros and cons of placing any considerable number of Marines in Da Nang area beyond those presently assigned, I develop grave reservations as to wisdom and necessity of so doing. Such action would be step in reversing long standing policy of avoiding commitment of ground combat forces in SVN. Once this policy is breached, it will be very difficult to hold line. If Da Nang needs better protection, so do Bien Hoa, Ton Son Nhut, Nha Trang and other key base areas. Once it becomes evident that we are willing assume such new responsibilities, one may be sure that GVN will seek to unload other ground force tasks upon us. Increased numbers of ground forces in SVN will increase points of friction with local population and create conflicts with RVNAF over command relationships. These disadvantages can be accepted only if there is clear and unchallenged need which can be satisfied only by US ground forces. Turning to possible uses for additional Marines in Da Nang area, I can see several which are worth examining. First, they could be used to reinforce protection of Da Nang airbase against Bien Hoa-type of attack by fire or against combined VC fire and ground attack.
>
> More ambitious mission would be readiness to engage in mobile operations against VC in Da Nang area to keep VC units at distance from base and make positive contribution to pacification of area. Such US forces would concurrently be available to join in conventional defense of area if DRV army moved southward in resumption of formal hostilities.
>
> In defense of the Da Nang airbase against surprise attack by fire, it would be necessary for Marines to be in place on ground in considerable strength. (MACV has estimated that about six battalions would be necessary to keep 81mm mortar fire off large airfield.) Even if whole MEB were deployed, they could not provide complete assurance that surprise mortar fire by small groups attacking at night would be kept off field. Protection of field against VC ground attack would be considerably simpler and would require fewer Marines. It is hard to imagine an attack on field by more than VC regiment and even an attack in those numbers would be extremely risky in face of superior friendly air and ground fire. To meet such an attack, battalion of Marines supported by local ARVN forces should be sufficient. On other hand, as indicated above, effective perimeter defense against mortar fire would require at least whole brigade of Marines.
>
> It has been suggested that an ancillary benefit to deployment of additional Marines to Da Nang would be freeing of ARVN units for use else-

where in mobile operations. While some ARVN troops of order of battalion might be so relieved, number would not be sufficient to constitute strong argument for bringing in Marines. Generally speaking, Marines would be performing task which has not been done adequately in past.

The use of Marines in mobile counter-VC operations has the attraction of giving them an offensive mission and one of far greater appeal than that of mere static defense. However, it would raise many serious problems which in past have appeared sufficiently formidable to lead to rejection of use of US ground troops in a counter-guerrilla role. White-faced soldier armed, equipped and trained as he is not suitable guerrilla fighter for Asian forests and jungles. French tried to adapt their forces to this mission and failed; I doubt that US forces could do much better. Furthermore, we would have vastly complicating factor of not running war and hence problem of arranging satisfactory command relationships with our Vietnamese allies. Finally, there would be ever present question of how foreign soldier would distinguish between a VC and friendly Vietnamese farmer. When I view this array of difficulties, I am convinced that we should adhere to our past policy of keeping our ground forces out of direct counterinsurgency role.

If there were any great likelihood of DRV forces crossing the Demilitarized Zone in conventional attack, there would be no question of need for strong US Ground force to assist ARVN in defense of coastal plain. However, this situation would not arise suddenly and we should have ample time to make our deployments before situation got out of hand.

In view of foregoing considerations, I conclude that only mission worth considering now for additional Marines in Da Nang area is to contribute to defense of base against mortar fire and ground attack. However, to defend against fire would require at least full brigade and I do not believe threat and possible consequences of mortar attack are so great as to warrant pinning down so valuable force in static defensive mission. However, in view of General Westmoreland's understandable concern for safety of this important base, I would be willing to recommend placing in Da Nang Marine battalion landing team. Such force would strengthen defense of base and, at same time, would be manageable force from point of view of accommodating it on base and absorbing it into Da Nang community. Such force with those Marines already present should remove any substantial danger of VC ground attack and in conjunction with available ARVN forces provide an acceptable level of security against attack by fire.

If Washington decision is to introduce additional Marines into [Vietnam, it should], of course, be made contingent upon getting concurrence of GVN. It would be useful and, I believe, not difficult to get GVN to initiate request for additional forces to which USG could then accede. Taylor.

3. CINCPAC's Support

CINCPAC cabled the JCS on 24 February and recommended immediate deployment of two Marine BLT's, one over the beach and one by air and surface. He advised, in addition, that a squadron of Marine F4's be deployed to Da Nang simultaneously. Those aircraft would be for close air support of the defenders and could be used "for other missions along with primary mission. . . . All CINCPAC contingency plans for SEA provide for employment of Marine aircraft from Da Nang." The tone of CINCPAC's cable was urgent.

He encouraged deployment *now* "before the tragedy," and he added that were the base to be attacked before the BLT's were put ashore, the landing force afloat would be unable, because of the time required to get forces to the scene, to influence the outcome. One of the references cited. in this lengthy CINCPAC cable was the Ambassador's message of 22 February. In addressing that reference, CINCPAC disagreed openly with Ambassador Taylor and cited the Marines' "distinguished record," saying:

> In ref F the Ambassador discusses the pros and cons of deploying the MEB to Da Nang. The Ambassador comments on the difficulty of providing complete assurance of security from surprise mortar fire even with the whole of MEB. This is true and consequently, what we are obliged to do here is to reduce within the limits of our capability the hazards to our people. I believe that the vulnerability of the U.S. investment in Da Nang is as apparent to the VC/DRV as it is to us. With a strong mobile force in the area providing a tight defense of the airfield complex and good security of U.S. outlying installations, I believe that two ancillary benefits will emerge. First, the RVNAF will be encouraged to use the forces thus freed for patrol and security operations, and second, the VC/DRV will be obliged to regard Da Nang as a tougher target. Finally, the Ambassador rejects the usefulness of U.S. ground elements in a counter-guerrilla war because of our color, armament, equipment and training. This stands athwart past performance in this function. The Marines have a distinguished record in counter-guerrilla warfare.

The JCS forwarded to the Secretary of Defense the substance of CINCPAC's recommendations in JCSM-130-65.

4. *Contingent Approval*

On 26 February the State Department cabled Ambassador Taylor that the Marines were on the way, and that he was to secure approval from the Government of Vietnam for their deployment to Da Nang. Ambassador Taylor cabled the State Department in reply on 28 February and said:

> After discussion of Ref A with Johnson and Throckmorton (Westmoreland was temporarily unavailable), we have decided to proceed as following.
>
> I shall seek an appointment with Quat at first opportunity (probably tomorrow March 1) and raise the matter of our concern (but not alarm) over the security of the Da Nang airfield and environs along following lines. It is the most important military installation in the country which is indispensable in air defense and in support of air and sea operations against the DRV. It must be at or near the top of the target list which the VC/DRV wish to destroy. I visited Da Nang on February 27 for the first time in several months and am deeply impressed with the increasing magnitude of the security problem as are General Westmoreland and his principal military colleagues.
>
> Except for the chronic shortage of GVN forces in I Corps, we would be inclined to urge GVN to allocate several additional battalions to the Da Nang area. But we know that such forces could not be made available except as prohibitive cost to the security of other areas in SVN. For these

reasons, we are driven to consider a solution which we have always rejected in the past, the introduction of US ground combat forces to reinforce the defense of Da Nang until GVN forces become available for the purpose. In spite of many cogent reasons against this solution, General Westmoreland and I are now reluctantly prepared to recommend it to Washington if the PM so desires and requests.

Quat may agree at once but is likely to want to take time to discuss the matter with Thieu and Minh. Even if he should acquiesce, I would suggest another meeting on the subject with Quat, Thieu, Minh and Thi at which Westmoreland and I would emphasize the limited mission of the Marines and their non-involvement in pacification.

If all goes well and concurrence is received, there should be no problem about a press release. We would envision this to be a short, joint GVN/US statement issued at once to the effect that, at the request of GVN, the USG is landing two battalions of Marines to strengthen the security of the Da Nang area until such time as they can be relieved by GVN forces. The first BLT could then land at once and the second on call from MACV.

I strongly urge a deferment of decision on landing in remainder of MEB until the first two BLT's are ashore and in place. By that time we will have around 7300 U.S. military personnel in the Da Nang area and I doubt ability to absorb or usefully employ the rest of the MEB. We can tell better after the two BLT's are shaken down. Taylor.

In a subsequent meeting with GVN officials, Ambassador Taylor secured their approval for the deployment. Generals Thieu and "Little" Minh expressed their concern about the possible reaction of the populace in the Da Nang area and asked that the Marines be "brought ashore in the most inconspicuous way feasible."

5. *Eleventh Hour Change*

One final obstacle to the Marine deployment was raised when Assistant Secretary of Defense McNaughton cabled the Ambassador in Saigon on 2 March stating that the 173rd Airborne Brigade, then stationed on Okinawa, would be substituted for the Marines. Other than exchange of cables, there is no documentary evidence in the files to indicate what might have been the rationale behind the belated attempt to deploy the 173rd Airborne to Da Nang in place of the Marines. One can only surmise the reasons behind such a move, but certain characteristics of the two forces may provide a clue. The Marines present *prima facie* a more formidable appearance upon arrival on the scene. They have organized a complement of heavy weapons, amphibious vehicles, and various other items of weighty hardware, including tanks, in contrast to the smaller and lighter airborne. Together with their accompanying armada of ships, the Marines might be seen as a more permanent force than the airborne. This, coupled with the common knowledge that the Marines have a long history of interventions in foreign countries for purposes of peacekeeping and stability, might have influenced someone in the decision apparatus to consider using the airborne in their stead as a positive signal that the Da Nang deployment was to be of short duration. If this was indeed the case, it suggests that there were still high-ranking people in Washington who were hoping to make the deployment of U.S. troops temporary and limited.

General Westmoreland objected to the proposed change on the grounds that the Marines were more self-sustaining and the Ambassador agreed with him. CINCPAC, in objecting to the proposed change, sent the following telegram to the JCS:

> The action outlined in Ref A, which would place the 173rd Airborne Brigade, a two-battalion brigade, at Da Nang, embodies several features which are undesirable. A light and flexible airborne force would be committed to a fixed task depriving CINCPAC of his air mobile reserve. It is the only airborne assault force in the theater. A comprehensive array of plans and logistic preparations which affect many of our forces, and the forces of other countries, would be undermined. The action would employ units which are less adequately constituted for the purpose.
>
> Since the origination of OPLAN 32 in 1959, the Marines have been scheduled for deployment to Da Nang. Seven CINCPAC and SEATO contingency plans and a myriad of supporting plans at lower echelons reflect this same deployment. As a result, there has been extensive planning, reconnaissance, and logistics preparation over the years. The CG, 9th MEB is presently in Da Nang finalizing the details of landing the MEB forces in such a way as to cause minimum impact on the civilian populace. The forces are present and ready to land, some now embarked, with plans for execution complete. The deployment has been thoroughly explored by Amb Taylor with Prime Minister Quat and the method in which the Marines would be introduced was mutually agreed upon as pointed out in Ref B.
>
> Another practical consideration is the fact that 1300 Marines are already at Da Nang. The Marines have been there in varying numbers for more than two years and thus have long since established the logistics and administrative base for future Marine deployments. They have a long standing and effective local relationship with the populace and the RVNAF. Then, there is the matter of adaptability for the task. Da Nang is on the sea coast. Each Marine BLT has its own amphibian vehicles, which are adaptable to continuing seaborne supply. Each one has a trained shore party to insure the flow of material across the beach in an area where port facilities are marginal. They embody amphibious bulk fuel systems which serve as a cardinal stand-by in case of interruption of commercial fuel supply. Their communications equipment and procedures are compatible with the hawks, helicopters and other Marine formations now in Da Nang and their organic heavy engineer equipment will be effective in developing the defensive works needed for accomplishing the task. The Marine MEB includes tanks and artillery. The airborne battalions, on the other hand, being designed for a different task, are deficient in each of these important particulars—in varying degrees—and are thus less desirable for the assignment.
>
> *The situation in Southeast Asia has now reached a point where the soundness of our contingency planning may be about to be tested.* The tasking has been completed. Logistic arrangements and lines of communication are establishing and operating. Command arrangements have been made and agreed upon and plans for landing and disposition of forces ashore have been made and these forces are ready to execute them. It therefore seems imprudent, at this time, to shift forces in a major sector and to force changes in contingency posture for other parts of Southeast Asia. [Emphasis added]

Whatever force is landed, its strength should be adequate for the job. The airborne force, if selected, would require substantial and diverse augmentation to achieve the desired combat capability.

If the final decision is to deploy and [sic] Army Brigade instead of the MEB to Da Nang, then I would recommend a one Brigade Task Force of the 25th Infantry Division. This would provide a ground combat capability reasonably similar to the ground elements of the MEB. The command and control elements and the initial light infantry elements of this task force could be airlifted to provide some early security at Da Nang. Achievement of a more adequate capability similar to the MEB would require air and sealift from Hawaii and CONUS augmentation of some support units for the task force. The DAFFD should not be used since it is an essential element of other contingency plans.

I recommend that the MEB be landed at Da Nang as previously planned.

6. *Final Approval*

The objections were sustained, and on 6 March 1965 the Pentagon issued the following news release:

TWO U.S. MARINE BATTALIONS TO BE DEPLOYED IN VIET NAM. After consultation between the governments of South Vietnam and the United States, the United States Government has agreed to the request of the Government of Vietnam to station two United States Marine Corps Battalions in the Da Nang area to strengthen the general security of the Da Nang Air Base complex.

The limited mission of the Marines will be to relieve Government of South Vietnam forces now engaged in security duties for action in the pacification program and in offensive roles against Communist guerrilla forces.

On the same day the Joint Chiefs of Staff ordered CINCPAC to commence the landing of the BLT's, and on 7 March Secretary of State Rusk told a national television and radio audience that the Marines would shoot back if shot at, but their mission was to put a tight security ring around Da Nang Air Base, thus freeing South Vietnamese forces for combat.

C. *THE SITUATION IN VIETNAM*

1. *Da Nang Local*

Prior to the landing of the Marines, Da Nang had yet to be attacked by the VC, but the official estimates of enemy intentions and capabilities in the I Corps area were none too encouraging. There were reported to be 12 battalions numbering some 6,000 men within striking distance of the base, and on the night of 7 March the town of Mieu Kong, three miles south of the airfield, had been probed by a VC unit of unknown size. General Throckmorton's estimate of ARVN lack of capability to prevent Viet Cong depradations against the sizeable and expensive stocks of U.S. equipment on the base was colored, no doubt, by recent Viet Cong attacks at Pleiku and Qui Nhon and by the raid on Bien Hoa airfield on 1 November 1964. In all of these attacks, the GVN security forces had not been able to prevent a determined Viet Cong attempt to penetrate the defenses around important installations. Moreover, it was apparent that U.S. personnel in South Vietnam were vulnerable. With the beginning of the Flaming Dart air strikes against North Vietnam in early February 1965, communist retaliation against the bases which supported those strikes became a distinct probability. In order to cope with possible communist reprisal air attacks on Da Nang, elements of a Marine HAWK Missile Battalion were ordered to that base on 7 February. However, communist air attacks were less probable and offered higher risk than a ground attack by Viet Cong forces in country, and Da Nang, which was heavily supporting air activity over North and South Vietnam, was a lucrative target. If, as General Westmoreland reported in his February 1965 Monthly Evaluation, the air strikes in North and South Vietnam were having a beneficial effect on morale in the GVN, then it was highly likely that the Viet Cong would at least make an effort to stop or slow down the frequency of the raids.

2. *GVN Instability*

Both the CIA and MACV were sober and somber in their estimates of the political situation in South Vietnam in early 1965. The fall of the Huong government in January and the confused events of 16–21 February which culminated in General Khanh's departure from Vietnam made any predictions difficult at best. The CIA thought Quat's government was shaky, and the Chairman of the Joint Chiefs of Staff in a message to General Westmoreland conveyed his fears that despite U.S. actions against North Vietnam, the GVN might collapse. General Westmoreland's reply to the Chairman stated in part:

> History may well record that the real significance of 1964 was not major VC advance and corresponding GVN retrogression but rather that South Vietnam's social and political institutions remained remarkably intact under the powerful disintegrating blows to which subjected—most of them not of VC making . . . Nonetheless, we do have the very real asset of a resilient people and this gives hope that there is more time available than we might think; time in which, if properly exploited, the needed national leadership could evolve . . .

CINCPAC added a telling note to General Westmoreland's comments when he said we needed the 9th MEB for insurance should the GVN be unable to resist collapse in the critical area of Da Nang where so much was already committed.

3. *Enemy Capabilities*

Despite some encouraging signs in January 1965, the official assessments of the military situation emanating from Saigon were bleak. The GVN armed forces had suffered a major defeat at Binh Gia, Phuoc Tuy Province, in late December–early January. There, the Viet Cong, fighting for the first time with coordinated units of regimental size, had stood off the best that ARVN could offer and held their ground. To many observers, including General Westmoreland, Binh Gia signaled the long-expected beginning of Phase III of the insurgency. The Viet Cong were confident enough to abandon their hit-and-run guerrilla tactics and engage the GVN armed forces in conventional ground combat.

Although the rate of Viet Cong activity in January was the lowest in 11 months, it was surmised that they were merely regrouping and planning their next steps. Sure enough, during the month of February the VC reappeared in force and carried out a series of successful raids and attacks, including those on the U.S. installations in Pleiku and Qui Nhon. The CIA in its February Sitrep was prompted to declare that the critical province of Binh Dinh in the II Corps area was just about lost to the Viet Cong. Binh Dinh is a key province for a number of reasons. Highway 1, the major north-south road artery connecting the I Corps with Saigon, runs the length of Binh Dinh. Of equal importance is Highway 19 which runs west from Qui Nhon through An Khe to the city of Pleiku. Qui Nhon, a coastal city at the eastern end of Highway 19, offers one of the few viable port alternatives to Saigon and is a major logistical base for resupply to the upland bases and camps. Loss of control of Highway 19 dictates that friendly forces in the highlands be resupplied entirely by air— a staggering prospect. Finally, the large population in Binh Dinh, numbering some 800,000, offers great prospects for manpower and sustenance to the side able to control the province.

Intelligence estimates began stating that the coming rainy season would be accompanied by a major Viet Cong attempt to cut the country in half in the II Corps. It was quite possible that the VC would attempt during such a campaign to seize complete control of one of the highland provinces, most probably Kontum, and would then proceed to set up a NLF government therein. The political and psychological effect of such a move might, some observers feared, sound the death knell for the GVN. General Westmoreland, in his February Monthly Evaluation added plaintively that he hoped the air activity in North and South Vietnam would help reverse the trend.

In October of 1964, the National Intelligence Board in Washington had published a grave picture of the situation in South Vietnam. In summary, they said that the political situation would continue to decay with a gradual petering out of the war effort. Coup after coup, intractable Buddhists, Montagnard revolt, and strikes were all evidence of the lack of leadership, and no charismatic leader was in sight. The Viet Cong were unlikely to make an overt bid to seize power as things were going their way, and they were looking for a neutralist coalition which they could easily dominate. The endurance of the people and the ability of the administration to carry on routine duties without any guidance from Saigon were cited as latent strengths as was the fact that no identifiable power group had yet called for an end to the fighting or had sought accommodation with the Viet Cong.

The events of the next few months added no new ingredients to this gloomy picture until the decision to initiate Rolling Thunder. In estimating probable communist reactions to the latter, the National Intelligence Board stated "we accordingly believe that the DRV/VC reaction to a few more air attacks like those of early February would probably be to continue their pressures in the South more or less on the scale of recent weeks . . . It is possible that they would, for a week or two, refrain from direct attacks on U.S. installations, but we cannot estimate that such restraint is probable."

McGeorge Bundy in his Memorandum to the President dated 7 February 1965 estimated that without additional U.S. action, the GVN would collapse within the next year. He saw latent anti-Americanism near the surface in South Vietnam and detected amongst the Vietnamese the attitude that the U.S. was going to quit. Bundy recommended the initiation of a policy of gradual and continuing reprisal, but he did not even mention the question of U.S. installation security nor did he mention the possibility of committing U.S. ground forces.

4. Contemporary Accounts

Contemporary accounts of the situation in South Vietnam from the non-official viewpoint are unanimous in their recognition of the continuing decay in the political and military capacity of the GVN to resist. The prospect for success if the U.S. did not change its approach to the war was nil. The Viet Cong were clearly winning. To writers like Halberstam and Mecklin, the choice for the U.S. boiled down to two alternatives; either get out or commit land forces to stem the tide. Neither of these writers was likely to view the arrival of the Marines as anything else but indication of a decision to take the second course. Shaplen treated the landing of the Marines as an isolated incident, but he did not accept the rationale that they were in Vietnam for strictly defensive reasons. In commenting on the subsequent arrival of more Marines and the concomitant expansion of their mission to include offensive patrol work, he says: ". . . and sooner or later, it was surmised, they would tangle directly with the Viet Cong; in fact, it was obvious from the outset that in an emergency they would be air-lifted to other areas away from their base."

A glance at some of the commentary of early March 1965 in newspapers and periodicals gives clear indication that the landing of the two Marine BLT's was seen as an event of major significance. Analysis of the import of the event varies, as would be expected, from writer to writer, but almost without exception they read more into the deployment than was made explicit by the brief Defense Department press release. By-lines from Saigon, where reporters had ready access to "reliable sources" in the U.S. Mission, give clear indication that there had been a major shift in attitude as regards the use of U.S. ground forces in Asia. Ted Sell, a Los Angeles Times staff writer, wrote on 10 March 1965. "The landing of the two infantry battalions is in its own way a far more significant act than were earlier attacks by U.S. airplanes, even though those attacks were directed against a country—North Vietnam—ostensibly not taking part in the direct war." Speaking after the Marines were ordered in, one high official said of the no-ground-troops-in-Asia shibboleth, "Sure, it's undesirable. But that doesn't mean we won't do it." It is especially significant that among the writers attempting to gauge the extent of U.S. resolve in the Vietnamese situation, the deployment of ground forces was somehow seen as a much more positive and credible indication of U.S. determination than any of the steps, including the air strikes on the DRV, previously taken.

D. THE DEVELOPING DEBATE ON THE DEPLOYMENT OF U.S. FORCES

1. Proposals for Actions Before the National Security Council Working Group, Late 1964

Events in the late 1964–early 1965 period moved at such a rapid pace as almost to defy isolated analysis. On 3 November 1964, just two days after the Viet Cong successfully attacked the U.S. air base and billetting at Bien Hoa, Assistant Secretary of State William Bundy convened the newly established NSC Working Group on SVN/SEA. Membership in the group included the State Department, OSD/

ISA, the JCS, and CIA. Debate within the group centered around three proposed courses of action, none of which contained a major U.S. ground troop commitment to SVN. Ground troop commitment was addressed in draft papers circulated within the group by the principals, but it does not appear that anyone was thinking in terms of a major U.S. effort on the ground in counterinsurgency operations. William Bundy's own papers mentioned CINCPAC OPLAN 32–64 and CINCPAC OPLAN 39–65, both of which contingency plans provided for the input of US ground combat forces into SEA in response to Chicom or DRV aggression or a combination of the two. In a draft dated 13 November 1964, Bundy discussed ground troop commitment and said in part that he did "not envisage the introduction of substantial ground forces into South Vietnam or Thailand in conjunction with these initial actions." The initial actions to which he referred were the three basic options under consideration at the time by the Working Group. Bundy went on in the same draft memorandum to state that the question of ground troop involvement needed further consideration, including the possibility of the introduction of a multilateral force into the northern provinces of South Vietnam. In discussing the pros and cons of ground troops, Bundy did not mention the security of bases but he did suggest that the presence of troops in South Vietnam might invite Viet Cong activity against them.

Other drafts circulated in the NSC Working Group dealt with ground forces. In a memorandum to the Working Group dated 30 November 1964, and entitled "Alternative to Air Attacks on North Vietnam: Proposals for the Use of U.S. Ground Forces in Support of Diplomacy in Vietnam," Messrs. Johnson and Kattenburg of the State Department proposed the introduction of a token ground force to provide proof of our resolve as a prelude to a major diplomatic offensive. The Joint Chiefs of Staff also made a proposal for the introduction of ground troops in their 23 November 1964 memo to the Secretary of Defense. In that JCSM, which was principally concerned with analysis of various courses of action to increase pressure on the DRV, the JCS recommended the collateral deployment of Marine units to Da Nang and other units from Okinawa to Ton Son Nhut Air Base for purposes of security and deterrence in accordance with CINCPAC OPLANS. There is no documentary evidence, however, that these drafts were in any way included in the memo sent to the President.

On 1 December 1964, the President approved the recommendations of Ambassador Taylor and the NSC Principals to proceed with the implementation of the Working Group's Course of Action A and, after 30 days or more and with some GVN progress along specified lines, to enter a second phase program consisting "principally of progressively more serious air strikes," as in Option C. Again, the U.S. focus was on the air war, not on the ground.

2. The Focus of the Joint Chiefs of Staff

In forwarding on 11 February 1965 their proposed program for the first eight weeks of military actions against North Vietnam, the JCS told the Secretary of Defense that their plan called primarily for airstrikes but also included the collateral deployment of a MEB to Da Nang and an Army Brigade to Thailand. Neither of these deployments were for purposes of counterinsurgency but rather were intended to deter any overt DRV/Chicom retaliation and to put us in a better posture in case the deterrent failed. The JCS forwarded this proposal to the Secretary again on 4 March 1965, still without mention of the possibility of ground combat action against the Viet Cong. The first proposal from the JCS that U.S. troop units be sent to SVN for active operations against the Viet Cong came on 20 March 1965, well after the landing of the Marines at Da Nang. That the JCS were considering such a proposal before the Marines were landed is indicated obliquely in Chairman Wheeler's cover letter to the Secretary of Defense of 1 March 1965, under which he forwarded the JSOP-70 and in which he said: "In arriving at the proposed force levels the present situation in Southeast Asia was only indirectly considered, and had little, if any, influence upon the JSOP-70 force levels. This is pointed out to identify a specific problem area that requires a near term and long term solution. By separate action the JCS are addressing the problem and will provide you with their views on this subject." While the Marines were landing at Da Nang, a key man from the Washington scene was a visitor in Saigon. Although his visit was unconnected with the Marine landings *per se,* his actions on return to Washington provided a fair measure of the attitudes prevalent in the U.S. community in Vietnam at that juncture.

General Johnson, Chief of Staff of the Army, was in Vietnam from the 5th through the 12th of March 1965. He was given a thorough briefing on the situation by General Westmoreland and other members of the United States mission, and he brought back to Washington detailed situation reports prepared by MACV and the Ambassador. The view from Saigon, as reflected in those reports, was very grave indeed. A succinct summation of the views of the entire U.S. Mission Council in Saigon appeared in the Ambassador's Sitrep forwarded to the State Department on 11 March 1965:

> Unless (and this is primary), NVN support is checked, GVN military and paramilitary resources increased, pacification goals and concepts refined, administrative efficiency improved, and an adequate political-psychological base created, there is little likelihood of stemming the tide of the VC insurgency. Only U.S. resources can provide the pressures on NVN necessary to check Hanoi's support, although some measure of SVN armed forces participation will be required for psychological reasons; the other measures and programs required to stem the tide of VC insurgency are largely internal to SVN, but even here success will require a marked increase in U.S. support and participation.

There is little doubt that General Johnson was impressed by the gravity of the situation in SVN as presented to him at the very time the Marines were landing at Da Nang. The report which he submitted to the Secretary of Defense on 14 March contains specific proposals, including some for deployment of additional U.S. ground combat forces, which Johnson felt should be implemented if the U.S. was to realize its objectives in SVN. Those objectives as seen by Johnson were: (1) to persuade the DRV to abandon its support and direction of the insurgency, (2) to defeat the Viet Cong insurgents, and (3) to create a stable GVN. In accord with the Ambassador, General Johnson called for U.S. action because "what the situation requires may exceed what the Vietnamese can be expected to do." To arrest the current deterioration Johnson presented a list of 21 specific actions to be taken. The upshot of these 21 points was greater U.S. involvement in terms of money, ships, aircraft, advisors, and assorted hardware, but no ground combat units were involved. They meant essentially more of the same, and all 21 points were approved by the President on 1 April 1965. There was more to the Johnson recommendations, however. To release RVNAF for offensive action, he proposed deploying a U.S. division either to defend the Bien Hoa/Ton Son Nhut airfield complex plus some coastal enclaves or to defend the highland provinces of Kontum, Pleiku and Darlac. Johnson obviously preferred the latter alternative because the enemy in the Montagnard populated highlands would be more easily identified by U.S. forces. The Secretary of Defense in commenting on the proposed deployment also preferred the second alternative although he thought neither afforded an efficient return in terms of RVNAF forces released per U.S. force input (alternative 1 called for 23,000 U.S. forces to release 5,000 ARVN; alternative 2 ratio was 15,000 U.S. to 6,000 ARVN). Secretary McNamara directed the JCS to consider the 2d alternative while emphasizing that he preferred an ROK division to one of our own. The culmination of General Johnson's report was his recommendation that the SEATO treaty be invoked to get allied participation in a four division force counter-infiltration cordon to be placed across the DMZ and the Laotian panhandle from the South China Sea to the Mekong River. In closing his report, General Johnson observed:

> In order for the USG to evaluate his [COMUSMACV's] requests properly when submitted, a policy determination must be made in the very near future that will assure the question: What should the Vietnamese be expected to do for themselves and how much more must the U.S. contribute directly to the security of South Vietnam?

In reference to this observation Secretary McNamara wrote that the "Policy is: anything that will strengthen the position of the GVN will be sent . . ."

3. *Attitudes West of CONUS*

Both CINCPAC and General Westmoreland were very much concerned during early 1965 with the possible implementation of existing contingency plans, at least two of which as already mentioned, called for the input into Southeast Asia of U.S. troop units. The alert (Phase I) of OPLAN 32–64 was in effect as of 1 January 1965. CINCPAC clearly indicated that his thinking was geared to contingency plans in his cabled objections to the proposed deployment of the 173rd Airborne *vice* the Marines into Da Nang. All of his OPLANs had buildup predicated on the Marines' use of Da Nang as a base. CINCPAC is equally clear in his cable traffic of this period, however, that he is not immediately thinking in terms of the commitment of U.S. ground forces in operations against the Viet Cong. In a cable to Chairman Wheeler on 5 March 1965 he said that "the single most important thing we can do quickly to improve the security situation in SVN is to make full use of our air power." He went on in the same cable to say that the MEB should be deployed to Da Nang as soon as possible for security and also to give the GVN a boost and the Viet Cong a warning.

General Westmoreland and his staff had been concerned with planning for the input of U.S. ground troops into South Vietnam in conjunction with the aforementioned CINCPAC contingency plans since late 1964. In view of the enemy's capabilities and the obvious deficiencies of the ARVN, both of which were all too apparent to observers in Vietnam (by early 1965), it is hard to see how the military planners in MACV could have disassociated the deployment of the Marines from further troop input. In the MACV Command History for 1965 there are several statements which would tend to confirm sequential thinking in the MACV staff. On the day the Marines were landing at Da Nang it is said in the History that "thus step one in the buildup of forces had been taken and subsequent steps appeared to be assured." The History also states that "the Phase II, RVN, portions of OPLAN 32–64 were essentially implemented by the U.S. buildup during 1965, although on a larger scale than planned." On 27 March 1965, General Westmoreland forwarded to CINCPAC his estimate of the situation in Vietnam and his recommendation for U.S. troop input for offensive action against the Viet Cong. In that cable COMUSMACV states that his staff commenced preparation of the estimate and troop recommendations on 13 March, five days after the Marines went into Da Nang, and the day after the Army Chief of Staff's departure from Saigon.

Ambassador Taylor was not enthusiastic about any continuation of troop buildup after the landing of the Marines. He had already stated his reasons in the lengthy cable of 22 February contained herein. On 3 March, in response to a Department of State query regarding the possible employment of an international force, Taylor conveyed the text of a conversation about the MLF between Ambassador Johnson and the Australian envoy to South Vietnam. The Australian had voiced fears similar to Taylor's in that he foresaw an increased manifestation of Vietnamese xenophobia with the input into South Vietnam of foreign troops, and he feared such a move would cause the GVN "to shuck off greater responsibility onto USG." Taylor told the Secretary of State in another cable on the same day that he had no idea what the GVN attitude toward a MLF might be and that there were many problems involved with such a move that had yet to be ironed out. The MLF was clearly only in the talking stage, while the Marine BLT's were a fact. The discussion of the MLF is included to illustrate that the Ambassador was consistent in looking beyond the immediate tactical need to support a faltering GVN—a need which Taylor saw just as clearly as did MACV—to analyze the long-term ramifications of the introduction into Vietnam of foreign combat troops. Taylor's warnings in this regard were, in light of the present situation in SVN, prophetic indeed.

E. FUTURE EXPECTATIONS

There seems to be sufficient evidence to conclude that General Westmoreland and his staff saw in the deployment of the Marines the beginning of greater things to come. The 1965 Command History says as much, and the rapidity with which the staff followed on the Marine BLT's with more proposals would tend to back up such a conclusion. It hardly seems a coincidence that General Johnson, immediately following his briefings by MACV, returned to Washington and recommended, among other things, that a U.S. division be deployed to SVN. CINCPAC, although obviously concerned with OPLANs and their focus on troop deployments, comes out clearly in his cable traffic for reliance on air power for the moment and for troop commitment to secure bases only. The JCS, because they had yet to address the overall question of U.S. ground force deployments, necessarily saw the Marine deployments as a stopgap measure to insure the security of U.S. lives and property in case of a partial or total GVN collapse. Traffic between the Embassy and the Department of State indicated that further ground force deployments as a deterrent to NVN invasion were in the thinking but were not yet in the proposal stage, and the Ambassador clearly had serious objections to further troop input. It appears that for the moment, with the possible exception of General Westmoreland, his staff, and perhaps an important ally in the person of General Johnson in Washington, the Marine deployment was taken at face value and that the official Washington hopes were pinned on early NVN response to the Rolling Thunder pressure, then just in its beginning stages.

F. ANALYSIS

This paper has raised basically two analytical questions. First, what was the significance of the landing of the two Marine battalions rather than other units, such as the 173rd Airborne? Second, what was the mix of objectives behind the deployment, and did the deployment meet these objectives?

The significance of putting the Marines into Da Nang turns on whether this deployment was intended or was viewed (1) as the first elements in a phased build-up of U.S. ground combat forces, or (2) as a one-shot response to a peculiar security need at Da Nang. There is evidence for both propositions.

There are two pieces of evidence in support of the phased build-up proposition. First, no less than seven CINCPAC contingency plans treated Da Nang as a base for U.S. Marine Corps activity, and at least two of those plans provided for major Marine ground forces in the I Corps tactical zone of South Vietnam. Except for Phase II of OPLAN 32-64, however, contingency plan build-ups of force were predicated on overt DRV or Chinese Communist action. At the time of the initial landings, such overt action was anticipated in the OPLAN but had not yet occurred. It was a fact, on the other hand, that some sort of action was needed in the South to halt the course of the insurgency there, and that two Marine BLT's would not do the trick.

The second piece of evidence was the last minute attempt by Ass't Secretary of Defense McNaughton to substitute the 173rd Airborne for the Marines, and CINCPAC's strong reaction against this attempt. The only apparent rationale for the McNaughton move is as a blocking measure against expected pressures for further build-ups as embodied in the contingency plans. The substitution would have created planning tangles for the Chiefs and CINCPAC and, therefore, would have delayed pressures for further deployment pending the development of new plans. CINCPAC's vigorous response, based on administrative and logistic arguments, coupled with concern for the loss of an airmobile reserve force, persuaded Washington and thwarted the McNaughton effort. It is interesting to note, in this regard, that McNaughton, at least on the record, did not receive any support for his attempt. Conceivably, Ambassador Taylor, who had expressed serious reservations about the implications of the ground force deployment, could have joined forces with McNaughton. Taylor's failure to do so was probably based on the fact that he did not believe the pressures could be significantly thwarted by the substitution, and that, therefore, it made much more military sense to proceed as planned.

The evidence against the phased build-up proposition and for the one-shot-security hypothesis rests on one major document, and paradoxically, on the absence of other documents. The major document is the McGeorge Bundy Memorandum for the President of February 7, 1965. In this memorandum, Bundy reviews the entire situation in Vietnam without any reference to future ground force deployment—even though the request for the Marine BLT's was only two weeks away. Moreover, the usual flood of documentation preceding a decision of significance is not to be found. In other words, it appears that the key decision-makers in Washington are not focusing hard on the importance of the deployment. The attention-getter, as the Bundy memo indicates, was the impending air war against North Vietnam.

The significance of the Marine BLT deployment must also be measured up to the objectives intended by the deployment. There were four distinguishable rationales:

(1) Freeing ARVN forces from static defense to base security;
(2) Providing added security for U.S. air bases being used in the air war against North Vietnam;
(3) Signaling Hanoi with increased U.S. determination to pay a higher price in meeting its commitments; and
(4) Bolstering GVN morale.

The first objective was the one most stressed publicly—to release RVNAF for offensive action against the Viet Cong. General Westmoreland cabled the JCS on 22 February saying that the deployment of the Marines to Da Nang would result ultimately in freeing four RF companies, one tank platoon, and another RF battalion then being formed. The MACV Monthly Evaluation of March 1965 stated that only two RF companies had in fact been released. It is apparent, then, that this objective could not have been taken very seriously. While it can be argued that any slight improvement in the local force ratios *vis-a-vis* the Viet Cong was desirable; even the most optimistic prediction of releasable RVNAF units would not have had much importance.

A second rationale was the notion of security for a major U.S. air base being used in bombing operations against North Vietnam. Da Nang was exposed and the probability of a Viet Cong attack on it could not be ignored. While the two Marine BLT deployment, by itself, was recognized as being insufficient for high level of confidence about base security, there can be little doubt that U.S. troops did make that important base more secure. In retrospect, it could be construed that this was the first sign of U.S. awareness of RVNAF inadequacy. There is, however, no documentary evidence available to support this view and, in fact, the real extent of this ineffectiveness was not recognized until a few months later.

A third objective may have been to signal Hanoi with the seriousness of the U.S. resolve in Vietnam. Notwithstanding the relatively minute combat power imposed in two battalions, the very fact that they were deployed would be a much clearer sign to Hanoi of U.S. determination in the fleeting appearance of a few jet aircraft or the shadowy presence offshore of a mighty fleet of ships. Taken in conjunction with the well-known U.S. shibboleth against involvement in a major Asian land war, the deployment should have been a highly visible step unequivocal in its meaning to Hanoi. Yet, there is no evidence that anyone in the U.S. government intended the deployment to convey such a signal and there was no discussion of what responses we expected from Hanoi. If this indeed were an unspoken objective, it made little dent on NVN designs. If anything, it may have aided those in Hanoi who wanted to send additional regular NVA units into SVN.

A fourth U.S. objective was bolstering morale within the GVN and the concomitant willingness to carry on the fight. It was quite reasonable to assume that the Marines, like the air strikes on NVN that preceded them, did have a beneficial effect on morale. It is equally obvious, however, that any such effects would be transitory. Long-term improvements in morale could only come with dramatic and lasting alteration of the situation, and the two Marine battalions did not have that capability by themselves.

It seems from this vantage point that only the objective of base security really made sense. The deployment of the Marines to Da Nang might have deterred an attack on the base by a regiment of main force Viet Cong. The Marine Infantry were dug in on commanding terrain facing the North and West along the most likely avenues of approach. The security of the base was by no means assured by their presence, however, as by their own admission they were in no position to prevent determined attack—or, especially, raids and mortar attacks—the kind that had done so much damage to Bien Hoa the year before. The U.S. forces only had responsibility for half of the base complex, and it was doubted that the RVNAF could prevent the Viet Cong infiltrating sabotage squads through the heavily populated areas on the GVN side. The Marines did not, as Secretary Rusk said they would, put a tight security ring around the base. The ring was not closed until considerably later, and even then, the Viet Cong successfully penetrated the defenses and caused considerable damage in a raid on 1 July 1965—the first of a series of raids that have continued up to the present.

The landing of the Marines at Da Nang was a watershed event in the history of the U.S. involvement in Vietnam. It represented a major decision made without much fanfare—and without much planning. Whereas the decision to begin bombing North Vietnam was the product of a year's discussion, debate, and a lot of paper, and whereas the consideration of pacification policies reached talmudic proportions over the years, this decision created less than a ripple. A mighty commandment of U.S. foreign policy—thou shall not engage in an Asian land war—had been breached. Besides CINCPAC and General Westmoreland who favored the deployment, Ambassador Taylor who concurred with deep reservation, and ASD McNaughton who apparently tried to add a monkey wrench, this is a decision without faces. The seeming ease with which the Marines were introduced and the mild reaction from Hanoi served to facilitate what was to come. It also weakened the position of those who were, a few scant months later, to oppose the landing of further U.S. ground combat forces.

II. PHASE I IN THE BUILD-UP OF U.S. FORCES, MARCH–JULY 1965

A. THE SITUATION IN VIETNAM, SPRING AND EARLY SUMMER, 1965

Vietnam in February, 1965, saw a brief flurry of enemy activity and the departure of the volatile General Nguyen Khanh as a result of another coup. The installation of Phan Huy Quat as Prime Minister and Phan Khac Suu as Chief of State was followed by a period of ominous quiescence. The drop in intensity of the fighting coincided with the dry season in the southern parts of the country, with the beginning of the United States Rolling Thunder program of continuous air strikes against North Vietnam, and with the arrival of the first U.S. ground combat troops committed to Asian soil since Korea.

1. The Political Situation

Despite its rather inauspicious beginning in February, the government had by early April convinced the CIA that for the first time the progressive deterioration in the South Vietnamese political situation had come to a halt. All the disruptive elements in the Vietnamese body politic remained, but Quat displayed considerable talent in placating dissidents and was setting about in his own quiet manner to tidy up the chaotic Saigon government. Quat was no charismatic leader. If anything, he was the opposite with his self-effacing, mild manner. But he impressed Ambassador Taylor with his businesslike approach, and the latter had high hopes for Quat's success.

By mid-May, to the dismay of the U.S. Mission, Quat's government began to manifest considerable strain. The Buddhists, a not always consistent pressure group, felt that Quat was too busy trying to please everyone instead of initiating a strong action program. The Catholics, on the other hand, were fearful of a Buddhist-dominated government and Saigon was full of rumors of the formation of Catholic paramilitary units. Colonel Pham Ngoc Thao, a familiar plotter, was said to have unsuccessfully attempted a coup on behalf of the Catholics around the 20th of May.

An apparently routine cabinet shuffle proposed by Premier Quat at the end of May precipitated a crisis which led to the fall of his government. Quat had intended to replace three cabinet ministers with southerners; but the incumbents, with the support of Chief of State Suu, refused to resign. All the dissident elements on the Saigon political scene seized on the incident as an excuse to rain invectives on Quat and, finding Suu all too ready to listen to their complaints, used him to effectively paralyze the government. The crisis came to a head on 9 June when Quat asked the senior generals of the RVNAF to mediate the dispute between himself and Suu. Instead, the generals forced Quat to resign and took over the government themselves.

Following the military takeover, a National Leadership Committee was formed. On 21 June, Major General Nguyen Van Thieu was installed as Chief of State with Air Vice Marshall Nguyen Cao Ky as the new Prime Minister. The accession of Thieu-Ky ended for the moment any hopes of Ambassador Taylor and others for the establishment of effective civilian government in Vietnam.

The sole bright spot in an otherwise very gloomy situation was the total absence of any violence associated with the military takeover. The new leaders came to office with an announced determination to maintain stability and to vigorously prosecute the war. Given the military situation at that time, little credence could be lent to their pronouncements.

2. The Military Situation

The Viet Cong were unusually inactive throughout March and April. There had been no major defeat of the enemy's forces and no signs of any major shift in strategy on his part. Hence it was assumed that he was merely pausing to regroup and to assess the effect of the changed American participation in the war embodied in air strikes and in the Marines.

During the spring months an emboldened ARVN displayed a new offensive spirit and scored a few successes at the expense of an elusive enemy. Most of the standard statistical indicators used by MACV to measure ARVN effectiveness showed favorable trends. The rate of enemy to friendly killed inclined in the government's favor, and for a brief but encouraging spell the rate of weapons lost to the enemy compared with weapons captured from him approached parity. A major effort by the GVN forces in March to open highway 19 from Qui Nhon in Binh Dinh Province to Pleiku in the highlands met with surprisingly light enemy resistance. Despite reports of heavy enemy force concentration and an impending offensive in that area, the road remained open. Incremental gains all over the country contributed to an air of euphoria manifested in the occasional expression of cautious optimism which crept into weekly or monthly situation reports, such as Ambassador Taylor's NODIS to the President (Saigon to Sec-State 3359, 13 April 1965) quoted below:

We have just completed another quite favorable week in terms of losses inflicted upon the Viet Cong, 643 of whom were killed in action to 135 on the government side. Binh Dinh Province which was considererd to be in critical condition two months ago has now been restored to what might be called normalcy; that is to say, the fear of the loss of major towns appears to be past although a large part of the province remains under Viet Cong control. The success in Binh Dinh is attributable to three factors; a new and aggressive division commander, the commitment of five general reserve battalions to the province, and the improved morale generated by the air actions in the North.

We still have the feeling that the Viet Cong are regrouping in the provinces in the northern half of the country and are probably preparing some kind of offensive action. However, there are a few indications that suggest that Viet Cong morale may be dropping. They have given up four major arms caches during the month without a sustained fight and the number of defectors during the week (129 Viet Cong military personnel and 23 political cadre) is the highest defection figure since weekly statistics were initiated in January 1964.

On the manpower side, unaudited figures indicate that government military and paramilitary forces increased by some 10,000 during the month of March of whom two-thirds were volunteers. This rate exceeds the target of 8,000 accessions per month which we had considered the best the government could do with a maximum effort.

Quat continued his program of provincial visits, making a tour of the Delta area from which he returned full of new ideas and bubbling with enthusiasm. He was quite impressed with the senior officers whom he met in the IV Corps and, as always, enjoyed talking to the country people who assembled to greet him.

His principal concern remains the unruly generals and the continued evidence of lack of unity in the senior officers corps. You have probably noted the case of insubordination in the Navy wherein several senior naval officers petitioned the removal of Admiral Cang, the Chief of Naval Operations. Quat is handling this matter routinely by a board of inquiry but is disturbed by this new evidence of lack of discipline in the armed forces. In his campaign to bring the generals under some kind of control, he is about to take the step of abolishing the position of Commander-in-Chief, while increasing the functions of the Minister of National Defense. This is a move in the right direction but his troubles will not end as long as the military command structure is clouded by the presence of the Armed Forces Council. Quat is fully aware of this problem and intends to resolve it, but slowly and cautiously.

Your Johns Hopkins speech and the reply to the 17-nation overture attracted much attention in Saigon where the reaction was generally very favorable. As one might expect, the phrase "unconditional discussion" brought forth considerable editorial comment, but the conclusion was that the term suggested no real difference in aims between the Vietnamese and the United States Government. On two occasions, I have urged Quat to sit down with Alex Johnson and me to discuss various alternative courses of international political action which may require consideration during the coming weeks and months. He has not responded affirmatively to this suggestion apparently because his own thoughts are not yet in order.

The mission has been very busy since my return with all agencies reviewing their programs to see that they are aligned with the recent decisions taken in Washington. USOM Director Killen has discussed the 41 point non-military program with Quat who has expressed particular interest in such projects as rural electrification, agricultural development, water supply and school construction. The Acting CAS Chief, Mr. Jorgensen, is giving priority attention to the 12 outline projects which Mr. McCone tabled during our Washington discussions and will soon have specific proposals for the Mission Council.

And the following excerpts from COMUSMACV's Monthly Evaluations for March and April 1965:

> *March, 1965:* Events in March were encouraging . . . RVNAF ground operations were highlighted by renewed operational effort . . . VC activity was considerably below the norm of the preceding six months and indications were that the enemy was engaged in the re-supply and re-positioning of units possibly in preparation for a new offensive, probably in the II Corps area . . . In summary, March has given rise to some cautious optimism. The current government appears to be taking control of the situation and, if the present state of popular morale can be sustained and strengthened, the GVN, with continued U.S. support, should be able to counter future VC offenses successfully.
>
> *April, 1965:* Friendly forces retained the initiative during April and a review of events reinforces the feeling of optimism generated last month . . . In summary, current trends are highly encouraging and *the GVN may have actually turned the tide at long last.* However, there are some disquieting factors which indicate a need to avoid overconfidence. A test of these trends should be forthcoming in the next few months if the VC launch their expected counter-offensive and the period may well be one of the most important of the war. [Emphasis added]

In view of the fact that nothing had basically changed in the South, it seems inconceivable that anyone was really fooled by the dramatic drop in enemy-initiated activity. Most official observers were hardheaded and realistic following the landing of the two Marine BLT's in March. COMUSMACV certainly was in the long and detailed Commander's Estimate of the Situation which he completed on 26 March and which will be analyzed at length later in this paper. In summary, General Westmoreland said in the Estimate that the program of air activity against the North, while it might ultimately succeed in causing the DRV to cease its support of the war, would not in the short run have any major effect on the situation in the South. The RVNAF, although at the moment performing fairly well, would not be able in the face of a VC summer offensive to hold in the South long enough for the bombing to become effective.

Realistic assessments of the situation in March notwithstanding, some of the parlance in cables and messages between Washington and Saigon expressed conviction that the situation in Vietnam was well in hand, and resisted radical changes or even urgent revision of ongoing U.S. programs. Ambassador Taylor, for example, reacted strongly to proposals that U.S. military-civil affairs personnel be introduced into the aid effort, and told McGeorge Bundy that the GVN was winning the war without such help. Taylor said:

> I am greatly troubled by DOD 152339Z April 15 [a cable from Mc-Naughton to Saigon containing a seven point program with "highest authority" sanction]. First, it shows no consideration for the fact that, as a result

of decisions taken in Washington during my visit, this mission is charged with securing implementation by the two month old Quat government of a 21 point military program, a 41 point non-military program, a 16 point Rowan USIS program and a 12 point CIA program. Now this new cable opens up new vistas of further points as if we can win here somehow on a point score. We are going to stall the machine of government if we do not declare a moratorium on new programs for at least six months.

Next, it shows a far greater willingness to get into the ground war than I had discerned in Washington during my recent trip. Although some additional U.S. forces should probably be introduced after we see how the Marines do in counterinsurgency operations, my own attitude is reflected in EMBTEL 3384, which I hope was called to the attention of the President.

My greatest concern arises over para 6 reftel which frankly bewilders me. What do the authors of this cable think the mission has been doing over the months and years? We have presumably the best qualified personnel the Washington agencies (State, AID, DOD, USIA, and CIA) can find working in the provinces seven days a week at precisely the tasks described in para 6. Is it proposed to withdraw these people and replace them by Army civil affairs types operating on the pattern of military occupation? If this is the thought, I would regard such a change in policy which will gain wide publicity, as disastrous in its likely efforts upon pacification in general and on US/GVN relations in particular.

Mac, can't we be better protected from our friends? I know that everyone wants to help, but there's such a thing as killing with kindness. In particular, we want to stay alive here *because we think we're winning—and will continue to win unless helped to death.* [Emphasis added]

The conferees who met in Honolulu three days later reached a joint agreement which was somewhat less optimistic than the Ambassador's pronouncement. Present in Honolulu were Secretary McNamara, Assistant Secretaries William Bundy of State and John McNaughton of Defense, Ambassador Taylor, Generals Wheeler and Westmoreland, and Admiral Sharp. Some of these men had helped produce the current optimism in situation reports and cables, and yet the consensus of their meeting was that *the then present level of Viet Cong activity was nothing but the lull before the storm.*

The situation which presented itself to the Honolulu conferees was in many ways the whole Vietnam problem in microcosm. What was needed to galvanize everyone into action was some sort of dramatic event within South Vietnam itself. Unfortunately, the very nature of the war precluded the abrupt collapse of a front or the loss of large chunks of territory in lightning strokes by the enemy. The enemy in this war was spreading his control and influence slowly and inexorably but without drama. The political infrastructure from which he derived his strength took years to create, and in most areas the expansion of control was hardly felt until it was a *fait accompli*. Only when he organized into units of battalion and regiment size, did the enemy voluntarily lend some dramatic elements to the war. Whenever these units appeared and engaged the RVNAF, the government and its U.S. helpers had something they could handle. Unfortunately at the time of the April 1965 Honolulu Conference the Viet Cong Main Force units were underground and the conferees had little or no tangible threat to which to react.

There were, however, plenty of indications in the early spring of 1965 of what was to come. There had been no major degradations in the Viet Cong strength nor in their order of battle. On the contrary, the enemy was recruiting apace and more than offsetting his losses. From throughout the country came reports that Viet Cong troops and cadre were moving into Central Vietnam and into areas adjacent to the ring of provinces comprising the "Hop Tac" area around Saigon.

Constant political turmoil involving many of the senior RVNAF officers and few significant victories combined to have a deleterious effect on the effectiveness of the GVN armed forces. The JCS on 20 March identified the degradation of RVNAF as a new phenomenon after months of *political* instability. They used the decline as justification to argue for the deployment of three divisions of reinforcements from the U.S. and Korea.

Finally and most ominous of all, a CIA-DIA memorandum dated 21 April 1965 reflected the acceptance into the enemy order of battle of one regiment of the 325th PAVN Division said to be located in Kontum Province. The presence of this regular North Vietnamese unit, which had been first reported as early as February, was a sobering harbinger of things to come.

The storm broke in earnest on 11 May when the Viet Cong attacked the capital of Phuoc Long Province, Song Be, using more than a regiment of troops. The enemy overran the town and its MACV advisory compound, causing heavy casualties among the U.S. and Vietnamese defenders. After holding the town for a day, the Viet Cong withdrew. Subsequent ARVN operations revealed that the enemy also had suffered heavily in the battle.

Significantly, while the Viet Cong were preparing their attack on Song Be, the GVN was pushing to completion a new Special Forces camp at Dong Xoai not far away on the NW corner of War Zone C. That camp was opened in May, and in less than a month the enemy was to reveal his interest in it.

Before May was over, however, the Viet Cong appeared again in strength, this time in Quang Ngai Province in the northern I Corps. Near the small outpost of Ba Gia a few kilometers west of Quang Ngai City, a battalion of the ARVN 51st Regiment was ambushed and overrun. Although the size of the enemy force was unknown, the ARVN commanders in the area rushed reinforcements out to the scene only to have them ambushed in turn. The battle dragged on for several days and ended in total defeat for the ARVN. Two battalions were completely decimated and, what was worse, the ARVN senior commanders on the scene had displayed tactical stupidity and cowardice in the face of large enemy forces. From Ba Gia came a sense of urgency, at least among some of the senior U.S. officers who had been witness to the battle. The very real possibility of ARVN collapse had been made manifest.

On the 7th of June, shortly after Ba Gia, General Westmoreland sent to CINCPAC this message (LIMDIS 19118, 07 Jun 65):

As indicated Ref A [COMUSMACV 04 NOTAL], a broad review of force requirements has been conducted in light of the changing situation in Southeast Asia and within RVN.

There are indications that the conflict in Southeast Asia is in the process of moving to a higher level. Some PAVN forces have entered SVN and more may well be on the way. Additional jet fighters and some jet light bombers have been deployed in the DRV.

Specifically, elements of the 325th PAVN Division are in the northern zone of II Corps. It is quite possible that the major portion, if not all, of the Division is now deployed in the Kontum, Pleiku, Phu Bon area. Elements of the 304th PAVN Division are suspected to be in the panhandle and, therefore, capable of following the 325th. The recent heavy actions in Phuoc Long and Quang Ngai, and VC initiatives in Pleiku, Kontum, Phu Bon and Thua Thien are demonstrations of VC strength and their apparent determination to employ their forces aggressively. Recent events as well as captured VC prisoners and documents suggest that a summer campaign is now underway to destroy govennment forces and, concurrently, to first isolate and then attack district and province towns.

So far, the VC have not employed their full capabilities in this campaign. Only two of the nine Viet Cong regiments have been heavily engaged (one in Phuoc Long and one in Quang Ngai), and probably only a similar proportion of their separate battalions has been committed. In most engagements, VC Main Force units have displayed improved training and discipline, heavier firepower from the new family of weapons with which most Main Force units have been equipped, and a willingness to take heavy losses in order to achieve objectives.

In pressing their campaign, the Viet Cong are capable of mounting regimental-size operations in all four ARVN Corps areas, and at least battalion-sized attacks in virtually all provinces. Known dispositions indicate major actions are likely in the near future in the Binh Duong–Phuoc Thanh–Phuoc Long area north of Saigon, in the Quang Ngai–Quang Tin area in Central Vietnam, and in Kontum, Pleiku, Phu Bon and Binh Dinh Provinces. Major attacks could occur also in other areas; the Viet Cong have shown that they are capable of concentrating in regimental strength with little or no warning. Whether or not the 304th Div is in, or moving toward SVN, the DRV has a "doorstep" capability to reinforce the VC with sizable forces.

ARVN forces on the other hand are already experiencing difficulty in coping with this increased VC capability. Desertion rates are inordinately high. Battle losses have been higher than expected; in fact, four ARVN battalions have been rendered ineffective by VC action in the I and II Corps zones. Therefore, effective fighting strength of many infantry and ranger battalions is unacceptably low. As a result, ARVN troops are beginning to show signs of reluctance to assume the offensive and in some cases their steadfastness under fire is coming into doubt. In order to bring existing battalions up to acceptable battlefield strength, it will be necessary to declare at least a temporary moratorium on the activation of new battalions. Thus, the GVN/VC force ratios upon which we based our estimate of the situation in March have taken an adverse trend. You will recall that I recommended the deployment of a U.S. division in II Corps to cover the period of the RVNAF buildup and to weight the force ratios in that important area. We assumed at that time that the ARVN battalions would be brought to full strength by now and that the force buildup would proceed on schedule. Neither of these assumptions has materialized.

The problem of low battlefield strength in ARVN has forced us to plan the use of personnel now training in 11 new battalions as fillers for old battalions. In effect, these 11 battalions will be deferred and during the period from mid-July to early November no new ARVN battalions will become available. Thus the gap to be filled is both deeper and wider.

In summary, the force ratios continue to change in favor of the VC. I believe that the DRV will commit whatever forces it deems necessary to tip the balance and that the GVN cannot stand up successfully to this kind of pressure without reinforcement. Even if DRV VC intentions are debatable, their capabilities must be acknowledged and faced. Additionally, it is prudent to consider possible enemy air action, leading to significant escalation and a broadening of the arena of conflict. We must be prepared to face such a contingency.

In order to cope with the situation outlined above, I see no course of action open to us except to reinforce our efforts in SVN with additional U.S. or Third Country forces as rapidly as is practical during the critical weeks ahead. Additionally, studies must continue and plans develop to deploy even greater forces, if and when required, to attain our objectives or counter enemy initiatives. Ground forces deployed to selected areas along the coast and inland will be used both offensively and defensively. U.S. ground troops are gaining experience and thus far have performed well. Although they have not yet engaged the enemy in strength, I am convinced that U.S. troops with their energy, mobility, and firepower can successfully take the fight to the VC. The basic purpose of the additional deployments recommended below is to give us a substantial and hard hitting [offen]sive capability on the ground to convince the VC that they cannot win. . . .

There were some who thought COMUSMACV's assessment of the situation was a bit precipitous, but the dissenters were effectively silenced the following week as the Viet Cong atttacked the aforementiond Special Forces camp and the adjoining district headquarters at Dong Xoai. ARVN reinforcements were committed piecemeal to the fray and were devoured by the enemy, who was on the scene with better than two regiments of troops. The battle, which lasted for five days and nearly saw the commitment of the U.S. 173rd Airborne Brigade to bail the ARVN out, marked the bitterest fighting of the war to date.

The GVN casualties of the second week in June were twice as high as any previous week of the war. The VC casualties, which were reported to exceed the ARVN total of 1,672, were a mute testimony to the enemy's regenerative capability and to his willingness to pay a heavy price in order to destroy the GVN's fighting power. The success of his efforts so far was made explicit on the 26th of June when COMUSMACV rated 5 ARVN regiments and 9 separate battalions combat ineffective. At the end of May the figure had been 2 regiments and 3 battalions.

By mid-June 1965, the Viet Cong summer offensive was in full stride. Shifting the emphasis away from the areas of their early successes on the periphery of "Hop Tac" and in the southern portion of I Corps, they began the long-expected offensive in the highlands of II Corps. On the 25th of June the district headquarters at Tou Morong in Kontum Province was invested and then taken by an enemy force said to be a PAVN regiment reinforced with some Viet Cong troops. Other remote district headquarters came under enemy pressure in the ensuing weeks until by 7 July a total of six of them had been abandoned or overrun. The Viet Cong were systematically forcing the GVN to yield what little control it still exercised in rural areas outside the Mekong Delta.

Summing up the situation at the end of the week of 14 July, the CIA said: "The initiative and momentum of military operations continue in favor of the Viet Cong. The impact of Viet Cong operations is being felt not only by the RVNAF but by the nation's internal economy as well. Nothing this week points to the RVN wresting the initiative from the VC."

A major part of counterinsurgency thinking and planning in early 1965 was based on the concept of force ratios. In order to defeat the insurgent, it was thought necessary to have a preponderance of force in favor of the GVN of somewhere around 10 to 1. The actual ratio for that time period was considerably less than 10 to 1 and was inclining in favor of the insurgents. In order to redress the situation, General Westmoreland advocated accelerating the build-up of the RVNAF. To accomplish this, he said, measures to increase induction and to curtail the shocking rates of desertion would have to be found. Unfortunately, any build-up strategy was obviated by the events of late May-early June. General Westmoreland informed CINCPAC on 7 June that the RVNAF build-up was to be suspended until November and that trainees would be used as fillers in heavily attrited units. If force ratios still were of paramount importance, then reinforcements for the GVN side would have to come from other than domestic Vietnamese sources.

The enemy side of the force ratio was open to question since historically Viet Cong strength tended to be understated. The enemy order of battle as reported on 17 March 1965 was as follows:

Confirmed strength— 37,000 Regular Troops
                100,000 Irregulars and Guerrillas (approx)
                      5 Regimental Headquarters
                   50 Battalions
                145 Separate Companies
                 35 Separate Platoons

All of these figures reflected substantial increases over the previous year. In fact, the confirmed strength had risen no less than 33% since 1964. After the Viet Cong had demonstrated rather bluntly that the March 1965 statistics were a trifle conservative, the order of battle was revised and on 21 July appeared as follows:

Confirmed strength— 53,000 Regular Troops
                100,000 Irregulars and Guerrillas (no change
                            from previous figure which was itself
                            an estimate)
                 10 Regional Headquarters
                 72 Battalions
              192 Separate Companies
              101 Separate Platoons

In light of subsequent information, even the above estimate, gloomy as it was, understated the enemy strength. Opposing the Viet Cong forces were the RVNAF Regular, Regional, and Popular Forces totaling some 570,000 men and boasting at best 133 infantry-type battalions. At a quick glance, the force ratios in July were seen to be about 3.8 to 1 in favor of the GVN in manpower (with the RVN Police and some paramilitary forces such as the Armed Combat Youth not being counted and about 1.9 to 1 in favor of the GVN in maneuver battalions. Undoubtedly the force ratios as seen in mid-1965 were far from optimum for theoretical counterinsurgency operations.

3. *Pacification*

The program to pacify, or extend government control over, the countryside never really recovered from the political turmoil of 1964 and early 1965. The 1965 master plan for "Rural Reconstruction" (one of many such euphemisms) was not approved by the RVNAF High Command until after the first quarter of the year. Situation reports, both MACV and CIA, described incremental plusses and minuses in what was obviously overall a stalled program.

On 6 April, a MACV military spokesman gave the following answers to questions from the press after a presentation summing up the month of March 1965:

Q.   Have the figures on VC control of territory and population changed appreciably?   A.   The statistic that counts is people, and in the month of March the statistics that are here do not have percentiles.

Q.   Can you give us figures on the number of people brought under government control in January and in March—or to the closest month?   A. It's not significant. I'd say it was a slow gain basically in the Hop Tac area. Any place else, you've had a trade-off.

Q.   Would it be a fair assumption to say that, outside of Hop Tac the government held its own?   A.   In the overall, held its own.

Q.   There was no significant progress, then. The government held its own? A.   That's correct.

Q.   It was a stalemate, then?   A.   No, I wouldn't call it a stalemate. I don't consider the fact that you pacified, or asserted control over 20 additional hamlets which might house as many as six or seven thousand people a stalemate.

Q.   At the same time we lost . . .   A.   No, you misunderstand me . . . the losses and the gains were counter balanced outside the Hop Tac area. In the Hop Tac area, there were gains.

CIA and MACV Situation Reports contained the following observations on pacification:

CIA Monthly Report, 21 January 1965:

"Pacification on a nationwide basis, has generally been stalled for the past month. Although there are pacification plans in effect in all provinces (except Con Son Island), there has been little significant progress; in some areas there has been an appreciable deterioration of governmental control. Even though South Vietnamese officials report continuing progress in the high priority Hop Tac effort around Saigon, it remains to be seen whether these are more than paper achievements. To date there has been no major effort by the Viet Cong to strike at areas which are now claimed as "secure," and therefore the validity of government claims remains untested. The Viet Cong have increased their numbers and the tempo of their operations in areas adjacent to Hop Tac and what is apparently an attempt to draw off government forces committed to this major pacification effort."

CIA Monthly Report, 17 February 1965:

"Nationwide, the pacification effort has barely moved ahead since 1 January; there has been a serious deterioration in some areas, mainly the I and II Corps. The slowdown in the pace of pacification is due to several factors which include: the preoccupation of some senior commanders with Saigon politics, the Tet holiday period, and VC strength, which in some areas has forced the GVN military forces into static or defensive roles."

MACV Monthly Evaluation Report for February 1965:

"The only pacification progress during February was registered in Hop Tac and other areas of III Corps, while other sections of the country either held earlier gains or showed deterioration. Contributing factors were increased VC activity, especially in the I and II Corps and the administrative confusion associated with the attempted coup of 19 February. At month's end, the 1965 pacification plans were still undergoing a review, with the result that pacification funds had not yet been released to the provinces. A stopgap allocation of 3 million $VN per province was made by the New Rural Life Directorate to permit programs to continue pending release of regular funds. Even so, many province chiefs are reluctant to push forward without more specific authorization and direction from higher authorities."

MACV Monthly Evaluation Report for March 1965:

"Although there was a lull in VC activity during the last half of the month, field commanders failed to capitalize on the situation and pursue pacification goals vigorously. During the month the pacification generally experienced regression in I and II CTZ while parts of III and IV Corps recorded slow but steady progress. In the Hop Tac area consistent gains were recorded throughout the month."

CIA Weekly Report, 24 March 1965:

"Pacification efforts during the past week remained stalled throughout most of the country. Some progress was seen in II Corps in pacification efforts."

MACV Monthly Evaluation for April 1965:

"Despite improved psychological conditions and the continued lull in VC activity, there was little tangible evidence of progress in rural reconstruction during the month . . . Overall, the slow but steady progress in III and IV Corps was offset by losses in I and II Corps. Contributing factors to this standstill were the GVN delay in approving provincial budgets and a continued lack of aggressiveness in operations directly supporting rural reconstruction. There was no appreciable increase in the number of refugees this month and relief measures taken by the Minister of Social Welfare and the province chiefs appear to be progressing satisfactorily, particularly in Binh Dinh and Quang Ngai provinces." The sole bright spot in all of this was the highly touted "Hop Tac" program which concentrated resources, human and material, on a few key provinces around the capital of Saigon. A lot of favorable things were being said about Hop Tac. McGeorge Bundy told the President in an apparently pivotal memorandum dated 7 February 1965 that although American air power would have to be used to buy time for us to break the Viet Cong hold on the countryside, the Hop Tac program offered hope for the future. (See Section I.A. in the Study on The Reemphasis of Pacification.) During the 6th of April press conference, the MACV spokesman told the press that "Hop Tac continues to move along a plus curve . . . "

Even without the dogged optimism, it is difficult in the absence of hard data to accurately assess the real situation in the countryside in early 1965, or to tell how much of the Hop Tac program was merely bluster and bravado. In regard to the latter, the Secretary of Defense sent to the Chairman of the JCS on 4 June 1965 the following query: "How did the Viet Cong mobilize a battalion to attack Binh Chanh district town only 10 miles from Saigon in the center of the Hop Tac area?" Whatever the case, the pacification program was overtaken by events of May and June. Prior to this, the II Corps, including the coastal provinces of Phu Yen and Binh Dinh and all of the highland provinces, was already in trouble.

4. *Economic Situation*

The staple food of the Vietnamese is rice, and Vietnam has in time of peace traditionally been an exporter of that commodity. The Viet Cong campaigned to control the countryside where the rice is grown and the routes of communication, land and water, over which it is moved to market. They were so successful that by 1965 the GVN was forced to contemplate massive imports of rice in order to feed the population and help stabilize prices. To illustrate the scope of the problem, the following statistics show rice exports from the district of Thanh Phu to the capital of its province Kien Hoa, one of the richest of the provinces in the Mekong Delta:

Metric tons of paddy rice exported from Thanh Phu to Kien Hoa 1960–1965:

1960	1,815 tons
1961	2,609 tons
1962	2,491 tons
1963	2,451 tons
1964	1,033 tons
1965	745 tons

By early 1965 the current crop of Delta rice had already been harvested, and it was obvious that the Viet Cong were not going to allow it to reach the urban markets. By the end of 1965 the retail price indices showed that for middle and working class families in Saigon the cost of food was 41% higher than a year earlier. The general price index, not including rent, for working class families was 33% higher and for the middle class, 30% higher. The upsurge in overt enemy military activity in May and June was accompanied by a major campaign to interfere with GVN lines of communication. Highway One and the railway which parallel one another through the coastal provinces in I and II Corps were both cut in numerous places. The road from Saigon to Da Lat, over which moved much vegetable produce, was constantly harassed. By the end of May, the town of Ben Cat in Binh Duong Province NW of Saigon was isolated. In May the Viet Cong cut the Danhiem-to-Saigon power-line and effectively prevented its repair.

Through increased control in the agricultural producing areas, very effective harassment of the primary means of communication within the GVN, and selective application of military pressure, the Viet Cong were waging a very successful campaign aimed at grinding the economy of the GVN to a halt.

There wasn't much the GVN could do about it. The 11 battalions of the RVNAF General Reserve were being "whipsawed" back and forth reacting to enemy military activity. By June the Reserve was already so heavily committed that there was little additional combat power available to the GVN with which to influence a rapidly deteriorating situation, military and economic.

B. *THE BRIEF TENURE OF THE STRATEGY OF SECURITY, AND SUBSEQUENT DEVELOPMENTS*

1. *Security as a Rationale*

The rationale that got two Marine BLT's into Da Nang in March 1965, which was publicly announced and which caused surprisingly little outcry, was plausibly advanced on several subsequent occasions as additional troops were deployed to various locations in Vietnam. Whether or not it was publicly offered as a rationale, the strategy of deploying troops for the security of bases was short-lived. The Marines hardly had their feet dry when several proposals were brought forward to get U.S. troops actively engaged in the ground war. These proposals, the first of which followed close on General Johnson's return from his Vietnam inspection trip of 5–12 March, were the center of much private debate in the spring and early summer of 1965. That debate went on largely behind the scene while the American public was in ignorance of the proceedings. The strategy of security effectively became a dead letter on the first of April, but the change in strategy was not revealed publicly until the 8th and 9th of June.

2. *NSC Meetings of 1–2 April 1965*

On the 17th of March, General Westmoreland sought Ambassador Taylor's concurrence in a proposal to deploy an additional USMC BLT to Phu Bai near Hue on the northern coast in I Corps. Westmoreland wanted to cut down some of the density of aircraft at Da Nang by moving helicopters to the strip at Phu Bai. The Marine BLT was needed to protect that strip. Taylor cabled to Washington: (EMBTEL 3003, 18 Mar 65)

> General Westmoreland has just sought my concurrence in his recommendation for the landing of the Third BLT of the 9th MEB at Phu Bai for the purpose of protecting the 8th RRU and the air strip there. He intends to move helicopters from Da Nang to the strip and thereby reduce field congestion at Da Nang. Because of the military advantages of thus rounding out the MEB, I have no reluctance in agreeing to the merit of his recommendation which, of course, should receive the concurrence of the GVN after that of Washington.
>
> This proposal for introducing the BLT is a reminder of the strong likelihood of additional requests for increases in U.S. ground combat forces in SVN. Such requests may come from the U.S. side, from the GVN side or from both. All of us here are keenly aware of the GVN trained military manpower shortage which will exist throughout 1965 and which probably can be rectified only in part by an accelerated mobilization. We will soon have to decide whether to try to get by with inadequate indigenous forces or to supplement them with Third Country troops, largely if not exclusively U.S. This matter was discussed with General Johnson during his recent visit who no doubt has raised it following his return to Washington. This message examines the pros and cons of such an action—specifically defined as the introduction of a U.S. division (appropriately modified) into SVN.
>
> The purpose of introducing of a division would be primarily to relieve the present shortage of ARVN units either by replacing ARVN in the defense of key installations or by engaging in active operations against the VC in conjunction with ARVN. Such a reinforcement would allow a strengthening of military efforts in the I and II Corps areas where the situation is deteriorating and would give a boost to GVN morale, military and civilian. Likewise, it should end any talk of a possible U.S. withdrawal and convince Hanoi of the depth of our resolve to see this thing through to a successful conclusion.
>
> This statement of the purpose of introducing a U.S. division is, in effect, a tabulation of the arguments in favor of so doing. However, there are

counter arguments on the other side of the case. The introduction of a U.S. division obviously increases U.S. involvement in the counterinsurgency, exposes greater forces and invites greater losses. It will raise sensitive command questions with our GVN allies and may encourage them to an attitude of "let the United States do it." It will increase our vulnerability to Communist propaganda and Third Country criticism as we appear to assume the old French role of alien colonizer and conqueror. Finally, there is considerable doubt that the number of GVN forces which our action would relieve would have any great significance in reducing the manpower gap.

It is possible to reach a conclusion with regard to the overall merit of this action without first examining in some detail the possible missions which could be assigned a U.S. division. There are two obvious possibilities: the first, the assignment of the division to one or more of the provinces of the high plateau where the climate is good, the terrain relatively open, and the Montagnard population more readily distinguishable from the alien Viet Cong. Here, our forces could utilize their mobility and firepower effectively and make an important contribution in cutting off the growing infiltration into and through this area. For the most part, the Montagnards are friendly to the U.S. and our forces would thus be operating in a relatively friendly environment.

On the other hand, such a mission in the highlands would place our forces in an area with highly exposed lines of communication leading to the coast. Their location in this area would create serious logistic problems because of the difficulty of the movement of land transport through areas infested by the Viet Cong. There would be problems both of reinforcement and of withdrawal because of this precariousness of land communications. Finally, the GVN may question the introduction of sizeable U.S. forces into the Montagnard area where we have often been accused of favoring the Montagnards over the Vietnamese and of encouraging Montagnard separatism.

The other role which has been suggested for U.S. ground forces is the occupation and defense of key enclaves along the coast such as Quang Ngai, Qui Nhon, Tuy Hoa and Nha Trang. Such a disposition would have the advantage of placing our forces in areas of easy access and egress with minimum logistic problems associated with supply and maintenance. The presence of our troops would assure the defense of these important key areas and would relieve some GVN forces for employment elsewhere. The troops would not be called upon to engage in counterinsurgency operations except in their own local defense and hence would be exposed to minimum losses.

On the other hand, they would be engaged in a rather inglorious static defensive mission unappealing to them and unimpressive in the eyes of the Vietnamese. Operating in major population areas would maximize the points of contact with Vietnamese and hence maximize the possible points of friction. The division would be badly fragmented to the extent that its command, control and supervision would be awkward.

The foregoing analysis leads me to the following tentative conclusions. First, it is not desirable to introduce a U.S. division into South Vietnam unless there are clear and tangible advantages outweighing the numerous disadvantages, many of which have been noted above. One must make a definite determination of the numbers and types of GVN forces relieved by the introduction of the U.S. unit and thus the effect of the increased U.S. presence in closing the manpower gap of 1965. Obviously, our division would make some contribution but it remains to be proved that it will be sufficient to reverse the downward trend and give such a lift to the GVN forces that they would perform better by the stimulation of the U.S. presence rather than worse in a mood of relaxation as passing the Viet Cong burden to the U.S.

If the evidence of the probable effectiveness of this U.S. contribution is convincing, then the matter of mission becomes the primary question. The inland mission in the highlands is clearly the more ambitious and, if well done, will make a greater contribution during the present critical period. On the other hand, it is the more exposed and even permits one to entertain the possibility of a kind of Dien Bien Phu if the coastal provinces should collapse and our forces were cut off from the coast except by air.

The coastal enclave mission is safer, simpler but less impressive and less productive than the inland mission. The contrast of the pros and cons of the two suggests the desirability of reexamining the question to see whether the advantages of the inland disposition could not be combined in some way with the retention of a base coastal area, linked with a position inland. In any case, considerable additional study is required before we are prepared to make a recommendation either for the introduction of a division or for the assignment of its mission. In the meantime, we should be giving much thought both in South Vietnam and in Washington as to the right course of action [if] and when this issue becomes pressing—as it shortly will.

CINCPAC forwarded General Westmoreland's Phu Bai proposal to the JCS on 19 March and further recommended that the remainder of the 9th MEB, one BLT plus headquarters elements, be landed at Da Nang within a month in order to consolidate command and control and build up the defense of that base. The JCS recommended both measures to the Secretary of Defense on 25 March, and they were discussed by the National Security Council and Ambassador Taylor during the latter's visit to the United States in late March-early April 1965. The President himself, in National Security Action Memorandum 328, approved the deployment of those two BLT's and at the same time, by changing the Marines' mission to include offensive operations, he ended the strategy of security. (For full text of NSAM 328, see Doc. 254)

NSAM 328 is a pivotal document. It marks the acceptance by the President of the United States of the concept that U.S. troops would engage in offensive ground operations against Asian insurgents. It indicates as well the anxiety of the President—his decision to proceed very slowly and carefully so that U.S. policy should appear to be wholly consistent. Thus the President only approved the deployment of two Marine BLT's, although he was doubtless aware of a JCS proposal favored by the Secretary of Defense and forwarded by the Chiefs on 20 March, which called for the deployment of a three division force, two U.S. and one Korean. At the President's request, all NSC members were admonished in NSAM 328 not to allow the release of any premature publicity for the actions dealing with the Marines and their mission. As a result, the change of mission was not publicized until it crept out almost by accident in a State Department release on 8 June.

Nor was the change of mission clearly defined in NSAM 328. The Marine BLT's were to be permitted more active use "under conditions to be established and approved by the Secretary of Defense in consultation with the Secretary of State" and, of course, their new mission was subject to the approval of the GVN. During his return trip to Saigon, Ambassador Taylor sent the following cable to the State Department:

In Washington discussions of new Marine mission in Da Nang-Phu Bai area, it was my understanding that SecDef would provide text of revised mission. If no guidance beyond language of reftel [Deptel 2184 containing the summarized guidance] is to be provided by Washington, I propose to describe the new mission to Quat as the use of Marines in a mobile counter-insurgency role in the vicinity of Da Nang for the improved protection of that base and also in a strike role as a reserve in support of ARVN operations anywhere within fifty miles of the base. This latter employment would follow acquisition of experience on local counterinsurgency missions.

It is pretty clear, then, that the President intended, after the early April NSC meetings, to cautiously and carefully experiment with U.S. forces in offensive roles. There was sober awareness that the North Vietnamese were not going to quit and that the U.S. was well on its way to being committed on the ground. The Rolling Thunder program, if it was going to bear any fruit at all, certainly was not going to do so in the next few months.

The U.S. decision-makers really were on what Assistant Secretary of Defense McNaughton described as "the horns of a trilemma." While addressing General Johnson's proposals for action in South Vietnam, McNaughton jotted down some notes on 24 March which accurately described the predicament facing the U.S. Government. The question, according to McNaughton, was: "Can the situation inside South Vietnam be bottomed out (a) without extreme measures against the DRV and (b) without deployment of large numbers of U.S. (and 3rd Country) combat troops inside SVN?" McNaughton's answer was "perhaps, but probably no." Because that was the case, he went on, the U.S. was faced with the "trilemma." Policy appeared to be drifting even though there was consensus that present action probably would not prevent collapse of the GVN. All three choices for remedial action so far presented had been rejected. These choices were (1) will-breaking strikes against the DRV which risked escalation flash and were thus too risky, (2) large U.S. troop input which raised the old spectre of an Asian land war and recalled memories of the French defeat, and (3) exit from the scene through negotiation which insured, because of the current situation, humiliation of the U.S. The alternatives, as described above by Mr. McNaughton, went into the National Security Council discussions which took place during the Ambassador's visit. What came out of those discussions was NSAM 328 and the decision to proceed ahead very slowly with ground force involvement.

Missing from NSAM 328 was the elucidation of a unified, coherent strategy. Ambassador Taylor, among others, had raised the question as to whether or not Western troops could fight effectively in Vietnam. No one could forget the French failure, and the Ambassador's reservations received due attention. Before devising a strategy for the use of U.S. ground forces, however, it was deemed necessary to experiment with small numbers of them to see how they would do. There was time to indulge the luxury of a leisurely build-up. The situation was bad, but currently the GVN was doing a bit better, and nothing pointed to immediate collapse.

The early April NSC meetings signalled the beginning of an enclave strategy. U.S. forces would operate within strictly limited boundaries (originally not to exceed 50 miles from base) and would have their backs to the sea. No Dien Bien Phu's would be presented for the enemy to exploit as supplies and reinforcements could be brought in with ease over sea LOC's controlled entirely by the U.S. Navy. As a corollary, the U.S. forces could be withdrawn with equal ease should the situation so dictate.

Although NSAM 328 only approved 2 Marine BLT's for deployment to Vietnam, there was also included an 18–20,000 man increase in U.S. forces in order to "fill out existing units and supply needed logistic personnel." Just what the President's intent was in approving that number of personnel became the subject of some debate. The Secretary of Defense on 21 April told the President that 11,000 of the approved increase was to augment various existing forces while a further 7,000 were logistic troops to support "previously approved forces." According to a memorandum from McNaughton to Vance dated 5 May, the JCS misconstrued the add-ons to mean logistic build-up for coastal enclaves and the possible later introduction of two to three divisions. It isn't entirely clear from the documents exactly what the President did have in mind for the support troop add-ons. What is clear, however, and was made explicit in a memorandum from the Secretary of Defense to the Chairman, Joint Chiefs of Staff, on 5 April was that the JCS were continuing to plan for the earliest possible introduction of two to three divisions into RVN. The Ambassador indicated to the State Department in a cable on 12 April that he too thought the 18–20,000 man increase was for something more than those forces already approved. Taylor said:

> I have been following with interest the logistic studies which are going on at PACOM and MACV in anticipation of the possible introduction of several divisions into SVN. Several comments occur to me which are passed on for what they are worth. There appears to be no question about the need for the 18,000–20,000 logistic build-up (the Category A force) recommended by General Westmoreland. The introduction of this force has been approved and should be implemented as rapidly as the elements can be moved and MACV can accept them. I am surprised to learn from MACV that May 1 is the earliest date for the arrival of the engineer element which paces the rate of arrival of the other components. If possible, this date should be advanced.
>
> The Category A package will provide support for about 50,000 U.S. personnel in-country, i.e., the present strength plus the additional Marines now landing in the Da Nang-Hue area and will permit some preliminary work in anticipation of the arrival of additional U.S. forces. To make any significant progress toward the establishment of a logistic base to support additional forces, it will be necessary to bring in rapidly about 5,000 more engineers (above those in Category A). MACV estimates they could arrive about August 1 (if the Category A engineers arrive on May 1). I would concur in the desirability of this reinforcement, feeling that these engineers can be very useful in SVN whether or not we ever introduce additional divisions.

Taylor went on in the same cable (as though he were summing up the results of the meetings which led to the NSAM):

> With regard to the imminence of the need for those divisions, I do not share the fear that the I and II Corps areas are about to fall apart which is expressed in some of the traffic bearing on the logistic build-up. In any case, if a debacle is going to take place in the next few months, the time factors developed in the logistic studies indicate that very little advance logistic preparation can be made in time. In such an unlikely contingency, U.S. combat reinforcements will have to deploy concurrently with their logistic units and build their base as they go.

While recognizing the importance of the current studies in developing the logistic facts of life as they bear on the reinforcement of SVN, I hope that they do not interfere with essential work in preparation for less ambitious but more probable developments. It was my understanding in Washington that, if the Marines demonstrate effectiveness in operating out of Da Nang in an offensive counterinsurgency role, other offensive enclaves may be established along the coast and garrisoned with brigade-sized contingents for employment similar to the Marines. General Westmoreland is very anxious to establish such a force as soon as possible in the Bien Hoa–Vung Tau area. Qui Nhon is also well situated for similar purposes. I would recommend that logistic preparations be initiated at once to permit each of these two areas to receive a U.S. brigade. Whatever is done for this purpose will assist in accommodating any larger forces which may be subsequently introduced. It is important that this lesser program be carried out rapidly enough to make a contribution to the situation which is now unfolding. This requires rapid action.

3. *The Additional Marines Land*

From the 11th through the 14th of April the two Marine BLT's approved by the President in NSAM 328 were deployed to Hue/Phu Bai and Da Nang. Their landing brought the total number of U.S. maneuver battalions in South Vietnam to four, all Marines. Although security was no longer the only authorized mission for these units, it certainly was their primary mission. The Marines set about consolidating and developing their two coastal base areas, and, although they pushed their patrol perimeters out beyond their tactical wire and thereby conducted active rather than passive defense, they did not engage in any offensive operations in support of ARVN for the next few months. (Major General "Rip" Collins, CG III MAF, was on the scene while ARVN was being beaten at Ba Gia at the end of May, and his Marine troops were almost committed to that fight.)

4. *Westmoreland Tries to Slide the 173rd in for Security*

As a kind of postscript to the strategy of security, it was used by General Westmoreland as justification for an attempt to get some Army ground troops on the stage in early April. Westmoreland had recommended in March that a separate Army Brigade (possibly the 173rd) be deployed to the Bien Hoa/Vung Tau areas "in order to secure vital U.S. installations." That recommendation accompanied Westmoreland's request for up to two divisions of forces and was contained in his "Commander's Estimate of the Situation," which will be considered later in some detail. On the 11th of April, Westmoreland cabled CINCPAC that he understood from news of the Taylor meetings in Washington that the requested divisions of forces were not immediately in the offing. Nevertheless, Westmoreland wanted a brigade in the Bien Hoa-Vung Tau area because "it was as necessary from a purely military standpoint as the deployments in the Da Nang–Phu Bai area which have already won acceptance." (Security of Bien Hoa/Vung Tau was not all COMUSMACV had in mind, however, for the same message mentioned the need to offset a Viet Cong threat embodied in two regiments and two separate battalions perched on the eastern flank of III Corps. He also wanted a light reserve force which could be airlifted to the Central Highlands in case of emergency.)

The 173rd, a two-battalion airborne brigade, was then located in Okinawa. It constituted CINCPAC's airmobile reserve. When an earlier attempt had been made to deploy the 173rd to Da Nang in place of the Marines, CINCPAC had stringently opposed the removal of his only quick-reaction force.

What followed General Westmoreland's request of 11 April, a request that Ambassador Taylor "had noted," was a rapid-fire series of cables, proposals, and false starts which, if nothing else, indicated that Washington was well ahead of Saigon in its planning and in its anxiety. The first event in the chain was a planning conference held in Honolulu 8–10 April and attended by representatives of PACOM and the Joint Staff. The conferees recommended the deployment of the 173rd and, in deference to CINCPAC's concern for his airmobile reserve, they also recommended that the 173rd be replaced by another brigade from CONUS as soon as practicable. The JCS ordered on 14 April that the 173rd be deployed temporarily to Bien Hoa/Vung Tau for security of air operations and logistical bases and at the same time tasked CINCSTRIKE to provide a brigade to replace the 173rd.

The decision to deploy the 173rd apparently caught the Ambassador flat-footed, for he had quite obviously not been privy to it. He cabled the State Department on the 14th and said:

> I have just learned by the reference JCS message to CINCPAC that the immediate deployment of the 173rd Airborne Brigade to Bien Hoa–Vung Tau has apparently been approved. This comes as a complete surprise in view of the understanding reached in Washington that we would experiment with the Marines in a counterinsurgency role before bringing in other U.S. contingents. . . . . This decision seemed sound to me at the time and continues to appear so. I recommend that this deployment be held up until we can sort out all matters relating to it.

Whatever was motivating those in Washington who had decided to make this deployment, the Ambassador held the trump card as he had to clear the move with the GVN before the troops could come in. The Prime Minister had not been told at this juncture about the proposed landing of more U.S. troops, and Taylor informed his superiors on 17 April that he did not intend to tell Quat without clearer guidance explaining Washington's intentions.

That Washington was determined, with the President's sanction, to go beyond what had been agreed to and formalized in NSAM 328 was manifested unmistakably in a cable sent under joint Defense/State auspices by Mr. McNaughton to the Ambassador on 15 April. That message, which will be treated in detail in a later section, contained the following preamble: "Hightest authority believes the situation in South Vietnam has been deteriorating and that, in addition to actions against the North, something new must be added in the South to achieve victory. As steps to that end, we believe the following actions should be undertaken . . ." The message goes on to list seven specific actions including the deployment of "a brigade force" to Bien Hoa/Vung Tau "to act as a security force for our installations and also to participate in counterinsurgency combat operations" according to plans to be prepared by General Westmoreland.

The documents do not reveal just exactly when Presidential sanction was obtained for the expanded scope of the above proposals. It is possible that the Ambassador may have caught the Defense Department and the JCS in a little cart-before-the-horsemanship. The day following the order from the JCS to deploy the 173rd and the Ambassador's reclama thereto, the JCS submitted a memorandum to the Secretary of Defense in which they addressed the Ambassador's objection to the deployment and offered their own position, which was that "the U.S. had need of the 173rd in Bien Hoa/Vung Tau to insure the security of air operations and logistics bases as had been recommended by COMUSMACV and by CINCPAC in CINCPAC to JCS DTG 13 April 1965." The 173rd was also needed, they said, for subsequent phasing into counterinsurgency operations. Whether or not the JCS wrote that memorandum with red faces, the Secretary of Defense dates approval for final deployment of the 173rd as of the 30th of April, which is considerably later. Even when the 173rd was finally ordered to deploy, it went on a temporary duty basis. It remained in that anomalous status well into the summer of 1965, expecting any day to be recalled to Okinawa and replaced by another unit. The troops continued to draw TDY pay, and their dependents remained at the permanent base on Okinawa instead of returning to the U.S.

With the 173rd successfully held in abeyance, the principals took that issue, along with the seven points of the 15 April cable, to Honolulu, where a conference convened on 20 April and structured the outlines of the ever popular enclave strategy.

5. Security as the Primary Mission for Most Phase 1 Units

The security of U.S. bases in mainland Southeast Asia may well have been dead as a basis for a strategy, but the bases nonetheless needed to be secured. The security rationale was consistently offered, along with other reasons, to justify the further deployment of ground combat units. In fact, looking back on the force deployments which were the main subject of this paper, the JCS in November 1965 stated that 21 of the original 44 "Phase I" U.S./3rd Country battalions, whose deployment to Vietnam was accomplished in the latter half of 1965, were committed to base and installation security.

C. THE STRATEGY OF EXPERIMENTATION: ENCLAVE STRATEGY

1. Geography

The geography of Vietnam lends itself to enclave thinking—that is, to operations based on coastal cities and with restricted extension of lines of communication inland. The central portion of Vietnam, encompassing the I and II Corps Tactical Zones and a portion of the III Corps, is long and narrow. The area near the coast is for the most part fairly flat and hospitable and contains the bulk of the population. The interior is mountainous and is sparsely populated throughout. In some places the mountains come right down to the coast, but the coastal plain is well defined for most of the length of Central Vietnam. Scattered along this coast are the mouths of numerous streams, each with a small delta which serves as an area for rice production and concentration of population, and as a focus for commercial activity.

Several cities, such as Da Nang, Qui Nhon, and Nha Trang, are located contiguous with the coastal population and have good deep water anchorages for ocean-going maritime activity. All three of these cities were, in early 1965, likely candidates for bases in an enclave strategy. There were other areas along the coast which did not have deep water anchorages but which were, nevertheless, readily accessible for amphibious resupply from the sea. Chu Lai, little more than a sandy hamlet, and Phu Bai fell into this category and were very much a part of enclave thinking.

In between the central coast and the Mekong Delta—which itself offered no good coastal access and egress and hence was never a part of any enclave strategy —was the port of Vung Tau. Located at the end of the Cap St. Jacques peninsula and easily defended, Vung Tau was the logical alternative to the port of Saigon, access to which required a risky trip up the Saigon River from a point not far from Vung Tau. Vung Tau could be called the southern limit of a chain of coastal enclaves beginning with Hue/Phu Bai in I Corps.

2. *Development of the Strategy*

General Johnson, Chief of Staff of the Army, brought back from his March 1965 inspection trip to Vietnam the germ of an idea to establish U.S. ground forces in coastal enclaves. The idea is included in one of two alternatives proposed by Johnson for the deployment of a U.S. division to Vietnam to supplant ARVN units in security missions and free them for offensive operations against the Viet Cong. One alternative proposed sending the division to secure bases at Bien Hoa/ Ton Son Nhut (near Saigon), Qui Nhon and Nha Trang (both coastal cities), and Pleiku (in the highlands). The other alternative proposed the deployment of a division to the highland provinces of Kontum, Pleiku, and Darlac. Significantly, the coastal city deployment and the second alternative were the two principal contenders for the location of the 1st Cavalry Division (Airmobile) debated later in the year. The second alternative was the one favored by both Johnson and JCS Chairman Wheeler.

By far the most dogged protagonist of the enclave strategy was Ambassador Taylor. He was consistent in his opposition to the initial involvement of U.S. forces in ground combat. As he saw his position being eroded on that question, it would seem natural for him to have fallen back in an only slightly less conservative posture. On 18 March 1965, in a cable already quoted in its entirety in Section II, Taylor brought up the question of the deployment of a U.S. division and presented the highland and coastal enclave alternatives. While not backing either alternative at that juncture, he did say that "the coastal enclave mission is safer, simpler but less productive than the inland mission." In regard to the latter, he said: "The inland mission in the highlands is clearly the more ambitious and, if well done, will make a greater contribution during the present critical period. On the other hand, it is the more exposed and even permits one to entertain the possibility of a kind of Dien Bien Phu if the coastal provinces should collapse and our forces were cut off from the coast except by air."

The Ambassador received no response from Washington to the cable quoted above. He sent another one on the 27th of March in which he reminded Washington that it was high time to make some decisions concerning U.S. strategy in Vietnam. According to Taylor, there were three choices: (1) to carry on with the present level of commitment and hope that Rolling Thunder would cause the DRV to cease its support, (2) to try and reverse the trend at least in a few key areas, and (3) to try and win as quickly as possible. If U.S. forces were to come, Taylor offered three alternatives for their mission: (1) defensive or offensive enclave, (2) territorial clear and hold, and (3) general reserve. For himself, Taylor preferred a combination of the offensive enclave plus reserve in case of an emergency. This was essentially the position that he carried into the NSC meetings in Washington of 1–2 April 1965.

Ambassador Taylor met with Secretary McNamara and the JCS in Washington just prior to the NSC meetings. He was shown the JCS's plan to introduce three divisions of U.S. and Korean troops into Vietnam for combat operations against the Viet Cong. That plan, which Taylor was inclined to oppose but which had the qualified support of McNamara, was undoubtedly also a focus of discussion within the NSC.

NSAM 328, the product of the NSC meetings of 1–2 April 1965, had its primary focus on air action against the DRV and Laos. In regard to that air activity the text of the NSAM said this:

> Subject to continuing review, the President approved the following general framework of continuing action against North Vietnam and Laos:
> We should continue roughly the present slowly ascending tempo of ROLLING THUNDER operations, being prepared to add strikes in response to a higher rate of VC operations, or conceivably to slow the pace in the unlikely event VC slacked off sharply for what appeared to be more than a temporary operational lull.
> The target systems should continue to avoid the effective GCI range of MIGs. We should continue to vary the types of targets, stepping up attacks on lines of communication in the near future, and possibly moving in a few weeks to attacks on the rail lines north and northeast of Hanoi.

And, also:

> Air operation in Laos, particularly route blocking operations in the Panhandle area, should be stepped up to the maximum remunerative rate."

In regard to action on the ground, NSAM 328 said in relation to force level increases:

> The President approved an 18–2.000 man increase in U.S. military support forces to fill out existing units and supply needed logistic personnel.
> The President approved the deployment of two additional Marine Battalions and one Marine Air Squadron and associated headquarters and support elements.

And, also:

> The President approved the urgent exploration, with the Korean, Australian, and New Zealand Governments, of the possibility of rapid deployment of significant combat elements from their armed forces in parallel with the additional Marine deployment approved. . . .

NSAM 328 sanctioned a change in mission for U.S. ground forces in Vietnam, but it did so in very cautious language:

> The President approved a change of mission for all Marine battalions deployed to Vietnam to permit their more active use under conditions to be established and approved by the Secretary of Defense in consultation with the Secretary of State.

This language may indicate that the President wanted to experiment very carefully with a small amount of force before deciding whether or not to accept any kind of ground war commitment. Implicit in the size of that force and in its location was the option to quickly evacuate it, should the U.S. so desire.

It appears that the Ambassador interpreted the NSAM change of mission as approval of his 27 March recommendation. He cabled Washington on the 4th of April that he would approach Quat with a proposal that the Marines be permitted to conduct mobile operations within their TAOR's and that they be used by the RVNAF as a reserve for operations up to 50 miles from their bases. The Vietnamese Prime Minister acquiesced in the deployment of the two Marine BLT's plus one Tactical Fighter Squadron (F4) on the 6th of April and in the change in mission on the 8th.

Taylor was at this juncture quite prepared to settle into a period of careful experimentation with the level of combat power fixed at four battalions. He said in a message dated 17 April that he had about 60 days in mind as the appropriate period for the experiment, and he indicated he was chagrined by some apparent anxiety in Washington to move considerably faster. In a message also dated 17 April he questioned the Washington panic manifested in a whole panoply of "hasty and ill-conceived" proposals for the deployment of more forces. In another message he again cautioned against precipitous action and offered the palliative that "things weren't going so badly" out there.

Four Marine battalions were enough for experimentation, but not so large as to alarm the xenophobic Vietnamese. In fact, the Ambassador's sensitivity to the proclivities of the Vietnamese Prime Minister on the question of foreign troops helps explain the Embassy's footdragging during this critical period of U.S. build-up debate. Thus, the Ambassador was surprised to discover that the Marines had come ashore with tanks, self-propelled artillery, and various other items of weighty equipment not "appropriate for counterinsurgency operations." That equipment, bland JCS explanations mentioning contingency plans and full TOE prudence notwithstanding, implied a permanence not communicated to Quat when clearance for their entry had been sought. Similarly, the decision to deploy the 173rd, had it been executed, would have placed Taylor in an exceedingly embarrassing position as he had not mentioned it to the GVN.

From analysis of the cable traffic of early April, it appears that Taylor was the only major figure opposed to further expansion of the U.S. combat role beyond what was agreed at the NSC meetings in Washington. His defense was tenacious, but as proposals from Washington got progressively more radical, his patience began to wear thin. Then Taylor communicated his ire to McGeorge Bundy in a message quoted in full in Section I of this paper and in which he maintained that Quat's government had quite enough to do without the addition of more U.S. programs or more U.S. forces. The chorus of suggestions and programs from Washington reached a crescendo with the joint State/Defense message of 18 April which, with the blessing of "highest authority" in Washington, proposed the following measures be considered to add "something new" to the equation:

(1) Experimental encadrement of U.S. troops into RVNAF either through the assignment of 50 U.S. soldiers to each of 10 ARVN battalions or through the "brigading" of ARVN and US battalions for operations;

(2) The introduction of a brigade force into Bien Hoa/Vung Tau for security of installations and later expansion into counterinsurgency operations under conditions to be spelled out by General Westmoreland;

(3) The introduction of several battalions into coastal enclaves such as Qui Nhon in accordance with proposals to be submitted by the Ambassador and COMUSMACV. The purpose was "to further experiment with US forces in the counterinsurgency role"; (*Sic*! The phrase "to further experiment" is misleading since up to the date of this cable, there had been *no* U.S. counterinsurgency operations worthy of the name.)

(4) Expansion of Vietnamese recruiting, using proven U.S. techniques;

(5) Expansion of the MEDCAP program using mobile dispensaries under guidelines to be worked out between COMUSMACV and the Surgeon General, U.S. Army;

(6) Experimentation in two or three provinces with a team of U.S. civil affairs personnel introduced into provincial government structure under conditions to be worked out between MG Peers and General Westmoreland;

(7) The supplement of low RVNAF pay through a program to provide some of the troops with a food ration. General Timmes would be seeing COMUSMACV to work out the details.

Although this cable was well-meaning in its intent, the Ambassador was amazed by its naivete and justifiably chargrined by its impertinence. Taylor's cable, [Doc. 6] one of many he sent to Washington during the tumultuous days just prior to the April Honolulu Conference, is worth quoting in its entirety as it contains the kind of guidance the Ambassador felt he should have been receiving from Washington.

Thus was the Ambassador propelled into the conference of 20 April 1965, only one step ahead of the Washington juggernaut, which was itself fueled by encouragement from Westmoreland in Saigon. Taylor was not opposed to the U.S. build-up per se, but rather was concerned to move slowly with combat troop deployments, which tended to cause alarm in an already delicate situation, while proceeding quietly with the prerequisite development of logistic bases to support later troop introduction. He was overtaken at Honolulu.

Honolulu brought the Saigon and Washington decision makers together to sanctify an expanded enclave strategy. In the preliminary discussions they agreed that:

(1) The DRV was not likely to quit within the next six months; and in any case, they were more likely to give up because of VC failure in the South than because of bomb-induced "pain" in the North. It could take up to two years to demonstrate VC failure.

(2) The level of air activity through Rolling Thunder was about right. The U.S. did not, in Ambassador Taylor's words, want "to kill the hostage." Therefore, Hanoi and environs remained on the restricted list. It was recognized that air activity would not do the job alone.

(3) Progress in the South would be slow, and great care should be taken to avoid dramatic defeat. The current lull in Viet Cong activity was merely *the quiet before a storm*.

(4) The victory strategy was to "break the will of the DRV/VC by denying them victory." Impotence would lead eventually to a political solution.

Going into the Honolulu Conference the level of approved U.S. forces for Vietnam was 40,200. In-country strength of 33,500 showed that not all the approved forces had closed. To accomplish the "victory strategy" described above, the conferees agreed that the following additional U.S. deployments should be made:

A. United States
  (1) An Army Brigade (3 Bns) to Bien Hoa–Vung Tau to close by 1 May
  (2) 3 USMC BLT's and 3 Tactical Fighter Squadrons to Chu Lai by 5 May
  (3) An Army Brigade (3 Bns) to Qui Nhon–Nha Trang to close by 15 June
  (4) Augmentations of existing forces and added logistical support

If approved, these recommended forces would have brought U.S. strength to a grand total of thirteen maneuver battalions and 82,000 men.

The U.S. Government also should approach the respective foreign governments and request:

B. Third Country
   (1) An Australian Army Battalion to Vung Tau to close by 21 May
   (2) A Korean Regimental Combat Team to Quang Ngai by 15 June

If approved, these recommended forces would bring Third Country strength to a grand total of 4 maneuver battalions and 7,250 men.

As an adjunct to the units above, the conferees mentioned, but did not recommend, the possible later deployment of:

C. United States
   (1) An Army Airmobile Division (9 Bns)
   (2) The remainder of the III MEF (2 Bns)
   (3) An Army Corps Headquarters
D. Third Country
   An ROK Division (–) consisting of 6 Battalions

The posited future add-ons comprised a further 17 maneuver battalions, which, if added to the approved totals, would have brought US/Third Country combat capability in South Vietnam to 34 battalions.

After they had dealt with the questions of troop deployments, the conferees then turned to the remaining points contained in the joint State/Defense 7-point program. It was decided to drop the idea of encadrement of U.S. forces in ARVN in favor of emphasis on combined operations. Recruiting, it was agreed, was less a problem of organization and method than it was a product of the limited manpower base and competing agencies (including the Viet Cong). The plan to improve MEDCAP was endorsed with enthusiasm, and it was agreed to experiment with a "single manager" concept in three pilot provinces. Finally, the proposed plan to distribute food to some RVNAF troops, an earlier version of which had merely encouraged greater corruption, was quietly deferred pending further study.

As a final note, the conferees considered the guidance which the Ambassador had prepared for himself in the event that more U.S. and Third Country forces were to be committed in Vietnam. The text remained essentially as Taylor had written it in his cable of 17 April. A few changes were made to reflect that the commitment was not limited to the current proposed deployments and that the U.S. was anxious to seize the initiative from the enemy. Taylor had said, "if the ground war is not to drag into 1966 and even beyond." That phrase was changed to read, "if the ground war is not to drag on *indefinitely*." [Emphasis added] The conferees appear to have realized not only that the forces they had recommended be deployed to Vietnam might not be enough, but also that it would be unwise to attempt to affix any time limit to the war.

The President received the Honolulu recommendations in a memorandum from Secretary McNamara on the 21st of April. Noted therein, but not recommended, were possible deployments of an Army Airmobile Division and the remainder of the III MEF.

The Honolulu Conference omitted to provide for reconstitution of CINC-PAC's airborne reserve after the deployment of the 173rd to Bien Hoa–Vung

Tau, largely because the designation and type of brigade which was to go to that location had not been specified. That the 173rd would go, however, was common knowledge and, indeed, had been recommended by the PACOM–JCS planning conference on 10 April and abortively approved by the JCS on the 14th. CINCPAC cabled the JCS on the 23rd to remind them that the 173rd should be replaced by a CONUS brigade as soon as possible.

Discussion and refinement of the Honolulu proposals continued on after the Conference. On 30 April, a JCSM summarized the planning as the Chiefs saw it and presented a detailed program for the deployment to Vietnam of some 48,000 U.S. and 5,250 Third Country forces, all of which were listed as approved. Included were all the units mentioned in the Honolulu recommendation plus a healthy support package. These forces were, according to the JCS, to "bolster GVN forces during their continued build-up, secure bases and installations, conduct counterinsurgency combat operations in coordination with the RVNAF, *and prepare for the later introduction of an airmobile division to the central plateau, the remainder of the III MEF to the Da Nang area, and the remainder of a ROK division to Quang Ngai."* [Emphasis added] Logistic forces of all services were "to strengthen support of in-country forces, provide support for the new forces, prepare bases and installations for possible future deployments, and be prepared to support those additional forces." From the thrust of this JCSM it is apparent that the enclave strategy was no stopping place as far as the Chiefs were concerned. They continued to push hard for the earliest possible input of three full divisions of troops. They were still well ahead of the pack in that regard.

None of the Honolulu recommendations had been approved at the time the 30 April JCSM was forwarded, although the 173rd was approved for Bien Hoa–Vung Tau and three Marine battalions for Chu Lai on the same day. Included in the logistics package listed by the JCS as "approved" were some 4,700 troops later identified by Mr. McNaughton as belonging to the three division program and definitely not approved. Secretary McNamara replied to the JCSM on the 15th of May, after the landing of the 173rd on the 5th and the Marines at Chu Lai on the 7th. The Secretary said that he considered as approved only so much of the remainder of the Honolulu recommendations as applied to the Australian Battalion, the ROK Regimental Combat Team and some MACV augmentations. He went on to approve: (1) movement of the I MEF from California to WESTPAC to reconstitute CINCPAC's floating reserve, and (2) preparation for the deployment of an Army brigade to Qui Nhon–Nha Trang with final decision on 21 May and closure on 27 June. This latter move, when approved, together with individual add-ons was to bring total *permanent* in-country strength to 69,143 (the 173rd having been deployed on a temporary basis). Secretary McNamara deferred decision on all JCS proposals dealing with the three division plan, thereby giving the enclave strategy temporary respite.

3.   *Difficulties in Experimentation*

As of the landings of the Marines at Chu Lai and the Airborne at Bien Hoa–Vung Tau, the U.S. forces in Vietnam with some nine maneuver battalions had yet to conduct a major offensive operation, with or without the RVNAF. The experimentation with U.S. forces in an offensive role, a large factor in the decision to accept the enclave concept, was delayed because some knotty problems involving command and contral remained to be ironed out with the Vietnamese.

In the early days when the Marines arrived to secure bases and installations, the control measure devised for their employment was the Tactical Area of Responsibility (TAOR). Under the overall suzerainty of the Vietnamese Corps Commander, the Marines were given a well-defined geographical area in which the U.S. exercised command authority over military forces and for which the U.S. accepted defensive responsibility. The original Marine TAOR consisted literally of their half of the Da Nang airfield and a portion of a couple of hills on which the Marines were entrenched and which they covered by the fields of fire of their small arms. Assured by this conservative assignation was minimum contact between U.S. troops and the Vietnamese population. In fact, there were only some 1,930 people living within the original Marine TAOR. From this humble beginning there followed a period of gradual expansion altogether compatible with the security mission until by the end of March the Da Nang TAOR was 12 square miles in size and incorporated some 11,141 Vietnamese souls.

Accompanying the NSAM 328 change of mission of U.S. forces to permit limited offensive operations was a dilemma. Mere expansion of the TAOR's would not suffice since U.S. forces did not have enough combat power to adequately secure an area the size of which they desired for offensive operations. Some arrangement was needed to allow U.S. commanders to share tactical responsibility with the Vietnamese.

Years of experience advising the Vietnamese armed forces was enough to convince knowledgeable U.S. officers that the U.S. did not want to relinquish command authority over its troops to the Vietnamese. Of equal import, it was felt, was the Vietnamese experience under the French and the resultant abhorrence of foreign command over their forces. As a further complication, the Viet Cong were ready to cry "imperialist puppet" at the first sign of GVN weakness. Washington was less sensitive to this problem than were the members of the Mission in Saigon. In May Secretary McNamara urged Westmoreland and Taylor to form a joint command structure with the GVN. Unfortunately, both of those gentlemen were well aware that the GVN was *very* cool to the idea. On the 23rd of April Taylor had visited with Prime Minister Quat for the first time since the Honolulu Conference. Although Quat was well aware of the Ambassador's intention to convey the text of the Honolulu recommendations, to Taylor's distress, he was reluctant to even discuss foreign reinforcements much less command arrangements.

In an attempt to get things unstuck, General Westmoreland produced a concept for the employment of U.S./Allied ground combat forces in support of RVNAF. With Ambassador Taylor's concurrence, he forwarded the concept through CINCPAC to Washington on 8 May. Westmoreland proposed that the "basic concept underlying command relations between U.S./Allied forces and RVNAF will be one of combat support through coordination and cooperation in the mutual self-interest of both commands." That this tenuous arrangement might break down in the face of imminent disaster was foreseen and included was an emergency escape clause whereby alternate arrangements could be made through mutual agreement of the tactical commanders on the ground. Westmoreland suggested that U.S./Allied forces would pass through three distinct stages of commitment to the war. Stage I (to which were already committed 9 U.S. battalions) entailed the security of base areas with TAOR's extended out to the range of light artillery. Stage II called for deep patrolling and offensive operations, both predicated on movement outside the TAOR in coordination with RVNAF. Finally, progress would be made into Stage III with long range search and destroy and reserve reaction operations in concert, of course, with Vietnamese wishes and desires.

Along with the concept Westmoreland presented, without any time frame, a crude sketch showing the evolution of strategies for U.S./Allied forces in the Vietnamese war. The war was to evolve through four phases. During Phase I coastal enclaves were to be secured and improved. In Phase II, operations would be conducted against the enemy from the above. In Phase III the forces would move inland to secure additional bases and areas, and finally in Phase IV would operate from the latter. At the time the concept was forwarded, the U.S. combat forces in Vietnam were in Phase I, Stage I. Progress to a more ambitious stage was stymied while negotiations went on with the GVN to refine the ground rules. In the meantime, the Ambassador observed that the troops would suffer from boredom and lose their edge.

The long official silence between the sanction for U.S. offensive operations contained in NSAM 328 and the final approval of the conditions under which U.S. troops could be committed was not without cost. The President had admonished each of the NSC members not to allow release of information concerning the provisions of the NSAM, but the unduly long interregnum inevitably led to leaks. The Marines incurred some 200 casualties, including 18 killed, as they went about tidying up their TAOR's in April and May. The Commandant of the Marine Corps raised the tempo of speculation by saying to the press during an inspection trip to Vietnam in April that the Marines were not in Vietnam to "sit on their dittyboxes"—they were there to "kill Viet Cong." An honest and superficially innocuous statement by Department of State Press Officer Robert McCloskey on 8 June to the effect that "American forces would be available for combat support together with Vietnamese forces when and if necessary" produced an immediate response. The press reaction to McCloskey's candor is best summed up in this New York Times clip of 9 June:

> The American people were told by a minor State Department official yesterday that, in effect, they were in a land war on the continent of Asia. This is only one of the extraordinary aspects of the first formal announcement that a decision has been made to commit American ground forces to open combat in South Vietnam: The nation is informed about it not by the President, not by a Cabinet member, not even by a sub-Cabinet official, but by a public relations officer.

The White House was hoisted by its own petard. In an attempt to quell the outcry, a statement was issued on the 9th of June which, because of its ambiguity, only served to further exacerbate the situation and to widen what was being described as "the credibility gap." The White House statement said in part:

> There has been no change in the mission of United States ground combat units in Vietnam in recent days or weeks. The President has issued no order of any kind in this regard to General Westmoreland recently or at any other time. The primary mission of these troops is to secure and safeguard important military installations like the air base at Da Nang. They have the associated mission of . . . patrolling and securing actions in and near the areas thus safeguarded.
>
> If help is requested by the appropriate Vietnamese commander, General Westmoreland also has authority within the assigned mission to employ these troops in support of Vietnamese forces faced with aggressive attack

when other effective reserves are not available and when, in his judgment, the general military situation urgently requires it.

The documents do not reveal whether or not the ground rules for engagement of U.S. forces had actually been worked out to everyone's satisfaction at the time of the White House statement. There is good indication that they had not. During at least two of the major battles in late May and early June, Ba Gia and Dong Xoai, the RVNAF were desperately in need of assistance. Although U.S. troops were available in both instances, the Marines at Ba Gia and the 173rd at Dong Xoai, they were not committed and the result in both cases was defeat for the RVNAF.

The first major ground combat operation by U.S. forces in the Vietnam War took place in War Zone D, NW of Saigon, from 27 to 30 June 1965. Participants were the 173rd Airborne Brigade, the 1st Battalion of the Royal Australian Regiment, two battalions from the ARVN Airborne Brigade, and the ARVN 48th Regiment. The operation could by no stretch of definition have been described as a reserve reaction. It was a search and destroy operation into Viet Cong base areas and its purpose was to deny to the enemy "freedom of action . . . in these safe havens." The War Zone D excursion was a direct result of the sanction given to General Westmoreland on the 26th of June to "commit U.S. troops to combat, independent of or in conjunction with GVN forces in any situation in which the use of such troops is requested by an appropriate GVN commander and when, in COMUSMACV's judgment, their use is necessary to strengthen the relative position of GVN forces."

At that juncture the 44 Battalion debate was in full swing and the enclave strategy, as a means to limit the amount and use of U.S. combat force in Vietnam, was certainly overcome by events. It was not until the 18th of August that an operation fitting the paradigm description of the Taylor enclave concept, Operation STARLIGHT, was conducted with dramatic success 15 miles south of the Chu Lai enclave. It established the viability of enclave operations limited to the northern coast of South Vietnam, a fact which no one disputed, but such operations were by that time only one facet of a much more ambitious strategy sanctioned by the President and in the process of being implemented by Westmoreland.

4.   *Where the U.S. Stood on 1 June 1965*

The beginning of the decisive month of June 1965 saw the U.S. in the infant stages of its enclave strategy. Established in coastal enclaves were Marine forces in Phu Bai, Da Nang and Chu Lai and Army forces in Vung Tau. Enclaves at Qui Nhon and Nha Trang were in the planning as locations for an Army brigade, and Korean troops were being considered for the defense of the provincial capital of Quang Ngai near the coast and as possible relief for the Marines at Chu Lai. The Secretary of Defense was also considering proposals from General Westmoreland and others to open up a major logistics base and enclave around the fine deep water harbor at Cam Ranh Bay.

As of the 1st of June 1965, the U.S. had *approved* for permanent deployment to South Vietnam forces which, when all had closed, would bring total combat strength to approximately 70,000 and the number of maneuver battalions, Army and Marine, to 13. Included in this total were 7 Marine BLT's already located at Phu Bai, Da Nang, and Chu Lai. Also included were 3 battalions in a brigade of the Army's 1st Division to be landed at Qui Nhon and

3 battalions in a brigade of the Army's 101st Airborne Division scheduled to replace the 173rd. In the planning stages but not yet approved were a further 11 maneuver battalions, the remaining 2 from the III MAF ("MEF" was changed to "MAF" because the word "Expeditionary" was offensive to the Vietnamese and was therefore changed to "Amphibious") and 9 battalions planned for the new Army Airmobile Division.

Third Country forces considered approved at this time amounted to 7,250 men of which 1,250 were already in-country in the 1st Battalion, Royal Australian Regiment, 2,000 were Korean service troops also already in-country, and the rest were to be deployed sometime later in a ROK Regimental Combat Team of 3 battalions. Still in the talking stages were a further 6 battalions of ROK troops totaling 12,000 men. The grand total of approved U.S./3rd Country forces was 17 maneuver battalions and approximately 77,250 men. If the additional forces then being discussed were thrown in, the total would have been 34 maneuver battalions and about 134,750 men. This, then, was the state of the build-up when General Westmoreland asked on 7 June for reinforcements from the U.S. and Third Countries "as rapidly as possible."

D. THE U.S. MOVES TO TAKE OVER THE LAND WAR: THE SEARCH AND DESTROY STRATEGY AND THE 44 BATTALION DEBATE

General Westmoreland's message #19118, of 7 June 1965, already quoted in part in Section I of this paper, punctuated a very grim period of ARVN defeats in Vietnam and stirred up a veritable hornet's nest in Washington. Up to that time, most of the Washington decision makers had been content to indulge in relatively low-key polemics about the enclave strategy and to advocate some experimentation with small numbers of U.S. troops in Vietnam. Westmoreland's request for reinforcements on a large scale, accompanied as it was by a strategy to put the troops on the offensive against the Viet Cong, did not contain any of the comfortable restrictions and safeguards which had been part of every strategy debated to date. Washington saw that it was Westmoreland's intention to aggressively take the war to the enemy with other than Vietnamese troops, and in such a move the spectre of U.S. involvement in a major Asian ground war was there for all to see. With no provision for quick withdrawal, and there was none, the long-term implications for the U.S. in terms of lives and money could not be averted. Temperatures rose rapidly after 7 June, and the debate was acrimonious and not without its casualties.

Just as Ambassador Taylor was consistent in his resistance to proposed involvement of U.S. forces in the Vietnamese War, so also was General Westmoreland equally determined to get enough US/3rd Country force into Vietnam to influence the situation. In addition to the level of force, Westmoreland was also bent on having a free hand in the use of it.

1.   Westmoreland Provides the Push

It has been suggested that COMUSMACV elected to interpret the landing of two Marine BLT's at Da Nang as the first step in a build-up of U.S. combat forces in Vietnam. It seems clear that General Westmoreland had reached the conclusion by early March that the RVNAF simply did not have the capability to overcome the Viet Cong by itself. Outside forces were going to be required to take up the slack until the GVN forces could be revamped and built up. It appears that General Westmoreland had a powerful ally in the person of General

Johnson, the Army Chief of Staff, who was in Saigon from the 5th through the 12th of March 1965, and who returned to Washington to submit the first of many recommendations that the U.S. send significant numbers of combat troops to Vietnam. Westmoreland was not far behind Johnson in submitting to Washington his own ideas on the subject.

The "Commander's Estimate of the Situation" prepared by General Westmoreland and his staff during the early weeks of March and completed on the 26th was a classic Leavenworth-style analysis, detailed and thorough in its consideration of possible U.S. courses of action. Copies of the Estimate, which in bulk amounted to a full half inch of foolscap paper, were delivered to Washington by Brigadier General De Puy, Westmoreland's J-3, who was traveling with Ambassador Taylor to the NSC meetings of 1–2 April. If the awesome bulk of the Estimate deterred anyone from giving it the careful study it merited, that is most unfortunate. As Westmoreland himself said:

> Recognizing recent marked changes in situation in SVN, we considered it appropriate to undertake a classical Commander's Estimate of the Situation to think through in a logical and precise manner strategy, objectives, enemy capabilities and our own possible courses of action before making what may prove to be in the light of history a momentous recommendation. In addition, by reducing the Estimate to writing we expose our thoughts to others, thus making possible careful review by higher authority and perhaps introduction of new considerations that were not apparent here.

The Estimate is as good as the Commander's word. The basic considerations to be analyzed are all laid out for the reader to see. First, the *Mission* as General Westmoreland interpreted it:

> Forces of the Government of Vietnam supported and assisted by forces of the U.S. Military Assistance Command, Vietnam, together with additional supporting U.S. and Free World forces, take as rapidly as possible those necessary actions to:
> A. Cause the DRV to cease its political and military support of the VC in SVN, and
> B. Enable an anti-communist GVN to survive so that ultimately it may defeat the VC insurgency inside SVN.

Secondly, the *Basic U.S. Strategy:*

> The analysis is predicated upon the assumption that basic strategy of retaliatory and punitive air strikes against NVN will, in time, bring about desired results, that is, supply and support of the insurgency will be terminated by DRV and hopefully DRV/VC High Command will direct the cessation of offensive operations. In any event, without external support the forces of RVNAF supported by U.S. would be able at first to contain and then to defeat VC. Therefore, Estimate addresses itself primarily to the interval in time between now and time at which basic strategy takes effect. If any time VC unilaterally cease fire and effect a cessation of incidents, this would mark end of the interval and end of pressure on GVN. Until pressure eases, stability of GVN is a prime concern and objective. Consequently, courses of action examined are measured as much in terms of their impact

on stability and effectiveness as upon their purely military value, although, of course, these two matters are closely interwoven.

As an adjunct to this, Westmoreland said:

> If basic strategy of punitive bombing in RVN (*sic!*) does not take effect by mid-year additional deployments of U.S. and 3rd Country forces should be considered, including introduction of full MEF into I Corps.

Third, *Main VC Capabilities:*

> A. Continue with present strategy and build-up and conduct large attacks whenever favorable.
> B. Above plus a major uprising to break the back of the GVN.
> C. By infiltration, commit PAVN up to a division in the I/II Corps.
> D. Create peace movement through subversion of existing organizations; get neutral government established, dominate it, and sue the North for peace and reunification.
> E. Unilaterally cease firing, causing the U.S. forces to leave and permitting the covert VC infrastructure to survive intact.

Courses of action in the Estimate were analyzed in relation to the main enemy capabilities outlined above. Maximum weight was given to the first three, which were considered to be the most likely. In addition, the following considerations formed part of the analysis matrix:

> A. Attainment of critical military objectives of
>   (1) Security of bases and ports,
>   (2) Denial of critical areas to the Viet Cong (areas such as the highlands of II Corps),
>   (3) Provision of a quick reaction reserve, and
>   (4) Provision of a basis for a combined command.
> B. Preservation of the stability and effectiveness of the GVN and of its armed forces.
> C. Improvement of force ratios as they changed with time,
> D. Remaining within the restrictions imposed by logistical limitations.

In order to achieve its objectives, the U.S. was presented, as Westmoreland saw it, essentially with three possible courses of action, there being several variations on one of the choices. The choices were:

> 1. Accelerate the build-up of RVNAF, commit the 7th Fleet to quarantine the coast against infiltration of men and arms, and continue U.S. logistical support as required. No outside combat power other than Naval and Air support would be provided the GVN under this option.
> 2. The above plus the commitment of up to two U.S. divisions with their support, either
>   a. to secure vital U.S. installations and defeat VC efforts to control the Kontum, Pleiku, Binh Dinh region, or
>   b. to secure critical enclaves in coastal regions, or
>   c. to do a combination of both of the above.
> 3. Both of the major choices above plus a cordon across SVN and the Laotian panhandle manned by up to three U.S. divisions coupled with ARVN, Thai and Laos forces.

In his subsequent analysis and comparison of courses of action, General Westmoreland gave each thorough coverage in light of all the considerations already enumerated. Course of Action 1, RVNAF build-up without outside ground force reinforcement, was certainly logistically feasible, but it failed to promise improvement in any of the other areas of consideration. Course of Action 3, the cordon plus the other courses, promised to attain all the military objectives, to provide a basis for improving GVN stability, and to improve force ratios in critical areas. Because of port and inland communications difficulties, however, the cordon force probably could not have been fully deployed before the end of Calendar Year 1965, which would have been too late to take up the slack during the critical phase of the RVNAF build-up. Also, if the basic strategy of punitive bombing had been successful, then the provision of a force of 165,000 men—132,000 of them from the U.S.—would have been out of proportion to the results expected. Should the bombing strategy fail or take effect only very slowly, then Westmoreland felt the cordon should be reconsidered.

The most propitious course of action to emerge from the analysis in the Estimate was the second one dealing with the commitment of up to two U.S. divisions, including 17 maneuver battalions, with support. Over and above what was in or authorized to be in Vietnam, Course of Action 2 called for an additional 33,000 men.

In order to illustrate trends in force ratios, Westmoreland postulated that one USMC BLT was the equivalent of three ARVN battalions, and one U.S. Army battalion was the equivalent of two ARVN battalions. Using that rationale, the combat battalions added on through Course of Action 2 would have amounted to 38 ARVN battalion-equivalents. Input on that scale would have had a fair effect on force ratios overall and a very dramatic effect locally in the areas where they were to operate.

Without the benefit of the increased battalion-equivalents provided by Course of Action 2, the ratio of ARVN (and the two Marine BLT's then in Vietnam) battalions to Viet Cong battalions would have degraded, according to the Estimate, from 1.7 to 1 in March 1965 to 1.6 to 1 in December of that year. This would have been the case despite an accelerated RVNAF build-up and only a modest rate of Viet Cong build-up as in 1964. With the input of Course of Action 2, the equivalent of a 10 month acceleration in the RVNAF build-up could have been accomplished by mid-year and by the end of the build-up period the forces could have been doubled—that is, assuming that the forces in Course of Action 2 were introduced during April, May, and June, a proposal which was barely feasible logistically and which was urged by General Westmoreland.

At the conclusion of his Estimate, General Westmoreland recommended that the U.S. build-up its combat force in Vietnam to 17 battalions by early June at the latest. He rejected the enclave alternative because it was too negative, because it brought U.S. troops into too intimate contact with the population, and because it posed some almost insurmountable problems in real estate acquisition. In the highlands the U.S. troops would have had no difficulty recognizing the enemy among the few montagnards who lived there, therefore Westmoreland recommended that a full U.S. division be deployed along the Qui Nhon–Pleiku axis with a brigade each at An Khe, Pleiku, and Kontum. This deployment would have altered the force ratios in the critical II Corps from 1.9:1 to 2.9:1 in favor of the RVNAF immediately. The ports of Qui Nhon and Nha Trang, rather than serving as enclave bases, would, according to the recommendation, have been developed as logistic support bases for the forces in the highlands and would have been provided with a battalion each for security. The rest of the 17 battalions were to provide base and installation security in the Da Nạng/Hue (4 USMC BLT's) and the Bien Hoa–Vung Tau (3 Army battalions) areas.

This was the position of COMUSMACV in March 1965. In concluding his Estimate, Westmoreland recognized the possibility that the GVN might infer from either Course of Action 2 or Course of Action 3 that the U.S. was determined to fight on alone. That possibility was outweighed in his eyes, however, by the tactical benefits to be gained plus the guarantee of a "more orderly buildup" than could have been the case under Course of Action 1.

In regard to the build-up of the RVNAF, MACV had in late 1964 two alternative proposals under discussion. Alternative 1 called for increases of 30,309 in the regular forces, plus 35,387 in the Regional Force and 10,815 in the Popular Force. Alternative 2 called for the same increases in RF/PF but for an accelerated figure for the regular forces of 47,556. Taking into account the limited leadership resources available to the GVN and the restricted training facilities, General Westmoreland in January 1965 recommended the more modest Alternative 1 build-up for Military Assistance Program funding. The Secretary of Defense approved the recommended increases on 23 January, thereby bringing the MAP supported RVNAF to levels of 275,058 for the regulars, plus 137,187 for RF and 185,000 for PF.

In response to COMUSMACV's Estimate of the Situation of March 1965 and a memorandum from the Joint Chiefs which followed it, the Secretary of Defense approved the accelerated Alternative 2 force level for the regulars and authorized MAP funding for an additional 17,247 spaces in RVNAF on 12 April 1965. Also provided was an increase in the MACV JTD of 160 spaces for advisors to work with the enlarged RVNAF.

In late May, the JCS asked the Secretary of Defense to authorize MAP support for another 2,369 spaces for ARVN. The purpose was to fatten out a division base for the eventual organization of a tenth ARVN division from existing separate regiments. The request was approved on the 4th of June.

Any further plans to build up the RVNAF were torpedoed by the extremely heavy losses suffered in combat during late May and early June. On 7 June, General Westmoreland told CINCPAC and Washington that a moratorium on RVNAF build-up was unavoidable as any trainees in the pipeline would have to be used as fillers in existing units. No new ARVN battalions would be coming on the scene until November of that year.

General Westmoreland was not in attendance at the NSC meetings of 1–2 April 1965. Having gone on record in his Estimate in favor of the earliest possible input of up to two division equivalents of U.S. forces, he was understandably disappointed with the very modest increases sanctioned by the President. He communicated to CINCPAC his concern that, while he understood that divisions were not immediately in the offing, he nevertheless felt a pressing need for a division in the highlands. Throughout the early part of April prior to the Honolulu Conference, Westmoreland also kept up the pressure to get an Army brigade into Bien Hoa–Vung Tau. The latter action happened to dovetail with the current Washington strategy options and hence was favorably considered at Honolulu while, as has already been noted, proposals to deploy divisions were not.

Only on one occasion through the spring of 1965 did General Westmoreland display any inclination to abandon his aggressive highlands campaign in favor of the more conservative enclave strategy. On 8 May he cabled to CINCPAC, with Ambassador Taylor's concurrence, his Concept of Operations by US/Allied Ground Combat Forces in Support of RVNAF. The Concept, as spelled out in that message, has already been discussed at length in an earlier section of this paper. Not discussed were some proposed deployments of U.S. and Third Country forces included by Westmoreland. Perhaps in deference to the Ambassador's known preference, Westmoreland suggested that the U.S. Airmobile Division be deployed to Qui Nhon and Nha Trang. In light of his previous recommendations and subsequent ones to be discussed, it is difficult to conclude that Westmoreland really seriously entertained this recommendation or that it was anything other than an aberration. On the 15th of the same month, Westmoreland sent a message to the Department of the Army indicating that, as far as he was concerned, the concept for employment of the Airmobile Division was still to be determined. Since he preferred an Airmobile Division, he asked the Department of the Army to send airmobile experts to Vietnam to assist him in the preparation of "a concept of operations for a division size force."

In his message #19118 of 7 June, General Westmoreland asked for U.S. and Third Country reinforcements after he had explained that redressing deteriorating force ratios was beyond the capability of the RVNAF. He said, "the force ratios continue to change in favor of the VC. I believe that the DRV will commit whatever force it deems necessary to tip the balance and that the GVN cannot stand up successfully to this kind of pressure without reinforcement." Westmoreland was convinced that U.S. troops could "successfully take the fight to the VC," and he explained that the forces he was requesting were "to give us a substantial and hard-hitting offensive capability on the ground *to convince the VC that they cannot win.*" [Emphasis added]

At the time Westmoreland submitted his recommendations in his 19118, which has erroneously been dubbed "the 44 Battalion request," there were, in addition to one Australian battalion, 7 U.S. Marine, and 2 U.S. Army battalions in Vietnam. In his message, Westmoreland said this:

> In sub-paragraph "A" below, deployments and actions are recommended on which decisions should be made now. In sub-paragraph "B" we have identified further actions on which planning should start and on which separate recommendations will be forthcoming.
>
> (3) One additional MAB to reinforce the III MAF.
>
> (4) Tactical air units for support of increased U.S. force (additional airfields in SVN and Thailand may be required).
>
> (5) Required combat and logistic support forces to include helicopter units to support the foregoing.
>
> Message has been discussed with Ambassador Taylor and Johnson. Ambassador Taylor is prepared to comment thereon during current visit to Washington.

In his subparagraph 'A' General Westmoreland did no more than request expeditious approval of forces which had been in the planning stages for some time. If his request had been approved as written, the grand total of maneuver battalions so provided would have been 33. This is one less than the total indicated in Section II of this paper as approved and planned because the Airmobile Division, when it was finally organized, had 8 rather than 9 airmobile battalions. If the 173d Airborne, which was only to be retained until the Airmobile Division was ready to begin operations, were counted, then the total of maneuver battalions requested by Westmoreland on 7 June was 35. In subparagraph 'B' he identified a further 9 battalions which might be needed and requested at some later date.

2. *CINCPAC Backs Into Enclaves*

The CINCPAC, Admiral Sharp, was by and large a consistent supporter of General Westmoreland in the latter's drive to get more forces into South Vietnam. With regard to the momentous recommendation of 7 June, CINCPAC concurred in General Westmoreland's evaluation of the situation and agreed also that Allied troops were needed to enable the friendly side to take the offensive. He said: "We will lose by staying in enclaves defending coastal bases." Having said that, Admiral Sharp then went on to disagree with Westmoreland as to the proper place for the Airmobile Division. Rather than have it deployed inland on the Qui Nhon–Pleiku axis as planned by Westmoreland, CINCPAC would have had it based on Qui Nhon with the primary mission of clearing Binh Dinh Province before moving inland. Sharp was very concerned that logistic backup for the Airmobile Division be assured before it be sent into the highlands. Securing one division's LOC with another division (Westmoreland intended to send the ROK's to Qui Nhon) was counterproductive, and Sharp felt that 600 to 800 tons of aerial resupply per day, should highway 19 be closed, would overtax the already limited airfield facilities in the highland areas where the Airmobile Division was to go.

Sharp's initial objections to Westmoreland's deployment plans smacked of conservatism and may well have played into the hands of those who continued to advocate the enclave strategy. The Ambassador was in Washington on 9 June, and one of the questions put to him by the Joint Chiefs was whether or not the Airmobile Division should go into the highlands. Taylor convinced them that it should not. Perhaps without Sharp's backing for the coastal deployment, the Joint Chiefs might not have been convinced.

It seems clear, however, that Admiral Sharp was not really an exponent of the enclave strategy. His insistence that the Airmobile Division stick to Binh Dinh was prompted by his conviction that the U.S. forces should operate in close proximity to the objective of the Viet war—the people. He was consistent in this approach when he pushed for deployment of the ROK RCT to Quang Ngai, where it was originally supposed to go and where there were plenty of people to be pacified, instead of to sparsely populated Cam Ranh for unremunerative security duty. He also recommended that the remaining ROK division (-), which would have been superfluous at Qui Nhon, be sent instead to Nha Trang or perhaps even into the Mekong Delta.

3. *The JCS Yields the Torch*

The JCS put the first major recommendation for ground troop commitment on the docket, as it were, on 20 March, shortly after Chief of Staff of the Army Johnson returned from Saigon. Because the Viet Cong were stronger and because the leaders of the RVNAF were overly involved in political matters, there had been, according to the JCS, for the first time a downward turn in what had been a relatively stable military situation. Unless the trend could be reversed, the Chiefs said, the war would be lost and it would be seen as a U.S. defeat. That would be intolerable; hence, the Chiefs recommended that U.S. and Allied forces be introduced with a new mission to stem the tide and assume the offensive. The Chiefs were manifestly not interested in any kind of holding action. As they said, "the requirement is not simply to withstand the Viet Cong, however, but to gain effective operational superiority and assume the offensive. To turn the tide of the war requires an objective of destroying the Viet Cong, not merely to keep pace with them, or slow down their rate of advance." The level of force which they recommended to carry out this aggressive mission and which they saw as an essential component of the broader program to put pressure on the DRV/VC and to deter Chinese Communist aggression, was three divisions, one ROK and two U.S.

In summary, the JCS recommended that one U.S. Marine division conduct, on order, offensive operations to kill Viet Cong with or without centralized GVN/US command structure. The Marines should operate out of their existing TAOR, and expand it as the force grew in size. The U.S. Army division should go to Pleiku, where it should operate with the RF/PF and CIDG troops there under U.S. command. The ARVN battalions thus released and shielded by a U.S. buffer along the Laotian border should then move to the populous coastal provinces. No location was specified for the ROK division, but the Chiefs recommended that its mission be similar to that of the U.S. divisions. They felt the Koreans' presence would have good "psychological effect."

This "three-division plan," as it was dubbed, was discussed with the Secretary of Defense and Ambassador Taylor on the 29th of March and was undoubtedly the topic of some discussion during the subsequent NSC meetings. In any case, even though the recommended deployments were not sanctioned in NSAM 328, the JCS continued to plan for ultimate implementation.

In earlier sections of this paper the possibility that the JCS may have gotten ahead of some of the other decision-makers in the U.S. Government was discussed. Thus, in early April they were forced to back down on the deployment they had ordered of the 173rd Airborne to Bien Hoa–Vung Tau, and in JCSM 321-65, 30 April 1965, they erroneously described as "approved" a package of some 4,700 logistical troops which were part of the three-division plan and still in the talking stage. The mission of forces listed in JCSM 321-65 as "approved" by the JCS was to be as follows:

> These forces are to bolster GVN forces during their continued build-up, secure bases and installations, conduct counterinsurgency combat operations in coordination with the RVNAF, and prepare for the later introduction of an airmobile division to the central plateau, the remainder of III MEF to the Da Nang area, and the remainder of a ROK division to Quang Ngai.
>
> Logistic forces of all services will strengthen support of in-country forces, provide support for the new forces, prepare bases and installations for possible future developments, and be prepared to support those additional forces.

The tone of JCSM 321-65 was consistent with the JCS' advocacy of a full three divisions of troops for Vietnam plus an aggressive mission for those troops. It was not in keeping, however, with the cautious language of the "Victory Strategy" sanctioned at the Honolulu Conference of 20 April. That strategy was the basis for the enclavists and it promised success through denial of victory to the Viet Cong. The enemy was to be denied victory because he would be unable to seize a certain number of decisive areas held by U.S. and Third Country forces, despite any successes he might enjoy throughout the rest of the country. Realizing his own impotence, the enemy would be moved to seek a negotiated settlement to the conflict. The level of commitment recommended to the President after the Honolulu Conference and in keeping with the "Victory Strategy" as described above was considerably less than three divisions as has been pointed out in earlier sections of this paper. The JCS should have been addressing the "Victory Strategy" in their 30 April memorandum, but preferred instead to continue the push for three divisions.

COMUSMACV's request of 7 June altered drastically the role of the JCS in the build-up debate. Up to that time the JCS had, if anything, been ahead of General Westmoreland in advocating Allied forces for Vietnam. The 27 battalions of their three-division plan were in themselves more than Westmoreland ever requested until 7 June. After that date, the big push came from Westmoreland in Saigon, and the JCS were caught in the middle between the latter and the powerful and strident opposition his latest request for forces had surfaced in Washington. The JCS memoranda of June and July 1965 were numerous and reflected, apparently without guiding, the 44 Battalion debate's progress. They showed the Airmobile Division in and out of Qui Nhon as the debate on the strategy for its employment ebbed and flowed. The 173rd Airborne Brigade and the brigade form 101st Airborne Division were first counted and then dropped and then counted again as the total permanent force to be deployed to Vietnam approached 44 maneuver battalions as a limit. On the 9th of June, the JCS favored the deployment of the Airmobile Division to the highlands. On the 11th they favored its going to Qui Nhon after discussing the matter with the Ambassador. On the 11th, the total recommended force was 33 battalions, 23 U.S. with the 173rd coming out, and 10 Third Country. On the 18th of June, the total had dropped to 22 and 10 as the 173rd was scheduled to stay but the brigade from the 101st was to leave. Final sanction for both airborne units to remain in Vietnam was not secured until August.

4. Search and Destroy as a Strategy and 44 Battalions as a Force

It was not at all clear that with the advent of the 44 battalion debate the vestiges of the enclave strategy and the conservatism which had characterized it had expired. On the contrary, enclave thinking was still very much alive. On the 11th of June, the JCS cabled CINCPAC and informed him that somewhat less than Westmoreland's 19118 was very close to being approved for deployment. The force described amounted to two Marine BLT's and three Army brigades, two of which had already been approved. The JCS wanted to know where Westmoreland intended to put this force in Vietnam. The implicit intention to keep a string on every unit going into Vietnam was obvious to General Westmoreland. In reply to this query and in response to the rising volume of criticism directed at his estimate of the seriousness of the situation and his proposed utilization of combat forces, Westmoreland sent the following cable to CINCPAC:

A. Actions recommended:
(1) Deploy at once to I CTZ the remaining two BLT's of the 3d Marine Division and appropriate supporting division and air elements (approximately 8,000 personnel). Reconstitute the SLF as a floating reserve.

(2) Deploy balance of increment 1 and all increment 2 (as defined in Reference C [Ref C was an earlier MACV message of 26 May 1965] of Army logistic and other support units in accordance with schedule set out in Reference D. [Ref D was a U.S. Army Support Command Vietnam message of 31 May] (Approximately 8,000 personnel)

(3) Deploy the U.S. Army Air Mobile Division (and logistic increment 3) through Qui Nhon to An Khe, Pleiku and Kontum (approxi-

mately 21,000 personnel). Qui Nhon will be ready to receive the division approximately 1 August upon the closure of increment 2 forces.

(4) Concurrently with the Air Mobile Division, deploy I Corps Headquarters (approximately 1,500 personnel).

(5) Deploy the ROK Marine RCT to Cam Ranh Bay as soon after 1 July as the unit can be readied for movement (approximately 4,000 personnel). Deploy balance of the ROK division force (approximately 14,500 personnel) plus U.S. logistic increment 4 (1,500 personnel); starting 15 September to the general area of Qui Nhon. (This answers Ref E [CINCPAC message of 5 June] in part—separate message. [Doc. 8])

(6) Deploy additional tactical fighter squadrons to Cam Ranh Bay when expeditionary landing field complete at that location. Also provide naval aircraft carried support of in-country operations as required; we believe the latter will engage one carrier full time.

(7) Hold the 173d Airborne Brigade in-country until the Air Mobile Division has deployed and is ready for operations.

(8) Continue air attacks against the DRV. (Reference F [MACV message of 20 May] applies)

B. *Additional deployment that may be required* and on which planning should begin: [Emphasis added]

(1) Three U.S. Army Hawk battalions to TSN Bien Hoa, Qui Nhon and Cam Ranh in that priority.

(2) The remainder of the 1st Infantry Division or the 101st Airborne Division beginning 1 October.

This message was extremely important, for in it COMUSMACV spelled out the concept of keeping U.S. forces away from the people. The search and destroy strategy for U.S. and Third Country forces which continues to this day and the primary focus of RVNAF on pacification both stem from that concept. In addition, Westmoreland made a big pitch in this cable for a free hand to maneuver the troops around inside the country. That is the prerogative of a major field commander—there is good indication that at this stage Westmoreland saw himself in that light rather than as advisor and assister to the Vietnamese armed forces.

Ambassador Taylor returned to Vietnam from Washington shortly after the battle at Dong Xoai, just as the new Thieu-Ky government was being installed. His first report confirmed the seriousness of the military situation as reported by General Westmoreland and also pointed up the very tenuous hold the new government had on the country. This report apparently helped to remove the last obstacles to consideration of all of the forces mentioned in Westmoreland's request of 7 June. On 22 June, the Chairman of the JCS cabled Westmoreland and CINCPAC to inform them that the ante had gone up from 35 to 44 battalions, counting all forces planned and programmed and including the 173rd. Westmoreland was asked if 44 battalions would be enough to convince the VC/DRV that they could not win. General Westmoreland replied that there was no evidence the VC/DRV would alter their plans regardless of what the U.S. did in the next six months. The 44 battalion force should, however, establish a favorable balance of power by the end of the year. If the U.S. was to seize the initiative from the enemy, then further forces would be required into 1966 and beyond.

On the 26th of June, as has already been noted, General Westmoreland was given the authority to commit U.S. forces to battle in support of RVNAF "in any situation . . . when, in COMUSMACV's judgment, their use is necessary to strengthen the relative position of GVN forces." This was about as close to a free hand in managing the forces as General Westmoreland was likely to get. The enclave strategy was finished, and the debate from then on centered on how much force and to what end. There were some attempts to snatch the chestnuts from the fire, however.

Westmoreland's opposition, while far from presenting a united front, had its day in court during late June and early July 1965. The Embassy in Saigon, while recognizing the seriousness of the situation in South Vietnam, was less than sanguine about the prospects for success if large numbers of foreign troops were brought in. Deputy Ambassador U. Alexis Johnson told Assistant Secretary of Defense McNaughton on 25 June that the U.S. should not bring in more troops. The situation, according to Johnson, was in many ways no more serious than the previous year. Even if it were more serious, he went on, massive input of U.S. troops was unlikely to make much difference. The best they could do would be to hold a few enclaves. Johnson pointed out that the Vietnamese were afraid they would lose authority if more U.S. troops were brought in. He advised that the U.S. allow the forces already in the country to settle. After some experimentation with them, the way would be much clearer. Once in, troops could not, without difficulty, be taken out again.

The views expressed by Johnson to McNaughton parallel those of Ambassador Taylor throughout the build-up debate. Both men were very much concerned with the effect of the proposed build-up on the Vietnamese. They were not directly opposed to the use of U.S. forces to help the GVN; they merely wanted to go very slowly to insure against loss of control.

At the opposite end of the spectrum from General Westmoreland was Under Secretary of State George Ball. Convinced that the U.S. was pouring its resources down the drain in the wrong place, Ball placed himself in direct opposition to the build-up. In a draft memorandum he circulated on the 28th of June, Ball stated that Westmoreland's intention was to go to Phase III combat (Phase III of the 8 May Concept of Operations which called for US/Allied forays inland to secure bases and areas for further operations). In Ball's view there was absolutely no assurance that the U.S. could with the provision of more ground forces achieve its political objectives in Vietnam. Instead, the U.S. risked involving itself in a costly and indeterminate struggle. To further complicate matters, it would be equally impossible to achieve political objectives by expanding the bombing of the North—the risks of involving the USSR and the CPR were too great, besides which such action would alienate friends. No combination of the two actions offered any better prospect for success. Since the costs to achieve its objectives if the U.S. embarked on an expanding program were indeterminate, the U.S. should, in Ball's view, not elect to follow such a course of action. It should instead "cut its losses" by restricting itself to the programmed 15 battalions and 72,000 men made public at a press conference in mid-June by the Secretary of Defense. By holding those forces to a very conservative Phase II strategy of base defense and reserve in support of RVNAF, U.S. combat losses could be held to a minimum while the stage was being set for withdrawal.

Ball was cold-blooded in his analysis. He recognized that the U.S. would not be able to avoid losing face before its Asian allies if it staged some form of conference leading to withdrawal of U.S. forces. The loss would only be of short term duration, however, and the U.S. could emerge from this period of travail as a "wiser and more mature nation." On 1 July, Ball sent to the President a memorandum entitled "A Compromise Solution for South Vietnam." In that memorandum, Ball presented his case for cutting losses essentially as it is described above.

Assistant Secretary of State William Bundy, like so many others, found himself in between Westmoreland and Ball. The U.S. needed to avoid the ultimatum aspects of the 44 battalions and also the Ball withdrawal proposal, both of which were undesirable in Bundy's estimation. On 1 July, Bundy suggested to the President that the U.S. should adopt a policy which would allow it to hold on without risking disasters of scale if the war were lost despite deployment of the full 44 battalions. For the moment, according to Bundy, the U.S. should complete planned deployments to bring in-country forces to 18 maneuver battalions and 85,000 men. The Airmobile Division and the remainder of the 1st Division should be brought to a high state of readiness, but the decision as to their deployment should be deferred. By so acting the U.S. would gain time in which to work diplomatically to realign Southeast Asia and thereby salvage its honor and credibility. The forces in Vietnam, which Bundy assumed would be enough to prevent collapse, would be restricted to reserve reaction in support of RVNAF. This would allow for some experimentation without taking over the war effort—a familiar theme. Bundy felt, as did Ambassador Taylor, that there remained considerable uncertainty as to how well U.S. troops would perform in the Vietnam environment. We needed to find out before going big.

5. *The Influence of the President and His Secretary of Defense*

It is difficult to be precise about the position of the Secretary of Defense during the build-up debate because there is so little of him in the files. In March, Ambassador Taylor sent to Saigon the following description of the Secretary's views regarding the JCS's three-division plan:

> a. The JCS has recommended to the Secretary of Defense the early deployment of a three division force with appropriate combat and logistic support. This force would include the entire MEF and I Corps area. An Army Division in the high plateau, and a Korean Division, location unspecified. The Chairman, JCS emphasized the urgent necessity to deploy a logistical command and the forward deployment of tactical fighter squadrons as well as the earliest possible construction of the airfield at Chu Lai and a runway at Da Nang.
>
> b. Ambassador Taylor indicated that 3 divisions seemed high; that Quat was not persuaded that more troops were necessary; that anti-American sentiment lies just below the surface and that finally there are two very real limitations on the number and rate of introduction of U.S. and Third Country forces. First is the absorptive capacity of the country and second logistical limitations.
>
> c. The Chairman, JCS outlined the importance of establishing a goal against which logistics planning could proceed.
>
> d. The Secretary of Defense indicated that further U.S. deployments must be accompanied by deployment of Koreans for reasons of domestic reaction.
>
> e. After an exchange of views on the missions and operating methods of U.S. forces the Secretary of Defense stated that he was impressed with the adverse force ratios and favored deployment of U.S. forces conditioned by:
>
> (1) political (psychological) absorption capacity

(2) logistical absorption capacity

(3) operational absorption—(that is operational requirements).

In his official reply to the JCS memorandum containing the three-division plan, the Secretary said this:

> I have considered the views of the JCS presented in referenced memorandum. As you are aware the substance of their recommendations was considered in the high-level discussions which took place in connection with the recent visit of Ambassador Taylor. I believe that the decisions made at that time reflect the views of the JCS to the extent required at this time.

It has already been pointed out that (after the NSC meetings of 1–2 April 1965) Mr. McNamara was interested in the JCS continuance of planning for the earliest possible introduction of the three divisions. In reply to the JCSM of 30 April in which the Chiefs summed up the results of the Honolulu Conference and subsequent discussions and in which they made another pitch for the three-division plan, the Secretary said in regard to the latter:

> The other deployments described will be considered in conjunction with continuing high-level deliberations on the Southeast Asia situation and as further requested by the JCS.

In the files are several other bits of information which, while perhaps not always directly attributable to the Secretary's personal philosophy, nevertheless are an indication of how he interpreted his guidance from the President. On 1 March he sent this memorandum to all departments:

> I want it clearly understood that there is an unlimited appropriation available for the financing of aid to Vietnam. Under no circumstances is lack of money to stand in the way of aid to that nation.

In response to a query by General Johnson, Army Chief of Staff, as to how much the U.S. must contribute directly to the security of South Vietnam, the Secretary said:

> Policy is: anything that will strengthen the position of the GVN will be sent.

On 2 April, the JCS sent the Secretary a bold memorandum in which they recommended clearing the decks of all "administrative and procedural impediments that hamper us in the prosecution of this war." They went on to list a whole panoply of problems which they felt were causing unnecessary headaches in providing support to General Westmoreland. The JCSM was a direct slap at some of the Secretary's management techniques and an appeal that the military staff be allowed to run the show. McNamara was silent for a long time. He replied to the memorandum on 14 May and addressed each of the JCS recommendations in turn. The gist of his reply was that he was not yet ready to yield the reins to the military. He said:

> I am sure it is recognized that many of these recommendations have received, or are now receiving, separate action review in appropriate

channels. Also, it appears clear that many of the actions recommended should be implemented only if execution of a major CINCPAC OPLAN were ordered.

There are plenty of other indications in the files that the Secretary was very carefully and personally insuring that the Defense Establishment was ready to provide efficient and sufficient support to the fighting elements in Vietnam. From the records, the Secretary comes out much more clearly for good management than he does for any particular strategy.

During the more heated debate following Westmoreland's request of 7 June, there is hardly a trace in the files of the Secretary's opinion. In a letter to Representative Mahon of the House Appropriations Committee on 9 June, McNamara indicated that the reserve stocks provided for combat consumption in the Fiscal Year 1966 Budget might have to be replenished as the situation in South Vietnam developed. He was not sure, however, and in any case could afford to wait and see. Perhaps there would be a request for a supplementary appropriation when the Congress reconvened *the following January.* (The President asked for a 1.7 billion supplementary appropriation in August of 1965 for military operations in Vietnam.)

Secretary McNamara went out to Vietnam for a firsthand look from 16 to 20 July. He wanted to hear Westmoreland's concept for the employment of the 44 battalions, and he sought the answers to a number of other questions including what forces Westmoreland thought would be required through January 1966 and beyond. When McNamara left Washington, the 44 battalion debate remained unresolved. While he was in Saigon, he received a cable from Deputy Secretary of Defense Vance informing him that the President had decided to go ahead with the plan to deploy all 34 of the U.S. battalions. The debate was over. McNamara left Saigon bearing Westmoreland recommendations for an even greater increase in forces which will be the subject of a later paper. "In many respects," McNamara told the press on leaving Vietnam, "it [the situation] has deteriorated since 15 months ago when I was last here."

There is no question that the key figure in the early 1965 build-up was the President of the United States. In NSAM 328, he only approved the modest input of two Marine battalions even though he was presented with a JCS recommendation that three full divisions be sent. The whole tone of the NSAM is one of caution. The President was determined that any changes authorized in that NSAM be understood as "being gradual and wholly consistent with existing policy." He was terribly concerned with control over release of information to the press, and a premature leak from Saigon of some of the details of the 1–2 April NSC meetings brought a sharp response from him. The subdued tones of NSAM 328 notwithstanding, the President apparently lent his sanction to the broader proposals contained in the joint State/Defense 7-point cable of 15 April, and in so doing he upset the Ambassador.

Most of the recommendations which came out of the Honolulu Conference received early attention by President Johnson, but during May things tended to slow down as his focus was diverted, no doubt, by the situation in the Dominican Republic.

On the 4th of May, the President sent a special message to the Congress in which he requested a supplemental appropriation of $700 million "to meet mounting military requirements in Vietnam." He described in that message the landing of U.S. Marines at Da Nang and Phu Bai the more recent arrival of the 173rd Airborne. He went on to say:

Nor can I guarantee this will be the last request. If our need expands I will turn again to the Congress. For we will do whatever must be done to insure the safety of South Vietnam from aggression. This is the firm and irrevocable commitment of our people and Nation.

And later in the same message:

I do ask for prompt support of our basic course: Resistance to aggression, moderation in the use of power, and a constant search for peace.

On 18 June, McGeorge Bundy sent this memorandum to the Secretary of Defense:

The President mentioned to me yesterday his desire that we find more dramatic and effective actions in South Vietnam. He also mentioned his desire for a report on the progress of his idea that we need more light planes for operations there. Finally, he asked if we have enough helicopters.

On the 16th of June Secretary McNamara had given the Army permission to proceed with the organization of an Airmobile Division using the assets of the 11th Air Assault Division and the 2nd Infantry Division. On the 22nd, four days after the Bundy Memorandum, the Secretary proceeded with readiness preparation of the Airmobile Division for deployment to South Vietnam, and the number of maneuver battalions being considered for eventual deployment rose from 23 U.S. to 34 U.S. or 44 U.S./3rd Country total. On the 23rd of June the deployments of one Marine BLT to Da Nang and one to Qui Nhon were approved. The latter move provided the needed security for the port of Qui Nhon in preparation for the arrival of the Airmobile Division and also allowed Westmoreland to divert the Army brigade originally scheduled for Qui Nhon to Cam Ranh Bay and Bien Hoa.

6. *Presidential Sanction for Phase I*

On 17 July, McNamara was in Saigon with the new Ambassador, Mr. Lodge, when he received the cable from Vance telling him that the President had decided to proceed with the deployment of all 34 U.S. battalions then under consideration. At that time, the Chief Executive was said by Vance to be favorably inclined toward calling up reserves to make the deployments a little less of a strain on the military establishment.

Upon his return from Vietnam, Secretary McNamara prepared a draft release to the press which stated that the total increase in U.S. forces with the latest approved add-ons would be about 100,000. That information was not given out. Instead, after a week of deliberation, the President held a press conference on the 28th of July in which he told the American people "the lesson of history" dictated that the U.S. commit its strength to resist aggression in South Vietnam. He said:

We did not choose to be the guardians at the gate, but there is no one else.

Nor would surrender in Vietnam bring peace, because we learned from Hitler at Munich that success only feeds the appetite of aggression. The battle would be renewed in one country and then another country, bringing with it perhaps even larger and crueler conflict, as we have learned from the lessons of history.

Moreover, we are in Vietnam to fulfill one of the most solemn pledges of the American Nation. Three Presidents—President Eisenhower, President Kennedy, and your present President—over 11 years have committed themselves and have promised to help defend this small and valiant nation.

Strengthened by that promise, the people of South Vietnam have fought for many long years. Thousands of them have died. Thousands more have been crippled and scarred by war. We just cannot now dishonor our word, or abandon our commitment, or leave those who believed us and who trusted us to the terror and repression and murder that would follow.

This, then, my fellow Americans, is why we are in Vietnam.

As far as increases in U.S. forces were concerned, the President said this:

First, we intend to convince the Communists that we cannot be defeated by force of arms or by superior power. They are not easily convinced. In recent months they have greatly increased fighting forces and their attacks and the number of incidents. I have asked the commanding general, General Westmoreland, what more he needs to meet this mounting aggression. He has told me. We will meet his needs.

I have today ordered to Vietnam the Airmobile Division and certain other forces which will raise our fighting strength from 75,000 to 125,000 men almost immediately. Additional forces will be needed later, and they will be sent as requested. This will make it necessary to increase our active fighting forces by raising the monthly draft call from 17,000 over a period of time to 35,000 per month, and for us to step up our campaign for voluntary enlistments.

After this past week of deliberations, I have concluded that it is not essential to order Reserve units into service now. If that necessity should later be indicated, I will give the matter most careful consideration and I will give the country due and adequate notice before taking such action, but only after full preparations.

We have also discussed with the Government of South Vietnam lately the steps that we will take to substantially increase their own effort, both on the battlefield and toward reform and progress in the villages. Ambassador Lodge is now formulating a new program to be tested upon his return to that area.

During the questioning period which followed the President's presentation, the following dialogue between the President and one of his interlocutors is recorded:

Question: Mr. President, does the fact that you are sending additional forces to Vietnam imply any change in the existing policy of relying mainly on the South Vietnamese to carry out offensive operations and using American forces to guard installations and to act as emergency backup?

The President: It does not imply any change in policy whatever. It does not imply change of objective.

The Annex to JCSM 590-65, forwarded by the JCS on 30 July 1965, reflected the final Phase I package approved for deployment as 44 maneuver battalions and a total strength in South Vietnam after all units had closed of 193,887 U.S. fighting men. During ensuing discussions concerning Phase II of the build-up, the Phase I package was further refined and increased. By 10 November, the Phase I package was fixed at 219,000 U.S. personnel.

The build-up progressed apace while the debate continued. In July two more Army brigades arrived followed closely by a corps headquarters. The 2d Brigade, 1st Infantry Division, which had originally been scheduled to protect Qui Nhon, went to Bien Hoa, leaving one battalion at Cam Ranh Bay for security. That battalion rejoined its parent unit when relieved at Cam Ranh by the 1st Brigade, 101st Airborne Division. In August the landing of the 7th Marine Regiment brought III MAF to a total strength of one Marine Division plus one regiment or 12 BLT's. The airmobile division, organized on 1 July as the 1st Air Cavalry Division, was fully deployed and responsible for its TAOR on 28 September. The remainder of the 1st Infantry Division closed on 7 October, and the ROK forces were fully deployed by 8 November, bringing the US/3rd Country forces in-country to a total fighting force of 44 maneuver battalions. U.S. strength in South Vietnam at the end of 1965 was 184,314 men.

E. EXPECTATIONS

The first four sections of this paper have presented the development of the situation in South Vietnam through the early months of 1965 and discussed the three strategies (1) Strategy of Security, 2) Enclave Strategy, and 3) Search and Destroy Strategy) which were considered during the same time span for the employment of United States ground forces. Each of the strategies had its heyday and its proponents, and each was associated in the minds of the decision-making principals who were weighing it with certain expectations.

1. The Strategy of Security

The short-lived strategy of security saw the deployments as a necessary evil to meet an immediate need—the bolstering of base security in South Vietnam for the air effort against North Vietnam. Few of the principals read any more into it than that.

The only intelligence estimate dealing with the ramifications of this strategy came when the intelligence community was tasked to predict probable communist reactions to the input of an entire Korean division for base security duty in South Vietnam. The SNIE resulting, dated 19 March 1965, indicated that input of Chinese or North Korean "volunteers" was very unlikely to occur. Inevitably there would be a great upsurge in propaganda and vilification directed against the Koreans and the U.S. for making such a move. In the main, however, communist reaction depended on how the signal was interpreted. They would almost certainly estimate that the input of a ROK division would "not in itself significantly alter the military situation. They might consider, however, that it portended a substantial further build-up of foreign forces . . . e.g., Nationalist Chinese, Thai, Philippines, and U.S. . . . for ground combat."

The strategy of security was intimately tied to the Rolling Thunder bombing program. It remained alive only so long as the decision-making principals were reasonably confident that the bombing was going to produce the desired effects on the DRV/VC will to persist. Expectations for the security strategy were quite modest if the foot-in-the-door aspects of it are discounted. No input of "volunteers" from China or other communist allies of the DRV was expected to occur in response to the provision of a few foreign troops to look after the bases in the South. It was merely expected that those bases would be better protected from attack.

2. The Enclave Strategy

At the NSC meetings of 1–2 April, those in attendance could see that Ho Chi Minh was not quite ready to throw in the towel. The McNaughton "trilemma" was addressed and it was decided to embark, albeit cautiously, on a program of ground troop deployments in excess of the requirements of base security. To insure control of troops untested in the environment of Asian insurgency, to provide security for the orderly construction of an expandable logistics base, and to provide for rapid and easy exit if the situation suddenly deteriorated, the forces were to be placed in coastal enclaves with their backs to the sea.

The proponents of the enclave strategy expected it to frustrate the DRV/VC by denying them victory. This denial of victory strategy spelled out at the Honolulu Conference, the high water mark of the enclave strategy, predicted that enemy impotence would lead eventually to a political solution. The enemy would be denied victory simply because a modicum of U.S. and 3rd Country force would enable the RVNAF to be expanded at a controlled rate without undue risk of collapse, loss of a key area, or a major defeat. The brunt of the war against the enemy's regular units would still be borne by the RVNAF. The Allied forces, operating from their secure bases, would be prepared to come to the aid of the Vietnamese if necessary. The relatively low intensity of operations to which the Allied forces would be exposed would permit low risk experimentation with them. The information gained from such experiments would be useful if the strategy failed and more forces had to be brought in. If the experiments verified that foreign soldiers could not fight effectively in the Vietnamese environment, a stronger case could be made for resisting any future attempts to get foreign troops enmeshed in the war.

Ambassador Taylor wanted to give the Vietnamese maximum opportunity to save themselves. He was quite sanguine about their prospects in the spring of 1965 and therefore was predisposed to hold the foreign troops down to the bare minimum. He thought things would remain stable enough to permit leisurely experimentation with four U.S. Marine battalions for two months before thought should be given to bringing in any more. As Taylor saw the situation at that time, the enclave strategy would buy enough time for the preparation of an entire logistics base. Any additional foreign reinforcements needed could be brought in later. As far as the few U.S. troops already in the country were concerned, Taylor expected their most serious problem would be boredom.

General Westmoreland expected, and CINCPAC supported him in this, that the war would be lost if the Allied forces were put into enclaves. The difference between Westmoreland and Taylor was the former's insistence on using U.S. and 3rd Country forces to take the war to the enemy. Taylor was quite content to let RVNAF do that with the occasional assist from the Allied forces if they got into difficulty. Westmoreland did not think they could do it, and he was convinced that no kind of victory could be had unless some pressure were put on the VC/DRV forces in South Vietnam.

Westmoreland was convinced that there would be an enemy offensive in the II Corps highlands sometime during the 1965 summer monsoon. If Allied forces weren't there to meet it, he was sure the highlands would be lost to the DRV/VC forces, who would then proceed to establish a front government there. Westmoreland expected this to happen if U.S. and 3rd Country forces went into coastal enclaves in lieu of moving directly into the interior.

CINCPAC expected the Airmobile Division to exhaust its supply lines if it were to move directly inland. He was not convinced that it could be supplied adequately by air as Westmoreland had suggested. The Ambassador expected the VC/DRV to try for another Dien Bien Phu if a U.S. division were to go inland to the highlands.

Westmoreland expected U.S. troops to have an abrasive effect on the Vietnamese population if they were in too close proximity to one another. The Ambassador was inclined to agree with him, but CINCPAC expected U.S. and 3rd Country forces to concentrate their efforts in areas where there were plenty of people, and he expected them to succeed. The Ambassador was prepared to put up with the prospect of poor relations between foreign troops and the Vietnamese in return for the low risk prospects offered by the enclave strategy.

It is not at all clear that the JCS ever endorsed the enclave strategy with any enthusiasm or that they expected much from it. From analysis of their recommendations it seems that they strove constantly to override the enclavists and get enough force into the country to do some good. In their three-division plan, they derided those who wanted to "merely keep pace" with the enemy or "slow down the rate" of his advance. The JCS said that to turn the tide of the war required "an objective of destroying the VC." The only way to win was to provide enough force to both stem the tide and assume the offensive. They recommended three divisions to accomplish the latter. The enclave strategists advocated neither the objective nor the amount of force.

Probably the last enclavist to be heard during the build-up debate was William Bundy. His "A Middle Way Course of Action in South Vietnam" memorandum was submitted to the President on the 1st of July. Bunudy expected 18 battalions and 85,000 men operating in conservative fashion from coastal enclaves to be enough to hold the whole facade together while the U.S. made concerted efforts to shore up Southeast Asia and extricate itself honorably from South Vietnam. He did not expect a victory from such a move, but he did not expect a loss either.

The reaction of the intelligence community to the enclave strategy was consistently less than optimistic. Immediately following the NSC meetings of the 1st of April, CIA Director McCone circulated a memorandum in which he argued that changing the mission of U.S. troops in Vietnam to offensive operations would merely lead to requests for more and more troops for a war the U.S. *"cannot win."* In the same memorandum, McCone argued that a marked increase in the tempo of air operations against NVN was an indispensable concomitant of a change in ground strategy. The NSAM which sanctioned the change of ground strategy called for no more than "slowly ascending tempo" for Rolling Thunder operations.

McCone circulated another memorandum on the day after the Honolulu Conference in which he estimated probable enemy reactions to greater U.S. involvement in the war. The enemy, McCone said, still saw things essentially going his way. An increased U.S. involvement on the ground would be seen by the enemy as an acceptance by the U.S. of a greater commitment, but he would also infer from the cautious enclave approach that the U.S. was quite reluctant to widen the war. It was probable that the VC would be reinforced with men and equipment, but direct intervention by the DRV or the Chinese Communists was unlikely.

On the 28th of April, a SNIE entitled "Communist Reactions to Certain U.S. Actions" described what could be expected of the enemy:

> The policies and tactics of the Communist powers engaged by the Vietnamese crisis have settled into a fairly definitive pattern. It appears that the

DRV, with strong Chinese encouragement, is determined for the present to ride out the U.S. bombardment. Both the DRV and Communist China have hardened their attitude toward negotiations, without categorically excluding the possibility under all conditions. They apparently calculate that the DRV can afford further punishment and that, in the meantime, U.S. determination to persist will weaken because of increasing DRV air defense capability, the threat of broader conflict, and the pressure of international and U.S. domestic opinion. Moreover, they consider that the tide is running in their favor in the South . . .

If the enemy's attitudes were as hard as described above, then a great deal of patience was going to be required of those who expected the Honolulu strategy to come to fruition.

3. The Search and Destroy Strategy

There are many aspects of the enclave strategy which were galling to professional military men. Many of those were brought out by the military men themselves in documents quoted in this paper. Probably the single most disturbing factor in the enclave approach was the implicit failure to try and seize the initiative from the enemy. Instead, it was proposed that the U.S. and the GVN try and ride out the war by denying the enemy a victory. The initiative to come to the conference table and thus end the fighting was left strictly to the enemy and depended on his appreciation of his own impotence. It looked as though the communists were to have all the options.

The JCS expected any strategy to fail if it did not include among its courses of action some provision for the seizure of the initiative. They said as much in each of their recommendations. General Westmoreland was of a similar bent, and he stated explicitly that the enclave strategy was "too negative." Nevertheless, both Westmoreland and the JCS are on record stating that 44 battalions would not be enough to seize the initiative from the enemy either. Westmoreland told the JCS on 24 June that he felt substantial increases of forces would be required over and above the 44 battalions in 1966. The U.S. would be too busy building up its forces in 1965 to seize the initiative from the enemy during that year. JCSM-515-65 of 2 July, which contained the JCS recommendation for the full 44 battalions, included the following paragraph:

> Pursuant to your discussions with the JCS on 28 June 1965, there is furnished in the Annex hereto a program for the deployment of such additional forces to South Vietnam at this time as are required to insure that the VC/DRV *cannot win in South Vietnam at their present level of commitment.* [Emphasis added]

The JCS went on to recommend the concurrent implementation of stepped-up air action against the DRV as "an indispensable component of this overall program." Thus, the JCS, who in March 1965 were recommending 27 battalions to "stem the tide and assume the offensive," were ready to admit in July of that year that 44 battalions would only be enough to hold the fort and that even greater effort would be required to seize the initiative.

When the Secretary of Defense came to Saigon during the third week of July 1965, he was introduced to General Westmoreland's latest ideas concerning the employment of U.S. and Free World Military Assistance Force (FWMAF) forces. Westmoreland laid out for the Secretary the force requirements projected into 1966. Force ratios based on estimates of enemy build-up capability and projections of the RVNAF rate of build-up called for the 44 US–FWMAF battalions through the end of 1965. In concert with Westmoreland's Concept of Operations, later formalized and published on 30 August, the 44 battalions were labeled Phase I forces. Secretary McNamara left Saigon with the first estimate by Westmoreland of the requirements for assuming the offensive in 1966. Phase II was anticipated by Westmoreland to require 24 additional maneuver battalions.

As an indication of Westmoreland's expectations for the 44 Phase I maneuver battalions which are the subject of this paper, there is no better source then his Concept of Operations. The Concept was developed through three distinct phases:

Phase I—The commitment of US/FWMAF forces necessary to halt the losing trend by the end of 1965.

Phase II—The resumption of the offensive by US/FWMAF forces during the first half of 1966 in high priority areas necessary to destroy enemy forces, and reinstitution of rural construction activities.

Phase III—If the enemy persisted, a period of a year to a year and a half following Phase II would be required for the defeat and destruction of the remaining enemy forces and base areas.

Withdrawal of US/FWMAF forces would commence following Phase III as the GVN became able to establish and maintain internal order and to defend its borders.

The overall Concept was based on some assumptions:

(1) That the VC would fight until convinced that military victory was impossible and then would not be willing to endure further punishment.

(2) That the Chinese Communists would not intervene except to provide aid and advice.

(3) That friendly forces would maintain control of the air over RVN.

The specific military tasks associated with each phase of the Concept were spelled out as follows:

Phase I

(1) Secure the major military bases, airfields and communications centers.

(2) Defend major political and population centers.

(3) Conduct offensive operations against major VC base areas in order to divert and destroy VC main forces.

(4) Provide adequate reserve reaction forces to prevent the loss of secure and defended areas.

(5) Preserve and strengthen the RVNAF.

(6) Provide adequate air support, both combat and logistic.

(7) Maintain an anti-infiltration screen along the coast and support forces ashore with naval gunfire and amphibious lift.

(8) Provide air and sea lifts necessary to transport the necessary but minimum supplies to the civil populace.

(9) Open up necessary critical lines of communication for essential military and civil purposes.

(10) Preserve and defend, to the extent possible, areas now under effective governmental control.

Phase II

(1) All Phase I measures.

(2) Resume and/or expand pacification operations. Priority will be given to the Hop Tac area around Saigon, to that part of the Delta along an east-west axis from Go Cong to Chau Doc, and in the provinces of Quang Nam, Quang Tri, Quang Ngai, Binh Dinh and Phu Yen.

(3) Participate in clearing, securing, reserve reaction and offensive operations as required to support and sustain the resumption of pacification.

Phase III

(1) All Phase I and II measures.

(2) Provide those additional forces necessary to extend and expand clearing and securing operations throughout the entire populated area of the country and those forces necessary to destroy VC forces and their base areas.

General Westmoreland went on in his Concept to lay out the tactics to be associated with the various military tasks and to list explicit tasks to be accomplished within each RVNAF Corps area. The above is sufficient for the needs of this paper, however, as it shows that General Westmoreland expected by the end of 1965 to have effectively stemmed the tide of the VC insurgency through the input of 44 US/FWMAF maneuver battalions and their accompanying support. It further shows that in the first half of 1966, with the input of more force, Westmoreland expected to shift his emphasis from the strategic defensive to the strategic offensive.

In his 25 June interview with McNaughton, Deputy Ambassador Johnson summed up the expectations for Ambassador Taylor and himself. In Johnson's view what was expected depended on how serious the situation actually was. If it were as bad as Westmoreland said it was, then large numbers of foreign troops could do little more than hold on to a few enclaves. If the situation were not significantly worse than the year before (and Johnson apparently felt in many ways it was not) then the U.S. was merely bringing in more foreign troops than were needed and could be expected to have difficulty getting them out again. Finally, Johnson expected the Vietnamese reaction to the massive input of foreign troops to be a major problem.

Under Secretary George Ball clearly felt that the U.S. was already engaged in an indeterminate struggle in Vietnam. Raising the US/FWMAF force levels to 44 battalions would, he expected, accomplish nothing more than raise the cost to the U.S. when it finally lost the war and pulled out.

Assistant Secretary Bundy saw in the 44 battalion request some ultimatum aspects that he felt were undesirable. Apparently, although he did not say so, he expected approval of that request and announcement of it to trigger some kind of dire response from the other side.

The person among the principals whose views can be found in the files dared to attach a probability to his expectations. Assistant Secretary McNaughton gave Secretary McNamara on the 13th of July a memorandum entitled "Analysis and Options for South Vietnam." McNaughton described three possible courses the war could take:

(1) Success for the US/GVN. (Actions one should expect to see in such a case were the extension of GVN control throughout the country, the disarming of the VC armed units, the cessation of infiltration and other DRV support, and

the relegation of the terror and other insurgent activity to little more than a rural police problem.)

(2) Inconclusive for either side (self-explanatory).

(3) GVN collapse and concomitant U.S. defeat (self-explanatory).

McNaughton recommended to Secretary McNamara that the U.S. deploy the 44 battalions and be prepared to send more force to try for a win as defined above. McNaughton's expectations for such a course, as expressed in probabilities, are laid out below. The assumed U.S. force level to develop these probabilities was between 200,000 and 400,000 men. With that amount of force, the probability of Success/Inconclusive/Collapse was

for the year 1966:   .2/.7/.1
for the year 1967:   .4/.45/.15 and
for the year 1968:   .5/.3/.2—no further projection being made.

It is noteworthy that while McNaughton expected the probability of success to increase with each year of investment, he also expected the probability of failure to increase, although not by as much. The probability that the war would end inconclusively was expected by McNaughton to shrink dramatically after the first year. In concluding his memorandum, McNaughton observed that the U.S. might decide at any time in mid-course to try for a compromise solution to the conflict. Such an option, while not assigned a probability of achievement, was defined as a situation in which the VC remained armed and in defense of areas they controlled in the country, the NLF was represented in the GVN, and the GVN agreed to keep hands off the VC areas.

Neither the President nor the Secretary of Defense is on record in 1965 with expectations as to the duration of the war or the impact of the 44 battalions. It looks as though they both were prepared for the moment to go along with General Westmoreland's predictions about the course of the war. The decision not to call up the Reserves, which was made some time during the week just prior to the President's press conference of 28 July, indicated that the President expected the war to last in Vietnam well beyond a year. No doubt the Secretary of Defense told him that without a declaration of national emergency—a move the President found politically unpalatable—the Reserves as an asset would be fully expended in one year, leaving the military establishment in worse shape than before if the war still continued.

The final element in the expectations matrix was provided by the NIB in a SNIE issued on 23 July entitled "Communist and Free World Reactions to a Possible U.S. Course of Action." The analysis was predicated on the following proposed action:

(1) The U.S. would increase its strength in SVN to 175,000 by 1 November,

(2) 225,000 U.S. Reserves would be called up,

(3) 20,000 tours of duty per month would be extended,

(4) The regular strength of the U.S. Armed Forces would be increased by 400,000 over the next year, and

(5) U.S. draft calls would be doubled.

In conjunction with the above, the U.S. would also make public statements reiterating its objectives and its readiness to negotiate. The forces going to Vietnam would be deployed so as not to threaten the 17th parallel. Also considered was a possible step-up of U.S. air activity against the DRV land lines of communication with China.

In reaction to the above, the Communists would probably see the U.S. moves as indication that the U.S. held little hope of negotiation. They would probably expect some increase in US/3rd Country forces anyway as they clearly felt they were winning. In order to offset the increases of US/3rd Country forces in South Vietnam, the Communists would probably build up their own strength with the input of 20,000 to 30,000 PAVN regulars by the end of 1965. This, of course, they were already in the process of doing.

It was seen as possible, but less probable, that the Communists might attack GVN forces and installations in hopes of achieving victory before the US/3rd Country build-up took effect. Barring that, they might avoid direct confrontation with U.S. forces and just peck away at them through harassing actions. By so doing, they might hope to demonstrate to the foreigner his own impotence in a Vietnamese war.

If the situation in South Vietnam were going badly for the VC, the DRV might show some interest in negotiations. If the U.S. did increase its air activity, the DRV was most likely to respond by asking the Soviets for more air defense hardware.

As far as the Chinese Communists were concerned, it was estimated that they were very unlikely to intervene in the air war over North Vietnam. They might put service troops into North Vietnam, but they would not be likely to introduce combat troops. The Chinese, the Estimate said, "would believe that the U.S. measures were sufficient only to postpone defeat while magnifying its eventual effect."

It could be expected that the Soviets would step up their aid to the DRV, especially in the field of air defense, and at the same time harden their attitude towards the U.S. without making any major challenge to U.S. interests around the world. It would come as no surprise if the Soviets raised the level of their military spending in response to this U.S. action.

It was felt that most of the allies of the United States realized that the U.S. was going to have to increase its commitment in Vietnam. It was recognized, however, that they would find it increasingly difficult to give U.S. policy any public support.

In order to mitigate somewhat the crisis atmosphere that would result from this major U.S. action, the Estimate concluded with the recommendation that announcements about it be made piecemeal with no more high level emphasis than necessary.

Predictably, the expectations of those outside of the official pale ran the gamut from supporters of Oregon Senator Wayne Morse ("the Administration policy is leading the United States to the abyss of total war"—"there are doubts beginning to show at the grass roots about our policy there, [in Vietnam] and when the coffins begin coming home those doubts will grow"—"the war in Asia cannot be won; . . . in the end the United States will be kicked out") to equally misguided zealots on the other end of the spectrum, such as Jack Foisie of the *Los Angeles Times* ("I foresee the day of mixed American–Vietnamese units under American command—to make our junior leadership stretch as far as possible"—"we are going to drive to the Laos border—lying only 50 to 75 miles inland in the central waist of Vietnam. Everything taken will be held, initially with firstline troops, and later—as a rear area—by second line militia").

Whatever their personal assessments of the ramifications of the 44 battalion decision might have been, all interested observers had one thing in common— they recognized the crossing of a major threshold and the embarkation on a major new course the end of which was not in sight.

Volume III   List of Documents

Document 181   (page 545)
Cable, Saigon 465 to State, on the problem in South Vietnam, 18 August 1964.

Document 182   (page 549)
Memorandum for the Secretary of Defense from Assistant Secretary of Defense
(Comptroller) re: review of USAF study: "Relationship of Tactical Air to
Ground Forces, Southeast Asia, 1964 and 1969," 24 August 1964.

Document 183   (page 550)
Memorandum for the Secretary of Defense from JCS re: recommended courses
of action in Southeast Asia, JCSM-746–64, 26 August 1964.

Document 184   (page 552)
State Department cable on SAR and T-28 missions (addressee unknown), 26
August 1964.

Document 185   (page 553)
Memorandum for William Bundy and J. T. McNaughton from JCS/SACSA, re:
September schedule for OPLAN 34A, 27 August 1964.

Document 186   (page 555)
Memorandum for the Sec. of Defense from John T. McNaughton, re: response to
JCS target study of North Vietnam, 29 August 1964.

Document 187   (page 555)
Memorandum for the Chairman, Joint Chiefs of Staff, from Robert McNamara,
on JCS target study of North Vietnam, 31 August 1964.

Document 188   (page 556)
Paper by McNaughton (2nd draft), *Plan of Action for South Vietnam,* 3 September 1964.

Document 189   (page 559)
Memorandum to Robert Manning from McGeorge Bundy on possible problems
in current form of Q&A booklet on Vietnam, 4 September 1964.

Document 190   (page 560)
Draft paper by Wm. Bundy, *Courses of Action for South Vietnam,* 8 September
1964.

Document 191   (page 561)
Memorandum recording Principals' consensus on courses of action for South
Vietnam, 8 September 1964.

Document 192   (page 563)
State/Defense message to Saigon, Vientiane, Bangkok re: Laos corridor operations, 9 September 1964.

Document 193   (page 563)
Memorandum for the Secretary of Defense from the JCS on 8 September Bundy
draft, CM-124–64, 9 September 1964.

Document 194   (page 565)
Rules of engagement, DeSoto Patrol, recommended by JCS, 9 September 1964.

Document 195 (*page 565*)
NSAM 314, 10 September 1964.

Document 196 (*page 566*)
Cable, Saigon 913 to State, summary of conclusions of meeting of three embassies held in Saigon on 11 September to review air and ground operations in the Lao corridor, 19 September 1964.

Document 197 (*page 568*)
Cable, CINCPAC to JCS re: DeSoto Patrols, 21 September 1964.

Document 198 (*page 569*)
Cable, CINCPAC to JCS re: planning for future contingencies, 25 September 1964.

Document 199 (*page 570*)
Cable, JCS 9117 to CINCPAC re rules of engagement applying to Laos, 28 September 1964.

Document 200 (*page 571*)
Memorandum to McNaughton from Deputy Secretary of Defense Vance re: 34A MAROPS procedures, 30 September 1964.

Document 201 (*page 571*)
Questions and answers on covert actions. Questions by J. T. McNaughton, answers by JCS and ISA, September 1964.

Document 202 (*page 575*)
Cable, CINCPAC to JCS on use of Thai-based U.S. air forces, 2 October 1964.

Document 203 (*page 576*)
Cable, Saigon to State on SEACOORD, 3 October 1964.

Document 204 (*page 576*)
State/Defense message to Vientiane authorizing commencement of air attacks against infiltration routes and facilities in the Laos Panhandle, 6 October 1964.

Document 205 (*page 577*)
Cable, State to Saigon re: convening organizing session for SEACOORD, 7 October 1964.

Document 206 (*page 578*)
Deptel 763 from Saigon on organizing session for SEACOORD, 9 October 1964.

Document 207 (*page 579*)
Cable, Saigon 1080 to State transmitting approved terms of reference for SEACOORD, 10 October 1964.

Document 208 (*page 580*)
Memorandum to J. A. Califano (author unknown) re: views of Lao Deputy Prime Minister on expanded military operations in Northern Laos, early October 1964.

[Document 156]

THE SECRETARY OF DEFENSE
Washington
21 December 1963

MEMORANDUM FOR THE PRESIDENT

Subject: Vietnam Situation

In accordance with your request this morning, this is a summary of my conclusions after my visit to Vietnam on December 19–20.

1. *Summary.* The situation is very disturbing. Current trends, unless reversed in the next 2–3 months, will lead to neutralization at best and more likely to a Communist-controlled state.

2. *The new government* is the greatest source of concern. It is indecisive and drifting. Although Minh states that he, rather than the Committee of Generals, is making decisions, it is not clear that this is actually so. In any event, neither he nor the Committee are experienced in political administration and so far they show little talent for it. There is no clear concept on how to re-shape or conduct the strategic hamlet program; the Province Chiefs, most of whom are new and inexperienced, are receiving little or no direction; military operations, too, are not being effectively directed because the generals are so preoccupied with essentially political affairs. A specific example of the present situation is that General Dinh is spending little or no time commanding III Corps, which is in the vital zone around Saigon and needs full-time direction. I made these points as strongly as possible to Minh, Don, Kim, and Tho.

3. *The Country Team* is the second major weakness. It lacks leadership, has been poorly informed, and is not working to a common plan. A recent example of confusion has been conflicting USOM and military recommendations both to the Government of Vietnam and to Washington on the size of the military budget. Above all, Lodge has virtually no official contact with Harkins. Lodge sends in reports with major military implications without showing them to Harkins, and does not show Harkins important incoming traffic. My impression is that Lodge simply does not know how to conduct a coordinated administration. This has of course been stressed to him both by Dean Rusk and myself (and also by John McCone), and I do not think he is consciously rejecting our advice; he has just operated as a loner all his life and cannot readily change now.

Lodge's newly-designated deputy, Davis Nes, was with us and seems a highly competent team player. I have stated the situation frankly to him and he has said he would do all he could to constitute what would in effect be an executive committee operating below the level of the Ambassador.

As to the grave reporting weakness, both Defense and CIA must take major steps to improve this. John McCone and I have discussed it and are acting vigorously in our respective spheres.

4. *Viet Cong progress* has been great during the period since the coup, with my best guess being that the situation has in fact been deteriorating in the countryside since July to a far greater extent than we realized because of our undue dependence on distorted Vietnamese reporting. The Viet Cong now control very high proportions of the people in certain key provinces, particularly those directly south and west of Saigon. The Strategic Hamlet Program was seriously over-extended in these provinces, and the Viet Cong has been able

to destroy many hamlets, while others have been abandoned or in some cases betrayed or pillaged by the government's own Self Defense Corps. In these key provinces, the Viet Cong have destroyed almost all major roads, and are collecting taxes at will.

As remedial measures, we must get the government to re-allocate its military forces so that its effective strength in these provinces is essentially doubled. We also need to have major increases in both military and USOM staffs, to sizes that will give us a reliable, independent U.S. appraisal of the status of operations. Thirdly, realistic pacification plans must be prepared, allocating adequate time to secure the remaining government-controlled areas and work out from there.

This gloomy picture prevails predominantly in the provinces around the capital and in the Delta. Action to accomplish each of these objectives was started while we were in Saigon. The situation in the northern and central areas is considerably better, and does not seem to have deteriorated substantially in recent months. General Harkins still hopes these areas may be made reasonably secure by the latter half of next year.

In the gloomy southern picture, an exception to the trend of Viet Cong success may be provided by the possible adherence to the government of the Cao Dai and Hoa Hao sects, which total three million people and control key areas along the Cambodian border. The Hoa Hao have already made some sort of agreement, and the Cao Dai are expected to do so at the end of this month. However, it is not clear that their influence will be more than neutralized by these agreements, or that they will in fact really pitch in on the government's side.

5. *Infiltration* of men and equipment from North Vietnam continues using (a) land corridors through Laos and Cambodia; (b) the Mekong River waterways from Cambodia; (c) some possible entry from the sea and the tip of the Delta. The best guess is that 1000–1500 Viet Cong cadres entered South Vietnam from Laos in the first nine months of 1963. The Mekong route (and also the possible sea entry) is apparently used for heavier weapons and ammunition and raw materials which have been turning up in increasing numbers in the south and of which we have captured a few shipments.

To counter this infiltration, we reviewed in Saigon various plans providing for cross-border operations into Laos. On the scale proposed, I am quite clear that these would not be politically acceptable or even militarily effective. Our first need would be immediate U–2 mapping of the whole Laos and Cambodian border, and this we are preparing on an urgent basis.

One other step we can take is to expand the existing limited but remarkably effective operations on the Laos side, the so-called Operation HARDNOSE, so that it at least provides reasonable intelligence on movements all the way along the Laos corridor; plans to expand this will be prepared and presented for approval in about two weeks.

As to the waterways, the military plans presented in Saigon were unsatisfactory, and a special naval team is being sent at once from Honolulu to determine what more can be done. The whole waterway system is so vast, however, that effective policing may be impossible.

In general, the infiltration problem, while serious and annoying, is a lower priority than the key problems discussed earlier. However, we should do what we can to reduce it.

6. *Plans for Covert Action into North Vietnam* were prepared as we had requested and were an excellent job. They present a wide variety of sabotage

and psychological operations against North Vietnam from which I believe we should aim to select those that provide maximum pressure with minimum risk. In accordance with your direction at the meeting, General Krulak of the JCS is chairing a group that will lay out a program in the next ten days for your consideration.

7. *Possible neutralization* of Vietnam is strongly opposed by Minh, and our attitude is somewhat suspect because of editorials by the *New York Times* and mention by Walter Lippmann and others. We reassured them as strongly as possible on this—and in somewhat more general terms on the neutralization of Cambodia. I recommend that you convey to Minh a Presidential message for the New Year that would repeat our position in the strongest possible terms and would also be a vehicle to stress the necessity of strong central direction by the government and specifically by Minh himself.

8. *U.S. resources and personnel* cannot usefully be substantially increased. I have directed a modest artillery supplement, and also the provision of uniforms for the Self Defense Corps, which is the most exposed force and suffers from low morale. Of greater potential significance, I have directed the Military Departments to review urgently the quality of the people we are sending to Vietnam. It seems to have fallen off considerably from the high standards applied in the original selections in 1962, and the JCS fully agree with me that we must have our best men there.

Conclusion. My appraisal may be overly pessimistic. Lodge, Harkins, and Minh would probably agree with me on specific points, but feel that January should see significant improvement. We should watch the situation very carefully, running scared, hoping for the best, but preparing for more forceful moves if the situation does not show early signs of improvement.

Robert S. McNamara

[Document 157]

THE JOINT CHIEFS OF STAFF
Washington 25, D.C.
JCSM–46–64
22 Jan 1964

MEMORANDUM FOR THE SECRETARY OF DEFENSE

Subject: Vietnam and Southeast Asia

1. National Security Action Memorandum No. 273 makes clear the resolve of the President to ensure victory over the externally directed and supported communist insurgency in South Vietnam. In order to achieve that victory, the Joint Chiefs of Staff are of the opinion that the United States must be prepared to put aside many of the self-imposed restrictions which now limit our efforts, and to undertake bolder actions which may embody greater risks.

2. The Joint Chiefs of Staff are increasingly mindful that our fortunes in South Vietnam are an accurate barometer of our fortunes in all of Southeast Asia. It is our view that if the US program succeeds in South Vietnam it will go far toward stabilizing the total Southeast Asia situation. Conversely, a loss of South Vietnam to the communists will presage an early erosion of the remainder of our position in that subcontinent.

3. Laos, existing on a most fragile foundation now, would not be able to endure the establishment of a communist—or pseudo neutralist—state on its eastern flank. Thailand less strong today than a month ago by virtue of the loss of Prime Minister Sarit, would probably be unable to withstand the pressures of infiltration from the north should Laos collapse to the communists in its turn. Cambodia apparently has estimated that our prospects in South Vietnam are not promising and, encouraged by the actions of the French, appears already to be seeking an accommodation with the communists. Should we actually suffer defeat in South Vietnam, there is little reason to believe that Cambodia would maintain even a pretense of neutrality.

4. In a broader sense, the failure of our programs in South Vietnam would have heavy influence on the judgments of Burma, India, Indonesia, Malaysia, Japan, Taiwan, the Republic of Korea, and the Republic of the Philippines with respect to US durability, resolution, and trustworthiness. Finally, this being the first real test of our determination to defeat the communist wars of national liberation formula, it is not unreasonable to conclude that there would be a corresponding unfavorable effect upon our image in Africa and in Latin America.

5. All of this underscores the pivotal position now occupied by South Vietnam in our world-wide confrontation with the communists and the essentiality that the conflict there be brought to a favorable end as soon as possible. However, it would be unrealistic to believe that a complete suppression of the insurgency can take place in one or even two years. The British effort in Malaya is a recent example of a counterinsurgency effort which required approximately ten years before the bulk of the rural population was brought completely under control of the government, the police were able to maintain order, and the armed forces were able to eliminate the guerrilla strongholds.

6. The Joint Chiefs of Staff are convinced that, in keeping with the guidance in NSAM 273, the United States must make plain to the enemy our determination to see the Vietnam campaign through to a favorable conclusion. To do this, we must prepare for whatever level of activity may be required and, being prepared, must then proceed to take actions as necessary to achieve our purposes surely and promptly.

7. Our considerations, furthermore, cannot be confined entirely to South Vietnam. Our experience in the war thus far leads us to conclude that, in this respect, we are not now giving sufficient attention to the broader area problems of Southeast Asia. The Joint Chiefs of Staff believe that our position in Cambodia, our attitude toward Laos, our actions in Thailand, and our great effort in South Vietnam do not comprise a compatible and integrated US policy for Southeast Asia. US objectives in Southeast Asia cannot be achieved by either economic, political, or military measures alone. All three fields must be integrated into a single, broad US program for Southeast Asia. The measures recommended in this memorandum are a partial contribution to such a program.

8. Currently we and the South Vietnamese are fighting the war on the enemy's terms. He has determined the locale, the timing, and the tactics of the battle while our actions are essentially reactive. One reason for this is the fact that we have obliged ourselves to labor under self-imposed restrictions with respect to impeding external aid to the Viet Cong. These restrictions include keeping the war within the boundaries of South Vietnam, avoiding the direct use of US combat forces, and limiting US direction of the campaign to rendering advice to the Government of Vietnam. These restrictions, while they may make our international position more readily defensible, all tend to make the task in Vietnam more complex, time consuming, and in the end, more costly. In ad-

dition to complicating our own problem, these self-imposed restrictions may well now be conveying signals of irresolution to our enemies—encouraging them to higher levels of vigor and greater risks. A reversal of attitude and the adoption of a more aggressive program would enhance greatly our ability to control the degree to which escalation will occur. It appears probable that the economic and agricultural disappointments suffered by Communist China, plus the current rift with the Soviets, could cause the communists to think twice about undertaking a large-scale military adventure in Southeast Asia.

9. In adverting to actions outside of South Vietnam, the Joint Chiefs of Staff are aware that the focus of the counterinsurgency battle lies in South Vietnam itself, and that the war must certainly be fought and won primarily in the minds of the Vietnamese people. At the same time, the aid now coming to the Viet Cong from outside the country in men, resources, advice, and direction is sufficiently great in the aggregate to be significant—both as help and as encouragement to the Viet Cong. It is our conviction that if support of the insurgency from outside South Vietnam in terms of operational direction, personnel, and material were stopped completely, the character of the war in South Vietnam would be substantially and favorably altered. Because of this conviction, we are wholly in favor of executing the covert actions against North Vietnam which you have recently proposed to the President. We believe, however, that it would be idle to conclude that these efforts will have a decisive effect on the communist determination to support the insurgency; and it is our view that we must therefore be prepared fully to undertake a much higher level of activity, not only for its beneficial tactical effect, but to make plain our resolution, both to our friends and to our enemies.

10. Accordingly, the Joint Chiefs of Staff consider that the United States must make ready to conduct increasingly bolder actions in Southeast Asia; specifically as to Vietnam to:

a. Assign to the US military commander responsibilities for the total US program in Vietnam.

b. Induce the Government of Vietnam to turn over to the United States military commander, temporarily, the actual tactical direction of the war.

c. Charge the United States military commander with complete responsibility for conduct of the program against North Vietnam.

d. Overfly Laos and Cambodia to whatever extent is necessary for acquisition of operational intelligence.

e. Induce the Government of Vietnam to conduct overt ground operations in Laos of sufficient scope to impede the flow of personnel and material southward.

f. Arm, equip, advise, and support the Government of Vietnam in its conduct of aerial bombing of critical targets in North Vietnam and in mining the sea approaches to that country.

g. Advise and support the Government of Vietnam in its conduct of large-scale commando raids against critical targets in North Vietnam.

h. Conduct aerial bombing of key North Vietnam targets, using US resources under Vietnamese cover, and with the Vietnamese openly assuming responsibility for the actions.

i. Commit additional US forces, as necessary, in support of the combat action within South Vietnam.

j. Commit US forces as necessary in direct actions against North Vietnam.

11. It is our conviction that any or all of the foregoing actions may be required to enhance our position in Southeast Asia. The past few months have disclosed that considerably higher levels of effort are demanded of us if US objectives are to be attained.

12. The governmental reorganization which followed the coup d'etat in Saigon should be completed very soon, giving basis for concluding just how strong the Vietnamese Government is going to be and how much of the load they will be able to bear themselves. Additionally, the five-month dry season, which is just now beginning, will afford the Vietnamese an opportunity to exhibit their ability to reverse the unfavorable situation in the critical Mekong Delta. The Joint Chiefs of Staff will follow these important developments closely and will recommend to you progressively the execution of such of the above actions as are considered militarily required, providing, in each case, their detailed assessment of the risks involved.

13. The Joint Chiefs of Staff consider that the strategic importance of Vietnam and of Southeast Asia warrants preparations for the actions above and recommend that the substance of this memorandum be discussed with the Secretary of State.

> For the Joint Chiefs of Staff:
> *Maxwell D. Taylor*
> Chairman
> Joint Chiefs of Staff

[Document 158]

> THE SECRETARY OF DEFENSE
> Washington
> 16 March 1964

MEMORANDUM FOR THE PRESIDENT

SUBJECT: South Vietnam

This report addresses two questions:

1. What is the present situation in Vietnam? (What is the trend of the counterinsurgency program, how stable is the Khanh government, and what is the effectiveness of our current policy of assisting the South Vietnamese Government by economic aid, military training and logistical support?)

2. How can we improve that situation? (What are the plans and prospects of the Khanh government and what more should they be doing, and what more should the U.S. be doing under present or revised policy, in South Vietnam or against North Vietnam?)

To answer the questions, the report will review: I. U.S. Objectives in South Vietnam; II. Present U.S. Policy in South Vietnam; III. The Present Situation; IV. Alternative Present Courses of Action; V. Possible Later Actions; VI. Other Actions Considered But Rejected; and VII. Recommendations.

I. U.S. OBJECTIVES IN SOUTH VIETNAM

We seek an independent non-Communist South Vietnam. We do not require that it serve as a Western base or as a member of a Western Alliance. South

Vietnam must be free, however, to accept outside assistance as required to maintain its security. This assistance should be able to take the form not only of economic and social measures but also police and military help to root out and control insurgent elements.

Unless we can achieve this objective in South Vietnam, almost all of Southeast Asia will probably fall under Communist dominance (all of Vietnam, Laos, and Cambodia), accommodate to Communism so as to remove effective U.S. and anti-Communist influence (Burma), or fall under the domination of forces not now explicitly Communist but likely then to become so (Indonesia taking over Malaysia). Thailand might hold for a period with our help, but would be under grave pressure. Even the Philippines would become shaky, and the threat to India to the west, Australia and New Zealand to the south, and Taiwan, Korea, and Japan to the north and east would be greatly increased.

All of these consequences would probably have been true even if the U.S. had not since 1954, and especially since 1961, become so heavily engaged in South Vietnam. However, that fact accentuates the impact of a Communist South Vietnam not only in Asia, but in the rest of the world, where the South Vietnam conflict is regarded as a test case of U.S. capacity to help a nation meet a Communist "war of liberation."

Thus, purely in terms of foreign policy, the stakes are high. They are increased by domestic factors.

II.   PRESENT U.S. POLICY IN SOUTH VIETNAM

We are now trying to help South Vietnam defeat the Viet Cong, supported from the North, by means short of the unqualified use of U.S. combat forces. We are not acting against North Vietnam except by a very modest "covert" program operated by South Vietnamese (and a few Chinese Nationalists)—a program so limited that it is unlikely to have any significant effect. In Laos, we are still working largely within the framework of the 1962 Geneva Accords. In Cambodia we are still seeking to keep Sihanouk from abandoning whatever neutrality he may still have and fulfilling his threat of reaching an accommodation with Hanoi and Peking. As a consequence of these policies, we and the GVN have had to condone the extensive use of Cambodian and Laotian territory by the Viet Cong, both as a sanctuary and as infiltration routes.

III.   THE PRESENT SITUATION IN SOUTH VIETNAM

The key elements in the present situation are as follows:

A. The military tools and concepts of the GVN/US effort are generally sound and adequate.* Substantially more can be done in the effective employment of military forces and in the economic and civic action areas. These improvements may require some selective increases in the U.S. presence, but it does not appear likely that major equipment replacement and additions in U.S. personnel are indicated under current policy.

B. The U.S. policy of reducing existing personnel where South Vietnamese are in a position to assume the functions is still sound. Its application will not

---

* Mr. McCone emphasizes that the GVN/US program can never be considered completely satisfactory so long as it permits the Viet Cong a sanctuary in Cambodia and a continuing uninterrupted and unmolested source of supply and reinforcement from NVN through Laos.

lead to any major reductions in the near future, but adherence to this policy as such has a sound effect in portraying to the U.S. and the world that we continue to regard the war as a conflict the South Vietnamese must win and take ultimate responsibility for. Substantial reductions in the numbers of U.S. military training personnel should be possible before the end of 1965. However, the U.S. should continue to reiterate that it will provide all the assistance and advice required to do the job regardless of how long it takes.

C. The situation has unquestionably been growing worse, at least since September:

1. In terms of government control of the countryside, about 40% of the territory is under Viet Cong control or predominant influence. In 22 of the 43 provinces, the Viet Cong control 50% or more of the land area, including 80% of Phuoc Tuy; 90% of Binh Duong; 75% of Hau Nghia; 90% of Long An; 90% of Kien Tuong; 90% of Dinh Tuong; 90% of Kien Hoa; and 85% of An Xuyen.

2. Large groups of the population are now showing signs of apathy and indifference, and there are some signs of frustration within the U.S. contingent:

a. The ARVN and paramilitary desertion rates, and particularly the latter, are high and increasing.

b. Draft dodging is high while the Viet Cong are recruiting energetically and effectively.

c. The morale of the hamlet militia and of the Self Defense Corps, on which the security of the hamlets depends, is poor and falling.

3. In the last 90 days the weakening of the government's position has been particularly noticeable. For example:

a. In Quang Nam province, in the I Corps, the militia in 17 hamlets turned in their weapons.

b. In Binh Duong province (III Corps) the hamlet militia were disarmed because of suspected disloyalty.

c. In Binh Dinh province, in the II Corps, 75 hamlets were severely damaged by the Viet Cong (in contrast, during the twelve months ending June 30, 1963, attacks on strategic hamlets were few and none was overrun).

d. In Quang Ngai province, at the northern edge of the II Corps, there were 413 strategic hamlets under government control a year ago. Of that number, 335 have been damaged to varying degrees or fallen into disrepair, and only 275 remain under government control.

e. Security throughout the IV Corps has deteriorated badly. The Viet Cong control virtually all facets of peasant life in the southernmost provinces and the government troops there are reduced to defending the administrative centers. Except in An Giang province (dominated by the Hoa Hao religious sect) armed escort is required for almost all movement in both the southern and northern areas of the IV Corps.

4. The political control structure extending from Saigon down into the hamlets disappeared following the November coup. Of the 41 incumbent province chiefs on November 1, 35 have been replaced (nine provinces had three province chiefs in three months; one province had four). Scores of lesser officials were replaced. Almost all major military commands have changed hands twice since the November coup. The faith of the peasants has been shaken by the disruptions in experienced leadership and the loss

of physical security. In many areas, power vacuums have developed causing confusion among the people and a rising rate of rural disorders.

5. North Vietnamese support, always significant, has been increasing:

a. Communications between Hanoi and the Viet Cong (see classified annex).

b. Since July 1, 1963, the following items of equipment, not previously encountered in South Vietnam, have been captured from the Viet Cong:

Chicom 75 mm. recoilless rifles.

Chicom heavy machine guns.

U.S. .50 caliber heavy machine guns on Chicom mounts.

In addition, it is clear that the Viet Cong are using Chinese 90 mm rocket launchers and mortars.

c. The Viet Cong are importing large quantities of munitions and chemicals for the production of explosives: Approximately 50,000 pounds of explosive-producing chemicals destined for the Viet Cong have been intercepted in the 12 months ending March 1964. On December 24, five tons of ammunition, of which one and one-half tons were 75 mm recoilless rifle ammunition, was captured at the Dinh Tuong Viet Cong arsenal. Ninety percent was of Chicom manufacture.

D. The greatest weakness in the present situation is the uncertain viability of the Khanh government. Khanh himself is a very able man within his experience, but he does not yet have wide political appeal and his control of the Army itself is uncertain (he has the serious problem of the jailed generals). After two coups, as was mentioned above, there has been a sharp drop in morale and organization, and Khanh has not yet been able to build these up satisfactorily. There is a constant threat of assassination or of another coup, which would drop morale and organization nearly to zero.* Whether or not French nationals are actively encouraging such a coup, de Gaulle's position and the continuing pessimism and anti-Americanism of the French community in South Vietnam provide constant fuel to neutralist sentiment and the coup possibility. If a coup is set underway, the odds of our detecting and preventing it in the tactical sense are not high.

E. On the positive side, we have found many reasons for encouragement in the performance of the Khanh government to date. Although its top layer is thin, it is highly responsive to U.S. advice, and with a good grasp of the basic elements of rooting out the Viet Cong. Opposition groups are fragmentary, and Khanh has brought in at least token representation from many key groups hitherto left out. He is keenly aware of the danger of assassination or coup and is taking resourceful steps to minimize these risks. All told, these evidences of energy, comprehension, and decision add up to a sufficiently strong chance of Khanh's really taking hold in the next few months for us to devote all possible energy and resources to his support.

IV. ALTERNATIVE PRESENT COURSES OF ACTION

A. NEGOTIATE ON THE BASIS OF "NEUTRALIZATION"

While de Gaulle has not been clear on what he means by this—and is probably deliberately keeping it vague as he did in working toward an Algerian settle-

---

* Mr. McCone does not believe the dangers of another coup (except as a result of a possible assassination) at this time are as serious as he believes this paragraph implies.

ment—he clearly means not only a South Vietnam that would not be a Western base or part of an alliance structure (both of which we could accept) but also withdrawal of all external military assistance and specifically total U.S. withdrawal. To negotiate on this basis—indeed without specifically rejecting it— would simply mean a Communist take-over in South Vietnam. Only the U.S. presence after 1954 held the South together under far more favorable circumstances, and enabled Diem to refuse to go through with the 1954 provision calling for nationwide "free" elections in 1956. Even talking about a U.S. withdrawal would undermine any chance of keeping a non-Communist government in South Vietnam, and the rug would probably be pulled before the negotiations had gone far.

B. *INITIATE GVN AND U.S. MILITARY ACTIONS AGAINST NORTH VIETNAM*

We have given serious thought to all the implications and ways of carrying out direct military action against North Vietnam in order to supplement the counterinsurgency program in South Vietnam. (The analysis of overt U.S. action is attached as Annex A.) In summary, the actions break down into three categories:

1. Border Control Actions. For example:
    a. An expansion of current authority for Laotian overflights to permit low-level reconnaissance by aircraft when such flights are required to supplement the currently approved U–2 flights.
    b. Vietnamese cross-border ground penetrations into Laos, without the presence of U.S. advisors or re-supply by U.S. aircraft.
    c. Expansion of the patrols into Laos to include use of U.S. advisors and re-supply by U.S. aircraft.
    d. Hot pursuit of VC forces moving across the Cambodian border and destruction of VC bases on the Vietnam/Cambodian line.
    e. Air and ground strikes against selected targets in Laos by South Vietnamese forces.
2. Retaliatory Actions. For example:
    a. Overt high and/or low level reconnaissance flights by U.S. or Farmgate aircraft over North Vietnam to assist in locating and identifying the sources of external aid to the Viet Cong.
    b. Retaliatory bombing strikes and commando raids on a tit-for-tat basis by the GVN against NVN targets (communication centers, training camps, infiltration routes, etc.).
    c. Aerial mining by the GVN aircraft (possibly with U.S. assistance) of the major NVN ports.
3. Graduated Overt Military Pressure by GVN and U.S. Forces.
    This program would go beyond reacting on a tit-for-tat basis. It would include air attacks against military and possibly industrial targets. The program would utilize the combined resources of the GVN Air Force and the U.S. Farmgate Squadron, with the latter reinforced by three squadrons of B–57s presently in Japan. Before this program could be implemented it would be necessary to provide some additional air defense for South Vietnam and to ready U.S. forces in the Pacific for possible escalation.
    The analysis of the more serious of these military actions (from 2(b)

upward) revealed the extremely delicate nature of such operations, both from the military and political standpoints. There would be the problem of marshalling the case to justify such action, the problem of communist escalation, and the problem of dealing with the pressures for premature or "stacked" negotiations. We would have to calculate the effect of such military actions against a specified political objective. That objective, while being cast in terms of eliminating North Vietnamese control and direction of the insurgency, would in practical terms be directed toward collapsing the morale and the self-assurance of the Viet Cong cadres now operating in South Vietnam and bolstering the morale of the Khanh regime. We could not, of course, be sure that our objective could be achieved by any means within the practical range of our options. Moreover, and perhaps most importantly, unless and until the Khanh government has established its position and preferably is making significant progress in the South, an overt extension of operations into the North carries the risk of being mounted from an extremely weak base which might at any moment collapse and leave the posture of political confrontation worsened rather than improved.

The other side of the argument is that the young Khanh government needs the reinforcement of some significant success against the North and without them the in-country program, even with the expansion discussed in Section C below, may not be sufficient to stem the tide.

On balance, except to the extent suggested in Section V below, I recommend against initiation at this time of overt GVN and/or U.S. military actions against North Vietnam.

C. INITIATE MEASURES TO IMPROVE THE SITUATION IN SOUTH VIETNAM

There were and are sound reasons for the limits imposed by present policy—the South Vietnamese must win their own fight; U.S. intervention on a larger scale, and/or GVN actions against the North, would disturb key allies and other nations; etc. In any case, it is vital that we continue to take every reasonable measure to assure success in South Vietnam. The policy choice is not an "either/or" between this course of action and possible pressures against the North; the former is essential without regard to our decision with respect to the latter. The latter can, at best, only reinforce the former.

The following are the actions we believe can be taken in order to improve the situation both in the immediate future and over a longer term period. To emphasize that a new phase has begun, the measures to be taken by the Khanh government should be described by some term such as "South Vietnam's Program for National Mobilization."

Basic U.S. Posture

1. The U.S. at all levels must continue to make it emphatically clear that we are prepared to furnish assistance and support for as long as it takes to bring the insurgency under control.

2. The U.S. at all levels should continue to make it clear that we fully support the Khanh government and are totally opposed to any further coups. The ambassador should instruct all elements, including the military

advisors, to report intelligence information of possible coups promptly, with the decision to be made by the ambassador whether to report such information to Khanh. However, we must recognize that our chances would not be great of detecting and preventing a coup that had major military backing.

3. We should support fully the Pacification Plan now announced by Khanh (described in Annex B), and particularly the basic theory—now fully accepted both on the Vietnamese and U.S. sides—of concentrating on the more secure areas and working out from these through military operations to provide security, followed by necessary civil and economic actions to make the presence of the government felt and to provide economic improvements. This so-called "oil spot" theory is excellent, and its acceptance is a major step forward. However, it is necessary to push hard to get specific instructions out to the provinces, so that there is real unity of effort at all levels. A related matter is to stabilize the assignment of province chiefs and senior commanders and clarify their responsibilities and relationships.

Many of the actions described in succeeding paragraphs fit right into the framework of the Plan as announced by Khanh. Wherever possible, we should tie our urging of such actions to Khanh's own formulation of them, so that he will be carrying out a Vietnamese plan and not one imposed by the U.S.

Civil and Military Mobilization

4. To put the whole nation on a war footing—to obtain the manpower for these efforts described below and to remedy present inequities and inadequacies in the use of manpower—a new National Mobilization Plan (to include a National Service Law) should be urgently developed by the Country Team in collaboration with the Khanh Government. The present structure of decrees, dating from the Diem Government, is haphazard and produces substantial injustices. The new Program for National Mobilization would both greatly increase the effectiveness of the war effort and be a strong visible sign of the Government's determination and will. Full attention should be given to the way it is presented so that it appears as a remedy for past injustices and not as a repressive or totalitarian act.

5. The strength of the Armed Forces (regular plus paramilitary) must be increased by at least 50,000 men. About 15,000 of these are required to fill the regular Armed Forces (ARVN) to their present authorized strength. Another 5,000 would fill the existing paramilitary forces to authorized strengths. The balance of 30,000 men is required to increase the strength of the paramilitary forces, in whatever form these may be organized (see paragraph 7 below). (All of the foregoing strength figures are illustrative and subject to review, which review I have directed General Harkins to make in consultation with General Khanh.)

6. A Civil Administrative Corps is urgently required to work in the provincial capitals, the district towns, the villages, and the hamlets. "Hamlet civic action teams" of five men each are now beginning to be trained, on a small scale, to go into hamlets after they have been cleared, start the rehabilitation process, and train hamlet leaders to carry on. School teachers and health technicians are now assigned in some hamlets, many more are needed, and those on the job need to be retrained to higher com-

petence. Many other types of technicians (e.g., agricultural workers) are needed, in varying numbers. Taking into account the fact that many hamlets are not now secure, and that adequate training is required, the initial goal during 1964 should be at least 7,500 additional persons; the ultimate target, at least 40,000 men for the 8,000 hamlets, in 2500 villages and 43 provinces. The administrators would come largely from the areas in which they serve and would be paid by the national government. The U.S. should work with the GVN urgently to devise the necessary recruiting plans, training facilities, financing methods, and organizational arrangements, and should furnish training personnel at once, under the auspices of the AID Mission. Further, maximum effort should be made to make use of the available trained personnel by assignment to provincial and village administration where needed.

Improved Military Forces

7. The paramilitary forces are now understrength and lacking in effectiveness. They must be improved and reorganized.

Specifically:

a. What remains of the present hamlet militia (and related forces of a part-time nature for hamlet defense) should be consolidated with the Self Defense Corps into a single force compensated by the national government.

b. Pay and collateral benefits must be substantially improved at once. A reasonable course of action would be to raise the pay scale of the Civil Guard approximately to that of the regular Armed Forces, and to raise the pay scale of a reorganized Self Defense Corps approximately to the present level of the Civil Guard. In addition, measures should be taken to improve the housing and allowances of the families of both forces, so that they can live decently in areas near where the forces are operating.

c. Strength should be maintained and expanded by conscription, effectively enforced, and by more centrally directed recruitment policies.

d. Additional U.S. personnel should be assigned to the training of all these paramilitary forces.

e. The National Police require special consideration. Their strength in the provinces should be substantially increased and consideration should be given to including them as part of an overall "Popular Defense Force." In expanding and improving the police, the AID Mission should make special arrangements to draw on the advice of the present British training mission under Brigadier Thompson because of its experience in Malaya. (Mr. Bell has instructed Mr. Brent, the USOM Chief, to accomplish this.)

8. An offensive Guerrilla force should be created to operate along the border and in areas where VC control is dominant. Such a force could be organized around present Ranger Companies and ARVN Special Forces and provided with special training and advice by U.S. Special Forces. The force should carry the fight to the VC on their own basis in advance of clear-and-hold operations on the conventional pattern.

Additional Military Equipment for the GVN

9. The Vietnamese Air Force should be strengthened at once by the substitution of 25 A–1H aircraft for the present 25 T–28s. The A–1H aircraft has a much greater bomb load and slightly better speed.*

10. Although there are no major equipment deficiencies in other forces, we should act at once to replace the present M–114 armored personnel carriers by 63 M–113s and to provide additional river boats. Additional lesser deficiencies should also be met at an estimated cost of approximately $10 million.

Economic Actions

11. The approved, but unannounced, Fertilizer Program should be particularly stressed and expanded and publicly announced. Its target of 85,000 tons for the present planting season (April–June) should probably be doubled for the next season and trebled the following season, both to provide immediate and direct benefits to peasants in secure areas and to improve the rice crops and export earnings. Estimates are that an additional ton of fertilizer costing around $70 can, if properly applied, produce additional yield of an equivalent two tons of rice, which might be sold for $110 per ton. Thus, the potential export improvement alone could be on the order of $20 million from this year's 85,000 ton input.

US and GVN Costs of the Above Actions

The above actions will involve a limited increase in U.S. personnel and in direct Defense Department costs. More significantly, they involve significant increase in Military Assistance Program costs and in the budget of the GVN itself, with the latter requiring additional US economic aid. The estimates of additional annual costs are as follows:

Action	*GVN Budget Costs*	*Cost to U.S.*
a. Raise military and paramilitary numbers and pay scales	5–6 billion piastres	$30–40 million†
b. Enlarge civil administrative cadre	250 million piastres (1st year)	$1,500,000 (first year)
c. Furnish additional military equipment		$20 million (one time)

* Concurrently, the effectiveness of the USAF's Farmgate operation will be increased by assignment of A–1E aircraft in replacement of B–26s and T–28s. Furthermore, in another important area, we are strengthening the U.S. intelligence and reporting system.

† Increases in GVN budget expenditures do not automatically require equal increases in U.S. economic aid. As a rough approximation, subject to later refinement, an increase of 5–6 billion piastres of GVN budget expenditures might require an increase of $30–40 million worth of imports financed through U.S. economic aid. Some of the imports undoubtedly could be obtained under P.L. 480.

Conclusion

If the Khanh Government can stay in power and the above actions can be carried out rapidly, it is my judgment that the situation in South Vietnam can be significantly improved in the next four to six months. The present deterioration may continue for a part of this period, but I believe it can be levelled out and some improvement will become visible during the period. I therefore believe that this course of action should be urgently pursued while we prepare such additional actions as may be necessary for success.

V. POSSIBLE LATER ACTIONS

If the Khanh government takes hold vigorously—inspiring confidence, whether or not noteworthy progress has been made—or if we get hard information of significantly stepped-up VC arms supply from the North, we may wish to mount new and significant pressures against North Vietnam. We should start preparations for such a capability now. (See Annex C for an analysis of the situation in North Vietnam and Communist China.) Specifically, we should develop a capability to initiate within 72 hours the "Border Control" * and "Retaliatory Actions" referred to on pages 5 and 6, and we should achieve a capability to initiate with 30 days' notice the program of "Graduated Overt Military Pressure." The reasoning behind this program of preparations for initiating action against North Vietnam is rooted in the fact that, even with progress in the pacification plan, the Vietnamese Government and the population in the South will still have to face the prospect of a very lengthy campaign based on a war-weary nation and operating against Viet Cong cadres who retain a great measure of motivation and assurance.

In this connection, General Khanh stated that his primary concern is to establish a firm base in the South. He favors continuation of covert activities against North Vietnam, but until such time as "rear-area security" has been established, he does not wish to engage in overt operations against the North.

In order to accelerate the realization of pacification and particularly in order to denigrate the morale of the Viet Cong forces, it may be necessary at some time in the future to put demonstrable retaliatory pressure on the North. Such a course of action might proceed according to the scenario outlined in Annex D.

VI. OTHER ACTIONS CONSIDERED BUT REJECTED

We have considered the following actions, but rejected them for the time being except to the extent indicated below:

1. *Return of Dependents.* We recommend that the present policy be continued of permitting dependents to return home on a voluntary basis, but not ordering them to do so. The security situation in Saigon appears to have improved significantly, and ordering dependents home would now, in the universal judgment of our senior people in Saigon, have a serious impact on South Vietnamese morale. It would also raise a serious question whether tours of duty for AID personnel would not have to be shortened. Thus, unless there are further serious incidents, or unless we were taking more drastic

---

* Authority should be granted immediately for covert Vietnamese operations into Laos, for the purposes of border control and of "hot pursuit" into Laos. Decision on "hot pursuit" into Cambodia should await further study of our relations with that country.

measures generally, we believe compulsory return should not be undertaken.

2. *Furnishing a U.S. Combat Unit to Secure the Saigon Area.* It is the universal judgment of our senior people in Saigon, with which we concur, that this action would now have serious adverse psychological consequences and should not be undertaken.

3. *U.S. Taking Over Command.* It has been suggested that the U.S. move from its present advisory role to a role that would amount in practice to effective command. Again, the judgment of all senior people in Saigon with which we concur, is that the possible military advantages of such action would be far outweighed by its adverse psychological impact. It would cut across the whole basic picture of the Vietnamese winning their own war and lay us wide open to hostile propaganda both within South Vietnam and outside. Moreover, the present responsiveness of the GVN to our advice—although it has not yet reduced military reaction time—makes it less urgent. At the same time, MACV is steadily taking actions to bring U.S. and GVN operating staffs closer together at all levels, including joint operating rooms at key command levels.

VII.   RECOMMENDATIONS

I recommend that you instruct the appropriate agencies of the U.S. Government:

1. To make it clear that we are prepared to furnish assistance and support to South Vietnam for as long as it takes to bring the insurgency under control.

2. To make it clear that we fully support the Khanh government and are opposed to any further coups.

3. To support a Program for National Mobilization (including a national service law) to put South Vietnam on a war footing.

4. To assist the Vietnamese to increase the armed forces (regular plus paramilitary) by at least 50,000 men.

5. To assist the Vietnamese to create a greatly enlarged Civil Administrative Corps for work at province, district and hamlet levels.

6. To assist the Vietnamese to improve and reorganize the paramilitary forces and to increase their compensation.

7. To assist the Vietnamese to create an offensive guerrilla force.

8. To provide the Vietnamese Air Force 25 A-1H aircraft in exchange for the present T-28s.

9. To provide the Vietnamese Army additional M-113 armored personnel carriers (withdrawing the M-114s there), additional river boats, and approximately $5–10 million of other additional material.

10. To announce publicly the Fertilizer Program and to expand it with a view within two years to trebling the amount of fertilizer made available.

11. To authorize continued high-level U.S. overflights of South Vietnam's borders and to authorize "hot pursuit" and South Vietnamese ground operations over the Laotian line for the purpose of border control. More ambitious operations into Laos involving units beyond battalion size should be authorized only with the approval of Souvanna Phouma. Operations across the Cambodian border should depend on the state of relations with Cambodia.

12. To prepare immediately to be in a position on 72 hours' notice to initiate the full range of Laotian and Cambodian "Border Control" actions

(beyond those authorized in paragraph 11 above) and the "Retaliatory Actions" against North Vietnam, and to be in a position on 30 days' notice to initiate the program of "Graduated Overt Military Pressure" against North Vietnam.

Robert S. McNamara

[Document 159]

Date: 18 March 1964

FM: JCS 5390
    (M/Gen F. T. Unger)

TO: CINCPAC

Refs: a. JCS 5375;
      b. OPLAN 34A;
      c. OPLAN 33;
      d. OPLAN 99;
      e. JCS 2343/326-6.

Subj: Planning Actions, Viet Nam

1. As a result of approval of recommendations in paragraph 12, section VII, reference a, planning for military actions in support of RVN has been identified in the following categories:
    a. Border control actions
    b. Retaliatory actions
    c. Graduated overt military pressures.
    In light of the above, planning for current and future military actions in support of the RVN must be aligned with the appropriate categories. It is appreciated that elements of several of these actions are contained in several extant plans (refs b, c, and d); however, these must now be drawn together in a cohesive plan or plans to permit sequential implementation as may be desired by higher authority within categories above. JCS views on operations in para c above are contained in ref e.
    2. The product of the new planning should include:
    a. Mission and objectives
    b. Time-phased US and GVN deployments, pre-positioning and augmentation required to implement envisaged operations, as well as to deter enemy reaction, within the time parameters of para 12, Section VII, ref a. (Time parameters are now under review and may be changed.)
    c. Complete target lists together with desired damage criteria as well as impact on enemy capability; or specific objective area.
    d. Actions to be taken in event of enemy escalation.
    e. US support required for unilateral RVNAF operations.
    f. Reconnaissance operations and planning.
    3. Planning should be in such detail as to permit review of individual actions or small increments in progressing through operations outlined above. As a matter of urgency, it is requested that planning be undertaken in the following order: border control actions, retaliatory actions, and graduated overt military pressures, and that elements of planning be forwarded to the JCS as completed. Request ASAP your schedule for completion of planning actions.

[Document 160]

Date: 20 March 1964

FM: State 1484 (The Secretary)

TO: Saigon

For Ambassador Lodge from the President

1. We have studied your 1776 and I am asking State to have Bill Bundy make sure that you get out latest planning documents on ways of applying pressure and power against the North. I understand that some of this was discussed with you by McNamara mission in Saigon, but as plans are refined it would be helpful to have your detailed comments. As we agreed in our previous messages to each other, judgment is reserved for the present on overt military action in view of the consensus from Saigon conversations of McNamara mission with General Khanh and you on judgment that movement against the North at the present would be premature. We have share General Khanh's judgment that the immediate and essential task is to strengthen the southern base. For this reason our planning for action against the North is on a contingency basis at present, and immediate problem in this area is to develop the strongest possible military and political base for possible later action. There is additional international reason for avoiding immediate overt action in that we expect a showdown between the Chinese and Soviet Communist parties soon and action against the North will be more practicable after than before a showdown. But if at any time you feel that more immediate action is urgent, I count on you to let me know specifically the reasons for such action, together with your recommendations for its size and shape.

2. On dealing with deGaulle, I continue to think it may be valuable for you to go to Paris after Bohlen has made his first try. (State is sending you draft instruction to Bohlen, which I have not yet reviewed, for your comment.) It ought to be possible to explain in Saigon that your mission is precisely for the purpose of knocking down the idea of neutralization wherever it rears its ugly head, and on this point I think that nothing is more important than to stop neutralist talk wherever we can by whatever means we can. I have made this point myself to Mansfield and Lippmann and I expect to use every public opportunity to restate our position firmly. You may want to convey our concern on this point to General Khanh and get his ideas on the best possible joint program to stop such talk in Saigon, in Washington, and in Paris. I imagine that you have kept General Khanh abreast of our efforts in Paris. After we see the results of the Bohlen approach you might wish to sound him out on Paris visit by you.

[Document 161]

Summary of JCSM-426-64, 19 May 1964

"North Vietnam Operations"

JCS appraised "achievements and limitations" of first 3 months of 34A operations: Overall objective cited as "to help convince NVN leadership that it is in its own self-interest to desist from its aggressive policies." "Ancillary objectives": (1) to gain more info (2) intensify current psychological war and resistance operations to weaken Hanoi's control of the population of NVN and commit regime to costly counter-measures.

Past three months indicate "slow beginning." "There are, however, indications that attempts at infiltration and continuing psychological activities, together with widespread press and radio speculation over the extension of the war, have had an effect /?/ on the DRV. Its reaction tends to substantiate the premise that Hanoi is expending substantial resources in defensive war."

JCS conclude: (1) GVN's general lack of program direction caused by 30 January coup; (2) program begun before special material and personnel required were assembled; (3) overflights of Laos essential to it for operational reasons; (4) bad weather and insufficient intelligence have hampered operations; (5) "potential of the program remains high."

JCS advocate continuing for Phase II period (Jan thru Sep) "at rate commensurate with growing operational capacities of MACV and GVN forces. (Electronic intelligence; sabotage teams; C-123 airlift; NASTY PT craft; all cited as new and invaluable resources available to program.) VNAF air strikes recommended.

[Document 162]

25 July 1964

From: Saigon 214

To: State

The GVN public campaign for "Marching North" (reported EMBTEL 201) may take several courses. In the face of US coolness and absence of evidence of real grass roots support outside certain military quarters, it may die down for a while although it is hardly likely to disappear completely. On the other hand, the proponents of a "Quick Solution" may be able to keep it alive indefinitely as an active issue, in which case it is likely to foment an increasing amount of dissatisfaction with the US, (assuming that we continue to give it no support) to the serious detriment of our working relations with the GVN and hence to the ultimate chances of success of the in-country pacification program. In such a case, Vietnamese leaders in and out of government, unable to find a vent to their frustration in "Marching North," may seek other panaceas in various forms of negotiation formulas. General Khanh may find in the situation an excuse or a requirement to resign.

Finally, this "March North" fever can get out of hand in an act of rashness —one Maverick pilot taking off for Hanoi with a load of bombs—which could touch off an extension of hostilities at a time and in a form most disadvantageous to US interests.

Faced with these unattractive possibilities, we propose a course of action designed to do several things.

We would try to avoid head-on collision with the GVN which unqualified US opposition to the "March North" campaign would entail. We could do this by expressing a willingness to engage in joint contingency planning for various forms of extended action against GVN. Such planning would not only provide an outlet for the martial head of steam now dangerously compressed but would force the generals to look at the hard facts of life which lie behind the neon lights of the "March North" slogans. This Planning would also gain time badly needed to stabilize this government and could provide a useful basis for military action if adjudged in our interest at some future time. Finally, it would also afford US an opportunity, for the first time, to have a frank discussion with GVN leaders concerning the political objectives which they would envisage as the purposes inherent in military action against the DRV. We do not really know whether they feel that Viet-nam can indeed be unified by military action, or whether such action is intended only to introduce a pressure which would be equivalent to Viet Cong terror in order to induce DRV to desist for aiding VC and to improve bargaining opportunities for a political negotiation wtih Hanoi.

It would be important, however, in initiating such a line of action that we make a clear record that we are not repeat not assuming any commitment to implement such plans. Therefore, I would recommend that I be authorized to give General Khanh the following written statement:

"The United States Government has noted recent public statements by various leaders of the Republic of Vietnam proposing military action against the sources of aggression in North Vietnam. The reasons which have prompted these statements are clear and the impatience of the people of the Republic of Vietnam in the face of continuing subversive warfare from the North is understandable.

"In considering ways and means to bring the Viet Cong insurgency under control, authorities in Washington have given serious study over a considerable period to the question of bringing military pressure to bear on the leaders of North Vietnam. It has been their conclusion that this is a complex problem involving judgments and decisions in both the political and military fields which neither the United States nor Vietnam can take independently. The current activity of the United States Government consists in the provision of massive assistance to your government in the extension of its ICRCNNTPI (as received) approved pacification programs in South Vietnam. The question of extending this assistance by the United States Government to a program of action outside the territorial limits of South Vietnam has not been seriously discussed up to now, but it is my belief that the time has come for giving the matter a thorough analysis.

"In the view of the United States Government, the best method of producing such an analysis would be in the form of a joint contingency planning study, undertaken by appropriate representatives of our two governments, without advance commitments by either side as to subsequent actions. If the government of the Republic of Vietnam agrees, the government of the United States has authorized me to appoint representatives who would be able to meet, under conditions of maximum discretion and security, with representatives of the Republic of Vietnam to undertake such discussions."

It is my opinion that such discussions, if initiated with responsible Vietnamese officials, would not only develop some of the fundamental political thinking which is currently motivating the Vietnamese leadership, but would also reveal the need for the completion of a number of preliminary actions which should be taken before serious consideration can be given to expanding the war. Such actions should include the absorption of the new AIH aircraft by November 1, the filling of the ranks of understrength ARVN units, air defense measures for urban centers and the establishment of a greater degree of control over the VC than now exists in order to secure the rear and flanks of fighting forces.

It would be most helpful if approval for the above statement can be received to permit its use at my next meeting with Khanh scheduled for 1600 July 27 (Saigon Time).

[Document 163]

26 July 1964

TO: Vientiane

FROM: State 89

1. Primarily for reasons of morale in South Vietnam and to divert GVN attention from proposal to strike North Vietnam, we are considering proposing to Ambassador Taylor that he discuss with Khanh air attacks on VC supply lines in the Laotian Panhandle. For meeting of Secretaries, request by 0600 our time Monday your views on such operations, your estimate of reaction of Souvanna and other Lao leaders, and your advice as to best way to obtain Souvanna's acquiescence.

2. Our preliminary views as to possible air attacks are as follows:

a. The military objective would be to interdict and destroy facilities supporting infiltration into SVN. (It is possible that the political objective might be achieved by fewer targets and/or sorties than indicated below.)

b. Initial targets, which would be programmed for moderate to severe damage, would probably be Muong Phine army barracks (12 sorties), Ban Thay military camp and 4 AAA gun emplacements (18 sorties), Ban Na Nhom military camp (12 sorties), Tchepone army barracks (68 sorties), Muong Nong military area (10 sorties), and Ban Trim barracks and supply area (34 sorties). Also considering Mu Gia border control point just inside North Vietnam (14 sorties). At same time, attacks of opportunity would be carried out on lines of communication by armed reconnaissance.

c. Aircraft would be either A1H with only GVN pilots, or A1H plus A1E with American instructors also aboard in case of A1Es. Our present thinking does not RPT not include use of Lao T-28s.

d. Armament would be napalm unless politically unacceptable, in which case armament would be less effective conventional bombs, rockets and 20 mm.

e. Estimate that attacks could begin in early August and could, without serious degration of air support for pacification in SVN, be carried out at rate of 20 sorties a day. Our proposal, however, may be that strikes be conducted on intermittent basis at a slower rate than indicated depending on political requirements.

f. Estimated aircraft losses at less than two per cent in early stages, meaning that some planes will probably be downed in Laos during attacks on initial targets.

g. We may recommend certain readiness measures in Laos and Thailand to cope with possible communist reaction or escalation (e.g., PL moves on Panhandle towns or even toward Mekong).

h. It is assumed that attacks would promptly become known and responsibility would be acknowledged by GVN; that if US instructors are on board, US would acknowledge this fact; that operation would be justified on grounds of infiltration of personnel and supplies through corridor in violation of Geneva Accords; and that we would publicize relevant evidence from photography and POW interrogation. We would hope Souvanna would publicly support such a rationale but at minimum would do or say nothing to undermine it.

3. As you know, joint US–GVN planning is underway not only for air attacks but also for ground operations up to battalion size in Panhandle. We may be querying you shortly for your reaction regarding such ground operations.

[Document 164]

27 July 1964

FM: Vientiane 170

TO: State

REF: Deptel 89

Air attacks on Viet Cong supply lines in Laotian Panhandle, while helping morale South Vietnam and diverting government there from its proposals to strike North Vietnam, would have only marginal effect on problem on infiltration via Laos and would greatly complicate Laotian situation which already threatens get out of hand as result Soviet threat withdraw from Co-Chairman role.

When various cross-border actions proposed earlier, also including air strikes, I pointed out fundamental attitude of Souvanna, which generally shared by Lao, that use of corridor, even though involving Lao territory, not primarily their problem, and anyway they have their hands full trying to protect heart of their country for defense of which corridor not essential. Our creating new military as well as inter-national political conflict over corridor will be regarded by them as another instance Laos being involuntarily involved in struggle among big powers on matter outside Laos' own prime interests. There is hope Souvanna's view (no doubt nurtured by French) that GVN is fighting a hopeless war.

Souvanna Phouma and other Lao leaders want help in immediate present to assure they can continue in secure possession of present territory of free Laos. If any new military initiatives are contemplated with attendant risk of escalation they would wish above all that they be directed at retaking Plaine des Jarres. More immediately they want maximum effort be made to cut route seven and they also wish be assured of fullest support for Muong Soui if again actively threatened, to say nothing of protection of routes toward Mekong if Muong Soui falls.

Likely reaction to proposals for air attacks in corridor would be: Why complicate our problem and risk creating dangerous military threat in central and southern areas where it does not now exist; why does not US apply its power to source of problem and bomb Hanoi or move effectively in some other way against North Vietnam? North Vietnam is cause of trouble and ought to be target; moreover we are not bound by international agreements there as we are in Laos. Department will recall this line of thinking has been pressed by Iking and Souvanna Phouma and is undoubtedly view even more strongly held by right wing leaders.

In this connection, wish point out with respect para g reftel that there are virtually no uncommitted Lao resources to deal with whatever PL/VM reaction may be. Energies and staff capacity as well as troops and planes are tied down in operation triangle and literally only reserve in country is two DNC para battalions which for political reasons unlikely leave Vientiane. Therefore preparedness measures in Laos would have to be taken by US.

Thus if we proceed with projected action Panhandle we must be prepared also to meet any responsible Lao request for help in defending what they regard as part of their country. If we hesitate under such circumstances Souvanna's occasional dissatisfaction with what he has regarded as foot dragging by US will be greatly accentuated and arguments on our part that certain actions should be avoided because of international complications or risks of escalation will not carry much weight. Nothing could illustrate point better than question Napalm, which being proposed for use in corridor operation at same time, I am obliged turn down request from Souvanna to use it in area he considers vital for defense his country.

In view foregoing I believe proposed action would probably bring to an end possibility our preserving even facade of government national union under Souvanna and Geneva Accords, keeping open possible road back to peaceful solution and avoiding resumption full scale civil war. There certainly has been no sign from Pathet Lao, DRV or Chicoms of any change in their attitude to encourage US to believe they are ready to start living by Geneva Accords and end their interference in Laos. Nevertheless it has been our hope that our recent assumption of stiffer political posture and careful application of stronger military measures would at least bring nibbling to an end. However, as result initiatives in corridor we may find ourselves turned entirely away from guiding principles of last two years under which we have accepted uneasy equilibrium of de facto division of Laos as best we could get for present and better than resumption large scale fighting. Following strikes in Panhandle we might even find ourselves being pressed hard into a major military effort aimed at pushing North Vietnamese out of Panhandle (when it becomes clear air attacks do not halt infiltration) and eventually entirely out of Laos and reestablishing authority of RLG throughout country.

I realize proposed action envisages employment primarily GVN personnel but from international point of view we must be prepared accept full responsibility. Action will also solidly link questions Laos and South Vietnam which at earlier date we appeared to be intent on keeping separate as possible, at least in context any international discussion.

From here it is difficult to see what all international repercussions of projected Panhandle action might be but I can foresee serious complications with British and Canadians on whom we depend for Co-Chairman and ICC help. They may well ask US to demonstrate that the installations to be hit have some important connection with infiltration problem and that strikes will appreciably improve situation South Vietnam. On other hand they will be most apprehensive about dangers of escalation as well as major complications in handling international aspects of problem as illustrated by Soviet note just received.

Souvanna's acquiescence in proposed action not be enough. If we proceed he will undoubtedly be beseiged by press and posture of PriMin of Laos can only be acquiescence in other countries' taking action on his territory. If we are to make effort to bring him along, his position would have to be supported in advance by build up of public evidence of use of corridor and its aggravation of problem in SVN. Public indications that corridor problem really much less than represented (for example see July 26 wireless file story by Robert Brunn, C. S. Monitor) must also be overcome. Against this background we might try sell Souvanna on line that action against corridor is fundamental to resolving what is basic cause of Laos' present plight, namely war in South Vietnam. In other words, block corridor so that GVN can again assume full authority over its territory at which point DRV can make no further use of corridor. Unless Souvanna can be persuaded action in Panhandle really serves his cause more than it endangers it, his support will be very hard to secure. Even if support is squeezed out (perhaps only as result of right wing pressure), his remaining on the job becomes problematical.

Specific comments follow:
(1) Delete Muong Phine from target list para 2B because of probable presence there of C-46 survivors.
(2) Foregoing reservations do not apply to Mu Gia control point or other points inside North Vietnam.
(3) Attacks of opportunity on convoys (if related to RECCE flights) and responsive strikes to ground fire would be less objectionable than proposed action, and this would be even truer of T-28 strikes.
In summary, I believe it would be exceptionally difficult to persuade Souvanna Phouma to approve stepped up military actions in Panhandle without triggering virtually irresistible pressures for similar escalation in this part of Laos, involving increased commitments here of sort we have thus far shied away from. Perhaps we can successfully withstand these pressures, but more likely outcome, in my judgment, would be heightened political instability and a situation in which we might well lose Souvanna and the international recognition has government commands, ending up with albatross around our neck in form of rightist regime lacking in international support and able to survive internal and external pressures only with our outright military support.

[Document 165]

5 Aug 64

RULES OF ENGAGEMENT

A. JCS 7700

B. CINCPAC INSTR 03710.2 OF 24 MAY 1961

C. CINCPAC 04

D. JCS 2084/80 OF 1 JUL 1964

E. JCS 3796 MAR 62

1. Events in Gulf of Tonkin accentuate need for clarification and changing rules of engagement under which US forces must operate in situations short of open hostilities.
2. Following are rules of engagement currently in effect as understood here:
A. Situation: unprovoked attack by hostile vessels against vessels in international waters.
(1) Rule: US vessels authorized to defend, pursue and destroy attacking vessels up to 11 miles from NVN coast and 4 miles from offshore islands. US aircraft authorized to pursue and destroy attacking vessels while operating in airspace up to 3 miles from NVN coast. Authorized by ref A.
B. Situation: unprovoked attack by hostile aircraft against U.S. vessels, aircraft, or personnel.
(1) Rule: US aircraft authorized to take immediate and aggressive protective measures, including immediate pursuit into hostile airspace if necessary and feasible. Authorized by ref B and C in case of attacks against any US forces; page 11 of reference D in case of attacks against US aircraft only. (Note: there are no geographic restrictions on U.S. aircraft in case of attacks by hostile aircraft).

C. Situation: overflight of RVN by hostile aircraft.

(1) Rule: US aircraft operating in RVN authorized to engage and destroy hostile aircraft within airspace over RVN territorial airspace. Authorized by ref E (original R/E for water glass/candy machine).

3. Above compilation of current rules indicates following voids which should be filled ASAP.

A. There are no R/E for intercept, pursuit and destruction of hostile aircraft which violate Thailand airspace.

B. US forces intercepting hostile aircraft over RVN are not authorized immediate pursuit outside of RVN territorial airspace.

4. Recommend following R/E be promulgated:

A. R/E to authorize US forces based in Thailand or operating within Thailand airspaces to intercept, engage and destroy hostile aircraft, to include immediate pursuit into hostile airspace if necessary and feasible. Such rules would, of course, require concurrence of rtg. R/E for RVN (ref E) could serve as model, with minor modifications.

B. Amend ref E to include immediate pursuit into hostile airspace.

5. General comments.

A. Hostile forces which initiate unprovoked attacks against our forces whether on the high seas or ashore should not be afforded sanctuary from which they can repeat the attack. The best way to preclude repeated attacks is to pursue and destroy the attackers. Such action is not punitive per se but primarily defensive. For self protection, US forces should be authorized immediate and unrestricted pursuit.

[Document 166]

TO: Vientiane   Aug 7 '64

FROM: State 136   ACTION: Amembassy VIENTIANE

LIMDIS

1. As pointed out in your 219, our objective in Laos is to stabilize the situation again, if possible within framework of the 1962 Geneva settlement. Essential to stabilization would be establishment of military equilibrium in the country. Moreover, we have some concern that recent RLG successes and reported low PL morale may lead to some escalation from Communist side, which we do not now wish to have to deal with.

2. Until now, Souvanna's and our position has been that military equilibrium would require Pathet Lao withdrawal from areas seized in PDJ since May 15 and that such withdrawal is also basic precondition to convening 14-nation conference. Question now arises whether territorial gains of Operation Triangle, provided they can be consolidated, have in practice brought about a situation of equilibrium and whether, therefore, it is no longer necessary to insist on Pathet Lao withdrawal from PDJ as precondition to 14-nation conference. This is in fact thought which has previously occurred to Souvanna (Vientiane's 191) and is also touched on in Secretary's letter to Butler (Deptel 88 to Vientiane). If Souvanna and we continued to insist on PDJ withdrawal other side would inevitably insist on our yielding Triangle gains, and our judgment is that such arrangement substantially worse than present fairly coherent geographical division. If withdrawal precondition were to be dropped, it could probably best be

done at tripartite meeting where it might be used by Souvanna as bargaining counter in obtaining satisfaction on his other condition that he attend conference as head of Laotian Government. Remaining condition would be cease-fire. While under present conditions cease-fire might not be of net advantage to Souvanna—we are thinking primarily of T–28 operations—Pathet Lao would no doubt insist on it. If so, Souvanna could press for effective ICC policing of cease-fire. Latter could be of importance in upcoming period.

3. Above is written with thought in mind that Polish proposals have effectively collapsed and that pressures continue for Geneva-type conference and will no doubt be intensified by current crisis brought on by DRV naval attacks. Conference on Laos might be useful safety valve for these generalized pressures while at same time providing some deterrent to escalation of hostilities on that part of the "front." We would insist that conference be limited to Laos and believe that it could in fact be so limited, if necessary by our withdrawing from the conference room if any other subject brought up, as we did in 1961–62. Side discussions on other topics could not be avoided but we see no great difficulty with this; venue for informal corridor discussions with PL, DRV, and Chicoms could be valuable at this juncture.

4. In considering this course of action, key initial question is of course whether Souvanna himself is prepared to drop his withdrawal precondition and whether, if he did, he could maintain himself in power in Vientiane. We gather that answer to first question is probably yes but we are much more dubious about the second. Request Vientiane's judgment on these points. Views of other addressees are so requested, including estimated reactions host governments. It is essential that these estimates take account of recent developments: military successes non-communist forces in Laos and latest demonstration US determination resist communist aggression in Southeast Asia.

END

RUSK

[Document 167]

Draft
8/7/64 McNaughton

EMBASSY OTTAWA IMMEDIATE EX DIS

You should ask Seaborn during August 10 visit to make following points (as having been conveyed to him by US Government since August 6):

A. Re Tonkin Gulf actions, which almost certainly will come up:

1. The DRV has stated that Hon Ngu and Hon Me islands were attacked on July 30. It should be noted that the USS MADDOX was, all of that day and into the afternoon of the next day, over 100 miles south of those islands, in international waters near the 17th Parallel, and that the DRV attack on the MADDOX took place on August 2nd, more than two days later. The destroyer was not in any way associated with any attack on the DRV islands.

2. Regarding the August 4 attack by the DRV on the two US destroyers, the Americans were and are at a complete loss to understand the DRV motive. They had decided to absorb the August 2 attack on the grounds that it very well might have been the result of some DRV mistake or miscalculation. The August 4 attack, however—from the determined nature of the attack as indicated by the radar, sonar, and eye witness evidence both from the ships and from their protecting aircraft—was, in the American eyes, obviously deliberate and planned and ordered in advance. In addition, premeditation was shown by the evidence

that the DRV craft were waiting in ambush for the destroyers. The attack did not seem to be in response to any action by the South Vietnamese nor did it make sense as a tactic to further any diplomatic objective. Since the attack took place at least 60 miles from nearest land, there could have been no question about territorial waters. About the only reasonable hypothesis was that North Vietnam was intent either upon making it appear that the United States was a "paper tiger" or upon provoking the United States.

3. The American response was directed solely to patrol craft and installations acting in direct support of them. As President Johnson stated: "Our response for the present will be limited and fitting."

4. In view uncertainty aroused by the deliberate and unprovoked DRV attacks this character, US has necessarily carried out precautionary deployments of additional air power to SVN and Thailand.

B. Re basic American position:

5. Mr. Seaborn should again stress that US policy is simply that North Vietnam should contain itself and its ambitions within the territory allocated to its administration by the 1954 Geneva Agreements. He should stress that US policy in South Vietnam is to preserve the integrity of that state's territory against guerrilla subversion.

6. He should reiterate that the US does not seek military bases in the area and that the US is not seeking to overthrow the Communist regime in Hanoi.

7. He should repeat that the US is fully aware of the degree to which Hanoi controls and directs the guerrilla action in South Vietnam and that the US holds Hanoi directly responsible for that action. He should similarly indicate US awareness of North Vietnamese control over the Pathet Lao movement in Laos and the degree of North Vietnamese involvement in that country. He should specifically indicate US awareness of North Vietnamese violations of Laotian territory along the infiltration route into South Vietnam.

8. Mr. Seaborn can again refer to the many examples of US policy in tolerance of peaceful coexistence with Communist regimes, such as Yugoslavia, Poland, etc. He can hint at the economic and other benefits which have accrued to those countries because their policy of Communism has confined itself to the development of their own national territories and has not sought to expand into other areas.

9. Mr. Seaborn should conclude with the following new points:

a. That the events of the past few days should add credibility to the statement made last time, that "US public and official patience with North Vietnamese aggression is growing extremely thin."

b. That the US Congressional Resolution was passed with near unanimity, strongly re-affirming the unity and determination of the US Government and people not only with respect to any further attacks on US military forces but more broadly to continue to oppose firmly by all necessary means, DRV efforts to subvert and conquer South Vietnam and Laos.

c. That the US has come to the view that the DRV role in South Vietnam and Laos is critical. If the DRV persists in its present course, it can expect to continue to suffer the consequences.

d. That the DRV knows what it must do if the peace is to be restored.

e. That the US has ways and means of measuring the DRV's participation, direction and control of, the war on South Vietnam and in Laos and will be carefully watching the DRV's response to what Mr. Seaborn is telling them.

[Document 168]

Canadians are urgently asked to have Seaborn during August 10 visit make following points (as having been conveyed to him by US Government since August 6):

A. Re Tonkin Gulf actions, which almost certainly will come up:

1. The DRV has stated that Hon Ngu and Hon Me islands were attacked on July 30. It should be noted that the USS MADDOX was, all of that day and into the afternoon of the next day, over 100 miles south of those islands, in international waters near the 17th parallel, and that the DRV attack on the MADDOX took place on August 2, more than two days later. Neither the MADDOX or any other destroyer was in any way associated with any attack on the DRV islands.

2. Regarding the August 4 attack by the DRV on the two US destroyers, the Americans were and are at a complete loss to understand the DRV motive. They had decided to absorb the August 2 attack on the grounds that it very well might have been the result of some DRV mistake or miscalculation. The August 4 attack, however—from the determined nature of the attack as indicated by the radar, sonar, and eye witness evidence both from the ships and from their protecting aircraft—was, in the American eyes, obviously deliberate and planned and ordered in advance. In addition, premeditation was shown by the evidence that the DRV craft were waiting in ambush for the destroyers. The attack did not seem to be in response to any action by the South Vietnamese, nor did it make sense as a tactic to further any diplomatic objective. Since the attack took place at least 60 miles from nearest land, there could have been no question about territorial waters. About the only reasonable hypothesis was that North Viet-Nam was intent either upon making it appear that the United States was a "paper tiger" or upon provoking the United States.

3. The American response was directed solely to patrol craft and installations acting in direct support of them. As President Johnson stated: "Our response for the present will be limited and fitting."

4. In view of uncertainty aroused by the deliberate and unprovoked DRV attacks this character, US has necessarily carried out precautionary deployments of additional air power to SVN and Thailand.

B. Re basic American position:

5. Mr. Seaborn should again stress that US policy is simply that North Viet-Nam should contain itself and its ambitions within the territory allocated to its administration by the 1954 Geneva Agreements. He should stress that US policy in South Viet-Nam is to preserve the integrity of that state's territory against guerrilla subversion.

6. He should reiterate that the US does not seek military bases in the area and that the US is not seeking to overthrow the Communist regime in Hanoi.

7. He should repeat that the US is fully aware of the degree to which Hanoi controls and directs the guerrilla action in South Viet-Nam and that the US holds Hanoi directly responsible for that action. He should similarly indicate US awareness of North Vietnamese control over the Pathet Lao movement in

Laos and the degree of North Vietnamese involvement in that country. He should specifically indicate US awareness of North Vietnamese violations of Laotian territory along the infiltration route into South Viet-Nam.

8. Mr. Seaborn can again refer to the many examples of US policy in tolerance of peaceful coexistence with Communist regimes, such as Yugoslavia, Poland, etc. He can hint at the economic and other benefits which have accrued to those countries because their policy of Communism has confined itself to the development of their own national territories and has not sought to expand into other areas.

9. Mr. Seaborn should conclude with the following new points:

a. That the events of the past few days should add credibility to the statement made last time, that "US public and official patience with North Vietnamese aggression is growing extremely thin."

b. That the US Congressional Resolution was passed with near unanimity, strongly re-affirming the unity and determination of the US Government and people not only with respect to any further attacks on US military forces but more broadly to continue to oppose firmly, by all necessary means, DRV efforts to subvert and conquer South Viet-Nam and Laos.

c. That the US has come to the view that the DRV role in South Viet-Nam and Laos is critical. If the DRV persists in its present course, it can expect to continue to suffer the consequences.

d. That the DRV knows what it must do if the peace is to be restored.

e. That the US has ways and means of measuring the DRV's participation in, and direction and control of, the war on South Viet-Nam and in Laos and will be carefully watching the DRV's response to what Mr. Seaborn is telling them.

[Document 169]

CINCPAC 176 FROM SAIGON AUG 9, 1964

LIMDIS

REF: DEPTEL 378

From our vantage point we can see positive disadvantages to our position in SEA in pursuing course of action outlined Reftel.

1. In first place rush to conference table would serve to confirm to Chicoms that US retaliation for destroyer attacks was transient phenomenon and that firm Chicom response in form of commitment to defend NVN has given us "paper tiger" second thoughts. Moreover, much of beneficial effects elsewhere resulting from our strong reaction to events in Gulf of Tonkin would be swiftly dissipated.

2. In Viet-Nam sudden backdown from previous strongly held US position on PDJ withdrawal prior to conf on Laos would have potentially disastrous effect. Morale and will to fight particularly willingness to push ahead with arduous pacification task and to enforce stern measures of Khanh's new emergency decree, would be undermined by what would look like evidence that US seeking to take advantage of any slight improvement in non-communist position as excuse for extricating itself from Indochina via conf rout. This would give strength to probable pro-Gaullist contention that GVN should think about following Laotian example by seeking negotiated solution before advantage of temporarily strengthened anti-communist position recedes.

3. General let down in Viet-Nam which would result from softening of our stand in Laos just after we had made great show of firmness vis-a-vis communists would undoubtedly erode Khanh's personal position, with prospects of increased political instability and coup plotting.

4. It should be remembered that our retaliatory action in Gulf of Tonkin is in effect an isolated US–DRV incident. Although this has relation, as Amb. Stevenson has pointed out, to larger problem of DRV aggression by subversion in Viet-Nam and Laos, we have not RPT not yet come to grips in a forceful way with DRV over the issue of this larger and much more complex problem. Instead, we are engaged, both in Viet-Nam and Laos, in proxy actions against proxy agents of DRV. If, as both Khanh and Souvanna hope, we are to parlay the consequences of our recent clash with the DRV into actions which specifically direct themselves against DRV violations of the 1954 and 1962 agreements, we must avoid becoming involved in political engagements which will tie our hands and inhibit our action. For example, any effort to undertake credible joint planning operations with GVN re interdictory air strikes upon infiltration network in southern DRV and especially in Panhandle would be completely undercut if we were engaged in conf discussing the Laos territory in question.

5. Similarly, it would seem to us that Souvanna's willingness to hold fast on pre-conditions or substantive negotiations bears direct relationship to his assessment of US willingness to meet the problem where it originates—in North Vietnam itself. This fact shines clearly through his recent brief letter to Pres Johnson. Moreover, it would be folly to assume that Khanh, who is now in fairly euphoric state as result of our Gulf of Tonkin action, would do anything other than slump into deepest funk if we sought to persuade him to send GVN del to conf. EMB prediction is that he would resign rather than send del.

Intensified pressures for Geneva-type conf cited in Reftel would appear to US to be coming almost entirely from those who are opposed to US policy objectives in SEA (except possibly UK which seems prepared jump on bandwagon). Under circumstances, we see very little hope that results of such conference would be advantageous to US. Moreover, prospects of limiting it to consideration of only Laotian problem appear at this time juncture to be dimmer than ever. Even though prior agreement reached to limit conf, we do not see how in actual practice we could limit discussion solely to Laos if others insist on raising other issues. To best our knowledge, we never "withdrew" from room when DRV attempted raise extraneous issues during 1961–1962 conf. Instead we insisted to chair on point of order and had DRV ruled out of order. Prospect of informal corridor discussions with PL, DRV and Chicoms is just what JGVN would fear most and may well increase pressures on GVN to undertake negotiated solution so as to avoid their fear of being faced with "fait accompli" by US.

7. Rather than searching for "safety valve" to dissipate current "generalized pressures" SEA, it seems to us we should be looking for means which will channel those pressures against DRV. Seems to us "safety valve," if needed (for example by Soviets), exists in current UNSC discussion. We should continue to focus attention in all forums on communist aggressive actions as root cause of tension in SEA and reinforce our current stance. In the final analysis, this stance would be more valid deterrent to escalation by PL/VM than attempt seek accommodation within context Laos problem alone.

While not RPT not specifically within our province, we would point out that PL/VM appear to have capability of retaking territory regained by RLG in operation triangle at any time of their choosing and that therefore "territorial swap" envisaged in Deptel may be highly illusory. Moreover, any territorial deal which seems to confirm permanent PL/VM control over corridor as an arrangement acceptable to US would be anathema to GVN and indicate our willingness accept infiltration network as tolerable condition on GVN frontiers. Such situation would in their and US mission opinions vitiate against any hope of successful pacification of GVN territory.

TAYLOR

[Document 170]

AUG 9 '64

ACTION: Amembassy Saigon 622
          Amembassy Vientiane 229
          Amembassy Bangkok 357

Joint State/Defense Message

Refs: Vientiane 296 and 305 to Bangkok
     Saigon 67 to Vientiane, repeated Dept 778

Meeting today approved in principle early initiation air and limited ground operations in Laos corridor as soon as politically and militarily feasible. Therefore believe meeting this week as proposed by Saigon would be useful way to clarify scope and timing possible operations. Following questions appear crucial:

    1. *Air operations.*

    a. Best targeting division as between GVN and RLAF, and what targets would be recommended for US suppressive strikes.

    b. Latest reading political acceptability GVN strikes and US suppressive strikes and whether we should inform Souvanna before undertaking, or go ahead without informing him. Related question is whether to publicize.

    2. *Ground operations.*

    a. Review of latest plans and possible timing of action especially for limited bridgehead along lines indicated Saigon 485.

    b. Requirement for US advisors and support. These not covered by today's decisions and might require another review when plans develop.

    c. Same political questions as to Souvanna and publicity.

    3. In light of answers to above what should be GVN, RLG, and US public stance re operations?

Believe that it would be desirable for Bangkok be represented at meeting, in view possible Thai involvement in some operations.

Ambassador Taylor concurs.

END

RUSK

[Document 171]

SECOND DRAFT
W. P. Bundy
August 11, 1964

NEXT COURSES OF ACTION IN SOUTHEAST ASIA

1. INTRODUCTION

This memorandum examines the courses of action the US might pursue, commencing in about two weeks, assuming that the Communist side does not react further to the events of last week.

We have agreed that the intervening period will be in effect a short holding phase, in which we would avoid actions that would in any way take the onus off the Communist side for escalation. We will not send the DESOTO patrol back; will hold up on new 34A operations (continuing only essential re-supply of air-dropped missions, plus relatively safe leaflet drops); continue intensive recon-naissance of the DRV and the Panhandle (PDJ if necessary) but hold up on U-2s over Communist China at least until we can use Chinat polots and unless we have evidence suggesting major military moves. Within Laos, the attempt to secure Phou Kout would continue, as would consolidation of the Triangle gains, but nothing further would be done or indicated.

We are not yet sure what the Communist side may do in this period. They have introduced aircraft into North Vietnam, and may well send in at least token ground forces. VC activity should step up markedly at any moment. Although the volume of Chicom propaganda and demonstrations is ominous, it does not yet clearly suggest any further moves; if they were made, we would act accordingly. This memorandum assumes the Communist side does not go beyond the above.

II.   ESSENTIAL ELEMENTS IN THE SITUATION

A. *South Vietnam* is not going well. The Mission's monthly report (Saigon 877) expresses the hope that there can be significant gains by the end of the year. But it also says Khanh's chances of staying in power are only 50–50, that the leadership (though not so much the people or the army) has symptoms of defeatism and hates the prospect of slugging it out within the country, that there will be mounting pressures for wider action which, if resisted, will create frictions and irritations which could lead local politicians to serious considera-tion of a negotiated solution or local soldiers to a military adventure without US "consent." In other words, even if the situation in our own view does go a bit better, we have a major problem of maintaining morale. Our actions of last week lifted that morale temporarily, but it could easily sag back again if the VC have some successes and we do nothing further.

B. *Laos,* on the other hand has righted itself remarkably—so much so that a Communist retaliatory move is a real possibility. If Phou Kout can be secured, the present military areas of control are if anything better for Souvanna than the line of last April. T-28 operations have been a major factor, and really hurt PL morale. Souvanna's internal position is also stronger, though the right-wing generals could make fools of themselves again at any time.

C. *Laos negotiations* may well start to move in the near future whatever we do. Souvanna has agreed to a tripartite meeting in Paris, and has suggested August 24th. With his gains in hand, he has already indicated he is likely not to insist on his previous precondition of Communist withdrawal from the PDJ before agreeing to a 14-nation conference. The USSR, India, and France—and the UK and Canada only slightly less so—are pressing for a conference or at least clear motion toward one. While it is not yet clear that Souphanouvang will accept the tripartite as proposed by Souvanna, we must recognize that if he does it will be a real step toward an eventual conference. We can and will urge Souvanna to go slow, but *our control will be limited.*

D. As of now, Hanoi and Peiping are certainly not persuaded that they must abandon their efforts in South Vietnam and Laos. The US response to the Viet-namese naval attacks has undoubtedly convinced the Communist side that we will act strongly where US force units are directly involved—as they have previously seen in our handling of Laos reconnaissance. But in other respects the Communist side may not be so persuaded that we are prepared to take stronger actions, either in response to infiltration into South Vietnam or VC activity. The Communists probably believe that we might counter air action in Laos quite firmly, but that we would not wish to be drawn into ground action there.

III.   ESSENTIAL ELEMENTS OF US POLICY

A. *South Vietnam* is still the main theater. Morale and momentum there must be maintained. This means:

> 1. We must devise means of action that get maximum results for minimum risks.
> 2. We must continue to oppose any Viet-Nam conference and must play the prospect of a Laos conference very carefully. We must particularly avoid any impression of rushing to a Laos conference, and must show a posture of general firmness into which an eventual Laos conference would fit without serious loss.
> 3. We particularly need to keep our hands free for at least limited measures against the Laos infiltration areas.

B. *Laos.* It is our interest to stabilize the Laos situation as between the Government forces and the PL/VM, and to reduce the chances of a Communist escalating move on this front. (If such a move comes, we must meet it firmly, of course. We should also be stepping up Thai support to deter and prevent any Communist nibbles.) However, Souvanna should not give up his strong cards, particularly T-28 operations, without getting a full price for them in terms of acceptance of his position and a really satisfactory military status. Moreover, we must seek to reduce as much as possible the inhibiting effect of any Laos talks on actions against the Panhandle.

C. *Solution.* Basically, a solution in both South Viet-Nam and Laos will require a combination of military pressure and some form of communication under which Hanoi (and Peiping) eventually accept the idea of getting out.* Negotiation without continued pressure, indeed without continued military action, will not achieve our objectives in the foreseeable future. But military pressure could be accompanied by attempts to communicate with Hanoi and perhaps Peiping—through third-country channels, through side conversations around a Laos conference of any sort—*provided* always that we make it clear both to the Communists and to South Viet-Nam that the pressure will continue until we have achieved our objectives. After, *but only after,* we have established a clear pattern of pressure, we could accept a conference broadened to include the Viet-Nam issue. (The UN now looks to be out as a communication forum, though this could conceivably change.)

---

* We have never defined precisely what we mean by "getting out"—what actions, what proofs, and what future guarantees we would accept. A small group should work on this over the next months.

TIMING AND SEQUENCE OF ACTIONS

A. PHASE ONE—"Military Silence" (through August) [see Sec. I]
PHASE TWO—Limited Pressures (September through December)

There are a number of limited actions we could take that would tend to maintain the initiative and the morale of the GVN and Khanh, but that would not involve major risks of escalation. Such actions could be such as to foreshadow stronger measures to come, though they would not in themselves go far to change Hanoi's basic actions.

1. *34A operations* could be overtly acknowledged and justified by the GVN. *Marine operations* could be strongly defended on the basis of continued DRV sea infiltration, and successes could be publicized. *Leaflet operations* could also be admitted and defended, again on the grounds of meeting DRV efforts in the South, and their impunity (we hope) would tend to have its own morale value in both Vietnams. *Air-drop operations* are more doubtful; their justification is good but less clear than the other operations, and their successes have been few. With the others admitted, they could be left to speak for themselves—and of course security would forbid any mention of specific operations before they succeeded.

2. Joint planning* between the US and the GVN already covers possible actions against the DRV and also against the Panhandle. It can be used in itself to maintain morale of the GVN leadership as well as to control and inhibit any unilateral GVN moves. With 34A surfaced, it could be put right into the same framework. We would not ourselves publicize this planning, but it could be leaked (as it probably would anyway) with desirable effects in Hanoi and elsewhere.

3. *Stepped-up training of Vietnamese on jet aircraft* should now be undertaken in any event in light of the presence of MIG's in North Vietnam. The JCS are preparing a plan, and the existence of training could be publicized both for its morale effect in the GVN and as a signal to Hanoi of possible future action.

4. *Cross-border operations into the Panhandle* could be conducted on a limited scale. To be successful, ground operations would have to be so large in scale as to be beyond what the GVN can spare, and we should not at this time consider major US or Thai ground action from the Thai side. But on the *air side,* there are at least a few worthwhile targets in the infiltration areas, and these could be hit by US and/or GVN air. Probably we should use both; probably we should avoid publicity so as not to embarrass Souvanna; the Communist side might squawk, but in the past they have been silent on this area. The strikes should probably be timed and plotted on the map to bring them to the borders of North Vietnam at the end of December.

5. *DESOTO patrols* could be reintroduced at some point. Both for present purposes and to maintain the credibility of our account of the events of last week, they *must* be clearly dissociated from 34A operations both in fact and in physical appearance. In terms of course patterns, we should probably avoid

---

* This is in Phase One also.

penetrations of 11 miles or so and stay at least 30 miles off; whatever the importance of asserting our view of territorial waters, it is less than the international drawbacks of appearing to provoke attack unduly.

6. *Specific tit-for-tat actions* could be undertaken for any VC or DRV activity suited to the treatment. These would be "actions of opportunity." As Saigon 877 points out, the VC have "unused dirty tricks" such as mining (or attacks) in the Saigon River, sabotage of major POL stocks, and terrorist attacks on US dependents. The first two, at least, would land themselves to prompt and precise reprisal, e.g., by mining the Haiphong channel and attacking the Haiphong POL storage. Terrorism against US dependents would be harder to find the right reprisal target, and reprisal has some disadvantages in that it could be asked why this was different from the regular pattern of terrorism.

C. PHASE THREE—More Serious Pressures (January 1965 and following).

All the above actions would be foreshadowing systematic military action against the DRV, and we might at some point conclude that such action was required either because of incidents arising from the above actions or because of deterioration in the situation in South Vietnam, particularly if there were to be clear evidence of greatly increased infiltration from the north. However, in the absence of such major new developments, we should probably be thinking of a contingency date, as suggested by Ambassador Taylor, of 1 January 1965. Possible categories of action beginning at about that time, are:

1. *Action against infiltration routes and facilities* is probably the best opening gambit. It would follow logically the actions in the Sept.–Dec. Phase Two. It could be strongly justified by evidence that infiltration was continuing and, in all probability, increasing. The family of infiltration-related targets starts with clear military installations near the borders. It can be extended almost at will northward, to inflict progressive damage that would have a meaningful cumulative effect, and would always be keyed to one rationale.

2. *Action in the DRV against selected military-related targets* would appear to be the next upward move. POL installations and the mining of Haiphong Harbor (to prevent POL import as its rationale) would be spectacular actions, as would action against key bridges and railroads. All of these could probably be designed so as to avoid major civilian casualties.

3. *Beyond these points* it is probably not useful to think at the present time.

D. Handling of Laos Negotiations.

1. We would wish to slow down any progress toward a conference and to hold Souvanna to the firmest possible position. Unger's suggestion of tripartite administration for the PDJ is one possibility that would be both advantageous and a useful delaying gambit. Insistence on full recognition of Souvanna's position is another point on which he should insist, and there would also be play in the hand on the question of free ICC operations. As to a cease-fire, we would certainly not want this to be agreed to at the tripartite stage, since it would remove Souvanna's powerful T-28 lever. But since Souvanna has always made a cease-fire one of his preconditions, we must reckon that the other side might insist on it before a conference were convened—which we would hope would not be until January in any case.

2. If, despite our best efforts, Souvanna on his own, or in response to third-

country pressures, started to move rapidly toward a conference, we would have a very difficult problem. If the timing of the Laos conference, in relation to the degree of pressures we had then set in motion against the DRV, was such that our attending or accepting the conference would have major morale drawbacks in South Viet-Nam, we might well have to refuse to attend ourselves and to accept the disadvantages of having no direct participation. In the last analysis, GVN morale would have to be the deciding factor.

[Document 172]

11 Aug 64

Honorable William P. Bundy
Assistant Secretary of State for
    Far Eastern Affairs
Department of State
Washington, D.C. 20520

Dear Bill:

Events in the Gulf of Tonkin and the subsequent decision to deploy additional forces to Southeast Asia accentuate the need for clarification and certain changes to the Rules of Engagement under which U.S. forces must operate in situations short of open hostilities.

A review of current rules indicates the following voids should be filled as soon as possible:

a. There are no Rules of Engagement for intercept, hot pursuit, and destruction of hostile aircraft which violate Thailand air space.

b. U.S. forces intercepting hostile aircraft over South Vietnam are not authorized hot pursuit outside of the South Vietnam territorial air space.

Hostile forces which initiate unprovoked attacks against our forces whether on the high seas or ashore should not be afforded sanctuary from which they can repeat the attack. The best way to preclude repeated attacks is to pursue and destroy the attackers. Such action is not punitive per se but primarily defensive for self-protection. U.S. forces should be authorized immediate and unrestricted pursuit.

The Joint Chiefs have recommended that the Rules of Engagement be handled as a matter of urgency. Their recommendations have been reviewed in a joint meeting with members of your staff and mine. Certain changes were tentatively agreed. The revised rules are attached in the form of a proposed message which the Joint Chiefs will be authorized to forward to CINCPAC subject to your concurrence.

I would appreciate your approval of the Rules of Engagement or your comments as soon as possible.

Sincerely,
John T. McNaughton

cc: Chan JCS w/Encl
[Enclosure missing]

[Document 173]

THE JOINT CHIEFS OF STAFF
WASHINGTON, D.C. 20301

OFFICE OF THE SPECIAL ASSISTANT FOR
COUNTERINSURGENCY AND SPECIAL ACTIVITIES

SACSA-M 400-64
14 August 1964

MEMORANDUM FOR COLONEL ALFRED J. F. MOODY
MILITARY ASSISTANT TO THE SECRETARY
OF DEFENSE

Subject: Ambassador Taylor's Initial Report from South Vietnam

1. Attached to this memorandum for Mr. McNamara's information is a brief of Ambassador Taylor's initial report from South Vietnam.

2. This brief was furnished to the Chairman, Joint Chiefs of Staff, and Secretary Vance as background material for their appearance before the Vinson Committee on Tuesday, 18 August 1964.

A. R. Brownfield
Colonel, USA
Acting Special Assistant

Attachment

[Document 174]

AMBASSADOR TAYLOR'S SITUATION REPORT ON THE RVN

10 Aug 1964

1. On 10 July 1964 the President requested Ambassador Taylor (Deptel 108) to furnish him a coordinated country team report at the end of the month.

2. On 10 August 1964 Ambassador Taylor complied with the President's request. A breakout of Ambassador Taylor's report follows:

General:

The report is not intended as a comparison, since the turmoil following the two coups and the invalidation of the earlier data base (Strategic Hamlet Program) provide no meaningful base on which a comparison could be made. However, this report is intended to establish a baseline from which future progress may be measured.

The basis of this report and monthly reports hereafter are the results of a country-wide canvass of responsible US advisors and observers. The canvass dealt with: Army and public morale, combat effectiveness of military units, US/GVN counterpart relationships, and effectiveness of GVN officials.

In broad terms, the canvass results are surprisingly optimistic at the operational levels of both the civil and military organizations. This feeling of optimism exceeds that of most senior US officials in Saigon. Future reports should determine who is right.

Viet Cong Situation:
  Strategy:
The communist strategy as defined by North Vietnam and the puppet National Liberation Front is to seek a political settlement favorable to the communists. This political objective to be achieved by stages, passing first through "neutralism," using the National Liberation Front machinery, and then the technique of a coalition government.

  Tactics:
The VC tactics are to harass, erode and terrorize the VN population and its leadership into a state of demoralization without an attempt to defeat the RVNAF or seize and conquer terrain by military means. US/GVN progress should be measured against this strategy and these tactics.

  Status:
In terms of equipment and training, the VC are better armed and led today than ever in the past.

VC infiltration continues from Laos and Cambodia.

No indication that the VC are experiencing any difficulty in replacing their losses in men and equipment.

No reason to believe the VC will risk their gains in an overt military confrontation with GVN forces, although they have a sizeable force with considerable offensive capability in the central highlands.

GVN Situation:
  Political:
The slow pace of the CI campaign and the weakness of his government has caused Khanh to use the March North theme to rally the homefront, and offset the war weariness.

US observers feel the symptoms of defeatism are more in the minds of the inexperienced and untried leadership in Saigon than in the people and the Army.

We may face mounting pressure from the GVN to win the war by direct attack on Hanoi which if resisted will cause local politicians to seriously consider negotiation or local soldiers to consider a military adventure without US consent.

For the present, the Khanh government has the necessary military support to stay in power.

It is estimated that Khanh has a 50/50 chance of lasting out the year.

The government is ineffective, beset by inexperienced ministers who are jealous and suspicious of each other.

Khanh does not have confidence or trust in most of his ministers and is not able to form them into a group with a common loyalty and purpose.

There is no one in sight to replace Khanh.

Khanh has, for the moment, allayed the friction between the Buddhists and Catholics.

Khanh has won the cooperation of the Hoa Hao and Cao Dai.

Khanh has responded to our suggestions for improved relations between GVN and US Mission.

The population is confused and apathetic.

Khanh has not succeeded in building active popular support in Saigon.

Population support in the countryside in directly proportionate to the degree of GVN protection.

There are grounds to conclude that no sophisticated psychological approach is necessary to attract the country people to the GVN at this time. The assurance of a reasonably secure life is all that is necessary.

The success of US attacks on North Vietnam, although furnishing a psychological lift to the GVN, may have whetted their appetite for further moves against the DRV.

Economic:

Prices are stable and inflation is under control.

Industrial production has shown a slight increase from 140% of the 1962 level on 1 April 1964 to 143% on 31 July 1964.

End CY 64 industrial production is projected to be 150% of the 1962 level.

Any increase in capital goods imports would, if not covered by US assistance, lead to a major balance of payments problem.

USOM is examining the GVN tax structure, import policy, present multiple exchange rate system, competence and effectiveness of government administration, and proper use of total resources in the prosecution of the war.

Pacification Support:

The inexperienced ministries of Police, Education, Public Works, Interior, Information, Rural Affairs, Health and Finance are not represented in follow-up actions in the areas that have been cleared by the armed forces. This advisory task is the responsibility of USOM and USIS.

USOM CY64 provincial manpower objective has been established as two Americans in each province, often reinforced with a third Public Safety Officer. A considerable increase from the current strength of 64.

USIS has 16 US personnel in the field and anticipates no increase.

GVN representation at the province and district level, although inexperienced, is reported by US observers to be performing effectively with good US/GVN working relationships.

Capitol Military District (CMD) Pacification Program (Hop Tac) is designed to induce the Vietnmese to:

Work together as a functioning government.

Build within both urban and rural areas a more sound administrative, social and economic platform.

Achieve some pragmatic military successes which will bolster Vietnamese morale, engage the energies of their best qualified personnel and drive the VC effectively away from the nation's heartland.

Military:

The regular and paramilitary personnel strengths are slowly rising and by January 1965 should reach 98% of the target strength of 446,000.

The RVNAF desertion rate has decreased to 5.72% or ½ the rate of last March.

Three VNAF squadrons of A-1H aircraft will be combat ready by 30 September 1964 and the fourth by 1 December 1964 with a two to one pilot to cockpit ratio.

The evaluation of RVNAF units reports the following number combat effective:

    28 of 30 regiments
    100 of 101 infantry, marine and airborne battalions
    17 of 20 ranger battalions
    19 of 20 engineer battalions

The principal defects are low present for duty strengths and weak leadership at the lower levels. Both are receiving corrective treatment.

Extensive intelligence programs are underway to improve our intelligence capability by the end of the year.

GVN Overall Objective:

Increase in percentage of population control represent progress toward stabilizing the in-country situation. Using July figures as a base, the following percentages should be attainable.

	Rural		Urban	
	31 July 64	*31 Dec 64*	*31 July 64*	*31 Dec 64*
GVN control	33%	40%	44%	47%
VC control	20%	16%	18%	14%
Contested	47%	44%	42%	39%

US Mission Objectives:

Do everything possible to bolster the Khanh Government.

Improve the in-country pacification campaign against the VC.

Concentrating efforts on strategically important areas such as the provinces around Saigon (The Hop Tac Plan).

Undertake "show-window" social and economic projects in secure urban and rural areas.

Be prepared to implement contingency plans against North Vietnam with optimum readiness by January 1, 1965.

Keep the US public informed of what we are doing and why.

3. Ambassador Taylor's report, because of its across the board approach to the counterinsurgency problem, should be of significant value to all governmental agencies in determining how much success their departmental programs are achieving.

[Document 175]

Date: 14 August 1964

FM: State

TO: Saigon 439
   Vientiane 157
   CINCPAC

Following are key points tentative high level paper on next courses of action in Southeast Asia. Request addressee comments by Tuesday morning for further review and refinement.

SUMMARY

I. INTRODUCTION

The next ten days to two weeks should be short holding phase in which we would avoid actions that would in any way take onus off Communist side for escalation.

We will not send DESOTO patrol back, will hold up on new 34A operations (continuing only essential re-supply of air-dropped missions, plus relatively safe leaflets drops), but will continue intensive reconnaissance of DRV and Panhandle (PDJ if necessary). Within Laos, attempt secure Phou Kout would continue (napalm use discretion of Unger) as would T-28 operations and consolidation Triangle gains, but no further military action would be done or indicated. In view possible Communist moves in Laos, road watch and other intelligence efforts should be intensified accepting some greater risks.

We not yet sure what Communist side may do in this period. They have introduced aircraft into North Viet Nam and may well send in at least token ground forces. VC activity could step up markedly any moment. Although volume Chicom propaganda and demonstrations ominous, it does not yet clearly suggest any further moves; if they were made, we would act accordingly. This paper assumes Communist side does not go beyond above.

II. ESSENTIAL ELEMENTS IN SITUATION

A. South Viet Nam not (rpt not) going well. Mission's monthly report (Saigon 377) expresses hope significant gains by end of year. But also says Khanh's chances of staying in power are only 50–50, that leadership (though not so much people or army) has symptoms defeatism and hates prospect of slugging it out within country, that there will be mounting pressures for wider action "which, if resisted, will create frictions and irritations which could lead local politicians to serious consideration negotiated solution or local soldiers to military adventure without US consent."

In other words, even if situation in our view does go bit better, we have major problem maintaining morale. Our actions of last week lifted that morale temporarily, but also aroused expectations, and morale could easily sag back again if VC have successes and we do nothing further.

B. Laos on other hand has shown real military progress—so much so that Communist retaliatory move is real possibility. If Phou Kout can be secured, present military areas of control are if anything better for Souvanna than line of last April. T-28 operations have been major factor and really hurt PL morale. Souvanna's internal position also stronger, though right-wing generals and colonels could make fools of themselves any time.

C. Laos negotiations may start to move in near future whatever we do. Souvanna has accepted tripartite meeting in Paris, and suggested August 24. With gains in hand, he already indicated he likely not insist on previous precondition of Communist withdrawal from PDJ before agreeing to 14-nation conference. USSR (at least publicly), India, and France—and UK and Canada only slightly less so—pressing for conference or at least clear motion toward one. Souvanouvong's silence and other indicators suggest Communist side may still not accept early tripartite meeting or push for conference but we must recognize that, if they do accept tripartite, it will be real step toward eventual conference. We can and will urge Souvanna go slow, but our control limited.

D. Hanoi and Peiping as of now certainly not persuaded they must abandon efforts in South Viet Nam and Laos. US response to North Vietnamese naval attacks undoubtedly convinced Communist side we will act strongly when US force units directly involved—as they have previously seen in our handling Laos reconnaissance. But in other respects Communist side may not be so persuaded we prepared take stronger actions, either in response infiltration into SVN or VC activity. Communists probably believe we might counter air action in Laos quite firmly but we would not wish be drawn into ground action there.

III. ESSENTIAL ELEMENTS OF US POLICY

A. South Viet Nam still main theater. Morale and momentum there must be maintained. This means:

1. There advantage devising best possible means of action that for minimum risks get maximum results in terms of SVN morale and pressure on DRV.

2. We must continue oppose any Viet Nam conference and must play prospect of Laos confernce very carefully. We must particularly avoid any impression rushing to Laos conference and must show posture general firmness into which eventual Laos conference might fit without serious loss.

3. We particularly need keep our hands free for at least limited measures against Laos infiltration areas.

B. It is in our interest stabilize Laos situation as between Government forces and Communist side, and reduce chances of Communist escalating move on this front. (If such move comes, we must meet it firmly. We should also be stepping up Thai support deter and prevent any Communist nibbles.) However, Souvanna should not give up his strong cards, particularly T-28 operations, without getting full price for them. Moreover, we must seek reduce as much as possible inhibiting effect any Laos talks on actions against Panhandle.

C. Basically solution in both South Viet Nam and Laos will require combination military pressure and some form of communication under which Hanoi (and Peiping) eventually accept idea of getting out. Negotiation without continued military action will not achieve our objectives in foreseeable future. But military pressures could be accompanied by attempts communicate with Hanoi and perhaps Peiping—through third-country channels, through side conversations around Laos negotiations of any sort—*provided* always that we make clear both to Communists and South Viet Nam that military pressure will continue until we have achieved our objectives. After, but only after, we have established clear pattern pressure hurting DRV and leaving no doubts in South Viet Nam of our resolve, we could even accept conference broadened to include Viet Nam issue. (UN now looks to be out as communication forum though this could conceivably change.)

IV. TIMING AND SEQUENCE OF ACTIONS

A. Limited Pressures (late August tentatively through December)

There are a number of limited actions we could take that would tend to maintain our initiative and morale of GVN and Khanh, but that would not involve major risks of escalation. Such actions could be such as to foreshadow stronger measures to come, though they would not in themselves go far to change Hanoi's basic actions.

1. *34A Operations* could be overtly acknowledged and justified by GVN. Marine operations could be strongly defended on basis of continued DRV sea infiltration, and successes could be publicized. Leaflet operations could also be admitted and defended, again on grounds of meeting DRV efforts in South, and their impunity (we hope) would tend to have its own morale value in both Vietnams. Air-drop operations are more doubtful; their justification is good but less clear than other operations, and successes have been few. With the others admitted, they could be left to speak for themselves—and of course security would forbid any mention of specific operations before they succeeded.

2. *Joint US/GVN planning* already covers possible actions against DRV and

the Panhandle. It can be used in itself to maintain morale of GVN leadership, as well as to control and inhibit any unilateral GVN moves. With 34A surfaced, it could be put right into same planning framework. We would not ourselves publicize this planning, but it could be leaked (as it probably would anyway) with desirable effects in Hanoi and elsewhere.

3. *Stepped-up training of Vietnamese on jet aircraft* should now be undertaken in any event in light of presence of MIG's in North Viet Nam. JCS are preparing a plan, and existence of this training could be publicized both for its morale effect in GVN and as a signal to Hanoi of possible future action.

4. *Cross-border operations into Panhandle* could be conducted on a limited scale. To be successful, ground operations would have to be so large in scale as to be beyond what GVN can spare, and we should not at this time consider major US or Thai ground action from Thai side. But for air operations there are at least a few worthwhile targets in infiltration areas, and these could be hit by GVN air US reconnaissance missions in Panhandle would of course continue in any event; suppressive missions might be considered at some point, but not until after GVN has acted in this area. (Our Panhandle reconnaissance does not have the justification of a request from Souvanna, as our PDJ operations do.) Probably we should avoid publicity on air operations so as not to embarrass Souvanna; Communist side might squawk, but in past they have been silent on this area.

5. DESOTO patrols could be reintroduced at some point. Both for present purposes and to maintain credibility of our account of events of last week, they *must* be clearly dissociated from 34A operations both in fact and in physical appearance. In terms of course patterns, we should probably avoid penetrations of 11 miles or so and stay at least 20 miles off; whatever the importance of asserting our view of territorial waters, it is less than international drawbacks of appearing to provoke attack unduly. The 20-mile distance would not appreciably change chances of a North Vietnamese reaction, while it would deprive them of a propaganda argument (since a great many other countries also assert a 12-mile territorial waters limit).

6. *Specific tit-for-tat actions* of opportunity could be undertaken for any special VC or DRV activity. As Saigon 377 points out, VC have "unused dirty tricks" such as mining (or attacks) in Saigon River, sabotage of major POL stocks, and terrorist attacks on US dependents. First two, at least, would lend themselves to prompt and precise reprisal, e.g., by mining Haiphong channel and attacking Haiphong POL storage.

7. *US Dependents.* This has two aspects. If there were substantial terrorism against our dependents, we should consider some specific reprisal against DRV; however, this has disadvantages in that it might appear that we were reacting only when US nationals were hit, and ignoring regular pattern of terrorism against South Vietnamese. Second aspect, whether or not there are terrorist attacks, is possible withdrawal of our dependents. If situation should reach another intense point, withdrawal might be useful in itself as signal to Hanoi that we were really getting ready for business.

8. *Sequence and mix of US and GVN actions* needs careful thought. At this point, we should emphasize both the GVN role in actions and rationales directly relating actions to what is being done to GVN. Overt 34A actions should be the first moves, and GVN would go first in air attacks against Panhandle. But there are advantages in other respects to actions related to US forces. If we lost an aircraft in Panhandle, we could act hard and fast, and of course similarly for any attack on DESOTO patrols. Probably sequence should be played somewhat

by ear, with aim of producing a slightly increased tempo but one that does not commit us prematurely to even stronger actions.

Summary. Above actions are in general limited and controllable. However, if we accept—as of course we must—necessity of prompt retaliation especially for attacks on our own forces, they *could* amount to at least a pretty high noise level that might stimulate some pressures for a conference. New DRV air and AA capability may also produce incidents.

These actions are not in themselves a truly coherent program of strong enough pressure either to bring Hanoi around or to sustain a pressure posture into some kind of discussion. Hence, we should continue absolutely opposed to any conference.

B. *More Serious Pressures*

All above actions would be foreshadowing systematic military action against DRV, and we might at some point conclude such action was required either because of incidents arising from above actions or because of deterioration in SVN situation, particularly if there were to be clear evidence of greatly increased infiltration from the north. However, in absence of such major new developments, we should be thinking of a contingency date for planning purposes, as suggested by Ambassador Taylor, of 1 January 1965.

End Summary

Among key questions above program are:

1. What is Saigon's best judgment whether it would maintain morale GVN leadership?

2. What is Vientiane's judgment how much Panhandle action Souvanna could accept without danger right-wing problems or his general position? Would it help to establish early pattern suppressive strikes and GVN air operations so that noise from this area became familiar background music, or would such early actions impair Souvanna's position? How much would Saigon like to see done in Panhandle to help GVN morale and achieve useful military results?

3. CINCPAC views on military aspects and specific action sequence should be conveyed JCS. Your general comments also welcome.

[Document 176]

15 Aug 64

FROM: JCS

TO: CINCJAC

JCS 7947

Subject: Rules of Engagement (U)

1. This message rescinds JCS 3976.

2. The JCS authorize the destruction of hostile aircraft and seaborne forces by US forces in Southeast Asia under the following rules of engagement:

a. US forces operating in Southeast Asia are authorized to attack and destroy any vessel or aircraft which attacks, or gives positive indication of intent to attack US forces operating in the international waters and air space over international waters of Southeast Asia. This includes hot pursuit into territorial waters or territorial air space as may be necessary and feasible.

b. US forces operating in Southeast Asia are authorized to engage and destroy hostile aircraft over South Vietnam and Thailand. Hot pursuit may be conducted as necessary and feasible over international waters or into North Vietnam, Laos, and Cambodia against hostile aircraft as defined in subpara 2 f (1) (b) below.

c. US forces operating in Laos are authorized to attack and destroy any aircraft which attacks or gives positive indication of intent to attack US forces. Hot pursuit may be conducted as necessary and feasible into North Vietnam, Cambodia, South Vietnam, and Thailand.

d. No pursuit is authorized at this time into the territorial waters or air space of Communist China.

e. US forces entering territorial waters and/or territorial air space as authorized by these rules are not authorized to attack other hostile forces or installations therein unless attacked first by them, and then only to the extent necessary for self defense.

f. Definitions:

(1) Hostile aircraft—A hostile aircraft is defined as one which is:

(a) Visually identified, or designated by the US director of a Joint Operations Center or his authorized US representatives, as a communist bloc aircraft over-flying RVN–Thailand territory without proper clearance from the government concerned;

(b) Observed in one of the following acts:

1. Attacking US or friendly ground forces or installations.

2. Attacking US or friendly aircraft.

3. Laying mines within friendly territorial waters.

4. Attacking US or friendly vessels.

5. Releasing parachutes or gliders over sovereign territory when obviously not in distress; or

6. Acting or behaving in a manner which is within reasonable certainty that air attack on US or forces is intended.

(2) Territorial waters include the territorial sea and waters. The territorial sea is the belt of sea adjacent to three miles in breadth measured from the low water mark [word missing]. Inland waters are waters to landward of the territorial sea.

These rules are not intended, in any manner, to infringe traditional responsibility of a military commander to guard against unprovoked armed attack. In the event of such attack, commander concerned will take immediate, aggressive action [word missing] attacking force with any available means at his command. Declaration of aircraft or vessels as hostile will be made with judgment and discretion. There may be cases where destruction of communist bloc forces would be contrary to US interests, examples of such cases are: due to navigation error, communist civilian aircraft over-fly RVN–Thailand territory; communist aircraft or vessels, manned by defectors attempting to land with the intention of surrendering themselves. All available intelligence should be considered in determining action to be taken in such cases.

[Document 177]

16 Aug 64

FM COMUSMACV

TO RUHPA/CINCPAC

CROSS BORDER OPERATIONS

A. MACJ312 JULY

B. JCS DTD 0420127

C. CINCPAC 1101527

1. Combined planning with JGS on cross border operations has reached a point where your approval or further guidance is necessary.

2. After a slow start and under the impetus of US actions against the DRV, the JGS is now energetically participating in combined cross border planning. . . . The liaison bureau headed by Lt Col Ho Tieu is the high command control headquarters for this operation, which has been entitled "Anh Dung." A war room is being set up at the liaison bureau headquarters in the old special forces compound. Radio communications are being established direct with Vietnamese special forces headquarters at Nha Trang and with I and II Corps.

4. Cross border mission type orders will be issued by the bureau over the signature of General Khiem, RVN Commander in chief. Detailed implementing plans will be prepared by I and II Corps, Hq VNSF and at a later date, VNAF, and submitted to the bureau for approval. JGS estimates from time the plan is approved it will take 10 days to get the operation underway.

5. The concept follows:

A. First Phase:

(1) Three bridgeheads to be established in Laos; one astride route 9 opposite Lao Bao, approximately 50 km wide by 15 km deep; one Ref C not held, will furnish on request, if obtainable the same size opposite Dak Prou; and one 20 kilometers wide by 11 km. deep opposite Dak To. VNSF to have responsibility for northern (Lao Bao) bridgehead, I Corps for central (Dak Prou), and II Corps for southern.

(2) VNSF to have available strike force of the CIDG camp at Kee Sanh, 4 ABN ranger companies, 3 recon teams from "Leaping Lena" group, and, in later stages one airborne battalion. The corps to use strike forces from CIDG camps at A Ro and Kham Duc (I Corps) and Dak Pek and Dak To (II Corps), plus one ranger battalion each and such infantry elements as can be spared from pacification effort, estimated at this time as not more than one battalion from each of corps involved.

(3) Reconnaissance patrols by squad and platoon elements initiate operations followed progressively and methodically by raids and ambushes of platoon and company size upon targets and infiltration routes developed by patrols. Larger scale and deeper penetrations of company and battalion size to follow hopefully to dominate the bridgehead area.

(4) Close air support missions and air strikes against known or strongly suspected critical targets to be blown (Ref C). . . . Preplanned air missions to require personal approval of . . . INCRVNAF and COMUSMACV.

B. Second Phase (as visualized by GVN):

1) Expand and connect bridgeheads. I and II Corps to be charged with responsibility for operating in and dominating a strip of the Laotian side of the border 40 km deep.

2) Within and beyond this strip, destruction operations to be mounted by air strikes, airborne ranger company and airborne battalion raids against major VC targets.

C. Because of extremely rugged terrain in the area of the bridgeheads operations will be slow in developing. After initiation of operation, troops will probably be limited to company size in each bridgehead for a period of several weeks. There will be ample opportunity to review and, if necessary, direct operations before substantially larger forces become involved.

It would be essential for US advisors to accompany CIDG, ranger, airborne ranger and airborne troops. Air strikes would . . . conducted VNAF. US Army and US Marine and VNAF helicopters would have to be used in supporting roles. US Air Force C-123's would be required for airborne operations. Considering the forces which could be made available this is . . . overly ambitious scheme. However, the desirability of getting such a program underway, coupled with GVN apparent willingness to . . . started now, argues for US encouragement and indorsement . . . first phase of concept. Although an effort will be made to build in US controls . . . should be recognized that once this operation is initiated . . . the GVN, US control may be marginal. While they would no doubt be willing to attack targets suggested by US or to mount intelligence and reconnaissance operations in areas desired by US, they may undertake operations at their own initiative and against targets of their choosing without our knowledge or consent. In other words, our control over their military actions in a compat situation could not be expected to change from the present. Advisory pattern. The VC are probably in the corridor in strength and there will be a number of tactical engagements requiring reinforcement and air support which from an operational standpoint must be controlled by the Corps CTOC/ASOC. Therefore, this type operation does not lend itself to single mission control from Saigon.

In view of the disrupting effect these operations could have . . . VC infiltration CAGTES and bases in Laos approval of the concept is recommended plan would be susceptible to execution in total or in part and can develop as experience is gained.

Coordination with Laotian government will be necessary and it is assumed Washington will take initiative in this matter at the appropriate time.

. . . combined cross border planning under the original terms of reference did not include the use of FARMGATE aircraft for airstrikes into the Panhandle. However, in view later authority to plan unilaterally for use of FARMGATE and in view fact that the use of FARMGATE would put COMUSMACV in position to insist on participation in decision making and combined control through the AOC, strongly recommend that FARMGATE be included within the scope of cross border operations outlined in this message.

12. Concept has been discussed with Ambassador Taylor who has not taken a position at this time.

[Document 178]

17 August 1964

From: Vientiane

To: State

Reference: EXDIS 157.

Very much appreciate REFTEL as guidance our actions over coming months. Once paper finally approved would appreciate being informed, including any amendments.

In reply to second key question I frankly find it difficult to say in abstract how much panhandle action Souvanna could and would accept. Principal danger as already noted in earlier messages, aside from his understandable preoccupation about provoking Communist escalation, is that stepped-up action in Panhandle makes it more difficult for U.S. to enforce counsels of moderation as regards his and Lao military actions in areas of country which are of more immediate concern to them.

As earlier noted I believe we could gradually establish pattern U.S. suppressive strikes in panhandle without adverse Souvanna reaction and this perhaps even truer of T-28 strikes. Even though strictly speaking suppressive strikes would not be in response to RLG request nevertheless believe Souvanna would back U.S. up if we represented them as being authorized by RLG. On other hand I would expect less ready acquiescence and certainly no support from him concerning GVN air operations in Laos. I of course appreciate importance panhandle action as help to GVN morale but continue question its achieving significant military results and I believe we should approach problem with this point realistically in mind.

With regard to introductory section of DRASO paper, I cannot guarantee "No further military action" in Laos. We are now assessing pressures for initiative against PDJ and if this confirms there is danger Lao adopting foolhardy plans we will move forcefully to persuade them abandon them, including visit by me to King in LUASG PRABANG if necessary. There may however be other more limited and rational military actions we would not wish to obstruct and therefore would prefer avoid categorical prohibition on this subject. Unfortunately also it would be our repression in this field that would most likely encourage right-wing generals and colonels to make fools of themselves.

Point A-3 under Section III again points up our contradictory position. I would conclude from this we should influence Souvanna to go very slow on any cease-fire agreement during forthcoming Paris talks. With regard Point B same section, what is full price . . . and if it is either withdrawal from PDJ (or unified administration PDJ) combined with ceasefire, how can we avoid inhibiting effect on panhandle actions?

With respect Section IV Point A-4 I thoroughly agree ground operations should not at this time be considered. Agree concerning suppressive measures, as already noted, but do not understand why this would have to follow GVN action. I also agree concerning wisdom avoiding publicity and would apply this same reasoning to point A-2 same section. Making public that U.S. and GVN planning actions in Laos objectionable: in first place on grounds this certainly also [words missing] and RLG should have voice in matter but presents even greater problem in that Souvanna and others would probably strongly resist such overt acknowledgment of intentions and plans, even while they might be prepared countenance activities which would be denied if Communists made public accusations.

In sum, if I read correctly between the lines, draft paper based on premise that resolution Laos problem depends fundamentally on resolution Vietnam and therefore our policy here (leaving aside corridor question) is necessarily an interim one of holding the line but trying avoid escalation of military contest.

[Document 179]

17 August 1964

From: CINCPAC

To: JCS

Next Courses of Action in Southeast Asia

A.   State 439 to Saigon, 14 August 8 PM

1.   This message responds to Ref A with coments and views on military assets and specific sequence of next courses of action in Southeast Asia. Para 2 following is my general assessment of the situation and course to be pursued. Para 3 and those thereafter follow same sequence of subjects as Ref A.

2.   Recent U.S. military actions in Laos and North Vietnam demonstrated our intent to move toward our objectives. Our operations and progress in Laos constitute one step along the route. Our directness and rapidity of reaction in bombing North Vietnamese installations and deploying U.S. combat forces to Southeast Asia were others. Each step played a part. (Their effect was to interrupt the continually improving Communist posture, catch the imagination of the Southeast Asian peoples, provide some lift to morale, however temporary, and force CHICOM/DRV assessment or reassessment of U.S. intentions.) But these were only steps along the way. What we have not done and must do is make plain to Hanoi and Peiping the cost of pursuing their current objectives and impeding ours. An essential element of our military action in this course is to proceed in the development of our physical readiness posture: deploying troops, ships, aircraft, and logistic resources in a manner which accords a maximum freedom of action. This is the thrust we should continue to pursue, one which is intended to provide more than one feasible course for consideration as the changed and changing Southeast Asian situation develops. Remarks in the paragraphs which follow are submitted in light of this assessment and with the view that pressures against the other side once instituted should not be relaxed by any actions or lack of them which would destroy the benefits of the rewarding steps previously taken in Laos and North Vietnam. These remarks are in same sequence as subjects and paragraphs in Ref A.

3.   Para I

The proposed two weeks suspension of operations is not in consonance with desire to get the message to Hanoi and Peiping. Pierce arrow showed both force and restraint. Further demonstration of restraint alone could easily be interpreted as period of second thoughts about pierce arrow and events leading thereto as well as sign of weakness and lack of resolve. Continous and effective pressure should be implied to the Communists in both the PDJ and panhandle. Consequently, concur in continued RECCE of DRV, panhandle and PDJ. Concur in attempt to secure Phou Kout and continued T-28 and triangle operations. Resumption of 34A actions and Desoto Patrols is considered appropriate. Each can be carefully conducted to avoid interference with the other.

Desired changes in situation South Vietnam can only occur as result of long, hard process. Quick, dramatic changes not possible. While South Vietnam operation not going well, effects of alternatives we have taken have not been realized yet and sufficient time has not passed to achieve an improved situation.

4. [missing]

5. Para II   B and C

Progress in Laos due almost entirely to T-28 operations and Thai artillery. Prime objective of Communists in any conference will be to arrange agreement to cease T-28 and other air operations. If operations cease as result of conference, Communists could then move back to their former positions, continue their nibbling process and we would have to live with agreement not to use T-28s. At that point, situation would be same as it formerly was. Related subject is stepup of air attacks in panhandle. Since we do not have ground capability to halt or severely interdict enemy surface movements in panhandle, air attacks in panhandle should be intensified, else we invite or insure uninterrupted flow of enemy units and material southward.

6. Para II   D

Concur. Hanoi and Peiping are not persuaded they must abandon efforts in Vietnam and Laos. On the contrary, reduction of military actions for two weeks may encourage them to expand their efforts in S.E. Asia.

7. Para III   A 1

Concur that South Vietnam is current hot spot and main concern in S.E. Asia. RVN cannot be reviewed apart from S.E. Asia. It is merely an area in a large theater occupied by the same enemy. Action to produce significant results in terms of pressure on DRV and improvements of morale in RVN must entail risk. Temptation toward zero action and zero risk must be avoided.

8. Para III   A 2

Concur.

9. Para III   A 3

Concur.

10. Para III   B

Concur, but stabilization by negotiation has failed in Laos with only one side following agreements.

11. Para III   C

Concur with the thesis set forth that we make clear to all that military pressure will continue until we achieve our objectives. Our actions must keep the Communists apprehensive of what further steps we will take if they continue their aggression. In this regard, we have already taken the large initial step of putting U.S. combat forces into Southeast Asia. We must maintain this posture; to reduce it would have a dangerous impact on the morale and will of all people in Southeast Asia. And we must face up to the fact that these forces will be deployed for some time and to their need for protection from ground or air attack. RVN cannot provide necessary ground security without degraduation of the counter-insurgency effort and has little air defense capability. A conference to include Vietnam, before we have overcome the insurgency, would lose U.S. our allies in Southeast Asia and represent a defeat for the United States.

12. Para IV   A 1

Knowledge of success of 34A operations would have a highly beneficial effect morale in the RVN. Suggest that these operations might be leaked to the press rather than overtly acknowledging them. 34A operations should be resumed to keep up external pressure on the DRV.

13. Para **IV   A** 2

While joint U.S./GVN planning is necessary, it cannot in itself maintain morale or control and inhibit unilateral GVN moves. Leaking this sort of peripheral activity is of little value and in the absence of action is unlikely to have quote desirable effects on Hanoi and elsewhere unquote.

14. Para **IV   A** 3

Training of RVN pilots in jet aircraft would work against the development of the kind of Air Force the RVN is able to support and maintain by diverting scarce pilots and maintenance resources to the training program.

The job of the Vietnamese Air Force is counterinsurgency. We are presently engaged in a program of converting the VNAF to A1HS. It is straining the resources of Vietnam to accomplish this program. The United States should reserve as its own task the operation of modern military jets against the Communists.

15. Para **IV   A** 4

Cross border air operations should commence as soon as possible, utilizing not only RVN but also U.S. aircraft. Shortly thereafter, RVN ground operations can commence as indicated in COMUSMACV 160943Z.

16. Para **IV   A** 5

We should have another Desoto Patrol in the Gulf of Tonkinsson.

17. Para **IV   A** 6

Concur that Tit-for-Tat operations should be undertaken. CINCPAC has not received Saigon 377 and thus cannot comment on the implications thereof.

18. Para **IV   A** 7

Withdrawal of dependents should be resisted as long as possible since it would be a psychological blow to the Vietnamese. While it might have some indication of a determination to act, it also indicates that Saigon is not secure.

19. Para **IV   A** 8

Concur that sequence and mix of U.S. and GVN actions need careful thought, and believe this being done. Our plans for graduated military pressures against NVN (OPlan 37–64 as example) have been submitted and are considered valid.

20. In considering more serious pressure, we must recognize that immediate action is required to protect our present heavy military investment in RVN. We have introduced large amounts of expensive equipment into RVN and a successful attack against Bien Hoa, Tan Ssn Nhut, Danang, or an installation such as a radar or communication site would be a serious psychological defeat for U.S. MACV reports that inability of GVN to provide requisite degree of security and therefore we must rely on U.S. troops. MACV has requested troops for defense of the three locations mentioned above. My comments on this request are being transmitted by separate message. In addition to the above, consideration should be given to creating a U.S. base in RVN. A U.S. base in RVN would provide one more indication of our intent to remain in S.E. Asia until our objectives are achieved. It could also serve as a U.S. command point or control center in event of the Caos which might follow another Coup. By an acknowledged concrete U.S. (as received) commitment, beyond the advisory effort, it informs the Communists that an overt attack on the RVN would be regarded as a threat to U.S. forces. Such a base should be accessible by air and sea, possessed of well developed facilities and installations, and located in an area from which U.S. operations could be launched effectively. Danang meets these criteria.

In summary, following actions should be taken in order to further the accomplishment of U.S. objectives in S.E. Asia. While maintaining current U.S. commitments in S.E. Asia and continuing present RECCE operations we should:

A. Resume 34A operations and Desoto Patrol.

B. Introduce sufficient U.S. units into South Vietnam to provide for adequate air and ground defense of deployed units.

C. Obtain rights to establish and occupy U.S. base in the Danang area.

D. Commence cross-border operations in accordance with combined U.S./ GVN plans.

These actions will help to maintain the strength of our present position and emphasize to Hanoi and Peiping the cost of pursuing their objectives and impeding ours.

22. In conclusion, our actions of August 5 have created a momentum which can lead to the attainment of our objectives in S.E. Asia. We have declared ourselves forcefully both by overt acts and by the clear readiness to do more. It is most important that we not lose this momentum.

[Document 180]

Extract: Memo for SecDef from CJCS "Combat Air Capability in North Vietnam" 17 AUG 64 (JCSM-707-64)

6. CINCPAC OPLANS 37-64 (Military Actions to Stabilize the Situation in RVN) and 99-64 (Military Actions to Stabilize the Situation in Laos) provide inter alia for the conduct of selected operations against NVN. Further, the JCS have directed that CINCPAC be prepared with the full range of action capabilities against NVN, including the readiness to execute selective strike or to initiate coordinated air campaign along the lines of OPLAN 37-64 or OPLAN 99-64 on the shortest possible notice, if and when directed. In addition, they have requested that CINCPAC complete as soon as possible detailed operational planning and preparations for employment of US and VNAF air resources, utilizing the "94 target list" as a basis, in order to facilitate obtaining decisions of higher authority as to the scale, tempo, and target categories to be struck, CINCPAC Fragmentary Operation Order No. 1-64 implements applicable portions of CINCPAC OPLANS 37-64 and 99-64, and provides a framework for selected air operations against NVN.

[Document 181]

FM: Saigon 465   Date: 18 August 1964

TO: State

Ref: Deptel 439

This is a US Mission message.

In preparing our reply, we have found it simpler to produce a new paper which undertakes to state the problem in South Viet Nam as we see it in two possible forms and then to provide course of action responding to each statement of the problem.

Underlying our analysis is the apparent assumption of Deptel 439 (which we believe is correct) that the present in-country pacification plan is not enough in itself to maintain national morale or to offer reasonable hope of eventual success. Something must be added in the coming months.

Statement of the problem—A. The course which US policy in South Viet Nam should take during the coming months can be expressed in terms of four objectives. The first and most important objective is to gain time for the Khanh government to develop a certain stability and to give some firm evidence of viability. Since any of the courses of action considered in this cable carry a considerable measure of risk to the US, we should be slow to get too deeply involved in them until we have a better feel of the quality of our ally. In particular, if we can avoid it, we should not get involved militarily with North Viet Nam and possibly with Red China if our base in South Viet Nam is insecure and Khanh's army is tied down everywhere by the VC insurgency. Hence, it is our interest to gain sufficient time not only to allow Khanh to prove that he can govern, but also to free Saigon from the VC threat which presently rigns (as received) it and assure that sufficient GVN ground forces will be available to provide a reasonable measure of defense against any DRV ground reaction which may develop in the execution of our program and thus avoid the possible requirement for a major US ground force commitment.

A second objective in this period is the maintenance of morale in South Viet Nam, particularly within the Khanh Government. This should not be difficult in the case of the government if we can give Khanh assurance of our readiness to bring added pressure on Hanoi if he provides evidence of ability to do his part. Thirdly while gaining time for Khanh, we must be able to hold the DRV in check and restrain a further buildup of Viet Cong strength by way of infiltration from the North. Finally, throughout this period, we should be developing a posture of maximum readiness for a deliberate escalation of pressure against North Viet Nam, using January 1, 1965 as a target D-Day. We must always recognize, however, that events may force US to advance D-Day to a considerably earlier date.

Course of action—A. If we accept the validity of the foregoing statement of the problem, we then need to design a course of action which will achieve the four objectives enumerated above. Such a course of action would consist of three parts; the first, a series of actions directed at the Khanh Government; the second, actions directed at the Hanoi Government; the third, following a pause of some duration, initiation of an orchestrated air attack against North Viet Nam.

In approaching the Khanh Government, we should express our willingness to Khanh to engage in planning and eventually to exert intense pressure on North Viet Nam, providing certain conditions are met in advance. In the first place before we would agree to go all out against the DRV, he must stabilize his government and make some progress in cleaning up his operational backyard. Specifically, he must execute the initial phases of the Hop Tac Plan successfully to the extent of pushing the Viet Cong from the doors of Saigon. The overall pacification program, including Hop Tac, should progress sufficiently to allow earmarking at least three division equivalents for the defense in I Corps if the DRV step up military operations in that area.

Finally, we should reach some fundamental understandings with Khanh and his government concerning war aims. We must make clear that we will engage in action against North Viet Nam only for the purpose of assuring the security and independence of South Viet Nam within the territory assigned by the 1954 agreements; that we will not (rpt not) join in a crusade to unify the north and south; that we will not (rpt not) even seek to overthrow the Hanoi regime provided the latter will cease its efforts to take over the south by subversive warfare.

With these understandings reached, we would be ready to set in motion the following:

(1) Resume at once 34A (with emphasis on Marine operations) and Desoto patrols. These could start without awaiting outcome of discussions with Khanh.

(2) Resume U-2 overflights over all NVN.

(3) Initiate air and ground strikes in Laos against infiltration targets as soon as joint plans now being worked out with the Khanh Government are ready. Such plans will have to be related to the situation in Laos. It appears to US that Souvanna Phouma should be informed at an appropriate time of the full scope of our plans and one would hope to obtain his acquiescence in the anti-infiltration actions in Laos. In any case we should always seek to preserve our freedom of action in the Laotian corridor.

By means of these actions, Hanoi will get the word that the operational rules with respect to the DRV are changing. We should perhaps consider message to DRV that shooting down of U-2 would result in reprisals. We should now lay public base for justifying such flights and have plans for prompt execution in contingency to shoot down.

One might be inclined to consider including at this stage tit-for-tat bombing operations in our plans to compensate for VC depredations in SVN. However, the initiation of air attacks from SVN against NVN is likely to release a new order of military reaction from both sides, the outcome of which is impossible to predict. Thus, we do not visualize initiating this form of reprisal as a desirable tactic in the current plan but would reserve the capability as an emergency response if needed.

Before proceeding beyond this point, we should raise the level of precautionary military readiness (if not already done) by taking such visible measures as introducing US Hawk units to Danang and Saigon, landing a Marine force at Danang for defense of the airfield and beefing up MACV's support base. By this time (assumed to be late fall) we should have some reading on Khanh's performance. Assuming that his performance has been satisfactory and that Hanoi has failed to respond favorably, it will be time to embark on the final phase of course of action A, a carefully orchestrated bombing attack on NVN, directed primarily at infiltration and other military targets. At some point prior thereto, it may be desirable to open direct communications with Hanoi if this not been done before. With all preparations made, political and military, the bombing program would begin, using US reconnaissance planes, VNAF/Farmgate aircraft against those targets which could be attacked safely in spite of the presence of the MIG's, and additional US combat aircraft if necessary for the effective execution of the bombing programs.

Pros and cons of course of action—A. If successful, course of action A will accomplish the objectives set forth at the outset as essential to the support of US policy in South Viet Nam. I will press the Khanh Government into doing its homework in pacification and will limit the diversion of interest to the out-of-country ventures it gives adequate time for careful preparation estimated at several months, while doing sufficient at once to maintain internal morale. It also provides ample warning to Hanoi and Peking to allow them to adjust their conduct before becoming over-committed.

On the other hand, course of action A relies heavily upon the durability of the Khanh government. It assumes that there is little danger of its collapse with notice or of its possible replacement by a weaker or more unreliable success. Also, because of the drawn-out nature of the program, it is exposed to the danger of international political pressure to enter into negotiations before NVN is really hurting from the pressure directed against it.

Statement of the Problem—B. It may well be that the problem of US policy in SVN is more urgent than that depicted in the foregoing statement. It is far from clear at the present moment that the Khanh Government can last until January 1, 1965, although the application of course of action A should have the effect of strengthening the government internally and of silencing [words missing] that we do not have the time available which is implicit in course of action A (several months), we would have to restate the problem in the following terms. Our objective avoid the possible consequences of a collapse of national morale. To accomplish these purposes, we would have to open the campaign against the DRV without delay, seeking to force Hanoi as rapidly as possible to resist from aiding the VC and to convince the DRV that it must cooperate in calling off the VC insurgency.

Course of Action—B. To meet this statement of the problem, we need an accelerated course of action, seeking to obtain results faster than under course of Action A. Such an accelerated program would include the following actions:

Again we must inform Khanh of our intentions, this time expressing a willingness to begin military pressures against Hanoi at once, providing that he will undertake to perform as in course of Action A. However, US action would not await evidence of performance.

Again we may wish to communicate directly on this subject with Hanoi or awaiting effect of our military actions. The scenario of the ensuing events would be essentially the same as under Course A but the execution would await only the readiness of plans to expedite, relying almost exclusively on US military means.

Pros and cons of Course of Action B. This course of action asks virtually nothing from the Khanh Government, primarily because it is assumed that little can be expected from it. It avoids the consequence of the sudden collapse of the Khanh Government and gets underway with minimum delay the punitive actions against Hanoi. Thus, it lessens the chance of an interruption of the program by an international demand for negotiation by presenting a fait accompli to international critics. However, it increases the likelihood of US involvement in ground action since Khanh will have almost no available ground forces which can be released from pacification employment to mobile resistance of DRV attacks.

CONCLUSION: It is concluded that Course of Action A offers the greater promised achievement of US policy objectives in SVN during the coming months. However, we should always bear in mind the fragility of the Khanh Government and be prepared to shift quickly to Course of Action B if the situation requires. In either case, we must be militarily ready for any response which may be initiated by NVN or by Chicoms.

MISCELLANEOUS: As indicated above, we believe that 34A operations should resume at once at maximum tempo, still on a covert basis; similarily, Desoto patrols should begin advance, operating outside 12-mile limit. We concur that a number of VNAF pilots should be trained on B-57's between now and first of year. There should be no change now with regard to policy on evacuation of US dependents.

RECOMMENDATION: It is recommended that USG adopt Course of Action A while maintaining readiness to shift to Course of Action B.

[Document 182]

ASSISTANT SECRETARY OF DEFENSE (COMPTROLLER)
WASHINGTON 25, D.C.

24 AUG 1964

MEMORANDUM FOR THE SECRETARY OF DEFENSE

SUBJECT: Review of USAF Study: "Relationship of Tactical Air to Ground Forces, Southeast Asia, 1964 and 1969"

The subject study examines the use of land-based tactical airpower as an alternative to the use of U.S. ground forces in the event of a large scale intervention in Southeast Asia by CHICOM/DRV forces. You have requested the Chairman, JCS, to review this study, with particular emphasis on the sections dealing with the use of non-nuclear ordnance in 1964. Completion of this review is expected by August 28. In the interim, my Systems Analysis office has completed a parallel and independent review.

The Air Force study contains the following sentence:

The evidence supports the conclusion that tactical air with nonnuclear munitions can prevent the takeover of Southeast Asia by CHICOM ground forces opposed by minimal friendly ground forces.

However, I cannot agree that the evidence presented in the report is sufficient to support (or deny) such a conclusion. I have attached a paper commenting in some detail on the study. Briefly, my objections are as follows:

Some critically important calculations are incorrect. These include weapons effectiveness and the resulting requirements for combat sorties.

Some significant issues are largely ignored. Among these are (1) the effects of weather, particularly with respect to non-average conditions; (2) the effects of aircraft losses due to enemy action; (3) the logistic support requirements for the proposed force; (4) the vulnerability of the friendly airbases to enemy ground and/or air forces; (5) the ability of the force to conduct the basic interdiction campaign in the event that suppression of enemy airbases should also be necessary; (6) the time required to deploy the proposed force, and the effects of a CHICOM/DRV intervention prior to completion of our build-up; and (7) the use of carrier-based tactical airpower.

Some assumptions are inadequately supported. Among these are (1) the adequacy of the existing airbases to support the large proposed force; and the lack of alternative modes of transport available to the enemy.

Some assumptions appear optimistic. Among these are (1) the high [word missing] rate achieved; and (2) the small number of flak suppression sorties [word missing].

In my opinion, the question of the relationship between tactical air and ground forces in Southeast Asia remains open. Not only is a far more [word missing] and comprehensive analysis needed, but the use of naval and, probably, Army forces, in addition to land-based tactical air, must be considered.

As to who might be the best candidate for such a study, I feel that there is much to be said for CINCPAC, who would ultimately have the operational responsibility for implementing his own analytical recommendations, should it come to that. However, I recommend that you discuss this problam with the Chairman of the Joint Chiefs of Staff. In the interim, I will take no formal action relating to the current Air Force study.

Charles J. Hitch

[Document 183]

THE JOINT CHIEFS OF STAFF
WASHINGTON, D.C. 20301

JCSM-746-64
26 AUG 1964

MEMORANDUM FOR THE SECRETARY OF DEFENSE

Subject: Recommended Courses of Action—Southeast Asia

1. In their memorandum to you dated 14 August 1964, the Joint Chiefs of Staff advised that they were analyzing the next military courses of action in Southeast Asia and that appropriate recommendations would be forwarded for your consideration before implementing actions are taken on the Bundy memorandum dated 13 August 1964. They also reiterated the views of the Joint Chiefs of Staff, less the Chairman, of 2 June 1964 that military courses of action should include attack of targets in the Democratic Republic of Vietnam (DRV) with the objective of destroying, as necessary, the DRV will and capabilities to continue support of insurgent forces in the Republic of Vietnam (RVN) and Laos.

2. In analyzing courses of action, the Joint Chiefs of Staff have considered the views of CINCPAC and Ambassadors Taylor and Unger. The Joint Chiefs of Staff also noted the DIA assessment dated 7 August 1964 of Asian communist capabilities and 15 probable courses of action following the 5 August retaliatory attack on North Vietnam and the current US buildup in the Western Pacific. This assessment indicates that the most likely course of action would be stepped up actions in RVN and Laos with attendant increased flow of men and supplies.

3. The Joint Chiefs of Staff have considered Ambassador Taylor's statements of objectives and courses of action. In recognition of recent events in SVN, however, they consider that his proposed course of action B is more in accord with the current situation and consider that such an accelerated program of actions with respect to the DRV is essential to prevent a complete collapse of the US position in Southeast Asia. Additionally, they do not agree that we should be slow to get deeply involved until we have a better feel for the quality of our ally. The United States is already deeply involved. The Joint Chiefs of Staff consider that only significantly stronger military pressures on the DRV are likely to provide the relief and psychological boost necessary for attainment of the requisite governmental stability and viability.

4. Recent US military actions in Laos and against the DRV have demonstrated our resolve more clearly than any other US actions in some time. These actions showed both force and restraint. Failure to resume and maintain a program of pressure through military actions could be misinterpreted to mean we have had second thoughts about Pierce Arrow and the events leading thereto, and could signal a lack of resolve. Accordingly, while maintaining a posture of increased readiness in the Western Pacific, the Joint Chiefs of Staff believed that the US program should have as concurrent objectives: (1) improvements in

South Vietnam, including emphasis on the Pacification Program and the Hop Tac plan to clear Saigon and its surroundings; (2) interdiction of the relatively unmolested VC lines of communication (LOC) through Laos by operations in the Panhandle and of the LOC through Cambodia by strict control of the waterways leading therefrom; (3) denial of Viet Cong (VC) sanctuaries in the Cambodia–South Vietnam border area through the conduct of "hot pursuit" operations into Cambodia, as required; (4) increased pressure on North Vietnam through military actions. As part of the program for increased pressures, the OPLAN 34A operations and also the Desoto patrols in the Gulf of Tonkin should be resumed, the former on an intensified but still covert basis.

5. The Joint Chiefs of Staff believe, however, that more direct and forceful actions than these will, in all probability, be required. In anticipation of a pattern of further successful VC and Pathet Lao (PL) actions in RVN and Laos, and in order to increase pressure on the DRV, the US program should also provide for prompt and calculated responses to such VC/PL actions in the form of air strikes and other operations against appropriate military targets in the DRV.

6. The Joint Chiefs of Staff recognize that defining what might constitute appropriate counteroperations in advance is a most difficult task. We should therefore maintain our prompt readiness to execute a range of selected responses, tailored to the developing circumstances and reflecting the principles in the Gulf of Tonkin actions, that such counter-operations will result in clear military disadvantage to the DRV. These responses, therefore, must be greater than the provocation in degree, and not necessarily limited to response in kind against similar targets. Air strikes in response might be purely VNAF; VNAF with US escort to provide protection from possible employment of MIGs; VNAF with US support in the offensive as well as the defensive role; or entirely US. The precise combination should be determined by the effect we wish to produce and the assets available. Targets for attack by air or other forces may be selected from appropriate plans including the Target Study for North Vietnam consisting of 94 targets, recently forwarded to you by the Joint Chiefs of Staff.

7. While a US program as discussed above will not necessarily provide decisive end results, the Joint Chiefs of Staff advocate its adoption and implementation at once. Anything less could be interpreted as a lack of resolve on the part of the United States. The military course of action which offers the best chance of success remains the destruction of the DRV will and capabilities as necessary to compel the DRV to cease providing support to the insurgencies in South Vietnam and Laos.

8. Attached as Appendices to this memorandum are discussions of the following:

    a. Operations in the Laos Panhandle—Appendix A.

    b. OPLAN 34A operations—Appendix B.

    c. Other possible actions against North Vietnam—Aerial mining against the DRV and resumptions of the Desoto patrol in the Gulf of Tonkin—Appendix C.

    d. Other actions in RVN—Strict control of waterborne traffic on the Mekong and Bassac rivers and direct action against Viet Cong leadership—Appendix D.

9. In summary, the Joint Chiefs of Staff recommend that:

    a. The following military actions receive priority (not necessarily in the order listed):

        (1) Continuation of the Pacification Program in RVN with emphasis on the Hop Tac program to establish the security of Saigon and its surroundings;

(2) Continuation of the present forward deployment of US combat units;

(3) Resumption and intensification of OPLAN 34A operations with emphasis on maritime operations and with initiation of air operations against selected targets when practicable. OPLAN 34 A operations should remain covert for the time being.

(4) Resumption of Desoto patrols in the Gulf of Tonkin;

(5) Operations against the VC LOC, including staging base areas and infiltration routes in the Laos Panhandle by:

(a) The RLAF;

(b) GVN and Thai forces in cross-border operations with US support as required;

(c) US Armed aerial reconnaissance, attacking infiltration installations.

(6) Retaliatory actions by GVN/US forces against appropriate targets in the DRV in response to stepped up Viet Cong/Pathet Lao actions should such occur.

(7) Institution of "hot pursuit" operations into Cambodia.

b. The following related actions be taken:

(1) Institution of strict controls on the Mekong and Bassac rivers;

(2) Direct action against the Viet Cong leadership in RVN.

c. Since the above actions will probably not in themselves accomplish our objectives of compelling the DRV to respond favorably, we should be prepared to:

(1) Commerce deployment of remaining Category III OPLAN 37-64 forces;

(2) Commence a US air strike program against targets in North Vietnam in accordance with current planning.

10. In light of recent developments in South Vietnam and the evaluations furnished by COMUSMACV, the Joint Chiefs of Staff conclude that accelerated and forceful action with respect to North Vietnam is essential to prevent a complete collapse of the US position in Southeast Asia. They consider that a decision as to specific actions and the timing of these actions is urgent and recommend that conversations with Ambassador Taylor focus on this issue with a view to its early resolution.

For the Joint Chiefs of Staff:

Curtis E. Le May
Acting Chairman
Joint Chiefs of Staff

Attachments

[Document 184]

Aug. 26, 1964

State Cable

[addressee missing]

We agree with your assessment of importance SAR operations that Air America pilots can play critically important role, and that SAR efforts should not discriminate between rescuing Americans, Thais and Lao. You are also hereby granted as requested discretionary authority to use AA pilots in T-28's for SAR operations when you consider this *indispensable* rpt indispensable to success of operation and with understanding that you will seek advance Washington authorization wherever situation permits.

At same time, we believe time has come to review scope and control arrangements for T-28 operations extending into future. Such a review is especially indicated view fact that these operations more or less automatically impose demands for use of US personnel in SAR operations. Moreover, increased AA capability clearly means possibilities of loss somewhat increased, and each loss with accompanying SAR operations involves chance of escalation from one action to another in ways that may not be desirable in wider picture. On other side, we naturally recognize T-28 operations are vital both for their military and psychological effects in Laos and as negotiating card in support of Souvanna's position. Request your view whether balance of above factors would call for some reduction in scale of operations and/or dropping of some of better-defended targets. (Possible extension T-28 operations to Panhandle would be separate issue and will be covered by septel.)

On control problem, our understanding is that Thai pilots fly missions strictly controlled by your Air Command Center with AIRA in effective control, but that this not true of Lao pilots. We have impression latter not really under any kind of firm control.

Request your evaluation and recommendations as to future scope T-28 operations and your comments as to whether our impressions present control structure correct and whether steps could be taken to tighten this.

End

RUSK

[Document 185]

THE JOINT CHIEFS OF STAFF
WASHINGTON, D.C. 20301
OFFICE OF THE SPECIAL ASSISTANT FOR
COUNTERINSURGENCY AND SPECIAL ACTIVITIES

27 August 1964

MEMORANDUM FOR MR. WILLIAM BUNDY
MR. J. T. McNAUGHTON

Subject: OPLAN 34A—September Schedule

Reference: MACSOG Message 8618 DTG 240855Z August

1. Attached hereto is COMUSMACV's proposed schedule of 34A actions for September.

2. All of the actions listed have either been specifically approved previously or are similar to such approved actions. For example, Action (3) (d) was specifically approved by consideration of JCSM-426-64 dated 19 May 1964, while Action (3) (b) is similar to a previously approved action against a security post.

3. The method of attack has been changed in some instances from destruction by infiltration of demolition teams to the concept of standoff bombardment from PTF's. These actions are so indicated in the attachment.

Rollen H. Anthis
Major General, USAF

Attachment

The proposed September 34A actions are as follows:

(1) *Intelligence Collection Actions*

(a) 1–30 September—Ariel photography to update selected targets along with pre- and post-strike coverage of approved actions.

(b) 1–30 September—Two junk capture missions; remove captives for 36–48 hours interrogation; booby trap junk with antidisturbance devices and release; captives returned after interrogation; timing depends upon sea conditions and current intelligence.

(2) *Psychological Operations*

(a) 1–30 September—In conjunction with approved overflights and maritime operations, delivery of propaganda leaflets, gift kits, and deception devices simulating resupply of phantom teams.

(b) 1–30 September—Approximately 200 letters of various propaganda themes sent through third country mail channels to North Vietnam.

(c) 1–30 September—Black Radio daily 30-minute programs repeated once, purports to be voice of dissident elements in North Vietnam.

(d) 1–30 September—White Radio broadcast of eight-and-one-half hours daily, propaganda "Voice of Freedom."

(3) *Maritime Operations*

(a) 1–30 September—Demolition of Route 1 bridge by infiltrated team accompanied by fire support teams, place short-delay charges against spans and caissons, place antipersonnel mines on road approaches. (This bridge previously hit but now repaired).

(b) 1–30 September—Bombard Cape Mui Dao observation post with 81 MM mortars and 40 MM guns from two PTFs.

(c) 1–30 September—Demolition of another Route 1 bridge (see map), concept same as (3) (a) above.

(d) 1–30 September—Bombard Sam Son radar, same as (3) (b).

(e) 1–30 September—Bombard Tiger Island barracks, same as (3) (b).

(f) 1–30 September—Bombard Hon Ngu Island, same as (3) (b).

(g) 1–30 September—Bombard Hon Matt Island, same as (3) (b) and run concurrently with (3) (f).

(h) 1–30 September—Destruction of section of Hanoi-Vinh railroad by infiltrated demolition team supported by two VN marine squads, by rubber boats from PTFs, place short-delay charges and anti-personnel mines around area.

(i) 1–30 September—Bombard Hon Me Island in conjunction with (3) (a) above, concept same as (3) (b).

(j) 1–30 September—Bombard Cape Falaise gun positions in conjunction with (3) (h) above, concept same as (3) (b).

(k) 1–30 September—Bombard Cape Mui Ron in conjunction with junk capture mission, concept same as (3) (b).

(4) *Airborne Operations*—Light-of-moon period 16–28 September

(a) Four missions for resupply of in-place teams.

(b) Four missions for reinforcement of in-place teams.

(c) Four missions to airdrop new psyops/sabotage teams depending upon development of drop zone and target information. These are low-key propaganda and intelligence gathering teams with a capability for small-scale sabotage on order after locating suitable targets.

(5) Dates for actual launch of maritime and airborne operations are contingent upon the intelligence situation and weather conditions.

[Document 186]

29 AUG 1964

MEMORANDUM FOR THE SECRETARY OF DEFENSE

SUBJECT: Response to JCSM-729-64: Target Study—North Vietnam (S)

1. JCSM 729-64 forwards to you, as Appendix A, the detailed JCS analysis of the 94 targets in North Vietnam. The JCSM sumarizes the types of targets included, the status of ordnance and POL requirements, aircraft availabilities and capabilities and sorties required. It also outlines the types of detailed strike plans now being developed by CINCPAC.

2. No response to the JCSM is required; it makes no specific recommendations and amounts to what is, in effect, an interim progress report. I think, however, that a word of appreciation is appropriate given the very substantial efforts devoted by the Joint Staff and DIA toward the compilation of what seem to me to be first-rate studies of the 94 targets. Such is the purpose of paragraph 1 of the attached response.

3. Paragraphs 2, 3 and 4, which request additional information from the Joint Chiefs of Staff, are self-explanatory.

4. Recommend signature.

Enclosure
Memo for Chairman, JCS

John T. McNaughton
Assistant Secretary of Defense
International Security Affairs

[Document 187]

31 AUG 1964

MEMORANDUM FOR THE CHAIRMAN, JOINT CHIEFS OF STAFF

SUBJECT: JCSM-729-64: Target Study—North Vietnam

1. I have examined with great interest and satisfaction your recent analysis of the 94 targets in North Vietnam. The detail and precision with which you have described and defined the targets, the attack objectives, and the weapons and sorties required to accomplish those objectives testify to the care with which you have undertaken your task and the weeks of effort which you have devoted to it. Earlier versions of your target studies have already proved to be of great value in connection with the recent reprisals against North Vietnam.

2. Would there be sufficient stocks of ordnance and POL in the theater to carry out OPLAN 32, Phase IV, *after* carrying out the largest pattern of attack shown in your memorandum (paragraph 8d)?

3. I should like to receive, within the next several weeks, your views concerning the economic and military effect upon North Vietnam of the patterns of attack contemplated. To put the matter more precisely, assume that attacks 8b, c and d were carried out and that the attacks resulted in the damage levels described in your target studies. In these circumstances, what would be your estimate:

    (a) Of the effects upon the capabilities of North Vietnam
        i. to support and assist the PL and VC.
        ii. to escalate through the use of DRV forces against SVN and Laos.

(b) Of the effects upon the economy of North Vietnam (in terms of such factors as internal transportation, imports and exports, industrial production and food production and distribution) within the short run (say three months) and in the long-run (say five years).

4. If the destruction of the 94 targets were not to succeed in its objective of destroying the DRV will and capability, what courses of action would you recommend? Would you recommend further attack on the 94 targets or the addition of more targets? What preparations would be necessary (e.g., target analysis, logistics) in order to carry out such attacks?

Signed
Robert S. McNamara

[Document 188]

2nd Draft
9/3/64

McNaughton
ISA

PLAN OF ACTION FOR SOUTH VIETNAM

1. *Analysis of the present situation.* The situation in South Vietnam is deteriorating. Even before the government sank into confusion last week, the course of the war in South Vietnam had been downward, with Viet Cong incidents increasing in number and intensity and military actions becoming larger and more successful, and with less and less territory meaningfully under the control of the government. Successful ambushes had demonstrated an unwillingness of the population even in what were thought to be pacified areas to run the risk of informing on the Viet Cong. War weariness was apparent. The crisis of the end of August—especially since the competing forces have left the government largely "faceless" and have damaged the government's ability to manage the pacification program—promises to lead to further and more rapid deterioration. Even if Khanh makes a recovery soon, the government is bound to be less effective at all levels for a time; South Vietnam will be a weakened target. Hanoi is certain to assess the situation this way, and it is quite likely that the Viet Cong in the next month or two will make an all-out effort to shake South Vietnam apart.

US policy has been to pacify South Vietnam by aid and advice and actions within the borders of South Vietnam. This policy will not work without a strong government in Saigon. It has become apparent that there is no likelihood that a government sufficiently strong to administer a successful pacification program will develop. It follows that our current US policy, which is based on such a program, will not succeed.

The odds are very great that if we do not inject some major new elements—and perhaps even if we do—the situation will continue to deteriorate; there is a substantial chance that the [words missing] completely apart, with dramatic VC military victories putting intolerable pressure on a weakened Saigon government. The result within a few months, or even a few weeks, could be a succession of governmental changes ending in a demand for a negotiated settlement.

The objective of the United States is to reverse the present downward trend.

Failing that, the alternative objective is to emerge from the situation with as good an image as possible in US, allied and enemy eyes.

2. *Inside South Vietnam.* We must in any event keep hard at work inside South Vietnam. This means, inter alia, immediate action:

    (a) to press the presently visible leaders to get a real government in operation;

    (b) to prevent extensive personnel changes down the line;

    (c) to see that lines of authority for carrying out the pacification program are clear.

New initiatives might include action:

    (d) to establish a US Naval base, perhaps at Danang;

    (e) to embark on a major effort to pacify one province adjacent to Saigon.

A separate analysis is being made of a proposal:

    (f) to enlarge significantly the US military role in the pacification program inside South Vietnam—e.g., large numbers of US special forces, divisions of regular combat troops, US air, etc., to "interlard" with or to take over functions or geographical areas from the South Vietnamese armed forces.

A combination of actions confined to the territory of South Vietnam, however, offers much promise to slow the deteriorating situation appreciably.

3. *Outside the borders of South Vietnam.* There is a chance that the downward trend can be reversed—or a new situation created offering new opportunities, or at least a convincing demonstration made of the great costs and risks incurred by a country which commits aggression against an ally of ours—if the following course of action is followed. The course of action is made up of actions outside the borders of South Vietnam designed to put increasing pressure on North Vietnam but designed also both to create as little risk as possible of the kind of military action which would be difficult to justify to the American public and to preserve where possible the option to have no US military action at all.

Timing. The scenario should begin approximately October 1. This date does not appear to be appreciably less desirable than a September date from the point of view of the deteriorating situation. Its advantages are that it allows time for consultation in Washington with Ambassador Taylor, and it allows time for some kind of a "voice" to emerge which can speak for South Vietnam (a prerequisite to the proposed course of action), and it postpones probably until November or December any decision as to serious escalation.

Objectives. The purpose of the course of action would be to improve our position in at least one of the following four ways:

    i. Increase the unity and therefore the effectiveness of the GVN government, thus facilitating pacification of South Vietnam.

    ii. Decrease DRV support for the Viet Cong, thus facilitating pacification of South Vietnam.

    iii. Increase the actual and portended cost of the war to DRV, thus improving our bargaining position in the event of negotiations.

    iv. Increase the actual and apparent cost of the war to the DRV and the actual and apparent contribution in risk and effort by the US, thus improving our image as a trustworthy ally no matter what the ultimate outcome.

Actions. The actions, in addition to present continuing "extra-territorial" actions (US U-2 recce of DRV, US jet recce of Laos, T-28 activity in Laos), would be by way of an orchestration of three classes of actions, all designed to meet these five desiderata—(1) From the US, GVN, and hopefully allied points of view, they should be legitimate things to do under the circumstances, (2) they should cause apprehension, ideally increasing apprehension, in the DRV, (3) they should be likely at some point to provoke a military DRV response, (4) the provoked response should be likely to provide good grounds for us to escalate if we wished, and (5) the timing and crescendo should be under our control, with the scenario capable of being turned off at any time. The three classes of actions are:

a. *South Vietnamese air attacks on the Laotian infiltration routes.* The strikes should begin in Laos near the South Vietnamese border and slowly "march" up the trails to and eventually across the North Vietnamese border. The case for action of this kind has already been made in the relevant bodies of opinion. The tacit consent of Souvanna would have to be and probably could be obtained. Ground fire at the VNAF aircraft would be sufficient but not necessary cause for US suppression of the AA batteries; MIG opposition to the VNAF aircraft would be encountered probably only late in the "march" up the trails and likewise would be sufficient but not necessary cause for US jet cap for the VNAF aircraft, hot pursuit of the MIGs, and even strikes at the MIG airfields in North Vietnam. The pace would be under our control.

b. *South Vietnamese sea attacks on North Vietnamese junks and shore facilities by bombardment and landings.* These operations can be fully justified as necessary to assist in interdiction of infiltration by sea. North Vietnamese opposition by sea or air could, but would not have to be, used by the US as grounds for giving sea or air protection for the South Vietnamese craft or even for undertaking such actions as the mining of certain North Vietnamese harbors. While the North Vietnamese would be able to select the time and place of their response to the South Vietnamese strikes, the US would in any instance retain the choice whether and how to escalate.

c. *De Soto patrols.* These patrols should be fully protected by naval and air units, disassociated from any South Vietnamese sea raids, and far out in international waters of the Gulf of Tonkin. There is a demonstrable and increasing military requirement for these patrols because of the likely changes in North Vietnamese equipment and procedures since August 5; and the US public is sympathetic to reasonable insistence on the right of the US Navy to ply international waters. We could not ignore a DRV sea or air attack on such a De Soto destroyer. Such an attack would require us either to apply the August 5 limited-retaliation formula again or, especially if a US ship were sunk, to commence a full-fledged squeeze on North Vietnam. (It is unlikely that the DRV will attack our ships if they are outside the "12-mile limit.")

4. *Actions of opportunity.* While the above course of action is being pursued, we should watch for other DRV actions which would justify a limited retaliation or the commencement of a squeeze on North Vietnam.

Among such DRV actions might be the following:

a. Downing of US recce or US rescue aircraft in Laos (likely by AA, unlikely by MIG).

b. MIG action in Laos or South Vietnam (unlikely).

c. Mining of Saigon Harbor (unlikely).

d. VC attacks on South Vietnamese POL storage, RR bridge, etc. (dramatic incident required).

e. VC attacks (e.g., by mortars on, or take-over of, air fields on which US aircraft are deployed (likely).

f. Some barbaric act of terrorism which inflames US and world opinion (unlikely).

5. *Graduated pressure on DRV.* The concept of the course of action described

above in essence is: by doing legimate things to provoke a DRV response and to be in a good position to seize on that response, or upon an unprovoked DRV action, to commence a crescendo of GVN-US military actions against the DRV. The escalating actions might be naval pressures, mining of harbors; or they might be made up of air strikes against North Vietnam moving from southern to northern targets, from targets associated with infiltration and by-then-disclosed DRV-VC radio command nets to targets of military then industrial importance, and from missions that could be handled by the VNAF alone to those which could be carried out only by the US. The effect of such escalation on Saigon and on other Vietnamese cities—the populations of which would be fearful of counter strikes—would have to be weighed. And the possibility that such actions would escalate further, perhaps bringing China into the war, would have to be faced. Substantial contingency deployments of ground, sea and air forces to Southeast Asia would have to be made at some point—at the latest, just before any overt US actions were taken against the territory of North Vietnam.

6. *Chances to resolve the situation.* Throughout the scenario, we should be alert to chances to resolve the situation:

  a. To back the DRV down, so South Vietnam can be pacified.

  b. To evolve a tolerable settlement:

    i. Explicit settlement (e.g., via a bargaining-from-strength conference, etc.).

    ii. Tacit settlement (e.g., via piecemeal live-and-let-live Vietnamese "settlements," a de facto "writing off" of indefensible portions of SVN, etc.).

  c. If worst comes and South Vietnam disintegrates or their behavior becomes abominable, to "disown" South Vietnam, hopefully leaving the image of "a patient who died despite the extraordinary efforts of a good doctor."

7. *Special considerations during next two months.* The relevant "audiences" of US actions are the Communists (who must feel strong pressures), the South Vietnamese (whose morale must be buoyed), our allies (who must trust us as "underwriters"), and the US public (which must support our risk-taking with US lives and prestige). During the next two months, because of the lack of "rebuttal time" before election to justify particular actions which may be distorted to the US public, we must act with special care—signaling to the DRV that initiatives are being taken, to the GVN that we are behaving energetically despite the restraints of our political season, and to the US public that we are behaving with good purpose and restraint.

[Document 189]

THE WHITE HOUSE
WASHINGTON

CONFIDENTIAL   September 4, 1964
MEMORANDUM TO: Mr. Robert Manning

Subject: Possible problems in the current form of the Q & A booklet on Vietnam

Yesterday when we agreed to hold up this booklet, I undertook to let you know what parts of it might give trouble as of now. Obviously, as the situation shifts the problem changes, but the following items occurred to me in a careful reading two days ago:

1. On page 4 in the last paragraph we use some adverbs about the new government that are a little hard to justify this week.

2. On page 9 we describe the military situation as "stabilized," which seems optimistic.

On page 10 the discussion of VC military activities seems a trifle dated, and the estimate of the improvement of government forces optimistic.

3. On pages 19 to 21, questions 21, 22, and 23 might be outdated by decisions in coming weeks. There is no certainty about this, but I doubt if we wish to be pinned to a course from which we might wish to shift.

4. On page 22, I doubt if it is enough to call the M-1 rifle "adequate."

5. On page 24, I think the Gulf of Tonkin action should not be quite so sharply separated from possible future operations. I would correct the paragraph by including the possibility of retaliation and counteraction against maritime infiltration, without giving the implication that any such force is definitely agreed on now.

6. In a similar way, on page 25, I think we ought to leave the door a little more open to appropriate action against the north, but a very marginal change would satisfy me.

McGeorge Bundy

[Document 190]

DRAFT—Bundy

COURSES OF ACTION FOR SOUTH VIETNAM

The Situation

1. Khanh will probably stay in control and may make some headway in the next 2–3 months in strengthening the government. The best we can expect is that he and the government will be able to maintain order, keeping the pacification program ticking over (but not progressing markedly), and keep up the appearance of a valid government.

2. Khanh and the GVN leaders are temporarily too exhausted to be thinking much about moves against the North. However, they do need to be reassured that the US continues to mean business, and as Khanh goes along in his government efforts, he will probably want more US effort visible.

3. The GVN over the next 2–3 months will be too weak for us to take any deliberate major risks of escalation that would involve any important contribution by South Vietnam. However, escalation arising from and directed against US action would tend to lift GVN morale. [Temporarily only; not worth US action for this purpose alone.]

4. The Communist side will probably avoid provocative action, and it is uncertain how much they will step up VC activity. They do need to be shown that we and the GVN are not simply sitting back after the Gulf of Tonkin.

Courses of Action

We should in any event:

1. Resume 34A operations very soon. The operations selected should be related to the case against VC infiltration by sea, and this case should be made publicly by the GVN to legitimize and surface—in a *general* sense—the maritime operations. Other 34A air drop operations should also be resumed but are secondary in importance. We should not consider air strikes under 34A for the present.

2. US naval patrols in the Gulf of Tonkin should be resumed very soon, initially beyond the twelve-mile limit and clearly dissociated from 34A maritime operations.

3. Limited GVN air and ground operations into the Corridor areas of Laos should be undertaken in the near future, together with Laos air strikes as soon as we can get Souvanna's permission. These operations will have only limited effect, however.

4. We should be prepared to respond on a tit-for-tat basis against the DRV in the event of any attack on US units or any special DRV/VC action against SVN.

The main further question is the extent to which we should add elements to the above actions that would tend to provoke a DRV reaction, and consequent retaliation by us. The main action to be considered would be running US naval patrols increasingly close to the North Vietnamese coast and/or associating them with 34A operations. Such extension might be undertaken if the initial US naval patrols had not aroused a reaction.

As to timing, the above actions would get underway late in September or early in October. The more provocative variations would be considered for insertion not earlier than mid-October.

W. P. Bundy/bmm
September 8, 1964

[Document 191]

8 September 1964

COURSES OF ACTION FOR SOUTH VIETNAM

This memorandum records the consensus reached in discussions between Ambassador Taylor and Secretary Rusk, Secretary McNamara, and General Wheeler, for review and decision by the President.

The Situation

1. Khanh will probably stay in control and may make some headway in the next 2–3 months in strengthening the government (GVN). The best we can expect is that he and the GVN will be able to maintain order, keep the pacification program ticking over (but not progressing markedly), and give the appearance of a valid government.

2. Khanh and the GVN leaders are temporarily too exhausted to be thinking much about moves against the North. However, they do need to be reassured that the US continues to mean business, and as Khanh goes along in his government efforts, he will probably want more US effort visible, and some GVN role in external actions.

3. The GVN over the next 2–3 months will be too weak for us to take any major deliberate risks of escalation that would involve a major role for, or threat to, South Vietnam. However, escalation arising from and directed against US action would tend to lift GVN morale at least temporarily.

4. The Communist side will probably avoid provocative action against the US, and it is uncertain how much they will step up VC activity. They do need to be shown that we and the GVN are not simply sitting back after the Gulf of Tonkin.

Courses of Action

We recommend in any event:

1. US naval patrols in the Gulf of Tonkin should be resumed immediately (about September 12). They should operate initially beyond the 12-mile limit and be clearly dissociated from 34A maritime operations. The patrols would comprise 2–3 destroyers and would have air cover from carriers; the destroyers would have their own ASW capability.

2. 34A operations by the GVN should be resumed immediately thereafter (next week). The maritime operations are by far the most important. North Vietnam is likely to publicize them, and at this point we should have the GVN ready to admit that they are taking place and to justify and legitimize them on the basis of the facts on VC infiltration by sea. 34A air drop and leaflet operations should also be resumed but are secondary in importance. We should not consider air strikes under 34A for the present.

3. Limited GVN air and ground operations into the corridor areas of Laos should be undertaken in the near future, together with Lao air strikes as soon as we can get Souvanna's permission. These operations will have only limited effect, however.

4. We should be *prepared* to respond on a tit-for-tat basis against the DRV in the event of any attack on US units or any *special* DRV/VC action against SVN. The response for an attack on US units should be along the lines of the Gulf of Tonkin attacks, against specific and related targets. The response to special action against SVN should likewise be aimed at specific and comparable targets.

The main further question is the extent to which we should add elements to the above actions that would tend deliberately to provoke a DRV reaction, and consequent retaliation by us. Examples of actions to be considered would be running US naval patrols increasingly close to the North Vietnamese coast and/or associating them with 34A operations. We believe such deliberately provocative elements should not be added in the immediate future while the GVN is still struggling to its feet. By early October, however, we may recommend such actions depending on GVN progress and Communist reaction in the meantime, especially to US naval patrols.

The aim of the above actions, external to South Vietnam, would be to assist morale in SVN and show the Communists we still mean business, while at the same time seeking to keep the risks low and under our control at each stage.

Further actions within South Vietnam are not covered in this memorandum. We believe that there are a number of immediate-impact actions we can take, such as pay raises for the police and civil administrators and spot projects in the cities and selected rural areas. These actions would be within current policy and will be refined for decision during Ambassador Taylor's visit. We are also considering minor changes in the US air role within South Vietnam, but these would not include decisions until November.

W. P. Bundy/bmm

[Document 192]

Amembassy SAIGON [number missing]   Sept. 9, 1964

Amembassy VIENTIANE 229

Amembassy BANGKOK 357

EXDIS

Joint State/Defense Message

Refs: Vientiane 296 and 305 to Bangkok
       Saigon 67 to Vientiane, repeated Dept 778

Meeting today approved in principle early initiation air and limited ground operations in Laos corridor as soon as politically and militarily feasible. Therefore believe meeting this week as proposed by Saigon would be useful way to clarify scope and timing possible operations. Following questions appear crucial:

1. *Air operations*
   a. Best targeting division as between GVN and RLAF, and what targets would be recommended for US suppressive strikes.
   b. Latest reading political acceptability GVN strikes and US suppressive strikes and whether we should inform Souvanna before undertaking, or go ahead without informing him. Related question is whether to publicize.
2. *Ground operations*
   a. Review of latest plans and possible timing of action especially for limited bridgehead along lines indicated Saigon 485.
   b. Requirement for US advisors and support. These not covered by today's decisions and might require another review when plans developed.
   c. Same political questions as to Souvanna and publicity.
3. In light of answers to above what should be GVN, RLG, and US public stance to operations?

Believe it would be desirable for Bangkok be represented at meeting, in view possible Thai involvement in some operations.

Ambassador Taylor concurs.

                         END   *RUSK*

[Document 193]

                                                        CM-124-64

                                                   9 September 1964

MEMORANDUM FOR THE SECRETARY OF DEFENSE

Subject: Courses of Action for South Vietnam

1. The Joint Chiefs of Staff have considered the draft paper prepared by Assistant Secretary William Bundy, subject as above, and have expressed the views set forth in subsequent paragraphs.

2. *De Soto patrols*—These patrols should be resumed shortly after the return (two to three days) of Ambassador Taylor to Saigon. The Joint Chiefs of Staff

believe that the first De Soto patrol should complete its operation and clear the Gulf of Tonkin before MAROPS are resumed. Rules of engagement, attached hereto, should be consonant with those earlier established to deal with hostile acts by DRV military forces.

3. *MAROPS*—Marine operations should be resumed as set forth above.

a. The Chief of Staff Army, the Chief of Naval Operations, the Chief of Staff Air Force, and the Commandant Marine Corps consider that MAROPS should not be made overt (legitimized) until these operations and De Soto patrol operations become so intertwined that they can be associated, or until the US is prepared openly to support MAROPS militarily.

b. The Chairman of the Joint Chiefs of Staff does not agree with *a* above. He considers that failure to legitimize MAROPS until the circumstances postulated above are realized could cause us to limit the scope and thereby the effectiveness of MAROPS and could inhibit the United States as to the nature and extent of our response to hostile attack on US forces on or over the high seas. In making this judgment, the Chairman considers that the fact the GVN is conducting maritime operations in the Gulf of Tonkin must not inhibit the mounting of De Soto patrols in those waters.

4. *Air and ground operations in Laos*—The JCS consider that the proposed actions should be somewhat expanded as follows: GVN air and ground operations should be undertaken in the near future against the VC LOC in the Laotian corridor to include attacks against staging bases and infiltration routes. US armed aerial reconnaissance flights should be used to supplement the foregoing actions. We should attempt to gain Thai participation in ground action in this area.

5. *Response to attack*—The Joint Chiefs of Staff believe that the term "tit for tat" could be interpreted to limit too narrowly our response to an attack on US units or any specific DRV/VC action against SVN. This action should be rephrased to state, "We should be prepared to respond as appropriate against the DRV in the event of any attack on US units or any special DRV/VC action against SVN."

6. The Joint Chiefs of Staff agree that the present in-country pacification plan, including the foregoing actions, is not enough in itself to maintain national morale or to offer reasonable hope of eventual success. Military action by GVN and US forces against the DRV will be required.

7. The Chief of Staff Air Force and Commandant of the Marine Corps believe that time is against us and military action against the DRV should be taken now. They concur that the American public should support any action taken by the United States Government against the DRV. They consider that, linked to the next significant incident, we should comence a retaliatory GVN and US air strike program against the DRV in accordance with the 94 target plan. In this regard, they consider that a battalion-size VC attack on South Vietnam should be construed as "significant."

8. The Chairman of the Joint Chiefs of Staff, the Chief of Staff, Army, and Chief of Naval Operations consider that, based upon Ambassador Taylor's recommendations, we should not purposely embark upon a program to create an incident immediately but that, as indicated above, we must respond appropriately against the DRV in the event of an attack on US units.

Attachment:
   Rules of Engagement,
   De Soto Patrol

                                     Earle G. Wheeler
                                     Chairman
                                     Joint Chiefs of Staff

[Document 194]

JOINT CHIEFS OF STAFF

9 September 1964

Rules of Engagement, De Soto Patrol

The following rules of engagement are recomended for De Soto patrols in the Gulf of Tonkin:

a. In the event of hostile attack, the patrol ships and aircraft are directed to fire upon the hostile attacker with the objective of insuring destruction. Ships are authorized to pursue the enemy to the recognized three mile territorial limit. Aircraft are authorized hot pursuit inside territorial waters (3 miles) against surface vessels and into hostile airspace (includes DRV, Hainan Island and Mainland China) against attacking aircraft when necessary to achieve destruction of identified attacking forces.

b. Ships and aircraft will confine their actions to the attacking ships and/or aircraft.

[Document 195]

September 10, 1964

NATIONAL SECURITY ACTION MEMORANDUM NO. 314

TO: The Secretary of State
The Secretary of Defense

The President has now reviewed the situation in South Vietnam with Ambassador Taylor and with other advisers and has approved the following actions:

1. U.S. naval patrols in the Gulf of Tonkin will be resumed promptly after Ambassador Taylor's return. They will operate initially well beyond the 12-mile limit and be clearly dissociated from 34A maritime operations. The patrols will comprise two to three destroyers and would have air cover from carriers; the destroyers will have their own ASW capability.

2. 34A operations by the GVN will be resumed after completion of a first De Soto patrol. The maritime operations are by far the most important. North Vietnam has already publicized them, and is likely to publicize them even more, and at this point we should have the GVN ready to admit that they are taking place and to justify and legitimize them on the basis of the facts of VC infiltration by sea. 34A air drop and leaflet operations should also be resumed but are secondary in importance. [We should not consider air strikes under 34A for the present.]

3. We should promptly discuss with the Government of Laos plans for limited GVN air and ground operations into the corridor areas of Laos, together with Lao air strikes and possible use of U.S. armed aerial reconnaissance. On the basis of these discussions a decision on action will be taken, but it should be recognized that these operations will in any case have only limited effect.

4. We should be prepared to respond as appropriate against the DRV in the event of any attack on US units or any special DRV/VC action against SVN.

5. The results of these decisions will be kept under constant review, and recommendations for changes or modifications or additions will be promptly considered.

6. The President reemphasizes the importance of economic and political actions having immediate impact in South Vietnam, such as pay raises for civilian personnel and spot projects in the cities and selected rural areas. The President emphasizes again that no activity of this kind should be delayed in any way by any feeling that our resources for these purposes are restricted. We can find the money which is needed for all worthwhile projects in this field. He expects that Ambassador Taylor and the country team will take most prompt and energetic action in this field.

7. These decisions are governed by a prevailing judgment that the first order of business at present is to take actions which will help to strengthen the fabric of the Government of South Vietnam; to the extent that the situation permits, such action should precede larger decisions. If such larger decisions are required at any time by a change in the situation, they will be taken.

McGeorge Bundy

[Document 196]

ACTION PRIORITY SECSTATE 913
SEPTEMBER 19, 5 PM, FROM AMEMBASSY SAIGON,
SIGNED TAYLOR.

STATE PASS DOD AND CINCPAC

SECTION ONE OF TWO

EXDIS

DEPTEL 622.

Following is a summary, coordinated with Vientiane and Bangkok, of the conclusions of the meeting of the three posts held at Saigon September 11 to review air and limited ground operations of the Lao corridor:

1. Air operations in Corridor. This involves attack of 22 targets for which folders available at Vientiane and Saigon. If objective is primarily military, i.e., to inflict maximum damage to targets, to prevent VN/PL dispersal and protective measures, and impede rapid VN/PL riposte, it was agreed that a series of sharp, heavy attacks must be made in a relatively short time span, which would involve substantial US and/or VNAF/FARMGATE attacks. If objective primarily psychological, military disadvantages of attacks over longer time frame would be acceptable and chief reliance could be placed on RLAF T-28s with some YANKEE TEAM strikes against harder targets, e.g., five bridges. Established sortie requirements for this second option 188 T 28 sorties and 80 USAF sorties. Time required 12 days. Vientiane representatives believe Souvanna would probably go along with second option but would probably wish to have such attacks spread out over considerable period of time. Also felt Souvanna would prefer VNAF not conduct air strikes in corridor. It was general consensus that best division of targeting for immediate future would be RLAF/YANKEE TEAM mix.

Vientiane is very reluctant to see VNAF participation such strikes and would hope that by keeping GVN informed of actions being taken by RLAF and US in corridor, psychological needs of GVN could reasonably be met. Saigon will seek to do this, but if there are compelling reasons for covert VNAF participation Vientiane would be given prior info on necessity, timing, and place of such strikes. Alternatively, it was agreed that, if possible, joint Lao, Thai, RVN, and US participation in a common effort against a common enemy would be desirable but, recognizing that, even if possible, arrangements for such an effort would take some time to achieve. If such negotiations are conducted, however, RLAF/ YANKEE TEAM strikes should not be precluded. Vientiane has since stated it does not consider that it would be desirable to seek to formalize such four country participation in corridor operations as to do so would raise question of degree of Souvanna Phouma's knowledge and involvement which Vientiane feels would jeopardize success of operations.

2. Ground operations.

A. Although it was agreed that northern Route 9 area offered most profitable targets, conference proceeded on assumption that Vientiane would find operations astride Route 9 politically unacceptable at this time. However, Vientiane's 448 to Dept, dispatched after return of conferees, now indicates that "shallow penetration raids (20 kilometers). . . . In Rte 9 area . . . by company-sized units" would be acceptable and would not require clearance by the RLG.

B. Conference also agreed that central and southern areas offered targets and terrain consistent with capabilities of current assets.

C. Saigon concept is that operations astride Rte 9 would be initiated by 8-man intelligence and reconnaissance teams infiltrated overland or by air. Exploitation of targets developed by these teams would be by airborne ranger companies (80– 100 men), committed by parachute, helicopter or overland. Operations in order two areas would be conducted by reconnaissance combat patrols of up to company size. In southernmost area operations would be characterized by limited but ever expanding overland ground probes; in central area combination overland and air launch methods probably required. In each area operations would be limited to 20 kilometers penetration not to exceed two companies at any one time. In addition airborne ranger companies, assets include CIDG strike companies and ARVN rangers.

D. Air supply for these operations can in normal foreseeable circumstances be handled exclusively within VNAF assets.

This would include not rpt not only air drop and air exfiltration requirements but also air strike support and SAR operations in the event of emergency. FARM-GATE and/or overt US support would be called upon only in the event of unforeseen contingency which would exceed available VNAF capability. No problem was foreseen in use of US jumpmasters/observers. Saigon group stated that under these operating rules, operations could be initiated within fifteen days of decision to execute.

E. It was the view of Saigon group that authority for US advisors to accompany units is a prerequisite to successful operations. Without this US participation probability of success is judged so low that the advisability of conducting cross border operations would be questionable. Vientiane representatives were strongly opposed to presence US advisors because of difficulty with current SAR operations in Laos and political importance of US maintaining credible stance of adhering to provisions Geneva Accords.

F. Embassy Vientiane had earlier indicated that they would insist on advanced clearance of cross border operations. All representatives agreed that this requirement would be met by VIENTIANE having opportunity to comment on all plans submitted to Washington for approval. Once approval to execute is received, Vientiane would be kept informed of day-to-day operations as information addressed on operational traffic between Saigon/Washington/CINCPAC.

[The remainder of this document was available only with the left-hand portion missing, as follows.]

stance. It was the unanimous opinion of the group
ould be preferable to have no publicity with regards
nal details, and that no comment should be made in
questions or accusations other than our unawareness
ch matters. Additionally, it was agreed that Souvanna
t be informed of any of these GVN/US actions. Use
ould, of course, have to be cleared by him.
mary, recommend we proceed as follows:
Team escort strike hard targets (5 bridges), RLAF
of 22-target list. Accordingly, VIENTIANE should be
d make approach to RLG on initiation T-28 strikes
H 2, Vientiane's 448 to department).
ize ground operations in all three areas, with timing
of employment of available assets as determined
te by COMUSMAC and CINCRVNAF, subject to provision
(19) relative depth of penetration and size of
be committed; para 2(D) relative air support;
2(F) relative coordination with Vientiane.
tions, ground and air, to be initiated as rapidly
ionally feasible.
licity and no public acknowledgement of any operational
ground or air. .
er to give some four nation "flavor" to operations,
Bangkok to approach TG for authority to use KORAT
or some of US aircraft participating in foregoing
am operations.
t earliest Washington decision as to use of US advisors,
ng Saigon's serious reservations as to changes of
if their suse is denied and Vientiane's concern over
political impact of capture by PL/VM of US military
in ALAOS.
Bangkok and Vientiane. Foregoing has been modified
ginal draft sent you in light your comments and:
's 448 to Dept.

[Document 197]

FM CINCPAC   21 Sept 64
TO RUEKDA/JCS

DESOTO Patrol OPS
A. COMUSMACV MAC 5147

1. Believe it urgent that we operate another DESOTO patrol in the immediate
future and certainly within a month. Failure to do so will, in my opinion,
materially increases the likelihood of enemy reaction to operations in the Gulf of
Tonkin later on. The DRV must not be given any reason to believe that the U.S.
considers the Gulf of Tonkin too hot for comfort. Much has been made both
publicly and in our own government's planning of our determination to get
the message to Hanoi and Peiping that continuation of their present course in
sea will cost them heavily. But to discontinue the DESOTO patrols now would
convey the opposite message.

2. Beyond that there are other substantial military advantages which can accrue to the U.S. and to the RVN by continuation of destroyer patrols in the Gulf of Tonkin. These are:

A. Determine DRV coastal defense posture including their capability to detect, track and intercept hostile targets. Of special significance are types/numbers of forces committed in reaction to DESOTO ships' presence and that point at which DRV forces attempt to harass aggressively or attack.

B. Identify visually and photograph naval units.

C. Collect sigint, including attempts at deception and jamming.

D. Determine possible relocation/repositioning of enemy naval forces.

E. Determine any revision to enemy operational procedures recent incidents.

F. Conduct area familiarization under QUASI-COMBAT conditions in a region of possible future naval combat operations. All personnel involved in the patrol are motivated to peak performance. The potentially hostile environment demands positive and realistic reaction to any indicated threat.

G. Divert attention of the DRV naval forces from an area where 34a maritime operations may be in progress.

H. Determine movements of DJV junk forces possibly employed for infiltration along the RVN coastline.

T. Deny the free, unobserved use of the Gulf of Tonkin to the DJV and CHICOM naval forces.

J. Determine the attitude of DRV toward US Navy maritime patrols by measuring their response to the patrol, i.e. establish the degree and success of delivering the "message to Hanoi."

3. There are still other justifications for the continuance of these patrols as COMUSMACV points out so clearly in REF A.

[Document 198]

FM: CINCPAC 25   Date: 25 September 1964

TO: JCS EXCLUSIVE FOR WHEELER

1. FYI, I have sent the following message to my component commanders: "For Gen. Waters, Adm. Moorer, Gen. Harris from Sharp

"1. The political situation in RVN is now so unstable as to raise some serious questions about our future courses of action. For example, we may find ourselves suddenly faced with an unfriendly government or no government at all. U.S. personnel in Vietnam, both dependent and military, may find themselves isolated and in danger. Saigon itself may become untenable.

"2. The above are illustrative contingencies which may develop in which event CINCPAC will be called on both for recommendations and for action. Conceivably the decision could be one of disengagement. In this case the problem would be how to go about it in such a way as to salvage the maximum in terms of safety of U.S. lives, recoupment of material and national pride.

"3. On the other hand the decision might be to remain in Vietnam in order to maintain a foothold on the mainland. This latter course would once again raise the question of a U.S. base in Vietnam and what it would take to man and hold it.

"4. Though we have not yet reached a point where these decisions might be made, events are moving rapidly and it is essential that we consider as a matter of urgency our future in RVN in the light of all possible contingencies, bearing in mind that any course of action we follow will have a direct and possibly final bearing on the U.S. role in Southeast Asia.

"5. Request your views on specific actions which we might take in event of:

    A. A national decision to disengage in RVN.

    B. A national decision to maintain a U.S. foothold in the country.

    C. A national decision to take a stronger hold on the SVN government together with increased U.S. participation in SVN and offensive actions against NVN.

"6. Any other thoughts you might have on other actions which might be taken."

[Document 199]

FROM: JCS   28 Sept 64

TO: CINCPAC

JCS   9117

Subj: Definitive Rules of Engagement Applying to Laos

Refs: a. JCS 7947, DTG 151318Z Aug; b. Vientiane 380 to State 29 Aug (NOTAL); and c. CINCPAC to JCS, DTG 041100Z Aug

1. Ref a remains in effect. This message supplements and provides specific guidance for friendly forces and installations—(See subpara 2c, ref a.)

2. Rules of Engagement for US air defense forces operating in Southeast Asia, as agreed to by Royal Laos Government (RLG), are:

    a. US air defense forces are authorized to engage and destroy hostile aircraft in Laos. Hot pursuit may be conducted as necessary and feasible over Thailand and South Vietnam.

    b. No pursuit is authorized at this time into North Vietnam or Cambodia except when actually engaged in air combat. No pursuit is authorized into Communist China.

    c. Unless specifically directed otherwise, US air defense forces are not authorized to attack other hostile forces or installations unless attacked first, and then only to extent necessary for self-defense.

3. Definitions

    a. Hostile aircraft—A hostile aircraft is defined as one which is:

        (1) Visually identified, or designated by the US Director of a Joint Operations Center or his authorized US representatives, as a communist bloc or Cambodian aircraft overflying Laos territory, and

        (2) Observed in one of the following acts:

            (a) Attacking US or friendly ground forces or installations;

            (b) Attacking US or friendly aircraft (including Air America or Bird and Son aircraft);

            (c) Laying mines within friendly territorial waters;

            (d) Attacking US or friendly vessels;

            (e) Releasing parachutes or gliders over friendly sovereign territory when obviously not in distress; or

            (f) Acting or behaving in a manner which indicates within reasonable certainty that air attack on US or friendly forces, installations, and aircraft (including Air America and Bird and Son aircraft) is intended.

4. These rules are not intended, in any manner, to infringe upon the traditional responsibility of a military commander to defend against unprovoked armed attack. In the event of such attack, the commander concerned will take immediate, aggressive action against the attacking force.

5. Declaration of aircraft as hostile will be tempered with judgement and discretion. There may be cases where the destruction of Cambodian or communist bloc forces would be contrary to US and allied interests. Examples of such cases are: due to navigational error, civilian aircraft which penetrate Laos sovereign territory; communist aircraft or vessels, manned by defectors attempting to land with the intention of surrendering themselves. All available intelligence should be considered in determining action to be taken in such cases.

6. Info on any action taken under this authority will be provided JCS by flash precedence.

[Document 200]

30 September 1964

MEMORANDUM FOR MR. McNAUGHTON

This will confirm the procedures to be used in connection with 34A maritime operations.

At the beginning of each month, I will coordinate with Mr. Bundy and Mr. Thompson the proposed schedule for the forthcoming month. This document will then be the agreed schedule for planning purposes. Thereafter, until further notice, each operation listed on the above-mentioned schedule will be approved in advance by State, Defense and the White House. General Anthis will be responsible for preparing the draft message and will submit it to me for initialling. Thereafter, you will be responsible for coordinating the message with State and the White House. In this connection, you or your designee will take with him General Anthis or his designee to answer any questions which State or the White House may have. Each such message will be initialled by Mr. Thompson and Mr. McGeorge Bundy or their respective designees.

Any changes in the schedule of maritime operations after it has been agreed upon must be approved by Mr. McNamara or me upon recommendation of General Wheeler.

Cyrus R. Vance

cc: General Wheeler

[Document 201]

Questions and Answers on Covert Activities, Sept. 1964

Questions by John T. McNaughton

Answers by JCS and ISA

1. What if the DRV and/or DRV air patrol boats attack our DeSoto patrols in the future?
2. What if Chicom air is involved in attacks on our DeSoto Patrols
3. What if DRV patrol boats engage 34A Marops in hot pursuit?

4. What if T-28s are attacked by North Vietnam fighters?

5. What if U.S. Yankee Team strikes in Laos are engaged by DRV fighters?

6. What if U.S. low-level reconnaissance in North Vietnam is attacked by ground fire and/or fighters?

7. What if Chinese redeploy offensive air to bases within strike distance of South Vietnam?

8. What if VC "spectaculars" in South Vietnam come as direct response to U.S. strikes in the Panhandle? Or U.S. strikes in North Vietnam?

9. What if North Vietnam aircraft attack targets in South Vietnam?

10. What if the Pathet-Lao reenforced by North Vietnamese units seize vulnerable targets such as Attopeu and Saravane?

11. What if the VC launch mortar attacks on Tan Son Nhut or Denau U.S. Embassy? Attack U.S. hotels, transportation facilities?

12. What if the DRV steps up infiltration sharply, including organized units?

13. What if there is a large-scale augmentation of North Vietnam units in Laos?

14. What if in response to U.S. attacks against targets in North Vietnam, the Communists make major forces movements on redeployments?

15. What if Chinese forces enter North Vietnam in strength?

16. What if the Chicoms along with the DRV move into Laos in strength?

17. What if Chinese "volunteers" are employed in Laos?

18. What if North Vietnam and/or Chinese air is employed in Laos?

19. What if the DRV responds to attacks on North Vietnam by full scale invasion of South Vietnam and Laos? And, then Laos alone? What if Chinese forces join this invasion?

20. What if the Chinese Communists launch attacks against Burma, Thailand?

21. What if the GVN collapses in the midst of the campaign against the North?

[JCS] Answers

1. Severe attacks might compel temporary withdrawal of DeSoto patrols from the gulf. U. S. would respond by attacking bases from which the attacks were mounted and associated targets.

2. Greater likelihood of damage. Hit Chinese bases from which attack was launched (Hainan).

3. In hot pursuit, employ all available air and naval to repulse the attack. Continue pursuit until attackers are destroyed.

4. Provide U. S. air caps for all T-28s strength. Include provisions for hot pursuit.

5. Such DRV attacks are likely to be of nuisance value only. U. S. assault fighters engage DRV fighters and employ hot pursuit as necessary. If attacks persist, hit bases from which DRV fighters came.

6. Suppressive fire and same as 5 above. North Vietnam attacks are not likely to be effective.

7. Alert U. S. forces to possible Chinese air attack. Have to press preparations for defense against Chinese air attack in South Vietnam to include augmentation of air defense radar, fighters and Hawks.

8. Materially increase severity of attacks in North Vietnam. Continue attacks in the Panhandle and attack certain targets in North Vietnam associated with infiltration.

9. Mount large scale South Vietnam and U. S. air attacks on all air facilities

in North Vietnam, with the intention of destroying North Vietnam air capability. North Vietnam air attacks are not likely to be militarily effective, but could have great psychological impact.

10. Respond by large-scale interdiction of Pathet-Lao and North Vietnamese supply routes employing T-28s and U. S. and South Vietnamese fighter bomber aircraft. Attempt to get Laotians to recapture towns when military situation permits.

11. Mount attacks against attacked targets on the 94 target list, and consider stepping up scale of U. S. activities in Laos. Evacuate remaining U. S. dependents, if any. Such attacks could be highly effective and could cause substantial loyal deterioration. Release U.S. air to support South Vietnamese anti-guerilla action. If high ranking U. S. personnel are associated, seek evidence of a North Vietnamese involvement and if established, direct reprisals against North Vietnam command and control facilities.

12. Mount heavy air strikes against infiltrated associated targets in Panhandle and South Vietnam.

13. Hit infiltration associated targets in the Panhandle and DRV LOC in North Vietnam.

14. Increase intelligence gathering activities, including high and low-level reconnaissance in North Vietnam and China. U. S. would be compelled to make counter-deployments in expectation of major Communist movements.

15. Commit U. S. ground forces to develop positions on border of North and South Vietnam. Increase reconnaissance activities to include low level.

16. If unopposed, Chinese forces could move into the Mekong in a relatively short period of time. Include initial air interdiction.

[ISA] ANSWERS

1. Patrol boats unlikely to cause damage; daytime air attack more likely to be damaging. US would respond by attacking bases from which the attacks were mounted and associated targets; on scale related to extent of damage.

2. Greater likelihood of damage. Hit Chinese bases from which attack was launched e.g. (Hainan).

3. Commit SVN air and naval forces plus FARMGATE to repulse the attack and destroy attackers.

4. Provide US cap for all T-28 strikes. Include provisions for hot pursuit.

5. Such DRV attacks are likely to be of nuisance value only. US assault fighters engage DRV fighters and employ hot pursuit as necessary. If attacks persist, hit bases from which DRV fighters launched.

6. Suppressive fire and same as 5 above. North Vietnam attacks are not likely to be effective.

7. Alert US forces to possible Chinese air attack. Press preparations for defense against Chinese air attack in South Vietnam to include augmentation of air defense radar, fighters and Hawks.

8. Continue attacks in the Panhandle and attack certain targets in southern North Vietnam associated with infiltration.

9. Mount large scale South Vietnam and US air attacks on all air facilities in North Vietnam, with the intention of destroying North Vietnam air capability. North Vietnam air attacks are not likely to be militarily effective, but could have great psychological impact.

10. Respond by large scale interdiction of Pathet-Lao and North Vietnamese supply routes employing T-28s and US and South Vietnamese fighter bomber

aircraft. Attempt to get Laotians to recapture towns when military situation permits.

11. Such attacks could be highly effective and could cause substantial deterioration of morale. Mount attacks against selected targets on the 94 target list. Release US air to support South Vietnamese anti-guerilla action. If high ranking US personnel are assassinated, seek evidence of a North Vietnamese involvement and if established, direct reprisals against North Vietnam command and control facilities.

12. Mount heavy air strikes against infiltration—associated targets in Panhandle and South Vietnam.

13. Hit infiltration associated targets in the Panhandle and DRV LOC in North Vietnam.

14. Increase intelligence gathering activities, including high and low-level reconnaissance in North Vietnam and China. Make counter-deployments in expectation of major Communist movements.

15. Commit US ground forces to defensive positions on border of North and South Vietnam. Increase reconnaissance activities to include low level recon.

16. If unopposed, Chinese forces could move into the Mekong in a relatively short period of time. Initiate air interdiction.

LESSER COMMUNIST RESPONSES TO US MILITARY PRESSURES

A. *DRV/Chicom Attacks on DeSoto Patrols*

US/GVN Responses.

a. Conduct one of 4 retaliatory punitive reprisal attack options against DRV targets from 94 target list (CINCPAC FRAG Order 3). Attack options represent graduated response according to level of damage to DeSoto. 1A and 1B with lowest order of response the options are—

    1A. Phouc Yen Airfield
        PT port facilities and associated POL
    1B. Key army barracks: supply and ammo depots, and major naval base and associated port facility.
    2A. Effected in 2 strike days and includes all targets in 1A plus. Secondary airfields, naval base and port facilities.
    2B. Effected in 2 days and includes all targets in 1A plus. Secondary airfields and 3 preselected highway bridges.

b. Pursue surface and air attackers in accordance with current rules of engagement for DeSoto, to be announced.

B. Pursue 34A MAROPS craft south of 17th Parallel.

In response, SVN air and naval forces to include Farmgate attack to repulse and destroy attackers (JCS msg 9109).

C. NVN air attacks X-Border air and/or YT aircraft in Laos.

In response, the US

1. Provides US CAP for all T-28 strikes (currently CAP is as requested by RLAF).

2. Hot pursuit (current rules of engagement for SEA and for Laos)

3. If attacks persist, strike DRV home and staging bases from 94 target list with increasing severity with the objective of destroying them and with them the DRV capabilities to continue air support of the Viet Cong and Pathet Lao. (Part VI, NSC working paper).

D. Introduce NVN air into Laos in attack of ground targets.
   The US response is the same as in paragraphs C2 and 3, above.
E. Introduce organized DRV units into Laos reinforcing P/L and seizing key
   objectives (Saravane, Attopeu). This could include covert or volunteer Chi-
Com support in Laos.
   The US/GVN forces:
   1. Interdict DRV and Pathet Lao LOC in Laos and NVN with US/VNAF;
air attacks of increasing severity on military and industrial targets selected from
94 target list (JCSM   in draft 16 Nov).
   2. Concurrently with a prior to initiating air strikes above. Implement
CINCPAC OPLAN 99-64.
   3. Reintroduce a MAAG-type supply and training mission (SATM) into Laos.
   4. Implement when required Phase II (Laos) OPLAN 32–64.
F. DRV effect air strikes on northern SVN air facilities.
   Initiate or continue in coordination with GVN an air strike campaign against
DRV bases and associated targets (OPLAN 37–64 and 94 target list); (Section
VI, para 2, NSC paper).

[Document 202]

FROM: CINCPAC   2 Oct 64

TO: JCS

Use of Thai Based US Air Forces

A. BANGKOK 2116 TO STATE, JUN 10, 2:25 PM NOTAL
B. CHJUSMAG THAILAND 061230Z AUG PASEP
C. CINCPAC 070424Z AUG NOTAL
D. DEPCOMUSMACTHAI 071402Z AUG PASEP
E. AMEMB BANGKOK 190625Z SEP NOTAL
F. JCS 7947 DTG 151318Z AUG NOTAL
G. JCS 9117 DTG 281438Z SEP NOTAL
   1. Ref A advises that armed strikes by Thai based US forces quote limited
repeat limited to SAR operations only and on further condition no public mention be made of use of Thai bases unquote.
   2. During early August Gulf of Tonkin incident, F–100's and F–105's were
deployed to Thailand. Ref B stated that country clearance did not repeat not
include clearance to launch sorties out of Thailand and in event this needed additional coordination was required, Ref C requested Amemb Bangkok guidance on
extent of our latitude in the operational use of US Thai based forces and limitations that may be imposed by necessity for prior clearance. In Ref D, DEPCOM-
USMACTHAI quoted Bangkok Embtel 157 which stated inter alia, the Dawee,
after considerable discussion agreed remove any restrictions on launch of combat
sorties out of Thailand by US aircraft on Thai bases in event this becomes necessary. Need for utmost discretion in exercising this authority was emphasized.
Para 3 of Ref D states, however, that authority granted unlimited repeat unlimited—except by request for lateral info at time of launch.
   3. Ref E stated that present authority from RTG to dispatch US aircraft from
Thai bases to strike points outside Thailand limited to armed escort for recce
missions and cap for SAR. In addition, they are available for any defense of Thai
airspace.
   4. Planning is currently underway to conduct Yankee team operations in Laos

north of 20 degrees latitude. Refs F and G provide adequate rules of engagement for US forces operating in Seasia. However, due to the above conflicting info, not clear here what latitude we have in use of US Thai Based Forces. Believe it militarily desirable to provide air defense effort which would implement Ref G from Thai bases. Also to provide escort for Yankee team missions in nothern Laos when they are approved for implementation. More flexible, effective and economical escort can be provided by US aircraft based in Thailand.

5. Prior to finalization of concept of operations and imitation of Yankee team missions in northern Laos, request clarification of current authorization re use of US Thai Based Aircraft for Yankee team escort SAR, and Air Defense of US and friendly forces in Laos.

[Document 203]

FROM: AMEMBASSY SAIGON   3 Oct 64

EXDIS

For Secretary Rusk

Embtel 870 and Deptel 727.

Mike Forrestal's State/RCI 30 raises an aspect of the coordination problem discussed in Embtel 870 and indicates belief that Emb Saigon Saigon should be coordination center.

I continue to favor the procedure contained in Embtel 870 which has the concurrence of Ambassadors Unger and Martin. In my opinion, the ad hoc methods mentioned in Deptel 727 are not likely to suffice to handle the growing requirements for prompt regional recommendations on politico-military matters affecting several embassies and CINCPAC. I would think it to the interest of State-Defense to fix responsibility for coordination in this field and not trust to the initiatives of the moment.

If you agree, I suggest issuance of a directive to embassies Saigon, Vientiane, and to CINCPACHO stablish in Saigon under Executive Agency of Embassy Saigon a committee for coordinating policy recommendations and military operational matters arising from the following activities: 34–A program (to include its coordination with DeSoto patrols); crossborder operations (air and ground) from SVN into Laos; air operations from SVN and Laos into NVN; Lucky Dragon; Yankee team; Blue Springs; Hardnose and any other operations in Laos requiring coordination with crossborder operations. Such a directive would indicate general approval of organization proposed in Embtel 870 and leave to principals of committee to work out the details.

TAYLOR

[Document 204]

Ref: Deptel 275 to Vientiane and Vientiane's   6 Oct 64
     545, 550, 568 and 581

JOINT STATE-DEFENSE MESSAGE

EXDIS

You are authorized to urge the RLG to begin air attacks against Viet Cong infiltration routes and facilities in the Laos Panhandle by RLAF T–28 aircraft as soon as possible. Such strikes should be spread out over a period of several weeks, and targets should be limited to these deemed suitable for attack by T–28s and listed Para. 8 Vientiane's 581, (excluding Mu Gia pass and any target which Lao will not hit without U.S. air cover or fire support) since decision this matter not yet made.

You are further authorized to inform Lao that YANKEE TEAM suppressive fire strikes against certain difficult targets in Panhandle, interspersing with further T–28 strikes, are part of the over-all concept and are to be anticipated later but that such US strikes are not repeat not authorized at this time.

Report soonest proposed schedule of strikes and, upon implementation, all actual commitments of RLG T–28s, including targets attacked, results achieved, and enemy opposition. Also give us any views in addition to those in Vientiane's 581 as to any targets which are deemed too difficult for RLG air strikes and on which US suppressive strikes desired.

FYI: Highest levels have not authorized YANKEE TEAM strikes at this time against Route 7 targets. Since we wish to avoid the impression that we are taking first step in escalation, we inclined defer decision on Route 7 strikes until we have strong evidence Hanoi's preparation for new attack in PDJ, some of which might come from RLAF operations over the Route. END FYI.

You may inform RLG, however, that US will fly additional RECCE over Route 7 to keep current on use being made of the Route by the PL and to identify Route 7 targets and air defenses. The subject of possible decision to conduct strikes on Route 7 being given study in Washington.

FYI: Cross border ground operations not repeat not authorized at this time. End FYI.

END

RUSK

[Document 205]

Amembassy SAIGON 783 IMMEDIATE   7 Oct 64

INFO: Amembassy BANGKOK FOR MARTIN 486
          Amembassy VIENTIANE FOR UNGER 306
          CINCPAC FOR ADMIRAL SHARP

FOR THE AMBASSADOR FROM THE SECRETARY

Ref: Embtel 1017 and 1032, Vientiane's 564

EXDIS

Concur convening organizing session as suggested reftels. We are completely sympathetic to need for coordinating politico-military recommendations affecting Vietnam through some regional arrangement and agree that this job would best be done by establishment group under chairmanship Alexis Johnson in Saigon.

We have, however, two concerns here. The first is that existence of this group remain completely confidential, since we do not wish give any impression at this time establishment of SLA political and military command structure in Saigon. In this connection wish avoid large movements military or civilian personnel from CINCPAC or other two posts.

Our second concern is that group should restrict itself to acting as clearing house for information on operations mentioned Saigon's 1017 and formulation of recommendations to Washington. Group should not repeat not exercise executive authority over other posts.

Perhaps at your meeting you and your colleagues could frame specific recommendation for terms of reference and method of operation which you consider desirable.

END

RUSK

[Document 206]

Action Priority Dept. 1063 from Saigon Oct 9, 7 PM

EXDIS

DEPTEL 763

Organizing session was held October 8 and terms of reference agreed and referendum to Ambassadors Unger and Martin. Agreed text will be transmitted Department.

Group also discussed all operations of common interest mentioned Saigon's 1017 with particular emphasis on rules of engagement for US aircraft three countries and SAR operations, particularly problems of SAR for OPLAN 34A crews that may be downed in Laos. Discussion rules of engagement disclosed possible grey area with respect to status of RTG clearance for Thai-based US aircraft to take-off on air defense mission over Laos prior to actual initiation of attacks over Laos by hostile aircraft. Bangkok will seek to clarify.

Very useful discussion of problem of SAR for OPLAN 34A crews clarified situation for Vientiane which will undertake definitive comments on Saigon's 1030 to Dept. as basis for Washington decision.

Bangkok will also seek to clarify situation with respect to Thai ranger cadres for Hard Nose as discussed at previous Udorn meeting.

There was also discussion of sharpening existing coordination and responsiveness of all intelligence assets to Viet Cong movements through Lao corridor, specifically, a military targeting sub-committee was formed to extend and improve the target list and reaction time.

In view of stand down on ground cross border operations and good possibility that ARVN will be unable afford detachment any significant ground combat capability for corridor in foreseeable future, air strikes are sole remaining dependable alternative.

Fixed targets (the 22 target list) will soon be destroyed if the RLAF performs as advertised and authorization received for Yankee Team strikes. Thus, the group discussed at length problem of acquisition additional targets in corridor and particularly problem of quick air reaction on targets of opportunity developed by ground observers. Saigon and Vientiane will further examine their assets and possibilities in this regard. Bangkok will explore availability and possibility of extending use of Thai assets in this connection.

There was also unanimous agreement that US participation in air operations in corridor is essential if such operations are to have desired military and psychological impact, particularly since initiative for operations came from us. US failure to participate could diminish US influence over these operations (whether we wish to expand or to limit them) and their continuation could well be jeopardized if Lao are expected to do job unassisted. Although Vientiane believes Lao prepared to go ahead with strikes against first twelve targets authorized DEPTEL 765 to Saigon, their initial enthusiasm may not survive loss of a few aircraft.

If so, if Lao do not hit those four targets for which US strikes [word illegible] and are discouraged from strikes on Mu Gia Pass, [words illegible] targets in the corridor will go unscathed. These omissions will grossly diminish the military benefits of these bombings. The group thus hoped that Washington would reconsider present ban on RLAF attack on Mu Gia Pass and approve soonest Yankee Team strike on other targets.

It was noted that Washington is still considering the Lao recommendations that the US provide CAP over RLAF strike aircraft. The present rules of engagement for US aircraft currently permit US attack on Communist Bloc aircraft attacking Laotian aircraft over Laos. Provisioning of a CAP would hence be a relatively minor extension of existing authority. Since the Lao have requested such CAP, it would have psychological value and group recommends early Washington approval. Vientiane anticipates RLAF would initiate operations October 14. Affirmative decision re CAP prior to that date would be most helpful.

Vientiane does not expect RLG will initiate any publicity on strikes but will probably acknowledge RLAF operations in response [words missing] to queries. Saigon and Bangkok will privately inform Khanh and Thanom prior to initiation operations. Vientiane will undertake keep Souvanna currently informed.

TAYLOR

[Document 207]

Date: 10 October 1964

FM: SAIGON 1080

TO: STATE

REF: Embtel 1068

Transmitted herewith are the approved Terms of Reference by Bangkok, Vientiane, and Saigon

"1. Group to be known as Coordinating Committee for US Mission Southeast Asia (SEACOORD).

"2. The objectives of the Committee are to coordinate policy recommendations and military operational matters affecting more than one mission.

"With respect to military and relating operational matters, the Committee will coordinate the operations and actions of their respective missions and component elements within the sphere of their competence and authority from Washington. The Committee will also act as a clearing house for the exchange of information on all military or other operations affecting more than one post.

"In making coordinated recommendations to Washington on proposed operations, the Committee will seek to take into account all relative political and military considerations.

"The Committee will not rpt not exercise executive authority over any mission or military command.

"3. Membership will normally consist of the US Missions in Saigon, Vientiane and Bangkok. Other US missions in Southeast Asia may be included in specific meetings if subject matter makes this desirable.

"4. Missions will normally be represented by the DCM's at Bangkok and Vientiane and by the Deputy Ambassador at Saigon, together with military and CAS representation as appropriate. Ambassadors may, of course, attend at their discretion. In addition to the representation provided CINCPAC through his military representatives in the area, CINCPAC and his subordinate commands may be represented as appropriate.

"5. Meetings will normally be held at Saigon not rpt not less than once a month and will be chaired by the Deputy Ambassador.

"Meetings may be called more frequently at the initiative of any of the three missions.

"6. The Chairman will be responsible for: [material missing]

  B) Proposing and circulating an Agenda prior to each meeting,

  C) Arranging appropriate briefings of participants,

  D) Transmitting to Washington such conclusions and recommendations as may be agreed.

"7. The Committee may form such other relating Committees as may be required.

"8. As an element of SEACOORD, a Standing Military Committee is hereby established composed of COMUSMACV, or his representative, as Chairman, Deputy COMUS MACTHAI or representative, and a Military Representative designated by the Ambassador Vientiane, and a CAS Saigon Representative. The Military Committee may form such Subcommittees as may be required. CINCPAC or subordinate CINCPAC Commands may participate as required, as well as political and CAS representation from Vientiane and Bangkok."

[Document 208]

MEMORANDUM FOR MR. JOSEPH A. CALIFANO, JR.

SUBJECT: Item for Weekly Report to the President

Lao Deputy Prime Minister Would Like to Expand Military Operations in the North.

General Phoumi Nosavan, Deputy Prime Minister in the coalition government of Laos, visited Washington from October 3 to 7. His chief objective in his talks in Washington seemed to be to sound out U.S. attitudes toward Laos, also toward possible changes in the government of National Union and, during conversations at the Department of Defense, to seek support for expending military operations largely of a clandestine, guerrilla type in Northern Laos. These proposed operations, which would cut deeply into territory held by the Pathet Lao at the time of the Geneva 1962 settlement, would seek to deny communist access from North Viet Nam to the strategic Plaine des Jarres. General Phoumi was informed that the U.S. would continue its efforts to gain adherence to the 1962 Geneva agreements and stabilize the situation in Laos.

[Document 209]

1st Draft (McNaughton) 10/13/64

AIMS AND OPTIONS IN SOUTHEAST ASIA

1. US aims in SEA are:

  a) To help SVN and Laos to develop as independent countries.

   b) To get DRV to leave its neighbors alone.

   c) To protect US power and prestige (see para 13 below).

2. In Laos, intermediate aims are:
   a) To preserve Souvanna's position (no coup).
   b) To prevent significant PL land grabs.

3. In SVN, intermediate aims are:
   a) To create and maintain a viable govt.
   b) To make progress in pacification (see no progress).

4. New efforts in SVN:
   a) Firmly based provisional government.
   b) Increased pay for civil servants.
   c) RAND initiatives in cities.
   d) Some responsibility dispersed to Corps.
   e) Large-scale Filipino participation.

5. To change DRV behavior (change can be tacit), US should "negotiate" by an optimum combination of words and deeds. Words across any conference table should be orchestrated with continuing military pressures. (In particular, there should be no one-way, Korea-type, cease fires.)

6. Likely *word* negotiations:
   a) UN Security Council debates (ending?).
   b) Paris talks re Laos (buying time).
   c) 14-Nation conference (Soviet threat to quit).
   d) US/DRV dialogue of some kind (slow and hard).

7. Actions for deed negotiations:
   a) 34A (MAROPS, black bomber?).
   b) DeSoto missions in Gulf of Tonkin.
   c) Recce
      high over Laos, DRV, China.
      medium over Laos, DRV.
      low (return-fire) over Laos, DRV.
      low (suppressive) over Laos, DRV.
   d) GVN ground attacks in Corridor (US advisers).
   e) MAAG, White Star teams in Laos.
   f) Air attacks
      T-28 in PDJ and Corridor.
      US "June 9" in PDJ and Corridor.
      VNAF in Corridor.
      VNAF (US?) in DRV.
      US on VC targets in SVN.
   g) Aerial mining of DRV harbors.
   h) Destroy DRV naval craft in international waters.
   i) Further US force deployments.

8. DRV must
   a) stop training and sending personnel to wage war in SVN and Laos.
   b) stop sending arms and supplies to SVN and Laos.
   c) stop directing and controlling military actions in SVN and Laos.
   d) order the VC and PL to stop their insurgencies and military actions.
   e) remove VM forces and cadres from SVN and Laos.

g) see that VC and PL cease resistance to government forces.
h) see that VC and PL turn in weapons and relinquish bases.
i) see that VC and PL surrender for amnesty or expatriation.

9. It is important that USSR and China understand the limited nature of our deeds—i.e., not for colony or base and not to destroy DRV, but only para 1 above.

10. Likely Communist deeds:
a) More jets to NVN with NVN or Chicom pilots.
b) AAA and radar gear to NVN.
c) Increased air and ground forces in South China.
d) Increased VC activities (kill top leaders, Americans?).
e) Major infiltrated VC unit activities (take a city?).
f) Cause major military or civilian defections in SVN.
g) PL land grabs in Laos.
h) "DRV" jet attacks on US DD's (and on Saigon?).
i) Other "defensive" DRV retaliation (shoot down U-2?).
j) Political drive for "neutralization" of Indo-china.
k) PL declaration of new government in Laos.
l) NOT invade South Vietnam.

11. Misc. problems:
a) Excuses for military actions in the future.
b) Get the deployed forces back out of SEA.
c) Watch for Saigon and Vientiane hanky panky with Reds.
d) Withdrawal of US dependents from Saigon.
e) More third-country participation in SEA effort.
f) Carrot and "golden bridge" for Hanoi.

12. Misc. ideas:
a) That we welcome a SEA conference with a two-way ceasefire (i.e., with a VC and PL stand-down).
b) That future pressures on DRV be overt.
c) That the theory of actions against DRV be "provocations of opportunity"—either (1) in response to such things as Aug 2 PT attacks on US DDs or (2) in response to fresh incidents and outrages in SVN and Laos.
d) That we start laying public-opinion base for reprisal against North justified, in particular, by VC outrages in South.

13. It is essential—however badly SEA may go over the next 2–4 years—that US emerge as a "good doctor." We must have kept promises, been tough, taken risks, gotten bloodied, and hurt the enemy very badly. We must avoid appearances which will affect judgments by, and provide pretexts to, other nations regarding US power, resolve and competence, and regarding how the US will behave in future cases of particular interest to those nations. The questions will be:

a. Has US policy of containment against overt and covert aggression changed, at least as to SEA? How will we behave in new confrontations a la South Vietnam, Korea (1950), Italy (1948) Berlin? (We want to be particularly careful that any loss in SVN is not generalized to overt aggression.)
b. Is US *power* to contain insufficient, at least at the fringes?
c. Is the US *hobbled by restraints* which might be relevant in future cases

(fear of illegality, of UN or neutral reaction, of domestic pressures, of US losses, of deploying US ground forces in Asia, of war with China or Russia, of use of nuclear weapons, etc.)?

It follows that care should be taken to attribute any set-backs to factors:

a. Which *cannot be generalized* beyond South Vietnam (i.e., weak government, religious dissention, uncontrollable borders, mess left by French, unfavorable terrain, distance from US, etc.).

b. Which are not US mis- or non-feasance (e.g., overexposure of "white faces" or unwise actions, or failure to take risks or provide sufficient aid of the right kind).

14. Recommended Military Scenario:

Phase One (November–December). Limited pressures not involving major risks of escalation, that would maintain GVN morale and initiative against the DRV:

Continue leaflet drops over DRV, and T-28 and recce over Laos.

Joint US–GVN planning proceeds covering all actions described below.

34A MAROPS (cutting sea infiltration) and leaflet drops (countering DRV radio-propaganda). These operations should be acknowledged.

Cross-border operations (air and ground) along the corridor.

Resume occasional desoto patrols (not within 12 miles of NVN).

Specify "opportunities" (responding to mining, POL sabotage, terrorism).

Phase Two (January et seq). More serious pressures—inside DRV:

Mine DRV harbors.

Strike infiltration routes, working in from border.

Strike other military targets.

Strike industrial targets.

[Document 210]

Date: October 14, 1964

FM: SAIGON 1129

TO: STATE

REF: Embtel 1046

My impressions this week are colored by the receipt of the monthly reports from the field for September. That month and October thus far have seen little or no progress in the overall situation (except possibly in the work of the High National Council) and some deterioration, particularly in the northern provinces. It has been a period characterized by government instability, civil disorders (now quieting down), indications of increased infiltration from the north, and a high level of military activity both on the part of the Viet Cong and the Government Forces.

During the past week, our attention and efforts have been focused primarily on the activities of the High National Council and its efforts to lay the foundation of a strong provisional government. We have been trying hard to influence it in the right direction and to bring about some understanding between the council and the military. I have been encouraged by the seriousness of purpose of the council and the evidence of having made considerable progress. We expect momentarily the announcement of a provisional charter which will provide for a Chief of State, a Prime Minister and eventually for a national assembly chosen at least in part by elections. It remains to be seen what kind of a reception the charter will receive from the public and interested minorities.

According to our contacts with members of the council, General Minh is the leading candidate for Chief of State, but there is no consensus as to the Prime Minister who, it is hoped, will be a strong civilian. The council members are worried about General Khanh's attitude toward their plans. They want him in the government but are afraid he will not take a reduction from Prime Minister to Minister of Defense or Commander-in-Chief as they would prefer. My talks with Khanh lead me to hope they are wrong in their misgivings and that both Minh and Khanh will undertake appropriate roles in the new government. There remains the unanswered questions of the selection of the civilian Prime Minister. Probably the principal obstacle now in the path of the new government.

On the military front, the Viet Cong appear to be holding down the number of attacks on military forces and concentrating on acts of sabotage and terrorism directed at impressing the civilian population. One reason for this emphasis is undoubtedly the heavy losses they have recently been taking in engagements with government forces. The cumulative effect of these losses must be creating man-power problems for them and probably explains the definite step-up in infiltration from North Vietnam, particularly in the northern provinces of South Vietnam. A recent analysis suggests that if the present rate of infiltration is maintained the annual figure for 1964 will be of the order of 10,000. Furthermore, as has probably been called to your attention, we are finding more and more "bona fide" North Vietnamese soldiers among the infiltrees. I feel sure that we must soon adopt new and drastic methods to reduce and eventually end such infiltration if we are ever to succeed in South Vietnam.

Pacification activities were sluggish during the week except in the Hop Tac area around Saigon where some progress is being made. In particular, the Hop Tac police are being somewhat more effective in controlling the movement of contraband intended for the use of the Viet Cong.

The psychological climate seems to be about the same, with some nervousness in Saigon over the outcome of the work of the High National Council. There are rumors Khanh may encourage demonstrations to maintain himself in office. I am inclined to doubt this but Khanh could be playing a deeper game than we presently think.

[Document 211]

23 OCT 1964

MEMORANDUM FOR THE SECRETARY OF DEFENSE

SUBJECT: US Search and Rescue Operations—Southeast Asia

COMUSMACV (Tab A) has requested the inclusion of 34A operations in ex-isting SAR plans for Laos and the Gulf of Tonkin. CINCPAC (Tab B) supports the MACV concept and recommends expanding SAR coverage to include cross-border operations into Laos. Ambassador Taylor (Tab C) concurs in SAR support for 34A crews downed in Laos. Ambassador Unger (Tab D & E) has expressed reservations with respect to use of his resources for SAR operations in support of VNAF or 34A personnel in Laos. The Joint Chiefs (JCSM 839-64) (Tab F) have proposed an expansion of existing SAR coverage along the lines advocated by CINCPAC and COMUSMACV.

The Joint Chiefs of Staff proposal would authorize US/SAR assistance to:

(a) RVNAF forces engaged in cross-border operations into Laos and also 34A aircraft in distress in Laos, and

(b) Both 34A surface and aircraft in the Gulf of Tonkin.

Regarding SAR support for RVN forces which might be involved in possible cross-border operations, the State Departement desires to defer decision. I suggest that we go along with State on this point for the time being.

With respect to SAR support for 34A operations, State Department (Tab G) has opposed any US support in either Laos or the Gulf of Tonkin, though it agrees to *GVN* SAR assistance to 34A *MAROPS*.

As a result of further discussions with Saigon on the question of SAR operations for 34A overflights of Laos, Ambassador Unger (Tab E) has now proposed that he be authorized to determine, on a case-by-case basis, whether to employ in-country assets available to him (RLAF, Air America, Bird & Sons) in SAR operations. State believes this is a more acceptable arrangement than the employment on field initiative of identifiable US SAR resources (i.e., Yankee Team and other US air assets in SEA) and would concur.

State also notes that, unlike the SAR problem for Yankee Team or RLAF (T-28) aircraft, the location of a downed 34A aircraft may be difficult to determine (i.e., radio silence, night flights, unaccompanied, etc.) and believes that the first effort should therefore be restricted to search for the aircraft. Once it is located, is identifiable US resources appear to be required for rescue, State would have Ambassador Unger refer the problem to Washington for decision.

In summary, resolution of the 34A question depends on the extent of recognition we wish to accord 34A forces. If they are characterized as "friendly", the existing Rules of Engagement would make them eligible *now* for US protection if attacked under all circumstances except when in or over DRV, and would entitle them to SAR assistance. Since it is current policy that 34A operations remain covert, US participation in their defense or rescue should be limited at this time. I recommend your signature to the attached self-explanatory memorandum to the Chairman, Joint Chiefs of Staff and your approval of the attached message which has been coordinated with the Department of State and White House staff.

John T. McNaughton
Assistant Secretary of Defense

Enclosures (2)
1. Memo to Ch/JCS
2. Draft Msg

[Document 212]

JOINT STATE-DEFENSE MESSAGE

ACTION: SAIGON
         VIETIANE
         JCS

INFORMATION: MACV   BANGKOK
                  CINCPAC

Consideration has been given to recommendations for the expansion of search and rescue (SAR) operations to cover OPLAN 34A operations and cross border operations into Laos by RVN forces.

In this connection it should be clearly understood that, since 34A operations are covert and not acknowledged by the United States, they are not entitled to be characterized as "friendly" under the US Rules of Engagement which have been promulgated for Southeast Asia and Laos. In the event of a 34A aircraft being downed in Laos, SAR operations are authorized as determined in the discretion of the United States Ambassador to Laos using only in-country resources available to him. In such a case, the Ambassador could employ (RLAF, Air America, and Bird and Sons assets) (including those based Udorn, as necessary) but would not be authorized to include other United States resources (i.e., Yankee Team and USAF aircraft). The question of employing such identifiable US resources will be referred in each instance to Washington for decision.

In the Gulf of Tonkin, SAR operations in behalf of 34A forces should be the responsibility of the RVN and should include no US forces without prior approval from Washington.

A decision regarding SAR operations in behalf of RVN forces involved in possible cross-border operations into Laos is deferred for consideration until such time as it may be decided to proceed with such operations.

[Document 213]

29 Oct 1964

AMEMBASSY

Jt State/Defense Msg fr OASD/ISA

EXCLUSIVE FOR AMBASSADOR TAYLOR

The JCS have proposed a program of military and supporing political actions with respect to the RVN envisaging accelerated forceful actions both inside and outside RVN. A copy of their memorandum, JCSM 902–64, has been transmitted to you this [word missing] via courier to arrive Saigon 31 October. In anticipation high level discussions, your comments on the JCS recommendations desired as soon as possible.

[Document 214]

ACTION: AMEMBASSY SAIGON PRIORITY 937   29 Oct, 1964

EXDIS

SAIGON FOR AMBASSADOR AND PASS TO COMUSMACV

JOINT STATE/DEFENSE MESSAGE

SUBJECT: Legitimation of OP34A

Refs: Saigon (a) 1221, Deptels (b) 678, (c) 680, Saigon 804
          (d) COMUSMACV 210147E Oct 64

Suggest your further exploration with Khanh the question of surfacing 34A MAROPS. His thinking is not clear here as to whose interests (US and/or GVN) he believes would be adversely affected, and how. It would be helpful too to have his rationale for acknowledging all 34A SABOTAGE OPS rather than MAROPS only.

FYI In view current situation SVN and possible need additional operations against NVN, public exposure of, and subsequent US support for, MAROPS could provide politically useful basis for expanded activities. END FYI

Desire you continue press for legitimizing 34A MAROPS, leave to your discretion however, whether you should press Khanh for public exposure of 34A MAROPS at next session or limit discussion to obtain his complete thinking on the subject.

END

BALL

[Document 215]

From: *JCS* 1451

To: *CINCPAC*

1 Nov 1964

PERSONAL FOR
ADMIRAL SHARP, GENERAL WESTMORELAND AND AMBASSADOR
TAYLOR FROM CJCS.

1. Highest level meeting to discuss courses of action related to Bien Hoa attack tentatively scheduled for 1300 hours Washington time 2 November.

2. At preliminary meeting same subject this date, concern was expressed that proposed US retaliatory/punitive actions could trigger North Vietnamese/CHICOM air and ground retaliatory acts. Highest authority desires to consider in conjunction with US military actions, increased security measures and precautionary moves of US air and ground units to protect US dependents, units and installations against North Vietnamese/CHICOM retaliation.

3. JCS are considering the following in connection with proposed US punitive actions against the DRV:

a. Outshipment of US dependents prior to or simultaneous with initiation of US air strikes.

b. Movement of SLF afloat to Da Nang airbase and two Army or Marine battalions by air to Saigon area to provide local security to US personnel and installations.

c. Movement one Marine HAWK battalion from 29 Palms, California to SVN.

d. Movement of augmentation land-based and carrier-based air required to optimize execution of course of action IA CINCPAC Frag Order 3.

e. Forward movement from CONUS or within PACOM of ground, sea, and air units to WESTPAC and alert of additional units in CONUS as might be required to implement appropriate portions of CINCPAC OPLAN 32–64 and/or CINCPAC OPLAN 39–65.

4. In addition to above, JCS are considering military utility of employing US aircraft in South Vietnam in country to augment VNAF and FARMGATE.

5. Request comments of addressees ASAP.

[Document 216]

November 3, 1964

PROJECT OUTLINE

Working Group on Courses of Action in Southeast Asia

(The following is an outline of inputs now being prepared. It will probably correspond closely to the outline of a final paper for high-level review, but the order and emphasis might vary. The main purpose of the outline is so that Working Group members will have a common index and be able to keep track of what is being prepared.)

I. *Situation in South Viet-Nam.*

    A. Prospects for political stability and effectiveness.

    B. Security situation and prospects.

    C. The DRV role and DRV policy. State of infiltration and probably VC tactics and actions.

    D. Chicom policy and present relevant actions.

    E. Soviet policy.

    F. Evaluation of prospects assuming present policies pursued (i.e., maximum US assistance and limited external actions in Laos and covertly against North Viet-Nam).

    G. Close analysis of the DRV role, directed to the question of what the prospects would be if that role were removed (1) wholly; (2) by superficial gestures of compliance that removed the more visible evidences of DRV participation.

Status: This paper will be prepared by an intelligence community special working group, for review by the major USIB members concerned. It will presumably be combined with a second section dealing with Communist and other reactions to the courses of action described in Option B below.

II. *US Objectives and Stakes in South Viet-Nam and Southeast Asia.*

    A. US objectives and the present basis of US action.

    B. Possible alternative objectives.

    C. Consequences of Communist control of South Viet-Nam in a worldwide sense.

    D. Consequences in Southeast Asia and Asia generally of Communist control in South Viet-Nam.

(Both C and D, in this paper, would deal with a generalized case of Communist control, noting the variations that would generally arise with different circumstances of loss, but aiming to put more precise evaluation into the concluding section on Conclusions and Recommendations.)

    E. The attitudes of major US allies and the general impact of various courses of action on the US leadership role with these countries.

    F. Attitudes in other relevant nations and the general impact of possible US courses of action on US capacity to affect their behavior in ways consistent with our worldwide objectives (i.e., not the US "image" but the reality of US relations and of the conduct of these countries).

Status: Mr. Bundy will prepare this section on the basis of the earlier draft already circulated to members of the Working Group. CIA also has an analysis, and various JCS papers cover highly important points. The CIA and JCS papers will be made available to Mr. Bundy and to the Working Group as soon as possible.

III. *The Broad Options.*

    A. Continue on present lines.
    B. Present policies plus a systematic program of military pressures against the north, meshing at some point with negotiation, but with pressure actions to be continued until we achieve our central present objectives.
    C. Present policies plus additional forceful measures and military moves, followed by negotiations in which we would seek to maintain a believable threat of still further military pressures but would not actually carry out such pressures to any marked degree during the negotiations.

Status: This would be a brief paper amplifying the above definitions only silghtly.

IV. *Alternative Forms of Negotiation.*

This paper would be an analysis of all the possible avenues of negotiation, including the UN, Geneva conferences, bilateral communications, use of intermediaries, etc. The analysis would be designed to be relevant to the negotiations that might ensue under any of the three options stated in Section III, but with greatest emphasis on the negotiating avenues relevant to Options B and C.

Status: First draft being prepared by State, S/P, in conjunction with IO and others in State.

V. *Analysis of Option A.*

This paper would virtually write itself in the light of Section I and the negotiating discussions in Section IV. It can be left to one side for the moment.

VI. *Analysis of Option B.*

    A. Initial military actions.
    B. Probably Communist response to such actions.
    C. Further actions in the event of Communist reaction of a strong character, to include the full possible gamut of DRV and Chicom reactions and how we would deal with each from a military standpoint.
    D. Political scenario to accompany all the above.

Status: The major initial input for this paper will come from JCS in consultation with DOD. The proposed line of action should then be subjected to an intelligence estimate of the likelihood of different types of Communist reactions—this being the second part of the intelligence initial input. The political scenario is being drafted in State to be meshed with the initial actions in a comprehensive scenario with dates fixed as exactly as possible in relation to a hypothetical date of decision.

VII. *Analysis of Option C.*

A more exact definition of this option will be derived from the paper on negotiating avenues (Section IV) and the analysis of military actions (Section VI). The preparation of this paper will follow the preparation of drafts of those two sections.

VIII. *Immediate Actions in the Period Prior to Decision.*

This is being urgently reviewed in State/FE. It will probably come up for decision before the project is completed, and it will then drop out of the final paper. In general, the Working Group has agreed that our aim should be to maintain present signal strength, showing no signs of determination but equally avoiding actions that would tend to pre-judge the basic decision.

IX. *Conclusion and Recommendations.*

This speaks for itself and might come at the end as a short paper synthesizing the whole project for the President.

FE:WPBundy:mk

[Document 217]

Nov. 3, 1964

FROM SAIGON FOR STATE

CINCPAC FOR POLAD

EXDIS

REF. DEF. 1342.

In compliance with request of DOD, I submit the following personal comments to JCSM 902-64 dated October 27, 1964. SNIE 53-2-64 is not RPT not available in Saigon and hence has not influenced my views. I assume that a political/psychological scenario is being prepared to support the military actions considered in the JCS study.

As indicated in EMBTEL 465 and elsewhere, I am in complete agreement with the thesis that the deteriorating situation in SVN requires the application of measured military pressures to DRV to induce that government to CEUE (sic) to provide support to VC and to use its authority to cause VC to cease or at least to moderate their depredations. The evidence of increased infiltration cited in EMBTEL 1189 [words missing] and effective action. The Bien Hoa incident of November 1, 1964 poses an even more pressing requirement for action under the retaliatory principle confirmed in NSAM 314.

EMBTEL 1357 contains the response to the Bien Hoa action which Embassy-MACV recommended. In effect, this recommendation is for retaliation bombing attacks on selected DRV targets by combined US/VNAF air forces and for a policy statement that we will act similarly in like cases in the future. If this recommendation is not RPT not accepted, I would favor intensifying 34-A operations and initiating air operations against selected targets as an interim substitute for more positive measures.

With ref to the JCS recommendations for the first five courses of action of Appendix A, they are all being implemented but the implementation has been weak in direct proportion to the ineffectiveness of the local government. This situation not RPT not likely to change for the better in time to effect the situation in the short term. The new government in its likely composition appears to have potentialities for improvement but it will be composed largely of men without governmental experience who will have to learn their trade on the job. It will take three to four months under favorable circumstances to get it functioning well.

Item 6 is new and I would have trouble in justifying it. It amounts to a departure for no RPT no clear gain from the principle that the Vietnamese fight their own war in SVN. Added air strength in-country is not RPT not going to have a significant effect on the outcome of the counterinsurgency campaign.

Under Appendix B, I see no RPT no advantage in resuming Desoto patrols [words missing] if we are seeking an excuse for action, it is to our interest to strike Hanoi for its malefactions in SVN and not RPT not for actions in the Bay of Tonkin against the US Navy. We need to tie our actions to Hanoi support of the VC, not RPT not to the defense of purely US interests. Hence, the excuse for our actions should ideally grow out of events in SVN and LAOS. Such events are available for our exploitation now in the form of infiltration activities in the Laotian Corridor and the DRV, the Bien Hoa incident and the increasing sabotage by the VC of the Saigon–Danang RY. With these [words missing] there is no RPT no need to seek others in the Tonkin Gulf where the second incident developed in such a way as to reduce our ability to use subsequent episodes as a credible basis for action.

Similarly, I see nothing but disadvantage in further stirring up the Cambodian border by implementing hot pursuit. We don't often catch the fleeing VC in the heart of SVN; I see little likelihood of doing better in Cambodia. Sihanouk does not RPT not have much in the way of ground forces but a few counter-incursions from his side could be very awkward in requiring the diversion of further ARVN to cover the frontier. We are presently short of trained SVN manpower and need to conserve it for essential purposes. The present unfriendly frontier is much preferable to one actively hostile.

With regard to low level reconnaissance probes, they are not RPT not needed as signals of intentions as, as I hope, we launch forth on a bombing program, overt or covert, against the north. In the latter case, low level RECCE should be flown [words missing]

Actions 7, 8, and 10 I tend to view as a package for concurrent implementation. In the aggregate, these actions constitute an attack on a coherent target system all of which may need to be progressively destroyed if infiltration is to be checked. [words missing] At some point, both would probably merge into a single pressure vector on the DRV.

As a final word, it is well to remind ourselves that "too much" in this matter of coercing Hanoi may be as bad as "too little." At some point, we will need a relatively cooperative leadership in Hanoi willing to wind up the VC insurgency on terms satisfactory to us and our SVN allies. What we don't want is an expanded war in sea and an unresolved guerrilla problem in SVN.

Taylor

[Document 218]

November 4, 1964

MEMORANDUM FOR: Mr. William Bundy—FE

FROM: Mr. Michael V. Forrestal—S/VN

SUBJECT: Comments on Your Input—II U.S. Objectives and Stakes in South Vietnam and Southeast Asia

It seems to me that there is an important flavor lacking in the excellent "hard look" of your week-end paper at our stakes in South Vietnam and Laos. It is the role of China. I think it would be helpful both to our thinking here and also as a basis for any discussion we may someday have with our European friends to weave into your exposé a paragraph or two on the nature and probable development of Chinese policy.

I think it is difficult to conceive of the effects of an American partial withdrawal in Southeast Asia without taking into account the effect this would have on Chinese policy. Putting it another way, (if China did not exist, the effect of our withdrawal from a situation in which the people we were trying to help seemed unable to help themselves might not be politically so pervasive in Asia).

As I see it, Communist China shares the same internal political necessity for ideological expansion today that the Soviet Union did during the time of the Comintern and the period just following the Second World War. Since China's problems with respect to her internal political and economic management are even greater than those of Russia, one would expect that the need to justify the sacrifices she demands of her people will continue for the plannable future. This will impel her, I suggest, to achieve ideological successes abroad, at least where these can be achieved without grave risk to the Mainland itself.

Since any ideological success will stimulate the need for further successes during the period of her internal tension, our objective should be to "contain" China for the longest possible period. We would realize, of course, that eventually China must be expected to exercise some degree of political pre-eminence on the fringes of Asia. But if we can delay the day when this happens and at the same time strengthen the political and economic structure of the bordering countries, we might indeed succeed in creating, at the very least, Titoist regimes on the periphery of China and at best Western oriented nations, who nevertheless maintain normal relationships with Peking. Somebody put this to me the other day in culinary terms. We should delay China's swallowing up Southeast Asia until (a) she develops better table manners and (b) the food is somewhat more indigestible.

I have been trying some of this reasoning on Lippman, and he appears to be toying with it, although I would not hope for much from that quarter.

[Document 219]

Draft

WPBundy
11–5–64

CONDITIONS FOR ACTION AND KEY ACTIONS SURROUNDING ANY DECISION

1. Bien Hoa may be repeated at any time. This would tend to force our hand, but would also give us a good springboard for any decision for stronger action. The President is clearly thinking in terms of maximum use of a Gulf of Tonkin rationale, either for an action that would show toughness and hold the line till we can decide the big issue, or as a basis for starting a clear course of action under the broad options.

2. Congress must be consulted before any major action, perhaps only by notification if we do a reprisal against another Bien Hoa, but preferably by careful talks with such key leaders as Mansfield, Dirksen, the Speaker, Albert, Halleck, Fulbright, Hickenlooper, Morgan, Mrs Bolton, Russell, Saltonstall, Rivers, (Vinson?), Arends, Ford, etc. He probably should wait till his mind is moving clearly in one direction before such a consultation, which would point to some time next week. Query if it should be combined with other topics (budget?) to lessen the heat.

3. We probably do not need additional Congressional authority, even if we decide on very strong action. A session of this rump Congress might well be the scene of a messy Republican effort.

4. We are on the verge of intelligence agreement that infiltration has in fact mounted, and Saigon is urging that we surface this by the end of the week or early next week. Query how loud we want to make this sound. Actually Grose in the *Times* had the new estimate on Monday, so the splash and sense of hot new news may be less. We should decide this today if possible. . . . In general, we all feel the problem of proving North Vietnamese participation is less than in the past, but we should have the Jorden Report updated for use as necessary.

5. A Presidential statement with the rationale for action is high on any check list. An intervening fairly strong Presidential noise to prepare a climate for an action statement is probably indicated and would be important in any event to counter any SVN fears of a softening in our policy. We should decide the latter today too if possible.

6. Secretary Rusk is talking today to Dobrynin. For more direct communication Seaborn can be revved up to go up the 15th if we think it wise. He is not going anyway, and we could probably hold him back so that the absence of any message was not itself a signal.

7. Our internal soundings appear to divide as follows:

   a. We should consult with the UK, Australia, New Zealand, and possibly Thailand *before* we reach a decision. We would hope for firm moral support from the UK and for participation in at least token form from the others.

   b. SEATO as a body should be consulted concurrently with stronger action. We should consult the Philippines a day or so before such action but not necessarily before we have made up our minds.

   c. The NATO Council should be notified on the Cuban model, i.e., concurrently, by a distinguished representative.

d. For negative reasons, France probably deserves VIP treatment also.

e. In the UN, we must be ready with an immediate affirmative presentation of our rationale to proceed concurrently either with a single reprisal action or with the initiation of a broader course of action.

f. World-wide, we should select reasonably friendly chiefs of state for special treatment seeking their sympathy and support, and should arm all our representatives with the rationale and defense of our action whether individual reprisal or broader.

8. USIA must be brought into the planning process not later than early next week, so that it is getting the right kind of materials ready for all our information media, on a contingency basis. The same is true of CIA's outlets.

[Document 220]

MEMORANDUM FOR MR. WILLIAM BUNDY   November 6, 1964

SUBJECT: Courses of Action in Viet Nam

I have read your memorandum outlining the options open to us in Viet Nam. It seems to me of the complete catalogue of the possibilities facing the President at this moment. I would offer the following comments derived from the recent perspective of Saigon.

First, I think it highly important that we recognize the anticipation which has built up in Viet Nam concerning the nature of the first U.S. actions after the election. All Vietnamese and other interested observers as well will be watching very closely to see what posture the newly mandated Johnson Administration will assume. I feel that the character, therefore, of our first action, no matter how limited that action in itself may be, will produce exaggerated reactions in many quarters.

Given this state of affairs, I think it is imperative that our first action be a positive one and one which gives the appearance of a determination to take risks if necessary to maintain our position in Southeast Asia. This posture is essential no matter which option the President chooses since we must indicate an attitude of strength if we are to take any of the steps open to us.

Secondly, I feel that it is important not only in terms of national policies but in terms of international attitudes that the Administration go on record fairly soon placing our policy in Viet Nam within the larger perspective of our policies in the Western Pacific, especially as they involve confrontation with Communist China. I have done a paper (attached as Tab A) which indicates the sort of statement that I feel is necessary. This paper was drafted as a possible article to be issued with authoritative anonymity in some mass circulation medium, such as the New York Times Magazine. It is a first draft and contains a number of statements which would probably give trouble to our "specialists" but which ought to be able to be said, with some editing, as a political document.

Having made these two generalized observations, I would move on to the following specific suggestions. For self-evident reasons, I have broken them into those matters which need immediate decision and those which have a somewhat longer time fuze.

A. IMMEDIATE DECISIONS

1. The Viet Cong maintain an ability to repeat the Bien Hoa performance at any one of a number of installations. Danang, the major communications in-

stallation at Nha Trang, and the facility at Phi Bai are only three of those which could be successfully damaged by the Viet Cong in the same sort of hit and run mortar attack. I believe a decision should be taken now that any action of this type meets with an immediate response tailored to an appropriate target of retaliation, taking into account such variable factors as the poor weather in North Viet Nam during the month or so ahead.

2. The build up of supplies coming in on Route 7 and the increase in infiltration units observed in the Panhandle indicate the need for a more active Yankee Team operation. As it is now we fly photo reconnaissance with armed escort. I think a decision should be made to convert these operations to genuine armed reconnaissance flights which will have the authority to destroy targets of opportunity, particularly truck convoys when sighted.

3. If we are to maintain our position in the Tonkin Gulf, we should renew de Soto patrols soonest. This introduces the prospect of a torpedo boat attack against the destroyers. (CINCPAC, at JCS direction, has developed a FRAG-ORDER for a retaliatory attack in the event of torpedo boat action against the destroyers.) In my opinion, the retaliation strike is of magnitude which would not be politically viable unless the destroyers were actually sunk or severely damaged. Since either of these is an unlikely possibility, it seems to me that the retaliation action ought to be reviewed on this side of the River to make it measure somewhat closer to political realities.

B. LONGER RANGE ACTIONS

All of the foregoing suggestions are actions which seem required by the immediate nature of the Viet Cong/North Viet Nam current operations. None of them crosses any particular threshold of decision beyond the level that we have generally taken in the past. However, if we are to contemplate actions designed to reverse the pattern of current difficulties in Viet Nam we ought to lay the ground work for longer-range actions moving toward a more decisive resolution. In this sense, it seems to me that the time has come for us to begin briefing responsible newspaper people on a background basis concerning both the degree of control which the North Vietnamese exercise over the Viet Cong and the nature of the infiltration process as derived from recent intelligence. I think both of these actions could be taken without breaching ultra-sensitive security information. Both of them, however, are essential if we are to make our case clearly understood that North Viet Nam is the responsible element in the Viet Cong campaign.

Once these facts have been better established in the public record, we can begin harassing action against the infiltration structure not only in Laos but more particularly in its operational roots in North Viet Nam. I am convinced that air attacks up and down this structure will produce a tremendous uproar but probably not anything in the way of a major military confrontation. Indeed, it is doubtful whether they will produce international political pressures of such a level that we would feel compelled to take responsive action.

Pressures mounted along this channel have two distinct advantages: 1) they are clearly reactions to an established and persistent threat; and 2) their intensity can be controlled at our discretion and initiative and doesn't rest upon Communist initiatives. Moreover, their nature would be such that for the moment all options continue to be preserved by the President. We do not need to stipulate our ultimate intentions in beginning this particular course of action.

I think this latter observation is important because of current variables. First, there is the quality of the new government in Viet Nam. While it is true that our own actions and our own decisions will have distinct effects upon the nature and determination of that Government, we do also need some assurances that the Government itself will be able to survive before we make definitive commitments beyond our current involvement. Secondly, there is the question of Sino-Soviet relations. We should know better in the next few weeks whether these are moving toward a rapprochement or whether the national and institutional factors of the dispute will persist.

This state of affairs, of course, decidedly effects the timing of any deliberate pressures we may undertake. The most important aspect of timing it seems to me is for us to maintain the appearance of a steady deliberative approach. Therefore, I would recommend that the set of decisions above be put into effect immediately so that their signal will reach the Communists soonest. At the same time, I believe an authoritative exposition of our position is needed in the immediate future.

As for movement toward the more deliberative pressure campaign, I would recommend that a meeting on this subject be held in Washington a couple of weeks from now, ostentatiously bringing in Ambassador Taylor and Admiral Sharp. (In this connection, the timing has to be fixed so as not to interfere with the CINCPAC weapons demonstration.) By the time that meeting is held, we should not only have been able to observe the effects of our initial and immediate attacks but also we should have a better reading of both the ability of the Saigon Government and the relations in the Sino-Soviet campaign.

William H. Sullivan

Attachment:

Tab A—Draft Article

[Document 221]

6 November 1964

CIA*DIA*INR PANEL DRAFT

SECTIONS VI-VII: PROBABLE REACTIONS TO OPTIONS B AND C.

A. COMMUNIST REACTIONS IN THE INDOCHINA AREA

(We refer the reader to SNIE 10-3-64, "Probable Reactions to Certain Possible US/GVN Courses of Action," of 9 October 1964. We feel that the judgments of this SNIE apply to the general levels of US military actions against the DRV which might be taken under the broad Options B or C of our present project outline—note especially the similarity with Category IV generalized US actions in pages 7–12 of the SNIE. Once Options B and C have been defined more precisely, the intelligence community, or intelligence community personnel, can estimate how Communist reactions would differ, if at all, from those in response to the assumed general US categories of action of SNIE 10-3-64.)

B. COMMUNIST MOVES ELSEWHERE IN THE WORLD

We believe that the USSR would be sufficiently concerned over the prospect of escalation of the crisis and of possible general war that it would not risk trying the American temper by provoking major crises in Berlin, Cuba, or else-where. We similarly doubt that Communist China would seek to create any major diversions outside of Southeast Asia during a US–DRV confrontation for fear of US nuclear retaliation.

C. REACTIONS IN SOUTH VIETNAM

1. The initial reaction would probably be one of elation, in the belief that the US was at last bringing its great power to bear against the enemy. Such attitudes would persist in the event that VC activity noticeably diminished or if the DRV soon indicated a serious interest in a cease-fire and negotiations. The South Viet-namese would be given a great psychological boost, and we would probably see at least a spurt of much more effective GVN military and administrative per-formance. Initial South Vietnamese elation and support would almost certainly quickly wane, however, if the war seemed to drag on despite the new US moves, and especially if the VC were able to increase their military and terrorist pres-sures.

2. In such event, the belief would almost certainly rapidly spread that eventual DRV/VC victory was inevitable, that the US was unable or unwilling to save the situation, and that prudence dictated an early accommodation. In such an atmosphere, VC exploitive efforts would bear considerable fruit. There would doubtless be some protest among South Vietnamese at the "inhuman" US actions against their kinsmen in the North. Deteriorating South Vietnamese morale, VC pressures, and perhaps French political action in South Vietnam could prob-ably succeed in soon casting up a new government committed to a cease-fire and a negotiated end to the war on almost any terms. The US would probably have the capability to install and protect a GVN subservient to US wishes, but the scene would have deteriorated to such an extent that there would be little nation-wide support for this government.

3. *VC tactics and capabilities.* The general level of VC activity—whether more, less, or about as at present—would of course be the result of Hanoi's basic decision of the moment as to how to respond to the US attacks. Involved in such decision would be Hanoi's estimate of the fragility of the political situa-tion in the South and whether "victory" might be quickly attained by a short, sudden burst. Available intelligence data do not warrant a confident estimate of VC "burst" capabilities, but we incline to the view that the VC does have mili-tary capabilities it has not yet committed. This may also be the case with VC terrorism, subversion, and political action, though we feel that any "unused" capabilities in these fields are less than in the case of the military. In any event, the VC would be hesitant to commit large-scale VC forces for fear that the GVN, with US assistance, could chew up such military units much more effec-tively than it has small VC groups. The VC, accordingly, would probably not attempt to administer such a coup de grace unless the demise of Saigon's author-ity appeared to be imminent.

D. NON-COMMUNIST REACTIONS

1. The reactions of the non-aligned states, and even of some US allies, to increased US military initiatives would tend to be adverse. The more severe the attacks were, and the longer they lasted, the greater and more articulate the the adverse reaction would be. Such reactions would be mitigated considerably if the moves appeared to achieve US objectives, and in any case some gov-

ernments would be privately more sympathetic to the US than would appear in their public stance or in public opinion media.

2. The most important non-Communist reactions would be those of the Asian states and of France and the UK.

a. In the Rep. of Korea, the Rep. of China, the Philippines, and Thailand there would be considerable elation that the US had adopted a tough new line which might check or cut back Communist expansion. These allies could probably be counted upon to lend some active support, use of bases, etc., to the US effort, but to balk at any US efforts to enlist their support for a negotiated settlement. The Japanese government, and considerable informed opinion in Japan, would be quietly pleased by the US action against the DRV. The Japanese government would probably attempt to stay fairly aloof from the question, however, for fear of provoking extreme domestic pressures or possible Chinese Communist action against Japan. In such process, the Japanese government, especially one headed by Kono, might seek to restrict certain US base rights in Japan.

b. The Indian government, and considerable informed opinion in India, would probably be quietly pleased by the US toughness, but the official Indian line would doubtless be one pressing for a quick end to hostilities and for US entry into negotiations. Prince Sihanouk would probably be the most troublesome neutralist, but his position would largely depend on his estimate of which was the stronger side. Sukarno can be confidently expected to lend at least verbal support to the Communist cause.

c. In the event US actions against the DRV were accompanied by an apparent US willingness to negotiate, *the UK* would probably prove our firmest political aide at this point, pressing for negotiations but resisting Communist efforts to make a mockery of them. The *French* would probably condemn US military action and associate themselves with Communist demands for negotiations without preconditions.

3. Longer-term world reactions would be influenced by success of the US sanctions: if they halted Communist expansion in Indochina and led to an easing of tensions, US firmness would be retrospectively admired, as in the Chinese offshore islands and Cuba missile showdowns.

4. The US would probably find itself progressively isolated in the event the US sanctions did not soon achieve either a Communist reduction of pressures in South Vietnam or some progress toward meaningful negotiations, and would almost certainly find itself isolated in the event that the crisis developed to the point where a US–Communist Chinese war seemed imminent. Some US allies, such as the GRC, the Philippines, and Thailand, would probably back the US wholeheartedly, with the GRC, at least, demanding to participate. Reactions of other US allies would depend in part upon the manner in which the situation had developed.

[Document 222]

Bundy Working Group

2nd Draft—11/6/64
McNaughton

ACTION FOR SOUTH VIETNAM

1. *US aims:*   (a) To protect US reputation as a counter-subversion guarantor.
   (b) To avoid domino effect especially in Southeast Asia.

    (c) To keep South Vietnamese territory from Red hands.
    (d) To emerge from crisis without unacceptable taint from methods.

2. *Present situation:* The situation in South Vietnam is deteriorating. Unless new actions are taken, the new government will probably be unstable and ineffectual, and the VC will probably continue to extend their hold over the population and territory. It can be expected that, soon (6 months? two years?), (a) government officials at all levels will adjust their behavior to an eventual VC take-over, (b) defections of significant military forces will take place, (c) whole integrated regions of the country will be totally denied to the GVN, (d) neutral and/or left-wing elements will enter the government, (e) a popular-front regime will emerge which will invite the US out, and (f) fundamental concessions to the VC and accommodations to the DRV will put South Vietnam behind the Curtain.

3. *Urgency:* "Bien Hoa" having passed, no urgent decision is required regarding military action against the DRV, but (a) such a decision, related to the general deteriorating situation in South Vietnam, should be made soon, and (b) in the event of another VC or DRV "spectacular," a decision (for at least a reprisal) would be urgently needed.

4. *Inside South Vietnam:* Progress inside SVN is important, but it is unlikely despite our best ideas and efforts (and progress, if made, will take at least several months). Nevertheless, whatever other actions might be taken, great efforts should be made within South Vietnam: (a) to strengthen the government, its bureaucracy, and its civil-military coordination and planning, (b) to dampen ethnic, religious, urban and civil-military strife by a broad and positive GVN program designed (with US Team help) to enlist the support of important groups, and (c) to press the pacification program in the countryside.

5. *Action against DRV:* Action against North Vietnam is to some extent a substitute for strengthening the government in South Vietnam. That is, a less active VC (on orders from DRV) can be matched by a less efficient GVN. We therefore should consider squeezing North Vietnam.

6. *Options open to us:* We have three options open to us (all envision reprisals in the DRV for DRV/VC "spectaculars" against GVN as well as US assets in South Vietnam):

OPTION A. *Continue present policies.* Maximum assistance within SVN and limited external actions in Laos and by the GVN covertly against North Vietnam. The aim of any reprisal actions would be to deter and punish large VC actions in the South, but not to a degree that would create strong international negotiating pressures. Basic to this option is the continued rejection of negotiating in the hope that the situation will improve.

OPTION B. *Fast/full squeeze.* Present policies plus a systematic program of military pressures against the North, meshing at some point with negotiation, but with pressure actions to be continued at a fairly rapid pace and without interruption until we achieve our central present objectives.

OPTION C. *Progressive squeeze-and-talk*. Present policies plus an orchestration of communications with Hanoi and a crescendo of additional military moves against infiltration targets, first in Laos and then in the DRV, and then against other targets in North Vietnam. The scenario would be designed to give the US the option at any point to proceed or not, to escalate or not, and to quicken the pace or not. The decisions in these regards would be made from time to time in view of all relevant factors.

7. *Analysis of OPTION A*. [To be provided.]

8. *Analysis of OPTION B*. [To be provided.]

9. *Analysis of OPTION C*.
   (a) *Military actions*. Present policy, in addition to providing for reprisals in DRV for DRV actions against US, envisions (1) 34A Airops and Marops, (2) deSoto patrols, for intelligence purposes, (3) South Vietnamese shallow ground actions in Laos when practicable, and (4) T28 strikes against infiltration-associated targets in Laos. Additional actions should be:

PHASE ONE (in addition to reprisals in DRV for VC "spectaculars" in South Vietnam):
   (5) US strikes against infiltration-associated targets in Laos.

PHASE TWO (in addition to reprisals in DRV against broader range of VC actions):
   (6) Low-level reconnaisance in southern DRV, (7) US/VNAF strikes against infiltration-associated targets in southern DRV.

PHASE THREE: Either continue only the above actions or add one or more of the following, making timely deployment of US forces: (8) Aerial mining of DRV ports, (9) Naval quarantine of DRV, and (10) Us/ VNAF, in "crescendo," strike additional targets on "94 target list."
South Vietnamese forces should play a role in any action taken against the DRV.
   (b) *Political actions*. Establish immediately a channel for bilateral US–DRV communication. This could be in Warsaw or via Seaborn in Hanoi. Hanoi should be told we do *not seek* to destroy North Vietnam or to acquire a colony or base, but that North Vietnam must:

   (1) Stop training and sending personnel to wage war in SVN and Laos.
   (2) Stop sending arms and supplies to SVN and Laos.
   (3) Stop directing and controlling military actions in SVN and Laos.
   (4) Order the VC and PL to stop their insurgencies and military actions.
   (5) Remove VM forces and cadres from SVN and Laos.
   (6) Stop propaganda broadcasts to South Vietnam.
   [(7) See that VC and PL stop attacks and incidents in SVN and Laos?]
   [(8) See that VC and PL cease resistance to government forces?]
   [(9) See that VC and PL turn in weapons and relinquish bases?]
   [(10) See that VC and PL surrender for amnesty of expatriation?]

US demands should be accompanied by offers (1) to arrange a rice-barter deal between the two halves of Vietnam and (2) to withdraw US forces from South Vietnam for so long as the terms are complied with.

We should not seek wider negotiations—in the UN, in Geneva, etc.—but we should evaluate and pass on each negotiating opportunity as it is pressed on us.

(c) *Information actions.* The start of military actions against the DRV will have to be accompanied by a convincing world-wide public information program. (The information problem will be easier if the first US action against the DRV is related in time and kind to a DRV or VC outrage or "spectacular," preferably against *SVN* as well as US assets.)

(d) *VC/DRV/Chicom/USSR reactions.* [To be elaborated later.] The DRV and China will probably *not* invade South Vietnam, Laos or Burma, nor is it likely that they will conduct air strikes on these countries. The USSR will almost certainly confine herself to political actions. If the DRV or China strike or invade South Vietnam, US forces will be sufficient to handle the problem.

(e) *GVN reactions.* Military action against the DRV could be counter-productive in South Vietnam because (1) the VC could step up its activities, (2) the South Vietnamese could panic, (3) they could resent our striking their "brothers," and (4) they could tire of waiting for results. Should South Vietnam disintegrate completely beneath us, we should try to hold it together long enough to permit us to try to evacuate our forces and to convince the world to accept the uniqueness (and congenital impossibility) of the South Vietnamese case.

(f) *Allied and neutral reactions.* [To be elaborated later.] (1) Even if OPTION C failed, it would, by demonstrating US willingness to go to the mat, tend to bolster allied confidence in the US as an ally. (2) US military action against the DRV will probably prompt military actions elsewhere in the world—e.g., Indonesia against Malaysia or Timor, or Turkey against Cyprus.

[Document 223]

3rd Draft—11/7/64—McNaughton

ACTION FOR SOUTH VIETNAM

1. *US aims:* (a) To protect US reputation as a counter-subversion guarantor.
(b) To avoid domino effect especially in Southeast Asia.
(c) To keep South Vietnamese territory from Red hands.
(d) To emerge from crisis without unacceptable taint from methods used.

2. *Present situation:* The situation in South Vietnam is deteriorating. "Bien Hoas" cannot be prevented; the new government will probably be unstable and ineffectual, and the VC will probably continue to extend their hold over the population and territory. It can be expected that soon (6 months? two years?) (a) government officials at all levels will adjust their behavior to an eventual VC take-over, (b) defections of significant military forces will take

place, (c) whole integrated regions of the country will enter as totally denied to the GVN, (d) neutral and/or left-wing elements will enter the government, (e) a popular-front regime will emerge which will invite the US out, and (f) fundamental concessions to the VC and accommodations to the DRV will put South Vietnam behind the Curtain.

3. *Urgency:* (a) For GVN morale, risky US action needed now (post-11/3) to prove mettle.
     (b) Reprisal for new DRV or VC "spectacular" would require urgent decision.
     (c) General deteriorating situation in SVN requires decision soon.

4. *Inside South Vietnam:* Progress inside SVN is important, but it is unlikely despite our best ideas and efforts (and progress, if made, will take at least several months). Nevertheless, whatever other actions might be taken, great efforts should be made within South Vietnam: (a) to strengthen the government, its bureaucracy, and its civil-military coordination and planning, (b) to dampen ethnic, religious, urban and civil-military strife by a broad and positive GVN program designed (with US Team help) to enlist the support of important groups, and (c) to press the pacification program in the countryside. [Separate paper on this subject needed.]

5. *Options against DRV:* Action against North Vietnam is to some extent a substitute for strengthening the government in South Vietnam. That is, a less active VC (on orders from DRV) can be handled by a less efficient GVN (which we expect to have). We have three options open to us (all envision reprisals in the DRV for DRV/VC "spectaculars" against GVN as well as US assets in South Vietnam):

OPTION A. *Continue present policies.* Maximum assistance within SVN and limited external actions in Laos and by the GVN covertly against North Vietnam. The aim of any reprisal actions would be to deter and punish large VC actions in the South (but not to a degree that would create strong international negotiating pressures). Basic to this option is the continued rejection of negotiating in the hope that the situation will improve.

OPTION B. *Fast/full squeeze.* Present policies plus a systematic program of military pressures against the North, meshing at some point with negotiation, but with pressure actions to be continued at a fairly rapid pace and without interruption until we achieve our central present objectives.

OPTION C. *Progressive squeeze-and-talk.* Present policies plus an orchestration of (a) communications with Hanoi and (b) a crescendo of additional military moves against infiltration targets, first in Laos and then in the DRV, and then against other targets in North Vietnam. The scenario should give the impression of a steady deliberate approach. It would be designed to give the US the option at any point to proceed or not, to escalate or not, and to quicken the pace or not. These decisions would be made from time to time in view of all relevant factors.

Analysis of OPTION A. [To be provided.]
Analysis of OPTION B. [To be provided.]
Analysis of OPTION C.

(a) *Military actions.* (South Vietnamese should play as large a role as possible.)

PRESENT (in addition to reprisals in DRV for DRV actions against US assets):

(1) High-level reconnaissance of North Vietnam.

(2) 34A Marops and Airops (legitimated? including "black bomber"?).

(3) DeSoto patrols, for intelligence purposes.

(4) South Vietnamese shallow ground actions in Laos when practicable.

(5) T28 strikes against infiltration-associated targets in Laos.

PHASE ONE (in addition to reprisals in DRV for VC "spectaculars" in South Vietnam):

(6) US armed-recce strikes against infiltration-associated targets in Laos.

PHASE TWO (in addition to reprisals in DRV against broader range of VC actions):

(7) Low-level reconnaissance in southern DRV.

(8) US/VNAF strikes against infiltration-associated targets in southern DRV.

PHASE THREE: Continue only the above actions or add one or more of the following, making timely evacuation of dependents and deployment of US forces:

(9) Aerial mining of DRV ports.

(10) Naval quarantine of DRV.

(11) US/VNAF, in "crescendo," strike additional targets on "94 target list."

(b) *Political side:* (1) After OPTION C decision, Taylor "noisily" to Washington.

(2) Before PHASE ONE, set up covert US–DRV talking channel.

(3) As larger forums (US, Geneva) pressed on us, judge them.

(c) *Terms:* (1) We do not seek to destroy North Vietnam or to acquire a base,

(2) We will arrange a rice-barter deal between the two Vietnams, and

(3) We will stop squeeze on DRV (no promise to withdraw from SVN),

but (4) DRV must stop training and sending personnel to SVN and Laos,

(5) DRV must stop sending arms and supplies into SVN and Laos,

(6) DRV must stop directing military actions in SVN and Laos,

(7) DRV must order the VC and PL to stop their insurgencies,

(8) DRV must stop propaganda broadcasts to South Vietnam, and

(9) DRV must remove VM forces and cadres from SVN and Laos,

[(10) DRV must see that VC and PL stop incidents in SVN and Laos?]

[(11) DRV must see that VC and PL cease resistance?]

[(12) DRV must see that VC and PL turn in weapons and bases?]

[(13) DRV must see that VC and PL surrender for amnesty of expatriation?]

(d) *Information actions.* The start of military actions against the DRV will have to be accompanied by a convincing world-wide public information program. Briefings of responsible newspaper people along "Jorden Report" lines (without disclosing sensitive information) should start before PHASE ONE. Our actions then would clearly be reactions to an established Communist perfidy, but the scenario would be under our control.

(e) *VC/DRV/Chicom/USSR reactions.* [to be elaborated later.] The DRV and China almost certainly will not invade South Vietnam, Laos or Burma, or conduct air strikes on these countries in response to PHASES ONE and TWO; and the same is probably true in response to PHASE THREE. The USSR will almost certainly confine herself to political actions. If the DRV or China strike or invade South Vietnam, US forces will be sufficient to handle the problem.

(f) *GVN reactions.* Military action against the DRV could be counter-productive in South Vietnam because (1) the VC could step up its activities, (2) the South Vietnamese could panic, (3) they could resent our striking their "brothers," and (4) they could tire of waiting for results. Should South Vietnam disintegrate completely beneath us, we should try to hold it together long enough to permit us to try to evacuate our forces and to convince the world to accept the uniqueness (and congenital impossibility) of the South Vietnamese case.

(g) *Allied and neutral reactions.* [To be elaborated later.] (1) Even if OPTION C failed, it would, by demonstrating US willingness to go to the mat, tend to bolster allied confidence in the US as an ally. (2) US military action against the DRV will probably prompt military actions elsewhere in the world—e.g., Indonesia against Malaysia or Timor, or Turkey against Cyprus.

(h) *Evaluation.* OPTION C, as compared with OPTION A, stands a better chance of coming out better (though, involving a somewhat larger chance of big escalation than OPTION A, it stands some chance of coming out very badly). If OPTION C is tried and fails, we are in no worse position than we would be under OPTION A; but whatever form a failure took, OPTION C would leave behind a better odor than OPTION A: It would demonstrate that US was a "good doctor" willing to keep promises, be tough, take risks, get bloodied, and hurt the enemy badly. OPTION C stands a better chance of avoiding appearances which will affect judgments by, and provide pretexts to, other nations regarding US power, resolve and competence, and regarding how the US will behave in future cases of particular interest to those nations.

[Document 224]

Draft
WPBundy:mk
11/7/64

III. The Broad Options

We believe there are three broad options as to our future course of action in reference to South VN.

Option A would be to continue present policies indefinitely. This would involve maximum assistance within South VN, together with limited external actions in Laos and by the GVN covertly against North VN. We would continue to seek every possible additional measure for expansion of the present effort that would fit within the present policy framework. We would also take specific individual reprisal actions not only against such incidents as the Gulf of Tonkin attack but also against any recurrence of VC "spectaculars" in South VN (particularly but not solely if such spectaculars were aimed at US installations). Under this option, the aim of such reprisal actions would be to deter and punish such VC actions in the south, but not to a degree that would create strong international negotiating pressures. Basic to this option is the continued rejection of negotiation in the hope that the situation will improve.

As to the basic forms of negotiation that might arise under this course of action there are two possibilities:

1. We would accept the risk that South Vietnamese elements would themselves open negotiations with the Liberation Front or with Hanoi directed probably to a cease-fire and a coalition government that would admit the Liberation Front.

2. We might ourselves initiate, or acquiesce in having others initiate, a negotiating track, probably through the convening of a Geneva Conference on VN or—if a Laos conference had otherwise come about—letting such a conference in practice extend itself to cover VN.

Option B would call for continuing present policies as above, but its key ingredient would be a systematic program of military pressures against the north, meshing at some point with negotiation, but with pressure actions to be continued at a fairly rapid pace and without interruption until we achieve our present objective of getting Hanoi completely out of South VN and an independent and secure South VN reestablished. This option can be labelled a "fast/full squeeze." Basic to it is that we would approach any discussions for negotiation with absolutely inflexible insistence on our present objectives.

Option C might be labelled "progressive squeeze and talk." It would consist of present policies, plus an orchestration of (1) communication with Hanoi and/or Peiping, and (2) additional graduated military moves against infiltration targets, first in Laos and then in the DRV, and then against other targets in North VN. The military scenario should give the impression of a steady deliberate approach, and should be designed to give the US the option at any time to proceed or not, to escalate or not, and to quicken the pace or not. These decisions would be made from time to time in view of all relevant factors.

The negotiating part of this course of action would have to be played largely by ear. But in essence we would be indicating from the outset a willingness to negotiate in an affirmative sense. We would at the outset clearly be sticking to our full present objectives, but we would have to accept the possibility that, as the whole situation developed, we might not achieve these full objectives unless we were prepared to take the greater risks envisaged under Option B. In essence, Option C is a medium risk/medium hope of accomplishment option.

A decision to go no further than Option A as our ultimate course of action would in itself rule out Option B or Option C. However, the opening military actions for Option B and Option C have much in common and it is theoretically possible to initiate these actions without having made a decision as to which option would ultimately be followed.

Nonetheless, we believe that in practice a breakpoint would very quickly be reached, at which we would have to make clear whether we did in fact mean to pursue our military actions in an unrelenting fashion, and whether we were pre-pared to negotiate in any sense other than inflexible insistence on our present full objectives. Hence, it is our view that a clear decision would in fact have to be made at the outset whether we were pursuing Option B or Option C. A decision favor of Option C would not foreclose the taking of some additional military measures as the situation unfolded, but the whole spirit and thrust of these operations would be different than under Option B.

[Document 225]

IMMEDIATE ACTIONS IN THE PERIOD PRIOR TO DECISION
(PART VIII OF THE BUNDY OUTLINE)

November 7, 1964

The US, together with the RLG and GVN, are involved in a number of operations—34A, Yankee Team, Recce, and RLAF T–28 ops—designed to warn and harass North Vietnam and to reduce enemy capabilities to utilize the Lao Panhandle for reinforcing the Viet Cong in South Vietnam and to cope with PL/VM pressures in Laos. The US also has under consideration DeSoto Patrols and Cross Border Ground Operations. The present status and outlook of these operations are described below, together with a checklist of outstanding problems relating to each of the field of operations.

In general the working group is agreed that our aim should be to maintain present signal strength and level of harassment, showing no signs of lessening of determination but also avoiding actions that would tend to prejudge the basic decision.

A.   OPLAN 34A

Although not all of Oplan 34A was suspended after the first Tonkin Gulf incident, in effect little was accomplishd during the remainder of August and the month of September. Several successful maritime and airborne operations have been conducted under the October schedule. A schedule for November is under discussion and will probably be approved November 7.

1. *Maritime Operations*

Since the resumption of Marops under the October schedule, the following have been completed:

Recon   L Day (Oct. 4) Probe to 12 miles of Vinh Sor.
Recon   L + 2 (Oct. 10)   "   " 3   "   "   "   "
Loki IV L + 5   Junk capture failed
32 & 45 E L + 8 (Oct. 28/29) Bombard Vinh Son radar and Mui Dao observa-
                             tion post.

The following operation was refused approval:

44C   L +10   Demolition by frog men supported by fire team of
                             bridge on Route 1.

Currently approved is:

34B   L + 12 (Nov. 4, on) Bombardment of barracks on Hon Matt
                            and Tiger Island.

The following maritime operations remain on the October schedule and presumably will appear on the November schedule along with some additional similar operations:

L + 13   Capture of prisoner by team from PTF
L + 15   Junk Capture
L + 19   Bombard Cap Mui Ron and Tiger Island
L + 25   Bombard Yen Phu and Sam Son radar
L + 28   Blow up Bridge Route 1 and bombard Cap Mui Dao
L + 30   Return any captives from L   15
L + 31   Bombard Hon Ne and Hon Me
L + 36   Blow up pier at Phuc Loi and bombard Hon Ngu
L + 38   Cut Hanoi–Vinh rail line
L + 41   Bombard Dong Hoi and Tiger Island
L + 24   Bombard Nightingale Island

2. *Airborne Operations*

Five teams and one singleton agent were in place at the beginning of October. Since then one of the teams has been resupplied and reinforced. The remaining four were scheduled to be resupplied and reinforced but weather prevented flights. These operations, plus the dropping of an additional team, will appear on the November schedule.

Two of the teams carried out successful actions during October. One demolished a bridge, the other ambushed a North Vietnamese patrol. Both teams suffered casualties, the latter sufficient to cast doubt on the wisdom of the action.

3. *Psychological Operations*

Both black and white radio broadcasts have been made daily. Black broadcasts have averaged eight to ten hours weekly,—white broadcasts sixty hours weekly.

Letters posted through Hong Kong have averaged about from 50 to 100 weekly.

During September and October only one leaflet delivery was made by air. This was done in conjunction with a resupply mission.

The November schedule will call for a large number of leaflet and deception operations.

4. *Reconnaissance Flights*

An average of four flights per week have covered the bulk of Oplan 34A targets.

Problems

1. *Surfacing of Marops*—The question of whether to surface Marops remains unresolved. While Washington has suggested this be done, General Khanh has been reluctant to do so. It is argued that surfacing the operations would enable

the US to offer some protection to them; the counter argument postulates US involvement in North Vietnam and consequent escalation.

2. *Security of Operations*—The postponement of an operation, whether because of unfavorable weather or failure of Washington to approve at the last moment, jeopardizes the operation. Isolation of teams presents hazards.

3. *Base Security*—After the Bien Hoa shelling some attention has been given to the security of the Danang base. Perimeter guard has been strengthened, but action remains to be taken for marine security, although a survey is underway.

4. *Team Welfare*—In-place teams Bell and Easy have been in dire need of supplies for several weeks. Weather has prevented resupply, which will be attempted again during the November moon phase.

5. *NVN Counteraction*—The capability of the North Vietnamese against Marops has improved somewhat, although not yet sufficiently to frustrate these operations.

B. YANKEE TEAM OPERATIONS

For several months now the pattern of Yankee Team Operations has . . . over a two-week period and about ten flights during the same time interval slated for Panhandle coverage. Additionally, we have recently been authorized a maximum of two shallow penetration flights daily to give comprehensive detailed coverage of cross border penetration. We have also recently told MACV that we have a high priority requirement for night photo recce of key motorable routes in Laos. At present about 2 night recce flights are flown along Route 7 areas within a two-week span.

YT supplies cap for certain T–28 corridor strikes. Cap aircraft are not authorized to participate in strike or to provide suppressive fire.

Pending questions include: (a) whether YT strikes should be made in support of RLAF T–28 corridor operations; (b) whether YT recce should be made of areas north of 20° parallel; (c) YT suppressive attacks against Route 7, especially Ban Ken Bridge; and (d) YT activity in event of large-scale ground offensive by PL (this issue has not arisen but undoubtedly would, should the PL undertake an offensive beyond the capabilities of Lao and sheep-dipped Thai to handle).

C. T–28 OPERATIONS

There are now 27 T–28 (including three RT–28) aircraft in Laos, of which 22 are in operation. CINCPAC has taken action, in response to Ambassador Unger's request to build this inventory back up to 40 aircraft for which a pilot capability, including Thai, is present in Laos.

The T–28's are conducting the following operations:

1. General harassing activities against Pathet Lao military installations and movements, primarily in Xieng Khouang and Sam Neua Provinces. This also includes efforts to interdict Route 7.

2. Tactical support missions for Operation Anniversary Victory No. 2 (Saleumsay), the FAR/Meo clearing operation up Route 4 and north of Tha Thom.

3. Tactical support for Operation Victorious Arrow (Sone Sai), a FAR clearing operation in southern Laos.

4. Strikes on targets of opportunity, including in support of FAR defensive actions such as at Ban Khen northwest of Thakhek.

5. Corridor interdiction program. The 13 original targets under this program have been hit and plans are now underway to hit four additional targets (including in the Tchepone area), plus restriking some of the original 13 targets. Ambassador Unger has submitted for approval under this program 6 additional targets.

6. The Ambassador has been authorized to discuss with the RLAF RT–28 reconnaissance in northwest Laos along the area just north of and to the east and west of the line from Vieng Phou Kha–Muong Sai.

In recent weeks, the T–28's have been dropping a large number of surrender leaflets on many of their missions. These have already led, in some cases, to PL defections.

US participation in SAR operations for downed T–28's is authorized. We are faced by the following problems in connection with the T–28's:

1. Authority for Yankee Team aircraft to engage in suppressive strikes in the corridor area, in support of the T–28 strike program there, has not been given as yet.

2. Also withheld is authorization for YT suppressive fire attack on Ban Ken Bridge on Route 7.

3. We are investigating reports of greatly increased truck movement along Route 7 as well as enemy build-up of tanks and other equipment just across the border in NVN. Counteraction may be required involving attack on Ban Ken.

4. Thai involvement. Hanoi claims to have shot down a T–28 over DRV territory on August 18 and to have captured the Thai pilot flying the plane. Although the information the North Vietnamese have used in connection with this case seems to be accurate, it is not clear the pilot is alive and can be presented to the ICC. The possibility cannot be excluded, however, nor that other Thai pilots might be captured by the PL.

5. The DRV claims T–28's have violated North Vietnamese airspace and bombed/strafed NVN villages on August 1 and 2, and on October 16 and 17 and again on October 28. The charges are probably accurate with respect to the first two dates (along Route 7) and the last one (Mu Gia Pass area). The October 16 and 17 strikes were actually in disputed territory which was recognized by the 1954 Geneva Agreement as being in Laos.

6. The Pathet Lao has called to the attention of the ICC T–28 strikes in the corridor area and called for the ICC to stop them and inform the Co-Chairmen. The ICC has already agreed to investigate another PL charge concerning alleged US/SVN activities in the corridor area in violation of the Geneva Agreements.

D. DeSOTO PATROLS

Further DeSoto Patrols have been held in abeyance pending top-level decision. Ambassador Taylor (Saigon's 1378) sees no advantage in resuming DeSoto Patrols except for essential intelligence purposes. He believes we should tie our actions to Hanoi's support of Viet Cong, not to the defense of purely US interests.

E. CROSS BORDER GROUND OPERATIONS

Earlier in the year several eight-man reconnaissance teams were parachuted into Laos as part of Operation Leaping Lena. All of these teams were located by the enemy and only four survivors returned to RVN. As a result of Leaping Lena Cross Border Ground Operations have been carefully reviewed and COMUSMACV has stated that he believes no effective Cross Border Ground Operations can be implemented prior to January 1, 1965 at the earliest.

F. COVERT OPERATIONS IN LAOS

Consideration is being given to improving Hardnose (including greater Thai involvement) and getting Hardnose to operate more effectively in the corridor infiltration areas.

No change in status of Kha.

G. OTHER SENSITIVE INTELLIGENCE OPERATIONS

These include "Queen Bee," "Box Top," "Lucky Dragon" and "Blue Springs."

FE:MGreen:ej
11/7/64

[Document 226]

November 10, 1964

MEMORANDUM FOR MEMBERS OF NSC WORKING GROUP

I am enclosing copies of draft Sections VII, IX, and X, which contain Mr. McNaughton's comments, for your general use. These should be considered working papers only and should not go outside the Working Group.

William P. Bundy

Enclosures:
Draft Sections VII, IX, and X.

D R A F T
W. P. Bundy/bmm
Nov. 8, 1964

VII. ANALYSIS OF OPTION C

A. RATIONALE AND PREPARATORY ACTIONS

1. *Rationale*

a. This course of action consists of progressive application of increasing military pressures, undertaken in concert with appropriate political pressures, to cause the DRV to terminate its support of the insurgency in South Vietnam (SVN) and Laos. It would be designed for maximum control at all stages, and to permit interruption at some appropriate point or points for negotiations, while seeking to maintain throughout a credible threat of further military pressures should such be required.

b. The object of negotiations would initially be the complete termination of DRV support to the insurgency in SVN and Laos, in order to re-establish an independent and secure SVN and the integrity of the 1962 Geneva Accords in Laos. However, the program would provide for the contingency that, as the result of politico–military evaluation of developments during its progress, it might become desirable to settle for less than complete assurances on our key objectives.

c. A stated basis for our actions would place maximum stress on the documented illegal infiltration of armed and trained insurgents from the DRV, and over-all DRV direction and control of VC insurgency all along. Our posture would be that these DRV activities had now reached an intolerable level requiring action against the DRV by the US and the GVN. Additional VC major actions in the south would be used to strengthen this posture, particularly if such actions included major further attacks on US installations.

2. *Preparatory Actions*

Substantial preparation for this course of action would already have been taken under the "Immediate Program" set forth in Section IX. The headings of preparatory action appear to be as follows:

a. A firm Presidential statement setting forth our rationale.

b. Key information actions addressed to the US public and to international audiences, notably the surfacing of all our useable information on infiltration.

c. Consultation with key leaders of Congress. We believe that the present Congressional Resolution provides an adequate legal basis for initiating this course of action.

d. With the GVN, we would make clear what we were planning to do, provide for GVN participation to the maximum degree militarily feasible, but above all take a very tough position insisting that the GVN set its own house in order, maintain political stability, and get ahead with the military and pacification programs.

e. Certain key allies—UK, Australia, New Zealand, Thailand, and the Philippines—would be fully informed in advance of our plans and would be asked to contribute in various ways to the maximum possible extent. A SEATO meeting might be used to obtain a strong general declaration of support, but the actions would not be placed on an explicit SEATO basis (unless perhaps France and Pakistan had in the meantime dropped out of SEATO).

f. Key involved nations such as Canada, India, and France, would require special individual treatment.

g. Laos would require practically full consultation.

h. In Asia and GRC and ROK would be informed in advance, but their active participation, except in limited GRC intelligence ways, would not be sought.

i. In NATO, we would make our basic position clear and seek their sympathy and moral support, but not seek to enlist them in military actions.

j. With non-aligned nations, we would make our position clear, combining individual approaches with our UN statements.

B. OPENING MILITARY ACTIONS

1. *Conditions of Action:* "cold blood" versus "hot blood"

There would be many advantages if the course of action could be initiated following either an additional VC "spectacular" or at least strong additional evidence of a major infiltration. However, we should be prepared to go ahead even without these, on the basis of a picture of over-all deterioration.

2. *Specific: Military Actions*

a. Intensified conduct of existing activities, such as 34–A MAROPS, De Soto patrols, Lao and US-armed recce strikes on infiltration-associated targets in Laos, high-level recce of the DRV, and shallow SVN ground actions in Laos to the degree practicable.

b. The key additional air actions in the first phase would be US/VNAF low-level reconnaissance in the southern DRV and the initiation of strikes against infiltration-associated targets in the southern DRV. These actions, actually hitting the DRV on an overt basis, would constitute the first real break-point in terms of both the beginning of real pressures on the DRV and international pressures for negotiation.

c. In conjunction with these air actions, we would be taking maximum security measures, with the GVN, in the south, and would also carry out a medium level of additional readiness deployments in the area. Dependents would already have been evacuated from SVN in the last stages of the "immediate program."

d. Reprisal actions at this point would be fitted into the larger script. We must recognize, however, that such reprisal actions might necessarily be more major individually than the attacks on the DRV contemplated under b. above.

e. Present military planning does not envisage the introduction of substantial ground forces into SVN or Thailand in conjunction with the first phase. We believe this needs further consideration. Among the proposals that should be considered would be the introduction of substantial ground forces into Thailand and, more dramatically, the introduction of a US or multilateral ground force into the northern provinces of South Vietnam. (Contributors to the multilateral force might include Australia, New Zealand, Thailand, and the Philippines. In other words, it would be a SEATO-member force prepared to act firmly on the ground, as opposed to a "neutralizing" force drawn from India, Canada, and similar nations. We believe the latter to be impracticable.)

f. The degree of action against Cambodia needs further thought. JCS plans would provide for hot pursuit at least. Others believe Cambodia should be treated on present lines unless Cambodia itself starts crossing the border.

g. Actions in Laos also need further thought. The military script now provides only for a more intensive application of present types of action. If the situation in Laos simply rocks along, without major Communist action, or if Laos negotiations have moved forward, this is probably the right course. However, the introduction of substantial ground forces to seal the Panhandle might be considered at some early military stage, especially if the Communist side had attacked in Laos. Such action would move us a very long way toward *de facto* partition of Laos; in effect, we would be adopting a strong blocking posture in Laos, necessarily balked by deployments in Thailand.

C. EARLY NEGOTIATING ACTIONS

This raises two questions: the inter-relation of various possible channels of communication and negotiating avenues, and the initial negotiating position to be taken by the US.

1. *Communication and Negotiating Avenues*

a. *Channels to Hanoi and Peiping*

(1) We would continue to use the existing channel to Hanoi.

(2) We could conceivably start direct conversations with Hanoi in some third country.

(3) Use of third countries as intermediaries for actual negotiations does not appear promising. We could hope that countries such as India, and perhaps Pakistan and France, would be useful in making clear the limited nature of our objectives. Moscow might likewise play a key role in this respect, and it is possible that Moscow would report back to us useful interpretations of the positions of Hanoi and Peiping. However, it seems most unlikely that Moscow would go so far as to serve as a useful intermediary. *In sum,* not much hope can be held that we would have useful negotiations through such channels. Hanoi and Peiping might give us indications of their position, but they would probably be pressing for some type of conference as an actual negotiating locale.

b. *The UN*

It is virtually certain that the initiation of attacks against the DRV would cause some form of UN discussion, and we believe it essential that we and the GVN take the initiative to explain our position and its justification, in the Security Council. It is just possible that we would have to fend off some condemnatory move in the General Assembly or the Security Council, and an affirmative initiative would be the best way to forestall this, as well as providing an essential forum for stating our position.

The question arises whether, beyond such use of the UN, we should seriously consider letting the UN become the scene of serious negotiations, either through inscription of a continuing item on the agenda or through *de facto* use of UN contacts. Here we encounter a major timing problem in relation to the issue of Chinese Communist representation. If a UN item were actually inscribed, before we had disposed of the Chinese issue in this General Assembly, there would be great pressures both to invite Hanoi and Peiping to the UN and to admit at least Peiping. Since we do not think the ChiRep issue will be disposed of before February, or perhaps even March, this timing factor argues almost insuperably against any formal inscription of the SVN problem, or the Southeast Asia problem generally, prior to that time.

c. *A Geneva Conference*

Once we had started attacks on the DRV, the USSR might well try to convene a Geneva Conference. Although the UK Government might be responsive to any pressures we exerted against doing so, UK public opinion would almost certainly exert enormous pressure for the UK to join in calling a conference. France would of course join in the hue and cry, and India would probably do likewise. In short, the aggregate pressure for a Geneva Conference would be very great in any event.

In these circumstances, we believe that the best course would be for the US to yield fairly early to such pressures, and in effect to accept a Geneva Conference as the best available negotiating forum. At the same time, we must recognize the difficulty inherent in such action—and indeed in the whole of Option C—that our early acceptance of negotiation would in itself have morale effects in South Vietnam, Thailand, and perhaps Laos. Thus, we would probably want to put on some show of resistance.

d.   *An Expanded Laos Conference*

The present prospects are that a Laos Conference will not be convened in the near future on the basis of satisfaction of Souvanna's present preconditions. We are trying out some variations that might ease these preconditions without hurting morale in Laos, and these might result in a conference—or at least make a record that the onus for rejecting one is on the Communist side. If a Laos Conference were in fact convened, it could be the locale for quiet negotiations with somewhat less disadvantage than the formal convening of a Geneva Conference on Vietnam itself. But we would have to weigh this advantage against the disadvantages of any interim concessions making a Laos Conference possible.

2.   *Initial US Negotiating Position*

Our initial position would be basically to insist on our present objectives, plus certain bargaining elements:

a. The 1954 settlement in South Vietnam must be restored. (We would duck the question of elections in all Vietnam, or insist that any such elections must be truly free, after a period of consolidation.) This means a South Vietnam not free to enter alliances, with any external military presence reduced to minimal "normal MAAG" levels, but free to accept external military equipment.

b. The DRV must observe the 1954 agreement by totally ceasing its support for the VC in SVN. We would specify an end to infiltration of arms and equipment, an end to propaganda, closing down of command and other communications, and removal of personnel from SVN.

c. The ending of DRV activity in SVN must be verified by some new enforcement machinery replacing the present ineffective ICC.

d. The DRV itself should be neutralized to the same extent as SVN, and this policed by effective [word illegible] enforcement machinery. This goes beyond 1954, and might later be traded out.

e. A new form of international guarantee should be provided against any violation of the above. This could take the form of declaration by all powers and the designation of some to provide forces in case of need.

In sum, we would use the negotiation in part as a propaganda forum to air the DRV violations and force other nations to endorse them. We also would set our sights high, so that "compromises" might still leave us in a defensible position.

D. PROBABLE COMMUNIST RESPONSES

There are three possible Communist responses:

1. Hanoi might start to yield visibly. This is unlikely.

2. Hanoi might retaliate militarily by some form of overt military action such as limited air attacks against South Vietnam, or an offensive in Laos. This is possible, but any major degree of military retaliation initially is less likely than:

3. Hanoi would hold firm, possibly avoiding major new attacks in South Vietnam but keeping up continued strong VC pressure. Hanoi and Peiping would do their utmost to stimulate condemnation of the attacks in world opinion and, if negotiations began, would take a tough initial position. This appears the most likely response.

E. IN THE EVENT OF THE THIRD TYPE OF COMMUNIST RESPONSE, LIKELY DEVELOPMENTS AND PROBLEMS

1. Within SVN, the initial reaction to attacks on the DRV would probably be one of clation, in the belief that the US was at last bringing its great power to bear against the enemy. The South Vietnamese would be given a substantial psychological boast, and we would quickly see at least a spurt of much more effective GVN military and administrative performance.

However, initial South Vietnamese elation and support would almost certainly quickly wane, if the war seemed to drag on despite the new US moves, and especially if the VC were able to increase their military and terrorist pressures.

In short, the appearance of a stalemate could easily produce a resumption in present deteriorating trends, and this could lead to a new government committed to a cease fire and a negotiated end of the war on almost any terms. The US would probably have the capability to install and protect a GVN subservient to US wishes, but the situation might have deteriorated to such an extent that there would be less nation-wide suport for this government.

If this somewhat gloomy prognosis of developments in South Vietnam proved correct, we could be driven at a fairly early point to consider:

2. Moving up to a second phase involving further increases of military pressure. Here the actions to consider would be extensions of the target system in the DRV to include additional targets on the "ninety-four target list," aerial mining of DRV ports, and a naval quarantine of the DRV. The aim of such actions would be to hold morale in South Vietnam and to increase the pressure on Hanoi.

3. Either in conjunction with such expanded action, or to some degree alternatively, the US might intensify its initial tough negotiating positions. Such modification would be a crucial break-point in the course of action. At this point, both the Communist side and such key nations as Thailand, as well as the GVN itself, would be tempted to conclude we were getting ready for a way out. Hence, the synchronizing of such modifying moves with our military actions would have to be extremely careful. In addition:

4. We should be conducting substantial actions to strengthen and reassure the nations of the area. Both for this purpose and to convey a continuing threat of further military action, we should probably [word illegible] consider major additional deployments to the area.

F. LIKELY DEVELOPMENTS AND PROBLEMS IF THE COMMU-NIST SIDE ENGAGED IN MAJOR MILITARY RETALIATIONS AT SOME POINT

1. Although we reckon this to be unlikely at the early stages, some sharp reprisal action, or Communist misreading of our intent, could change this calculation.

2. In the second phase of military actions, there would be a progressively increasing chance of some major Communist military response. This might take the form of:

a. Air attacks against the south. Effective air defense measures probably should be taken as part of the initial deployment, in any event prior to the second phase.

b. DRV ground action in South Vietnam or Laos. This would call for retaliatory air and ground action that underscores the need for ground deployments either early or in the second phase.

c. Chinese Communist ground action does not seem likely in Vietnam, but might conceivably take place into Laos or even elsewhere. While we believe this very unlikely, it cannot be excluded as a response to the hitting of major targets in the DRV. It would call for very substantial US deployments and a major scale of military action.

G. POSSIBLE OVER-ALL OUTCOMES

The variable factors are too great to permit a confident evaluation of how this course of action would come out.

1. At best, we might (judo) our way to a settlement that would involve some modification but that would give South Vietnam a fair chance to survive and get going.

2. At worst, South Vietnam might come apart while we were pursuing the course of action so that we had to fight a military action for a non-existent client or the conflict might escalate to war with China.

H. PROS AND CONS OF OPTION C

Pros

1. Option C is more hopeful than Option A, more controlable and less risky of major military action than Option B.

2. If the outcome were in the end the loss of South Vietnam to Communist control, our having taken stronger measures would still leave us a good deal better off than under Option A with respect to the confidence and willingness to stand firm of the nations in the next line of defense in Asia. This would apply particularly to Thailand, where much might depend on the course events had taken in Laos. Another factor would be the degree of military deployments we had taken to Thailand.

3. On a worldwide basis, we would be on the whole reasonably well off with our European allies for having made an effort but at the same time not having become inextricably involved in major action.

Cons

1. This course of action is inherently likely to stretch out and to be subject to major pressures both within the US and internationally. As we saw in Korea, an "in-between" course of action will always arouse a school of thought that believes things should be tackled quickly and conclusively. On the other side, the continuation of military action and a reasonably firm posture will arouse sharp criticism in other political quarters. Internationally, the latter line of criticism would be more prevalent, but the first would be the position of key Asian nations such as Thailand, the GRC, and the ROK.

2. The course of action probably cannot achieve our full objectives even in the best case.

3. The course of action has lesser risks of military actions than Option B, but such risks cannot by any means be eliminated.

IX. IMMEDIATE ACTIONS OVER THE NEXT FEW WEEKS

To meet the problem of sustaining South Vietnamese morale, and to convey a firm signal to Hanoi and Peiping as a prelude to the carrying out of Option C, the following program could be adopted during the coming weeks. Basic to this program would be an immediate decision that Option C was our preferred course of action, and that we would move into that course of action, probably early in the new year, unless Hanoi showed clear signs of yielding.

The basic ingredients of the program would be:

A. [words illegible] communications to Hanoi and Peiping in the same way.

B. Military build up and other measures clearly foreshadowing stronger action.

C. Vigorous actions within present policy, with reference to actions in South Viet-Nam, actions within Laos, and overt actions against North Viet-Nam.

D. Reprisals against any repetition here of the Gulf of Tonkin incident or any major VC "spectacular" such as the Bien Hoa attack, in South Viet-Nam.

Specific actions under the above headings would be as follows:

A. *Talking Tough.*

1. A continued picture of intense government activity and concern, leading up to the return of Ambassador Taylor for consultation about November 18.

2. Issuance of a public statement, following an NSC meeting at which Ambassador Taylor reported, that would convey the general flavor that North Viet-Nam had been continuing and increasing its activity in the South and that we were getting fed up with it. This statement would not commit us to a specific date for stronger action, but would carry the unmistakable threat of such action.

3. A generalized strong message to Hanoi through the existing channel, to be conveyed about November 15. This would definitely foreshadow the Washington statement expected about November 18, but would not wholly scoop it.

4. As a part of the above specific actions, we would in some way convey on a background basis that our objectives and our position on negotiation were unchanged, i.e., that we would accept a negotiated settlement if but only if Hanoi got out and the situation was restored.

B. *Miscellaneous Actions.*

1. Order a strengthening of our naval, air, and ground readiness posture in the area, not at a crash tempo but so as to be clearly spotted by the other side.

2. As to US dependents, an early order stopping the sending of additional dependents, followed by the orderly removal, probably at some time in December, first of families with children and finally of all dependents from South Viet-Nam.

3. Tough conversations with GVN civilian and military leaders indicating, on the one hand, that we were preparing to move to stronger action, but making it perfectly clear, on the other hand, that the GVN must set its house in order. This would include such specific GVN measures as intensifying the Hop Tac program, putting its military forces on a totally wartime operations basis, tightening security in Saigon and elsewhere, etc.

C. *Vigorous Actions within Current Policy.*

1. A strong 34A MAROPS schedule (already approved). Consider US air cover if required for specific operations. Surfacing of MAROPS probably not to be pressed, unless GVN itself indicates willingness.

2. Continued strong air activity in the Panhandle area of Laos, including at least a few US armed reconnaissance strikes.

3. Continued strong air activity in central Laos, both Lao T–28's and US reconnaissance, possibly including—if evidence of the Communist build-up continues—a major armed reconnaissance strike on Route 7.

4. A DESOTO patrol, probably in early December, dissociated from any specific MAROPS.

5. Consider explicit use of US air in South Viet-Nam if a lucrative target appears. (This could be part of the reprisals under D below or new.)

D. *Reprisals.*

1. In case of another Gulf of Tonkin incident, extend the reprisal to Haiphong facilities and other major naval-related targets.

2. In case of another Bien Hoa, attack infiltration-related targets in the southern part of South Viet-Nam, using GVN and FARMGATE aircraft.

In addition, this program must include the following *collateral actions:*

a. Early discussion with Congressional leaders.

b. Early discussion with major allies, probably through the immediate creation of a special consultative group to include the UK, Australia, New Zealand, Thailand, and possibly the Philippines.

c. Early surfacing in Saigon of the usable evidence of greatly-increased DRV infiltration into the south. Pending a decision to adopt this program, together with Option C at a later date, this material should not be surfaced in any formal fashion (even on a background basis), although of course we should not deny or contradict accurate indications in this direction that may be starting to come out of the GVN almost at once.

Among the *problems* that this program may raise, and with which we would have to deal, would be the following:

a. Possible Communist reaction to our stronger signal, including the possibility of additional military deployments. This needs an intelligence judgment.

b. Possible pressures for early negotiations before we start on Option C. Such pressures will come in any event from the French and perhaps others, and we should be prepared to fight them off.

X.   CONCLUSIONS AND RECOMMENDATIONS

We recommend that the President:

A. Approve the program for immediate actions within the next few weeks stated in Section IX;

B. Make the decision that, if the Communist side does not respond favorably to the Section IX program, the US will initiate early in the new year a course of action along the lines of Option C.

[Document 227]

ENCLOSURE (to Joint Staff memo, 10 Nov 64)
WORKING PAPER

NSC WORKING GROUP PROJECT—COURSES OF ACTION IN SOUTHEAST ASIA

Subject: Comments on CIA-DIA-INR Panel Draft Section I—The Situation

1. Introductory Note: The subject draft, dated 6 Nov. 1964, has been circulated as a proposed Section I of the NSC Working Group project, subject as above. In the following paragraphs are comments on the draft which have been developed as the result of Joint Staff judgments assisted by DIA advice in premises.

2. Para 3, last sentence: This sentence notes that "pressures and open criticism" of the new government have already appeared, stated in a context such that this seems intended as an additional sign of weakness in the situation. We suggest that the fact that these matters are open may instead be a favorable sign —the pressures and criticisms in our own country are certainly open.

3. Para 6, last sentence: This sentence takes note of the view that hopes for government stability now appear to have improved somewhat, though the chances for real stability are still less than even. This is one of the key factors behind the recommendations by the Joint Chiefs of Staff for early and positive actions in SVN. It would appear that the point should be made more prominent in this paper than it is in its present rather obscure position.

4. Para 7: This paragraph appears to address the wrong point. The new government may help improve GVN esprit and thus effectiveness, but its principal task is to afford the platform upon which the RVN armed forces, with US assistance, prosecute the war. Its capabilities in this area have not been tested, but appear reasonably favorable. The paragraph as written appears to pre-judge contrarily. We recognize there are substantial internal political interactions in the question of over-all counterinsurgency success; there seems to be a valid question about governmental capacities in that regard, which do not appear to be addressed by the paragraph.

5. Para 8: This paragraph appears to overstate the basic problem, in that it identifies the minimum essential US achievement as total destruction of both the

DRV will and capabilities to support the VC insurrection, and then proceeds to develop estimates of our capability to accomplish these ends. We believe that a better expression of the problem would result from an examination which included the following considerations:

a. The actual US requirement with respect to the DRV is reduction of the *rate of delivery* of support to the VC, to levels below their minimum necessary sustaining level. After that is accomplished, effective corollary actions in SVN can end the insurgency, which is the US objective.

b. In the present unstable situation something far less than total destruction may be all that is required to accomplish the above. A very modest change in the government's favor, accomplished through positive measures with US assistance, *may* be enough to turn the tide and lead to a successful solution. Of course it is not possible to predict in advance with complete assurance the precise level of measures which will be required to achieve the above. This is the reason for designing a program of progressively increasing squeeze.

c. Obviously that program may have to continue through substantial levels of military, industrial, and governmental destruction in the DRV.

d. It is informative to estimate the influence of progressive levels of the above destruction upon the will and capabilities of the DRV internally in their own country. It is more pertinent to our problem, however, to estimate the corresponding rates of delivery of support in South Vietnam, which remain attainable after US attacks, in relation to what the VC require. Even this cannot be estimated with high precision in advance, so that judgments would have to be applied progressively during the development of the squeeze program, a point which appears to merit recognition in this paragraph:

6. Para 8d, fourth sentence: Here is another example of what appears to be unwarranted emphasis on the negative side of the problem. DRV capability to continue to operate from the bush, as against the French, is not a valid basis for estimation. What is pertinent, instead, would be continued VC capability to operate against a national population (a different problem from operating against foreign colonialists).

7. Para 9b, last sentence: This notes that Hanoi and Peiping are probably anxious not to become involved in a war in which greatly superior US weaponry would be brought to bear against them; and that they almost certainly feel that they can win without having to undertake the risk of that occurring. The sentence includes two important thoughts bearing upon proposals for US action:

a. Its first thought forms the basis for the effectiveness of our deterrence to Communist adventures, through powerful visible deployments of the kind of weaponry they should indeed fear. We believe that this deterrent factor has a substantial probability of success. The draft, however, appears to include no reckonings with respect either to deterrence or the chances it will work.

b. The second thought is the Communist judgment that they can continue a winning program without much risk of having to feel the weight of US response. To revise their thinking in this respect is among the main reasons for the recommended program of military pressures. Hence it seems that the thought should be brought out more prominently amongst the pertinent basic considerations.

8. Para 10a, last sentence: It is unclear what is meant by expressing Hanoi's estimate that the election results give Washington greater policy "flexibility." If this means that Hanoi thinks we are now in position to accept world-wide

humiliation, with respect to our formerly stated objectives in Vietnam, this is another reason why it is desirable that we take early measures to disabuse their thinking.

9. Para 10c, last sentence: This expression of judgment, negative in implications, appears to be beyond the scope of the paper and an unwarranted inference with which we do not concur.

10. Para 11: This paragraph, on the subject of DRV ability and willingness to sustain damage, does not provide a valid measure of their capability to support the necessary level of VC action against the government and people of SVN. It should be substantially revised to refocus upon the problem at hand. In particular, its illusion to the results of aerial operations in the Korean and French-Viet Minh wars is invalid.

11. Para 13: (DRV judgment of the weight to attach to world pressures against the United States). It could be postulated that the DRV believe that pressures might be developed from quarters we would respect (as distinguished from the familiar communist-neutralist bray), and that the United States would back down and sacrifice its vital world issues in response to these pressures. Such an image of a United States which will back down from defense of its vital interests in response to mere words (the paper tiger) would be one of the strongest encouragements to further communist adventures, in Southeast Asia and everywhere else. If this estimate of Hanoi views is valid, it emphasizes the importance of our taking actions to insure against the spread of such a notion.

12. Para 15: This paragraph appears to overstate the implications of Chicom capabilities to support NVN in respects which concern the United States. Chicom air defense and naval capabilities are inadequate in their entirety against existing PACOM resources (a circumstance which we believe is understood in Peiping). Foreseeable diversions of these inadequate resources to the assistance of North Vietnam should have little significant bearing upon the situation. Thus we believe there should be added to this paragraph a sentence to the effect "These changes will not alter significantly the communist defensive posture against potential US actions."

[Document 228]

10 November 1964

MEMORANDUM FOR THE CHAIRMAN, NSC WOKING GROUP ON SOUTHEAST ASIA (Mr. William P. Bundy, Department of State)

Subject: Comment on Draft for Part II of Project Outline on Courses of Action in Southeast Asia—"US Objectives and Stakes in SVN and SEA"

1. Furnished herewith are comments on the subject draft, which earlier you requested.

2. The draft, which provides a well-written examination of a broad range of considerations, has been studied carefully within the Joint Staff. Principal conclusions are:

   a. It appears to understate rather substantially the gravity to the United States of the possible loss of SVN to the communists, under whatever circumstances, and

b. It appears to overstate rather markedly the magnitude, difficulty, and potential risks in measures by the United States to prevent that loss.

3. The attached copy of the draft, with line-by-line insertion of comments, will indicate wherein the above impressions tend to be formed.

L. M. MUSTIN
Vice Admiral, USN
Working Group Member

Enclosure
  As Stated

ENCLOSURE

WORKING PAPER

NSC WORKING GROUP PROJECT—
COURSES OF ACTION, SOUTHEAST ASIA

Subject: Comments on Draft Section II—US Objectives and Stakes in South Vietnam and Southeast Asia

INTRODUCTORY NOTE: In an early working-group meeting Mr. Bundy provided drafts of material intended for Section II of the NSC working group project, subject as above, and asked for comments. Below is reproduced, in quotes, the current version of Section II, with interspersed comments developed from a search of related JCS expressions of views in the premises.

II. *US Objectives and Stakes in South Viet-Nam and Southeast Asia*

A. *US Objectives and the Present Basis of US Action*

In South Viet-Nam we are helping a government defend its independence. In Laos, we are working to preserve, in its essence, an international neutralized settlement willfully flouted by the communist side. Paradoxically, while American opinion weights the former well ahead of the latter, there are some quarters—such as Britain and India—where the latter is a more appealing cause both legally and practically. But our basic rationale is defensible in both cases.

> *Comment:* I believe the United States is committed in the eyes of the world to both of these tasks as matters of national prestige, credibility, and honor with respect to world-wide pledges. Later material in the paper seems to agree. This then would not appear to be a subject on which we should permit ourselves to be swayed unduly by other nations' views, paradoxical or other, and possibly more useful than noting that our rationale "is defensible" would be to affirm that it needs no defense.

Behind our policy have been three factors:
  a. The general principle of helping countries that try to defend their own freedom against communist subversion and attack.
  b. The specific consequences of communist control of South Viet-Nam and Laos for the security of, successively, Cambodia, Thailand (most seriously), Malaysia, and the Philippines—and resulting increases in the threat

to India and—more in the realm of morale effects in the short term—the threat to South Korea and perhaps the GRC, and the effect on Japanese attitudes through any development that appears to make Communist China and its allies a dominant force in Asia that must be lived with.

c. South Viet-Nam, and to a lesser extent, Laos, as test cases of communist "wars of national liberation" world-wide.

> *Comment:* The third factor above, which is broadly stated, is related to but appears distinguishable from what may be considered a fourth, more specific issue: Now that we are publicly, officially, and heavily committed in SVN, US prestige has been rather specifically put at issue, and requires successful defense if we are to retain a measure of free-world leadership. This thought is brought out later in the paper; it could well be listed here as part of the subject introduction.

In other words, our policy toward South Viet-Nam and Laos is an integral part of our over-all policy of resisting Communist expansion world-wide, and a particularly close part of our policy of resisting the expansion of Communist China and its allies, North Viet-Nam and North Korea.

Thus, the loss of South Viet-Nam to Communist control, in any form, would be a major blow to our basic policies. US prestige is heavily committed to the maintenance of a non-Communist South Viet-Nam, and only less heavily so to a neutralized Laos.

Yet we must face the fact that, on any analysis we can now make, we cannot guarantee to maintain a non-Communist South Viet-Nam short of committing ourselves to whatever degree of military action would be required to defeat North Viet-Nam and probably Communist China militarily. Such a commitment would involve high risks of a major conflict in Asia, which could not be confined to air and naval action but would almost inevitably involve a Korean-scale ground action and possibly even the use of nuclear weapons at some point. Even if all these things were done, South Vietnam might still come apart under us.

> *Comment:* The above paragraph appears to overstate rather markedly the degree of difficulty associated with success for our objectives in SVN. Our first objective is to cause the DRV to terminate support of the SEA insurgencies. Once this is done, then we have a period of stabilization and maturing in SVN, during which we can consider what next we need do. To achieve this objective does not necessarily require that we "defeat North Viet-Nam," and it almost certainly does not require that we defeat Communist China. Hence our commitment to SVN does not involve a high probability let alone "high risks," of a major conflict in Southeast Asia. One reason it does not is our capability to show the CHICOMs that if there's a "risk" of such a war, the main "risk" is theirs. Certainly no responsible person proposes to go about such a war, if it should occur, on a basis remotely resembling Korea. "Possibly even the use of nuclear weapons at some point" is of course why we spend billions to have them. If China chooses to go to war against us she has to contemplate their possible use, just as does anyone else—this is more of the "risk" to *them*. And of course SVN *might* nevertheless come apart under us, but an alert initiative commensurate with the stakes should make the likelihood of this quite remote.

Hence, we must consider realistically what our over-all objectives and stakes are, and just what degree of risk and loss we should be prepared to make to hold South Vietnam, or alternatively to gain time and secure our further lines of defense in the world and specifically in Asia.

> *Comment:* Here again is emphasis on "risk" and "loss" to us, as though the harder we try the more we stand to risk and to lose. On the contrary, a resolute course of action in lieu of half measures, resolutely carried out instead of dallying and delaying, offers the best hope for minimizing *risks, costs,* and *losses* in achieving our objectives. The paragraph also implies there is some alternative to our holding South Viet-Nam. There is none.

B. *Possible Alternate US Objectives*

Bluntly stated, our fall-back objectives in South Viet-Nam would be:
1. To hold the situation together as long as possible, so that we have time to strengthen other areas of Asia.
2. To take forceful enough measures in the siutation so that we emerge from it, even in the worst case, with our standing as the principal helper against Communist expansion as little impaired as possible.
3. To make clear to the world, and to nations in Asia particularly, that failure in South Viet-Nam, if it comes, was due to special local factors that do not apply to other nations we are committed to defend—that, in short, our will and ability to help those nations defend themselves is not impaired.

> *Comment:* We have no further fall-back position in Southeast Asia in the stated view of the Joint Chiefs of Staff. The three courses outlined above add emphasis to that reality:
>
> (1) Strengthening other areas of Asia, in the context of our having been pushed out of SVN, would be a thoroughly non-productive effort militarily, and politically it seems dubious we'd even be offered the opportunity to attempt it.
>
> (2) It is difficult to conceive of how our "standing as the principal helper against communist expansion" could suffer a more abject humiliation, trumpeted more widely to the world, than for us now to lose SVN.
>
> (3) Course number three is a slight paraphrase of Aesop's fox and grapes story. No matter how we talk it up amongst ourselves it could only be completely transparent to intelligent outside observers.

The first two of these speak for themselves. The third calls for a review of the elements in the South Vietnamese situation that do truthfully lend themselves to this thesis.

The honest fact is that South Viet-Nam and Laos have not really been typical cases from the beginning, which accounts in part for our inability to enlist the kind of international support we had in Korea and for our having to carry the load so largely alone. Most of the world had written off both countries in 1954, and our ability to keep them going—while an extraordinary and praiseworthy effort—has never given them quite the standing of such long-established national entities as Greece, Turkey, and Iran, or the special ward-of-the-UN status that South Korea had in 1950.

Comment: This is illusory. First, we had no significant support in Korea, other than verbal. Except for the South Koreans themselves, the US did essentially all the fighting, took all the casualties, and paid all the bills. Second, regardless of how many or what kinds of countries had written off Laos and SVN in 1954, *we* did not—and we've committed ourselves accordingly. It is *our* judgment, skill, capability, prestige, and national honor which are at stake, and we put them there. And it doesn't seem particularly pertinent, in that context, how these countries may compare with Greece, etc.

Moreover, the recent courses of events has already highlighted—and could be brought even more to highlight—the atypical features that in sum have made South Viet-Nam and Laos so difficult. A bad colonial heritage of long standing, totally inadequate preparation for self-government by the colonial power, a colonialist war fought in half-baked fashion and lost, a nationalist movement taken over by Communist ruling in the other half of an ethnically and historically united country, the Communist side inheriting much the better military force and far more than its share of the talent—these are the facts that dog us to this day.

Comment: This seems mainly to be more in the sour grapes vein. Because things may be atypical or difficult doesn't afford a very persuasive basis for giving up on them with standards unblemished.

The basic point, of course, is that we have never thought we could defend a government or a people that had ceased to care strongly about defending themselves, or that were unable to maintain the fundamentals of government. And the overwhelming world impression is that these are lacking elements in South Viet-Nam, and that its loss will be due, if it comes, to their lack.

Comment: A resolute United States would ensure, amongst other things, that this lack were cured, as the alternative to accepting the loss.

To get across these points, there would be much merit to non-government information activity getting across this picture, primarily of past French errors.

Comment: French errors also included major political delays and indecisions, which amongst other things tolerated if not enforced a military fiasco. Rather than now lamely resurrecting the story of how the French couldn't do the job, it seems to me we should instead make sure we don't repeat their mistakes. (The French also tried to build the Panama Canal).

C. *Consequences of Communist Control of South Viet-Nam in a Worldwide Sense.*

How badly would the loss of South Viet-Nam shake the faith and resolve of other non-Communist nations that face the threat of Communist aggression or subversion and rely on us for major help?

Comment: In JCS view, near-disastrously, or worse.

Within NATO, probably not at all, provided we had carried out any military actions in Southeast Asia without taking forces from NATO for this purpose, and provided further that adverse developments in Southeast Asia had not produced a wave of revulsion in American public opinion against [words illegible] commitments overseas. The latter possibility raises a [words illegible] question, that probably cannot now be estimated with any precision; too much would depend on the US casualties and the total circumstances of the loss.

> *Comment:* This paragraph appears to be predicated on an assumed campaign of such magnitude we have to draw on CINCLANT/ CINCEUR resources for it (which is in excess of anything on the books), heavy casualties in that campaign, but nevertheless, its loss. This seems so remote a postulate that it only confuses the basic question as to the NATO evaluation, with which we do not agree.

Greece and Turkey might be affected to some degree, and this would call our taking reassuring action there.

Iran and India appear to be the next problem cases outside the Far East. Iran has not concerned itself at all with Southeast Asia, and India has been from time to time deeply concerned, but has done little about it. Yet we must face the chance that, as a US defeat sank in, there could be serious adverse repercussions in these countries. We do not have alliance commitments to either; yet in fact both rely on us in the background of all their calculations. Again, we would have to consider reassuring action, but the effects do not appear beyond reach.

> *Comment:* In the context here concerned, actions that would be truly "reassuring" seem beyond our physical and fiscal capabilities. As to words, they could only be regarded by others as starkly empty, and much propaganda would be devoted to pointing that out.

In other areas of the world, notably the Middle East, Africa, and Latin America, either the nature of the Communist threat, or the degree of US commitment, or both, are so radically different than in Southeast Asia that it is difficult to assess the impact. Almost everything would depend on whether the US was in fact able to go on with its present policies. If it did so, the results would probably not be too serious.

> *Comment:* We do not share the feeling of reassurance implied by the last sentence.

D. *Consequences in Southeast Asia and in Asia Generally of Communist Control in South Vietnam.*

1. In Southeast Asia.

The so-called domino theory implies that Cambodia, Thailand, possibly Burma, and Malaysia, would fall almost automatically to Communist domination if South Vietnam does.

> *Comment:* We hold this to be the most realistic estimate for Cambodia and Thailand, probably Burma, possibly Malaysia.

> *Comment:* Perhaps the British could save Malaysia if they undertook resolutely to do so, but we estimate that Thailand goes if SVN is lost.

These are the key pressure points that would immediately become crucial. If either Thailand or Malaysia were lost, or went badly sour in any way, then the rot would be in real danger of spreading all over mainland Southeast Asia.

> *Comment:* Since we are convinced Thailand would indeed go, this underscores the especially grave concern relative to SVN on the part of the Joint Chiefs of Staff.

2. *In Asia generally:*

Both the initial and ultimate effects would depend heavily on the circumstances in which South Vietnam was lost, and on whether the loss did in fact greatly weaken or lead to the early loss of other areas in Southeast Asia.

> *Comment:* We do not agree with the reasoning leading to this reasoning relative to SVN, and estimate the results would be most grave almost regardless of foreseeable variants as to circumstance.

Yet the initial effects would be substantial in any event. There is already something of a crisis of confidence in the GRC, arising from the Chinese Communist nuclear explosion and possibly to be accentuated by developments in the ChiRep situation in the UN. In South Korea, there is a tremendous sense of dependence on the US, and some discouragement at the failure to make as much progress politically and economically as North Korea (from a much more favorable initial position) has made. And in the Philippines, there is also a strong sense of dependence on the US.

All three of these would need maximum reassurance in any case.

We must also weigh the effects on Japan, where the set is already in the direction of closer ties with Communist China, with a clear threat of early recognition. While Japan's faith in our military posture and determination might not be shaken, the growing feeling that Communist China must somehow be lived with might well be accentuated.

Beyond this point—if the rest of Southeast Asia did in fact succumb over time—these effects would be multiplied many times over. This is not to say that there would not be a great deal we could still do to reassure these countries. But the picture of a defense line clearly breached could have serious effects, and could easily, over time, tend to unravel the whole Pacific defense structure.

> *Comment:* We do not share the views indicated above as to the potential value of "reassurance" to others if we lose SVN. There would be no words left that won't have been shown to be hollow, and there would be few deeds left, short of general war, that will be within our capabilities. We agree with the last sentence, and estimate the time concerned to be short.

3. *Summary*

In sum, there are enough "ifs" and enough possibilities of offsetting action in the above analysis so that it cannot be concluded that the loss of South Vietnam would soon have the totally crippling effect in Southeast Asia and Asia generally that the loss of Berlin would have in Europe. Nonetheless, the loss would be extremely serious, and it *could* be as bad as Berlin, driving us to the progressive loss of other areas or to taking a stand at some point where there would almost certainly be major conflict and perhaps the great risk of nuclear war.

> *Comment:* We do not agree. Berlin *per se* means much symbolically, but little militarily. SVN means just as much symbolically, and is a military keystone.

[Document 229]

Nov 14, 1964

EXDIS

EMBTEL 1438

In reply to his query Johnson told Seaborn today that we had not yet received any indication as to whether dept would have message for him on his next trip but that if convenient thought it would be preferable for Seaborn to postpone trip until Nov 30 as if there was to be message it would be more likely at that time than on Nov 23. Seaborn said postponement to Nov 30 presented no problem if he did it now and that he would.

Do so. He expressed hope that if we had message he could receive it as long before Nov 30 as possible in order that he could absorb it and have opportunity discuss any obscure points.

He said Ottawa had strongly endorsed point he had made to Johnson previously, that is, that general theme of last two messages had been played as far as they could go and if we had anything to deliver on next trip it was hoped that it would be something specific. He also said Ottawa does not plan to approach dept but will await dept initiative.

TAYLOR

[Document 230]

14 November 1964

JCSM 955-64

[first section missing]

4. The Joint Chiefs of Staff do not concur with a concept of "tit-for-tat" reprisals nor with Ambassador Taylor's recommendation that the United States and the Government of Vietnam (GVN) jointly announce such a policy which ties our action to equivalency. "Tit for tat" is considered unduly restrictive, inhibits US initiative, and implies an undesirable lack of flexibility both as to the nature and level of response. Adoption and announcement of a policy of a "tit-for-tat" basis only would serve to pass to the DRV substantial initiatives with respect to the nature and timing of further US actions.

5. On 1 November, the Joint Chiefs of Staff recommended and hereby confirm that the following specific actions be taken:

a. Within 24–36 hours, Pacific Command (PACOM) forces take initial US military actions as follows:

(1) Conduct air strikes in Laos against targets #3 (Tchepone barracks, northwest), #4 (Tchepone military area), #19 (Ban Thay military area), #8 (Nape highway bridge), and the Ban Ken bridge on Route 7.

(2) Conduct low-level air reconnaissance of infiltration routes and of targets in North Vietnam south of Latitude 19 degrees.

b. Prior to air attacks on the DRV, land the Marine special landing force at Da Nang and airlift Army or Marine units from Okinawa to the Saigon/Tan Son Nhut/Bien Hoa area, to provide increased security for US personnel and installations.

c. Use aircraft engaged in airlift (subparagraph b, above) to assist in evacuation of US dependents from Saigon, to commence concurrently with the daylight air strikes against the DRV (subparagraph d, below).

d. Assemble and prepare necessary forces so that:

(1) Within 60 to 72 hours, 30 B-52s from Guam conduct a night strike on DRV target #6 (Phuc Yen airfield).

(2) Commencing at first light on the day following subparagraph (1), above, PACOM air and naval forces conduct air strikes against DRV targets #6 (Phuc Yen airfield) (daylight follow-up on the above night strike), #3 (Hanoi Gia Lam airfield), #8 (Haiphong Cat Bi airfield), #48 (Haiphong POL), and #49 (Hanoi POL).

(3) Concurrently with subparagraph (2), above, the Vietnamese Air Force (VNAF) will strike DRV target #36 (Vit Thu Lu barracks).

(4) Combat air patrols (CAP), flak suppressive fire, strike photographic reconnaissance, and search and rescue operations (SAR) are conducted as appropriate.

(5) The above actions are followed by:

(a) Armed reconnaissance on infiltration routes in Laos.

(b) Air strikes against infiltration routes and targets in the DRV.

(c) Progressive PACOM and SAC strikes against the targets listed in the 94 Target Study.

e. Thai bases be used as necessary in connection with the foregoing, with authority to be obtained through appropriate channels.

6. As to the specific actions recommended above, the Joint Chiefs of Staff consider that initiation of our response by attacking targets in Laos and conducting low-level reconnaissance in the southern DRV will provide militarily useful operations within the immediate capabilities of forces in place and, at the same time, will serve to divert notice from the preparations and force deployments necessary for the ensuing stronger actions. Recognizing that security of this plan is of critical importance, they consider that external agencies, such as the VNAF, should be apprised only of those parts of the plan necessary to insure proper and effective coordination. The same limited revelation of plans should govern discussions with the Thais in securing authority for unlimited use of Thai bases.

7. The night B-52 strike on Phuc Yen airfield as the first major military response is designed to destroy a major component of present and potential DRV air capability, by use of an all-weather weapon system. The specific strikes recom-

mended for PACOM forces during the next daylight will destroy additional DRV capabilities, including facilities otherwise available for CHICOM reinforcing actions, and set the stage for the follow-on US and VNAF operations. The recommended VNAF strike provides GVN participation and is within VNAF capability.

8. The Joint Chiefs of Staff consider that the approximately 1600 US Government dependents should be evacuated from SVN in connection with the foregoing, to commence concurrently with the first daylight US strike against the DRV. In this regard, they note that there are an additional 3100 nonmilitary US nationals and US-sponsored personnel in country. Objections to their evacuation have been made primarily because of the adverse psychological impact upon the Government and people of SVN. It is considered that these impacts will be more than offset by the results of military actions now proposed. The demonstrated vulnerability to VC actions of carefully-secured areas makes retention of US dependents after the start of overt US military operations no longer prudent. Their withdrawal is appropriate in light of the proposed increased tempo and scale of activity.

9. The Joint Chiefs of Staff have requested and will consider CINCPAC's recommendations for any augmentation forces required, to include increased air defense, a Marine light antiair missile battalion from CONUS to Da Nang, and any tactical air or CVA augmentation. A follow-on memorandum on this will be forwarded to you.

10. In summary, the Joint Chiefs of Staff believe that:

a. We have reached a major decision point in Southeast Asia;

b. The United States should continue to pursue its stated objective of keeping Laos, Thailand, and SVN free from communist domination. Military actions such as recommended herein are necessary contributions to this objective; and

c. Early US military action against the DRV would lessen the possibility of misinterpretation by the DRV and Communist China of US determination and intent and thus serve to deter further VC attacks such as that at Bien Hoa.

> For the Joint Chiefs of Staff:
>
> *Earle G. Wheeler*
> Chairman
> Joint Chiefs of Staff

[Document 231]

14 November 1964

MEMORANDUM FOR THE CHAIRMAN, NSC WORKING GROUP ON SOUTHEAST ASIA (Mr. William P. Bundy, Department of State)

Subject: Additional Material for Project on Courses of Action in Southeast Asia

References: a. Your Memorandum of 13 November 1964
to the NSC Working Group
b. JCSM 932-64, dated 27 October 1964
c. JCSM 933-64, dated 4 November 1964
d. JCSM 955-64, dated 14 November 1964

1. Reference a requests JCS views spelling out Option "B" as a preferred alternative, with something like Option "C" as a fall-back alternative. Because of the

way in which formal JCS views in the premises have been developed and expressed, this requires some degree of interpretation.

2. Reference b is the most recent recommendation by the Joint Chiefs of Staff for courses of action with respect to South Vietnam, framed in the context of initiation "in cold blood." Various JCS papers, the most recent dated 22 October 1964, identify the corresponding recommendations with respect to Laos. Reference b specifically identifies certain of its listed actions to begin now, with the balance of them "implemented as required to achieve US objectives in Southeast Asia."

3. Reference c formalized the most recent JCS recommendation for reprisal (hot blood) actions and reference d provided an analysis of DRV/CHICOM reactions to these strikes, and the probable results thereof. The proposed actions are essentially the same as in reference c except for the principal difference that the "hot blood" actions are initiated at a substantial higher level of military activity.

4. Only in that the courses of action in either of these sets of documents can be completed in minimum time consistent with proper conduct of military operations do they match Option "B" as defined for purposes of the NSC Working Group study. The distinction is that while the Joint Chiefs of Staff offer the capability for pursuing Option "B" as defined, they have not explicitly recommended that the operations be conducted on a basis necessarily that inflexible. All implementing plans do in fact explicitly recognize a controlled phase which would permit suspension whenever desired by national authority.

5. I believe my draft contribution to PART VI provides a reasonable application of the JCS recommendations to Option "B" as defined for the study, but this does not mean that the Joint Chiefs of Staff have recommended Option "B" as defined in the study.

6. There is in an advanced state of completion a JCS fall-back recommendation for a course of action which, subject to possible further modifications by the Joint Chiefs of Staff, will provide essentially the same military actions listed in my draft input to PART VII. These include the same military actions listed in the above, but without the stress upon starting forthwith, and with more specific emphasis on some extension of the over-all time for execution of the complete list. Thus it imposes what amount to some arbitrary delays, which would provide additional intervals for diplomatic exchanges.

7. Because of the time delays which it reflects, it is specifically the JCS fall-back position.

8. For information, the analysis in reference d develops and supports the conclusion that the United States and its Allies can deal adequately with any course of action the DRV and/or CHICOMs decide to pursue. You may note that this conclusion is developed in the context of the most intense of all courses of action proposed by the Joint Chiefs of Staff. This reflects a position less pessimistic than some which have appeared in project drafts.

9. A final over-all comment by the Joint Staff member of the Working Group:

We recognize quite clearly that any effective military action taken by the United States will generate a hue and cry in various quarters. The influence that this kind of "pressure" may have upon the United States acting in support of its national interests will be no more than what we choose to permit it to be. There are repeated expressions in various project draft materials indicating that this influence will necessarily be great. We do not agree. There are too many current examples of countries acting in what they presumably believe to be their own enlightened self-interest, in utter disregard for "world opinion," for us to accept the position that the United States must at all times conduct all its affairs on the basis of a world popularity contest. In short, we believe that certain strong US actions are required in Southeast Asia, that we must take them regardless of opinion in various other quarters, and that results of our failing to take them would be substantially more serious to the United States than would be any results of world opinions if we did take them. And as far as that goes, we do not believe that if we took the necessary actions the adverse pressures from other countries would prove to be very serious after all—at least from countries that matter to us.

L. M. Mustin
Vice Admiral, USN
Working Group Member

[Document 232]

November 16, 1964

PERSONAL

TO: Secretary McNamara

FROM: W. W. Rostow

SUBJECT: *Military Dispositions and Political Signals*

Following on our conversation of last night I am concerned that too much thought is being given to the actual damage we do in the North, not enough thought to the signal we wish to send.

The signal consists of three parts:
a) damage to the North is now to be inflicted because they are violating the 1954 and 1962 Accords;
b) we are ready and able to go much further than our initial act of damage;
c) We are ready and able to meet any level of escalation they might mount in response; if they are so minded.

Four points follow.
1. I am convinced that we should not go forward into the next stage without a US ground force commitment of some kind:

a. The withdrawal of those ground forces could be a critically important part of our diplomatic bargaining position. Ground forces can sit during a conference more easily than we can maintain a series of mounting air and naval pressures.
b. We must make clear that counter escalation by the Communists will run directly into US strength on the ground; and, therefore, the possibility of radically extending their position on the ground at the cost of air and naval damage alone, is ruled out.
c. There is a marginal possibility that in attacking the airfield they were thinking two moves ahead; namely, they may be planning a pre-emptive ground force response to an expected US retaliation for the Bien Hoa attack.

2. The first critical military action against North Vietnam should be designed merely to install the principle that they will, from the present forward, be vul-

nerable to retaliatory attack in the north for continued violations for the 1954 and 1962 Accords. In other words, we would signal a shift from the principle involved in the Tonkin Gulf response. This means that the initial use of force in the north should be as limited and as unsanguinary as possible. It is the installation of the principle that we are initially interested in, not tit for tat.

3. But our force dispositions to accompany an initial retaliatory move against the north should send three further signals lucidly:

a. that we are putting in place a capacity subsequently to step up direct and naval pressure on the north, if that should be required;

b. that we are prepared to face down any form of escalation North Vietnam might mount on the ground; and

c. that we are putting forces into place to exact retaliation directly against Communist China, if Peiping should join in an escalatory response from Hanoi. The latter could take the form of increased aircraft on Formosa plus, perhaps, a carrier force sitting off China as distinguished from the force in the South China Sea.

4. The launching of this track, almost certainly, will require the President to explain to our own people and to the world our intentions and objectives. This will also be perhaps the most persuasive form of communication with Ho and Mao. In addition, I am inclined to think the most direct communication we can mount (perhaps via Vientiane and Warsaw) is desirable, as opposed to the use of cut-outs. They should feel they now confront an LBJ who has made up his mind. Contrary to an anxiety expressed at an earlier stage, I believe it quite possible to communicate the limits as well as the seriousness of our intentions without raising seriously the fear in Hanoi that we intend at our initiative to land immediately in the Red River Delta, in China, or seek any other objective than the re-installation of the 1954 and 1962 Accords.

[Document 233]

Part VI (Analysis of Option B), Section F. *Likely Developments and Problems if the Communist Side Engaged in Major Retaliation at Some Point.*

Right from the outset, this course of action would entail some chance of a Communist military response against the south. Furthermore, as we move to the stage of "further increases of military pressure," the chance of the more severe types of response would increase. We need a more precise judgment of just how likely various contingencies discussed below are, but each must be considered from the standpoint of what it would require on our side to deal with it.

Four classes of serious Communist responses to increased military pressures will be discussed here: a VC offensive in South Vietnam; DRV or Chicom air attacks in South Vietnam; DRV ground offensives into South Vietnam; and Chicom/DRV offensives into South Vietnam or Laos. These could occur in combinations. Extensive planning is applicable to the latter two cases and we shall summarize the force requirements implied by current plans. We shall not discuss here the circumstances—considered in SNIE 10-3-64 and in other sections of this paper—that would make these various Communist actions more or less probable; it is enough to assume that pressures upon the North have progressed to a point that makes the respective Communist military reactions significantly likely.

1. *VC Offensive in South Vietnam.* Under a wide range of US/RVN pressures, Hanoi might direct greatly intensified VC operations in South Vietnam. These could take various forms:

a. Increased sabotage and terrorism countrywide;
b. Assaults upon US personnel, including high diplomatic figures, or their dependents;
c. Terrorism and attacks in and around Saigon, or in provincial capitols;
d. Attacks up to regimental strength, on airfields, particularly Danang, Bien Hoa and Tan Son Nhut;
e. Facilities such as communications, POL or transportation facilities (including roads, bridges, railroad lines and inland waterways).

US ground forces—such as the Marine SLF afloat and Army or Marine units from Okinawa—will have been deployed to defend bases in the Da Nang and Saigon areas prior to undertaking air operations against the DRV. The positioning of US forces at these major bases and population centers releases ARVN forces for security duty at other locations and for combat in the field against the VC, which are primary responsibilities of the RVNAF.

Prior to or concurrently with the introduction of US ground forces, US dependents will be evacuated.

Depending on developments, further security measures and US forces may be required. US fixed-wing aircraft could be committed to direct support within South Vietnam.

For purposes of such a burst of operations, the VC is believed to have military capabilities it has not yet committed and may, to a lesser extent, have unused capabilities for terrorism and subversion. As in the mortar attack on Bien Hoa, the VC could inflict serious damage on US materiel and personnel based within South Vietnam, though this would not affect the major US resources in the area on carriers or based outside South Vietnam. Large-scale, protracted combat operations by the VC would expose them to heavy and possibly disastrous counterattack by RVN regular forces, perhaps directly supported by US air. But against this risk would be the hope that intense VC operations could produce mass defections, government shifts toward "neutralism," or an atmosphere of public demoralization and war-weariness such that US advisors and support could remain in South Vietnam only against strong popular wish.

2. *Chicom or DRV Air Attacks.* North Vietnam would be limited to fighter strikes against the south. Of their 117 military aircraft, 36 are MIG 15-17 jet fighters, all now located at Phuc Yen Airfield northwest of Hanoi, out of range of targets in South Vietnam. If relocated to Dong Hoi airfield, these fights could reach targets in northern South Vietnam, such as Danang and Hue.

Significant air actions would have to originate with Communist China, which has in addition to jet fighters (including 80 MIG-19s and about 15 MIG-21s, which can reach the 17th parallel from Hanoi or Hainan Island) 290 11-28s, 2 TU-16s and 13 TU-4s. The 11-28 light jet bomber can reach Danang from Phuc Yen on a two-way mission. With a normal bomb load, it could reach Saigon only on a one-way sortie—unless Dong Hoi airfield is improved, or Hainan's Lingshui used. From Hainan, the 11-28 can cover Laos, Cambodia, South Vietnam and western Thailand.

DRV attacks would be essentially nuisance raids, and even the Chicom attacks would have primarily psychological rather than military effort.

The US response to DRV air action in SVN would be to initiate or to continue in coordination with the RVN forces an air strike campaign against DRV air bases and associated targets. In case of Chicom air attacks, including attacks on a US aircraft carrier US forces would attack air bases, nuclear production facilities and other selected military targets in Communist China.

DRV OFFENSIVE IN SOUTH VIETNAM: LAOS

1. *DRV capabilities:*

   a. Attack across the Demarcation Zone (DMZ) with two infantry divisions (20,000 troops) within 48 hours after initiation of strikes on DRV.

   b. In conjunction with the attack into SVN, move into southern Laos with two infantry divisions and two infantry brigades, supported by one tank regiment and eight artillery regiments (total 45,000 troops).

2. CHICOMs could provide support to the DRV offensive with increased shipments of military weapons and equipment, food and medical supplies and provide the DRV with covert or "volunteer" air defense, engineer, ordnance and medical personnel.

3. US response to defend the area under attacks and to push back the communist offensive would require implementation of CINCPAC OPLAN 32-64, Phase III. US force deployments into mainland Southeast Asia, totaling nearly five divisions with supporting air and naval units, are summarized as follows:

   a. *Into South Vietnam—*
   D + 1   III Marine Expeditionary Force Hq. (Da Dang)
   D + 2   One Marine Division (Da Dang)
   to   One Marine Air Wing (Da Dang)
   D + 35 One Army Airborne Brigade
   D + 15 Hq. COMUSSFASIA (augmented)
           One Army Corps Hq.
   D + 60 One Army Infantry Division
           Army Combat and Combat Support Units

   b. *Into Thailand—*
   D + 15 One Army Corps Hq.
   to   One Army Infantry Division
   D + 35 One Army Airborne Brigade
   One Army Logistic Command Hq.
   D + 40 One Army Mechanized Infantry Brigade (Reinforced)
   D + 60 Army Combat and Combat Support Units

   c. Air and air support units as required in addition to forces presently in place.

   d. Naval forces available for direct support or to reinforce COMUSSEASIA—
      1–2 Attack Carrier Groups
      1 ASW Carrier Group
      2 Patrol Squadrons
      2 Submarines
      3 Minesweep Divisions
      3–4 Amphibious Squadrons
      2–3 Landing Ship Squadrons
      2–3 LCU Divisions
      1 Marine Expeditionary Force

4. The mission of CINCPAC OPLAN 32-64 Phase III is to bring about an early cessation of hostilities under conditions representing a net advantage to the Free World. In conjunction with the campaign of the above deployed forces in the areas under invasion, air and naval strikes against the DRV and a naval blockade will contribute toward bringing the superior allied military power into play against the enemy. The plan envisages further an early ground attack northward to seize, liberate and occupy North Vietnam.

CHICOM OFFENSIVE IN SOUTHEAST ASIA

1. *CHICOM capabilities*

a. Reinforce a DRV attack into southern Laos with six infantry divisions. These divisions could close the Vinh area in about seven days.

b. Attack against indigenous forces in South Vietnam, Laos and Thailand with a combined CHICOM/DRV force equivalent to up to 31 divisions, supported by one tank regiment, 13 artillery regiments and combat support and service support troops of five Army headquarters. Against US/Allied opposition an attack could be launched with the equivalent of 22 infantry divisions supported by five artillery regiments.

c. The above estimates are for dry season operations. During the wet season, the increased problems of movement through a difficult terrain and of maintaining logistic support could reduce effective combat forces up to fifty per cent.

d. In conjunction with the above ground attacks the CHICOM/DRV could support the employment of 540 jet fighters and 120 jet light bombers and attack US/RVN forces with a sustained sortie rate of 650 air defense/combat patrol and 85 bomber sorties per day. It is most likely that over 50 per cent of the 540 jet fighters would be used to control air space and to perform air defense missions over south/southwest China and North Vietnam. From south/southwest China bases jet light bombers could deliver 4,400 pound bomb loads to targets northward of Saigon and Bangkok. FAGOT/FRESCO jet fighters, with external fuel and guns only, would have the same combat radii as the jet light bombers. In a ground support role FAGOT/FRESCOs, with guns only, operating from southern Hainan Island could cover little more than the northern part of South Vietnam and northeastern Thailand. If jet fighters were operated from Dong Hoi airfield, they could penetrate farther into South Vietnam.

e. At sea the CHICOMs could attack US/RVN naval forces in the Tonkin Gulf and South China Sea with 45 motor torpedo boats and 20 motor gunboats. Transfer of submarines from the North and East Sea Fleets could be accomplished, with an estimated limit of six submarines on station in the South China Sea area.

2. US response to meet a CHICOM drive into Southeast Asia would require implementation of CINCPAC OPLAN 39-65 and/or OPLAN 32-64 Phase IV.

a. CINCPAC OPLAN 39-65 is designed to employ massive US naval and air power against Communist China and her satellites at times and places of our choice to force termination of the aggression. It visualizes minimum use of US ground forces and maximum use of indigenous forces. The plan can, however, be implemented in conjunction with, or preliminary to, other contingency plans for the area concerned; such as, for Southeast Asia, OPLAN 32-64, Phase IV (see below). Deployments under OPLAN 39-65 provide for a significant increase in US strength in the Western Pacific, mostly naval and air, by movements from the Continental US and the Eastern Pacific. Forces will be positioned initially throughout WestPac, from Japan and Korea to the Philippines and Thailand, with adjustments to be made within the area for best effective employment. The following summarizes the major force increases visualized to meet the Southeast Asia situation:

	NORMAL WEST-PAC STRENGTH	*INCREASE*
US AIR FORCE		
TAC FTR SQDNS	9	30
TAC BOMB SQDNS	2	—
FTR INTERC SQDNS	5	2
MED BOMB SQDNS (B-47)	—	3
HVY BOMB SQDNS (B-52)	—	2
TROOP CARRIER SQDNS	8	6

Plus reconnaissance, refueling and support units.

US NAVY		
ATTACK CARRIERS (CVA)	3	3

Plus following embarked squadrons

FIGHTER	7	6
ATTACK	9	9
HVY ATTACK	1½	1½

Plus reconnaissance and airborne early warning units.

ASW CARRIERS (CVS)	1	1
CRUISERS	2	2
DESTROYER TYPES	30–32	20–28
SUBMARINES	8–9	6–7
AMPHIBIOUS SHIPS	22	30

Plus reconnaissance and patrol squadrons, minecraft and support units.

US MARINE CORPS		
DIV/WING TEAMS	1	1
FTR SQDNS	1	4
FTR/ATTACK SQDNS	2	2
ATTACK SQDNS	2	4

Plus reconnaissance, refueling and support units.

US ARMY		
DIVISIONS	2 (Korea)	1 (from Hawaii to Thailand)
ABN DIVISIONS	1 ABN BDE (Okinawa)	1 (to Hawaii)

Plus air defense, missile artillery, aviation and support forces.

CONUS Army forces to be alerted: 1 ABN DIVISION
2 INF DIVISIONS
2 MECH BRIGADES

b. CINCPAC OPLAN 32-64 Phase IV is designed to counter aggression by Communist China in Southeast Asia, either independently or in conjunction with North Vietnam. The objective is to bring about an early cessation of hostilities under conditions representing a net advantage to the Free World, including liberation and control of North Vietnam and reunification of Vietnam under a government aligned with the Free World. US forces are increased to nearly six divisions, and air strike and blockade actions are extended to south China. Major force deployments to mainland Southeast Asia are summarized as follows:

To South Vietnam—

D + 1   III Marine Expeditionary Force Hq. (Da Nang)
        One Air Force Control Center Hq. (Saigon)
D + 5   1st ANGLICO (Da Nang)
D + 15 Army Hq. COMUSSEASIA (augmented)
        One Army Corps Hq.
D + 9   One Army Airborne Brigade
to
D + 20
D + 2   One Marine Division
to   One Marine Air Wing
D + 35
D + 60 One Army Infantry Division

To Thailand—

D + 15 One Army Corps Hq.
        One Army Logistics Command Hq. (augmented)
D + 8   One Army Airborne Division
to
D + 45 Two Army Infantry Divisions
        One Army Mech. Infantry Brigade (Reinforced)

Follow on to Vietnam and Thailand—

Army air defense, combat and combat support and logistics support units.
Navy and Marine Corps construction battalion units.

Back-Up Forces—

Back-up forces include one Army airborne division from CONUS to Hawaii, one Marine division from CONUS to Okinawa, and one Marine Air Wing from CONUS to Japan.

Air Forces—

Air Force units are assumed to be largely in place as result of implementation of earlier phases of OPLAN 32-64 or preparations for implementation of OPLAN 39-65. Supporting augmentation units to be deployed to West Pac include:
    Combat and service support units.
    Logistic support units.
    Composite air strike force units.
    Two C-123 squadrons.

Naval Forces—

Following forces are available for direct support in Southeast Asia area or to reinforce COMUSSEASIA:

1–3 Attack carrier groups
1–2 ASW Carrier Group
3 Patrol Squadrons
4–6 Submarines
6 Minesweep Divisions
3–4 Amphibious Squadrons
2–3 Landing Ship Squadrons
2–3 LCU Divisions
1 Marine Expeditionary Force combat and service support units as required

3. In Initial operations against CHICOM aggression the serious enemy air threat, his naval capability, and the potential threat of his ponderous ground forces will require the greatest magnitude of over-all US effort. Priority of effort will be directed toward gaining and maintaining air superiority in the area, preventing the advance of enemy troops and their supplies, and altering the enemy's intent to continue the aggression. As operations develop, air and naval attacks will be increased in scope and in intensity against Chinese forces and into southern China to increase the pressure on the Chinese communists. Both OPLANs 32-64 and 39-65 provide for either non-nuclear or nuclear options. Strategic Air Command forces are to be utilized to strike selected targets within China using nuclear and/or non-nuclear weapons, as directed by the Joint Chiefs of Staff.

As early as practicable, counteroffensive operations to regain friendly territory and to liberate North Vietnam will be initiated. Amphibious forces will launch a major assault in North Vietnam to seize the initiative, cut enemy supply lines and routes of withdrawal, and facilitate the ground offensive. Concurrently, US/ Allied ground forces will mount a major offensive along the coastal axis northward from Da Nang; forces in other areas will launch simultaneous attacks; and air and naval attacks will be intensified. The magnitude and intensity of operations will be increased until favorable conditions are achieved to force the enemy to accept terms for the cessation of hostilities, the reunification of Vietnam, and the curtailment of communist influence in Southeast Asia.

[Document 234]

DOCUMENT 234

18 NOV 1964

MEMORANDUM FOR THE SECRETARY OF DEFENSE

Subject: Courses of Action in Southeast Asia

1. This memorandum derives from your conversation with the Chairman, Joint Chiefs of Staff, on 10 November 1964 concerning a possible US program of actions in Southeast Asia comprising a controlled program of systematically increased military pressures against the Democratic Republic of Vietnam (DRV) applied in coordination with appropriate political pressures.

2. It is desirable that a clear set of military objectives be agreed upon before further military involvement in Southeast Asia is undertaken. In this connection, the Joint Chiefs of Staff consider that JCSM-955-64 dated 14 November 1964, sets forth their preferred course of action to reverse the unfavorable trend in the Republic of Vietnam (RVN) and Laos with the objective of causing the DRV to cease supporting and directing the insurgencies in those countries. However, should a controlled program of systematically increased pressures referred to in paragraph 1 above be directed, the views of the Joint Chiefs of Staff are set forth herein on how such a program should be implemented.

3. For a program of graduated military pressures, the following objectives are appropriate:

a. Signal the willingness and determination of the United States to employ increasing force in support of national objectives with respect to RVN and Laos; namely, an independent and stable noncommunist government in RVN and a free and neutral Laos under the terms of the Geneva Accords of 1962.

b. Reduce, progressively, DRV support of the insurgencies in RVN and Laos to the extent necessary to tip the balance clearly in favor of the Governments of RVN and Laos by:

(1) Reduction of the amount of support available through destruction of men, material, and supporting facilities;

(2) Reduction of the amount of support available through diversion of DRV resources to increased homeland defenses and alerts; and

(3) Reduction of the rate of delivery of the available support through destruction of bridges and other LOC choke points; staging facilities and transport; and through interruption of movements by attacks on selected fixed targets, armed route reconnaissance, raids, and waterborne interdictions.

c. Punish the DRV for DRV-supported military actions by the Viet Cong/ Pathet Lao (VC/PL) against the Governments of RVN and Laos, including the US casualties which have resulted from those actions.

d. Terminate the conflicts in Laos and RVN only under conditions which would result in the achievement of US objectives.

4. In JCSM-955-64, the Joint Chiefs of Staff analyzed certain possible enemy reactions to US air strikes against North Vietnam and appropriate US/allied responses thereto. The Joint Chiefs of Staff reaffirm the salient conclusion which arose from that analysis, which is equally applicable to this program, that the United States and its allies can deal adequately with any course of action the DRV and/or CHICOMs decide to pursue. The logistic, personnel, and intelligence considerations contained in the above memorandum are also applicable to this program.

5. Should a course of action to apply controlled, systematically increased pressures against the DRV be directed, the Joint Chiefs of Staff recommend the program of actions contained in the Appendix and the objectives contained in paragraph 3, above.

For the Joint Chiefs of Staff:

Earle G. Wheeler
Chairman
Joint Chiefs of Staff

Attachment

[Document 235]

ASSISTANT SECRETARY OF DEFENSE
WASHINGTON, D. C. 20301

18 NOV 1964

INTERNATIONAL SECURITY AFFAIRS

MEMORANDUM FOR THE SECRETARY OF DEFENSE

SUBJECT: Immediate Resumption of the DESOTO Patrols

The Joint Chiefs of Staff, in JCSM 894-64 (Tab A), recommended a resumption of the DESOTO Patrols which have been suspended since mid-September. Action on the memorandum in question was deferred pending State-Defense review of all proposed future courses of action for Southeast Asia. In the interim, the Joint Chiefs of Staff incorporated a general recommendation for the resumption of DESOTO patrols in their memorandum, JCSM 902-64, which you will recall was forwarded for Ambassador Taylor's review and comment. Ambassador Taylor's views on this subject as reported in message Saigon 1378 to State (Tab B) stated that he perceived no advantage in resuming DESOTO patrols unless they be for essential intelligence gathering purposes. However, as this course of action, among others, is under current consideration, I shall keep it in mind for possible use. Recommend your signature to the attached self-explanatory memorandum addressed to the Chairman, Joint Chiefs of Staff.

Peter Solbert
Deputy Assistant Secretary

Enclosure:
Memo to Ch/JCS

Your reference:
JCSM 894-64

MEMORANDUM FOR THE CHAIRMAN, JOINT CHIEFS OF STAFF

Subject: Immediate Resumption of the DESOTO Patrols

I have noted the recommendation by the Joint Chiefs of Staff, as expressed in the referenced memorandum for the resumption of DESOTO Patrols. Their views were stated again in a subsequent memorandum (JCSM 902-64) as a proposed future course of action for Southeast Asia.

This proposal of the Joint Chiefs of Staff, among other recommendations for courses of action in Southeast Asia, is under active consideration.

Robert S. McNamara

[Sent 20 November 1964 as drafted]

[Document 236]

OFFICE OF THE ASSISTANT SECRETARY OF DEFENSE

23 Nov 1964

TO: Mr. Bundy

FROM: Mr. Rowen

Bill:

These comments are partly McNaughton's and partly mine. If John disagrees with any of them, he'll let you know later in the day.

(Signed)
Harry

23 November 1964

MEMORANDUM FOR MR. WILLIAM P. BUNDY

Subject: Comments due Monday Noon, November 23, 1964

I make the following suggestions relevant to your draft paper:
1. Add to the "US Objectives and Stakes" this factor: "The desire of the US to emerge from the crisis without an unacceptable taint because of the methods it used."
2. With respect to Option A in "Broad Options," restore the concept you had in your original draft to the effect that "We would accept the risk that South Vietnamese elements would themselves open negotiations with the liberation front or with Hanoi directly probably to a cease fire and to a coalition government that would admit the liberation front."
3. With respect to Option C in "Broad Options," the negotiating part of the definition should be changed to indicate that the United States would *not* be a party to negotiations in the early stages. Talks of some kind should start fairly early but they should be carried on by the South Vietnamese.
4. We think that the following three points should be made in connection with the advocacy of the Option A position:
   a. It gives us more time than Option C before actions are taken against North Vietnam and before any US negotiations are begun. I suspect that, taking account of the possibility that the new Government may surprise us all by achieving some success, this increased delay may be a good thing.
   b. It is more consistent with the image of a "Vietnamese war" with only US "requested help." This minimizes the price that the United States will pay if, despite our efforts, an unfavorable outcome results.
   c. Specifically, it lends itself better than Option C to the Vietnamese doing their own negotiating—which, as indicated above, is better than a course of action in which the United States is doing the negotiating.
5. Regarding the analysis of Option B, we have no comments other than that this option appears highly undesirable—(a) it is quite unlikely to work, (b) it involves substantial risks of escalation, (c) it will appear to the world to be an "extremist" course of action, (d) it commits much more of the prestige of the US to a highly dubious course of action.
6. Regarding the analysis of Option C:

a. Our main point is the one regarding negotiations made in para 3 above. Course C (and even more Course B) involves an increase in the US stake in Vietnam without having a high probability of success. If it turns out badly, it may be quite important for the GVN to have negotiated its future with the US being in the position of a good friend willing to take risks of a major war in SEA; the US should not put itself in a position where it can be plausibly accused of having "sold out Southeast Asia."

b. We doubt the wisdom of any "firm Presidential statement" at the beginning of such a moderate course of military actions. The deeds themselves should carry the freight.

c. Somewhere in the analysis of Option C should appear the concept that we might achieve a *level* of harassment of North Vietnam that would be adequate for our purpose; this is the "Corcoran" idea.

d. We must, somewhere, wrestle with the JCS problem regarding the DRV air capability. That is, they have stated that, as a military matter, the DRV airfields and POL have to be taken out very soon in any sequence of strikes against North Vietnam. This is a problem with both Options B and C.

e. The issue on US ground deployments to SVN should flag the point that this would increase the sense of US commitment without contributing much directly to the conduct of the war.

f. Option C should state clearly our judgment that the DRV would probably "hold firm" not only through our initial military actions but also well into and perhaps through all the way of a second phase of US actions.

g. Reprisals should be given a special paragraph—one which (i) notes that we could have an escalation of reprisals, and (ii) may make much more "noise" than the controlled squeeze that we are trying to apply to North Vietnam. As for the first of these two observations, there may be some merit in being able to pursue this route in harassing North Vietnam; it avoids US commitment to a *program* unrelated to any specific acts by the VC.

7. As for "Immediate Actions," some of the above comments apply:

a. We think the United States should avoid "tough public statements," but should rely rather on its deeds.

b. Although it is not stated in your draft, we think it should be understood that there will be no US negotiations going on during this phase.

8. I suggest that your Recommendations section be something like the following:

The choice between Options B and C on the one hand and Option A on the other turns largely on the degree of confidence we have in six estimates:

1. That the situation in South Vietnam is in fact very bad and that it will continue to deteriorate rapidly, despite the best we can do under the present ground rules (or any ground rules not allowing at least some strikes on North Vietnam).

2. That we can devise and will be able politically and militarily to carry out a scheme of military pressure on North Vietnam sufficient to cause the DRV leadership to knuckle and to diminish meaningfully its assistance and direction to the VC.

3. That VC activities in South Vietnam will be meaningfully reduced by such a DRV reduction in assistance and direction.

4. That the GVN would remain intact during a campaign against the North and would make profitable use of a respite in VC activities.

5. That the risk is not high of escalation to major conflict or of having to disengage later when we have even more chips on the table.

6. That the US would not be tainted too much because of the methods used

or because a compromise settlement coming out of Option C might be widely interpreted as a US "sell out" of Southeast Asia.

It is our judgment that the odds are better than even that all six of the above propositions are true if a moderate course of pressure on North Vietnam is pursued. We, therefore, recommend that Options A and B be rejected in favor of Option C.

[Document 237]

[This duplication of Document 218 was noted late in the manufacturing process.]

Position Papers
Nov 23, 1964

MEMORANDUM FOR: Mr. William Bundy—FE

FROM: Mr. Michael V. Forrestal—S/VN

It seems to me that there is an important flavor lacking in the excellent "hard look" of your weekend paper at our stakes in SVN and Laos. It is the role of China. I think it would be helpful both to our thinking here and also as a basis for any discussion we may someday have with our European friends to weave into your expose a paragraph or two on the nature and probable development of Chinese policy.

I think it is difficult to conceive of the effects of an American partial withdrawal in Southeast Asia without taking into account the effect this would have on Chinese policy. Putting it another way, if China did not exist, the effect of our withdrawal from a situation in which the people we were trying to help seemed unable to help themselves might not be politically so pervasive in Asia.

As I see it, Communist China shares the same internal political necessity for ideological expansion today that the Soviet Union did during the time of the Comintern and the period just following the Second World War. Since China's problems with respect to her internal political and economic management are even greater than those of Russia, one would expect that the need to justify the sacrifices she demands of her people will continue for the plannable future. This will impel her, I suggest, to achieve ideological successes abroad, at least where these can be achieved without grave risk to the Mainland itself.

Since any ideological success will stimulate the need for further successes during the period of her internal tension, our objective should be to "contain" China for the longest possible period. We would realize, of course, that eventually China must be expected to exercise some degree of political pre-eminence on the fringes of Asia. But if we can delay the day when this happens and at the same time strengthen the political and economic structure of the bordering countries, we might indeed succeed in creating, at the very least, Titoist regimes on the periphery of China and at best Western oriented nations who nevertheless maintain normal relationships with Peking. Somebody put this to me the other day in culinary terms. We should delay China's swallowing up Southeast Asia until (a) she develops better table manners and (b) the food is somewhat more indigestible.

I have been trying some of this reasoning on Lippman, and he appears to be toying with it, although I would not hope for much from that quarter.

[Document 238]

DEPARTMENT OF STATE
Counselor and Chairman
Policy Planning Council
Washington

November 23, 1964

TO: The Secretary

THROUGH: S/S

FROM: S/P—W. W. Rostow

SUBJECT: *Some Observations As We Come to the Crunch in Southeast Asia*

I leave for Lima this Saturday for the CIAP and CIES meetings. I presume that in early December some major decisions on Southeast Asia will be made. I should, therefore, like to leave with you some observations on the situation. I have already communicated them to Bill Bundy.

1. We must begin by fastening our minds as sharply as we can around our appreciation of the view in Hanoi and Peiping of the Southeast Asia problem. I agree almost completely with SNIE 10-3-64 of October 9. Here are the critical passages:

> While they will seek to exploit and encourage the deteriorating situation in Saigon, they probably will avoid actions that would in their view unduly increase the chances of a major US response against North Vietnam (DRV) or Communist China. We are almost certain that both Hanoi and Peiping are anxious not to become involved in the kind of war in which the great weight of US weaponry could be brought against them. Even if Hanoi and Peiping estimated that the US would not use nuclear weapons against them, they could not be sure of this. . . .
>
> In the face of new US pressures against the DRV, further actions by Hanoi and Peiping would be based to a considerable extent on their estimate of US intentions, i.e., whether the US was actually determined to increase its pressures as necessary. Their estimates on this point are probably uncertain, but we believe that fear of provoking severe measures by the US would lead them to temper their responses with a good deal of caution. . . .
>
> If, despite Communist efforts, the US attacks continued, Hanoi's leaders would have to ask themselves whether it was not better to suspend their support of Viet Cong military action rather than suffer the destruction of their major military facilities and the industrial sector of their economy. In the belief that the tide has set almost irreversibly in their favor in South Vietnam, they might calculate that the Viet Cong could stop its military attacks for the time being and renew the insurrection successfully at a later date. Their judgment in this matter might be reinforced by the Chinese Communist concern over becoming involved in a conflict with US air and naval power.

Our most basic problem is, therefore, how to persuade them that a continuation of their present policy will risk major destruction in North Viet Nam; that a preemptive move on the ground as a prelude to negotiation will be met by US strength on the ground; and that Communist China will not be a sanctuary if it assists North Viet Nam in counter-escalation.

2. In terms of force dispositions, the critical moves are, I believe, these.

a. The introduction of some ground forces in South Viet Nam and, possibly, in the Laos corridor.

b. A minimal installation of the principle that from the present forward North Viet Nam will be vulnerable to retaliatory attack for continued violation of the 1954–1962 Accords.

c. Perhaps most important of all, the introduction into the Pacific Theater of massive forces to deal with any escalatory response, including forces evidently aimed at China as well as North Viet Nam, should the Chinese Communists enter the game. I am increasingly confident that we can do this in ways which would be understood—and not dangerously misinterpreted—in Hanoi and Peiping.

3. But the movement of forces, and even bombing operations in the north, will not, in themselves, constitute a decisive signal. They will be searching, with enormous sensitivity, for the answer to the following question: Is the President of the United States deeply committed to reinstalling the 1954–1962 Accords; or is he putting on a demonstration of force that would save face for, essentially, a US political defeat at a diplomatic conference? Here their judgment will depend not merely on our use of force and force dispositions but also on the posture of the President, including commitments he makes to our own people and before the world, and on our follow-through. The SNIE accurately catches the extent of their commitments and their hopes in South Viet Nam and Laos. They will not actually accept a setback until they are absolutely sure that we really mean it. They will be as searching in this matter as Khrushchev was before he abandoned the effort to break our hold on Berlin and as Khrushchev was in searching us out on the Turkish missiles before he finally dismantled and removed his missiles from Cuba. Initial rhetoric and military moves will not be enough to convince them.

4. Given the fundamental assessment in this SNIE, I have no doubt we have the capacity to achieve a reinstallation of the 1954–1962 Accords if we enter the exercise with the same determination and staying power that we entered the long test on Berlin and the short test on the Cuba missiles. But it will take that kind of Presidential commitment and staying power.

5. In this connection, the SNIE is quite sound in emphasizing that they will seek, if they are permitted, either to pretend to call off the war in South Viet Nam, without actually doing so; or to revive it again when the pressure is off. (We can see Castro doing this now in Venezuela.) The nature of guerrilla war, infiltration, etc., lends itself to this kind of ambiguous letdown and reacceleration. This places a high premium on our defining precisely what they have to do to remove the pressure from the north. It is because we may wish to maintain pressure for some time to insure their compliance that we should think hard about the installation of troops not merely in South Viet Nam south of the seventeenth parallel, but also in the infiltration corridor of Laos. The same consideration argues for a non-sanguinary but important pressure in the form of naval blockade which will be easier to maintain during a negotiation or quasi-negotiation phase than bombing operations.

6. The touchstones for compliance should include the following: the removal of Viet Minh troops from Laos; the cessation of infiltration of South Viet Nam from the north; the turning off of the tactical radio network; and the overt statement on Hanoi radio that the Viet Cong should cease their operations and pursue their objectives in South Viet Nam by political means. On the latter point, even if contrary covert instructions are given, an overt statement would have important political and psychological impact.

7. As I said in my memorandum to the President of June 6, no one can be or should be dogmatic about how much of a war we still would have—and for how long—if the external element were thus radically reduced or eliminated. The odds are pretty good, in my view, that, if we do these things in this way, the war will either promptly stop or we will see the same kind of fragmentation of the Communist movement in South Viet Nam that we saw in Greece after the Yugoslav frontier was closed by the Tito-Stalin split. But we can't proceed on that assumption. We must try to gear this whole operation with the best counter-insurgency effort we can mount with our Vietnamese friends outside the country; and not withdraw US forces from Viet Nam until the war is truly under control. (In this connection, I hope everyone concerned considers carefully the RAND proposal of November 17, 1964, entitled "SIAT: *Single Integrated Attack Team, A Concept for Offensive Military Operations in South Viet-Nam.*")

8. I do not see how, if we adopt this line, we can avoid heightened pressures from our allies for either Chinese Communist entrance into the UN or for a UN offer to the Chinese Communists on some form of two-China basis. This will be livable for the President and the Administration if—but only if—we get a clean resolution of the Laos and South Viet Nam problems. The publication of a good Jorden Report will help pin our allies to the wall on a prior reinstallation of the 1954 and 1962 Accords.

9. Considering these observations as a whole, I suspect what I am really saying is that our assets, as I see them, are sufficient to see this thing through if we enter the exercise with adequate determination to succeed. I know well the anxieties and complications on our side of the line. But there may be a tendency to underestimate both the anxieties and complications on the other side and also to underestimate that limited but real margin of influence on the outcome which flows from the simple fact that at this stage of history we are the greatest power in the world—if we behave like it.

10. In the President's public exposition of his policy, I would now add something to the draft I did to accompany the June 6 memorandum to the President. I believe he should hold up a vision of an Asian community that goes beyond the Mekong passage in that draft. The vision, essentially, should hold out the hope that if the 1954 and 1962 Accords are reinstalled, these things are possible:

    a. peace;

    b. accelerated economic development;

    c. Asians taking a larger hand in their own destiny;

    d. as much peaceful coexistence between Asian Communists and non-Communists as the Communists wish.

11. A scenario to launch this track might begin as follows:

    A. A Presidential decision, communicated to but held by the Congressional leaders. Some leakage would not be unhelpful.

    B. Immediate movement of relevant forces to the Pacific.

    C. Immediate direct communication to Hanoi to give them a chance to back down before faced with our actions, including a clear statement of the limits of our objectives but our absolute commitment to them.

    D. Should this first communication fail (as is likely) installation of our ground forces and naval blockade, plus first attack in North, to be accompanied by publication up-dated Jorden Report and Presidential speech.

[Document 239]

November 24, 1964

MEMORANDUM FOR: Secretary Rusk
                   Secretary McNamara
                   Mr. McCone
                   General Wheeler
                   Mr. Ball
                   Mr. McGeorge Bundy

SUBJECT: Issues Raised by Papers on Southeast Asia

Although the official comments are not all in at this writing, I think it will be useful for your meeting this afternoon to have a list of the issues that appear to one mind to warrant priority discussion. Some are explicitly disagreed, others have been lurking and should be surfaced in my judgment.

I.   BASIC ISSUES AS BETWEEN THE OPTIONS

A. Is it true that *the South Vietnam situation* would deteriorate further under Option A even with reprisals, but stands a significant chance of improving under Option B or Option C?

Comment: Advocates of A maximize the chances of decay even under B and C, advocates of B and C think the lift from greater action *could* really take hold and move us forward in South Vietnam, whereas A is doomed. All concede there is *some* chance that the GVN would come apart under any Option.

B. Is the *negotiating outcome* under Option A (with or without US negotiating participation) likely to be clearly worse than under Option C?

Comment: Advocates of A doubt that it would be.

C. What are the best estimates of the *risks of major conflict* under Option B and Option C? If, as the intelligence paper states, they are about the same as between Option B and Option C *at its highest,* is there enough chance that C would succeed before it reached this point to make a real difference on the risk factor?

D. Is it true, as the draft paper states, that Option B has the best chance of attaining our full objectives?

E. As to *our stakes in SEA,* is the paper valid as written, or should it be revised in the direction of the Joint Staff comments that loss of SVN would be *necessarily* catastrophic? Is the analysis of the attitudes of non-Asian key allies right, and what weight should we give to this?

Comment: The point of the Joint Staff comments really is that greater risks of major conflict are worth accepting in view of their view of the stakes. The Joint Staff view would also implicitly assign less weight to key non-Asian allies, and still less to the non-aligned countries.

F. *Can Option C be carried out in practice* under the klieg lights of a democracy, in view of its requirement that we maintain a credible threat of major action while at the same time seeking to negotiate, even if quietly?

Comment: This is a key point raised by advocates of A. The parallel to Korea in 1951–53 is forbidding. Even advocates of C concede the difficulties.

G. Are we safe in assuming that SVN can only come apart for morale reasons, and not in a military sense as well?

Comment: The intelligence estimate is not confident on VC "burst capabilities." The President's repeated concern on protecting the south has not really been met in these papers, but we have all felt that the purely military aspects of the VC could be contained. This is a first question to ask of Ambassador Taylor.

II. ISSUES RELATING TO THE IMMEDIATE COURSES OF ACTION (SECTION VII)

A. Is our reprisal planning in proper shape to produce varied options on demand? Does it provide adequately for GVN participation?

Comment: CINCPAC Frag Order No. 3 is the current basis of planning. It provides for optional clusters of targets, but no one option calls for less than about 175 strikes, under very high damage criteria. Such a high order of action could throw off all calculations based on the theory of "squeeze" under Option C and even under Option B. As to GVN participation, the latest plans do crank this in, at some sacrifice of destructiveness.

B. What *do* we mean to take as a basis for reprisal?

Comment: We all agree that another Bien Hoa would call for reprisal, but it would help to refine our thinking somewhat further. Incidents not solely directed at the US would be desirable for political reasons. What kind might these be?

C. What sort of high-level statement is needed if we adopt the immediate program?

Comment: Should it be generalized, with the infiltration evidence speaking for itself separately, or should it make express use of the infiltration evidence? Is the latter wholly ready for surfacing? Is the new Jorden Report?

III. ISSUES CONCERNING THE EXECUTION OF OPTION A

A. Can this Option really be extended to include continued (non-reprisal) actions against the DRV even at a low scale?

Comment: The longer draft had so extended it. Most of us think this is a mistake in definition, in that any continued actions against the DRV create international and other pressures and are in effect the early stages of Option C.

B. Could or should ground forces be put into northern SVN even under this Option?

Comment: Advocates of A urge this as a bargaining counter. Most of us think that, apart from lacking any military necessity in the absence of attacks on the DRV, it would appear as a bluff and not help any negotiation.

C. Assuming the situation does deteriorate under this Option, should we let Vietnamese negotiations develop, or ourselves seek a forum?

Comment: This is a less urgent issue, and perhaps cannot be answered now.

IV. ISSUES CONCERNING THE EXECUTION OF OPTION B

A. Should we hit major targets, especially airfields, at once, or only after and if the DRV has hurt us from them?

Comment: Even under this Option, many of us feel the actions should be progressive, with the prospect of more to come at least as important psychologically as present damage. We all accept the *will* of the DRV as the real target.

B. Is ground invasion of the DRV (at Vinh per present plans) a military necessity or advantage that outweighs the increased risks the Chicoms would then come in force? (This applies to C as well as B.)

Comment: The intelligence estimate (p. 9 of "Probable Communist Reactions," dated 19 November) highlights this as significantly raising the odds. It would also tend to change our objectives in the eyes of the world. Is it worth it?

C. At what stage, if ever, might nuclear weapons be required, and on what scale? What would be the implications of such use?

Comment: This is clearly a sensitive issue. The President may want a more precise answer than appears in the papers.

V. ISSUES CONCERNING THE EXECUTION OF OPTION C

A. Should ground forces be introduced into northern SVN at the *early* stages?

Comment: The pros and cons of this are argued in Section VII of the *long* draft.

B. Is our early targeting properly thought through?

Comment: This is partly the question of whether to hit Phuc Yen early. But also some individual comment has highlighted the possible utility of focussing *at length* on low-key targets, not so much for the sake of damage as to show how helpless the DRV is, to cause it to strain its security apparatus, and ask for help from the Chicoms in ways the Chicoms may not be able to give effectively. Also to keep our losses low. Such an *un*dramatic "water-drip" technique would, in the opinion of many Chicom experts, both hit the DRV will harder than more dramatic attacks and strain the key DRV-Chicom relationships more. Put differently, this school of thought argues that dramatic acts, with probably higher US losses, would tend to knit the DRV people and the DRV and Chicoms; US losses are also a key factor in DRV morale, as their propaganda has shown for months. If we were acting with impunity, this would have a major effect, and the falseness of their propaganda would become a major weakness in their hold over their people.

C. How do we handle any early negotiations?

Comment: This is the least satisfactory part of the present script. To keep up our show of determination and at the same time listen for nibbles is a tough job in any case. We need to consider use of third countries at the outset perhaps more.

D. Do we even listen to nibbles till we have established a clear "common law" pattern of attacks?

Comment: The point is not made as clear as it should be. I think not.

VI. ACTIVE ISSUES APPLICABLE TO ANY DECISIONS

A. White House statement.

B. High-level speech.

C. Congressional consultation, including whether Ambassador Taylor should testify if Committees ask.

D. Key Allies—UK, Australia, New Zealand, Thailand, Philippines. Individually or would we now form a group as in Korea? (I am inclined against a formal group, with or without publicity—the interests are too diverse.) SEATO?

E. US Government machinery. Do we not need a designated ExCom *now*, with a subordinate working group?

William P. Bundy

cc: Members of Working Group (for individual use only until directed otherwise).

[Document 240]

24 November 1964

NSC WORKING GROUP ON VIETNAM

SECTION 1: INTELLIGENCE ASSESSMENT: THE SITUATION
IN VIETNAM*

A. SOUTH VIETNAM

1. As compared with sharply accelerated political deterioration last August, adverse political trends appear at least to have slowed. There has been no repetition of the flurry of riots and demonstrations of serious proportions, or of labor strikes, armed revolts, urban lawlessness, and coup plotting that seemed to be bringing South Vietnam close to the brink of internal chaos and disintegration, although pressures and open criticism have already appeared from various sectors in response to the new civilian government. The outlook for the government is still uncertain. Its success so far in avoiding open mass opposition is encouraging, but even if the government can avoid a direct public confrontation, the lack of positive support from various key segments of the populace seems certain to hamper its effectiveness. The generally strong stand of Huong so far, however, may make his government more viable than his critics now predict. Finally, although General Khanh has given up his position as Prime Minister, his power position does not appear to have been weakened as a result of the civilian cabinet and indeed may have improved somewhat.

2. The political situation, nonetheless, remains critical and extremely fragile. Direction and a sense of purpose are still lacking. Administration in both Saigon and the provinces remains seriously plagued by confusion, apathy, and poor morale. A cohesive leadership or even a modus operandi between the various power forces has not been established. The present government is composed primarily of technicians and has about it a caretaker aura. Basic differences have not been resolved and, despite the restraint exhibited in recent weeks, open conflict could emerge at any moment.

3. The military leadership remains factionalized, and even the extent of Khanh's support among these factions is uncertain. Khanh and some of his military colleagues, while supporting the new government, have made it clear that they intend to remain the real power in South Vietnam and that they will not countenance any interference from the civilians in the conduct of the war.

The Security Situation

4. The security situation in the countryside has continued to deteriorate. The Viet Cong retain the initiative and are applying increasing pressure on a nationwide scale, from the northern coastal lowlands to the Camau peninsula. They have improved their firepower and capabilities for large operations and have demonstrated increased daring and improved coordination and planning in their attacks, ambushes, and sabotage. They have strengthened their armed forces

---

* Note: The judgments of this Section are based as closely as possible on existing National Estimates: SNIE 53-2-64, "The Situation in South Vietnam," dated 1 October 1964; SNIE 10-3-64, "Probable Communist Reactions to Certain Possible US/GVN Courses of Action," dated 9 October 1964; and SNIE 50-2-64, "Probable Consequences of Certain US Actions with Respect to Vietnam and Laos," dated 25 May 1964.

and military organization, in part from increased infiltration, particularly in the northern provinces. Finally, Viet Cong control is spreading over areas heretofore controlled by the government, and the insurgent military presence is now closer than ever before to an increasing number of urban centers, major installations, and transportation lines.

5. By and large, government military operations continue to be reactions to Viet Cong initiatives and the government has not been able to disrupt the overall Viet Cong effort. The total number of military operations making contact with the Viet Cong remains small. The GVN does seem presently capable of curbing or repelling major military initiatives on the part of the VC. Furthermore, there are recurrent instances of encouraging initiative and success on the part of individual GVN units. Meanwhile, however, political stresses, factionalism and power struggles within the military leadership, and numerous military command changes have adversely affected military morale and organization. South Vietnamese field commanders are finding it increasingly difficult to engender wholehearted interest in military matters and pacification operations. The pacification effort itself, limited in scope and effectiveness over the past months, is now showing a noticeable slackening of momentum in many areas. The Embassy has noted in a recent assessment that the deleterious effects of political turmoil, administrative and military disruptions, and growing Viet Cong capabilities have been greater than heretofore appeared.

Present Prospects, Assuming No Major Changes in US Policies

6. Arrest or reversal of the deteriorating military trend will in part depend on the ability of the new government to hold together, gain a base of popular support, and energize the administration. It is too early to assess the prospect that the present untested leadership can achieve these goals.

7. It is possible that the new government can improve GVN esprit and effectiveness, though on the basis of present indications this appears unlikely. It is also possible that GVN determination and authority could virtually give way suddenly in the near future, in response to VC pressures or South Vietnamese defeatism, though the chances seem better than even that the new GVN can hang on for the near future and thus afford a platform upon which its armed forces can, with US assistance, prosecute the war and attempt to turn the tide. Success in this effort requires that, at least, the Saigon Government not be so unstable and inept as to increase the difficulties of the counterinsurgency campaign in the countryside. Even under the best of circumstances, however, reversal of present military trends will be extremely difficult. Moreover, given the extent of Viet Cong capabilities and control of the countryside, failure to reverse existing military trends within the next few months will increasingly reduce the prospects for survival of the present or any successor anti-Communist government.

B. THE DRV/VC

8. Lasting success in South Vietnam depends upon a substantial improvement in the energy and effectiveness of the RVN government and pacification machinery. The nature of the war in Vietnam is such that US ability to compel the DRV to end or reduce the VC insurrection rests essentially upon the effect of US sanctions on the will of DRV leadership to sustain and enlarge that insurrection, and to a lesser extent upon the effect of sanctions on the capabilities of the DRV to do so.

a. The basic elements of Communist strength in South Vietnam remain indigenous: South Vietnamese grievances, war-weariness, defeatism, and political disarray; VC terror, arms capture, disciplined organization, highly developed intelligence systems, and ability to recruit locally; and the fact that the VC enjoys some status as a nationalist movement. The high VC morale is sustained by successes to date and by the receipt of outside guidance and support.

b. The DRV contribution is substantial. The DRV manages the VC insurrection. It gives it general tactical direction, maintaining a steady flow of communications between Hanoi and senior VC echelons. It exercises similar control over the political/propaganda activities of the "National Liberation Front." It provides the VC senior officers, key cadre, military specialists and certain key military and communications equipment. The tactical direction of VC efforts is in effect provided by Vietnamese who are North Vietnamese officers on a detached duty. Consequently, we believe that any orders from Hanoi—to step up or to desist from further military action—would in large measure be obeyed by Communist forces in South Vietnam.

c. The DRV contribution may now be growing. There appears to be a rising rate of infiltration, providing additional DRV stiffening to VC units. This may be reflected in a raised level of VC aggressiveness and in further VC exploitation of political disarray in the cities.

d. US-inflicted destruction in North Vietnam and Laos would reduce these supporting increments and damage DRV/VC morale. It might give the GVN/ARVN a breathing spell and opportunity to improve. However, it would almost certainly not destroy DRV capability to continue supporting the insurrection in the South, although at a lessened level, should Hanoi so wish. Much would depend on whether any DRV "removal" of its direction and support of the VC were superficial or whole. If the latter situation obtained, the South Vietnamese could in time probably develop enough military and political dynamism themselves to reduce the VC threat to manageable proportions—assuming the DRV did not thereafter attempt once more to subvert their country. If any DRV "removal" were superficial or permitted to become so, however, limited to gestures to compliance that removed only the more visible evidences of the DRV increment, it would probably not be possible to develop sufficient GVN/ARVN capability—*and,* most importantly, will—to establish and maintain a viable and free government in South Vietnam.

9. *DRV POLICY and the DRV View of the Situation in South Vietnam*

a. The Communist leaders in Hanoi undoubtedly feel that present trends in South Vietnam are much in their favor. They anticipate that a political vacuum is forming which they can probably soon fill with a "neutralist" coalition eventually designed [words missing] Communist elements. They see . . . [words missing] . . . become more favorable to them as soon as South Vietnam slips a bit more; in the meantime their major concern in Laos is to keep the corridor and the areas bordering North Vietnam and China in Communist hands.

b. The North Vietnamese regime (DRV) is intensely committed to the final aim of bringing South Vietnam under its control, an outcome which for Hanoi's leaders would mark the completion of their revolution. In pursuing its ends in South Vietnam the DRV has been patient, careful to avoid the costs and risks of direct involvement. Both Hanoi and Peiping are almost certainly anxious not to become involved in the kind of war in which the great weight of superior US weaponry might be brought to bear against them, and they almost certainly feel —under present circumstances at least—that they will not have to initiate actions carrying great risk of such US response in order to win the day in time.

c. The recent mortar attack on US equipment and personnel at Bien Hoa airfield may indicate a willingness to take somewhat greater risk of increased US counteraction. In any case, it is obvious that DRV leaders had decided that the humiliation to the US, the damage to RVN morale, and the boost to the morale of their own forces justified running such risks as they estimated were entailed.

d. The DRV leaders probably believe that victory may be near through a collapse of anti-Communist government in South Vietnam. They probably feel that the GVN's will to continue the fight is waning, that the South Vietnamese are uncertain of the extent of future US support, and that blows such as that at Bien Hoa can further this doubt and perhaps critically depress South Vietnamese will to resist. To this extent the DRV/VC operations may be entering a new stage involving carefully selected blows against US units. It is not likely however, that Hanoi believes the time has arrived for launching upon General Giap's "third stage"—engagement of the ARVN in conventional (i.e., non-guerrilla) warfare. Indeed, as a means of averting heavier US involvement in Indochina, Hanoi may soon opt to make a serious call for negotiations, perhaps using the vehicle of Sihanouk's repeated demands for an international conference to guarantee Cambodia's neutral status.

10. *Hanoi's comprehension of US intentions.*

a. The course of actions the Communists have pursued in South Vietnam over the past few years implies a fundamental estimate on their part that the difficulties facing the US are so great that US will and ability to maintain resistance in that area can be gradually eroded—without running high risks that the US would wreak heavy destruction on the DRV or Communist China. Hanoi's immediate estimate is probably that the passing of the US election gives Washington the opportunity to take new military actions against the DRV and/or new diplomatic initiatives.

b. Initiation of new levels of military pressure against the DRV with the declared aim of getting Hanoi to stop its support of the VC in the South and the PL in Laos would confront Hanoi's leaders with a basic question. Is the US determined to continue escalating its pressures to achieve its announced objectives regardless of the danger of war with Communist China and regardless of the international pressures that could be brought to bear against it, or is the US escalation essentially a limited attempt to improve the US negotiating position? They would also have to decide whether US aims were indeed limited. Their decision on these questions would be affected by the US military posture in the area, by the extent and nature of the US escalation, the character of the US communication of its intentions, and their reading of domestic US and international reactions to the inauguration of US attacks on the North. In any event, comprehension of the other's intentions would almost certainly be difficult on both sides, and especially so as the scale of hostilities mounted. 10c. (removed) (JCS criticism)

11. *DRV ability and willingness to sustain damage.* We have many indications that the Hanoi leadership is acutely and nervously aware of the extent to which North Vietnam's transportation system and industrial plant is vulnerable to attack. On the other hand, North Vietnam's economy is overwhelmingly agricultural and, to a large extent, decentralized in a myriad of more or less economically self-sufficient villages. Interdiction of imports and extensive destruction of transportation facilities and industrial plants would cripple DRV industry. These actions would also seriously restrict DRV military capabilities, and would degrade, though to a lesser extent, Hanoi's capabilities to support guerrilla warfare in South Vietnam and Laos. We do not believe that such actions would have a

crucial effect on the daily lives of the overwhelming majority of the North Vietnamese population. We do not believe that attacks on industrial targets would so greatly exacerbate current economic difficulties as to create unmanageable control problems. It is reasonable to infer that the DRV leaders have a psychological investment in the work of reconstruction they have accomplished over the last decade. Nevertheless, they would probably be willing to suffer some damage to the country in the course of a test of wills with the US over the course of events in South Vietnam.

12. *DRV appraisal of the value and hazards of Chinese Communist rescue.* Strong US pressures on North Vietnam would pose painful questions for the DRV leadership and doubtless occasion sharp debates within the upper echelons of the hierarchy. We believe, however, that Hanoi would refrain as long as possible from requesting such Chinese assistance as might endanger DRV independence: for example, large-scale ground force "volunteer" intervention. This hesitancy would of course be overcome if DRV leaders considered the existence of their regime to be at stake.

13. *DRV judgment of the weight to attach to world pressure against the US.* Hanoi probably believes that considerable international pressure would develop against a US policy of expanding the war to the North and that this might impel the US to relax its attacks and bring the US to an international conference on Vietnam. With both open and covert USSR and Communist Chinese propaganda and political action support, Hanoi would endeavor to intensify such free world sentiments—probably overestimating their impact on the US. Hanoi would probably be confident that in any case—while this game was being played or while an international conference was being held—the VC and Pathet Lao could continue to undermine non-Communist authority in South Vietnam and Laos.

C. THE INTERESTS AND CAPABILITIES OF COMMUNIST CHINA IN THE AREA

14. Although there is little evidence on the matter, we believe that close cooperation exists between Hanoi and Peiping and that Hanoi consults Peiping on major decisions regarding South Vietnam. Peiping clearly supports Hanoi's decision to maintain pressure in the South even at the risk of US attacks on North Vietnam. Pieping's interests in undermining the US position in Asia is well served by Hanoi and the Viet Cong. Preoccupation with the security of their frontiers also has been a factor behind the Chinese leaders' announcement of their readiness to assist in North Vietnam's defense, despite their evident desire to avoid provoking a direct clash with the US. The Sino-Soviet relationship provides added incentive for Peiping to honor its commitments to Hanoi. Despite any current efforts to modify the polemics, the Chinese Communists still will feel compelled to demonstrate their readiness to support "wars of natural liberation," particularly in the case of Vietnam.

15. Short of large-scale introduction of ground forces, Chinese Communist capabilities to augment DRV offensive and defensive capabilities are slight, certainly as compared with US forces at hand. Peiping could provide the DRV some air defense equipment. It could send additional jet fighters and naval patrol craft in limited numbers, though at some cost to its own defensive posture. Recent Chinese Communist deployments into South China indicate that improvements are being made in their defense posture which would also strengthen their offensive capabilities.

D. THE INTERESTS, ROLE AND CAPABILITIES OF THE USSR IN THE AREA

16. In the wake of Khrushchev's ouster there are some tenuous indications that Khrushchev's successors may intend to pursue a somewhat more active policy in Indochina. Nevertheless, Moscow's role in Vietnam is likely to remain a relatively minor one. In general the Soviets remain committed to a Communist government in the North and continuing efforts to undermine South Vietnam, but they are unwilling to run substantial risks to bring it about. Soviet influence in North Vietnam is based upon Moscow's ability to provide strategic nuclear protection and upon the North Vietnamese desire for continuing Soviet military and economic aid. Moscow's ability to influence decisions in Hanoi tends consequently to be proportional to the North Vietnamese regime's fears of American action against it, rising in moments of crisis and diminishing in quieter periods. Moscow's willingness to give . . . seems to be in inverse proportion . . . to North Vietnamese . . .

[Document 241]

Revised Draft 11/21/64
WPBundy/JMcNaughton

Revised page 11/26/64

Summary

COURSES OF ACTION IN SOUTHEAST ASIA

I. INTELLIGENCE ASSESSMENT: THE SITUATION IN SOUTH VIETNAM

A. *South Vietnam.* The political situation remains critical and extremely fragile. The security situation in the countryside has continued to deteriorate.

It is possible that the new government in Saigon can improve South Vietnamese esprit and effectiveness, though on the basis of current indications this appears unlikely. It is also possible that GVN determination and authority could virtually give way suddenly in the near future, though the chances seem better than even that the new GVN can hang on for this period and thus afford a platform upon which its armed forces, with US assistance, can prosecute the war and attempt to turn the tide. Even under the best of circumstances, however, reversal of present military trends will be extremely difficult.

B. *The VC and the North Vietnamese Role.* The basic elements of Communist strength in South Vietnam remain indigenous, but the North Vietnamese (DRV) contribution is substantial and may now be growing. There appears to be a rising rate of infiltration.

We believe any orders from Hanoi would in large measure be obeyed by Communist forces in South Vietnam. US ability to compel the DRV to end or reduce the VC insurrection rests essentially upon the effect of US sanctions on the will of the DRV leadership, and to a lesser extent on the effect of such sanction on DRV capabilities. US-inflicted destruction in North Vietnam and Laos would reduce the elements of DRV support and damage DRV/VC morale. It might give the GVN a breathing spell and chance to improve. However, it would almost certainly not destroy DRV capabilities to continue, although at a lessened level.

If the DRV did in fact remove *wholly* its direction and support to the VC, the South Vietnamese could in time probably reduce the VC threat to manageable proportions. But if any DRV "removal" were superficial only, the South Vietnamese probably could not develop the capability to establish and maintain a workable and free government in South Vietnam.

Despite a large and growing North Vietnamese contribution to the Viet Cong insurrection, the primary sources of Communist strength in the South remain indigenous. Even if severely damaged, North Vietnam—should it choose—could still direct and support the Viet Cong insurrection at a reduced level. Increased US pressures on North Vietnam would be effective only if they persuaded Hanoi that the price of maintaining the insurrection in the South would be too great and that it would be preferable to reduce its aid to the Viet Cong and direct at least a temporary reduction of Viet Cong activity.*

II. U.S. OBJECTIVES AND STAKES IN SOUTH VIETNAM AND SOUTHEAST ASIA

A. US objectives and the Present Basis of US Action. Behind our policy in South Vietnam and Laos have been three factors, all closely related to our overall policy of resisting Communist expansion:

1. The general principle of helping countries that try to defend their own freedom against Communist subversion and attack.

2. The specific consequences of Communist control of South Vietnam and Laos on the security of other nations in Asia.

3. The implications worldwide of South Vietnam, and, to a lesser extent, Laos as test cases of Communist "wars of national liberation."

Essentially, the loss of South Vietnam to Communist control, in any form would be a major blow to our basic policies. US prestige is heavily committed to the maintenance of a non-Communist South Vietnam, and only less heavily so to a neutralized Laos.

Yet we must face the facts that (a) there is some chance that South Vietnam might come apart under us whatever course of action we pursue; (b) strong military action necessarily involves some risks of an enlarged and even conceivably major conflict in Asia. These problems force us to weigh in our analysis the drawbacks and possibilities of success of various options, including the drawbacks of accepting only the fallback objectives set forth below.

B. Possible Alternate US Objectives. Our fall-back objectives in South Vietnam would be:

1. To hold the situation together as long as possible, so that we have time to strengthen other areas of Asia.

2. To take forceful enough measures in the situation so that we emerge from it, even in the worst case, with our standing as the principal helper against Communist expansion as little impaired as possible.

3. To make clear to the world, and to nations in Asia particularly, that failure in South Vietnam, if it comes, was due to special local factors—such as a bad colonial heritage and a lack of will to defend itself—that do not apply to other nations.

* DIA reserves its position on the final two sentences, believing that they understate the importance of reduced North Vietnamese capabilities.

C. Consequences of Communist Control of South Vietnam

1. *In Southeast Asia.* The so-called "domino" theory is oversimplified. It might apply if, but only if, Communist China entered Southeast Asia in force and/or the US was forced out of South Vietnam in circumstances of military defeat. Nonetheless, Communist control of South Vietnam would almost immediately make Laos extremely hard to hold, have Cambodia bending sharply to the Communist side, place great pressure on Thailand (a country which has an historic tendency to make "peace" with the side that seems to be winning), and embolden Indonesia to increase its pressure on Malaysia. We could do more in Thailand and with the British in Malaysia to reinforce the defense of these countries, but the initial shock wave would be great.

2. *In Asia Generally.* The effects in Asia generally would depend heavily on the circumstances in which South Vietnam was lost and on whether the loss did in fact greatly weaken or lead to the early loss of other areas in Southeast Asia. Nationalist China (shaken already by the Chicom nuclear explosion and the UN membership crisis), South Korea, and the Philippines would need maximum reassurance. While Japan's faith in our military posture and determination might not be shaken, the growing feeling that Communist China must somehow be lived with might well be accentuated. India and Iran appear to be the Asian problem cases outside the Far East. A US defeat could lead to serious repercussions in these countries. There is a great deal we could still do to reassure these countries, but the picture of a defense line clearly breached could have serious effects and could easily, over time, tend to unravel the whole Pacific and South Asian defense structures.

3. *In the World at Large.* Within NATO (except for Greece and Turkey to some degree), the loss of South Vietnam probably would not shake the faith and resolve to face the threat of Communist aggression or confidence in us for major help. This is so provided we carried out any military actions in Southeast Asia without taking forces from NATO and without generating a wave of "isolationism" in the US. In other areas of the world, either the nature of the Communist threat or the degree of US commitment or both are so radically different than in Southeast Asia that it is difficult to assess the impact. The question would be whether the US was in fact able to go on with its present policies.

4. *Summary.* There are enough "ifs" in the above analysis so that it cannot be concluded that the loss of South Vietnam would soon have the totally crippling effect in Southeast Asia and Asia generally that the loss of Berlin would have in Europe; but it could be that bad, driving us to the progressive loss of other areas or to taking a stand at some point so that there would almost certainly be major conflict and perhaps the great risk of nuclear war.*

D. *ATTITUDES OF OTHER NATIONS REGARDING US ACTIONS*

1. *Major US Allies.* We must maintain, particularly to our key NATO allies, the picture of a nation that is strong and at the same time wise in the exercise

---

* The Joint Staff believes that early loss of Southeast Asia and the progressive unraveling of the wider defense structures would be almost inevitable results of the loss of South Vietnam in any circumstances.

of its power. As for France, we are damned either way we go. Both Britain and, to a lesser extent, Germany sympathize in principle with our whole policy of seeking to restrain Communist Chinese expansion, and the British recognize their own specific parallel stake in the closely related problem of Malaysia. All European countries could be affected in their view of the US and their willingness to accept continued US leadership by the way we handle Southeast Asia. Despite the fact that their Far East "experts" tend to believe that Western influence in Asia is on the wane in any case, our key European allies probably would now understand our applying an additional measure of force to avoid letting the ship sink; but they could become seriously concerned if we get ourselves involved in a major conflict that degraded our ability to defend Europe and produced anything less than an early and completely satisfactory outcome.

2. *"Nonaligned" Nations.* In these countries, the issue is our continued ability to exert influence on these countries, to keep the peace in and among them, and to keep the waverers from wavering clear over to Communist answers. The "nonaligned" nations, with the possible exception of India, would by and large be opposed to any stronger action we might take. Indeed, they cannot be expected to support any course of action we follow in South Vietnam and Laos. A program of systematic attacks against the DRV would find many of these nations supporting a condemnatory resolution in the UN. But, as we saw in the Cuban missile crisis, the nonaligned and Afro-Asian nations will accept and even admire and be grateful for actions that achieve the result we want in a strong and wise way.

3. *Summary.* As for likely foreign reactions to our three possible courses of action in Part III below, it appears that Option A (continue present course indefinitely) would cause no adverse reactions but if it failed it would leave a considerable after-taste of US failure and ineptitude; Option B (fast unyielding pressure) would run major risks of sharply expressed condemnation which would be erased only if the course of action succeeded quite clearly and in a reasonable time; Option C (progressive pressure-and-talk) would probably be in-between in both respects.

III. THE BROAD OPTIONS

A. Option A would be to continue present policies indefinitely: Maximum assistance within South Vietnam, limited external actions in Laos and by the GVN covertly against North Vietnam, specific individual reprisal actions not only against such incidents as the Gulf of Tonkin attack but also against any recurrence of VC "spectaculars" such as Bien Hoa. Basic to this option is the continued rejection of negotiations.

B. Option B would add to present actions a systematic program of military pressures against the north, with increasing pressure actions to be continued at a fairly rapid pace and without interruption until we achieve our present stated objectives. The actions would mesh at some point with negotiation, but we would approach any discussions or negotiations with absolutely inflexible insistence on our present objectives.

C. Option C would add to present actions on orchestration of (1) communications with Hanoi and/or Peiping, and (2) additional graduated military moves against infiltration targets, first in Laos and then in the DRV, and then against other targets in North Vietnam. The military scenario should give the impression of a steady deliberate approach, and should be designed to give the US the option at any time to proceed or not, to escalate or not, and to quicken the pace or not. These decisions would be made from time to time in view of all relevant factors. The negotiating part of this course of action would have to be played largely by ear, but in essence we would be indicating from the outset a willingness to negotiate in an affirmative sense, accepting the possibility that we might not achieve our full objectives.

IV (old V) ANALYSIS OF OPTION A

Option A is a continuation of present policies, with the additional element of deciding to have reprisal action not only against another Gulf of Tonkin incident, but against any repetition of a spectacular attack by the VC within South Vietnam, particularly but not solely an attack involving US forces or installations.

As far as they go, Option A actions are in fact common to all three Options, and would be pursued with equal force under Option B or Option C. It is basic that the situation in the south be improved by all possible means whatever else we do.

A. *Actions within South Vietnam.* There is a great deal that can be done to improve GVN performance and to strengthen the whole pacification program. We must continue to seek additional third-country contributions (though these will probably remain limited). We are working to improve the key police program, military tactics, the air effort, the economic program including a stronger emphasis on the cities, etc. We continue to reject the introduction of US combat forces or a US taking over of command—but short of such changes in policy we are working as hard as we can on all major avenues for improvement.

The point is that the effectiveness of all such measures depends on having an increasingly effective GVN, with sustained government and popular morale. We do not yet have this, though we have hopes that the present government will settle down and become effective over a period of 2–4 months. The issue is whether this can happen if we do no more than Option A over this period.

B. *Actions Outside South Vietnam.* We would in any event continue and intensify the various covert forms of action against North Vietnam, and the various Lao and US actions in Laos, adding GVN air and ground action in Laos on a limited scale. We would also conduct reprisals as indicated above.

C. *Prognosis.* The above actions will not physically affect the DRV scale of infiltration, nor do we believe they would affect Hanoi's determination and will. They might, however, keep the DRV from engaging in further spectaculars, and thus keep the scale of the conflict in the south within some limits.

The question is whether the GVN could start to make real and visible headway on these terms, with no indication on the US side that we were prepared to go further. We think that reprisal actions would tend to lift GVN morale and performance for a time, but their lifting effect would decline with each successive case. For a period of time, perhaps some months, this Option might keep the GVN afloat and even get it moving slowly toward effectiveness. Most of us doubt that it can do more than that.

D. *Negotiating Avenues.* We ourselves would be rejecting negotiation, as at present, at the outset.

But this still leaves the chance that the GVN itself, or individual South Vietnamese in potentially powerful positions, might at any time start discussions with Hanoi or the Liberation Front. If the situation continued to deteriorate, the chances of this taking place would increase. If it did, Hanoi might not insist on early US withdrawal, but the way would be paved for a Vietnamese "deal" that would end up with the US being withdrawn and a coalition government with Communist representation installed in Saigon. The odds would be heavy that over time such a government—as in Poland in 1946–47—would be taken over by the Communist element, and eventually merged with the north into a unified Communist Vietnam.

We might stand aside in such a process, which would at least avoid our name going into the deal. Alternatively, if the situation was deteriorating beyond repair, we might seek to cover a retreat by accepting negotiations, most likely through a Geneva conference that would improve the above deal by adding elements of international supervision that might stretch out the process of Communist control and buy time.

E. *Pros and Cons of Option A.* There is clearly a case for Option A as a means of buying a short period of time. We would have gone the last mile in restraint, and in putting the show up to the Vietnamese. We would be giving the Sino-Soviet relationship time to clarify—which we think would be a reaffirmed deep split. And we could hope for some improved GVN performance before we did more. *But* the odds are against the latter, and on balance it seems more likely we would later have to decide whether to take Options B or C under even worse circumstances.

As an indefinite course of action, Option A appears to offer little hope of getting Hanoi out or an independent South Vietnam re-established. Its sole advantages would be that (a) defeat would be clearly due to GVN failure, and we ourselves would be less implicated than if we tried Option B or Option C, *and failed;* (b) the most likely result would be a Vietnamese-negotiated deal, under which an eventually unified Communist Vietnam would reassert its traditional hostility to Communist China and limit its own ambitions to Laos and Cambodia. In such a case . . . whether the rot spread to Thailand would be hard to judge; it seems likely that the Thai would conclude we simply could not be counted on, and would accommodate somehow to Communist China even without any marked military move by Communist China.

V (old VI) ANALYSIS OF OPTION B

a. *Rationale and Preparatory Actions.*

The basic headings of preparatory action are the same as for Option C.

b. *Opening Military Actions.*

The opening military actions under Option B would be major air attacks on key targets in the DRV, starting with the major Phuc Yen airfield.

c. *Early Negotiating Actions.*

Even though we would be taking a totally inflexible position on negotiating, we would have to deal with channels of communication, the UN, and perhaps— despite our strong opposition—a re-convened Geneva conference of some sort.

d. *Probable Communist Responses.*

The possible Communist responses again fall under three headings, but with different orders of likelihood than under Option C.

1. It is still considered unlikely that Hanoi would really yield, at least in the early stages.

2. The chances are significantly greater than under Option C that Hanoi might retaliate at least by limited air attacks in South Vietnam, possibly an offensive in Laos, conceivably a ground offensive into South Vietnam, and—least likely but necessarily to be considered—Chicom ground action into Laos primarily.

3. The most likely general course of action would still be for Hanoi to hold firm, doing its utmost to stimulate condemnation of our actions, but possibly trying to pretend that it had reduced its activity in the south.

e. *In the Event of the Third Type of Communist Response, Likely Developments and Problems.*

1. Within South Vietnam, the initial reaction to attacks on the DRV would probably be one of elation, and there would probably be a spurt of more effective GVN performance.

However, as in Option C, there would be offsetting factors that would come into play, and still leave us with a continuing danger that the situation would resume its present deteriorating course. The Vietnamese people are clearly war-weary. Probably they would hold fairly firm under Option B, perhaps firmer than under Option C once the latter became entwined with real negotiations. But there is the lesser chance that things would weaken.

Either for this reason, or because Hanoi was not caving—the latter in almost any event—we would be driven to up the ante militarily.

2. Our further increases in military pressure would then be the same generally as under Option C, but applied considerably more rapidly and toughly. And at this point, the odds would necessarily start to increase that Hanoi, no longer able to temporize, would either start to yield by some real actions to cut down, or would move itself to a more drastic military response.

3. Our position internationally could become very difficult at this point. We must face the fact that we would incur a really serious barrage of criticism including the dominant public opinion in some of our key allies such as the UK. Our influence might not be drastically affected on such issues as MLF and NATO, where the issues are less affected by popular opinion, but the effect could be much more serious on such opinion-related issues as the Kennedy Round, African views on Communist China, etc., etc.

f. *Likely Developments and Problems if the Communist Side Engaged in Major Retaliation At Some Point.*

Right from the outset, this course of action would entail some chance of a Communist military response against the south. Furthermore, as we move to the stage of "further increases of military pressure," the chance of the more severe types of response would increase. These, and the required responses, are covered in the Military Annex.

g. *Possible Over-all Outcomes.*

1. *At best,* conceivably in the early stages, but much more likely only after

we had engaged in the further military pressures covered under E above, Hanoi might decide that the pain it was incurring was greater than the gains of continuing its present strategy in South Vietnam. They might be ready to sit down and work out a settlement in some form that would give us a restoration of the 1954 agreements, hopefully supplemented by more effective international machinery and guarantees to maintain such a settlement.

2. *At worst,* South Vietnam might come apart while we were pursuing the course of action. In such a case, we would be in the position of having got into an almost irreversible sequence of military actions, but finding ourselves fighting on behalf of a country that no longer wished to continue the struggle itself.

3. *Between these two outcomes,* there is much less chance than under Option C that the struggle would continue indecisively for a considerable period. We could find ourselves drawn into a situation where such military actions as an amphibious landing in the DRV—proposed as one of our further actions— moved us very far toward continuing occupation of DRV soil. Alternatively, the volume of international noise and desire for a peaceful settlement could reach the point where, in the interest of our world-wide objectives, we would have to consider accepting a negotiation on terms that would be relatively but not necessarily wholly favorable to the attainment of our full objectives.

h. *Pros and Cons of Option B.*

Pros

1. Option B probably stands a greater chance than either of the other two of attaining our objectives vis-a-vis Hanoi and a settlement in South Vietnam.

2. Our display of real muscle in action would undoubtedly have a salutary effect on the morale of the rest of non-Communist Asia.

3. The course of military events vis-a-vis Communist China *might* give us a defensible case to destroy the Chinese Communist nuclear production capability.

Cons

1. This course of action has considerably higher risks of major military conflict with Hanoi and possibly Communist China.

2. If we found ourselves thus committed to a major military effort the results could be extremely adverse to our position in other areas, and perhaps to American resolve to maintain present world-wide policies, *unless* we achieved a clearly satisfactory outcome in a fairly short time.

VI (old VII) ANALYSIS OF OPTION C

A. *Rationale and Preparatory Actions.* The rationale of Option C is explained in para III C above. The stated basis for our action would be that documented DRV illegal infiltration of armed and trained insurgents, and over-all DRV direction and control of VC insurgency, had now reached an intolerable level and that it was now necessary to hit at the infiltration from the DRV and to bring pressure on Hanoi to cease this infiltration and direction. The immediate preparatory actions (consistent with all three options) are set out in Part VII (old IX) below. Under this Option C, the following preparatory action should be taken:

1. A firm Presidential statement setting forth our rationale.

2. Information actions, surfacing useable information on DRV infiltration and direction.

3. Consultation with leaders of Congress (no new Resolution needed).

4. Talks with the GVN explaining our plans, providing for GVN participation, and insisting that the GVN "shape up."

5. Appropriate consultation and talks with allies and neutrals—especially the UK, Australia, New Zealand, Thailand, the Philippines and Laos.

B. *Early Military Actions.* There would be advantages if Option C could be initiated following either another "Bien Hoa" or at least strong additional evidence of major infiltration. Absent these "pegs," the actions, in addition to any reprisal actions required from time to time, would be these:

1. Intensification of GVN sea harassment, one or more US destroyer patrols, Lao strikes on infiltration targets in Laos, high-level recce of the DRV, and shallow GVN ground actions in Laos.

2. US air strikes on infiltration targets in Laos, including Route 7.

3. US/VNAF low-level reconnaissance in southern DRV.

4. US/VNAF air strikes against infiltration targets in southern DRV (after removal of US dependents and taking security measures in SVN). In addition to such actions, there is an issue whether we should at an early stage make a significant ground deployment to the northern part of South Vietnam, either in the form of a US combat force (perhaps a division) or a SEATO-members force including at least token contingents from Australia, New Zealand, the UK, Thailand, and the Philippines. Such a force is not a military requirement—at least until or unless the DRV threatened a ground move to the south—but there is a strong political argument that it would demonstrate resolve and also give us a major bargaining counter in negotiations.

C. *Early Negotiating Actions.*

1. *UN.* We would have to defend our position in the Security Council in any case. We would hope that this could be a brief proceeding and we believe that the reactions would be such as to make it crystal clear that the UN could not *act* usefully. (The latter point would be useful to meet critics in the US.)

2. We would resist any formal Geneva conference on Vietnam, since the mere convening of such a conference would have serious morale effects.

3. We would use all available channels to Hanoi and Peiping to make clear our objectives and our determination.

4. At the same time, we would watch and listen closely for reactions from Hanoi and Peiping. If these showed any signs of weakening in their positions, we would then try to follow up as quietly as possible to see what they had in mind. At this stage we would be insisting on three fundamentals: (a) that the DRV cease its assistance to and direction of the VC; (b) that an independent and secure GVN be reestablished; and (c) that there be adequate international supervising and verification machinery. (These fundamentals would not be fully spelled out; in practice they leave room for minor concessions at later stages.)

D. *Probable Communist Responses to Initial Military Actions.*

There are three possible Communist responses to the above initial military actions:

1. Yield visibly (quite unlikely).
2. Retaliate militarily—e.g., by air attacks against South Vietnam or by an offensive in Laos (initially unlikely).
3. Hold firm while stimulating condemnation of US by world opinion, and, if in negotiations, take a tough position (most likely).

E. *If Hanoi Holds Firm.* The initial reaction in South Vietnam to attacks on the DRV would probably be one of elation and might cause a spurt of more effective performance. We would try to capitalize on any improvement in the GVN situation by pressing harder for acceptance of our initial negotiating position, continuing (not needing to step up) our military pressures and trying to establish a "common law" justification for attacks on infiltration and other limited targets in the DRV. But the elation in South Vietnam would probably wane if the war dragged on, and deteriorating trends would probably resume.* In this case, we would have to decide whether to intensify our military actions, modify our negotiating positions, or both. A second phase in our military pressure would here include (5) extension of the target system in the DRV to include additional targets on the "94 target list," (6) aerial mining of DRV ports, and (7) a naval quarantine of the DRV. Any visible modification of our negotiating position at this point would create a major problem, in that key nations on both sides would suspect that we were getting ready for a way out. Hence, any such modifying moves would have to be synchronized with military actions. (Simultaneously, we should strengthen and reassure the nations of the area, possibly involving major additional deployments there.)

Meanwhile, even if the Communists did not attack South Vietnam, they might take steps to reduce our initial advantage by improving air defenses in North Vietnam, deploying Chinese ground forces southward, and hardening their propaganda (thus hardening their public commitment).

F. *If the Communist Side Engaged in Major Military Retaliation.* We reckon major Communist retaliation to be unlikely in the early stages, although a sharp US/GVN reprisal or a Communist misreading of our intent could change this estimate. In the second phase of military action, there would be a progressively increasing chance of major Communist military response.

The more serious Communist responses are (1) stepped-up VC activities in South Vietnam, (2) air attacks on South Vietnam, (3) DRV ground offensive in South Vietnam or Laos, and (4) Chicom ground offensive in Southeast Asia. The US plans and capabilities to counter these Communist responses are contained in the Military Annex to this memorandum.

G. *Possible Over-all Outcomes.* The variable factors are too great to permit a confident evaluation of how the Option C course of action would come out. *At best:* To avoid heavy risk and punishment, the DRV might feign compliance and settle for an opportunity to subvert the South another day. That is, a respite might be gained. *At worst:* South Vietnam might come apart while we were pursuing the course of action. *In between:* We might be faced with no improvement in the internal South Vietnam situation and with the difficult decision whether to escalate on up to major conflict with China.

H. *Pros and Cons of Option C.* Option C is more controllable and less risky of major military action than Option B. Being a "stretched out" course of action,

---

* The Joint Staff believes there is less chance that deterioration would resume and more chance that a listing upward trend in SVN would come about.

however, it is likely to generate criticism in some quarters. It is more likely than Option A to achieve at least part of our objectives, and, even if it ended in the loss of South Vietnam, our having taken stronger measures would still leave us a good deal better off than under Option A with respect to the confidence and willingness to stand firm of the nations in the next line of defense in Asia.

VII   (old IX) IMMEDIATE ACTIONS OVER THE NEXT FEW WEEKS

To bolster South Vietnamese morale and to convey a firm signal to Hanoi and Peiping, we need in any event a program of immediate actions during the coming weeks. The following program could be conducted for a period of four weeks or might be extended to eight weeks or longer as desired:

A.   *A strong White House or Presidential statement* following the meeting with Ambassador Taylor, with the disclosure of the evidence of increased DRV infiltration to be included or to follow promptly.

B.   An order stopping the sending of further dependents to Vietnam.

C.   Stepped-up air operations in Laos against infiltration targets particularly.

D.   Increased high-level reconnaissance of the DRV.

E.   Starting low-level reconnaissance of the DRV.

F.   A small number of strikes just across the DRV border against the infiltration routes.

G.   A destroyer patrol in the Tonkin Gulf and also (but separately) intensified GVN maritime operations along present lines.

H.   Major air deployments to the Philippines and at sea, in position to hit North Vietnam.

I.   At any time, reprisal air strikes against the DRV might be undertaken for a spectacular DRV or VC action whether against US personnel or not. Reprisals would be linked to DRV activity, and the scale of the reprisal action would be determined on a flexible basis in accordance with the magnitude of the hostile action.

In conjunction with the above sequence of actions, we would consult with the GVN to "shape up" in every possible way, through intensifying all present programs, putting military forces on a totally wartime operations basis, tightening security in Saigon and elsewhere, etc.

Congress and our major allies would have to be consulted at an early stage. Our basic rationale would be that the increasing DRV infiltration required this degree of action.

None of these actions are inconsistent in theory with a decision to stick with Option A at least for the next few months. Nonetheless, to the degree they foreshadow stronger action, they would tend to have diminishing effect on GVN performance unless taken concurrently with at least an internal US government decision that we were ready to move to Option C early in 1965 unless the situation changed.

[Document 242]

Taylor briefing 27 Nov 64

Subject: The Current Situation in South Vietnam—November 1964

After a year of changing and ineffective government, the counter-insurgency program country-wide is bogged down and will require heroic treatment to assure revival. Even in the Saigon area, in spite of the planning and the special treatment accorded the Hop Tac plan, this area also is lagging. The northern provinces of South Vietnam which a year ago were considered almost free of Viet Cong are now in deep trouble. In the Quang Ngai–Binh Dinh area, the gains of the Viet Cong have been so serious that once more we are threatened with a partition of the country by a Viet-Cong salient driven to the sea. The pressure on this area has been accompanied by continuous sabotage of the railroad and of Highway 1 which in combination threaten an economic strangulation of the northern provinces.

This deterioration of the pacification program has taken place in spite of the very heavy losses inflicted almost daily on the Viet-Cong and the increase in strength and professional competence of the Armed Forces of South Vietnam. Not only have the Vietcong apparently made good their losses, but of late, have demonstrated three new or newly expanded tactics: The use of stand-off mortar fire against important targets, as in the attack on the Bien Hoa airfield; economic strangulation on limited areas; finally, the stepped-up infiltration of DRV military personnel moving from the north. These new or improved tactics employed against the background of general deterioration offer a serious threat to the pacification program in general and to the safety of important bases and installations in particular.

Perhaps more serious than the downward trend in the pacification situation, because it is the prime cause, is the continued weakness of the central government. Although the Huong government has been installed after executing faithfully and successfully the program laid out by the Khanh government for its own replacement, the chances for the long life and effective performance of the new line-up appear small. Indeed, in view of the factionalism existing in Saigon and elsewhere throughout the country, it is impossible to foresee a stable and effective government under any name in anything like the near future. Nonetheless, we do draw some encouragement from the character and seriousness of purpose of Prime Minister Huong and his cabinet and the apparent intention of General Khanh to keep the Army out of politics, at least for the time being.

As our programs plod along or mark time, we sense the mounting feeling of war weariness and hopelessness which pervade South Vietnam, particularly in the urban areas. Although the provinces for the most part appear steadfast, undoubtedly there is chronic discouragement there as well as in the cities. Although the military leaders have not talked recently with much conviction about the need for "marching North," assuredly, many of them are convinced that some new and drastic action must be taken to reverse the present trends and to offer hope of ending the insurgency in some finite time.

The causes for the present unsatisfactory situation are not hard to find. It stems from two primary causes, both already mentioned above, the continued ineffectiveness of the central government, the increasing strength and effectiveness of the Vietcong and their ability to replace losses.

While in view of the historical record of South Vietnam, it is not surprising to have these governmental difficulties, this chronic weakness is a critical liability to future plans. Without an effective central government with which to mesh the US effort, the latter is a spinning wheel unable to transmit impulsion to the machinery of the GVN. While the most critical governmental weaknesses are in Saigon, they are duplicated to a degree in the provinces. It is most difficult to find adequate provincial chiefs and supporting administrative personnel to carry forward the complex programs which are required in the field for successful pacification. It is true that when one regards the limited background of the provincial chiefs and their associates, one should perhaps be surprised by the results which they have accomplished, but unfortunately, these results are generally not adequate for the complex task at hand or for the time schedule which we would like to establish.

As the past history of this country shows, there seems to be a national attribute which makes for factionalism and limits the development of a truly national spirit. Whether this tendency is innate or a development growing out of the conditions of political suppression under which successive generations have lived is hard to determine. But it is an inescapable fact that there is no national tendency toward team play or mutual loyalty to be found among many of the leaders and political groups within South Vietnam. Given time, many of these conditions will undoubtedly change for the better, but we are unfortunately pressed for time and unhappily perceive no short-term solution for the establishment of stable and sound government.

The ability of the Vietcong continuously to rebuild their units and to make good their losses is one of the mysteries of this guerrilla war. We are aware of the recruiting methods by which local boys are induced or compelled to join the Viet Cong ranks and have some general appreciation of the amount of infiltration of personnel from the outside. Yet taking both of these sources into account, we still find no plausible explanation of the continued strength of the Vietcong if our data on Viet Cong losses are even approximately correct. Not only do the Viet Cong units have the recuperative powers of the phoenix, but they have an amazing ability to maintain morale. Only in rare cases have we found evidences of bad morale among Viet Cong prisoners or recorded in captured Viet Cong documents.

Undoubtedly one cause for the growing strength of the VietCong is the increased direction and support of their campaign by the government of North Vietnam. This direction and support take the form of endless radioed orders and instructions, and the continuous dispatch to South Vietnam of trained cadre and military equipment, over infiltration routes by land and by water. While in the aggregate, this contribution to the guerrilla campaign over the years must represent a serious drain on the resources of the DRV, that government shows no sign of relaxing its support of the Viet Cong. In fact, the evidence points to an increased contribution over the last year, a plausible development, since one would expect the DRV to press hard to exploit the obvious internal weaknesses in the south.

If, as the evidence shows, we are playing a losing game in South Vietnam, it is high time we change and find a better way. To change the situation, it is quite clear that we need to do three things: first, establish an adequate government in SVN; second, improve the conduct of the counter insurgency campaign; and, finally, persuade or force the DRV to stop its aid to the Viet Cong and to use its directive powers to make the Viet Cong desist from their efforts to overthrow the government of South Vietnam.

With regard to the first objective, it is hard to decide what is the minimum government which is necessary to permit reasonable hope for the success of our efforts. We would certainly like to have a government which is capable of maintaining law and order, of making and executing timely decisions, of carrying out approved programs, and generally of leading its people and gearing its efforts effectively with those of the United States.

As indicated above, however, it seems highly unlikely that we will see such a government of South Vietnam in the time frame available to us to reverse the downward trend of events. It seems quite probable that we will be obliged to settle for something considerably less.

However, it is hard to visualize our being willing to make added outlays of resources and to run increasing political risks without an allied government which, at least, can speak for and to its people, can maintain law and order in the principal cities, can provide local protection for the vital military bases and installations, can raise and support Armed Forces, and can gear its efforts to those of the United States. Anything less than this would hardly be a government at all, and under such circumstances, the United States Government might do better to carry forward the war on a purely unilateral basis.

The objective of an improved counter insurgency program will depend for its feasibility upon the capacity of the South Vietnamese government. We cannot do much better than what we are doing at present until the government improves. However, we need to have our plans and means organized on the assumption that some improvement will occur and will permit intensified efforts toward the pacification of the country.

In any case, we feel sure that even after establishing some reasonably satisfactory government and effecting some improvement in the counterinsurgency program, we will not succeed in the end unless we drive the DRV out of its reinforcing role and obtain its cooperation in bringing an end to the Viet Cong insurgency.

To attain these three objectives, we must consider what are the possible courses of action which are open to us. To improve the government we will, of course, continue to aid, advise and encourage it much as we are doing at the present time. We will try to restrain, insofar as we can, the minority groups bent upon its overthrow. We will indicate clearly the desire of the United States Government to see an end to the succession of weak and transitory governments and we will throw all of our influence on the side of stabilizing programs both for organizations and for personnel.

As these efforts in themselves will probably be inadequate, we should also consider ways and means to raise the morale and restore the confidence both of the government and of the South Vietnamese people. One way to accomplish this lift of morale would be to increase the covert operations against North Vietnam by sea and air and the counter-infiltration attacks within the Laotian corridor. While the former would be covert in the sense of being disavowed, nonetheless the knowledge of their occurrence could be made known in such a way as to give the morale lift which is desired. Additionally, we could engage in reprisal bombings, to repay outrageous acts of the Vietcong in South Vietnam, such as the attack on Bien Hoa.

All these actions, however, may not be sufficient to hold the present government upright. If it fails, we are going to be in deep trouble, with limited resources for subsequent actions. It is true that we could try again with another civilian government but the odds against it would be even higher than those which have confronted the Huong government. We might try in a second civilian government to take over operational control by US officials if indeed the GVN would agree to this change. However, there are more objections to this form of US intervention than there are arguments in favor of it. Another alternative would be to invite back a military dictatorship on the model of that headed of late by General Khanh. However, Khanh did very poorly when he was on the spot and we have little reason to believe that a successor military government could be more effective. Finally, we always have the option of withdrawing, leaving the internal situation to the Vietnamese, and limiting our contribution to military action directed at North Vietnam. Such action, while assuring that North Vietnam would pay a price for its misdeeds in the South, would probably not save South Vietnam from eventual loss to the Viet Cong.

There is little to say about the ways and means of intensifying the in-country counterinsurgency program except to recognize again that this program depends entirely upon the government. If we can solve the governmental problem, we can improve the in-country program.

In bringing military pressure to bear on North Vietnam, there are a number of variations which are possible. At the bottom of the ladder of escalation, we have the initiation of intensified covert operations, anti-infiltration attacks in Laos, and reprisal bombings mentioned above as a means for stiffening South Vietnamese morale. From this level of operations, we could begin to escalate progressively by attacking appropriate targets in North Vietnam. If we justified our action primarily upon the need to reduce infiltration, it would be natural to direct these attacks on infiltration-related targets such as staging areas, training facilities, communications centers and the like. The tempo and weight of the attacks could be varied according to the effects sought. In its final forms, this kind of attack could extend to the destruction of all important fixed targets in North Vietnam and to the interdiction of movement on all lines of communication.

Before making a final decision on any of the courses of action, it will be necessary to have a heart-to-heart talk with Prime Minister Huong and General Khanh to find out their reaction to the alternatives which we are considering. They will be taking on risks as great or greater than ours so that they have a right to a serious hearing. We should make every effort to get them to ask our help in expanding the war. If they decline, we shall have to rethink the whole situation. If, as is likely, they urge us with enthusiasm, we should take advantage of the opportunity to nail down certain important points such as:

a. The GVN undertakes (1) to maintain the strength of its military and police forces; (2) to replace incompetent military commanders and province chiefs and to leave the competent ones in place for an indefinite period; (3) to suppress disorders and demonstrations; (4) to establish effective resources control; and (5) to obtain US concurrence for all military operations outside of South Vietnam.

b. The US undertakes responsibility for the air and maritime defense of South Vietnam.

c. The GVN takes responsibility for the land defense of South Vietnam to include the protection of all US nationals and installations.

d. The GVN accepts the US statement (to be prepared) of war aims and circumstances for negotiations.

Shortly after initiating an escalation program it will be important to communicate with the DRV and the CHICOMS to establish certain essential points in the minds of their leaders. The first is that under no circumstances will the United States let the DRV go unscathed and reap the benefits of its nefarious actions in South Vietnam without paying a heavy price. Furthermore, we will not accept any statement from the DRV to the effect that it is not responsible for the Viet Cong insurgency and that it cannot control the Viet Cong actions. We know better and will act accordingly. However, the enemy should know that the United States objectives are limited. We are not seeking to unify North and South Vietnam; we are seeking no permanent military presence in Southeast Asia. But on the other hand, we do insist that the DRV let its neighbors, South Vietnam and Laos, strictly alone.

Furthermore, we are not trying to change the nature of the government in Hanoi. If the North Vietnamese prefer a Communist government, that is their choice to make. If the DRV remain aloof from the CHICOMS in a Tito-like state, we would not be adverse to aiding such a government provided it conducted itself decently with its neighbors.

But with all, we are tired of standing by and seeing the unabashed efforts of the DRV to absorb South Vietnam into the Communist orbit against its will. We know that Hanoi is responsible and that we are going to punish it until it desists from this behavior.

Just how and when such a communication should be transmitted should be a subject of careful study. But, some such transmission is required to assure that the Communists in the North know exactly what is taking place and will continue to take place.

We can be reasonably sure that the DRV, and Viet Cong will not take such offensive actions on our part without a reaction. Already the Viet Cong, assisted from Hanoi, are doing many things to hamper and harass the central and local governments of South Vietnam, to encourage minorities to resist Saigon and to foster the spirit of neutralism and defeatism everywhere. They are quite capable of intensifying such actions, of raising the level of harassments of people and officials, of mounting mortar attacks on the model of Bien Hoa, and of continuing to try to effect the economic strangulation of many areas within South Vietnam.

There are several courses of action which they could adopt which are presently not on their program. They can call for international intervention to force us to desist from our pressures. They can engage in limited air and ground attacks in South Vietnam using formed units of the armies of North Vietnam and perhaps volunteers from Red China. It is quite likely that they will invite some CHICOM military forces into the DRV if only to reinforce its air defense. Furthermore, they have some limited seaborne capability for raids against the South Vietnamese coast.

If their counter actions failed and our pressures became unbearable, the DRV might feign submission and undertake to lie low for a time. They would probably, however, insist that they do not have the capability of compelling the Viet Cong to lay down their arms and become law-abiding citizens. Any temporary reduction of their support of the Viet Cong could, of course, be resumed at any time after the United States had been cajoled into leaving the scene of action.

In view of the foregoing considerations, we reach the point where a decision must be taken as to what course or courses of action we should undertake to change the tide which is running against us. It seems perfectly clear that we must work to the maximum to make something out of the present Huong government or any successor thereto. While doing so, we must be thinking constantly of what we would do if our efforts are unsuccessful and the government collapses. Concurrently, we should stay on the present in-country program, intensifying it as possible in proportion to the current capabilities of the government. To bolster the local morale and restrain the Viet Cong during this period, we should step up the 34-A operations, engage in bombing attacks and armed recce in the Laotion corridor and undertake reprisal bombing as required. It will be important that United States forces take part in the Laotian operations in order to demonstrate to South Vietnam our willingness to share in the risks of attacking the North.

If this course of action is inadequate, and the government falls, then we must start over again or try a new approach. At this moment, it is premature to say exactly what these new measures should be. In any case, we should be prepared for emergency military action against the North if only to shore up a collapsing situation.

If, on the other hand as we hope, the government maintains and proves itself, then we should be prepared to embark on a methodical program of mounting air attacks in order to accomplish our pressure objectives vis-a-vis the DRV and at the same time do our best to improve in-country pacification program. We will leave negotiation initiatives to Hanoi. Throughout this period, our guard must be up in the Western Pacific, ready for any reaction by the DRV or of Red China. Annex I suggests the train of events which we might set in motion.

Whatever the course of events, we should adhere to three principles:

a. Do not enter into negotiations until the DRV is hurting.

b. Never let the DRV gain a victory in South Vietnam without having paid a disproportionate price.

c. Keep the GVN in the forefront of the combat and the negotiations.

Maxwell D. Taylor

ANNEX I

SUGGESTED SCENARIO FOR CONTROLLED ESCALATION

(The following suggests a sequence of events without at this time attempting to establish precise time intervals. It assumes that 34-A operations and corridor strikes including armed reconnaissance in Laos have been continuing for some period prior to initiating scenario. It also assumes that background briefing on infiltration has been given in both Saigon and Washington.)

1. Definitive discussions with GVN to obtain firm GVN request for joint action against DRV and to reach agreement on the framework of demands to be made on the DRV as well as on general negotiating procedures. (See 15 below)

2. Initiate discussions with Thai Government.

3. Initiate discussions with other selected friendly governments.

4. Quietly initiate necessary preparatory military moves that have thus far not been taken. (Preparatory military moves should have included or include stationing of Hawk battalion and F-105's at Danang, a MEB afloat off Danang and the alerting of the 173rd ABG).

5. Initiate discussions with RLG.

6. Cease travel to Vietnam of additional dependents, but take no action to evacuate dependents already in Vietnam pending further developments.

7. An appropriate intermediary tells Hanoi nothing has been heard from the US; he is concerned over the situation; and does Hanoi have anything to pass on to the US?

8. Yankee Team strikes Route Seven targets in Laos.

9. RLAF attack on DRV side of Mua Gia Pass with US air CAP.

10. A single VNAF air strike against an infiltration target in DRV just north of DMZ.

11. A significant MAROP supported by US air cover.

12. GVN–US air strike on an infiltration target just north of DMZ.

13. Continue limited military actions in the foregoing categories sequentially with not more than a few days gap between each, while being prepared promptly to make higher level responses to attacks from MIGs or V-C spectaculars in SVN.

14. Throughout the foregoing, in absence of public statements by DRV, initiate no public statement or publicity by ourselves or GVN. If DRV does make public statements, confine ourselves and GVN to statements that GVN is exercising right of self-defense and we are assisting.

15. In light of developments, disclose to selected allies, and possibly USSR, US/GVN terms for cessation of attacks as follows: (It will be important to assure that one of these channels undertakes accurately and fully to communicate these terms to both Hanoi and Peking)

    A. Demands:

        1. DRV return to strict observance of 1954 Accords with respect to SVN—that is, stop infiltration and bring about a cessation of VC armed insurgency. (Query—should demand include DRV observance of 1962 accords with respect to Laos and how should such demand be framed so as to give ICC Laos effective role in monitoring infiltration through Laos?)

    B. In return:

        1. US will return to 1954 Accords with respect to military personnel in GVN and GVN would be willing to enter into trade talks looking toward normalization of economic relations between DRV and GVN.

        2. Subject to faithful compliance by DRV with 1954 Accords, US and GVN would give assurances that they would not use force or support the use of force by any other party to upset the Accords with respect to the DRV.

        3. Within the framework of the 1954 Accords, the GVN would permit VC desiring to do so to return to the DRV without their arms or would grant amnesty to those peacefully laying down their arms and desiring to remain in SVN.

    C. If and when Hanoi indicates its acceptance of foregoing conditions, careful considerations must be given to immediate subsequent procedures which will avoid dangers of (a) becoming involved in a cease fire vis-a-vis the DRV and/or the VC accompanied by strung-out negotiations; (b) making conditions so stringent as to be unworkable from practical point of view. Probably best procedure would be to have the GVN and DRV meet in the DMZ under ICC auspices with US observers to reach agreement on mechanics of carrying out understanding while action against the VC and DRV continues, at least in principle.

[Document 243]

27 November 1964

SUMMARY OF RECENT MACV AND CIA CABLES
ON INFILTRATION

1. The working team in Saigon has examined the MACV materials and methods and concludes that the 31 October MACV study of infiltration is essentially correct in reporting a larger number of infiltrators than was reported by MACV in its April 1964 study.

2. The team concluded that on the "basis of the presently available information, it considers 19,000 infiltrators from 1959 to the present as a firm (confirmed) minimum. In regard to the estimated figure given in the MACV 31 October study for the total number of infiltrators since 1959 (approximately 34,000), the team believes that it represents a maximum on the basis of present information.

3. The team broke the PW interrogation reports and captured documents into several categories: Category A consists of sources and documents which have been confirmed in whole or in part by other sources or documents; Category B consists of sources whose information is probably true but not yet confirmed by other sources; Category C is all others. The total for Category A from 1959 to the present is 21,889 (of these some 2,756 may be duplications, leaving the firm (confirmed)) total of 19,133 infiltrators . . . Category B consists of 7,433 infiltrators which the team considers probable. Another 4,646 are in Category C as possible infiltrators.

4. The totals reported in the MACV October 1964 study are based on a compilation of evaluated reports selected on the same standards as the reports used to prepare previous MACV infiltration studies. The drastic increase reported in infiltrators in the October study results primarily, according to the team, from the greater number of prisoner interrogation reports. The April 1964 study, for example, was based on 85 interrogees, and the October study on 187. Previous MACV studies had been based on less than 30 prisoners.

5. For the most part, MACV has used a conservative approach, according to the team, in analyzing the available data. They note that as additional data continues to become available, upward refinements are likely. Furthermore, there almost certainly have been other groups of infiltrators of which there is no present knowledge.

6. The team concluded that in view of the wide difference between confirmed, probable and possible infiltrators, the significance of the infiltration to the insurgency cannot be defined with precision. However, it is clear that most of the leadership of the VC has been provided by infiltration, and it appears that infiltrated personnel constitute the bulk of the main and local force units in the Communist Military Region 5 in the northern part of South VN.

7. The team investigated the possibility that the GVN was doctoring the interrogation reports for its own purpose, and was assured by MACV that there was very little indication that this had occurred.

[Document 244]

DEPARTMENT OF STATE ** ASSISTANT SECRETARY

Nov 27, 1964

MEMORANDUM OF MEETING ON SOUTHEAST ASIA

November 27, 1964

Present: Sec Rusk   Mssrs. Ball
         Sec McNamara   McGeorge Bundy
         Amb Taylor   William Bundy
         Mr. McCone   McNaughton
         Gen. Wheeler   Forrestal

1. The question was raised of what message to the GVN would make them perform better. Ambassador Taylor thought that he must have a strong message but that any threat of "withdrawal unless" would be quite a "gamble." It was noted that it was still possible to stress that we could not help as we would like unless the GVN did shape up.

2. There was discussion of whether we could carry on "unilateral" military

actions if the GVN collapsed or told us to get out. The consensus was that it was hard to visualize continuing in these circumstances, but that the choice must certainly be avoided if at all possible.

3. Ambassador Taylor noted that "neutralism" as it existed in Saigon appeared to mean throwing the internal political situation open and thus inviting Communist participation. There was discussion of neutralism in the sense of withdrawal of external assistance, and the opinion was expressed that external assistance would remain essential unless the VC was defeated and that neutralism either in the sense of no more external assistance or in the sense of a free political system could not be maintained unless this was done.

4. Ambassador Taylor, upon being asked about the problem of administrative cumbersomeness, said that some progress had been made and that this problem could be handled if the GVN itself got going. He expressed the general view that newspaper reports exaggerated the weakness of the present government, that Huong had many fine qualities, and that he, Vien, and Khanh could mesh into a reasonably effective team if they could handle sniping from the Buddhists and students. The Ambassador noted that there was no prospect of a widely based Assembly for some months, but that such an Assembly, if it came, could be serious in causing general static and possibly leading to some Communist representation. In answer to a question, Ambassador Taylor said that General Khanh was performing quite effectively, was out in the field except for weekends, and had made many military command changes of which General Westmoreland approved. Khanh had said that he would make no more changes.

5. Ambassador Taylor noted that General Westmoreland had prepared a report of the military situation, which he would distribute to the group. Westmoreland was generally more optimistic than he, Taylor, and saw many signs and possibilities of improvement on the military side. Westmoreland would be inclined to wait six months to have a firmer base for stronger actions. However, the Ambassador said that he himself did not believe that we could count on the situation holding together that long, and that we must do something sooner than this. Secretary McNamara noted his disagreement with General Westmoreland's views. The view was expressed that the political situation was not likely to become stronger but that nonetheless the US was justified in taking measures along the lines of Option C. Ambassador Taylor noted that stronger action would definitely have a favorable effect on GVN and South Vietnamese performance and morale, but he was not sure this would be enough really to improve the situation. Others in the group agreed with this evaluation, and the view was expressed that the strengthening effect of Option C could at least buy time, possibly measured in years.

It was urged that over the next two months we adopt a program of Option A plus the first stages of Option C. The likelihood of improvement in the government seemed so doubtful that to get what improvement we could it was thought that we should move into some parts of C soon.

6. Ambassador Taylor gave details of the kind of message he would propose giving to the GVN. (This will be incorporated into the draft scenario for discussion at the next meeting.)

7. There was discussion of the infiltration evidence, and it was agreed that State and Defense should check statements made by Secretary Rusk, Secretary McNamara, and General Wheeler on this subject, so that these could be related to the previous MACV and other estimates and a full explanation developed of how these earlier estimates had been made and why they had been wrong in the light of fuller evidence.

8. Ambassador Taylor stressed the importance of police forces and said that we would recommend holding the Popular Forces at the present level but stressing additional police. He noted that the police had better pay and perquisites than the armed forces and thought that this was right.

Ambassador Taylor raised a series of questions which he did not think had been adequately covered in the papers. (This list will be circulated separately.)

9. It was agreed that we needed a more precise and fully spelled out scenario of what would be proposed if a decision were taken to adopt a general program along the lines of Section VII of the Draft Summary (Immediate Actions), with or without a decision to move into the full Option C program at some time thereafter. Mr. Wm. Bundy undertook to produce a draft scenario along these lines for discussion at the next meeting of the group, which was scheduled for 11:00 am on Sat., Nov. 28.

FE:WPBundy:mk

[Document 245]

November 28, 1964

MEMORANDUM FOR SOUTHEAST ASIA PRINCIPALS

Subject: Scenario for Immediate Action Program

I have gone over with the Working Group the problem of a scenario for carrying out the Immediate Action Program (Section VII of the draft summary) or Ambassador Taylor's recommended sequence, which comes very close to the same ingredients. We have tried to work on this on the alternative assumption, that a decision is *or is not* taken to go on with Option C thereafter if Hanoi does not bend or the GVN come apart. Frankly, the Working Group inclines more and more to the view that at least a contingent decision to go on *is* now required.

The problem is a difficult one, a real jigsaw puzzle in which you have to weigh at every point the viewpoints of:

a. The American Congress and public.
b. Saigon.
c. Hanoi and Peiping.
d. Key interested nations.

At this point, I don't see how all can be met at all points, but I have attacked it by listing the actions that might be included and setting up worksheets for each, with an indication of their possible timing and substance. So much depends on the actual terms of the President's decision that we should in any case avoid getting too firmly fixed on all elements. This will need a lot of work before the Tuesday meeting, and quite possibly after as well.

William P. Bundy

CHECKLIST FOR SCENARIO ACTIONS

I. *US Public Actions*
   A. White House statement following Tuesday meeting
   B. Background briefing on infiltration in both Saigon and Washington
   C. Congressional Consultation

D. Major speech
E. Jorden Report
II. *GVN*
A. Consultation with GVN
B. GVN statement
III. *Key Allies*
A. Consultation with RLG
B. Consultation with Thai
C. Consultation with UK, Australia, New Zealand, and Philippines.
D. SEATO Council statement (?)
IV. *Communist Nations*
A. Signals and messages to Hanoi and Peiping
B. What to say to Soviets (and Poles?)
V. *Other Nations*
A. Canada, India, and France
B. UN is required
VI. *Existing Categories of Military Actions*
A. US Laos reconnaissance
B. RLAF attacks in Laos
C. GVN MAROPS
D. US high-level reconnaissance of DRV
VII. *Reprisal Actions*
A. Renewed DESOTO patrol
B. Another Bien Hoa or other spectacular
VIII. *Added Military or Other Actions*
A. Stopping flow of dependents
B. YT strikes in Laos: infiltration areas, Route 7
C. US low-level reconnaissance over DRV
D. Strikes across the border into DRV: GVN and US roles

[Document 246]

November 29, 1964

DEPARTMENT OF STATE
Assistant Secretary

MEMORANDUM FOR SOUTHEAST ASIA PRINCIPALS:

I attach a draft action paper for review at the meeting at 1:30 on Monday in Secretary Rusk's Conference Room. Secretary Rusk has generally approved the format of these papers, and they have been given a preliminary review for substance by Ambassador Taylor and Messrs. McNaughton and Forrestal. However, I am necessarily responsible for the way they are now drafted.

William P. Bundy

Attachment:

Draft action paper.

FE:WPBundy:mk

DRAFT
WPBundy:mk
11/29/64

DRAFT POSITION PAPER ON SOUTHEAST ASIA

I. *Concept*

A. US objectives in South Vietnam (SVN) are unchanged. They are to:

1. Get Hanoi and North Vietnam (DRV) support and direction removed from South Vietnam, and, to the extent possible, obtain DRV cooperation in ending Viet Cong (VC) operations in SVN.

2. Re-establish an independent and secure South Vietnam with appropriate international safeguards, including the freedom to accept US and other external assistance as required.

3. Maintain the security of other non-Communist nations in Southeast Asia including specifically the maintenance and observance of the Geneva Accords of 1962 in Laos.

B. We will continue to press the SVN Government (GVN) in every possible way to make the government itself more effective and to push forward with the pacification program.

C. We will join at once with the South Vietnamese and Lao Governments in a determined action program aimed at DRV activities in both countries and designed to help GVN morale and to increase the costs and strain on Hanoi, foreshadowing still greater pressures to come. Under this program the first phase actions (see Tab. D) within the next thirty days will be intensified forms of action already under way, plus (1) US armed reconnaissance strikes in Laos, and (2) GVN and possibly US air strikes against the DRV, as reprisals against any major or spectacular Viet Cong action in the south, whether against US personnel and installations or not.

D. Beyond the thirty-day period, first phase actions may be continued without change, or additional military measures may be taken, including the withdrawal of dependents and the possible initiation of strikes a short distance across the border against the infiltration routes from the DRV. In the latter case this would become a transitional phase.

E. Thereafter, if the GVN improves its effectiveness to an acceptable degree and Hanoi does not yield on acceptable terms, [or if the GVN can only be kept going by stronger action] the US is prepared—at a time to be determined—to enter into a second phase program, in support of the GVN and RLG, of graduated military pressures directed systematically against the DRV. Such a program would consist principally of progressively more serious air strikes, of a weight and tempo adjusted to the situation as it develops (possibly running from two to six months). Targets in the DRV would start with infiltration targets south of the 19th parallel and work up to targets north of that point. This could eventually lead to such measures as air strikes on all major military-related targets, aerial mining of DRV ports, and a US naval blockade of the DRV. The whole sequence of military actions would be designed to give the impression of a steady, deliberate approach, and to give the US the option at any time (subject to enemy reaction) to proceed or not, to escalate or not, and to quicken the pace or not. Concurrently, the US would be alert to any sign of yielding by Hanoi, and would be prepared to explore negotiated solutions that attain US objectives in an acceptable manner. [The US would seek to control any negotiations and would oppose any independent South Vietnamese efforts to negotiate.]

Note

The Joint Chiefs of Staff recommend immediate initiation of sharply intensified military pressures against the DRV, starting with a sharp and early attack in force on the DRV, subsequent to brief operations in Laos and US low-level reconnaissance north of the boundary to divert DRV attention prior to the attack in force. This program would be designed to destroy in the first three days Phuc Yen airfield near Hanoi, other airfields, and major POL facilities, clearly to establish the fact that the US intends to use military force to the full limits of what military force can contribute to achieving US objectives in Southeast Asia, and to afford the GVN respite by curtailing DRV assistance to and direction of the Viet Cong. The follow-on military program—involving armed reconnaissance of infiltration routes in Laos, air strikes on infiltration targets in the DRV, and then progressive strikes throughout North Vietnam—could be suspended short of full destruction of the DRV if our objectives were earlier achieved. The military program would be conducted rather swiftly, but the tempo could be adjusted as needed to contribute to achieving our objectives.

DRAFT STATEMENT TO GVN

During the recent review in Washington of the situation in SVN, it came out clearly that the unsatisfactory progress being made in the pacification of the Viet Cong was the result of two primary causes from which many secondary causes stemmed; first, the governmental instability in Saigon and the second, the continued reinforcement and direction of the VC by the DRV. To change the downward trend of events, it will be necessary to deal adequately with both of these factors.

It is clear, however, that these factors are not of equal importance. There must be a stable, effective government to conduct a successful campaign against the VC even if the aid of the DRV for the VC should end. While the elimination of DRV intervention will raise morale on our side and make it easier for the government to function, it is not an end in itself but rather an important contributory factor to the creation of conditions favoring a successful counterinsurgency campaign. But to obtain this contribution, we do not believe that we should incur the risks which are inherent in any expansion of hostilities without first assuring that there is a government in Saigon capable of handling the serious problems involved in such an expansion and of exploiting the favorable effects which may be anticipated from the elimination of the DRV.

It is this consideration which has borne heavily on the recent deliberations in Washington and has conditioned the conclusions reached. There have been many expressions of admiration for the courage being shown by the Huong government which has the complete support of the USG in its resistance to the minority pressure groups which are attempting to drag it down. However, the difficulties which it is encountering raise inevitable questions as to its viability and as to its readiness to discharge the responsibilities which would devolve upon it if some of the new measures under consideration were taken.

There has been discussion of the minimum criteria for governmental performance which would justify or, indeed, make possible, the taking of these new measures. At a minimum, the government should be able to speak for and to its people who will need guidance and leadership throughout the coming critical period. It should be capable of maintaining law and order in its principal centers of population, make plans for the conduct of operations and assure their effective execution by military and police forces completely responsive to its authority. It must have the means to cope with the enemy reactions which must be expected to result from any change in the pattern of our operations. Throughout, it will be essential that the GVN and the USG cooperate closely and effectively as loyal allies dedicated to the attainment of the same objectives. These objectives in the broadest terms are to cause the DRV to respect the rights of its neighbors, to terminate the Viet Cong insurgency and to effect a return to the conditions of the 1954 agreement.

Until we are reasonably sure that such a government is in place in Saigon, the USG considers it unwise for itself and its allies to commit themselves to a deliberate expansion of operations against the territory of the DRV. It is willing, however, to take an important step in that direction by striking harder at the infiltration routes leading out of the DRV both by land and by sea. In conjunction with the RLG, it is prepared to add US air power as needed to restrict the use of Laotian territory as an infiltration route into SVN. At sea, it is ready to reinforce the so-called covert MAROPS using US aircraft to cover these operations. To provide this cover, it will be necessary to divest MAROPS of their present covert character and, sooner or later, the USG will be obliged to explain its actions to its own people.

While these intensive operations are going on, the armed forces of the GVN and the USG must be ready to execute prompt reprisals for any unusual hostile action such as the attack on U.S. vessels in the Gulf of Tonkin or on the airfield at Bien Hoa. The U.S. Mission is authorized to work out with the GVN appropriate plans and procedures to this end.

It is hoped that this phase will prove to be merely preliminary to direct military pressure on the DRV after the GVN has shown itself firmly in control. Indeed, the actions undertaken in this first phase should provide encouragement and enlist popular support for the government and thus facilitate its task. The time provided by this phase can be used to advantage in filling up the strength of the RVNAF and the police, in making operational the four VNAF squadrons, in assuring that the most competent officials and officers are in the key positions of the government and the Armed Forces, and in preparing for the next phase— direct pressure on the DRV.

This second phase, in general terms, would constitute a series of air attacks progressively mounting in scope and intensity for the purpose of convincing the leaders of the DRV that it is to their interest to cease to aid the VC and to restore the conditions contemplated in the agreements of 1954. The participants in these attacks, as we visualize them, would be the air forces of the GVN, of the USG and, we hope, of the RLG. The USG would participate (as at present) in support of the RVNAF and at the request of the GVN. We would work out joint plans and, prior to implementation, would agree on war aims, joint declarations, and the manner of conducting operations outside of SVN. The U.S. Mission is authorized to initiate such planning now with the GVN with the understanding that the USG does not commit itself now to any form of implementation.

The USG would be grateful to receive as soon as possible the reaction of the GVN to the foregoing expression of views.

A. A White House Statement will be issued following the meeting with Ambassador Taylor, with the text as in Tab A, attached.

B. Ambassador Taylor will consult with the GVN promptly on his return, making a general presentation in accordance with the draft instructions in Tab

B, attached. He will further press for action on specific measures such as those listed in Tab B.

C. At the earliest feasible date, we will publicize the evidence of increased DRV infiltration. This action will be coordinated by Mr. Chester Cooper in order to insure that the evidence is sound and that senior government officials who have testified on this subject in the past are in a position to defend and explain the differences between the present estimates and those given in the past. The publicizing will take four forms:

1. An on-the-record presentation will be made to the press in Washington, concurrently with an on-the-record or background presentation to the press in Saigon.

2. Available Congressional leaders will be given special briefings. (No special leadership meeting will be convened for this purpose.)

3. The Ambassadors of key allied nations will be given special briefings.

4. A written report will be prepared and published within the next ten days giving greater depth and background to the evidence.

D. *Laos and Thailand.* The US Ambassadors in these countries will inform the government leaders in general terms of the concept we propose to follow and of specific actions requiring their concurrence or participation. In the case of Laos, we will obtain RLG approval of an intensified program of US armed reconnaissance strikes both in the Panhandle area of Laos and along the key infiltration routes in central Laos. These actions will not be publicized except to the degree approved by the RLG. It is important, however, for purposes of morale in SVN, that their existence be generally known.

Thailand will be asked to support our program fully, to intensify its own efforts in the north and northeast, and to give further support to operations in Laos, such as additional pilots and possibly artillery teams.

E. *Key Allies.* We will consult immediately with the UK, Australia, New Zealand and the Philippines.

1. *UK.* The President will explain the concept and proposed actions fully to Prime Minister Wilson, seeking full British support, but without asking for any additional British contribution in view of the British role in Malaysia.

2. Australia and New Zealand will be pressed, through their Ambassadors, not only for support, but for . . .

3. The Philippines will be particularly pressed for additional contributions along the lines of the program for approximately 1800 men already submitted to President Macapagal.

F. We will press generally for more third country aid, stressing the gravity of the situation and our deepening concern. A summary of existing third country aid and of the types of aid that might now be obtained is in Tab C, attached.

G. *Communist Countries.*

1. We will convey to Hanoi our unchanged determination and our objec-. tives, and that we have a growing concern at the DRV role, to see if there is any sign of change in Hanoi's position.

2. We will make no special approaches to Communist China in this period.

3. We will convey our determination and grave concern to the Soviets, not in the expectation of any change in their position but in effect to warn them to stay out, and with some hope they will pass on the message to Hanoi and Peiping.

H. *Other Countries.*

1. We will convey our grave concern to key interested governments such as Canada, India, and France, but avoid spelling out the concept fully.

2. In the event of a reprisal action, we will explain and defend our action in the UN as at the time of the Gulf of Tonkin incident. We do not plan to raise the issue otherwise in the UN. (The Lao Government may stress the DRV infiltration in Laos in its speech, and we should support this and spread the information.)

I. *Intensified Military Actions.*

1. GVN maritime operations (MAROPS) will be intensified, including US air protection of GVN vessels from attacks by Migs or DRV surface vessels. We will urge the GVN to surface and defend these as wholly justified in response to the wholly illegal DRV actions.

2. Lao air operations will be intensified, especially in the corridor areas and close to the DRV border. US air cover and flak suppression may be supplied if needed.

3. US high-level reconnaissance over the DRV will be stepped up.

4. US armed air reconnaissance and air strikes will be carried out in Laos, first against the corridor area and within a short time against Route 7 and other infiltration routes in a major operation to cut key bridges. (These actions will be publicized only to the degree agreed with Souvanna.)

J. *Reprisal Actions.* For any VC provocation similar to the following, a reprisal will be undertaken, preferably within 24 hours, against one or more selected targets in the DRV. GVN forces will be used to the maximum extent, supplemented as necessary by US forces. The exact reprisal will be decided at the time, in accordance with a quick-reaction procedure which will be worked out.

The following may be appropriate occasions for reprisals, but we should be alert for any appropriate occasion:

1. Attacks on airfields.
2. Attack on Saigon.
3. Attacks on provincial or district capitals.
4. Major attacks on US citizens.
5. Attacks on major POL facilities.
6. Attacks on bridges and railroad lines after the presently damaged facilities have been restored and warning given.
7. Other "spectaculars" such as earlier attack on a US transport carrier at a pier in Saigon.

In these or similar cases, the reprisal action would be linked as directly as possible to DRV infiltration, so that we have a common thread of justification.

A flexible list of reprisal targets has been prepared running from infiltration targets in the southern part of the DRV up to airfields, ports, and naval bases also located south of the 19th parallel.

K. *US/GVN Joint Planning* will be initiated immediately both for reprisal actions and for possible later air strikes across the border into the DRV.

L. *Major Statement or Speech.* Depending on US public reaction, a major statement or speech may be undertaken by the President during this period. This will necessarily be required if a reprisal action is taken, but some other significant action, such as the stopping of the flow of US dependents, might be the occasion. Such a statement or speech would re-state our objectives and our determination, why we are in South Vietnam, and how gravely we view the situation. It should in any event follow the full publicizing of infiltration evidence.

M. *Dependents.* The flow of dependents to South Vietnam will be stopped [at an early date, probably immediately after Ambassador Taylor has consulted with the GVN] [at the start of the second phase], and this will be publicly announced.

N. *Deferred Actions.* (see Tab D)

The following actions will not be taken within the thirty-day period, but will be considered for adoption in the transitional or second phases of the program:

1. Major air deployments to the area.

2. Furnishing US air cover for GVN MAROPS.

3. Be prepared to resume destroyer patrols in the Gulf of Tonkin. If attacked, these would be an alternative basis for reprisals, and should be considered primarily in this light.

4. US low-level reconnaissance into the DRV.

5. GVN/US air strikes across the borders, initially against the infiltration routes and installations and then against targets south of the 19th parallel.

6. Be prepared to evacuate US dependents.

[Document 247]

DRAFT: January 4, 1965—Observations Re South Vietnam—JTM

1) (Scarcely needs to be said: Pique should not be allowed to make policy.) [This is a comment on Max Taylor's attitude toward Khanh and his dissolution of the high national council.] [Author of bracketed material not known.]

2) Our stakes in South Vietnam are:

   (a) Buffer real estate near Thailand and Malaysia and
   (b) Our reputation.

The latter is more important than the former; the latter is sensitive to how, as well as whether, the area is lost.

3) The best present estimate is that South Vietnam is being "lost." From the point of view of the real estate this means that a government not unfriendly to the DRV will probably emerge within two years; from the point of view of our reputation, it will suffer least if we continue to support South Vietnam and if Khanh and company continue to behave like children if the game is lost.

4) The situation could change for the better over night, however. This happened in the Philippines. This is another reason for d - - - - - - perseverance.

5) We should continue to try to do better inside South Vietnam. ("The people do not support the government; their indication is that the GVN treats prisoners badly; etc.")

6) Essentials of U.S. conduct: (a) continue to take risks on behalf of South Vietnam. A reprisal should be carried out soon. (Dependents could be removed at that time.) [This attitude reflected my own arguments, for better or worse.]; (b) keep slugging away. Keep help flowing but do not increase the number of U.S. men in South Vietnam. (Additional U.S. soldiers are as likely to be counterproductive as productive.) [MACV and the JCS were pushing for a logistic command and increased logistic support troops in Vietnam; McNaughton withholding the line on total U.S. troops at this time.] (c) do not appear to lead in any negotiations. Chances of reversing the tide will be better and, if we don't reverse the tide, our reputation will emerge in better condition; (d) if we leave,

be sure it is a departure of the kind which would put everyone on our side, wondering how we stuck it and took it so long.

7) If things slip, have, plans to shore up Thailand and Malaysia.

Note from a McNaughton Draft in 1964:

There has been no decision taken putting on the same value scale (a) desirability of various outcomes, (b) undesirability of various efforts and (c) undesirability of having tried and failed. For example:

(1) Is a collapse at a 75,000 level worse than an inclusive situation at a 200,000–400,000+ level? Probably yes;

(2) Is a 60 percent chance of a compromise better than a 40 percent chance of winning? Probably yes if the compromise is tolerable;

(3) Is a 40 percent chance of compromise in 1966 better than a 40 percent chance of winning in 1967? Query.

[Document 248]

January 6, 1965

MEMORANDUM FOR THE SECRETARY

SUBJECT: Notes on the South Vietnamese Situation and Alternatives

For your meeting this afternoon with the President, and even though Ambassador Taylor's incoming messages have not been released by the President except to yourself and Mr. Ball, I thought it might be helpful to have notes prepared among Mike Forrestal, Len Unger, and myself.

1. I think we must accept that Saigon morale in all quarters is now very shaky indeed, and that this relates directly to a widespread feeling that the US is not ready for stronger action and indeed is possibly looking for a way out. We may regard this feeling as irrational and contradicted by our repeated statements, but Bill Sullivan was very vivid in describing the existence of such feelings in October, and we must honestly concede that our actions and statements since the election have not done anything to offset it. The blunt fact is that we have appeared to the Vietnamese (and to wide circles in Asia and even in Europe) to be insisting on a more perfect government than can reasonably be expected, before we consider any additional action—and that we might even pull out our support unless such a government emerges. We have not yet been able to assess the over-all impact of the continuing political crises and of the Binh Gia military defeat, but there are already ample indications that they have had a sharp discouraging effect just in the last two weeks.

2. By the same token, it is apparent that Hanoi is extremely confident, and that the Soviets are being somewhat tougher and the Chinese Communists are consolidating their ties with Hanoi. All three have called for a Laos conference without preconditions but have refrained from mentioning a conference on Vietnam. We think the explanation is extremely simple: that they are not too happy with the way things have gone in Laos, but that they see Vietnam falling into their laps in the fairly near future. At the same time, as to Laos, none of us think that the Communist side would concede in any meaningful fashion on any of the preconditions; they probably hope that Souvanna or we would abandon these preconditions, and they probably share our judgment that for

Souvanna to do so would drastically weaken his own position in Vientiane if not destroy it.

3. In key parts of the rest of Asia, notably Thailand, our present posture also appears weak. As such key parts of Asia see us, we looked strong in May and early June, weaker in later June and July, and then appeared to be taking a quite firm line in August with the Gulf of Tonkin. Since then we must have seemed to be gradually weakening—and, again, insisting on perfectionism in the Saigon government before we moved. With all the weaknesses that we all recognize in the Saigon political situation, the fact is that it is not an unusual or unfamiliar one to an Asian mind, and that our friends in Asia must well be asking whether we would support them if they too had internal troubles in a confrontation situation.

4. The sum total of the above seems to us to point—together with almost certainly stepped-up Viet Cong actions in the current favorable weather—to a prognosis that the situation in Vietnam is now likely to come apart more rapidly than we had anticipated in November. We would still stick to the estimate that the most likely form of coming apart would be a government of key groups starting to negotiate covertly with the Liberation Front or Hanoi, perhaps not asking in the first instance that we get out, but with that necessarily following at a fairly early stage. In one sense, this would be a "Vietnam solution," with some hope that it would produce a Communist Vietnam that would assert its own degree of independence from Peiping and that would produce a pause in Communist pressure in Southeast Asia. On the other hand, it would still be virtually certain that Laos would then become untenable and that Cambodia would accommodate in some way. Most seriously, there is grave question whether the Thai in these circumstances would retain any confidence at all in our continued support. In short, the outcome would be regarded in Asia, and particularly among our friends, as just as humiliating a defeat as any other form. As events have developed, the American public would probably not be too sharply critical, but the real question would be whether Thailand and other nations were weakened and taken over thereafter.

5. The alternative of stronger action obviously has grave difficulties. It commits the US more deeply, at a time when the picture of South Vietnamese will is extremely weak. To the extent that it included actions against North Vietnam, it would be vigorously attacked by many nations and disapproved initially even by such nations as Japan and India, on present indications. Most basically, its stiffening effect on the Saigon political situation would not be at all sure to bring about a more effective government, nor would limited actions against the southern DRV in fact sharply reduce infiltration or, in present circumstances, be at all likely to induce Hanoi to call it off.

6. Nonetheless, on balance we believe that such action would have some faint hope of really improving the Vietnamese situation, and, above all, would put us in a much stronger position to hold the next line of defense, namely Thailand. Accepting the present situation—or any negotiation on the basis of it —would be far weaker from this latter key standpoint. If we moved into stronger actions, we should have in mind that negotiations would be likely to emerge from some quarter in any event, and that under existing circumstances, even with the additional element of pressure, we could not expect to get an outcome that would really secure an independent South Vietnam. Yet even on an outcome that produced a progressive deterioration in South Vietnam and an eventual Communist takeover, we would still have appeared to Asians to have done a lot more about it.

7. In specific terms, the kinds of action we might take in the near future would be:

    a. An early occasion for reprisal action against the DRV.

    b. Possibly beginning low-level reconnaissance of the DRV at once.

    c. Concurrently with a or b, an early orderly withdrawal of our dependents.

We all think this would be a grave mistake in the absence of stronger action, and if taken in isolation would tremendously increase the pace of deterioration in Saigon. If we are to clear our decks in this way—and we are more and more inclined to think we should—it simply *must* be, for this reason alone, in the context of *some* stronger action.

    d. Intensified air operations in Laos may have some use, but they will *not* meet the problem of Saigon morale and if continued at a high level, may raise significant possibilities of Communist intervention on a substantial scale in Laos with some plausible justification. We have gone about as far as we can go in Laos by the existing limiting actions, and, apart from cutting Route 7, we would not be accomplishing much militarily by intensifying US air actions there. This form of action thus has little further to gain in the Laos context, and has no real bearing at this point on the South Vietnamese context.

    e. Introduction of limited US ground forces into the northern area of South Vietnam still has great appeal to many of us, concurrently with the first air attacks into the DRV. It would have a real stiffening effect in Saigon, and a strong signal effect to Hanoi. On the disadvantage side, such forces would be possible attrition targets for the Viet Cong. For your information, the Australians have clearly indicated (most recently yesterday) that they might be disposed to participate in such an operation. The New Zealanders are more negative and a proposal for Philippine participation would be an interesting test.

William P. Bundy

[Document 249]

DRAFT: 27 January 1965 by J. T. McNaughton—Observations Re South Vietnam After Khanh's "Re-Coup"

1) Khanh has given the U.S. a pretext to "dump" South Vietnam. This option should not be exercised.

2) The new Khanh government could be a "good" one but history is against it.

3) Max Taylor's effectiveness, with Khanh government, is doubtful.

4) The situation in South Vietnam in general continues to deteriorate.

5) Steady efforts inside South Vietnam can, probably, only slow that deterioration.

6) U.S. objective in South Vietnam is not to "help friend" but to contain China.

7) Loss in South Vietnam would merely move the conflict to Malaysia or Thailand (marginal comment by McNamara—These will go fast). U.S. won't repeat South Vietnam there! Continue with side effects of accommodation elsewhere in Asia.

8) The three options:

(a) Strike the DRV;
(b) "Negotiate"; or
(c) Keep plugging.

RSM comment: "Drifting."

9) Negotiation, with so few counters, is no way to improve the actual situation; it might serve to diffuse and confuse to some extent the psychological impact of loss.

McNamara comment: "This is better than drifting."

10) (The Fulbright-Mansfield Church School, for example, has written off South Vietnam; they are seeking solely to cut the damage to our prestige as South Vietnam goes down the drain.)

11) Striking DRV might, but probably won't. RSM comment: Dissent. Help the actual situation. The most serious RSM comment: Dissent. Risk is that the U.S. public will not support a squeeze unless results show soon.

12) Strikes against DRV should be done anyway, first as reprisals. RSM comment to reprisals: "Too narrow. Can use 34A, Desoto, infiltration data, etc. Feel way from there.

13) It is essential that we keep plugging in South Vietnam in any event. Immediate action: (a) Ride along with the new government, make no adverse comments; (b) continue vigorous advisory effort, but add no more U.S. men. RSM comment: "They are in for 6500 more.!"; (c) get dependents out; (d) authorize Westmoreland to use jets. RSM comment: Yes, in emergencies in South Vietnam; (e) React promptly and firmly to next reprisal opportunity; (f) start re-educating U.S. public that Southeast Asia confrontation will last years.

(*Note:* I handed this to RSM 0745, on January 27, 1965, and discussed it for twenty-five minutes. He commented as indicated.)

[Document 250]

McG. Bundy
7 Feb 1965

A POLICY OF SUSTAINED REPRISAL

I. INTRODUCTORY

We believe that the best available way of increasing our chance of success in Vietnam is the development and execution of a policy of *sustained reprisal* against North Vietnam—a policy in which air and naval action against the North is justified by and related to the whole Viet Cong campaign of violence and terror in the South.

While we believe that the risks of such a policy are acceptable, we emphasize that its costs are real. It implies significant U.S. air losses even if no full air war is joined, and it seems likely that it would eventually require an extensive and costly effort against the whole air defense system of North Vietnam. U.S. casualties would be higher—and more visible to American feelings—than those sustained in the struggle in South Vietnam.

Yet measured against the costs of defeat in Vietnam, this program seems cheap. And even if it fails to turn the tide—as it may—the value of the effort seems to us to exceed its cost.

II. OUTLINE OF THE POLICY

1. In partnership with the Government of Vietnam, we should develop and exercise the option to retaliate against *any* VC act of violence to persons or property.

2. In practice, we may wish at the outset to relate our reprisals to those acts of relatively high visibility such as the Pleiku incident. Later, we might retaliate against the assassination of a province chief, but not necessarily the murder of a hamlet official; we might retaliate against a grenade thrown into a crowded cafe in Saigon, but not necessarily to a shot fired into a small shop in the countryside.

3. Once a program of reprisals is clearly underway, it should not be necessary to connect each specific act against North Vietnam to a particular outrage in the South. It should be possible, for example, to publish weekly lists of outrages in the South and to have it clearly understood that these outrages are the cause of such action against the North as may be occurring in the current period. Such a more generalized pattern of reprisal would remove much of the difficulty involved in finding precisely matching targets in response to specific atrocities. Even in such a more general pattern, however, it would be important to insure that the general level of reprisal action remained in close correspondence with the level of outrages in the South. We must keep it clear at every stage both to Hanoi and to the world, that our reprisals will be reduced or stopped when outrages in the South are reduced or stopped—and that we are *not* attempting to destroy or conquer North Vietnam.

4. In the early stages of such a course, we should take the appropriate occasion to make clear our firm intent to undertake reprisals on any further acts, major or minor, that appear to us and the GVN as indicating Hanoi's support. We would announce that our two governments have been patient and forbearing in the hope that Hanoi would come to its senses without the necessity of our having to take further action; but the outrages continue and now we must react against those who are responsible; we will not provoke; we will not use our force indiscriminately; but we can no longer sit by in the face of repeated acts of terror and violence for which the DRV is responsible.

5. Having once made this announcement, we should execute our reprisal policy with as low a level of public noise as possible. It is to our interest that our acts should be seen—but we do not wish to boast about them in ways that make it hard for Hanoi to shift its ground. We should instead direct maximum attention to the continuing acts of violence which are the cause of our continuing reprisals.

6. This reprisal policy should begin at a low level. Its level of force and pressure should be increased only gradually—and as indicated above it should be decreased if VC terror visibly decreases. The object would not be to "win" an air war against Hanoi, but rather to influence the course of the struggle in the South.

7. At the same time it should be recognized that in order to maintain the power of reprisal without risk of excessive loss, an "air war" may in fact be necessary. We should therefore be ready to develop a separate justification for energetic flak suppression and if necessary for the destruction of Communist air power. The essence of such an explanation should be that these actions are intended solely to insure the effectiveness of a policy of reprisal, and in no sense represent any intent to wage offensive war against the North. These distinctions should not be difficult to develop.

8. It remains quite possible, however, that this reprisal policy would get us

quickly into the level of military activity contemplated in the so-called Phase II of our December planning. It may even get us beyond this level with both Hanoi and Peiping, if there is Communist counter-action. We and the GVN should also be prepared for a spurt of VC terrorism, especially in urban areas, that would dwarf anything yet experienced. These are the risks of any action. They should be carefully reviewed—but we believe them to be acceptable.

9. We are convinced that the political values of reprisal require a *continuous* operation. Episodic responses geared on a one-for-one basis to "spectacular" outrages would lack the persuasive force of sustained pressure. More important still, they would leave it open to the Communists to avoid reprisals entirely by giving up only a small element of their own program. The Gulf of Tonkin affair produced a sharp upturn in morale in South Vietnam. When it remained an isolated episode, however, there was a severe relapse. It is the great merit of the proposed scheme that to stop it the Communists would have to stop enough of their activity in the South to permit the probable success of a determined pacification effort.

III.   EXPECTED EFFECT OF SUSTAINED REPRISAL POLICY

1. We emphasize that our primary target in advocating a reprisal policy is the improvement of the situation in *South* Vietnam. Action against the North is usually urged as a means of affecting the will of Hanoi to direct and support the VC. We consider this an important but longer-range purpose. The immediate and critical targets are in the South—in the minds of the South Vietnamese and in the minds of the Viet Cong cadres.

2. Predictions of the effect of any given course of action upon the states of mind of people are difficult. It seems very clear that if the United States and the Government of Vietnam join in a policy of reprisal, there will be a sharp immediate increase in optimism in the South, among nearly all articulate groups. The Mission believes—and our own conversations confirm—that in all sectors of Vietnamese opinion there is a strong belief that the United States could do much more if it would, and that they are suspicious of our failure to use more of our obviously enormous power. At least in the short run, the reaction to reprisal policy would be very favorable.

3. This favorable reaction should offer opportunity for increased American influence in pressing for a more effective government—at least in the short run. Joint reprisals would imply military planning in which the American role would necessarily be controlling, and this new relation should add to our bargaining power in other military efforts—and conceivably on a wider plane as well if a more stable government is formed. We have the whip hand in reprisals as we do not in other fields.

4. The Vietnamese increase in hope could well increase the readiness of Vietnamese factions themselves to join together in forming a more effective government.

5. We think it plausible that effective and sustained reprisals, even in a low key, would have a substantial depressing effect upon the morale of Viet Cong cadres in South Vietnam. This is the strong opinion of CIA Saigon. It is based upon reliable reports of the initial Viet Cong reaction to the Gulf of Tonkin episode, and also upon the solid general assessment that the determination of Hanoi and the apparent timidity of the mighty United States are both major items in Viet Cong confidence.

6. The long-run effect of reprisals in the South is far less clear. It may be that

like other stimulants, the value of this one would decline over time. Indeed the risk of this result is large enough so that we ourselves believe that a very major effort all along the line should be made in South Vietnam to take full advantage of the immediate stimulus of reprisal policy in its early stages. Our object should be to use this new policy to effect a visible upward turn in pacification, in governmental effectiveness, in operations against the Viet Cong, and in the whole U.S./ GVN relationship. It is changes in these areas that can have enduring long-term effects.

7. While emphasizing the importance of reprisals in the South, we do not exclude the impact on Hanoi. We believe, indeed, that it is of great importance that the level of reprisal be adjusted rapidly and visibly to both upward and downward shifts in the level of Viet Cong offenses. We want to keep before Hanoi the carrot of our desisting as well as the stick of continued pressure. We also need to conduct the application of the force so that there is always a prospect of worse to come.

8. We cannot assert that a policy of sustained reprisal will succeed in changing the course of the contest in Vietnam. It may fail, and we cannot estimate the odds of success with any accuracy—they may be somewhere between 25% and 75%. What we can say is that even if it fails, the policy will be worth it. At a minimum it will damp down the charge that we did not do all that we could have done, and this charge will be important in many countries, including our own. Beyond that, a reprisal policy—to the extent that it demonstrates U.S. willingness to employ this new norm in counter-insurgency—will set a higher price for the future upon all adventures of guerrilla warfare, and it should therefore somewhat increase our ability to deter such adventures. We must recognize, however, that that ability will be gravely weakened if there is failure for any reason in Vietnam.

IV.   PRESENT ACTION RECOMMENDATIONS

1. This general recommendation was developed in intensive discussions in the days just before the attacks on Pleiku. These attacks and our reaction to them have created an ideal opportunity for the prompt development and execution of sustained reprisals. Conversely, if no such policy is now developed, we face the grave danger that Pleiku, like the Gulf of Tonkin, may be a short-run stimulant and a long-term depressant. We therefore recommend that the necessary preparations be made for continuing reprisals. The major necessary steps to be taken appear to us to be the following:

(1) We should complete the evacuation of dependents.

(2) We should quietly start the necessary westward deployments of back-up contingency forces.

(3) We should develop and refine a running catalogue of Viet Cong offenses which can be published regularly and related clearly to our own reprisals. Such a catalogue should perhaps build on the foundation of an initial White Paper.

(4) We should initiate joint planning with the GVN on both the civil and military level. Specifically, we should give a clear and strong signal to those now forming a government that we will be ready for this policy when they are.

(5) We should develop the necessary public and diplomatic statements to accompany the initiation and continuation of this program.

(6) We should insure that a reprisal program is matched by renewed public commitment to our family of programs in the South, so that the central importance of the southern struggle may never be neglected.

(7) We should plan quiet diplomatic communication of the precise meaning of what we are and are not doing, to Hanoi, to Peking and to Moscow.

(8) We should be prepared to defend and to justify this new policy by concentrating attention in every forum upon its cause—the aggression in the South.

(9) We should accept discussion on these terms in any forum, but we should *not* now accept the idea of negotiations of any sort except on the basis of a stand down of Viet Cong violence. A program of sustained reprisal, with its direct link to Hanoi's continuing aggressive actions in the South, will not involve us in nearly the level of international recrimination which would be precipitated by a go-North program which was not so connected. For this reason the International pressures for negotiation should be quite manageable.

[Document 251]

February 10, 1965

MEMORANDUM FOR MR. McGEORGE BUNDY

SUBJECT: Additional Military and Diplomatic Possibilities

Ambassador Thompson and I discussed the status of planning last night, and he came up with two thoughts that should be very much in our minds.

1. In light of the very mild official Soviet reaction to date, but their obvious concern at any immediate repetition of our action, he believes that we should take serious account of the March 1 date of the Communist Party meeting. He thinks that the Soviets would be put even more sharply on the spot by any US action taken prior to March 1.

Comment: I realize that this would defer our next action well beyond the 4–10 days discussed in your group last night. However, we need to see whether that gap might not be filled in by a predominantly GVN action related directly to some action against the South Vietnamese—e.g., railroad atrocity. I think we would all agree—and you may be interested to know that this was stressed to me by several senators yesterday, as well as by the Chinese Ambassador on Sunday— that we have a terrific problem to avoid appearing to be reacting just when the US is hit and turning this into a US/DRV situation exclusively.

2. On the diplomatic track, Ambassador Thompson noted that the Soviets would be much more ready to play some kind of moderately constructive role in relation to Laos. He therefore wondered if we could somehow get Laos negotiations going and make this a test of DRV willingness to negotiate, in effect arguing that if they were not ready to see the 1962 Accords observed, how could we possibly expect anything from them in Vietnam negotiations.

Comment: I have hitherto thought Laos negotiations were so fraught with internal problems in Vietnam that that alone argued strongly against making this our negotiating initiative—although it could well play in its own way. The dust has not settled from the latest troubles in Vientiane, and we probably should check with Sullivan to see what he now thinks Souvanna's position would be. More basically, however, I would have grave doubt about whether Laos negotiations could in fact be pressed to the point of doing anything effective about the corridor, which as a practical matter Souvanna regards more as our issue than his. Finally, any Lao negotiations would be likely to get tied into knots in which a lot of our own activities would be pilloried as just about as bad as anything the Communists have done.

In short, I am very skeptical that we can really make use of this gambit either for profit in itself or as a plausible way of holding off Vietnamese negotiations.

However, I think it needs further study, and I am asking my staff to look at it hard today, with of course crucial advice from Len.

William P. Bundy

Copies to: Ambassador Thompson
Mr. McNaughton
Mr. Green
Mr. Unger
Mr. Cooper
Mr. Trueheart

[Document 252]

DRAFT
FE:WPBundy:mk
2/18/65

Where Are We Heading?

This memorandum examines possible developments and problems if the US pursues the following policy with respect to South Viet-Nam:

a. Intensified pacification within South Viet-Nam. To meet the security problem, this might include a significant increase in present US force strength.

b. A program of measured, limited, and spaced air attacks, jointly with the GVN, against the infiltration complex in the DRV. Such attacks would take place at the rate of about one a week, unless spectacular Viet Cong action dictated an immediate response out of sequence. The normal pattern of such attacks would comprise one GVN and one US strike on each occasion, confined to targets south of the 19th parallel, with variations in severity depending on the tempo of VC action, but with a slow upward trend in severity as the weeks went by.

c. That the US itself would take no initiative for talks, but would agree to cooperate in consultations—*not* a conference—undertaken by the UK and USSR as Co-Chairmen of the Geneva Conferences. As an opening move, the British would request an expression of our views, and we would use this occasion to spell out our position fully, including our purposes and what we regard as essential to the restoration of peace. We would further present our case against the DRV in the form of a long written document to be sent to the President of the United Nations Security Council and to be circulated to members of the UN.

*   *   *

1. *Communist responses.*

a. *Hanoi* would almost certainly not feel itself under pressure at any early point to enter into fruitful negotiations or to call off its activity in any way. They would denounce the continued air attacks and seek to whip up maximum world opposition to them. Within South Viet-Nam, they might avoid spectacular actions, but would certainly continue a substantial pattern of activity along past lines, probably with emphasis on the kind of incidents we have seen this week, in which Communist agents stirred up a village "protest" against government air attacks, and against the US. Basically, they would see the situation in South Viet-Nam as likely to deteriorate further ("crumble," as they have put it), and would be expecting that at some point someone in the GVN will start secret talks with them behind our backs.

b. *Communist China* might supply additional air defense equipment to the DRV, but we do not believe they would engage in air operations from Communist China, at least up to the point where the MIGs in the DRV were engaged and we had found it necessary to attack Fukien or possibly—if the MIGs had been moved there—Vinh.

c. *The Soviets* would supply air defense equipment to the DRV and would continue to protest our air attacks in strong terms. However, we do not believe they would make any new commitment at this stage, and they would probably not do so even if the Chicoms became even more deeply involved—provided that we were not ourselves attacking Communist China. At that point, the heat might get awfully great on them, and they would be in a very difficult position to continue actively working as Co-chairmen. However, their approach to the British on the Co-chairmanship certainly suggests that they would find some relief in starting to act in that role, and might use it as a hedge against further involvement, perhaps pointing out to Hanoi that the Co-chairmen exercise serves to prevent us from taking extreme action and that Hanoi will get the same result in the end if a political track is operating and if, in fact, South Viet-Nam keeps crumbling. They might also argue to Hanoi that the existence of the political track tends to reduce the chances of the Chicoms having to become deeply involved—which we believe Hanoi does not want unless it is compelled to accept it.

2. *Within South Viet-Nam* the new government is a somewhat better one, but the cohesive effects of the strikes to date have at most helped things a bit. The latest MACV report indicates a deteriorating situation except in the extreme south, and it is unlikely that this can be arrested in any short period of time even if the government does hold together well and the military go about their business. We shall be very lucky to see a leveling off, much less any significant improvement, in the next two months. In short, we may have to hang on quite a long time before we can hope to see an improving situation in South Viet-Nam—and this in turn is really the key to any negotiating position we could have at any time.

3. *On the political track* we believe the British will undertake their role with vigor, and that the Soviets will be more reserved. The Soviets can hardly hope to influence Hanoi much at this point, and they certainly have no leverage with Communist China. In the opening rounds, the Soviets will probably fire off some fairly sharp statements that the real key to the situation is for us to get out and to stop our attacks, and the opposing positions are so far apart that it is hard to see any useful movement for some time to come. We might well find the Soviets —or even the Canadians—sounding us out on whether we would stop our attacks in return for some moderation in VC activity. This is clearly unacceptable, and the very least we should hold out on is a verified cessation of infiltration (and radio silence) before we stop our attacks. Our stress on the cessation of infiltration may conceivably lead to the Indians coming forward to offer policing forces—a suggestion they have made before—and this would be a constructive move we could pick up. But, as noted above, Hanoi is most unlikely to trade on this basis for a long time to come.

4. In sum—the most likely prospect is for a prolonged period without major risks of escalation but equally without any give by Hanoi. If, contrary to our present judgment, the GVN should start to do better,

[material missing]

[Document 253]

JTM to MCN   3/24/65 (first draft)

PROPOSED COURSE OF ACTION RE VIETNAM

1. *Assessment and prognosis.* The situation in Vietnam is bad and deteriorating. Even with great, imaginative efforts on the civilian as well as military sides inside South Vietnam, the decline probably will not "bottom out" unless major actions are taken.

2. *The "trilemma."* US policy appears to be drifting. This is because, while there is near-consensus that efforts inside SVN will probably fail to prevent collapse, all 3 of the possible remedial courses of action have been rejected for one reason or another: (a) Will-breaking strikes on DRV; (b) large troop deployments; (c) exit by negotiations.

3. *Urgency.* Even with a stretched-out strike-North program, we could reach flash points within a few weeks (e.g., confrontation with DRV MIGs, hot pursuit of Chicom MIGs, DRV air attack on SVN, massive VC attack on Danang, sinking of US naval vessel, etc.). Furthermore, there is now a hint of flexibility on the Red side: The Soviets are struggling to find a Gordian knot-cutter; the Chicoms may be wavering (PARIS 5326).

4. *Actions:*
   (1) Redouble and redouble efforts inside SVN (get better organized for it!).
   (2) Prepare to deploy US combat troops, first to Pleiku (and more to Danang).
   (3) Continue distended strike-North program, postponing Phuc Yen until June.
   (4) Initiate quiet talks along the following lines:
PHASE ONE:
   (A) *When?* Now, before a flash point.
   (B) *Who?* US–USSR, perhaps US–China in Warsaw or Moscow, or US–DRV via Seaborn in Hanoi. (Not with Liberation Front or through UK, France, India or UN; be alert for GVN officials talking under the table.)
   (C) *How?* With GVN consent; private and quiet. (Refuse formal talks until *Phase Two.*)
   (D) *What?*
      (1) Offer to stop strikes on DRV and to withhold deployment of division-size US forces in exchange for DRV withdrawal of named units in SVN, and stoppage of infiltration, communications to VC, and VC attacks, sabotage and terrorism.
      (2) Compliance would be policed unilaterally. If, as is likely, complete compliance by the DRV is not forthcoming, we would carry out occasional strikes.
      (3) Do not demand stoppage of propaganda or public renunciation of doctrines.
      (4) Regarding "defensive" VC attacks—i.e., VC defending VC-held areas from encroaching ARVN forces—we take the *public* position that

ARVN forces must be free to operate throughout SVN, especially in areas where amnesty is offered (but in fact, restraint and discretion will be exercised by the ARVN).

(5) Terrorism and sabotage, however, must be dampened markedly throughout SVN—e.g., civilian administrators must be able to move and operate freely, certainly in so-called contested areas, and roads and railroads must be open.

PHASE TWO:

(A) *When?* At the end of *Phase One.*

(B) *Who?* All interested nations.

(C) *How?* Publicly in large Geneva-type conference.

(D) *What?*

(1) Offer to remove US combat forces from South Vietnam in exchange for repatriation (or regroupment?) of DRV infiltrators and hardcore sympathizers and for erection of international machinery to verify the end of infiltration and coded communication.

(2) Offer to seek to determine the will of the people under international supervision, with an appropriate reflection of those who favor the VC.

(3) Any recognition of the Liberation Front would have to be accompanied by disarming the VC and at least avowed VC independence from DRV control.

NOTE: If the DRV will not "play" the above game, we must be prepared (1) to risk passing some flash points in the Strike-North program, (2) to put more US troops into SVN, and/or (3) to reconsider our minimum acceptable outcome.

5. *Outcomes.* In between "victory" and "defeat" in SVN lie (a) a Laos-like "government of national unity" attempting to rule all of SVN; (b) a live-and-let-live stand-down (ceasefire) tacitly recognizing current, or recent, areas of influence; (c) a "semi-equilibrium" or "slow-motion war" with slowly shifting GVN–VC areas of control.

3/24/65 (first draft)

ANNEX—PLAN OF ACTION FOR SOUTH VIETNAM

1. *US aims:*

70%—To avoid a humiliating US defeat (to our reputation as a guarantor).

20%—To keep SVN (and then adjacent) territory from Chinese hands.

10%—To permit the people of SVN to enjoy a better, freer way of life.

ALSO—To emerge from crisis without unacceptable taint from methods used.

NOT—To "help a friend," although it would be hard to stay in if asked out.

2. *The situation:* The situation in general is bad and deteriorating. The VC have the initiative. Defeatism is gaining among the rural population, somewhat in the cities, and even among the soldiers—especially those with relatives in rural areas. The Hop Tac area around Saigon is making little progress; the Delta stays bad; the country has been severed in the north. GVN control is shrinking to enclaves, some burdened with refugees. In Saigon we have a remission: Quat is giving hope on the civilian side, the Buddhists have calmed, and the split generals are in uneasy equilibrium.

3. *The preliminary question:* Can the situation inside SVN be bottomed out (a) without extreme measures against the DRV and/or (b) without deployment of large numbers of US (and other) combat troops inside SVN? The answer is perhaps, but probably no.

4. *Ways GVN might collapse:*

    (a) VC successes reduce GVN control to enclaves, causing:
        (1) insurrection in the enclaved population,
        (2) massive defections of ARVN soldiers and even units,
        (3) aggravated dissension and impotence in Saigon,
        (4) defeatism and reorientation by key GVN officials,
        (5) entrance of left-wing elements into the government,
        (6) emergence of a popular-front regime,
        (7) request that US leave,
        (8) concessions to the VC, and
        (9) accommodations to the DRV.
    (b) VC with DRV volunteers concentrate on I & II Corps,
        (1) conquering principal GVN-held enclaves there,
        (2) declaring Liberation Government,
        (3) joining the I & II Corps areas to the DRV, and
        (4) pressing the course in (a) above for rest of SVN.
    (c) While in a temporary funk, GVN might throw in sponge:
        (1) dealing under the table with the VC,
        (2) asking the US to cease at least military aid,
        (3) bringing left-wing elements into the government,
        (4) leading to a popular-front regime, and
        (5) ending in accommodations to the VC and DRV.
    (d) In a surge of anti-Americanism, GVN could ask the US out and pursue course otherwise similar to (c) above.

5. *The "trilemma":* US policy appears to be drifting. This is because, while there is consensus that efforts inside SVN (para 6) will probably fail to prevent collapse, all three of the possible remedial courses of action have so far been rejected:

    a. *Will-breaking strikes on the North* (para 7) are balked (1) by flash-point limits, (2) by doubts that the DRV will cave and (3) by doubts that the VC will obey a caving DRV. (Leaving strikes only a political and anti-infiltration nuisance.)
    b. *Large US troop deployments* (para 8) are blocked by "French-defeat" and "Korea" syndromes, and Quat is queasy. (Troops could be net negatives, and be besieged.)
    c. *Exit by negotiations* (para 9) is tainted by the humiliation likely to follow.

6. *Efforts inside South Vietnam:* Progress inside SVN is our main aim. Great, imaginative efforts on the civilian political as well as military side must be made, bearing in mind that progress depends as much on GVN efforts and luck as on added US efforts. While only a few of such efforts can pay off quickly enough to affect the present ominous deterioration, some may, and we are dealing here in small critical margins. Furthermore, such investment is essential to provide a foundation for the longer run.

a. *Improve spirit and effectiveness.* [fill out further, drawing from State memo to the President]
   (1) Achieve governmental stability.
   (2) Augment the psy-war program.
   (3) Build a stronger pro-government infrastructure.
b. *Improve physical security.* [fill out]
c. *Reduce infiltration.* [fill out]

7. *Strikes on the North* (*program of progressive military pressure*).

a. *Purposes:*
   (1) To reduce DRV/VC activities by affecting DRV will.
   (2) To improve the GVN/VC relative "balance of morale."
   (3) To provide the US/GVN with a bargaining counter.
   (4) To reduce DRV infiltration of men and materiel.
   (5) To show the world the lengths to which US will go for a friend.
b. *Program:* Each week, 1 or 2 "mission days" with 100-plane high-damage US–VNAF strikes each "day" against important targets, plus 3 armed recce missions—all moving upward in weight of effort, value of target or proximity to Hanoi and China.
   ALTERNATIVE ONE: 12-week DRV-wide program shunning only "population" targets.
   ALTERNATIVE TWO: 12-week program short of taking out Phuc Yen (Hanoi) airfield.
c. *Other actions:*
   (1) Blockade of DRV ports by VNAF/US-dropped mines or by ships.
   (2) South Vietnamese-implemented 34A MAROPS.
   (3) Reconnaissance flights over Laos and the DRV.
   (4) Daily BARREL ROLL armed recce strikes in Laos (plus T-28s).
   (5) Four-a-week BARREL ROLL choke-point strikes in Laos.
   (6) US/VNAF air & naval strikes against VC ops and bases in SVN.
   (7) Westward deployment of US forces.
   (8) No deSoto patrols or naval bombardment of DRV at this time.
d. *Red "flash points."* There are events which we can expect to imply substantial risk of escalation:
   [(1) Air strikes north of 17°. (This one already passed.)]
   (2) First US/VNAF confrontation with DRV MIGs.
   (3) Strike on Phuc Yen MIG base near Hanoi.
   (4) First strikes on Tonkin industrial/population targets.
   (5) First strikes on Chinese railroad or near China.
   (6) First US/VNAF confrontation with Chicom MIGs.
   (7) First hot pursuit of Chicom MIGs into China.
   (8) First flak-suppression of Chicom- or Soviet-manned SAM.
   (9) Massive introduction of US ground troops into SVN.
   (10) US/ARVN occupation of DRV territory (e.g., Ile de Tigre).
   (11) First Chi/Sov–US confrontation or sinking in blockade.
e. *Blue "flash points."* China/DRV surely are sensitive to events which might cause *us* to escalate:
   (1) All of the above "Red" flash points.
   (2) VC ground attack on Danang.
   (3) Sinking of a US naval vessel.
   (4) Open deployment of DRV troops into South Vietnam.

    (5) Deployment of Chinese troops into North Vietnam.
    (6) Deployment of FROGs or SAMs in North Vietnam.
    (7) DRV air attack on South Vietnam.
    (8) Announcement of Liberation Government in I/II Corps area.
  f. *Major risks:*
    (1) Losses to DRV MIGs, and later possibly to SAMs.
    (2) Increased VC activities, and possibly Liberation Government.
    (3) Panic or other collapse of GVN from under us.
    (4) World-wide revulsion against us (against strikes, blockade, etc.).
    (5) Sympathetic fires over Berlin, Cyprus, Kashmir, Jordan waters.
    (6) Escalation to conventional war with DRV, China (and USSR?).
    (7) Escalation to the use of nuclear weapons.
  g. *Other Red moves:*
    (1) More jets to NVN with DRV or Chicom pilots.
    (2) More AAA (SAMs?) and radar gear (Soviet-manned?) to NVN.
    (3) Increased air and ground forces in South China.
    (4) Other "defensive" DRV retaliation (e.g., shoot-down of a U-2).
    (5) PL land grabs in Laos.
    (6) PL declaration of new government in Laos.
    (7) Political drive for "neutralization" of Indo-China.
  h. *Escalation control.* We can do three things to avoid escalation too-much or too-fast:
    (1) *Stretch out.* Retard the program (e.g., 1 not 2 fixed strikes a week).
    (2) *Circuit breaker.* Abandon at least temporarily the theory that our strikes are intended to break DRV will, and "plateau" them below the "Phuc Yen airfield" flash point on one or the other of these tenable theories:
      [a] That we strike as necessary to interdict infiltration.
      [b] That our level of strikes is generally responsive to the level of VC/DRV activities in South Vietnam.
    (3) *Shunt.* Plateau the air strikes per para (2) and divert the energy into:
      [a] A mine- and/or ship-blockade of DRV ports.
      [b] Massive deployment of US (and other?) troops into SVN (and Laos?):
        [1] To man the "enclaves," releasing ARVN forces.
        [2] To take over Pleiku, Kontum, Darlac provinces.
        [3] To create a 16+° sea-Thailand infiltration wall.
  i. *Important miscellany:*
    (1) Program should appear to be relentless (i.e., possibility of employing "circuit-breakers" should be secret).
    (2) Enemy should be kept aware of our limited objectives.
    (3) Allies should be kept on board.
    (4) USSR should be kept in passive role.
    (5) Information program should preserve US public support.

8. *Program of large US ground effort in SVN and SEA.*

  a. *Purposes:*
    (1) To defeat the VC on the ground.
    (2) To improve GVN/VC relative "morale balance."
    (3) To improve US/GVN bargaining position.
    (4) To show world lengths to which US will go to fulfil commitments.

b. *Program:*

(1) Continue strike-North "crescendo" or "plateau" (para 7 above).

(2) Add any "combat support" personnel needed by MACV;
and

(3) Deploy remainder of the III Marine Expeditionary Force to Danang;
and

(4) Deploy one US (plus one Korean?) division to defeat VC in Pleiku-Kontum-Darlac area,
or

(5) Deploy one US (plus one Korean?) division to hold enclaves (Bien Hoa/ Ton Son Nhut, Nha Trang, Qui Non, Pleiku);
and/or

(6) Deploy 3–5 US divisions (with "international" elements) across Laos–SVN infiltration routes and at key SVN population centers.

c. *Advantages:*

(1) Improve (at least initially) manpower ratio vs. the VC.

(2) Boost GVN morale and depress DRV/VC morale.

(3) Firm up US commitment in eyes of all Reds, allies and neutrals.

(4) Deter (or even prevent) coups in the South.

d. *Risks:*

(1) Deployment will suck Chicom troops into DRV.

(2) Deployment will suck counterbalancing DRV/Chinese troops into SVN.

(3) Announcement of deployment will cause massive DRV/Chicom effort pre-emptively to occupy new SVN territory.

(4) US losses will increase.

(5) Friction with GVN (and Koreans?) over command will arise.

(6) GVN will tend increasingly to "let the US do it."

(7) Anti-US "colonialist" mood may increase in- and outside SVN.

(8) US forces may be surrounded and trapped.

e. *Important miscellany:*

(1) There are no obvious circuit-breakers. Once US troops are in, it will be difficult to withdraw them or to move them, say, to Thailand without admitting defeat.

(2) It will take massive deployments (many divisions) to improve the GVN/US:VC ratio to the optimum 10+:1.

(3) In any event, our Project 22 planning with the Thais for defense of the Mekong towns must proceed apace.

9. *Exit by negotiations.*

a. *Bargaining counters.*

(1) *What DRV could give:*

[a] Stop training and sending personnel to SVN/Laos.

[b] Stop sending arms and supplies into SVN/Laos.

[c] Stop directing military actions in SVN/Laos.

[d] Order the VC/PL to stop their insurgencies.

[e] Stop propaganda broadcasts to South Vietnam.

[f] Remove VM forces and cadres from SVN and Laos.

[g] See that VC/PL stop incidents in SVN and Laos.

[h] See that VC/PL cease resistance.

[i] See that VC/PL turn in weapons and bases.

[j] See that VC/PL surrender for amnesty/expatriation.

(2) *What GVN/US could give:*

[a] Stop (or not increase) air strikes on DRV.

[b] Remove (or not increase) US troops in SVN.

[c] Rice supply to DRV.

[d] Assurance that US/GVN have no designs on NVN.

[e] Assurance that US/GVN will not demand public renunciation by DRV of Communist goals.

[f] Assurance that "peaceful coexistence" (e.g., continuation of Red propaganda in SVN) is acceptable.

[g] Capitulation: Leftists in GVN, coalition government, and eventual incorporation of SVN into DRV.

b. *Possible outcomes.*

(1) Pacified non-Communist South Vietnam.

(2) "Laotian" solution, with areas of de facto VC dominion, a "government of national unity," and a Liberation Front ostensibly weaned from DRV control.

(3) Explicit partition of SVN, with each area under a separate government.

(4) A "semi-equilibrium"—a slow-motion war—with slowly shifting GVN–VC lines.

(5) Loss of SVN to the DRV.

c. *Techniques to minimize impact of bad outcomes.* If/when it is estimated that even the best US/GVN efforts mean failure ("flash" or defeat), it will be important to act to minimize the after-damage to US effectiveness and image by steps such as these:

(1) Publicize uniqueness and congenital impossibility of SVN case (e.g., Viet Minh held much of SVN in 1954, long sieve-like borders, unfavorable terrain, no national tradition, few administrators, mess left by French, competing factions, Red LOC advantage, late US start, etc.).

(2) Take opportunity offered by next coup or GVN anti-US tantrum to "ship out" (coupled with advance threat to do so if they fail to "shape up"?).

(3) Create diversionary "offensives" elsewhere in the world (e.g., to shore up Thailand, Philippines, Malaysia, India, Australia; to launch an "anti-poverty" program for underdeveloped areas).

(4) Enter multi-nation negotiations calculated to shift opinions and values.

d. *Risks:* With the physical situation and the trends as they are, the risk is overwhelming that an exit negotiated now would result in humiliation for the US.

10. *Evaluation:* It is essential—however badly SEA may go over the next 1–3 years—that US emerge as a "good doctor." We must have kept promises, been tough, taken risks, gotten bloodied, and hurt the enemy very badly. We must avoid harmful appearances which will affect judgments by, and provide pretexts to, other nations regarding how the US will behave in future cases of particular interest to those nations—regarding US policy, power, resolve and competence to deal with their problems. In this connection, the relevant audiences are the Communists (who must feel strong pressures), the South Vietnamese (whose

morale must be buoyed), our allies (who must trust us as "underwriters") and the US public (which must support our risk-taking with US lives and prestige).

a. *Urgency.* If the strike-North program (para 7) is not altered: we will reach the MIG/Phuc Yen flash point in approximately one month. If the program is altered only to stretch out the crescendo: up to 3 months may be had before that flash point, at the expense of a less persuasive squeeze. If the program is altered to "plateau" or dampen the strikes: much of their negotiating value will be lost. (Furthermore, there is now a hint of flexibility on the Red side: The Soviets are struggling to find a Gordian knot-cutter; the Chicoms may be wavering (Paris 5326).)

b. *Possible course:*

(1) Redouble efforts inside SVN (get better organized for it).

(2) Prepare to deploy US combat troops in phases, starting with one Army division at Pleiku and a Marine MEF at Danang.

(3) Stretch out strike-North program, postponing Phuc Yen until June (exceed flash points only in specific retaliations).

(4) Initiate talks along the following lines, bearing in mind that formal partition, or even a "Laos" partition, is out in SVN; we must break the VC back or work out an accommodation.

PHASE ONE TALKS:

(A) *When:* Now, before an avoidable flash point.

(B) *Who:* US–USSR, perhaps also US–India. (Not with China or Liberation Front; not through UK or France or U Thant; keep alert to possibility that GVN officials are talking under the table.)

(C) *How:* With GVN consent, private, quiet (refuse formal talks).

(D) *What:*

(1) Offer to stop strikes on DRV and withhold deployment of large US forces in trade for DRV stoppage of infiltration, communications to VC, and VC attacks, sabotage and terrorism, and for withdrawal of named units in SVN.

(2) Compliance would be policed unilaterally. If, as is likely, complete compliance by the DRV is not forthcoming, we would carry out occasional strikes.

(3) We make clear that we are not demanding cessation of Red propaganda nor a public renunciation by Hanoi of its doctrines.

(4) Regarding "defensive" VC attacks—i.e., VC defending VC-held areas from encroaching ARVN forces—we take the public position that ARVN forces must be free to operate throughout SVN, especially in areas where amnesty is offered (but in fact, discretion will be exercised).

(5) Terrorism and sabotage, however, must be dampened markedly throughout the country, and civilian administrators must be free to move and operate freely, certainly in so-called contested areas (and perhaps even in VC base areas).

PHASE TWO TALKS:

(A) *When:* At the end of *Phase One.*

(B) *Who:* All interested nations.

(C) *How:* Publicly in large conference.

(D) *What:*

(1) Offer to remove US combat forces from South Vietnam in exchange for repatriation (or regroupment?) of DRV infiltra-

tors and for erection of international machinery to verify the
end of infiltration and communication.

   (2) Offer to seek to determine the will of the people under international supervision, with an appropriate reflection of those
who favor the VC.

   (3) Any recognition of the Liberation Front would have to be
accompanied by disarming the VC and at least avowed VC independence from DRV control.

PHASE THREE TALKS: Avoid any talks regarding the future of all
of Southeast Asia. Thailand's future should
not be up for discussion; and we have the
1954 and 1962 Geneva Accords covering the
rest of the area.

  c. *Special Points:*

   (1) Play on DRV's fear of China.

   (2) To show good will, suspend strikes on North for a few days if requested by Soviets during efforts to mediate.

   (3) Have a contingency plan prepared to evacuate US personnel in case
a para-9-type situation arises.

   (4) If the DRV will not "play" the above game, we must be prepared
[a] to risk passing some flash points, in the Strike-North program,
[b] to put more US troops into SVN, and/or [c] to reconsider our
minimum acceptable outcome.

[Document 254]

THE WHITE HOUSE

WASHINGTON

April 6, 1965

NATIONAL SECURITY ACTION MEMORANDUM NO. 328

MEMORANDUM FOR

THE SECRETARY OF STATE
THE SECRETARY OF DEFENSE
THE DIRECTOR OF CENTRAL INTELLIGENCE

On Thursday, April 1, the President made the following decisions with respect to
Vietnam:

   1. Subject to modifications in the light of experience, and to coordination and
direction both in Saigon and in Washington, the President approved the 41-point
program of non-military actions submitted by Ambassador Taylor in a memorandum dated March 31, 1965.

   2. The President gave general approval to the recommendations submitted by
Mr. Rowan in his report dated March 16, with the exception that the President
withheld approval of any request for supplemental funds at this time—it is his
decision that this program is to be energetically supported by all agencies and
departments and by the reprogramming of available funds as necessary within
USIA.

   3. The President approved the urgent exploration of the 12 suggestions for
covert and other actions submitted by the Director of Central Intelligence under
date of March 31.

4. The President repeated his earlier approval of the 21-point program of military actions submitted by General Harold K. Johnson under date of March 14 and re-emphasized his desire that aircraft and helicopter reinforcements under this program be accelerated.

5. The President approved an 18–20,000 man increase in U.S. military support forces to fill out existing units and supply needed logistic personnel.

6. The President approved the deployment of two additional Marine Battalions and one Marine Air Squadron and associated headquarters and support elements.

7. The President approved a change of mission for all Marine Battalions deployed to Vietnam to permit their more active use under conditions to be established and approved by the Secretary of Defense in consultation with the Secretary of State.

8. The President approved the urgent exploration, with the Korean, Australian, and New Zealand Governments, of the possibility of rapid deployment of significant combat elements from their armed forces in parallel with the additional Marine deployment approved in paragraph 6.

9. Subject to continuing review, the President approved the following general framework of continuing action against North Vietnam and Laos:

We should continue roughly the present slowly ascending tempo of ROLLING THUNDER operations, being prepared to add strikes in response to a higher rate of VC operations, or conceivably to slow the pace in the unlikely event VC slacked off sharply for what appeared to be more than a temporary operational lull.

The target systems should continue to avoid the effective GCI range of MIGs. We should continue to vary the types of targets, stepping up attacks on lines of communication in the near future, and possibly moving in a few weeks to attacks on the rail lines north and northeast of Hanoi.

Leaflet operations should be expanded to obtain maximum practicable psychological effect on the North Vietnamese population.

Blockade or aerial mining of North Vietnamese ports needs further study and should be considered for future operations. It would have major political complications, especially in relation to the Soviets and other third countries, but also offers many advantages.

Air operation in Laos, particularly route blocking operations in the Panhandle area, should be stepped up to the maximum remunerative rate.

10. Ambassador Taylor will promptly seek the reactions of the South Vietnamese Government to appropriate sections of this program and their approval as necessary, and in the event of disapproval or difficulty at that end, these decisions will be appropriately reconsidered. In any event, no action into Vietnam under paragraphs 6 and 7 above should take place without GVN approval or further Presidential authorization.

11. The President desires that with respect to the actions in paragraphs 5 through 7, premature publicity be avoided by all possible precautions. The actions themselves should be taken as rapidly as practicable, but in ways that should minimize any appearance of sudden changes in policy, and official statements on these troop movements will be made only with the direct approval of the Secretary of Defense, in consultation with the Secretary of State. The President's desire is that these movements and changes should be understood as being gradual and wholly consistent with existing policy.

McGeorge Bundy

[Document 255]

Reprinted from New York *Times*

April 17, 1965

FM: AMEMBASSY SAIGON

TO: SECSTATE IMMEDIATE 3423

EXDIS

This message undertakes to summarize instructions which I have received over the last ten days with regard to the introduction of third-country combat forces and to discuss the preferred way of presenting the subject to the GVN.

As the result of the meeting of the President and his advisors on April 1 and the NSC meeting on the following day, I left Washington and returned to Saigon with the understanding that the reinforcement of the Marines already ashore by two additional BLT's and a F-4 squadron and the progressive introduction of IIAWPNPPP support forces were approved but that decision on the several proposals for bringing in more U.S. combat forces and their possible modes of employment was withheld in an offensive counterinsurgency role. State was to explore with the Korean, Australian and New Zealand govts the possibility of rapid deployment of significant combat elements in parallel with the Marine reinforcement.

Since arriving home, I have received the following instructions and have taken the indicated actions with respect to third-country combat forces.

April 6 and 8. Received GVN concurrence to introduction of the Marine reinforcements and to an expanded mission for all Marines in Danang-Phu Bai area.

April 8. Received Deptel 2229 directing approach to GVN, suggesting request to Australian govt for an infantry battalion for use in SVN. While awaiting a propitious moment to raise the matter, I received Deptel 2237 directing approach be delayed until further orders. Nothing further has been received since.

April 14. I learned by JCS 009012 to Cincpac of apparent decision to deploy 173rd airborne brigade immediately to Bien Hoa-Vung Tau. By Embtel 3373, delay in this deployment was urgently recommended but no reply has been received. However, Para 2 of Doc 152339 apparently makes reference to this project in terms which suggest that is something less than as an approved immediate action. In view of the uncertainty of its status, I have not broached the matter with Quat.

April 15. Received Deptel 2314 directing that embassy Saigon discuss with GVN introduction of Rok regimental combat team and suggest GVN request such a force Asap. Because of Quat's absence from Saigon, I have not been able to raise matter. As matter of fact, it should not be raised until we have a clear concept of employment.

April 16. I have just seen state-defense message Dod 152339 cited above which indicates a favorable attitude toward several possible uses of U.S. combat forces beyond the NSC decisions of April 2. I am told to discuss these and certain other non-military matters urgently with Quat. The substance of this cable will be addressed in a separate message. I can not raise these matters with Quat without further guidance.

Faced with this rapidly changing picture of Washington desires and intentions with regard to the introduction of third-country (as well as U.S.) combat forces, I badly need a clarification of our purposes and objectives. Before I can present our case to GVN, I have to know what that case is and why. It is not going to be easy to get ready concurrence for the large-scale introduction of foreign troops unless the need is clear and explicit.

Let me suggest the kind of instruction to the AMB which it would be most helpful to receive for use in presenting to GVN what I take to be a new policy of third-country participation in ground combat.

"The USG has completed a thorough review of the situation in SVN both in its national and international aspects and has reached certain important conclusions. It feels that in recent weeks there has been a somewhat favorable change in the overall situation as the result of the air attacks on DRV, the relatively small but numerous successes in the field against the VC and the encouraging progress of the Quat govt. However, it is becoming increasingly clear that, in all probability, the primary objective of the GVN and the USG of changing the will of the DRV to support the VC insurgency can not be attained in an acceptable time-frame by the methods presently employed. The air campaign in the North must be supplemented by signal successes against the VC on the South before we can hope to create that frame of mind in Hanoi which will lead to the decisions we seek.

"The JCS have reviewed the military resources which will be available in SVN by the end of 1965 and have concluded that even with an attainment of the highest feasible mobilization goals, ARVN will have insufficient forces to carry out the kind of successful campaign against the VC which is considered essential for the purposes discussed above. If the ground war is not to drag into 1966 and even beyond, they consider it necessary to reinforce GVN ground forces with about 23 battalion equivalents in addition to the forces now being recruited in SVN. Since these reinforcements can not be raised by the GVN, they must inevitably come from third-country sources.

"The USG accepts the validity of this reasoning of the JCS and offers its assistance to the GVN to raise these additional forces for the purpose of bringing the VC insurgency to an end in the shortest possible time. We are prepared to bring in additional U.S. ground forces provided we can get a reasonable degree of participation from other third countries. If the GVN will make urgent representations to them, we believe it entirely possible to obtain the following contributions; Korea, one regimental combat team; Australia, one infantry battalion; New Zealand, one battery and one company of tanks; PI, one battalion. If forces of the foregoing magnitude are forthcoming, the USG is prepared to provide the remainder of the combat reinforcements as well as the necessary logistic personnel to support the third-country contingents. Also it will use its good offices as desired in assisting the GVN approach to these govts.

"You (the Ambassador) will seek the concurrence of the GVN to the foregoing program, recognizing that a large number of questions such as command relationships, concepts of employment and disposition of forces must be worked out subsequently." Armed with an instruction such as the foregoing, I would feel adequately equipped to initiate what may be a sharp debate with the GVN. I need something like this before taking up the pending troop matters with Quat.

[Document 256]

21 April 1965: W. Bundy, JTM and I met with Amb Taylor, Wheeler, Sharp and Westmoreland in Honolulu on April 20. Following is my report of that meeting.

1. None of them expects the VC to capitulate or to come to a position acceptable to us, in less than six months. This is because they believe that a settlement

will come as much or more from VC failure in the South as from DRV pain in the North, and that it will take more than six months, perhaps a year or two, to demonstrate VC failure in the South.

2. With respect to strikes against the North, they all think that the present tempo is about right, that sufficient increasing pressure is provided by repetition and continuation. All of them envisioned a strike program continuing at least six months, perhaps a year or more, avoiding the Hanoi-Haiphong-Phuc Yen areas during that period. There might be fewer fixed targets, or more restrikes, or more armed reconnaissance missions. Amb Taylor stated what appears to be a shared view; that it is important not to "kill the hostage" by destroying the NVNese assets inside the "Hanoi donut." They all believe that the strike program is essential to our campaign—both psychologically and physically—but that it cannot be expected to do the job alone. They all considered it very important that strikes against the North be continued during any talks.

3. None of them sees a dramatic improvement in the South in the immediate future. Their strategy for "victory" over time, is to break the will of the DRV/VC by depriving them of victory. Amb Taylor put it in terms of a demonstration of Communist impotence, which will lead eventually to a political solution. They see slow improvement in the South, but all emphasized the critical importance of holding on and avoiding—for psychological and morale reasons—a spectacular defeat of GVN or US forces. And they all suspect that the recent VC lull is but the quiet before a storm.

4. To bolster the GVN forces while they are building up, they all recommend the following deployments in addition to the 2000 Koreans and 33,500 US troops already in-country (including the 4 Marine battalions at Danang-Hue):

(13 US battalions: 82,000; ROK and ANZAC 4 bns: 7250. Possible later deployments, not recommended now; US Airmobile div (15,800), rest of Korean division, rest of MEF 24,800).

McNamara

Justification of the War—Public Statements

CONTENTS

JOHNSON ADMINISTRATION

1964

the attack on the *Maddox* and our established policy of assisting countries victimized by aggression as leading to U.S. actions.

Public Statement 10   *(page 720)*
President Johnson recalls SEATO commitment to South Vietnam in address to Congress; he stressed consistency in U.S. policy as enunciated on June 2 (D-7).

Public Statement 11   *(page 721)*
Secretary Rusk explains swiftness of U.S. response to Gulf of Tonkin attack as necessitated by act of war and the importance of conveying to Hanoi the seriousness of the situation.

Public Statement 12   *(page 722)*
Gulf of Tonkin resolution cites the attack on an American ship in combination with aggressive acts of NVN in SVN as justifying "all necessary measures to repel any armed attack against the forces of the U.S. and to prevent further aggression."

Public Statement 13   *(page 722)*
Secretary Rusk states, ". . . South Vietnam is a critical test-case for new Communist strategy."

Public Statement 14   *(page 723)*
William Bundy relates the fall of SVN and the success of the wars of liberation strategy to the future of other Asian countries, including India and Japan, Australia and the underdeveloped nations throughout the world.

Public Statement 15   *(page 723)*
Secretary Rusk suggests that U.S. security is threatened by persistent aggression which remains unchecked; while not supporting the "domino theory" designation, he points out the Communist appetite for revolution as expressed in their proclamations.

1965

Public Statement 16   *(page 725)*
Secretary Rusk again suggests one does not need the domino theory to predict Communist threat; Peiping proclamations and actions provide ample evidence of expansionist doctrine; relates validity of NATO commitment to U.S. response to aggressive acts to a SEATO protocol state.

Public Statement 17   *(page 725)*
President Johnson emphasizes again U.S. presence in response to request from SVN to help meet aggression and its relation to U.S. security interests.

Public Statement 18   *(page 725)*
William Bundy relates actions in Korea to VN; spells out action initiated in 1954 by President Eisenhower and the support provided by Congress in terms of SEATO ratification and budget approvals. He cites effect of the outcome of VN struggle on neighboring states and on the prestige and power of the Communist movement's new strategy, wars of liberation.

Public Statement 19   *(page 727)*
William Bundy cites the U.S.'s intent to permit nations to develop freely the potential consequences to neighboring countries if SVN should fall under Communist

control and the importance of demonstrating that "wars of liberation" are not to be tolerated as paramount among U.S. concerns.

Public Statement 20 (page 727)
Secretary Rusk states the legal basis of U.S. bombing to be "self defense of SVN and the commitments of U.S. with respect to the security and self-defense of SVN."

Public Statement 21 (page 727)
Ambassador Stevenson cites record of aggression in SVN in communication to UN.

Public Statement 22 (page 729)
Secretary Rusk refers to lessons of World War II and SEATO pact as important reasons for meeting aggression in SVN before it spreads further.

Public Statement 23 (page 729)
Department of State statement cites Constitutional authority of President to meet obligation under SEATO in response to aggression in SVN.

Public Statement 24 (page 730)
President Johnson relates aggression in SVN as "part of wider pattern of aggressive purposes" urged on by Peiping; vows to fulfill U.S. commitment supported by his three predecessors.

Public Statement 25 (page 731)
Leonard Unger emphasizes strategic significance of region to U.S. and "test case for wars of liberation" strategy in explaining U.S. concerns in VN.

Public Statement 26 (page 733)
Secretary Rusk defines "wars of liberation" as endorsed by Communist leaders, explains SVN's right of self-defense in legal terms and details the nature of the struggle in SVN.

Public Statement 27 (page 736)
President Johnson cites aggression as requiring firm stand by U.S. Secretary McNamara in response to a question defines the "wars of liberation" strategy as urged by Communist leaders.

Public Statement 28 (page 737)
Secretary Ball cites "wars of liberation" as threatening the existence of small states everywhere.

Public Statement 29 (page 738)
President Johnson states the Communist aim in VN is to show the "American commitment is worthless"; success in that effort, he predicts, would remove the one obstacle standing between "expanding communism and independent Asian nations."

Public Statement 30 (page 738)
William Bundy explains myths surrounding the question of "reunification election" and the relationship between the opposition to Diem and the Viet Cong; he documents U.S. concerns regarding the "wars of liberation" threat.

Public Statement 31 (page 741)
President Johnson states Communist China's "target is not merely SVN, it is

Asia" and their objective in VN is "to erode and to discredit America's ability to help prevent Chinese domination over all of Asia."

Public Statement 32   (page 741)
William Bundy discusses the threat of Communist China which underlies the American presence in Asia, and the relationship of Hanoi to the Communist movement.

Public Statement 33   (page 743)
President Johnson states our failures in the 1930's resulted from inaction rather than action.

JOHNSON ADMINISTRATION

Summary

1964

President Johnson succeeded to the Presidency upon the assassination of President Kennedy in November 1963 only three weeks after the *coup d'etat* which saw the Ngo Dinh Diem regime crushed and Diem himself murdered. Confronted with a crisis, the U.S. renewed its pledge to support the military junta and the free government of Vietnam. The U.S. increased its support even as the GVN wavered through a series of government changes each reflecting the control retained by the military. U.S. involvement deepened with the increased advisory strength and the introduction of combat troops in 1964. The Tonkin Gulf crisis and the subsequent resolution became benchmarks for the U.S. commitment. The new Administration emphasized the following points:

a. Organized aggression from the North obligated the United States to fulfill its commitments under the SEATO treaty.

b. The strategic importance of Southeast Asia to the security of the United States and the test of "wars of liberation" there as important to the future peace and freedom of South Vietnam.

c. The Gulf of Tonkin action showed that "aggression by terror" had been joined by "open aggression on the high seas" against the United States and the resolution which followed justified measures to "repel any armed attack."

d. The communist "appetite for aggression" through "wars of liberation" threatened not only other Asian countries, but also the United States if left unchecked. The U.S. seeks no wider war.

e. Four basic themes govern U.S. policy, essentially unchanged since 1954: America keeps her word; the future of Southeast Asia is the issue; "our purpose is peace; and, this war is a "struggle for freedom."

1965

The level of war was escalated by introduction of increased U.S. combat troop strength and the initiation of air strikes against targets in North Vietnam. The Administration justified the escalation on the basis of increased infiltration of North Vietnamese units into South Vietnam and, in general, justified U.S. involvement using much the same rationale as the Kennedy Administration. The "domino theory," however, was de-emphasized in light of communist proclamations and predictions for success. The role of Communist China was given more publicity. The Administration's public pronouncements stressed the following:

a. The U.S. had been committed ten years before and had pledged help to the people of South Vietnam. "Three Presidents have supported that pledge" and it would not be broken. The "integrity of the American commitment" is at the heart of the problem as a point of national honor.

b. The security of the U.S. was tied closely to the expansion of communism in Southeast Asia: if the American counterinsurgency efforts are defeated in Vietnam, they can be defeated anywhere in the world. Failure to halt aggression through "wars of national liberation" would see increasing communist pressure on neighboring states and subsequently greater aggression. "These are big stakes indeed."

c. The basic issue of the conflict was "letting the nations of the area develop as they see fit"; if South Vietnam fell to communist control it would be difficult to prevent the fall of neighboring states. The "domino theory" was not considered a suitable explanation for the SEA situation.

d. "The confused nature of this conflict cannot mask the fact that it is the new face of an old enemy. Over this war—and all Asia—is another reality: the deepening shadow of Communist China. The rulers in Hanoi are urged on by Peiping."

e. South Vietnam represented a major test of communism's new strategy of "wars of liberation." Veiled aggression under this strategy had its source in North Vietnam—previously a privileged sanctuary—and free nations had to defend themselves. "The simple issue is that military personnel and arms have been sent across an international demarcation line contrary to international agreements and law . . ."

Johnson Administration

1. *Secretary Rusk Interviewed on Voice of America, 15 February 1964, Department of State Bulletin, 2 March 1964, p. 333:*

* * *

Mr. O'Neill: "Well, Hanoi has just publicly now identified itself as supporting the guerrillas in South Vietnam and also threatening that Red China would intervene in any action against North Vietnam. Do you see any connection between that and the French recognition, or do you think this is an isolated development?"

Secretary Rusk: "I haven't seen anything that would lead me to say there was an organic connection between what Hanoi has just said and what Paris has done. It is true that Hanoi has made no secret of this policy since 1959. They have publicly declared that they are out to take over South Vietnam, and in this same statement to which you are referring they made it very clear that North Vietnam is not going to be neutralized and that their interest in South Vietnam is not so much neutrality as taking it over. So I think the issues have been drawn very clearly out there."

Mr. O'Neill: "While we are on that area, how is the fighting in South Vietnam? Are we going to be able to win out, and do you have any idea as to how soon that might be?"

Secretary Rusk: "Well, I think we will have to wait a bit before we can speak with complete confidence about it in the short run. In the long run, I have no doubt that the resources, the will, the material are present in South Vietnam to enable the South Vietnamese to do this job. We are determined that Southeast Asia is not going to be taken over by the communists. We must insist that these basic accords be adhered to. And so we are in this to the point where the South Vietnamese are going to be independent and secure."

* * *

Mr. Ward: "Mr. Secretary, I wish you'd say something about this word 'neutralization'—not whether Southeast Asia or some parts thereof should be neutralized, but what the word itself means. It seems to me there is a great deal of misunderstanding that flows from varied uses of the word."

Secretary Rusk: "Well, the word gets confused because it has meant so many different things to different people. I suppose in the strictest sense a neutral is, in time of peace, a so-called 'unaligned' country, that it is not committed to one of the two major power blocs in the world, the NATO bloc or the communist bloc.

"Well, now, we don't object to neutrals or policies of neutrality or neutralization in that sense. There are a great many countries who are unaligned with whom we have very close and friendly relations. We are not looking for allies. We are not looking for military bases out in Southeast Asia. We are not even looking for a military presence in that part of the world.

"Our troops are there assisting the South Vietnamese because people in the north have been putting pressures on Southeast Asia. If those pressures did not exist, those troops wouldn't be there. But when one talks about neutralizing South Vietnam in the present context, this means, really, getting the Americans out. That is all that that means.

"Now, North Vietnam is not going to be neutralized. It's going to remain a member of the communist camp. And from the time that it was established, North Vietnam has broken agreements and has applied pressure on its neighbors, particularly Laos and South Vietnam. So that if anyone has in mind that South Vietnam should be neutralized, meaning that Americans should simply go home and leave it exposed to takeover from the north, then this isn't going to happen.

"Now, if South Vietnam were independent and secure, it would be perfectly free to pursue its own policy. It can be unaligned, as far as we are concerned."

*   *   *

2. *TV Interview with President Johnson, 15 March 1964, Public Papers of The Presidents, Johnson, 1963–64, p. 370:*

Mr. Sevareid: "Mr. Kennedy said, on the subject of Vietnam, I think, that he did believe in the 'falling domino' theory, that if Vietnam were lost, that other countries in the area would soon be lost."

The President: "I think it would be a very dangerous thing, and I share President Kennedy's view, and I think the whole of Southeast Asia would be involved and that would involve hundreds of millions of people, and I think it's—it cannot be ignored, we must do everything that we can, we must be responsible, we must stay there and help them, and that is what we are going to do."

*   *   *

3. *"United States Policy in Vietnam," by Robert S. McNamara, Secretary of Defense, 26 March 1964, Department of State Bulletin, 13 April 1964, p. 562:*

*   *   *

"At the Third National Congress of the Lao Dong (Communist) Party in Hanoi, September 1960, North Vietnam's belligerency was made explicit. Ho Chi Minh stated, 'The North is becoming more and more consolidated and transformed into a firm base for the struggle for national reunification.' At the same congress it was announced that the party's new task was 'to liberate the South from the atrocious rule of the U.S. imperialists and their henchmen.' In brief, Hanoi was about to embark upon a program of wholesale violations of the Geneva agreements in order to wrest control of South Vietnam from its legitimate government.

"To the communists, 'liberation' meant sabotage, terror, and assassination: attacks on innocent hamlets and villages and the coldblooded murder of thousands of schoolteachers, health workers, and local officials who had the misfortune to oppose the communist version of 'liberation.' In 1960 and 1961 almost 3,000 South Vietnamese civilians in and out of government were assassinated and another 2,500 were kidnaped. The communists even assassinated the colonel who served as liaison officer to the International Control Commission.

"This aggression against South Vietnam was a major communist effort, meticulously planned and controlled, and relentlessly pursued by the government in Hanoi. In 1961 the Republic of Vietnam, unable to contain the menace by itself, appealed to the United States to honor its unilateral declaration of 1954. President Kennedy responded promptly and affirmatively by sending to that country additional American advisers, arms, and aid.

U.S. Objectives:

"I turn now to a consideration of United States objectives in South Vietnam. The United States has no designs whatever on the resources or territory of the area. Our national interests do not require that South Vietnam serve as a Western base or as a member of a Western alliance. Our concern is threefold.

"First, and most important, is the simple fact that South Vietnam, a member of the free world family, is striving to preserve its independence from communist attack. The Vietnamese have asked our help. We have given it. We shall continue to give it.

"We do so in their interest; and we do so in our own clear self-interest. For basic to the principles of freedom and self-determination which have sustained our country for almost two centuries is the right of peoples everywhere to live and develop in peace. Our own security is strengthened by the determination of others to remain free, and by our commitment to assist them. We will not let this member of our family down, regardless of its distance from our shores.

"The ultimate goal of the United States in Southeast Asia, as in the rest of the world, is to help maintain free and independent nations which can develop politically, economically, and socially and which can be responsible members of the world community. In this region and elsewhere many peoples share our sense of the value of such freedom and independence. They have taken the risks and made the sacrifices linked to the commitment to membership in the family of the free world. They have done this in the belief that we would back up our pledges to help defend them. It is not right or even expedient—nor is it in our nature—to abandon them when the going is difficult.

"Second, Southeast Asia has great strategic significance in the forward defense of the United States. Its location across east-west air and sea lanes flanks the Indian subcontinent on one side and Australia, New Zealand, and the Philippines on the other and dominates the gateway between the Pacific and Indian Oceans. In communist hands this area would pose a most serious threat to the security of the United States and to the family of free-world nations to which we belong. To defend Southeast Asia, we must meet the challenge in South Vietnam.

"And third, South Vietnam is a test case for the new communist strategy. Let me examine for a moment the nature of this strategy.

"Just as the Kennedy administration was coming into office in January 1961, Chairman Khrushchev made one of the most important speeches on communist strategy of recent decades. In his report on a party conference entitled 'For New Victories of the World Communist Movement,' Khrushchev stated: 'In modern conditions, the following categories of wars should be distinguished: world wars, local wars, liberation wars and popular uprising.' He ruled out what he called 'world wars' and 'local wars' as being too dangerous for profitable indulgence in a world of nuclear weapons. But with regard to what he called 'liberation wars,' he referred specifically to Vietnam. He said, 'It is a sacred war. We recognize such wars . . .' "

*   *   *

"President Kennedy and President Johnson have recognized, however, that our forces for the first two types of wars might not be applicable or effective against what the communists call 'wars of liberation,' or what is properly called covert aggression or insurgency. We have therefore undertaken and continue to press a variety of programs to develop skilled specialists, equipment, and techniques to enable us to help our allies counter the threat of insurgency.

"Communist interest in insurgency techniques did not begin with Khrushchev, nor for that matter with Stalin. Lenin's works are full of tactical instructions, which were adapted very successfully by Mao Tse-tung, whose many writings on guerrilla warfare have become classic references. Indeed, Mao claims to be the true heir of Lenin's original prescriptions for the worldwide victory of communism. The North Vietnamese have taken a leaf or two from Mao's book—as well as Moscow's—and added some of their own.

"Thus today in Vietnam we are not dealing with factional disputes or the remnants of a colonial struggle against the French but rather with a major test case of communism's new strategy. That strategy has so far been pursued in Cuba, may be beginning in Africa, and failed in Malaya and the Philippines only because of a long and arduous struggle by the people of these countries with assistance provided by the British and the United States.

"In Southeast Asia the communists have taken full advantage of geography— the proximity to the communist base of operations and the rugged, remote, and heavily foliated character of the border regions. They have utilized the diverse ethnic, religious, and tribal groupings and exploited factionalism and legitimate aspirations wherever possible. And, as I said earlier, they have resorted to sabotage, terrorism, and assassination on an unprecedented scale.

"Who is the responsible party—the prime aggressor? First and foremost, without doubt, the prime aggressor is North Vietnam, whose leadership has explicitly undertaken to destroy the independence of the South. To be sure, Hanoi is encouraged on its aggressive course by Communist China. But Peiping's interest is hardly the same as that of Hanoi.

"For Hanoi, the immediate objective is limited: conquest of the South and national unification, perhaps coupled with control of Laos. For Peiping, however, Hanoi's victory would be only a first step toward eventual Chinese hegemony over the two Vietnams and Southeast Asia and toward exploitation of the new strategy in other parts of the world.

"Communist China's interests are clear: It has publicly castigated Moscow for betraying the revolutionary cause whenever the Soviets have sounded a cautionary note. It has characterized the United States as a paper tiger and has insisted that the revolutionary struggle for 'liberation and unification' of Vietnam could be conducted without risks by, in effect, crawling under the nuclear and conventional defense of the free world. Peiping thus appears to feel that it has a large stake in demonstrating the new strategy, using Vietnam as a test case. Success in Vietnam would be regarded by Peiping as vindication for China's views in the worldwide ideological struggle.

"Taking into account the relationship of Vietnam to Indochina—and of both to Southeast Asia, the Far East, and the free world as a whole—five U.S. Presidents have acted to preserve free-world strategic interests in the area. President Roosevelt opposed Japanese penetration in Indochina; President Truman resisted communist aggression in Korea; President Eisenhower backed Diem's efforts to save South Vietnam and undertook to defend Taiwan; President Kennedy stepped up our counterinsurgency effort in Vietnam; and President Johnson, in addition to reaffirming last week that the United States will furnish assistance and support to South Vietnam for as long as it is required to bring communist aggression and terrorism under control, has approved the program that I shall describe in a few minutes.

"The U.S. role in South Vietnam, then, is *first*, to answer the call of the South Vietnamese, a member nation of our free-world family, to help them save their country for themselves; *second*, to help prevent the strategic danger which would exist if communism absorbed Southeast Asia's people and resources; and *third*, to prove in the Vietnamese test case that the free-world can cope with communist 'wars of liberation' as we have coped successfully with communist aggression at other levels."

*　　*　　*

4. *"U.S. Calls for Frontier Patrol to Help Prevent Border Incidents Between Cambodia and Vietnam." Statement by Adlai Stevenson to Security Council, 21 May 1964, Department of State Bulletin, 8 June 1964, p. 908:*

*　　*　　*

First, the United States had no, repeat *no*, national military objective anywhere in Southeast Asia. United States policy for Southeast Asia is very simple. It is the restoration of peace so that the peoples of that area can go about their own independent business in whatever associations they may freely choose for themselves without interference from the outside.

I trust my words have been clear enough on this point.

Second, the United States Government is currently involved in the affairs of the Republic of Vietnam for one reason and one reason only: because the Republic of Vietnam requested the help of the United States and of other governments to defend itself against armed attack fomented, equipped, and directed from the outside.

"This is not the first time that the United States Government has come to the aid of peoples prepared to fight for their freedom and independence against armed aggression sponsored from outside their borders. Nor will it be the last time unless the lesson is learned once and for all by *all aggressors* that armed aggression does not pay—that it no longer works—that it will not be tolerated. The record of the past two decades makes it clear that a nation with the will for self-preservation can outlast and defeat overt or clandestine aggression—even when that internal aggression is heavily supported from the outside, and even after significant early successes by the aggressors. I would remind the members that in 1947, after the aggressors had gained control of most of the country, many people felt that the cause of the Government of Greece was hopelessly lost. But as long as the people of Greece were prepared to fight for the life of their own country, the United States was not prepared to stand by while Greece was overrun.

This principle does not change with the geographical setting. Aggression is aggression; organized violence is organized violence. Only the scale and the scenery change; the point is the same in Vietnam today as it was in Greece in 1947 and in Korea in 1950. The Indochinese Communist Party, the parent of the present Communist Party in North Vietnam, made it abundantly clear as early as 1951 that the aim of the Vietnamese Communist leadership is to take control of all of Indochina. This goal has not changed—it is still clearly the objective of the Vietnamese Communist leadership in Hanoi.

Hanoi seeks to accomplish this purpose in South Vietnam through subversive guerrilla warfare directed, controlled, and supplied by North Vietnam. The communist leadership in Hanoi has sought to pretend that the insurgency in South Vietnam is a civil war, but Hanoi's hand shows very clearly. Public statements by the Communist Party in North Vietnam and its leaders have repeatedly demonstrated Hanoi's direction of the struggle in South Vietnam. For example, Le Duan, First Secretary of the Party, stated on September 5, 1960, "At present our Party is facing [a] momentous task: . . . to strive to complete . . . revolution throughout the country . . ." He also said this: "The North is the common revolutionary base of the whole country." Three months after the Communist Party Congress in Hanoi in September 1960, the so-called "National Front for the Liberation of South Vietnam" was set up pursuant to plans outlined publicly at that Congress.

The International Control Commission in Vietnam, established by the Geneva accords of 1954, stated in a special report which it issued in June 1962 that there is sufficient evidence to show that North Vietnam has violated various articles of the Geneva accords by its introduction of armed personnel, arms, munitions, and other supplies from North Vietnam into South Vietnam with the object of supporting, organizing, and carrying out hostile activities against the Government and armed forces of South Vietnam.

Infiltration of military personnel and supplies from North Vietnam to South Vietnam has been carried out steadily over the past several years. The total number of military cadres sent into South Vietnam via infiltration routes runs into the thousands. Such infiltration is well documented on the basis of numerous defectors and prisoners taken by the armed forces of South Vietnam.

Introduction of communist weapons into South Vietnam has also grown steadily. An increasing amount of weapons and ammunition captured from the Viet Cong has been proven to be of Chinese Communist manufacture or origin. For example, in December 1963 a large cache of Viet Cong equipment captured in one of the Mekong Delta provinces in South Vietnam included recoilless rifles, rocket launchers, carbines, and ammunition of Chinese Communist manufacture.

The United States cannot stand by while Southeast Asia is overrun by armed aggressors. As long as the peoples of that area are determined to preserve their own independence and ask for our help in preserving it, we will extend it. This, of course, is the meaning of President Johnson's request a few days ago for additional funds for more economic as well as military assistance for Vietnam.

And if anyone has the illusion that my Government will abandon the people of Vietnam—or that we shall weary of the burden of support that we are rendering these people—it can only be due to ignorance of the strength and the conviction of the American people.

*   *   *

5. *"The Defense of the Free World,"* Robert S. McNamara, Secretary of Defense, before the National Ind Conf Bd, 21 May 1964, Department of State Bulletin, 8 June 1964, p. 895:

*   *   *

The "Forward Defense" Nations:

Our military assistance program today is oriented mainly toward those countries on the periphery of the major communist nations where the threats are greatest and in which the indigenous resources are least. In the fiscal year 1965 program now before the Congress, about two-thirds of the total amount is scheduled to go to the 11 nations on the southern and eastern perimeters of the Soviet and Red Chinese blocs. These sentinels of the free world, in a sense, are in double jeopardy from potential military aggression from without and from attempted subversion from within. These countries are under the Red shadow. They face the major threat, and they are the ones most affected by the modernization of communist forces. For this group we requested $745 million in military assistance. They best illustrate the points I want to make.

Imagine a globe, if you will, and on that globe the Sino-Soviet bloc. The bloc is contained at the north by the Arctic. To the west are the revitalized nations of Western Europe. But across the south and to the east you find the 11 "forward defense" nations—Greece, Turkey, Iran, Pakistan, India, Laos, Thailand, South Vietnam, the Philippines, and the Republics of China and Korea. These nations, together with stretches of the Pacific Ocean bearing the U.S. Fleet, describe an arc along which the free world draws its frontlines of defense.

The frontlines are there in the interests of those 11 nations; the lines are there also in the interests of the United States and the rest of the free world. The areas which this 11-nation arc protects are of obvious strategic importance to the United States. More significant, however, is the importance of the arc to the principle that nations have a right to be independent—a right to develop in peace, in freedom, and according to the principle of self-determination. United States support of these rights at the frontiers thickens the blood of the free-world family; it strengthens our security at home.

We must recognize, however, that the United States does not have the resources to maintain a credible force by itself along all of this great arc of forward positions. Such a strategy would be unbearably costly to us in both money and human resources. The United States maintains major combat units ashore in forward positions only in Europe and in parts of the Far East. Such deployments are costly and hurt our balance-of-payments position. We do not now contemplate additional semipermanent deployments of forces abroad.

*   *   *

6. *"Laos and Viet-Nam—A Prescription for Peace,"* Address by Secretary Rusk before the American Law Institute, Washington, D.C., 22 May 1964, Department of State Bulletin, 8 June 1964, p. 890:

*   *   *

Four Alternatives in Vietnam:

You are all aware of the four principal alternatives in South Vietnam which have been referred to in recent discussion. The first would be to withdraw and forget about Southeast Asia. That would mean not only grievous losses to the free world in Southeast and southern Asia but a drastic loss of confidence in the will and capacity of the free world to oppose aggression. It would also bring us much closer to a major conflagration. Surely we have learned, in the course of the last 35 years, that a course of aggression means war and that the place to stop it is at its beginning.

*   *   *

At the meeing of the Council of the Southeast Asia Treaty Organization in Manila last month, seven of the eight members joined in declaring the defeat of the aggression against South Vietnam to be "essential not only to the security of the Republic of Vietnam, but to that of Southeast Asia." And, they said, its defeat will also be convincing proof that communist expansion by such tactics will not be permitted.

*   *   *

7. *"President Outlines Basic Themes of U.S. Policy in Southeast Asia," Statement by President Johnson at his News Conference on June 2, 1964, Department of State Bulletin, 22 June 1964, p. 953:*

It may be helpful to outline four basic themes that govern our policy in Southeast Asia.
First, America keeps her word.
Second, the issue is the future of Southeast Asia as a whole.
Third, our purpose is peace.
Fourth, this is not just a jungle war, but a struggle for freedom on every front of human activity.
On the point that America keeps her word, we are steadfast in a policy which has been followed for 10 years in three administrations.

*   *   *

8. *"Address to the Nation by President Johnson," 4 August 1964, Department of State Bulletin, 24 August 1964, p. 259:*

*   *   *

In the larger sense this new act of aggression, aimed directly at our own forces, again brings home to all of us in the United States the importance of the struggle for peace and security in Southeast Asia. Aggression by terror against the peaceful villagers of South Vietnam has now been joined by open aggression on the high seas against the United States of America.

*   *   *

9. *"Address by the President, Syracuse University, 5 August 1964," Department of State Bulletin, 24 August 1964, p. 260:*

*   *   *

Aggression—deliberate, willful, and systematic aggression—has unmasked its face to the entire world. The world remembers—the world must never forget—that aggression unchallenged is aggression unleashed.

We of the United States have not forgotten. That is why we have answered this aggression with action.

America's course is not without long provocation.

For 10 years, three American Presidents—President Eisenhower, President Kennedy, and your present President—and the American people have been actively concerned with threats to the peace and security of the peoples of Southeast Asia from the communist government of North Vietnam.

President Eisenhower sought—and President Kennedy sought—the same objectives that I still seek:

—That the governments of Southeast Asia honor the international agreements which apply in the area;

—That those governments leave each other alone;

—That they resolve their differences peacefully;

—That they devote their talents to bettering the lives of their peoples by working against poverty and disease and ignorance.

In 1954 we made our position clear toward Vietnam.

In July of that year we stated we would view any renewal of the aggression in violation of the 1954 agreements "with grave concern and as seriously threatening international peace and security."

In September of that year the United States signed the Manila Pact, on which our participation in SEATO is based. That pact recognized that aggression by means of armed attack on South Vietnam would endanger the peace and the safety of the nations signing that solemn agreement.

In 1962 we made our position clear toward Laos. We signed the Declaration on the Neutrality of Laos. That accord provided for the withdrawal of all foreign forces and respect for the neutrality and independence of that little country.

The agreements of 1954 and 1962 were also signed by the government of North Vietnam.

In 1954 that government pledged that it would respect the territory under the military control of the other party and engage in no hostile act against the other party.

In 1962 that government pledged that it would "not introduce into the Kingdom of Laos foreign troops or military personnel."

That government also pledged that it would "not use the territory of the Kingdom of Laos for interference in the internal affairs of other countries."

That government of North Vietnam is now willfully and systematically violating those agreements of both 1954 and 1962.

To the south, it is engaged in aggression aagainst the Republic of Vietnam.

To the west, it is engaged in aggression against the Kingdom of Laos.

To the east, it has now struck out on the high seas in an act of aggression against the United States of America.

There can be and there must be no doubt about the policy and no doubt about the purpose.

So there can be no doubt about the responsibilities of men and the responsibilities of nations that are devoted to peace.

Peace cannot be assured merely by assuring the safety of the United States destroyer MADDOX or the safety of other vessels of other flags.

Peace requires that the existing agreements in the area be honored.

Peace requires that we and all our friends stand firm against the present aggressions of the government of North Vietnam.

The government of North Vietnam is today flouting the will of the world for peace. The world is challenged to make its will against war known and to make it known clearly and to make it felt and to make it felt decisively.

So, to our friends of the Atlantic alliance, let me say this this morning. The challenge that we face in Southeast Asia today is the same challenge that we have faced with courage and that we have met with strength in Greece and Turkey, in Berlin and Korea, in Lebanon and in Cuba, and to any who may be tempted to support or to widen the present aggression I say this: There is no threat to any peaceful power from the United States of America. But there can be no peace by aggression and no immunity from reply. That is what is meant by the actions that we took yesterday.

*   *   *

10. *"President's Message to Congress, 5 August 1964," Department of State Bulletin, 24 August 1964, p. 261:*

*   *   *

These latest actions of the North Vietnamese regime have given a new and grave turn to the already serious situation in Southeast Asia. Our commitments in that area are well known to the Congress. They were first made in 1954 by President Eisenhower. They were further defined in the Southeast Asia Collective Defense Treaty approved by the Senate in February 1955.

This treaty with its accompanying protocol obligates the United States and other members to act in accordance with their constitutional processes to meet communist aggression against any of the parties or protocol states.

Our policy in Southeast Asia has been consistent and unchanged since 1954. I summarized it on June 2 in four simple propositions:

1. *America keeps her word.* Here as elsewhere, we must and shall honor our commitments.

2. *The issue is the future of Southeast Asia as a whole.* A threat to any nation in that region is a threat to all, and a threat to us.

3. *Our purpose is peace.* We have no military, political, or territorial ambitions in the area.

4. *This is not just a jungle war, but a struggle for freedom on every front of human activity.* Our military and economic assistance to South Vietnam and Laos in particular has the purpose of helping these countries to repel aggression and strengthen their independence.

The threat to the free nations of Southeast Asia has long been clear. The North Vietnamese regime has constantly sought to take over South Vietnam and Laos. This communist regime has violated the Geneva accords for Vietnam. It has systematically conducted a campaign of subversion, which includes the direction, training, and supply of personnel and arms for the conduct of guerrilla warfare in South Vietnamese territory. In Laos, the North Vietnamese regime has maintained military forces, used Laotian territory for infiltration into South Vietnam, and most recently carried out combat operations—all in direct violation of the Geneva agreements of 1962.

In recent months, the actions of the North Vietnamese regime have become steadily more threatening. In May, following new acts of communist aggression in Laos, the United States undertook reconnaissance flights over Laotian territory, at the request of the Government of Laos. These flights had the essential mission of determining the situation in territory where communist forces were preventing inspection by the International Control Commission. When the communists attacked these aircraft, I responded by furnishing escort fighters with instructions to fire when fired upon. Thus, these latest North Vietnamese attacks on our naval vessels are not the first direct attack on armed forces of the United States.

As President of the United States I have concluded that I should now ask the Congress, on its part, to join in affirming the national determination that all such attacks will be met, and that the United States will continue in its basic policy of assisting the free nations of the area to defend their freedom.

As I have repeatedly made clear, the United States intends no rashness, and seeks no wider war. We must make it clear to all that the United States is united in its determination to bring about the end of communist subversion and aggression in the area. We seek the full and effective restoration of the international agreements signed in Geneva in 1954, with respect to South Vietnam, and again in Geneva in 1962, with respect to Laos.

*   *   *

11. *"Secretary Rusk Discusses Asian Situation on NBC Program," 5 August 1964, Department of State Bulletin, 24 August 1964, p. 268:*

Following is the transcript of an interview of Secretary Rusk by NBC correspondent Elie Abel, broadcast over nationwide television on August 5.

Mr. Abel: "Mr. Secretary, are we going to get through this situation without touching off a bigger war?"

Secretary Rusk: "Well, Mr. Abel, one can't be a reliable prophet when the other side helps to write the scenario. But I do want to insist upon one point, that the purpose of the United States in Southeast Asia for these past 10 years or more has been a part of a general policy of the United States since World War II, that is, to organize a decent world community in which nations will leave their neighbors alone and in which nations can have a chance to live at peace with each other and cooperate on a basis of their common interests.

"Now, in Southeast Asia we have been saying over and over again, in conferences such as the Geneva conference of 1962 and elsewhere, that there is only one problem with peace in Southeast Asia and that is these pressures from the north, that if the north would leave their neighbors to the south alone, these peoples of that area could have their peace and could have a chance to work out their own lives in their own way. That is the problem, and to come to the decision to leave their neighbors alone is a necessary decision which Hanoi and anyone supporting Hanoi must reach."

Q. "Why was it necessary, Mr. Secretary, for us to strike as swiftly and abruptly as we did without taking time even to notify our allies?"

A. "Well, in the first place, we had some ships in the Gulf of Tonkin who were under attack, and they were dodging torpedoes. Here is a vast expanse of international waters in which we have a perfect right to be. We had to strike immediately because we didn't expect to ask those ships to run a continuing gauntlet of torpedoes on their way back to the Gulf of Tonkin when their mission was completed, nor were we prepared to have them denied international waters in the Gulf of Tonkin.

"Further than that, if under these attacks there had not been an immediate and appropriate response, then Hanoi and those who might be standing behind Hanoi in this might well have come to a very formidable mistaken judgment about what is possible in the Southeast Asian situation."

Q. "You mean their view that we are a paper tiger might have been confirmed?"

A. "That's correct. They could have made a basic miscalculation about what the commitment of the United States means in a situation of this sort."

*   *   *

12. *Text of Joint Resolution, August 7, Department of State Bulletin, 24 August 1964, p. 268:*

"To promote the maintenance of international peace and security in Southeast Asia.

"Whereas naval units of the communist regime in Vietnam, in violation of the principles of the Charter of the United Nations and of international law, have deliberately and repeatedly attacked United States naval vessels lawfully present in international waters, and have thereby created a serious threat to international peace; and

"Whereas these attacks are part of a deliberate and systematic campaign of aggression that the communist regime in North Vietnam has been waging against its neighbors and the nations joined with them in the collective defense of their freedom; and

"Whereas the United States is assisting the peoples of Southeast Asia to protect their freedom and has no territorial, military or political ambitions in that area, but desires only that these peoples should be left in peace to work out their own destinies in their own way: Now, therefore, be it

"*Resolved by the Senate and House of Representatives of the United States of America in Congress assembled,* That the Congress approves and supports the determination of the President, as Commander in Chief, to take all necessary measures to repel any armed attack against the forces of the United States and to prevent further aggression.

"Sec. 2. The United States regards as vital to its national interest and to world peace the maintenance of international peace and security in Southeast Asia. Consonant with the Constitution of the United States and the Charter of the United Nations and in accordance with its obligations under the Southeast Asia Collective Defense Treaty, the United States is, therefore, prepared, as the President determines, to take all necessary steps, including the use of armed force, to assist any member or protocol state of the Southeast Asia Collective Defense Treaty requesting assistance in defense of its freedom.

"Sec. 3. This resolution shall expire when the President shall determine that the peace and security of the area is reasonably assured by international conditions created by action of the United Nations or otherwise, except that it may be terminated earlier by concurrent resolution of the Congress."

*   *   *

13. *"Freedom in the Postwar World," by Secretary Rusk before American Veterans of WW II and Korea, Philadelphia, 29 August 1964, Department of State Bulletin, 14 September 1964, p. 365:*

*   *   *

"In Southeast Asia the free world suffered a setback in 1954 when, after the defeat at Dien Bien Phu, Vietnam was divided and a communist regime was consolidated in Hanoi. We helped South Vietnam to get on its feet and to build its military defenses. It made remarkable progress for a few years—which is perhaps why Communist North Vietnam, with the backing of Communist China, renewed its aggression against South Vietnam in 1959. In 1961 President Kennedy reviewed the situation, concluded that the assault from the north had been underestimated, and substantially increased our assistance to the Government and people of South Vietnam."

* * *

"Hanoi and Peiping have not yet learned that they must leave their neighbors alone. But this is a decision which they must reach. We and our SEATO allies have declared that the communist aggressions in Southeast Asia must be defeated. As you said, Commander Gulewicz, in your statement to the platform committees of the two major parties, '. . . we cannot afford to abandon the free people of Vietnam. The world watches because South Vietnam is a critical test-case for new communist strategy.' "

* * *

14. *"Progress and Problems in East Asia: An American Viewpoint," by William P. Bundy, Assistant Secretary for Far Eastern Affairs, Address made before the Research Institute of Japan at Tokyo, 29 September 1964, Department of State Bulletin, 19 October 1964, p. 537:*

* * *

"A word further about the situation in Southeast Asia, especially in South Vietnam. Here the aim of our policy is to assist the Government of South Vietnam in maintaining its independence and its control over the territory allotted to it by the Geneva accords of 1954. We do not aim at overthrowing the communist regime of North Vietnam but rather at inducing it to call off the war it directs and supports in South Vietnam.

"We believe it essential to the interests of the free world that South Vietnam not be permitted to fall under communist control. If it does, then the rest of Southeast Asia will be in grave danger of progressively disappearing behind the Bamboo Curtain and other Asian countries like India and even in time Australia and your own nation in turn will be threatened. If Hanoi and Peiping prevail in Vietnam in this key test of the new communist tactics of 'wars of national liberation,' then the communists will use this technique with growing frequency elsewhere in Asia, Africa, and Latin America."

* * *

15. *Secretary Rusk's News Conference of December 23, Press Release dated 23 December 1964, Department of State Bulletin, 11 January 1965, p. 37:*

* * *

American Interest in Vietnamese Independence:

Q. "Mr. Secretary, it is sometimes stated that one of the reasons for American assistance to Vietnam is the fact that vital Western interests are involved in the situation there. Now that we are once again confronted with what apparently is a critical situation, could you define for us the precise nature and extent of those vital Western interests, as you see them?"

A. "Well, our interest in Southeast Asia has been developed and expressed throughout this postwar period. Before SEATO (Southeast Asia Treaty Organization) came into existence, we and Britain and France were in very close touch with that situation. SEATO underlined the importance we attached to the security of the countries of that area.

"But actually the American interest can be expressed in very simple terms. Where there is a country which is independent and secure and in a position to work out its own policy and be left alone by its neighbors, there is a country whose position is consistent with our understanding of our interests in the world. It's just as simple as that.

"If we have military personnel in Southeast Asia, it is because we feel that they are needed to assist South Vietnam at the present time to maintain its security and independence. If South Vietnam's neighbors would leave it alone, those military people could come home.

"We have no desire for any bases or permanent military presence in that area. We are interested in the independence of states. That is why we have more than 40 allies. That is why we are interested in the independence and security of the nonaligned countries. Because, to us, the general system of states represented in the United Nations Charter is our view of a world that is consistent with American interests. So our own interest there is very simple.

"But it is very important, because we feel that we have learned in the last many decades that a persistent course of aggression left to go unchecked can only lead to a general war and therefore that the independence of particular countries is a matter of importance to the general peace."

Peiping's Militant Doctrine:

Q. "Mr. Secretary, could I put that question slightly differently? In the last decade or so, over three or four administrations, this Government has taken the position that the Indochina peninsula had an importance to this country beyond the actualities of the countries involved; that is, that it had a relationship to the American problem with China, and out of this developed, over a long period of time, the so-called falling-domino theory. Could you tell us whether you subscribe to that theory and whether you look upon our interest in Vietnam and Laos—or how you look upon our interest in Vietnam and Laos in relation to China?"

A. "Well, I would not myself go to the trouble of trying to outline a 'domino' theory. The theory of the problem rests in Peiping. It rests in a militant approach to the spread of the world revolution as seen from the communist point of view. And we know, given their frequently and publicly proclaimed ambitions in this respect and what they say not only about their neighbors in Asia but such continents as Africa—Africa is ripe for revolution, meaning to them ripe for an attempt on their part to extend their domination into that continent —there is a primitive, militant doctrine of world revolution that would attempt to destroy the structure of international life as written into the United Nations Charter.

"Now, these are appetites and ambitions that grow upon feeding. In 1954 Vietnam was divided. North Vietnam became communist. The next result was pressures against Laos, contrary to those agreements; pressures against South Vietnam, contrary to those agreements. In other words, until there is a determination in Peiping to leave their neighbors alone and not to press militantly their notions of world revolution, then we are going to have this problem.

"And it's the same problem we have had in another part of the world in an earlier period in this postwar period in such things as the Berlin blockade, the pressures against Greece. Those things had to be stopped. They were stopped in the main.

"Now the problem is out in the Pacific. And we have a large interest in the way these problems evolve in the Pacific, because we have allies and we have interests out there. Southeast Asia is at the present time the point at which this issue of militant aggression against one's neighbors for ideological reasons is posed."

*   *   *

16. *A Conversation with Dean Rusk, NBC News Program on January 3, 1965, Department of State Bulletin, January 18, 1965, p. 64.*

*   *   *

Secretary Rusk: . . . Now, when North Viet-Nam was organized as a Communist country, almost immediately its neighbor, Laos, and its neighbor, South Viet-Nam, came under direct pressure from North Viet-Nam. Now, this is the nature of the appetite proclaimed from Peiping. One doesn't require a 'domino' theory to get at this. Peiping has announced the doctrine. It is there in the primitive notion of a militant world revolution which has been promoted by these veterans of the long march who now control mainland China. So we believe that you simply postpone temporarily an even greater crisis if you allow an announced course of aggression to succeed a step at a time on the road to a major catastrophe.

*   *   *

Now, there are some in other countries, for example, who seem to be relatively indifferent to problems of this sort in Southeast Asia, and yet they are the first ones to say that if we were to abandon Southeast Asia, this would cause them to wonder what our commitments under such arrangements as NATO would mean. Do you see?

In other words, the issue here is the capability of halting a course of aggression at the beginning, rather than waiting for it to produce a great conflagration.

*   *   *

17. *The State of the Union Address of the President to the Congress, January 4, 1965, Public Papers of the Presidents, Johnson, 1965, p. 3.*

*   *   *

We are there, first, because a friendly nation has asked us for help against the Communist aggression. Ten years ago our President pledged our help. Three Presidents have supported that pledge. We will not break it now.

Second, our own security is tied to the peace of Asia. Twice in one generation we have had to fight against aggression in the Far East. To ignore aggression now would only increase the danger of a much larger war.

Our goal is peace in Southeast Asia. That will come only when aggressors leave their neighbors in peace.

*   *   *

18. *America Policy in South Viet-Nam and Southeast Asia, William P. Bundy, Remarks Made Before the Washington (Mo.) Chamber of Commerce on January 23, 1965, Department of State Bulletin, February 8, 1965, p. 168.*

*   *   *

In retrospect, our action in Korea reflected three elements:

—a recognition that aggression of any sort must be met early and head-on or it will have to be met later and in tougher circumstances. We had relearned the lessons of the 1930's—Manchuria, Ethiopia, the Rhineland, Czechoslovakia.

—a recognition that a defense line in Asia, stated in terms of an island perimeter, did not adequately define our vital interests, that those vital interests could be affected by action on the mainland of Asia.

—an understanding that, for the future, a power vacuum was an invitation to aggression, that there must be local political, economic, and military strength in being to make aggression unprofitable, but also that there must be a demonstrated willingness of major external power both to assist and to intervene if required.

*   *   *

Such was the situation President Eisenhower and Secretary Dulles faced in 1954. Two things were clear: that in the absence of external help communism was virtually certain to take over the successor states of Indochina and to move to the borders of Thailand and perhaps beyond, and that with France no longer ready to act, at least in South Viet-Nam, no power other than the United States could move in to help fill the vacuum. Their decision, expressed in a series of actions starting in late 1954, was to move in to help these countries. Besides South Viet-Nam and more modest efforts in Laos and Cambodia, substantial assistance was begun to Thailand.

The appropriations for these actions were voted by successive Congresses, and in 1954 the Senate likewise ratified the Southeast Asia Treaty, to which Thailand and the Philippines adhered along with the United States, Britain, France, Australia, New Zealand, and Pakistan. Although not signers of the treaty, South Viet-Nam, Laos, and Cambodia could call on the SEATO members for help against aggression.

So a commitment was made, with the support of both political parties, that has guided our policy in Southeast Asia for a decade now. It was not a commitment that envisaged a United States position of power in Southeast Asia or United States military bases there. We threatened no one. Nor was it a commitment that substituted United States responsibility for the basic responsibility of the nations themselves for their own defense, political stability, and economic progress. It *was* a commitment to do what we could to help these nations attain and maintain the independence and security to which they were entitled—both for their own sake and because we recognized that, like South Korea, Southeast Asia was a key area of the mainland of Asia. If it fell to Communist control, this would enormously add to the momentum and power of the expansionist Communist regimes in Communist China and North Viet-Nam and thus to the threat to the whole free-world position in the Pacific.

*   *   *

. . . In simple terms, a victory for the Communists in South Viet-Nam would inevitably make the neighboring states more suceptible to Communist pressure and more vulnerable to intensified subversion supported by military pressures. Aggression by 'wars of national liberation' would gain enhanced prestige and power of intimidation throughout the world, and many threatened nations might well become less hopeful, less resilient, and their will to resist undermined. These are big stakes indeed.

*   *   *

19. *William Bundy Discusses Vietnam Situation, February 7, 1965, Department of State Bulletin, March 8, 1965, p. 292.*

* * *

. . . Why are we there? What is our national interest? I think it was pretty well stated by Congress last August when it passed a resolution, following the Gulf of Tonkin affair, in which it stated that the United States "regards as vital to its national interest and world peace the maintenance of international peace and security in southeast Asia." And that's the basic reason right there—peace in the area, letting the nations of the area develop as they see fit and free from Communist external infiltration, subversion, and control.

Secondly, it's obvious on the map that if South Viet-Nam were to fall under Communist control it would become very much more difficult—I'm not using what's sometimes called 'the domino theory,' that anything happens automatically or quickly—but it would become very much more difficult to maintain the independence and freedom of Thailand, Cambodia, of Malaysia, and so on. And the confidence of other nations in the whole perimeter of Southeast Asia would necessarily be affected, and the Communists would think they had a winning game going for them. So that's a very important, strategic reason in addition to the fact that we're helping a nation under aggression.

And thirdly, this technique they're using—they call it "wars of national liberation"—is a technique that will be used elsewhere in the world if they get away with this one, and they'll be encouraged to do that.

So those are the three basic reasons why our national interest—and basically our national interest in peace in this whole wide Pacific area with which we have historically had great concern and for which we fought in World War II and in Korea—are deeply at stake in this conflict.

* * *

20. *Secretary Rusk's News Conference of February 25, 1965, Department of State Bulletin, March 15, 1965, p. 367.*

* * *

Q. Mr. Secretary, what kind of legal basis did the United States have to bomb the targets of North Viet-Nam?

A. Self-defense of South Viet-Nam and the commitments of the United States with respect to the security and the self-defense of South Viet-Nam."

* * *

21. *Statement Submitted by Adlai Stevenson to U.N. Summarizing a Significant Report Entitled, "Aggression from the North, the Record of North Vietnam's Campaign to Conquer South Vietnam." It was released as Department of State Publication 7839, February 27, 1965.*

EXCELLENCY: For the information of the Members of the Security Council, I am transmitting a special report entitled *Aggression from the North, the Record of North Viet-Nam's Campaign to Conquer South Viet-Nam*, which my Government is making public today. It presents evidence from which the following conclusions are inescapable:

First, the subjugation by force of the Republic of Viet-Nam by the regime in northern Viet-Nam is the formal, official policy of that regime; this has been stated and confirmed publicly over the past five years.

Second, the war in Viet-Nam is directed by the Central Committee of the Lao Dong Party (Communist) which controls the government in northern Viet-Nam.

Third, the so-called People's Revolutionary Party in the Republic of Viet-Nam is an integral part of the Lao Dong Party in North Viet-Nam.

Fourth, the so-called liberation front for South Viet-Nam is a subordinate unit of the Central Office for South Viet-Nam, an integral part of the governmental machinery in Hanoi.

Fifth, the key leadership of the Viet-Cong—officers, specialists, technicians, intelligence agents, political organizers and propagandists—has been trained, equipped and supplied in the north and sent into the Republic of Viet-Nam under Hanoi's military orders.

Sixth, most of the weapons, including new types recently introduced, and most of the ammunition and other supplies used by the Viet-Cong, have been sent from North to South Viet-Nam.

Seventh, the scale of infiltration of men and arms, including regular units of the armed forces of North Viet-Nam, has increased appreciably in recent months.

Eighth, this entire pattern of activity by the regime in Hanoi is in violation of general principles of international law and the Charter of the United Nations, and is in direct violation of the Geneva Accords of 1954. Such a pattern of violation of the treaty obligations undertaken at Geneva was confirmed by a special report of the International Control Commission in 1962 and it has been greatly intensified since then.

These facts about the situation in Viet-Nam make it unmistakably clear that the character of that conflict is an aggressive war of conquest waged against a neighbor—and make nonsense of the cynical allegation that this is simply an indigenous insurrection.

I request that you circulate copies of the Report, together with copies of this letter, to the Delegations of all Member States as a Security Council document.

In making this information available to the Security Council, my Government wishes to say once more that peace can be restored quickly to Viet-Nam by a prompt and assured cessation of aggression by Hanoi against the Republic of Viet-Nam. In that event, my Government—as it has said many times before— would be happy to withdraw its military forces from the Republic of Viet-Nam and turn promptly to an international effort to assist the economic and social development of Southeast Asia.

In the meantime, my Government awaits the first indication of any intent by the government in Hanoi to return to the ways of peace and peaceful resolution of this international conflict.

Accept, Excellency, the assurance of my highest consideration.

ADLAI E. STEVENSON.

*   *   *

22. *"Some Fundamentals of American Policy," Address by Secretary Rusk Before the U.S. Council of the International Chamber of Commerce at New York, March 4, 1965, Department of State Bulletin, March 22, 1965, p. 401.*

* * *

The defeat of these aggressions is not only essential if Laos and South Viet-Nam are to remain independent; it is important to the security of Southeast Asia as a whole. You will recall that Thailand has already been proclaimed as the next target by Peiping. This is not something up in the clouds called the domino theory. You don't need that. Listen to the proclamation of militant, world revolution by Peiping, proclaimed with a harshness which has caused deep division within the Communist world itself, quite apart from the issues posed for the free world.

The U.S. Stake in Viet-Nam

So what is our stake? What is our commitment in that situation? Can those of us in this room forget the lesson that we had in this issue of war and peace when it was only 10 years from the seizure of Manchuria to Pearl Harbor; about 2 years from the seizure of Czechoslovakia to the outbreak of World War II in Western Europe? Don't you remember the hopes expressed in those days: that perhaps the aggressor will be satisfied by this next bite, and perhaps he will be quiet? Remember that? You remember that we thought that we could put our Military Establishment on short rations and somehow we needn't concern ourselves with peace in the rest of the world. But we found that ambition and appetite fed upon success and the next bite generated the appetite for the following bite. And we learned that, by postponing the issue, we made the result more terrible, the holocaust more dreadful. We cannot forget that experience.

We have a course of aggression proclaimed in Peiping, very clear for all to see, and proclaimed with a militancy which says that their type of revolution must be supported by force and that much of the world is ripe for that kind of revolution. We have very specific commitments—the Manila Pact, ratified by the Senate by a vote of 82 to 1, a pact to which South Viet-Nam is a protocol state. We have the decision of President Eisenhower in 1954 to extend aid. . . ."

* * *

23. *"Viet-Nam Action Called 'Collective Defense Against Armed Aggression,' "* [Department Statement read to news correspondents on March 4, 1965 by Robert J. McCloskey, Director, Office of News], *Department of State Bulletin, March 22, 1965, p. 403.*

The fact that military hostilities have been taking place in Southeast Asia does not bring about the existence of a state of war, which is a legal characterization of a situation rather than a factual description. What we have in Viet-Nam is armed aggression from the North against the Republic of Viet-Nam. Pursuant to a South Vietnamese request and consultations between our two Governments, South Viet-Nam and the United States are engaged in collective defense against that armed aggression. The inherent right of individual and collective self-defense is recognized in article 51 of the United Nations Charter.

If the question is intended to raise the issue of legal authority to conduct the actions which have been taken, there can be no doubt that these actions fall within the constitutional powers of the President and within the congressional resolution of August 1964.

*   *   *

24. *"Pattern for Peace in Southeast Asia," Address by President Johnson at Johns Hopkins University, Baltimore, Maryland on April 7, 1965, Department of State Bulletin, April 26, 1965, p. 607.*

*   *   *

The confused nature of this conflict cannot mask the fact that it is the new face of an old enemy.

Over this war—and all Asia—is another reality: the deepening shadow of Communist China. The rulers in Hanoi are urged on by Peiping. This is a regime which has destroyed freedom in Tibet, which has attacked India, and has been condemned by the United Nations for aggression in Korea. It is a nation which is helping the forces of violence in almost every continent. The contest in Viet-Nam is part of a wider pattern of aggressive purposes.

Why Are We in South Viet-Nam?

Why are these realities our concern? Why are we in South Viet-Nam?

We are there because we have a promise to keep. Since 1954 every American President has offered support to the people of South Viet-Nam. We have helped to build, and we have helped to defend. Thus, over many years, we have made a national pledge to help South Viet-Nam defend its independence.

And I intend to keep that promise.

To dishonor that pledge, to abandon this small and brave nation to its enemies, and to the terror that must follow, would be an unforgivable wrong.

We are also there to strengthen world order. Around the globe, from Berlin to Thailand, are people whose well-being rests in part on the belief that they can count on us if they are attacked. To leave Viet-Nam to its fate would shake the confidence of all these people in the value of an American commitment and in the value of America's word. The result would be increased unrest and instability, and even wider war.

We are also there because there are great stakes in the balance. Let no one think for a moment that retreat from Viet-Nam would bring an end to conflict. The battle would be renewed in one country and then another. The central lesson of our time is that the appetite of aggression is never satisfied. To withdraw from one battlefield means only to prepare for the next. We must say in Southeast Asia—as we did in Europe—in the words of the Bible: "Hitherto shalt thou come, but no further."

There are those who say that all our effort there will be futile—that China's power is such that it is bound to dominate all Southeast Asia. But there is no end to that argument until all of the nations of Asia are swallowed up.

There are those who wonder why we have a responsibility there. Well, we have it there for the same reason that we have a responsibility for the defense of Europe. World War II was fought in both Europe and Asia, and when it ended we found ourselves with continued responsibility for the defense of freedom.

Our objective is the independence of South Viet-Nam and its freedom from attack. We want nothing for ourselves—only that the people of South Viet-

Nam be allowed to guide their own country in their own way. We will do everything necessary to reach that objective, and we will do only what is absolutely necessary.

In recent months attacks on South Viet-Nam were stepped up. Thus it became necessary for us to increase our response and to make attacks by air. This is not a change of purpose. It is a change in what we believe that purpose requires.

We do this in order to slow down aggression.

We do this to increase the confidence of the brave people of South Viet-Nam who have bravely borne this brutal battle for so many years with so many casualties.

* * *

25. *Address by Leonard Unger, Deputy Assistant Secretary for Far Eastern Affairs, before the Detroit Economic Club, "Present Objectives and Future Possibilities in Southeast Asia," April 19, 1965, Department of State Bulletin, May 10, 1965, p. 712.*

* * *

These objectives are not just pious generalities, nor is Southeast Asia just a configuration on a map. Distant though it may seem from Detroit, that area has great strategic significance to the United States and the free world. Its location across east-west air and sea lanes flanks the Indian subcontinent on one side and Australia, New Zealand, and the Philippines on the other, and dominates the gateway between the Pacific and Indian Oceans.

In Communist hands this area would pose a most serious threat to the security of the United States and to the family of free-world nations to which we belong. To defend Southeast Asia, we must meet the challenge in South Viet-Nam.

Communist 'Wars of Liberation'

Equally important, South Viet-Nam represents a major test of communism's new strategy of 'wars of liberation.' "

* * *

After the Communists' open aggression failed in Korea, they had to look for a more effective strategy of conquest. They chose to concentrate on 'wars of national liberation'—the label they use to describe aggression directed and supplied from outside a nation but cloaked in nationalist guise so that it could be made to appear an indigenous insurrection.

That strategy was tried on a relatively primitive scale, but was defeated in Malaya and the Philippines only because of a long and arduous struggle by the people of those countries, with assistance provided by the British and the United States. In Africa and Latin America such 'wars of liberation' are already being threatened. But by far the most highly refined and ambitious attempt at such aggression by the Communists is taking place today in Viet-Nam. . . .

* * *

In order to cope with this veiled aggression, free nations must determine the real source of the aggression and take steps to defend themselves from this source. In Viet-Nam this has meant ending privileged sanctuary heretofore afforded North Viet-Nam—the true source of the Viet Cong movement.

The "wars of national liberation" approach has been adopted as an essential element of Communist China's expansionist policy. If this technique adopted by Hanoi should be allowed to succeed in Viet-Nam, we would be confirming Peiping's contention that militant revolutionary struggle is a more productive Communist path than Moscow's doctrine of peaceful coexistence. We could expect "wars of national liberation" to spread. Thailand has already been identified by Communist China as being the next target for a so-called "liberation struggle." Peiping's Foreign Minister Chen Yi has promised it for this year. Laos, Malaysia, Burma—one Asian nation after another—could expect increasing Communist pressures. Other weakly defended nations on other continents would experience this new threat of aggression by proxy.

Even the Asian Communists have acknowledged that Viet-Nam represents an important test situation for indirect aggression. North Viet-Nam's Premier Pham Van Dong recently commented that:

"The experience of our compatriots in South Viet-Nam attracts the attention of the world, especially the peoples of *South America*."

General [Vo Nguyen] Giap, the much-touted leader of North Viet-Nam's army, was even more explicit. In another recent statement, he said that,

"South Viet-Nam is the model of the national liberation movement of our time. . . . If the special warfare that the U.S. imperialists are testing in South Viet-Nam is overcome, then it can be defeated everywhere in the world."

Our strong posture in Viet-Nam then seeks peace and security in three dimensions: for South Viet-Nam, for the sake of Southeast Asia's independence and security generally, and for the other small nations that would face the same kind of subversive threat from without if the Communists were to succeed in Viet-Nam. . . .

*   *   *

All this, of course, is contrary to the 1954 Geneva accords on Viet-Nam and the 1962 agreement on Laos. I mention the latter because it is an established fact that Hanoi has been both threatening Laos and using Laos as a corridor for supplying personnel and arms to the Viet Cong.

Our State Department has documented the character and intensity of North Viet-Nam's aggressive efforts since 1959 in the recent white paper, and in the similar report issued in 1961. The 1962 report of the International Control Commission for Viet-Nam also spelled out North Viet-Nam's aggressive actions in flagrant violation of the 1954 and 1962 agreements.

*   *   *

The Communists are fond of saying that whether the Viet Cong are born in the North or South, they are still Vietnamese and therefore an indigenous revolt must be taking place. Certainly, they are Vietnamese, and the North Koreans who swept across their boundary in 1950 to attack South Korea were also Koreans. However, this did not make the Korean war an indigenous revolt from the point of view of either world security or in terms of acceptable standards of conduct.

By the same token, if West Germany were to take similar action against East Germany, it is doubtful that the East Germans, the Soviet Union, and the rest of the Communist bloc would stand aside on the grounds that it was nothing more than an indigenous affair.

The simple issue is that military personnel and arms have been sent across an international demarcation line (just as valid a border as Korea or Germany)

contrary to international agreements and law to destroy the freedom of a neighboring people."

*   *   *

. . . . It is for that reason, and because Hanoi has stepped up its aggression, that the Government of South Viet-Nam and the United States have been forced to increase our response and strike through the air at the true source of the aggression—North Viet-Nam. This does not represent a change of purpose on our part but a change in the means we believe are necessary to stem aggression.

And there can be no doubt that our actions are fully justified as an exercise of the right of individual and collective self-defense recognized by article 51 of the United Nations Charter and under the accepted standards of international law.

*   *   *

26. *Address by Secretary Rusk, Made before the American Society of International Law on April 23, 1965, "The Control of Force in International Relations," Department of State Bulletin, May 10, 1965, p. 697.*

*   *   *

What Is a "War of National Liberation"?

What is a "war of national liberation"? It is, in essence, any war which furthers the Communist world revolution—what, in broader terms, the Communists have long referred to as a "just" war. The term "war of national liberation" is used not only to denote armed insurrection by people still under colonial rule—there are not many of those left outside the Communist world. It is used to denote any effort led by Communists to overthrow by force any non-Communist government.

Thus the war in South Viet-Nam is called a "war of national liberation." And those who would overthrow various other non-Communist governments in Asia, Africa, and Latin America are called the "forces of national liberation."

Nobody in his right mind would deny that Venezuela is not only a truly independent nation but that it has a government chosen in a free election. But the leaders of the Communist insurgency in Venezuela are described as leaders of a fight for "national liberation"—not only by themselves and by Castro and the Chinese Communists but by the Soviet Communists.

A recent editorial in Pravada spoke of the "peoples of Latin America . . . marching firmly along the path of struggle for their national independence" and said, ". . . the upsurge of the national liberation movement in Latin American countries has been to a great extent a result of the activities of Communist parties." It added:

"The Soviet people have regarded and still regard it as their sacred duty to give support to the peoples fighting for their independence. True to their international duty the Soviet people have been and will remain on the side of the Latin American patriots."

In Communist doctrine and practice, a non-Communist government may be labeled and denounced as "colonialist," "reactionary," or a "puppet," and any state so labeled by the Communists automatically becomes fair game—while Communist intervention by force in non-Communist states is justified as "self-defense" or part of the "struggle against colonial domination." "Self-determination" seems to mean that any Communist nation can determine by itself that any non-Communist state is a victim of colonialist domination and therefore a justifiable target for a "war of liberation."

As the risks of overt aggression, whether nuclear or with conventional forces, have become increasingly evident, the Communists have put increasing stress on the "war of national liberation." The Chinese Communists have been more militant in language and behavior than the Soviet Communists. But the Soviet Communist leadership also has consistently proclaimed its commitment in principle to support wars of national liberation. This commitment was reaffirmed as recently as Monday of this week by Mr. Kosygin [Aleksai N. Kosygin, Chairman of the U.S.S.R. Council of Ministers].

International law does not restrict internal revolution within a state or revolution against colonial authority. But international law does restrict what third powers may lawfully do in support of insurrection. It is these restrictions which are challenged by the doctrine, and violated by the practice, of "wars of liberation."

It is plain that acceptance of the doctrine of "wars of liberation" would amount to scuttling the modern international law of peace which the charter prescribes. And acceptance of the practice of "wars of liberation," as defined by the Communists, would mean the breakdown of peace itself.

South Viet-Nam's Right of Self-Defense

Viet-Nam presents a clear current case of the lawful versus the unlawful use of force. I would agree with General Giap [Vo Nguyen Giap, North Vietnamese Commander in Chief] and other Communists that it is a test case for "wars of national liberation." We intend to meet that test.

Were the insurgency in South Viet-Nam truly indigenous and self-sustained, international law would not be involved. But the fact is that it receives vital external support—in organization and direction, in training, in men, in weapons and other supplies. That external support is unlawful for a double reason. First, it contravenes general international law, which the United Nations Charter here expresses. Second, it contravenes particular international law: the 1954 Geneva accords on Viet-Nam and the 1962 Geneva agreements on Laos.

In resisting the aggression against it, the Republic of Viet-Nam is exercising its right of self-defense. It called upon us and other states for assistance. And in the exercise of the right of collective self-defense under the United Nations Charter, we and other nations are providing such assistance.

The American policy of assisting South Viet-Nam to maintain its freedom was inaugurated under President Eisenhower and continued under Presidents Kennedy and Johnson. Our assistance has been increased because the aggression from the North has been augmented. Our assistance now encompasses the bombing of North Viet-Nam. The bombing is designed to interdict, as far as possible, and to inhibit, as far as may be necessary, continued aggression against the Republic of Viet-Nam.

When that aggression ceases, collective measures in defense against it will cease. As President Johnson has declared:

". . . if that aggression is stopped, the people and Government of South Viet-Nam will be free to settle their own future, and the need for supporting American military action there will end."

The fact that the demarcation line between North and South Viet-Nam was intended to be temporary does not make the assault on South Viet-Nam any less of an aggression. The demarcation lines between North and South Korea and between East and West Germany are temporary. But that did not make the North Korean invasion of South Korea a permissible use of force.

Let's not forget the salient features of the 1962 agreements on Laos. Laos was to be independent and neutral. All foreign troops, regular or irregular, and other military personnel were to be withdrawn within 75 days, except a limited number of French instructors as requested by the Lao Government. No arms were to be introduced into Laos except at the request of that Government. The signatories agreed to refrain "from all direct or indirect interference in the internal affairs" of Laos. They promised also not to use Lao territory to intervene in the internal affairs of other countries—a stipulation that plainly prohibited the passage of arms and men from North Viet-Nam to South Viet-Nam by way of Laos. An International Control Commission of three was to assure compliance with the agreements.

What happened? The non-Communist elements complied. The Communists did not. At no time since that agreement was signed have either the Pathet Lao or the North Viet-Nam authorities complied with it. The North Vietnamese left several thousand troops there—the backbone of almost every Pathet Lao battalion. Use of the corridor through Laos to South Viet-Nam continued. And the Communists barred the areas under their control both to the Government of Laos and the International Control Commission.

Nature of Struggle in Viet-Nam

To revert to Viet-Nam: I continue to hear and see nonsense about the nature of the struggle there. I sometimes wonder if the gullibility of educated men and the stubborn disregard of plain facts by men who are supposed to be helping our young to learn—especially to learn how to think.

Hanoi has never made a secret of its designs. It publicly proclaimed in 1960 a renewal of the assault on South Viet-Nam. Quite obviously its hopes of taking over South Viet-Nam from within had withered to close to zero—and the remarkable economic and social progress of South Viet-Nam contrasted, most disagreeably for the North Vietnamese Communists, with their own miserable economic performance.

The facts about the external involvement have been documented in white papers and other publications of the Department of State. The International Control Commission has held that there is evidence "beyond reasonable doubt" of North Vietnamese intervention.

There is no evidence that the Viet Cong has any significant popular following in South Viet-Nam. It relies heavily on terror. Most of its reinforcements in recent months have been North Vietnamese from the North Vietnamese Army.

Let us be clear about what is involved today in Southeast Asia. We are not involved with empty phrases or conceptions which ride upon the clouds. We are talking about the vital national interests of the United States in the peace of the Pacific. We are talking about the appetite for aggression—an appetite which grows upon feeding and which is proclaimed to be insatiable. We are talking about the safety of nations with whom we are allied—and the integrity of the American commitment to join in meeting attack.

It is true that we also believe that every small state has a right to be unmolested by its neighbors even though it is within reach of a great power. It is true that we are committed to general principles of law and procedure which reject the idea that men and arms can be sent freely across frontiers to absorb a neighbor. But underlying the general principles is the harsh reality that our own security is threatened by those who would embark upon a course of aggression whose announced ultimate purpose is our own destruction.

Once again we hear expressed the views which cost the men of my generation a terrible price in World War II. We are told that Southeast Asia is far away—but so were Manchuria and Ethiopia. We are told that, if we insist that someone stop shooting, that is asking them for unconditional surrender. We are told that perhaps the aggressor will be content with just one more bite. We are told that, if we prove faithless on one commitment, perhaps others would believe us about other commitments in other places. We are told that, if we stop resisting, perhaps the other side will have a change of heart. We are asked to stop hitting bridges and radar sites and ammunition depots without requiring that the other side stop its slaughter of thousands of civilians and its bombings of schools and hotels and hospitals and railways and buses.

Surely we have learned over the past three decades that the acceptance of aggression leads only to a sure catastrophe. Surely we have learned that the aggressor must face the consequences of his action and be saved from the frightful miscalculation that brings all to ruin. It is the purpose of law to guide men away from such events, to establish rules of conduct which are deeply rooted in the reality of experience.

*   *   *

27. *Statement by President Johnson at a News Conference at the White House on April 27, 1965 and Transcript of Secretary of Defense Robert S. McNamara's News Conference of April 26, 1965 on the Situation in Viet-Nam, Department of State Bulletin, May 17, 1965, p. 78.*

Statement by President Johnson

*   *   *

Independent South Viet-Nam has been attacked by North Viet-Nam. The object of that attack is conquest.

Defeat in South Viet-Nam would be to deliver a friendly nation to terror and repression. It would encourage and spur on those who seek to conquer all free nations within their reach. Our own welfare and our own freedom would be in danger.

This is the clearest lesson of our time. From Munich until today we have learned that to yield to aggression brings only greater threats—and more destructive war. To stand firm is the only guarantee of lasting peace.

*   *   *

Viet Cong Weapons from External Sources

The latest step has been the covert infiltration of a regular combat unit of the North Vietnamese Army into South Viet-Nam. Evidence accumulated within the last month now confirms the presence in northwest Kontum Province —that is in the central highland area of South Viet-Nam, around Pleiku and north of Pleiku—recent evidence which we have received confirms the presence in that northwest Kontum Province of the 2d Battalion of the 325th Division of the regular North Vietnamese Army. It is important to recognize, I think, that the great bulk of the weapons which the Viet Cong are using and with which they are supplied come from external sources.

* * *

[Secretary McNamara]

Communist Strategy

Q. "Mr. Secretary, a personal question. As the fighting has increased in Viet-Nam, more and more of the U.S. critics of the administration's policy have been referring to this as 'McNamara's war.' What is your reaction? Does this annoy you?"

A. "It does not annoy me because I think it is a war that is being fought to preserve the freedom of a very brave people, an independent nation. It is a war which is being fought to counter the strategy of the Communists, a strategy which Premier Khrushchev laid out very clearly in the very famous speech which he made on January 6, 1961.

"You may recall that at that time he divided all wars into three categories. He spoke of world wars, meaning nuclear wars; he spoke of local wars, by which he meant large-scale conventional wars; and then he spoke of what he called 'wars of liberation.'

"He ruled out world wars as being too dangerous to the existence of the Communist states. He ruled out local wars because he said they could very easily escalate into nuclear wars which would lead to the ultimate destruction of the Communist states. But he strongly endorsed 'wars of liberation' and made it perfectly clear that it would be through application of that strategy that the Communists would seek to subvert independent nations throughout the world, seek to extend their domination, their political domination, of other nations.

"It is very clear that that is the Communist Chinese strategy in Southeast Asia. It is a strategy I feel we should oppose, and, while it is not my war, I don't object to my name being associated with it."

* * *

28. *Statement by Secretary Ball on May 3, 1965 at the Opening Session of the SEATO Council Ministers' 10th Meeting at London, Department of State Bulletin, June 7, 1965, p. 922.*

* * *

We have, however, come to realize from the experience of the past years that aggression must be dealt with wherever it occurs and no matter what mask it may wear. Neither we nor other nations of the free world were always alert to this. In the 1930's Manchuria seemed a long way away, but it was only 10 years from Manchuria to Pearl Harbor. Ethiopia seemed a long way away. The rearmament of the Rhineland was regarded as regrettable but not worth a shooting war. Yet after that came Austria. And after Austria, Czechoslovakia. Then Poland. Then the Second World War.

The central issue we face in South Viet-Nam should, I think, be clear for all to see. It is whether a small state on the periphery of Communist power should be permitted to maintain its freedom. And that is an issue of vital importance to small states everywhere.

Moreover, it is an issue that affects the security of the whole free world.

Never has that point been more succinctly stated than by one of the greatest of all Englishmen, Sir Winston Churchill. "The belief," he said, "that security can be obtained by throwing a small state to the wolves is a fatal illusion." And let us not forget that General [Vo Nguyen] Giap, the head of the North Vietnamese armed forces, has said quite explicitly that if the so-called "war of liberation" technique succeeds in Viet-Nam, it can succeed "everywhere in the world."

*   *   *

29. *Remarks by President Johnson at White House Before House and Senate Committees on May 4, 1965, "Congress Approves Supplemental Appropriation for Vietnam," Department of State Bulletin, May 24, 1965, p. 817.*

*   *   *

This is not the same kind of aggression which the world has long been used to. Instead of the sweep of invading armies there is the steady and the deadly attack in the night by guerrilla bands that come without warning, that kill people while they sleep.

In Viet-Nam we pursue that same principle which has infused American action in the Far East for a quarter of a century. There are those who ask why this responsibility should be ours. The answer, I think, is simple. There is no one else who can do the job. Our power alone, in the final test, can stand between expanding communism and independent Asian nations.

Thus, when India was attacked, it looked to us for help, and we gave it immediately. We believe that Asia should be directed by Asians. But that means that each Asian people must have the right to find is own way, not that one group or one nation should overrun all the others.

Now make no mistake about it, the aim in Viet-Nam is not simply the conquest of the South, tragic as that would be. It is to show that American commitment is worthless, and they would like very much to do that, and once they succeed in doing that, the gates are down and the road is open to expansion and to endless conquest. Moreover, we are directly committed to the defense of South Viet-Nam beyond any question.

In 1954 we signed the Southeast Asia Collective Defense Treaty and that treaty committed us to act to meet aggression against South Viet-Nam. . . .

*   *   *

30. *Address by William P. Bundy Before Dallas Council on World Affairs on May 13, 1965, "Reality and Myth Concerning South Vietnam," Department of State Bulletin, June 7, 1965, p. 893.*

*   *   *

Myths on the South Viet-Nam Story

"This is the simple basic story of what has happened in South Viet-Nam since 1954. Let me now turn to certain myths that have arisen concerning that story.

"First, there is the question of the attitude of the South Vietnamese Government and ourselves toward the reunification of Viet-Nam through free elections. The 1954 Geneva accords had provided for free elections by secret ballot in 1956, and it has been alleged that the failure to proceed with these elections in some way justified Hanoi's action in resorting to military measures, first slowly and then by the stepped-up infiltration beginning in 1959 and 1960.

The facts are quite otherwise. The Eisenhower administration had fully supported the principle of free elections under international supervision, in Viet-Nam as in other situations where a country was divided, Korea and Germany.

A similar position was taken by President Diem of South Viet-Nam. For example, in January 1955 Diem made it clear to an American correspondent that:

"The clauses providing for the 1956 elections are extremely vague. But at one point they are clear—in stipulating that the elections are to be free. Everything will now depend on how free elections are defined. The President said he would wait to see whether the conditions of freedom would exist in North Viet-Nam at the time scheduled for the elections. He asked what would be the good of an impartial counting of votes if the voting had been preceded in North Viet-Nam by the ruthless propaganda and terrorism on the part of a police state."

I do not think any of us would dissent from this description of what is required for free elections. And the simple fact is that, when the issue arose concretely in 1956, the regime in Hanoi—while it kept calling for elections in its propaganda—made no effort to respond to the call of the Soviet Union and Great Britain, as cochairmen of the 1954 Geneva conference, for the setting up of the appropriate machinery for free elections.

The reason is not far to seek. For North Viet-Nam in 1956—and indeed today—is a Communist state and in 1956 North Viet-Nam was in deep trouble. Its own leaders admitted as much in their party congress in the fall of 1956 in a statement by General [Vo Nguyen] Giap referring to widespread terror, failure to respect the principles of faith and worship in the so-called land reform program, the use of torture as a normal practice, and a whole list of excesses which even the Communists had come to realize went too far.

So the answer is, I repeat, simple. There was no chance of free elections in North Viet-Nam in 1956. We shall wait to see whether there will ever be such a chance in the future.

Second, there is the myth that the Viet Cong movement has any significant relationship to the political opposition to President Diem. I have referred already to the unfortunate trends that developed after 1959 in President Diem's rule. There was unquestionably opposition to him within South Viet-Nam, and that opposition included many distinguished South Vietnamese, some of whom went into exile as a result. Others stayed in Saigon, and some were imprisoned.

But the point is this. The men who led the opposition to Diem are not today in the Viet Cong. On the contrary, the present Prime Minister, Dr. [Phan Huy] Quat, and his group of so-called Caravellistes, all of whom opposed Diem, are today the leaders of the Government. These men, and their followers, are nationalists and strongly anti-Communist; not one of them, of any significance, went over to the Viet Cong.

This brings me to the question of the so-called National Liberation Front, which is the political facade, made in Hanoi, for the Viet Cong movement. I doubt if any of you can name a single leader of the National Liberation Front. But these are faceless men installed by Hanoi to give the appearance of bourgeois and truly South Vietnamese support for the operation.

Lest you think I exaggerate, I refer you to the excellent recent account by Georges Chaffard, a French correspondent for *L'Express* in Paris, who recently visited the Viet Cong and interviewed some of its "leaders." Chaffard describes vividly what these men are, including their strong desire to find a replacement for the obscure lawyer named Tho who is the titular head of the front and who apparently is the only figure Hanoi can find who was even in Saigon or participating in South Vietnamese political life during the latter Diem period. Chaffard's conclusion, which I quote, is that:

"The Front for National Liberation structure is the classic structure of a 'National Front' before the taking over of power by the Communists."

So there should be no doubt of the true nature of the Viet Cong and its Liberation Front, or that they are a completely different movement from the political opposition to Diem. As to the latter, and its present emergence into a truly nationalistic amalgam of forces—regional, religious, military, and civilian—I can perhaps best refer you to the excellent lead article by Mr. George Carver, an American with long experience in Saigon, in the April issue of Foreign Affairs. Mr. Carver tells a fascinating story of the emergence of these new nationalistic forces in South Viet-Nam, with all their difficulties and weaknesses, but with the fundamental and overriding fact that they are the true new voice of South Viet-Nam and that they have never had anything to do with the Viet Cong.

*   *   *

The Korean War also had an important message for the Communists—and as a result we may have seen the last of the old classical war of open invasions. Korea proved to the Communists that they had to find a more effective strategy of conquest. They chose to refine a technique that they had used on a primitive scale and to their ultimate defeat in Greece, Malaya, and the Philippines. I am referring to the so-called "war of national liberation." This is the label Khrushchev employed in 1961 to describe Communist strategy for the future—aggression directed and supplied from outside a nation, but disguised in nationalist trappings so that it might pass as an indigenous insurrection.

*   *   *

The Communists have expanded upon their "wars of liberation" technique. Africa and Latin America are already feeling the threat of such thrusts. But by far the most highly sophisticated and ambitious attempt at such aggression by the Communists is taking place today in Viet-Nam.

*   *   *

The "wars of liberation" strategy is at this time an essential element of the expansionist policy of Communist China and her Asian ally, North Viet-Nam. If we allow it to succeed in Viet-Nam, we would be confirming Peiping's assertion that armed struggle is a more productive Communist course than Moscow's doctrine of peaceful coexistence. "Wars of national liberation" would most certainly spread. Red China has already identified Thailand as the next target for a so-called "liberation struggle," and its Foreign Minister Chen Yi has promised that it will be launched before the end of this year.

The major test to date of this new Communist strategy is taking place today in Viet-Nam. Even the Asian Communists have acknowledged the larger implications of this confrontation. Not long ago General Giap, the well-known leader of North Viet-Nam's army, declared that,

"South Viet-Nam is the model of the national liberation movement of our time. . . . If the special warfare that the U.S. imperialists are testing in South Viet-Nam is overcome, then it can be defeated everywhere in the world."

In another recent comment, North Viet-Nam's Premier Pham Van Dong said that:

"The experience of our compatriots in South Viet-Nam attracts the attention of the world, especially the peoples of South America."

The *People's Daily,* Peiping's official newspaper, echoed those statements in an editorial on May Day of this year. It said:

"The Vietnamese people's struggle against U.S. imperialism has become the focal point of the international class struggle at this moment. This is an acid test for all political forces in the world."

Our firm posture in Viet-Nam, then, seeks peace and security in three related dimensions: for South Viet-Nam, for the sake of Southeast Asia's independence and security generally, and for the other small nations everywhere that would face the same kind of subversive threat from without if the Communists were to succeed in Vietnam. . . .

*　　*　　*

31. *Address by President Johnson Before the Association of American Editorial Cartoonists at the White House on May 13, 1965, "Viet-Nam: The Third Face of the War," Department of State Bulletin, May 31, 1965, p. 838.*

*　　*　　*

. . . . Communist China apparently desires the war to continue whatever the cost to their allies. Their target is not merely South Viet-Nam; it is Asia. Their objective is not the fulfillment of Vietnamese nationalism; it is to erode and to discredit America's ability to help prevent Chinese domination over all of Asia.

*　　*　　*

32. *Address by William P. Bundy, Assistant Secretary for Far Eastern Affairs, Before the Faculty Forum of the University of California at Berkeley on May 27, 1965, "A Perspective on U.S. Policy in Viet-Nam," Department of State Bulletin, June 21, 1965, p. 1001.*

*　　*　　*

For the underlying fact is that there cannot be a balance of power in Asia without us. Under the control of a Communist regime still at the peak of its ideological fervor, a unified mainland China today does threaten the outnumbered newly independent nations of Asia, not merely in the sense of influence but in the sense of domination and the denial of national self-determination and independence—not necessarily drastically or at once, for the Chinese Communist leaders are patient; not necessarily, or even in their eyes preferably, by conventional armed attack, but surely and inexorably, as they see it, through the technique of spurious national movements deriving their real impetus and support from external and Communist sources.

And in this central Communist effort, the other Communist nations of Asia, North Viet-Nam and North Korea, are willing partners. They have their national character, they are not true satellites—indeed, deep down, they too fear Chinese domination. Yet, so long as the spoils are fairly divided, they are working together with Communist China toward a goal the opposite of the one we seek, subjugation of the true national independence of smaller countries, an Asia of spheres of domination."

*　　*　　*

For South Viet-Nam is the outcome of a very particular slice of recent Asian history. Only in Viet-Nam was a genuine nationalist movement taken over by Communist leaders and transmuted into the Communist state of North Viet-Nam. And so the French, instead of yielding gradually or with the fullest possible preparation for self-government, as the British wisely did in India, Pakistan, and Malaysia, were effectively driven out in 1954 and Viet-Nam was divided.

*   *   *

By 1956, to paraphrase the same eminent scholar, Communist China and North Viet-Nam, all propaganda to the contrary notwithstanding, simply were not willing to risk the loss of South Viet-Nam in elections, and, perhaps most crucial, the conditions for free elections did not prevail in either North or South Viet-Nam. So the date passed, and the dividing line between the two Viet-Nams became a political division as in Germany and Korea, with reunification left to the future. And in the course of time another 30-odd nations recognized South Viet-Nam, and recognize it today.

(By the way, the eminent scholar I have just been citing was Professor Hans J. Morgenthau, writing in a pamphlet entitled "America's Stake in Viet-Nam," published in 1956. One of the other participants in that conference was the then junior Senator from Massachusetts. He was a bit more downright than the professor, saying that "neither the United States nor Free Viet-Nam is ever going to be a party to an election obviously stacked and subverted in advance.")

Since 1956 two different strands have dominated developments in South Viet-Nam. One is a genuine nationalist internal political ferment, in which the South Vietnamese themselves are seeking a lasting political base for their country—in the face of the same problems other new nations have faced, but compounded by the colonial heritage of lack of training and divide-and-rule tactics. That ferment should not surprise us; almost every new nation has gone through it—for example, Korea and Pakistan. Under Diem it drove many distinguished South Vietnamese to exile or prison, from 1962 until early this year it seriously weakened the defense of the nation, and it now has brought into power a regime led by men who were the real opponents of Diem and are something close to the true voice of South Vietnamese nationalism—men, too, who are already widening the base of support and holding local elections.

*   *   *

The other, and entirely different, strand has been Hanoi's effort to take over the South by subversive aggression. On this the facts are plain and have been fully set out, though still in summary form, in the white papers published in December of 1961 and February 1965. If these do not convince you, read Hanoi's own pronouncements over the years, the eyewitness accounts of the tons of weapons found just in recent months, the personal interrogation of a typical infiltrated Viet Cong by Seymour Topping in Sunday's New York Times, or the recent accounts by the Frenchman, George Chaffard, who concluded that the so-called National Liberation Front was a classic example of the type of Communist organization used to take over another country.

In short, North Viet-Nam has been from the start, quite proudly and unashamedly, what President Johnson has called the heartbeat of the Viet Cong. As in Greece, the Viet Cong have won control of major areas of the country, playing in part on propaganda and the undoubted weaknesses of Diem and his successors, but relying basically on massive intimidation of civilians. Over the years, the rate of civilian casualties—deliberate action casualties, killed, wounded and kidnapped—has been about 40 a day in South Viet-Nam; civilian officials have been particular targets, with the obvious aim of crippling the government structure.

*   *   *

I come now to the choice of methods. Till 1961 President Eisenhower and President Kennedy limited our help to a massive economic effort and to the supply of military equipment under the terms of the Geneva accords. When, after 2 years of intensified effort from the North, the situation had become serious in late 1961, President Kennedy made the decision to send thousands of our military men for advisory and other roles short of the commitment of combat units. President Johnson intensified this effort in every possible way and only in February of this year took the further decision, urged by the South Vietnamese themselves, to do what would have been justified all along—and had never been excluded—engage in highly selective and measured military bombing of the North itself, still coupled with every possible effort to assist in the South in the struggle which only the South Vietnamese can win there.

*   *   *

33. *Address by President Johnson in Chicago, Illinois on June 3, 1965, "The Peace of Mankind," Department of State Bulletin, June 21, 1965, p. 987.*

*   *   *

In the 1930's we made our fate not by what we did but what we Americans failed to do. We propelled ourselves and all mankind toward tragedy, not by decisiveness but by vacillation, not by determination and resolution but by hesitancy and irresolution, not by action but by inaction.

The failure of free men in the 1930's was not of the sword but of the soul. And there just must be no such failure in the 1960's.

*   *   *

Glossary

AAA   Antiaircraft Artillery
ACR   Armored Cavalry Regiment
ABM   Antiballistic Missile
ABN   Airborne
ADP   Automatic Data Processing
AFB   Air Force Base
AID   Agency for International Development
AIROPS   Air Operations
AM   Airmobile
AMB   Ambassador
ANG   Air National Guard
APB   Self-propelled barracks ship
ARL   Landing craft repair ship
ARVN   Army of the Republic of [South] Vietnam
ASA   U.S. Army Security Agency
ASAP   As soon as possible
ASD   Assistant Secretary of Defense
BAR   Browning automatic rifle
BDE   Brigade
BLT   Battalion Landing Team
BN   Battalion
BOB   Bureau of the Budget
B-52   U.S. heavy bomber
B-57   U.S. medium bomber
CAP   Combined Action Platoon
CAS   Saigon Office of the U.S. Central Intelligence Agency
CDC   Combat Development Command
CG   Civil Guard
CHICOM   Chinese Communist
CHMAAG   Chief, Military Assistance Advisory Group
CI   Counterinsurgency
CIA   Central Intelligence Agency
CIDG   Civilian Irregular Detachment Group
CINCPAC   Commander in Chief, Pacific
CIP   Counterinsurgency Plan
CNO VNN   Chief of Naval Operations, Vietnamese Navy
CJCS   Chairman, Joint Chiefs of Staff
CMD   Capital Military District
COMUS   U.S. Commander
COMUSMACV   Commander, U.S. Military Assistance Command, Vietnam

CONARC   Continental Army Command
CONUS   Continental United States
CORDS   Civil Operations and Revolutionary Development Support [pacification]
COS   Chief of Station, CIA
CPR   Chinese Peoples Republic
CPSVN   Comprehensive Plan for South Vietnam
CTZ   Corps tactical zone
CY   Calendar year
DCM   Deputy Chief of Mission
DCPG   Defense Command Planning Group
DEPTEL   [State] Department telegram
DESOTO   Destroyer patrols off North Vietnam
DIA   Defense Intelligence Agency
DMZ   Demilitarized Zone separating North and South Vietnam
DOD   Department of Defense
DPM   Draft Presidential Memorandum [from the Secretary of Defense]
DRV   Democratic Republic of [North] Vietnam
DULTE   Cable identifier, from Secretary of State Dulles to addressee
ECM   Electronic Countermeasures
EXDIS   Exclusive (high level) distribution
FAL and FAR   Royal Armed Forces of Laos
FARMGATE   Clandestine U.S. Air Force unit in Vietnam, 1964
FE and FEA   Bureau of Far Eastern Affairs in the State Department
FEC   French Expeditionary Corps
FLAMING DART   Code name of bombing operations, in reprisal for attacks on U.S. forces
FOA   Foreign Operations Administration
FWMA   Free World Military Assistance
FWMAF   Free World Military Assistance Force

FY   Fiscal Year
FYI   For your information
GRC   Government of the Republic of China (Nationalist China)
GVN   Government of [South] Vietnam
G-3   U.S. Army General Staff, Branch for Plans and Operations
HES   Hamlet Evaluation System
HNC   High National Council
Hop Tac   Program to clear and hold land around Saigon, 1964
IBP   International Balance of Payments
ICA   International Cooperation Administration
ICC   International Control Commission
IDA   Institute for Defense Analyses
IMCSH   Inter-ministerial Committee for Strategic Hamlets
INR   Bureau of Intelligence and Research in the Department of State
ISA   Office of International Security Affairs in the Department of Defense
I Corps   Northern military region of South Vietnam
II Corps   Central military region in South Vietnam
III Corps   Military region in South Vietnam surrounding Saigon
IV Corps   Southern military region in South Vietnam
JCS   Joint Chiefs of Staff
JCSM   Joint Chiefs of Staff Memorandum
JGS   Vietnamese Joint General Staff
JOC   Joint Operations Center
Joint Staff   Staff organization for the Joint Chiefs of Staff
JUSPAO   Joint United States Public Affairs Office, Saigon
J-2   Intelligence Branch, U.S. Army
KANZUS   Korean, Australian, New Zealand, and U.S.
KIA   Killed in action
LANTFLT   Atlantic Fleet
LOC   Lines of communications (roads, bridges, rail)
LST   Tank Landing Ship
LTC   Lt. Col.
MAAG   Military Assistance Advisory Group
MAB   Marine Amphibious Brigade
MAC   Military Assistance Command
MACCORDS   Military Assistance Command, Civil Operations and Revolutionary Development Support
MAF   Marine Amphibious Force
MAP   Military Assistance Program

MAROPS   Maritime Operations
MEB   Marine Expeditionary Brigade
MEF   Marine Expeditionary Force
MIA   Missing in action
MDAP   Mutual Defense Assistance Program
MOD   Minister of Defense
MORD   Ministry of Revolutionary Development
MRC   Military Revolutionary Committee
MR5   Highland Area
NATO   North Atlantic Treaty Organization
NCO   Non-commissioned officer
NFLSV   National Front for the Liberation of South Vietnam
NIE   National Intelligence Estimate
NLF   National Liberation Front
NODIS   No distribution (beyond addressee)
NSA   National Security Agency (specializes in electronic intelligence, i.e. monitoring radio communications)
NSAM   National Security Action Memorandum (pronounced nas-sam; described presidential decisions under Kennedy and Johnson)
NSC   National Security Council
NVA   North Vietnamese Army
NVN   North Vietnam
OB   Order of battle
OCO   Office of Civil Operations [pacification]
O&M   Operations and Management
Opcon   Operations Control
OPLAN   Operations Plan
Ops   Operations
OSA   Office of the Secretary of the Army
OSD   Office of the Secretary of Defense
PACFLT   Pacific Fleet
PACOM   Pacific Command
PAT   Political Action Team
PAVN   People's Army of [North] Vietnam
PBR   River Patrol Boat
PDJ   Plaine Des Jarres, Laos
PF   Popular Forces
PFF   Police Field Force
PL   Pathet Lao
PNG   Provisional National Government
POL   Petroleum, oil, lubricants
POLAD   Political adviser (usually, State Department representative assigned to a military commander)
PRV   People's Republic of Vietnam

PSYOP   Psychological Operations
qte   Quote
RAS   River Assault Squadron
RCT   Regimental Combat Team
RD   Rural (or Revolutionary) Development
RECCE   Reconnaissance
Reclama   Protest against a cut in budget or program
RF   Regional Forces
RLAF   Royal Laotian Air Force
RLG   Royal Laotian Government
RLT   Regimental Landing Team
ROK   Republic of [South] Korea
Rolling Thunder   Code name for sustained bombing of North Vietnam
rpt   Repeat
RSSZ   Rung Sat Special Zone (east of Saigon)
RT   Rolling Thunder Program
RTA   Royal Thai Army
RVN   Republic of [South] Vietnam
RVNAF   Republic of Vietnam Air Force or Armed Forces
RVNF   Republic of Vietnam Forces
SA   Systems Analysis Office in the Department of Defense
SAC   Strategic Air Command
SACSA   Special Assistant [to the JCS] for Counterinsurgency and Special [covert] Activities
SAM   Surface-to-air missile
SAR   Search and Rescue
SDC   Self Defense Corps
SEA   Southeast Asia
SEACOOR   Southeast Asia Coordinating Committee
SEATO   Southeast Asia Treaty Organization
SecDef   Secretary of Defense
SECTO   Cable identifier, from Secretary of State to addressee
Sitrep   Situation Report
SMM   Saigon Military Mission
SNIE   Special National Intelligence Estimate
SQD   Squadron
STRAF   Strategic Army Force

SVN   South Vietnam
TAOR   Tactical Area of Responsibility
TCS   Tactical Control System
TEDUL   Cable identifier, overseas post to Secretary of State Dulles
TERM   Temporary Equipment Recovery Mission
TF   Task force
TFS   Tactical Fighter Squadron
TO&E   Table of organization and equipment (for a military unit)
TOSEC   Cable identifier, from overseas post to Secretary of State
TRIM   Training Relations and Instruction Mission
TRS   Tactical Reconnaissance Squadron
34A   1964 operations plan covering covert actions against North Vietnam
T-28   U.S. fighter-bomber
UE   Unit equipment allowance
UH-1   Helicopter
UK   United Kingdom
USAF   U.S. Air Force
USARAL   U.S. Army, Alaska
USAREUR   U.S. Army, Europe
USASGV   U.S. Army Support Group, Vietnam
USG   United States Government
USIA   U.S. Information Agency
USIB   U.S. Intelligence Board
USIS   U.S. Information Service
USOM   U.S. Operations Mission (for economic assistance)
VC   Viet Cong
VM   Viet Minh
VN   Vietnam
VNA   Vietnamese National Army
VNAF   [South] Vietnamese Air Force or Armed Forces
VNQDD   Vietnam Quocdandang (pre-independence, nationalistic political party)
VNSF   [South] Vietnamese Special Forces
VOA   Voice of America
WESTPAC   Western Pacific Command
WIA   Wounded in action